ローマ字	ひらがな	カタカナ	ローマ字	ひらがな	カタカナ	ローマ字	ひらがな	カタカナ	ローマ字	ひらがな	カタカナ
o	お	オ									
ko	こ	コ	kya	きゃ	キャ	kyu	きゅ	キュ	kyo	きょ	キョ
so	そ	ソ	sha	しゃ	シャ	shu	しゅ	シュ	sho	しょ	ショ
to	と	ト	cha	ちゃ	チャ	chu	ちゅ	チュ	cho	ちょ	チョ
no	の	ノ	nya	にゃ	ニャ	nyu	にゅ	ニュ	nyo	にょ	ニョ
ho	ほ	ホ	hya	ひゃ	ヒャ	hyu	ひゅ	ヒュ	hyo	ひょ	ヒョ
mo	も	モ	mya	みゃ	ミャ	myu	みゅ	ミュ	myo	みょ	ミョ
yo	よ	ヨ									
ro	ろ	ロ	rya	りゃ	リャ	ryu	りゅ	リュ	ryo	りょ	リョ
o	を	ヲ									
go	ご	ゴ	gya	ぎゃ	ギャ	gyu	ぎゅ	ギュ	gyo	ぎょ	ギョ
zo	ぞ	ゾ	ja	じゃ	ジャ	ju	じゅ	ジュ	jo	じょ	ジョ
do	ど	ド									
bo	ぼ	ボ	bya	びゃ	ビャ	byu	びゅ	ビュ	byo	びょ	ビョ
po	ぽ	ポ	pya	ぴゃ	ピャ	pyu	ぴゅ	ピュ	pyo	ぴょ	ピョ

ローマ字つづりの注意事項

(1) はねる音はすべて "n" で表した。
　　新聞 *shinbun*　天気 *tenki*

(2) はねる音の "n" の次にすぐ母音字または "y" が続く場合には、"n" の次にアポストロフィー "'" を入れた。
　　原因 *gen'in*　金曜日 *kin'yōbi*

(3) つまる音は次に来る子音字を重ねて表した。ただし、子音字が "ch" の場合には "tch" とした。
　　学校 *gakkō*　マッチ *matchi*

(4) "あっ" のような感動詞の場合、つまる音はアポストロフィーをつけて表した。
　　あっ、たいへんだ。 *A'! Taihen da.*

(5) 長音は母音字の上に長音符号をつけて表した。ただし、"i" の場合には、"ii" とした。
　　セーター *sētā*　コーヒー *kōhii*

THE JAPAN FOUNDATION

BASIC
JAPANESE−ENGLISH
DICTIONARY

Second edition

基礎日本語学習辞典　第二版

OXFORD
UNIVERSITY PRESS

BONJINSHA

OXFORD
UNIVERSITY PRESS

Great Clarendon Street, Oxford OX2 6DP

Oxford University Press is a department of the University of Oxford.
It furthers the University's objective of excellence in research, scholarship,
and education by publishing worldwide in

Oxford New York

Auckland Bangkok Buenos Aires Cape Town Chennai
Dar es Salaam Delhi Hong Kong Istanbul Karachi Kolkata
Kuala Lumpur Madrid Melbourne Mexico City Mumbai Nairobi
São Paulo Shanghai Taipei Tokyo Toronto

Oxford is a registered trade mark of Oxford University Press
in the UK and in certain other countries

Published in the United States
by Oxford University Press Inc., New York

British Library Cataloguing in Publication Data

Data available

Library of Congress Cataloging in Publication Data

Data available

ISBN-13: 978-0-19-860859-2
ISBN-10: 0-19-860859-4
ISBN-13: 978-4-89358-554-7
ISBN-10: 4-89358-554-1
(Bonjinsha edition)

4

Printed in Great Britain by
Clays Ltd, Bungay, Suffolk
Bonjinsha Co, Ltd.
1-3-13 Hirakawacho, Chiyoda-ku
Tokyo 102-0093, Japan

Preface

As international exchange deepens, the role of language as a means for mutual understanding becomes larger. The Japanese language is no exception, and with the importance of Japan worldwide, the number of people studying Japanese in foreign countries has been steadily rising.

However, at present there are hardly any easy-to-use dictionaries in their own language for foreigners starting their study of Japanese. Therefore most foreign students of Japanese are forced to make do with dictionaries — Japanese-English, Japanese-French, etc.— compiled for Japanese students of European languages. These dictionaries may be useful for intermediate and advanced students of Japanese who know such European languages well, but they are very difficult for beginners to use. That is, the example sentences are written in *kanji* with no *furigana* or romanization, and the lack of translations in their own language makes these sentences difficult to understand for those whose native language is not English, French, or the like.

We at the Japan Foundation thus felt that there was a need for a dictionary that was easy to use by such students of Japanese, with editions in various foreign languages. Therefore we embarked on the compilation of this dictionary. A selection of basic vocabulary has been made from words in everyday use, an analysis of the different senses in which these words are used has been carried out, and the different senses have been shown through example phrases and sentences. *Furigana* and romanization have been included so that this work can be used by beginners.

Since an English translation has been added on the right-hand side of each page, this edition should be easy for English speakers to understand. The study of language is in effect the attempt to understand by overcoming cultural differences, and in the translation when no exact equivalent exists the closest approximation has been chosen; cultural explanations have been added as necessary.

This dictionary will have served its purpose if through its use the student finds it even a little easier to understand this basic vocabulary and to use it in the actual speaking and writing of Japanese. We would be happy to receive comments and suggestions for use in later editions.

We would also like to express our thanks here to all the individuals who have participated in the planning, compilation, translation, and checking of this dictionary.

The Japan Foundation
July 2004

About This Dictionary

1. This dictionary has been compiled for use by foreigners studying Japanese who are still at a relatively early stage in their studies. In addition, in 2003 an overall review of the dictionary has been conducted; new entries have been added, some examples with low frequency have been eliminated, and example sentences have been rewritten. Also, with the change of the form of entries from roman letters to *hiragana*, an index written in *Romaji* has been added for the students' reference and *katakana* words and their English translations, which are dealt in Japanese textbooks for beginners, have been provided.

2. There are 2,981 separate entries, chiefly centering around vocabulary used by Japanese language teaching institutions at an introductory level. The choice of entries was based on Japanese language teaching materials, studies of vocabulary in common use, dictionaries, and consultations with people involved in teaching Japanese as a foreign language. In addition, all the vocabulary included in the 3rd and 4th grade of Japanese Language Proficiency Test issued by the Japan Foundation is covered.

3. The entries are written in *hiragana* so that learners can get accustomed to Japanese script (*hiragana*) at an early stage, and this is followed by the standard writing in *kanji* and/or *kana*. Romanization has also been provided for example expressions, compounds, and sentences; and *furigana* is provided for *kanji* in the entries and the example expressions, compounds, and sentences.

4. In order to clarify the meaning and usage of entry words and to aid in the formation of one's own sentences, example sentences have been provided; compounds and idiomatic expressions using the word are also included. In addition, as necessary, different senses of the word have been shown and explanations of usage given. Indication has also been made of words of contrasting and similar meaning which should be consulted.

5. An English translation accompanies the Japanese text so that the student can compare the two.

6. The different senses given for the entries, in accordance with the nature of this dictionary, have been restricted to the basic ones but at times they are quite detailed so that they will be useful at a relatively high level of study.

Using This Dictionary

This dictionary consists of Japanese text on the left-hand side of the page with a corresponding English translation on the right-hand side of the page.

I. The entries

(1) The form of the entry

    (a) The entry is written first in *hiragana* and then in standard Japanese writing in *kanji* and/or *kana* followed by an abbreviation indicating part or parts of speech.

    (b) The entry is given in the dictionary or citation form. Adjective-verbs are given in the stem form.

    (c) The hyphens with prefixes and suffixes indicate where they are attached to other words.

$$\text{だい - 第 - 〔頭〕 \quad - ぶ - 部 〔尾〕}$$

    (d) In the case of compounds, the symbol ～ indicates the omission of some word or element.

$$\text{（～て）あげる 〔連〕}$$

    (e) More than one part of speech has been indicated where appropriate.

$$\text{たいへん 〔副、形動〕}$$

    Nouns and adverbs that can be used with *suru* as Type III verbs have been indicated as such.

$$\text{べんきょう 勉強 〔名、～する〕}$$
$$\text{はっきり 〔副、～する〕}$$

(2) The arrangement of entries

    (a) The entries are in *hiragana* order.

    (b) In the case of different entries with the same spelling, those written in *kanji* come before those written in *kana*.

$$\text{ふく 吹く 〔動 I〕}$$
$$\text{ふく 〔動 I〕}$$

    (c) Words with the same pronunciation usually differentiated by *kanji* are treated as separate entries. There is no particular rule of order in such a case.

あたたか	暖か 〔形動〕	あてる	当てる 〔動 II〕
あたたか	温か 〔形動〕	あてる	充てる 〔動 II〕

II. The form of writing in Japanese

(1) The use of *tōyōkanji*, *kana*, and inflectional *kana* follows standards established by the Japanese government.

(2) *Furigana* is included for all *kanji* in the entries, example compounds, example expressions, and example sentences. *Kanji* have been used as much as possible for words usually written in *kanji* while words generally written in *hiragana* have been written in *hiragana*. Thus in some cases a word may be written in both *kanji* and *hiragana* in the example sentences for a single entry.

絵を掛ける   (e o *kakeru*)
心配をかける   (shinpai o *kakeru*)

(3) Numbers are written in kanji in the entries but, as the text is written in horizontal form, they generally appear in Arabic numerals in the text itself.

(4) The romanization generally follows that of the second table in the Japanese government's *Rōmaji no tsuzurikata* (The Romanization of Japanese). See also the table at the front of this volume.

III. The example sentences

(1) Example sentences for the entry are indicated by the sign ¶ .

¶ はがきを5枚ください。   (*Hagaki* o gomai kudasai)

(2) Sentences spoken by different speakers are indicated by「 」in the Japanese text.

¶「これは日本語の本ですか。」(Kore wa Nihongo no hon desu ka?)
「はい、そうです。」   (*Hai*, sōdesu.)

(3) Within the example expressions and sentences, the entry word is indicated by boldface type in the Japanese and italics in the romanization.

はは 母〔名〕
¶ 母は今年60歳です。   (*Haha* wa kotoshi rokujissai desu.)

IV. The explanations of meaning and usage

(1) When judged advisable, different senses of the entry are indicated by the numbers ① , ② , ③ , etc.; the individual meanings appear within brackets.

(2) The senses are generally listed with those used most frequently appearing first.

(3) Where more than one part of speech is applicable, separate explanations have been provided if there is a significant difference in meaning.

じっさい　実際〔名、副〕

1〔名〕

¶彼の話は**実際**とはだいぶ違います。

(Kare no hanashi wa *jissai* to wa daibu chigaimasu.)

2〔副〕

¶この問題には**実際**困っています。

(Kono mondai ni wa *jissai* komatte imasu.)

(4) Usage notes are indicated by a boldface asterisk (＊). Where the note only applies to that one particular sense of the word, a small asterisk (*) has been used.

V. Words of contrasting meaning and other related words

(1) Words of contrasting meaning to an entry are indicated by ⇔. When the word applies to only one sense of the entry ‹ › is used.

(2) A cross-reference to a word with a related meaning is indicated by ⇒. A cross-reference to a related word applying to a single sense of the entry is indicated by →.

(3) When the entry appears under a different form the reader is referred to the correct entry by ☞.

VI. The abbreviations used for the parts of speech

The abbreviations used for the parts of speech in the entries are:

〔名〕	[n]	noun
〔代〕	[pron]	pronoun
〔動Ⅰ〕	[vI]	Type I verb (*godan* verb; -u verb)
〔動Ⅱ〕	[vII]	Type II verb (*-ru* verb)
〔動Ⅲ〕	[vIII]	Type III verb
〔形〕	[adj]	adjective
〔形動〕	[adj-v]	adjective-verb
〔副〕	[adv]	adverb
〔連体〕	[attrib]	attributive
〔接〕	[conj]	conjunction
〔感〕	[interj]	interjection
〔助動〕	[auxil]	auxiliary
〔助〕	[part]	particle
〔頭〕	[pref]	prefix
〔尾〕	[suf]	suffix
〔連〕	[compd]	compound

VII. Proprietary terms

The inclusion in this dictionary of any words which are, or are asserted to be, proprietary names or trademarks does not imply they have acquired for legal purposes a non-proprietary or general significance, nor is any other judgment implied concerning their legal status.

Concerning the English-Language Edition

I. The entries

(1) The form of the entry

    (a) To help beginners, there are entries for verb endings (-*ba*, -*mashō*, -*masu*, -*nai*, -*nakereba naranai*, -*nasai*, -*rareru*, -*reru*, -*saseru*, -*seru*, -*ta*, -*tara*, -*te*, -*te mo*, -*te wa*, -*yō*, -*zu*, etc.) not usually found in other Japanese-English dictionaries. Entries for expressions with a verb in the -te form plus a helping verb are found under the helping verb ([-*te*] *ageru*, [-*te*] *ikenai*, [-te*te*] *kuru*, [-*te*] *miru*, [-*te*] *oku*, [-*te*] *shimau*, etc.). Entries for expressions with a verb in the stem form plus a second verb are also found under the second verb (-*au*, -*dasu*, -*komu*, -*sugiru*, etc.).

    (b) Words often used with the prefix *o*- are generally found under the base form (*cha*, *rei*, *tagai*, *tearai*, etc.).

    (c) Idiomatic expressions can generally be found listed as separate senses under both of the key words. For example, *hara ga tatsu* can be found under both the entries for *hara* and for *tatsu*.

(2) The arrangement of entries and romanization

    (a) The hiragana order is letter-by-letter, not word-by-word.

なな	七	nara
なmy	七つ	nanatsu
ななめ	斜め	naname
なに (-)	何 (-)	nani(-)
なにか	何か	nani ka
なん (-)	何 (-)	nan(-)
なんでも	何でも	nandemo

    (b) Long vowels are transcribed with a macron except for "i," which is written "ii."

        セーター   sētā   ビール biiru

    (c) Certain words have been transcribed with a double vowel in accordance with how they are written in Japanese: *baai*, *hoo*, *koori*, *kooru*, *kuu*, *nuu*, *oo*-, *ooi*, *ookii*, *ookina*, *ookisa*, *ooku*, *oozei*, *too*, *tooi*, *tooka*, *tooku*, *toori*, -*toori*, *tooru*, and *toosu*.

    (d) No distinction is made in the hiragana order between short vowels and long vowels written with a macron.

ゆ	湯	yu
ゆう	夕-	yū-
ゆうべ		yūbe
ゆび	指	yubi
ようやく		yōyaku
よやく	予約	yoyaku
よゆう	余裕	yoyū
よわい	弱い	yowai

(e) Words written with a doubling of the vowel are alphabetized accordingly.

ば		ba	ビール		biiru
ばあい	場合	baai	びじゅつ	美術	bijutsu
(-) ばい	(-) 倍	(-)bai	びっくりする		bikkuri suru
ばか		baka	べつに	別に	betsu ni

II. The English translation

(3) The definitions

    (a) Different senses of the word in the definition at the head of the entry are separated by semicolons.

    (b) The definitions for different senses found in brackets are often not a direct translation of the Japanese definition but rather the English equivalent of the word being defined.

> ちかく③ [数量などがそれより少し足りないが
> それとほとんど同じくらいであること]
>
> (literally, an amount, etc., being a little less but almost the same) →
> [nearly, almost]

(4) The translations of the example phrases and sentences

    (a) The translations have been kept as close to the Japanese original as possible, and a literal translation is generally given if a natural English sentence close to the Japanese is not possible.

    (b) In some cases one Japanese sentence may become two sentences in English and vice versa. The part of speech may also change in the translation. For this reason, the reader will notice that the words in boldface type in the English translations may not correspond exactly to what is in boldface in the Japanese text.

    (c) The choice of the singular or the plural or of the definite or indefinite article in the English translation is often arbitrary, as Japanese does not make these dis-

tinctions. Thus "Kodomo ga niwa de asonde imasu" could be "A child is playing in the yard," "The child is playing in the yard," "Children are playing in the
yard," or "The children are playing in the yard." The most likely possibility
has been chosen.

(d) An attempt has been made to indicate major alternative possibilities in sense,
tense, and meaning of individual vocabulary items, but these are not exhaustive.

(e) The translations are in American English, and an effort has been made to make
them easy to understand for non-native as well as native speakers of English.

(5) Symbols used in the English translation

(a) // separates different example compounds or phrases.

(b) [ ] indicates items specified in English but not in Japanese.

あ、あれは上田さんです。

Oh, that's [Mr.] Ueda.

(c) ( ) indicates items specified in Japanese but not in English.

姉は洗たく物にアイロンをかけています。

My (elder) sister is ironing the laundry.

お茶をどうぞ。

Please have some (green) tea.

(d) 〚 〛indicates alternative possibilities.

成績が上がる

one's grades 〚business results〛 improve

雨が降り出しました。

It has started to rain 〚It started to rain〛.

(e) * indicates incorrect or ungrammatical sentences.

(6) The reader is also referred to the "Introduction to Japanese Grammar" found at the
back of this volume.

は　し　が　き

　国際間の交流が一層深まるに従って、意思疎通の手段として言語の果たす役割は大きくなってきています。日本語もその例外ではなく、日本の国際的な役割が増大するにつれ、海外で日本語を学ぶ人の数は増大の一途をたどっています。

　ところが、日本語の学習を始めようとする外国人にとって、自国語の訳がついた使いやすい辞書がほとんどないのが現状です。従って多くの外国人学習者は、日本人の外国語学習用に編集された「和英辞典」や「和仏辞典」を代用している場合が多いようです。これらの辞典は英語やフランス語が良くできる中・上級の学習者には有益であったとしても、初級学習者にとっては非常に使いにくいといわれています。というのは、文例中の漢字に振りがながなく、ローマ字表記もついていないし、英語等以外の言語を母国語とする学習者にとって自国語の対訳もなく、解りにくいからです。

　国際交流基金では、こうした初級の日本語学習者にとって使いやすい辞典を各国語版で刊行する必要があると考え、本「基礎日本語学習辞典」の編集を進めてまいりました。日常使われる言葉から基礎語いを選定し、その語のもつ意味の分類を行い、それぞれの意味ごとに語の使われ方を語例や文例の中で明示しました。振りがなおよびローマ字表記も添えましたので、初めての学習者も利用できるものと確信しております。

　ページの右側には対照に英語訳をつけましたので、英語を母国語とする学習者にとって解りやすいはずです。ことばの学習は文化の違いを超えて理解しようとする試みでもあるわけですが、英語訳をつけるにあたっては、日本語の意味にぴったりとする訳語がない場合にはその近似値を選び、必要に応じて文化的説明を加えて理解を助けました。

　本辞典を利用することにより基本語いの理解が少しでも容易になり、また文例の中でどう用いられるかを学ぶことによって、実際に話したり書いたりする時に役立てられれば、本辞典の役割は果たされたことになります。本辞典についてご意見・ご批判をお寄せいただければ、改訂の際に参考にさせていただきます。

　最後に、本辞典の企画・編集に参画された編集委員の先生方、翻訳、校閲の諸先生およびご協力頂いた方々に心より感謝の意を表したいと存じます。

　平成 16 年 7 月

独立行政法人　国際交流基金

はじめに（第二版出版にあたって）

1. この辞典は、日本語を学習する外国人が、比較的初期の段階において使用することを目的として編集されたものです。

   また、平成15年に、全面的な見直しを行い、新規見出し語の追加と一部使用頻度の低くなった語例の削除、用例の変更を行いました。また、見出し語をローマ字からひらがなに変更したことにともなうローマ字インデックスの追加、初級日本語の教科書に取り上げられているカタカナ語とその英訳を追加いたしました。

2. 見出し語として、2981語を収録いたしました。各日本語教育機関などにおいて初期の段階で多く取り扱われる語が中心になっています。

   見出し語は日本語の教材や語い調査、辞書などを参考にして、日本語教育に関係している方々の合意によって決めました。

   また、国際交流基金発行の日本語能力試験出題基準の3級、4級に取り上げられている語いはすべてカバーいたしました。

3. 学習者が早い段階で日本語表記になれるように見出し語はひらがなで示し、それに日本語の標準的な表記を併記しました。

   語例および用例には、すべてローマ字の表記を併記し、また漢字にはすべて振りがなをつけました。

4. 見出し語の意味や用法がよく理解できるように、また、文章を書くときに役立つように、用例をかかげ、さらにその語に関連した複合語や慣用的な語句もあげました。また、必要に応じて、意味分類をするとともに注をふしてその用法について解説を加えました。

   なお、反対語や参照語なども示しました。

5. 学習者が日本語を英語と比較して学習できるように、日本語に対応する英語による翻訳を添えました。

6. 見出し語の意味分類は、この辞典の性格から基礎的なものに限りましたが、やや高い段階の学習にも利用できるように少し詳しい分類を行ったものもあります。

凡　例

　この辞典は、左側には日本語、右側にはそれに対応する英語による訳文が載せてあります。

I．見出し語

(1) 書き表し方

　(a)　初めにひらがなで示し、次に日本語の標準的な表記を示して、その品詞名などを略語で添えました。

　(b)　活用語は「終止の形」で示しました。ただし、形容動詞は語幹の形で示しました。

　(c)　見出し語のうち、接頭語・接尾語については、次のように、つく語の位置にハイフン「 - 」を置きました。

　　　　だい - 第 -〔頭〕　　 - ぶ - 部〔尾〕

　(d)　連語については、前に語がつくものは、それを「〜」で示し、次のようにしました。

　　　　（〜て）あげる〔連〕

　(e)　二つ以上の品詞にわたるものは、それを併記しました。

　　　　たいへん〔副、形動〕

　　また、名詞、副詞などで動Ⅲの動詞として用いられるものは〔名、〜する〕〔副、〜する〕などして示しました。

　　　　べんきょう　勉強〔名、〜する〕
　　　　はっきり〔副、〜する〕

(2) 配　列

　(a)　見出し語はひらがな順に配列しました。

　(b)　見出し語に同音異義語が二つ以上ある場合は、漢字表記の語を先に、かな表記の語をあとにあげました。

　　　　ふく　吹く〔動Ⅰ〕
　　　　ふく〔動Ⅰ〕

　(c)　同音の語で普通漢字によって書き分けられているものについては、別の見出し語として取り扱いました。その先後については、特に問いませんでした。

あたたか	暖か〔形動〕	あてる	当てる〔動Ⅱ〕
あたたか	温か〔形動〕	あてる	充てる〔動Ⅱ〕

Ⅱ. 日本語の表記について

(1) 当用漢字 (内閣告示の当用漢字表・同音訓表・同字体表)、現代かなづかい (内閣告示)、送りがなのつけ方 (内閣告示) を基準としました。

(2) 見出し語および語例、用例の漢字にはすべて振りがなをつけました。広く漢字による表記が行われているものは、できるだけ漢字による表記をとりましたが、一般的にひらがなで表記されることが多いと思われるものはひらがなにしました。したがって、同じ見出し語の中の用例でも漢字によって表記したものとひらがなによって表記したものとがある場合があります。

絵を掛ける　　　　　　　(e o *kakeru*)
心配をかける　　　　　　(shinpai o *kakeru*)

(3) 数詞については、見出し語は漢数字で示してありますが、本文が横書きなので、適宜、算用数字を使用しました。

(4) ローマ字の表記は、おおむね内閣告示「ローマ字のつづり方」の「第2表」によりました。

　なお、表のとびらの「ローマ字・ひらがな・カタカナ対照表」を参照してください。

Ⅲ. 用例について

(1) 見出し語を実際に用いた語例、用例のうち、用例は¶で示しました。

　　　¶はがきを5枚ください。　　(*Hagaki o gomai kudasai*)

(2) 会話文の用例は、「　」で示しました。

　　　¶「これは日本語の本ですか。」(*Kore wa Nihongo no hon desu ka?*)
　　　　「はい、そうです。」　　(*Hai*, sōdesu.)

(3) 語例、用例中の見出し語に当たる語は、ゴチック体で示し、ローマ字表記は、イタリック体で示しました。

はは　母〔名〕
　¶母は今年60歳です。　　(*Haha* wa kotoshi rokujissai desu.)

Ⅳ. 意味・用法の説明

(1) 見出し語の意味を分類したほうがよいと認めた場合は、①、②、③‥‥と分類し、[ ] の中にその意味の説明をしました。

(2) 意味分類の配列は、普通によく使われるものを先にしました。

(3) 二つ以上の品詞などにわたるもので、意味の上で必要な場合は、それぞれ品詞別の項目を立てて記述しました。

> **じっさい 実際**〔名、副〕
>
> 1 〔名〕
> ¶彼の話は**実際**とはだいぶ違います。
>
> (Kare no hanashi wa *jissai* to wa daibu chigaimasu.)
>
> 2 〔副〕
> ¶この問題には**実際**困っています。
>
> (Kono mondai ni wa *jissai* komatte imasu.)

(4) 見出し語の用法について説明する必要があると認めた場合は、＊をつけて説明しました。

また、意味分類の中の各項の用法について説明する場合は、＊をつけて説明しました。

Ⅴ. 反対語・参照語など

(1) 見出し語に対する反対語がある場合は、⇔で示しました。

また、意味分類の中の各項における反対語は‹ ›で示しました。

(2) 見出し語に対して関係のある語を参照語としてあげましたが、見出し語全体に対する参照語は⇒で示しました。

また、意味分類の中の各項における参照語は→で示しました。

(3) 他の見出し語を参照する場合は、☞で示しました。

Ⅵ. 品詞名などの略語

〔名〕	名詞	〔副〕	副詞
〔代〕	代名詞	〔連体〕	連体詞
〔動Ⅰ〕	Ⅰ型の動詞（五段活用）	〔接〕	接続詞
〔動Ⅱ〕	Ⅱ型の動詞（上一段活用・下一段活用）	〔感〕	感動詞
		〔助動〕	助動詞
〔動Ⅲ〕	Ⅲ型の動詞（カ行変格活用・サ行変格活用）	〔助〕	助詞
		〔頭〕	接頭語
〔形〕	形容詞	〔尾〕	接尾語
〔形動〕	形容動詞	〔連〕	連語

Ⅶ. 英語への翻訳について

(1) 定義

(a) 見出しの初めに併記した定義のうち、意味に差異のある語については、；を用いて区分しました。

(b) 意味分類をした定義のうち、[　] の中には、日本語による定義の直訳ではなく、英語における同義語を示しました。

ちかく③ [数量などがそれより少し足りないが
それとほとんど同じくらいであること]
(literally, an amount, etc., being a little less but almost the same）→
[nearly, almost]

(2) 語例及び用例の翻訳

(a) 翻訳はできるだけ日本語の原文に近づけるよう努めましたが、英文の表現として不自然になる場合には、通常、文字通りの訳文も別に記しました。

(b) 翻訳の際、1 つの和文に対応する英文が 2 つになる場合や、その逆の場合、また、品詞が変わる場合があります。このため、英文中でボールド体で表記した語が、和文中のゴシック体で表記した語と一字一句そのまま対応しているとは限りません。

(c) 日本語の原文においては、単数・複数あるいは、定冠詞・不定冠詞の区別がないので、英語に翻訳する際には適宜選択しました。

(d) 文意や時制、個々の語いの意味等の点において言い換えが可能な表現を示すように試みましたが、すべてを網羅しているわけではありません。

(e) 翻訳にあたってはアメリカ英語を採用し、英語を母国語とする学習者はもちろん、それ以外の学習者にも理解しやすいように努めました。

(3) 英語訳で用いた記号について

(a) // は語例を併記する際区分するのに用いました。

(b) [　] の中には、英語においてのみ区別のある語いを示しました。

あ、あれは上田（うえだ）さんです。
Oh, that's [Mr.] Ueda.

(c) （　） の中には日本語においてのみ区別のある語いを示しました。
姉（あね）は洗（せん）たく物（もの）にアイロンをかけています。
My (elder) sister is ironing the laundry.

(d) 〖　〗 の中には言い換えが可能な表現を示しました。
成績（せいせき）が上（あ）がる
one's grades 〖business results〗 improve

(e) ＊は間違ったあるいは非文法的な文例を示しました。

(4) 学習者の参考となるよう巻末に "Introduction to Japanese Grammar" を編集しました。

Ⅷ. 商品名・商標について

　この辞典には商品名または商標と認識される固有名詞が含まれています。出版者は、現在の日本社会においてこれらの語が日常頻繁に使われていることから、日本語学習者の利便のためここに収録したものですが、これらの商品ないしは商標に関する何らの価値判断を有しているものではありません。念のため付記いたします。

あ

あ 〔感〕

¶あ、富士山が見えます。(*A* ! Fujisan ga miemasu.)

¶あ、あれは上田さんです。(*A* ! Are wa Ueda san desu.)

¶あっ、地震だ。(*A'* ! Jishin da.)

ああ 〔副〕

¶ああいう人は見たことがありません。(*Ā*iu hito wa mita koto ga arimasen.)

¶ああ忙しくては、ゆっくり食事をする暇もないでしょう。(*Ā* isogashikute wa, yukkuri shokuji o suru hima mo nai deshō.)

＊話し手にとっても話し相手に対してともに隔たりのあるものごとの様子をさし示すのに使う。

⇒こう **kō** そう **so** どう **dō**

ああ 〔感〕

¶ああ、うれしい。(*Ā*, ureshii.)

¶ああ、そうですか。わかりました。(*Ā*, sō desu ka. Wakarimashita.)

あい 愛 〔名、〜する〕

母の愛 (haha no *ai*) 神の愛 (kami no *ai*) 平和を愛する (heiwa o *ai*suru)

¶あの人は親切なので、みんなに愛されています。(Ano hito wa shinsetsu na node, minna ni *ai*sarete imasu.)

あいさつ 〔名、〜する〕

¶日本では、朝「お早うございます。」とあいさつをします。(Nihon de wa,

---

a 〚interj〛 **Oh!**

¶**Oh** look! You can see Mount Fuji.

¶**Oh**, that's [Mr.] Ueda.

¶**Oh**! It's an earthquake!

ā 〚adv〛 **that, so**

¶I've never seen **that** sort of person before.

¶[They] look **so** busy [they] probably don't have time to eat leisurely.

＊Used for something at a distance from both the speaker and the listener.

ā 〚interj〛 **Oh!, Ah!**

¶**Oh**, I'm so glad!

¶**Oh**, is that so? I understand.

ai 〚n, 〜*suru*〛 **love, affection**

a mother's **love** // divine **love** // **to love** peace

¶Since that person is kind, [he] is **loved** by all.

aisatsu 〚n, 〜*suru*〛 **greeting**

¶In Japan, one **greets** people in the morning with ohayō gozaimasu 〚good morning〛.

1

asa "Ohayō gozaimasu." to *aisatsu* o shimasu.)

¶ わたしがあいさつしたのに、山田さんは返事をしませんでした。(Watashi ga *aisatsu* shita noni, Yamada san wa henji o shimasen deshita.)

¶ Although I **greeted** [her], [Mrs.] Yamada gave no response.

あいじょう　愛情 〔名〕

¶ 子供に対する親の愛情はなによりも強いです。(Kodomo ni taisuru oya no *aijō* wa nani yori mo tsuyoi desu.)

¶ 二人の愛情はますます深くなっていきました。(Futari no *aijō* wa masumasu fukaku natte ikimashita.)

aijō 〔n〕 **love, affection**

¶ **The love** of parents for their children is stronger than anything else.

¶ **The affection** between the two deepened further.

あいず　合図 〔名、〜する〕

¶ ピストルの音を合図に子供たちは駆けだしました。(Pisutoru no oto o aizu ni kodomotachi wa kakedashimashita.)

¶ 手を挙げて合図しても、タクシーは止まりませんでした。(Te o agete aizu shite mo, takushii wa tomarimasen deshita.)

aizu 〔n, 〜*suru*〕 **signal**

¶ The children started to run at **the signal** of a pistol shot.

¶ The taxi didn't stop even though [I] **signaled** it by raising [my] hand.

アイスクリーム 〔名〕

¶ アイスクリームは牛乳と砂糖と卵で作ります。(*Aisukuriimu* wa gyūnyū to satō to tamago de tsukurimasu.)

aisukuriimu 〔n〕 **ice cream**

¶ **Ice cream** is made from milk, sugar and eggs.

あいだ　間 〔名〕

① [空間的な隔たり、二つの物にはさまれた所]

¶ 机と机の間をもう少し広くしてください。(Tsukue to tsukue no *aida* o mō sukoshi hiroku shite kudasai.)

¶ 銀行と郵便局の間の道をまっすぐ行くと、学校の前に出ます。(Ginkō to yūbinkyoku no *aida* no michi o massugu iku to, gakkō no mae ni demasu.)

② [限られた一続きの時間]

aida 〔n〕 **space; interval; relations**

① [physical space, the space between two things]

¶ Please move the desks a little farther **apart**.

¶ When you go straight along the street **between** the bank and the post office, you come out in front of the school.

② [a certain interval of time]

¶１時から２時までの間にここへ来てください。(Ichiji kara niji made no *aida* ni koko e kite kudasai.)

¶ Please come here **between** one and two o'clock.

¶ずいぶん長い間お目にかかりませんでしたね。(Zuibun nagai *aida* ome ni kakarimasen deshita ne.)

¶ I haven't seen you for such a long **time**.

¶わたしが留守の間にだれか訪ねてきたようです。(Watashi ga rusu no *aida* ni dare ka tazunete kita yō desu.)

¶ It seems that someone came to visit **while** I was out.

③ [間がら・関係など]

③ [relations, etc.]

¶近ごろ、山田さんは奥さんとの間がうまくいっていないようです。(Chikagoro, Yamada san wa okusan to no *aida* ga umaku itte inai yō desu.)

¶ It seems that Mr. Yamada and his wife aren't getting along well recently.

¶Ａ国とＢ国との間についに戦争が起こりました。(Ē-koku to Bii-koku to no *aida* ni tsuini sensō ga okorimashita.)

¶ In the end war broke out **between** Country A and Country B.

あいて 相手 〔名〕

aite 〔n〕 **the other party, the object of**

¶わたしは結婚の相手を探しています。(Watashi wa kekkon no *aite* o sagashite imasu.)

¶ I am looking for **someone** to marry.

¶わたしには困ったときの相談相手がいません。(Watashi ni wa komatta toki no sōdan *aite* ga imasen.)

¶ I have **no one** to consult when I have a problem.

¶この店は外国人を相手に商売をしています。(Kono mise wa gaikokujin o *aite* ni shōbai o shite imasu.)

¶ This shop does most of its business with foreigners 〚This shop **caters to** foreigners〛.

アイロン 〔名〕

airon 〔n〕 **iron**

¶姉は洗たく物にアイロンをかけています。(Ane wa sentakumono ni *airon* o kakete imasu.)

¶ My (elder) sister is **ironing** the laundry.

あう 会う 〔動Ⅰ〕

au 〔vⅠ〕 **meet**

¶またあした会いましょう。(Mata ashita aimashō.)

¶ **Let's meet** again tomorrow.

3

¶昨日、わたしは山田さんに会いました。(Kinō, watashi wa Yamada san ni aimashita.)

＊目上の人には、丁寧な言い方「お目にかかる（ome ni kakaru）」を使う。

⇒別れる **wakareru**

あう 遭う〔動Ⅰ〕

¶田中さんは交通事故に遭ったそうです。(Tanaka san wa kōtsū-jiko ni atta sō desu.)

¶雨に降られて、ひどい目にあいました。(Ame ni furarete, hidoi me ni aimashita.)

あう 合う〔動Ⅰ〕

① [適合する、適当である]

¶このくつは大きすぎて、わたしには合いません。(Kono kutsu wa ookisugite, watashi ni wa aimasen.)

¶この眼鏡は、わたしに合っていません。(Kono megane wa, watashi ni atte imasen.)

② [合致する、同じである]

¶わたしは、山田さんとはよく意見が合います。(Watashi wa, Yamada san to wa yoku iken ga aimasu.)

③ [調和する]

¶ネクタイと服が合っていません。(Nekutai to fuku ga atte imasen.)

¶あの壁にはこの色のカーテンが合います。(Ano kabe ni wa kono iro no kāten ga aimasu.)

④ [正しいものと一致する]

¶あなたの時計は合っていますか。(Anata no tokei wa atte imasu ka?)

¶ I **met** [Miss] Yamada yesterday.

＊ When referring to persons of higher status, a more polite expression, *ome ni kakaru*, is used.

au 〔vⅠ〕 encounter, be subjected to

¶ I hear that [Mrs.] Tanaka **was in** a traffic accident.

¶ I was caught in the rain and **had an** awful time.

(-)au 〔vⅠ〕 fit; coincide; match; be correct

① [fit]

¶ These shoes **do not fit** me; they are too big.

¶ These glasses **are not right** for me (that is, the lenses are incorrect).

② [agree with, coincide with]

¶ [Mr.] Yamada and I often **have the same** opinions.

③ [match, go together, be in harmony]

¶ [His] necktie and suit **do not go together**.

¶ This color curtain **goes well** ⟦**would go well**⟧ with those walls.

④ [be correct, match something that is correct]

¶ Is your watch **correct**?

¶ この計算は合っています。(Kono keisan wa atte imasu.)

¶ These calculations **are correct**.

¶ 答えが合っている人は、手を挙げてください。(Kotae ga atte iru hito wa, te o agete kudasai.)

¶ Would those with the **correct** answer please raise their hands.

⑤ [いくつかのものが互いに同じことをする]

⑤ [do something together with someone]

話し合う (hanashi*au*) 愛し合う (aishi*au*)

talk **with** // love **each other**

¶ 困ったときは、お互いに助け合いましょう。(Komatta toki wa, otagai ni tasukeaimashō.)

¶ **Let's help each other** when we have a problem.

* 「動詞(基幹の形)＋合う(*au*)」の形で使う。

*Used in the pattern "verb (stem form) + -*au*."

あお 青 〔名〕

ao 〔n〕 blue, green

青色 (*ao*iro)

the color **blue**

¶ 信号が青になったら、道を渡りましょう。(Shingō ga *ao* ni nattara, michi o watarimashō.)

¶ Let's cross the street when the light turns **green**.

＊ 「青信号(*ao*shingō)」「青葉(*ao*ba)」などのように、緑色も「青(*ao*)」と言うことがある。

＊Although it usually means "blue," *ao* is sometimes used for "green" as in *aoshingo* (a green light) and *aoba* (green leaves).

あおい 青い 〔形〕

aoi 〔adj〕 blue, green; pale

① [青の色をしている様子]

① [blue, green]

青い空 (*aoi* sora) 青い海 (*aoi* umi)

the **blue** sky // the **blue** sea

¶ 田中さんは青いセーターを着ています。(Tanaka san wa *aoi* sētā o kiteimasu.)

¶ [Mrs.] Tanaka is wearing a **blue** sweater.

* 「青い草(*aoi* kusa)」「青いりんご(*aoi* ringo)」などのように緑色も「青い(*aoi*)」と言うことがある。

*Although it usually means "blue," *aoi* is sometimes used for the color green as in *aoi kusa* (green grasses) and *aoi ringo* (green apple).

② [顔に血の気がなく元気のない様子]

② [pale]

¶ 山田さんは病気で青い顔をしています。(Yamada san wa byōki de *aoi* kao o shite imasu.)

¶ [Mr.] Yamada is **pale** from [his] illness.

あか　赤〔名〕

赤鉛筆（*aka*enpitsu）

¶信号が赤に変わりました。（Shingō ga *aka* ni kawarimashita.）

aka 〔n〕 **red**

a **red** pencil

¶ The traffic light turned **red**.

あかい　赤い〔形〕

赤いシャツ（*akai* shatsu）赤いりんご（*akai* ringo）

¶庭に赤い花が咲きました。（Niwa ni *akai* hana ga sakimashita.）

¶山田さんはビールを飲むと、すぐ顔が赤くなります。（Yamada san wa biiru o nomuto, sugu kao ga akaku narimasu.）

akai 〔adj〕 **red**

a **red** shirt 〚T-shirt, etc.〛 // a **red** apple

¶ A **red** flower is in bloom in the garden.

¶ When [Mr.] Yamada drinks beer, [his] face soon becomes **flushed**.

あかちゃん　赤ちゃん〔名〕

男の赤ちゃん（otoko no *akachan*）かわいい赤ちゃん（kawaii *akachan*）

＊「赤ん坊（akanbō）」の丁寧な言い方。

⇒赤ん坊 akanbō

akachan 〔n〕 **baby**

a **baby** boy // a cute **baby**

＊The polite way of saying *akanbō*.

あかり　明かり〔名〕

①[電燈などの光]

明かりをつける（*akari* o tsukeru）明かりを消す（*akari* o kesu）

¶隣の部屋はまだ明かりがついています。（Tonari no heya wa mada *akari* ga tsuite imasu.）

¶丘の上から港の明かりが見えます。（Oka no ue kara minato no *akari* ga miemasu.）

②[日や月の光]

¶月の明かりで波が光っています。（Tsuki no *akari* de nami ga hikatte imasu.）

akari 〔n〕 **light**

① [electric light, etc.]

turn on **the light** // turn off **the light**

¶ **The lights** are still on in the next room 〚in the next-door apartment〛.

¶ From the top of the hill you can see the harbor **lights**.

② [sunlight, moonlight]

¶ The waves are glimmering in the moon**light**.

あがる　上がる〔動 I〕

①[上へ行く、高い所へ行く]

二階へ上がる（nikai e *agaru*）階段を上がる（kaidan o *agaru*）

agaru 〔v I〕 **go up; rise; eat, drink**

① [go up, climb]

go up to the second floor // **climb** the stairs

¶いすに上がって、たなの上の本を取ってください。(Isu ni agatte, tana no ue no hon o totte kudasai.)

¶ Please **stand** on the chair and reach down the book on the shelf.

¶どうぞ、こちらへお上がりください。(Dōzo, kochira e oagari kudasai.)

¶ Please come in (that is, up from the lowered entryway).

②[値段・価値・程度などが高くなる] 物価が上がる (bukka ga *agaru*) 温度が上がる (ondo ga *agaru*) 成績が上がる (seiseki ga *agaru*) 月給が上がる (gekkyū ga *agaru*)

② [rise in price, value, degree, etc.] prices **rise** // the temperature **rises** // one's grades 〖business results〗 **improve** // one's (monthly) salary **rises**

¶来月から、バス代が20円上がるそうです。(Raigetsu kara, basudai ga nijūen *agaru* sō desu.)

¶ I hear that bus fares are **going up** 20 yen from next month.

↔下がる **sagaru**

③[食べる、飲む]

③ [eat, drink]

¶どうぞ、お茶をおあがりください。(Dōzo, ocha o oagari kudasai.)

¶ Please **have** some tea.

*「食べる(taberu)」「飲む(nomu)」の尊敬語。

Aparu is the honorific form of *taberu* and *nomu*.

あかるい 明るい〔形〕

akarui 〔adj〕 **bright**

¶この部屋はたいへん明るいですね。(Kono heya wa taihen *akarui* desu ne.)

¶ This room **is** very **sunny** 〖well lighted; cheerrul〗.

¶この電球は暗いから、もっと明るいのに取り替えたほうがいいですよ。(Kono denkyū wa kurai kara, motto *akarui* no ni torikaeta hō ga ii desu yo.)

¶ This light bulb is too weak. You should replace it with a **brighter** one.

¶雨がやんで、空が明るくなってきました。(Ame ga yande, sora ga akaruku natte kimashita.)

¶ The rain has stopped and the sky is now **clear** 〖The rain stopped and the sky became **clear**〗.

⇔暗い **kurai**

あかんぼう 赤ん坊〔名〕

akanbō 〔n〕 **baby**

¶赤ん坊が泣いています。(Akanbō ga naite imasu.)

¶ **The baby** is crying.

¶赤ん坊のお守りをしてください。(Akanbō no omori o shite kudasai.)

¶ Please look after **the baby** for me.

7

＊他人の赤ん坊は「赤ちゃん
(akachan)」と言うほうがよい。
⇒赤ちゃん akachan

＊It is best to use *akachan* to refer to a
baby which is not one's own.

あき 秋〔名〕

¶日本では九月と十月と十一月は秋で
す。(Nihon de wa kugatsu to jūgatsu to
jūichigatsu wa *aki* desu.)

aki〔n〕**autumn**

¶In Japan **autumn** is September,
October and November.

あき 空き〔名〕

空き家 (*aki*ya) 空き箱 (*aki*bako) 空き
びん (*aki*bin)

aki〔n〕**being empty**

a **vacant** house // an **empty** box // an
empty bottle

あきらか 明らか〔形動〕

明らかな事実 (*akiraka* na jijitsu)
¶あの人がうそをついているのは明ら
かです。(Ano hito ga uso o tsuiteiru no
wa *akiraka* desu.)
¶その考えは明らかに間違っていま
す。(Sono kangae wa *akiraka* ni machigatte imasu.)
¶この物語は、だれが作ったのか明ら
かでは、ありません。(Kono monoga-
tari wa, dare ga tsukutta no ka *akiraka* de
wa arimasen.)

akiraka〔adj-v〕**clear, plain,
evident**
an **obvious** fact
¶It is obvious that [he] is lying.

¶That notion is **plainly** mistaken.

¶**It is not clear** who wrote this tale.

あきらめる〔動Ⅱ〕

¶なくした時計はもうあきらめなさ
い。(Nakushita tokei wa mō
akiramenasai.)
¶わたしは日本への留学をあきらめま
した。(Watashi wa Nihon e no ryūgaku
o akiramemashita.)

akirameru〔vⅡ〕**give up (doing
something), resign oneself to**
¶You'd better reconcile yourself to
the loss of your watch.

¶I have given up on the idea of
studying in Japan.

あきる 飽きる〔動〕

①〔じゅうぶんに満足する〕
飽きるほど食べる (*akiru* hodo taberu)

akiru〔vⅡ〕**be satiated; tire of**
①〔be satiated, be completely satisfied〕
eat **to one's heart's content**

¶毎日、魚ばかり食べていたので、もう飽きました。（Mainichi, sakana bakari tabete ita node, mō akimashita.）
②［ものごとを続けて行うのがいやになる］
仕事にあきる（shigoto ni *akiru*）
¶この絵は何度見てもあきません。（Kono e wa nando mite mo akimasen.）

¶ Since I've eaten nothing but fish every day, **I've had my fill of it**.
② [tire of, lose interest in]
be tired of a job
¶ **I never tire of** this picture no matter how many times I look at it.

あく 開く ［動 I］

¶窓が開いています。（Mado ga aite imasu.）
¶風で戸が開きました。（Kaze de to ga akimashita.）
¶かぎが掛かっていて、ドアが開きません。（Kagi ga kakatte ite, doa ga akimasen.）
¶朝早くて、まだ店が開いていません。（Asa haya*aku*te, mada mise ga aite imasu.）
⇔閉まる shimaru

aku 〔v I〕 **open, be opened**
¶ The window **is open**.
¶ The wind blew the door **open**.
¶ The door **won't open** because it's locked.
¶ It's early in the morning and the stores **aren't open** yet.

あく 空く ［動 I］

¶このアパートには、今空いた部屋はありません。（Kono apāto ni wa, ima aita heya wa arimasen.）
¶汽車がこんでいて、空いている席はありませんでした。（Kisha ga konde ite, aite iru seki wa arimasen deshita.）

aku 〔v I〕 **become empty, not be in use**
¶ There arc no **vacant** apartments now in this apartment building.
¶ The train was crowded, and there were no **empty** seats.

あくしゅ 握手 ［名、〜する］
友達と握手する（tomodachi to akushu suru）

akushu 〔n, 〜*suru*〕 **a handshake**
shake hands with a friend

あける 開ける ［動 II］
かばんを開ける（kaban o *akeru*）かぎを開ける（kagi o *akeru*）口を開ける（kuchi o *akeru*）本を開ける（hon o *akeru*）

akeru 〔v II〕 **open**
open a bag 〘suitcase, briefcase, etc.〙 // **open** a lock // **open** one's mouth // **open** a book

¶暑いから窓を開けてください。
（Atsui kara mado o akete kudasai.）

¶このびんのふたを開けてくださいませんか。（Kono bin no futa o akete kudasaimasen ka？）

¶ゆうべ、3時間しか寝なかったので、眠くて目を開けていられません。（Yūbe, sanjikan shika nenakatta node, nemukute me o akete iraremasen.）

⇔閉める shimeru　閉じる tojiru

¶ It's hot—please **open** the window.

¶ Would you please **open** this bottle for me?

¶ Since I only slept three hours last night, I'm so sleepy I can hardly **keep** my eyes **open**.

あける　空ける〔動Ⅱ〕

席を空ける（seki o *akeru*）　時間を空ける（jikan o *akeru*）

¶今日の午後は家を空けます。（Kyō no gogo wa ie o akemasu.）

akeru 〔v Ⅱ〕 leave vacant, keep open

make room (for someone to sit down) // **keep** a time **open** (for someone)

¶ **I will not be** at home this afternoon.

あける　明ける〔動Ⅱ〕

①［明るくなる、朝になる］
¶夜が明けて、辺りが明るくなってきました。（Yo ga akete atari ga akaruku natte kimashita.）

②［一年が終わって新年になる］

¶明けましておめでとうございます。（Akemashite omedetō gozaimasu.）

akeru 〔v Ⅱ〕 dawn; open, begin

① [become light, to dawn]
¶ **With the dawn** it has become 〚it became〛 light all around.

② [one year ends and the new year begins]

¶ Happy **New Year!**

あげる　挙げる〔動Ⅱ〕

①［下から上へ持ち上げる］
¶答えがわかった人は手を挙げてください。（Kotae ga wakatta hito wa te o agete kudasai.）

②［並べて人に示す］
¶先生は例を挙げて説明してくださいました。（Sensei wa rei o agete setsumei shite kudasaimashita.）

③［式などを行う］

ageru 〔v Ⅱ〕 raise; give; hold (a ceremony)

① [raise]
¶ Will those who know the answer please **raise** their hands.

② [give, offer]
¶ The teacher explained by **giving** an example.

③ [hold a ceremony, etc.]

¶わたしたちは教会で結婚式を挙げました。(Watashitachi wa kyōkai de kekkonshiki o agemashita.)

¶ We **had** our wedding ceremony in a church.

あげる 上げる〔動Ⅱ〕

① [下から上へ移す]

¶この荷物をたなに上げましょうか。(Kono nimotsu o tana ni agemashō ka？)

② [値段・価値・程度などを高める]

値段を上げる (nedan o *ageru*) 温度を上げる (ondo o *ageru*) 月給を上げる (gekkyū o *ageru*)

¶政府は来年から税金を上げるそうです。(Seifu wa rainen kara zeikin o *ageru* sō desu.)

↔下げる **sageru**

③ [やる、与える]

結婚のお祝いを上げる (kekkon no oiwai o *ageru*)

¶この本をあなたに上げましょう。(Kono hon o anata ni agemashō.)

¶どれでも好きな物を上げるから、持って行きなさい。(Dore demo suki na mono o *ageru* kara, motte ikinasai.)

*「やる (yaru)」「与える (ataeru)」の謙譲語であるが、最近はむしろ上品な言葉として使う。普通、対等または目下の人にある物を与えるときに使う。目上の人の場合も使うが、直接目上の人に言う場合には使わない。直接目上の人に向かって言うときには「差し上げる (sashi*ageru*)」を使う。「この本を先生に差し上げます。(Kono hon o sensei ni sashiagemasu.)」

→やる **yaru** 差し上げる **sashi*ageru***

ageru 〔v II〕 raise; give

① [raise something]

¶ **Shall I put** this bag **up** on the shelf for you?

② [raise prices, value, degree, etc.]

raise prices // **raise** the temperature // **raise** (monthly) wages

¶ I hear that the government is going to **raise** taxes from next year.

③ [give]

give a wedding present

¶ **I'll give** you this book.

¶ **I want you to have** whichever you like; please take it with you.

Ageru is the humble form of *yaru*, *ataeru*; recently used as refined language. Usually used when giving something to someone of equal or lower status. Also used in the case of superiors but not in direct address. When directly addressing a person of higher status, such as one's teacher, *sashiageru* is used: "*Kono hon o sensei ni sashiagemasu*" (This book is for you, sir).

（〜て）あげる〔連〕

¶わたしはその人に駅へ行く道を教えてあげました。(Watashi wa sono hito ni eki e iku michi o oshiete agemashita.)

¶その荷物を持ってあげましょうか。(Sono nimotsu o motte agemashō ka？)

¶わたしは友達に漢字を教えてあげました。(Watashi wa tomodachi ni kanji o oshiete agemashita.)

＊「（〜て）やる（[〜te] yaru）」の謙譲の言い方であるが、むしろ上品な言い方として使われる。一般に、動作をする人が相手の人のためにある動作をするという意味を表す。動作をする人の側に立って言うときに使う。普通、目上の人に直接向かって言うときには使わない。例えば、先生が大きな荷物を持っているような場合に「そのお荷物を持ってあげましょう。(Sono onimotsu o motte agemashō.)」とは言わない。そのような場合には「そのお荷物をお持ちしましょう。(Sono onimotsu o omochi shimashō.)」と言う。

⇒（〜て）やる（〜te) yaru

あさ 朝〔名〕

朝御飯（asagohan）朝日（asahi）毎朝（maiasa）

¶あなたは朝何時に起きますか。(Anata wa asa nanji ni okimasu ka？)

あさい 浅い〔形〕

¶深い方へ行かないで、浅い所で遊びなさい。(Fukai hō e ikanaide, asai tokoro de asobinasai.)

(-te)ageru 〔compd〕 **do someone the favor of -ing**

¶ I **told** that person the way to the station.

¶ **Let me carry** that bag for you.

¶ I **taught** my friend kanji.

＊The humble form of (-te) *yaru* but now often used as refined language. Generally expresses the meaning of the speaker performing some action for the benefit of the listener. It is not usually used when directly addressing a person of higher status. For example, when one's teacher is carrying a large bag or package, one should not say * "*Sono onimotsu o motte agemashō.*" In such a case one would say "*Sono onimotsu o omochi shimashō.*"

asa 〔n〕 **morning**

breakfast // the **morning** sun; Asahi (proper noun) // every **morning**

¶ What time do you get up in the **morning**?

asai 〔adj〕 **shallow**

¶ Don't go to the deep end but play where **it's shallow**.

¶この池は浅くて、底が見えます。
（Kono ike wa asakute, soko ga
miemasu.）
⇔深い fukai

¶ This pond 〚pool〛 **is shallow;** one
can see the bottom.

あさって〔名〕

asatte 〔n〕 **the day after tomorrow**

¶あさっては何曜日ですか。（Asatte
wa nan'yōbi desu ka？）

¶ What day of the week is **the day
after tomorrow?**

¶あさって、あなたのうちに行っても
いいですか。（Asatte, anata no uchi ni
itte mo ii desu ka？）

¶ Is it all right if I come to your home
the day after tomorrow?

あさねぼう 朝寝坊〔名、〜する〕

asanebō 〔n, 〜suru〕 **late riser,
sleepyhead**

¶朝寝坊をして、学校に遅刻してしま
いました。（Asanebō o shite, gakkō ni
chikoku shite shimaimashita.）

¶ **I overslept** and was late for school.

あし 足〔名〕

ashi 〔n〕 **foot, leg; walking**

①[歩くときに使う体の一部]

① [foot, leg; part of the body used
when walking]

足が強い（ashi ga tsuyoi）足が弱い
（ashi ga yowai）

be a good **walker** // be a poor **walker**

¶少し歩くと、すぐ足が疲れます。
（Sukoshi arukuto, sugu ashi ga
tsukaremasu.）

¶ **My legs** soon tire after walking just a
little.

¶だれかの足音が聞こえてきました。
（Dare ka no ashioto ga kikoete
kimashita.）

¶ [I] can 〚could〛 hear someone
coming 〚someone's **footsteps**〛.

②[歩くこと]
足が遅い（ashi ga osoi）

② [walking]
be a slow walker

¶山田さんは足が速いですね。もう、
あんなに遠くへ行ってしまいました。
（Yamada san wa ashi ga hayai desune.
Mō anna ni tooku e itte shimaimashita.）

¶ [Mr.] Yamada is a fast **walker**. [He]
has already moved that far away.

あし 脚〔名〕

ashi 〔n〕 **leg**

¶机の脚が折れてしまいました。
（Tsukue no ashi ga orete shimaimashita.）

¶ The desk **leg** is broken.

あじ 味 〔名〕

味がいい (*aji* ga ii) 味が濃い (*aji* ga koi) 味が薄い (*aji* ga usui) 味をみる (*aji* o miru)

¶ このスープはとてもいい味ですね。(Kono sūpu wa totemo ii *aji* desu ne.)

¶ この料理は砂糖やしょう油などで味をつけます。(Kono ryōri wa satō ya shōyu nado de *aji* o tsukemasu.)

あした 〔名〕

¶ あしたは何日ですか。(*Ashita* wa nannichi desu ka?)

¶ あした映画を見に行きませんか。(*Ashita* eiga o mi ni ikimasen ka?)

あす 明日 〔名〕 ☞あした ashita

あずかる 預かる 〔動Ⅰ〕

¶ この荷物を預かってくれる所はないでしょうか。(Kono nimotsu o azukatte kureru tokoro wa nai deshō ka?)

¶ 銀行では1円以上のお金を預かります。(Ginkō de wa ichien ijō no okane o azukarimasu.)

あずける 預ける 〔動Ⅱ〕

¶ 友達に荷物を預けてきました。(Tomodachi ni nimotsu o azukete kimashita.)

¶ 銀行に10万円預けてあります。(Ginkō ni jūman'en azukete arimasu.)

¶ わたしは近所の人に赤ん坊を預けて、働きに行っています。(Watashi wa kinjo no hito ni akanbō o azukete, hataraki ni itte imasu.)

---

aji 〔n〕 **flavor, taste**

taste good // be strongly **flavored** // be weakly **flavored** // to taste (something)

¶ This soup is delicious.

¶ This dish is mainly **flavored** with sugar and soy sauce.

ashita 〔n〕 **tomorrow**

¶ What is the date **tomorrow?**

¶ Won't you go with [me] to see a movie **tomorrow?**

asu 〔n〕 ☞**ashita**

azukaru 〔v I〕 **take charge of, be entrusted with**

¶ Isn't there somewhere that **will look after** this package 〖bag, etc.〗 for me?

¶ Banks **will receive on deposit** money from one yen up.

azukeru 〔v II〕 **place in someone's charge, entrust to**

¶ **I left** my bag 〖luggage, package, etc.〗 **with** a friend.

¶ **I have** a hundred thousand yen **deposited** in the bank.

¶ **I go to work leaving** my baby **in the care of** a neighbor.

あせ　汗〔名〕

汗が出る (ase ga deru) ハンカチで汗をふく (hankachi de ase o fuku)

¶階段を急いで上ったら、汗をかきました。(Kaidan o isoide nobottara, ase o kakimashita.)

ase〔n〕**sweat, perspiration**

to sweat, perspire // wipe off **sweat** with a handkerchief

¶ I hurried up the stairs and got all **sweaty**.

あそこ〔代〕

① [話し手にとっても話し相手に対してもともに隔たりのある関係にある所をさし示す]

¶「あそこでテレビを見ている人はだれですか。」(Asoko de terebi o mite iru hito wa dare desu ka?)「あの人は上田さんです。」(Ano hito wa Ueda san desu.)

¶「どこが玄関ですか。」(Doko ga genkan desu ka?)「あそこが玄関です。」(Asoko ga genkan dcsu.)

② [話し手にとっても話し相手に対してもともに隔たりのある関係にあるものごとの状態や問題の点などをさし示す]

¶山田さんの病気があそこまで進んでいたとはだれも気づきませんでした。(Yamada san no byōki ga asoko made susunde ita to wa dare mo kizukimasen deshita.)

¶中村さんがあそこまで知っているとは思いませんでした。(Nakamura san ga asoko made shitte iru to wa omoimasen deshita.)

⇒ここ **koko**　そこ **soko**　どこ **doko**

asoko〔pron〕**there, over there**

① [indicates a place physically distant from both the speaker and the listener]

¶ "Who is that person watching televison **over there?**"
"That is [Mrs.] Ueda."

¶ "Where is the entryway?"
"The entryway is **over there**."

② [indicates a condition, problem point, etc., psychologically distant from both the speaker and the listener]

¶ No one noticed that [Miss] Yamada's illness had advanced to **that point**.

¶ I didn't think that [Mr.] Nakamura knew **that much** about it.

あそび　遊び〔名〕

¶今度、私の家に遊びに来てください。(Kondo, watashi no ie ni asobi ni kite kudasai.)

asobi〔n〕**play, game**

¶ Please come and visit our home next time.

15

あそぶ 遊ぶ 〔動Ⅰ〕

¶子供が庭で遊んでいます。(Kodomo ga niwa de asonde imasu.)

¶ときどき、トランプをして遊びます。(Tokidoki, toranpu o shite asobimasu.)

¶昨日、新宿へ遊びに行きました。(Kinō, Shinjuku e asobi ni ikimashita.)

¶わたしのうちへ遊びに来てください。(Watashi no uchi e asobi ni kite kudasai.)

あたえる 与える 〔動Ⅱ〕

① [あるものをほかの人にやってその人のものにする]
金を与える (kane o *ataeru*) ほうびを与える (hōbi o *ataeru*)

② [やるべきことを割り当てる]
¶先生は一人一人の学生に別々の問題を与えて答えさせました。(Sensei wa hitorihitori no gakusei ni betsubetsu no mondai o ataete kotaesasemashita.)

¶わたしは与えられた仕事をいつもきちんとします。(Watashi wa ataerareta shigoto o itsumo kichinto shimasu.)

③ [損害などを被らせる]
¶今度の台風は各地に大きな被害を与えました。(Kondo no taifū wa kakuchi ni ookina higai o ataemashita.)

あたたか 温か 〔形動〕

温かな心 (*ataraka* na kokoro) 温かな家庭 (*ataraka* na katei) 温かなコーヒー (*ataraka* na kōhii)
⇒温かい *atatakai*

あたたか 暖か 〔形動〕

暖かな毛布 (*ataraka* na mōfu)

---

asobu 〔vⅠ〕 **play, amuse oneself**

¶ The children **are playing** in the garden 〚yard〛.

¶ Sometimes [we] play cards (literally, **enjoy ourselves** playing cards).

¶ Yesterday I **enjoyed myself** in Shinjuku. Please come and **visit** me.

¶ Please come and **visit** me.

ataeru 〔vⅡ〕 **give; assign; inflict**

① [give, bestow]

give away money // **give** a reward

② [assign]

¶ The teacher **gave** each of the students a different problem to answer.

¶ I always do carefully the work I am **assigned to do**.

③ [inflict, suffer (damage, etc.)]

¶ Each area **suffered** much damage in the last typhoon.

atataka 〔adj-v〕 **warm; kindly**

a **warm** 〚**kindly**〛 heart // a **happy** home // **hot** coffee

atataka 〔adj-v〕 **warm**

a **warm** blanket

¶昨日は穏やかで暖かな日でした。
（Kinō wa odayaka de *atataka* na hi deshita.）

¶ Yesterday was a mild, **warm** day.

¶風邪を引いたので、暖かにして寝ました。（Kaze o hiita node, *atataka* ni shite nemashita.）

¶ Since I caught 〚had caught〛 a cold, I bundled up **warmly** and went to bed.

⇒暖かい *atataka***i**

あたたかい 暖かい〔形〕

atatakai〔adj〕**warm**

暖かい日（*atatakai* hi）暖かい毛布（*atatakai* mōfu）

a **warm** day // a **warm** blanket

¶春が来て、暖かくなりました。（Haru ga kite, atatakaku narimashita.）

¶ Spring has come and it has become **warmer**.

⇒暖か *atataka*

あたたかい 温かい〔形〕

atatakai〔adj〕**warm; kindly**

温かいスープ（*atatakai* sūpu）温かい家庭（*atatakai* katei）

hot soup // a **happy** home, a **happy** family

¶このプールの水は温かいですね。（Kono pūru no mizu wa *atatakai* desu ne.）

¶ The water in this pool **is warm**, isn't it?

¶一郎さんは心の温かい人です。（Ichirō san wa kokoro no *atatakai* hito desu.）

¶ Ichirō is a **warmhearted** person.

⇒温か *atataka*

あたためる 暖める〔動Ⅱ〕

atatameru〔v Ⅱ〕**heat, warm**

¶ストーブをたいて、部屋を暖めました。（Sutōbu o taite, heya o atatamemashita.）

¶ 〚I〛 lighted the (wood or coal) heater and **warmed up** the room.

あたためる 温める〔動Ⅱ〕

atatameru〔v Ⅱ〕**warm, heat up**

¶牛乳を温めて飲みました。（Gyūnyū o atatamete nomimashita.）

¶ 〚I〛 **heated** some milk and drank it.

あたま 頭〔名〕

atama〔n〕**head; brains**

①〔頭部〕
頭を洗う（*atama* o arau）頭を下げる（*atama* o sageru）

① 〔head〕
wash **one's hair** // lower 〚bow〛 **one's head**

¶頭が痛いので、学校を休みました。
(*Atama* ga itai node, gakkō o yasumimashita.)

¶ I stayed home from school because I
have a headache.

② [頭脳、頭の働き]
頭が悪い (*atama* ga warui) 頭を使う
(*atama* o tsukau)

② [brains, intelligence]
be slow **witted** // use **one's head**, think

¶あの学生はとても頭がいいですよ。
(Ano gakusei wa totemo *atama* ga ii desu
yo.)

¶ That student is very **intelligent**.

あたらしい 新しい〔形〕

atarashii 〔adj〕 new; fresh

①[ものごとができたり始まったりし
てから間のない様子]
新しい家 (*atarashii* ie)

① [brand-new]

a **new** house

¶このくつは買ったばかりで、まだ新
しいです。(Kono kutsu wa katta bakari
de, mada *atarashii* desu.)

¶ These shoes are still **new**—I just
bought them.

② [新鮮ないきいきしている様子]
新しい魚 (*atarashii* sakana)

② [fresh]
fresh fish

¶新しい野菜を生で食べるのは、体に
たいへんいいそうです。(*Atarashii*
yasai o nama de taberu no wa, karada ni
taihen ii sō desu.)

¶ They say it's very good for one's
health to eat **fresh**, raw vegetables.

③ [今までにないものが初めてできあ
がる様子]
新しい型の自動車 (*atarashii* kata no
jidōsha)

③ [novel, the latest thing]

a **new**-model car

¶山田さんは新しく家を建てました。
(Yamada san wa atarashiku ie o
tatemashita.)

¶ [Mr.] Yamada built a **new** house.

⇔古い **furui**

あたり 辺り〔名〕

atari 〔n〕 vicinity

¶この辺りは夜になると、寂しくなり
ます。(Kono *atari* wa yoru ni naru to,
sabishiku narimasu.)

¶ It is lonely **around** here after dark.

¶学校の辺りにいい部屋はないでしょ
うか。(Gakkō no *atari* ni ii heya wa
naideshō ka？)

¶ Are there any good rooms available
near the school?

18

＊いつも「この辺り（kono *atari*）」「その辺り（sono *atari*）」「あの辺り」（ano *atari*）」「どの辺り（dono *atari*）」「名詞＋の（no）＋辺り（*atari*）」の形で使う。

＊Always used in the patterns "noun + *no* + *atari*", "*kono atari*" (around here), "*sono atari*" (around there), "*ano atari*" (around there), and "*dono atari*" (whereabouts).

-あたり〔尾〕

-atari 〚suf〛 about, around; per

① [時・所などを表す言葉のあとにつけてだいたいを言うときに使う]

¶次の日曜あたりはどうですか。（Tsugi no nichiyō atari wa dō desu ka？）

① [about, around, approximately (after words expressing time, place, etc.)]

¶ How about next Sunday **or thereabouts** (when making an appointment, etc.)?

¶去年あたりは野菜が安かったのですが、今年は高くなりました。（Kyonen atari wa yasai ga yasukatta no desu ga, kotoshi wa takaku narimashita.）

¶ Last year **or so** vegetables were cheap, but this year they've become expensive.

¶今度、新宿あたりでいっしょに食事をしましょう。（Kondo, Shinjuku atari de issho ni shokuji o shimashō.）

¶ Let's have dinner together next time **somewhere in the** Shinjuku **area**.

② [数や単位などを表す言葉につけて割合や平均を言うときに使う]

¶会費は一人あたり3,000円です。（Kaihi wa hitori atari sanzen'en desu.）

② [per (when added to numbers, units, etc.)]

¶ The dues 〚fee for a group party or outing〛 are three thousand yen **per person**.

¶このひもは1メートルあたりいくらですか。（Kono himo wa ichimētoru atari ikura desu ka？）

¶ How much is this cord 〚string, lace, tape, thong, ribbon, etc.〛 **per** meter?

あたりまえ〔形動、〜の〕

atarimae 〚adj-v, 〜no〛 matter of course; proper

あたりまえのこと（*atarimae* no koto）

a matter of course

¶借りた物を返すのはあたりまえです。（Karita mono o kaesu no wa atarimae desu.）

¶ **It goes without saying** that one should return borrowed articles.

⇒当然 tōzen

あたる 当たる〔動Ⅰ〕

ataru 〚vⅠ〛 hit, touch; hit the mark

①[ぶつかる、触れる]

¶ボールが頭に当たりました。（Bōru ga atama ni atarimashita.）

① [hit, touch]

¶ The ball **hit** [his] head.

② [日の光がそこまで及ぶ]

¶この部屋はよく日が当たって暖かいです。（Kono heya wa yoku hi ga atatte atatakai desu.）

③ [日・光・熱・風などを体に受ける]

¶寒いから、火に当たりましょう。（Samui kara, hi ni atarimashō.）

④ [予想などがそのとおりになる]

¶今日の天気予報は当たりました。（Kyō no tenki-yohō wa atarimashita.）

↔外れる hazureru

⑤ [的中する]

¶ピストルの弾がちょうど真ん中に当たりました。（Pisutoru no tama ga chōdo mannaka ni atarimashita.）

↔外れる hazureru

⑥ [くじで金や賞品などをもらえることになる]

¶くじで100万円当たりました。（Kuji de hyakuman'en atarimashita.）

↔外れる hazureru

あちら 〔代〕

① [話し手にとっても話し相手に対してもともに隔たりのある関係にある方向をさし示す]

¶あちらに見えるのが富士山です。（Achira ni mieru no ga Fujisan desu.）

¶「新宿へ行く電車のホームはどちらですか。」（Shinjuku e iku densha no hōmu wa dochira desu ka?）「あちらのホームです。」（Achira no hōmu desu.）

*話し手・話し相手のどちらにも身近な関係にない方向をさし示すのに使う。

② [話し手にとっても話し相手に対してもともに隔たりのある関係にある方向に存在する所をさし示す]

---

② [sunlight reaches a certain point]

¶ This room is warm as it gets much sun.

③ [be in the path of sunlight, light, heat, wind, etc.]

¶ As it's cold **let's warm ourselves** at the fire.

④ [a prediction, etc., is proven right]

¶ Today's weather report **was correct**.

⑤ [hit the mark]

¶ The pistol bullet **hit** exactly in the middle.

⑥ [win money, a prize, etc., in a lottery]

¶ [I] **won** 1 million yen in a lottery.

achira 〔pron〕 there; that

① [indicates a direction distant from both the speaker and the listener]

¶ The mountain you can see **over there** is Mount Fuji.

¶ "Which is the platform for the train going to Shinjuku?" "It's **that** platform **over there**."

*Used to indicate a direction not close physically to either the speaker or the listener.

② [indicates a place distant from both the speaker and the listener]

¶ここは危ないですから、あちらで遊びなさい。(Koko wa abunai desu kara, *achira* de asobinasai.)

¶北海道の山田さんからのお便りによると、あちらはまだときどき雪が降るそうです。(Hokkaidō no Yamada san kara no otayori ni yoru to, *achira* wa mada tokidoki yuki ga furu sō desu.)

*話し手・話し相手のどちらにも身近な関係にない方向に存在する所をさし示す。東京にいる話し手が同じ東京にいる話し相手に対して北海道のことについて言う場合は「あちら(*achira*)」と言う。

③[話し手にとっても話し相手に対してもともに隔たりのある関係にある方向に存在する人をさし示す]

¶こちらは山田さんで、あちらは田中さんです。(Kochira wa Yamada san de, *achira* wa Tanaka san desu.)

¶このことについては、あちら様では何とおっしゃっていますか。(Kono koto ni tsuite wa, *achira* sama de wa nan to osshatte imasu ka?)

*話し手・話し相手のどちらにも身近な関係にない方向にいる人をさし示すのに使う。現に話題になっている先方の人も「あちら(*achira*)」または「あちら様(*achira* sama)」と言う。

④[話し手にとっても話し相手に対してもともに隔たりのある関係にある方向に存在するものをさし示す]

¶こちらは山田さんので、あちらは田中さんのです。(Kochira wa Yamada san no de, *achira* wa Tanaka san no desu.)

¶ Play **over there** because it's dangerous here.

¶ According to what I hear from [Miss] Yamada in Hokkaido, it still snows **there** sometimes.

*Indicates a place not close physically to either the speaker or the listener. A speaker in Tokyo talking to someone who is also in Tokyo will refer to Hokkaido as *achira*.

③ [indicates a person distant from both the speaker and the listener]

¶ This is [Mrs.] Yamada and that is [Mr.] Tanaka.

¶ What do **they** have to say concerning this matter (very polite)?

*Used to indicate a person not close physically to either the speaker or the listener. A person not present whose identity is known to both the speaker and the listener can also be referred to as *achira* or *achira sama*.

④ [indicates something distant from both the speaker and the listener]

¶ This is [Mrs.] Yamada's and **that** is [Mr.] Tanaka's.

¶あちらのほうがおいしそうですから、あちらを5個ください。(*Achira* no hō ga oishisō desu kara, *achira* o goko kudasai.)

¶ Those over there look better; give me five of **them**.

＊「あっち（atchi）」とも言うが、「あちら（achira）」のほうが丁寧な言葉である。

＊*Atchi* is also used in conversation, but *achira* is more polite.

⇒こちら **kochira** そちら **sochira** どちら **dochira**

あつい 暑い〔形〕

atsui 〔adj〕 **hot, warm**

¶今日は暑いですね。(Kyō wa *atsui* desu ne.)

¶ **It's hot** today, isn't it?

¶昼間は暑かったが、夕方から涼しくなりました。(Hiruma wa atsukatta ga, yūgata kara suzushiku narimashita.)

¶ **It was hot** during the day, but it's cooled off this evening 〚it cooled off during the evening〛.

⇔寒い **samui**

あつい 熱い〔形〕

atsui 〔adj〕 **hot, heated**

¶熱いお茶を一杯ください。(*Atsui* ocha o ippai kudasai.)

¶ Please give me a cup of **hot** (green) tea.

¶おふろが熱かったら、水を入れてください。(Ofuro ga atsukattara, mizu o irete kudasai.)

¶ If the bath **is too hot**, please add some cold water.

⇔冷たい **tsumetai**

あつい 厚い〔形〕

atsui 〔adj〕 **thick**

厚い本 (*atsui* hon) 厚い壁 (*atsui* kabe)

a **thick** book // a **thick** wall; a **major** obstacle

¶この辞書はずいぶん厚いですね。(Kono jisho wa zuibun *atsui* desu ne.)

¶ This dictionary **is** very **thick**.

¶冬は厚いセーターを着ます。(Fuyu wa *atsui* sētā o kimasu.)

¶ In the winter everyone wears 〚I wear〛 **heavy** sweaters.

⇔薄い **usui**

あつかう 扱う〔動 I〕

atsukau 〔v I〕 **handle; deal with**

①[受け付ける、仕事としてそれをする]

① [handle, accept, transact (business)]

¶郵便局では貯金も扱っています。
（Yūbinkyoku de wa chokin mo atsukatte imasu.）
②[操作する、取り扱う]
¶わたしはこの機械の扱い方がわかりません。（Watashi wa kono kikai no atsukaikata ga wakarimasen.）
③[待遇する]
客を丁寧に扱う（kyaku o teinei ni *atsukau*）扱いにくい人（atsukainikui hito）

¶ Post offices **handle** savings accounts too.

② [handle, work (something)]
¶ I don't know how **to work** this machine.

③ [treat, deal with]
treat a customer 〚guest〛 politely // a person hard **to deal with**, a difficult person

あっち〔代〕 ☞あちら achira

あつまる 集まる〔動Ⅰ〕

¶あした10時に駅前に集まってください。（Ashita jūji ni ekimae ni atsumatte kudasai.）
¶ここは夏になると、人がたくさん集まってきます。（Koko wa natsu ni naruto, hito ga takusan atsumatte kimasu.）
¶会費は全部集まりました。（Kaihi wa zenbu atsumarimashita.）

atchi〔pron〕 ☞achira

atsumaru〔v Ⅰ〕**gather together, be collected**

¶ Please **assemble** in front of the station at ten o'clock tomorrow.

¶ In summer lots of people **flock to** this place.

¶ The dues 〚fees〛 have all **been collected**.

あつめる 集める〔動Ⅱ〕
お金を集める（okane o *atsumeru*）
¶わたしは切手を集めています。（Watashi wa kitte o atsumete imasu.）
¶友達を集めて、パーティーを開きました。（Tomodachi o atsumete, pātii o hirakimashita.）

atsumeru〔v Ⅱ〕**gather, collect**
collect 〚raise〛 money
¶ I **collect** stamps.

¶ [We] **got** [our] friends **together** and had a party.

あてな あて名〔名〕

手紙にあて名を書く（tegami ni atena o kaku）

atena〔n〕**recipient's name (on an envelope or postcard)**
to address a letter (that is, write **the recipient's name**)

23

あてる　充てる〔動II〕

¶夜は勉強の時間に充てています。
（Yoru wa benkyō no jikan ni atete imasu.）
¶月給の2割を家賃に充てています。
（Gekkyū no niwari o yachin ni atete imasu.）

ateru 〔v II〕 **assign, allocate**

¶[My] evenings **are set aside** for study.

¶Twenty percent of [my] (monthly) wages is allocated to rent.

あてる　当てる〔動II〕

① [あるものをほかのものに触れさせる]
額に手を当てる（hitai ni te o *ateru*）

② [言い当てる]
¶この箱の中に何が入っているか、当ててごらんなさい。（Kono hako no naka ni nani ga haitte iru ka, atete goran nasai.）
③ [割り当てる]
¶先生は一人一人に当てて本を読ませました。（Sensei wa hitorihitori ni atete hon o yomasemashita.）
④ [日や風などに触れさせる]
布団を日に当てる（futon o hi ni *ateru*）
風に当てて乾かす（kazeni atete kawakasu）
¶フィルムは日に当てないようにしてください。（Firumu wa hi ni atenai yō ni shite kudasai.）

ateru 〔v II〕 **apply, strike; guess; call on; expose to**

① [apply, strike; touch something to something]
lay one's hand on one's 〚someone else's〛 forehead

② [guess]
¶Try **to guess** what's in this box!

③ [call on]
¶The teacher **called on** them to read the book one by one.

④ [expose to the sun, wind, etc.]
air out bedding in the sun // **dry** (something) in the breeze

¶Please **keep** the film **from being exposed** to sunlight.

あと〔名〕

① [後ろ]
あとを振り返る（*ato* o furikaeru）
¶わたしのあとから犬がついてきました。（Watashi no *ato* kara inu ga tsuite kimashita.）
→後ろ ushiro

ato 〔n〕 **back, rear; after, later; the rest**

① [back, rear]
look **back**

¶A dog **followed** me.

② [のち]

¶わたしはあとで行きます。（Watashi wa *ato* de ikimasu.）

¶四、五日あとにまた来てください。（Shi, gonichi *ato* ni mata kite kudasai.）

③ [残り、し残したこと]

¶あとはまたあしたやりましょう。（*Ato* wa mata ashita yarimashō.）

¶必要な物だけ残して、あとは捨ててください。（Hitsuyō na mono dake nokoshite, *ato* wa sutete kudasai.）

② [after, **later**]

¶ I'll come later.

¶ Please come again **in** four or five days.

③ [**the rest**]

¶ Let's do **the rest** tomorrow.

¶ Please set aside only what you need and throw away **the rest**.

あな 穴 〔名〕

① [物の表面からくぼんでいる空間]

¶穴を掘って、木を植えました。（*Ana* o hotte, ki o uemashita.）

② [物の向こう側までつきぬけている空間]

¶シャツに穴があきました。（Shatsu ni *ana* ga akimashita.）

¶くつの底に穴があいてしまいました。（Kutsu no soko ni *ana* ga aite shimaimashita.）

ana 〔n〕 **hole**

① [a depression in a surface]

¶ I dug **a hole** and planted a tree.

② [a hole in something]

¶ There is **a hole** in the shirt 〖undershirt〗.

¶ I have **a hole** in the bottom of my shoe.

あなた 〔代〕

あなたがた（*anata*gata）あなたたち（*anata*tachi）

¶あなたは田中さんですか。（*Anata* wa Tanaka san desu ka？）

¶あなたのお国はどちらですか。（*Anata* no okuni wa dochira desu ka？）

¶これをあなたに上げましょう。（Kore o *anata* ni agemashō.）

＊目上の人に対してはあまり言わない。例えば先生などに対しては「あなた（*anata*）」と言わないで、「先生（sensei）」と言うほうがよい。「あなた（*anata*）」は、自分と同じ程度の人、または目下の人に対して使う。「-がた（-

anata 〔pron〕 **you**

you (plural) // **you** (plural)

¶ Are **you** [Miss] Tanaka?

¶ What country are **you** from?

¶ I am giving this to **you**.

＊Not used so much toward persons of higher status. For example, one should address a teacher or doctor as s*ensei rather than anata. Anata* is used toward those of the same or lower status but is usually omitted if

gata）」「-たち（-tachi）」は複数を表
す。「-たち（tachi）」より「-がた（-
gata）」のほうが丁寧な言い方である。

understood from context. For the
plural, *-gata* and *-tachi* are used; the
former is more polite.

あに 兄〔名〕

¶わたしには兄が二人います。
（Watashi ni wa *ani* ga futari imasu.）
¶上の兄は医者で、二番めの兄は大学
の先生をしています。（Ue no *ani* wa
isha de, nibanme no *ani* wa daigaku no
sensei o shite imasu.）
＊自分の兄のことを他人に話す場合に
使う。直接、兄に呼びかける場合や、
他人の兄のことを言う場合は、「お兄
さん（oniisan）」と言う。
⇔弟 otōto
⇒お兄さん oniisan

ani 〔n〕 **elder brother**

¶I have two **older brothers**.

¶My eldest **brother** is a doctor and my
next eldest is a university professor.

＊Used to refer to one's own brother
when talking with others. When
directly addressing one's elder brother
or referring to someone else's elder
brother, *oniisan* is used.

あね 姉〔名〕

¶わたしには姉が三人います。
（Watashi ni wa *ane* ga sannin imasu.）
¶いちばん上の姉は銀行に勤めていま
す。（Ichiban ue no *ane* wa ginkō ni
tsutomete imasu.）
＊自分の姉のことを他人に話す場合に
使う。直接、姉に呼びかける場合や、
他人の姉のことを言う場合は、「お姉
さん（onēsan）」と言う。
⇔妹 imōto
⇒お姉さん onēsan

ane 〔n〕 **elder sister**

¶I have three **older sisters**.

¶My oldest **sister** works at a bank.

＊Used to refer to one's own sister
when talking to others. When directly
addressing one's elder sister or when
referring to someone else's elder sister,
onēsan is used.

あの〔連体〕

①［話し手にとっても話し相手に対し
てもともに隔たりのあるものごととの
関係をさし示す］
あの人（*ano* hito）あの方（*ano* kata）

ano 〔attrib〕 **that, those**

① [indicates something distant from
both the speaker and the listener]

that person // **that** person
(more polite)

26

¶「あの机の上に何がありますか。」
（*Ano* tsukue no ue ni nani ga arimasu
ka？）「かばんがあります。」（Kaban
ga arimasu.）

¶ "What is on **that** desk?"
"A bag 〖briefcase, etc.〗."

¶「あの人はだれですか。」（*Ano* hito
wa dare desu ka？）「あの人は中村さん
です。」（*Ano* hito wa Nakamura san
desu.）

¶ "Who is **that** person over there?"
"**That** is [Miss] Nakamura."

¶「あの方はどなたですか。」（*Ano*
kata wa donata desu ka？）「あの方は上
田先生です。」（*Ano* kata wa Ueda sensei
desu.）

¶ "Who is **that** person over there?"
(more polite).
"**That** is Professor Ueda."

*話し手・話し相手にともに身近では
ないものごととの関係をさし示すのに
使う。

*Used for something not physically
close to either the speaker or the
listener.

② [文脈の上で前に述べたものごとと
話し手・話し相手との隔たりのある関
係をさし示す]

② [indicates something mentioned
earlier that is distant from both the
speaker and the listener]

¶「中村さんや田中さんもお金が足り
なくて困っていますか。」（Nakamura
san ya Tanaka san mo okane ga tarinakute
komatte imasu ka？）「いいえ、あの人
たちはお金には困っていません。」
（Iie, *ano* hitotachi wa okane ni wa
komatte imasen.）

¶ "Are [Mr.] Nakamura and [Miss]
Tanaka troubled by a lack of money?"
"No, they (literally, those people) have
enough money."

¶戦争中は物がなくてずいぶん苦労し
ました。あの時のことは忘れられませ
ん。（Sensōchū wa mono ga nakute
zuibun kurō shimashita. *Ano* toki no koto
wa wasureraremasen.）

¶ During the war we suffered greatly
from the scarcity of goods. I will never
forget **that** time.

*文脈的に前に述べたものごととの関
係を話し手・話し相手ともに身近な関
係にはないものとしてさし示すのに使
う。

*Used to indicate that something
mentioned previously is not
psychologically close to either the
speaker or the listener.

③ [話し手にとっても話し相手に対し
てもともに隔たりのある関係にあって
共通に了解されているものごととの関
係をさし示す]

③ [indicates something known to both
the speaker and the listener that is
distant from both of them]

¶「あのことはどうなりましたか。」（*Ano* koto wa dō narimashita ka？）「ああ、あのことはもう解決しましたよ。」（Ā, *ano* koto wa mō kai-ketsu shimashita yo.）

¶ "What happened in regard to that matter?"
"Oh, **that** has already been resolved."

¶去年の夏、北海道で親切な人に会いましたね。あの方は今どうしていらっしゃるかしら。（Kyonen no natsu, Hokkaidō de shinsetsu na hito ni aimashita ne. *Ano* kata wa ima dōshite irassharu kashira？）

¶ Last summer we met that kind person in Hokkaido. I wonder how [he] is now.

⇒この **kono**　その **sono**　どの **dono**

あのう〔感〕

¶あのう、この漢字の意味を教えていただけますか。（Anō, kono kanji no imi o oshiete itadake masu ka?）

anō〔interj〕sir, uh, uhm, er, well

¶ Sir (Madam), can you tell me the meaning of this kanji?

アパート〔名〕

¶わたしはアパートに住んでいます。（Watashi wa apāto ni sunde imasu.）

apāto〔n〕apartment, apartment building

¶ I am living in **an apartment**.

あびる　浴びる〔動Ⅱ〕

湯を浴びる（yu o *abiru*）川で水を浴びる（kawa de mizu o *abiru*）日光を浴びる（nikkō o *abiru*）

¶わたしは毎朝シャワーを浴びます。（Watashi wa maiasa shawā o abimasu.）

abiru〔v Ⅱ〕pour on oneself; bathe in

take a bath // **take** a dip in a river // be **bathed** in sunlight

¶ I **take** a shower every morning.

あぶない　危ない〔形〕

¶危ないから、道の真ん中を歩かないでください。（*Abunai* kara, michi no mannaka o arukanaide kudasai.）

¶ガソリンスタンドの近くでたばこを吸うのは危ないです。（Gasorin-sutando no chikaku de tabako o suu no wa *abunai* desu.）

abunai〔adj〕dangerous

¶ Don't walk in the middle of the street—**it's dangerous**.

¶ **It's dangerous** to smoke near a gasoline station.

あぶら　油 〔名〕

¶機械に油をさしてください。(Kikai ni *abura* o sashite kudasai.)

¶機械を直したので、手が油で汚れました。(Kikai o naoshita node, te ga *abura* de yogoremashita.)

¶料理には油をよく使います。(Ryōri ni wa *abura* o yoku tsukaimasu.)

abura 〔n〕 **oil, grease**

¶ Please **oil** the machine.

¶ [My] hands are all **greasy** because [I] fixed the machine.

¶ One often uses **oil** in cooking.

あふれる 〔動II〕

¶大雨が降って、池の水があふれました。(Ooame ga futte, ike no mizu ga afuremashita.)

¶ビールがコップからあふれてしまいました。(Biiru ga koppu kara afurete shimaimashita.)

afureru 〔v II〕 **overflow**

¶ It rained heavily and the pond **overflowed** its banks.

¶ The beer **ran over** the top of the glass.

あまい　甘い 〔形〕

¶このお菓子はとても甘いです。(Kono okashi wa totemo *amai* desu.)

¶わたしは甘い物より辛い物のほうが好きです。(Watashi wa *amai* mono yori karai mono no hō ga suki desu.)

⇔辛い **karai**

amai 〔adj〕 **to be sweet**

¶ This candy 〖cake, etc.〗 **is** very sweet.

¶ I like salty 〖sharply flavored〗 foods better than **sweet** ones.

あまり　余り 〔名〕

¶魚の余りをねこにやりました。(Sakana no *amari* o neko ni yarimashita.)

amari 〔n〕 **the remaining, the rest, surplus**

¶ I gave the **leftover** fish to the cat.

あまり 〔副〕

① [そんなに、それほど]

¶このバナナはあまりおいしくありません。(Kono banana wa *amari* oishiku arimasen.)

¶わたしはあまりラジオを聞きません。(Watashi wa *amari* rajio o kikimasen.)

amari 〔adv〕 **(not)very; too much**

① [(not) very, (not) so]

¶ This banana does not taste **very** good.

¶ I don't listen to the radio **very much**.

*あとに打ち消しの言葉が来る。「あまり〜ない（amari〜nai）」の形で使う。

②［とても、非常に］

¶あまり急いだので、かぎを忘れてきました。（Amari isoida node, kagi o wasurete kimashita.）

¶あまり無理をすると、病気になりますよ。（Amari muri o suru to, byōki ni narimasu yo.）

¶あまり悲しい映画を見ると、彼女はすぐに泣いてしまいます。（Amari kanashii eiga o miruto, kanojo wa suguni naite shimaimasu.）

*あとに肯定の言葉が来る。

＊「あんまり（anmari）」とも言う。

あまる 余る〔動 I〕

¶まだお金は余っています。（Mada okane wa amatte imasu.）

¶紙を配りますから、余ったら先生に返してください。（Kami o kubarimasu kara, amattara sensei ni kaeshite kudasai.）

あみ 網〔名〕

¶子供たちが網で魚を捕っています。（Kodomotachi ga ami de sakana o totte imasu.）

¶海岸で漁師が網を編んでいます。（Kaigan de ryōshi ga ami o ande imasu.）

あむ 編む〔動 I〕

¶お母さんが子供のセーターを編んでいます。（Okāsan ga kodomo no sātā o ande imasu.）

¶竹を編んで、かごを作ります。（Take o ande, kago o tsukurimasu.）

*Used with the negative. Used in the pattern "amari 〜 -nai."

② [too much, very, extremely]

¶ I was in **such** a hurry that I forgot my key.

¶ You will become ill if you do **so much**.

¶ She starts crying in no time when she sees a really sad movie.

*Used with the positive.

＊Variant: anmari.

amaru 〚v I〛 **remain, be in excess**

¶ There is still some money **left over**.

¶ I am going to hand out paper; **if there is any extra**, please return it to the teacher.

ami 〚n〛 **net**

¶ Children are catching fish in **a net**.

¶ Along the shore fishermen are weaving **nets**.

amu 〚v I〛 **knit, braid, weave**

¶ The mother **is knitting** a sweater for her child.

¶ [They] **weave** bamboo to make baskets.

あめ 雨 〔名〕

¶昨日は雨が降りました。（Kinō wa *ame* ga furimashita.）

¶今日も朝から雨です。（Kyō mo asa kara *ame* desu.）

¶午後になって、雨がやみました。（Gogo ni natte, *ame* ga yamimashita.）

¶雨に降られて、ぬれてしまいました。（*Ame* ni furarete, nurete shimaimashita.）

ame 〔n〕 rain

¶**It rained** yesterday.

¶**It's been raining** from the morning today too.

¶It stopped **raining** in the afternoon.

¶I got wet when I was caught in **the rain**.

あやしい 怪しい 〔形〕

¶この辺で怪しい男を見ませんでしたか。（Kono hen de *ayashii* otoko o mimasen deshita ka?）

ayashii 〔adj〕 questionable, suspicious

¶Didn't you see a **suspicious-looking** man around here?

あやまる 謝る 〔動Ⅰ〕

¶田中さんは「わたしが悪かった。」と言って謝りました。（Tanaka san wa "Watashi ga warukatta." to itte ayamarimashita.）

¶いくら謝っても、山田さんは許してくれませんでした。（Ikura ayamattemo, Yamada san wa yurushite kuremasen deshita.）

ayamaru 〔vⅠ〕 apologize

¶[Mr.] Tanaka **apologized** by saying, "I was at fault."

¶No matter how much **I apologized**, [Miss] Yamada wouldn't forgive me.

あらい 荒い 〔形〕

①〔穏やかでない〕

¶今日は波が荒いので泳げません。（Kyō wa nami ga *arai* node oyogemasen.）

②〔乱暴な様子〕

¶上田さんは道具の使い方が荒いので、何でもすぐ壊してしまいます。（Ueda san wa dōgu no tsukaikata ga *arai* node, nan demo sugu kowashite shimaimasu.）

arai 〔adj〕 rough

① [rough; not calm, gentle, or soft]

¶[We] cannot swim today because the waves **are rough**.

② [rough, rude]

¶Because [Mr.] Ueda is so **rough**, everything [he] uses soon breaks.

あらう 洗う 〔動Ⅰ〕

¶わたしは朝起きて顔を洗います。
（Watashi wa asa okite kao o araimasu.）
¶シャツが汚れたから、洗ってくださ
い。（Shatsu ga yogoreta kara, aratte
kudasai.）

あらそう 争う 〔動Ⅰ〕

① [けんかをする、言い合いをする]
¶兄弟が互いに争うのはよくありませ
ん。（Kyōdai ga tagai ni arasou no wa
yoku arimasen.）
② [競争する]
優勝を争う（yūshō o arasou）
¶田中さんと山田さんはクラスで一番
を争っています。（Tanaka san to
Yamada san wa kurasu de ichiban o
arasotte imasu.）

あらためる 改める 〔動Ⅱ〕

規則を改める（kisoku o *aratameru*）欠
点を改める（ketten o *aratameru*）
¶今年から交通規則が改められまし
た。（Kotoshi kara kōtsū-kisoku ga
aratameraremashita.）
¶その悪い癖は改めたほうがいいです
よ。（Sono warui kuse wa aratameta hō
ga ii desu yo.）

あらわす 現す 〔動Ⅰ〕

¶雲の間から太陽が顔を現しました。
（Kumo no aida kara taiyō ga kao o
arawashimashita.）
¶山田さんはその会議に最後まで姿を
現しませんでした。（Yamada san wa
sono kaigi ni saigo made sugata o
arawashimasen deshita.）

arau 〔vⅠ〕 **wash**

¶I get up in the morning and **wash** my
face.

¶Please **wash** my shirt 〚undershirt〛 as
it is dirty.

arasou 〔vⅠ〕 **argue; compete**

① [argue, quarrel]
¶It is not good for brothers **to quarrel**
with each other.

② [compete]
compete for victory
¶[Mr.] Tanaka and [Miss] Yamada **are
competing for** first place in the class.

aratameru 〔vⅡ〕 **change, reform**

revise the regulations // **mend** one's
faults

¶Traffic regulations **are revised** from
this year.

¶You should **correct** that bad habit.

arawasu 〔vⅠ〕 **show, reveal**

¶The sun **is looking** 〚looked〛 out
from between the clouds.

¶[Mrs.] Yamada **never showed** [her]
self at that meeting.

あらわす　表す〔動Ⅰ〕

¶感謝の気持ちをどのように表したらよいかわかりません。(Kansha no kimochi o dono yō ni arawashitara yoi ka wakarimasen.)

¶この文章には、作者の気持ちがよく表されています。(Kono bunshō ni wa, sakusha no kimochi ga yoku arawasarete imasu.)

arawasu 〔v Ⅰ〕 **show, express**

¶ I don't know how **to express** my gratitude.

¶ The feelings of the author **are** fully **revealed** in these sentences.

あらわれる　現れる〔動Ⅱ〕

¶この辺には、ときどきくまが現れるそうです。(Kono hen ni wa, tokidoki kuma ga *arawareru* sō desu.)

¶舞台の右の方から、一人の漁師が現れました。(Butai no migi no hō kara, hitori no ryōshi ga arawaremashita.)

arawareru 〔v Ⅱ〕 **appear, emerge**

¶ I hear that sometimes bears **come out** in this area.

¶ A fisherman **appeared** from the right side of the stage.

ありがたい〔形〕

¶親切にしていただき、本当にありがたいと思っています。(Shinsetsu ni shite itadaki, hontō ni *arigatai* to omotte imasu.)

arigatai 〔adj〕 **grateful, thankful**

¶ You've been so kind to me; I'm really **grateful**.

ありがとう〔連〕

¶今日は、どうもありがとう。本当に楽しかったです。(Kyō wa, dōmo *arigatō*. Hontō ni tanoshikatta desu.)

¶「けっこうな物をいただきまして、ありがとうございました。」(Kekkō na mono o itadakimashite *arigatō* go-zaimashita.)「いいえ、どういたしまして。」(Iie, dō itashimashite.)

⇒ありがたい **arigatai**

arigatō 〔compd〕 **Thank you**

¶ **Thank you** for today. It was really pleasant.

¶ "**Thank you** very much for this fine gift."
"No, not at all."

ある〔動Ⅰ〕

①[ものなどがある所に存在する]
¶机の上に本があります。(Tsukue no ue ni hon ga arimasu.)

aru 〔v Ⅰ〕 **be, exist; be located; have, possess; take place**

① [there is, there are, exist, be found]
¶ **There is** a book on the desk.

¶どこかに貸家はありませんか。
（Doko ka ni kashiya wa arimasen ka？）

② [ものなどがある所に位置する]

¶富士山は東京の西にあります。
（Fujisan wa Tōkyō no nishi ni arimasu.）

¶家の後ろに川があります。（Ie no ushiro ni kawa ga arimasu.）

③ [あるものがあるものに付属して存在する]

¶その家には広い庭があります。
（Sono ie ni wa hiroi niwa ga arimasu.）

¶この家にはふろ場がありません。
（Kono ie ni wa furoba ga arimasen.）

④ [あるものがあるものに含まれている]

¶この本にはおもしろい話がたくさんあります。（Kono hon ni wa omoshiroi hanashi ga takusan arimasu.）

⑤ [時間・距離・重さ・広さなどがどの程度あるかを表す]

¶時間がありませんから、急いでください。（Jikan ga arimasen kara, isoide kudasai.）

¶夏休みはどのくらいありますか。
（Natsuyasumi wa dono kurai arimasu ka？）

¶この荷物は何キロぐらいあるでしょうか。（Kono nimotsu wa nankiro gurai *aru* deshō ka？）

¶部屋の広さはどのくらいありますか。（Heya no hirosa wa dono kurai arimasu ka？）

⑥ [人があるものを持っている]
¶わたしはお金がありません。
（Watashi wa okane ga arimasen.）

¶ **Isn't there** a house to rent somewhere?

② [be located, stand, lie, etc.]

¶ Mount Fuji **lies** to the west of Tokyo.

¶ A river **runs** behind the house.

③ [have, possess, be equipped with]

¶ That house **has** a large garden 〚yard〛.

¶ This house **doesn't have** a Japanese bath.

④ [be contained in, be included in]

¶ This book **contains** many interesting stories.

⑤ [number, weigh, measure (in regard to time, distance, weight, width, etc.)]

¶ There **isn't** any time to spare so please hurry.

¶ How long **is** the summer vacation?

¶ How many kilograms does this package **weigh**?

¶ How big **is** the room?

⑥ [possess, be blessed with]
¶ I **don't have** any money.

¶私の部屋には本がたくさんありま
す。（Watashi no heya ni wa hon ga
takusan *ari*masu.）

¶ There are many books in my room.

¶彼は音楽の才能があります。（Kare
wa ongaku no sainō ga arimasu.）

¶ He **is endowed with** musical talent.

⑦［あることが行われる］

⑦ [take place]

¶あしたは試験があります。（Ashita
wa shiken ga arimasu.）

¶ [We] **have** a test tomorrow.

¶学校は4時まであります。（Gakkō wa
yoji made arimasu.）

¶ [We] **have** school until four o'clock.

¶今日は、午前中に会議がありまし
た。（Kyō wa, gozenchū ni kaigi ga
arimashita.）

¶ [I] **had a** meeting this morning.

⑧［あることが発生する、ある事態な
どが起こる］

⑧ [happen, occur]

¶昨日、ここで交通事故がありまし
た。（Kinō, koko de kōtsū-jiko ga
arimashita.）

¶ A traffic accident **took place** here
yesterday.

¶ゆうべ、大きな地震がありました。
（Yūbe, ookina jishin ga arimashita.）

¶ **There was** a large earthquake last
night.

¶山田さんからさっき電話がありまし
たよ。（Yamada san kara sakki denwa ga
arimashita yo.）

¶ **There was** a telephone call from
[Mr.] Yamada a little while ago.

⑨［ときどきあることをする、ときど
きある状態になる］

⑨ [occasional occurrence]

¶おふろに入る前に御飯を食べること
があります。（Ofuro ni hairu mae ni
gohan o taberu koto ga arimasu.）

¶ **There are times** when [I] eat before
taking a bath.

¶外国に一人で住んでいると、寂しい
ことがあります。（Gaikoku ni hitori de
sunde iru to, sabishii koto ga arimasu.）

¶ When one lives alone in a foreign
country, **sometimes** one is lonely.

＊「動詞・形容詞（連体の形）＋こと
が（も）ある（koto ga〔mo〕 *aru*）」
の形で使う。

＊Used in the pattern "verb or adjective
(dictionary form) + *koto ga*〖*mo*〗aru."

⑩［あることがらの経験がある］

⑩ [have the experience of]

35

¶あの人には、前に一度会ったことが
あります。(Ano hito ni wa, mae ni
ichido atta koto ga arimasu.)

¶I **have** met [him] once before.

¶わたしは日本へ行ったことがありま
せん。(Watashi wa Nihon e itta koto ga
arimasen.)

¶I **have never** been to Japan.

*「動詞・形容詞（たの形）＋ことが
（も）ある（koto ga［mo］ *aru*)」の形
で使う。

*Used in the pattern "verb or adjective
(-*ta* form) + *koto ga*〚*mo*〛*aru*."

ある 〔連体〕
ある日（*aru* hi）ある人（*aru* hito）

aru 〔attrib〕 **a certain, some**
one day〚a **certain** day〛// **some**one〚a
certain person〛

¶田中さんはある学校で数学を教えて
います。(Tanaka san wa *aru* gakkō de
sūgaku o oshiete imasu.)

¶[Miss] Tanaka is teaching
mathematics at a school **somewhere**
〚at a **certain** school〛.

（〜て）ある 〔連〕

(-te)aru 〔compd〕 **being in the
state of -ing**

¶壁に絵が掛けてあります。(Kabe ni e
ga kakete arimasu.)

¶There **is** a picture **hanging** on the
wall.

¶暑いので、戸が開けてあります。
(Atsui node, to ga akete arimasu.)

¶The door **is standing open** be-cause
it's so hot.

*「他動詞（ての形）＋ある（aru)」
の形で使う。

*Used in the pattern "transitive verb (-
te form) + *aru*."

⇒（〜て）いる（〜**te**) **iru**

あるく　歩く 〔動Ⅰ〕

aruku 〔v Ⅰ〕 **walk**

¶ここから駅まで歩いて10分かかりま
す。(Koko kara eki made, aruite jippun
kakarimasu.)

¶It takes 10 minutes **to walk** from here
to the station.

¶日本では、人は道の右側を歩きま
す。(Nihon de wa, hito wa michi no
migigawa o arukimasu.)

¶In Japan people **walk** on the right-
hand side of the road.

アルバイト 〔名、〜する〕

arubaito 〔n〕 **part-time job, side
job**

¶私はアルバイトをしながら大学に
通っています。(Watashi wa *arubaito* o
shinagara daigaku ni kayotte imasu.)

¶I go to college while doing a part-
time job.

あれ 〔代〕

① [話し手からも話し相手からもともに隔っていると認められるものごとをさし示す]

¶「あれは何ですか。」（*Are* wa nan desu ka？）「あれは郵便局です。」（*Are* wa yūbinkyoku desu.）

¶「壁に掛けてあるのはだれの写真ですか。（Kabe ni kakete aru no wa d*are* no shashin desu ka？）「あれはわたしの両親の写真です。」（*Are* wa watashi no ryōshin no shashin desu.）

*話し手が「あれ（*are*）」でさし示すものは話し相手も「あれ（*are*）」でさし示す。

② [話題に上ったある人を対等以下の人としてさし示すのに使う]

¶山田君、あれは信用ができない男ですよ。（Yamada kun？*Are* wa shin'yō ga dekinai otoko desu yo.）

*その場にいない人をさし示すことが多い。

③ [文脈の上で前に述べたものごとを心理的・時間的に隔たりのある関係にあるものとして回想的にさし示す]

¶去年山に登った時、深い谷へ落ちそうになりました。あれを思うと、もう山へは登る気がしません。（Kyonen yama ni nobotta toki, fukai tani e ochisō ni narimashita. *Are* o omoutto, mō yama e wa noboru ki ga shimasen.）

④ [文脈の上で前に述べた心理的・時間的に隔たりのある過去のことがらの成立した時をさし示す]

¶上田さんとは3年前に京都で別れました。あれから一度も会っていません。（Ueda san to wa sannen mae ni

are 〔pron〕 **that, that one**

① [indicates something judged to be physically distant from both the speaker and the listener]

¶ "What is **that**?"
"**That** is the post office."

¶ "Whose photograph is that hanging on the wall?"
"**That** is a photograph of my parents."

*When the speaker refers to something as *are*, the listener also refers to it as *are*.

② [used to indicate that someone who comes up in conversation is a person of equal or lower status]

¶ Yamada? **That's** a man who can't be trusted.

*Usually used to refer to someone who is not present.

③ [used to indicate that something mentioned earlier is distant psychologically or in terms of time]

¶ When I was mountain climbing last year I almost fell into a deep ravine. When I think about **that**, I don't feel like climbing mountains any more.

④ [indicates a certain time in the past referred to earlier that is distant psychologically or in terms of time]

¶ I parted from [Mr.] Ueda three years ago in Kyoto. I haven't met [him] at all since **that time**.

Kyōto de wakaremashita. *Are* kara ichido
mo atte imasen.)

⑤ [話し手にとっても話し相手に対し
てもともに隔たりのある関係にあって
共通に了解されているものごとをさし
示す]

¶「先日お願いしたあれはどうなりま
したか。」(Senjitsu onegai shita *are* wa
dō narimashita ka？)「あの本ですか。
あれはまだ田中さんが返してくれませ
ん。もう少し待ってください。」(Ano
hon desu ka？ *Are* wa mada Tanaka san
ga kaeshite kuremasen. Mō sukoshi matte
kudasai.)

⇒これ **kore** それ **sore** どれ **dore**

あれる 荒れる〔動Ⅱ〕

① [穏やかでなくなる]
¶台風が近づいたので、海が荒れてい
ます。(Taifū ga chikazuita node, umi ga
arete imasu.)
② [手入れなどをしなくてひどい状態
になる]
手が荒れる (te ga *areru*) 肌が荒れる
(hada ga *areru*)
¶この家はずいぶん荒れていますね。
(Kono ie wa zuibun arete imasune.)

あわせる 合わせる〔動Ⅱ〕

① [二つ以上のものを一つにする]

手を合わせる (te o *awaseru*) 声を合わ
せる (koe o *awaseru*) 心を合わせる
(kokoro o *awaseru*)
¶橋を架けるために、みんなが力を合
わせて働きました。(Hashi o kakeru
tame ni, minna ga chikara o awasete
hatarakimashita.)

⑤ [indicates something known to both
the listener and the speaker that is
distant from them]

¶ "What happened in regard to **that
matter** that I asked you to take care of
the other day?"
"That book? [Mrs.] Tanaka hasn't
returned it to me yet. Please wait a
little longer."

areru 〔v Ⅱ〕 **become rough; fall
   into decay**

① [become rough, cease being calm]
¶ The sea **is rough** because a typhoon
is approaching.

② [fall into decay, fall into a bad state
from neglect, etc.]
get roughened 〚**chapped**〛 **hands** //
get roughened 〚**chapped**〛 **skin**
¶ This house **has** really **been neglected**.

awaseru 〔v Ⅱ〕 **combine; adjust;
   compare**

① [combine; put together two or more
things]
put one's hands **together** (in worship,
etc.) // speak **as one**; sing **in chorus** //
cooperate warmly, **be united**
¶ Everyone **combined** their strength to
raise the bridge.

② [あるものに適合させる、一致させる]

¶時計の針を駅の時計に合わせました。(Tokei no hari o eki no tokei ni awasemashita.)

¶ピアノに合わせて歌いましょう。(Piano ni awasete utaimashō.)

③ [二つのものを比べる、照らし合わせる]

¶答えを合わせてみました。(Kotae o awasete mimashita.)

② [adjust, set, adapt]

¶ [I] **set** [my] watch by the station clock (past action).

¶ Let's sing **accompanied by** the piano.

③ [compare two things]

¶ [They] **checked** [their] answers 〚**compared** their answers among themselves〛.

あわてる 〔動 II〕

¶どろぼうはあわてて逃げました。(Dorobō wa awatete nigemashita.)

¶あまりあわてたので、財布を忘れました。(Amari awateta node, saifu o wasuremashita.)

¶そんなにあわてなくても、時間はじゅうぶんあります。(Sonna ni awate-nakute mo, jikan wa jūbun arimasu.)

awateru 〔v II〕 **be flustered, be hurried**

¶ The thief **panicked** and ran.

¶ **I was in** such **a hurry** 〚**I was** so **flustered**〛 that I forgot my wallet.

¶ There is plenty of time so you don't need to be **in** such **a hurry**.

あんがい 案外 〔副、形動〕

案外に安い (*angai* ni yasui)

¶この本は案外安いですね。(Kono hon wa *angai* yasui desu ne.)

¶この計画は案外うまくいくかもしれません。(Kono keikaku wa *angai* umaku iku ka mo shiremasen.)

angai 〔adv, adj-v〕 **contrary to expectation, unexpectedly**

surprisingly inexpensive

¶ This book is cheaper **than one would expect**.

¶ This plan might work out **surprisingly** well.

あんしん 安心 〔名、〜する〕

¶いい報告を聞いて安心しました。(Ii hōkoku o kiite *anshin* shimashita.)

¶合格の発表を見るまでは安心できません。(Gōkaku no happyō o miru made wa *anshin* dekimasen.)

anshin 〔n, 〜*suru*〕 **ease, relief, complacency, be at ease**

¶ I am relieved to hear the good news.

¶ **I'll have no peace** until I've seen the announcement of those who have passed the examination.

あんぜん　安全〔名、形動〕

交通安全（kōtsū-anzen）

¶彼の方が運転が上手なので、私よりも彼が運転した方が安全です。（Kare no hō ga unten ga jōzuna node watashi yorimo kare ga untenshita hō ga *anzen* desu.）

⇔危険 kiken

---

anzen〔n, adj-v〕**safety**

traffic safety

¶**It will be safe** if [they] play in the park.

あんてい　安定〔名、〜する〕

¶次第に物価が安定してきました。（Shidai ni bukka ga *antei* shite kimashita.）

---

antei〔n, 〜*suru*〕**stability, stabiliza-tion**

¶Prices have gradually stabilized〖Prices gradually **stabilized**〗.

あんな〔連体〕

①[話し手にとっても話し相手に対してもともに隔たりのある関係にあるものごとの状態をさし示す]

¶あんないい家に住んでみたいです。（*Anna* ii ie ni sunde mitai desu.）

*話し手・話し相手にともに身近な関係にないものごとの状態をさし示すのに使う。

②[文脈の上で前に述べたものごとの状態を話し手にとっても話し相手に対してもともに隔たりのある関係でさし示す]

¶上田さんは田中さんにとてもひどいことを言うんです。上田さんがあんな人だとは思いませんでした。（Ueda san wa Tanaka san ni totemo hidoi koto o iu n desu. Ueda san ga *anna* hito da to wa omoimasen deshita.）

⇒こんな konna　そんな sonna
どんな donna

---

anna〔attrib〕**such, that sort of**

① [indicates something distant from both the speaker and the listener]

¶I would like to live in **that sort** of nice house.

*Used to indicate a condition not psychologically close for either the speaker or the listener.

② [indicates something mentioned earlier that is distant from both the speaker and the listener]

¶[Mr.] Ueda said some terrible things to [Mr.] Tanaka. I didn't think that [he] was **that sort** of person.

あんない 案内〔名、〜する〕

案内人（*annai*nin）案内所（*annai*jo）
道を案内する（michi o *annai* suru）

¶京都を案内していただけませんか。
（Kyōto o *annai* shite itadakemasenka？）

annai〔n, 〜*suru*〕 guidance; information

a guide // an information office 〚desk, counter〛 // show (someone) the way

¶ Won't you show [us] around Kyoto?

あんなに〔副〕

¶山田さんはあんなに金持ちなのに、とてもけちです。（Yamada san wa *anna ni* kanemochi na noni, totemo kechi desu.）
¶あんなに驚いたのは初めてです。（*Anna ni* odoroita no wa hajimete desu.）
¶あんなに謝っているのですから、今度だけは許してあげましょう。（*Anna ni* ayamatte iru no desu kara, kondo dake wa yurushite agemashō.）
＊話し手にとっても話し相手に対してもともに隔たりのある関係にあるものごとの程度や状態をさし示すのに使う。
⇒こんなに **konnani** そんなに **sonnani** どんなに **donna ni**

anna ni〔adv〕 in that way, to that extent

¶ Even though [Mrs.] Yamada is so rich, [she] is very stingy.

¶ I've never been so surprised.

¶ Since [he] has apologized so much, let's forgive [him] this one time.

＊Used to indicate the degree or condition of something at a distance from both the speaker and the listener.

あんまり〔副〕　☞**あまり amari**

anmari〔adv〕　☞**amari**

い

い 胃 〔名〕
胃腸 (ichō)
¶最近、少し胃の調子が悪いです。
(Saikin, sukoshi i no chōshi ga warui
desu.)
¶あの子は胃が丈夫です。(Ano ko wa
i ga jōbu desu.)

いい 〔形〕

① [正しい立派な様子]
¶困っている人を助けることはいいこ
とですよ。(Komatte iru hito o tasukeru
koto wa ii koto desu yo.)
¶いいと思ったことは、勇気を出して
おやりなさい。(Ii to omotta kotowa,
yūki o dashite oyarinasai.)
⇔悪い warui
→よい yoi

② [善良である様子]
¶上田さんは親切ないい人です。
(Ueda san wa shinsetsu na ii hito desu.)
⇔悪い warui
→よい yoi

③ [親しい様子]
¶山田さんと中村さんは仲がいいで
す。(Yamada san to Nakamura san wa
naka ga ii desu.)
*普通「仲がいい (naka ga ii)」の形で
使う。
⇔悪い warui
→よい yoi

④ [ものごとの優れている様子]
いい声 (ii koe) いい品物 (ii
shinamono) いい習慣 (iishūkan)

i 〔n〕 stomach

stomach and intestines
¶ [I] have recently been having some
stomach trouble.

¶ That child has a strong stomach
〖good digestion〗.

ii 〔adj〕 good, right; excellent,
fine; suitable
① [good, right]
¶ It is good to help those who are in
trouble.

¶ Be brave and do what you think is
right.

② [good, good-natured]
¶ [Mrs.] Ueda is a kind and good
person.

③ [good, close, intimate]
¶ [Mr.] Yamada and [Mr.] Nakamura
are on good terms with each other.

*Usually used in the pattern "naka ga
ii."

④ [good, excellent, fine]
a fine voice // good merchandise // a
good custom 〖habit〗

42

¶あの子はたいへん頭がいいです。
（Ano ko wa taihen atama ga iidesu.）

¶中村さんは2学期はたいへんいい成績
でした。（Nakamura san wa nigakki wa
taihen ii seiseki deshita.）

⇔悪い **warui**

→よい **yoi**

⑤ [好ましい様子、気持ちのよい様子]
景色がいい（keshiki ga ii）気分がいい
（kibun ga ii）

¶今日はいい天気です。（Kyō wa ii
tenki desu.）

¶この店は感じのいい店ですね。
（Kono mise wa kanji no ii mise desu ne.）

¶少しお酒を飲んで、いい気持ちにな
りました。（Sukoshi osake o nonde, ii
kimochi ni narimashita.）

⇔悪い **warui**

→よい **yoi**

⑥ [感情的に望ましい様子]

¶お母さんの病気が早くよくなるとい
いですね。（Okāsan no byōki ga hayaku
yoku naru to ii desu ne.）

⑦ [適当で望ましいと思う様子]

¶あんな所へは二度と行かないほうが
いいですよ。（Anna tokoro e wa nido to
ikanai hō ga ii desu yo.）

¶わたしはこちらのほうがいいです。
（Watashi wa kochira no hō ga ii desu.）

*普通「ほうがいい（hō ga ii）」の形で
使う。

⑧ [好都合な様子、ほどよい様子]

¶ That child is very **bright**.

¶ [Miss] Nakamura got very **good**
grades the second semester.

⑤ [good. fine, pleasing, nice]
a **nice** view // be in a **good** mood, feel
good

¶ It's a **beautiful** day today.

¶ This shop 〖restaurant, bar, etc.〗 has a
nice feel about it.

¶ [I] drank a little and felt **good**.

⑥ [it would be good if ～, I hope, I
wish]

¶ **I hope** your mother recovers quickly
from her illness

⑦ [be better, prefer]

¶ **It would be best** not to go to that
sort of place a second time.

¶ **I prefer** this one.

*Usually used in the pattern "～ *hō ga
ii*."

⑧ [good, proper, suitable]

¶この辞書は小さくて、持って歩くのにはちょうどいいです。（Kono jisho wa chiisakute, motte aruku no ni wa chōdo ii desu.）

¶このシャツはあなたにちょうどいい大きさです。（Kono shatsu wa anata ni chōdo ii ookisa desu.）

⑨ [じゅうぶんである様子]

¶今度の旅行には、どのぐらいお金を持って行けばいいでしょう。（Kondo no ryokō ni wa, dono gurai okane o motte ikeba ii deshō？）

→よい **yoi**

⑩ [あるものごとに対して効果がある様子]

健康にいい体操（kenkō ni ii taisō）

¶この薬は風邪にたいへんいいですよ。（Kono kusuri wa kaze ni taihen ii desu yo.）

⇔悪い **warui**

＊「いい（ii）」は「終止の形」「連体の形」が使われる。「ないの形」は「よくない（yokunai）」「たの形」は「よかった（yokatta）」などと「よい（yoi）」が使われる。

（〜ても）いい [連]

① [許可の意味を表す]

¶試験はボールペンで書いてもいいです。（Shiken wa bōrupen de kaite mo *ii* desu.）

¶「ここでたばこを吸ってもいいですか。」（Koko de tabako o sutte mo *ii* desu ka？）「いいえ、吸ってはいけません。」（Iie, sutte wa ikemasen.）

② [不必要の意味を表す]

¶This dictionary is small and just **right** for carrying about with one.

¶This shirt is exactly the **right** size for you.

⑨ [will do, be enough, serve the purpose]

¶How much money **should** one bring on the trip?

⑩ [good for, efficacious]

exercise **that is good** for one's health

¶This medicine **is** very **good** for a cold 〚the flu〛.

＊*Ii* is the sentence-final and dictionary form. *Yoi* is used for other forms: the negative form is *yoku nai* and the *-ta* form is *yokatta*.

(-te mo)ii 〚compd〛 may 〜, be all right to 〜; do not have to 〜

① [may 〜, be all right to 〜]

¶**One may** use a ballpoint pen for the test.

¶**"Is it all right** to smoke here?" "No, it isn't."

② [do not have to 〜, need not 〜]

¶そんなに急がなくてもいいです。
(Sonna ni isoganakute mo *ii* desu.)
¶「薬を飲まなくてもいいですか。」
(Kusuri o nomanakute mo *ii* desu ka？)
「いいえ、飲まなくてはいけません。」
(Iie, nomanakute wa ikemasen.)
＊「〜なくてもいい（〜nakute mo ii）」
の形で使う。
⇔（〜ては）いけない（〜**te wa**）
ikenai
⇒（〜ても）かまわない（〜**te mo**）
kamawanai

¶ [You] **don't have to** hurry so.

¶ **"Is it all right** not to take any
medicine?"
"No, you have to take some."

*Used in the pattern "-*nakute mo ii*."

いいえ〔感〕

¶「あれはあなたの本ですか。」（Arc
wa anata no hon desu ka？）「いいえ、違
います。」（Iie, chigaimasu.）
¶「あなたは日本語が話せますか。」
（Anata wa Nihongo ga hanasemasu
ka？）「いいえ、話せません。」（Iie,
hanasemasen.）
⇔はい **hai**

iie〔interj〕no

¶ "Is that your book?"
"**No**, it's not."

¶ "Can you speak Japanese?"
"**No**, I can't."

いいわけ 言い訳〔名〕

¶彼はいつもいろいろと言い訳をしま
す。（Kare wa itsu mo iroiro to *iiwake* o
shimasu.）
¶そんな言い訳は聞きたくありませ
ん。（Sonna *iiwake* wa kikitaku
arimasen.）

iiwake〔n〕explanation, excuse, apology

¶ He always has various **excuses**.

¶ I don't want to hear that kind of
excuse.

いいん 委員〔名〕

委員長（*iin*chō）委員会（*iin*kai）

¶クラスの新しい委員を選びました。
（Kurasu no atarashii *iin* o erabimashita.）

iin〔n〕committee member, delegate

the **committee** chairman // a
committee, commission, board, panel
¶ [We] chose a new class
representative.

45

¶その問題について委員の報告を聞き
ました。（Sono mondai ni tsuite *iin* no
hōkoku o kikimashita.）

¶ [I] listened to **the commissioner's**
report concerning that problem.

いう　言う〔動 I〕
iu 〔v I〕 say, state, express;
besaid; be called, named

① [思ったことや考えたことなどを言
葉で表す]

① [say, speak, state, remark, express]

¶中村さんは「今度の旅行には行きた
くない。」と言っていました。
（Nakamura san wa "Kondo no ryokō ni
wa ikitaku nai." to *itte* imashita.）

¶ [Miss] Nakamura **said**, "I don't want
to go on the trip this time."

¶あの人はその問題について何と言っ
ていましたか。（Ano hito wa sono
mondai ni tsuite nan to *itte* imashita
ka？）

¶ What did [he] **say** concerning that
problem?

②[ものごとの評価を表すときに使う]

② [expresses an evaluation]

¶山田さんは中村さんのことをあまり
よく言いません。（Yamada san wa
Nakamura san no koto o amari yoku
iimasen.）

¶ [Mrs.] Yamada doesn't have much
good **to say** about [Mrs.] Nakamura.

＊普通「よく言う（yoku iu）」「悪く言
う（waruku iu）」の形で使う。

＊Usually used in the patterns "*yoku iu*"
and "*waruku iu*."

③[おおぜいの人がそう称する]

③ [be said, be called, be talked about,
people say]

¶彼は学生時代は秀才と言われていま
した。（Kare wa gakusei-jidai wa shūsai
to *iwarete* imashita.）

¶ He **was said to be** 〚known as〛 a
bright boy in his student days.

④[そう呼ばれる、そう称される]

④ [be called, be named, be termed]

¶さっき田中さんという人が来ました
よ。（Sakki Tanaka san to *iu* hito ga
kimashita yo.）

¶ **A** [Mr.] Tanaka was here earlier.

¶これは何という花ですか。（Kore wa
nan to *iu* hana desu ka？）

¶ What is this flower **called**?

＊「～という（～to iu）」の形で使う。

＊Used in the pattern "～ *to iu*."

⑤[ものごとの様子などを例示するの
に使う]

⑤ [used to describe a condition]

¶こういうぐあいにすると、うまくいきますよ。(Kō*iu* guai ni suruto, umaku ikimasu yo.)

¶そういう問題はわたしにはよくわかりません。(Sō*iu* mondai wa watashi ni wa yoku wakarimasen.)

¶ああいう人はどうしても好きになれません。(Ā*iu* hito wa dōshite mo suki ni naremasen.)

¶これはどういう意味ですか。(Kore wa dō*iu* imi desu ka？)

*「こう (kō)」「そう (sō)」「ああ (ā)」「どう (dō)」などの言葉につく。「こういうふうに (kōiu fū ni)」「こういったふうに (kōitta fū ni)」などの形でも使う。

いえ 家 [名]

① [住居]

¶あの人の家はこの近くです。(Ano hito no ie wa kono chikaku desu.)

¶彼は最近立派な家を建てました。(Kare wa saikin rippa na ie o tatemashita.)

② [家庭]

¶田中さんの家にはピアノがあります。(Tanaka san no ie ni wa piano ga arimasu.)

¶彼は貧しい家に生まれました。(Kare wa mazushii ie ni umaremashita.)

⇒うち uchi

いか 以下 [名]

① [ある数量・時間などよりも少ないこと]

¶ It will go better if you do it **like** this.

¶ I don't understand that **sort of** problem well.

¶ Somehow I just can't like that **sort of** person.

¶ **What** does this mean?

*Used with the words *kō*, *sō*, *ā*, *dō*, etc. Used in the patterns "*kō iu fū ni* ," "*kō itta fū ni* ," etc.

ie [n] house, home; household, family

① [house, home, residence]

¶ [His] **home** is near here.

¶ He recently built a lovely **house**.

② [household, family]

¶ **The Tanakas** have a piano.

¶ He was born into a poor **family**.

ika [n] and less, less than; under, below; the following

① [and less, less than, under, below]

¶今朝は零度以下まで気温が下がりました。(Kesa wa reido *ika* made kion ga sagarimashita.)

¶Temperatures fell to zero **and below** this morning.

¶19歳以下の人はたばこを吸ってはいけません。(Jūkyūsai *ika* no hito wa tabako o sutte wa ikemasen.)

¶Those 19 years of age **and below** aren't allowed to smoke.

*「19歳以下（jūkyūsai ika）」という場合は19歳も含む。

*When used with a figure, *ika* means that figure and less. Thus, strictly speaking, *jhkyiisai ika* means "19 years and below" and not simply "less than 19 years."

②[ある状態などよりも程度が低いこと]

②[under, below]

平均以下（heikin *ika*）

below average

¶今年の米の収穫は予想以下でした。(Kotoshi no kome no shūkaku wa yosō *ika* deshita.)

¶The rice harvest this year was **smaller** than expected.

③[これまでに言ったことよりあとのこと]

③[the following, the hereafter, mentioned below]

¶以下は彼の言葉です。(Ika wa kare no kotoba desu.)

¶**The following** is in his own words.

¶以下は省略します。(Ika wa shōryaku shimasu.)

¶**The rest** is omitted.

⇔以上 **ijō**

いがい 以外 〔名〕

igai 〔n〕 **except for, other than**

¶生の魚以外は何でも食べます。(Nama no sakana *igai* wa nan demo tabemasu.)

¶I eat everything **with the exception** of raw fish.

¶そこへ行くには歩く以外に方法がありません。(Soko e iku ni wa aruku *igai* ni hōhō ga arimasen.)

¶One can **only** go there on foot〖There is no way to get there **other than** on foot〗.

いがい 意外 〔形動〕

igai 〔adj-v〕 **unexpected, surprising**

意外な事件（*igai* na jiken）意外な結果（*igai* na kekka）

a **surprising** incident // an **unexpected** outcome

¶試験は意外に易しかったです。(Shiken wa *igai* ni yasashikatta desu.)

¶The test was **surprisingly** easy.

¶試験に失敗したと思っていたら、意外なことにいい成績でした。(Shiken ni shippai shita to omotte itara, *igai* na koto ni ii seiseki deshita.)

¶ I thought I had failed the test, but **to my surprise** I got a good grade on it.

いかが〔副〕

¶お体のぐあいはいかがですか。(Okarada no guai wa *ikaga* desu ka？)

¶コーヒーをもう一杯いかがですか。(Kōhii o mō ippai *ikaga* desu ka？)

＊「どう(dō)」より丁寧な言葉。

⇒どう dō

ikaga 〔adv〕 **how, what**

¶ **How** do you feel (literally, **What** is the condition of your body)?

¶ Would you like another cup of coffee?

＊*Ikaga* is more polite than *dō*.

いがく 医学〔名〕

医学博士(*igaku*-hakushi)

¶わたしは医学の勉強をしたいと思っています。(Watashi wa *igaku* no benkyō o shitai to omotte imasu.)

¶あの国の医学はたいへん進んでいます。(Ano kuni no *igaku* wa taihen susunde imasu.)

igaku 〔n〕 **medicine, medical science**

a doctor **of medicine**, an MD

¶ I want to study **medicine**.

¶ **Medicine** is very advanced in that country.

いかす 生かす〔動Ⅰ〕

¶川で捕った魚は、あの池の中で生かしておきましょう。(Kawa de totta sakana wa, ano ike no naka de *ikashite* okimashō.)

ikasu 〔v Ⅰ〕 **revive, keep alive**

¶ Let's put the fish [we] caught in the river into the pond 〖pool〗 (literally, Let's put the fish we caught in the river into the pond and **keep them alive**).

いき 息〔名〕

息をする(*iki* osuru) 息をはく(*iki* o haku)

¶走ったので息が切れました。(Hashitta node *iki* ga kiremashita.)

¶深く息を吸ってください。(Fukaku *iki* o sutte kudasai.)

iki 〔n〕 **a breath, breathing**

to breathe // breathe out, exhale

¶ [I] am **out of breath** as [I] have been running 〖was **out of breath** as I had been running〗.

¶ Please take a deep **breath**.

いき 行き〔名〕

行き帰り(*iki* kaeri) 行き先(*iki* saki)

iki 〔n〕 **going, bound for**

going and returning, coming and **going** // destination

¶行きの切符は買えましたが、帰りの切符は買えませんでした。(Iki no kippu wa kaemashita ga, kaeri no kippu wa kaemasen deshita.)

¶ [I] was able to buy a ticket **for the trip there** but couldn't get a return ticket.

¶東京行きの電車に乗りました。(Tōkyō *iki* no densha ni norimashita.)

¶ [I] got on the train **for** Tokyo.

⇒行き yuki

いきおい 勢い〔名〕

ikioi 〔n〕 vigor, energy, power, force

¶この村の農業は非常な勢いで発展しました。(Kono mura no nōgyō wa hijō na *ikioi* de hatten shimashita.)

¶ Agriculture has advanced **in a spurt** in this village.

¶子供は勢いよく走っていきました。(Kodomo wa *ikioi* yoku hashitte ikimashita.)

¶ The children ran off **energetically**.

いきなり〔副〕

ikinari 〔adv〕 suddenly, abruptly, all of a sudden, without notice

¶道路にいきなり子供が飛び出してきました。(Dōro ni *ikinari* kodomo ga tobidashite kimashita.)

¶ A child **suddenly** ran out into the road 〚A child has **suddenly** run out into the road〛.

¶いきなり質問されても答えられません。(Ikinari shitsumon sarete mo kotaeraremasen.)

¶ [I] can't answer when **suddenly** asked something.

いきる 生きる〔動〕

ikiru 〔v II〕 live, be alive

¶百歳まで生きる人は少ないです。(Hyakusai made *ikiru* hito wa sukunai desu.)

¶ Few people **live** to the age of one hundred.

¶この虫は何を食べて生きていますか。(Kono mushi wa nani o tabete *ikite* imasu ka?)

¶ What does this insect **subsist** on?

いく 行く〔動〕

iku 〔v I〕 go, come; proceed

① [ある目的の所へ向かって進む]

① [go, come, advance toward a particular target]

¶昨日はどこへ行きましたか。(Kinō wa doko e *ikimashita* ka?)

¶ Where **did you go** yesterday?

¶このバスは飛行場へ行きますか。
（Kono basu wa hikōjō e *ikimasu* ka？）
⇔来る **kuru**

②[ものごとが行われる]
¶今度の計画はうまくいきそうです。
（Kondo no keikaku wa umaku *ikisō*
desu.）
¶この仕事はあなたが考えているよう
にはいかないと思いますよ。（Kono
shigoto wa anata ga kangaete iru yō ni wa
ikanai to omoimasu yo.）

③[結婚して他家に入る]
¶春子さんは去年の春お嫁にいきまし
た。（Haruko san wa kyonen no haru
oyome ni *ikimashita*.）
＊「行く（yuku）」とも言う。

（〜て）いく〔連〕

①[動作がある方向へ進むことを表す]
¶鳥が北の方へ飛んでいきます。（Tori
ga kita no hō e tonde *ikimasu*.）
¶子供はお弁当を持っていきました。
（Kodomo wa obentō o motte *ikimashita*.）
②[ある動作・状態などが継続する様
子を表す]
¶この本は読んでいくうちに、だんだ
んおもしろくなるでしょう。（Kono
hon wa yonde *iku* uchi ni, dandan
omoshiroku naru deshō.）
¶これからは親と離れて一人で生活し
ていかなければなりません。（Kore
kara wa oya to hanarete hitori de seikatsu
shite *ikanakereba* narimasen.）
③[ある状態に変化する様子を表す]

¶ Does this bus **go** to the airport?

②[proceed]
¶ **It looks like** this project **will turn
out** well.

¶ I don't think this work **will proceed**
in the way you think.

③[marry and enter another household]
¶ Haruko **married** last spring.

＊Variant: *yuku*.

(-te)iku 〔compd〕 **an expression
indicating movement,
progression, change, etc.**
① [indicates movement]
¶ Some birds **are flying off** to the
north.

¶ The children **took** their lunches with
them.
② [indicates the continuation of an
action or state]
¶ You will probably find this book
more and more interesting **as you read**
it.

¶ [I] **must** leave home and live alone
from now on.

③ [indicates change in a state of
affairs]

¶これからますます寒くなっていきますから、風邪を引かないように気をつけてください。（Kore kara masumasu samuku natte *ikimasu* kara, kaze o hikanai yō ni ki o tsukete kudasai.)

¶みんなの努力で町がだんだんきれいになっていきます。（Minna no doryoku de machi ga dandan kirei ni natte *ikimasu*.)

⇔（〜て）くる（〜te) **kuru**

いくつ 幾つ〔名〕

①[何歳]

¶お子さんはお幾つですか。（Okosan wa o*ikutsu* desu ka?)

②[何個]

¶そこに卵が幾つありますか。（Soko ni tamago ga *ikutsu* arimasu ka?)

¶兄は時計を幾つも持っています。（Ani wa tokei o *ikutsu* mo motte imasu.)

いくら〔名、副〕

1〔名〕

①[不明な数量・値段などを表す]

¶これはいくらですか。（Kore wa *ikura* desu ka?)

¶そのくつは、いくらで買いましたか。（Sono kutsu wa *ikura* de kaimashita ka?)

¶この荷物の目方はいくらぐらいありますか。（Kono nimotsu no mekata wa *ikura* gurai arimasu ka?)

②[ものごとのわずかであることを表す]

¶今月はもうお金はいくらも残っていません。（Kongetsu wa mō okane wa *ikura* mo nokotte imasen.)

¶ As it **will get** colder and colder from now on please be careful not to catch a cold.

¶ The town is gradually **becoming** cleaner due to everyone's efforts.

ikutsu 〔n〕 **how old; how many**

① [how old]

¶ **How old** is your child?

② [how many; several]

¶ **How many** eggs are there there?

¶ My older brother owns **several** watches.

ikura 〔n, adv〕 **how much, how many; hardly any, not much; however 〜, no matter how 〜**

1 〔n〕

① [how much, how many]

¶ **How much** is this?

¶ **How much** did you pay for those shoes?

¶ **How much** does this luggage 〚freight, load, cargo, etc.〛 weigh?

② [not much, not many, very few]

¶ [I] have **hardly any** money left for this month.

¶費用はいくらもかかりませんから、今度の旅行に参加しませんか。(Hiyō wa *ikura* mo kakarimasen kara, kondo no ryokō ni sanka shimasen ka?)

＊「いくらも〜ない（ikura mo〜nai）」の形で使う。

2 〔副〕

¶いくら高くても買います。(Ikura takakute mo kaimasu.)

¶いくら呼んでも返事がありません。(Ikura yonde mo henji ga arimasen.)

＊「いくら〜ても（ikura〜te mo）」の形で使うことが多い。

いく- 幾- 〔頭〕

幾度 (*iku*do) 幾日 (*iku*nichi) 幾人 (*iku*nin)

＊「何-（nan-）」より少しかたい感じで、いっしょに使われる語もあまり多くない。

⇒何- nan-

いけ 池 〔名〕

¶庭に池があって、金魚が泳いでいます。(Niwa ni *ike* ga atte, kingyo ga oyoide imasu.)

¶今朝は池の水が凍りました。(Kesa wa *ike* no mizu ga koorimashita.)

いけない 〔連〕

¶あなたの言い方がいけなかったので、あの人は怒ったのです。(Anata no iikata ga *ikenakatta* node, ano hito wa okotta no desu.)

¶Won't you come on the trip? It won't cost **very much**.

＊Used in the pattern "*ikura mo* 〜 -*nai*."

2 〖adv〗 however 〜, no matter how 〜

¶[I] will buy it **no matter how** expensive it may be.

¶There is no response **no matter how much** one calls.

＊Usually used in the pattern "*ikura* 〜 -*te mo*."

iku- 〖pref〗 **how many; several**

how many times; **several** times // **how many** days; **what** day of the month; **several** days // **how many** people; **several** people

＊The prefix *iku*- is somewhat more formal than *nan*- and can only be used with a restricted set of words.

ike 〖n〗 **pond, pool, basin**

¶There's **a pool** in the garden where goldfish are swimming.

¶**The pond** froze this morning.

ikenai 〖compd〗 **bad, wrong, to blame**

¶[He] got angry because the way you talked to [him] **was out of line**.

¶風邪を引くといけないから、もう一枚シャツを着ました。(Kaze o hiku to *ikenai* kara, mō ichimai shatsu o kimashita.)

¶ [I] wore one more shirt as [I] **didn't want to** catch a cold.

(〜ては) いけない 〔連〕

(-te wa)ikenai 〔compd〕 **must not, should not, be forbidden**

¶この中へ入ってはいけません。(Kono naka e haitte wa *ikemasen*.)

¶ここでたばこを吸ってはいけません。(Koko de tabako o sutte wa *ikemasen*.)

⇔ (〜ても) いい (〜**te mo**) **ii**

⇔ (〜ても) かまわない (〜**te mo**) **kamawanai**

¶ **No** admittance 〖Keep out; **Don't** come into this place; etc.〗

¶ This is a **no**-smoking area.

いけばな 生け花 〔名〕

ikebana 〔n〕 **Japanese flower arrangement, ikebana**

¶生け花を習っていますか。(Ikebana o naratte imasu ka?)

¶田中さんは生け花の歴史を研究しています。(Tanaka san wa *ikebana* no rekishi o kenkyū shite imasu.)

¶ Are you studying *ikebana*?

¶ [Mrs.] Tanaka is researching the history of *ikebana*.

いけん 意見 〔名、〜する〕

iken 〔n, 〜*suru*〕 **opinion, view; advice, admonition**

① [あるものごとについての考え]
意見を言う (*iken* o iu) 意見を述べる (*iken* o noberu)

¶わたしもあなたと同じ意見です。(Watashi mo anata to onaji *iken* desu.)

¶あなたとはよく意見が合いますね。(Anata to wa yoku *iken* ga aimasu ne.)

¶みんなその意見に従いました。(Minna sono *iken* ni shitagaimashita.)

② [教えるように言って聞かせること]
¶勉強しないので、子供に意見しました。(Benkyō shinai node, kodomo ni *iken* shimashita.)

① [opinion, view, idea]
give 〖express〗 one's opinion // give 〖express〗 **one's opinion**

¶ I agree with your **opinion**.

¶ We often hold the same **opinion**, don't we?

¶ Everyone accepted that **opinion**.

② [advice, admonition]
¶ [I] **scolded** the children for not studying.

いご 以後 [名]

① [その時からのち]
¶午後5時以後はうちにいます。(Gogo goji *igo* wa uchi ni imasu.)
⇔以前 izen
② [今からのち、今後]

¶すみません。以後じゅうぶん気をつけます。(Sumimasen. Igo jūbun ki o tsukemasu.)

igo [n] **after that, afterward; after this, from now on**

① [after that, afterward, thereafter]
¶I will be at home **after** 5 PM.

② [after this, from now on, hereafter, in the future]

¶I'm sorry. I'll be very careful **from now on**.

いし 石 [名]

¶この橋は石でできています。(Kono hashi wa *ishi* de dekite imasu.)
¶池に石を投げないでください。(Ike ni *ishi* o nagenaide kudasai.)

ishi [n] **stone, rock, pebble**

¶This bridge is made of **stone**.

¶Please don't throw **stones** 〖**pebbles**〗 into the pond 〖pool〗.

いし 意志 [名]

意志が弱い (*ishi* ga yowai) 意志が堅い (*ishi* ga katai) 自由意志 (jiyū*ishi*)
¶彼は意志が強いですね。(Kare wa *ishi* ga tsuyoi desu ne.)

ishi [n] **will**

be weak **willed** // be firm **willed** // of one's own free **will**

¶He is a man **of strong character,** isn't he?

いし 意思 [名]

¶彼にわたしの意思をはっきり伝えてください。(Kare ni watashi no *ishi* o hakkiri tsutaete kudasai.)
¶手紙ではなかなか意思が通じません。(Tegami de wa nakanaka *ishi* ga tsūjimasen.)

ishi [n] **intent, purpose, intention**

¶Please clearly convey my **intentions** to him.

¶It is difficult to communicate one's **intentions** in a letter.

いじめる [動]

¶動物をいじめてはいけません。(Dōbutsu o *ijimete* wa ikemasen.)
¶男の子が女の子をいじめています。(Otoko no ko ga onna no ko o *ijimete* imasu.)

ijimeru [v II] **tease, annoy, illtreat, torment, persecute**

¶One mustn't **tease** 〖**torment**〗 animals.

¶A boy is **teasing** 〖**annoying**〗 a girl.

いしゃ 医者〔名〕

医者に診てもらう（isha ni mite morau）

¶早く医者を呼んでください。
（Hayaku isha o yonde kudasai.）

¶どこの医者にかかっていますか。
（Doko no isha ni kakatte imasu ka？）

＊丁寧に言うときは「お医者さん（oishasan）」と言う。

isha〔n〕doctor, physician, surgeon

see **a doctor**

¶ Please call **a doctor** right away.

¶ Who is **your doctor**?

＊When one has to be polite one should use *oishasan* to refer to a doctor. In direct address a doctor is called *sensei*.

いじょう 異常〔名、形動〕

¶機械を調べてみましたが、何も異常はありません。（Kikai o shirabete mimashita ga, nani mo ijō wa arimasen.）

¶今年の夏は異常に暑かったです。
（Kotoshi no natsu wa ijō ni atsukatta desu.）

ijō〔n, adj-v〕unusual, abnormal

¶ [I] have examined the machinery but there is nothing **wrong** with it.

¶ Summer was **abnormally** hot this year.

いじょう 以上〔名〕

①[ある数量・時間などよりも多いこと]

¶毎日8時間以上働きます。（Mainichi hachijikan ijō hatarakimasu.）

¶この地方では一年間に千ミリ以上の雨が降ります。（Kono chihō de wa ichinenkan ni senmiri ijō no ame ga furimasu.）

＊「8時間以上（hachijikan ijō）」という場合は8時間を含む。

⇔以下 **ika**

②[ある状態などよりも程度が高いこと]

ijō〔n〕or more, more than; beyond, above; the abovementioned; since, seeing that

① [or more, more than, not less than]

¶ [I] work **more than** eight hours〚eight hours **or more**〛every day.

¶ One thousand millimeters **or more** of rain falls a year in this area.

*When *ijō* is used with a figure, it means that figure and more. Thus, strictly speaking, *hachijikan ijō* means "eight hours or more" and not simply "more than eight hours."

② [beyond, above, past]

平均以上 (heikin ijō)

above average

¶試験は予想以上に難しかったです。
(Shiken wa yosō *ijō* ni muzukashikatta desu.)

¶ The exam was **more** difficult than expected.

¶もうこれ以上我慢できません。(Mō kore *ijō* gaman dekimasen.)

¶ I can't stand **any more** than this 〚This is all I can take〛.

⇔以下 **ika**

③[これまでに言ったことなど]

③ [the above-mentioned, the foregoing]

¶私の言いたいことは以上です。
(Watakushi no iitai koto wa *ijō* desu.)

¶ **That** is all I had to say.

¶以上、どうぞよろしくお願いします。(Ijō, dōzo yoroshiku onegai shimasu.)

¶ I now commend **this matter** to you.

⇔以下 **ika**

④[前のことがらによってあとのことがらが当然成立するという関係を表す]

④ [since, so long as, seeing that]

¶約束した以上、守らなければなりません。(Yakusoku shita *ijō*, mamoranakereba narimasen.)

¶ You must keep a promise **once** you have made it.

¶お世話になった以上、お礼を言うのは当然です。(Osewa ni natta *ijō*, orei o iu no wa tōzen desu.)

¶ It is only fitting to thank people **after** being helped by them.

いす 〔名〕

isu 〔n〕 **chair, sofa**

いすに腰掛ける (*isu* ni koshikakeru) いすに座る (*isu* ni suwaru)

sit down on **a chair** // sit down on **a chair**

¶どうぞ、そのいすにお掛けください。(Dōzo, sono *isu* ni okake kudasai.)

¶ Please take **a chair** 〚a seat〛 there.

いぜん 以前 〔名〕

izen 〔n〕 **in advance, before; ago, formerly**

①[ある時より前]
¶出発は2月10日以前にしましょう。
(Shuppatsu wa nigatsu tooka *izen* ni shimashō.)

① [in advance, before a certain time]
¶ Let's make the departure **prior to** February 10.

⇔以後 **igo**

②[今からしばらく前、昔]

② [ago, formerly]

¶この辺は以前とても静かでした。
(Kono hen wa *izen* totemo shizuka
deshita.)

¶ **It used to be** very quiet around here.

いそがしい 忙しい〔形〕

¶今日は忙しい日でした。(Kyō wa
isogashii hi deshita.)

¶勉強が忙しくて、遊ぶ暇がありませ
ん。(Benkyō ga *isogashikute*, asobu hima
ga arimasen.)

isogashii 〔adj〕 **be busy, be engaged**

¶ Today has been a **busy** day.

¶ [I]'m **busy** with studying and have no
time for play.

いそぐ 急ぐ〔動Ⅰ〕

¶時間がないから急ぎましょう。
(Jikan ga nai kara *isogimashō*.)

¶遅刻しそうなので、急いで出かけま
した。(Chikoku shisō na node, *isoide*
dekakemashita.)

¶急がないと遅れますよ。(*Isoganai* to
okuremasu yo.)

¶急げばまだ12時の汽車に間に合うで
しょう。(*Isogeba* mada jūniji no kisha ni
maniau deshō.)

isogu 〔vⅠ〕 **hurry, be in a hurry, make haste**

¶ **Let's hurry** as time is getting short.

¶ [I] left **in a hurry** as it looked like [I]
would be late.

¶ You'll be late if **you don't hurry**.

¶ **If [you] hurry** [you] can probably
still make the twelve o'clock train.

いた 板〔名〕

まな板 (mana*ita*)

¶板を組み立てて、本箱を作りまし
た。(Ita o kumi*ta*tete, honbako o
tsukurimashi*ta*.)

ita 〔n〕 **board, plank**

a chopping **board** 〖block〗

¶ [I] built a bookcase out of **boards**.

いたい 痛い〔形〕

¶少し頭が痛いです。(Sukoshi atama
ga *itai* desu.)

¶急に歯が痛くなりました。(Kyū ni
ha ga *itaku* narimashita.)

¶昨日はおなかが痛かったので、学校
を休みました。(Kinō wa onaka ga
itakatta node, gakkō o yasumimashita.)

itai 〔adj〕 **be painful, be sore, hurts**

¶ I have a slight head**ache**.

¶ My teeth suddenly started **to ache**.

¶ I stayed home from school yesterday
as I had a stomach**ache**.

いたす 致す〔動Ⅱ〕
¶ この仕事は私が致します。(Kono shigoto wa watakushi ga *itashi* masu.)

いたずら〔名、形動、〜する〕

¶ うちの子はいたずらで困ります。(Uchi no ko wa *itazura* de komarimasu.)
¶ 子供がいたずらして、時計を壊しました。(Kodomo ga *itazura* shite, tokei o kowashimashita.)

いただく〔動Ⅰ〕
① [もらう]
¶ 先生に本をいただきました。(Sensei ni hon o *itadakimashita*.)
¶ お見舞いにきれいな花をいただきました。(Omimai ni kirei na hana o *itadakimashita*.)
* 「もらう (morau)」の謙譲語。ある人が目上の人から与えられたものを受け取るという意味を表す。受け取る人の側に立って言うときに使う。与える人が対等か目下の人などである場合には「もらう (morau)」を使う。
→もらう morau
② [食べる、飲む]
¶ 「どうぞ、おあがりください。」(Dōzo, oagari kudasai.)「では、いただきます。」(Dewa, *itadakimasu*.)
¶ 「もう少しお召し上がりになりませんか。」(Mō sukoshi omeshiagari ni narimasen ka?)「ありがとうございます。もうじゅうぶんにいただきました。」(Arigatō gozaimasu. Mō jūbun ni *itadakimashita*.)
* 「食べる (taberu)」「飲む (nomu)」の謙譲語。
③ [食事の前のあいさつの言葉]

itasu 〔vⅡ〕 **do**
¶ I will do this task.

itazura 〔n, adj-v, 〜*suru*〕 **mischief, trick, prank**
¶ Our child **is always up to mischief** and we don't know what to do.
¶ The children **were fooling around** and broke the clock〚watch〛.

itadaku 〔vⅠ〕 **receive; eat, drink**
① [receive]
¶ **I received** a book from my teacher 〚My teacher gave me a book〛.
¶ **I received** some pretty flowers as a gct-well present.

Itadaku is the humble form for *morau*; it expresses the meaning of someone receiving something from someone of higher status. It is used from the point of view of the recipient. When the giver is of equal orlower status, *morau* is used.
② [eat, drink]
¶ "Please go ahead and eat."
"Thank you, **I will**."

¶ "Won't you have some more?"
"No, thank you. I couldn't **eat** another thing."

*This *itadaku* is the humble form for *taberu, nomu*.
③ [set expression used before a meal]

¶ いただきます。（*Itadakimasu.*）

¶ Thank you for this food I am about **to eat**.

（〜て）いただく 〔連〕

¶ わたしは田中先生に日本語を教えていただきました。（Watashi wa Tanaka sensei ni Nihongo o oshiete *itadakimashita.*）

¶ Professor Tanaka **kindly** taught me Japanese 〚**was kind enough** to teach me Japanese〛.

¶ 旅行の写真を見せていただきたいんですが。（Ryokō no shashin o misete *itadakitai* n desu ga.）

¶ **Could I please** see the photographs of the trip?

＊普通ある人が動作をする人の動作によって利益や恩恵などを受けたり、または依頼してある動作をさせるようにしたりする意味を表す。利益を受けたり、依頼したりする人の側に立って言うときに使う。動作をする人が利益などを受ける人より目上の人であるときに使う。動作をする人が対等か目下の人などである場合には「（〜て）もらう（〔〜te〕morau）」を使う。
⇒（〜て）もらう（〜te）**morau**

＊Usually (*-te*) *itadaku* expresses the meaning of receiving some benefit from the actions of another or of requesting and having some action done for one. It is used from the standpoint of the person receiving the benefit or making the request and when the person doing the action is of higher status than the recipient. When the person doing the favor is of equal or lower status, (*-te*) *morau* is used.

(-te)itadaku 〔compd〕 **receive the favor of something being done**

いち 一 〔名〕

ichi 〔n〕 **one**

いち 位置 〔名、〜する〕

ichi 〔n, 〜*suru*〕 **location, position**

¶ この部屋の家具の位置を変えましょう。（Kono heya no kagu no *ichi* o kaemashō.）

¶ Let's change **the position** of the furniture in this room.

¶ わたしの学校は東京の東に位置しています。（Watashi no gakkō wa Tōkyō no higashi ni *ichi* shite imasu.）

¶ My school **is located** to the east of Tokyo 〚in east Tokyo〛.

いちおう 一応 〔副〕

ichiō 〔adv〕 **once, in outline, in genral, tentatively, for the time being**

¶ できるかどうかわかりませんが、一応やってみましょう。（Dekiru ka dō ka wakarimasen ga, *ichiō* yatte mimashō.）

¶ I'm not sure whether it can be done or not but I'll just give it a try **anyway**.

¶決める前に一応あの人に相談してください。（Kimeru mae ni *ichiō* ano hito ni sōdan shite kudasai.）

¶Before deciding please consult with [him] **once** about it.

¶上田さんは旅行には行かないと思いますが、一応話してみましょう。（Ueda san wa ryokō ni wa ikanai to omoimasu ga, *ichiō* hanashite mimashō.）

¶I don't think [Mr.] Ueda will be going on the trip but let's talk to him about it **just in case**.

いちがつ　一月〔名〕

ichigatsu〔n〕**January**

いちご〔名〕

ichigo〔n〕**strawberries**

いちじ　一時〔名〕

ichiji〔n〕**for a time, temporarily; once, at one time; one o'clock**

①［短い時間、しばらくの間］
一時停止（*ichiji*-teishi）

①［for a time, temporarily］
momentary stop (of a train, car, etc.)

¶工事のため一時店を閉めます。（Kōji no tame *ichiji* mise o shimemasu.）

¶The shop will be closed **temporarily** due to construction.

¶子供が病気で、一時はとても心配でした。（Kodomo ga byōki de, *ichiji* wa totemo shinpai deshita.）

¶**For a time** [we] were very worried by [our] child's illness.

②［過去のある時、その当時］

②［once, at one time］

¶あの歌は一時たいへんはやりました。（Ano uta wa *ichiji* taihen hayarimashita.）

¶**At one time** that song was very popular.

いちじに　一時に〔副〕

ichiji ni〔adv〕**at once, at one time, all together**

¶一時にそんなにたくさんのことはできません。（*Ichijii ni* sonna ni takusan no koto wa dekimasen.）

¶[I] cannot do that much 〚that many things〛 **all at one time**.

⇒一度に ichido ni

いちど　一度〔名〕

ichido〔n〕**once**

¶この本は一度、読んだことがあります。（Kono hon wa *ichido*, yonda koto ga arimasu.）

¶I have read this book once before.

いちどに 一度に〔副〕

¶電車のドアが開くと、一度にたくさんの人が降りてきました。(Densha no doa ga aku to, *ichido ni* takusan no hito ga orite kimashita.)

¶こんなにたくさんの仕事を一度にやろうと思っても無理です。(Konna ni takusan no shigoto o *ichido ni* yarō to omotte mo muri desu.)

⇒一時に ichiji ni

ichido ni 〔adv〕 **at once, at one time, simultaneously**

¶ When the train doors opened, lots of people poured out **all at once**.

¶ It is impossible to think of doing this much work **at one time**.

いちにち 一日〔名〕

¶雨が降っていたので、今日は一日じゅう家にいました。(Ame ga futte ita node, kyō wa *ichinichi*jū ie ni imashita.)

¶これでやっと一日の仕事が終わりました。(Kore de yatto *ichinichi* no shigoto ga owarimashita.)

⇒-日 -nichi

ichinichi 〔n〕 **one day, all day**

¶ As it was raining, [I] stayed at home **all day** today.

¶ With this the **day's** work is finally finished.

いちば 市場〔名〕

¶母は市場へ買い物に行きました。(Haha wa *ichiba* e kaimono ni ikimashita.)

¶市場はいつもこんでいます。(Ichiba wa itsu mo konde imasu.)

ichiba 〔n〕 **market, marketplace**

¶ My mother went to **the market** to shop.

¶ The **market** is always crowded.

いちばん〔副〕

¶いちばん好きな食べ物は何ですか。(Ichiban suki na tabemono wa nan desu ka?)

¶東京は日本でいちばん大きい都会です。(Tōkyō wa Nihon de *ichiban* ookii tokai desu.)

ichiban 〔adv〕 **most, best, number one, first**

¶ What foods do you like **the best**?

¶ Tokyo is the **largest** city in Japan.

いちぶ 一部 〔名〕

¶一部の人はその計画に反対です。
(Ichibu no hito wa sono keikaku ni hantai desu.)

¶台風で村の一部に被害が出ました。
(Taifū de mura no *ichibu* ni higai ga demashita.)

⇒全部 zenbu

いちぶぶん 一部分 〔名〕

¶宿題はまだ一部分しか終わっていません。(Shukudai wa mada *ichibubun* shika owatte imasen.)

¶昨夜の火事で、町は一部分を残してほとんど焼けてしまいました。
(Sakuya no kaji de, machi wa *ichibubun* o nokoshite hotondo yakete shimaimashita.)

⇒大部分 daibubun

いつ 〔名〕

¶いつ日本へ来ましたか。(Itsu Nihon e kimashita ka?)

¶この宿題はいつまでですか。(Kono shukudai wa *itsu* made desu ka?)

¶彼はいつ行っても留守です。(Kare wa *itsu* itte mo rusu desu.)

¶夜はいつでも家にいます。(Yoru wa *itsu* demo ie ni imasu.)

いつか 五日 〔名〕

①[日付を表す]
¶五月五日は子供の日です。(Gogatsu *itsuka* wa kodomo no hi desu.)

②[日数を表す]
五日間 (*itsuka*kan)

---

ichibu 〔n〕 **part, section**

¶ **Some** are opposed to that plan.

¶ **Part** of the village was damaged in the typhoon.

ichibubun 〔n〕 **part, section**

¶ Only **part** of the homework is done.

¶ Almost all of the town burned down in the fire last night; only **a part** of it remains.

itsu 〔n〕 **when**

¶ **When** did you come to Japan?

¶ **When** is this homework due?

¶ **Whenever** [I] go to his home he is out.

¶ I am at home **anytime** in the evenings.

itsuka 〔n〕 **the fifth of the month; five days**

① [the fifth of the month]

¶ The **fifth** of May is Children's Day.

② [five days]

for **five days**, a period of **five days**

¶ 風邪で五日も学校を休みました。
(Kaze de *itsuka* mo gakkō o
yasumimashita.)
⇒-日 -ka

¶ [I] stayed home from school **for five days** with a cold 〖the flu〗.

いつか 〔副〕

itsu ka 〔adv〕 **sometime, at one time**

¶ いつかうちへ遊びに来てください。
(Itsuka uchi e asobi ni kite kudasai.)

¶ Please come and visit me **sometime**.

¶ 彼にはいつか会ったことがあります。(Kare ni wa itsu ka atta koto ga
arimasu.)

¶ [I] have met him **at some time or other**.

いっか 一家 〔名〕

ikka 〔n〕 **a family, a household**

¶ 田中さん一家は音楽がたいへん好きです。(Tanaka san *ikka* wa ongaku ga
taihen suki desu.)

¶ The Tanaka **family** is very fond of music.

¶ 昨日は一家そろって買い物に出かけました。(Kinō wa *ikka* sorotte kaimono
ni dekakemashita.)

¶ Yesterday the whole **family** went out shopping together.

いっしょう 一生 〔名〕

isshō 〔n〕 **lifetime, one's whole life**

¶ 彼は一生結婚しませんでした。
(Kare wa *isshō* kekkon shimasen
deshita.)

¶ He remained single **all his life**.

¶ 人の一生は短いものです。(Hito no
isshō wa mijikai mono desu.)

¶ **Human life** is short.

いっしょうけんめい 一生懸命
〔副、形動〕

isshōkenmei 〔adv, adj-v〕 **as hard as one can, wholeheartedly, with all one's might**

¶ 一生懸命働いても、生活が楽になりません。(Isshōkenmei hataraite mo,
seikatsu ga raku ni narimasen.)

¶ Even if one works **as hard as one can**, it's still difficult to make a good living.

¶ あの学生は一生懸命に勉強しています。(Ano gakusei wa *isshōkenmei* ni
benkyō shite imasu.)

¶ That student is studying **hard**.

¶ 早く日本語が上手になろうと、みんな一生懸命です。(Hayaku Nihongo ga
jōzu ni narō to, minna *isshōkenmei* desu.)

¶ All **are intent** on becoming good in Japanese quickly.

いっしょに〔副〕

¶みんなでいっしょに言ってください。(Minna de *issho ni* itte kudasai.)

¶友達といっしょに映画へ行きます。(Tomodachi to *issho ni* eiga e ikimasu.)

issho ni〔adv〕**together**

¶Will everyone please say it **together**.

¶[I] am going to go to a movie **with** a friend.

いっそう〔副〕

¶8月は今よりいっそう暑くなります。(Hachigatsu wa ima yori *issō* atsuku narimasu.)

¶勉強が前よりいっそうおもしろくなりました。(Benkyō ga mae yori *issō* omoshiroku narimashita.)

issō〔adv〕**more, much more, still more**

¶It becomes **much** hotter in August than it is now.

¶[My] studies have become **much more** interesting now than before.

いったい〔副〕

¶そんなにあわてて、いったいどうしたのですか。(Sonna ni awatete, *ittai* dō shita no desu ka?)

¶彼はいったい何を考えているのかわたしにはわかりません。(Kare wa *ittai* nani o kangaete iru no ka watashi ni wa wakarimasen.)

ittai〔adv〕**what 【how, why】 in the world, what 【how, why】 on earth**

¶**What on earth** is the matter that you are so flustered?

¶I don't know **what in the world** he can be thinking of.

いっち 一致〔名、〜する〕

¶二人の意見が一致しました。(Futari no iken ga *itchi* shimashita.)

¶彼は言うこととすることが一致していません。(Kare wa iu koto to suru koto ga *itchi* shite imasen.)

itchi〔n, 〜*suru*〕**be in accord, be consistent, correspond with**

¶The views of the two **are 〖were〗 in accord**.

¶His acts **are not in accordance** with his words.

いつつ 五つ〔名〕

①[5個]
¶みかんを五つください。(Mikan o *itsutsu* kudasai.)

②[5歳]

itsutsu〔n〕**five items; five years of age**

①[five items]
¶Please give me **five** mandarin oranges.

②[five years of age]

¶ この子は五つです。（Kono ko wa *itsutsu* desu.）

¶ This child is **five years old**.

いっぱい〔副、形動〕

ippai〔adv, adj-v〕**full; all, the whole of**

① [満ちている様子、あるものの中に何かが限度まである様子]
腹いっぱい食べる（hara *ippai* taberu）

① [full]

to eat until **full**

¶ もうおなかがいっぱいです。（Mō onaka ga *ippai* desu.）

¶ [I]'m **full**.

¶ デパートは人でいっぱいでした。（Depāto wa hito de *ippai* deshita.）

¶ The department store **was filled** with people.

② [全部、限りを尽くす様子]
時間いっぱい（jikan *ippai*）精いっぱい（sei *ippai*）

② [all, the whole of]
until one's time **is up**, using **all** the time available for some task // with **all** one's might. **to the best of** one's abilities

¶ 今月いっぱい東京にいます。（Kongetsu *ippai* Tōkyō ni imasu.）

¶ [I] will be in Tokyo **all** this month.

いっぱん 一般〔名〕
一般的（*ippan*teki）

ippan〔n〕**general, common general, in general**

¶ そんな専門的なことは一般の人にはわからないでしょう。（Sonna senmonteki na koto wa *ippan* no hito ni wa wakaranai deshō.）

¶ The **average** person probably can't understand such a specialized matter.

¶ この本は一般の本屋にはありません。（Kono hon wa *ippan* no hon'ya ni wa arimasen.）

¶ This book will not be found in the **average** bookstore.

¶ この商品はまだ一般には売られていません。（Kono shōhin wa mada *ippan* ni wa urarete imasen.）

¶ This product is not yet on **general** sale.

いっぱんに 一般に〔副〕

ippan ni〔adv〕**generally, in general, on the whole, commonly, usually**

¶ 今度の試験は一般に難しかったです。（Kondo no shiken wa *ippan ni* muzukashikatta desu.）

¶ **On the whole,** the exam this time was difficult.

¶最近の映画は一般にあまりおもしろくありません。（Saikin no eiga wa *ippan ni* amari omoshiroku arimasen.）

¶ **Generally speaking,** recent movies haven't been very interesting.

いっぽう 一方 〔名〕

① [片方、一つの方面]
一方通行（*ippō*-tsūkō）

¶一方の言うことだけで判断するのは危険です。（Ippō no iu koto dake de handan suru no wa kiken desu.）

¶もう一方の人たちは、この問題についてどう言っていますか。（Mō *ippō* no hitotachi wa kono mondai ni tsuite dō itte imasu ka？）

② [一つの傾向が強くなるばかりであること]

¶収入は減る一方です。（Shūnyū wa heru *ippō* desu.）

¶交通事故は増える一方です。（Kōtsū-jiko wa fueru *ippō* desu.）

ippō 〔n〕 **one side; one-way, only**

① [one side]
one-way traffic

¶ It is risky to make judgments based on just **one side** of the story.

¶ What do **others** have to say about this problem?

② [one-way, only]

¶ Income **goes on** declining (that is, it never increases).

¶ Traffic accidents **steadily** increase (that is, they never decrease).

いつも 〔副〕

¶妹の電話はいつも長いです。
（Imōto no denwa wa *itsumo* nagai desu.）

¶彼はいつも本を読んでいます。
（Kare wa *itsumo* hon o yonde imasu.）

itsu mo 〔adv〕 **always**

¶ My younger sister **always** talks for a long time on the telephone.

¶ He is **always** reading a book.

いと 糸 〔名〕

毛糸（ke*ito*）絹糸（kinu*ito*）木綿糸（momen*ito*）

¶この糸はとても丈夫です。（Kono *ito* wa totemo jōbu desu.）

¶針と糸を貸してください。（Hari to *ito* o kashite kudasai.）

ito 〔n〕 **thread, yarn, string, line, filament, etc.**

yarn, wool **yarn** // silk **thread** // cotton **thread,** cotton **yarn**

¶ This **thread** 〚**string, line**〛 is very strong.

¶ Please lend me a needle and **thread.**

いど 井戸 〔名〕

井戸を掘る（*ido* o horu）

ido 〔n〕 **a well**

dig **a well**

¶この地方では井戸の水を使っていま
す。(Kono chihō de wa *ido* no mizu o
tsukatte imasu.)

¶In this region **well**-water is used.

いとこ〔名〕

itoko〔n〕**cousin**

¶彼はわたしのいとこです。(Kare wa
watashi no *itoko* desu.)

¶He is my **cousin**.

¶わたしにはいとこがたくさんいま
す。(Watashi ni wa *itoko* ga takusan
imasu.)

¶I have many **cousins**.

いない 以内〔名〕

inai〔n〕**within, no more than**

¶この本は1週間以内に返してくださ
い。(Kono hon wa isshūkan *inai* ni
kaeshite kudasai.)

¶Please return this book **within** one
week.

¶この建物の10メートル以内で火を
使ってはいけません。(Kono tatemono
no jūmētoru *inai* de hi o tsukatte wa
ikemasen.)

¶It is forbidden to have a fire 〚to
smoke, etc.〛 **within** 10 meters of this
building.

いなか 田舎〔名〕

inaka〔n〕**country, countryside;
one's native place**

¶たくさんの人が田舎から都会へ出て
働いています。(Takusan no hito ga
inaka kara tokai e dete hataraite imasu.)

¶Many people have left **the country**
and gone to the city to work.

¶冬休みには田舎へ帰ります。
(Fuyuyasumi ni wa *inaka* e kaerimasu.)

¶[I] will return **home to the
countryside** during winter vacation.

⇒都会 **tokai**

いぬ 犬〔名〕

inu〔n〕**dog**

¶門の前に犬がいます。(Mon no mae
ni *inu* ga imasu.)

¶There is **a dog** in front of the gate.

¶彼は犬を2匹飼っています。(Kare wa
inu o nihiki katte imasu.)

¶He keeps two **dogs**.

いね 稲〔名〕

ine〔n〕**rice plant**

稲刈り (*ine*kari)

rice reaping, harvesting **rice**

¶稲がよく実っています。(Ine ga yoku
minotte imasu.)

¶**The rice plants** are doing well.

いのち　命〔名〕

命を助ける（*inochi* o tasukeru）命が助
かる（*inochi* ga tasukaru）

¶ひどいけがですが、命は大丈夫で
す。（Hidoi kega desu ga, *inochi* wa
daijōbu desu.）

¶毎年たくさんの人が交通事故で命を
落としています。（Mainen takusan no
hito ga kōtsū-jiko de *inochi* o otoshite
imasu.）

inochi 〔n〕 **life**

save〚spare〛**someone's life**, save
〚spare〛**a creature's life** // escape
death, survive

¶It's a bad injury but not a **mortal** one.

¶Every year a great many people lose
their lives in traffic accidents.

いのる　祈る〔動Ⅰ〕

¶御健康をお祈りします。（Gokenkō o
oinorishimasu.）
¶神に平和を祈りました。（Kami ni
heiwa o *inorimashita*.）

inoru 〔vⅠ〕 **pray; wish**

¶[I] **hope** for your continued good
health.
¶[I] **prayed** to God for peace.

いはん　違反〔名、～する〕

規則違反（kisoku-*ihan*）交通違反
（kōtsū-*ihan*）選挙違反（senkyo-*ihan*）
スピード違反（supiido-*ihan*）契約に違
反する（keiyaku ni *ihan* suru）

¶そんなことをすると法律に違反しま
す。（Sonna koto o suru to hōritsu ni *ihan*
shimasu.）

ihan 〔n, ～*suru*〕 **violation,
infraction**

a **violation** of regulations, **an
infraction** of the rules // a traffic
violation // an election law **violation** //
a speeding **violation**, speeding //
violate a contract

¶That sort of thing **is against** the law.

いま　今〔名〕

①［現在］
¶今、何時ですか。（Ima, nanji
desuka？）
¶この本は今から50年ぐらい前に書か
れました。（Kono hon wa *ima*kara
gojūnen gurai mae ni kakaremashita.）
②［現在を中心にごく近い前後の時］
¶わたしは今来たばかりです。
（Watashi wa *ima* kita bakari desu.）

ima 〔n〕 **now, at present; just
now, soon**

① [now, at present]
¶What time is it **now**?

¶This book was written about 50 years
ago.

② [just now, soon]
¶I have **just now** arrived.

¶今行きますから、ちょっと待ってください。(Ima ik*ima*su kara, chotto matte kudasai.)

¶ I will come **right away** so please wait for me.

いみ 意味〔名、〜する〕

imi 〔n, 〜*suru*〕 **meaning, sense; significance**

① [言葉などの表しているものごと・内容]

① [meaning, sense (of a word, etc.)]

¶この言葉の意味がわかりません。(Kono kotoba no *imi* ga wakarimasen.)

¶ [I] don't know **the meaning** of this word.

¶この印は何を意味していますか。(Kono shirushi wa nani o *imi* shite imasu ka?)

¶ What is **the meaning** of this mark?

②[ねうち・ためになることなど]

② [significance, meaning, value]

¶この仕事はたいへん意味があると思います。(Kono shigoto wa taihen *imi* ga aru to omoimasu.)

¶ I think this job is very **meaningful**.

いも 芋〔名〕

imo 〔n〕 **potato**

じゃが芋 (jaga*imo*) 里芋 (sato*imo*) さつま芋 (satsuma*imo*) 山芋 (yama*imo*)

potato, white **potato** // taro // sweet **potato** // yam

いもうと 妹〔名〕

imōto 〔n〕 **younger sister**

¶わたしには妹が二人います。(Watashi ni wa *imōto* ga futari imasu.)

¶ I have two **younger sisters**.

¶妹さんはお元気ですか。(Imōtosan wa ogenki desu ka?)

¶ How is your **sister** (literally, Is your **younger sister** well)?

⇔姉 ane

いや〔形動〕

iya 〔adj-v〕 **disagreeable, unpleasant, distasteful, offensive**

¶あの人はいつも不満ばかり言っていて、いやな人です。(Ano hito wa itsu mo fuman bakari itte ite, *iya* na hito desu.)

¶ [He] is a **disagreeable** person who is always complaining.

¶都会の生活はもういやになりました。(Tokai no seikatsu wa mō *iya* ni narimashita.)

¶ I have gotten **fed up** with city life.

いよいよ 〔副〕

① [ますます、よりいっそう]

¶台風が近づいて、風はいよいよ激しくなりました。(Taifū ga chikazuite, kaze wa *iyoiyo* hageshiku narimashita.)

¶問題はいよいよ複雑になってきました。(Mondai wa *iyoiyo* fukuzatsu ni natte kimashita.)

② [予定されていたことなどがついに起こる様子、とうとう]

¶いよいよ出発の日が来ました。(*Iyoiyo* shuppatsu no hi ga kima shita.)

¶いよいよ今日が卒業式ですね。(*Iyoiyo* kyō ga sotsugyōshiki desu ne.)

いらい 以来 〔名〕

¶日本に来て以来、ずっと東京に住んでいます。(Nihon ni kite *irai*, zutto Tōkyō ni sunde imasu.)

¶先月以来田中さんに会っていません。(Sengetsu *irai* Tanaka san ni atte imasen.)

いらっしゃる 〔動 I〕

① [来る]

¶よくいらっしゃいました。(Yoku *irasshaimashita*.)

¶こちらにいらっしゃい。(Kochira ni *irasshai*.)

*「来る (kuru)」の尊敬語。

② [行く]

¶これから会議にいらっしゃいますか。(Kore kara kaigi ni *irasshaimasu* ka?)

¶先生は旅行にいらっしゃいました。(Sensei wa ryokō ni *irasshaimashita*.)

iyoiyo 〔adv〕 ever more, more and more; at last

① [ever more, more and more, increasingly]

¶ With the approaching typhoon, the winds have become 〚the winds became〛 **increasingly** violent.

¶ The problem has gotten **more and more** complicated.

② [at last, finally]

¶ Well, the day of departure has arrived.

¶ Well, today is **finally** graduation day, isn't it?

irai 〔n〕 since, after that

¶ [I] have lived in Tokyo **ever since** coming to Japan.

¶ [I] haven't seen [Miss] Tanaka **since** last month.

irassharu 〔v I〕 come; go; be

① [come]

¶ Welcome. [I'm] glad **you could come**.

¶ **Come** over here please.

*This *irassharu* is the honorific form of *kuru*.

② [go]

¶ **Are you going** to the meeting 〚conference〛 now?

¶ The professor 〚teacher, doctor, etc.〛 **has left** on a trip.

＊「行く（iku）」の尊敬語。

③ [いる]

¶「先生は研究室にいらっしゃいますか。」(Sensei wa kenkyūshitsu ni *irasshaimasu* ka？)「はい、いらっしゃいます。」(Hai, *irasshaimasu*.)

¶あそこで新聞を読んでいらっしゃる方はどなたですか。(Asoko de shinbun o yonde *irassharu* kata wa donata desu ka？)

＊「いる（iru）」の尊敬語。

④ [である]

¶あの方は上田さんの奥さんでいらっしゃいます。(Ano kata wa Ueda san no okusan de *irasshaimasu*.)

¶その後お元気でいらっしゃいますか。(Sono go ogenki de *irasshaimasu* ka？)

＊「である（de aru）」の尊敬語。

＊「ますの形」は「いらっしゃいます（irasshaimasu）」となる。

いりぐち 入り口 〔名〕

¶この建物の入り口はどこですか。(Kono tatemono no *iriguchi* wa doko desu ka？)

¶入り口はあちらです。(Iriguchi wa achira desu.)

⇔出口 deguchi

いる 要る 〔動 I〕

¶この計画を実現するにはいくらぐらいお金が要りますか。(Kono keikaku o jitsugen suru ni wa ikura gurai okane ga *irimasu* ka？)

---

*This *irassharu* is the honorific form of *iku*.

③ [be, exist, be present]

¶ " Is the professor in the office 〚laboratory〛?"
"Yes, [he] **is**."

¶ Who is that gentleman 〚lady〛 reading a newspaper over there?

*This *irassharu* is the honorific form of *iru*.

④ [be]

¶ That lady **is** Mr. Ueda's wife.

¶ How **have you been** since then?

*This *irassharu* is the honorific form of *de aru*.

＊The *-masu* form of *irassharu* is *irasshaimasu*.

iriguchi 〚n〛 entrance

¶ Where is **the entrance** of this building?

¶ **The entrance** is over there.

iru 〚v I〛 need, be necessary

¶ How much money **will be needed** to carry out this project?

¶ この雑誌はもう要りませんから捨ててください。（Kono zasshi wa mō *irimasen* kara sutete kudasai.）

¶ [I] **don't need** these magazines any longer; please throw them out.

いる〔動II〕

① [人や動物などがある所に存在する]
¶ 父は今部屋にいます。（Chichi wa ima heya ni *imasu*.）

¶ 今そこにはだれもいません。（Ima soko ni wa dare mo *imasen*.）

② [滞在する、住んでいる]
¶ あの外国人はもう5年も日本にいます。（Ano gaikokujin wa mō gonen mo Nihon ni *imasu*.）

（〜て）いる〔連〕

① [動作・作用の進行の状態を表す]

¶ 子供が庭で遊んでいます。（Kodomo ga niwa de asonde *imasu*.）

¶ 兄は部屋で本を読んでいます。（Ani wa heya de hon o yonde *imasu*.）

② [職業などに従事している状態を表す]

¶ 姉は銀行で働いています。（Ane wa ginkō de hataraite *imasu*.）

¶ 弟は大学で教えています。（Otōto wa daigaku de oshiete *imasu*.）

③ [ある動作の結果の状態を表す]

¶ 窓が開いています。（Mado ga aite *imasu*.）

¶ この時計は壊れています。（Kono tokei wa kowarete *imasu*.）

¶ 彼は帽子をかぶっています。（Kare wa bōshi o kabutte *imasu*.）

→（〜て）ある（〜te) **aru**

iru 〔v II〕 be, exist; live, reside

① [be, exist]
¶ My father **is** now in his room.

¶ No one **is** there now.

② [live, reside, dwell]
¶ That foreigner **has** already **been** in Japan for five years.

(-te)iru 〔compd〕 an expression indicating continuing action or a resultant state

① [be 〜ing, keep 〜ing; indicates continuing action]
¶ The children **are playing** in the garden 〚yard〛.

¶ My (older) brother **is reading** a book in his room.

② [indicates the state of being engaged in an occupation, etc.]
¶ My older sister **works** at a bank.

¶ My younger brother **is teaching** at a college.

③ [be 〜; indicates a state resulting from an action]
¶ The window **is open**.

¶ This watch 〚clock〛 **is broken**.

¶ He **is wearing** a hat.

いれる　入れる〔動Ⅱ〕

① [ものを何かの中に移す]

¶ コーヒーに砂糖を入れますか。
（Kōhii ni satō o *iremasu* ka？）

¶ 窓を開けて、新しい空気を入れま
しょう。（Mado o akete, atarashii kūki o
iremashō.）

⇔出す dasu

② [学校や病院などに入らせる]

¶ 今年、子供を小学校に入れました。
（Kotoshi, kodomo o shōgakkō ni
iremashita.）

¶ 母が病気になったので、駅の前の病
院に入れました。（Haha ga byōki ni
natta node, eki no mae no byōin ni
iremashita.）

③ [含める、いっしょに計算する]
¶ 結婚した兄も入れて兄弟は5人で
す。（Kekkon shita ani mo *irete* kyōdai
wa gonin desu.）

④ [お茶やコーヒーなどが飲めるよう
に用意する]
¶ お茶を入れましょう。（Ocha o
iremashō.）

いろ　色〔名〕

茶色（cha*iro*）灰色（hai*iro*）黄色
（ki*iro*）緑色（midori*iro*）桃色
（momo*iro*）

¶ あなたはどんな色が好きですか。
（Anata wa donna *iro* ga suki desu ka？）

¶ 濃い色がいいですか、薄い色がいい
ですか。（Koi *iro* ga ii desu ka, usui *iro*
ga ii desu ka？）

ireru 〔v Ⅱ〕 **put in, add; send; include; prepare (hot drinks)**

① [put in, add, insert]

¶ Do you **take** sugar **in** your coffee?

¶ Let's open the window to **let in** some fresh air.

② [be admitted to a hospital, school, etc.]

¶ My child **started** elementary school this year.

¶ My mother is sick and **was admitted** to the hospital in front of the station.

③ [include]
¶ **Counting** my married (elder) brother, there are five of us children.

④ [prepare (coffee, tea, etc.)]

¶ **I'll fix** some tea now.

iro 〔n〕 **color**

light brown, brown // gray // yellow // green // pink

¶ What **colors** do you like?

¶ Do you want a dark **color** or a light **color?**

いろいろ 〔副、形動、〜の〕

¶ この問題についていろいろ考えてみましたが、どうしたらよいかわかりません。(Kono mondai ni tsuite *iroiro* kangaete mimashita ga, dō shitara yoi ka wakarimasen.)

¶ デパートではいろいろな物を売っています。(Depāto de wa *iroiro* na mono o utte imasu.)

¶ 学生の意見はいろいろです。(Gakusei no iken wa *iroiro* desu.)

＊副詞は「いろいろと（iroiro to)」の形でも使う。また、「いろいろな（iroiro na)」は、「いろんな（ironna)」とも言う。

⇒さまざま **samazama**

いわ 岩 〔名〕

¶ 山で岩から落ちてけがをしました。(Yama de *iwa* kara ochite kega o shimashita.)

¶ あの岩の上に鳥がいます。(Ano *iwa* no ue ni tori ga imasu.)

いわう 祝う 〔動 I 〕

¶ みんなで友達の誕生日を祝いました。(Minna de tomodachi no tanjōbi o *iwaimashita*.)

¶ 友達の結婚を祝って、プレゼントしました。(Tomodachi no kekkon o *iwatte*, purezento shimashita.)

-いん -員 〔尾〕

駅員

¶ 私の父は会社員です。(Watashi no chichi wa kaishain desu.)

---

iroiro 〔adv, adj-v, 〜no〕 **various, several.**

¶ [I] have thought about this problem **from various angles,** but [I] don't know what to do.

¶ Department stores sell **a variety** of items.

¶ Student opinion **is divided.**

＊The adverbial *iroiro* is also used in the form *iroiro* to. *Iroiro na* sometimes becomes *ironna.*

iwa 〔n〕 **rock, crag**

¶ [I] fell from **some rocks** in the mountains and hurt [my]self.

¶ There is a bird on that **rock** over there.

iwau 〔v I 〕 **congratulate, celebrate**

¶ [We] all **celebrated** a friend's birthday together.

¶ [I] gave my friend a wedding present.

-in 〔suf〕 **person, worker**

station worker

¶ My father is a white-collar worker.

インク 〔名〕

¶ペンとインクをください。(Pen to *inku* o kudasai.)

¶万年筆にインクを入れました。(Mannenhitsu ni *inku* o iremashita.)

いんさつ 印刷 〔名、〜する〕

印刷物 (*insatsu*butsu) 印刷所 (*insatsu*jo)

¶この本は印刷が悪くて読みにくいです。(Kono hon wa *insatsu* ga warukute yominikui desu.)

¶この本は日本で印刷されました。(Kono hon wa Nihon de *insatsu* saremashita.)

いんしょう 印象 〔名〕

第一印象 (daiichi-*inshō*) 印象的 (*inshō*teki)

¶新しい先生はみんなにいい印象を与えました。(Atarashii sensei wa minna ni ii *inshō* o ataemashita.)

¶あのレストランはサービスが悪くて、たいへん印象が悪かったです。(Ano resutoran wa sābisu ga warukute, taihen *inshō* ga warukatta desu.)

¶あの人はあまり印象に残っていません。(Ano hito wa amari *inshō* ni nokotte imasen.)

inku 〔n〕 ink

¶ A pen and **ink**, please.

¶ [I] put **ink** in the fountain pen.

insatsu 〔n, 〜suru〕 printing, presswork

printed matter // a press, a **print** shop

¶ **The printing** in this book is poor so it is hard to read.

¶ This book **was printed** in Japan.

inshō 〔n〕 impression

one's first **impression** // **impressive, memorable, striking, dramatic**

¶ The new teacher **impressed** everyone favorably.

¶ The service was bad in that restaurant, giving a very poor **impression**.

¶ [He] didn't make a very strong **impression** on me.

う

う〔助動〕

① [意志を表す]

¶君にこのお菓子をやろう。(Kimini kono okashi o yarō.)

¶来年、日本へ行こうと思っています。(Rainen, Nihon e ikō to omotte imasu.)

¶どんなテレビを買おうとお思いですか。(Donna terebi o kaō to oomoi desu ka?)

¶上田さんは来年日本へ帰ろうと考えているそうです。(Ueda san wa rainen Nihon e kaerō to kangaete iru sō desu.)

*「～と思う (～to omou)」「～と考える (to kangaeru)」などといっしょに使うことが多い。

② [勧誘を表す]

¶仕事が終わったから帰ろう。(Shigoto ga owatta kara kaerō.)

¶勉強が終わったら、映画を見に行こう。(Benkyō ga owattara, eiga o mini ikō.)

③ [ある動作・作用がこれから行われるという意味を表す]

¶手紙を書こうとしたら、電話がかかってきました。(Tegami o kakō to shitara, denwa ga kakatte kimashita.)

¶エレベーターが閉まろうとしたので、急いで乗りました。(Erebētā ga shimarō to shita node, isoide norimashita.)

-u 〔auxil〕 **a verb ending indicating intent, urging, etc.**

① [experesses intent]

¶ Here, **have** this candy 〚sweet, cake, etc.〛 (literally, **I will give** you this candy).

¶ **I am thinking of going** to Japan next year.

¶ What sort of television **are you thinking of buying?**

¶ I hear that [Mr.] Ueda **is thinking of returning** to Japan next year.

*Generally used together with ～ *to omou,* ～ *to kangaeru,* etc.

② [expresses urging]

¶ We've finished the job so **let's go home**.

¶ **Let's go see** a movie after studying.

③ [indicates that some action or process is about to occur]

¶ The phone rang **just as I was about to write** a letter.

¶ [I] hurriedly got in the elevator **just as the doors were about to close**.

＊「〜うとする（〜u to suru）」の形で使うことが多い。
＊「う（u）」はⅠ型動詞につき、その他の動詞には「よう（yō）」がつく。
⇒よう **yō**

＊Generally used in the pattern "-ō *to suru*."
＊When added to Type I verbs -ō is used, but for other verbs -yō is used.

ウイスキー〔名〕

¶わたしはウイスキーもビールも飲みます。（Watashi wa *uisukii* mo biiru mo nomimasu.）

uisukii〔n〕**whiskey**

¶ I drink both **whiskey** and beer.

うえ 上〔名〕

① [位置が高い所]
¶富士山の頂上は雲の上にあります。（Fujisan no chōjō wa kumo no *ue* ni arimasu.）
¶3ページの上から7行めを見てください。（Sanpēji no *ue* kara nanagyōme o mite kudasai.）
② [物の表面]
¶テーブルの上をふいてください。（Tēburu no *ue* o fuite kudasai.）
¶床の上に紙くずが落ちています。（Yuka no *ue* ni kamikuzu ga ochite imasu.）
③ [年齢・地位・程度などが高いこと]
¶いちばん上の姉は結婚しています。（Ichiban *ue* no ane wa kekkon shite imasu.）
¶英語を話す力は、山田さんのほうがわたしより上です。（Eigo o hanasu chikara wa, yamada san no hō ga watashi yori *ue* desu.）
⇔下 **shita**

ue〔n〕**up, upward, above; top; higher, superior, older**

① [up, upward, above; the upper part]
¶ The top of Mount Fuji is **above** the clouds.

¶ Please look at the seventh line from **the top** on page 3.

② [top]
¶ Please wipe off the table.

¶ Some paper scraps have fallen **onto** the floor.

③ [higher, superior, older, more than]
¶ My **oldest** sister is married.

¶ [Miss] Yamada can speak English **better** than I can.

うえる 植える〔動Ⅱ〕

¶庭に木を植えました。（Niwa ni ki o *uemashita*.）

ueru〔v Ⅱ〕**plant, raise, grow**

¶ [I] **planted** a tree in the yard.

うかがう　伺う〔動Ⅰ〕

① [きく、尋ねる]

¶すみません。ちょっと伺います
が…。(Sumimasen. Chotto *ukagaimasu
ga...*)

¶田中さんの御意見を伺いたいのです
が。(Tanaka san no goiken o *ukagaitai
no desuga...*)

*「きく (kiku)」「尋ねる (tazuneru)」
の謙譲語。

② [聞く、耳にする]

¶先生のおうわさはたびたび伺ってお
ります。(Sensei no ouwasa wa tabitabi
ukagatte orimasu.)

¶中村さんは来月アメリカへ行かれる
と伺っております。(Nakamura san wa
raigetsu Amerika e ikareru to *ukagatte*
orimasu.)

*「聞く (kiku)」の謙譲語。

③ [訪問する]

¶あした、先生のお宅へ伺ってもよろ
しいでしょうか。(Ashita, sensei no
otaku e *ukagatte* mo yoroshii deshō
ka？)

¶何時ごろ伺ったらよろしいでしょう
か。(Nanji goro *ukagattara* yoroshii
deshōka？)

*「訪問する (hōmon suru)」の謙譲
語。

うかぶ　浮かぶ〔動Ⅰ〕

① [水面・空中などに物がとどまって
いる]

¶木の葉が水に浮かんでいます。
(Konoha ga mizu ni *ukande* imasu.)

---

ukagau 〔vⅠ〕 **ask, inquire; hear;
visit, call on**

① [ask, inquire]

¶Excuse me. Could you tell me 〜?

¶Could you give [us] your view, [Mr.]
Tanaka?

*This *ukagau* is the humble form of
kiku and of *tazuneru*.

② [hear]

¶**I have heard** a lot about you, sir
〚ma'am〛 (said to one's teacher, doctor,
etc.).

¶**I hear** that [Mr.] Nakamura is going
to the United States next month.

*This *ukagau* is the humble form of
kiku.

③ [visit, call on]

¶**May I call** on you at home tomorrow
(said to one's teacher, doctor, etc.)?

¶About what time **should I come**?

*This *ukagau* is the humble form of
hōmon suru.

ukabu 〔vⅠ〕 **float; rise to the
surface, appear; occur to one**

① [float]

¶Leaves **are floating** on top of the
water.

¶この海は、油が浮かんでいて汚いですね。(Kono umi wa, abura ga *ukande* ite kitanai desu ne.)

¶ The water in this sea **is oily** and dirty.

¶青い空に白い雲が浮かんでいます。(Aoi sora ni shiroi kumo ga *ukande* imasu.)

¶ White clouds **are floating** in a blue sky.

→浮く uku

② [あるものがものの表面に現れる]

② [rise to the surface, appear]

¶悲しくて目に涙が浮かんできました。(Kanashikute me ni namida ga *ukande* kimashita.)

¶ [I] was so sad tears **came to** [my] eyes.

③ [考えなどが頭などの中に現れる]

③ [occur to one, strike one]

¶いい考えが頭に浮かびました。(Ii kangae ga atama ni *ukabimashita*.)

¶ **A** good idea **came** to me [**popped** into my mind]].

うく 浮く [動 I]

uku [v I] **float, rise to the surface**

¶木の葉が水に浮いたり沈んだりして流れていきます。(Konoha ga mizu ni *uitari* shizundari shite nagarete ikimasu.)

¶ Leaves are being carried along by the current, now **rising** and now sinking below the surface.

¶湖には死んだ魚がたくさん浮いていました。(Mizuumi ni wa shinda sakana ga takusan *uite* imashita.)

¶ Numerous dead fish **were floating** on the lake.

⇔沈む shizumu

うけつけ 受付 [名]

uketsuke [n] **acceptance, receipt; reception desk; receptionist, usher**

¶御用の方は受付へおいでください。(Goyō no kata wa *uketsuke* e oide kudasai.)

¶ Visitors are directed to **the reception desk** (a written sign).

¶受付時間は午前9時から午後5時までです。(Uketsuke-jikan wa gozen kuji kara gogo goji made desu.)

¶ **Reception** office hours are from 9 AM to 5 PM.

うけつける 受け付ける [動 II]

uketsukeru [v II] **accept, receive**

¶入学の申し込みは、今月の十日まで受け付けています。(Nyūgaku no mōshikomi wa kongetsu no tooka made *uketsukete* imasu.)

¶ Applications for admittance to this school **will be accepted** until the tenth of this month.

¶会員になりたい人はここで受け付けていますから、申し込んでください。
(Kaiin ni naritai hito wa koko de *uketsukete* imasu kara, mōshikonde kudasai.)

¶ Will those who wish to become members please apply here.

うけとり 受取 〔名〕

¶この荷物の受取人はだれですか。
(Kono nimotsu no *uketori*nin wa dare desu ka?)

uketori 〔n〕 receipt

¶ Who is this package addressed to?

うけとる 受け取る 〔動 I〕

¶今日、母からの手紙を受け取りました。(Kyō, haha kara no tegami o uketorimashita.)

¶お金を払って、品物を受け取るのを忘れました。(Okane o haratte, shinamono o *uketoru* no o wasuremashita.)

uketoru 〔v I〕 receive, take delivery of

¶ **I received** a letter from my mother today.

¶ [I] paid but forgot **to take** my purchase with [me].

うける 受ける 〔動 II〕

① [自分の方に向かってくるものを支え止める]
¶山田さんは飛んできたボールを左手で受けました。(Yamada san wa tonde kita bōru o hidarite de *ukemashita*.)

¶滝の水を手で受けて飲みました。
(Taki no mizu o te de *ukete* nomimashita.)

② [他からの働きかけに対して応じたり認めたりする]
質問を受ける (shitsumon o *ukeru*) 手術を受ける (shujutsu o *ukeru*)

¶わたしは来年、大学の入学試験を受けます。(Watashi wa rainen, daigaku no nyūgaku-shiken o *ukemasu*.)

ukeru 〔v II〕 catch, take; receive, accept, undergo; suffer, be subjected to; be given
① [catch, take]

¶ [Mr.] Yamada **caught** the ball in [his] left hand.

¶ [I] **took** water from the waterfall in [my] cupped hand(s) and drank it.

② [receive, accept, undergo]

take a question, **answer** a question // **undergo** a surgical operation, be operated upon
¶ **I will take** university entrance exams next year.

¶わたしは山田さんから結婚について相談を受けました。（Watashi wa yamada san kara kekkon ni tsuite sōdan o *ukemashita*.）

¶[Miss] Yamada **consulted me** about getting married.

③[ほかからの働きかけがあるものに及ぶ]

③[suffer, be subjected to]

傷を受ける（kizu o *ukeru*）影響を受ける（eikyō o *ukeru*）

be wounded, be injured // be influenced

¶この地方は台風で大きな被害を受けました。（Kono chihō wa taifū de ookina higai o ukemashita.）

¶This region **suffered** extensive damage in the typhoon.

④[ほかから何かを与えられる]
許可を受ける（kyoka o *ukeru*）

④[be given]
obtain permission, be authorized

うごかす 動かす〔動 I〕

ugokasu 〔v I〕 **move, change the position of; set in motion, operate**

①[ある物の位置を移す]
¶重い石を一人で動かしました。（Omoi ishi o hitori de *ugokashimashita*.）

①[move, change the position of, shift]
¶[I] **moved** the heavy rock all by [My] self.

②[機械などを働かせる]
¶この機械を動かすのは難しいですよ。（Kono kikai o *ugokasu* no wa muzukashii desu yo.）

②[set in motion, operate]
¶It is difficult **to operate** this machine 〚apparatus, etc.〛.

うごき 動き〔名〕

ugoki 〔n〕 **movement, motion; trend, movement**

①[運動・動作・行動など]
¶寒くなると、体の動きが鈍くなります。（Samuku naruto, karada no *ugoki* ga nibuku narimasu.）

①[movement, motion, activity]
¶[We] are loath **to move** when it is cold.

②[ものごとの移り変わり]
¶テレビやラジオのおかげで、世界の動きがよくわかるようになりました。（Terebi ya rajio no okagede, sekai no *ugoki* ga yoku wakaru yō ni narimashita.）

②[trend, movement]
¶World **trends** have become easy to follow thanks to television and radio.

うごく 動く〔動 I〕

ugoku 〔v I〕 **move, stir; work, run, go**

①[あるものの位置が移る]

①[move, stir]

¶写真を撮りますから、動かないでください。(Shashin o torimasu kara, *ugokanaide* kudasai.)

¶ **Don't move**—I'm going to take the photo now!

②[機械などが働く]

②[work, run, go]

¶この時計は動いていません。(Kono tokei wa *ugoite* imasen.)

¶ This clock 〚watch〛 **isn't running**.

¶大雪で電車が動かなくなりました。(Ooyuki de densha ga *ugokanaku* narimashita.)

¶ The trains have been 〚weret〛 **brought to a standstill** by the heavy snows.

うし 牛 [名]

牛小屋 (*ushi*goya)

ushi 〔n〕 **cow, cattle**

a **cow**shed, a **cattle** barn

うしなう 失う [動 I]

ushinau 〔v I〕 **lose, be deprived of**

¶田中さんは職を失って、生活に困っています。(Tanaka san wa shoku o *ushinatte*, seikatsu ni komatte imasu.)

¶ [Mr.] Tanaka **has lost** [his] job and is having a hard time making ends meet.

¶山田さんはついに外国へ行く機会を失ってしまいました。(Yamada san wa tsuini gaikoku e iku kikai o *ushinatte* shimaimashita.)

¶ In the end [Mr.] Yamada **missed out** on the chance to go abroad.

うしろ 後ろ [名]

ushiro 〔n〕 **the back, the rear; behind, in back of**

¶先生の後ろに黒板があります。(Sensei no *ushiro* ni kokuban ga arimasu.)

¶ There is a blackboard **in back** of the teacher.

¶道を歩いていたら、後ろから犬がついてきました。(Michi o aruite itara, *ushiro* kara inu ga tsuite kimashita.)

¶ As [I] walked down the Street a dog started following [me].

⇒前 mae

うすい 薄い [形]

usui 〔adj〕 **thin; weak**

①[厚くない]

①[thin, not thick]

¶夏には薄いシャツを着ます。(Natsu ni wa *usui* shatsu o kimasu.)

¶ [We] wear **thin** shirts in summer.

¶辞書には薄い紙が使ってあります。(Jisho ni wa *usui* kami ga tsukatte arimasu.)

¶ **Thin** paper is used in dictionaries.

↔厚い atsui

② [程度などが少ない]

¶コーヒーは、薄いのと濃いのとどちらがいいですか。(Kōhii wa, *usui* no to koi no to dochira ga ii desu ka?)

↔濃い **koi**

② [weak, thin, light, scanty]

¶ How do you like your coffee—**weak** or strong?

うそ 〔名〕

うそをつく (*uso* o tsuku)

¶あの人が言ったことはうそです。(Ano hito ga itta koto wa *uso* desu.)

¶うそを言わないで、本当のことを言いなさい。(*Uso* o iwanaide, hontō no koto o iinasai.)

⇒本当 **hontō**

uso 〔n〕 a lie, falsehood

tell **a lie**

¶ What [he] said **isn't true**.

¶ Don't **lie** now, tell the truth.

うた 歌 〔名〕

歌を歌う (*uta* o utau)

¶春子さんは歌が上手です。(Haruko san wa *uta* ga jōzu desu.)

uta 〔n〕 a song, singing

sing **a song**

¶ Haruko is a good **singer**.

うたう 歌う 〔動 I〕

¶さあ、みんなで歌いましょう。(Sā, minna de *utaimashō*.)

¶子供が歌を歌っています。(Kodomo ga uta o *utate* imasu.)

utau 〔v I〕 sing

¶ Well, **let's** all sing now.

¶ The children **are singing**.

うたがう 疑う 〔動 I〕

¶山田さんは、わたしがうそをついているのではないかと疑っています。(Yamada san wa watashiga uso o tsuite iru no de wa nai ka to *utagatte* imasu.)

⇔信じる **shinjiru**

utagau 〔v I〕 doubt, be doubtful; suspect, be suspicious

¶ [Mr.] Yamada **thinks** I might be lying.

うち 内 〔名〕

① [何かで区切られた中側]
内側 (*uchi*gawa)

uchi 〔n〕 inside, the interior; one's home, one's family; within, while; between, among

① [inside, the interior]
the inside, the **inner** part; within, inside

¶電気が消えて、内も外も真っ暗です。(Denki ga kiete, *uchi* mo soto mo makkura desu.)

¶ The lights went out so it is now pitch black both **inside** and out.

¶ドアには内からかぎが掛かっていて開きません。(Doa ni wa *uchi* kara kagi ga kakatte ite akimasen.)

¶ The door won't open as it is locked from **inside**.

↔外 soto

②[自分の所属しているところ]

② [one's home, family, etc.]

¶うちの会社は駅の近くにあります。(*Uchi* no kaisha wa eki no chikaku ni arimasu.)

¶ **My** 〚**office**〛 is near the station.

¶うちの父は小学校の先生です。(*Uchi* no chichi wa shōgakkō no sensei desu.)

¶ **My** father is an elementary school teacher.

③[ある一定の時間の間]

③ [within, while, in the course of, before; during a set period of time]

¶暗くならないうちに帰りましょう。(Kuraku naranai *uchi* ni kaerimashō.)

¶ Let's start for home **before** it gets dark.

¶この本は、読んでいるうちにだんだんおもしろくなってきました。(Kono hon wa, yonde iru *uchi* ni dandan omoshiroku natte kimashita.)

¶ This book gradually became more interesting **as** I read more of it 〚This book has gradually become more interesting **as** I have read more of it〛.

*普通「~うちに (~uchi ni)」の形で使う。

*Usually used in the pattern " ~*uchi ni*."

④[ある範囲を表す]

④ [between, among, out of, of]

¶試験問題十のうち半分しか答えられませんでした。(Shiken-mondai too no *uchi* hanbun shika kotaeraremasen deshita.)

¶ [I] could only answer half **of** the 10 test questions.

¶5人のうちで、わたしがいちばん背が低いです。(Gonin no *uchi* de, watashi ga ichiban se ga hikui desu.)

¶ I am the shortest **of** the five of us.

うち〔名〕

uchi〔n〕**a house; a household**

①[住居]

① [a house]

¶田中さんは最近うちを建てました。(Tanaka san wa saikin *uchi* o tatemashita.)

¶ [Mr.] Tanaka built **a house** recently.

¶この辺には、大きくて立派なうちがたくさんあります。（Kono hen ni wa, ookikute rippa na *uchi* ga takusan arimasu.）

¶There are many fine, large **homes** around here.

②［家庭］

②[a household]

¶あなたのうちは、何人家族ですか。（Anata no *uchi* wa, nannin kazoku desu ka？）

¶How many are there in **your** faimily?

¶わたしのうちでは父も母も働いています。（Watashi no *uchi* de wa chichi mo haha mo hataraite imasu.）

¶Both **my** mother and father work.

⇒家 ie

うちあわせる 打ち合わせる ［動 II］

uchiawaseru 〚v II〛 **make arrange ments with, work out in advance**

¶田中さんと電話で仕事について打ち合わせました。（Tanaka san to denwa de shigoto ni tsuite *uchiawasemashita.*）

¶[Mr.] Tanaka and I **decided** on the phone **how to do** the work.

¶旅行のことで友達とこれから打ち合わせなければなりません。（Ryokō no koto de tomodachi to kore kara *uchiawasenakereba* narimasen.）

¶I must go now to **work out the details** of the trip with my friends.

うつ 打つ ［動 I］

utsu 〚v I〛 **strike, hit**

①［ある物を他の物に瞬間的に強く当てる］

①[strike, hit, beat, knock]

ボールをラケットで打つ（bōru o raketto de *utsu*）くぎを打つ（kugi o *utsu*）

hit a ball with a racket // **strike** a nail

¶田中さんは転んで、頭を強く打ちました。（Tanaka san wa koronde, atama o tsuyoku *uchimashita.*）

¶[Mrs.] Tanaka fell and **got a** bad **knock** on the head.

②［たたくような動作で何かをする］
電報を打つ（denpō o *utsu*）

②[strike, tap, touch, do]
send a telegram

¶わたしはタイプを打ったことがありません。（Watashi wa taipu o *utta* koto ga arimasen.）

¶I have never **typed** anything.

③［たたいて鳴らす］
鐘を打つ（kane o *utsu*）

③[strike, beat, ring, sound]
ring a bell

¶時計が3時を打ちました。(Tokei ga sanji o *uchimashita*.)

¶ The clock **struck** three o'clock.

うつ 撃つ 〔動 I 〕

utsu 〔v I〕 **fire, shoot**

¶鉄砲で鳥を撃ちました。(Teppō de tori o *uchimashita*.)

¶ [I] **shot** a bird with a gun.

うつくしい 美しい 〔形〕

utsukushii 〔adj〕 **beautiful, lovely, pretty**

¶この辺がいちばん景色の美しい所です。(Kono hen ga ichiban keshiki no *utsukushii* tokoro desu.)

¶ The scenery **is at its best** around here.

¶会場は花で美しく飾られていまた。(Kaijō wa hana de *utsukushiku* kazararete imashita.)

¶ The hall was **prettily** decorated with flowers.

うつす 写す 〔動 I 〕

utsusu 〔v I〕 **take (a photograph), film; copy**

¶写真を写しますから、集まってください。(Shashin o *utsushimasu* kara atsumatte kudasai.)

¶ Please move together so [I] **can take** your picture.

¶先生が黒板に書いた字を学生がノートに写しています。(Sensei ga kokuban ni kaita ji o gakusei ga nōto ni *utsusite imasu*.)

¶ The students **are copying** in their notebooks the characters that their teacher wrote on the blackboard.

うつす 映す 〔動 I 〕

utsusu 〔v I〕 **reflect, project**

¶先生が映画を映して見せてくださいました。(Sensei ga eiga o *utsushite* misete kudasaimashita.)

¶ The teacher **showed** us a film.

¶姉は自分の姿を鏡に映して見てます。(Ane wa jibun no sugata o kagami ni *utsushite* mite imasu.)

¶ My (older) sister is looking at **her reflection** in the mirror.

うつす 移す 〔動 I 〕

utsusu 〔v I〕 **move, transfer**

¶本箱を机のそばへ移しました。(Honbako o tsukue no soba e *utsushimashita*.)

¶ [I] **moved** the bookcase to beside the desk.

¶卵をかごから冷蔵庫の中へ移しました。(Tamago o kago kara reizōko no naka e *utsushimashita*.)

¶ [I] **transferred** the eggs from the basket to the refrigerator.

うつる 移る〔動Ⅰ〕

¶わたしは昨日から二階の部屋へ移りました。（Watashi wa kinō kara nikai no heya e *utsurimashita*.）

¶その会社は1か月前、東京から大阪に移りました。（Sono kaisha wa ikkagetsu mae, Tōkyō kara Oosaka ni *utsurimashita*.）

utsuru〔vⅠ〕**move**

¶I **moved** to a room〖apartment〗on the second floor yesterday.

¶That company **moved** from Tokyo to Osaka a month ago.

うつる 映る〔動Ⅰ〕

¶湖に白い雲が映っています。（Mizuumi ni shiroi kumo ga *utsutte* imasu.）

¶鏡に外の景色が映っています。（Kagami ni soto no keshiki ga *utsutte* imasu.）

utsuru〔vⅠ〕**be reflected**

¶One can see a white cloud **reflected** in the lake.

¶**There is a reflection** of the scene outside in the mirror.

うつる 写る〔動Ⅰ〕

¶このカメラはとてもよく写ります。（Kono kamera wa totemo yoku *utsurimasu*.）

¶部屋が暗いから、写真がよく写らないと思います。（Heya ga kurai kara, shashin ga yoku *utsuranai* to omoimasu.）

utsuru〔vⅠ〕**be taken (a photo, etc.), come out**

¶This camera **takes** good **pictures**.

¶This room is dark so I **don't think pictures will come out** well.

うで 腕〔名〕

腕時計（*ude*dokei）腕を組む（*ude* o kumu）

¶重い物を持っていたので、腕が痛いです。（Omoi mono o motte ita node, *ude* ga itai desu.）

ude〔n〕**arm**

a **wrist**watch //fold **one's arms** in front of one; link **one's arm** through another's

¶**My arms** are sore from holding something heavy.

うどん〔名〕

¶御飯よりうどんのほうが好きです。（Gohan yori *udon* no hō ga suki desu.）

udon〔n〕**udon, udon noodles**

¶I like **udon** better than rice.

うなずく〔動Ⅰ〕

¶彼女に結婚を申し込んだ時、彼女はぼくの顔をじっと見て、うなずいてくれました。(Kanojo ni kekkon o mōshikonda toki, kanojo wa boku no kao o jitto mite, *unazuite* kuremashita.)

¶あの人は、電話で話しながら何度もうなずいていました。(Ano hito wa, denwa de hanashinagara nando mo *unazuite* imashita.)

うま 馬〔名〕

¶馬に乗ってこの広い野原を走ってみたいです。(*Uma* ni notte kono hiroi nohara o hashitte mitai desu.)

うまい〔形〕

①[上手、いい]
¶あの女の人は歌がうまいですね。(Ano onna no hito wa uta ga *umai* desune.)
¶この言葉は発音が難しくてうまく言えません。(Kono kotoba wa hatsuon ga muzukashikute *umaku* iemasen.)
↔下手 heta
→上手 jōzu

②[おいしい]
¶あの店の料理はとてもうまいよ。(Ano mise no ryōri wa totemo *umai* yo.)
¶やはり新鮮な果物はうまいね。(Yahari shinsen na kudamono wa *umai* ne.)
*女性は「うまい（umai）」のかわりに「おいしい（oishii）」のほうをよく使う。
↔まずい mazui
→おいしい oishii

unazuku 〔vⅠ〕 nod, nod assent

¶ When I asked her to marry me, she looked at me intently and then **nodded yes**.

¶ [He] **nodded** several times while talking on the telephone.

uma 〔n〕 a horse

¶ I would like to go **horseback** riding on this wide plain 〚in this large field〛.

umai 〔adj〕 skillful, good at; delicious

① [skillful, expert, good at]
¶ She is a **good** singer.

¶ This word is hard to say—[I] can't pronounce it **well**.

② [delicious, good]
¶ The food is very **good** there 〚in that restaurant, coffee shop, etc.〛.
¶ When all is said and done, fresh fruit **does taste the best**, doesn't it?

*Women usually use *oishii* rather than *umai*.

うまれ 生まれ〔名〕

¶彼は大阪の生まれです。(Kare wa Oosaka no *umare* desu.)

¶上田さんは生まれは東京ですが、育ったのは北海道だそうです。(Ueda san wa *umare* wa Tōkyō desu ga, sodatta no wa Hokkaidō da sō desu.)

umare 〔n〕 **birth, origin, birthplace**

¶He's **a native** of Osaka.

¶I hear that [Mr.] Ueda **was born** in Tokyo but raised in Hokkaido.

うまれる 生まれる〔動Ⅱ〕

¶わたしは京都で生まれました。(Watashi wa Kyōto de *umaremashita*.)

¶わたしが生まれたのは 1950 年です。(Watashi ga *umareta* no wa senkyūhyaku-gojūnen desu.)

umareru 〔v Ⅱ〕 **be born, come into existence**

¶I **was born** in Kyoto.

¶I **was born** in 1950.

うみ 海〔名〕

¶わたしの家は海の近くにあるので、夏には毎日海で泳ぎます。(Watashi no ie wa *umi* no chikaku ni aru node, natsu ni wa mainichi *umi* de oyogimasu.)

umi 〔n〕 **sea, ocean**

¶Since my home is near **the sea**, I go swimming every day in the summer.

うむ 産む〔動Ⅰ〕

¶妹が男の赤ちゃんを産みました。(Imōto ga otoko no akachan o *umimashita*.)

¶この鶏は毎日卵を産みます。(Kono niwatori wa mainichi tamago o *umimasu*.)

umu 〔v Ⅰ〕 **give birth to; produce**

¶My younger sister **gave birth** to a boy.

¶This chicken **lays** eggs every day.

うめる 埋める〔動Ⅱ〕

¶うちで飼っていた鳥が死んだので、庭に穴を掘って埋めてやりました。(Uchi de katte ita tori ga shinda node, niwa ni ana o hotte *umete* yarimashita.)

¶この辺は海を埋めて造った土地だそうです。(Kono hen wa umi o *umete* tsukutta tochi da sō desu.)

umeru 〔v Ⅱ〕 **bury; fill up, plug up**

¶[Our] pet bird died so [we] dug a hole in the yard〚garden〛and **buried** it.

¶I hear that the land around here **has been reclaimed** from the sea.

うら 裏〔名〕

① [表面の反対側]

足の裏（ashi no *ura*）裏側（*ura*gawa）
¶質問は表だけでなく裏にも書いてあ
ります。（Shitsumon wa omte dake de
naku *ura* ni mo kaite arimasu.）

② [家などのうしろの場所・入口]
裏門（*ura*mon）
¶子供達は裏の空き地で遊んでいま
す。（Kodomotachi wa *ura* no akichi de
asonde imasu.）

¶表はかぎが掛かっていますから、裏
から入ってください。（Omote wa kagi
ga kakatte imasu kara, *ura* kara haitte
kudasai.）
⇔表 omote

うらやましい〔形〕

¶わたしはあの人の成功がうらやまし
いです。（Watashi wa ano hito no seikō
ga *urayamashii* desu.）
¶あなたはお金も暇もたくさんあっ
て、うらやましいですね。（Anata wa
okane mo hima mo takusan atte,
urayamashii desu ne.）

うりば 売り場〔名〕

¶ネクタイ売り場はどこですか。
（Nekutai-*uriba* wa doko desu ka？）

うる 売る〔動Ⅰ〕

¶これはデパートで売っていますか。
（Kore wa depāto de *utte* imasu ka？）

¶あの店で売っているお菓子は、あま
りおいしくありません。（Ano mise de
utteiru okashi wa, amari oishiku
arimasen.）

---

ura 〔n〕 **the reverse, wrong side; the back, the rear**

① [the reverse, the wrong side, the back side, the other side]
the sole of the foot // the **back** side
¶ The questions are written on **the back** of the paper as well as the front.

② [the back, the rear (of a house, etc.)]
the **back** gate
¶ The children are playing in the vacant lot at **the back**.

¶ The front is locked so please enter at **the rear**.

urayamashii 〔adj〕 **be envious**

¶ **I envy** [his] success.

¶ **I envy you** for having so much money and free time.

uriba 〔n〕 **sales counter, store**

¶ Where is the necktie **counter**?

uru 〔v I〕 **sell**

¶ **Is** this **sold** at department stores 〚Can one buy this at a department store〛?

¶ The sweets 〚candy, cakes, etc.〛 **sold** at that store aren't very good.

⇔買う kau

うるさい〔形〕

¶ラジオの音がうるさくて、勉強ができません。（Rajio no oto ga *urusakute*, benkyō ga dekimasen.）

¶隣の部屋に病人がいるから、うるさくしないでください。（Tonari no heya ni byōnin ga iru kara, *urusaku* shinaide kudasai.）

⇒静か shizuka

urusai 〔adj〕 **noisy**

¶The radio **is so noisy** [I] can't study.

¶Please **be quiet** as there is someone sick in the next room.

うれしい〔形〕

¶うれしそうですね。何かいいことがあったんですか。（*Ureshisō* desu ne. Nani ka ii koto ga atta n desu ka？）

¶試験の成績がよかったので、うれしかったです。（Shiken no seiseki ga yokatta node, *ureshikatta* desu.）

⇔悲しい kanashii

ureshii 〔adj〕 **be happy, glad, pleased, joyful**

¶**You look happy**. Has something good happened?

¶[I] **was happy** because [I] got a good mark on the exam.

うわぎ 上着〔名〕

¶暑いので、上着を脱ぎました。（Atsui node *uwagi* o nugimashita.）

uwagi 〔n〕 **coat, suit jacket, upper garment, outerwear**

¶As it was hot [I] took off [my] jacket.

うわさ〔名、〜する〕

¶山田さんが結婚するといううわさは本当ですか。（Yamada san ga kekkon suru to iu *uwasa* wa hontō desu ka？）

¶うわさによると、今度山田さんは会社を辞めるそうです。（*Uwasa* ni yoru to, kondo Yamada san wa kaisha o yameru sō desu.）

uwasa 〔n, 〜*suru*〕 **rumor, gossip, report, talk, hearsay**

¶Is **the rumor** that [Mr.] Yamada is going to get married true?

¶**Rumor** has it that [Mr.] Yamada is going to quit [his] job soon.

うん 運〔名〕

運がいい（*un* ga ii）運が悪い（*un* ga warui）

un 〔n〕 **destiny, fate, chance, fortune, luck**

be lucky, be fortunate // be unlucky, be unfortunate

¶昨日、わたしが乗っていたタクシーが交通事故を起こしたのですが、わたしは運よくけがもしませんでした。(Kinō, watashi ga notte ita takushii ga kōtsū-jiko o okoshita no desuga, watashi wa *un* yoku kega mo shimasen deshita.)

¶The taxi I took yesterday caused an accident, but **fortunately** I escaped injury.

うん〔感〕

¶わたしが「いっしょに行こう。」と誘ったら、彼は「うん。」と言ってうなずきました。(Watashi ga "Issho ni ikō." to sasottara, kare wa "*un*." to itte unazukimashita.)

¶「みんなといっしょに話そうよ。」(Mina to issho ni hanasō yo.)「うん、そうしよう。」(*Un*, sō shiyō.)

＊「はい (hai)」「ええ (ee)」と同じ意味であるが、丁寧な言葉ではないから、目上の人などにはあまり使わない。

un〔interj〕**yes, yeah**

¶When I invited him to go with us, he nodded and said **OK**.

¶"Let's go talk with everyone." "**Yes**, let's."

＊*Un* has the same meaning as *hai* or *ee*, but since it is not polite language it is rarely used toward persons of higher status.

うんてん 運転〔名、〜する〕

運転手 (*unten*shu)

¶あなたは自動車の運転ができますか。(Anata wa jidōsha no *unten* ga dekimasu ka？)

¶雨の日は道が滑りやすいので、運転に気をつけなければなりません。(Ame no hi wa michi ga suberiyasui node, *unten* ni ki o tsukenakereba narimasen.)

unten〔n, 〜*suru*〕**driving (a car), operating (a machine)**
driver, operator

¶Can you **drive** a car?

¶The roads are slippery on rainy days so one must be particularly careful when **driving** then.

うんどう 運動〔名、〜する〕

①[健康のために体を動かすこと]

運動会 (*undō*kai) 運動選手 (*undō*-senshu)

undō〔n, 〜*suru*〕**motion, movement, exercise, sports; a movement, a campaign**
① [motion, movement, exercise, sports]
an **athletic** meet, a **field** meet // **an athlete, a sportsman**

¶あなたは何か運動をしていますか。
（Anata wa nani ka *undō* o shite imasu ka？）

¶最近は運動不足のため体の調子があまりよくないです。(Saikin wa *undō*-busoku no tame karada no chōshi ga amari yoku nai desu.)

② [ある目的のために人々に働きかけること]

政治運動（seiji-*undō*）選挙運動（senkyo-*undō*）

¶彼は学生時代から世界を平和にしようという運動に参加しています。
(Kare wa gakusei-jidai kara sekai o heiwa ni shiyō to iu *undō* ni sanka shite imasu.)

¶ Do you take any **exercise** 〚Do you play some **sport**〛?

¶ Recently I've been feeling a little off due to a lack of **exercise**.

② [a movement, campaign, drive]

a political **movement** // an election **campaign**

¶ He has been a participant in **the movement** for world peace since his student days.

え

え 絵〔名〕
絵はがき (ehagaki) 絵本 (ehon) 絵の具 (enogu) 絵をかく (e o kaku)

¶田中さんは絵が上手です。(Tanaka san wa e ga jōzu desu.)
¶どんな絵が好きですか。(Donna e ga suki desu ka?)

え〔感〕
¶え、何ですか。(E! Nan desu ka?)
¶えっ、それは本当ですか。(E'! Sore wa hontō desu ka?)

えいが 映画〔名〕
映画館 (eigakan) ニュース映画 (nyūsu-eiga)
¶今晩、映画を見に行きましょう。(Konban, eiga o mi ni ikimashō.)
¶あの映画はおもしろいですか。(Ano eiga wa omoshiroi desu ka?)

えいきょう 影響〔名、～する〕
¶子供は友達の影響を受けやすいです。(Kodomo wa tomodachi no eikyō o ukeyasui desu.)
¶仏教は日本の文化に大きな影響を与えました。(Bukkyō wa Nihon no bunka ni ookina eikyō o ataemashita.)

えいご 英語〔名〕
¶英語の本を買いました。(Eigo no hon o kaimashita.)
¶英語で手紙を書きました。(Eigo de tegami o kakimashita.)

---

e〔n〕 **picture, painting, drawing**
a **picture** postcard // a **picture** book // pigments, paints // draw 〚paint〛 **a picture**
¶[Mrs.] Tanaka can **draw** 〚**paint**〛 well.
¶ What sort of **pictures** 〚**paintings**〛 do you like?

e〔interj〕 **Oh!, What!; eh?, what?**
¶ What did you say?
¶ **What!** Is that really so?

eiga〔n〕 **movie, motion picture**
a **movie** theater // a news**reel**, news **film**
¶ Let's go to see **a movie** tonight.
¶ Is that **movie** interesting?

eikyō〔n, ～suru〕 **influence, effect**
¶ Children are easily **influenced** by their friends.
¶ Buddhism exerted a great **influence** on Japanese culture.

eigo〔n〕 **English, the English language**
¶[I] bought a book written in **English**.
¶[I] wrote a letter in **English**.

えいせい　衛生〔名〕

公衆衛生（kōshū-*eisei*）衛生的
（eiseiteki）

¶あの店の衛生状態はたいへんいいで
す。（Ano mise no *eisei*-jōtai wa taihen ii
desu.）

eisei 〔n〕 **hygiene, sanitation**

public **health** // **sanitary, hygienic**

¶The **sanitary** conditions in that store
〚restaurant, bar, etc.〛are very good.

えいよう　栄養〔名〕

栄養が足りない（*eiyō* ga tarinai）

¶この食べ物はたいへん栄養がありま
す。（Kono tabemono wa taihen *eiyō* ga
arimasu.）

¶じゅうぶんに栄養を取ってくださ
い。（Jūbun ni *eiyō* o totte kudasai.）

eiyō 〔n〕 **nutrition, nourishment**

be under**nourished**

¶This food is very **nutritious**.

¶Please be sure to get adequate
nutrition.

ええ〔感〕

¶「この本を貸してください。」（Kono
hon o kashite kudasai.）「ええ、いいで
すよ。」（*Ee*, ii desu yo.）

¶「お元気ですか。」（Ogenki desu
ka？）「ええ、おかげさまで。」（*Ee*,
okagesama de.）

＊「はい（hai）」のほうが丁寧な言葉
である。

⇒はい **hai**

ee 〔interj〕 **yes, yeah**

¶"Please lend me this book 〚Please let
me use this book for a while〛."
"**Yes**, certainly."

¶"How are you?"
"Fine, thank you."
(More literally, "Are you healthy?"
"**Yes**, thanks to you.")

＊*Hai* is more polite than *ee*.

えき　駅〔名〕

駅長（*eki*chō）駅員（*eki*in）

¶駅から家まで歩いて5分です。（*Eki*
kara ie made aruite gofun desu.）

¶駅のそばに銀行があります。（*Eki* no
soba ni ginkō ga arimasu.）

eki 〔n〕 **station**

a **station**master // a **station** employee

¶It is a five-minute walk from **the
station** to the house.

¶There is a bank near **the station**.

えきたい　液体〔名〕

¶あのびんの中の液体は何ですか。
（Ano bin no naka no *ekitai* wa nan desu
ka？）

ekitai 〔n〕 **liquid (state), fluid**

¶What is **the liquid** in that bottle?

¶危険な液体には色がつけてあります。(Kiken na *ekitai* ni wa iro ga tsu-kete arimasu.)
⇒気体 kitai　固体 kotai

¶ Dangerous **liquids** have had coloring added.

エスカレーター 〔名〕
¶1階から3階までエスカレーターで行きました。(Ikkai kara sangai made *esukarētā* de ikimashita.)

esukarētā 〔n〕 escalator
¶ [I] went from the first to the third floor on **the escalator**.

えだ 枝 〔名〕
木の枝 (ki no *eda*) 枝を折る (*eda* o oru)

eda 〔n〕 branch, bough, twig
a tree **branch** 〚**twig**〛 // break off a **branch** 〚**twig**〛

えび 〔名〕

ebi 〔n〕 shrimp, lobster, prawn

えらい 偉い 〔形〕

erai 〔adj〕 great, excellent; eminent

①[人物・能力などが優れている]
¶上田博士は偉い学者です。(Ueda hakushi wa *erai* gakusha desu.)
¶あの学生は将来偉くなるでしょう。
(Ano gakusei wa shōrai *eraku* naru deshō.)

① [great, excellent, outstanding]
¶ Dr. Ueda is a **great** scholar.

¶ That student should **make** [**his**] **mark** in the future.

②[地位などが上である]

¶会社の偉い人に会いました。(Kaisha no *erai* hito ni aimashita.)
¶彼は偉くないのに、いばっています。(Kare wa *eraku* nai noni, ibatte imasu.)

② [eminent, celebrated, famous, of high position]
¶ [I] met a person **high up** in the company.

¶ He puts on airs even though **he's nobody important**.

えらぶ 選ぶ 〔動Ⅰ〕
¶好きな飲み物を選んでください。
(Suki na nomimono o *erande* kudasai.)
¶田中さんは社長に選ばれました。
(Tanaka san wa shachō ni *eraba-remashita*.)

erabu 〔vⅠ〕 choose, select
¶ Please **choose** what you would like to drink.

¶ [Mr.] Tanaka **was chosen** president of the company.

エレベーター 〔名〕

¶エレベーターで5階まで行きました。
(*Erebētā* de gokai made ikimashi-ta.)
¶階段よりエレベーターのほうが楽です。(Kaidan yori *erebētā* no hō ga raku desu.)

erebētā 〔n〕 **elevator**

¶[I] went up to the fifth floor in **the elevator**.

¶Taking **the elevator** is easier than walking up the stairs.

(-)えん (-)円 〔名、尾〕

1 〔名〕
円をかく (*en* o kaku) 円形の建物
(*en*kei no tatemono)
2 〔尾〕
100円 (hyaku*en*) 1万円 (ichi-man'*en*)

(-)en 〔n, suf〕 **circle; yen**

1 〔n〕 a circle
draw **a circle** // a **round** building

2 〔suf〕 the counter for yen
one hundred **yen** // ten thousand **yen**

えんき 延期 〔名、～する〕

¶試験は延期になりました。(Shiken wa *enki* ni narimashita.)
¶雨のために旅行を延期しました。
(Ame no tame ni ryokō o *enki* shimashita.)

enki 〔n, ～*suru*〕 **postponement**

¶The exam **has been postponed**.

¶[They] **postponed** [their] trip because of rain.

えんし 遠視 〔名〕

¶遠視の眼鏡を作りました。(*Enshi* no megane o tsukurimashita.)
⇔近視 kinshi

enshi 〔n〕 **farsightedness, longsightedness**

¶I had glasses made for my **farsightedness**.

えんじょ 援助 〔名、～する〕

¶この計画を実現するには、政府の援助が必要です。(Kono keikaku o jitsugen suru ni wa, seifu no *enjo* ga hitsuyō desu.)
¶たくさんの学生が経済的な援助を希望しています。(Takusan no gakusei ga keizaiteki na *enjo* o kibō shite imasu.)

enjo 〔n, ～*suru*〕 **assistance, aid**

¶Government **assistance** will be necessary to realize this project.

¶Many students are hoping for financial **aid**.

エンジン 〔名〕

¶あの車のエンジンはたいへんいいです。(Ano kuruma no *enjin* wa taihen ii desu.)

enjin 〔n〕 **engine**

¶That car's **engine** is very good.

¶新しいエンジンの調子はどうですか。（Atarashii *enjin* no chōshi wa dō desu ka？）

How is the new **engine** running?

えんそう　演奏〔名、〜する〕

ensō〔n, 〜*suru*〕**musical performance, recital**

ギターを演奏する（gitā o *ensō* suru）ピアノ曲を演奏する（Pianokyoku o *ensō* suru）

perform on the guitar // **perform** a piece on the piano

¶今晩、ピアノの演奏会があります。（Konban, piano no *ensō*kai ga arimasu.）

¶ There is a piano **recital** tonight.

えんちょう　延長〔名、〜する〕

enchō〔n, 〜*suru*〕**continuation, extension**

¶ビザを延長しました。（Biza o *enchō* shimashita.）

¶ [I] extended [my] visa.

¶留学の期間を1年間延長したいです。（Ryūgaku no kikan o ichinenkan *enchō* shitai desu.）

¶ I want **to extend** my studies abroad for a year.

えんとつ　煙突〔名〕

entotsu〔n〕**chimney, smokestack**

¶あの工場には煙突が何本も立っています。（Ano kōjō ni wa *entotsu* ga nanbon mo tatte imasu.）

¶ There are many **smokestacks** at that factory.

¶煙突から煙がたくさん出ています。（*Entotsu* kara kemuri ga takusan dete imasu.）

¶ A lot of smoke is coming out of **the chimney**.

えんぴつ　鉛筆〔名〕

enpitsu〔n〕**pencil**

赤鉛筆（aka*enpitsu*）色鉛筆（iro-*enpitsu*）鉛筆削り（*enpitsu*kezuri）

a red **pencil** // a colored **pencil** // a **pencil** sharpener

¶この鉛筆は一本いくらですか。（Kono *enpitsu* wa ippon ikura desu ka？）

¶ How much are these **pencils** apiece?

¶ここは鉛筆で書いてください。（Koko wa *enpitsu* de kaite kuda-sai.）

¶ Please write this part here in **pencil**.

えんりょ 遠慮 〔名、～する〕

¶ どうぞ遠慮しないでください。
（Dōzo *enryo* shinaide kudasai.）

¶ 彼はたいへん遠慮深いです。（Kare wa taihen *enryo*bukai desu.）

enryo 〔n, ～*suru*〕 **reserve, diffidence**

¶ Please **don't hold back** 〖Please **don't stand on ceremony**; Please **don't be shy**〗.

¶ He is a very **reserved** person.

お

おい〔名〕
⇔めい **mei**

oi〔n〕**nephew**

おいしい〔形〕

¶このお菓子はおいしいです。(Kono okashi wa *oishii* desu.)
¶テーブルの上に、おいしそうな料理が並んでいます。(Tēburu no ue ni, *oishisō* na ryōri ga narande imasu.)
⇔まずい **mazui**
⇒うまい **umai**

oishii〔adj〕**good-tasting, delicious**

¶This sweet **is very good.**

¶There is a **good-looking** spread of food on the table.

おいつく 追いつく〔動Ⅰ〕

¶急いで歩いたら、途中で山田さんに追いつきました。(Isoide aruitara, tochū de Yamada san ni *oitsukimashita.*)
¶病気で休んでいても、一生懸命勉強すれば、すぐみんなに追いつきます。(Byōki de yasunde ite mo, isshōkenmei benkyō sureba, sugu minna ni *oitsukimasu.*)

oitsuku〔v Ⅰ〕**overtake, catch up with**

¶Walking fast, **I caught up** with [Mrs.] Yamada on the way.

¶Even if you did miss school when you were sick, you will soon **catch up** with everyone if you study hard.

おいで〔連、名〕

1〔連〕
①〔行く〕
¶先生は先ほどあちらへおいでになりました。(Sensei wa sakihodo achira e *oide* ni narimashita.)
②〔来る〕
¶こちらへおいでください。(Kochira e *oide* kudasai.)
¶先生がおいでになりました。(Sensei ga *oide* ni narimashita.)

oide〔compd, n〕**go; come; be, be present**

1〔compd〕
①[go]
¶The professor 〚doctor〛 **went** there a little while ago.

②[come]
¶Please **come** here.

¶The professor 〚doctor〛 **has come**.

101

③ [いる]

¶お父さんはおいでですか。(Otōsan wa *oide* desu ka？)

2 〔名〕

¶先生のおいでをお待ちいたしております。(Sensei no *oide* o omachi itashite orimasu.)

③ [be, be present]

¶ **Is** your father **there** 〖**home**〗?

2 〖n〗 going, coming, being present

¶ I am waiting for the professor 〖doctor〗 **to come** 〖I am looking forward to **your visit**, sir〗.

おいわい お祝い 〔名〕

¶わたしは春子さんの誕生日のお祝いに花を上げました。(Watashi wa Haruko san no tanjōbi no *oiwai* ni hana o agemashita.)

⇒祝う **iwau**

oiwai 〖n〗 **congratulations, celebration**

¶ I gave Haruko flowers **for** her birthday.

おう 追う 〔動 I 〕

① [追い払う]

¶手ではえを追いました。(Te de hae o *oimashita*.)

② [追いかける]

¶警官がどろぼうを追っていきました。(Keikan ga dorobō o *otte* ikimashita.)

③ [急がされる]

¶仕事に追われて休む暇がありません。(Shigoto ni *owarete* yasumu hima ga arimasen.)

ou 〖v I〗 **drive away; pursue, chase; be pressed, be driven**

① [drive away, shoo away]

¶ [He] **shooed away** a fly with [his] hand.

② [pursue, chase]

¶ The policeman **chased after** the thief.

③ [be pressed, be driven, be overtasked]

¶ [I] **have so much** work [I] have no time to rest.

おうえん 応援 〔名、〜する〕

① [人手がなくて困っているときなどに助ける]

¶人が足りないそうですから、応援に行きましょう。(Hito ga tarinai sō desu kara, *ōen* ni ikimashō.)

② [声援する]

応援団 (*ōen*dan)

ōen 〖n, 〜*suru*〗 **aid, assistance; cheer on, support**

① [aid, assistance]

¶ I hear they are shorthanded—let's go **help**.

② [cheer on, support, root for]

cheerleaders, a **cheering** section

102

¶昨日、野球の応援に行きました。
(Kinō, yakyū no ōen ni ikimashita.)

¶ [I] went **to cheer on** our baseball team yesterday.

おうせつま 応接間 〔名〕

ōsetsuma 〔n〕 **reception room**

¶こちらの応接間でしばらくお待ちください。(Kochira no ōsetsuma de shibaraku omachi kudasai.)

¶ Please wait here in this reception room for a while.

おうふく 往復 〔名、〜する〕

ōfuku 〔n, 〜*suru*〕 **going and returning, coming and going, round trip**

往復切符 (ōfuku-kippu) 往復はがき (ōfuku-hagaki)

a **round-trip** ticket // a postcard with an attached **return** card

¶ここから東京まで往復で1200円です。(Koko kara Tōkyō made ōfuku de sennihyakuen desu.)

¶ The **round-trip** fare between here and Tokyo is 1,200 yen.

⇔片道 katamichi

おうよう 応用 〔名、〜する〕

ōyō 〔n, 〜*suru*〕 **practice, practical application**

応用問題 (ōyō-mondai) 理論を実際に応用する (riron o jissai ni ōyō suru)

exercises (in a textbook), an **applied** question (on an exam) // put a theory into actual **practice**

おえる 終える 〔動 II〕

(-)oeru 〔v II〕 **finish, complete; finish doing something**

① [終了する]

① [finish, complete, end]

¶これで今日の仕事を全部終えました。(Kore de kyō no shigoto o zenbu oemashita.)

¶ This **finishes** all the work for today.

¶兄は来年、大学を終えます。(Ani wa rainen, daigaku o oemasu.)

¶ My older brother **completes** college next year.

② [ある動作が終了することを表す]

② [finish doing something]

¶御飯を食べ終えたら、すぐ出かけましょう。(Gohan o tabeoetara, sugu dekakemashō.)

¶ Let's leave right after we **finish** eating.

¶やっと論文を書き終えました。(Yatto ronbun o kakioemashita.)

¶ [I]'ve finally **finished** writing [my] thesis 〚I finally **finished** writing my thesis〛.

*「動詞（基幹の形）＋終える
（oeru）」の形で使う。
⇔始める hajimeru
⇒終わる owaru

*Used in the pattern "verb (stem form)
+ -oeru."

おおい　多い〔形〕

¶あなたのクラスは、どこの国の学生
が多いですか。（Anata no kurasu wa,
doko no kuni no gakusei ga *ooi* desu
ka？）
¶このごろ、自動車の事故が多くなり
ました。（Konogoro, jidōsha no jiko ga
ooku narimashita.）
⇔少ない sukunai

ooi 〔adj〕 **many, numerous, much**

¶ What nationalities are **heavily**
represented in your class?

¶ The number of automobile accidents
has increased recently.

おおきい　大きい〔形〕

¶この大きいくつは山田さんのです。
（Kono *ookii* kutsu wa Yamada san no
desu.）
¶中村さんはわたしよりずっと大きい
です。（Nakamura san wa watashi yori
zutto *ookii* desu.）
¶ラジオの音をあまり大きくしないで
ください。（Rajio no oto o amari *ookiku*
shinaide kudasai.）
⇔小さい chiisai
⇒大きな ookina

ookii 〔adj〕 **big, large, great**

¶ These **large** shoes belong to [Mr.]
Yamada.

¶ [Mr.] Nakamura is much **larger** than
I am.

¶ Please don't have the radio on too
loud.

おおきさ　大きさ〔名〕

¶その木の実の大きさは卵ぐらいで
す。（Sono ki no mi no *ookisa* wa tamago
gurai desu.）
⇒-さ -sa

ookisa 〔n〕 **size, dimensions,**
magnitude, volume

¶ That fruit is about **the size** of an egg.

おおきな　大きな〔連体〕

大きな荷物（*ookina* nimotsu）大きな声
（*ookina* koe）
⇔小さな chiisana
⇒大きい ookii

ookina 〔attrib〕 **big, large, great**

a **large** load 〚package, etc.〛// a **loud**
voice

おおく 多く〔名〕

多くの人（*ooku* no hito）

¶この学校には多くの国から留学生が勉強に来ています。（Kono gakkō ni wa *ooku* no kuni kara ryūgakusei ga benkyō ni kite imasu.）

ooku 〔n〕 **many, a number of, much**

many people; **most** people

¶This school has foreign students from **many different** countries.

おおぜい〔名〕

¶東京には外人がおおぜい住んでいます。（Tōkyō ni wa gaijin ga *oozei* sunde imasu.）

¶おおぜいで旅行するのは、とても楽しいです。（*Oozei* de ryokō suru no wa, totemo tanoshii desu.）

＊動物や物などの場合には「おおぜい（oozei）」は使わない。

oozei 〔n〕 **a great number of people, a crowd**

¶**A great many** foreigners live in Tokyo.

¶It is very pleasant to travel in **a large group**.

＊*Oozei* is only used to refer to people.

オートバイ〔名〕

¶日本では 16 歳になると、オートバイの運転免許を取ることができます。（Nihon de wa jūrokusai ni naru to, *ōtobai* no untenmenkyo wo toru koto ga deki masu.）

ōtobai 〔n〕 **motorcycle, autobicycle**

¶In Japan, you can obtain a motorcycle license when you are 16.

オーバー〔名〕

ōbā 〔n〕 **overcoat**

おお- 大-〔頭〕

大雨（*oo*ame）大通り（*oo*doori）大急ぎ（*oo*isogi）大騒ぎ（*oo*sawagi）

oo- 〔pref〕 **large, great**

a **heavy** rain, a downpour // a **main** thoroughfare // in **great** haste, urgent // a **great** commotion, an uproar

おか 丘〔名〕

oka 〔n〕 **hill, rise, hillock**

おかあさん お母さん〔名〕

¶お母さんはうちにいらっしゃいますか。（*Okāsan* wa uchi ni irasshaimasu ka？）

okāsan 〔n〕 **mother**

¶Is **your mother** at home?

＊他人の母親について話す場合、または自分の母親に呼びかけたり、家族の者に母親のことを言う場合に使う。他人に自分の母親のことを話す場合には、普通「お母さん（okāsan）」と言わないで「母（haha）」と言う。

⇔お父さん otōsan
⇒母 haha

＊*Okāsan* is used when talking about someone else's mother, in direct address to one's own mother, and when talking about one's own mother with other family members. When talking about one's own mother with nonfamily members, one usually uses *haha* rather than *okāsan*.

おかげ〔名〕

¶「お元気ですか。」（Ogenki desu ka?）「おかげさまで、元気です。」（*Okage*sama de, genki desu.）

¶一生懸命勉強したおかげで成績が上がりました。（Isshōkenmei benkyō shita *okage* de seiseki ga agarimashita.）

okage 〔n〕 **thanks to, owing to, by grace of**

¶ "How are you?" "Fine, **thank you.**"

¶ [My] grades improved **as a result of** hard study.

おかしい〔形〕

① [こっけいだ、おもしろい]
¶山田さんはおかしい話をして、みんなを笑わせました。（Yamada san wa *okashii* hanashi o shite, minna o warawasemashita.）

→おもしろい omoshiroi

② [普通でなくて変だ]
¶おかしいですね。約束したのに、中村さんはまだ来ません。（*Okashii* desune. Yakusoku shita noni, Nakamura san wa mada kimasen.）

＊「おかしな（okashina）」（連体）という言葉もある。「おかしな話（okashina hanashi）」

okashii 〔adj〕 **funny, amusing; funny, strange**

① [funny, amusing, comic]
¶ [Mr.] Yamada told a **funny** story and made everyone laugh.

② [funny, strange, odd, queer]
¶ That's **odd**. [Miss] Nakamura hasn't come yet for [our] date 〚appointment〛.

＊The form *okashina* is sometimes used as a modifier before a noun, as in *okashina hanashi* (a funny story, an odd story).

おがむ　拝む〔動 I〕

¶おおぜいの人がお寺の前で手を合わせて拝んでいました。（Oozei no hito

ogamu 〔v I〕 **worship, pray**

¶ A great number of people were standing in front of the temple with their hands pressed together **in prayer**.

ga otera no mae de te o awasete *ogande*
imashita.)

-おき〔尾〕

¶ わたしは1日<ruby>日<rt>にち</rt></ruby>おきに<ruby>事務所<rt>じむしょ</rt></ruby>へ<ruby>行<rt>い</rt></ruby>きま
す。(Watashi wa ichinichi *oki* ni jimusho
e ikimasu.)
¶ 5メートルおきに<ruby>木<rt>き</rt></ruby>を<ruby>植<rt>う</rt></ruby>えました。
(Gomētoru *oki* ni ki o uemashita.)

おきる 起きる〔動Ⅱ〕

① [目を覚ます、寝床から出る]
¶ あなたは<ruby>朝<rt>あさ</rt></ruby><ruby>何時<rt>なんじ</rt></ruby>ごろ<ruby>起<rt>お</rt></ruby>きますか。
(Anata wa asa nanji goro *okimasu* ka？)
¶ <ruby>赤<rt>あか</rt></ruby>ん<ruby>坊<rt>ぼう</rt></ruby>が<ruby>起<rt>お</rt></ruby>きるから、<ruby>静<rt>しず</rt></ruby>かにしてく
ださい。(Akanbō ga *okiru* kara, shizuka
ni shite kudasai.)
② [寝ないでいる]
¶ <ruby>上田<rt>うえだ</rt></ruby>さんは<ruby>毎晩<rt>まいばん</rt></ruby><ruby>遅<rt>おそ</rt></ruby>くまで<ruby>起<rt>お</rt></ruby>きて<ruby>勉強<rt>べんきょう</rt></ruby>
しています。(Ueda san wa maiban
osoku made *okite* benkyō shite imasu.)
③ [事件などが生じる]
<ruby>事件<rt>じけん</rt></ruby>が<ruby>起<rt>お</rt></ruby>きる (jiken ga *okiru*) <ruby>戦争<rt>せんそう</rt></ruby>が
<ruby>起<rt>お</rt></ruby>きる (sensō ga *okiru*)
→<ruby>起<rt>お</rt></ruby>こる okoru

おく <ruby>奥<rt>おく</rt></ruby>〔名〕

<ruby>山<rt>やま</rt></ruby>の<ruby>奥<rt>おく</rt></ruby> (yama no *oku*)

¶ <ruby>大切<rt>たいせつ</rt></ruby>な<ruby>物<rt>もの</rt></ruby>は<ruby>引<rt>ひ</rt></ruby>き<ruby>出<rt>だ</rt></ruby>しの<ruby>奥<rt>おく</rt></ruby>にしまって
あります。(Taisetsu na mono wa
hikidashi no *oku* ni shimatte arimasu.)
¶ <ruby>玄関<rt>げんかん</rt></ruby>では<ruby>話<rt>はなし</rt></ruby>ができませんから、どう
ぞ<ruby>奥<rt>おく</rt></ruby>へお<ruby>入<rt>はい</rt></ruby>りください。(Genkan de
wa hanashi ga dekimasen kara, dōzo *oku* e
ohairi kudasai.)

-oki 〔suf〕 **at intervals of ~, ~
apart**

¶ I go to the office **every other** day.

¶ [I] planted the trees at intervals of
five meters 〖five meters **apart**〗.

okiru 〔v II〕 **wake up, get up; be
up, be awake; take place, occur**

① [wake up, get up]
¶ What time do you **get up** in the
morning?

¶ Please be quiet—you'll **wake up** the
baby (literally, the baby **will wake up**).

② [be up, be awake]
¶ [Miss] Ueda **stays up** late every
night studying.

③ [take place, occur]
an incident **takes place** // war **breaks
out**

oku 〔n〕 **interior, recesses, depths
the heart** of a mountain, **deep in the
mountains**
¶ The valuables are shut away towards
the back of the drawer.

¶ Please come **inside**; we can't talk
comfortably here in the entryway.

おく 億 〔名〕

1億 （ichi*oku*） 10億 （jū*oku*） 100億
（hyaku*oku*）

oku 〔n〕 **100 million**

100,000,000 // 1,000,000,000; one
billion // 10,000,000,000; ten billion

おく 置く 〔動 I〕

¶ 机の上に本を置きます。（Tsukue no
ue ni hon o *okimasu*.）

荷物はここに置いてください。
（Nimotsu wa koko ni *oite* kudasai.）

oku 〔v I〕 **put, place, lay, leave**

¶ [I] **will put** the book on the desk.

¶ Please **put** [your] things 〚load, bags,
packages, etc.〛 here.

（〜て）おく 〔連〕

① [ある動作が終わったままの状態に
する]

¶ わたしはいつも部屋のかぎを掛けて
おきます。（Watashi wa itsumo heya no
kagi o kakete *okimasu*.）

¶ ここに置いておいた辞書を知りませ
んか。（Koko ni oite *oita* jisho o
shirimasen ka？）

② [あらかじめ準備したりする]

¶ お客さんが来ますから、部屋を掃除
しておきましょう。（Okyakusan ga
kimasu kara, heya o sōji shite *okimashō*.）

¶ 行く前に電話をかけておいたほうが
いいですよ。（Iku mae ni denwa o
kakete *oita* hō ga ii desu yo.）

(-te)oku 〔compd〕 **an expression
indicating something being left
in a certain state or something
being done in preparation**

① [leave, let, keep; leave or keep
something in a certain state]

¶ I always **keep** my room locked.

¶ Do you know what happened to the
dictionary **that was here?**

② [make preparations, do in advance]

¶ **Let's clean** the room—a guest is
coming.

¶ You had better **telephone** before you
go there.

おくさま 奥様 〔名〕
☞奥さん okusan

okusama 〔n〕　☞okusan

おくさん 奥さん 〔名〕

¶ 中村さんの奥さんは英語の先生で
す。（Nakamura san no *okusan* wa Eigo
no sensei desu.）

¶ 奥さん、このりんごはおいしいです
よ。（*Okusan*, kono ringo wa oishii desu
yo.）

okusan 〔n〕 **wife, married woman**

¶ Mr. Nakamura's **wife** teaches English.

¶ These apples are good today, **ma'am**.

＊他人の妻に直接呼びかけたり、他人
の妻のことを話す場合に使う。丁寧に
言う場合には「奥様（okusama）」と言
う。
⇒家内 kanai　妻 tsuma

おくじょう　屋上〔名〕
ビルの屋上（biru no okujō）
¶あのデパートの屋上には、子供のた
めの遊び場があります。（Ano depāto
no okujō ni wa, kodomo no tame no
asobiba ga arimasu.）

おくびょう　おく病〔名、形動〕

¶この子はおく病で、夜一人では歩け
ません。（Kono ko wa okubyō de, yoru
hitori de wa arukemasen.）
¶一度失敗すると、次からはおく病に
なります。（Ichido shippai suru to, tsugi
kara wa okubyō ni narimasu.）

おくりもの　贈り物〔名〕
¶友達のうちに赤ちゃんが生まれたの
で、お祝いの贈り物を持って行きまし
た。（Tomodachi no uchi ni akachan ga
umareta node, oiwai no okurimono o
motte ikimashita.）
⇒プレゼント purezento

おくる　送る〔動Ⅰ〕

①[物をある所から他の所まで届ける]
¶田舎の母がりんごを送ってくれまし
た。（Inaka no haha ga ringo o okutte
kuremashita.）
¶あなたは家から毎月いくらぐらいお
金を送ってもらいますか。（Anata wa
ie kara maitsuki ikura gurai okane o okutte
moraimasu ka？）

＊Used in direct address to someone
else's wife or when referring to
someone else's wife. When speaking
politely, *okusama* is used.

okujō〔n〕**roof, housetop, rooftop**
the rooftop of a building
¶There is a play area for children on
the roof of that department store.

okubyō〔n, adj-v〕**cowardice,
timidity**
¶This child **is timid** and is afraid to
walk alone at night.

¶One **loses one's nerve** after failing
once.

okurimono〔n〕**present, gift**
¶My friends had a baby so I took them
a present.

okuru〔v Ⅰ〕**send; see off, see
home**
①[send]
¶My mother **sent me** some apples
from the country.

¶How much money does your family
send you each month?

109

②[見送る、ある所までつき添ってい
く]

¶あした、わたしは飛行場へ友達を送
りに行きます。(Ashita, watashi wa
hikōjō e tomodachi o *okuri* ni ikimasu.)

¶道が暗いから、わたしが駅まで送り
ましょう。(Michi ga kurai kara, watashi
ga eki made *okurimashō*.)

② [see off, see home]

¶ Tomorrow I'm going to the airport **to
see off** a friend.

¶ I'll **walk with you** to the station as
the streets are dark now.

おくる 贈る 〔動 I〕

¶わたしは田中さんにクリスマスのプ
レゼントを贈りました。(Watashi wa
Tanaka san ni kurisumasu no purezento o
okurimashita.)

okuru 〔v I〕 **give as a present,
present with**

¶ I **gave** a Christmas present to [Miss]
Tanaka.

おくれる 遅れる 〔動 II〕

¶早くしないと、学校に遅れますよ。
(Hayaku shinai to, gakkō ni *okuremasu*
yo.)

¶田中さんは約束の時間に 30 分も遅れ
てきました。(Tanaka san wa yakusoku
no jikan ni sanjippun mo *okurete*
kimashita.)

okureru 〔v II〕 **be late, be tardy**

¶ If you don't hurry **you'll be late** for
school.

¶ [Mr.] Tanaka **was** 30 minutes **late** for
[our] appointment 〖date〗.

おくれる 後れる 〔動 II〕

¶3 か月も学校を休んだので、勉強が
後れてしまいました。(Sankagetsu mo
gakkō o yasunda node, benkyō ga *okurete*
shimaimashita.)

¶その時計は5分後れています。(Sono
tokei wa gofun *okurete* imasu.)

okureru 〔v II〕 **be behind, fall back**

¶ [I] was out of school for three months
so [I] **am** 〖**was**〗 **behind** in [my]
studies.

¶ That clock **is** five minutes **slow**.

おこさん お子さん 〔名〕

¶お子さんは何人いらっしゃいます
か。(Okosan wa nannin irasshai masu
ka?)

okosan 〔n〕 **child, children**

¶ How many children do you have?

おこす 起こす 〔動 I〕

①[目を覚まさせる]

okosu 〔v I〕 **wake up; raise, set
up; give rise to, cause**

① [wake up, rouse]

¶あしたの朝、6時に起こしてください。（Ashita no asa, rokuji ni *okoshite* kudasai.）

②[立たせる]

¶子供が転んだので、起こしてやりました。（Kodomo ga koronda node, *okoshite* yarimashita.）

③[生じさせる]

¶上田さんは事故を起こして、警察で調べられています。（Ueda san wa jiko o *okoshite*, keisatsu de shiraberarete imasu.）

おこなう 行う〔動 I〕

¶これから今日の授業を行います。（Kore kara kyō no jugyō o *okonaimasu*.）

¶その祭りは今でもこの地方で行われています。（Sono matsuri wa ima demo kono chihō de *okonawarete* imasu.）

おこる 怒る〔動 I〕

①[腹を立てる]

¶父が怒った顔をしています。（Chichi ga *okotta* kao o shite imasu.）

¶山田さんは、あなたが約束を破ったことを怒っていますよ。（Yamada san wa, anata ga yakusoku o yabutta koto o *okotte* imasu yo.）

②[しかる]

¶わたしは子供のころ、よく母に怒られました。（Watashi wa kodomo no koro, yoku haha ni *okoraremashita*.）

¶ Please **wake me up** tomorrow morning at six o'clock.

② [raise, set up, set upright]

¶ **I helped up** the child who had fallen down.

③ [give rise to, cause]

¶ [Mr.] Ueda **caused** an accident and is being interrogated by the police.

okonau 〔v I〕 **hold, perform, do, carry out**

¶ Today's class **will start** now.

¶ That festival **is** still **observed** in this region even today.

okoru 〔v I〕 **get angry, be angered; scold**

① [get angry, be angered, lose one's temper]

¶ My father looks **angry**.

¶ [Mr.] Yamada **is angry** at you for not keeping your word.

② [scold]

¶ When I was a child **I was** often **scolded** by my mother.

おこる 起こる [動 I]

¶ 昨日、ここで交通事故が起こりました。(Kinō, koko de kōtsū-jiko ga *okorimashita*.)

¶ 戦争が起こった時、わたしは外国にいました。(Sensō ga *okotta* toki, watashi wa gaikoku ni imashita.)

⇒起きる **okiru**

okoru [v I] happen, occur, take place

¶ A traffic accident **took place** here yesterday.

¶ I was abroad when war **broke out**.

おさえる 押さえる [動 II]

¶ 手で紙を押さえて、飛ばないようにしました。(Te de kami o *osaete*, tobanai yō ni shimashita.)

¶ 犬を押さえているから、こわがらなくてもいいです。(Inu o *osaete* iru kara, kowagaranakute mo ii desu.)

osaeru [v II] hold down, press down; suppress, control, restrain

¶ [I] **held down** the paper with [my] hand(s) so that it wouldn't blow away.

¶ [I] **have hold** of the dog so you needn't be afraid.

おさめる 納める [動 II]

¶ 今月の末までに税金を納めなければなりません。(Kongetsu no sue made ni zeikin o *osamenakereba* narimasen.)

¶ 授業料はいつまでに納めればいいですか。(Jugyōryō wa itsu made ni *osamereba* ii desu ka?)

osameru [v II] settle, pay

¶ Taxes **must be paid** by the end of this month.

¶ What is the final date **for paying** tuition?

おじ [名]

¶ わたしのおじは医者です。(Watashi no *oji* wa isha desu.)

⇔おば **oba**

⇒おじさん **ojisan**

oji [n] uncle

¶ My **uncle** is a doctor.

おしい 惜しい [形]

① [残念だ]

¶ 父に買ってもらった時計をなくして、惜しいことをしました。(Chichi

oshii [adj] disappointing, regrettable; a waste, a shame

① [disappointing, regrettable]

¶ **I feel bad** that I lost the watch my father bought me.

ni katte moratta tokei o nakushite, *oshii* koto o shimashita.)

②[もったいない]

¶そのくつはまだはけます。捨てるのは惜しいですよ。(Sono kutsu wa mada hakemasu. Suteru no wa *oshii* desu yo.)

②[a waste, a shame]

¶ Those shoes are still good. **It's a shame** to throw them away.

おじいさん〔名〕

①[他人の祖父を尊敬しまたは自分の祖父を親しんで言う言葉]

¶あなたのおじいさんは今年おいくつですか。(Anata no *ojiisan* wa kotoshi oikutsu desu ka?)

*他人に自分の祖父のことを話す場合には、普通「おじいさん(ojiisan)」と言わないで「祖父(sofu)」と言う。

→祖父 **sofu**

②[よその年寄りの男の人]

¶おじいさん、お元気ですね。(Ojiisan, ogenki desu ne.)

⇔おばあさん **obāsan**

ojiisan〔n〕 **grandfather; an old man**

① [grandfather; used when referring to someone else's grandfather with respect or to one's own grandfather with affection]

¶ How old is your **grandfather** this year?

*When talking about one's grandfather with someone outside one's family, one usually uses *sofu* rather than *ojiisan*.

② [an old man]

¶ You seem very spry, **sir**.

おしいれ 押し入れ〔名〕

¶押し入れには布団がしまってあります。(Oshiire ni wa futon ga shimatte arimasu.)

oshiire〔n〕 **closet**

¶ The futon is kept in the closet.

おしえる 教える〔動Ⅱ〕

①[知識や技術などを人に与える]

¶上田さんは中学で数学を教えています。(Ueda san wa chūgaku de sūgaku o *oshiete* imasu.)

②[知っていることを人に知らせる]

¶駅へ行く道を教えてください。(Eki e iku michi o *oshiete* kudasai.)

oshieru〔v Ⅱ〕 **teach; tell, inform**

① [teach, instruct, show how]

¶ [Miss] Ueda **teaches** math in a junior high school.

② [tell, inform]

¶ Please **tell me** the way to the station.

おじぎ 〔名、〜する〕

¶わたしは先生に「お早うございます。」と言っておじぎをしました。（Watashi wa sensei ni "Ohayō gozaimasu." to itte *ojigi* o shimashita.）

ojigi 〔n, 〜*suru*〕 **bow, curtsy**

¶ I **bowed** to our teacher and said, "*Ohayō gozaimasu.*"

おじさん 〔名〕

① [他人のおじを尊敬しまたは自分のおじを親しんで言う言葉]

¶あなたのおじさんは何をなさっていますか。（Anata no *ojisan* wa nani o nasatte imasu ka？）
*他人に自分のおじのことを話す場合には、普通「おじさん（ojisan）」と言わないで「おじ（oji）」と言う。
→おじ **oji**
② [よその中年の男の人]
¶魚屋のおじさんはいつも元気です。（Sakanaya no *ojisan* wa itsu mo genki desu.）
⇔おばさん **obasan**

ojisan 〔n〕 **uncle; a middle-aged man**

① [uncle; used to refer to someone else's uncle with respect or to one's own uncle with affection]

¶ What does your **uncle** do?

*When talking about one's own uncle with someone outside one's family, one usually uses *oji* rather than *ojisan*.

② [a middle-aged man]
¶ The fish store **man** is always in good spirits.

おじょうさん お嬢さん 〔名〕

¶先生のお嬢さんは今、大学生です。（Sensei no *ojōsan* wa ima, daigakusei desu.）

ojōsan 〔n〕 **daughter**

¶ The professor's **daughter** is a college student now.

おす 雄 〔名〕

雄犬（*osu*inu） 雄ねこ（*osu*neko）
*動物について言い、人間には使わない。
⇔雌 **mesu**

osu 〔n〕 **male (animal)**

a **male** dog // a **male** cat, a tomcat
Osu is used only for animals.

おす 押す 〔動 I〕

① [力を加えて物などを向こうへ動かす]

¶ドアを押して開けました。（Doa o *oshite* akemashita.）

osu 〔v I〕 **push; stamp, seal**

① [push, shove, press]

¶ [I] **pushed** open the door.

¶危ないから、後ろから押さないでください。(Abunai kara, ushiro kara *osanaide* kudasai.)

↔引く **hiku**

② [力を加えて印などをつける]

¶ここに判を押してください。(Koko ni han o *oshite* kudasai.)

¶ Please **don't push**—it's dangerous (said to people in a crowd, etc.).

② [stamp, seal, impress]

¶ Please **stamp** your personal seal here.

おそい 遅い 〔形〕

① [時刻が早くない]

¶山田さんはいつも夜遅く帰って来ます。(Yamada san wa itsu mo yoru *osoku* kaette kimasu.)

¶遅いですね。中村さんはまだ来ませんか。(*Osoi* desu ne. Nakamura san wa mada kimasen ka?)

↔早い **hayai**

② [速度が速くない]

¶この汽車はずいぶん遅いですね。(Kono kisha wa zuibun *osoi* desu ne.)

↔速い **hayai**

osoi 〔adj〕 **late; slow**

① [late]

¶ [Mr.] Yamada always returns home **late** at night.

¶ Hasn't [Miss] Nakamura come yet? [She]'s **so late!**

② [slow]

¶ This train is really **slow-moving**, isn't it?

おそらく 恐らく 〔副〕

¶恐らく上田さんは今日は来ないでしょう。(*Osoraku* Ueda san wa kyō wa konai deshō.)

¶恐らくあしたは雨でしょう。(*Osoraku* ashita wa ame deshō.)

＊普通あとに「だろう (darō)」「でしょう (deshō)」などの推量の言い方が来る。

osoraku 〔adv〕 **probably**

¶ [Mrs.] Ueda **probably** isn't coming today.

¶ It will **probably** rain tomorrow 〚**Chances are** it will rain tomorrow〛.

＊Usually followed by an expression of conjecture such as *darō*, *deshō*, etc.

おそれ 〔名〕

¶台風が来ているので、大雨のおそれがあります。(Taifū ga kite iru node, ooame no *osore* ga arimasu.)

osore 〔n〕 **fear, concern, danger, risk, chance**

¶ There is **a threat** of heavy rains as a typhoon is on its way here.

¶このテレビの番組は子供たちに悪い影響を与えるおそれがあります。
（Kono terebi no bangumi wa kodomotachi ni warui eikyō o ataeru *osore ga arimasu*.）

¶There is **concern** that this television program might have a bad influence on children.

おそれる　恐れる〔動Ⅱ〕

①［こわがる］
¶死を恐れない人はいません。（Shi o *osorenai* hito wa imasen.）

②［心配する］
¶間違いを恐れていては、日本語が上手になりません。（Machigai o *osorete* ite wa, Nihongo ga jōzu ni narimasen.）

osoreru〔v Ⅱ〕 **fear, be frightened; be apprehensive, be fearful**

① [fear, be frightened, be afraid]
¶Everyone **fears** death (literally, There is no one who **doesn't fear** death).

② [be apprehensive, be fearful, dread]
¶You will not become good at Japanese if **you are afraid** of making mistakes.

おそろしい　恐ろしい〔形〕

¶わたしはゆうべ恐ろしい夢を見ました。（Watashi wa yūbe *osoroshii* yume o mimashita.）
¶恐ろしくてひざが震えました。（*Osoroshikute* hiza ga furuemashita.）

osoroshii〔adj〕 **terrible, fearsome, horrible, dreadful**

¶I had a **terrible** nightmare last night.

¶[I] **was so frightened** [my] knees were knocking.

おたがい　お互い〔名〕
☞互い tagai

otagai〔n〕 ☞**tagai**

おたく　お宅〔名〕

¶先生のお宅はどちらですか。（Sensei no *otaku* wa dochira desu ka?）

otaku〔n〕 **your home, your house, residence**

¶Where do you live, sir?

おだやか　穏やか〔形動〕

①［静かな様子］
穏やかな気候（*odayaka* na kikō）
¶今日は風もなくて、海が穏やかです。（Kyō wa kaze mo nakute, umi ga *odayaka* desu.）

②［静かで落ち着いている様子］

odayaka〔adj-v〕 **quiet, peaceful; gentle, tranquil**

① [quiet, peaceful, calm, mild]
a **mild** climate
¶There's no wind today and the sea is **calm**.

② [gentle, tranquil, mild]

116

¶中村さんは性格の穏やかな人です。
（Nakamura san wa seikaku no *odayaka* na hito desu.）

¶ [Mr.] Nakamura is **mild-mannered**.

おちつく 落ち着く 〔動Ⅰ〕

ochitsuku 〔v Ⅰ〕 **calm down, become composed, settle down**

¶試験の結果が心配で落ち着きません。（Shiken no kekka ga shinpai de *ochitsukimasen*.）

¶ [I]'m so nervous about the exam results that [I] **can't settle down**.

¶地震のときには、落ち着いて行動しなければなりません。（Jishin no toki ni wa, *ochitsuite* kōdō shinakereba narimasen.）

¶ One must **keep one's head** during an earthquake.

おちゃ お茶 〔名〕 ☞茶 cha

ocha 〔n〕 ☞**cha**

おちる 落ちる 〔動Ⅱ〕

ochiru 〔v Ⅱ〕 **fall, drop; fall, go down; fail**

①[あるものが上から下へ自然に移動する]

① [fall, drop]

¶秋になると、木の葉が落ちます。（Aki ni naru to, ki no ha ga *ochimasu*.）

¶ Trees **shed** their leaves in the fall.

¶弟が階段から落ちてけがをしました。（Otōto ga kaidan kara *ochite* kega o shimashita.）

¶ My (younger) brother **fell down** the stairs and hurt himself.

②[程度が下がる、低くなる]
速度が落ちる（sokudo ga *ochiru*）

② [fall, go down]
the speed **falls**

¶勉強しなかったので、成績が落ちました。（Benkyō shinakatta node, seiseki ga *ochimashita*.）

¶ [My] grades **fell** because [I] didn't study.

③[落第する、試験に失敗する]

③ [fail]

¶田中さんは大学の試験に落ちました。（Tanaka san wa daigaku no shiken ni *ochimashita*.）

¶ [Mr.] Tanaka **failed** [his] university entrance exams.

おっしゃる 〔動Ⅰ〕

ossharu 〔v Ⅰ〕 **say**

¶先生が「あした試験をする。」とおっしゃいました。（Sensei ga "Ashita shiken o suru." to *osshaimashita*.）

¶ The teacher **said**, "There will be a test tomorrow."

¶お名前は何とおっしゃいますか。
（Onamae wa nan to *osshaimasu* ka？）
＊「言う（iu）」の尊敬語。「ますの形」は「おっしゃいます（osshaimasu）」となる。

¶ What **is** your name please? (very polite)

＊*Ossharu* is the honorific form of *iu*. The -*masu* form is *osshaimasu*.

おっと　夫〔名〕

otto 〔n〕 **husband**

¶妻は寝ないで夫の帰りを待っていました。（Tsuma wa nenaide *otto* no kaeri o matte imashita.）

¶ The wife waited up for **her husband**.

＊結婚した男女の男のほうをさす言葉。自分の夫のことを他人に話す場合には普通「主人（shujin）」と言う。
⇔妻 tsuma
⇒主人 shujin

＊*Otto* is used to indicate a male spouse. When talking with others about one's own husband, one usually uses *shujin*.

おてあらい　お手洗い〔名〕

otearai 〔n〕 **toilet, washroom**

¶すみませんが、お手洗いはどこですか。（Suimasen ga, *otearai* wa doko desu ka?）

¶ Excuse me, where is the toilet?

おと　音〔名〕

oto 〔n〕 **sound, noise**

音を立てる（*oto* o tateru）

make **a sound**, make **a noise**

¶庭の方で大きな音がしました。
（Niwa no hō de ookina *oto* ga shimashita.）

¶ There was a large **crash** 〘great **noise**〙 in the yard 〘garden〙.

¶ラジオの音をもう少し小さくしてください。（Rajio no *oto* o mō sukoshi chiisaku shite kudasai.）

¶ Please turn the radio down a little.

おとうさん　お父さん〔名〕

otōsan 〔n〕 **father**

¶あなたはお父さんに手紙を書きましたか。（Anata wa *otōsan* ni tegami o kakimashita ka？）

¶ Have you written a letter to **your father?**

¶お父さん、お母さんが呼んでいますよ。（*Otōsan*, okāsan ga yonde imasu yo.）

¶ **Dad**, Mom is calling you.

＊他人の父親について話す場合、または自分の父親に呼びかけたり、家族の者に父親のことを言う場合に使う。他人に自分の父親のことを話す場合には、普通「お父さん（otōsan）」と言わないで「父（chichi）」と言う。

⇔お母さん okāsan
⇒父 chichi

＊*Otōsan* is used when talking about someone else's father, in direct address to one's own father, or when talking about one's father with other family members. When talking with nonfamily members about one's own father, one usually uses *chichi* rather than *otōsan*.

おとうと 弟 〔名〕

¶わたしの弟は小学生です。
(Watashi no *otōto* wa shōgakusei desu.)
¶あなたの弟さんはおいくつですか。
(Anata no *otōto*san wa oikutsu desu ka？)
⇔兄 ani

otōto 〔n〕 **younger brother**

¶ My **younger brother** is an elementary school student.
¶ How old is your **younger brother?**

おとこ 男 〔名〕

男の子（*otoko* no ko）男の人（*otoko* no hito）
¶これは男のくつです。(Kore wa *otoko* no kutsu desu.)
¶このクラスには男の学生が少ないです。(Kono kurasu ni wa *otoko* no gakusei ga sukunai desu.)
⇔女 onna

otoko 〔n〕 **man, male**

a boy // a man

¶ These are **men's** shoes.

¶ There are few **male** students in this class.

おとす 落とす 〔動 I〕

① [落下させる]
¶コップを落として、割ってしまいました。(Koppu o *otoshite*, watte shimaimashita.)
② [なくす、失う]
¶電車の中でお金を落としました。(Densha no naka de okane o *otoshimashita*.)
③ [程度などを低い状態にする]
速度を落とす（sokudo o *otosu*）

otosu 〔v I〕 **drop; lose; decrease, lessen**

① [drop, let fall]
¶ [I] **dropped** the glass tumbler and it broke.
② [lose]
¶ [I] **lost** [my] money in the train.
③ [decrease, lessen, lower]
reduce one's speed, slow down

おととい〔名〕

¶おとといは何日でしたか。(Ototoi wa nannichi deshita ka?)

¶おとといの晩、近所で火事がありました。(Ototoi no ban, kinjo de kaji ga arimashita.)

ototoi 〔n〕 **the day before yesterday**

¶ What was the date **the day before yesterday?**

¶ There was a fire in the neighborhood **the night before last**.

おととし〔名〕

¶わたしはおととしの2月に日本へ来ました。(Watashi wa ototoshi no nigatsu ni Nihon e kimashita.)

ototoshi 〔n〕 **the year before last**

¶ I came to Japan in February **the year before last**〚**two years ago**〛.

おとな 大人〔名〕

¶電車賃は大人100円、子供50円です。(Denshachin wa otona hyakuen, kodomo gojūen desu.)

¶その映画は大人だけしか見られません。(Sono eiga wa otona dake shika miraremasen.)
⇔子供 kodomo

otona 〔n〕 **an adult, a grown-up**

¶ The train fare is a hundred yen **for adults** and fifty yen for children.

¶ Admission to that movie is restricted to **adults**.

おとなしい〔形〕

¶山田さんはおとなしい人です。(Yamada san wa otonashii hito desu.)

¶「おとなしくしていれば、お菓子を上げます。」と、お母さんが子供に言いました。("Otonashiku shite ireba, okashi o agemasu." to, okāsan ga kodomo ni iimashita.)

otonashii 〔adj〕 **gentle, docile, quiet, well-behaved, reserved, mild-mannered, even-tempered**

¶ [Mrs.] Yamada is **mild-mannered**.

¶ The mother said to her children, "**If you're good** I'll give you a sweet."

おどり 踊り〔名〕

¶わたしたちはみんなで日本の踊りを踊りました。(Watashitachi wa minna de Nihon no odori o odorimashita.)

odori 〔n〕 **dance, dancing**

¶ We all did some Japanese **dances** together.

おどる 踊る〔動 I〕

¶わたしと踊ってくださいませんか。(Watashi to odotte kudasaimasen ka?)

odoru 〔v I〕 **to dance**

¶ Could I please **have this dance?**

120

おどろく 驚く〔動Ⅰ〕

① [びっくりする]
¶「火事だ。」という声を聞いて、驚いて外へ飛び出しました。("Kaji da!"to iu koe o kiite, *odoroite* soto e tobidashimashita.)
② [感心する]
¶あの人は歌がとても上手なので驚きました。(Ano hito wa uta ga totemo jōzu na node *odorokimashita*.)

おなか〔名〕
おなかが痛い（*onaka* ga itai）おなかがすく（*onaka* ga suku）
¶もう、おなかがいっぱいです。(Mō, *onaka* ga ippai desu.)
⇒腹 hara

おなじ 同じ〔形動〕
¶どの品物も値段は皆同じです。(Dono shinamono mo nedan wa mina *onaji* desu.)
¶わたしもあなたと同じ30歳です。(Watashi mo anata to *onaji* sanjissai desu.)
¶あの人はわたしと同じシャツを着ています。(Ano hito wa watashi to *onaji* shatsu o kite imasu.)
＊名詞などを修飾する場合は、「同じ（onaji）」の形で使う。

おにいさん お兄さん〔名〕
¶お兄さんは今年おいくつですか。(*Oniisan* wa kotoshi oikutsu desu ka？)
＊他人に自分の兄のことを話す場合には、普通「お兄さん（oniisan）」と言わないで「兄（ani）」と言う。
⇒兄 ani

odoroku 〔v Ⅰ〕 be surprised; be amazed

① [be surprised, be startled]
¶ **Startled** by the cry of "Fire!" [I] ran outside.

② [be amazed, marvel at]
¶ [We] **marveled** at how good a singer [he] is.

onaka 〔n〕 stomach
have a **stomach**ache, have **stomach** pains // be hungry
¶ I'm **full** now.

onaji 〔adj-v〕 the same, alike
¶ All of the merchandise costs the **same**.

¶ I am also 30 years old, **the same** as you.

¶ He is wearing the **same** shirt as I am.

＊ Used in the form *onaji* when modifying a noun, etc.

oniisan 〔n〕 older brother
¶ How old is **your elder brother** this year?

＊ When talking with nonfamily members about one's own elder brother, one usually uses *ani* rather than *oniisan*.

おねえさん　お姉さん〔名〕

¶お姉さんはどこに勤めていらっしゃいますか。（*Onēsan* wa doko ni tsutomete irasshaimasu ka？）

＊他人に自分の姉のことを話す場合には、普通「お姉さん（onēsan）」と言わないで「姉（ane）」と言う。
⇒姉 ane

onēsan〔n〕**older sister**

¶ Where does **your older sister** work?

＊When talking with nonfamily members about one's own elder sister, one usually uses *ane* rather than *onēsan*.

おねがい　お願い〔名〕
☞願い negai

onegai〔n〕　☞**negai**

おば〔名〕

¶わたしのおばは田舎にいます。（Watashi no *oba* wa inaka ni imasu.）
⇔おじ oji
⇒おばさん obasan

oba〔n〕**aunt**

¶ My **aunt** lives in the country.

おばあさん〔名〕

①［他人の祖母を尊敬しまたは自分の祖母を親しんで言う言葉］

¶あなたのおばあさんは今年おいくつですか。（Anata no *obāsan* wa kotoshi oikutsu desu ka？）

＊他人に自分の祖母のことを話す場合は、普通「おばあさん（obāsan）」と言わないで「祖母（sobo）」と言う。
→祖母 sobo

②［よその年寄りの女の人］
¶おばあさん、ここにお掛けなさい。（*Obāsan*, oko ni okakenasai.）
⇔おじいさん ojiisan

obāsan〔n〕**grandmother; an elderly lady**

①［grandmother; used to refer to someone else's grandmother with respect or to one's own grandmother with affection］

¶ How old is your **grandmother** this year?

＊One usually uses *sobo* rather than *obāsan* when talking about one's grandmother with someone outside of one's family.

②［an elderly woman］
¶ **Ma'am**, please have this seat 〖Here's a seat for you, **ma'am**〗.

おばさん〔名〕

①［他人のおばを尊敬しまたは自分のおばを親しんで言う言葉］

obasan〔n〕**aunt; a middle-aged woman, a lady**

①［aunt; used to refer to another's aunt with respect or to one's own aunt with affection］

¶あなたのおばさんはどこに住んでいますか。(Anata no *obasan* wa doko ni sunde imasu ka？)

*他人に自分のおばのことを話す場合には、普通「おばさん（obasan）」とは言わないで「おば（oba）」と言う。

→おば **oba**

②[よその中年の女の人]

¶八百屋のおばさんがわたしにりんごをくれました。(Yaoya no *obasan* ga watashi ni ringo o kuremashita.)

⇔おじさん **ojisan**

おはよう　お早う〔連〕

¶朝、人に会ったら、「お早うございます。」とあいさつします。(Asa, hito ni attara, "*Ohayō* gozaimasu." to aisatsu shimasu.)

＊丁寧に言う場合は「お早うございます（ohayō gozaimasu）」と言う。

おぼえる　覚える〔動Ⅱ〕

①[頭にとめておく]

¶あなたはわたしのことを覚えていますか。(Anata wa watashi no koto o *oboete* imasu ka？)

¶日本の歌をたくさん覚えていたのですが、もうだいぶ忘れました。(Nihon no uta o takusan *oboete* ita no desu ga, mō daibu wasuremashita.)

②[習得する]

¶早く仕事を覚えようとがんばっています。(Hayaku shigoto o *oboeyō* to ganbatte imasu.)

¶ Where does your **aunt** live?

*One usually uses *oba* rather than *obasan* when talking about one's aunt with someone outside of one's family.

② [a middle-aged woman, a lady]

¶ The **lady** in the fruit and vegetable store gave me an apple.

ohayō 〔compd〕 **Good morning**

¶ One greets people in the morning by saying *ohayō gozaimasu* 〖**good morning**〗.

＊One uses *ohayō gozaimasu* rather than *ohayō* when speaking politely.

oboeru 〔v Ⅱ〕 **memorize, remember, know; learn, master**

① [memorize, remember, know]

¶ Do you **remember** me?

¶ I once **knew** many Japanese songs but I've forgotten most of them.

② [learn, master]

¶ I'm working hard **to master** the job as quickly as possible.

おぼれる 〔動Ⅱ〕

¶台風で船が沈んで、人がおおぜいおぼれました。(Taifū de fune ga shizunde, hito ga oozei *oboremashita*.)

¶わたしは川で泳いでいる時、おぼれそうになりました。(Watashi wa kawa de oyoide iru toki, *oboresō* ni narimashita.)

おまつり お祭り 〔名〕

¶この辺りでは毎年8月中旬にお祭りがあります。(Kono atari de wa maitoshi hachigatsu chūjun ni *omatsuri* ga arimasu.)

おまわりさん お巡りさん 〔名〕

¶道がわからないので、交番のお巡りさんにききました。(Michi ga wakaranai node, kōban no *omawarisan* ni kikimashita.)

⇒警官 keikan

おみまい お見舞い 〔名〕

¶入院中に友達がお見舞いに来てくれました。(Nyūinchū ni tomodachi ga *omimai* ni kite kuremashita.)

おめでとう 〔連〕

¶明けましておめでとうございます。(Akemashite *omedetō* gozaimasu.)

¶誕生日おめでとう。(Tanjōbi *omedetō*.)

¶御結婚おめでとうございます。(Gokekkon *omedetō* gozaimasu.)

＊丁寧に言う場合は、「おめでとうございます（omedetō gozaimasu）」と言う。

⇒めでたい medetai

---

oboreru 〔v Ⅱ〕 **drown, be drowned**

¶A ship went down in the typhoon and many lives **were lost**.

¶**I came close to drowning** while swimming in the river.

omatsuri 〔n〕 **festival, gala, carnival**

¶The matsuri festival is held every year in mid August in this area.

omawarisan 〔n〕 **policeman**

¶[I] didn't know the way so [I] went to a police box and asked **the policeman** for directions.

omimai 〔n〕 **inquiry, visiting someone in the hospital**

¶My friend visited me while I was hospitalized.

omedetō 〔compd〕 **Congratulations**

¶**Happy** New Year!

¶**Happy** birthday!

¶**Congratulations** on your marriage!

＊When speaking politely, *Omedetō gozaimasu* is used.

おも 主 〔形動〕

¶日本の主な輸出品は工業製品です。（Nihon no *omo* na yushutsuhin wa kōgyō-seihin desu.）

¶あの学校の留学生は東南アジアの学生が主です。（Ano gakkō no ryūgakusei wa Tōnan-ajia no gakusei ga *omo* desu.）

omo 〔adj-v〕 chief, main, principal

¶ The **principal** exports of Japan are manufactured goods.

¶ The foreign students at that school are **chiefly** from Southeast Asia.

おもい 重い 〔形〕

① ［目方が多い］

¶この荷物は重くて、一人では持てません。（Kono nimotsu wa *omokute*, hitori de wa motemasen.）

② ［程度がはなはだしい］

¶上田さんは重い病気で3か月も入院しています。（Ueda san wa *omoi* byōki de sankagetsu mo nyūin shite imasu.）

⇔軽い karui

omoi 〔adj〕 heavy; severe, grave

① ［heavy］

¶ This load 〚package, bag. etc.〛 **is too heavy** for a single person to carry.

② ［severe, grave, serious］

¶ [Mrs.] Ueda is **seriously** ill and has been in the hospital for three months.

おもいだす 思い出す 〔動 I〕

¶わたしはときどき、小さいころのことを思い出します。（Watashi wa tokidoki, chiisai koro no koto o *omoidashimasu*.）

¶あの人の名前がどうしても思い出せません。（Ano hito no namae ga dōshite mo *omoidasemasen*.）

omoidasu 〔v I〕 recall, remember

¶ Every now and then **I think back** to when I was small.

¶ I just **can't remember** [his] name for the life of me.

おもいで 思い出 〔名〕

¶だれでも皆、子供のころのいろいろな思い出を持っています。（Daredemo mina, kodomo no koro no iroiro na *omoide* o motte imasu.）

¶今日の会は日本でのいい思い出になるでしょう。（Kyō no kai wa Nihon de no ii *omoide* ni naru deshō.）

omoide 〔n〕 memory, recollection

¶ All of us have various **memories** of our childhood.

¶ I **will** fondly **remember** today's gathering as one of my best times in Japan.

おもう　思う〔動Ⅰ〕

① [考える]
¶あなたはこの計画をどう思いますか。（Anata wa kono keikaku o dō *omoimasu* ka？）

② [推量する]
¶あの人は 40 歳ぐらいだと思います。（Ano hito wa yonjissai gurai da to *omoimasu*.）

③ [信じる]
¶あなたはきっとその仕事に成功すると思います。（Anata wa kitto sono shigoto ni seikō suru to *omoimasu*.）

④ [予期する]
¶山田さんは8時には来ると思います。（Yamada san wa hachiji ni wa kuru to *omoimasu*.）

⑤ [感じる]
¶あなたの国より日本のほうが寒いと思いますか。（Anata no kuni yori Nihon no hō ga samui to *omoimasu* ka？）

⑥ [望む]
¶わたしはその映画を見に行きたいと思っています。（Watashi wa sono eiga o mi ni ikitai to *omotte* imasu.）

⑦ [あることをするつもりである]
¶わたしは2週間ぐらい日本にいようと思っています。（Watashi wa nishūkan gurai Nihon ni iyō to *omotte* imasu.）

おもさ　重さ〔名〕
¶この荷物の重さを量ってください。（Kono nimotsu no *omosa* o hakatte kudasai.）

---

omou 〔v I〕 **think; suppose; believe; expect; feel; want; intend**

① [think]
¶ What **do you think** of this plan?

② [suppose, guess, imagine]
¶ **I suppose** [he's] around 40.

③ [believe]
¶ **I am sure** you will be a success at that job.

④ [expect]
¶ **I expect** [Miss] Yamada will be here at eight o'clock.

⑤ [feel]
¶ **Do you find** that Japan is colder than your native country?

⑥ [want, desire, wish]
¶ **I would like** to go see that movie.

⑦ [intend to, plan to, think of]
¶ **I am planning** to stay in Japan for about two weeks.

omosa 〔n〕 **weight**
¶ Please **weigh** this package 〚load, bag, etc.〛.

¶その小包の重さはどのぐらいですか。(Sono kozutsumi no *omosa* wa dono gurai desu ka?)

⇒-さ -sa

おもしろい〔形〕

① [おかしくて笑いたくなる様子]
¶中村さんはいつもおもしろい話をして、みんなを笑わせます。(Nakamura san wa itsu mo *omoshiroi* hanashi o shite, minna o warawasemasu.)

→おかしい okashii

② [楽しい]
¶旅行はとてもおもしろかったです。(Ryokō wa totemo *omoshirokatta* desu.)

③ [興味深い]
¶この小説はおもしろいです。(Kono shōsetsu wa *omoshiroi* desu.)

おもちゃ〔名〕

¶子供がおもちゃで遊んでいます。(Kodomo ga *omocha* de asonde imasu.)

おもて 表〔名〕

① [表面]
¶封筒の表に、相手の住所と名前を書きます。(Fūtō no *omote* ni, aite no jūsho to namae o kakimasu.)

⇔裏 ura

② [家の外]
¶家の中にばかりいないで、表で遊びなさい。(Ie no naka ni bakari inaide, *omote* de asobinasai.)

¶ How much does that parcel **weigh?**

omoshiroi 〔adj〕 **amusing, funny; pleasant, entertaining; interesting**

① [amusing, funny]
¶ [Mr.] Nakamura always makes everyone laugh with [his] **funny** stories.

② [pleasant, entertaining, enjoyable]
¶ The trip **was** a lot of **fun.**

③ [interesting]
¶ This novel **is interesting.**

omocha 〔n〕 **toy**
¶ The children are playing with **toys.**

omote 〔n〕 **face, surface; outside, outdoors**

① [face, surface, right side, front]
¶ One writes the name and address of the recipient on **the front** of an envelope.

② [outside, outdoors]
¶ Don't stay inside all the time—go play **outside.**

おもに 主に 〔副〕

¶この会には主に学生が集まります。
（Kono kai ni wa *omoni* gakusei ga
atsumarimasu.）
¶夜は主にラジオの音楽番組を聞いて
います。（Yoru wa *omoni* rajio no
ongaku-bangumi o kiite imasu.）

omoni 〔adv〕 **mainly, for the most part, generally**

¶These meetings **mainly** attract students.

¶**For the most part** [I] listen to music on the radio in the evening.

おや 親 〔名〕

父親（chichi*oya*）母親（haha*oya*）
¶この子はよく病気をして親に心配を
かけます。（Kono ko wa yoku byōki o
shite *oya* ni shinpai o kakemasu.）
⇔子 **ko**

oya 〔n〕 **parents, a parent**

a father // a mother

¶This child is a worry to **its parents** as it is frequently ill.

おや 〔感〕

¶おや、あの人は田中さんじゃないで
すか。（Oya, ano hito wa tanaka san ja
nai desu ka.）

oya 〔interj〕 **gee, oho**

¶Oh! Isn't that Mr Tanaka?

おやこ 親子 〔名〕

¶あの人たちは親子のようによく似て
います。（Ano hitotachi wa *oyako* no yō
ni yoku nite imasu.）

oyako 〔n〕 **parent and child**

¶Those two resemble each other as closely as if they were **parent and child**.

おやすみなさい お休みなさい 〔連〕

¶「お休みなさい」は、寝るときのあ
いさつです。（"*Oyasumi nasai*"wa, neru
toki no aisatsu desu.）

oyasumi nasai 〔compd〕 **Good night; set expression exchanged when parting for the last time that evening or when retiring for the night**

¶*Oyasumi nasai* is the expression used to someone at bedtime.

およぐ 泳ぐ 〔動 I〕

¶あなたは泳ぐことができますか。
（Anata wa *oyogu* koto ga dekimasu
ka？）

oyogu 〔v I〕 **swim**

¶Do you know how **to swim**?

128

¶池の中には魚がたくさん泳いでいます。(Ike no naka ni wa sakana ga takusan *oyoide* imasu.)

⇒水泳 suiei

おりもの 織物〔名〕

織物工場 (*orimono-kōjō*)

¶日本は昔から織物が盛んです。(Nihon wa mukashi kara *orimono* ga sakan desu.)

おりる 降りる〔動 II〕

¶バスを降りて少し歩きました。(Basu o *orite* sukoshi arukimashita.)

おりる 下りる〔動 II〕

¶足が痛いので、階段をゆっくり下りました。(Ashi ga itai node, kaidan o yukkuri *orimashita*.)

おる 織る〔動 I〕

¶この地方の人たちは布を織って生活しています。(Kono chihō no hitotachi wa nuno o *otte* seikatsu shite imasu.)

おる 折る〔動 I〕

①［曲げて取ったり傷めたりする］
¶公園の木の枝を折ってはいけません。(Kōen no ki no eda o *otte* wa ikemasen.)
¶転んで足の骨を折ってしまいました。(Koronde ashi no hone o *otte* shimaimashita.)

②［たたむ、曲げて重ねる］
¶紙を二つに折れば、この封筒に入ります。(Kami o futatsu ni *oreba*, kono fūtō ni hairimasu.)

¶ There are many fish **swimming** in the pond 〚pool〛.

orimono〔n〕 **cloth, textile**

a **textile** mill

¶ **Textiles** have flourished in Japan from ancient times.

oriru〔v II〕 **get off, disembark**

¶ [I] **got off** the bus and walked a little ways.

oriru〔v II〕 **come down, descend**

¶ As my leg 〚feet〛 hurt〚was sore〛, I **went down** the stairs slowly.

oru〔v I〕 **weave**

¶ The people in this region make their living from **weaving**.

oru〔v I〕 **break, break off; fold, bend**

① [break, break off, snap]

¶ One mustn't **break** branches **off** the trees in the park.

¶ [I] fell and **broke** [my] leg 〚a bone in my foot〛.

② [fold, bend]

¶ **If you fold** the paper in half it will fit into this envelope.

129

おれる 折れる 〔動Ⅱ〕

¶チョークが折れました。(Chōku ga oremashita.)

¶風で木の枝が折れそうです。(Kaze de ki no eda ga oresō desu.)

oreru 〔v Ⅱ〕 **break, be broken**

¶The chalk **broke in two**.

¶The tree branch **is close to breaking off** in the wind.

おろす 降ろす 〔動Ⅰ〕

¶次の交差点の所で降ろしてください。(Tsugi no kōsaten no tokoro de oroshite kudasai.)

¶荷物をたなから降ろしてください。(Nimotsu o tana kara oroshite kudasai.)

orosu 〔v Ⅰ〕 **take down, lower; let off, unload**

¶Please **let me off** at the next intersection.

¶Please **lift** the packages 〚bags, etc.〛 **down off** the shelf.

おろす 下ろす 〔動Ⅰ〕

貯金を下ろす (chokin o orosu)

¶わたしは銀行へお金を下ろしに行きました。(Watashi wa ginkō e okane o oroshi ni ikimashita.)

orosu 〔v Ⅰ〕 **withdraw money from a bank account**

withdraw one's savings

¶I went to the bank **to take out** some money.

おわり 終わり 〔名〕

¶夏休みも今週で終わりです。(Natsuyasumi mo konshū de owari desu.)

¶今日の授業はこれで終わりです。(Kyō no jugyō wa kore de owari desu.)

⇔始め hajime

owari 〔n〕 **end, close, conclusion**

¶Summer vacation **ends** this week.

¶This **concludes** class for today.

おわる 終わる 〔動Ⅰ〕

① 〔終了する〕
¶日本語の授業は9時に始まって4時に終わります。(Nihongo no jugyō wa kuji ni hajimatte yoji ni owarimasu.)

¶もう仕事は終わりましたか。(Mō shigoto wa owarimashita ka？)

¶これで今日の授業を終わります。(Kore de kyō no jugyō o owarimasu.)

(-)owaru 〔v Ⅰ〕 **to end; to finish doing something**

① 〔end, finish, be finished〕
¶Japanese classes begin at nine o'clock and **end** at four o'clock.

¶**Are you through** with work for today now 〚**Is** the work **done** already〛?

¶This **concludes** class for today.

*普通、自動詞として使うが、他動詞
として使うこともある。

②[ある動作が終了することを表す]
¶その本はもう読み終わりました。
(Sono hon wa mō yomi*owarimashita*.)
¶答えを書き終わったら、出してくだ
さい。(Kotae o kaki*owattara*, dashite
kudasai.)
*「動詞（基幹の形）＋終わる
(owaru)」の形で使う。
⇔始まる hajimaru
⇒終える oeru

Owaru is usually an intransitive verb,
but it can also be used as a transitive
verb.

②[finish doing something]
¶[I]'ve already **finished** reading that
book.
¶Please hand in your answers when
you're **finished**.

*Used in the pattern "verb (stem form)
+ -*owaru*."

おんがく 音楽〔名〕

音楽家（*ongak*ka）音楽会（*ongak*kai）
¶わたしは毎晩ラジオで音楽を聞きま
す。(Watashi wa maiban rajio de *ongaku*
o kikimasu.)
¶あの人は中学の音楽の先生です。
(Ano hito wa chūgaku no *ongaku* no
sensei desu.)

ongaku 〔n〕 **music**
a musician // a concert, recital
¶I listen to **music** on the radio every
night.

¶[He] is a junior high school **music**
teacher.

おんせん 温泉〔名〕

¶日本には温泉がたくさんあります。
(Nihon ni wa *onsen* ga takusan arimasu.)

onsen 〔n〕 **a hot spring, a spa**
¶There are many **hot springs** in Japan.

おんど 温度〔名〕

温度計（*ondo*kei）温度が上がる
（*ondo* ga agaru）温度が下がる（*ondo*
ga sagaru）温度が高い（*ondo* ga takai）
温度が低い（*ondo* ga hikui）
¶部屋の中の温度は、今 20 度ぐらいで
す。(Heya no naka no *ondo* wa, ima
nijūdo gurai desu.)

ondo 〔n〕 **temperature, heat**
a thermometer // **the temperature**
rises // **the temperature** falls // **the
temperature** is high // **the
temperature** is low
¶The room **temperature** is presently
around 20 degrees.

おんな 女〔名〕

¶これは女の時計です。(Kore wa *onna*
no tokei desu.)

onna 〔n〕 **woman, female**
¶This is a **woman's** watch.

¶部屋の中に女の人が二人います。
(Heya no naka ni *onna* no hito ga futari imasu.)

¶There are two **women** in the room.

⇔男 otoko

おんなのこ 女の子〔名〕

onna no ko 〔n〕 girl

¶あの女の子は新しいおもちゃが欲しいようです。(Ano onna no ko wa atarashii omocha ga hoshii yō desu.)

¶That **little girl** seems to want a new toy.

お-〔頭〕

o- 〔pref〕 a prefix expressing respect, humility, or politeness

① [尊敬の気持ちを表す]
お考え (okangae) お元気 (ogenki)

① [used to express respect]
(your) idea, (your) thinking // (your) being healthy

¶お名前は何とおっしゃいますか。
(Onamae wa nan to osshaimasu ka？)

¶What is your name?

¶このごろお忙しいようですね。
(Kono goro oisogashii yō desu ne.)

¶You seem to be busy these days.

¶社長は、今新聞をお読みになっています。(Shachō wa, ima shinbun o oyomi ni natte imasu.)

¶The company president is reading the newspaper now.

¶あなたの手紙を読んで、ご家族の方はお喜びなさるでしょう。(Anata no tegami o yonde, gokazoku no kata wa oyorokobi nasaru deshō.)

¶Your family will undoubtedly be happy to receive your letter.

¶上田先生がわたしたちに英語をお教えくださいました。(Ueda sensei ga watashitachi ni Eigo o ooshie kudasaimashita.)

¶Professor Ueda taught us English.

*動詞の場合、「お (o) ＋動詞 (基幹の形) ＋になる (ni naru)」、「お (o) ＋動詞 (基幹の形) ＋なさる (nasaru)」、「お (o) ＋動詞 (基幹の形) ＋くださる (kudasaru)」などの形で使う。

*o- expressing respect is used with verbs in the patterns "*o-* + verb (stem form) + *ni naru* ," "*o-* + verb (stem form) + *nasaru* ," "*o-* + verb (stem form) + *kudasaru* ," etc.

② [謙譲の気持ちを表す]

② [used to express humility]

¶あとでお電話するか、お手紙を差し上げます。（Ato de *o*denwa suru ka, *o*tegami o sashiagemasu.）

¶ I will call or write later.

¶その荷物をお持ちしましょう。
(Sono nimotsu o *o*mochi shimashō.)

¶ Shall I carry that package 〚bag, etc.〛 for you?

¶先生に旅行の写真をお見せいたしました。（Sensei ni ryokō no shashin o *o*mise itashimashita.）

¶ I showed my teacher 〚doctor〛 photos from the trip.

*動詞の場合、「お（o）＋動詞（基幹の形）＋する（suru）」、「お（o）＋動詞（基幹の形）＋いたす（itasu）」などの形で使う。

*o- expressing humility is used with verbs in the patterns "*o*- + verb (stem form) + *suru* ," "*o*- + verb (stem form) + *itasu* ," etc.

③ [丁寧の気持ちを表す]
お酒（*o*sake）お寒い（*o*samui）

③ [used to express politeness]
sake, liquor // cold, it's cold

¶お茶とお菓子を買ってきました。
(*O*cha to *o*kashi o katte kimashita.)

¶ I bought (literally, bought and brought) some tea and sweets.

＊外来語にはつきにくい。また、「応接間（ōsetsuma）」などのように「お（o）」で始まる言葉にもつきにくい。
⇒御- **go-**

＊*o*- is seldom added to borrowed words written in *katakana* or to words beginning in "o" such as *ōsetsuma* (parlor, reception room).

か

か　蚊 〔名〕

蚊に食われる (ka ni kuwareru) 蚊帳
(kaya)

¶この辺は夏になると、蚊が多いで
す。(Kono hen wa natsu ni naru to, *ka* ga
ooi desu.)

か 〔助〕

¶あなたはあしたどこかへ行きます
か。(Anata wa ashita doko *ka* e ikimasu
ka？)

¶何か欲しいものがありますか。
(Nani *ka* hoshii mono ga arimasu ka？)

¶山田さんの誕生日はいつか知ってい
ますか。(Yamada san no tanjōbi wa itsu
ka shitte imasu ka？)

¶隣の部屋にだれかいますか。(Tonari
no heya ni dare *ka* imasu ka？)

¶ゆうべ食べた魚が悪かったためか、
おなかが痛いです。(Yūbe tabeta
sakana ga warukatta tame *ka*, onaka ga itai
desu.)

か 〔助〕

①[いくつかあるもののうち一つを選
ぶときに使う]

¶来週の土曜日か日曜日に海へ泳ぎに
行きます。(Raishū no doyōbi *ka*
nichiyōbi ni umi e oyogi ni ikimasu.)

¶正しい答えはAかBかわかりますか。
(Tadashii kotae wa ē *ka* bii *ka*
wakarimasu ka？)

ka 〔n〕 **mosquito**

be bitten by **a mosquito** // a **mosquito**
net

¶ There are many **mosquitoes** in this
area in the summer.

ka 〔part〕 **the interrogative particle**

¶ Are you going **anywhere** tomorrow?

¶ Is there **something** you want 〚you'd
like〛?

¶ Do you know **when** [Mrs.] Yamada's
birthday is?

¶ Is there **anyone** in the room next
door?

¶ My stomach aches, **probably**
because the fish I ate last night was bad.

ka 〔part〕 **or**

① [or; used when two different
alternatives are possible]

¶ I will go to the ocean to swim next
Saturday **or** Sunday.

¶ Do you know if the correct answer is
A **or** B?

¶大学に進むか社会に出て働くか、まだ決めていません。(Daigaku ni susumu *ka* shakai ni dete hataraku *ka*, mada kimete imasen.)

¶ [I] haven't decided yet whether to go to college **or** to go out into the world and get a job.

② [二つの可能性のうちどちらかはっきりしないときに使う]

② [or; used when one alternative and its opposite are possible]

¶あしたハイキングに行くか行かないか早く決めてください。(Ashita haikingu ni iku *ka* ikanai *ka* hayaku kimete kudasai.)

¶ Please hurry up and make up your mind whether you are going hiking tomorrow **or** not.

¶あの人は今日来るかどうかわかりません。(Ano hito wa kyō kuru *ka* dō *ka* wakarimasen)

¶ I don't know if [he] is coming today **or** not.

¶学校があした休みかどうかきいてください。(Gakkō ga ashita yasumi *ka* dō *ka* kiite kudasai.)

¶ Please inquire whether there is school tomorrow **or** not.

¶このりんごはおいしいかどうか食べてみましょう。(Kono ringo wa oishii *ka* dō *ka* tabete mimashō.)

¶ Let's try these apples and see if they're good tasting **or** not.

③ [あるものごとを例として挙げる]

③ [or; used when offering something as one possibility]

¶のどが渇いたから、コーヒーか何かを飲みましょう。(Nodo ga kawaita kara, kōhii *ka* nani ka o nomimashō.)

¶ I'm thirsty. Let's have some coffee **or** something.

¶この仕事は山田さんかだれかに頼みましょう。(Kono shigoto wa Yamada san *ka* dare ka ni tanomimashō.)

¶ Let's ask [Mr.] Yamada **or** someone to do this work.

¶それはデパートかどこかで売っていると思います。(Sore wa depāto *ka* doko ka de utte iru to omoimasu.)

¶ I think that's on sale 〚one can buy that〛 at a department store **or** the like.

*「～か何か（～ka nani ka）」「～かだれか（～ka dare ka）」「～かどこか（～ka doko ka）」の形で使う。また、あとのほうの「か（ka）」につく助詞の

*Used in the patterns "~ *ka nani ka* ," "~ *ka dare ka* ," and "~ *ka doko ka*." After the second *ka*, the particle *ga* and *o* are sometimes omitted.

「が（ga）」「を（o）」は省略すること
ができる。

か〔助〕

① [質問の意味を表す]
¶あれは何^{なん}ですか。（Are wa nan desu
ka？）
¶あなたは学生^{がくせい}ですか。（Anata wa
gakusei desu *ka*？）
¶ここはどこですか。（Koko wa doko
desu *ka*？）
② [歓誘・依頼などを表す]
¶映画^{えいが}を見に行きませんか。（Eiga o mi
ni ikimasen *ka*？）
¶ちょっと、その本^{ほん}を見^みせてください
ませんか。（Chotto, sono hon o misete
kudasaimasen *ka*？）
③ [相手の意向をうかがうのに使う]

¶私^{わたくし}がその本を買^かってきましょうか。
（Watakushi ga sono hon o katte kimashō
ka？）
¶この仕事^{しごと}はわたしがいたしましょう
か。（Kono shigoto wa watashi ga
itashimashō *ka*？）
④ [疑念の意味を表す]
¶あれは何^{なん}だろうか。（Are wa nan darō
ka？）
¶こんな難^{むずか}しい問題^{もんだい}がわたしにできる
だろうか。（Konna muzukashii mondai
ga watashi ni dekiru darō *ka*？）
¶こんな小^{ちい}さな舟^{ふね}に5人^{ごにん}も乗^のって大丈
夫^{だいじょう}だろうか。（Konna chiisana fune ni
gonin mo notte daijōbu darō *ka*？）
⑤ [自問自答の形で事実を確かめるの
に使う]

ka〚part〛 **the sentence-final
interrogative particle**
① [indicates a question]
¶ What's that?

¶ Are you a student?

¶ Where is this 〚Where am I〛?

② [indicates an invitation or request]
¶ Won't you come to a movie with
[me]?
¶ Would you let me see that book for a
moment, please?

③ [used to inquire about the desires of
the listener]
¶ Would you like me to buy that book?

¶ Shall I do this job 〚How about my
doing this work〛?

④ [indicates doubt]
¶ What do you suppose that is 〚I
wonder what that is〛?
¶ I'm not sure I can do such a difficult
problem.

¶ Can five people fit into this small
boat all right?

⑤ [used to confirm something in the
form of a rhetorical question]

¶「山田さんは試験に失敗したそうで
す。」(Yamada san wa shiken ni shippai
shita sō desu.)「やはりそうでしたか。
全然勉強しませんでしたからね。」
(Yahari sō deshita ka. Zenzen benkyō
shimasen deshita kara ne.)

¶ "I hear [Miss] Yamada failed [her]
exam."
"Really? That's just what I expected.
[She] didn't study at all."

が〔助〕

ga 〔part〕 **but, and**

① [前件から当然予想される結果が後
件において成立しないという関係を表
す]

① [but, and yet; indicates that what
would naturally follow the first clause
is lacking]

¶種をまきましたが、とうとう芽が出
ませんでした。(Tane o makimashita *ga*,
tōtō me ga demasen deshita.)

¶ [I] planted 〚sowed〛 some seeds, **but**
in the end they did not come up.

¶頭が痛いので薬を飲みましたが、少
しもよくなりません。(Atama ga itai
node kusuri o nomimashita *ga*, sukoshi
mo yoku narimasen.)

¶ I took some medicine for my
headache, **but** it hasn't gotten any
better at all.

② [前件が後件に対して対比的・対立
的な関係にあることを表す]

② [but; indicates that the second
clause is in contrast or opposition to
the first clause]

¶ペンはありますが、インクがありま
せん。(Pen wa arimasu *ga*, inku ga
arimasen.)

¶ There's a pen, **but** there isn't any ink.

¶わたしは海は好きですが、山はあま
り好きではありません。(Watashi wa
umi wa suki desu *ga*, yama wa amari suki
de wa arimasen.)

¶ I like the ocean, **but** I don't
particularly like the mountains.

¶わたしは約束どおり早く行きました
が、山田さんはずいぶん遅れて来まし
た。(Watashi wa yakusokudōri hayaku
ikimashita *ga*, yamada san wa zuibun
okurete kimashita.)

¶ I came on time, **but** [Mrs.] Yamada
came very late.

¶去年の冬はずいぶん寒かったです
が、今年は暖かでたいへん楽です。
(Kyonen no fuyu wa zuibun samukatta
desu *ga*, kotoshi wa atataka de taihen raku
desu.)

¶ It was a very severe winter last year,
but this year it's a very warm and easy
one.

③[前件が後件に対する前置きなどの関係にあることを表す]

¶すみませんが、水を一杯ください。(Sumimasen *ga*, mizu o ippai kudasai.)
¶こちらは山田でございますが、中村さんでしょうか。(Kochira wa Yamada de gozaimasu *ga*, Nakamura san deshō ka？)
¶駅へ行きたいのですが、どう行ったらよいでしょう。(Eki e ikitai no desu *ga*, dō ittara yoi deshō ka？)

④[前件のことがらが後件のことがらに対して共存的な関係にあることを表す]

¶山田さんは体も大きいが、力もあります。(Yamada san wa karada mo ookii *ga*, chikara mo arimasu.)
¶去年の冬も寒かったですが、今年もやはり寒いですね。(Kyonen no fuyu mo samukatta desu ga, kotoshi mo yahari samui desu ne.)
¶山田さんは医者ですが、息子さんもやはり医者になりました。(Yamada san wa isha desu ga, musukosan mo yahari isha ni narimashita.)
⇒けれども keredomo

が〚助〛

①[動作や存在や状態などの主体を表す]
¶「そこに何がありますか。」(Soko ni nani *ga* arimasu ka？)「ここに本があります。」(Koko ni hon *ga* arimasu.)
¶丘の上には桜の花がきれいに咲いていました。(Oka no ue ni wa sakura no hana *ga* kirei ni saite imashita.)

③ [but, and; indicates that the first clause is preliminary or introductory to the second clause]

¶ Excuse me, **but** could I have a glass of water please?

¶ This is [Mr.] Yamada calling. Is this [Mr.] Nakamura?

¶ I want to go to the station. Could you please tell me the way?

④ [and; indicates the coexistence of the first and second clauses]

¶ [Mr.] Yamada is large, **and** [he] is strong too.

¶ Last winter was cold, **and** it's cold this winter too.

¶ [Mrs.] Yamada is a doctor, **and** [her] son became a doctor too.

ga 〚part〛 **a particle acting as a subject marker**

① [indicates the subject of an action, state, condition, etc.]
¶ "What is there?"
"There is a book here."

¶ Beautiful cherry blossoms were in bloom on the hilltop.

¶昨日は一日じゅう雨が降っていました。(Kinō wa ichinichijū ame *ga* futte imashita.)

¶ It rained all day yesterday.

¶だれが窓ガラスを割ったのですか。(Dare *ga* madogarasu o watta no desu ka？)

¶ Who broke the window?

¶公園の桜の花がとてもきれいです。(Kōen no sakura no hana *ga* totemo kirei desu.)

¶ The cherry blossoms in the park are very pretty.

¶海は波が静かでした。(Umi wa nami *ga* shizuka deshita.)

¶ The ocean waves were gentle.

¶どれがあなたの万年筆ですか。(Dore *ga* anata no mannenhitsu desu ka？)

¶ Which one is your fountain pen?

② [希望や好ききらいなどの感情の対象を表す]

② [indicates the object of feelings of desire, like, dislike, etc.]

¶わたしは山登りが好きです。(Watashi wa yamanobori *ga* suki desu.)

¶ I like mountain climbing.

¶兄は運動がきらいです。(Ani wa undō *ga* kirai desu.)

¶ My (elder) brother dislikes exercise.

¶「あなたは何が欲しいですか。」(Anata wa nani *ga* hoshii desu ka？)「わたしはカメラが欲しいです。」(Watashi wa kamera *ga* hoshii desu.)

¶ "What do you want?"
"I want a camera."

¶わたしは水が飲みたいです。(Watashi wa mizu *ga* nomitai desu.)

¶ I want a drink of water.

¶わたしは頭が痛いです。(Watashi wa atama *ga* itai desu.)

¶ I have a headache.

*「動詞（基幹の形）＋たい（tai）」の形で希望を表す場合には「を（o）」も使われる。「わたしは田舎に家を建てたいです。(Watashi wa inaka ni ie o tatetai desu.)」

*The particle *o* can also be used in the pattern "verb (stem form) + *-tai*": "*Watashi wa inaka ni ie o tatetai desu*" (I want to build a house in the country).

③ [能力・可能不可能・上手下手などの対象を表す]

③ [indicates the object of ability, possibility, impossibility, skill, lack of skill, etc.]

¶中村さんは上手に英語が話せます。
（Nakamura san wa jōzu ni Eigo *ga*
hanasemasu.)

¶ [Mr.] Nakamura can speak English
well.

¶わたしは中国語がよくわかりませ
ん。(Watashi wa Chūgokugo *ga* yoku
wakarimasen.)

¶ I can't understand Chinese very well.

¶わたしはまだ泳ぐことができませ
ん。(Watashi wa mada oyogu koto *ga*
dekimasen.)

¶ I still can't swim.

¶中村さんはスキーがとても上手で
す。(Nakamura san wa sukii *ga* totemo
jōzudesu.)

¶ [Miss] Nakamura can ski very well.

が〔助〕

ga 〔part〕 **but, and**

① [ものごとをはっきり断定的に言う
のを避けて柔らかく言い相手の反応を
待つ気持ちを表す]

① [used to soften a statement and to
indicate that one is waiting for the
listener's response]

¶実はお金を少しお借りしたいのです
が。(Jitsu wa okane o sukoshi okari
shitai no desu *ga*.)

¶ Actually I would like to borrow a
little money....

¶父は今外出しておりますが。(Chichi
wa ima gaishutsu shite orimasu *ga*.)

¶ My father is out now....

② [望ましいことがらの成立を願う気
持ちや実現しなかったことがらを回想
してそれが成立していればどんなによ
かったかというような気持ちなどを表
す]

② [expresses a desire for something to
happen or regret that something didn't
happen]

¶今日じゅうにあの峠を越えることが
できればよいが。(Kyōjū ni ano tōge o
koeru koto *ga* dekireba yoi *ga*.)

¶ It would be nice if we could get over
that ridge sometime today〖If only we
could get over that ridge sometime
today〗....

¶学生の時に海外旅行をしておけばよ
かったのだが。(Gakusei no toki ni
kaigai-ryokō o shite okeba yokatta no da
ga.)

¶ If only I had traveled abroad when I
was a student....

⇒けれども **keredomo**

(-)か (-)科〔名、尾〕

(-)ka 〖n, suf〗 **course; branch, department, faculty**

1〔名〕
科目（*ka*moku）
¶あなたは文学部のどの科に進むつもりですか。（Anata wa bungakubu no dono *ka* ni susumu tsumori desu ka？）

1 〖n〗 course
subject, course (in school)
¶ What **course** do you plan to major in within the faculty of literature?

2〔尾〕
学科（gak*ka*）文科（bun*ka*）理科（ri*ka*）内科（nai*ka*）外科（ge*ka*）眼科（gan*ka*）歯科（shi*ka*）

2 〖suf〗
branch, department, faculty school
subject; course of study, curriculum // **dept.** of liberal arts // science; the science **course** // internal medicine, internal **dept.** (of a hospital) // surgery, **dept.** of surgery // ophthalmology, **dept.** of opthalmology // dentistry

(-)か (-)課〔名、尾〕

(-)ka 〖n, suf〗 **division, section; lesson**

1〔名〕
①［役所・会社などの事務組織の区別の一つ］
課長（*ka*chō）学生課（gakusei*ka*）

1 〖n〗
① [division, section]
a **section** chief // the student **division**

②［教科書などの一区切りを表す］
¶昨日習った課を復習してください。（Kinō naratta *ka* o fukushū shite kudasai.）

② [lesson (in a textbook)]
¶ Please review the **chapter(s)** [we] studied yesterday.

2〔尾〕
¶今日は第5課から始めましょう。（Kyō wa daigo*ka* kara hajimemashō.）

2 〖suf〗 lesson, section
¶ Let's start today with **Lesson** 5.

-か -家〔尾〕

-ka 〖suf〗 **the suffix for a person carrying on a given profession**

政治家（seiji*ka*）小説家（shōsetsu*ka*）芸術家（geijutsu*ka*）専門家（senmon*ka*）音楽家（ongaku*ka*）作曲家（sakkyoku*ka*）画家（ga*ka*）評論家（hyōron*ka*）

a politic**ian** // a nove**list** // an art**ist** // a special**ist**, expert // a music**ian** // a compos**er** // a painter // a critic, commentat**or**

-か -化〔尾〕

電化 (den*ka*) 自動化 (jidō*ka*) オート
メーション化 (ōtomēshon*ka*) 具体化
(gutai*ka*) 映画化 (eiga*ka*) 合理化
(gōri*ka*) 近代化 (kindai*ka*) 民主化
(minshu*ka*)

¶最近の日本の農業は機械化されてい
ます。(Saikin no Nihon no nōgyō wa
kikai*ka* sarete imasu.)

-か -日〔尾〕

① [日付を表す]
二日 (futsu*ka*) 三日 (mik*ka*) 四日
(yok*ka*) 五日 (itsu*ka*) 六日 (mui*ka*)
七日 (nano*ka*) 八日 (yō*ka*) 九日
(kokono*ka*) 十日 (too*ka*) 十四日
(jūyok*ka*) 二十日 (hatsu*ka*) 二十四日
(nijūyok*ka*)

¶三月三日は女の子のお祭りの日で
す。(Sangatsu mik*ka* wa onna no ko no
omatsuri no hi desu.)
② [日数を表す]
¶あと三日で夏休みです。(Ato mik*ka*
de natsuyasumi desu.)
¶上田さんは十日間も学校を休んでい
ます。(Ueda san wa too*ka*kan mo gakkō
o yasunde imasu.)
＊「一日」は、日付を表すときは普通
「ついたち (tsuitachi)」と言い、日数
を表すときは「いちにち (ichinichi)」
と言う。
⇒-日 **-nichi**

-か〔尾〕

1か所 (ik*ka*sho) 3か月 (san*ka*getsu)
5か国 (go*ka*koku)

-ka〔suf〕 **-ize, -zation**

electrifica**tion** // automa**tion**,
automati**zation** // automa**tion**,
automati**zation** // embodiment,
actuali**zation**, giving concrete form
to // **making into** a film //
rationali**zation** // moderni**zation** //
democrati**zation**

¶ In recent times Japanese agriculture
is becoming **mechanized**.

-ka〔suf〕 **days**

① [the counter for days of the month]
the second (of the month) // the third //
the fourth // the fifth // the sixth // the
seventh // the eighth // the ninth // the
tenth // the fourteenth // the twentieth //
the twenty-fourth

¶ The **third** of March is Girls' Day.

② [the counter for number of days]
¶ In three **days** it will be summer
vacation.

¶ [Mr.] Ueda has been absent from
school for 10 **days**.

＊The compound "一日" is read
tsuitachi when referring to the first of
the month and *ichinichi* when referring
to one day.

-ka-〔suf〕 **the suffix used for counting**

one place // three months // five
countries

¶ 1年は 12 か月です。(Ichinen wa jūni*kagetsu* desu.)

＊数字のあとにつけて年月・所などを数えるのに使う。

¶ One year is 12 months.

＊Used between the numeral and the unit when counting units of time, places, etc.

カーテン〔名〕

カーテンを掛ける（*kāten* o kakeru）カーテンを引く（*kāten* o hiku）

¶ 窓に白いレースのカーテンが掛かっています。(Mado ni shiroi rēsu no *kāten* ga kakatte imasu.)

kāten〔n〕**curtains**

hang up **curtains** // pull **a curtain** closed

¶ There are white lace **curtains** hanging at the window(s).

かい 貝〔名〕

貝がら（*kai*gara）

¶ 海岸で珍しい貝を拾いました。(Kaigan de mezurashii *kai* o hiroimashita.)

¶ 昔、中国では貝がお金の役目をしていました。(Mukashi, Chūgoku de wa *kai* ga okane no yakume o shite imashita.)

kai〔n〕**shellfish, shell**

a shell

¶ [I] found a rare **seashell** at the shore.

¶ **Shells** were used for money in the past in China.

がい 害〔名、〜する〕

害虫（*gai*chū）公害（kō*gai*）水害（sui*gai*）

¶ たばこは健康に害があります。(Tabako wa kenkō ni *gai* ga arimasu.)

gai〔n, 〜*suru*〕**injury, harm**

a **harmful** insect // pollution // flood **damage**

¶ Smoking is **bad for** one's health.

(-)かい (-)回〔名、尾〕

1〔名〕
回を重ねる（*kai* o kasaneru）

¶ 今回は出席できませんが、次回は必ず出席します。(Kon*kai* wa shusseki dekimasen ga, ji*kai* wa kanarazu shusseki shimasu.)

2〔尾〕

(-)kai〔n, suf〕**time, round, game, inning**

1〔n〕
do many **times**

¶ I can't attend this **time**, but I'll be there without fail next **time**.

2〔suf〕

¶「日本へ何回行きましたか。」
(Nihon e nan*kai* ikimashita ka？)「一回
も行ったことがありません。」(Ik*kai*
mo itta koto ga arimasen.)

¶委員会は1か月に2回開かれます。
(Iinkai wa ikkagetsu ni ni*kai*
hirakaremasu.)

¶ "How many **times** have you been to
Japan?"
"I've never been there even **once**."

¶ The committee 〚commission,
council〛 meets **twice** a month.

(-)かい (-)会 〔名、尾〕

(-)kai 〚n, suf〛 **meeting, assembly;
society, association**

1〔名〕
会を開く (*kai* o hiraku) 会を閉じる
(*kai* o tojiru) 会に出席する (*kai* ni
shusseki suru) 会合 (*kai*gō)
¶今日は3時からお茶の会がありま
す。(Kyō wa sanji kara ocha no *kai* ga
arimasu.)

1 〚n〛 meeting, assembly, gathering
open **a meeting** 〚party〛 // close **a
meeting** 〚party〛 // attend **a meeting**
〚party〛 // a meeting, a gathering
¶ There's a tea ceremony **meeting** 〚tea
party〛 from three o'clock today.

2〔尾〕
①[ある目的のために人々が集まるこ
と]
送別会 (sōbetsu*kai*) 委員会 (iin*kai*)

2 〚suf〛
① [a gathering of persons for a
certain purpose]
a farewell **party** // a committee, a
commission; a committee **meeting**

¶あした、上田先生の歓迎会をしま
す。(Ashita, Ueda sensei no kangei*kai* o
shimasu.)
¶音楽会は7時から始まります。
(Ongaku*kai* wa shichiji kara
hajimarimasu.)
②[関係のある人々の作った団体]
¶わたしたちは日本文化研究会を作り
ました。(Watashitachi wa Nihon-bunka-
kenkyū*kai* o tsukurimashita.)

¶ A welcome **party** 〚welcoming
reception〛 will be held tomorrow for
[Mr.] Ueda.
¶ **The concert** 〚recital〛 starts at seven
o'clock.

② [society, association, group]
¶ We formed a Japanese culture study
group.

(-)かい (-)階 〔名、尾〕

(-)kai 〚n, suf〛 **floor, story**

1〔名〕
¶おもちゃは、この上の階で売ってい
ます。(Omocha wa, kono ue no *kai* de
utte imasu.)

1 〚n〛
¶ Toys are sold on the next **floor** up.

2〔尾〕

2 〚suf〛

1階（ik*kai*）3階（san*gai*）6階（rok*kai*）8階（hak*kai*［hachi*kai*］）10階（jik*kai*）何階（nan*gai*）2階建ての家（ni*kai*date no ie）

¶わたしはこの建物の5階に住んでいます。（Watashi wa kono tatemono no go*kai* ni sunde imasu.）

the first **floor** // the third **floor** // the sixth **floor** // the eighth **floor** // the tenth **floor** // which **floor**, how many **floors** // a two-story house

¶ I live on the fifth **floor** of this building.

かいがい　海外 ［名］

¶来年、海外旅行をするつもりです。（Rainen, *kaigai*-ryokō o suru tsumori desu.）

¶新聞で国内のニュースはもちろん、海外のニュースもよく読んでいます。（Shinbun de kokunai no nyūsu wa mochiron, *kaigai* no nyūsu mo yoku yonde imasu.）

kaigai 〖n〗 **overseas, abroad**

¶ I plan to travel **abroad** next year.

¶ [I] often read the **international** news in the newspaper; of course [I] read the domestic news, too.

かいがん　海岸 ［名］

¶今朝、海岸を散歩しました。（Kesa, *kaigan* o sanpo shimashita.）

¶汽車は海岸に沿って走っています。（Kisha wa *kaigan* ni sotte hashitte imasu.）

kaigan 〖n〗 **seashore, coast, beach**

¶ [I] strolled along **the beach** this morning.

¶ The train runs along **the coast**.

かいぎ　会議 ［名］

会議室（*kaigi*shitsu）会議場（*kaigi*-jō）国際会議（kokusai*kaigi*）会議を開く（*kaigi* o hiraku）会議に出席する（*kaigi* ni shusseki suru）会議に欠席する（*kaigi* ni kesseki suru）

¶今日、2時から会議があります。（Kyō, niji kara *kaigi* ga arimasu.）

¶今、社長は会議中です。（Ima, shachō wa *kaigi*chū desu.）

kaigi 〖n〗 **meeting, conference**

a **conference** room, **assembly** room // a **conference** hall // an international **conference** 〚**congress**〛 // hold a **conference** 〚**meeting**〛 // attend a **meeting** 〚**conference**〛 // be absent from a **meeting** 〚**conference**〛

¶ There is a **meeting** 〚**conference**〛 today at two o'clock.

¶ The president (of the company) is now **in conference**.

かいきょう 回教 〔名〕

回教国 (*kaikyō*koku) 回教徒
(*kaikyō*to)

kaikyō 〔n〕 **Mohammedanism, Islam**

a **Moslem** land // a **Moslem**

かいけい 会計 〔名〕

① [お金の出し入れを計算・管理すること]

会計検査 (*kaikei*-kensa) 会計簿
(*kaikei*bo)

¶会計課の窓口へ行って、お金を払ってください。(*Kaikei*ka no mado-guchi e itte, okane o haratte kudasai.)

②[レストランなどでの代金の勘定・支払い]

¶今日の会計はわたしがします。(Kyō no *kaikei* wa watashi ga shimasu.)

¶会計をお願いします。(*Kaikei* o onegai shimasu.)

→勘定 kanjō

kaikei 〔n〕 **accounts; bill**

① [accounts]

an audit, auditing // an **account** book

¶ Please proceed to the **accounts** window 〚**cashier**〛 and pay.

② [bill (at a restaurant, etc.)]

¶ I'll **pay** today.

¶ **The bill**, please.

かいけつ 解決 〔名、～する〕

未解決の問題 (mi*kaiketsu* no mondai)

¶わたしたちは問題の解決に努力しています。(Watashitachi wa mondai no *kaiketsu* ni doryoku shite imasu.)

¶この問題の解決がつくまでには時間がかかりそうです。(Kono mondai no *kaiketsu* ga tsuku made ni wa jikan ga kakarisō desu.)

¶あの事件はまだ解決していません。(Ano jiken wa mada *kaiketsu* shite imasen.)

kaiketsu 〔n、～*suru*〕 **solution, settlement**

an un**solved** problem, a pending question

¶ We are working **to solve** the problem.

¶ It looks like it will be some time before this matter **is settled**.

¶ That case **hasn't been solved** yet.

がいこう 外交 〔名〕

外交官 (*gaikō*kan) 外交問題 (*gaikō*-mondai) 外交政策 (*gaikō*-seisaku)

gaikō 〔n〕 **diplomacy**

a **diplomat**, the **diplomatic** service // a **diplomatic** question // a **diplomatic** policy

146

¶それは外交上の秘密です。(Sore wa *gaikō*jō no himitsu desu.)

¶ That is a **diplomatic** secret.

¶A国とB国との間には現在外交関係がありません。(Ē-koku to Bii-koku to no aida ni wa genzai *gaikō*-kankei ga arimasen.)

¶ At present, Country A does not have **diplomatic** relations with Country B.

がいこく 外国 〔名〕

gaikoku 〔n〕 **foreign country**

外国人 (*gaikoku*jin) 外国語 (*gaikoku*go)

a **foreigner** // a **foreign** language

¶わたしはまだ外国へ行ったことがありません。(Watashi wa mada *gaikoku* e itta koto ga arimasen.)

¶ I've never been to a **foreign country**.

かいしゃ 会社 〔名〕

kaisha 〔n〕 **company, business firm**

会社員 (*kaisha*in) 株式会社 (kabu-shiki-*gaisha*)

a **company** employee, an **office** worker // a joint-stock **company**, a corporation

¶大学を卒業して、貿易会社に入りました。(Daigaku o sotsugyō shite, bōeki-*gaisha* ni hairimashita.)

¶ [I] graduated from college and went to work for a trading **company**.

¶わたしの弟は建築会社に勤めています。(Watashi no otōto wa kenchiku-*gaisha* ni tsutomete imasu.)

¶ My younger brother works for a construction **firm**.

¶先月、上田さんは会社を辞めました。(Sengetsu, Ueda san wa *kaisha* o yamemashita.)

¶ [Mrs.] Ueda quit [her] **job** last month.

かいじょう 会場 〔名〕

kaijō 〔n〕 **venue**

¶今度の日本語の試験の会場は家からとても遠いです。(Kondo no nihongo no shiken no *kaijō* wa ie kara totemo tooi desu.)

¶ The next Japanese examination venue is a long way from my house.

がいじん 外人 〔名〕

gaijin 〔n〕 **foreigner, alien**

¶あの外人は日本語が上手ですね。(Ano *gaijin* wa Nihongo ga jōzu desu ne.)

¶ That **foreigner** speaks Japanese well.

147

¶観光のため、たくさんの**外人**が京都
へ行きます。（Kankō no tame, takusan
no *gaijin* ga Kyōto e ikimasu.）

＊「外国人（gaikokujin）」とも言う。

¶ Many **foreigners** go to Kyoto to
sightsee.

＊Variant: *gaikokujin*.

かいだん　階段〔名〕

kaidan 〔n〕 stairs, stairway, flight of stairs

階段を上る（*kaidan* o noboru）階段を
降りる（*kaidan* o oriru）

¶階段が急だから、気をつけてくださ
い。（*Kaidan* ga kyū da kara, ki o tsukete
kudasai.）

go up **the stairs**, go upstairs // go
down **the stairs**, go downstairs

¶ Please be careful as **the stairs** are
very steep.

かいふく　回復〔名、～する〕

kaifuku 〔n, ~*suru*〕 recovery

¶天候の回復を待って、出発しましょ
う。（Tenkō no *kaifuku* o matte,
shuppatsu shimashō.）

¶上田さんは1か月休んで、ようやく
健康を回復しました。（Ueda san wa
ikkagetsu yasunde, yōyaku kenkō o
kaifuku shimashita.）

¶一度失った信用を回復するのはたい
へんです。（Ichido ushinatta shin'yō o
kaifuku suru no wa taihen desu.）

¶ Let's wait for the weather **to improve**
before setting out.

¶ After staying at home a month, [Mr.]
Ueda has finally **regained** [his] health.

¶ It is difficult **to restore** trust once it
has been lost.

かいもの　買い物〔名〕

kaimono 〔n〕 shopping, a purchase

¶わたしは毎週日曜日に買い物をしま
す。（Watashi wa maishū nichiyōbi ni
kaimono o shimasu.）

¶母はデパートへ買い物に行きまし
た。（Haha wa depāto e *kaimono* ni
ikimashita.）

¶買い物をしてから、映画を見まし
た。（*Kaimono* o shite kara, eiga o
mimashita.）

¶ I go **shopping** every week on Sunday.

¶ My mother has gone **shopping** at a
department store.

¶ After **shopping**, [I] went to a movie.

かいわ　会話〔名、～する〕

英会話（eikaiwa）

¶学校では、文法だけでなく会話も習っています。（Gakkō de wa, bunpō dake de naku *kaiwa* mo naratte imasu.）

¶わたしは日本人と初めて日本語で会話してみました。（Watashi wa Nihonjin to hajimete Nihongo de *kaiwa* shite mimashita.）

kaiwa 〔n, ～*suru*〕 **conversation, talk**

English **conversation, conversation** in English

¶ In school [we] are studying not only grammar but **conversational skills** as well.

¶ I tried for the first time **to converse** with a Japanese in Japanese.

かう　買う〔動 I〕

¶わたしは八百屋で野菜を買いました。（Watashi wa yaoya de yasai o *kaimashita*.）

¶わたしはデパートへ服を買いに行きます。（Watashi wa depāto e fuku o *kai* ni ikimasu.）

¶ノートを買いたいのですが、どこで売っていますか。（Nōto o *kaitai* no desu ga, doko de utte imasu ka？）

⇔売る **uru**

kau 〔v I〕 **buy**

¶ I **bought** vegetables at the vegetable store.

¶ I am going to the department store **to buy** some clothes.

¶ **I want to buy** a notebook—where are they sold?

かう　飼う〔動 I〕

¶わたしのうちでは、ねこを飼っています。（Watashi no uchi de wa, neko o *katte* imasu.）

kau 〔v I〕 **raise, rear**

¶ Wc **keep** a cat 〖cats〗 at my home.

かえす　返す〔動 I〕

¶この前借りたお金はあした返します。（Kono mae karita okane wa ashita *kaeshimasu*.）

¶今、図書館へ本を返しに行くところです。（Ima, toshokan e hon o *kaeshi* ni iku tokoro desu.）

kaesu 〔v I〕 **return, give back**

¶ Tomorrow [I] **will pay back** the money [I] borrowed from [you].

¶ [I]'m now on my way to the library **to return** a book.

かえり 帰り〔名〕

¶学校の帰りにデパートで買い物をしようと思っています。(Gakkō no *kaeri* ni depāto de kaimono o shiyō to omotte imasu.)

kaeri 〔n〕 **going back, getting back, return**

¶ On my way back from school, I intend to go shopping at the department store.

かえる 帰る〔動Ⅰ〕

¶山田さんは昨日外国から帰ってきました。(Yamada san wa kinō gaikoku kara *kaette* kimashita.)

¶わたしは8時までにうちへ帰らなければなりません。(Watashi wa hachiji made ni uchi e *kaeranakereba* narimasen.)

¶お母さんは何時ごろお帰りになりますか。(Okāsan wa nanji goro o*kaeri* ni narimasu ka?)

kaeru 〔vⅠ〕 **return, go 【come】 back home**

¶ [Miss] Yamada **returned home** from abroad yesterday.

¶ I **must return home** by eight o'clock.

¶ What time will your mother **arrive home**?

かえる 返る〔動Ⅰ〕

¶時計が無事に持ち主に返りました。(Tokei ga buji ni mochinushi ni *kaerimashita*.)

kaeru 〔vⅠ〕 **return to, be returned to**

¶ The watch 〚clock〛 **was returned** to its owner all right.

かえる 変える〔動Ⅱ〕

¶熱は氷を水に変えます。(Netsu wa koori o mizu ni *kaemasu*.)

¶都合が悪くなったので、出発の日を変えました。(Tsugō ga waruku natta node, shuppatsu no hi o *kaemashita*.)

¶飛行機は方向を変えて、南に向かいました。(Hikōki wa hōkō o *kaete*, minami ni mukaimashita.)

kaeru 〔vⅡ〕 **change, alter**

¶ Heat **converts** ice to water.

¶ [I] **changed** the departure date as it had become inconvenient.

¶ The plane **altered** direction and headed south.

かえる 替える 〔動 II〕

¶池の水が汚れたので替えました。
(Ike no mizu ga yogoreta node
kaemashita.)
¶パーティーがあるので、洋服を替え
て出かけました。(Pātii ga aru node,
yōfuku o *kaete* dekakemashita.)

kaeru 〔v II〕 **change, exchange, substitute**

¶ [I] **changed** the water in the pool as it was dirty.

¶ [I] **changed** my clothes and left for the party.

かえる 代える 〔動 II〕

¶今度の試合には田中選手に代えて上
田選手を出すことにしました。(Kon-
do no shiai ni wa Tanaka senshu ni *kaete*
Ueda senshu o dasu koto ni shimashita.)
¶わたしの命に代えても、子供の命を
助けたいと思います。(Watashi no
inochi ni *kaete* mo, kodomo no inochi o
tasuketai to omoimasu.)

kaeru 〔v II〕 **change, substitute**

¶ [I] have decided **to substitute** Ueda for Tanaka in the next game.

¶ I want to save the life of my child even **at the expense** of my own.

かえる 換える 〔動 II〕

¶窓を開けて、部屋の空気を換えま
しょう。(Mado o akete, heya no kūki o
kaemashō.)
¶電車を降りて、バスに乗り換えまし
た。(Densha o orite, basu ni nori-
kaemashita.)

kaeru 〔v II〕 **change, exchange**

¶ Let's open the window and **get some fresh** air in the room.

¶ [I] got off the train and **transferred** to a bus.

かお 顔 〔名〕

顔つき (*kaotsuki*) 顔を洗う (kao o
arau) 悲しそうな顔をする (kana-shisō
na *kao* o suru)
¶恥ずかしくて顔が真っ赤になりまし
た。(Hazukashikute *kao* ga makka ni
narimashita.)
¶上田さんはびっくりした顔でわたし
を見ました。(Ueda san wa bikkuri shita
kao de watashi o mimashita.)

kao 〔n〕 **face**

look, expression (on one's face) //
wash **one's face** // **look** sad

¶ **My face** turned bright red from embarrassment 〚shame〛.

¶ [Miss] Ueda looked at me with a surprised expression on [her] face.

151

¶顔色が悪いですね。どこかぐあいが悪いのですか。(Kaoiro ga warui desu ne. Doko ka guai ga warui no desu ka？)

¶ You **look** pale. Do you feel ill?

かかえる　抱える〔動Ⅱ〕

kakaeru〔v Ⅱ〕**carry; bear a burden**

① [腕で支えてわきの下・胸の前などで物を持つ]

① [carry in or under one's arms]

¶上田さんは研究室からたくさんの本を抱えて出てきました。(Ueda san wa kenkyūshitsu kara takusan no hon o *kakaete* dete kimashita.)

¶ [Miss] Ueda came out of the professor's office **carrying** many books.

② [負担になるものを持っている]

② [bear a burden]

¶田中さんは5人の子供を抱えて、苦しい生活をしています。(Tanaka san wa gonin no kodomo o *kakaete*, kurushii seikatsu o shite imasu.)

¶ [Mr.] Tanaka has a hard time making ends meet with five children **to feed**.

¶山田さんはたくさんの仕事を抱えて忙しそうです。(Yamada san wa takusan no shigoto o *kakaete* isogashisō desu.)

¶ [Miss] Yamada seems very busy with the many jobs [she] **has to do**.

かかく　価格〔名〕

kakaku〔n〕**price, value, cost**

¶米の価格が20パーセント上がりました。(Kome no *kakaku* ga nijippāsento agarimashita.)

¶ **The price** of rice rose 20 percent.

¶上田さんは家を500万円の価格で売りました。(Ueda san wa ie o gohyaku-man'en no *kakaku* de urimashita.)

¶ [Mr.] Ueda sold [his] house **for** 5 million yen.

かがく　科学〔名〕

kagaku〔n〕**science**

科学者 (*kagaku*sha) 人文科学 (jin-bun-*kagaku*) 自然科学 (shizen-*kagaku*) 社会科学 (shakai-*kagaku*) 科学的 (*kagaku*teki) 科学博物館 (*kagaku*-hakubutsukan)

a scientist // cultural **sciences**, humanities // natural **science(s)** // social **science(s)** // **scientific** // a **science** museum

¶20世紀になって、科学は非常に進歩しました。(Nijisseiki ni natte, *kagaku* wa hijō ni shinpo shimashita.)

¶ **Science** has advanced greatly since the beginning of the 20th century.

¶その考えは非科学的だと思います。
（Sono kangae wa hi*kagaku*teki da to omoimasu.）

¶ [I] think that way of thinking 〚idea〛 is **unscientific**.

かがく　化学〔名〕

応用化学（ōyō-*kagaku*）化学肥料（*kagaku*-hiryō）化学変化（*kagaku*-henka）化学作用（*kagaku*-sayō）化学反応（*kagaku*-hannō）化学記号（*kagaku*-kigō）

kagaku 〔n〕 **chemistry**

applied **chemistry** // artificial 〚**chemical**〛 fertilizer // a **chemical** change // **chemical** action // **chemical** reaction // a **chemical** symbol

かがみ　鏡〔名〕

鏡を見る（*kagami* o miru）
¶あなたの姿が鏡に映っています。
・（Anata no sugata ga *kagami* ni utsutte imasu.）
¶鏡がないと、ネクタイが締められません。（*Kagami* ga nai to, nekutai ga shimeraremasen.）

kagami 〔n〕 **mirror**

look in **a mirror**
¶ Your image is reflected in **a mirror**.

¶ [I] can't tie [my] necktie without **a mirror**.

かがやく　輝く〔動 I〕

① [明るく光る]
¶空には星が輝いています。（Sora ni wa hoshi ga *kagayaite* imasu.）
¶山の上の雪が朝日を受けて輝いています。（Yama no ue no yuki ga asahi o ukete *kagayaite* imasu.）
② [明るく晴れやかに見える]
目が輝く（me ga *kagayaku*）
¶上田さんの顔は喜びに輝いています。（Ueda san no kao wa yorokobi ni *kagayaite* imasu.）

kagayaku 〔v I〕 **shine; sparkle, light up**

① [shine, sparkle, gleam, etc.]
¶ Stars **are shining** in the sky.

¶ The snow on top of the mountain is **glittering** in the morning sun.

② [sparkle, light up]
one's eyes **sparkle**
¶ [Miss] Ueda's face **is lit up** 〚**beaming**〛 with joy.

(-)かかり　(-)係〔名、尾〕

1〔名〕
係長（*kakari*chō）係員（*kakari*in）

(-)kakari 〔n, suf〕 **charge, duty, subsection, person in charge**

1〔n〕
an **assistant section** chief, chief **clerk** // the clerk **in charge**, an attendant

¶係の者がいないので、よくわかりません。(*Kakari* no mono ga inai node, yoku wakarimasen.)

¶ The person **in charge** of that isn't here right now, and I'm not familiar with that 〚and I'm afraid I can't help you〛.

2 〔尾〕
案内係 (annai*gakari*)

2 〚suf〛

a **clerk** at an information desk, desk **clerk**, usher

かかる 掛かる 〔動 I 〕

kakaru 〚v I〛 hang, be suspended; require, take; be placed on something ; be covered; catch, work

① [壁などに下がる]
¶壁にきれいな絵が掛かっています。(Kabe ni kirei na e ga *kakatte* imasu.)
¶この部屋の窓にはカーテンが掛かっていません。(Kono heya no mado ni wa kāten ga *kakatte* imasen.)

① [hang, be suspended]
¶ There is a pretty picture **hanging** on the wall.
¶ The windows in this room **have not been hung** with curtains.

② [かぎがしてある]
¶この部屋にはかぎが掛かっていて入れません。(Kono heya ni wa kagi ga *kakatte* ite hairemasen.)

② [be locked]
¶ This room **is locked** so [we] can't enter.

③ [時間・費用などが必要である]
¶学校まで何分ぐらいかかりますか。(Gakkō made nanpun gurai *kakarimasu* ka？)
¶交通費は一か月いくらぐらいかかりますか。(Kōtsūhi wa ikkagetsu ikura gurai *kakarimasu* ka？)

③ [require (time, money, etc.)]
¶ How many minutes **does it take** to go to school from here 〚**take you** to go to school〛?
¶ How much **is** carfare a month?

④ [電話が通じる]
¶さっき山田さんから電話がかかってきましたよ。(Sakki Yamada san kara denwa ga *kakatte* kimashita yo.)

④ [be telephoned]
¶ **There was** a call from [Miss] Yamada earlier.

⑤ [会う]
¶いつかまたお目にかかりたいと思います。(Itsu ka mata ome ni *kakaritai* to omoimasu.)
*いつも「お目にかかる (ome ni kakaru)」の形で使う。

⑤ [meet]
¶ **I hope we can meet** again sometime.

*Always used in the pattern "*ome ni kakaru*."

⑥ [医者に診てもらう]

¶ わたしは丈夫なので、今まで医者にかかったことがありません。(Watashi wa jōbu na node, ima made isha ni *kakatta* koto ga arimasen.)

⑥ [consult a doctor]

¶ I'm robust so that I've never **been to see** a doctor.

⑦ [水などがふりかかる]

¶ 自動車がすぐそばを通ったので、ズボンにどろ水がかかって汚れました。(Jidōsha ga sugu soba o tootta node, zubon ni doromizu ga *kakatte* yogoremashita.)

⑦ [be splashed by water, etc.]

¶ The car went by right next to me so that my trousers **were splattered** with dirty water.

⑧ [税金が加わる]

¶ この品物には税金がかかっていません。(Kono shinamono ni wa zeikin ga *kakatte* imasen.)

⑧ [be taxed]

¶ This merchandise is tax-**free**.

⑨ [心配になる]

¶ 試験の結果が気にかかって、何も食べられません。(Shiken no kekka ga ki ni *kakatte*, nani mo taberaremasen.)

*いつも「気にかかる (ki ni kakaru)」の形で使う。

⑨ [worry, be anxious]

¶ [I]'m **so nervous** about the results of the test that [I] can't eat.

*Always used in the pattern "*ki ni kakaru*."

⑩ [こんろなどの上に置かれたりしている]

¶ ガスこんろになべがかかっています。(Gasu-konro ni nabe ga *kakatte* imasu.)

⑩ [be placed on top of a burner, etc.]

¶ There **is** a pot on the gas burner.

⑪ [霧などが立ちこめる]

¶ 霧がかかって、周りの景色がよく見えません。(Kiri ga *kakatte*, mawari no keshiki ga yoku miemasen.)

⑪ [covered with fog, etc.]

¶ The surrounding area can't be seen very well as it **is enveloped** in fog 〚mist〛.

⑫ [悪いこと・好ましくないことなどが人に及ぶ]

手数がかかる (tesū ga *kakaru*)

¶ 先生に御迷惑がかかっては申し訳ありません。(Sensei ni gomeiwaku ga *kakatte* wa mōshiwake arimasen.)

⑫ [have something bad befall one]

(a task) **is** bothersome

¶ I'm sorry **to trouble** you, sir 〚ma'am〛 (said to one's teacher or professor).

⑬ [機械が働き始める]

ブレーキがかかる (burēki ga *kakaru*)

⑬ [catch, work]

brakes **work**

155

¶寒いので、自動車のエンジンがなかなかかかりません。(Samui node, jidōsha no enjin ga nakanaka *kakarimasen*.)

¶ As it's cold, the engine **doesn't start** right away.

¶目覚まし時計がかかっていなかったので、起きられませんでした。(Mezamashidokei ga *kakatte* inakatta node, okiraremasen deshita.)

¶ [I] overslept as the alarm clock **wasn't set**.

かかる 架かる〔動Ⅰ〕

kakaru 〔vⅠ〕 **be built across, be constructed over**

¶この川には木の橋が架かっています。(Kono kawa ni wa ki no hashi ga *kakatte* imasu.)

¶ There **is** a wooden bridge across this river.

かぎ〔名〕

kagi 〔n〕 **key, lock**

かぎを掛ける (*kagi* o kakeru) かぎを閉める (*kagi* o shimeru) かぎを開ける (*kagi* o akeru) 合いかぎ (ai*kagi*)

lock up // lock up // unlock // a duplicate **key**, pass**key**

¶部屋の戸には必ずかぎを掛けてから、出かけてください。(Heya no to ni wa kanarazu *kagi* o kakete kara, dekakete kudasai.)

¶ Please be sure to always **lock** your door when going out.

かきとめ 書留〔名〕

kakitome 〔n〕 **registered (mail)**

書留郵便 (*kakitome*-yūbin) 現金書留 (genkin-*kakitome*)

registered mail // sending cash by **registered mail**

¶この手紙を書留で出してください。(Kono tegami o *kakitome* de dashite kudasai.)

¶ Please have this letter sent by **registered mail**.

¶この手紙を書留にしてください。(Kono tegami o *kakitome* ni shite kudasai.)

¶ I'd like to send this letter by **registered mail**.

かぎり 限り〔名〕

kagiri 〔n〕 **limits, bounds; as far as; as long as, unless**

①[ものごとの限界を表す]
¶人の力には限りがあります。(Hito no chikara ni wa *kagiri* ga arimasu.)

① [limits, bounds]
¶ There's **a limit** to human strength.

¶船は限りなく広い海を進んでいきました。(Fune wa *kagiri* naku hiroi umi o susunde ikimashita.)

¶申し込みは3月10日限りで締め切ります。(Mōshikomi wa sangatsu tooka *kagiri* de shimekirimasu.)

② [ものごとの範囲を表す]

¶わたしの知っている限りのことを話しましょう。(Watashi no shitte iru *kagiri* no koto o hanashimashō.)

¶この辺りは見渡す限り畑が広がっています。(Kono atari wa miwatasu *kagiri* hatake ga hirogatte imasu.)

③ [ある条件の限界を表す]

¶あの人が謝らない限り、わたしは許しません。(Ano hito ga ayamaranai *kagiri*, watashi wa yurushimasen.)

かぎる 限る [動I]

① [範囲を限定する]

¶この劇場は小さいので、入場者は100名以内に限られています。(Kono gekijō wa chiisai node, nyūjōsha wa hyakumei inai ni *kagirarete* imasu.)

¶わたしは毎日復習の時間を2時間と限っています。(Watashi wa mainichi fukushū no jikan o nijikan to *kagitte* imasu.)

② [それだけはほかと違って特別であると限定する]

¶あの人に限って、そんなことはしないでしょう。(Ano hito ni *kagitte*, sonna koto wa shinai deshō.)

¶この店は土曜日に限り、一割引きで売っています。(Kono mise wa doyōbi ni *kagiri*, ichiwaribiki de utte imasu.)

¶ The ship moved over the **boundlessly** vast ocean.

¶ Applications will not be accepted after March 10 〖after the **cut-off** date, March 10〗.

② [as far as, as much as; indicates the furthermost extent of something]

¶ I will tell you **as much as** I know about it.

¶ Fields stretch out here **as far as** the eye can see.

③ [as long as, unless; indicates the bounds of a condition on something]

¶ I won't forgive [him] **unless** [he] apologizes to me.

kagiru 〔v I〕 limit, restrict

① [limit, restrict]

¶ As this theater is small, admittance **is limited** to a hundred persons.

¶ I **restrict** my time spent reviewing lessons each day to two hours.

② [used to define one thing as special and different from others]

¶ [He], **at least**, wouldn't do such a thing 〖He would be the last person in the world to do such a thing〗.

¶ This shop is offering a 10 percent discount on Saturday **alone**.

157

*いつも「〜に限って（ni kagitte）」「〜に限り（〜ni kagiri）」の形で使う。

*Always used in the patterns " 〜 *ni kagitte*" and "〜 *ni kagiri*."

かく 書く〔動Ⅰ〕

¶わたしは友達に手紙を書きました。(Watashi wa tomodachi ni tegami o *kakimashita*.)

¶ここに名前を書いてください。(Koko ni namae o *kaite* kudasai.)

¶この万年筆はとても書きやすいです。(Kono mannenhitsu wa totemo *kakiyasui* desu.)

kaku 〔v I〕 **write, compose**

¶ I **wrote** a letter to a friend.

¶ Please **write** your name here.

¶ This fountain pen **is** very **easy to write with**.

かく〔動Ⅰ〕

地図をかく（chizu o *kaku*）

¶子供たちが花の絵をかいています。(Kodomotachi ga hana no e o *kaite* imasu.)

kaku 〔v I〕 **draw, paint**

draw a map

¶ The children **are drawing** 〚**painting**〛 pictures of flowers.

かく〔動Ⅰ〕

①[ひっかく]

¶背中がかゆいからかいてください。(Senaka ga kayui kara *kaite* kudasai.)

¶あの人は頭をかく癖があります。(Ano hito wa atama o *kaku* kuse ga arimasu.)

②[汗を出す]

¶急いで来たので、汗をかきました。(Isoide kita node, ase o *kakimashita*.)

kaku 〔v I〕 **scratch ; sweat**

① [scratch]

¶ My back itches; please **scratch it** for me.

¶ [He] has a habit of **scratching** [his] head.

② [sweat, perspire]

¶ **I am sweaty** as I hurried here.

かぐ 家具〔名〕

¶テーブルは家具の一つです。(Tēburu wa *kagu* no hitotsu desu.)

kagu 〔n〕 **furniture, household furnishings**

¶ A table is a piece of **furniture**.

-がく -学〔尾〕

物理学（butsuri*gaku*）地理学（chiri*gaku*）言語学（gengo*gaku*）語学（go*gaku*）法律学（hōritsu*gaku*）人類学（jinrui*gaku*）化学（ka*gaku*）経済学

-gaku 〔suf〕 **study, science, learning**

physics, physical **science** // geography // linguistics, philology // foreign language **study** // jurisprudence, // anthropology // chemistry //

（keizai*gaku*）農学 （nō*gaku*）歴史学
（rekishi*gaku*）生物学 （seibutsu*gaku*）
政治学 （seiji*gaku*）社会学
（shakai*gaku*）宗教学 （shūkyō*gaku*）水
産学 （suisan*gaku*）薬学 （yaku*gaku*）

economics, // (the **science** of)
agriculture // history, // biology //
political **science** // sociology, social
studies // the **science** of religion //
fishery **science** // pharmacy,
pharmacology

がくしゃ 学者 〔名〕

¶あの人は有名な学者です。（Ano hito
wa yūmei na *gakusha* desu.）
¶おおぜいの学者がこの問題を研究し
ています。（Oozei no *gakusha* ga kono
mondai o kenkyū shite imasu.）

gakusha 〔n〕 **scholar**

¶ [He] is a celebrated **scholar**.

¶ A great number of **scholars** are
studying this problem.

がくしゅう 学習 〔名、〜する〕

¶語学の学習には辞書が必要です。
（Gogaku no *gakushū* ni wa jisho ga
hitsuyō desu.）
¶この本を使って日本語を学習しまし
た。（Kono hon o tsukatte Nihongo o
gakushū shimashita.）

gakushū 〔n, 〜*suru*〕 **learning,
study**

¶ Dictionaries are necessary in
language **study**.

¶ [I] **studied** Japanese using this book.

かくす 隠す 〔動 I〕

① [人の目につかないようにする]
¶どろぼうは盗んだ財布を木の下に隠
しました。（Dorobō wa nusunda saifu o
ki no shita ni *kakushimashita*.）
¶隠しておいた手紙を母に読まれてし
まいました。（*Kakushite* oita tegami o
haha ni yomarete shimaimashita.）
② [人に知られないようにする、秘密
にする]
欠点を隠す （ketten o *kakusu*）
¶山田さんはそのことを隠さないでみ
んな話してくれました。（Yamada san
wa sono koto o *kakusanaide* minna
hanashite kuremashita.）

kakusu 〔v I〕 **hide, conceal**

① [hide, conceal, keep from sight]
¶ The thief **hid** the stolen wallet
beneath a tree.

¶ My mother read the letter **I had
hidden**.

② [hide, conceal, keep secret]

hide weak points
¶ [Miss] Yamada **didn't hide** that but
told [us] everything about it.

¶彼は真実をわたしたちに隠そうとしました。(Kare wa shinjitsu o watashitachi ni *kakusō* to shimashita.)

¶He **tried to keep** the truth from us.

がくせい 学生 〔名〕

学生服 (*gakusei*fuku) 学生運動 (*gakusei*-undō)

¶わたしは学生です。(Watashi wa *gakusei* desu.)

¶この大学には何人学生がいますか。(Kono daigaku ni wa nannin *gakusei* ga imasu ka？)

＊高等学校の生徒は「高校生 (kōkōsei)」と言う。

＊普通「学生 (gakusei)」は「大学生 (daigakusei)」を指し、「高校生 (kōkōsei)」「中学生 (chūgakusei)」は「生徒 (seito)」、「小学生 (shōgakusei)」は「児童 (jidō)」と言う。

gakusei 〔n〕 **student**

a **student** uniform // the **student** movement

¶I am a **student**.

¶How many **students** are there at this university?

＊High-school students are called *kōkōsei*.

＊*Gakusei* usually refers to college students (*daigakusei*). High-school students (*kōkōsei*) and junior-high students (*chūgakusei*) are called *seito*, and elementary school students (*shōgakusei*) are called *jidō*.

かくど 角度 〔名〕

①〔角の度数〕
角度を測る (*kakudo* o hakaru)

¶正三角形のそれぞれの角度は60度です。(Seisankakkei no sorezore no *kakudo* wa rokujūdo desu.)

②〔ものごとを見たり考えたりする立場〕

¶その問題をいろいろな角度から考えてみました。(Sono mondai o iroiro na *kakudo* kara kangaete mimashita.)

kakudo 〔n〕 **angle; viewpoint**

① [angle, degrees of an angle]
compute **an angle**

¶Each **angle** of an equilateral triangle is 60 degrees.

② [viewpoint, angle]

¶I considered that problem from various **angles**.

がくねん 学年 〔名〕

¶あなたの大学は一学年何人ぐらいですか。(Anata no daigaku wa ichi*gakunen* nannin gurai desu ka？)

gakunen 〔n〕 **school year, academic year; class**

¶How many students are there **in each year** at your university?

¶学年末試験はいつですか。
（Gakunenmatsu-shiken wa itsu desu
ka？）

¶ When are the **final** exams?

がくぶ 学部〔名〕

学部長（*gakubu*chō）文学部
（bun*gakubu*）法学部（hō*gakubu*）医学
部（i*gakubu*）工学部（kō*gakubu*）理学
部（ri*gakubu*）政治経済学部
（seijikeizai*gakubu*）商学部
（shō*gakubu*）

gakubu 〖n (university or college)〗
department, faculty

dean, head of a **department** or
faculty // **faculty** of letters // law
school, law **faculty** // medical **school** //
school of engineering // **department**
of science and mathematics //
department of political science and
economics // **department** of
commercial science

がくもん 学問〔名、～する〕

¶ずっと学問を続けていきたいと思っ
ています。（Zutto *gakumon* o tsuzukete
ikitai to omotte imasu.）
¶これは学問的にも立派な研究です。
（Kore wa *gakumon*teki ni mo rippa na
kenkyū desu.）

gakumon 〔n, ～suru〕 **learning,
scholarship**

¶ I would like to keep **studying** as long
as possible.

¶ This is a fine piece of research
academically speaking as well.

かくれる 隠れる〔動Ⅱ〕

①［物にさえぎられて直接見えなくな
る］
¶太陽が雲に隠れてしまいました。
（Taiyō ga kumo ni *kakurete*
shimaimashita.）
¶船が島の陰に隠れて見えなくなりま
した。（Fune ga shima no kage ni
kakurete mienaku narimashita.）
②［人目につかないように身を隠して
おく］
隠れ家（*kakure*ga）
¶危険が過ぎるまで、隠れているほう
がいいですよ。（Kiken ga sugiru made,
kakurete iru hō ga ii desu yo.）

kakureru 〔v Ⅱ〕 **be lost to sight;
hide**

① ［be lost to sight, disappear from
view］

¶ The sun **is** 〖**was**〗 **hidden** behind
some clouds.

¶ The ship **has become** 〖**became**〗 **lost
to sight** behind the island.

② ［hide, conceal oneself］

a **hide**out, a **hide**away, a retreat
¶ You had better **hide** until the danger
is past.

かく- 各- 〔頭〕

各国 (*kak*koku) 各人 (*kaku*jin)

¶わたしはこの夏日本の各地を旅行しました。(Watashi wa kono natsu Nihon no *kaku*chi o ryokō shimashita.)

¶各クラス2名の委員を選びました。(*Kaku*kurasu nimei no iin o erabimashita.)

kaku- 〔pref〕 **each, every**

each country, **various** countries, **all** countries // **each** person, **every**body

¶ This summer I traveled in **various** districts throughout Japan.

¶ **Each** class chose two representatives.

かげ 陰 〔名〕

① [光線の当たらない所]

¶この家はビルの陰になっているので、日当たりが悪いです。(Kono ie wa biru no *kage* ni natte iru node, hiatari ga warui desu.)

¶暑いから日陰で休みましょう。(Atsui kara hi*kage* de yasumimashō.)

② [物にさえぎられて直接見えない所]

電柱の陰に隠れる (denchū no *kage* ni kakureru)

¶船が島の陰に隠れて見えなくなりました。(Fune ga shima no *kage* ni kakurete mienaku narimashita.)

kage 〔n〕 **shade; the back, the other side**

① [shade, shadows]

¶ As this house is in **the shade** of an office building it doesn't get much sun.

¶ It's hot — let's go rest in **the shade**.

② [the back, the other side]

hide **behind** a telephone pole

¶ The ship can't be seen now as it is hidden **behind** the island.

かげ 影 〔名〕

① [水や鏡などに映って見える人や物の形]

¶湖に富士山の影が映っています。(Mizuumi ni Fujisan no *kage* ga utsutte imasu.)

② [光をさえぎったときにできる暗い部分の形]

¶ガラス戸に人の影が映っています。(Garasudo ni hito no *kage* ga utsutte imasu.)

kage 〔n〕 **reflection; shadow**

① [reflection (in a mirror, water, etc.)]

¶ Mount Fuji **is reflected** in the lake.

② [shadow, silhouette]

¶ Someone's **silhouette** can be seen behind the glass door.

-かげつ -か月 〔尾〕

¶日本に来てから、もう３か月たちました。(Nihon ni kite kara, mō sankagetsu tachimashita.)

かける 欠ける 〔動Ⅱ〕

①[物の一部分が壊れる]

¶このさらは少し欠けています。(Kono sara wa sukoshi *kakete* imasu.)

¶硬い物を切ったので、ナイフの刃が欠けてしまいました。(Katai mono o kitta node, naifu no ha ga *kakete* shimaimashita.)

②[不足する]

¶あの人は常識に欠けていますね。(Ano hito wa jōshiki ni *kakete* imasu ne.)

¶今日の会議はメンバーが二人欠けていますね。(Kyō no kaigi wa menbā ga futari *kakete* imasu ne.)

かける 掛ける 〔動Ⅱ〕

①[いすなどに腰を下ろす]

ベンチに腰を掛ける (benchi ni koshi o *kakeru*)

¶どうぞ、このいすにお掛けください。(Dōzo, kono isu ni o*kake* kudasai.)

②[壁などに下げる]

¶壁にきれいな絵が掛けてあります。(Kabe ni kirei na e ga *kakete* arimasu.)

③[かぎをする]

¶わたしはいつもドアにかぎを掛けておきます。(Watashi wa itsu mo doa ni kagi o *kakete* okimasu.)

④[物の上にかぶせる]

-kagetsu 〔suf〕 **month**

¶ It has already been three months since I arrived in Japan.

kakeru 〔vⅡ〕 **be broken off; lack**

① [be broken off, chipped]

¶ This dish **is** a little **chipped**.

¶ As I cut something hard, the blade of the knife **got nicked**.

② [lack, be short, be missing]

¶ [He] **is lacking** in common sense.

¶ Today's meeting **is missing** two members.

kakeru 〔vⅡ〕 **sit down; hang up; put on; multiply; spend; place on; turn on; sprinkle on; extending over**

① [sit down]

sit down on a bench

¶ Please **sit down** here in this chair.

② [hang up, suspend]

¶ A pretty picture **has been hung** on the wall.

③ [lock]

¶ I always **lock** my door.

④ [put on, cover with]

163

¶寒いから布団をたくさん掛けて寝ました。（Samui kara futon o takusan *kakete* nemashita.）

¶As it was cold I slept with many covers **on**.

⑤[ある数を何倍かする]

¶2に3を掛けると6になります。（Ni ni san o *kakeru* to roku ni narimasu.）

⑤[multiply]

¶Two **times** three (literally, three **times** two) is six.

⑥[費用・時間などを費やす]

時間をかける（jikan o *kakeru*）お金をかける（okane o *kakeru*）

⑥[spend time, money, etc.]

spend time (on something) // **spend** money (on something)

⑦[電話をする]

¶友達に電話をかけました。（Tomodachi ni denwa o *kakemashita*.）

⑦[make a telephone call]

¶[I] **telephoned** a friend.

⑧[眼鏡をつける]

¶あの眼鏡をかけた女の人はだれですか。（Ano megane o *kaketa* onnano hito wa dare desu ka？）

⑧[wear glasses]

¶Who is that woman **wearing** glasses?

⑨[こんろなどの上にのせる]

¶ガスこんろになべがかけてあります。（Gasu-konro ni nabe ga *kakete* arimasu.）

⑨[place on a burner, etc.]

¶A pot **has been placed** on 〚**is on**〛 the gas burner.

⑩[機械などを働かせる]

ブレーキをかける（burēki o *kakeru*）レコードをかける（rekōdo o *kakeru*）

¶ラジオをかけてもいいですか。（Rajio o *kakete* mo ii desu ka？）

⑩[turn on, start]

put on the brakes // **play** a record

¶Is it all right if **I turn on** the radio?

⑪[目方を量る]

はかりにかける（hakari ni *kakeru*）

⑪[weigh]

weigh on a scale

⑫[ふりかける]

¶味が薄いですから、塩をかけて食べてください。（Aji ga usui desu kara, shio o *kakete* tabete kudasai.）

⑫[sprinkle, pour on, dash]

¶It's lightly seasoned 〚**It may be on the bland side**〛 so please **add** salt if you like.

⑬[心配させる]

¶両親に心配をかけないようにしなさい。（Ryōshin ni shinpai o *kakenai* yō ni shinasai.）

⑬[cause worry]

¶Don't do anything **to worry** your parents (literally, Act so as **not to worry** your parents).

⑭[ある時・場所からある時・場所に及ぶ]

⑭[extending over, from ～ to ～]

¶わたしは先週の土曜日から日曜日にかけて旅行しました。(Watashi wa senshū no doyōbi kara nichiyōbi ni *kakete* ryokō shimashita.)

¶わたしは奈良から京都にかけて、お寺を見て歩きました。(Watashi wa Nara kara Kyōto ni *kakete*, otera o mite arukimashita.)

*いつも「〜から〜にかけて(〜kara 〜ni kakete)」の形で使う。

¶ I took a trip on Saturday **and** Sunday last week.

¶ I visited temples from Nara **to** Kyoto.

*Always used in the pattern "〜 *kara* 〜 *ni kakete*."

かける 架ける〔動Ⅱ〕

¶この川には木の橋が架けてあります。(Kono kawa ni wa ki no hashi ga *kakete* arimasu.)

kakeru 〔v Ⅱ〕 **build, construct**

¶ A wooden bridge **has been built** over this river.

かける 駆ける〔動Ⅱ〕

¶遅刻しそうなので、学校まで駆けていきました。(Chikoku shisō na node, gakkō made *kakete* ikimashita.)
⇒走る hashiru

kakeru 〔v Ⅱ〕 **run**

¶ [I] **ran** to school as it looked like [I] would be late.

かこ 過去〔名〕

¶彼はできるだけ過去のことを思い出さないようにしています。(Kare wa dekiru dake *kako* no koto o omoidasanai yō ni shite imasu.)

¶わたしは過去3年間、外国で生活をしていました。(Watashi wa *kako* sannenkan, gaikoku de seikatsu o shite imashita.)

¶次の動詞の過去形は何ですか。(Tsugi no dōshi no *kako*kei wa nan desu ka?)
⇒現在 genzai 未来 mirai

kako 〔n〕 **the past**

¶ He makes it a practice to forget **the past** as much as possible.

¶ **In the past** I lived abroad for three years.

¶ What is the **past** tense of the next verb?

かご〔名〕

かごを編む(*kago* o amu) くずかご(kuzu*kago*) 虫かご(mushi*kago*)

kago 〔n〕 **cage; basket**

weave **a basket** // a wastepaper **basket**, waste**basket**, trash **basket** // an insect **cage**

¶鳥かごの中で小鳥が鳴いています。
(Tori*kago* no naka de kotori ga naite
imasu.)

¶ A bird is singing in **its cage**.

¶そのかごの中に果物がありますよ。
(Sono *kago* no naka ni kudamono ga
arimasu yo.)

¶ There's fruit in that **basket**.

かこむ 囲む 〔動 I〕

kakomu 〔v I〕 enclose, surround, ring, encircle

¶先生を囲んで、一晩楽しく話しまし
た。(Sensei o *kakonde*, hitoban tanoshiku
hanashimashita.)

¶ **Sitting around** our teacher, we
passed a pleasant evening in
conversation.

¶日本は海に囲まれた国です。(Nihon
wa umi ni *kakomareta* kuni desu.)

¶ Japan is a country **surrounded** by
the sea.

¶次の言葉のうち正しいものを○で囲
みなさい。(Tsugi no kotoba no uchi
tadashii mono o maru de *kakominasai*.)

¶ **Circle** the correct choice(s) among
the following words.

かさ 〔名〕

kasa 〔n〕 umbrella

雨がさ (ama*gasa*) 日がさ (hi*gasa*) か
さをさす (*kasa* o sasu) かさをひろげ
る (*kasa* o hirogeru) かさをつぼめる
(*kasa* o tsubomeru)

a (rain) **umbrella** // a parasol // put up
an umbrella // open **an umbrella** //
close **an umbrella**

¶電車の中にかさを忘れてきました。
(Densha no naka ni *kasa* o wasurete
kimashita.)

¶ I left **my umbrella** in the train.

かさなる 重なる 〔動 I〕

kasanaru 〔v I〕 be piled up; occur one after another

① [物の上に物がのる]
¶机の上にたくさんの本が重なってい
ます。(Tsukue no ue ni takusan no hon
ga *kasanatte* imasu.)

① [(things are) piled up]
¶ Many books **are piled up** on the
desk.

¶電車が急に止まったので、乗客が重
なって倒れました。(Densha ga kyū ni
tomatta node, jōkyaku ga *kasanatte*
taoremashita.)

¶ The train stopped abruptly and the
passengers fell over **on top of each
other**.

②[ものごとが次々に起こる]

② [(events) occur one after another]

¶あの人は不幸が重なってお気の毒ですね。(Ano hito wa fukō ga kasanatte okinodoku desu ne.)

¶ Isn't it unfortunate how [he] has suffered **one** misfortune **after another!**

かさねる 重ねる〔動Ⅱ〕

kasaneru〔v Ⅱ〕**pile up, lay one on top of another; repeat**

① [物の上に物をのせる]
¶寒いからシャツを重ねて着ました。(Samui kara shatsu o *kasanete* kimashita.)

① [pile up, lay one on top of another]
¶ It's cold so [I]'m wearing **two layers** of shirts.

②[ものごとを繰り返す]
¶失敗を重ねましたが、やっと成功しました。(Shippai o *kasanemashita*ga, yatto seikō shimashita.)

② [repeat]
¶ After **a series** of failures at last [I]'ve succeeded〚I succeeded〛.

かざり 飾り〔名〕

kazari〔n〕**ornament, decoration**

首飾り (kubi*kazari*)
¶町はお祭りのための飾りでいっぱいです。(Machi wa omatsuri no tame no *kazari* de ippai desu.)

a necklace
¶ There are **decorations** up all over town for the festival.

かざる 飾る〔動Ⅰ〕

kazaru〔v Ⅰ〕**decorate, ornament**

¶客が来るので、部屋に花を飾りました。(Kyaku ga kuru node, heya ni hana o *kazari*mashita.)

¶ [I] **put** flowers **out** in the room because a guest was coming.

¶部屋をきれいに飾って、ダンス・パーティーをしました。(Heya o kirei ni *kazatte*, dansu-pātii o shimashita.)

¶ [We] **decorated** the room nicely and had a dance party.

かざん 火山〔名〕

kazan〔n〕**volcano**

¶日本には火山がたくさんあります。(Nihon ni wa *kazan* ga takusan arimasu.)

¶ There are many **volcanoes** in Japan.

かし 菓子〔名〕

kashi〔n〕**sweets, confectionary, cake, pastry**

菓子屋 (*kashi*ya)
¶このお菓子はとてもおいしいです。(Kono o*kashi* wa totemo oishii desu.)

a **confectionary** store, **candy** store
¶ This **candy**〚sweet〛is very good.

かじ 火事 〔名〕

火事になる（*kaji* ni naru）火事が起きる（*kaji* ga okiru）火事を消す（*kaji* o kesu）

¶昨日の火事はたばこの火が原因だそうです。（Kinō no *kaji* wa tabako no hi ga gen'in da sō desu.）

¶上田さんの家は火事で焼けました。（Ueda san no ie wa *kaji* de yakemashita.）

kaji 〔n〕 fire

a fire takes place // a fire takes place // put out a fire

¶ I hear the cause of **the fire** yesterday was a cigarette butt.

¶ [Mrs.] Ueda's house **burned down.**

かしこまりました 〔連〕

¶「この品物を包んでください。」（Kono shinamono o tsutsunde ku-dasai.）「はい、かしこまりました。」（Hai, *kashikomarimashita*.）

kashikomarimashita 〔compd〕 a set expression of understanding or agreement usually used by an employee toward a customer

¶ "Please wrap this merchandise." "**Certainly**, sir〚ma'am〛."

かす 貸す 〔動 I〕

本を貸す（hon o *kasu*）

¶千円ほど貸してくださいませんか。（Sen'en hodo *kashite* kudasaimasen ka？）

¶わたしは田中さんにお金を貸してあげました。（Watashi wa Tanaka san ni okane o *kashite* agemashita.）

⇔借りる **kariru**

kasu 〔v I〕 lend, loan, rent out

lend a book

¶ Could you please **lend** me a thousand yen?

¶ I **loaned** [Mr.] Tanaka some money.

かず 数 〔名〕

数を数える（*kazu* o kazoeru）

¶自動車の数が年ごとに増えています。（Jidōsha no *kazu* ga toshigoto ni fuete imasu.）

¶数多くの人がその意見に賛成しています。（*Kazu* ooku no hito ga sono iken ni sansei shite imasu.）

kazu 〔n〕 number

to count

¶ **The number** of cars on the roads increases each year.

¶ **A great many** people have expressed their agreement with that view.

ガス 〔名〕

ガス爆発 (*gasu*-bakuhatsu) ガス中毒 (*gasu*-chūdoku) ガスストーブ (*gasu*-sutōbu) プロパンガス (puropan-*gasu*)

¶ガスのにおいがしたので、窓を開けました。(Gasu no nioi ga shita node, mado o akemashita.)

gasu [n] a gas

a **gas** explosion // **gas** poisoning // a **gas** heater // propane **gas**

¶ There was a smell of **gas** so [I] opened the window.

かぜ 風邪 〔名〕

風邪薬 (*kaze*gusuri)

¶ゆうべ寒かったので、風邪を引いてしまいました。(Yūbe samukatta node, *kaze* o hiite shimaimashita.)

kaze [n] a cold, the flu

cold medicine

¶ It was cold last night and [I] caught a **cold**.

かぜ 風 〔名〕

風が吹く (*kaze* ga fuku) 風がやむ (*kaze* ga yamu)

¶午前中は風が強かったが、午後からは弱くなりました。(Gozenchū wa *kaze* ga tsuyokatta ga, gogo kara wa yowaku narimashita.)

kaze [n] wind, breeze, draft

the **wind** blows // the **wind** dies down

¶ **The wind** was strong during the morning but fell off in the afternoon.

かぞえる 数える 〔動Ⅱ〕

数を数える (kazu o *kazoeru*)

¶日本語で1から10まで数えてください。(Nihongo de ichi kara jū made *kazoete* kudasai.)

¶本は1冊、2冊と数えます。(Hon wa issatsu, nisatsu to *kazoemasu*.)

kazoeru [v Ⅱ] count

to **count**

¶ Please **count** from one to ten in Japanese.

¶ Books **are counted** *issatsu, nisatsu*, and so on in Japanese.

かぞく 家族 〔名〕

家族制度 (*kazoku*-seido) 大家族 (dai*kazoku*) 核家族 (kaku*kazoku*)

¶御家族の皆さんはお元気ですか。(Go*kazoku* no minasan wa ogenki desu ka?)

¶夏休みには家族そろって旅行するつもりです。(Natsuyasumi ni wa *kazoku* sorotte ryokō suru tsumori desu.)

kazoku [n] family

the **family** system // an extended **family** // a nuclear **family**

¶ How is **your family?**

¶ I plan to take a trip with the whole **family** during summer vacation.

ガソリン〔名〕

ガソリンスタンド（*gasorin*-sutando）

¶車にガソリンを入れました。

（Kuruma ni *gasorin* o iremashita.）

gasorin 〔n〕 **gasoline**

a **gas** station, service station

¶ [I] had **gas** put in the car.

かた 肩〔名〕

肩がこる（*kata* ga koru）肩に担ぐ

（*kata* ni katsugu）

¶わたしはおばあさんの肩をたたいて

あげました。（Watashi wa obāsan no

kata o tataite agemashita.）

¶上田さんは胸が厚く、肩幅が広いで

す。（Ueda san wa mune ga atsuku,

*kata*haba ga hiroi desu.）

kata 〔n〕 **shoulder (s)**

have a stiff **shoulder(s)** // carry on

one's shoulder

¶ I massaged my grandmother's

shoulders by hitting them lightly with

my fists.

¶ Mr. Ueda is thick-chested and broad-

shouldered.

かた 型〔名〕

大型（oo*gata*）小型（ko*gata*）

¶この自動車は 1980 年型です。

（Kono jidōsha wa senkyūhyaku-

hachijūnen*gata* desu.）

¶この洋服は型が古いですね。（Kono

yōfuku wa *kata* ga furui desu ne.）

kata 〔n〕 **model, pattern, make,
style**

large-**size**, king-**size**, over**size** // small-

size, pocket-**size**, miniature

¶ This is a **1980** car.

¶ **The cut** of this piece of clothing is

old-fashioned.

(-)かた (-)方〔名、尾〕

1〔名〕

¶あの方はどなたですか。（Ano *kata*

wa donata desu ka？）

¶上田さんという方がいらっしゃいま

した。（Ueda san to iu *kata* ga

irasshaimashita.）

*人を丁寧に呼ぶときの言葉。

2〔尾〕

話し方（hanashi*kata*）泳ぎ方（oyo-

gi*kata*）教え方（oshie*kata*）

(-)kata 〔n, suf〕 **person; method,
way of doing something**

1 〔n〕 person

¶ Who is that **gentleman**〚**lady**〛?

¶ **A** [Mr.] Ueda is here〚came〛.

*Used to refer to persons politely; the

polite form of *hito*.

2 〔suf〕 method, way of doing

something

way of speaking // **way** of swimming,

how to swim // **method** of teaching,

how to teach

¶この漢字の読み方がわかりません。
（Kono kanji no yomi*kata* ga wakarimasen.）

¶[I] don't know **the reading** for this *kanji*.

かたい　硬い〔形〕

katai 〔adj〕 **hard**

¶ダイヤモンドは非常に硬い物質です。（Daiyamondo wa hijō ni *katai* busshitsu desu.）

¶A diamond is an extremely **hard** substance.

かたい　固い〔形〕

katai 〔adj〕 **firm, steady; tight; stubborn; hard**

①[しっかりとして変わらない様子]

① [firm, steady, strong]

¶わたしは上田さんと固い約束をしました。（Watashi wa Ueda san to *katai* yakusoku o shimashita.）

¶I made a **firm** promise to [Mr.] Ueda.

¶もう、お酒を飲まないと固く決心しました。（Mō, osake o nomanai to *kataku* kesshin shimashita.）

¶I have made a **firm** resolution not to drink anymore.

②[力が入ってゆるみのない様子]

② [tight, with no looseness]

固い握手（*katai* akushu）固く結ぶ（*kataku* musubu）

a **firm** handshake // tie **tightly**

¶この荷物のひもを固くしばってください。（Kono nimotsu no himo o *kataku* shibatte kudasai.）

¶Please tie up this parcel **tightly**.

③[融通のきかなない様子、がんこな様子]

③ [stubborn, obstinate]

¶山田さんは頭の固い人です。（Yamada san wa atama no *katai* hito desu.）

¶[Mr.] Yamada is quite **stubborn**.

④[やわらかくない様子]

④ [hard, not soft]

¶パンがかたくなってしまいました。（Pan ga *kataku* natte shimaimashita.）

¶The bread has gotten **hard**.

かたい　堅い〔形〕

katai 〔adj〕 **hard, stiff; steady, reliable, upright**

①[材質などがしっかりしている様子]

① [hard, stiff, tough]

¶この机は堅い木で作ってあります。（Kono tsukue wa *katai* ki de tsukutte arimasu.）

¶This desk is made of **hard** wood.

¶このくつの革は堅いですね。（Kono kutsu no kawa wa *katai* desu ne.）

¶The leather of these shoes **is stiff**.

②［まじめである様子、まちがいなどない様子］

堅い人（*katai* hito）

②［steady, reliable, upright, serious, dry］

a **reliable** 〚**upright, unbending, straitlaced**〛 person

¶パーティーですから、堅い話ではなくおもしろい話をしてください。（Pātii desu kara, *katai* hanashi de wa naku omoshiroi hanashi o shite kudasai.）

¶This is a party so please talk about something interesting and less **dry** 〚**serious**〛.

カタカナ〔名〕

katakana 〔n〕 the *katakana* syllabary for writing Japanese

¶外国語を日本語で書き表す場合は、カタカナで書きます。（Gaikokugo o Nihongo de kakiarawasu baai wa, *katakana* de kakimasu.）

¶In the Japanese language foreign words are written with *katakana*.

⇒かな kana　ひらがな hiragana

かたち　形〔名〕

katachi 〔n〕 shape, form

四角い形をした入れ物（shikakui *katachi* o shita iremono）

a square container

¶あの山は富士山のような形をしています。（Ano yama wa Fujisan no yō na *katachi* o shite imasu.）

¶That mountain is similar **in shape** to Mount Fuji.

¶上田さんはいろいろな形の石を集めています。（Ueda san wa iroiro na *katachi* no ishi o atsumete imasu.）

¶[Mrs.] Ueda collects rocks of various **shapes**.

かたづける〔動Ⅱ〕

katazukeru 〔v Ⅱ〕 put in order, straighten up; dispose of, finish up

①［整理してきちんとする］

①［put in order, straighten up, put away, clear off］

¶机の上をかたづけなさい。（Tsukue no ue o *katazukenasai*.）

¶**Tidy up** your desk.

②［処理すべきものごとをやってしまう］

②［dispose of, finish up］

¶わたしはこの仕事をかたづけてから帰ります。(Watashi wa kono shigoto o *katazukete* kara kaerimasu.)

¶ I will go home after I **finish up** this piece of work.

かたまる 固まる〔動Ⅰ〕

¶このセメントはすぐ固まります。(Kono semento wa sugu *katamarimasu*.)

katamaru〔vⅠ〕**become hard, harden, solidity, congeal**

¶ This cement **hardens** quickly.

かたみち 片道〔名〕

片道切符 (*katamichi*-kippu)
¶小学生のころ片道5キロの道を毎日歩いて通いました。(Shōgakusei no koro *katamichi* gokiro no michi o mainichi aruite kayoimashita.)
⇔往復 ōfuku

katamichi〔n〕**one-way**

a **one-way** ticket
¶ When in elementary school, [I] walked to school every day, a trip of five kilometers **each way**.

かたむく 傾く〔動Ⅰ〕

①[斜めになる]
¶地震で家が傾いてしまいました。(Jishin de ie ga *katamuite* shimaimashita.)

¶この柱は10度も傾いています。(Kono hashira wa jūdo mo *katamuite* imasu.)

②[太陽や月が地平線に近づく]
¶太陽が西に傾いてきました。(Taiyō ga nishi ni *katamuite* kimashita.)

katamuku〔vⅠ〕**tilt, slant; sink, set**

① [tilt, slant, incline]
¶ The house **is tilting** as a result of the earthquake.

¶ This pillar **is slanting** at an angle of 10 degrees.

② [sink, set]
¶ The sun **is**〚**was**〛low in the west.

かためる 固める〔動Ⅱ〕

①[粉や土などをかたくする]
¶この人形は土を固めて作ったものです。(Kono ningyō wa tsuchi o *katamete* tsukutta mono desu.)
②[しっかりとしたものにする]
¶わたしは国へ帰る決心を固めました。(Watashi wa kuni e kaeru kesshin o *katamemashita*.)

katameru〔vⅡ〕**harden, make hard; strengthen**

① [harden, make hard]
¶ This doll is made of **hardened** earth.

② [strengthen]
¶ I am〚was〛**firmly** resolved to return to my native country.

かち 価値 〔名〕

価値がある（kachi ga aru）価値がない（kachi ga nai）価値が高い（kachi ga takai）価値が低い（kachi ga hikui）

¶あの人にこの絵の価値がわかるでしょうか。（Ano hito ni kono e no kachi ga wakaru deshō ka？）

¶あの映画は見る価値があります。（Ano eiga wa miru kachi ga arimasu.）

kachi 〘n〙 **value, worth**

valuable, worthy, of **value** // worthless, of no **value** // of great **value**, invaluable // of little **value**

¶ Does [he] comprehend **the value** 〖**true worth**〗 of this painting?

¶ That movie **is worth** seeing.

かつ 勝つ 〔動Ⅰ〕

¶わたしたちはその試合に4対3で勝ちました。（Watashitachi wa sono shiai ni yon tai san de kachimashita.）

⇔負ける makeru

katsu 〘vⅠ〙 **win**

¶ We **won** that match by a score of 4 to 3.

-がつ -月 〔尾〕

1月（ichigatsu）2月（nigatsu）3月（sangatsu）4月（shigatsu）5月（gogatsu）6月（rokugatsu）7月（shichigatsu）8月（hachigatsu）9月（kugatsu）10月（jūgatsu）11月（jūichigatsu）12月（jūnigatsu）

-gatsu 〘suf〙 **month**

January // February // March // April // May // June // July // August // September // October // November // December

がっかりする 〔動Ⅲ〕

¶入学試験に落ちてがっかりしました。（Nyūgaku-shiken ni ochite gakkari shimashita.）

¶失敗してもがっかりしないでください。（Shipparshite mo gakkari shinaide kudasai.）

gakkari suru 〘vⅢ〙 **be discouraged, be disappointed**

¶ I am 〖**was**〗 **disheartened** over failing the school entrance exam.

¶ **Don't lose heart** even if you should suffer a failure.

がっき 学期 〔名〕

¶学期の終わりには試験があります。（Gakki no owari ni wa shiken ga arimasu.）

gakki 〘n〙 **academic term, school term, semester**

¶ There's an exam at the end of **the term**.

¶ 1学期に漢字を 400 勉強しました。
(Ichi*gakki* ni kanji o yonhyaku benkyō shimashita.)

¶ [I] learned four hundred *kanji* in one **semester**.

がっき 楽器〔名〕 gakki〔n〕 musical instrument

¶ あなたは何か楽器が弾けますか。
(Anata wa nani ka *gakki* ga hikemasu ka?)

¶ Can you play **a musical instrument?**

¶ あの店にはいろいろな楽器があります。(Ano mise ni wa iroiro na *gakki* ga arimasu.)

¶ That shop has various **musical instruments**.

かっこう〔名〕 kakkō〔n〕 appearance, shape

¶ この自動車はスマートで、かっこうがいいですね。(Kono jidōsha wa sumāto de, *kakkō* ga ii desu ne.)

¶ This car is smart and stylish **looking**.

がっこう 学校〔名〕 gakkō〔n〕 school

小学校（shō*gakkō*）中学校
(chū*gakkō*）高等学校（kōtō*gakkō*）専門学校（senmon-*gakkō*）公立学校（kōritsu-*gakkō*）私立学校（shiritsu-*gakkō*）

elementary **school** // junior high **school**, lower secondary **school** // high **school**, upper secondary **school** // technical **school**, professional **school** // public **school** // private **school**

¶ 病気で学校を休みました。(Byōki de *gakkō* o yasumimashita.)

¶ [I] stayed home from **school** due to illness.

¶ どこの学校を卒業しましたか。
(Doko no *gakkō* o sotsugyō shimashita ka?)

¶ What **school** did you graduate from?

かって 勝手〔名〕 katte〔n〕 kitchen

¶ 母は今お勝手にいます。(Haha wa ima o*katte* ni imasu.)
⇒台所 daidokoro

¶ My mother is in **the kitchen** now.

かって〔形動〕 katte〔adj-v〕 one's own convenience, selfishness, willfulness

¶ あの人は自分かってなことばかりします。(Ano hito wa jibun*katte* na koto bakari shimasu.)

¶ [He] only acts **to please [him]self** [He never thinks of others].

¶人の物をかってに使っては困りま
す。(Hito no mono o *katte* ni tsu*katte* wa
komarimasu.)

¶ It will not do to help yourself to the
possessions of others **as if they were
your own**.

かつどう 活動 〔名、〜する〕

政治活動 (seiji-*katsudō*) 活動的な人
(*katsudō*teki na hito)
¶この学校は課外活動が盛んです。
(Kono gakkō wa kagai-*katsudō* ga sakan
desu.)
¶休火山が再び活動し始めました。
(Kyūkazan ga futatabi *katsudō*
shihajimemashita.)

katsudō 〔n, 〜*suru*〕 **activity,
activities**
political **activity** // an **active**
〖energetic〗 person
¶ Extracurricular **activities** are popular
at this school.

¶ A dormant volcano has become
active once again.

かてい 家庭 〔名〕

家庭を持つ (*katei* o motsu) 家庭教師
(*katei*-kyōshi) 家庭教育 (*katei*-
kyōiku)
¶上田さんのうちはたいへん明るい家
庭です。(Ueda san no uchi wa taihen
akarui *katei* desu.)
¶上田さんの奥さんはとても家庭的な
方です。(Ueda san no okusan wa totemo
*katei*teki na kata desu.)

katei 〔n〕 **home, family, household**
be married and settled down // a tutor,
private teacher // **home** training
¶ [Mr.] Ueda has a very happy **home**.

¶ Mr. Ueda's wife is a very **domestic**
woman.

かど 角 〔名〕

① [とがったところ]
¶子供が机の角に頭をぶつけて、けが
をしました。(Kodomo ga tsukue no
kado ni atama o butsukete, kega o
shimashita.)
② [道の折れ曲がったところ]
角の店 (*kado* no mise)
¶その角を右に曲がった所に交番があ
ります。(Sono *kado* o migi ni magatta
tokoro ni kōban ga arimasu.)

kado 〔n〕 **corner, edge; corner,
turning**
① [corner, edge]
¶ The child hit [his] head on **the
corner** of the desk and hurt [him]self.

② [corner, turning]
a **corner** shop
¶ If you turn right at that **corner**, you
will find a police box.

かな〔名〕

ひらがな（hira*gana*）カタカナ
（kata*kana*）振りかな（furi*gana*）かな
遣い（*kana*zukai）

¶外国人の名前はカタカナで書きま
す。（Gaikokujin no namae wa kata*kana*
de kakimasu.）
¶次の漢字にかなをつけなさい。
（Tsugi no kanji ni *kana* o tsukenasai.）
⇒ひらがな **hiragana**　カタカナ
katakana

かない　家内〔名〕

¶これは家内が作った料理です。
（Kore wa *kanai* ga tsukutta ryōri desu.）
¶これがわたしの家内です。どうぞ、
よろしく。（Kore ga watashi no *kanai*
desu. Dōzo, yoroshiku.）
＊他人に自分の妻のことを話す場合に
使う。
⇒妻 **tsuma**　奥さん **okusan**

かなしい　悲しい〔形〕

¶去年死んだ母のことを思うと悲しく
なります。（Kyonen shinda haha no koto
o omou to *kanashiku* narimasu.）
¶あの少女は悲しそうな顔をしていま
すね。（Ano shōjo wa *kanashisō* na kao o
shite imasu ne.）
⇔うれしい **ureshii**

かならず　必ず〔副〕

¶あしたの朝6時に必ず来てくださ
い。（Ashita no asa rokuji ni *kanarazu*
kite kudasai.）

kana 〔n〕 the Japanese syllabary alphabets

hiragana // *katakana* // *furigana*
(**kana** printed to the side of *kanji*
giving the reading) // **kana**
orthography, rules for the use of **kana**

¶ The names of foreigners are written
in *katakana*.

¶ Write down the pronunciation of the
following *kanji* in **kana**.

kanai 〔n〕 one's wife

¶ This dish was cooked by **my wife**.

¶ This is **my wife**. I'd like you to meet
her.

＊*Kanai* is used when talking about
one's own wife with others.

kanashii 〔adj〕 sad, unhappy, sorrowful, mournful

¶ I become **sad** when I think about my
mother who died last year.

¶ That young girl looks **sad**, doesn't
she?

kanarazu 〔adv〕 certainly, without fail

¶ Please **be sure** to come tomorrow
morning at six o'clock.

¶約束は必ず守ります。（Yakusoku wa *kanarazu* mamorimasu.）

¶ [I] **never fail** to keep [my] promises.

かなり〔副、形動、〜の〕

kanari〔adv, adj-v, 〜*no*〕**fairly, quite, considerably**

¶上田さんの病気はかなり重いようです。（Ueda san no byōki wa *kanari* omoi yō desu.）

¶ [Mr.] Ueda's illness seems to be **quite** serious.

¶わたしは日本語を読むことはかなりできますが、話すことはまだ下手です。（Watashi wa Nihongo o yomu koto wa *kanari* dekimasu ga, hanasu koto wa mada heta desu.）

¶ I can read Japanese **fairly** well, but I'm still poor at speaking.

¶田中さんはかなりの収入があります。（Tanaka san wa *kanari* no shūnyū ga arimasu.）

¶ [Mr.] Tanaka has a **handsome** income.

かに〔名〕

kani〔n〕**crab**

かね 金〔名〕

kane〔n〕**money**

金を払う（*kane* o harau）金がない（*kane* ga nai）金をなくす（*kane* o nakusu）

to pay **money** // have no **money**, have little **money** // lose **some money**

¶今度の旅行には、ずいぶんお金がかかりました。（Kondo no ryokō ni wa zuibun o*kane* ga kakarimashita.）

¶ The last trip was very **expensive**.

¶お金を千円貸してください。（O*kane* o sen'en kashite kudasai.）

¶ Please loan me a thousand yen.

かね 鐘〔名〕

kane〔n〕**bell, gong**

鐘を鳴らす（*kane* o narasu）

ring **a bell**

¶お寺の鐘が鳴りました。（Otera no *kane* ga narimashita.）

¶ The temple **bell** sounded.

¶教会の鐘の音が聞こえてきました。（Kyōkai no *kane* no ne ga kikoete kimashita.）

¶ One can 〖could〗 hear the sound of church **bells**.

かねもち 金持ち〔名〕

kanemochi〔n〕**a rich person**

¶彼は一生懸命に働いてお金持ちになりました。（Kare wa isshōkenmei ni hataraite o*kanemochi* ni narimashita.）

¶ He worked very hard and **made his fortune**.

¶上田さんはお金持ちの家に生まれました。(Ueda san wa o*kanemochi* no ie ni umaremashita.)

¶[Miss] Ueda was born into a **wealthy** family.

かのう 可能〔名、形動〕

kanō〔n, adj-v〕**possibility, possible**

不可能（fu*kanō*）

im**possible, im**possibility

¶日本語がわからなくても、日本の大学に入ることは可能でしょうか。
（Nihongo ga wakaranakute mo, Nihon no daigaku ni hairu koto wa *kanō* deshō ka？）

¶**Is it possible** to become a student at a Japanese university even if one doesn't know Japanese?

¶火星に生物が住んでいる可能性はほとんどないでしょう。(Kasei ni seibutsu ga sunde iru *kanō*sei wa hotondo nai deshō.)

¶There is little **chance** of life on Mars.

かのじょ 彼女〔代〕

kanojo〔pron〕**she, her**

¶彼女はどこへ行きましたか。
（*Kanojo* wa doko e ikimashita ka？）
⇒彼 **kare**

¶Where did **she** go?

カバー〔名〕

kabā〔n〕**a cover**

まくらカバー（makura-*kabā*）本にカバーを掛ける（hon ni *kabā* o kakeru）

a pillow**case** // put a book **cover** on a book

かばん〔名〕

kaban〔n〕**bag, briefcase, satchel, suitcase, trunk**

¶山田さんはいつも黒いかばんを提げて歩いています。(Yamada san wa itsu mo kuroi *kaban* o sagete aruite imasu.)

¶[Mr.] Yamada always carries a black **briefcase**.

かびん 花びん〔名〕

kabin〔n〕**vase, flower vase**

¶花びんに花が生けてあります。
（*Kabin* ni hana ga ikete arimasu.）

¶There is an arrangement of flowers in **the vase**.

かぶる〔動Ⅰ〕

kaburu〔vⅠ〕**wear (on the head); pour over; cover**

①[ある物で頭・顔などをおおう]

①[wear or put something on the head or face]

¶赤い帽子をかぶっている人はだれで
すか。(Akai bōshi o *kabutte* iru hito wa
dare desu ka?)

¶ Who is the person **wearing** a red hat
〚ski cap, etc.〛?

¶寒いので、毛布を頭からかぶって寝
ました。(Samui node, mōfu o atama
kara *kabutte* nemashita.)

¶ As it was cold [I] slept with the
covers **up over** [my] head.

② [頭の上から浴びる]

② [pour over the head or top of
something]

波をかぶる (nami o *kaburu*)

covered with waves

¶あまり暑かったので、水をかぶりま
した。(Amari atsukatta node, mizu o
kaburi mashita.)

¶ Since it was so hot, I splashed water
over my head.

③ [物の表面をおおう]

③ [cover something]

¶1週間も掃除をしなかったので、机
はほこりをかぶっています。(Isshū
kan mo sōji o shinakatta node, tsukue wa
hokori o *kabutte* imasu.)

¶ As [I] haven't cleaned for a week, the
desk **is covered** with dust.

かべ 壁 〔名〕

kabe 〔n〕 **wall**

¶壁に絵が掛けてあります。(*Kabe* ni e
ga kakete arimasu.)

¶ There is a painting hanging on **the
wall**.

¶壁を白く塗りました。(*Kabe* o
shiroku nurimashita.)

¶ [I] painted **the wall(s)** white.

(～ても) かまわない 〔連〕

(-te mo)kamawanai 〔compd〕
**don't mind, don't care, it's all
right**

① [許可の意味を表す]

① [indicates permission]

¶「ボールペンで書いてもかまいませ
んか。」(Bōrupen de kaite mo
kamaimasen ka?)「ええ、どうぞ。」
(Ee, dōzo.)

¶ "**Is it all right** to write it with a ballpoint pen?"
"Yes, that will be fine."

¶「ここでたばこを吸ってもかまいま
せんか。」(Koko de tabako o sutte mo
kamaimasen ka?)「いいえ、吸っては
いけません。」(Iie, sutte wa ikemasen.)

¶ "**Is it all right** to smoke here?"
"No, it's not."

② [不必要の意味を表す]

② [indicates something is unnecessary]

180

¶お金は今すぐ払わなくてもかまいません。(Okane wa ima sugu harawanakute mo *kamaimasen*.)

¶「あした、買い物に行かなくてもかまいませんか。」(Ashita, kaimono ni ikanakute mo *kamaimasen* ka？)「いいえ、行かなくてはいけません。」(Iie, ikanakute wa ikemasen.)

＊「〜なくてもかまわない（〜nakute mo kamawanai)」の形で使う。

⇔（〜ては）いけない（〜**te wa**）**ikenai**

⇒（〜ても）いい（〜**te mo**）**ii**

¶ **It's all right** if you don't pay right away.

¶ **"Is it all right** if [I] don't go shopping tomorrow?" "No, [you] must go."

*Used in the pattern "-*nakute mo kamawanai*."

がまん 我慢〔名、〜する〕

¶あの人の態度にはもう我慢ができません。(Ano hito no taido ni wa mō *gaman* ga dekimasen.)

¶もう少し我慢してください。(Mō sukoshi *gaman* shite kudasai.)

gaman 〔n, 〜*suru*〕 **patience, endurance**

¶ **I've run out of patience** with [his] attitude.

¶ Please **be patient** a little longer.

かみ 神〔名〕

¶あなたは神を信じますか。(Anata wa *kami* o shinjimasu ka？)

¶あなたの無事を神に祈っています。(Anata no buji o *kami* ni inotte imasu.)

＊「神様（kamisama)」とも言う。

kami 〔n〕 **God, a god, a deity**

¶ Do you believe in **God**?

¶ [I] will pray for your safety.

*Variant: *kamisama*.

かみ 紙〔名〕

紙くず（*kami*kuzu）紙包み（*kami*-zutsumi）紙袋（*kami*bukuro）紙芝居（*kami*shibai）

¶その紙を1枚ください。(Sono *kami* o ichimai kudasai.)

kami 〔n〕 **paper**

waste**paper, paper** scraps // a **paper**-wrapped parcel // a **paper** bag // a **picture-card** show

¶ Please give me a sheet of that **paper**.

かみ 髪 〔名〕

髪をとかす（*kami* o tokasu）髪を分ける（*kami* o wakeru）髪を刈る（*kami* o karu）髪を伸ばす（*kami* o nobasu）髪を洗う（*kami* o arau）

¶髪が伸びたので、床屋へ行きました。(*Kami* ga nobita node, tokoya e ikimashita.)

¶髪の毛をもう少し短くしてください。(*Kami*noke o mō sukoshi mijikaku shite kudasai.)

かみそり 〔名〕

安全かみそり（anzen-*kamisori*）

¶毎朝、電気かみそりでひげをそります。(Maiasa, denki-*kamisori* de hige o sorimasu.)

¶このかみそりはあまりよく切れませんね。(Kono *kamisori* wa amari yoku kiremasen ne.)

かみなり 雷 〔名〕

¶雷が鳴って、強い雨が降ってきました。(*Kaminari* ga natte, tsuyoi ame ga futte kimashita.)

¶どこかに雷が落ちたらしいです。(Doko ka ni *kaminari* ga ochita rashii desu.)

かむ 〔動Ⅰ〕

¶御飯をよくかんで食べなさい。(Gohan o yoku *kande* tabenasai.)

¶わたしは犬にかまれて、けがをしました。(Watashi wa inu ni *kamarete*, kega o shimashita.)

カメラ 〔名〕

¶これは日本製のカメラです。(Kore wa Nihonsei no *kamera* desu.)

kami 〔n〕 hair

comb **one's hair** // part **one's hair** // cut **someone's hair**, have **one's hair** cut // let **one's hair** grow // wash **one's hair**

¶ [I] went to the barber as **[my] hair** had grown out.

¶ Please cut **it** a little shorter (said to someone cutting one's hair).

kamisori 〔n〕 **razor**

a safety **razor**

¶ [I] shave every morning with an electric **shaver**.

¶ This **razor** doesn't shave very well.

kaminari 〔n〕 **thunder, thunderbolt**

¶ It **thundered** and started 〖has started〗 raining heavily.

¶ It seems that **lightning** struck somewhere.

kamu 〔v I〕 **bite, chew**

¶ **Chew** your food 〖rice〗 well.

¶ I was injured when a dog **bit** me.

kamera 〔n〕 **camera**

¶ This **camera** was made in Japan.

かもく 科目 〔名〕

選択科目 （sentaku-*kamoku*） 必修科目
（hisshū-*kamoku*）

¶ 大学の入学試験には、どんな科目が
ありますか。（Daigaku no nyūgaku-
shiken ni wa, donna *kamoku* ga arimasu
ka？）

kamoku 〔n〕 **subject, course,
curriculum**

an elective, an optional **course** // a
required **course**

¶ What sort of **subjects** are covered in
the university entrance examination?

かもしれない 〔連〕

¶ 雨が降るかもしれないから、かさを
持って行ったほうがいいですよ。
（Ame ga furu *ka mo shirenai* kara, kasa o
motte itta hō ga ii desu yo.）
¶ 彼は時間に遅れるかもしれません。
（Kare wa jikan ni okureru *ka mo
shiremasen*.）
¶ 彼の話は本当かもしれません。
（Kare no hanashi wa hontō *ka mo
shiremasen*.）

ka mo shirenai 〔compd〕 **maybe,
perhaps**

¶ You'd better take an umbrella as it
may rain.

¶ He **might** be late.

¶ His story **might** be true.

かゆい 〔形〕

¶ 虫に刺された所がかゆいので、薬を
つけました。（Mushi ni sasareta tokoro
ga *kayui* node, kusuri o tsukemashita.）
¶ 夏は汗をかくので、体がかゆくなり
ます。（Natsu wa ase o kaku node, karada
ga *kayuku* narimasu.）

kayui 〔adj〕 **itchy**

¶ As the spot where I had been bitten
〚stung〛 by an insect **itched**, I put on
some medicine.

¶ One's body becomes **itchy** in the
summer when one sweats a lot.

かよう 通う 〔動 I〕

① ［何度も同じ所を通る］

¶ わたしは自転車で学校に通っていま
す。（Watashi wa jitensha de gakkō ni
kayotte imasu.）

kayou 〔v I〕 **commute, run
(between); be conveyed**
① ［commute, visit frequently, go to
and from, run (between)］
¶ I **commute** to school by bicycle.

¶わたしの生まれた所は、バスも通わないほどの田舎です。（Watashi no umareta tokoro wa, basu mo *kayowanai* hodo no inaka desu.）

② [心が通じる]

¶お互いの心が通い合っていなければ、いっしょに生活できません。（Otagai no kokoro ga *kayoi*atte inakereba, issho ni seikatsu dekimasen.）

¶ My birthplace is in such an out-of-the-way place that it **isn't** even **served by** a bus.

② [be conveyed, be communicated]

¶ People can't live together if they can't **understand** each other's feelings.

かよう（び） 火曜（日）〔名〕

kayō (bi) 〔n〕 **Tuesday**

から 空 〔名〕

kara 〔n〕 **empty, vacant**

空びん（*kara*bin）空箱（*kara*bako）

¶この箱は空です。（Kono hako wa *kara* desu.）

an **empty** bottle // an **empty** box

¶ This box is **empty**.

から 〔助〕

kara 〔part〕 **because**

① [前件が理由・根拠をなし、後件がその帰結となっているという関係を表す]

① [because; indicates the second clause is a consequence of the first one]

¶暑いから、窓を開けてください。（Atsui *kara*, mado o akete kudasai.）

¶ It's hot. Please open the window.

¶遅くなったから、タクシーで帰りましょう。（Osoku natta *kara*, takushii de kaerimashō.）

¶ **As** it's late, let's take a taxi home.

¶危ないから、道路で遊んではいけません。（Abunai *kara*, dōro de asonde wa ikemasen.）

¶ One mustn't play in the street **because** it's dangerous.

¶ゆっくりしていては汽車に乗り遅れるから、早く行きなさい。（Yukkuri shite ite wa kisha ni noriokureru *kara*, hayaku ikinasai.）

¶ Go quickly **as** you will miss the train if you don't.

*後件には、「〜でしょう（deshō）」などの推量、「〜う［よう］（〜u ［yō］）」などの意志、「〜なさい（nasai）」などの命令、「〜てください（〜te kudasai）」などの依頼、「〜ては

*Subjective expressions can also be used in the second clause such as inferences with *deshō*, expressions of intent or will with -ō 〚-yō〛, imperatives with -*nasai*, requests with -*te kudasai*, and prohibitions with -*te wa ikenai*.

いけない（〜te wa ikenai）」などの禁止
などの主観的な言い方も来る。

→ので node

② [前件の成立する理由や根拠などを
後件によって説明するのに使う]

¶山田さんが休んだのは風邪を引いた
からです。（Yamada san ga yasunda no
wa kaze o hiita *kara* desu.）

¶みんな夜遅くまで勉強しています。
試験が近づいたからです。（Minna
yoru osoku made benkyō shite imasu.
Shiken ga chikazuita *kara* desu.）

*「〜からだ（〜kara da）」「〜からで
す（〜kara desu）」の形で使う。

② [because; indicates the first clause is
explained by the second clause]

¶[Mrs.] Yamada was absent **because**
[she] caught a cold.

¶Everyone is studying until late at
night. That's **because** exams are
approaching.

*Used in the patterns "〜 *kara da*" and
"〜 *kara desu*."

から 〔助〕

① [時・所などの起点を表す]

¶学校は8時から始まります。（Gakkō
wa hachiji *kara* hajimarimasu.）

¶うちから駅まで歩いて10分です。
（Uchi *kara* eki made aruite jippun desu.）

¶父は昨日外国から帰ってきました。
（Chichi wa kinō gaikoku *kara* kaette
kimashita.）

② [経由する所を表す]

¶わたしの部屋の窓から港が見えま
す。（Watashi no heya no mado *kara*
minato ga miemasu.）

¶戸のすき間から冷たい風が入ってき
ます。（To no sukima *kara* tsumetai kaze
ga haitte kimasu.）

③ [動作の出どころなどを表す]

¶友達からお祝いの品物をもらいまし
た。（Tomodachi *kara* oiwai no
shinamono o moraimashita.）

kara 〔part〕 from; after

① [from, at (a given time or place)]

¶School starts **at** eight o'clock.

¶It's a 10-minute walk **from** my home
to the station.

¶My father returned home **from**
overseas yesterday.

② [from, out of (an intermediary
place)]

¶You can see the harbor **from** the
window of my room.

¶A cold draft is coming in **from**
around the door.

③ [from (a source of an action, etc.)]

¶[I] received a present **from** a friend.

¶わたしは山田先生から日本語を教えていただきました。（Watashi wa Yamada sensei *kara* Nihongo o oshiete itadakimashita.）

¶図書館から借りた本をなくしてしまいました。（Toshokan *kara* karita hon o nakushite shimaimashita.）

④ [原料・材料などを表す]

¶日本の酒は米から作ります。（Nihon no sake wa kome *kara* tsukuri-masu.）

¶石油からいろいろな物が作られます。（Sekiyu *kara* iroiro na mono ga tsukuraremasu.）

⑤ [原因・理由・根拠となるものごとを表す]

¶この事故は運転手の不注意から起こったものです。（Kono jiko wa untenshu no fuchūi *kara* okotta mono desu.）

⑥ [順序・順番の初めを表す]

¶このページの1番から順に読んでください。（Kono pēji no ichiban *kara* jun ni yonde kudasai.）

¶あなたから始めてください。（Anata *kara* hajimete kudasai.）

⑦ [ある動作・作用が終わったあとに他の動作・作用が行われることを表す]

¶あなたはうちへ帰ってから何をしますか。（Anata wa uchi e kaette *kara* nani o shimasu ka？）

¶御飯を食べてからテレビを見ます。（Gohan o tabete *kara* terebi o mimasu.）

¶学校を卒業してから10年たちました。（Gakkō o sotsugyō shite *kara* jūnen tachimashita.）

＊「動詞（ての形）＋から（kara）」の形で使う。

¶ I was taught Japanese **by** Professor Yamada.

¶ [I] lost a library book.

④ [from, out of (some raw material)]

¶ Japanese *sake* is made **from** rice.

¶ Various things can be made **from** petroleum.

⑤ [from, out of, due to (some cause or reason)]

¶ This accident was caused **by** careless driving.

⑥ [from (the beginning or the first one)]

¶ Start reading this page **from** number one.

¶ We'll start **with** you.

⑦ [after (doing something)]

¶ What do you do 〚will you do〛 **after** returning home?

¶ [I] watch television **after** eating dinner.

¶ Ten years have 〚had〛 passed **since** [I] graduated from school.

＊Used in the pattern "verb (*-te* form) + *kara*."

カラー〔名〕

カラーテレビ（*karā*-terebi）カラー写真（*karā*-shashin）カラーフィルム（*karā*-firumu）

¶あなたのテレビはカラーですか、白黒ですか。（Anata no terebi wa *karā* desu ka, shirokuro desu ka？）

からい 辛い〔形〕

①[香辛料の味]

¶そんなにからしをつけたら辛いですよ。（Sonna ni karashi o tsuketara *karai* desu yo.）

¶あの店のカレーは辛かったですね。（Ano mise no karē wa *karakatta* desu ne.）

②[塩味が強い]

¶この魚料理は塩辛いですね。（Kono sakanaryōri wa shio*karai* desu ne.）

⇔甘い amai

ガラス〔名〕

ガラスのコップ（*garasu* no koppu）

¶子供が窓ガラスを割りました。（Kodomo ga mado*garasu* o warimashita.）

からだ 体〔名〕

①[身体]

¶上田さんはずいぶん体の大きい人ですね。（Ueda san wa zuibun *karada* no ookii hito desu ne.）

¶柔道の練習で体じゅうが痛くなりました。（Jūdō no renshū de *karada*jū ga itaku narimashita.）

②[健康の状態]

¶体のぐあいが悪いので、学校を休みました。（*Karada* no guai ga warui node, gakkō o yasumimashita.）

karā 〔n〕 color

color television // a **color** photo // **color** film

¶ Is your television set **color** or black and white?

karai 〔adj〕 hot (taste); salty

① [hot, sharp]

¶ It will be **very hot** if you put on so much mustard.

¶ That restaurant's curry **was really hot**, wasn't it?

② [salty]

¶ This fish is **very salty**, isn't it?

garasu 〔n〕 glass

a glass, a **glass** tumbler

¶ The children broke the window 〚the window **glass**〛.

karada 〔n〕 body; health

① [body]

¶ [Mr.] Ueda is **a big man**, isn't he?

¶ I ache 〚ached〛 all over **my body** from practicing judo.

② [health]

¶ [I] **didn't feel well** so [I] stayed home from school.

¶体にはじゅうぶん気をつけてください。(*Karada* ni wa jūbun ki o tsukete kudasai.)

¶ Please take good care of **yourself**.

かりる 借りる〔動Ⅱ〕

金を借りる (kane o *kariru*) 部屋を借りる (heya o *kariru*)

¶わたしは上田さんから1万円借りました。(Watashi wa Ueda san kara ichiman'en *karimashita*.)

¶借りた本はあした返します。(*Karita* hon wa ashita kaeshimasu.)

¶電話をお借りできますか。(Denwa o o*kari* dekimasu ka?)

⇔貸す **kasu**

kariru 〔v Ⅱ〕 borrow; hire, rent

borrow money // **rent** a room

¶ **I borrowed** ten thousand yen from [Miss] Ueda.

¶ Tomorrow I will return the book **I borrowed**.

¶ Do you have a telephone **I could use?**

-がる〔尾〕

行きたがる (ikita*garu*) うれしがる (ureshi*garu*) いやがる (iya*garu*)

¶子供がお菓子を欲しがっています。(Kodomo ga okashi o hoshi*gatte* imasu.)

¶暖房がないので、みんな寒がっています。(Danbō ga nai node, minna samu*gatte* imasu.)

＊「-がる (-garu)」は形容詞・形容動詞の語幹および「たい (tai)」の「た (ta)」に続き、そのように感じる、またはそのような様子にみせるなどの意味を表す。普通は話し手や聞き手以外の人について言う場合に使う。

⇒たがる **tagaru**

-garu 〔suf〕 feel -, want to -, be apt to

want to go, **be anxious** to go // be glad // dislike, be unwilling to

¶ Children **crave** sweets.

¶ There's no heating so everyone **is feeling** the cold.

＊The suffix *-garu* is added to the stem form of adjectives and adjective-verbs or to the *-ta-* of *-tai*. It expresses how someone feels or appears to feel. It is usually used to refer to someone other than the speaker or the listener.

かるい 軽い〔形〕

①[目方が少ない]

¶この荷物は軽いから、片手で持てます。(Kono nimotsu wa *karui* kara, katate de motemasu.)

②[たいした程度ではない]

karui 〔adj〕 light; trifling

① [light, not heavy]

¶ As this package 〚luggage, bag〛 **is light** it can be carried in one hand.

② [trifling, slight]

¶上田さんの病気は軽いそうです。
(Ueda san no byōki wa *karui* sō desu.)

¶子供が大学を卒業したので、わたしの責任も軽くなりました。(Kodomo ga daigaku o sotsugyō shita node, watashi no sekinin mo *karuku* narimashita.)

⇔重い omoi

¶ I hear that [Mrs.] Ueda's illness **isn't serious**.

¶ As my children have graduated from college, my responsibility has become **lighter**.

かれ 彼 〔代〕

¶彼の名前は上田です。(*Kare* no namae wa Ueda desu.)

⇒彼女 kanojo

kare 〔pron〕 **he, his**

¶ **His** name is Ueda.

かれら 彼ら 〔代〕

¶今日の仕事は彼らが手伝ってくれます。(Kyō no shigoto wa *karera* ga tetsudatte kuremasu.)

karera 〔pron〕 **they**

¶ **They** will help me with today's work.

かれる 枯れる 〔動 II〕

枯れ木（*kare*ki）枯れ葉（*kare*ha）

¶水をやらなかったので、木が枯れてしまいました。(Mizu o yaranakatta node, ki ga *kare*te shimaimashita.)

kareru 〔v II〕 **wither, die**

a **dead** tree // a **dead** leaf

¶ The tree **died** because it hadn't been watered.

カレンダー 〔名〕

カレンダーをめくる（*karendā* o mekuru）

¶来月の 15 日は何曜日か、カレンダーで調べてください。(Raigetsu no jūgonichi wa nan'yōbi ka, *karendā* de shirabete kudasai.)

karendā 〔n〕 **calendar**

turn over **a calendar**, tear a sheet off **a calendar**

¶ Please look at **the calendar** and see what day of the week the fifteenth is next month.

かわ 川 〔名〕

ナイル川（Nairu*gawa*）川幅（*kawa*-haba）

¶家の前に川が流れています。(Ie no mae ni *kawa* ga nagarete imasu.)

¶川岸にホテルが 1 軒建っています。(*Kawa*gishi ni hoteru ga ikken tatte imasu.)

kawa 〔n〕 **river, stream**

the Nile **River** // the width of **a river**

¶ There is **a river** 〚**stream**〛 running in front of the house.

¶ There is a single hotel standing on the **river**bank.

かわ 皮〔名〕

kawa 〔n〕 skin, hide, fur, peel, shell

毛皮 (kegawa)
¶みかんは皮をむいて食べます。
(Mikan wa kawa o muite tabemasu.)

fur
¶ **One peels** a mandarin orange before eating it.

かわ 革〔名〕

kawa 〔n〕 leather

革ぐつ (kawagutsu) 革のカバン
(kawa no kaban)
¶このベルトは革でできています。
(Kono beruto wa kawa de dekite imasu.)

leather shoes // a **leather** bag
〖briefcase, suitcase, etc.〗
¶ This belt is made of **leather**.

-がわ -側〔尾〕

-gawa 〔suf〕 side; part

こちら側 (kochiragawa) 向こう側
(mukougawa) 中側 (nakagawa) 外側
(sotogawa)
¶道の両側に木が植えてあります。
(Michi no ryōgawa ni ki ga uete arimasu.)
¶日本では人は右側を、車は左側を通ります。(Nihon de wa hito wa migigawa o, kuruma wa hidarigawa o toori masu.)

this **side** //the other **side**, the opposite **side** //the in**side** //the out**side**

¶ There are trees planted on both **sides** of the street.

¶ In Japan people walk on the righthand **side** and cars run on the lefthand **side** of the road.

かわいい〔形〕

kawaii 〔adj〕 cute, sweet, charming

¶とてもかわいい人形ですね。
(Totemo kawaii ningyō desu ne.)
¶田中さんからかわいい子犬をもらいました。(Tanaka san kara kawaii koinu o moraimashita.)

¶ This is a very **cute** doll, isn't it?

¶ I received a **cute** little puppy from [Mrs.] Tanaka.

かわいがる〔動Ⅰ〕

kawaigaru 〔vⅠ〕 love, pet, show affection to, be attached to

¶おじいさんはわたしをとてもかわいがってくれました。(Ojiisan wa watashi o totemo kawaigatte kuremashita.)
¶上田さんは犬をたいへんかわいがっています。(Ueda san wa inu o taihen kawaigatte imasu.)

¶ I **was a special favorite** of my grandfather.

¶ [Mr.] Ueda **is very fond** of [his] dog.

かわいそう〔形動〕

¶両親のいない子供はかわいそうです。(Ryōshin no inai kodomo wa *kawaisō* desu.)

¶あの子はかわいそうに目が見えないのです。(Ano ko wa *kawaisō* ni me ga mienai no desu.)

kawaisō 〔adj-v〕 **poor, pitiful, pathetic**

¶Children without parents **are to be pitied**.

¶**Sadly enough** that child is blind.

かわかす　乾かす〔動 I〕

¶ぬれた服を火で乾かしました。(Nureta fuku o hi de *kawakashimashita*.)

kawakasu 〔v I〕 **dry, dry out**

¶[I] **dried** the wet clothes at the fire.

かわく　乾く〔動 I〕

¶天気がいいので、洗たく物がすぐ乾きます。(Tenki ga ii node, sentakumono ga sugu *kawakimasu*.)

kawaku 〔v I〕 **dry, become dry**

¶As it's a nice day laundry 〖the laundry〗 will soon **dry**.

かわく　渇く〔動 I〕

¶のどが渇いたから、水を一杯ください。(Nodo ga *kawaita* kara, mizu o ippai kudasai.)

kawaku 〔v I〕 **be thirsty**

¶**I'm thirsty** — please give me a glass of water.

かわせ　為替〔名〕

¶お金を為替にして送りました。(Okane o *kawase* ni shite okurimashita.)

kawase 〔n〕 **money order, (currency) exchange**

¶[I] sent the money by **money order**.

かわり　代わり〔名〕

¶父の代わりにわたしが来ました。(Chichi no *kawari* ni watashi ga kimashita.)

¶上田先生が病気なので、代わりに山田先生が教えてくださいました。(Ueda sensei ga byōki na node, *kawari* ni Yamada sensei ga oshiete kudasaimashita.)

kawari 〔n〕 **substitute, in place of**

¶I've come **in place of** my father.

¶Professor Ueda was sick so Professor Yamada taught **in [his] place**.

かわり 替わり〔名〕

¶あまりおいしかったので、コーヒーのお替わりをしました。(Amari oishikatta node, kōhii no okawari o shimashita.)

¶御飯のお替わりはいかがですか。(Gohan no okawari wa ikaga desu ka？)

kawari 〔n〕 **another helping, a refill**

¶ As it was so good, I had **another cup** of coffee.

¶ Would you like **another helping** 〚**serving**〛 of rice?

かわる 変わる〔動Ⅰ〕

¶信号が赤から青に変わりました。(Shingō ga aka kara ao ni kawarimashita.)

¶このごろのお天気は変わりやすいです。(Konogoro no otenki wa kawariyasui desu.)

＊前の状態とは違った状態になる場合に使う。

kawaru 〔vⅠ〕 **change**

¶ The light **changed** from red to green.

¶ The weather **is very changeable** lately.

＊This *kawaru* is used when the existing situation or condition has changed to a new one.

かわる 替わる〔動Ⅰ〕

¶最近、あの会社は経営者が替わりました。(Saikin, ano kaisha wa keieisha ga kawarimashita.)

＊ある地位や役割を占めていた人がほかの人と交替する場合に使う。

kawaru 〔vⅠ〕 **change**

¶ The manager 〚chief executive〛 of that company **has changed** recently.

＊This *kawaru* is used when a person holding a certain position or role is replaced by someone else.

かわる 代わる〔動Ⅰ〕

¶これからのエネルギーは、石油に代わって原子力になるでしょう。(Kore kara no enerugii wa, sekiyu ni kawatte genshiryoku ni naru deshō.)

＊別の人や物が、その役割をする場合に使う。

kawaru 〔vⅠ〕 **take the place of, replace, substitute for**

¶ In the future nuclear power will probably **replace** oil as our principal source of energy.

＊This *kawaru* is used when a different person or thing substitutes in or fulfills a given function or role.

-かん -間〔尾〕

① [ある一定の長さ]

-kan 〔suf〕 **interval, period; between**

① [interval, period]

1時間（ichijikan）1週間（isshūkan）短期間（tankikan）

¶疲れましたから、10分間休憩しませんか。（Tsukaremashita kara, jippunkan kyūkei shimasen ka？）

¶わたしは高校の3年間、1日も休みませんでした。（Watashi wa kōkō no sannenkan, ichinichi mo yasumimasen deshita.）

②[ある地点からある地点までの隔たり]

¶東京・大阪間の距離は 550 キロメートルです。（Tōkyō - Oosakakan no kyori wa gohyaku-gojikkiromētoru desu.）

③[間がら、関係]

¶夫婦間の問題はほかの人にはわかりにくいです。（Fūfukan no mondai wa hoka no hito ni wa wakarinikui desu.）

¶A、Bの両国間には今貿易上の問題がいろいろあります。（Ē, Bii no ryōkokukan ni wa ima bōekijō no mondai ga iroiro arimasu.）

one hour // one week // a short **period** of time

¶ [I]'m tired. Let's take a **10-minute** break.

¶ I wasn't absent even a single day in the **three years** of high school.

② [between two points, from ～ to ～]

¶ The distance **between** Tokyo and Osaka is 550 kilometers.

③ [between, among]

¶ Problems **between** husbands and wives are difficult for outsiders to understand.

¶ There are presently various trade problems **between** countries A and B.

かんがえ　考え〔名〕

¶わたしにいい考えがあります。（Watashi ni ii kangae ga arimasu.）

¶あの人の考えには賛成できません。（Ano hito no kangae ni wa sansei dekimasen.）

kangae 〔n〕 thought, thinking, idea, opinion, way of thinking

¶ I have a good **idea**.

¶ I can't agree with **[his]** way of **thinking**.

かんがえる　考える〔動Ⅱ〕

¶あなたは今、何を考えているのですか。（Anata wa ima, nani o kangaete iru no desu ka？）

¶この計画についてどう考えますか。（Kono keikaku ni tsuite dō kangaemasu ka？）

kangaeru 〔v Ⅱ〕 think, consider

¶ What are you **thinking about?**

¶ What **do you think** of this project?

¶よく考えてから返事をします。
（Yoku *kangaete* kara henji o shimasu.）

¶ I'd like **to think** about it before giving you my answer.

かんきょう 環境〔名〕

社会環境（shakai-*kankyō*）家庭環境（katei-*kankyō*）環境衛生（*kankyō*-eisei）
¶子供はよい環境で育てなければなりません。（Kodomo wa yoi *kankyō* de sodatenakereba narimasen.）

kankyō 〔n〕 **environment, surroundings**
social **environment** // home **environment** // **environmental** hygiene〚sanitation〛
¶ Children should be raised in a good home **environment**.

かんけい 関係〔名、〜する〕

¶あなたと上田さんとは、どういう関係ですか。（Anata to Ueda san to wa, dōiu *kankei* desu ka？）
¶A国とB国との関係が悪化しました。（Ē-koku to Bii-koku to no *kankei* ga akka shimashita.）
¶わたしはその会には関係していません。（Watashi wa sono kai ni wa *kankei* shite imasen.）

kankei 〔n、〜*suru*〕 **relation, relationship**
¶ What is your **connection** with [Mr.] Ueda?

¶ **Relations** worsened between countries A and B.

¶ I have **nothing to do** with that association〚club, etc.〛.

かんげい 歓迎〔名、〜する〕

¶あなたを心から歓迎します。（Anata o kokoro kara *kangei* shimasu.）
¶山田さんのために歓迎会を開きました。（Yamada san no tame ni *kangei*kai o hirakimashita.）

kangei 〔n、〜*suru*〕 **welcome**
¶ I **welcome** you from the bottom of my heart.
¶ [We] held a **welcoming** party〚reception〛 for [Mrs.] Yamada.

かんこう 観光〔名〕

観光地（*kankō*chi）観光バス（*kankō*-basu）観光客（*kankō*kyaku）観光旅行（*kankō*-ryokō）
¶京都は観光都市として有名です。（Kyōto wa *kankō*-toshi to shite yūmei desu.）

kankō 〔n〕 **sightseeing**
a **resort** area, a **sightseeing** place // a **sightseeing** bus // **a tourist** // a **sightseeing** trip
¶ Kyoto is famous as a **tourist** city.

かんごふ　看護婦〔名〕

¶わたしの姉は看護婦をしています。
（Watashi no ane wa *kangofu* o shite
imasu.）
¶看護婦さん、頭が痛いんですが…。
（*Kangofu* san, atama ga itai n desu ga...）

kangofu 〔n〕 **nurse**

¶My elder sister is **a nurse**.

¶**Nurse**, my head aches.

かんさつ　観察〔名、〜する〕

¶わたしの子供は虫の観察に興味を
持っています。（Watashi no kodomo wa
mushi no *kansatsu* ni kyōmi o motte
imasu.）
¶植物の生長を観察しています。
（Shokubutsu no seichō o *kansatsu* shite
imasu.）

kansatsu 〔n, 〜*suru*〕 **observation**

¶My children are interested in
observing insects.

¶[He] **is studying** the growth of plants.

かんじ　感じ〔名〕

①[感覚]
¶氷を長い間持っていると、冷たくて
指の感じがなくなってきます。（Koori
o nagai aida motte iru to, tsumetakute yubi
no *kanji* ga nakunatte kimasu.）
②[ものごとから受ける感情・印象]
¶あの人はとても感じのいい人です。
（Ano hito wa totemo *kanji* no ii hito
desu.）
¶この絵は明るい感じの絵ですね。
（Kono e wa akarui *kanji* no e desu ne.）

kanji 〔n〕 **feeling, sensation;
impression, feeling**

① [feeling, sensation]
¶When one holds ice for a long time,
the cold makes one lose **the sensation**
in one's fingers.

② [impression, feeling, effect]
¶[He] is a very **nice** person.

¶This is a **cheerful** picture〚painting〛,
isn't it?

かんじ　漢字〔名〕
当用漢字（tōyō*kanji*）

¶あした、漢字の試験があります。
（Ashita, *kanji* no shiken ga arimasu.）
¶日本人の名前はほとんど漢字で書か
れています。（Nihonjin no namae wa
hotondo *kanji* de kakarete imasu.）

kanji 〔n〕 **Chinese characters**
the *tōyō* **kanji** (the Chinese
characters designated for daily use)
¶There's a **kanji** test tomorrow.

¶Almost all Japanese personal names
are written in **kanji**.

かんしゃ 感謝 〔名、〜する〕

¶クラスを代表して、先生に感謝の言葉を述べたいと思います。(Kurasu o daihyō shite, sensei ni *kansha* no kotoba o nobetai to omoimasu.)

¶御親切を心から感謝します。(Goshinsetsu o kokoro kara *kansha* shimasu.)

kansha 〔n, 〜*suru*〕 thanks, gratitude

¶ Representing the class, I would like to express **our gratitude** to you, sir 〚ma'am〛 (said to one's teacher or professor).

¶ **I am** deeply **grateful** for your kindness to me.

かんじょう 勘定 〔名、〜する〕

① [計算]
お金を勘定する (okane o *kanjō* suru)
¶箱の中にりんごがいくつあるか勘定してください。(Hako no naka ni ringo ga ikutsu aru ka *kanjō* shite kudasai.)
② [支払い]
¶お勘定をお願いします。(*Okanjō* o onegai shimasu.)

¶今日の勘定はわたしが払います。(Kyō no *kanjō* wa watashi ga haraimasu.)

¶勘定を済ませて、ホテルを出ました。(*Kanjō* o sumasete, hoteru o demashita.)
→会計 **kaikei**

kanjō 〔n, 〜*suru*〕 counting, calculation, computation; payment, settlement of accounts

① [counting, calculation, computation]
count money
¶ Please **count** how many apples are in the box.

② [payment, settlement of accounts]
¶ **The bill**, please.

¶ I'll pay today (for dinner, etc.).

¶ [I] paid **the bill** and checked out of the hotel.

かんじょう 感情 〔名〕

¶あの人は、あまり感情を顔に表しません。(Ano hito wa, amari *kanjō* o kao ni arawashimasen.)
¶人間は感情の動物です。(Ningen wa *kanjō* no dōbutsu desu.)

kanjō 〔n〕 feeling, emotion

¶ [He] doesn't show [his] feelings very much in [his] face.

¶ Humans are **emotional** creatures.

かんじる 感じる 〔動 II〕

① [感覚を生じる]

kanjiru 〔v II〕 feel, experience; feel, be struck by

① [feel, experience]

¶手術をしましたが、あまり痛みは感じませんでした。(Shujutsu o shimashita ga, amari itami wa *kanjimasen*deshita.)

¶ I had an operation but **I didn't feel** much pain.

②[ものごとに対してある気持ちを抱く]

② [feel, be struck by, be affected by]

¶外国語の必要を感じて、勉強を始めました。(Gaikokugo no hitsuyō o *kanjite*, benkyō o hajimemashita.)

¶ **I realized** the necessity of knowing foreign languages and started studying one.

かんしん 感心 〔名、形動、～する〕

kanshin 〔n, adj-v, ～*suru*〕 **admiration, wonder**

¶まだ子供なのに、よく働いて感心ですね。(Mada kodomo nanoni, yoku hataraite *kanshin* desu ne.)

¶ **I'm impressed** at how hard [he] works even though still a child.

¶あの犬は、どろぼうを捕まえた感心な犬です。(Ano inu wa, dorobō o tsukamaeta *kanshin* na inu desu.)

¶ That's **some** dog! It caught a thief.

¶上田さんは山田さんの上手な話し方にたいへん感心したようです。(Ueda san wa Yamada san no jōzu na hanashikata ni taihen *kanshin* shita yō desu.)

¶ [Mr.] Ueda seems **to have been** very **impressed** by [Mr.] Yamada's skillful way of talking.

かんせい 完成 〔名、～する〕

kansei 〔n, ～*suru*〕 **completion**

¶わたしの研究も完成に近づいてきました。(Watashi no kenkyū mo *kansei* ni chikazuite kimashita.)

¶ My research is nearing **completion**.

¶この建物は去年の10月に完成しました。(Kono tatemono wa kyonen no jūgatsu ni *kansei* shimashita.)

¶ This building **was completed** in October of last year.

かんせつ 間接 〔名〕

kansetsu 〔u〕 **indirectness, indirect**

間接税 (*kansetsuzei*) 間接話法 (*kansetsu*-wahō) 間接的な影響 (*kansetsu*teki na eikyō)

an **indirect** tax, **indirect** taxation // **indirect** narration // an **indirect** influence

¶上田さんとは直接話したことはありませんが、友人を通して間接に知っています。(Ueda san to wa choku-setsu hanashita koto wa arimasen ga, yūjin o tooshite *kansetsu* ni shitte imasu.)

¶ I've never spoken directly with [Mr.] Ueda but I know of [him] **at second hand** through friends.

⇔直接 **chokusetsu**

かんぜん　完全 〔名、形動〕

完全無欠 (*kanzen*-muketsu) 不完全 (fu*kanzen*)

¶今度の実験は完全に失敗しました。(Kondo no jikken wa *kanzen* ni shippai shimashita.)

¶この建物はまだ完全にでき上がっていません。(Kono tatemono wa mada *kanzen* ni dekiagatte imasen.)

kanzen 〔n, adj-v〕 **perfection, perfect, completeness, complete absolute** perfection // im**perfect**, in**complete**

¶ This experiment was a **complete** failure.

¶ This building is not yet **completely** finished.

かんたん　簡単 〔形動〕

①[ものごとが単純・簡略である様子]

¶時間がないので、簡単に説明します。(Jikan ga nai node, *kantan* ni setsu-mei shimasu.)

¶これは簡単な機械ですから、だれにでも動かせますよ。(Kore wa *kantan* na kikai desu kara, dare ni demo ugokasemasu yo.)

→複雑 **fukuzatsu**

②[ものごとが平易でわかりやすい様子]

¶こんな簡単な問題がわからないのですか。(Konna *kantan* na mondai ga wakaranai no desu ka?)

¶試験は意外に簡単でした。(Shiken wa igai ni *kantan* deshita.)

kantan 〔adj-v〕 **simple**

① [simple, uncomplicated, brief]

¶ Since there isn't much time, [I]'ll explain **briefly**.

¶ This is a **simple** machine that anyone can operate.

② [simple, easy]

¶ You mean you don't understand this sort of **simple** problem?

¶ The test was surprisingly **easy**.

かんづめ　かん詰め〔名〕

¶これは牛肉のかん詰めです。(Kore wa gyūniku no *kanzume* desu.)

⇒-詰め -zume

kanzume 〔n〕 **canned goods, canned food**

¶This is **a can** of beef.

がんばる〔動Ⅰ〕

¶試験が近いので、夜遅くまでがんばって勉強しています。(Shikenga chikai node, yoru osoku made *ganbatte* benkyō shite imasu.)

¶がんばってください。(*Ganbatte* kudasai)

ganbaru 〔v Ⅰ〕 **persist, hold firm**

¶The exam is close so [I]'m **staying up** and studying until late at night.

¶**Don't give up**〖**Never say die; Keep on fighting;** etc.〗.

かんばん　看板〔名〕

酒屋の看板 (sakaya no *kanban*)

¶映画館の看板はほかの看板と比べて大きいです。(Eigakan no *kanban* wa hoka no *kanban* to kurabete ookii desu.)

kanban 〔n〕 **signboard, sign**

a liquor shop **sign**

¶**The signboards** for movie theaters are large compared to other **signboards**.

199

き

き 木 〔名〕

¶庭に桜の木を植えました。(Niwa ni sakura no *ki* o uemashita.)

¶都会には木が少ないです。(Tokai ni wa *ki* ga sukunai desu.)

¶日本には木でできた家が多いです。(Nihon ni wa *ki* de dekita ie ga ooi desu.)

ki 〔n〕 tree, shrub, wood

¶ [I] planted a cherry **tree** in the garden 〖yard〗.

¶ There are few **trees** 〖is little **foliage**〗 in the city.

¶ There are many houses made of **wood** in Japan.

き 気 〔名〕

① [注意する]

¶病気にならないように気をつけてください。(Byōki ni naranai yō ni *ki* o tsukete kudasai.)

¶気をつけないと、自動車にひかれますよ。(*Ki* o tsukenai to, jidōsha ni hikaremasu yo.)

*いつも「気をつける (ki o tsukeru)」「気をつけない (ki o tsukenai)」の形で使う。

② [あることがらを意識するようになる]

¶電車を降りてから、かばんがないのに気がつきました。(Densha o orite kara, kaban ga nai no ni *ki* ga tsukimashita.)

¶わたしがあいさつをしたのに、上田さんは気がつきませんでした。(Watashi ga aisatsu o shita noni, Ueda san wa *ki* ga tsukimasen deshita.)

*いつも「気がつく (ki ga tsuku)」「気がつかない (ki ga tsukanai)」の形で使う。

→気づく kizuku

③ [ものごとに対してある感じを持つ]

ki 〔n〕 spirit, mood, feeling, mind

① [be careful, take care, pay attention to]

¶ Please **take care** not to become ill.

¶ **Look out** or you will be hit by a car!

*Always used in the patterns "*ki o tsukeru*" and "*ki o tsukenai*."

② [notice, become aware of, perceive]

¶ After getting off the train **I noticed** that I didn't have my bag 〖suitcase, briefcase, etc.〗.

¶ Although I greeted [him], [Mr.] Ueda **didn't notice** me.

*Always used in the patterns "*ki ga tsuku*" and "*ki ga tsukanai*."

③ [feel, think, have the feeling that ～]

200

¶ 日本に来てまだ2週間しかたってい
ませんが、もう2か月もたったような
気がします。(Nihon ni kite mada
nishūkan shika tatte imasen ga, mō
nikagetsu mo tatta yō na *ki* ga shimasu.)

¶ I have the feeling that a big
earthquake is coming one of these days.

¶ そのうち大きな地震が来そうな気が
します。(Sonouchi ookina jishin ga kisō
na *ki* ga shimasu.)

¶ I have the feeling that a big
earthquake is coming one of these days.

¶ ここにいると、外国にいるような気
がしません。(Koko ni iru to, gaikoku ni
iru yō na *ki* ga shimasen.)

¶ When I'm here I don't feel like I'm in
a foreign country.

*いつも「気がする (ki ga suru)」「気
がしない (ki ga shinai)」の形で使う。

*Always used in the patterns "*ki ga
suru*" and "*ki ga shinai*."

④ [あることをいつも考えて心配した
り心を煩わしたりする]

④ [mind, be concerned about, worry
about]

¶ 中村さんは試験の点ばかり気にして
います。(Nakamura san wa shiken no
ten bakari *ki* ni shite imasu.)

¶ [Mr.] Nakamura is only concerned
about test marks.

¶ お金のことは気にしないで勉強だけ
しなさい。(Okane no koto wa *ki*ni
shinaide benkyō dake shinasai.)

¶ Just study and don't concern
yourself with money matters.

*いつも「気にする (ki ni suru)」「気に
しない (ki ni shinai)」の形で使う。

*Always used in the patterns "*ki ni
suru*" and "*ki ni shinai*."

⑤ [あることが頭から離れないで落ち
着かない]

⑤ [be bothered about, weigh on one's
mind, get on one's nerves]

¶ 試験のことが気になって、眠れませ
んでした。(Shiken no koto ga *ki*ni natte,
nemuremasen deshita.)

¶ I couldn't sleep for worrying about
the exam.

¶ 隣の部屋の音が気になって勉強でき
ません。(Tonari no heya no oto ga *ki* ni
natte benkyō dekimasen.)

¶ I'm bothered by the noise 〚sounds〛
next door so that I can't study 〚I can't
study with those sounds going on next
door〛.

¶わたしは周りがうるさくても気になりません。(Watashi wa mawari ga urusakute mo *ki* ni narimasen.)

¶隣に座った美人が気になって、落ち着いて本が読めませんでした。(Tonari ni suwatta bijin ga *ki* ni natte, ochitsuite hon ga yomemasen deshita.)

*いつも「気になる (ki ni naru)」「気にならない (ki ni naranai)」の形で使う。

⑥ [安全や健康などが心配になる]

¶病気で寝ている母のことがいつも気にかかっています。(Byōki de nete iru haha no koto ga itsu mo *ki* ni kakatte imasu.)

¶飛行機が予定の時間を過ぎても到着しないので、気にかかります。(Hikōki ga yotei no jikan o sugite mo tōchaku shinai node, *ki* ni kakarimasu.)

*いつも「気にかかる (ki ni kakaru)」の形で使う。

⑦ [満足する、好きになる]

¶この部屋が気に入ったので、借りることにしました。(Kono heya ga *ki* ni itta node, kariru koto ni shimashita.)

¶壁の色が気に入らないので、塗り替えることにしました。(Kabe no iro ga *ki* ni iranai node, nurikaeru koto ni shimashita.)

*いつも「気に入る (ki ni iru)」「気に入らない (ki ni iranai)」の形で使う。

⑧ [何かをしようと思う]

¶ **It doesn't bother me** if it's noisy around me.

¶ **I was so conscious** of the beautiful woman sitting next to me that I couldn't concentrate on my book.

*Always used in the patterns "*ki ni naru*" and "*ki ni naranai*."

⑥ [worry about, be anxious about]

¶ **I am** always **anxious** about my mother who is ill in bed.

¶ **I am worried** because the plane hasn't arrived yet even though it's past its scheduled time of arrival.

*Always used in the pattern "*ki ni kakaru*."

⑦ [be pleased with, like, take a liking to]

¶ I've decided to rent this room 〖apartment〗 as **it's to my liking**.

¶ I decided to repaint the walls 〖have the walls repainted〗 as **I don't like** the present color.

*Always used in the patterns "*ki ni iru*" and "*ki ni iranai*."

⑧ [feel like ～ing, be disposed to]

¶この会社で働く気があるなら、社長に紹介してあげましょう。(Kono kaisha de hataraku *ki ga aru nara*, shachō ni shōkai shite agemashō.)

¶勉強する気がないのに、大学へ行ってもむだです。(Benkyō suru *ki ga nai* noni, daigaku e itte mo muda desu.)

¶あまり暑いので、仕事をする気がしません。(Amari atsui node, shigoto o suru *ki ga shimasen*.)

¶日本に一度行ってみたい気がします。(Nihon ni ichido itte mitai *ki ga* shimasu.)

*いつも「～する気がある（～suru ki ga aru)」「～する気がない（～suru ki ga nai)」「～する気がする（～suru ki ga suru)」「～する気がしない（～suru ki ga shinai)」の形で使う。

¶ If you think **you'd like** to work at this company, I'll introduce you to the president.

¶ It's useless to go to college if **you don't want** to study.

¶ **I don't feel like** working as it's so hot.

¶ **I'd like** to go to Japan at least once.

*Always used in the patterns "~ *suru ki ga aru* ," "~ *suru ki ga nai* ," "~ *suru ki ga suru* ," and "~ *suru ki ga shinai*."

-き -器〔尾〕

① [器具]
食器（shok*ki*）洗面器（senmen*ki*）電熱器（dennetsu*ki*）消火器（shōka*ki*）受話器（juwa*ki*）楽器（gak*ki*）

② [器官]
消化器（shōka*ki*）呼吸器（kokyū*ki*）

-ki 〔suf〕 utensil, tool, apparatus; bodily organ

① [utensil, tool, apparatus]
tableware, a dinner **set** // a wash**basin**, wash**bowl** // an electric hot **plate** // a fire **extinguisher** // a telephone **receiver** // a musical **instrument**

② [bodily organ]
digestive **organs** // respiratory **organs**

-き -機〔尾〕

① [機械]
写真機（shashin*ki*）印刷機（insatsu*ki*）扇風機（senpū*ki*）洗たく機（sentaku*ki*）

② [飛行機]
ジェット機（jetto*ki*）旅客機（ryo-kak*ki*）

③ [飛行機などの数を表す]

-ki 〔suf〕 machine; aircraft

① [machine, mechanism]
a camera // a printing **machine**, press // an electric fan // a washing **machine**

② [aircraft]
a jet **plane** // a passenger **plane**, an airliner

③ [the counter for aircraft]

1機 (ik*ki*) 2機 (ni*ki*) 3機 (san*ki*) 6機 (rok*ki*) 何機 (nan*ki*)

one **plane** 〖helicopter, etc.〗 // two **planes** // three **planes** // six **planes** // how many **planes**

きいろ 黄色 〔名〕

¶田中さんは黄色のシャツを着ています。(Tanaka san wa *kiiro* no shatsu o kite imasu.)

kiiro 〔n〕 **yellow**

¶[Mr.] Tanaka is wearing a **yellow** shirt 〖knit shirt, T-shirt, etc.〗.

きいろい 黄色い 〔形〕

¶あの黄色い本が、あなたの探している本ですよ。(Ano *kiiroi* hon ga, anata no sagashiteiru hon desu yo.)

kiiroi 〔adj〕 **yellow**

¶That yellow book is the one you are looking for.

きえる 消える 〔動Ⅱ〕

① [明かりや火などがなくなる]
¶風でろうそくの火が消えました。(Kaze de rōsoku no hi ga *kiemashita*.)
¶電気が突然消えました。(Denki ga totsuzen *kiemashita*.)
② [ものの形や姿などが見えなくなる]
¶飛行機が夜空に消えていきました。(Hikōki ga yozora ni *kiete* ikimashita.)

kieru 〔v Ⅱ〕 **go out, be extinguished; vanish, disappear**
① [go out, be extinguished]
¶The candle **went out** in the wind 〖draft〗.
¶The lights suddenly **went out**.
② [vanish, disappear]
¶The airplane **disappeared** in the night sky.

きおく 記憶 〔名、〜する〕

記憶力 (*kioku*ryoku)
¶わたしは一度あの人に会った記憶があります。(Watashi wa ichido ano hito ni atta *kioku* ga arimasu.)
¶小さい時のことはほとんど記憶していません。(Chiisai toki no koto wa hotondo *kioku* shite imasen.)

kioku 〔n, 〜*suru*〕 **memory recollection**
memory, one's powers of **memory**
¶I have a **memory** of once meeting [him].
¶[I] **remember** hardly anything of when [I] was small.

きおん 気温 〔名〕

気温が上がる (*kion* ga agaru) 気温が下がる (*kion* ga sagaru)

kion 〔n〕 **(atmospheric) temperature**
the **temperature** rises // the **temperature** falls

¶一日のうちで気温がいちばん高くなるのは午後の2時ごろです。(Ichi-nichi no uchi de *kion* ga ichiban takaku naru no wa gogo no niji goro desu.)

¶The highest **temperature** of the day comes at around two o'clock in the afternoon.

きかい 機会〔名〕

kikai 〔n〕 **opportunity, chance, occasion**

¶わたしの国には日本人がほとんどいないので、日本語を話す機会がありません。(Watashi no kuni ni wa Nihonjin ga hotondo inai node, Nihongo o hanasu *kikai* ga arimasen.)

¶As there are hardly any Japanese in my country, there are no **opportunities** for me to speak Japanese.

¶わたしは機会があれば、日本へ行きたいと思います。(Watashi wa *kikai* ga areba, Nihon e ikitai to omoimasu.)

¶I'd like to go to Japan if I had **the chance**.

きかい 機械〔名〕

kikai 〔n〕 **machine, machinery, mechanism, device, apparatus**

¶この機械は日本製です。(Kono *kikai* wa Nihonsei desu.)

¶This **machinery** was made in Japan.

¶わたしはこの機械の動かし方がわかりません。(Watashi wa kono *kikai* no ugokashikata ga wakarimasen.)

¶I don't know how to operate this **machine**.

きかえる 着替える〔動Ⅱ〕

kikaeru 〔v Ⅱ〕 **change clothes**

¶雨にぬれたので、洋服を着替えました。(Ame ni nureta node, yōfuku o *kikaemashita*.)

¶[I] **changed** the clothes that had gotten wet in the rain.

＊「着替える（kigaeru)」とも言う。

＊Variant: *kigaeru*.

きかん 期間〔名〕

kikan 〔n〕 **term, period of time**

¶あなたが外国にいた期間はどのくらいですか。(Anata ga gaikoku ni ita *kikan* wa dono kurai desu ka？)

¶How long was **your stay** abroad?

¶東京での滞在期間は1週間の予定です。(Tōkyō de no taizai-*kikan* wa isshūkan no yotei desu.)

¶The scheduled **time** of stay in Tokyo is one week.

きかん 機関〔名〕

kikan 〔n〕 **engine; institution**

①[エンジン]

①[engine]

蒸気機関車 (jōki-*kikan*sha) 電気機関車 (denki-*kikan*sha)

a steam **locomotive** // an electric **locomotive**

② [ある目的を持った組織]

② [institution, facilities, system; an organization with a set purpose]

教育機関 (kyōiku-*kikan*)

an educational **institution**

¶ 都市は交通機関が発達しています。(Toshi wa kōtsū-*kikan* ga hattatsu shite imasu.)

¶ Transportation **facilities** are advanced in the city.

きぎょう 企業 〔名〕

kigyō 〔n〕 **business, enterprise, undertaking**

中小企業 (chūshō-*kigyō*)

small and medium **enterprises**, minor **enterprises**

¶ 大企業で働いている人は労働条件がいいです。(Dai*kigyō* de hataraite iru hito wa rōdō-jōken ga ii desu.)

¶ Working conditions are good for those working for big **business**.

¶ 個人企業の経営はなかなかたいへんです。(Kojin-*kigyō* no keiei wa nakanaka taihen desu.)

¶ Private **enterprises**〚One-man **businesses**〛are quite difficult to run.

きく 聞く 〔動Ⅰ〕

kiku 〔vⅠ〕 **hear, listen to; obey**

① [音や声を耳に入れて理解する]

① [hear, listen to]

話を聞く (hanashi o *kiku*)

listen to a story, **listen to** someone talking

¶ 山田さんは今部屋で音楽を聞いています。(Yamada san wa ima heya de ongaku o *kiite* imasu.)

¶ [Miss] Yamada **is listening to** music in [her] room now.

¶ あなたは上田さんが病気だということをだれから聞きましたか。(Anata wa Ueda san ga byōki da to iu koto o dare kara *kikimashita* ka?)

¶ Who **did you hear** about [Mr.] Ueda's illness from〚Who told you about Mr. Ueda's illness〛?

② [要求・注意などを受け入れる]

② [obey, comply]

¶ あの子は両親の言うことをよく聞きます。(Ano ko wa ryōshin no iu koto o yoku *kikimasu*.)

¶ That child **minds** its parents.

きく 利く 〔動Ⅰ〕

kiku 〔vⅠ〕 **work, act**

¶ この車はブレーキが利きません。(Kono kuruma wa burēki ga *kiki-masen*.)

¶ This car's〚cart's, etc.〛brakes **don't work**.

きく 効く 〔動 I〕

¶この薬は風邪にとてもよく効きます。(Kono kusuri wa kaze ni totemo yoku *kikimasu*.)

kiku 〔v I〕 **be effective, be good for**

¶This medicine **is** very **effective** for colds.

きく 菊 〔名〕

¶日本では、秋になると菊の花が咲きます。(Nihon de wa, aki ni naru to *kiku* no hana ga sakimasu.)

kiku 〔n〕 **chrysanthemum**

¶**Chrysanthemums** bloom in the autumn in Japan.

きく 〔動 I〕

¶交番で駅へ行く道をききました。(Kōban de eki e iku michi o *kikimashita*.)

¶わからないことは何でも先生にききなさい。(Wakaranai koto wa nan demo sensei ni *kikinasai*.)

kiku 〔v I〕 **ask, inquire**

¶[I] **asked** for directions to the station at a police box.

¶**Ask** your teacher about anything at all that you don't understand.

きけん 危険 〔名、形動〕

¶危険だから、触らないでください。(*Kiken* da kara, sawaranaide kudasai.)

¶危険な所へ行ってはいけません。(*Kiken* na tokoro e itte wa ikemasen.)

¶大水のために、この辺は危険になってきました。(Oomizu no tame ni, kono hen wa *kiken* ni natte kimashita.)

⇔安全 anzen

kiken 〔n, adj-v〕 **danger, risk, hazard**

¶Don't touch it — **it's dangerous**.

¶You shouldn't go to **dangerous** places.

¶Flooding has made this area **unsafe**.

きげん 期限 〔名〕

¶このキップは期限が切れていますよ。(Kono kippu wa *kigen* ga kirete imasu yo.)

¶借りた本は期限内に返してください。(Karita hon wa *kigen*nai ni kaeshite kudasai.)

¶2年の期限つきで家を借りました。(Ninen no *kigen*tsuki de ie o karimashita.)

kigen 〔n〕 **term, period, time limit**

¶This ticket has **expired**.

¶Please return borrowed books within **the time limit**.

¶[I] rented a house for **a term** of two years.

きげん〔名〕

① [快・不快などの心の状態]
¶山田さんは試験で100点を取ったので、とてもきげんがいいです。
(Yamada san wa shiken de hyaku-ten o totta node, totemo *kigen* ga ii desu.)
¶わたしが遅れてきたので、田中さんはきげんが悪いです。(Watashi ga okurete kita node, Tanaka san wa *kigen* ga warui desu.)
¶上田さんは、わたしにきげんよく会ってくれました。(Ueda san wa, watashi ni *kigen* yoku atte kuremashita.)
② [他人の健康・気分の状態]
¶ごきげんいかがですか。(Go*kigen* ikaga desu ka？)
*あいさつの言葉として「ごきげん（gokigen)」の形で使う。

きこう 気候〔名〕
¶わたしの国は、一年じゅうあまり気候の変化がありません。(Watashi no kuni wa, ichinenjū amari *kikō* no henka ga arimasen.)

きこえる 聞こえる〔動Ⅱ〕

① [音や声が耳に入る]
¶聞こえませんから、もっと大きい声で話してください。(Kikoemasen kara, motto ookii koe de hanashite kudasai.)
② [そのように思える、そのように理解される]
¶上田さんの話は本当らしく聞こえますが、ほとんどうそです。(Ueda san no hanashi wa, hontō rashiku *kikoemasu* ga, hotondo uso desu.)

kigen 〔n〕 **humor, temper, mood; state of health or mind**

① [humor, temper, mood]
¶ [Miss] Yamada is in a very good **mood** as [she] scored 100 on the test.

¶ [Mr.] Tanaka is in a bad **mood** as I came late.

¶ [Mrs.] Ueda met me in a good **mood**.

② [state of health or mind]
¶ How are you?

*Used in the form *gokigen* in greetings.

kikō 〔n〕 **climate, weather**
¶ In my country there is little variation in **climate** throughout the year.

kikoeru 〔v Ⅱ〕 **hear, be heard; sound ～, seem ～**
① [hear, be heard, be audible]
¶ [I] **can't hear** you. Please speak up.

② [sound ～, seem ～]

¶ What [Mr.] Ueda says **sounds** true but is almost all false.

きこく 帰国 〔名、〜する〕

¶だんだん帰国の日が近づいてきましたね。(Dandan *kikoku* no hi ga chikazuite kimashita ne.)

¶1年間の留学が終わって、間もなく帰国します。(Ichinenkan no ryū-gaku ga owatte, mamonaku *kikoku* shimasu.)

kikoku 〔n, 〜*suru*〕 **return to one's country**

¶ The day of **[your] return home** is getting closer and closer, isn't it?

¶ [My] year of study abroad is ending and soon [I] **will be returning to [my] own country**.

きし 岸 〔名〕

¶船が岸に近づいてきました。(Fune ga *kishi* ni chikazuite kimashita.)

¶川岸で子供が遊んでいます。(Kawa-*gishi* de kodomo ga asonde imasu.)

kishi 〔n〕 **banks, shore, coast**

¶ The boat is nearing 〚neared〛 **the shore**.

¶ Children are playing along the river**bank**.

きじ 記事 〔名〕

新聞記事 (shinbun-*kiji*)

¶今朝の新聞におもしろい記事が出ていました。(Kesa no shinbun ni omoshiroi *kiji* ga dete imashita.)

kiji 〔n〕 **news story, article (in a newspaper or magazine)**

newspaper **article** 〚**account**〛

¶ There was an interesting **item** in this morning's newspaper.

きじ 生地 〔名〕

¶このワイシャツの生地は木綿です。(Kono waishatsu no *kiji* wa momen desu.)

kiji 〔n〕 **cloth**

¶ **The material** of this shirt is cotton.

きしゃ 記者 〔名〕

新聞記者 (shinbun-*kisha*) 雑誌記者 (zasshi-*kisha*)

kisha 〔n〕 **reporter, journalist**

a newspaper **reporter** // a magazine **writer**, journalist

きしゃ 汽車 〔名〕

汽車に乗る (*kisha* ni noru) 汽車を降りる (*kisha* o oriru) 東京行きの汽車 (Tōkyō yuki no *kisha*) 東京発の汽車 (Tōkyō hatsu no *kisha*) 汽車賃 (*kisha*chin)

kisha 〔n〕 **train**

take **a train**, ride in **a train**, board a **train** // get off **a train** // **a train** bound for Tokyo, the Tokyo **train** // **the train** from Tokyo, **a train** starting in Tokyo // **a railroad** fare

ぎじゅつ 技術〔名〕

技術者 (gijutsusha) 工業技術
(kōgyō-gijutsu) 技術の進歩 (gijutsu
no shinpo)
¶この国の農業技術はたいへん進んで
います。(Kono kuni no nōgyō-gijutsu
wa taihen susunde imasu.)

gijutsu 〔n〕 **technique, skill,
technology**

a technicalexpert, **technician,
engineer** // industrial **technology** // the
advance of **technology**

¶ The agricultural **techniques** of this
country are very advanced.

きず 傷〔名〕

① [けがなどをして体についたあと]

¶その足の傷はどうしたのですか。
(Sono ashi no kizu wa dō shita no
desuka？)
¶わたしは医者へ行って、傷の手当て
をしてもらいました。(Watashi wa isha
e itte, kizu no teate o shite moraimashita.)
② [品物が傷んでいること]

¶このりんごにはきずがありますよ。
(Kono ringo ni wa kizu ga arimasu yo.)
¶この花びんはきずがついているから
安いです。(Kono kabin wa kizu ga tsuite
iru kara yasui desu.)

kizu 〔n〕 **wound, injury; flaw,
disfigurement**

① [wound, injury, cut, scratch, bruise,
scar ; refers to living creatures]

¶ How did you get that leg〚foot〛
injury〚**scar**〛?

¶ I went to the doctor and had my
injury treated.

② [flaw, disfigurement, defect, crack,
scratch, bruise ; refers to objects]

¶ This apple **is bruised**.

¶ This vase is cheap because it **is
defective**〚**is scratched**〛.

きすう 奇数〔名〕

¶1、3、5という数は奇数と言い、2、
4、6は偶数と言います。(Ichi, san, go
to iu sū wa kisū to ii, ni, shi, roku wa gūsū
to iimasu.)
⇔偶数 **gūsū**

kisū 〔n〕 **odd number, uneven
number**

¶ One, three and five are called **odd
numbers**, and two, four and six are
called even numbers.

きせつ 季節〔名〕

¶桜の咲く季節になりました。
(Sakura no saku kisetsu ni narimashita.)

kisetsu 〔n〕 **season, time of the
year**

¶ The cherry blossom **season** has
〚had〛 started.

¶日本では四つの季節がはっきりしています。(Nihon de wa yottsu no *kisetsu* ga hakkiri shite imasu.)

¶ Japan has four distinct **seasons**.

きそ 基礎〔名〕

① [建物の土台]

¶この家は基礎がしっかりしています。(Kono ie wa *kiso* ga shikkari shite imasu.)

② [学問などのもとになるたいせつな部分]

¶どんな勉強でも基礎が大切です。(Donna benkyō demo *kiso* ga taisetsu desu.)

kiso〔n〕 **foundation, base**

① [foundation (of a building)]

¶ This house has a solid **foundation**.

② [base, foundation (of learning, etc.)]

¶ A firm grounding in **the basics** is important in any field of study.

きそく 規則〔名〕

交通規則（kōtsū-*kisoku*）規則を守る（*kisoku* o mamoru）規則を破る（*kisoku* o yaburu）

¶学生は学校の規則に従わなければなりません。(Gakusei wa gakkō no *kisoku* ni shitagawanakereba narimasen.)

¶わたしは毎日規則正しい生活をしています。(Watashi wa mainichi *kisoku* tadashii seikatsu o shite imasu.)

¶中村さんは不規則な生活をしたので、病気になってしまいました。(Nakamura san wa fu*kisoku* na seikatsu o shita node, byōki ni natte shimaimashita.)

¶会は1か月に2回、規則的に開かれています。(Kai wa ikkagetsu ni nikai, *kisoku*teki ni hirakarete imasu.)

kisoku〔n〕 **rule, regulations**

traffic **regulations** // obey **the rules** // break **the rules**

¶ Students must observe school **regulations**.

¶ I live a **regular** life〚keep **regular** hours〛.

¶ [Mr.] Nakamura became ill because [he] led an **irregular** life.

¶ The club〚association, group〛meets **regularly** twice a month.

きた 北〔名〕

北風（*kita*kaze）北側（*kita*gawa）北向き（*kita*muki）

kita〔n〕 **north**

north wind, **northerly** wind // the **north** side // **northern** exposure, facing **north**

¶北国ではもう雪が降っています。　　　¶ Snow is already falling in **the North**.
(*Kita*guni de wa mō yuki ga futte imasu.)
⇔南 **minami**

ギター〔名〕　　　　　　　　　　**gitā** 〔n〕 **guitar**
ギターを弾く (*gitā* o hiku)　　　　play **the guitar**
¶彼はギターが上手です。(Kare wa　　¶ He plays **the guitar** well.
gitā ga jōzu desu.)
¶ギターに合わせて、みんなで歌いま　　¶ All sang accompanied by **a guitar**.
した。(*Gitā* ni awasete, mina de
utaimashita.)

きたい　期待〔名、〜する〕　　　**kitai** 〔n, 〜*suru*〕 **expectation,**
　　　　　　　　　　　　　　　　　anticipation, hope
¶あの青年は将来を期待されていま　　¶ **Much is expected** of that youth in
す。(Ano seinen wa shōrai o *kitai* sarete　the future.
imasu.)
¶その音楽会は期待していたとおりす　　¶ That concert 〚recital〛 was as
ばらしいものでした。(Sono ongakukai　marvelous **as expected**.
wa *kitai* shite ita toori subarashii mono
deshita.)

きたい　気体〔名〕　　　　　　　**kitai** 〔n〕 **a gaseous body, gas,**
　　　　　　　　　　　　　　　　　vapor
¶空気は気体です。(Kūki wa *kitai*　　¶ The air is **gaseous**.
desu.)
⇒液体 **ekitai**　固体 **kotai**

きたない　汚い〔形〕　　　　　　**kitanai** 〔adj〕 **dirty**
¶汚い手で触らないでください。　　　¶ Please don't touch it 〚me〛 with **dirty**
(*Kitanai* te de sawaranaide kudasai.)　hands.
¶掃除をしないので、部屋が汚くなっ　　¶ The room has gotten **dirty** as [I]
ています。(Sōji o shinai node, heya ga　haven't been cleaning it.
kitanaku natte imasu.)

きちんと〔副〕　　　　　　　　**kichinto** 〔adv〕 **exactly; neatly**
① [正確な様子]　　　　　　　　　① [exactly, accurately, carefully,
　　　　　　　　　　　　　　　　　regularly]
¶上田さんは、約束どおりきちんと3　　¶ [Miss] Ueda came **punctually** at
時に来ました。(Ueda san wa, yaku-　three o'clock **sharp**.
soku doori *kichinto* sanji ni kimashita.)

② [整っている様子]

¶部屋の中をきちんと整理してください。(Heya no naka o *kichinto* seiri shite kudasai.)

¶田中さんはいつもきちんとしたかっこうをしています。(Tanaka san wa itsu mo *kichinto* shita kakkō o shite imasu.)

⇒ちゃんと **chanto**

きづく 気づく〔動 I〕

¶田中さんは自分が悪かったということに気づきました。(Tanaka san wa jibun ga warukatta to iu koto ni *kizukimashita*.)

¶山田さんはわたしに気づかないで、通り過ぎていきました。(Yamada san wa watashi ni *kizukanaide*, toorisugite ikimashita.)

＊普通「～に気づく（～ni kizuku)」の形で使う。

⇒気 **ki**

きっさてん 喫茶店〔名〕

¶わたしたちは喫茶店でコーヒーを飲みました。(Watashitachi wa *kissaten* de kōhii o nomimashita.)

きって 切手〔名〕

記念切手（kinen-*kitte*）切手をはる（*kitte* o haru）

きっと〔副〕

あの人はきっと来ますよ。(Ano hito wa *kitto* kimasu yo.)

¶いくら呼んでも返事がないから、きっと留守ですよ。(Ikura yonde mo henji ga nai kara, *kitto* rusu desu yo.)

② [neatly, tidily]

¶ Please **tidy up** the room.

¶ [Mr.] Tanaka is always **neatly dressed**〚**well-groomed**〛.

kizuku〔v I〕**notice, perceive, realize**

¶ [Mr.] Tanaka later **realized** that [he] had been at fault.

¶ [Miss] Yamada went by **without noticing** that I was there.

＊Generally used m the pattern "～ *ni kizuku*."

kissaten〔n〕**tearoom, coffee shop, cafe**

¶ We drank coffee in **a coffee shop**.

kitte〔n〕**(postage) stamp**

a commemorative **stamp** // paste a **stamp** on

kitto〔adv〕**certainly, undoubtedly**

¶ [He]'ll come **for sure**.

¶ [She] **must** not be at home as there's no reply no matter how much one calls to [her].

きっぷ 切符 〔名〕

¶東京までの切符を買いました。
（Tōkyō made no *kippu* o kaimashita.）
¶音楽会の切符はもう売り切れました。（Ongakukai no *kippu* wa mō urikire-mashita.）

kippu 〔n〕 **ticket**

¶ [I] bought **a ticket** to Tokyo.

¶ **The tickets** for the concert are already sold out.

きぬ 絹 〔名〕

絹のネクタイ（*kinu* no nekutai）

kinu 〔n〕 **silk**

a **silk** necktie

きねん 記念 〔名、〜する〕

記念日（*kinen*bi）記念品（*kinen*hin）
記念写真（*kinen*-shashin）

¶わたしたちは卒業を記念して、木を植えました。（Watashitachi wa sotsu-gyō o *kinen* shite, ki o uemashita.）

kinen 〔n, 〜*suru*〕 **commemoration**

a **memorial** day, an anniversary // a souvenir, memento, keepsake // a **souvenir** photograph

¶ We planted a tree **in commemoration** of our graduation.

きのう 昨日 〔名〕

¶昨日は何曜日でしたか。（*Kinō* wa nan'yōbi deshita ka？）
¶これは昨日の新聞です。（Kore wa *kinō* no shinbun desu.）

kinō 〔n〕 **yesterday**

¶ What day of the week was it **yesterday?**

¶ This is **yesterday's** newspaper.

きのどく 気の毒 〔形動〕

① [他人の不幸などに同情する様子]

¶あの人は火事で家が焼けて気の毒ですね。（Ano hito wa kaji de ie ga yakete *kinodoku* desu ne.）
② [迷惑をかけてすまないと思う様子]

¶昨日山田さんがわざわざ来てくれたのに、留守で気の毒なことをしました。（Kinō Yamada san ga wazawaza kite kureta noni, rusu de *kinodoku* na koto o shimashita.）

kinodoku 〔adj-v〕 **pitiful, poor, unfortunate, regrettable, too bad**

① [used in sympathy toward the misfortune of others]

¶ **What a pity it is** that [he] lost [his] house in a fire.

② [used to express one's regret at having inconvenienced others]

¶ **I feel bad** that I wasn't at home yesterday when [Miss] Yamada came to see me.

きびしい 厳しい〔形〕

① [厳格な]
¶あの先生はとても厳しいです。(Ano sensei wa totemo *kibishii* desu.)
¶わたしは子供を厳しく育てました。(Watashi wa kodomo o *kibishiku* sodatemashita.)
② [激しい、程度がはなはだしい]
¶二月になってから、寒さが厳しくなりました。(Nigatsu ni natte kara, samusa ga *kibishiku* narimashita.)

kibishii 〔adj〕 **severe, strict; intense, severe**

① [severe, strict, rigorous, harsh]
¶ That teacher is very **strict**.
¶ I raised my children **strictly**.

② [intense, severe, hard]
¶ The cold became **much more severe** from February.

きぶん 気分〔名〕

① [心の状態、気持ち]
¶元気がありませんね。気分が悪いのではありませんか。(Genki ga arimasen ne. *Kibun* ga warui no de wa arimasen ka?)
¶シャワーを浴びたあとはとてもいい気分です。(Shawā o abita ato wa totemo ii *kibun* desu.)
② [ふんいき]
¶町はお祭りで楽しい気分にあふれています。(Machi wa omatsuri de tanoshii *kibun* ni afurete imasu.)

kibun 〔n〕 **mood, feeling; atmosphere**

① [mood, feeling, frame of mind]
¶ You don't seem well. Do you **feel** ill?

¶ **One feels** really good after taking a shower.

② [atmosphere]
¶ The city has a merry festival **air**.

きぼう 希望〔名、～する〕

¶わたしの希望は、将来医者になることです。(Watashi no *kibō* wa, shōrai isha ni naru koto desu.)
¶あの人は日本留学を希望しています。(Ano hito wa Nihon-ryūgaku o *kibō* shite imasu.)

kibō 〔n, ～*suru*〕 **hope, desire, wish, aspiration**

¶ My **aspiration** is to become a doctor someday.

¶ [He] **hopes** to study in Japan.

きほん 基本〔名〕

基本的人権 (*kihon*teki-jinken)

kihon 〔n〕 **foundation, basis, standard**

fundamental human rights

215

¶何をするのにも基本が大事です。(Nani o suru no ni mo *kihon* ga daiji desu.)

¶何をするのにも基本を学ばなければなりません。(Nani o suru no ni mo *kihon* o manabanakereba narimasen.)

¶首相は外交についての基本的な考えを述べました。(Shushō wa gaikō ni tsuite no *kihon*teki na kangae o nobemashita.)

¶ **The fundamentals** 〚**basics**〛 are important no matter what one does.

¶ One must learn **the fundamentals** 〚**basics**〛 no matter what one does.

¶ The prime minister talked about [his] **fundamental** views on international relations.

きまり 決まり 〔名〕

kimari 〔n〕 **rule, regulation; settlement, conclusion**

① [決められていることがら、規則]

① [rule, regulation]

¶学校の決まりは守らなければなりません。(Gakkō no *kimari* wa mamoranakereba narimasen.)

¶ One must obey the school **rules**.

②[ものごとのしめくくり]

② [settlement, conclusion]

¶わたしはこの仕事に決まりをつけてから帰ります。(Watashi wa kono shigoto ni *kimari* o tsukete kara kaerimasu.)

¶ I will go home after **concluding** this piece of work.

*「決まりがつく (kimari ga tsuku)」「決まりをつける (kimari o tsukeru)」の形で使う。

*Used in the patterns "*kimari ga tsuku*" and "*kimari o tsukeru*."

きまる 決まる 〔動 I〕

kimaru 〔v I〕 **be decided, be settled, be fixed, be arranged**

¶会は来週開かれることに決まりました。(Kai wa raishū hirakareru koto ni *kimarimashita*.)

¶ **It has been decided** to hold the party 〚meeting, conference〛 next week.

¶出発の日が決まったら、知らせてください。(Shuppatsu no hi ga *ki-mattara*, shirasete kudasai.)

¶ Please inform me when the date of departure **has been fixed**.

¶田中さんには決まった仕事がありません。(Tanaka san ni wa *kimatta* shigoto ga arimasen.)

¶ [Mr.] Tanaka doesn't have a **regular** job.

きみ 君〔代〕

¶君はぼくの本がどこにあるか知らない。(*Kimi* wa boku no hon ga doko ni aru ka shiranai？)

¶君、いっしょに映画を見に行こう。(*Kimi*, issho ni eiga o mi ni ikō.)

＊普通、親しい男どうしの間で使う。

kimi 〔pron〕 you

¶ Do **you** know where my book is?

¶ Let's go to a movie together.

＊*Kimi* is generally used among males who know each other well.

ぎむ 義務〔名〕

義務を果たす (*gimu* o hatasu)

¶国民は税金を払う義務があります。(Kokumin wa zeikin o harau *gimu* ga arimasu.)

¶日本の義務教育は 9 年間です。(Nihon no *gimu*-kyōiku wa kyūnenkan desu.)

⇔権利 kenri

gimu 〔n〕 duty, obligation

fulfill **one's obligations**, discharge one's duties

¶ Citizens have **an obligation** to pay taxes.

¶ **Compulsory** education is for nine years in Japan.

きめる 決める〔動Ⅱ〕

¶今度の大会に参加することに決めました。(Kondo no taikai ni sanka suru koto ni *kimemashita*.)

¶飛行機の手荷物は20キロ以下と決められています。(Hikōki no tenimotsu wa nijikkiro ika to *kimerarete* imasu.)

kimeru 〔v Ⅱ〕 decide, settle, fix, arrange, determine

¶ [I] **decided** to participate in the next convention 〖rally, tournament, meet, etc.〗.

¶ Airplane baggage **is set** at no more than 20 kilograms.

きもち 気持ち〔名〕

①[心の感じ方]

¶この部屋は明るくて、気持ちがいいですね。(Kono heya wa akarukute, *kimochi* ga ii desu ne.)

¶あなたは子供を亡くしたお母さんの気持ちがわかりますか。(Anata wa kodomo o nakushita okāsan no *kimochi* ga wakarimasu ka？)

②[体のぐあいによって感じる気分]

kimochi 〔n〕 feeling, sensation

① [feeling, sensation, mood]

¶ This room is bright and **pleasant**, isn't it?

¶ Can you understand how a mother **feels** when she has lost a child?

② [feeling or sensation caused by one's physical condition]

¶田中さんは気持ちが悪くなったの
で、家に帰りました。（Tanaka san wa *kimochi* ga waruku natta node, ie ni kaerimashita.）

¶ [Mr.] Tanaka went home as [he] **was feeling sick**.

きもの　着物〔名〕

¶あのきれいな着物を着ている女の人はだれですか。（Ano kirei na *kimono* o kite iru onna no hito wa dare desu ka？）

kimono 〔n〕 **kimono, clothes, clothing**

¶ Who is that woman wearing a beautiful **kimono?**

ぎもん　疑問〔名〕

¶疑問があったら、おっしゃってください。（Gimon ga attara, osshatte kudasai.）

¶彼が成功するかどうかは疑問です。（Kare ga seikō suru ka dōka wa *gimon* desu.）

gimon 〔n〕 **doubt, question**

¶ If you have **any doubts**, please tell [us] about them.

¶ **It's doubtful** whether he will succeed or not.

きゃく　客〔名〕

① [招かれて来る人、訪ねて来る人]
観光客（kankō*kyaku*）お客を呼ぶ（o*kyaku* o yobu）

¶あしたはお客さんが3人来ます。（Ashita wa o*kyaku*san ga sannin kimasu.）

¶部屋が汚れているのに、お客が突然訪ねてきてあわてました。（Heya ga yogorete iru noni, o*kyaku* ga totsuzen tazunete kite awatemashita.）

② [物を買ったり食べたりしてお金を払う人]

¶あの店はいつも客が多いです。（Ano mise wa itsu mo *kyaku* ga ooi desu.）

¶デパートの店員は、客に対してたいへん丁寧な言葉を使います。（Depāto no ten'in wa, *kyaku* ni taishite taihen teinei na kotoba o tsukaimasu.）

kyaku 〔n〕 **guest; customer**

① [guest, caller, visitor, company] a tourist, sightseer // invite **a guest**

¶ Three **visitors** 〚**guests**〛 will be coming tomorrow.

¶ [My] apartment 〚room〛 was dirty so [I] was flustered when **someone** unexpectedly **came to visit**.

② [customer, client, passenger]

¶ That shop 〚restaurant, bar, etc.〛 is always filled with **customers**.

¶ Department store employees use very polite language toward **customers**.

ぎゃく　逆〔名、形動〕

¶時計の針を逆に回さないでください。(Tokei no hari o *gyaku* ni mawasanaide kudasai.)

¶あの人の考えはその逆です。(Ano hito no kangae wa sono *gyaku* desu.)

gyaku〔n, adj-v〕**reverse, inverse, the contrary**

¶Please don't move the hands of the watch〚clock〛**backwards**.

¶[His] opinion is **the complete opposite** of that.

きゃっかんてき　客観的〔形動〕

¶ものごとは客観的に見なければいけません。(Monogoto wa *kyakkanteki* ni minakereba ikemasen.)

⇔主観的 shukanteki

kyakkanteki〔adj-v〕**be objective**

¶One must take an **objective** view of things.

きゅう　九〔名〕

十九世紀 (ju*kyū*seiki)　九階 (*kyū*kai)

⇒九 ku

kyū〔n〕**nine**

the 19th century // the **ninth** floor

きゅう　急〔名、形動〕

① [緊急な様子]

救急車 (*kyūkyū*sha)

¶急な用事ができたので、すぐ帰らなければなりません。(*Kyū* na yōji ga dekita node, sugu kaeranakereba narimasen.)

② [ものごとが突然に起こる様子]

¶電車が急に止まりました。(Densha ga *kyū* ni tomarimashita.)

③ [傾斜が大きい様子]

¶この階段はずいぶん急ですね。(Kono kaidan wa zuibun *kyū* desu ne.)

④ [ものごとの速い様子]

急行列車 (*kyū*kō-ressha)

¶この川の流れは急です。(Kono kawa no nagare wa *kyū* desu.)

kyū〔n, adj-v〕**emergency, urgent; sudden; steep, sharp; rapid**

① [emergency, urgent, pressing]

an ambulance

¶[I] must go home right away as something **urgent** has come up.

② [sudden, abrupt]

¶The train stopped **suddenly**.

③ [steep, sharp]

¶These are very **steep** stairs〚steps〛, aren't they?

④ [rapid, swift]

an **express** train

¶This river has a **swift** current.

きゅう- 旧-〖頭〗

旧暦（*kyū*reki） 旧正月（*kyū*shō-gatsu） 旧市内（*kyū*shinai） 旧漢字（*kyū*kanji） 旧式（*kyū*shiki）
⇒新- shin-

kyū-〖pref〗 **old, former, ex-**

the **old** calendar, the lunar calendar // the New Year according to the **old** calendar, the lunar New Year // within the **old** city // the **older** *kanji*, the **old** forms of *kanji* // **old**-style, out-of-date, **old**-fashioned

---

きゅうか 休暇〖名〗

¶休暇をとって旅行に出ます。（*Kyūka* o totte ryokō ni demasu.）
¶休暇中は仕事のことはあまり考えません。（*Kyūka*chū wa shigoto no koto wa amari kangaemasen.）

kyūka〖n〗 **holiday (s), vacation, time off**

¶ [I] am taking **some time off** and going on a trip.
¶ While on **vacation** [I] rarely think about work.

きゅうぎょう 休業〖名、～する〗

臨時休業（rinji-*kyūgyō*） 夏期休業（kaki-*kyūgyō*）
¶このデパートは毎週木曜日が休業日です。（Kono depāto wa maishū mokuyōbi ga *kyūgyō*bi desu.）
¶あの床屋には「本日休業」の札が出ています。（Ano tokoya ni wa "honjitsu *kyūgyō*"no fuda ga dete imasu.）

kyūgyō〖n, ～*suru*〗 **suspension of business, being closed, a day off**

a special **holiday**; **Closed** Today (sign) // summer **holidays**

¶ This department store **is closed** every Thursday.
¶ That barbershop has a sign out reading "**Closed** Today."

きゅうけい 休憩〖名、～する〗

¶10分間の休憩をしてから、また始めましょう。（Jippunkan no *kyūkei* o shite kara, mata hajimemashō.）
¶会議は休憩しないで続けられました。（Kaigi wa *kyūkei* shinaide tsuzukeraremashita.）

kyūkei〖n, ～*suru*〗 **rest, recess, break, intermission**

¶ Let's take a 10-minute **break** and then start again.

¶ The meeting continued without a **break**.

きゅうこう 急行〖名〗

急行列車（*kyūkō*-ressha） 急行券（*kyūkō*ken）

kyūkō〖n〗 **an express, express train**

an **express train** // an **express ticket**

220

¶午後7時に京都行特別急行が発車します。（Gogo shichiji ni Kyōto yuki tokubetsu-*kyūkō* ga hassha shimasu.）

¶ The limited **express** for Kyoto leaves at 7 PM.

きゅうじつ　休日〔名〕

kyūjitsu 〔n〕 **holiday, day off**

¶今度の休日には家族で旅行します。（Kondo no *kyūjitsu* ni wa kazoku de ryokō shimasu.）

¶ I am going on a trip with my family over the coming **holiday**.

ぎゅうにく　牛肉〔名〕

gyūniku 〔n〕 **beef**

¶牛肉を買って、すきやきをしました。（*Gyūniku* o katte, sukiyaki o shimashita.）

¶ [I] bought **beef** and fixed *sukiyaki*.

¶牛肉と豚肉とどちらが好きですか。（*Gyūniku* to butaniku to dochira ga suki desu ka？）

¶ Which do you like better, **beef** or pork?

ぎゅうにゅう　牛乳〔名〕

gyūnyū 〔n〕 **(cow's) milk**

牛乳びん（*gyūnyū*bin）牛乳配達（*gyūnyū*-haitatsu）牛乳屋（*gyūnyū*ya）

a **milk** bottle // a **milk** delivery // a **dairy**man, **milk**man, **milk** shop

¶朝御飯はいつもパンと牛乳です。（Asagohan wa itsu mo pan to *gyūnyū* desu.）

¶ [I] always have bread [toast, a croissant, a pastry, etc.] and **milk** for breakfast.

⇒ミルク **miruku**

きゅうびょう　急病〔名〕

kyūbyō 〔n〕 **sudden illness, a sudden attack**

急病人（*kyūbyō*nin）

an **emergency** patient

¶上田さんは急病で来られなくなりました。（Ueda san wa *kyūbyō* de korarenaku narimashita.）

¶ [Mr.] Ueda can't 〖couldn't〗 come because [he] **was suddenly taken ill**.

きゅうよう　急用〔名〕

kyūyō 〔n〕 **urgent matter, pressing business**

¶上田さんは急用ができたので、今朝早く国へ帰りました。（Ueda san wa *kyūyō* ga dekita node, kesa hayaku kuni e kaerimashita.）

¶ **Something urgent** came up so [Mr.] Ueda left for his hometown early this morning.

¶田中さん、急用ですからすぐ来てください。（Tanaka san, *kyūyō* desu kara sugu kite kudasai.）

¶ [Mr.] Tanaka, please come here immediately; **it's urgent**.

きゅうりょう　給料　〔名〕

¶わたしの会社の給料日は毎月 25 日
です。（Watashi no kaisha no *kyū-ryō*bi
wa maitsuki nijūgonichi desu.）
¶給料には月給、週給、日給、自給
の4種類があります。（*Kyūryō* ni wa
gekkyū, shūkyū, nikkyū, jikyū no
yonshurui ga arimasu.）

kyūryō 〔n〕 **pay, wages, salary**

¶ **Payday** at my company is the twenty-fifth of the month.

¶ There are four types of salary:
monthly, weekly, daily and hourly.

きょう　今日　〔名〕

¶今日は何曜日ですか。（*Kyō* wa
nan'yōbi desu ka？）
¶今日から夏休みです。（*Kyō* kara
natsuyasumi desu.）
¶今日、銀行へ行くつもりです。（*Kyō*,
ginkō e iku tsumori desu.）

kyō 〔n〕 **today**

¶ What day of the week is it **today**?

¶ Summer vacation starts **today**.

¶ I plan to go to the bank **today**.

(-)ぎょう　(-)行　〔名、尾〕

1〔名〕
行をかえる（*gyō* o kaeru）
2〔尾〕
¶1行ずつ読んでください。（Ichi*gyō*
zutsu yonde kudasai.）
¶下から3行めの漢字が読めません。
（Shita kara san*gyō*me no kanji ga
yomemasen.）

(-)gyō 〔n, suf〕 **line of type, row of type**

1 〔n〕 a line of type
begin a new **line** (on a page)
2 〔suf〕 the counter for lines of type
¶ Please read aloud one **line** each.

¶ I can't read the *kanji* in the third **line**
from the bottom.

きょういく　教育　〔名、～する〕

義務教育（gimu-*kyōiku*）職業教育
(shokugyō-*kyōiku*）家庭教育（katei-
kyōiku）教育費（*kyōiku*hi）教育映画
(*kyōiku*-eiga）教育者（*kyōiku*sha）

¶この国の教育程度はかなり高いで
す。（Kono kuni no *kyōiku*-teido wa
kanari takai desu.）

kyōiku 〔n, ～*suru*〕 **education, instruction, training**

compulsory **education** // vocational
training // home **training** //
educational expenses // an
educational film, **instructional** film //
an educator, a schoolteacher
¶ The level of **education** in this
country is quite high.

¶国の発展のためには教育が最も大切
です。(Kuni no hatten no tame ni wa
kyōiku ga mottomo taisetsu desu.)

¶ **Education** is the most important
element in the development of a nation.

きょうかい 教会 〔名〕

kyōkai 〔n〕 **church**

¶日曜日の朝は教会へ行くことにして
います。(Nichiyōbi no asa wa *kyōkai* e
iku koto ni shite imasu.)

¶ I make it a practice to go to **church**
on Sunday morning.

きょうかしょ 教科書 〔名〕

kyōkasho 〔n〕 **textbook,
schoolbook, manual**

¶教科書の10ページを開いてくださ
い。(*Kyōkasho* no jippēji o hiraite
kudasai.)

¶ Please open **your books** to page 10.

¶あなたの学校では、どんな日本語の
教科書を使っていますか。(Anata no
gakkō de wa, donna Nihongo no *kyōkasho*
o tsukatte imasu ka?)

¶ What Japanese-language **textbooks**
do they use at your school?

きょうぎ 競技 〔名〕

kyōgi 〔n〕 **match, contest,
competition, game, sport,
sports event**

競技会 (*kyōgi*kai) 競技場 (*kyōgi*-jō)

an **athletic** meet, **track-and-field**
meet; **a contest, competition** // a
sports ground, stadium

¶水泳競技が間もなく始まります。
(Suiei-*kyōgi* ga mamonaku hajimarimasu.)

¶ The swimming **events** will start
momentarily.

きょうさんしゅぎ 共産主義 〔名〕

kyōsanshugi 〔n〕 **communism**

きょうし 教師 〔名〕

kyōshi 〔n〕 **teacher, instructor,
schoolteacher**

¶兄は数学の教師をしています。(Ani
wa sūgaku no *kyōshi* o shite imasu.)
⇒先生 sensei

¶ My older brother **teaches**
mathematics.

ぎょうじ 行事 〔名〕

gyōji 〔n〕 **event, function**

¶2学期の行事の予定を教えてくださ
い。(Nigakki no *gyōji* no yotei o oshiete
kudasai.)

¶ Please inform me of **the events**
scheduled for the second term.

¶日本の年中行事についてレポートを
書きます。(Nihon no nechū-*gyōji* ni
tsuite repōto o kakimasu.)

¶ [I] am writing a report on annual
events〚rites〛 in Japan.

きょうしつ 教室〔名〕

kyōshitsu 〔n〕 **classroom,
schoolroom**

¶教室の中では静かにしてください。
(*Kyōshitsu* no naka de wa shizuka ni shite
kudasai.)

¶ Please be quiet while in **the
classroom**.

きょうじゅ 教授〔名、～する〕

kyōju 〔n, ～*suru*〕 **teaching,
instruction; professor**

①[教えること]
¶あの人はピアノの個人教授をしてい
ます。(Ano hito wa piano no kojin-*kyōju*
o shite imasu.)

① [teaching, instruction]
¶ [He] **gives** private piano **lessons**.

②[大学の先生]
¶あの方は東京大学の教授です。
(Ano kata wa Tōkyō-daigaku no *kyōju*
desu.)

② [professor]
¶ [He] is **a professor** at Tokyo
University.

きょうそう 競争〔名、～する〕

kyōsō 〔n, ～*suru*〕 **competition,
contest, rivalry**

競争に勝つ (*kyōsō* ni katsu) 競争に負
ける (*kyōsō* ni makeru)

win **a race**, be victorious in **a
competition** // lose **a race**, be defeated
in **a competition**

¶田中さんと山田さんはいつも競争で
勉強しています。(Tanaka san to
Yamada san wa itsu mo *kyōsō* de benkyō
shite imasu.)

¶ [Mr.] Tanaka and [Mr.] Yamada are
always **competing** with each other in
their studies.

¶この辺は店が多いので、どの店も競
争して安く売っています。(Kono hen
wa mise ga ooi node, dono mise mo *kyōsō*
shite yasuku utte imasu.)

¶ There are many stores around here so
they all sell cheaply **in competition
with each other**.

きょうだい 兄弟〔名〕

kyōdai 〔n〕 **brothers, brothers
and sisters, siblings**

¶あなたは兄弟が何人いますか。
(Anata wa *kyōdai* ga nannin imasu ka？)

¶ How many **brothers and sisters** do
you have?

¶兄弟は五人です。兄が二人、姉が二人、わたしはいちばん下です。(Kyōdai wa gonin desu. Ani ga futari, ane ga futari, watashi wa ichiban shita desu.)
⇒姉妹 shimai

¶ There are five of **us children**—my two older brothers, my two older sisters and me, the youngest.

きょうつう　共通〔名、〜する〕

kyōtsū 〔n, ~*suru*〕 **common, shared**

共通点（kyōtsūten）留学生にとって共通の問題（ryūgakusei ni totte kyōtsū no mondai）

something **in common**, a **shared** similarity // a problem **in common** of foreign students

¶中国語と日本語は、漢字を使うという点で共通しています。(Chūgokugo to Nihongo wa, kanji o tsukau to iu ten de kyōtsū shite imasu.)

¶ The Chinese and Japanese languages have the use of Chinese characters **in common**.

きょうどう　共同〔名〕

kyōdō 〔n〕 **common, communal, joint, united, public**

共同生活（kyōdō-seikatsu）共同便所（kyōdō-benjo）共同経営（kyōdō-keiei）共同墓地（kyōdō-bochi）

collective life, **co**habitation // a **public** 〚**shared**〛 toilet // **joint** management // a **public** cemetery

¶わたしたちはこの部屋を共同で使っています。(Watashitachi wa kono heya o kyōdō de tsukatte imasu.)

¶ We **are sharing** this room.

きょうみ　興味〔名〕

kyōmi 〔n〕 **interest**

¶日本の茶道に興味を持っている外国人が多いです。(Nihon no sadō ni kyōmi o motte iru gaikokujin ga ooi desu.)

¶ Many foreigners have **an interest** in the Japanese tea ceremony.

¶わたしは日本文学に興味があります。(Watashi wa Nihon-bungaku ni kyōmi ga arimasu.)

¶ I'm **interested** in Japanese literature.

きょうりょく　協力〔名、〜する〕

kyōryoku 〔n, ~*suru*〕 **cooperation, collaboration**

¶多くの人の協力によってダムは完成しました。(Ooku no hito no kyōryoku ni yotte damu wa kansei shimashita.)

¶ The dam was 〚has been〛 completed through **the united efforts** of a great many people.

¶兄と協力して事業を始めました。
（Ani to *kyōryoku* shite jigyō o
hajimemashita.）

¶ [I]'ve started a business **in
collaboration** with my elder brother.

きょか 許可 〔名、〜する〕

kyoka 〔n, 〜*suru*〕 **permission,
approval, authorization**

入学許可 （nyūgaku-*kyoka*）

admission (to a school)

¶出国許可がもらえないので、まだ出
発できません。（Shukkoku-*kyoka* ga
moraenai node, mada shuppatsu
dekimasen.）

¶ [I] can't leave yet because [I] haven't
been able to obtain a departure **permit**.

¶社長は山田さんの外国旅行を許可し
ました。（Shachō wa Yamada san no
gaikoku-ryokō o *kyoka* shimashita.）

¶ The company president **approved**
[Mr.] Yamada's overseas trip.

ぎょぎょう 漁業 〔名〕

gyogyō 〔n〕 **fishing industry**

漁業組合 （*gyogyō*-kumiai）

fishermen's union

¶日本は漁業がたいへん盛んです。
（Nihon wa *gyogyō* ga taihen sakan desu.）

¶ **The fishing industry** is very active
in Japan.

(-)きょく (-)曲 〔名、尾〕

(-)kyoku 〔n, suf〕 **tune, melody,
piece of music, musical
composition**

1 〔名〕

1 〔n〕

¶わたしはこの曲が大好きです。
（Watashi wa kono *kyoku* ga daisuki
desu.）

¶ I love this **piece** 〚**song, tune**〛.

¶この曲は上田さんが作りました。
（Kono *kyoku* wa Ueda san ga
tsukurimashita.）

¶ [Mr.] Ueda wrote this **piece**.

2 〔尾〕

2 〔suf〕

¶あなたの国の歌を一曲歌ってくださ
い。（Anata no kuni no uta o ik*kyoku*
utatte kudasai.）

¶ Please sing **a song** from your country
for us.

-きょく -局 〔尾〕

-kyoku 〔suf〕 **department, bureau**

郵便局 （yūbin*kyoku*）電話局 （den-
wa*kyoku*）放送局 （hōsō*kyoku*）

a post **office** // a telephone **office** // a
broadcasting 〚radio, TV〛 **station**

きょくせん 曲線 〔名〕
⇔直線 chokusen

kyokusen 〔n〕 **curved line, curve**

きょねん 去年〔名〕

¶わたしは去年の10月に日本へ行って
きました。（Watashi wa *kyonen* no
jūgatsu ni Nihon e itte kimashita.）

¶わたしは去年大学を卒業しました。
（Watashi wa *kyonen* daigaku o sotsugyō
shimashita.）

きょり 距離〔名〕

¶わたしの家から駅までの距離は約3
キロです。（Watashi no ie kara eki made
no *kyori* wa yaku sankiro desu.）

¶タクシーの料金は距離によって計算
されます。（Takushii no ryōkin wa *kyori*
ni yotte keisan saremasu.）

きらい〔形動〕

¶食べ物できらいな物はありません。
（Tabemono de *kirai* na mono wa
arimasen.）

¶わたしはうそをつく人が大きらいで
す。（Watashi wa uso o tsuku hito ga
dai*kirai* desu.）

⇔好き **suki**

きらう〔動 I〕

¶あなたは、なぜあの人をそんなにき
らうのですか。（Anata wa, naze ano hito
o sonna ni *kirau* no desu ka？）

¶あの人はみんなにきらわれていま
す。（Ano hito wa minna ni *kirawarete*
imasu.）

きり 霧〔名〕

夜霧（yogiri）霧が深い（*kiri* ga fukai）
霧がかかる（*kiri* ga kakaru）霧が晴れ
る（*kiri* ga hareru）

---

kyonen 〔n〕 **last year**

¶ I took a trip to Japan in October of
last year.

¶ I graduated from college **last year**.

kyori 〔n〕 **distance, interval, gap**

¶ **The distance** from my house to the
station is approximately three
kilometers.

¶ Taxi fares are calculated according to
distance.

kirai 〔adj-v〕 **dislike, aversion,
hatred**

¶ There are no foods that I **dislike** 〚I
like all foods〛.

¶ I **hate** people who lie.

kirau 〔v I〕 **to dislike, hate**

¶ Why do you **dislike** [him] so?

¶ [He] **is disliked** by all.

kiri 〔n〕 **fog, mist, spray**

a night **fog**, a night **mist** // be **foggy**, be
misty // **a fog** 〚**mist**〛 gathers // **a fog**
lifts, **a mist** clears

キリストきょう キリスト教〔名〕
キリスト教を信じる（*kirisutokyō* o shinjiru）キリスト教徒（*kirisuto-kyō*to）

kirisutokyō〔n〕 **Christianity**
believe in **Christianity** // a **Christian**

きる　着る〔動Ⅱ〕
¶寒いので、セーターを着ました。（Samui node, sētā o *kimashita*.）
¶暑いから、上着を着ないで会社へ行きます。（Atsui kara, uwagi o *kinaide* kaisha e ikimasu.）
¶あなたの着ている洋服はどこで買ったのですか。（Anata no *kite* iru yōfuku wa doko de katta no desu ka？）
⇔脱ぐ **nugu**

kiru〔v Ⅱ〕 **put on, wear**
¶[I] **wore** a sweater because it was cold.
¶[I] go to work **without** a suit coat because it's so hot.

¶Where did you buy the clothes you're **wearing?**

きる　切る〔動Ⅰ〕

①[ナイフなどで物を傷つけたりいくつかの部分に分けたりする]
¶大きなりんごを四つに切って食べました。（Ookina ringo o yottsu ni *kitte* tabemashita.）
¶ナイフで手を切ってしまいました。（Naifu de te o *kitte* shimaimashita.）
②[電気などを止める]
¶テレビのスイッチを切ってください。（Terebi no suitchi o *kitte* kudasai.）
③[続いている行為・関係などをやめる]
¶電話を切らないで、そのまま待っていてください。（Denwa o *kiranaide*, sono mama matte ite kudasai.）

kiru〔v Ⅰ〕 **cut; switch off; break off, cut off**

① [cut, chop, carve]

¶[I] **cut** a large apple into four pieces and ate it.

¶[I] **cut** [my] hand on a knife.

② [switch off, turn off]
¶Please **turn off** the television.

③ [break off, cut off, break with, sever connections]
¶Please **hold the line** (said on the telephone).

-きる〔尾〕

①[あることを全部終える、最後まであることをやる]

-kiru〔suf〕 **finish; completely ~; dare to**
① [finish, end]

¶ この小説を一晩で読みきってしまいました。（Kono shōsetsu o hitoban de yomi*kitte* shimaimashita.）

¶ 一つの料理を食べきらないうちに、もう次の料理が出てきました。（Hitotsu no ryōri o tabe*kiranai* uchi ni, mō tsugi no ryōri ga dete kimashita.）

② [完全にその状態になる]
枯れきった木（kare*kitta* ki）

¶ 食べすぎたり飲みすぎたりするのが体によくないことはわかりきっています。（Tabesugitari nomisugitari suru no ga karada ni yoku nai koto wa wakari*kitte* imasu.）

③ [それ以上のひどい状態はない]
困りきる（komari*kiru*）弱りきる（yowari*kiru*）

¶ 疲れきって、もう一歩も歩けません。（Tsukare*kitte*, mō ippo mo arukemasen.）

④ [勇気を出してあることをする、はっきりあることをする]

¶ 高い所から思いきって飛び降りました。（Takai tokoro kara omoi*kitte* tobiorimashita.）

¶ いやなことはいやだと言いきる勇気を持たなければいけません。（Iya na koto wa iya da to ii*kiru* yūki o motanakereba ikemasen.）

きれ〔名〕

¶ この本の表紙にはきれがはってあります。（Kono hon no hyōshi ni wa *kire* ga hatte arimasu.）

きれい〔形動〕

① [美しい]

¶ [I] **finished** reading this book in one evening.

¶ The next dish came **before [I] could finish** eating the previous one.

② [completely reach a certain state]
a **completely** dead tree

¶ [I] am **fully** aware that eating and drinking too much are bad for the health.

③ [a completely bad condition]
be **greatly** embarrassed, be at one's wit's ends, be at a loss // be run down, break down; be at a loss, be floored

¶ [I]'m **completely** exhausted; [I] can't take another step.

④ [dare to, be able to]

¶ [I] **summoned [my] courage** and leaped down from that high place.

¶ You must have the courage to **come out and say so** when you don't want to do something.

kire 〔n〕 **cloth**

¶ This is a **cloth** bound book.

kirei 〔adj-v〕 **beautiful; clean; tidy; neat; completely, thoroughly**

① [beautiful, pretty, good-looking]

¶ このきれいな花を一本ください。
（Kono *kirei* na hana o ippon kudasai.）

¶ あの女の人は本当にきれいですね。
（Ano onna no hito wa hontō ni *kirei* desu ne.）

② ［よごれていない、清潔だ］
きれいな水（*kirei* na mizu）
¶ 窓を開けてきれいな空気を入れましょう。（Mado o akete *kirei* na kūki o iremashō.）

③ ［きちんとしている様子］
¶ あなたの部屋はいつもきれいですね。（Anata no heya wa itsu mo *kirei* desu ne.）

④ ［すっかり、完全に］
¶ たくさんあった料理をきれいに食べてしまいました。（Takusan atta ryōri o *kirei* ni tabete shimaimashita.）

＊「きれいに（kirei ni）」の形で副詞的に使う。

きれる　切れる ［動 II］

① ［一つながりのものが途中でいくつかに分かれてしまう］
¶ つり糸が切れて、魚が逃げてしまいました。（Tsuriito ga *kirete*, sakana ga nigete shimaimashita.）

② ［裂ける、傷がつく］
¶ ズボンの後ろが切れていますよ。
（Zubon no ushiro ga *kirete* imasu yo.）

¶ ガラスで手が切れました。（Garasu de te ga *kiremashita*.）

③ ［続いていたものが一時終わる］

¶ Please give me one of these **pretty** flowers.

¶ That woman is really **beautiful**, isn't she?

② [clean, pure, clear]

clear water, **pure** water

¶ Let's open the window and let in some **fresh** air.

③ [tidy, neat, in good order]

¶ Your room is always **nice and neat**, isn't it?

④ [completely, thoroughly]

¶ [We] finished off **all** of the many dishes of food.

*Used adverbially in the form *kirei ni*.

kireru 〔v II〕 **break; split, rip; break off, be cut off; run out, be exhausted, be sold out; expire, run out; cut well, be sharp**

① [break, give way]

¶ The fishing line **snapped** and the fish got away.

② [split, rip]

¶ There's **a rip** in the seat of your trousers.

¶ [I] **cut** [my] hand on some glass.

③ [break off, be cut off, be disconnected]

¶話をしている途中で、電話が切れてしまいました。(Hanashi o shite iru tochū de, denwa ga *kirete* shimaimashita.)

¶ We were **cut off** in the middle of our telephone conversation.

④[使ったり売ったりして品物が一時なくなる]

④ [run out, be exhausted, be sold out]

¶油が切れたらしく、機械が動かなくなりました。(Abura ga *kireta* rashiku, kikai ga ugokanaku narimashita.)

¶ The machine seems to have stopped running because it **ran out** of oil.

¶紙が切れていますから、買っておいてください。(Kami ga *kirete* imasu kara, katte oite kudasai.)

¶ We've **run out** of paper. Please buy some more.

⑤[ある期間が過ぎる]
期限が切れる (kigen ga *kireru*)

⑤ [expire, run out]
a time limit **expires**

¶この定期券は、もう切れていますよ。(Kono teikiken wa, mō *kirete* imasu yo.)

¶ This pass 〖train pass〗 **has expired**.

⑥[よく切ることができる]

⑥ [cut well, be sharp]

¶このナイフはよく切れます。(Kono naifu wa yoku *kiremasu*.)

¶ This knife **cuts** well 〖is sharp〗.

-きれる〔尾〕

-kireru〔suf〕 be able to do to the end; be able to do all

①[最後まですることができる]

① [be able to do to the end]

¶隣のラジオがあまりうるさいので、我慢しきれないで文句を言いに行きました。(Tonari no rajio ga amari urusai node, gaman shi*kirenaide* monku o ii ni ikimashita.)

¶ The radio was so loud next door that I **couldn't stand it any longer** and went to complain.

*あとに打ち消しの言葉を伴って、不可能の意味を表す。

*This -kireru is used in the negative and expresses impossibility.

②[完全にすることができる、すっかりすることができる]

② [be able to finish, be able to do all of something]

¶こんなにたくさんの料理はとても食べきれません。(Konna ni takusan no ryōri wa totemo tabe*kiremasen*.)

¶ [I] **can't possibly eat** this much food.

¶明日までにはこの本は読み切れません。(Asu made ni wa kono hon wa yomi*kiremasen*.)

¶ [I] **can't read all** of this book by tomorrow.

-キロ 〔尾〕

-kiro 〔suf〕 **a kilo, kilometer, kilogram, kilowatt, kilocycle, kiloliter, etc.**

5キログラム (go*kiroguramu*) 6キロメートル (rok*kirom*ētoru)

five **kilograms** // six **kilometers**

きろく 記録 〔名、〜する〕

kiroku 〔n, 〜*suru*〕 **record, document; record, record time**

①[書いておくこと、またその文書]
¶図書館には、この町についての古い記録が残っています。(Toshokan ni wa, kono machi ni tsuite no furui *kiroku* ga nokotte imasu.)

① [record, document]
¶ Ancient **documents** concerning this city are preserved in the library.

¶会議でみんなが言ったことを記録してください。(Kaigi de minna ga itta koto o *kiroku* shite kudasai.)

¶ Please keep **a record** of what everyone says at the meeting.

②[競技などの成績]
¶上田さんは水泳で世界記録をつくりました。(Ueda san wa suiei de sekai*kiroku* o tsukurimashita.)

② [record, record time]
¶ [Mr.] Ueda set a world **record** in swimming.

ぎろん 議論 〔名、〜する〕

giron 〔n, 〜*suru*〕 **argument, discussion, debate**

¶それについては、いろいろ議論があります。(Sore ni tsuite wa, iroiro *giron* ga arimasu.)

¶ There is much that is **debatable** concerning that matter.

¶わたしたちはゆうべ遅くまで日本の政治について議論しました。
(Watashitachi wa yūbe osoku made Nihon no seiji ni tsuite *giron* shimashita.)

¶ We **discussed** Japanese politics until late last night.

きわめて 極めて 〔副〕
¶この問題の解決は極めて難しいです。(Kono mondai no kaiketsu wa *kiwamete* muzukashii desu.)

kiwamete 〔adv〕 **extremely, very**
¶ This problem will be **extremely** difficult to resolve.

¶この計画に反対する人は極めて少ないです。（Kono keikaku ni hantai suru hito wa *kiwamete* sukunai desu.）

¶ **Very** few are opposed to this plan.

きん 金 〔名〕

kin 〔n〕 **gold**

金ペン（*kin*pen）金時計（*kin*dokei）金貨（*kin*ka）金色（*kin*'iro）金髪（*kin*patsu）

a **gold** pen // a **gold** watch // a **gold** coin, **gold** currency // **gold, golden, gold** color // **fair** hair

¶秋子さんは金の指輪をはめています。（Akiko san wa *kin* no yubiwa o hamete imasu.）

¶ Akiko is wearing a **gold** ring.

¶父は金縁の眼鏡をかけています。（Chichi wa *kin*buchi no megane o kakete imasu.）

¶ My father wears a pair of **gold**-rimmed glasses.

ぎん 銀 〔名〕

gin 〔n〕 **silver (the metal)**

銀色（*gin*iro）銀貨（*gin*ka）

silver, silver colored // silver coins

きんえん 禁煙 〔名、～する〕

kin'en 〔n, ～*suru*〕 **prohibition of smoking, No Smoking (sign)**

¶上映中は禁煙です。（Jōeichū wa *kin'en* desu.）

¶ **Smoking is prohibited** during the showing of the film.

¶体の調子が悪いので、禁煙しています。（Karada no chōshi ga warui node, *kin'en* shite imasu.）

¶ [I] **am refraining from smoking** because [I] don't feel in very good shape 〖quite up to par〗.

ぎんこう 銀行 〔名〕

ginkō 〔n〕 **bank**

銀行員（*ginkō*in）

bank employee

¶銀行にお金を預けておきます。（*Ginkō* ni okane o azukete okimasu.）

¶ I put my money in **the bank** for safekeeping.

¶銀行からお金を下ろします。（*Ginkō* kara okane o oroshimasu.）

¶ [I] withdraw money from **the bank**.

きんし 禁止 〔名、～する〕

kinshi 〔n, ～*suru*〕 **prohibition**

通行禁止（tsūkō-*kinshi*）駐車禁止（chūsha-*kinshi*）立ち入り禁止（tachiiri-*kinshi*）

No Passage // **No** Parking // **Keep Out, No** Admittance, **No** Trespassing

¶夜は外出禁止です。（Yoru wa gaishutsu-*kinshi* desu.）

¶ There's an evening **curfew** in effect.

¶政府は米の輸出を禁止しました。
（Seifu wa kome no yushutsu o *kinshi*
shimashita.）

¶ The government **has prohibited** the
exporting of rice.

きんし 近視 〔名〕

kinshi 〔n〕 **nearsightedness,
shortsightedness**

¶上田さんは近視なので、眼鏡をかけ
ています。（Ueda san wa *kinshi* na node,
megane o kakete imasu.）
＊「近眼（kingan）」とも言う。
⇔遠視 enshi

¶ [Mr.] Ueda wears glasses because
[he] is **nearsighted**.

＊Variant: *kingan*.

きんじょ 近所 〔名〕

kinjo 〔n〕 **neighborhood, vicinity**

¶この近所に交番はありませんか。
（Kono *kinjo* ni kōban wa arimasen ka？）
¶上田さんは学校の近所に住んでいま
す。（Ueda san wa gakkō no *kinjo* ni
sunde imasu.）
⇒近く chikaku

¶ Is there a police box **near** here?

¶ [Mrs.] Ueda lives **near** the school.

きんぞく 金属 〔名〕

kinzoku 〔n〕 **metal**

¶木の机より金属製の机のほうが丈夫
です。（Ki no tsukue yori *kinzoku*sei no
tsukue no hō ga jōbu desu.）

¶ **Metal** desks are more durable than
wooden ones.

きんだい 近代 〔名〕

kindai 〔n〕 **modern ages, recent
times**

近代化（*kindai*ka）近代史（*kindai-
shi*）近代思想（*kindai-shisō*）
¶近代的な建物が次々と建築されてい
ます。（*Kindai*teki na tatemono ga
tsugitsugi to kenchiku sarete imasu.）

modernization // **modern** history //
modern thought

¶ **Modern** buildings are being put up
one after another.

きんよう(び) 金曜(日) 〔名〕

kin'yō (bi) 〔n〕 **Friday**

く

く　九 〔名〕
九人 (kunin)　九時 (kuji)
⇒九 kyū

ku 〔n〕 **nine**
nine people // nine o'clock

ぐあい 〔名〕
① [体などの調子・状態]
¶お体のぐあいはいかがですか。
(Okarada no *guai* wa ikaga desu ka？)
② [ものごとのありさま・やり方]
¶おはしはこういうぐあいに使います。(Ohashi wa kōiu *guai* ni
tsukaimasu.)

guai 〔n〕 **physical condition,
　health; condition, state**
① [physical condition, health]
¶ How are you feeling?

② [condition, state]
¶ Chopsticks are used in this **manner**.

くう　食う 〔動 I 〕
① [食べる]
えさを食う (esa o *kuu*)

¶木の葉がこんなに虫に食われています。(Ki no ha ga konnani mushi ni
kuwarete imasu.)
*「食べる (taberu)」に比べて、あまり丁寧な言葉ではない。
② [虫などがかんだり刺したりする]
¶蚊に食われて、手がかゆくてたまりません。(Ka ni *kuwarete*, e ga ka-yukute
tamarimasen.)
③ [消費する]
¶この車はずいぶんガソリンを食いますね。(Kono kuruma wa zuibun gasorin
o *kuimasu* ne.)

kuu 〔v I〕 **eat; bite; consume**
① [eat]
(an animal) **eats** its food, (a fish) **takes**
the bait
¶ The tree leaves are all **eaten up** by
insects!

Kuu is less polite than *taberu*.

② [(insects, etc.) bite]
¶ [My] hand is all itchy now from a
mosquito **bite**.

③ [consume, eat up]
¶ This car **uses** a lot of gas 〚is a real
gas **guzzler**〛.

くうき　空気 〔名〕
¶都会は空気が汚れています。(Tokai
wa *kūki* ga yogorete imasu.)

kūki 〔n〕 **air, atmosphere**
¶ The air is dirty in the city.

¶タイヤの空気が抜けていますよ。
（Taiya no *kūki* ga nukete imasu yo.）

¶ Hey, your tire is going flat (literally, is losing **air**)!

くうこう 空港〔名〕

kūkō〔n〕**airport**

¶空港から飛行機が次々に飛び立っていきます。（*Kūkō* kara hikōki ga tsugitsugi ni tobitatte ikimasu.）
⇒飛行場 **hikōjō**

¶ Airplanes are taking off from **the airport** one after the other.

ぐうすう 偶数〔名〕

gūsū〔n〕**an even number, the even numbers**

¶2、4、6は偶数で、1、3、5は奇数です。（Ni, shi, roku wa *gūsū* de, ichi, san, go wa kisū desu.）

¶ Two, four and six are **even numbers**; and one, three and five are odd numbers.

¶偶数の札を持っている人は、こちら側に座ってください。（*Gūsū* no fuda o motte iru hito wa, kochiragawa ni suwatte kudasai.）
⇔奇数 **kisū**

¶ Will those having **even-numbered** tickets〖tags〗please sit on this side.

ぐうぜん 偶然〔名、副、形動〕

gūzen〔n, adv, adj-v〕**chance, accident**

¶デパートで偶然田中さんに会いました。（Depāto de *gūzen* Tanaka san ni aimashita.）

¶ I **run into** [Mrs.] Tanaka at a department store.

¶それは本当に偶然の一致です。（Sore wa hontō ni *gūzen* no itchi desu.）

¶ That is really **a coincidence**.

クーラー〔名〕

kūrā〔n〕**air conditioner**

¶暑いときにはクーラーがあるといいですね。（Atsui toki ni wa *kūrā* ga aru to ii desu ne.）

¶ It would be nice〖It's nice〗to have **an air conditioner** when it's hot.

くがつ 九月〔名〕

kugatsu〔n〕**September**

くぎ〔名〕
くぎを打つ（*kugi* o utsu）くぎを抜く（*kugi*onuku）

kugi〔n〕**a nail, tack, rivet**
nail, drive in **a nail** // extract **a nail**

くさ 草〔名〕

草を刈る (kusa o karu) 枯草 (karekusa) 草原 (kusahara) 草花 (kusabana)

¶庭に草が生えたので、草取りをしました。(Niwa ni kusa ga haeta node, kusatori o shimashita.)

kusa 〔n〕 **grass, herb, weed**

cut **the grass** // dried **grass**, dry **herbs** // a **grassy** plain, a meadow // a flowering **plant**, a flower

¶ I **weeded** the garden because it needed it (literally, because **weeds** had grown in).

くさい 臭い〔形〕

汗臭い (asekusai) 酒臭い (sakekusai)

¶この川はみんながごみを捨てるので、とても臭いです。(Kono kawa wa minna ga gomi o suteru node, totemo kusai desu.)

kusai 〔adj〕 **bad-smelling, stinking, smelly, smell of ~**

smell of sweat // smell of liquor, **have** liquor **on one's breath**

¶ As everyone throws garbage in this river **it smells** very **bad**.

くさる 腐る〔動 I〕

① [腐敗する]

¶腐った魚を食べて、おなかをこわしました。(Kusatta sakana o tabete, onaka o kowashimashita.)

¶夏は食べ物が腐りやすいです。(Natsu wa tabemono ga kusariyasui desu.)

¶腐らないようにこれを冷蔵庫に入れておきましょう。(Kusaranai yō ni kore o reizōko ni irete okimashō.)

② [木などが悪くなって役に立たなくなる]

¶この家はたいへん古くて、柱が腐っています。(Kono ie wa taihen furukute, hashira ga kusatte imasu.)

kusaru 〔v I〕 **rot; go bad**

① [rot, go bad, decay]

¶ [I] ate some fish that **had gone bad** and got an upset stomach.

¶ Food **spoils** very easily in the summer.

¶ Let's put this in the refrigerator so **it won't spoil**.

② [become bad and no longer useful]

¶ This house is very old, and the pillars 〚posts〛 **are rotten**.

くし〔名〕

¶わたしは毎朝くしで髪の毛をとかします。(Watashi wa maiasa kushi de kaminoke o tokashimasu.)

kushi 〔n〕 **comb**

¶ I comb my hair every morning (with **a comb**).

くしゃみ〔名〕

くしゃみをする (*kushami* o suru)

¶風邪を引いているので、くしゃみが
出て困ります。(Kaze o hiite iru node,
kushami ga dete komarimasu.)

くしん 苦心〔名、〜する〕

¶苦心の末、ようやく論文を書き終え
ました。(*Kushin* no sue, yōyaku ronbun
o kakioemashita.)
¶彼はたいへん苦心して、その詩を書
きました。(Kare wa taihen *kushin* shite,
sono shi o kakimashita.)

くず〔名〕

紙くず (kami*kuzu*) くずかご
(*kuzu*kago)
¶くずを散らかさないようにしてくだ
さい。(*Kuzu* o chirakasanai yō ni shite
kudasai.)

くずす 崩す〔動 I〕

①[形あるものを壊す]
¶山を崩して道路を作っています。
(Yama o *kuzushite* dōro o tsukutte
imasu.)
②[字画などを省いたり続けたりして
書く]
¶くずした字は読みにくいです。
(*Kuzushita* ji wa yominikui desu.)
③[小銭にする]
¶千円札を百円玉にくずしてくださ
い。(Sen'ensatsu o hyakuendama ni
kuzushite kudasai.)

kushami 〔n〕 **a sneeze**

to sneeze

¶ [I] have caught a cold and have an
annoying **sneeze**.

kushin 〔n, ~*suru*〕 **pains, efforts,
labor, hard work**

¶ After **much hard labor** [I] have
finally finished 〚I finally finished〛
writing [my] thesis.

¶ He **put a lot** into the writing of that
poem.

kuzu 〔n〕 **rubbish, waste,
garbage, trash, junk, rags, etc.**
wastepaper // a **waste**basket, **trash** can

¶ Please don't **litter**.

kuzusu 〔v I〕 **destroy, demolish;
simplify; change money**

① [destroy, demolish, pull down, level]
¶ They **are leveling** a hill in building
the road.

② [simplify (a written character, etc.)]

¶ Characters **written in a cursive style**
are hard to read.

③ [break or change money]
¶ Please **give me** hundred-yen **coins**
for this thousand-yen bill.

くすり　薬〔名〕

薬屋（kusuriya）風邪薬（kaze-gusuri）薬代（kusuridai）薬びん（kusuribin）

¶今夜は薬を飲んで早く寝たほうがいいですよ。（Kon'ya wa kusuri o nonde hayaku neta hō ga ii desu yo.）

¶この薬はあまり効きませんね。（Kono kusuri wa amari kikimasen ne.）

くずれる　崩れる〔動II〕

①［形のある物が壊れて下に落ちる］

¶大雨で山が崩れました。（Ooame de yama ga kuzuremashita.）

②［整っているもの・安定しているものなどが乱れる］

¶この帽子は形がくずれていますね。（Kono bōshi wa katachi ga kuzurete imasu ne.）

¶今晩から天気がくずれそうです。（Konban kara tenki ga kuzuresō desu.）

③［小銭に替えることができる］

¶一万円札がくずれますか。（Ichiman'ensatsu ga kuzuremasu ka？）

くせ　癖〔名〕

¶あの人はうそをつく癖があります。（Ano hito wa uso o tsuku kuse ga arimasu.）

¶寝る前に本を読むのが癖になってしまいました。（Neru mae ni hon o yomu no ga kuse ni natte shimaimashita.）

kusuri 〖n〗 medicine, drug, medication, chemical

a drugstore, a pharmacy // cold medicine // a charge for medicine // a medicine bottle, a vial, a phial

¶ You'd better take some medicine and go to bed early tonight.

¶ This medicine doesn't seem to be very effective.

kuzureru 〖v II〗 crumble, collapse, fall down; break down, get out of shape, decline; can change money

① [crumble, collapse, fall down]

¶ There were landslides due to the heavy rains.

② [break down, get out of shape, decline]

¶ This hat has lost its shape.

¶ It looks like the weather will deteriorate from this evening.

③ [can break or change money]

¶ Can you give me change for a ten-thousand-yen bill?

kuse 〖n〗 personal habit, mannerism, quirk, foible, weakness, vice

¶ [He] is a habitual liar.

¶ [I] have 〖had〗 fallen into the habit of reading before going to sleep.

ください 〔動Ⅰ〕

¶うちに着いたら、すぐ電話をください。(Uchi ni tsuitara, sugu denwa o *kudasai*.)

¶何か飲み物をくださいませんか。(Nani ka nomimono o *kudasaimasen* ka?)

（お〜）ください 〔連〕

¶もっとゆっくりお話しください。(Motto yukkuri ohanashi *kudasai*.)

（ご〜）ください （御〜）ください 〔連〕

¶その問題は山田先生に御相談ください。(Sono mondai wa Yamada sensei ni gosōdan *kudasai*.)

＊普通「御 (go)」のあとには「研究 (kenkyū)」「紹介 (shōkai)」などの漢語が来る。

（〜て）ください 〔連〕

¶もっとゆっくり話してください。(Motto yukkuri hanashite *kudasai*.)

¶第3課をみんなで読んでください。(Daisanka o minna de yonde *kudasai*.)

¶寒いから、窓を開けないでください。(Samui kara, mado o akenaide *kudasai*.)

くださる 〔動Ⅰ〕

¶先生はわたしに本をくださいました。(Sensei wa watashi ni hon o *kudasaimashita*.)

¶これは田中先生がくださったペンです。(Kore wa Tanaka sensei ga *kudasatta* pen desu.)

kudasai 〔ⅴⅠ〕 **give**

¶ **Please call me** as soon as you arrive home.

¶ Could you **please give me** something to drink?

(o- 〜)kudasai 〔compd〕 **please 〜**

¶ **Please** speak more slowly.

(go- 〜)kudasai 〔compd〕 **please 〜**

¶ **Please** consult Professor Yamada concerning that problem.

＊Generally a Sino-Japanese compound such as *kenkyū* or *shōkai* follows *go-*.

(-te)kudasai 〔compd〕 **please 〜**

¶ **Please** speak more slowly.

¶ **Please** read Lesson 3 aloud, everyone.

¶ **Please** don't open the window: it's too cold.

kudasaru 〔ⅴⅠ〕 **give**

¶ My teacher 〚professor〛 **gave** me a book.

¶ This is the pen that Professor 〚Doctor〛 Tanaka **gave** me.

＊「くれる（kureru）」「与える（ataeru）」の尊敬語。「ますの形」は「くださいます（kudasaimasu）」となる。ある人が話し手や話し手側の者にある物を与えるという意味を表す。その物を受け取る人の側に立って言うときに使う。一般に、与える人が受け取る人より目上の人であるときに使う。同等か目下の人である場合には「くれる（kureru）」を使う。

⇒くれる kureru

（〜て）くださる〔連〕

¶上田先生がわたしたちに日本語を教えてくださいました。（Ueda sensei ga watashitachi ni Nihongo o oshiete *kudasaimashita*.）

¶病気で寝ていたら、先生がお見舞いに来てくださいました。（Byōki de nete itara, sensei ga omimai ni kite *kudasaimashita*.）

＊「ますの形」は「（〜て）くださいます（[〜te] kudasaimasu）」となる。ある人が話し手や話し手側の者のためにある動作をするという意味を表す。話し手の側に立って言うときに使う。一般に、動作をする人が話し手などよりも目上の人であるときに使う。同等か目下の人である場合には「（〜て）くれる（[〜te] kureru）」を使う。

⇒（〜て）くれる（〜te）kureru

くだもの 果物〔名〕

¶あなたはどんな果物が好きですか。（Anata wa donna *kudamono* ga suki desu ka？）

＊*Kudasaru* is the honorific form of *kureru* and *ataeru*. The *-masu* form is *kudasaimasu*. This verb expresses the meaning of someone giving something to the speaker or to someone close to the speaker. It is used from the standpoint of the recipient and is generally used when the donor is of higher status than the recipient. When the donor is of equal or lesser status, *kureru* is used instead.

(-te)kudasaru 〔compd〕 do someone the favor of 〜ing, be kind enough to 〜

¶ Professor Ueda taught us 〖**was kind enough** to teach us〗 Japanese.

¶ My teacher *was kind enough* to pay me a get-well visit when I was sick in bed.

＊The *-masu* form is (*-te*) *kudasaimasu*. This pattern is used to express the meaning of someone doing something for the speaker or for someone close to the speaker. It is used from the standpoint of the speaker, generally when the performer of the action is of higher status than the recipient of that action. When the performer is of equal or lesser status, (*-te*) *kureru* is used instead.

kudamono 〔n〕 fruit

¶ What **fruits** do you like?

¶果物屋でみかんとりんごを買いました。(*Kudamono*ya de mikan to ringo o kaimashita.)

¶ [I] bought some mandarin oranges and apples at a **fruit** store.

くだり 下り〔名〕

kudari 〔n〕 **descent, going down; outbound**

① [上から下に移ること、下り坂]
上り下りの船 (nobori *kudari* no fune)

① [descent, going down]
downstream and upstream boats

¶山道の上りはたいへんですが、下りは楽です。(Yamamichi no nobori wa taihen desu ga, *kudari* wa raku desu.)

¶ Going up mountain trails is arduous but **coming down** is easy.

¶あそこからは坂が下りになりますから楽です。(Asoko kara wa saka ga *kudari* ni narimasu kara raku desu.)

¶ From over there it **slopes downhill** and so is easier going.

② [中心からその他の所へ行く汽車・電車]

② [outbound trains]

¶上りの電車はこんでいましたが、下りの電車はすいていました。(Nobori no densha wa konde imashita ga, *kudari* no densha wa suite imashita.)

¶ The train going in was crowded but **coming out** there was plenty of room.

⇔上り **nobori**

くだる 下る〔動I〕

kudaru 〔vI〕 **descend, come down, go down**

¶雨になったので、わたしたちは急いで山を下りました。(Ame ni natta node, watashitachi wa isoide yama o *kudarimashita*.)

¶ It started raining so we hurriedly **descended** the mountain.

¶この坂を下った所に本屋があります。(Kono saka o *kudatta* tokoro ni hon'ya ga arimasu.)

¶ There is a bookstore **at the bottom** of this hill.

⇔上る **noboru**

くち 口〔名〕

kuchi 〔n〕 **mouth**

くちびる〔名〕

kuchibiru 〔n〕 **lip (s)**

くつ〔名〕

くつ屋 (*kutsu*ya) 長ぐつ (naga-*gutsu*) 運動ぐつ (undō*gutsu*) くつみがき (*kutsu*migaki) くつをはく (*kutsu* o haku) くつを脱ぐ (*kutsu* o nugu)

kutsu 〔n〕 **shoes, boots**

a **shoe** store, a **shoe**maker // **boots**, high **boots** // basketball 〖tennis, running〗 **shoes**, // **shoe** polishing, a **shoe**shine man // wear 〖put on〗 **shoes**, // take off **one's shoes**

くつした くつ下〔名〕

ナイロンのくつ下 (nairon no *kutsu-shita*) 毛のくつ下 (ke no *kutsu-shita*) ¶このくつ下は婦人用です。(Kono *kutsushita* wa fujin'yō desu.)

kutsushita 〔n〕 **socks, stockings**

nylon **stockings**, nylon **socks** // wool **socks**

¶ These are women's **socks**.

くに 国〔名〕

① 〔国家〕
¶わたしのクラスの学生は、いろいろな国から来ています。(Watashi no kurasu no gakusei wa, iroiro na *kuni* kara kite imasu.)
② 〔自分の生まれた所〕

¶わたしはお正月には国へ帰ります。(Watashi wa oshōgatsu ni wa *kuni* e kaerimasu.)

kuni 〔n〕 **country, nation; one's native place**

① 〔country, nation〕
¶ The students in my class are from many different **countries**.

② 〔one's native place, one's hometown, one's birthplace〕
¶ I always go back to **my hometown** during the New Year's holidays.

くばる 配る〔動 I〕

新聞を配る (shinbun o *kubaru*)
¶そのパンフレットを皆さんに配ってください。(Sono panfuretto o minasan ni *kubatte* kudasai.)

kubaru 〔v I〕 **distribute, pass out, deliver**

deliver newspapers

¶ Please **give** everyone one of those pamphlets.

くび 首〔名〕

kubi 〔n〕 **neck, head**

くふう 工夫〔名、～する〕

¶工夫に工夫を重ねて、ついに新製品を完成しました。(*Kufū* ni *kufū* o

kufū 〔n, ～*suru*〕 **device, invention, plan, means, expedient**

¶ 〔We〕 **worked and worked** and finally invented a new product.

kasanete, tsuini shinseihin o kansei
shimashita.)

¶いろいろ工夫しながらお菓子を作る
のは楽しいです。（Iroiro *kufū* shinagara okashi o tsukuru no wa tanoshii
desu.）

¶ It is fun to make candy 〖sweets,
cakes, etc.〗 trying out different **ideas**
as one goes along.

くべつ 区別〔名、〜する〕

¶子供にはよいことと悪いことの区別
をはっきり教えなければなりません。
（Kodomo ni wa yoi koto to warui koto no
kubetsu o hakkiri oshienakereba
narimasen.）
¶あの兄弟は区別できないほどよく似
ています。（Ano kyōdai wa *kubetsu*
dekinai hodo yoku nite imasu.）

kubetsu 〔n, 〜*suru*〕 **distinction,
difference**
¶ One must clearly teach children **the
difference** between good and bad
〖right and wrong〗.

¶ Those brothers look so much alike
that it's hard **to tell them apart**.

(-)くみ (-)組〔名、尾〕

1〔名〕
¶わたしたちの組は全部で15名です。
（Watashitachi no *kumi* wa zenbu de
jūgomei desu.）
2〔尾〕
¶3年生はA組からE組まであります。
（Sannensei wa Ē-*gumi* kara Ii-*gumi* made
arimasu.）

(-)kumi 〔n, suf〕 **class, band,
squad, team, pair, group**
1〔n〕
¶ There are 15 in all in our **squad**
〖group〗.

2〔suf〕
¶ The third-year students are divided
into five **squads**, from A to E.

くみあい 組合〔名〕

労働組合（rōdō-*kumiai*）協同組合
（kyōdō-*kumiai*）
¶この会社には組合があります。
（Kono kaisha ni wa *kumiai* ga arimasu.）
¶この売店は組合員だけが利用できま
す。（Kono baiten wa *kumiai*in dake ga
riyō dekimasu.）

kumiai 〔n〕 **association, league**
a labor **union** // a cooperative
association, a cooperative
¶ This company **is unionized**.

¶ Only **co-op members** can use this
store.

くみたてる 組み立てる 〔動Ⅱ〕

¶このラジオは自分で組み立てました。(Kono rajio wa jibun de *kumitate-mashita*.)

¶材料を組み立てて、本だなを作りました。(Zairyō o *kumitatete*, hondana o tsukurimashita.)

くむ 組む 〔動Ⅰ〕

① [からみ合わせる]
¶田中さんは腕を組んで考え込んでいます。(Tanaka san wa ude o *kunde* kangaekonde imasu.)

② [あることをするために仲間になる]
¶わたしは田中さんと組んでテニスの試合に勝ちました。(Watashi wa Tanaka san to *kunde* tenisu no shiai ni kachimashita.)

くむ 〔動Ⅰ〕

¶バケツに水をくんで持って来てください。(Baketsu ni mizu o *kunde* motte kite kudasai.)

¶川から水をくんできて、畑にまきます。(Kawa kara mizu o *kunde* kite, hatake ni makimasu.)

くも 雲 〔名〕

¶今日は雲一つない、いい天気です。(Kyō wa *kumo* hitotsu nai, ii tenki desu.)

くもり 曇り 〔名〕

¶あしたは曇りで、風も強いそうです。(Ashita wa *kumori* de, kaze mo tsuyoi sōdesu.)
⇒晴れ hare

kumitateru 〔v Ⅱ〕 **put together, construct, assemble**

¶ I **put together** this radio myself.

¶ [I] **made** a bookcase from scratch.

kumu 〔v Ⅰ〕 **cross, braid, fold; unite, band together, join forces**

① [cross, braid, fold]
¶ [Mr.] Tanaka is deep in thought with [his] arms **folded** across [his] chest.

② [unite, band together, join forces]
¶ [Miss] Tanaka and I **teamed up** and won the tennis match.

kumu 〔v Ⅰ〕 **draw, ladle, pump**

¶ Please **fill** a bucket with water and bring it here.

¶ [They] **take** water from the river and water the fields with it.

kumo 〔n〕 **cloud (s)**

¶ It's a nice day today without a single **cloud** in sight.

kumori 〔n〕 **cloudiness, cloudy weather**

¶ They say that tomorrow it will be **cloudy** with strong winds.

くもる 曇る〔動Ⅰ〕

¶今日は朝から曇っています。(Kyō
wa asa kara *kumotte* imasu.)
⇒晴れる hareru

kumoru〔vⅠ〕**become cloudy,
become overcast**

¶ Today **has been overcast** from the
morning on.

くらい 暗い〔形〕

¶この部屋は昼間でも暗いです。
(Kono heya wa hiruma demo *kurai*
desu.)
¶暗くなったから、家へ帰りましょ
う。(*Kuraku* natta kara, ie e kaerimashō.)
⇔明るい akarui

kurai〔adj〕**dark, dim, gloomy**

¶ This room **is dark** even during the
daytime.

¶ It's gotten **dark**—let's go home.

くらい〔助〕

① [だいたいの数量や程度などを表す]

¶「ここからあなたの家まで歩いてど
のくらいかかりますか。」(Koko kara
anata no ie made aruite dono *kurai*
kakarimasu ka？)「15分ぐらいで
す。」(Jūgofun *gurai* desu.)
¶「あなたのうちは駅からどのくらい
ありますか。」(Anata no uchi wa eki
kara dono *kurai* arimasu ka？)「10キロ
ぐらいあります。」(Jikkiro *gurai*
arimasu.)
¶「本代は一か月いくらぐらいかかり
ますか。」(Hondai wa ikkagetsu ikura
gurai kakarimasu ka？)「三千円ぐらい
かかります。」(Sanzen'en *gurai*
kakarimasu.)
② [ある例を挙げてそれとだいたい同
じ程度であることを表す]

kurai〔part〕**about; as 〜 as 〜; at
least; nothing as 〜 as 〜**

① [about, 〜 or so; expresses an
approximate amount or degree]
¶ **"How long** does it take to walk to
your house from here?"
"About 15 minutes."

¶ **"How far** is your home from the
station?"
"About 10 kilometers. "

¶ **"How much** will be required for
books per month?"
"About three thousand yen."

② [as 〜 as 〜, like 〜, so 〜 that;
indicates that something is of
approximately the same degree as
something else being cited]

¶ 上田さんの部屋は、ちょうどこれくらいの広さです。(Ueda san no heya wa, chōdo kore *kurai* no hirosa desu.)

¶ [Mr.] Ueda's room 〚apartment〛 is just **about** the same size **as** this one.

¶ 山田さんくらい英語が上手に話せればいいのですが…。(Yamada san *kurai* Eigo ga jōzu ni hanasereba ii no desu ga...)

¶ I wish I could speak English **as** well **as** [Miss] Yamada does.

¶ もう一歩も歩けないくらい疲れてしまいました。(Mō ippo mo arukenai *kurai* tsukarete shimaimashita.)

¶ I was **so** tired **that** I couldn't take another step 〚I am **so** tired **that** I can't take another step〛.

③ [あるものごとを簡単なもの・やさしいもの・程度の低いものなどの例として示す]

③ [at least, at any rate; cites something as being simple, easy, of low degree, etc.]

¶ 子供でもこのくらいのことは知っていますよ。(Kodomo demo kono *kurai* no koto wa shitte imasu yo.)

¶ Even a child knows **that**.

¶ こんな易しい漢字くらいだれだって書けますよ。(Konna yasashii kanji *kurai* dare datte kakemasu yo.)

¶ Anyone can write a *kanji* **as easy as** this one.

¶ 日本語を半年も勉強しているのですから、もうひらがなぐらいは書けるでしょう。(Nihongo o hantoshi mo benkyō shite iru no desu kara, mō hiragana *gurai* kakeru deshō.)

¶ [He] has been studying Japanese for half a year so [he] should be able to write *hiragana* **at least**.

¶ お金がないといっても、百円くらいは持っているでしょう。(Okane ga nai to itte mo, hyakuen *kurai* wa motte iru deshō.)

¶ You say you don't have any money, but you must have **at least** one hundred yen.

④ [ほかに同じ程度のものがなくそれがいちばんであるということを表す]

④ [nothing as ～ as ～; indicates that something is number one, that nothing else is of the same degree]

¶ あの人くらい親切な人はいません。(Ano hito *kurai* shinsetsu na hito wa imasen.)

¶ You couldn't find anyone **kinder than** [him] (literally, There is no one **as kind as** him).

¶ 山に登ったとき飲む水くらいおいしいものはありません。(Yama ni nobotta toki nomu mizu *kurai* oishii mono wa arimasen.)

¶ Nothing tastes **better than** cold water drunk while mountain climbing.

＊「〜くらい〜はない（〜kurai〜wa nai）」の形で使う。

＊「ぐらい（gurai）」とも言う。

ぐらい 〔助〕

くらす　暮らす 〔動 I〕

¶1か月5万円で暮らすのは無理です。（Ikkagetsu goman'en de *kurasu* no wa muri desu.）

¶家族は皆元気に暮らしていますから、御安心ください。（Kazoku wa mina genki ni *kurashite* imasu kara, goanshin kudasai.）

クラス 〔名〕

¶わたしのクラスでは、上田さんがいちばん背が高いです。（Watashi no *kurasu* de wa, Ueda san ga ichiban sei ga takai desu.）

くらべる　比べる 〔動 II〕

¶この紙とその紙を比べると、この紙のほうが質がいいです。（Kono kami to sono kami o *kuraberu* to, kono kami no hō ga shitsu ga ii desu.）

¶今年は去年に比べて雨が少ないです。（Kotoshi wa kyonen ni *kurabete* ame ga sukunai desu.）

⇒比較 **hikaku**

-グラム 〔尾〕

¶牛肉を500グラム買いました。（Gyūniku o gohyaku*guramu* kaimashita.）

¶これは100グラムいくらですか。（Kore wa hyaku*guramu* ikura desu ka？）

クリーニング 〔名〕

洋服をクリーニングに出す（yōfuku o *kuriiningu* ni dasu.）

＊Used in the pattern "〜 *kurai* 〜 *wa nai*."

＊Variant: *gurai*.

gurai 〔part〕　☞**kurai**

kurasu 〔v I〕 **live, make a living, get along**

¶ It is impossible **to live** on fifty thousand yen a month.

¶ **We are** all in fine health so please don't worry about us 〚I am glad to assure you that **we are** all in good health〛.

kurasu 〔n〕 **class**

¶ [Mr.] Ueda is the tallest person in my **class**.

kuraberu 〔v II〕 **compare, contrast**

¶ If [we] **compare** this type of paper with that one, this one is of better quality.

¶ There has been less rain this year **than** last year.

-guramu 〔suf〕 **gram (s)**

¶ [I] bought five hundred **grams** of beef.

¶ How much is one hundred **grams** of this?

kuriiningu 〔n〕 **cleaning, dry cleaning, laundry**

send clothing to **the cleaners**

¶ワイシャツが汚れたので、クリーニング屋へ持っていきました。
（Waishatsu ga yogoreta node, *kuriininguya* e motte ikimashita.）

¶ [My] shirts were dirty so I took them to **the cleaners**.

くりかえす 繰り返す〔動Ⅰ〕

¶教科書を繰り返して読みましたが、わかりませんでした。（Kyōkasho o *kurikaeshite* yomimashita ga, wakarimasen deshita.）

¶その発音を何度も繰り返して練習しましたが、うまく言えませんでした。（Sono hatsuon o nando mo *kurikaeshite* renshū shimashita ga, umaku iemasen deshita.）

kurikaesu 〔v Ⅰ〕 **repeat, do over again**

¶ [I] read about it in the textbook **many times** but [I] still didn't understand it.

¶ [I] practiced that pronunciation **over and over again** but still couldn't say it exactly right.

クリスマス〔名〕

¶12月24日の夜にクリスマスパーティーを開きました。（Jūnigatsu nijūyokka no yoru ni *kurisumasu* pātii o hirakimashita.）

kurisumasu 〔n〕 **Christmas**

¶ [We] had a **Christmas** party on the evening of December 24.

くる 来る〔動Ⅲ〕

¶もうすぐ春が来ます。（Mō sugu haru ga *kimasu*.）

¶山田さんはまだ来ませんか。（Yamada san wa mada *kimasen* ka？）

¶今度日本へ来るときには、奥さんも連れてきてください。（Kondo Nihon e *kuru* toki ni wa, okusan mo tsurete kite kudasai.）

⇔行く iku

kuru 〔v Ⅲ〕 **come, arrive**

¶Spring **will** soon **be here**.

¶ **Hasn't** [Miss] Yamada **arrived** yet?

¶The next time **you come** to Japan please bring your wife along with you.

（〜て）くる〔連〕

①［こちらへ近づく、あることをしてからこちらにもどる］

(-te)kuru 〔compd〕 **an expression indicating various conditions**

① [approach; come having done something]

（〜て）くる

¶向こうから大きなトラックが走って
きました。(Mukō kara ookina torakku
ga hashitte *kimashita*.)

¶すみません。今日は宿題をしてきま
せんでした。(Sumimasen. Kyō wa
shukudai o shite *kimasen deshita*.)

¶A large truck **came**〚**is coming**〛
from the opposite direction.

¶I'm sorry. I haven't done the
homework (literally, **I haven't come**
today with the homework done; **I've
come** today **without** having done the
homework).

¶その問題について、昨日図書館へ
行って調べてきました。(Sono mondai
ni tsuite, kinō toshokan e itte shirabete
kimashita.)

⇔（〜て）いく（〜**te**）**iku**

② [動作・作用が継続してある時点に
至る]

¶[I] **went** to the library yesterday **and
did** some research on that question.

② [indicates that an action or
operation has continued and has
reached a certain point]

¶この1年間毎日日本語を勉強してき
ました。(Kono ichinenkan mainichi
Nihongo o benkyō shite *kimashita*.)

¶今までこの会社に20年間勤めてきま
した。(Imamade kono kaisha ni
nijūnenkan tsutomete *kimashita*.)

⇔（〜て）いく（〜**te**）**iku**

③ [動作・作用が始まる]

¶This past year **I've studied** Japanese
every day.

¶**I've worked** for this company 20
years now.

③ [indicates that an action or
operation has begun]

¶あっ、雨が降ってきた。(A'! Amega
futte *kita*.)

¶急におなかが痛くなってきました。
(Kyū ni onaka ga itaku natte *kimashita*.)

¶Oh, **it's started** to rain!

¶My stomach **has** suddenly **started** to
ache〚My stomach suddenly **started** to
ache〛.

④ [だんだんにある状態に変わる]

¶大雨が降って、川の水が増えてきま
した。(Ooame ga futte, kawa no mizu ga
fuete *kimashita*.)

¶最近、物価が高くなってきて、人々
は困っています。(Saikin, bukka ga

④ [indicates that something gradually
changes to a certain condition]

¶With the heavy rains, the river **has
risen**〚**rose**〛.

¶Recently prices **have gone up**, and
people are having a hard time.

takaku natte *kite*, hitobito wa komatte imasu.)

¶ 霧がはれて、星がはっきり見えてきました。 (Kiri ga harete, hoshi ga hakkiri miete *kimashita*.)

⇔ （〜て）いく （〜**te**) **iku**

⑤ [ものごとが出現する]

¶ いい考えが頭に浮かんできました。 (Ii kangae ga atama ni ukande *kimashita*.)

¶ うちからの手紙を読んでいたら、妹の顔が浮かんできました。 (Uchi kara no tegami o yonde itara, imōto no kao ga ukande *kimashita*.)

くるしい 苦しい 〔形〕

① [体のぐあいが悪くて我慢できない様子]

¶ 病人はとても苦しそうです。 (Byō-nin wa totemo *kurushisō* desu.)

② [お金や物などがなくて困っている様子]

¶ 月給が安いから生活が苦しいです。 (Gekkyū ga yasui kara seikatsu ga *kurushii* desu.)

くるしむ 苦しむ 〔動 I 〕

① [体のぐあいが悪くて我慢できない]

¶ 田中さんは長い間病気で苦しんでいます。 (Tanaka san wa nagai aida byōki de *kurushinde* imasu.)

② [お金や物などがなくて困る]

¶ With the lifting of the fog, the stars **have become** clearly visible 〚**became** clearly visible〛.

⑤ [indicates that something makes an appearance]

¶ A good idea **has come** to me 〚I hit upon a good idea〛.

¶ As I read a letter from home the face of my younger sister **flitted** across my mind.

kurushii 〔adj〕 **painful; trying, taxing, hard, difficult**

① [painful, tormenting, (physically) trying]

¶ The patient **seems to be in** much **pain** 〚very **uncomfortable**〛.

② [trying, taxing, hard, difficult (financially, etc.)]

¶ As [my] wages are low [I] **have a hard time** making ends meet.

kurushimu 〔v I〕 **suffer, be in pain; be troubled, be distressed**

① [suffer, be in pain, be afflicted (physically)]

¶ [Mr.] Tanaka **has** long **been ill** (literally, **has** long **been suffering** with an illness, disease, etc.).

② [be troubled, be distressed (financially, etc.)]

¶世界には食べ物がなくて苦しんでいる人がおおぜいいます。(Sekai ni wa tabemono ga nakute *kurushinde* iru hito ga oozei imasu.)

¶都会の人たちは住宅の不足に苦しんでいます。(Tokai no hitotachi wa jūtaku no fusoku ni *kurushinde* imasu.)

¶ Many people in the world don't have enough to eat (literally, don't have enough to eat and **are suffering**).

¶ Urban dwellers **suffer** from the shortage of housing.

くるま 車 〔名〕

kuruma 〔n〕 **wheel (s); (wheeled) vehicle, car**

① [車輪]

① [wheels, castors]

¶この旅行かばんには車がついています。(Kono ryokō-kaban ni wa *kuruma* ga tsuite imasu.)

¶ This suitcase has attached **wheels**.

¶馬車の車が壊れてしまったから、直してください。(Basha no *kuruma* ga kowarete shimatta kara, naoshite kudasai.)

¶ One of **the wheels** of the cart 〚carriage, coach〛 is broken. Please fix it.

② [乗り物、自動車]
車に乗る (*kuruma* ni noru) 車を降りる (*kuruma* o oriru)

② [(wheeled) vehicle, car, taxi]
ride in **a car** 〚taxi, carriage, wagon, etc.〛 // get out of **a car** 〚taxi, carriage, wagon, etc.〛

¶ここから駅まで車で10分です。(Koko kara eki made *kuruma* de jippun desu.)

¶ It is 10 minutes by **car** from here to the station.

くれる 暮れる 〔動 II〕

kureru 〔v II〕 **get dark end come to a close**

① [日が沈んで暗くなる]

① [get dark]

¶日が暮れる前に仕事を終えましょう。(Hi ga *kureru* mae ni shigoto o oemashō.)

Let's finish this job before **it gets dark**.

② [時が経過して年や季節などが終わりになる]

② [end, (years, days, etc.) come to a close]

¶あと数日で今年も暮れますね。(Ato sūjitsu de kotoshi mo *kuremasu* ne.)

¶ In a few days this year **will draw to a close**.

くれる 〔動II〕

¶ 父がわたしにお金をくれました。
(Chichi ga watashi ni okane o
kuremashita.)

¶ 上田さんが弟に誕生日のお祝いを
くれました。(Ueda san ga otōto ni
tanjōbi no oiwai o *kuremashita*.)

＊普通、ある人が話し手や話し手側の
者にある物を与えるという意味を表
す。その物を受け取る人の側に立って
言うときに使う。一般に、与える人が
受け取る人と同等か目下の人または身
内の人であるときに使う。目上の人で
ある場合には「くださる（kudasaru）」
を使う。「先生がこの本をくださいま
した。（Sensei ga kono hon o
kudasaimashita.）」

⇒くださる kudasaru

（～て）くれる 〔連〕

¶ 母がわたしにシャツを買ってくれま
した。(Haha ga watashi ni shatsu o katte
kuremashita.)

¶ このことについては上田さんにきけ
ば、詳しく教えてくれると思います。
(Kono koto ni tsuite wa Ueda san ni
kikeba kuwashiku oshiete *kureru* to
omoimasu.)

＊ある人が話し手のためにある動作を
するという意味を表す。話し手の側に
立って言うときに使う。一般に、動作
をする人が、話し手などと同等か目下
の人であるときに使う。動作をする人
が話し手などより目上である場合に
は、「（～て）くださる（[～te]
kudasaru）」を使う。「先生に伺えば、

kureru 〔v II〕 give

¶ My father **gave** me some money.

¶ [Mrs.] Ueda **gave** my younger
brother a birthday present.

＊*Kureru* usually expresses the
meaning of someone giving something
to the speaker or to someone close to
the speaker. It is used from the
standpoint of the recipient, generally
when the donor is of equal or lesser
status than the recipient or is within the
recipient's inner circle. When the donor
is of higher status, *kudasaru* is used
instead, as in "*Sensei ga kono hon o
kudasaimashita*" (My teacher gave me
this book).

(-te)kureru 〔compd〕 do someone the favor of ～, be kind enough to ～

¶ My mother bought me a shirt.

¶ If you ask [Mr.] Ueda about this
matter, I'm sure that [he] **will be kind
enough** to tell you about it in some
detail.

＊This pattern expresses the meaning
of someone doing something for the
speaker. It is used from the standpoint
of the speaker, generally when the
performer of the action is of equal or
lesser status than the recipient. When
the performer of the action is of higher
status, (-te) *kudasaru* is used instead,

詳しく教えてくださると思います。
（Sensei ni ukagaeba, kuwashiku oshiete
kudasaru to omoimasu.）」

⇒（〜て）くださる（〜**te**）**kudasaru**

くろ 黒〔名〕

黒インク（*kuro*inku）白黒フィルム
（shiro*kuro*-firumu）黒髪（*kuro*-kami）
黒砂糖（*kuro*zatō）黒ビール
（*kuro*biiru）

kuro 〔n〕 **black**

black ink // **black**- and -white film //
black hair // **brown** sugar, **unrefined**
sugar // **dark** beer, **black** beer

くろい 黒い〔形〕

¶田中さんは黒いくつをはいていま
す。（Tanaka san wa *kuroi* kutsu o haite
imasu.）
¶日に焼けて顔が黒くなりました。
（Hi ni yakete kao ga *kuroku*
narimashita.）

kuroi 〔adj〕 **black, dark**

¶ [Mr.] Tanaka is wearing **black** shoes.

¶ [My] face has 〖had〗 gotten **brown** in
the sun.

くろう 苦労〔名、〜する〕

¶御苦労さまでした。（Gokurōsama
deshita.）
¶よい辞書がないので、勉強するのに
苦労しました。（Yoi jisho ga nai node,
benkyō suru no ni *kurō* shimashita.）
¶父が早く死んだので、母は苦労して
わたしたちを育てました。（Chichi ga
hayaku shinda node, haha wa *kurō* shite
watashitachi o sodatemashita.）
＊「御苦労さま。（Gokurōsama.）「御苦
労さまでした。（Gokurōsama
deshita.）」というあいさつの言葉は目
上の者が目下の者に対して使う。

kurō 〔n, 〜*suru*〕 **trouble,
hardship, suffering, toil, labor,
pains, cares, worry, anxiety**

¶ **Thank you very much** 〖Many
thanks **for your trouble**〗.

¶ I **had a hard time** studying that as
there isn't any good dictionary for it
〖as I didn't have a good dictionary〗.

¶ Since my father died young, my
mother **had a hard time of it** raising
us.

＊The set expressions *Gokurōsama*
and *Gokurōsama deshita* are used by
persons of higher status towards those
of lower status.

くわえる 加える〔動Ⅱ〕

① [数量を増やす、足す]

kuwaeru 〔v Ⅱ〕 **add, add up;
increase; include; inflict, apply**

① [add, add up, add to]

¶2に3を加えると、5になります。（Ni ni san o *kuwaeru* to, go ni narimasu.）

¶この料理にはもう少し塩を加えてください。（Kono ryōri ni wa mō sukoshi shio o *kuwaete* kudasai.）

②[程度を大きくする]

¶汽車はだんだんスピードを加えていき、とうとう見えなくなってしまいました。（Kisha wa dandan supiido o *kuwaete* iki, tōtō mienaku natte shimaimashita.）

③[仲間に入れる]

仲間に加える（nakama ni *kuwaeru*）

¶その研究会にわたしも加えてください。（Sono kenkyūkai ni watashi mo *kuwaete* kudasai.）

④[ある動作・作用を与える]

力を加える（chikara o *kuwaeru*）

¶ナイロンに熱を加えると、溶けてしまいます。（Nairon ni netsu o *kuwaeru* to, tokete shimaimasu.）

くわしい 詳しい〔形〕

①[詳細な]

¶もっと詳しく話してください。

（Motto *kuwashiku* hanashite kudasai.）

¶その辞書よりもこの辞書の説明のほうが詳しいです。（Sono jisho yori mo kono jisho no setsumei no hō ga *kuwashii* desu.）

②[よく知っている]

¶あの人は日本の歴史に詳しいですね。（Ano hito wa Nihon no rekishi ni *kuwashii* desu ne.）

¶彼はこの辺の地理に詳しいです。

（Kare wa kono hen no chiri ni *kuwashii* desu.）

¶ Two **plus** three is five.

¶ Please **add** a little more salt to this dish.

②[increase]

¶ The train gradually **speeded up** and disappeared into the distance.

③[include, count in, incorporate]

take into one's circle, **let join**

¶ Please **add** me to that study group.

④[inflict, apply, give]

apply force

¶ Nylon melts when **heated**.

kuwashii〔adj〕 **detailed, minute; know well, be well versed**

①[detailed, minute, full]

¶ Please **elaborate**.

¶ This dictionary gives **fuller** explanations than that one.

②[know well, be well versed]

¶ [He] **knows a lot** about Japanese history.

¶ He **is well acquainted** with this neighborhood.

*普通「〜に詳しい（〜ni kuwashii）」
の形で使う。

-くん -君〔尾〕

田中君（Tanaka *kun*）
＊普通、男の人が男の友達や目下の男
の人を呼ぶときに名前のあとにつけて
使う。

ぐんじん 軍人〔名〕

¶父は軍人でした。（Chichi wa *gunjin*
deshita.）

ぐんたい 軍隊〔名〕

¶この国では、若い男の人はみんな軍
隊に入ります。（Kono kuni de wa,
wakai otoko no hito wa minna *guntai* ni
hairimasu.）
¶軍隊での経験は役に立ちますか。
（Guntai de no keiken wa yaku ni
tachimasu ka？）

*Generally used in the pattern "〜 *ni
kuwashii*."

-kun 〔suf〕 a suffix added to names

Mr. Tanaka
＊Generally added to names when men
address their male friends or men lower
in status than themselves.

gunjin 〔n〕 soldier, serviceman, member of the armed forces

¶My father was **in the military**.

guntai 〔n〕 troops, army, the military

¶In this country all young men have to
serve in **the military**.

¶Is one's **military** experience of any
use? 〖Will my **military** experience be
of any use?〗

け

け 毛 [名]

① [動物の体や頭などに生える細かい糸のような物]

髪の毛 (kaminoke) 毛が生える (ke ga haeru) 毛が抜ける (ke ga nukeru) 毛深い (kebukai)

¶ このブラシは豚の毛でできています。(Kono burashi wa buta no ke de dekite imasu.)

② [織物などの原料としての羊毛、またそれで作ったもの]

毛織物 (keorimono) 毛糸 (keito)

¶ 毛のシャツはとても暖かいです。(Ke no shatsu wa totemo atatakai desu.)

-けい -系 [尾]

文科系 (bunkakei) 理科系 (rikakei) 太陽系 (taiyōkei) 日系人 (nikkei-jin)

けいえい 経営 [名、～する]

経営者 (keeisha) 個人経営 (kojin-keiei) 多角経営 (takakukeiei) 経営学 (keieigaku)

¶ この町には中国人経営のレストランが3軒あります。(Kono machi ni wa Chūgokujin keiei no resutoran ga sangen arimasu.)

ke [n] hair, feather, fur; wool

① [hair, feather, fur, down]

(human) **hair** // **hair** grows in // **hair** falls out, lose **one's hair** // be **hairy**

¶ This brush is made from hog **bristles**.

② [wool]

woolen cloth, **woolen** goods // **woolen** yarn, knitting yarn
¶ **Wool** shirts are very warm.

-kei [suf] system; descent; faction, clique

of 〖a graduate of〗 the department of liberal arts // of 〖a graduate of〗 the science department // the solar **system** // a person of Japanese **descent** (and born outside of Japan)

keiei [n, ～suru] management, administration, operation

a manager, executive, operator, proprietor // private **management** // multiple **operation** // business **administration**
¶ There are three restaurants under Chinese **management** in this town.

¶上田さんはホテルを経営しています。(Ueda san wa hoteru o *keiei* shite imasu.)

¶ [Mr.] Ueda **runs** a hotel.

けいかく 計画〔名、〜する〕

keikaku〔n, 〜*suru*〕**plan, project, scheme**

計画経済（*keikaku*-keizai）計画者（*keikaku*sha）都市計画（toshi-*keikaku*）

a **planned** economy // **a promoter, planner** // city **planning**

¶政府は経済5か年計画を立てました。(Seifu wa keizai gokanen *keikaku* o tatemashita.)

¶ The government drew up a five year economic **plan**.

¶研究は計画どおりに進んでいます。(Kenkyū wa *keikaku* doori ni susunde imasu.)

¶ Research is proceeding according to **plan**〚**schedule**〛.

¶この犯罪は計画的に行われたようですね。(Kono hanzai wa *keikaku*teki ni okonawareta yō desu ne.)

¶ It appears that this was a **premeditated** crime.

けいかん 警官〔名〕

keikan〔n〕**police officer, policeman, the police**

婦人警官（fujin-*keikan*）警官隊（*keikan*tai）

policewoman // **police** force〚**squad**〛

¶どろぼうは警官に捕まりました。(Dorobō wa *keikan* ni tsukamari-mashita.)

¶ The thief was caught by **the police**.

¶道がわからないときは警官に尋ねます。(Michi ga wakaranai toki wa *keikan* ni tazunemasu.)

¶ [I] ask **a policeman** when [I] don't know the way.

⇒お巡りさん omawarisan

けいけん 経験〔名、〜する〕

keiken〔n, 〜*suru*〕**experience**

経験がある（*keiken* ga aru）経験がない（*keiken* ga nai）経験が深い（*keiken* ga fukai）経験を積む（*keiken* o tsumu）

have **experience**, be experienced // have no **experience**, be inexperienced // have much 〚**extensive**〛 **experience** // gain **experience**, add to **one's experience**

¶わたしはまだ日本で生活した経験はありません。(Watashi wa mada Nihon de seikatsu shita *keiken* wa arimasen.)

¶ I don't yet have **any experience** of life in Japan.

¶わたしは外国に行った時、言葉がわからなくてつらい経験をしました。（Watashi wa gaikoku ni itta toki, kotoba ga wakaranakute tsurai *keiken* o shimashita.）

¶ Not knowing the language(s), I had painful **experiences** when I went abroad.

けいこう 傾向〔名〕

keikō 〔n〕 **tendency, inclination**

¶都市の人口は次第に増える傾向にあります。（Toshi no jinkō wa shidai ni fueru *keikō* ni arimasu.）

¶ There is **a tendency** for the population of cities to gradually increase.

¶あの人は何でも大げさに言う傾向があります。（Ano hito wa nan demo oogesa ni iu *keikō* ga arimasu.）

¶ [He] **tends** to exaggerate everything.

けいこうとう けい光燈〔名〕

keikōtō 〔n〕 **a fluorescent light**

¶最近では、どの家庭でもけい光燈を使っています。（Saikin de wa, dono katei demo *keikōtō* o tsukatte imasu.）

¶ Recently all households have come to use **fluorescent lights**.

けいざい 経済〔名〕

keizai 〔n〕 **economy, economics; finance; saving, economy**

①〔社会生活に必要なものを生産したり分配したり消費したりする活動〕

① [economy, economics]

¶第二次大戦後、日本の経済は大きく発展しました。（Dainiji-taisengo, Nihon no *keizai* wa ookiku hatten shimashita.）

¶ Japan's **economy** made great strides after World War II.

②〔お金のやりくり、財政状態〕

② [finance]

¶田中さんは今仕事がないので、経済的に苦しいようです。（Tanaka san wa ima shigoto ga nai node, *keizai*teki ni kurushii yō desu.）

¶ As [Mr.] Tanaka is presently out of work, it seems [he]'s having a hard time **financially**.

③〔お金などがあまりかからないこと〕

③ [saving, economy]

¶タクシーよりも電車のほうが経済的です。（Takushii yori mo densha no hō ga *keizai*teki desu.）

¶ The train is more **economical** than a taxi.

けいさつ 警察〔名〕

keisatsu 〔n〕 **the police**

警察官（*keisatsu*kan）警察署（*keisatsu*sho）警察犬（*keisatsu*ken）

a **police** officer // a **police** station // a **police** dog

¶お金を拾ったので、警察に届けました。(Okane o hirotta node, *keisatsu* ni todokemashita.)

¶ [I] found some money and turned it over to **the police**.

けいさん 計算 〔名、〜する〕

keisan 〔n, 〜*suru*〕 **calculation, computation, accounts**

計算が合う (*keisan* ga au) 計算を間違える (*keisan* o machigaeru) 計算が早い (*keisan* ga hayai)

the figures add up, the figures prove to be correct // miscalculate, do **a sum** wrong // be quick at **figures**

¶山田さんはこんな易しい計算もできません。(Yamada san wa konna yasashii *keisan* mo dekimasen.)

¶ [Mr.] Yamada can't do even a simple **calculation** like this one.

¶一か月の食費がどのくらいになるか計算してください。(Ikkagetsu no shokuhi ga dono kurai ni naru ka *keisan* shite kudasai.)

¶ Please **calculate** how much one month's food expenses come to.

けいしき 形式 〔名〕

keishiki 〔n〕 **form, formalities; external form**

① [ものごとを行うときの一定の型]

① [form, formalities]

¶この小説は手紙の形式で書かれています。(Kono shōsetsu wa tegami no *keishiki* de kakarete imasu.)

¶ This novel is written in **the form** of a series of letters.

② [ものごとの内容の伴わない表面的なあり方]

② [external form]

形式的 (*keishiki*teki)

formal, a matter of **form**

¶形式よりも内容が大切です。(Keishiki yori mo naiyō ga taisetsu desu.)

¶ Content is more important than **external form** 〚Substance is more important than **form**〛.

げいじゅつ 芸術 〔名〕

geijutsu 〔n〕 **(fine)art, an art, the arts**

芸術品 (*geijutsu*hin) 芸術家 (*geijutsu*ka)

a work of **art**, an **art** object // **an artist**

¶わたしは日本の芸術に興味を持っています。(Watashi wa Nihon no *geijutsu* ni kyōmi o motte imasu.)

¶ I am interested in **the fine arts and performing arts** of Japan.

けいと　毛糸〔名〕

¶毛糸で編んだくつ下は暖かいです
ね。(*Keito* de anda kutsushita wa atatakai
desu ne.)

けいやく　契約〔名、〜する〕

契約書（*keiyaku*sho）契約を結ぶ
（*keiyaku* o musubu）契約を守る
（*keiyaku* o mamoru）契約を破る
（*keiyaku* o yaburu）
¶一か月二万円で家を借りる契約をし
ました。(Ikkagetsu niman'en de ie o
kariru *keiyaku* o shimashita.)
¶来年の３月で契約が切れます。
(Rainen no sangatsu de *keiyaku* ga
kiremasu.)

ゲーム〔名〕

¶みんなでゲームをしましょう。
(Minna de *gēmu* o shimashō.)
¶日本の子供はどんなゲームをして遊
びますか。(Nihon no kodomo wa donna
gēmu o shite asobimasu ka？)

けが〔名、〜する〕

けが人（*kega*nin）大けが（oo*kega*）

¶転んで足にけがをしました。
(Koronde ashi ni *kega* o shimashita.)
¶彼はけがが原因で死にました。
(Kare wa *kega* ga gen'in de shini-
mashita.)

げき　劇〔名〕

悲劇（hi*geki*）喜劇（ki*geki*）

keito 〔n〕 **woolen yarn, knitting wool**

¶Knitted **wool** socks are warm, aren't they?

keiyaku 〔n, 〜*suru*〕 **contract, agreement**

a (written) **contract** // conclude a **contract** // abide by **a contract** // break **a contract**

¶[I] signed **a contract** to rent a house for twenty thousand yen a month.

¶**The contract** expires in March of next year.

gēmu 〔n〕 **a game**

¶Let's all play **a game**.

¶What sort of **games** do Japanese children play for fun?

kega 〔n, 〜*suru*〕 **injury, wound**

an **injured** person, the wounded // a serious **injury**

¶[I] fell and **hurt** [my] leg 〚foot〛.

¶He died of **his wound(s)**.

geki 〔n〕 **drama, play, theatrical performance**

tragedy // comedy

¶外国人の学生が日本語で劇をしました。(Gaikokujin no gakusei ga Nihongo de *geki* o shimashita.)

¶あなたも劇に出ますか。(Anata mo *geki* ni demasu ka?)

¶ The foreign students performed **a play** in Japanese.

¶ Are you going to be in **the play?**

げきじょう 劇場〔名〕

gekijō 〔n〕 **theater**

¶あの劇場では今何をやっていますか。(Ano *gekijō* de wa ima nani o yatte imasu ka?)

¶ What's on now at that **theater?**

¶劇場は満員で入れませんでした。(Gekijō wa man'in de hairemasen deshita.)

¶ **The theater** was full and [we] weren't able to get in.

けさ 今朝〔名〕

kesa 〔n〕 **this morning**

¶わたしは今朝6時に起きました。(Watashi wa *kesa* rokuji ni okimashita.)

¶ I got up at six o'clock **this morning**.

けしき 景色〔名〕

keshiki 〔n〕 **scenery, view**

¶北海道には景色のいい所がたくさんあります。(Hokkaidō ni wa *keshiki* no ii tokoro ga takusan arimasu.)

¶ There is much beautiful **scenery** in Hokkaido.

¶ここから見る富士山の景色は本当にすばらしいです。(Koko kara miru Fujisan no *keshiki* wa hontō ni subarashii desu.)

¶ **The view** of Mount Fuji from here is really wonderful.

けしゴム 消しゴム〔名〕

keshigomu 〔n〕 **(rubber) eraser**

¶間違えた字を消しゴムで消しました。(Machigaeta ji o *keshigomu* de keshimashita.)

¶ [I] erased the mistaken letter with **an eraser**.

げしゅく 下宿〔名、～する〕

geshuku 〔n, ～*suru*〕 **lodging, a boardinghouse, a rooming house**

¶いい下宿を探しています。(Ii *geshuku* o sagashite imasu.)

¶ [I] am looking for a good **room**.

¶わたしは学校のそばに下宿しています。(Watashi wa gakkō no soba ni *geshuku* shite imasu.)

¶ I am living in a **rooming house** near school.

げじゅん 下旬 〔名〕

¶今月の下旬に引っ越します。
(Kongetsu no *gejun* ni hikkoshimasu.)
¶3月の下旬から4月の上旬にかけて
旅行します。(Sangatsu no *gejun* kara
shigatsu no jōjun ni kakete ryokō
shimasu.)
⇒上旬 jōjun 中旬 chūjun

gejun 〔n〕 **the last third of the month**

¶ [I]'m going to move **late** this month
〖**towards the end** of this month〗.
¶ [I] will be traveling from **late** March
through early April 〖from **the last part**
of March through the early part of
April〗.

けしょう 化粧 〔名、〜する〕

化粧品 (*keshō*hin)
¶姉は今お化粧をしています。(Ane
wa ima o*keshō* o shite imasu.)
¶あの人は化粧しなくてもきれいで
す。(Ano hito wa *keshō* shinakute mo
kirei desu.)

keshō 〔n, 〜*suru*〕 **makeup, (one's) toiletry**
cosmetics

¶ My (elder) sister is now putting on
her makeup.
¶ She is beautiful even without
makeup.

けす 消す 〔動Ⅰ〕

① [明かりや火などをなくす]

火を消す (hi o *kesu*)
¶ゆうべは電気を消さないで寝てしま
いました。(Yūbe wa denki o *kesanaide*
nete shimaimashita.)
② [スイッチを切って音などをなくす]
ラジオを消す (rajio o *kesu*)
¶見ないときは、テレビを消しなさ
い。(Minai toki wa, terebi o
keshinasai.)
③ [物の形などを見えなくする]
¶黒板の字を消してください。
(Kokuban no ji o *keshite* kudasai.)
¶間違ったところを消しゴムで消して
書き直しました。(Machigatta tokoro o

kesu 〔v Ⅰ〕 **put out, extinguish; turn off; erase; disappear, vanish**

① [put out, extinguish (lights, fire, etc.)]
put out a fire
¶ [I] fell asleep last night **without turning off** the lights.

② [turn off (a switch, etc.)]
turn off the radio
¶ **Turn off** the television when you are not watching it.

③ [erase, rub out, delete]
¶ Please **erase** the words on the blackboard.
¶ I corrected it, **erasing** the mistaken parts with an eraser.

263

keshigomu de *keshite*
kakinaoshimashita.)

④ [姿などが見られなくなる]

¶ この動物は昔はたくさんいたんです
が、最近はすっかり姿を消してしまい
ました。(Kono dōbutsu wa mukashi wa
takusan ita n desu ga, saikin wa sukkari
sugata o *keshite* shimaimashita.)

④ [disappear, vanish]

¶ This animal was plentiful in the past
but recently has completely
disappeared.

けずる　削る〔動 I〕

① [物の表面を薄くそぎとる]

¶ ナイフで鉛筆を削ります。(Naifu de
enpitsu o *kezurimasu*.)

② [必要でない部分を取り除く]

¶ 余分なところを削って、文章を短く
しました。(Yobun na tokoro o *kezutte*,
bunshō o mijikaku shimashita.)

kezuru 〔v I〕 **shave, sharpen,
whittle; cut down, reduce**

① [shave, sharpen, whittle; remove the
surface of an object]

¶ One **sharpens** a pencil with a knife.

② [cut down, reduce, cross out, delete;
remove an unnecessary part]

¶ [I] shortened the text by **taking out**
the unnecessary parts.

けち〔形動〕

¶ あの人はけちだから、お金を貸して
くれないと思います。(Ano hito wa
kechi da kara, okane o kashite kurenai to
omoimasu.)

¶ 人間は、お金がたまるとますますけ
ちになると言われています。(Ningen
wa, okane ga tamaru to masumasu *kechi* ni
naru to iwarete imasu.)

kechi 〔adj-v〕 **stingy, miserly**

¶ I don't think [he] will loan [us] any
money because [he]'s **so stingy**.

¶ It's said that people become **stingier**
the more money they have.

けっか　結果〔名〕

¶ 試験の結果はいつ発表されますか。
(Shiken no *kekka* wa itsu happyō
saremasu ka?)

¶ 長い間努力した結果、ついに実験に
成功しました。(Nagai aida doryoku
shita *kekka*, tsuini jikken ni seikō
shimashita.)
⇔原因 gen'in

kekka 〔n〕 **result, outcome**

¶ When will **the results** of the exam be
annouced?

¶ Long-term efforts at last **resulted** in
the success of the experiment.

げっきゅう　月給 〔名〕

¶今度月給をもらったら、レコードを
買うつもりです。（Kondo *gekkyū* o
morattara, rekōdo o kau tsumori desu.）

けっきょく　結局 〔副〕

¶いろいろ話し合いましたが、結局い
い考えは出てきませんでした。（Iroiro
hanashiaimashita ga, *kekkyoku* ii kangae
wa dete kimasen deshita.）
¶このフットボールの試合は、結局A
チームが勝ちました。（Kono futtobōru
no shiai wa, *kekkyoku* Ē-chīmu ga
kachimashita.）

けっこう 〔副、形動〕

1 〔副〕
¶このカメラは古いが、けっこうよく
撮れます。（Kono kamera wa furui ga,
kekkō yoku toremasu.）
2 〔形動〕
①［よい、立派だ］
¶けっこうな贈り物をありがとうござ
いました。（*Kekkō* na okurimono o
arigatō gozaimashita.）
②［じゅうぶんだ］
¶「お茶をもう一杯いかがですか。」
（Ocha o mō ippai ikaga desu ka？）「も
う、けっこうです。」（Mō *kekkō* desu.）

けっこん　結婚 〔名、～する〕
結婚式（*kekkon*shiki）結婚生活
（*kekkon*-seikatsu）結婚届（*kekkon*-
todoke）国際結婚（kokusai*kekkon*）

gekkyū 〔n〕 **monthly salary,
wages**

¶I plan to buy some records when I **get
paid** next.

kekkyoku 〔adv〕 **finally,
ultimately, in the end**

¶We talked about various possibilities
but **in the end** had no good ideas.

¶**Ultimately** Team A won this football
〖soccer〗 match.

kekkō 〔adv, adj-v〕 **quite, fairly
well, good, fine; well enough,
fine as is**

1 〔adv〕 **quite, fairly well**
¶This camera is old but works **quite
well**.

2 〔adj-v〕
① [**good, fine, nice, excellent**]
¶Thank you for the **lovely** present.

② [**well enough, fine as is**]
¶"Would you like another cup of
(green) tea?"
"No, this is **fine** 〖No, thank you〗.

kekkon 〔n, ～*suru*〕 **marriage**
a **marriage** ceremony, wedding //
married life // registration of **one's
marriage** // **marriage** between those
of different nationalities

¶上田さんは秋子さんに結婚を申し込みました。(Ueda san wa Akiko san ni *kekkon* o mōshikomimashita.)

¶ Mr. Ueda **proposed** to Akiko.

¶上田さんと秋子さんは来月結婚します。(Ueda san to Akiko san wa raigetsu *kekkon* shimasu.)

¶ Mr. Ueda and Akiko **are going to get married** next month.

¶御結婚おめでとうございます。(Go*kekkon* omedetō gozaimasu.)

¶ Congratulations on **your marriage**.

けっして　決して〔副〕

kesshite〔adv〕**never, by no means**

¶御親切は決して忘れません。(Go-shinsetsu wa *kesshite* wasuremasen.)

¶ I will **never** forget your kindness.

¶その問題の解決は決して簡単ではありません。(Sono mondai no kaiketsu wa *kesshite* kantan de wa arimasen.)

¶ Solving that problem will **by no means** be easy.

＊あとに打ち消しの言葉が来る。

＊*Kesshite* is used with the negative.

けっしん　決心〔名、～する〕

kesshin〔n, ～*suru*〕**determination, resolution**

¶わたしは今日からたばこをやめる決心をしました。(Watashi wa kyō kara tabako o yameru *kesshin* o shimashita.)

¶ I **have resolved** to quit smoking from today on.

¶行こうかどうしようか、まだ決心がつきません。(Ikō ka dō shiyō ka, mada *kesshin* ga tsukimasen.)

¶ [I] haven't **made up my mind** yet whether to go or not.

けっせき　欠席〔名、～する〕

kesseki〔n, ～*suru*〕**absence, non-attendance**

欠席者（*kesseki*sha)　欠席届（*kesseki*-todoke)

an absentee // a report of **absence**

¶試験が終わると、急に欠席者が多くなります。(Shiken ga owaru to, kyū ni *kesseki*sha ga ooku narimasu.)

¶ After exams are over, the number of students **missing class** suddenly goes up.

¶上田さんは病気で今日は欠席です。(Ueda san wa byōki de kyō wa *kesseki* desu.)

¶ [Miss] Ueda **is absent** today due to illness.

¶急用ができましたので、今日の会議は欠席します。(Kyūyō ga dekimashita de, kyō no kaigi wa *kesseki* shimasu.)

¶ As some urgent business has arisen, [I] **will be absent** from today's meeting.

⇔ 出席 shusseki

けってい　決定 〔名、〜する〕

¶わたしは皆さんの決定に従います。
(Watashi wa minasan no *kettei* ni
shitagaimasu.)
¶出発の日はもう決定しましたか。
(Shuppatsu no hi wa mō *kettei* shimashita
ka？)

kettei 〔n, 〜*suru*〕 **a decision, a
determination, a conclusion**
¶ I will abide by **the decision** of all.

¶ **Have you set** the departure date yet?

けってん　欠点 〔名〕

¶上田さんの欠点は約束を守らないこ
とです。(Ueda san no *ketten* wa
yakusoku o mamoranai koto desu.)
¶このレストランは、料理はおいしい
のですが、いつもこんでいるのが欠点
です。(Kono resutoran wa, ryōri wa
oishii no desu ga, itsu mo konde iru no ga
ketten desu.)
⇒短所 tansho

ketten 〔n〕 **fault, defect, flaw,
weak point**
¶ [Mr.] Ueda's **major weak point** is
not keeping [his] promises.

¶ The food is good at this restaurant,
but its always being crowded is **a
drawback.**

げつよう(び)　月曜(日) 〔名〕

getsuyō (bi) 〔n〕 **Monday**

けつろん　結論 〔名〕

¶何回も話し合いましたが、なかなか
結論が出ませんでした。(Nankai mo
hanashiaimashita ga, nakanaka *ketsuron*
ga demasen deshita.)
¶この工事を今年じゅうに完成するの
は無理だという結論に達しました。
(Kono kōji o kotoshijū ni kansei suru no
wa muri da to iu *ketsuron* ni
tasshimashita.)

ketsuron 〔n〕 **conclusion**
¶ [We] talked together many times but
couldn't arrive at **any conclusion.**

¶ [They] came to **the conclusion** that it
was impossible to complete this
construction work before the end of the
year.

けど ☞けれども

kedo ☞**keredomo**

けむり　煙 〔名〕
たばこの煙 (tabako no *kemuri*)

kemuri 〔n〕 **smoke, fumes**
cigarette **smoke,** tobacco **fumes**

¶工場の煙突から煙が出ています。
（Kōjō no entotsu kara *kemuri* ga dete
imasu.）

¶**Smoke** is being emitted from the
factory smokestack(s).

けもの　獣〔名〕

¶あの森にはいろいろな獣がいます。
（Ano mori ni wa iroiro na *kemono* ga
imasu.）

kemono 〔n〕 **beast, animal, wild
animal**

¶There are various **wild animals** in
that forest.

ける〔動Ⅰ〕

¶ボールをけって遊びましょう。
（Bōru o *kette* asobimashō.）
¶上田さんは馬にけられて、けがをし
ました。（Ueda san wa uma ni *kerarete*,
kega o shimashita.）

keru 〔v I〕 **kick**

¶Let's play **kicking** the ball.

¶[Mr.] Ueda was injured when [he]
was kicked by a horse.

けれども〔接〕

¶わたしは田中さんを知っています。
けれども、田中さんはわたしを知らな
いでしょう。（Watashi wa Tanaka san o
shitte imasu. *Keredomo*, Tanaka san wa
watashi o shiranai deshō.）
¶わたしは大学へ行きたいんです。け
れども、お金がないんです。（Watashi
wa daigaku e ikitai n desu. *Keredomo*,
okane ga nai n desu.）
＊前のことがらを受けて、それから予
想される結果に合わないことや対比
的・対立的なことなどをあとに言うと
きに使う。「けれど（keredo）」「けども
（kedomo）」「けど（kedo）」とも言う。
⇒しかし **shikashi**

keredomo 〔conj〕 **however, but**

¶I know [Mr.] Tanaka. **However**,
[Mr.] Tanaka probably doesn't know
me.

¶I want to go to college. **However**, I
don't have the money for it.

＊*Keredomo* is used when the second
sentence doesn't agree with what would
be expected to follow the first sentence
or when it is in contrast or opposition
to it. Variants are *keredo*, *kedomo* and
kedo.

けれども〔助〕

①[ものごとをはっきり断定的に言う
のを避けて柔らかく言い相手の反応を
待つ気持ちを表す]

keredomo 〔part〕 **but**

① [but; employed to soften one's
speech and avoid saying something
directly and conclusively and also to
indicate that one is awaiting the
listener's response]

¶あなたがどういう意味でおっしゃっているのかわからないんですけれども。(Anata ga dōiu imi de osshatte iru no ka wakaranai n desu *keredomo*.)

¶I'm not sure what you mean by that... (omitted: please make it clearer, etc.).

¶あの方のお名前が思い出せないんですけれども。(Ano kata no onamae ga omoidasenai n desu *keredomo*.)

¶I can't remember that person's name... (omitted: could you tell me what it is?).

②[望ましいことがらの成立を願う気持ちや実現しなかったことがらを回想してそれが成立していればどんなによかったかというような気持ちを表す]

②[but; used to express the wish that something could happen or to express how nice it would have been if something could have been realized]

¶父が生きていたら、大学へも行けたんですけれども。(Chichi ga ikite itara, daigaku e mo iketa n desu *keredomo*.)

¶If my father had lived I could have gone to college... (omitted: **but** he died and I couldn't).

¶試験に合格していればいいのですけれども。(Shiken ni gōkaku shite ireba ii no desu *keredomo*.)

¶[I] hope [I] passed the exam (omitted: **but** I'm not sure I did).

＊「けれど (keredo)」「けども (kedomo)」「けど (kedo)」とも言う。

＊Variants: *keredo*, *kedomo* and *kedo*.

⇒が **ga**

けれども〔助〕

keredomo 〔part〕 but, although; however, nevertheless

①[前件から当然予想される結果が後件において成立しないという関係を表す]

①[but, although, even though; indicates the disappointment in the second clause of what would be expected as a natural result of the first clause]

¶やっと家を建てたのですけれども、また引っ越さなければならなくなりました。(Yatto ie o tateta no desu *keredomo*, mata hikkosanakereba naranaku narimashita.)

¶[We] were finally able to build a house, **but** then [we] had to move again.

¶一生懸命勉強したけれども、試験には受かりませんでした。(Isshōkenmei benkyō shita *keredomo*, shiken ni wa ukarimasen deshita.)

¶**Although** I studied very hard, I failed the exam.

② [前件が後件に対して対比的・対立的な関係にあることを表す]

¶ 車を買いたいけれども、お金がないので買えません。（Kuruma o kaitai *keredomo*, okane ga nai node kaemasen.）

¶ わたしは田中さんを知っていますけれども、田中さんはわたしを知らないでしょう。（Watashi wa Tanaka san o shitte imasu *keredomo*, Tanaka san wa watashi o shiranai deshō.）

③ [前件が後件に対する前置きなどの関係にあることを表す]

¶ もしもし、上田ですけれども、田中さんはいらっしゃいますか。（Moshi moshi, Ueda desu *keredomo*, Tanaka san wa irasshaimasu ka？）

¶ すみませんけれど、上田さんのお宅はどの辺でしょうか。（Sumimasen *keredo*, Ueda san no otaku wa dono hen deshō ka？）

¶ 時計を買いたいのですけれど、どこの店で買ったらいいでしょうか。（Tokei o kaitai no desu *keredo*, doko no mise de kattara ii deshō ka？）

¶ バスで行こうと思いましたけれども、あまり天気がいいので、歩いていくことにしました。（Basu de ikō to omoimashita *keredomo*, amari tenki ga ii node, aruite iku koto ni shimashita.）

④ [前件のことがらが後件のことがらに対して共存的な関係にあることを表す]

¶ わたしはテレビも欲しいけれど、ラジオもやはり欲しいです。（Watashi wa terebi mo hoshii *keredo*, rajio mo yahari hoshii desu.）

② [but, however, nevertheless; indicates that the first clause is in contrast or opposition to the second clause]

¶ I want to buy a car **but** can't because I don't have the money.

¶ I know [Miss] Tanaka. **However**, [Miss] Tanaka probably doesn't know me.

③ [but, and; indicates the first clause introduces the second one]

¶ Hello, this [Mr.] Ueda. Is [Mr.] Tanaka there?

¶ Excuse me. Whereabouts is the Ueda residence?

¶ I want to buy a watch 〚clock〛. Where is a good store to buy it?

¶ I thought I would go by bus, **but** it was such a nice day that I decided to walk instead.

④ [but, however; indicates the coexistence of the first and second clauses]

¶ I want a television **but** I also want a radio.

¶北海道へも行きたいけれど、沖縄へ
も行ってみたいです。(Hokkaidō e mo
ikitai *keredo*, Okinawa e mo itte mitai
desu.)

＊「けれど (keredo)」「けども (ke-
domo)」「けど (kedo)」とも言う。

⇒が **ga**

¶ I want to go to Hokkaido **but** I'd also
like to go to Okinawa.

＊Variants: *keredo*, *kedomo* and *kedo*.

けん 県〔名〕
広島県 (Hiroshima-*ken*) 県庁 (*ken-
chō*) 県知事 (*ken*chiji)

ken 〔n〕 **prefecture**
Hiroshima **Prefecture** // **prefectural**
office // **prefectural** governor

けん 券〔名〕
乗車券 (jōsha*ken*) 定期券 (teiki-*ken*)
急行券 (kyūkō*ken*) 入場券
(nyūjō*ken*) 前売り券 (maeuri*ken*) 診察
券 (shinsatsu*ken*) 招待券 (shōtai*ken*)
割引券 (waribiki*ken*) 食券 (shok*ken*)
旅券 (ryo*ken*) 株券 (kabu*ken*)

ken 〔n〕 **ticket, coupon, bond**
a passenger **ticket** // a commuting
pass, season **pass** // an express **ticket** //
an admission **ticket**, platform **ticket** //
an advance **ticket** // a clinic registration
card // a complimentary **ticket**,
invitation **card** (for an exhibition,
etc.) // a discount **coupon** // a meal
ticket, food **coupon** // a passport // a
stock **certificate**

¶券を買わなければ入場できません。
(*Ken* o kawanakereba nyūjō dekimasen.)

¶ You cannot enter without **a ticket**.

¶音楽会の券が2枚ありますから、いっ
しょに行きませんか。(Ongakukai no
ken ga nimai arimasu kara, issho ni
ikimasen ka？)

¶ I have two **tickets** to a concert
〚recital〛. Won't you come with me?

-けん -軒〔尾〕
1軒 (ik*ken*) 3軒 (san*gen*) 6軒
(rok*ken*) 8軒 (hak*ken*) 何軒
(nan*gen*)

-ken 〔suf〕 **the counter for houses**
one **house** // three **houses** // six
houses // eight **houses** // how many
houses

¶川の向こうに家が二、三軒見えま
す。(Kawa no mukō ni ie ga ni-san*gen*
miemasu.)

¶ Two or three **houses** can be seen on
the other side of the river.

げんいん 原因〔名〕

¶今、事故の原因を調べています。
(Ima, jiko no *gen'in* o shirabete imasu.)
¶火事の原因はたばこの火でした。
(Kaji no *gen'in* wa tabako no hi deshita.)
⇔結果 kekka

けんか〔名、〜する〕

兄弟げんか(kyōdai-*genka*) 夫婦げん
か(fūfu-*genka*)

¶子供たちがけんかをしています。
(Kodomotachi ga *kenka* o shite imasu.)
¶わたしは上田さんとけんかしてしま
いました。(Watashi wa Ueda san to
kenka shite shimaimashita.)

けんがく 見学〔名、〜する〕

見学旅行(*kengaku*-ryokō)

¶学校から工場見学に行きました。
(Gakkō kara kōjō-*kengaku* ni
ikimashita.)

げんかん 玄関〔名〕

¶玄関にだれか来たようです。
(Genkan ni dare ka kita yō desu.)
¶日本では玄関でくつを脱いで上がり
ます。(Nihon de wa *genkan* de kutsu o
nuide agarimasu.)

げんき 元気〔名、形動〕

①[活動力があっていきいきしている
こと]

gen'in 〔n〕 **cause, source, origin**

¶ **The cause** of the accident is
presently under investigation.

¶ **The cause** of the fire was a cigarette
butt.

kenka 〔n, 〜*suru*〕 **quarrel,
argument, fight, coming to
blows**

a quarrel between brothers // **a
quarrel** between husband and wife,
domestic **strife**

¶ The children **are arguing** 〚**fighting**〛.

¶ I **quarreled** 〚**had a fight**〛 with
[Mrs.] Ueda.

kengaku 〔n, 〜*suru*〕 **study by
inspection, field trip**

an **inspection** trip, a **study** tour, a
school trip

¶ [I] went on **a school trip** to a factory.

genkan 〔n〕 **vestibule, entryway,
entrance hall**

¶ It looks like someone has come **to
the door**.

¶ In Japan one takes off one's shoes
inside the front door.

genki 〔n, adj-v〕 **energy, vitality;
health**

① [energy, vitality]

元気がある (*genki* ga aru) 元気がいい (*genki* ga ii) 元気な子供 (*genki* na kodomo)

② [体の状態がよくて健康であること]

¶「お元気ですか。」(Ogenki desu ka？)「はい、おかげさまで元気です。」(Hai, okagesama de *genki* desu.)

¶彼はもうすぐ元気になって退院するでしょう。(Kare wa mō sugu *genki* ni natte taiin suru deshō.)

be **in good spirits**, be **in good vigor** // be **in high spirits**, be **in good vigor** // an **active** child

② [health, vigor]

¶ "How are you?"
"Fine, thank you." (literally, "Are you **in good health?**" "Yes, **I am** thanks to you.")

¶ He should soon **be up and about** and be able to leave the hospital.

けんきゅう 研究 〔名、〜する〕

研究室 (kenkūshitsu) 研究所 (*kenkyū*jo) 研究会 (*kenkyū*kai) 研究費 (*kenkyū*hi) 研究活動 (*kenkyū*katsudō)

¶最近、わたしたちの国でも日本研究が盛んになってきました。(Saikin, watashitachi no kuni de mo Nihon-*kenkyū* ga sakan ni natte kima-shita.)

¶あなたは日本で何を研究するつもりですか。(Anata wa Nihon de nani o *kenkyū* suru tsumori desu ka？)

kenkyū 〔n, 〜*suru*〕 **study, research, investigation**

a study, office, laboratory // a **research** laboratory, **research** institute // a **study** group, society for the **study** of a certain subject // **research** funds, **research expenses** // **research** activities

¶ Recently **the study** of Japan has become popular in our country.

¶ What do you plan **to study** in Japan?

げんきん 現金 〔名〕

現金で払う (*genkin* de harau)

¶今、現金でいくら持っていますか。(Ima, *genkin* de ikura motte imasu ka？)

¶現金を持っていると、すぐ使ってしまいます。(Genkin o motte iru to, sugu tsukatte shimaimasu.)

genkin 〔n〕 **cash**

pay in cash

¶ How much **money** do you have with you now?

¶ When [I] carry **cash** with [me], [I] soon spend it all.

けんこう 健康 〔名、形動〕

健康診断 (*kenkō*-shindan) 健康状態 (*kenkō*-jōtai) 健康保険 (*kenkō*-ho-ken) 健康を害する (*kenkō* o gaisuru)

kenkō 〔n, adj-v〕 **health**

a **physical** checkup, a **medical** examination // the condition of **one's health** // **health** insurance // injure **one's health**

¶健康にじゅうぶん注意してください。(Kenkō ni jūbun chūi shite kudasai.)

¶ Please take good care **of yourself**.

¶たばこの吸いすぎは健康に悪いです。(Tabako no suisugi wa *kenkō* ni warui desu.)

¶ Smoking too much is bad for **one's health**.

¶父はもうすっかり健康を回復しました。(Chichi wa mō sukkari *kenkō* o kaifuku shimashita.)

¶ My father is completely **recovered** now.

¶健康な人なら、一日 30 キロは歩けますよ。(*Kenkō* na hito nara, ichinichi sanjikkiro wa arukemasu yo.)

¶ A person **in good health** should be able to walk 30 kilometers in one day.

けんさ 検査〔名、〜する〕

kensa 〔n, 〜*suru*〕 **inspection, examination, test**

検査を受ける (*kensa* o ukeru) 身体検査 (shintai-*kensa*)

be **examined** // a physical **examination**, a checkup, a physical

¶この機械は検査に合格しています。(Kono kikai wa *kensa* ni gōkaku shite imasu.)

¶ This machine has passed **inspection**.

¶わたしは空港で荷物を厳しく検査されました。(Watashi wa kūkō de nimotsu o kibishiku *kensa* saremashita.)

¶ My bags were subjected to a rigorous **inspection** at the airport.

げんざい 現在〔名〕

genzai 〔n〕 **now, presently**

¶現在、わたしは東京に住んでいます。(Genzai, watashi wa Tōkyō ni sundeimasu.)

¶ I am **presently** living in Tokyo.

¶現在でも電気のない村があります。(Genzai demo denki no nai mura ga arimasu.)

¶ Even **now** there are villages which are not electrified.

⇒過去 kako　未来 mirai

げんじつ 現実〔名〕

genjitsu 〔n〕 **actuality, reality**

¶理想と現実は違います。(Risō to *genjitsu* wa chigaimasu.)

¶ The ideal and **the real**〔**actual**〕are two different things.

¶現実は厳しいですよ。(Genjitsu wa kibishii desu yo.)

¶ **Reality** is a harsh taskmaster〔**Life** is hard〕.

けんしゅう　研修〔名、〜する〕

研修生（kenshūsei）研修所
（kenshūjo）研修期間（kenshū-kikan）
¶あしたから技術研修が始まります。
（Ashita kara gijutsu-kenshū ga
hajimarimasu.）
¶学校を卒業して、すぐ工場で研修す
るつもりです。（Gakkō o sotsugyō shite,
sugu kōjō de kenshū suru tsumori desu.）

kenshū 〔n, 〜*suru*〕 training, study
and training, on-the-job training
a trainee // an in-service training
institute // a term of **training**
¶ Technical **training** starts from
tomorrow.

¶ I plan to enter **on-the-job training** at
a factory soon after graduating from
school.

げんしょう　減少〔名、〜する〕

¶この国の人口は次第に減少していま
す。（Kono kuni no jinkō wa shidai ni
genshō shite imasu.）
¶今年の夏は天気が悪かったので、米
の生産が減少しました。（Kotoshi no
natsu wa tenki ga warukatta node, kome
no seisan ga genshō shimashita.）
⇔増加 zōka
⇒減る heru

genshō 〔n, 〜*suru*〕 decrease,
decline
¶ The population of this country **is**
gradually **declining**.

¶ Rice production **has dropped** due to
the bad weather this past summer.

げんしょう　現象〔名〕

不思議な現象（fushigi na genshō）
¶それは世界的な現象です。（Sore wa
sekaiteki na genshō desu.）
¶高い山では珍しい自然現象が見られ
ます。（Takai yama de wa mezurashii
shizen-genshō ga miraremasu.）

genshō 〔n〕 phenomenon
a strange **phenomenon**〚happening〛
¶ That is a worldwide **phenomenon**.

¶ Rare natural **phenomena** can be
observed on high mountains.

けんせつ　建設〔名、〜する〕

建設工事（kensetsu-kōji）建設費
（kensetsuhi）建設会社（kensetsu-
gaisha）
¶政府は高速道路の建設を計画してい
ます。（Seifu wa kōsoku-dōro no
kensetsu o keikaku shite imasu.）

kensetsu 〔n, 〜*suru*〕 construction,
erection, building,
establishment
construction work // the cost of
construction, **construction**
expenses // a **construction** firm
¶ The government is planning **the**
construction of an expressway.

¶今年じゅうに10万戸の住宅を建設する予定です。（Kotoshijū ni jūmanko no jūtaku o *kensetsu* suru yotei desu.）

¶ One hundred thousand houses are scheduled **to be built** before the year is out.

げんだい　現代 〔名〕

現代的（*gendai*teki）現代日本文学（*gendai*-Nihonbungaku）

¶現代は科学の時代です。（Gendai wa kagaku no jidai desu.）

gendai 〔n〕 **the present age, today modern, up-to-date** // **contemporary** Japanese literature

¶ **This** is the age of science.

けんちく　建築 〔名、～する〕

建築家（*kenchiku*ka）建築様式（*kenchiku*-yōshiki）建築材料（*kenchiku*-zairyō）建築工事（*kenchiku*-kōji）建築技術（*kenchiku*-gijutsu）建築学（*kenchiku*gaku）木造建築（mokuzō-kenchiku）コンクリート建築（konkuriito-*kenchiku*）

¶古い時代の日本の建築はたいへん美しいです。（Furui jidai no Nihon no *kenchiku* wa taihen utsukushii desu.）

¶このお寺は百年前に建築されたそうです。（Kono otera wa hyakunen mae ni *kenchiku* sareta sō desu.）

kenchiku 〔n, ～*suru*〕 **construction, building, architecture**

an architect // style of **building**, **architectural** style // **construction** materials // **construction** work // **construction** techniques // **architecture** // a wooden **building** // a concrete **building**

¶ Ancient Japanese **architecture** is 〘Ancient Japanese **buildings** are〙 very beautiful.

¶ This temple is said to **have been constructed** a hundred years ago.

けんぶつ　見物 〔名、～する〕

¶来週、わたしたちは京都見物に行きます。（Raishū, watashitachi wa Kyōto-*kenbutsu* ni ikimasu.）

¶今晩、歌舞伎を見物するつもりです。（Konban, kabuki o *kenbutsu* suru tsumori desu.）

kenbutsu 〔n, ～*suru*〕 **sightseeing, visit**

¶ We are going to go **see the sights** in Kyoto next week.

¶ I plan to **go see** *kabuki* tonight.

けんぽう　憲法 〔名〕

憲法を制定する（*kenpō* o seitei suru）
憲法を改正する（*kenpō* o kaisei suru）

kenpō 〔n〕 **a constitution**

establish **a constitution** // revise **a constitution**

¶5月3日は日本の憲法記念日です。（Gogatsu mikka wa Nihon no *kenpō-kinenbi desu.*）

¶ The third of May is **Constitution** Day in Japan.

けんり　権利〔名〕

kenri〔n〕**a right, a claim**

¶第二次大戦後、女性にも男性と同じ権利が与えられました。（Dainiji-taisengo, josei ni mo dansei to onaji *kenri* ga ataeraremashita.）

¶ After World War II women were granted the same **rights** as men.

¶国民は教育を受ける権利と義務があります。（Kokumin wa kyōiku o ukeru *kenri* to gimu ga arimasu.）

¶ Citizens have **the right** and obligation of receiving an education.

⇔義務 **gimu**

げんりょう　原料〔名〕

genryō〔n〕**raw material (s)**

¶日本の酒の原料は米です。（Nihon no sake no *genryō* wa kome desu.）

¶ **The raw material** of Japanese sake is rice.

¶石油を原料にして、いろいろな物ができます。（Sekiyu o *genryō* ni shite, iroiro na mono ga dekimasu.）

¶ Various products are made from **the raw material** petroleum.

こ 子〔名〕

① [親から生まれたもの]
¶うちの子は今年小学校に入学します。(Uchi no *ko* wa kotoshi shōgakkō ni nyūgaku shimasu.)
¶ねこが子を産みました。(Neko ga *ko* o umimashita.)
⇔親 oya

② [幼い者]
¶あの子の名前は何と言いますか。(Ano *ko* no namae wa nan to iimasu ka?)
¶庭で男の子と女の子が遊んでいます。(Niwa de otoko no *ko* to onna no *ko* ga asonde imasu.)
⇔大人 otona
⇒子供 kodomo

ko 〔n〕 one's child (ren), offspring; children, the young

① [one's child(ren), offspring]
¶ Our **child** enters elementary school this year.

¶ The cat had **kittens**.

② [children, the young]
¶ What is the name of that **child**?

¶ A **boy** and a **girl** are playing in the yard.

-ご -後〔尾〕

1時間後 (ichijikan*go*) 数日後 (sūjitsu*go*) 戦後 (sen*go*) 帰国後 (kikoku*go*)

¶母の死後、父は寂しそうです。(Haha no shi*go*, chichi wa sabishisō desu.)
¶数年後に日本へ行く予定です。(Sūnen*go* ni Nihon e iku yotei desu.)

-go 〔suf〕 after, later, since

after one hour, one hour **later** // **after** several days, several days **later** // **after** the war, **post**war // **after** returning to one's native country

¶ My father seems lonely **since** my mother's death.

¶ I plan to go to Japan **in** a few years.

ご- 御-〔頭〕

① [尊敬の意味を表す]
¶両親はお元気ですか。(*Go*ryōshin ... enki desu ka?)

go- 〔pref〕 an honorific prefix

① [indicates respect toward the listener]
¶ How are your parents 〚Are your parents in good health〛?

¶御旅行はいかがでしたか。（*Go*ryokō wa ikaga deshita ka？） ¶ How was your trip?

② [謙譲の意味を表す]

② [indicates humility on the part of the speaker]

¶あした御連絡します。（Ashita *go*renraku shimasu.）

¶ I'll be in touch with you tomorrow.

¶あとで御説明します。（Ato de *go*setsumei shimasu.）

¶ I'll explain later.

⇒お- **o-**

ご 五 〔名〕

go 〔n〕 **five**

(-)ご (-)語 〔名、尾〕

(-)go 〔n, suf〕 **word; language**

1 〔名〕

1 〔n〕 word

¶次の語は何と読みますか。（Tsugi no *go* wa nan to yomimasu ka？）

¶ How is the next **word** read?

2 〔尾〕
中国語（Chūgoku*go*）ドイツ語（Doitsu*go*）英語（Ei*go*）フランス語（Furansu*go*）日本語（Nihon*go*）スペイン語（Supein*go*）現代語（gendai*go*）近代語（kindai*go*）

2 〔suf〕 language
Chinese (**language**) // German (**language**) // English (**language**) // French (**language**) // Japanese (**language**) // Spanish (**language**) //the present-day **language** //the modern **language**

-こ -個 〔尾〕

-ko 〔suf〕 **a piece, an item; the counter for small objects**

¶1個50円のりんごを5個買いました。（Ik*ko* gojūen no ringo o go*ko* kaimashita.）

¶ I bought **five** apples at fifty yen **each**.

¶この卵は10個でいくらですか。（Kono tamago wa jik*ko* de ikura desu ka？）

¶ How much are **10** of these eggs?

こい 濃い 〔形〕

koi 〔adj〕 **dark in color, deep in color; strong in taste; thick, heavy (in density)**

① [色の程度が強い様子]
¶あの濃い茶色の服を着ているのが、わたしの兄です。（Ano *koi* chairo no fuku o kite iru no ga, watashi no ani desu.）

① [dark in color, deep in color]
¶ The man in the **dark** brown suit i* my older brother.

¶ここの部分だけ濃く塗ってください。(Koko no bubun dake *koku* nutte kudasai.)

② [味の程度が強い様子]
濃いお茶 (*koi* ocha)
¶わたしは料理は濃い味のほうが好きです。(Watashi wa ryōri wa *koi* aji no hō ga suki desu.)
¶わたしは濃いコーヒーは飲めませんから、薄くしてください。(Watashiwa *koi* kōhii wa nomemasen kara, usuku shite kudasai.)

③ [密度が高い様子]
ひげが濃い (hige ga *koi*)
¶濃い霧のため、電車が遅れました。(*Koi* kiri no tame, densha ga okuremashita.)
⇔薄い usui

こい 恋 〔名、〜する〕
初恋 (hatsu*koi*) 恋人 (*koi*bito)

¶恋は人間を美しくします。(*Koi* wa ningen o utsukushiku shimasu.)
¶上田さんは田中さんの妹に恋をしています。(Ueda san wa Tanaka san no imōto ni *koi* o shite imasu.)
⇒恋愛 ren'ai

こう 〔副〕
① [話し手に身近な関係にあるものごとの様子をさし示す]
¶その漢字はこう書くんです。(Sono kanji wa *kō* kaku n desu.)
¶こう忙しくては、ゆっくり新聞も読めません。(*Kō* isogashikute wa, yukkuri shinbun mo yomemasen.)

¶ Please paint just this part **dark**.

② [strong in taste, strong in flavor]
strong green tea
¶ I prefer **strongly** flavored dishes.

¶ I can't drink **strong** coffee so please make mine on the weak side.

③ [thick, heavy (in density)]
a **heavy** moustache 〖beard〗
¶ The train was late due to **heavy** fog.

koi 〔n, 〜*suru*〕 **love**
one's first **love**, puppy **love** // a **lover**, **boyfriend, girlfriend**
¶ **Love** makes people beautiful.

¶ Mr. Ueda **is in love** with [Mr.] Tanaka's younger sister.

kō 〔adv〕 **like this, this way**
① [like this, this way; indicates something close to the speaker]
¶ That *kanji* is written **like this**.

¶ When [I] am **this** busy [I] can't read a newspaper leisurely.

② [文脈の上で前に述べたものごとの
状態などを話し手に身近な関係にある
ものとしてさし示したりまたあとから
述べる話し手の考えなどを前もってさ
し示したりする]

② [like this, this way; indicates that
something already mentioned is close
to the speaker or introduces an opinion,
etc., of the speaker]

¶ 人々は板の上で木の棒をもんで、火
を出すことを発明しました。その後、
石と石とを打ち合わせて火を出すこと
を考えました。こうして、火が発明さ
れてから世界はどんどん開けてきまし
た。(Hitobito wa ita no ue de ki no bō o
monde, hi o dasu koto o hatsumei
shimashita. Sono go, ishi to ishi to o
uchiawasete hi o dasu koto o
kangaemashita. *Kō* shite, hi ga hatsumei
sarete kara sekai wa dondon hirakete
kimashita.)

¶ Humans discovered producing fire by
rubbing a stick on top of a board. After
that they thought of striking rocks
together to start a fire. **In this way**
their world was rapidly opened up after
the discovery of fire.

¶ わたしはこう思います。いくら学問
があっても、人に対する思いやりがな
くてはいけません。(Watashi wa *kō*
omoimasu. Ikura gakumon ga atte mo,
hito ni taisuru omoiyari ga nakute wa
ikemasen.)

¶ **This** is what I think. However
learned someone may be, he or she
should still show consideration toward
others.

⇒そう **sō**　ああ **ā**　どう **dō**

-ごう -号 〔尾〕
1号車 (ichi*gō*sha) 2月号 (nigatsu*gō*)

-gō 〔suf〕 **number, issue**
Car **No**. 1 (of a train) //the February
issue (of a magazine or journal)

こうえん 公園 〔名〕
¶ 公園へ散歩に行きましょう。(*Kōen* e
sanpo ni ikimashō.)

kōen 〔n〕 **park, public garden**
¶ Let's go for a walk in **the park**.

こうか 効果 〔名〕
¶ この方法で勉強すれば、効果が上が
りますよ。(Kono hōhō de benkyō
sureba, *kōka* ga agarimasu yo.)

kōka 〔n〕 **effect, effectiveness,
efficiency, result**
¶ You will have better **results** if you
study with this method.

¶漢字の効果的な勉強法を教えてくだ
さい。（Kanji no *kōka*teki na benkyōhō o
oshiete kudasai.)

¶ Please teach [us] an **efficient**
〖**effective, good**〗way to study *kanji*.

こうかい　後悔〔名、〜する〕

¶学生時代にもっと勉強しておけばよ
かったと後悔しています。
（Gakusei-jidai ni motto benkyō shite
okeba yokatta to *kōkai* shite imasu.)
¶今になって後悔しても遅いですよ。
（Ima ni natte *kōkai* shite mo osoi desu
yo.)

kōkai〔n, 〜*suru*〕**regret, remorse,
repentance**
¶ **I regret** that I didn't study harder in
my student days.

¶ It's too late for **regrets** now.

こうがい　郊外〔名〕

¶わたしは東京の郊外に住んでいま
す。（Watashi wa Tōkyō no *kōgai* ni
sunde imasu.)

kōgai〔n〕**suburbs, environs,
outskirts**
¶ I live in **the suburbs** of Tokyo.

こうがい　公害〔名〕

¶飛行機や汽車の騒音は公害の一種で
す。（Hikōki ya kisha no sōon wa *kōgai*
no isshu desu.)
¶この町の人々は、工場から出る煙
の公害で苦しんでいます。（Kono
machi no hitobito wa, kōjō kara deru
kemuri no *kōgai* de kurushinde imasu.)

kōgai〔n〕**environmental pollution**
¶ The noise of planes and trains is one
form of **pollution**.

¶ The people of this city suffer **air
pollution** caused by factory emissions.

ごうかく　合格〔名、〜する〕

不合格（fu*gōkaku*）

¶彼は入学試験に合格しました。
（Kare wa nyūgaku-shiken ni *gōkaku*
shimashita.)
¶この製品は検査に合格しています。
〜no seihin wa kensa ni *gōkaku* shite

gōkaku〔n, 〜*suru*〕**passing an
examination, being declared
eligible, passing an inspection**
failure, disqualification, elimination,
rejection
¶ He **passed** the school entrance
examination.

¶ This product **has passed** inspection.

こうかん　交換 〔名、〜する〕

¶お金と交換に品物を渡します。
(Okane to *kōkan* ni shinamono o watashimasu.)
¶わたしたちは留学生を招いて意見の交換をしました。(Watashitachi wa ryūgakusei o maneite iken no *kōkan* o shimashita.)

kōkan 〔n, 〜*suru*〕 **exchange, interchange, barter**

¶One hands over merchandise **in exchange** for money.

¶We invited foreign students and **had an exchange of** views.

こうぎ　講義 〔名、〜する〕
¶今日は日本語の助詞についての講義があります。(Kyō wa Nihongo no joshi ni tsuite no *kōgi* ga arimasu.)
¶あしたは田中先生が上田先生の代わりに講義します。(Ashita wa Tanaka sensei ga Ueda sensei no kawari ni *kōgi* shimasu.)

kōgi 〔n, 〜*suru*〕 **lecture**

¶There is **a lecture** today about the use of particles in Japanese.

¶Tomorrow Professor Tanaka **will lecture** in place of Professor Ueda.

こうぎょう　工業 〔名〕

重工業 (jū*kōgyō*) 軽工業 (kei*kōgyō*) 工業専門学校 (*kōgyō*-senmongakkō) 工業地帯 (*kōgyō*-chitai)
¶この国は工業が発達しています。
(Kono kuni wa *kōgyō* ga hattatsu shite imasu.)

kōgyō 〔n〕 **an industry, the manufacturing industry**

heavy **industry** // light **industry** // a **technical** school // an **industrial** area, a **manufacturing** district

¶This country is advanced **industrially**.

こうくうびん　航空便 〔名〕
¶ジャカルタから東京まで航空便なら三日で届きます。(Jakaruta kara Tōkyō made *kōkūbin* nara mikka de todokimasu.)
⇔船便 funabin

kōkūbin 〔n〕 **airmail**

¶Mail sent **airmail** from Jakarta takes three days to get to Tokyo.

ごうけい　合計 〔名、〜する〕
¶「参加者は合計何人ですか。」
(Sankasha wa *gōkei* nannin desu ka？)
「合計 35 人です。」(Gōkei sanjūgonin desu.)

gōkei 〔n, 〜*suru*〕 **total, sum total**

¶"How many participants are there altogether?"

"There are **a total** of 35 participants."

¶ 食事代と交通費を合計するといくら
になりますか。(Shokujidai o kōtsūhi o
gōkei suru to ikura ni narimasu ka？)

¶ How much do meal and travel
expenses **come to?**

こうげき 攻撃 〔名、〜する〕

敵から攻撃を受ける (teki kara *kōgeki* o
ukeru) 敵を攻撃する (teki o *kōgeki*
suru)

kōgeki 〔n, 〜*suru*〕 **attack**
be attacked by an enemy, be under
enemy **attack** // **attack** an enemy,
make an attack on the enemy

こうこく 広告 〔名、〜する〕

新聞広告 (shinbun-*kōkoku*)

¶ 新聞に新しい自動車の広告が出てい
ます。(Shinbun ni atarashii jidōsha no
kōkoku ga dete imasu.)

kōkoku 〔n, 〜*suru*〕
**advertisement, notice,
announcement, publicity**
a newspaper **advertisement**, classified
ad in the newspaper
¶ There are **ads** in the newspaper for
the new cars.

こうさい 交際 〔名、〜する〕

¶ 山田さんは交際範囲が広いので、友
達がおおぜいいます。(Yamada san wa
kōsai-han'i ga hiroi node, tomodachi ga
oozei imasu.)
¶ 外国人と交際したいのですが、紹介
していただけませんか。(Gaikokujin to
kōsai shitai no desu ga, shōkai shite
itadakemasen ka？)

kōsai 〔n, 〜*suru*〕 **associating
with, keeping company with,
having social relations with,
mixing with, dating**
¶ [Mr.] Yamada has a wide **circle of
acquaintances** and many friends.

¶ I would like **to become friends** with
a foreigner. Could you introduce me to
someone?

こうさてん 交差点 〔名〕

¶ 交差点に立って、信号が変わるのを
待ちました。(*Kōsaten* ni tatte, shingō
ga kawaru no o machimashita.)
¶ この交差点で、交通事故がよく起こ
ます。(Kono *kōsaten* de, kōtsū-jiko ga
u okorimasu.)

kōsaten 〔n〕 **intersection,
crossroads, crossing**
¶ [I] stood at **the crossing** waiting for
the light to change.

¶ Accidents are frequent at this
intersection.

こうじ 工事 〔名、～する〕

工事中 (kōjichū)
¶この道は道路工事のため通れません。(Kono michi wa dōro-kōji no tame tooremasen.)
¶この工事はいつ完成しますか。
(Kono kōji wa itsu kansei shimasu ka？)

kōji 〔n, ～*suru*〕 **Construction, construction work**
under construction
¶This street is closed to traffic due to road **repairs**.

¶When will this **construction work** be completed?

こうしょう 交渉 〔名、～する〕

団体交渉 (dantai-kōshō)
¶交渉がなかなかまとまりません。
(Kōshō ga nakanaka matomarimasen.)
¶労働条件について会社と交渉した結果、少しよくなりました。(Rōdō-jōken ni tsuite kaisha to kōshō shita kekka, sukoshi yoku narimashita.)

kōshō 〔n, ～*suru*〕 **negotiations, bargaining, talks**
collective **bargaining**
¶**The negotiations** aren't near a conclusion.
¶Working conditions have improved somewhat as a result of **talks** with the management.

こうじょう 工場 〔名〕

自動車工場 (jidōsha-kōjō)
¶この工場では、何人の工員が働いていますか。(Kono kōjō de wa, nannin no kōin ga hataraite imasu ka？)
¶工場の煙突から出る煙が空気を汚しています。(Kōjō no entotsu kara deru kemuri ga kūki o yogoshite imasu.)
⇒工場 **kōba**

kōjō 〔n〕 **factory, plant**
an automobile **manufacturing plant**
¶How many workers are employed at this **factory?**

¶The smoke coming out of the **factory** smokestacks is dirtying the air.

こうぞう 構造 〔名〕

¶この機械は構造が簡単です。(Kono kikai wa kōzō ga kantan desu.)
¶日本の社会構造は複雑です。(Nihon no shakai-kōzō wa fukuzatsu desu.)

kōzō 〔n〕 **structure, framework, constitution, organization**
¶This machine is simple **in design**.

¶The social **structure** of Japan is complex.

こうたい　交替〔名、〜する〕

¶あのスーパーマーケットの店員は8時間ずつ交替で働いています。(Ano sūpāmāketto no ten'in wa hachijikan zutsu *kōtai* de hataraite imasu.)

¶フットボールの試合で山田さんがけがをしたので、田中さんと交替しました。(Futtobōru no shiai de Yamada san ga kega o shita node, Tanaka san to *kōtai* shimashita.)

kōtai 〔n, 〜*suru*〕 **alternative, change, shift, relief, relay**

¶ The employees at that supermarket work in eight-hour **shifts**.

¶ Since [Mr.]Yamada was injured in the football 〚soccer〛 match, he **was relieved** by [Mr.]Tanaka.

こうちゃ　紅茶〔名〕

¶紅茶がいいですか。コーヒーがいいですか。(*Kōcha* ga ii desu ka? Kōhii ga ii desu ka?)

kōcha 〔n〕 **(black) tea**

¶ Which would you like—**tea** or coffee?

こうちょう　校長〔名〕

¶上田さんのお父さんは小学校の校長です。(Ueda san no otōsan wa shōgakkō no *kōchō* desu.)

kōchō 〔n〕 **principal, headmaster**

¶ [Miss] Ueda's father is an elementary school **principal**.

こうつう　交通〔名〕

交通事故 (*kōtsū*-jiko) 交通信号 (*kōtsū*-shingō) 交通費 (*kōtsū*hi)

¶この道は交通が激しいから注意してください。(Kono michi wa *kōtsū* ga hageshii kara chūi shite kudasai.)

¶この辺は交通の便がいいですね。(Kono hen wa *kōtsū* no ben ga ii desu ne.)

kōtsū 〔n〕 **traffic, transport, transportation**

a **traffic** accident // a **traffic** signal // **travel** expenses, **car**fare

¶ Please be careful as **the traffic** is very heavy on this street.

¶ **Public transportation** is convenient in this area.

こうてい　肯定〔名、〜する〕

¶山田さんはその質問に対して否定も肯定もしませんでした。(Yamada san sono shitsumon ni taishite hitei mo ～ mo shimasen deshita.)

→ **hitei**

kōtei 〔n, 〜*suru*〕 **affirmative, affirmation**

¶ [Mr.] Yamada didn't give any definite answer to that question (literally, didn't say no or **yes**).

こうどう　講堂〔名〕

¶この講堂は１８９０年に建てられました。(Kono kōdō wa senhappyakukyūjū nen ni tateraremashita.)

kōdo〔n〕 auditorium

¶This auditorium was built in 1890.

こうどう　行動〔名、～する〕

¶団体で行動しているとき自分勝手な行動をすると、他人に迷惑をかけます。(Dantai de *kōdō* shite iru toki jibunkatte na *kōdō* o suru to, tanin ni meiwaku o kakemasu.)
¶上田さんはたいへん行動的な人です。(Ueda san wa taihen *kōdō*teki na hito desu.)

kōdō〔n, ～*suru*〕 action, movement, behavior

¶When **acting** together with others in a group, **acting** only to please oneself will inconvenience others.

¶[Mr.] Ueda is a **take-charge** person〚Mr. Ueda never hesitates to **take action**〛.

こうとうがっこう　高等学校〔名〕

¶日本の高等学校は３年です。(Nihon no *kōtōgakkō* wa sannen desu.)
＊略して「高校（kōkō）」とも言う。

kōtōgakkō〔n〕 high school, senior high school, upper secondary school

¶**High school** is three years long in Japan.

＊The abbreviated form *kōkō* is also used.

こうば　工場〔名〕

工場で働く（*kōba* de hataraku）
＊「工場（kōba）」は小さい個人経営の作業場を主として言う。
⇒工場 **kōjō**

kōba〔n〕 factory, workshop

work in **a factory**

＊*Kōba* chiefly refers to a small, privately managed workplace.

こうばん　交番〔名〕

¶交番のお巡りさんが丁寧に道を教えてくれました。(*Kōban* no omawarisan ga teinei ni michi o oshiete kuremashita.)

kōban〔n〕 police box

¶The policeman at **the police box** gave me careful directions.

こうふく　幸福〔名、形動〕

¶わたしは今とても幸福です。(Watashi wa ima totemo *kōfuku* desu.)

kōfuku〔n, adj-v〕 happiness, good fortune

¶I am very **happy** now.

¶幸福な家庭に育って幸せですね。
(*Kōfuku* na katei ni sodatte shiawase desu ne.)

¶You are fortunate to have grown up in a **happy** home.

¶田中さんは結婚して幸福に暮らしています。(Tanaka san wa kekkon shite *kōfuku* ni kurashite imasu.)

¶[Mr.] Tanaka is living in wedded **bliss**.

⇔不幸 **fukō**

こうふん　興奮〔名、〜する〕

kōfun 〔n, 〜*suru*〕 **excitement, agitation**

¶山田さんは会議で田中さんと大声で議論していましたが、その時の興奮がまだ続いているようです。(Yamada san wa kaigi de Tanaka san to oogoe de giron shite imashita ga, sono toki no *kōfun* ga mada tsuzuite iru yō desu.)

¶[Mr.] Yamada raised [his] voice and argued with [Mr.] Tanaka at the meeting, and **the aroused emotions** of that time seem to still be alive.

¶試合を見ていた人たちは興奮して立ち上がりました。(Shiai o mite ita hitotachi wa *kōfun* shite tachiagarimashita.)

¶The people watching the game 〚match〛 came to their feet **in their excitement**.

こうへい　公平〔名、形動〕

kōhei 〔n, adj-v〕 **impartiality, fairness, justice**

¶上田先生はすべての学生に公平です。(Ueda sensei wa subete no gakusei ni *kōhei* desu.)

¶Professor Ueda **is impartial** toward all students.

¶このお菓子を公平に分けてください。(Kono okashi o *kōhei* ni wakete kudasai.)

¶Please divide this candy 〚sweet〛 **evenly**.

こうむいん　公務員〔名〕

kōmuin 〔n〕 **public servant**

¶経済状態が良くないので、公務員は今、とても人気がある職業です。(Keizaijōtai ga yokunai node *kōmuin* wa ima totemo ninki ga aru shokugyō desu.)

¶The occupation of public servant is very popular because the economic situation is very slow.

こうりつ 公立〔名〕

¶田中さんの子供は公立の小学校に通っています。(Tanaka san no kodomo wa *kōritsu* no shōgakkō ni kayotte imasu.)
⇒国立 kokuritsu 私立 shiritsu

kōritsu 〔n〕 public, public institution

¶[Mrs.] Tanaka's children go to a **public** elementary school.

こえ 声〔名〕

¶声が小さくて聞こえません。(*Koe* ga chiisakute ki*koe*masen.)
¶田中先生はいつも大きい声で話します。(Tanaka sensei wa itsu mo ookii *koe* de hanashimasu.)

koe 〔n〕 voice

¶[Your] voice is low and I can't hear what [you]'re saying.

¶Professor 〖Doctor〗 Tanaka always speaks in a loud **voice**.

こえる 越える〔動Ⅱ〕

¶この山を越えた所にわたしの村があります。(Kono yama o *koeta* tokoro ni watashi no mura ga arimasu.)

koeru 〔v Ⅱ〕 cross, go across

¶My village lies **on the other side** of this mountain.

こえる 超える〔動Ⅱ〕

¶昨日は 40 度を超える暑さでした。(Kinō wa yonjūdo o *koeru* atsusa deshita.)
¶この狭い国に一億を超える人が住んでいます。(Kono semai kuni ni ichioku o *koeru* hito ga sunde imasu.)

koeru 〔v Ⅱ〕 exceed, be over

¶Yesterday the heat **exceeded** 40 degrees.

¶**Over** 100 million people live in this small country.

コート〔名〕

¶今朝はとても寒かったので、コートを着て出かけました。(Kesa wa totemo samukatta node, *kōto* o kite dekakemashita.)

kōto 〔n〕 coat

¶I wore a coat out this morning as it was so cold.

コーヒー〔名〕

¶コーヒーを飲みに行きましょう。(*Kōhii* o nomi ni ikimashō.)
¶コーヒーに砂糖とミルクを入れてください。(*Kōhii* ni satō to miruku o irete kudasai.)

kōhii 〔n〕 coffee

¶Let's go have **a cup of coffee**.

¶Please put sugar and milk in my coffee.

こおり　氷〔名〕

¶池に氷が張っています。（Ike ni *koori* ga hatte imasu.）

¶暑いから、ジュースに氷を入れてください。（Atsui kara, jūsu ni *koori* o irete kudasai.）

koori〔n〕**ice**

¶ The pool〚pond〛**is frozen over**.

¶ Could you please put **ice** in the juice? It's such a hot day!

こおる　凍る〔動Ⅰ〕

¶冬の間は池の水が凍ります。（Fuyu no aida wa ike no mizu ga *koorimasu*.）

¶夏は物が腐りやすいので、凍らせて保存します。（Natsu wa mono ga kusariyasui node, *koorasete* hozon shimasu.）

kooru〔vⅠ〕**freeze, be frozen over**

¶ The pond **freezes** during the winter.

¶ Food goes bad easily during the summer so it is preserved **by freezing**.

ごかい　誤解〔名、～する〕

¶それは誤解です。（Sore wa *gokai* desu.）

¶つまらない誤解のため、あの二人はけんかしてしまいました。（Tsumaranai *gokai* no tame, ano futari wa kenka shite shimaimashita.）

gokai〔n, ～*suru*〕**misunderstanding, misapprehension**

¶ That is **a misunderstanding**.

¶ Those two quarreled because of a trifling〚foolish〛**misunderstanding**.

ごがつ　五月〔名〕

gogatsu〔n〕**the month of May**

こぎって　小切手〔名〕

¶現金ではなく、小切手で支払います。（Genkin de wa naku, *kogitte* de shiharaimasu.）

kogitte〔n〕**(bank) check**

¶ [I] will pay by **check** rather than in cash.

こきゅう　呼吸〔名、～する〕

¶高い山に登ると、呼吸が苦しくなります。（Takai yama ni noboru to, *kokyū* kurushiku narimasu.）

ラソンをしたあとで、何回も深呼ました。（Marason o shita ato de, ● shin*kokyū* o shimashita.）

kokyū〔n, ～*suru*〕**breath, breathing, respiration**

¶ One experiences difficulty **in breathing** when climbing a high mountain.

¶ [He] **breathed** deeply in and out several times after completing the marathon.

こくがい 国外 〔名〕

¶上田さんは主に国外で活躍していま
す。(Ueda san wa omo ni *kokugai* de
katsuyaku shite imasu.)
⇔国内 kokunai

こくご 国語 〔名〕

① [日本語]
国語辞典 (*kokugo*-jiten) 国語学
(*kokugo*gaku)
¶上田先生は中学校で国語を教えてい
ます。(Ueda sensei wa chūgakkō de
kokugo o oshiete imasu.)
② [国の公的言語]
¶オーストラリアの国語は英語です。
(Ōsutoraria no *kokugo* wa Eigo desu.)

こくさい 国際 〔名〕

国際関係 (*kokusai*kankei) 国際連合
(*kokusai*rengō) 国際協力
(*kokusai*kyōryoku) 国際問題
(*kokusai*mondai) 国際電話
(*kokusai*denwa) 国際結婚
(*kokusai*kekkon)
¶東京で漁業についての国際会議が開
かれました。(Tōkyō de gyogyō ni tsuite
no *kokusai*kaigi ga hirakaremashita.)
¶英語は国際的な言葉です。(Eigo wa
*kokusai*teki na kotoba desu.)
＊いつも他の言葉といっしょに使う。

kokugai 〔n〕 **overseas, outside the country**
¶ [Mr.] Ueda's activities are predominantly conducted **overseas**.

kokugo 〔n〕 **the Japanese language; the language of a nation**
① [the Japanese language]
a **Japanese-language** dictionary // the linguistic study of **Japanese**
¶ [Miss] Ueda teaches **Japanese** in middle school.
② [the language of a nation]
¶ **The national language** of Australia is English.

kokusai 〔n〕 **international, international intercourse**
international relations // the United Nations // **international** cooperation // an **international** problem, a diplomatic issue // an **overseas** telephone call // marriage between persons **of differing nationality**
¶ An **international** conference on fishing has opened 〖was held〗 in Tokyo.
¶ English is an **international** language.
＊*Kokusai* is always used in compounds with other words.

こくせき　国籍〔名〕

¶国籍と名前をこのカードに書いてください。（*Kokuseki* to namae o kono kādo ni kaite kudasai.）
¶わたしの国籍は日本です。（*Watashi no kokuseki* wa Nihon desu.）

kokuseki 〔n〕 **nationality, citizenship**

¶ Please write **your nationality** and name on these cards.

¶ I am a Japanese **national**.

こくない　国内〔名〕

¶郵便料金は国内どこでも同じです。（*Yūbin-ryōkin* wa *kokunai* doko demo onaji desu.）
⇔国外 kokugai

kokunai 〔n〕 **interior, domestic, inside a country**

¶ Postage rates are the same anywhere **in the country**.

こくばん　黒板〔名〕

¶黒板に今習った漢字を書きなさい。（*Kokuban* ni ima naratta kanji o kakinasai.）

kokuban 〔n〕 **blackboard**

¶ Write the *kanji* we've just studied on **the blackboard**.

こくみん　国民〔名〕

国民感情（*kokumin*-kanjō）国民生活（*kokumin*-seikatsu）国民性（*kokumin*sei）
¶国民は税金を納める義務があります。（*Kokumin* wa zeikin o osameru gimu ga arimasu.）

kokumin 〔n〕 **a nation, a people, a citizen**

national sentiment // **national** life // the **national** character, **national** traits

¶ **Citizens** have a duty to pay taxes.

こくりつ　国立〔名〕

国立大学（*kokuritsu*-daigaku）国立公園（*kokuritsu*-kōen）国立劇場（*kokuritsu*-gekijō）国立病院（*ko-kuritsu*-byōin）
¶この建物は国立博物館です。（Kono tatemono wa *kokuritsu*-hakubutsukan ...u.）
...立 kōritsu　私立 shiritsu

kokuritsu 〔n〕 **national, state-run**

a **national** university // a **national** park // a **national** theater, the **National** Theater // a **national** hospital

¶ This building is the **National** Museum.

ごくろうさま　御苦労さま〔連〕

¶御苦労さまでした。（Gokurōsama deshita.）

＊目上の人に対しては使わない。

gokurōsama 〔compd〕 **an expression used to someone who is doing or has just finished some task for the speaker**

¶ **Thank you very much** 〚Thank you for your trouble; Good-bye〛.

＊Not used toward persons of higher status.

こげる　焦げる〔動Ⅱ〕

¶魚が真っ黒に焦げてしまいました。（Sakana ga makkuro ni *kogete* shimaimashita.）

¶パンを焼くとき、焦げないように気をつけてください。（Pan o yaku toki, *kogenai* yō ni ki o tsukete kudasai.）

kogeru 〔v Ⅱ〕 **burn, scorch**

¶ The fish **is** 〚**was**〛 **burnt** to a cinder.

¶ When toasting bread, please be careful **not to burn it**.

ここ〔代〕

① [空間的に話し手に身近な関係にある所などをさし示す]

¶「鉛筆はどこにありますか。」（Enpitsu wa doko ni arimasu ka？）「ここにあります。」（*Koko* ni arimasu.）

¶「ここは銀座ですか。」（*Koko* wa Ginza desu ka？）「いいえ、ここは銀座ではありません。銀座はこの次です。」（Iie, *koko* wa Ginza de wa arimasen. Ginza wa kono tsugi desu.）

¶「あなたはいつからこの寮に住んでいますか。」（Anata wa itsu kara kono ryō ni sunde imasu ka？）「去年の四月に日本に来てから、ずっとここに住んでいます。」（Kyonen no shigatsu ni Nihon ni kite kara, zutto *koko* ni sunde imasu.）

＊話し手と話し相手が同じ所にいる場合には、話し手が「ここ（koko）」でさし示す所は、話し相手も「ここ（koko）」でさし示す。

koko 〔pron〕 **here, this place; this**

① [here, this place; indicates a place physically close to the speaker]

¶ "Where is my pencil?" "**Here** it is."

¶ "Is **this** Ginza?" "No **this** isn't Ginza. Ginza is the next stop."

¶ "How long have you been living in this dormitory?" "I've been living **here** ever since I came to Japan last April (that is, last year in April)."

*When the speaker and listener are both in the same place, the listener will also use *koko* for a place the speaker refers to as *koko*.

②[話し手が指さして説明する場合などにそのさし示している所などを表す]

¶「名前はどこに書いたらいいですか。」(Namae wa doko ni kaitara ii desu ka?)「ここに書いてください。」(*Koko* ni kaite kudasai.)

¶この地図を見てください。ここが東京で、ここが大阪です。(Kono chizu o mite kudasai. *Koko* ga Tōkyō de, *koko* ga Oosaka desu.)

③[話し手が現に取り上げているものごとの範囲・部分・点などをさし示す]

¶今日の勉強はここまでです。(Kyō no benkyō wa *koko* made desu.)

¶ここが特に大切なところです。(*Koko* ga toku ni taisetsu na tokoro desu.)

④[話し手の当面する時間を基準としてその前後の時間のある範囲をさし示す]

¶ここ二、三日はまだ雨が降り続くそうです。(*Koko* ni, sannichi wa mada ame ga furitsuzuku sō desu.)

¶ここ一週間はずっと風邪で寝ていました。(*Koko* isshūkan wa zutto kaze de nete imashita.)

⇒そこ soko　あそこ asoko　どこ doko

ごご　午後 〔名〕

¶あしたの午後、デパートへ買い物に行きます。(Ashitano *gogo*, depāto e kaimono ni ikimasu.)

¶午後から雨が降るでしょう。(*Gogo* kara ame ga furu deshō.)

⇒午前 gozen

② [here, this place; a place indicated by the speaker when pointing while explaining, etc.]

¶ "Where should I write my name?" "Please write it **here**."

¶ Please look at this map. Tokyo is **here** and Osaka is **here** 〖**This** is Tokyo and **this** is Osaka〗.

③ [here, this; indicates a section, a point, the environment, etc., of whatever the speaker is talking about at the time]

¶ **This** concludes our studies for today 〖That's all for today〗.

¶ **This** is an especially important part.

④ [this; takes the present time of the speaker as the standard and indicates a period before or after that]

¶ It looks like the rain will continue for **the next** two or three days.

¶ [I] have been in bed **this past** week with a cold 〖the flu〗.

gogo 〔n〕 **afternoon, PM**

¶ [I]'m going to go shopping at a department store tomorrow **afternoon**.

¶ It will probably rain from **midday**.

ここのか　九日〔名〕

① [日付を表す]
一月九日　(ichigatsu *kokonoka*)

② [日数を表す]
¶病気で九日も学校を休みました。
(Byōki de *kokonoka* mo gakkō o
yasumimashita.)
⇒-日 **-ka**

kokonoka 〔n〕 **the ninth of the
month; nine days**

① [the ninth of the month]
January **9**

② [nine days]
¶[I] was absent from school for **nine
days** due to illness.

ここのつ　九つ〔名〕

① [9 個]
¶ここにみかんが九つあります。
(Koko ni mikan ga *kokonotsu* arimasu.)

② [9 歳]
¶今年、この子は九つです。(Kotoshi,
kono ko wa *kokonotsu* desu.)

kokonotsu 〔n〕 **nine; nine years
old**

① [nine, nine items]
¶There are **nine** mandarin oranges
here.

② [nine years old]
¶This child is **nine years old** this year.

こころ　心〔名〕

心細い　(*kokoro*bosoi)

¶あの人は心の優しい人です。(Ano
hito wa *kokoro* no yasashii hito desu.)
¶御親切を心から感謝いたします。
(Goshinsetsu o *kokoro* kara kansha
itashimasu.)
¶心をこめてお礼の手紙を書きまし
た。(*Kokoro* o komete orei no tegami o
kakimashita.)

kokoro 〔n〕 **heart, mind, spirit,
feeling**

forlorn, down**hearted**, lonely,
discouraging
¶[He] is a **kindhearted** person.

¶I thank you for your kindness from
the bottom of **my heart**.

¶[I] wrote a **heartfelt** letter of thanks.

ございます〔連〕

¶何か御用がございますか。(Nani ka
goyō ga *gozaimasu* ka？)

¶お変わりございませんか。(Okawari
gozaimasen ka？)

gozaimasu 〔compd〕 **there is,
there are, be, have**

¶**Is there** something I can do for you
〚Did you want to see me about
something〛?
¶How have you been doing (literally,
Aren't there any changes)?

¶遅くなりまして、申し訳ございません。(Osokunarimashite, mōshiwake *gozaimasen*.)

¶I'm very sorry to be late.

¶ありがとうございます。(Arigatō *gozaimasu*.)

¶Thank you very much.

¶お早うございます。(Ohayō *gozaimasu*.)

¶Good morning.

¶御結婚、おめでとうございます。(Gokekkon, omedetō *gozaimasu*.)

¶Congratulations on your wedding.

¶あれが博物館でございます。(Are ga hakubutsukan de *gozaimasu*.)

¶That **is** the museum.

＊「ある（aru）」の丁寧語。

＊*Gozaimasu* is the polite form of *aru*.

こし 腰 〔名〕

koshi 〔n〕 **waist, hip, small of the back**

腰を下ろす（*koshi* o orosu）腰を掛ける（*koshi* o kakeru）

sit down // sit down

¶わたしのおばあさんは年を取っているので、腰が曲がっています。(Watashi no obāsan wa toshi o totte iru node, *koshi* ga magatte imasu.)

¶My grandmother is elderly and **bent** with age.

こしかける 腰掛ける 〔動Ⅱ〕

koshikakeru 〔v Ⅱ〕 **sit down, take a seat**

¶わたしは山田さんと並んで腰掛けました。(Watashi wa Yamada san to narande *koshikakemashita*.)

¶I **sat down** next to [Mrs.] Yamada.

こしょう 故障 〔名、～する〕

koshō 〔n, ～*suru*〕 **trouble, breakdown, malfunction, defect, accident**

¶電車の故障で学校に遅れました。(Densha no *koshō* de gakkō ni okuremashita.)

¶[I] was late for school because of a train **breakdown** 〖**accident**〗.

¶この機械は故障しています。(Kono kikai wa *koshō* shite imasu.)

¶This machine **is out of order**.

こしょう〔名〕

¶肉料理にこしょうをかけると、味が
もっとよくなります。(Nikuryōri ni
koshō o kakeru to, aji ga motto yoku
narimasu.)

koshō〔n〕 **pepper**

¶Meat dishes taste better if one adds
pepper.

こじん 個人〔名〕

個人主義 (*kojin*-shugi)
¶個人の権利を守らなければなりませ
ん。(*Kojin* no kenri o mamoranakereba
narimasen.)
¶これはわたしの個人的な意見です。
(Kore wa watashi no *kojin*teki na iken
desu.)

kojin〔n〕 **individual, persons in
their private capacity**
individualism

¶The rights of **the individual** must be
protected.

¶This is my **personal** opinion.

ごぜん 午前〔名〕

¶学校は午前9時に始まります。
(Gakkō wa *gozen* kuji ni hajimarimasu.)
¶土曜の午前中は家にいます。(Doyō
no *gozen*chū wa ie ni imasu.)
⇔午後 gogo

gozen〔n〕 **morning, AM**

¶School starts at 9 **AM**.

¶I will be at home Saturday **morning**
〚I am at home Saturday **mornings**〛.

ごぞんじ ご存じ〔名〕

¶あの二人が最近、結婚したことをご
存知ですか。(Ano futari ga saikin
kekkon shita koto o *gozonji* desu ka?)

gozonji〔n〕 **knowledge**

¶Did you know that the couple got
married recently?

こたい 固体〔名〕

¶氷は水が固体になったものです。
(Koori wa mizu ga *kotai* ni natta mono
desu.)
⇒液体 ekitai 気体 kitai

kotai〔n〕 **solid, solid body**

¶Ice is **the solid form** of water.

こたえ 答え〔名〕

① [返事]
¶部屋の外からいくら呼んでも答えが
ありませんでした。(Heya no soto kara
ikura yonde mo *kotae* ga arimasen
deshita.)

kotae〔n〕 **answer, reply; answer,
solution, result**

① [answer, reply, response]
¶There was no **response** from inside
the room no matter how much [we]
called from outside.

② [解答]

¶ その答えは間違っています。(Sono *kotae* wa machigatte imasu.)

こたえる 答える 〔動Ⅱ〕

① [返事する]
¶ わたしが名前を呼んだら、「はい。」と答えてください。(Watashi ga namae o yondara, "Hai." to *kotaete* kudasai.)

② [解答する]
¶ 次の質問に答えなさい。(Tsugi no shitsumon ni *kotaenasai*.)

ごちそう 〔名、〜する〕

¶ テーブルの上には、ごちそうがたくさん並んでいました。(Tēburu no ue ni wa, *gochisō* ga takusan narande imashita.)

¶ 先生のお宅で夕食をごちそうになりました。(Sensei no otaku de yūshoku o *gochisō* ni narimashita.)

¶ 先日はごちそうさまでした。
(Senjitsu wa *gochisō*sama deshita.)

こちら 〔代〕

① [話し手に身近な関係にある方向をさし示す]

¶ どうぞ、こちらへ。
(Dōzo, *kochira* e.)
¶ 皆さん、写真を撮りますから、こちらを見てください。(Minasan, shashin o torimasu kara, *kochira* o mite kudasai.)

② [answer, solution, result (for a question or problem)]

¶ That **answer** is wrong.

kotaeru 〔v Ⅱ〕 **answer, reply; answer, solve**

① [answer, reply, respond]
¶ Please **reply** *hai* 〖Here!〗 when I call your name.

② [answer, solve, do (a problem)]
¶ **Answer** the following questions.

gochisō 〔n, 〜*suru*〕 **hospitality, treat, delicacies; an expression used to express gratitude for food or drink served or paid for by the listener**

¶ Many **delicacies** were laid out on the table.

¶ I **was invited** to dinner at the home of my teacher 〖professor〗.

¶ Thank you for **your hospitality**

kochira 〔pron〕 **this way, here; this place; this person; this one; this side, I, we**

① [this way, here ; indicates a direction physically close to the speaker]
¶ **This way**, please.

¶ Will everyone please look **this way** so that I can take the photograph.

② [話し手に身近な関係にある方向に
存在する所などをさし示す]

¶わたしがこちらへ来てから10年にな
ります。(Watashi ga *kochira* e kitekara
jūnen ni narimasu.)

¶「トイレはどこにありますか。」
(Toire wa doko ni arimasu ka？)「トイ
レはこちらです。」(Toire wa *kochira*
desu.)

③ [話し手に身近な関係にある方向に
いる人をさし示す]

¶御紹介します。こちらは山田さんで
す。(Goshōkai shimasu. *Kochira* wa
Yamada san desu.)

*話し手にとって対等または目上の人
に対して使う。「こちらの方（kochira
no kata）」とも言う。

④ [話し手に身近な関係にある方向に
存在するものをさし示す]

¶「どちらの時計になさいますか。」
(Dochira no tokei ni nasaimasu ka？)「そ
うですね。こちらのほうにしましょ
う。(Sō desu ne. *Kochira* no hō ni
shimashō.)

¶そちらよりこちらのほうがいいで
す。こちらをください。(Sochira yori
kochira no hō ga ii desu. Kochira o
kudasai.)

⑤ [話し手自身や話し手側の者を表
す、わたし、わたしたち]

¶もしもし、上田さんですか。こちら
は中村です。(Moshimoshi, Ueda san
desu ka？ *Kochira* wa Nakamura desu.)

¶おかげさまで、こちらはみんな元気
に暮らしております。(Okagesama de,
kochira wa minna genki ni kurashite
orimasu.)

② [this place, here; indicates a place,
etc., physically close to the speaker]

¶ Ten years have passed since I came
here.

¶ "Where are the rest rooms?"
"The rest rooms are **here**."

③ [this person; indicates a person
physically close to the speaker]

¶ Let me introduce you. **This** is [Mrs.]
Yamada.

*Kochira is used to refer to someone
of equal or higher status than the
speaker. *Kochira no kata* is also used.

④ [this one; indicates something
physically close to the speaker]

¶ "Which watch 〖clock〗 would you
like?"
"Well, let's see. I'll take **this one**."

¶ I like **this one** better than that one.
Please give me **this one**.

⑤ [this side, I, we; indicates the
speaker or those on the speaker's side]

¶ Hello. Is that [Mr.] Ueda? **This** is
[Mr.] Nakamura calling.

¶ **I and my family** are all well, thank
you.

＊「こっち (kotchi)」とも言うが、「こちら (kochira)」のほうが丁寧な言葉である。

＊*Kotchi* is also used, but *kochira* is more polite.

⇒そちら **sochira** あちら **achira** どちら **dochira**

こっか 国家〔名〕

¶第二次大戦後、世界に新しい国家が次々に誕生しました。(Dainiji-taisengo, sekai ni atarashii *kokka* ga tsugitsugi ni tanjō shimashita.)

¶国家の安全を守るために条約を結びます。(*Kokka* no anzen o mamoru tame ni jōyaku o musubimasu.)

kokka 〔n〕 **state, country, nation**

¶After World War II new **nations** entered the world community one after the other.

¶Treaties are concluded in order to protect the security of **the state**.

こっか 国歌〔名〕

kokka 〔n〕 **national anthem**

こづかい 小遣い〔名〕

¶あなたの小遣いは一か月いくらですか。(Anata no *kozukai* wa ikkagetsu ikura desu ka？)

kozukai 〔n〕 **pocket money, spending money, allowance**

¶How much is your **allowance** each month?

こっき 国旗〔名〕

¶オリンピック会場には世界各国の国旗が飾られます。(Orinpikku-kaijō ni wa sekai-kakkoku no *kokki* ga kazararemasu.)

kokki 〔n〕 **national flag**

¶When the Olympics are held, **the national flags** of countries around the world are on display.

こづつみ 小包〔名〕

¶これは小包にして送りましょう。(Kore wa *kozutsumi* ni shite okurimashō.)

kozutsumi 〔n〕 **parcel, package**

¶Let's do this up in **a parcel** and mail it.

コップ〔名〕

¶そのコップに水を一杯ください。(Sono *koppu* ni mizu o ippai kudasai.)

koppu 〔n〕 **glass, tumbler**

¶Please give me water in that **glass**.

こと〔名〕

①[ことがら、事実、問題]

koto 〔n〕 **matter, affair**

① [matter, affair, fact, question]

¶わたしのことは心配しないでください。(Watashi no *koto* wa shinpai shinaide kudasai.)

¶ Please don't worry **on my account**.

¶日本のことが新聞に出ています。(Nihon no *koto* ga shinbun ni dete imasu.)

¶ There is **something** about Japan in the newspaper.

¶そんなことは知りませんでした。(Sonna *koto* wa shirimasen deshita.)

¶ I had no knowledge of that **matter**.

②[可能を表す]

② [can, cannot; expresses ability]

¶あなたは日本語を話すことができますか。(Anata wa Nihongo o hanasu *koto* ga dekimasu ka?)

¶ **Can** you speak Japanese?

¶お金がないので買うことができません。(Okane ga nai node kau *koto* ga dekimasen.)

¶ [I] **can't** buy it since [I] don't have the money for it.

*「動詞(連体の形)+ことができる(koto ga dekiru)」の形で使う。

*Used in the pattern "verb (dictionary form) + *koto ga dekiru*."

③[場合を表す]

③ [expresses circumstances or a case]

¶わたしは朝御飯を食べないで学校へ行くことがあります。(Watashi wa asagohan o tabe naide gakkō e iku *koto* ga arimasu.)

¶ **There are times** when I go to school without eating breakfast.

*「動詞(連体の形)+ことがある(koto ga aru)」の形で使う。

*Used in the pattern "verb (dictionary form) + *koto ga aru*."

④[経験を表す]

④ [expresses experience]

¶あなたは京都へ行ったことがありますか。(Anata wa Kyōto e itta *koto* ga arimasu ka?)

¶ **Have you ever** been to Kyoto?

*「動詞(たの形)+ことがある(koto ga aru)」の形で使う。

Used in the pattern "verb (-ta* form) + *koto ga aru*."

⑤[決定を表す]

⑤ [expresses decision]

¶わたしは今日からたばこを吸わないことにしました。(Watashi wa kyō kara tabako o suwanai *koto* ni shimashita.)

¶ I **have decided** to stop smoking from today on.

*「動詞(連体の形)+ことにする(koto ni suru)」の形で使う。

*Used in the pattern "verb (dictionary form) + *koto ni suru*."

⑥ [習慣を表す]

¶わたしは毎晩10時に寝ることにしています。(Watashi wa maiban jūji ni neru *koto* ni shite imasu.)
*「動詞（連体の形）＋ことにしている（koto ni shite iru)」の形で使う。

⑦ [結果を表す]
¶わたしは来年、日本へ行くことになりました。(Watashi wa rainen, Nihon e iku *koto* ni narimashita.)
*「動詞（連体の形）＋ことになる（koto ni naru)」の形で使う。

⑧ [必要を表す]
¶そんなに急ぐことはないですよ。(Sonna ni isogu *koto* wa nai desu yo.)
*「動詞（連体の形）＋ことはない（koto wa nai)」の形で使う。

⑨ [命令を表す]
¶図書館の本は1週間以内に返すこと。(Toshokan no hon wa isshūkan inai ni kaesu *koto*.)
*「動詞（連体の形）＋こと（koto)」の形で文末に使う。

-ごと〔尾〕

¶日曜ごとにつりに行きます。
(Nichiyō *goto* ni tsuri ni ikimasu.)
¶1メートルごとに木を植えました。
(Ichimētoru *goto* ni ki o uemashita.)

ことし　今年〔名〕
¶今年は雨が多いですね。(*Kotoshi* wa ame ga ooi desu ne.)
¶わたしは今年じゅうにこの仕事を終わらせるつもりです。(Watashi wa *kotoshi*jū ni kono shigoto o owaraseru tsumori desu.)

⑥ [make it a rule to 〜; expresses habitual action]
¶ **I make it a practice** to go to bed every night at ten o'clock.

*Used in the pattern "verb (dictionary form) + *koto ni shite iru*."

⑦ [expresses a result]
¶ I **am going to** go to Japan next year.

*Used in the pattern "verb (dictionary form) + *koto ni naru*."

⑧ [expresses necessity]
¶ **There is no need** to be in such a hurry.

*Used in the pattern "verb (dictionary form) + *koto wa nai*."

⑨ [expresses an order]
¶ Library books **are to be** returned within one week.

*Used in the pattern "verb (dictionary form) + *koto*."

-goto 〔suf〕 **every 〜, at an interval of**

¶ [He] goes fishing **every** Sunday.

¶ [I] planted trees at one-meter **intervals**.

kotoshi 〔n〕 **this year**

¶ It's rained a lot **this year**, hasn't it?

¶ I plan to finish up this work before **the year** is out.

¶わたしは今年大学を卒業します。
（Watashi wa *kotoshi* daigaku o sotsugyō
shimasu.）

ことば 言葉 〔名〕

¶あなたの国の言葉で本は何と言いま
すか。（Anata no kuni no *kotoba* de hon
wa nan to iimasu ka？）
¶今日は、あいさつの言葉を勉強しま
しょう。（Kyō wa, aisatsu no *kotoba* o
benkyō shimashō.）

こども 子供 〔名〕

① [親から生まれたもの]
¶わたしの子供は3人とも女です。
（Watashi no *kodomo* wa sannin tomo
onna desu.）
⇔親 oya
② [幼い者]
¶公園で子供たちが遊んでいます。
（Kōen de *kodomo*tachi ga asonde imasu.）
⇔大人 otona
⇒子 ko

ことり 小鳥 〔名〕
¶私の家では小鳥を飼っています。
（Watashi no ie dewa *kotori* o katte
imasu.）

ことわる 断る 〔動 I〕

① [相手の願いを受け付けない]
¶仕事を頼まれましたが、忙しいので
断りました。（Shigoto o
tanomaremashita ga, isogashii
node *koto-warimashita*.）
② [前もって了解を求める]

¶ I graduate from college **this year**.

kotoba 〔n〕 speech, language,
 word, phrase, expression

¶ What is **the word** for "book" in your
native language?

¶ Today we will study **greetings**.

kodomo 〔n〕 one's child (ren);
 children, the young

① [one's child(ren), offspring]
¶ My three **children** are all girls.

② [children, the young]
¶ **Children** are playing in the park.

kotori 〔n〕 small bird
¶ I have a pet bird.

kotowaru 〔v I〕 decline, refuse;
 tell, give notice, ask permission
① [decline, refuse]
¶ I was asked to do a job but **refused**
because I'm too busy.

② [tell, give notice, ask permission,
apologize]

¶用事があったので、課長に断って会社を休みました。(Yōji ga atta node, kachō ni *kotowatte* kaisha o yasumimashita.)

¶ I had something to attend to so I took some time off work **after informing** my section chief.

こな 粉 〔名〕

kona 〔n〕 **flour, meal, powder, dust**

粉ミルク (*kona*miruku) 粉薬 (*kona*gusuri) 粉石けん (*kona*sekken)

powdered milk, **dry** milk // **powdered** medicine // soap **powder**, soap **flakes**, washing **powder**

¶この菓子は米の粉で作ります。(Kono kashi wa kome no *kona* de tsukurimasu.)

¶ This sweet is made from rice **flour**.

この 〔連体〕

kono 〔attrib〕 **this, these**

① [話し手とものごととの身近な関係をさし示す]

① [this, these; indicates that someone or something is physically close to the speaker]

この人 (*kono* hito) この方 (*kono* kata)

this person // **this** lady 〚gentleman〛

¶「このかばんはだれのですか。」(*Kono* kaban wa dare no desuka?)「そのかばんは山田さんのです。」(Sono kaban wa Yamada san no desu.)

¶ "Whose bag 〚suitcase, briefcase, etc.〛 is **this**?"
"That bag is [Mr.] Yamada's."

¶「この建物の中には教室がいくつありますか。」(*Kono* tatemono no naka ni wa kyōshitsu ga ikutsu arimasu ka?)「この建物の中には教室が 20 あります。」(*Kono* tatemono no naka ni wa kyōshitsu ga nijū arimasu.)

¶ "How many classrooms are there in **this** building?"
"There are 20 classrooms in **this** building."

*話し手と話し相手とが同じ所にいて、話し手にとっても話し相手にとっても身近な範囲の所にあるものごとは、話し手も話し相手も「この (kono)」でさし示す。

*The speaker and listener both use *kono* when they are in the same location and when the object or person is physically close to both of them.

② [文脈の上で前に述べたものごとを話し手にとって身近な関係にあるものとしてさし示す]

② [this, these; refers to something mentioned earlier as something that is close to the speaker]

¶昨日、ホテルに着きました。このホテルは林の中にあるので、たいへん涼しいです。(Kinō hoteru ni tsukimashita. *Kono* hoteru wa hayashi no naka ni aru node, taihen suzushii desu.)

¶試験の成績が60点以上でなければ、上のクラスには進めません。このことは、あなたも知っていたはずです。(Shiken no seiseki ga rokujitten ijō de nakereba, ue no kurasu ni wa susumemasen. *Kono* koto wa, anata mo shitte ita hazu desu.)

③[話し手の当面する時間を基準としてその前後の時間のある範囲をさし示す]

¶山田さんはこの二、三日元気がないです。(Yamada san wa *kono* ni'sannichi genki ga nai desu.)

⇒その **sono** あの **ano** どの **dono**

このあいだ この間 〔名〕

¶わたしはこの間、上田さんに会いました。(Watashi wa *konoaida*, Ueda san ni aimashita.)

＊「こないだ (konaida)」とも言う。

⇒先日 **senjitsu**

このごろ 〔名〕

¶このごろは忙しくて、新聞も読めません。(*Konogoro* wa isogashikute, shinbun mo yomemasen.)

¶このごろの若者は髪の毛を長く伸ばしています。(*Konogoro* no wakamono wa kaminoke o nagaku nobashite imasu.)

¶ [I] arrived at the hotel yesterday. As **this** hotel is in the middle of the woods, it is very cool here.

¶ One cannot advance to the next class unless one has a grade of 60 or better on the exam. You must have known **this**.

③ [this, these, past, next; indicates a time before or after the present time of the speaker, which is taken as the standard]

¶ [Miss] Yamada has been in low spirits **these past** two or three days.

konoaida 〔n〕 **the other day, recently**

¶ I met [Mr.] Ueda **the other day**.

＊Variant: *konaida*.

konogoro 〔n〕 now, nowadays, recently, lately

¶ I'm so busy **these days** I can't even read the newspaper.

¶ Young people wear their hair long **these days**.

このつぎ この次〔連〕

¶この次の日曜日にテニスをしませんか。(*Kono tsugi* no nichiyōbi ni tenisu o shimasen ka?)

¶この次は20ページから始めます。(*Kono tsugi* wa nijippēji kara hajimemasu.)

kono tsugi 〔compd〕 **next, next time, another time**

¶ Won't you play tennis with me **next** Sunday?

¶ **Next time** we will start from page 20.

このまえ この前〔連〕

¶この前、日本へ行った時は春でした。(*Kono mae*, Nihon e itta toki wa haru deshita.)

¶この前の日曜日は家族と銀座へ行きました。(*Kono mae* no nichiyōbi wa kazoku to Ginza e ikimashita.)

⇒前 mae

kono mae 〔compd〕 **last, last time, before this, previously**

¶ It was spring when [I] went to Japan **the last time**.

¶ **Last** Sunday [I] went with my family to Ginza.

ごはん 御飯〔名〕

① [食事]
朝御飯 (asa*gohan*) 昼御飯 (hiru*gohan*) 晩御飯 (ban*gohan*)
夕御飯 (yū*gohan*)

② [米を炊いた食べ物]
御飯を炊く (*gohan* o taku)

¶朝は御飯とパンとどちらがいいですか。(Asa wa *gohan* to pan to dochira ga ii desu ka?)

gohan 〔n〕 **a meal; boiled rice**

① [a meal]
breakfast // lunch // dinner, supper // dinner, supper

② [boiled rice]
to cook **rice**

¶ Which would you prefer for breakfast, **rice** or bread 〚toast, a croissant, etc.〛?

ごぶさた 〔名、〜する〕

¶長い間ごぶさたしました。(Nagai aida *gobusata* shimashita.)

¶ごぶさたしていますが、皆さんお元気ですか。(Gobusata shite imasu ga, minasan ogenki desu ka?)

gobusata 〔n, 〜*suru*〕 **an expression used in apology when one has been out of contact with the other person for some time**

¶ Please excuse me **for my** long **silence**.

¶ Sorry to **have been out of touch**. I hope everyone is well.

こぼす 〔動 I〕

¶ 机の上に水をこぼしてしまいました。（Tsukue no ue ni mizu o *koboshite* shimaimashita.）

¶ あの映画を見て、涙をこぼさない人はいないでしょう。（Ano eiga o mite, namida o *kobosanai* hito wa inai deshō.）

こまかい 細かい 〔形〕

① [形や金額が小さい]
¶ 目が悪いので、細かい字は読めません。（Me ga warui node, *komakai* ji wa yomemasen.）

¶ 1万円を細かくしてください。
（Ichiman'en o *komakaku* shite kudasai.）

② [内容が詳しい]
¶ このことについて、もっと細かく説明しましょう。（Kono koto ni tsuite, motto *komakaku* setsumei shimashō.）

＊「細か（komaka）」（形動）という言葉もある。「細かな字（komaka na ji）」

こまる 困る 〔動 I〕

¶ この国の人たちは食糧に困っています。（Kono kuni no hitotachi wa shokuryō ni *komatte* imasu.）

¶ 工場がうるさくて、近所の人が困っています。（Kōjō ga urusakute, kinjo no hito ga *komatte* imasu.）

¶ 難しい質問をされて、返事に困りました。（Muzukashii shitsumon o sarete, henji ni *komarimashita*.）

---

kobosu 〔v I〕 spill, shed, drop

¶ [I] **spilled** water on the top of the desk.

¶ No one can see that movie **without shedding** some tears 〖The person doesn't exist who can see that movie **without crying**〗.

komakai 〔adj〕 small, fine; detailed

① [small, fine, minute]
¶ [My] eyes are bad so [I] can't read **small** print.

¶ Please give me **change** for this ten-thousand-yen bill.

② [detailed, minute]
¶ Let me explain **in** more **detail** about this matter.

＊The word *komaka* (an adjective-verb) can also be used, as in *komaka na ji* (small print).

komaru 〔v I〕 be in difficulties; be badly off; be at a loss, be bothered

¶ The people in this country **are short** of food.

¶ The neighborhood people **are inconvenienced** by the noise of the factory.

¶ [I] was asked a difficult question and **was hard put** for an answer.

ごみ〔名〕

ごみ箱（*gomi*bako）ごみ袋
（*gomi*bukuro）ごみ捨て場
（*gomi*suteba）

¶ここにごみを捨てないでください。
（Koko ni *gomi* o sutenaide kudasai.）
¶東京では、一日にどのぐらいごみが
出ますか。（Tōkyō de wa, ichinichi ni
dono gurai *gomi* ga demasu ka？）

こむ〔動 I〕

¶日曜日なので、映画館はたいへんこ
んでいました。（Nichiyōbi na node,
eigakan wa taihen *konde* imashita.）

ゴム〔名〕

消しゴム（keshi*gomu*）ゴムひも
（*gomu*himo）輪ゴム（wa*gomu*）

¶このひもはゴムのように伸びます
ね。（Kono himo wa *gomu* no yō ni
nobimasu ne.）

-こむ -込む〔尾〕

①〔中に入る、入れる〕
プールに飛び込む（pūru ni tobi*komu*）
¶雨が降ってきたので、軒下に駆け込
みました。（Ame ga futte kita node,
nokishita ni kake*komimashita*.）
¶この欄に国籍と名前を書き込んでく
ださい。（Kono ran ni kokuseki to namae
o kaki*konde* kudasai.）
②〔すっかりそういう状態になる〕
¶あの人は何を考え込んでいるので
しょう。（Ano hito wa nani o
kangae*konde* iru no deshō.）

gomi 〔n〕 **dust, litter, garbage,
trash**

a **trash** container // a **trash** bag // a
garbage dump

¶ Please don't throw away **trash** here
〖No littering; No dumping〗.
¶ How much **garbage** is produced in
Tokyo a day?

komu 〔v I〕 **be crowded**

¶ The movie theater **was** very **crowded**
as it was Sunday.

gomu 〔n〕 **rubber, gum (elastic)**
(rubber) eraser // **elastic** band //
rubber band

¶ This string stretches like **elastic**.

-komu 〔suf〕 **come in, put in;
completely ～**

① [come in, put in]
jump 〖**dive, plunge**〗 into the pool
¶ It started raining so [I] **ran under** the
eaves.

¶ Please **fill in** this column with your
nationality and name.

② [completely ～]
¶ I wonder what [he] **is so lost in
thought** about.

¶中村さんはお酒を飲んで、眠り込んでしまいました。(Nakamura san wa osake o nonde, nemuri*konde* shimaimashita.)

*動詞のあとについて、その動詞の意味を強める。

¶ [Mr.] Nakamura was drinking and **fell fast asleep.**

*-*komu* intensifies the meaning of the verb it is added to.

こむぎ 小麦 〔名〕

¶小麦粉でパンを作ります。(*Komugi*ko de pan o tsukurimasu.)

komugi 〔n〕 wheat

¶ Bread is made from (**wheat**) flour.

こめ 米 〔名〕

¶日本では米が主食です。(Nihon de wa *kome* ga shushoku desu.)

kome 〔n〕 rice

¶ **Rice** is the staple food of Japan.

ごめんください 〔連〕

gomen kudasai 〔compd〕 **an expression used to call attention to oneself if no one is in sight or when parting from or ending a telephone conversation with a person of higher status**

¶玄関で「ごめんください。」と言う声がしました。(Genkan de "Gomen kudasai." to iu koe ga shimashita.)

¶奥さんは、「では、ごめんください。」と言って電話を切りました。(Okusan wa, "Dewa, *gomen kudasai*." to itte denwa o kirimashita.)

¶ Someone at the door called out, "*Gomen kudasai*."

¶ The wife ended the telephone conversation with the words, "*Dewa, gomen kudasai*."

ごめんなさい 〔連〕

gomen nasai 〔compd〕 **I'm sorry; excuse me**

¶遅くなって、ごめんなさい。(Osoku natte, *gomen nasai*.)

¶わたしが悪かったです。ごめんなさい。(Watashi ga warukatta desu. Gomen nasai.)

⇒すみません sumimasen

¶ **I'm sorry** to be late.

¶ It was my fault. **I'm very sorry.**

こよみ 暦 〔名〕
☞カレンダー karendā

koyomi 〔〕 ☞**karendā**

309

（〜て）ごらんなさい 〔連〕

¶ちょっと食べてごらんなさい。
(Chotto tabete *goran nasai*.)
¶来てごらんなさい。きれいな鳥がいますよ。（Kite *goran nasai*. Kirei na tori ga imasu yo.）

ごらんになる　ご覧になる 〔動Ⅰ〕

¶あの映画はもうご覧になりましたか。(Ano eiga wa mō goran ni narimashita ka?)

これ 〔代〕

① [話し手に身近な関係にあるものごとをさし示す]

¶「これはだれの本ですか。」（*Kore* wa dare no hon desu ka?）「それは上田さんの本です。」（Sore wa Ueda san no hon desu.）
¶「そのりんごはおいしいですよ。」（Sono ringo wa oishii desu yo.）「では、これを五つください。」（Dewa, *kore* o itsutsu kudasai.）
¶「東京の地図はこれですか。」（Tōkyō no chizu wa *kore* desu ka?）「いいえ、東京の地図はそれではありません。」（Iie, Tōkyō no chizu wa sore de wa arimasen.）
② [話し手が当面している時間をさし示す、今]
¶「あなたはこれからどこへ行きますか。」（Anata wa *kore* kara doko e ikimasu ka?）「わたしはこれからデパートへ行きます。」（Watashi wa *kore* kara depāto e ikimasu.）

(-te)goran nasai 〔compd〕 **try and ~ (cannot be used toward those of higher status)**
¶ **Have a taste** of it.
¶ **Come** here a minute! There's a pretty bird.

goranninaru 〔vI〕 **see, look**
¶ Have you already seen that movie?

kore 〔pron〕 **this, these; now; this person**
① [this, these, this one; indicates something physically close to the speaker]
¶ "Whose book is **this**?"
"That is [Mr.] Ueda's book."
¶ "Those apples are good."
"Well then, give me five of **them**."
¶ "Is **this** a map of Tokyo?"
"No, that isn't a map of Tokyo."
② [this, now; indicates the present time of the speaker]
¶ "Where are you going **now**?"
"I'm going to the department store **now**."

¶「あなたはこれから何をしますか。」（Anata wa *kore* kara nani o shi-masu ka?）「わたしはこれから図書館で勉強します。」（Watashi wa *kore* kara toshokan de benkyō shimasu.）

¶「What are you going to do **now?**」 "I'm going to study at the library **now**."

¶この前の試験は、これまででいちばんいい成績でした。（Kono mae no shiken wa, *kore* made de ichiban ii seiseki deshita.）

¶ [My] mark on the last exam was the highest [I]'ve had up to **now**.

*「これから（kore kara）」「これまで（kore made）」などの形で使う。

*Used in the patterns "*kore kara*," "*kore made*," etc.

③ [話し手の家族や友人などで話し手の身近にいる者をさし示す]

③ [this, this person; indicates a person close to the speaker such as a family member or friend]

¶これが今年大学に入った弟です。（*Kore* ga kotoshi daigaku ni haitta otōto desu.）

¶ **This** is my younger brother, who has started college this year.

¶これがわたしの家内です。どうぞよろしく。（*Kore* ga watashi no kanai desu. Dōzo yoroshiku.）

¶ **This** is my wife. Let me introduce you.

④ [文脈の上で前に述べたものごとを話し手に身近な関係にあるものとしてさし示す]

④ [this; refers to something mentioned earlier as something that is close to the speaker]

¶わたしのうちでは犬を飼っています。これはどろぼうが入るのを防ぐためです。（Watashi no uchi de wa inu o katte imasu. *Kore* wa dorobō ga hairu no o fusegu tame desu.）

¶ We keep a dog at my house. **This** is to prevent thieves from breaking in.

¶工場の煙突から出る煙は炭のような粒が集まったものです。石油が燃えるときに出る煙もこれと同じです。（Kōjō no entotsu kara deru kemuri wa sumi no yō na tsubu ga atsumatta mono desu. Sekiyu ga moeru toki ni deru kemuri mo *kore* to onaji desu.）

¶ The smoke coming from the factory smokestack is like charcoal soot. The smoke produced when oil burns is the same as **this**.

⑤ [話し手が当面している今の状態をさし示す]

⑤ [this, now; indicates the present situation of the speaker]

¶今日の勉強はこれまでにします。
（Kyō no benkyō wa *kore* made ni
shimasu.）

¶ **This** ends the lesson for today.

¶これで今日の授業は終わります。
（*Kore* de kyō no jugyō wa owarimasu.）

¶ **This** concludes today's class.

¶これからが大切ですから、よく聞い
ていてください。（*Kore* kara ga tai-
setsu desu kara, yoku kiite ite kudasai.）

¶ The **next** part is especially important
so please listen carefully.

¶では、これで失礼します。（Dewa,
kore de shitsurei shimasu.）

¶ Well, **with this** I'll take my leave
〚Well, I'll say good-bye **now**〛.

*「これまで（kore made）」「これで
（kore de）」「これから（kore kara）」な
どの形で使う。

*Used in the patterns "*kore made*,"
"*kore de*," "*kore kara*," etc.

⇒それ **sore**　あれ **are**　どれ **dore**

これから〔連〕

kore kara 〚compd〛 **from now on,
after this, in future**

¶これからだんだん寒くなります。
（*Kore kara* dandan samuku narimasu.）

¶ **From now on** it will become colder
and colder.

¶これから気をつけます。（*Kore kara*
ki o tsukemasu.）

¶ I'll be careful **in future**.

¶わたしはこれから学校へ行くところ
です。（Watashi wa *kore kara* gakkō e
iku tokoro desu.）

¶ I am on the point of leaving for
school **now**.

ころ〔名〕

koro 〚n〛 **time, about, around**

¶子供のころ、よく川へ魚を捕りに行
きました。（Kodomo no *koro*, yoku
kawa e sakana o tori ni ikimashita.）

¶ **When** [I] was a child [I] often went
fishing in the river.

¶父はもう帰ってくるころだと思いま
す。（Chichi wa mō kaette kuru *koro* da
to omoimasu.）

¶ I think it's **about time** for my father
to come home.

-ごろ〔尾〕

-goro 〚suf〛 **about, around**

¶毎朝6時ごろ起きます。（Maiasa
rokuji *goro* okimasu.）

¶ [I] get up every morning **around** six
o'clock.

¶わたしたちは今年の10月ごろ結婚し
ます。（Watashitachi wa kotoshi no
jūgatsu *goro* kekkon shimasu.）

¶ We are going to get married this year
around October.

ころがる 転がる 〔動Ⅰ〕

① [回りながら進む]
¶山の上から石が転がってきました。
(Yama no ue kara ishi ga *korogatte*
kimashita.)
¶卵がテーブルの上から転がり落ちま
した。(Tamago ga tēburu no ue kara
*korogari*ochimashita.)
② [横たわる]
¶わたしたちは草の上に寝転がって休
みました。(Watashitachi wa kusa no ue
ni *nekorogatte* yasumimashita.)

ころす 殺す 〔動Ⅰ〕

¶これはねずみを殺す薬です。(Kore
wa nezumi o *korosu* kusuri desu.)
¶その人は自分の部屋で殺されていま
した。(Sono hito wa jibun no heya de
korosarete imashita.)

ころぶ 転ぶ 〔動Ⅰ〕

¶転んで足にけがをしました。
(*Koronde* ashi ni kega o shimashita.)
¶道が悪いから、転ばないように注意
してください。(Michi ga warui kara,
korobanai yō ni chūi shite kudasai.)

こわい 怖い 〔形〕

① [厳しい]
¶山田先生はとても怖い先生です。
(Yamada sensei wa totemo *kowai* sensei
desu.)
¶父が怖い顔でしかりました。(Chichi
ga *kowai* kao de shikarimashita.)
② [恐ろしい]

(-)korogaru 〔v Ⅰ〕 roll, roll over, tumble, fall; lie down

① [roll, roll over, tumble, fall]
¶A rock **came tumbling down** from
the mountaintop.

¶An egg **fell off** the table.

② [lie down]
¶We **lay down** on the grass and rested.

korosu 〔v Ⅰ〕 kill, murder

¶This is a chemical for **killing** rats.

¶[He] was found **murdered** in [his]
room.

korobu 〔v Ⅰ〕 fall down, have a fall

¶[I] **fell down** and injured [my] leg
〖foot〗.

¶The road is bad so please be careful
not to fall.

kowai 〔adj〕 terrible, dreadful; frightened, fearful

① [terrible, dreadful, grim]
¶Professor Yamada **is very forbidding**.

¶My father scolded me with a **terrible**
expression on his face.

② [frightened, fearful]

¶ゆうべ近所で火事があり、とても怖かったです。(Yūbe kinjo de kaji ga ari, totemo *kowakatta* desu.)

¶There was a fire nearby last night; **I was** quite **frightened**.

¶この辺は昔からお化けが出るといわれているので、夜は怖くて通れません。(Kono hen wa mukashi kara obake ga deru to iwarete iru node, yoru wa *kowakute* tooremasen.)

¶It has long been said that this area is haunted by ghosts so that **I'm afraid** to walk through it at night.

こわす 壊す 〔動 I〕

kowasu 〔v I〕 **break, destroy; injure**

① [破壊する]

① [break, destroy, demolish]

¶この箱を壊したのはだれですか。(Kono hako o *kowashita* no wa dare desu ka?)

¶Who **broke** this box?

② [体を悪くする]

② [injure, damage (one's health)]

¶わたしはおなかをこわしているので、何も食べられません。(Watashi wa onaka o *kowashite* iru node, nani mo taberaremasen.)

¶I'm **having stomach trouble** and can't eat anything.

¶上田さんは働きすぎて、体をこわしてしまいました。(Ueda san wa hatarakisugite, karada o *kowashite* shimaimashita.)

¶[Mr.] Ueda **ruined [his] health** through overwork.

こわれる 壊れる 〔動 II〕

kowareru 〔v II〕 **be broken, be wrecked; be broken, be out of order**

① [もとの形がなくなる]

① [be broken, be wrecked, come to pieces]

¶地震で家がたくさん壊れました。(Jishin de ie ga takusan *kowaremashita*.)

¶Many houses **were destroyed** in the earthquake.

② [機械などが働かなくなる]

② [be broken, be out of order]

¶このラジオは壊れています。(Kono rajio wa *kowarete* imasu.)

¶This radio **is broken**.

コンクリート 〔名〕
¶この建物はコンクリート建築です。
(Kono tatemono wa *konkuriito*- kenchiku desu.)

konkuriito 〔n〕 **concrete**
¶ This is a **concrete** building.

こんげつ 今月 〔名〕
¶わたしは今月の末に京都へ行きます。(Watashi wa *kongetsu* no sue ni Kyōto e ikimasu.)
¶田中さんは今月アメリカから帰ってきます。(Tanaka san wa *kongetsu* Amerika kara kaette kimasu.)

kongetsu 〔n〕 **this month**
¶ I am going to go to Kyoto at the end of **this month**.

¶ [Miss] Tanaka returns from the United States **this month**.

こんご 今後 〔名〕

¶同じ間違いをしないように、今後は気をつけます。(Onaji machigai o shinai yō ni, *kongo* wa ki o tsuke-masu.)
¶今後ともよろしくお願いします。(*Kongo* tomo yoroshiku onegai shimasu.)

kongo 〔n〕 **after this, from now on, hereafter, in the future**
¶ I will be careful **from now on** not to make the same mistake again.

¶ I hope I can **continue** to receive your good offices.

コンサート 〔名〕
¶コンサートの招待券が２枚あるんだけど、一緒に聞きに行きませんか。(Konsāto no shōtaiken ga nimai aru n dakedo ishoni ikimasen ka.?)

konsāto 〔n〕 **concert**
¶ I have two free tickets for the concert; would you like to go with me?

こんしゅう 今週 〔名〕
¶今週の土曜日にうちに来てください。(*Konshū* no doyōbi ni uchi ni kite kudasai.)
¶今週、わたしは京都へ行くつもりです。(*Konshū*, watashi wa Kyōto e iku tsumori desu.)

konshū 〔n〕 **this week**
¶ Please come to visit me **this** Saturday.

¶ I plan to go to Kyoto **this week**.

こんど 今度 〔名〕

① [この次、近い将来]

kondo 〔n〕 **next time; this time; recently**
① [next time, soon]

¶今度の日曜日に映画を見に行きましょう。(*Kondo* no nichiyōbi ni eiga o mi ni ikimashō.)

¶今度日本に行くときは、両親も連れていくつもりです。(*Kondo* Nihon ni iku toki wa, ryōshin mo tsurete iku tsumori desu.)

② [今回]

¶今度の実験は成功しました。(*Kondo* no jikken wa seikō shimashita.)

¶入学試験のため一生懸命勉強しましたが、今度もだめでした。(Nyū-gaku-shiken no tame isshōkenmei benkyō shimashita ga, *kondo* mo dame deshita.)

*何回か繰り返されるものごとのうち、いちばん最近のことについて言うときに使う。

③ [最近]

¶今度、新しく来た先生のお名前は何と言いますか。(*Kondo*, tarashiku kita sensei no onamae wa nan to iimasu ka？)

¶わたしは今度初めて日本へ来ました。(Watashi wa *kondo* hajimete Nihon e kimashita.)

*新しく起こったものごとについて言うときに使う。

こんな 〔連体〕

① [話し手にとって身近な関係にあるものごとの様子をさし示す]

¶こんなひどい雨でも行くのですか。(*Konna* hidoi ame demo iku no desuka？)

¶難しい試験に通って、こんなうれしいことはありません。(Muzukashii shiken ni tootte, *konna* ureshii koto wa arimasen.)

¶ Let's go to see a movie **next** Sunday.

¶ I plan to take my parents with me **the next time** I go to Japan.

② [this time, now]

¶ The experiment succeeded **this time**.

¶ [I] studied hard for the school entrance exam but failed **this time** too.

*Used for the most recent of a series of repeated events.

③ [recently]

¶ What is the name of the **new** teacher?

¶ I **recently** came to Japan for the first time.

*Used for something taking place not long before.

konna 〔attrib〕 **such, this, like this**

① [such, this, like this; indicates something close to the speaker]

¶ Are you going even in **such** a heavy rain?

¶ Nothing could afford greater happiness than this passing of a difficult exam.

¶こんなふうにすると、うまくいきますよ。(*Konna* fū ni suru to, umaku ikimasu yo.)

②[文脈の上で前に述べたことがらの内容・状態などを話し手に身近な関係にあるものとしてさし示したりまたあとから述べる話し手の考えなどを前もってさし示したりする]

¶「もうあんな所へは二度と行きたくない。」と、子供はこんなことを言うのです。("Mō anna tokoro e wa nido to ikitaku nai." to, kodomo wa *konna* koto o iu no desu.

¶わたしはこんなふうに考えます。子供にはあまりきびしくしても自由にさせてもよくないと思うのです。(Watashi wa *konna* fū ni kangaemasu. Kodomo ni wa amari kibishiku shite mo jiyū ni sasete mo yoku nai to omou no desu.)

⇒そんな **sonna**　あんな **anna**
どんな **donna**

こんなに〔副〕

¶この問題がこんなに複雑だとは思いませんでした。(Kono mondai ga *konna ni* fukuzatsu da to wa omoimasen deshita.)

¶こんなに楽しいパーティーは初めてです。(*Konna ni* tanoshii pātii wa hajimete desu.)

¶こんなにたくさんいただいて、ありがとうございます。(*Konna ni* taku-san itadaite, arigatō gozaimasu.)

＊話し手が身近に認めるものごとの状態・程度・数量などをさし示すのに使う。強調的にさし示すこともある。
⇒そんなに **sonna ni**　あんなに
anna ni　どんなに **donna ni**

¶ It will work better if you do it **like this**.

②[this, like this; indicates that something mentioned earlier is close to the speaker or introduces an opinion, etc., of the speaker]

¶ The child had **this** to say: "I never want to go to that sort of place again."

¶ **This** is what I think. I think it's bad to be either too strict or too easy-going with one's children.

konna ni〔adv〕**so, so much, like this**

¶ I didn't think that this problem was **so** complicated.

¶ I have never before been to **such** an enjoyable party.

¶ Thank you for giving me **all this**.

＊*Konna ni* is used to indicate the condition, extent, amount, etc., of things recognized as close by the speaker. It is sometimes used as an intensifier.

こんなん　困難〔名、形動〕

konnan 〔n, adj-v〕 difficulty, trouble, suffering, distress, hardship

¶今月中に論文を完成するのは困難です。(Kongetsuchū ni ronbun o kansei suru no wa *konnan* desu.)

¶ **It will be difficult** to finish the thesis by the end of the month.

¶上田さんは困難な仕事をとうとうやり遂げました。(Ueda san wa *konnan* na shigoto o tōtō yaritogemashita.)

¶ [Mr.] Ueda finally finished that **difficult** task.

¶物価が上がって、生活が困難になってきました。(Bukka ga agatte, seikatsu ga *konnan* ni natte kimashita.)

¶ With the rise in prices it has become 〖it became〗 **difficult** to make ends meet.

こんにち　今日〔名〕

konnichi 〔n〕 today, these days, nowadays, at present

¶今日の日本は民主国家として発展しています。(*Konnichi* no Nihon wa minshukokka to shite hatten shite imasu.)

¶ **Present-day** Japan is an advanced democracy.

こんにちは　今日は〔連〕

konnichi wa 〔compd〕 a greeting used during the day

¶今日は。(*Konnichi wa !*)

¶ **Good day** 〖Good morning; Good afternoon; Hello〗

こんばん　今晩〔名〕

konban 〔n〕 this evening, tonight

¶今晩6時から音楽会があります。(*Konban* rokuji kara ongakukai ga arimasu.)

¶ There is a concert 〖recital〗 **tonight** at six o'clock.

⇒今夜 kon'ya

こんばんは　今晩は〔連〕

konban wa 〔compd〕 a greeting used in the evening

¶今晩は。(*Konban wa !*)

¶ **Good evening**.

こんや　今夜〔名〕

kon'ya 〔n〕 this evening, tonight

¶今夜はこのホテルに泊まりましょう。(*Kon'ya* wa kono hoteru ni tomarimashō.)

¶ Let's stay at this hotel **tonight**.

¶今夜、わたしのうちに来てください。(*Kon'ya*, watashi no uchi ni kite kudasai.)

¶ Please come to visit me **this evening**.

⇒今晩 konban

こんやく　婚約〔名、〜する〕

婚約指環（*kon'yaku*-yubiwa）婚約期間
（*kon'yaku*-kikan）婚約者
（*kon'yaku*sha）

¶一郎さんと春子さんは昨日婚約しま
した。(Ichirō san to Haruko san wa kinō
kon'yaku shimashita.)

kon'yaku〔n, 〜*suru*〕
engagement, betrothal

an **engagement** ring // an **engagement**
period // **a fiancé, fiancée**

¶ Ichirō and Haruko **became engaged**
yesterday.

さ 差 〔名〕

¶この辺りは、昼と夜とではかなり温度の差があります。(Kono atari wa, hiru to yoru to de wa kanari ondo no *sa* ga arimasu.)

¶昨日の試験では、1点の差で1番になれませんでした。(Kinō no shiken de wa, itten no *sa* de ichiban ni naremasen deshita.)

sa 〔n〕 **difference, disparity, margin**

¶ There are considerable **changes** of temperature between the day and night in this area.

¶ [I] was only one point **from being** first on yesterday's exam.

-さ 〔尾〕

暑さ (atsu*sa*) 寒さ (samu*sa*) 美しさ (utsukushi*sa*) 白さ (shiro*sa*) 苦しさ (kurushi*sa*) 明るさ (akaru*sa*) 重さ (omo*sa*) 長さ (naga*sa*) 速さ (haya*sa*) 深さ (fuka*sa*) 正確さ (seikaku*sa*) すなおさ (sunao*sa*)

＊形容詞・形容動詞の語幹に続いて名詞を作り、ものごとの性質・状態やその程度を表す。

-sa 〔suf〕 **a suffix for making adjectives and adjective-verbs into nouns**

heat, warm**th** // cold**ness**, the cold // beauty // white**ness** // anguish, distress // bright**ness** // weight // length // quick**ness**, speed // depth // accuracy, preci**sion** // frank**ness**, lack of guile

＊-sa is added to the stem of an adjective or adjective-verb to form a noun; it expresses nature, condition, degree, etc.

さあ 〔感〕

①[人を促すときに使う]

¶さあ、行きましょう。(*Sā*, ikimashō.)

②[ためらうときに使う]

sā 〔interj〕 **come, come now; well, well now**

① [come, come now; used when urging some course of action]
¶ Let's be off now!

② [well, well now, let me see; used when one is hesitant or unsure about something]

320

¶「あの人はだれですか。」(Ano hito wa dare desuka？)「さあ、知りません。」(*Sā*, shirimasen.)

¶ "Who is that person?" "Well, I don't really know."

サービス〔名、〜する〕

sābisu〔n, 〜*suru*〕 **service; special price, special service**

① [世話をすること]
セルフサービス（serufu*sābisu*）サービスが悪い（*sābisu* ga warui）
¶あのホテルはとてもサービスがいいですよ。(Ano hoteru wa totemo *sābisu* ga ii desu yo.)

① [service]
self-**service** // the **service** is poor, have poor **service**
¶ You get excellent **service** at that hotel.

②[値段を引くこと、おまけ]

¶シャツを買ったら、サービスにハンカチをくれました。(Shatsu o kattara, *sābisu* ni hankachi o kuremashita.)

② [special price, special service, something included free of charge]
¶ When [I] bought a shirt they gave me a handkerchief **free of charge**.

-さい -歳〔尾〕

-sai〔suf〕 **age, years**

¶わたしは今月の10日で30歳になります。(Watashi wa kongetsu no tooka de sanjis*sai* ni narimasu.)

¶ I will be 30 **years old** on the tenth of this month.

さいきん 最近〔名〕

saikin〔n〕 **the latest, recent; recently, lately**

¶最近、あの人は学校へ来ません。(*Saikin*, ano hito wa gakkō e kimasen.)
¶最近は物の値段が上がる一方です。(*Saikin* wa mono no nedan ga agaru ippō desu.)

¶ [He] hasn't been coming to school **lately**.
¶ **Recently** prices just keep going up and up.

さいご 最後〔名〕

saigo〔n〕 **last, final, ultimate**

¶最後にこの部屋を出た人はだれですか。(*Saigo* ni kono heya o deta hito wa dare desu ka？)
¶どんなに苦しくても、最後までがんばってください。(Donna ni kurushikute mo, *saigo* made ganbatte kudasai.)
⇔最初 saisho

¶ Who was the **last** person to leave this room?

¶ Please stick it out to **the end**, no matter how difficult it may be.

さいこう　最高 〔名〕

最高裁判所 (*saikō*-saibansho) 最高記録 (*saikō*-kiroku) 最高点 (*saikō*-ten)

¶昨日の最高気温は 30 度でした。
(Kinō no *saikō*-kion wa sanjūdo deshita.)

saikō 〔n〕 **highest, maximum, supreme; the greatest**
the **Supreme** Court // the **best** record (for a sports event, etc.) // the **highest** mark scored
¶ Yesterday's **high** temperature was 30 degrees.

ざいさん　財産 〔名〕

¶山田さんは土地や建物などずいぶん財産を持っているようです。(Yamada san wa tochi ya tatemono nado zuibun *zaisan* o motte iru yō desu.)

zaisan 〔n〕 **estate, assets, property, fortune**
¶ It seems that [Mr.] Yamada owns much **property**—land, buildings, etc.

さいじつ　祭日 〔名〕

¶3月 21 日は祭日なので、学校は休みです。(Sangatsu nijūichinichi wa *saijitsu* na node, gakkō wa yasumi desu.)
¶来週は日曜と祭日が続くから、旅行する人が多いでしょう。(Raishū wa nichiyō to *saijitsu* ga tsuzuku kara, ryokō suru hito ga ooi deshō.)

saijitsu 〔n〕 **a national holiday**
¶ There's no school on March 21 as it's **a national holiday**.

¶ Monday is **a holiday** (more literally, **a holiday** comes after Sunday) next week so probably many people will be traveling over the three-day weekend.

さいしょ　最初 〔名〕

¶授業の最初にいつも発音の練習をします。(Jugyō no *saisho* ni itsumo hatsuon no renshū o shimasu.)
¶この本は最初はつまらなかったが、だんだんおもしろくなってきました。(Kono hon wa *saisho* wa tsumaranakatta ga, dandan omoshiroku natte kimashita.)
⇔最後 saigo

saisho 〔n〕 **the first, the beginning; at first, originally**
¶ At **the beginning** of class [we] always have pronunciation drill.

¶ **At first** this book was boring but it has gradually gotten more interesting.

さいそく　催促 〔名、〜する〕

¶学校から授業料の催促を受けました。(Gakkō kara jugyōryō no *saisoku* o ukemashita.)

saisoku 〔n, 〜*suru*〕 **urging, demand**
¶ [I] got a letter from the school **requesting** payment of [my] tuition.

322

¶早く本を返してくれるように、友達に催促しました。(Hayaku hon o kaeshite kureru yō ni, tomodachi ni *saisoku* shimashita.)

¶ [I] **urged** [my] friend to return the borrowed book soon.

さいだい 最大 〔名〕

saidai 〔n〕 **greatest, largest, maximum**

¶世界最大の都市はどこですか。(Sekai *saidai* no toshi wa doko desu ka？)

¶ What is the **largest** city in the world?

¶健康であることは最大の幸福です。(Kenkō de aru koto wa *saidai* no kōfuku desu.)

¶ The **greatest** blessing is to have one's health.

さいのう 才能 〔名〕

sainō 〔n〕 **talent, ability, aptitude**

¶この子は音楽の才能があります。(Kono ko wa ongaku no *sainō* ga arimasu.)

¶ This child has **a talent** for music.

¶才能がなくても、努力すればすぐ上手になります。(*Sainō* ga nakute mo, doryoku sureba sugu jōzu ni narimasu.)

¶ Even if you don't have **any aptitude** for it, you will soon become good at it if you work hard.

さいばん 裁判 〔名、～する〕

saiban 〔n, ～*suru*〕 **trial, hearing, judgment**

裁判官（*saiban*kan）裁判所（*saiban*sho）

a judge, the judiciary // a court of law; a courthouse

¶この事件の裁判は来月二日に行われます。(Kono jiken no *saiban* wa raigetsu futsuka ni okonawaremasu.)

¶ **The trial** in this case will be held 〖This case will be brought **to trial**〗 on the second of next month.

さいふ 財布 〔名〕

saifu 〔n〕 **wallet**

¶この財布には、あまりお金が入っていません。(Kono *saifu* ni wa, amari okane ga haitte imasen.)

¶ There isn't much money in this **wallet.**

ざいもく 材木 〔名〕

zaimoku 〔n〕 **wood, lumber, timber**

¶この家にはいい材木が使われています。(Kono ie ni wa ii *zaimoku* ga tsukawarete imasu.)

¶ High-quality **lumber** has been used in this house.

323

¶山道を歩いていたら、材木をたくさん積んだ車に出会いました。
(Yamamichi o aruite itara, *zaimoku* o takusan tsunda kuruma ni deaimashita.)

¶ While I was walking along a mountain road, a truck loaded up with **timber** came toward me.

ざいりょう 材料〔名〕

zairyō〔n〕**material, raw materials, ingredients, data**

¶この料理の材料は、肉と野菜と豆腐です。(Kono ryōri no *zairyō* wa, niku to yasai to tōfu desu.)

¶ **The ingredients** of this dish are meat, vegetables, and *tōfu*.

¶いい材料を使わないと、こんな立派な家具はできませんね。(Ii *zairyō* o tsukawanai to, konna rippa na kagu wa dekimasen ne.)

¶ Good **materials** are necessary to produce fine furniture like this.

サイン〔名、～する〕

sain〔n, ～*suru*〕**sign, signal; signature, autograph**

①[合図]

① [sign, signal]

¶手を振ってサインを送りました。
(Te o futte *sain* o okurimashita.)

¶ [He] **signaled** by waving [his] hand.

②[署名]

② [signature, autograph]

¶この書類にサインをしてください。
(Kono shorui ni *sain* o shite kudasai.)

¶ Please **sign** these papers.

¶あの俳優のサインが欲しいです。
(Ano haiyū no *sain* ga hoshii desu.)

¶ I'd like to have that actor's 〚actress's〛 **autograph**.

さい- 最-〔頭〕

sai-〔pref〕**the most, the maximum, ultra-**

最終 (*sai*shū) 最強 (*sai*kyō) 最古 (*sai*ko) 最上 (*sai*jō) 最小 (*sai*shō) 最低 (*sai*tei) 最善 (*sai*zen) 最愛 (*sai*ai) 最新式 (*sai*shinshiki) 最年長者 (*sai*nenchōsha)

the last, the ultimate // the strongest // the oldest // the best, the finest, supreme // the smallest, the minimum, the least // the lowest, the minimum; the worst // one's best, the best // dearest, beloved // the latest style // the oldest person

さえ〔助〕

① [極端な例を挙げて他の場合はもちろんであるという意味を表す]

¶わたしの子供は漢字はもちろん、ひらがなさえまだ読めません。(Watashi no kodomo wa kanji wa mochiron, hiragana *sae* mada yomemasen.)

¶そんな易しい問題は、小学生でさえできます。(Sonna yasashii mondai wa, shōgakusei de *sae* dekimasu.)

② [その条件だけでじゅうぶんであるという意味を表す]

¶少しぐらい天気が悪くても、大雨さえ降らなければ行きましょう。(Sukoshi gurai tenki ga warukute mo, ooame *sae* furanakereba ikimashō.)

¶食べ物さえあれば、ほかには何もいりません。(Tabemono *sae* areba, hoka ni wa nani mo irimasen.)

*「〜さえ〜ば (〜sae〜ba)」「〜さえ〜たら (〜sae〜tara)」などの形で使う。

さか 坂〔名〕

坂道 (*saka*michi) 上り坂 (nobori*zaka*) 下り坂 (kudari*zaka*)

¶あの辺は坂が多いから、自転車で行くのはたいへんですよ。(Ano hen wa *saka* ga ooi kara, jitensha de iku no wa taihen desu yo.)

¶この坂は急ですから、気をつけて下りてください。(Kono *saka* wa kyū desu kara, ki o tsukete orite kudasai.)

sae 〔part〕 **even, besides, on top of; if only, so long as**

① [even, besides, on top of; used when giving an extreme example and indicating something else is a matter of course]

¶ My children 〚child〛 can't **even** read *hiragana* yet, much less *kanji*.

¶ **Even** an elementary school student could do such a simple problem.

② [if only, so long as; indicates that a certain condition is enough by itself]

¶ Let's go even if the weather isn't so good **as long as** it's not raining heavily.

¶ [I] don't need **anything but** food.

*Used in the patterns "〜 *sae* 〜 *-ba*" "〜 *sae* 〜 *-tara*," etc.

saka 〔n〕 **slope, incline, hill**

an uphill road, a **sloping** road // an ascent, an up**hill** road, a rising **grade** // a descent, a down**hill** road, a downward **grade**

¶ There are many **hills** in that area so it is hard to go there on a bicycle.

¶ This **slope** is steep so please be careful going down it.

さかい 境 〔名〕

¶ここが隣の土地との境です。(Koko ga tonari no tochi to no *sakai* desu.)

¶この川を境に、向こうがA国です。(Kono kawa o *sakai* ni, mukō ga Ē-koku desu.)

sakai 〔n〕 border, boundary

¶ This is **the border line** with the neighboring land.

¶ This river forms **the boundary** — the other side is Country A.

さがす 探す 〔動Ⅰ〕

仕事を探す (shigoto o *sagasu*)

¶わたしは安くて静かなアパートを探しています。(Watashi wa yasukute shizuka na apāto o *sagashite* imasu.)

sagasu 〔v I〕 search for, look for, try to obtain

look for a job

¶ I'm **hunting for** a cheap and quiet apartment.

さがす 捜す 〔動Ⅰ〕

¶田中さんがあなたを捜していましたよ。(Tanaka san ga anata o *sagashite* imashita yo.)

¶いくら捜しても、時計が見つかりません。(Ikura *sagashite* mo tokei ga mitsukarimasen.)

sagasu 〔v I〕 search for, look for, try to locate

¶ [Mrs.] Tanaka **was looking for** you.

¶ [I] can't find [my] watch no matter how much [I] **search**.

さかな 魚 〔名〕

魚を捕る (*sakana* o toru) 魚をつる (*sakana* o tsuru)

¶この池には魚がたくさんいます。(Kono ike ni wa *sakana* ga takusan imasu.)

¶この魚は焼いて食べましょう。(Kono *sakana* wa yaite tabemashō.)

sakana 〔n〕 fish

catch **a fish**, catch **fish** // to fish

¶ There are many **fish** in this pond 〚pool〛.

¶ Lets eat this **fish** grilled.

さがる 下がる 〔動Ⅰ〕

① [低い方へ移る]
温度が下がる (ondo ga *sagaru*) 物価が下がる (bukka ga *sagaru*) 熱が下がる (netsu ga *sagaru*)

sagaru 〔v I〕 fall, drop, decline; hang, hang down; step back

① [fall, drop, decline, go down]
the temperature **falls** // prices **drop** // a fever **goes down**

¶ 勉強しなかったので、成績が下がってしまいました。(Benkyō shinakatta node, seiseki ga *sagatte* shimaimashita.)
↔ 上がる **agaru**

② [下の方へ垂れる]
¶ 窓に白いカーテンが下がっています。(Mado ni shiroi kāten ga *sagatte* imasu.)

③ [後ろへ退く]
¶ 危ないですから、後ろへ下がってください。(Abunai desu kara, ushiro e *sagatte* kudasai.)

さかん 盛ん 〔形動〕

¶ この国は工業が盛んです。(Kono kuni wa kōgyō ga *sakan* desu.)
¶ この国ではサッカーが盛んです。(Kono kuni de wa sakkā ga *sakan* desu.)
¶ 火が盛んに燃えています。(Hi ga *sakan* ni moete imasu.)
¶ 首相は空港で盛んな出迎えを受けました。(Shushō wa kūkō de *sakan* na demukae o ukemashita.)

(-)さき (-)先 〔名、尾〕

1 〔名〕
① [先端]
¶ この鉛筆の先は丸くなっています。(Kono enpitsu no *saki* wa maruku natte imasu.)

② [前方]
¶ 銀行はこの先にあります。(Ginkō wa kono *saki* ni arimasu.)

¶ [My] grades **fell** 〚**have fallen**〛 because [I] didn't study.

② [hang, hang down, be suspended]
¶ There **is** a white curtain at the window.

③ [step back, draw back]
¶ Please **step back** as it's dangerous to stand right there.

sakan 〔adj-v〕 **prosperous, flourishing, thriving; vigorous, lively; enthusiastic, keen; popular**

¶ This country is **highly** industrialized.

¶ Soccer **is popular** in this country.

¶ The fire is burning **briskly**.

¶ The prime minister received a **warm** reception at the airport.

(-)saki 〔n, suf〕 **point, tip; ahead, beyond; in front, the head, the first; earlier than, before; future, coming; objective, destination**

1 〚n〛
① [point, tip]
¶ **The point** of this pencil is blunt.

② [ahead, beyond]
¶ The bank is **straight ahead**.

327

¶20ページの問題が終わったら、その先に進んでください。(Nijippēji no mondai ga owattara, sono *saki* ni susunde kudasai.)

③ [先頭]

¶山田さんは先に立って、みんなを案内しました。(Yamada san wa *saki* ni tatte, minna o annai shimashita.)

④ [時間的に前、それ以前]

¶田中さんはわたしより先に来ていました。(Tanaka san wa watashi yori *saki* ni kite imashita.)

¶今日は用事があるので、お先に失礼します。(Kyō wa yōji ga aru node, o*saki* ni shitsurei shimasu.)

⑤ [将来]

¶これから十年先、日本はどうなっているでしょう。(Kore kara jūnen *saki*, Nihon wa dō natte iru deshō.)

2 〖尾〗
送り先 (okuri*saki*) 届け先 (todoke*saki*) 連絡先 (renraku*saki*)

¶田中さんの行き先がわかりません。(Tanaka san no iki*saki* ga wakarimasen.)

さく 咲く 〖動 I〗

¶庭に花が咲いています。(Niwa ni hana ga *saite* imasu.)

¶東京では、だいたい4月の初めに桜が咲きます。(Tōkyō de wa, daitai shigatsu no hajime ni sakura ga *sakimasu*.)

¶ When you have finished the problems on page 20, please go on **from there**.

③ [in front, the head, the first]

¶ [Mrs.] Yamada stood **in front** and acted as guide.

④ [earlier than, before, previous, prior]

¶ [Miss] Tanaka came **before** me.

¶ As I have an errand to do 〖other business to attend to〗, I will have to take my leave **before [you]**.

⑤ [future, coming]

¶ I wonder what Japan will be like 10 years **from now**.

2 〖suf〗 objective, destination **the address, the destination** (of something being sent) // the receiver's **address, the destination** (of something being sent or delivered); **the person** or **place** to which a report is to be given // the contact **address, telephone, person**, etc.

¶ [I] don't know **where** [Mr.] Tanaka went.

saku 〖v I〗 **to bloom, blossom, flower**

¶ Flowers **are in bloom** in the garden.

¶ In Tokyo the cherry blossoms generally **come out** in early April.

さくしゃ 作者 〔名〕

小説の作者 (shōsetsu no *sakusha*)
¶この絵は 15 世紀にかかれたものですが、作者はわかりません。(Kono e wa jūgoseiki ni kakareta mono desuga, *sakusha* wa wakarimasen.)

sakusha 〔n〕 **author, artist, composer, etc.**
the author of a novel
¶ This picture dates from the 15th century but **the artist** is unknown.

さくひん 作品 〔名〕

文学作品 (bungaku-*sakuhin*) 芸術作品 (geijutsu-*sakuhin*)
¶生徒の作品の展覧会を開きました。(Seito no *sakuhin* no tenrankai o hirakimashita.)
¶この絵は山田さんの若いころの作品です。(Kono e wa yamada san no wakai koro no *sakuhin* desu.)

sakuhin 〔n〕 **a work, a production, a creation**
a literary **work, a piece** of literature // an art**work**
¶ An exhibition of student **works** opened 〖has opened〗.
¶ This picture is an early **work** of [Mr.] Yamada's.

さくぶん 作文 〔名〕

¶この時間は、「わたしの一日」という題で作文を書いてください。(Kono jikan wa, "Watashi no ichinichi" to iu dai de *sakubun* o kaite kudasai.)

sakubun 〔n〕 **composition, writing; an essay, a theme**
¶ This class hour please write **a composition** on the topic: "My day."

さくら 桜 〔名〕

¶桜が咲きました。(*Sakura* ga sakimashita.)
¶桜の花を見ながらごちそうを食べることを、お花見と言います。(*Sakura* no hana o minagara gochisō o taberu koto o, ohanami to iimasu.)

sakura 〔n〕 **a cherry tree, cherry blossoms**
¶ **The cherry blossoms** are 〖were〗 in bloom.
¶ Eating delicacies while viewing **the cherry blossoms** is called *ohanami*.

さく- 昨- 〔頭〕

昨日 (*saku*jitsu) 昨晩 (*saku*ban) 昨夜 (*saku*ya) 昨年 (*saku*nen)

saku- 〔pref〕 **last**
yesterday // **last** night, yesterday evening // **last** night, yesterday evening // **last** year

さけ 酒 〔名〕

① [アルコール分を含んだ飲み物]
¶ あなたは酒を飲みますか。（Anata wa *sake* o nomimasu ka？）
② [日本酒]
¶ 酒は米から造ります。（*Sake* wa kome kara tsukurimasu.）
¶ ビールにしますか、お酒にしますか。（Biiru ni shimasu ka, o*sake* ni shimasu ka？）

さけぶ 叫ぶ 〔動 I〕

① [大きな声を出す]
¶ だれかが「助けて。」と叫んでいます。（Dare ka ga "Tasukete！" to *sakende* imasu.）
② [あることを実現させるため世間の人々に強く訴える]
¶ あの人たちは戦争反対を叫んでいます。（Ano hitotachi wa sensō-hantai o *sakende* imasu.）

さける 避ける 〔動 II〕

¶ あの人はわたしと会うのを避けているようです。（Ano hito wa watashi to au no o *sakete* iru yō desu.）
¶ 暗い道は避けて、明るい道を帰ったほうがいいですよ。（Kurai michi wa *sakete*, akarui michi o kaetta hō ga ii desu yo.）

さげる 下げる 〔動 II〕

① [低い方へ移す]
温度を下げる（ondo o *sageru*）熱を下げる（netsu o *sageru*）

---

sake 〔n〕 liquor, alcoholic beverage; sake, Japanese rice wine
① [liquor, alcoholic beverage]
¶ Do you drink **alcohol?**
② [*sake*, Japanese rice wine]
¶ *Sake* is made from rice.

¶ Which will you have—beer or *sake?*

sakebu 〔v I〕 shout, yell, cry out; clamor for, advocate
① [shout, yell, cry out]
¶ Someone **is crying out** for help.

② [clamor for, advocate]

¶ Those people **are active** in their antiwar stand.

sakeru 〔v II〕 avoid, evade, shirk
¶ It seems [he] **is avoiding** me.

¶ You had better **keep away** from dark streets and take well-lit ones on your way home.

sageru 〔v II〕 lower, let down, drop; hang, wear
① [lower, let down, drop]
lower the temperature // **bring down** a fever

¶山田さんは丁寧に頭を下げてお礼を言いました。（Yamada san wa teinei ni atama o *sagete* orei o iimashita.）

¶値段を下げれば、買う人もいるでしょう。（Nedan o *sagereba*, kau hito mo iru deshō.）

↔上げる **ageru**

②［下の方へ垂らす］

¶肩からカメラを下げている人が中村さんです。（Kata kara kamera o *sagete* iru hito ga Nakamura san desu.）

ささえる　支える〔動Ⅱ〕

¶木が風で倒れないように、棒で支えてあります。（Ki ga kaze de taorenai yō ni, bō de *sasaete* arimasu.）

¶けが人は友達に支えられながら病院へ入っていきました。（Keganin wa tomodachi ni *sasaerarenagara* byōin e haitte ikimashita.）

さしあげる　差し上げる〔動Ⅱ〕

①［持ち上げる］

¶中村さんは重い石を頭の上まで差し上げました。（Nakamura san wa omoi ishi o atama no ue made *sashiagemashita*.）

②［与える］

¶お客様にお茶を差し上げてください。（Okyakusama ni ocha o *sashiagete* kudasai.）

¶あなたにこの本を差し上げましょう。（Anata ni kono hon o *sashiagemashō*.）

＊「与える（ataeru）」「やる（yaru）」の謙譲語で、「上げる（ageru）」より更に丁寧な言い方である。「（〜て）さしあげる（［〜te］sashiageru）」という言い

¶ [Mr.] Yamada politely **lowered** [his] head and thanked [them].

¶ **If [we] lower** the price it will probably sell.

② [hang, wear]

¶ The person **with** the camera over [his] shoulder is [Mr.] Nakamura.

sasaeru 〔v Ⅱ〕 **support, hold up, prop, maintain, sustain**

¶ The tree **is reinforced** with poles 〖stakes, sticks, etc.〗 so it won't be blown over by the wind.

¶ The injured person walked into the hospital **supported** by a friend.

sashiageru 〔v Ⅱ〕 **lift, raise; give**

① [lift, raise, hold up]

¶ [Mr.] Nakamura **lifted** a heavy rock **up** over [his] head.

② [give]

¶ Please **serve** some tea to [our] guest 〖customer〗.

¶ I'd like **to give** you this book.

*Sashiageru is the humble form of ataeru or yaru; it is more polite than ageru. It is also used in the form (-te) sashiageru, as in "Sensei no onimotsu

方もある。「先生のお荷物を持ってさ
しあげました。(Sensei no onimotsu o
motte sashiagemashita.)」
⇒上げる **ageru** (〜て) あげる
(〜**te**) **ageru**

o motte sashiagemashita" (I carried the
professor's 〚doctor's〛 things 〚bags〛 for
him 〚her〛).

ざしき 座敷 〔名〕

¶お客様を奥の座敷に御案内してくだ
さい。(Okyakusama o oku no *zashiki* ni
goannai shite kudasai.)

zashiki 〔n〕 **room, reception
room, parlor; usually a tatami,
Japanese-style room**

¶ Please show our customer 〚guest〛 to
the room in the back.

さしみ 〔名〕

¶さしみはまだ食べたことがありませ
ん。(*Sashimi* wa mada tabeta koto ga
arimasen.)

sashimi 〔n〕 **sashimi, slices of
raw fish**

¶ I haven't eaten *sashimi* yet.

さす 指す 〔動 I〕

① [指などで示す]
¶先生は黒板に書いた字を一つ一つ指
しながら、学生に読ませます。
(Sensei wa kokuban ni kaita ji o hitotsu
hitotsu *sashinagara*, gakusei ni
yomasemasu.)
¶時計の針がちょうど 12 時を指してい
ます。(Tokei no hari ga chōdo jūniji o
sashite imasu.)
② [指名する]
¶急に先生に指されたので、答えられ
ませんでした。(Kyū ni sensei ni
sasareta node, kotaeraremasen deshita.)

sasu 〔v I〕 **point to, indicate;
designate**

① [point to, point at, indicate]
¶ The teacher **points** one by one **at** the
characters written on the blackboard
and has [her] students read them aloud.

¶ The hands of the clock **are standing**
exactly at twelve 〚The clock **reads**
exactly twelve o'clock〛.
② [designate, name]
¶ The teacher **called on** me suddenly,
and I was not able to answer.

さす 刺す 〔動 I〕

① [突く、突き通す]
¶針で指を刺してしまいました。(Hari
de yubi o *sashite* shimaimashita.)
② [虫がかんだり針を刺したりする]
はちに刺される (hachi ni *sasareru*)

sasu 〔v I〕 **pierce, stab; bite, sting**

① [pierce, stab, prick]
¶ [I] **pricked** [my] finger on the needle.

② [bite, sting]
be stung by a bee

¶わたしは虫に足を刺されました。
（Watashi wa mushi ni ashi o
sasaremashita.)

さす 〔動 I〕

① [注ぐ]
目薬をさす（megusuri o *sasu*）やかん
に水をさす（yakan ni mizu o *sasu*）
¶機械を掃除して、油をさしました。
（Kikai o sōji shite, abura o
sashimashita.)

② [かさなどを開いて持つ]
¶雨がやんだのに、あの人はかさをさ
しています。（Ame ga yanda noni, ano
hito wa kasa o *sashite* imasu.)

さすが 〔副、〜に、〜の〕

① [そうはいうもののやはり]
¶社長の命令なので、さすがに「いや
だ。」とは言えませんでした。（Shachō
no meirei na node, *sasuga* ni "Iyada." to
wa iemasen deshita.)

② [予想どおり、やはり]

¶田中さんはイギリスに留学していた
ので、さすがに英語が上手です。
（Tanaka san wa Igirisu ni ryūgaku shite
ita node, *sasuga* ni Eigo ga jōzu desu.)
¶朝から何も食べていないので、さす
がにおなかがすきました。（Asa kara
nani mo tabete inai node, *sasuga* ni onaka
ga sukimashita.)

ざせき 座席 〔名〕
座席に着く（*zaseki* ni tsuku）

¶ I **was bitten** on the leg 〖foot〗 by an
insect.

sasu 〔v I〕 pour in, fill, insert; hold
up an umbrella
① [pour in, fill, insert]
put in eye drops // **fill** a kettle with
water
¶ [I] cleaned the machine and **oiled** it.

② [hold up an umbrella, etc.]
¶ [She] **has** [her] umbrella **up** even
though it has stopped raining.

sasuga 〔adv, 〜*ni*, 〜*no*〕 after all;
as might be expected, like the
〜 it is
① [after all]
¶ As it was, **after all**, the order of the
company president, [I] could not say
that [I] didn't want to do it.

② [as might be expected, like the〜 it
is]
¶ [Mr.] Tanaka speaks English well, **as
might be expected** of someone who
has studied in England.

¶ **It is only natural** that [I] am hungry
as [I] haven't eaten anything all day.

zaseki 〔n〕 a seat, seating
take **a seat**, be seated

¶山田さんが、わたしの座席を取って
おいてくれました。(Yamada san ga,
watashi no *zaseki* o totte oite
kuremashita.)
⇒席 seki

¶ [Miss] Yamada saved **a seat** for me.

させる〔助動〕

① [他に対してある行為を実現するよ
うに仕向ける意味を表す]
¶先生が質問して、学生に答えさせま
す。(Sensei ga shitsumon shite, gakusei
ni kotae*sasemasu*.)

¶わたしが来られなければ、弟 を来さ
せます。(Watashi ga korarenakereba,
otōto o ko*sasemasu*.)

② [他の人がある行為をするのを許容
あるいは黙認する意味を表す]
¶子供にあんなに夜遅くまでテレビを
見させておいてはいけませんよ。
(Kodomo ni anna ni yoru osoku made
terebi o mi*sasete* oite wa ikemasen yo.)

¶子供にお菓子をあんなにたくさん食
べさせていいのですか。(Kodomo ni
okashi o anna ni takusan tabe*sasete* ii no
desu ka?)

＊Ⅱ型動詞とⅢ型動詞の「来る
(kuru)」につく。
⇒せる seru

-saseru 〔auxil〕 **a verb ending
indicating the causative, etc.**

① [make someone do something, have
someone do something]
¶ The teacher asks questions for the
students **to answer.**

¶ If I can't come, I'll **have** my (younger)
brother come.

② [let someone do something, allow
someone to do something]
¶ You shouldn't **let** the children watch
television until so late at night.

¶ **Should** the children be eating so
many sweets?

＊ *-saseru* is added to Type II verbs and
the Type III verb *kuru* (→*kosaseru*).

さそう 誘う〔動Ⅰ〕

¶わたしは山田さんを誘って、映画を
見に行きました。(Watashi wa Yamada
san o *sasotte*, eiga o mi ni ikimashita.)

¶京都へ行こうと誘われましたが、断
りました。(Kyōto e ikō to
sasowaremashita ga, kotowarimashita.)

sasou 〔vⅠ〕 **invite, ask**

¶ I **invited** [Mr.] Yamada and we went
to see a movie together.

¶ **I was invited** to go to Kyoto but I
declined.

-さつ -札〔尾〕

千円札 (sen'en*satsu*) 一万円札
(ichiman'en*satsu*)

-satsu〔suf〕**the counter for paper money**
a thousand yen **bill** // a ten thousand yen **bill**

-さつ -冊〔尾〕

4冊 (yon*satsu*) 8冊 (has*satsu*)

¶このノートは1冊100円です。(Kono nōto wa is*satsu* hyakuen desu.)

-satsu〔suf〕**the counter for bound books, magazines, etc.**
four **volumes**, four **copies** // eight **volumes**, eight **copies**
¶ These notebooks are a hundred yen **each**.

さつえい 撮影〔名、〜する〕

¶ここはよく映画の撮影に使われます。(Koko wa yoku eiga no *satsuei* ni tsukawaremasu.)
¶夜撮影するのは難しいです。(Yoru *satsuei* suru no wa muzukashii desu.)

satsuei〔n, 〜*suru*〕**photographing, filming**
¶ This spot is often used **in films**.
¶ Night **filming** is difficult〔It is hard **to take photographs** at night〕.

さっか 作家〔名〕

流行作家 (ryūkō-*sakka*)
¶わたしはあの作家の書いた小説は、全部読みました。(Watashi wa ano *sakka* no kaita shōsetsu wa, zenbu yomimashita.)

sakka〔n〕**author, writer, novelist**
a best-selling **writer**
¶ I have read all of that **author's** books.

さっき〔副〕

¶わたしは田中さんとさっき会ったばかりです。(Watashi wa Tanaka san to *sakki* atta bakari desu.)
¶子供たちはさっきまで遊んでいたのに、もう寝てしまいました。
(Kodomotachi wa *sakki* made asonde ita noni, mō nete shimaimashita.)
＊改まった場合には「さきほど (sakihodo)」と言う。

sakki〔adv〕**a little while ago, just now, some time ago**
¶ I met [Mrs.] Tanaka just **a little while ago**.
¶ The children were playing until **a little while ago** but they're sleeping now.
＊When speaking formally, *sakihodo* is used in place of *sakki*.

ざっし 雑誌〔名〕

週刊雑誌 (shūkan-*zasshi*)

zasshi〔n〕**magazine, periodical**
a weekly, a weekly magazine

¶この雑誌は毎月 15 日に発行されます。(Kono *zasshi* wa maitsuki jūgonichi ni hakkō saremasu.)

¶ This **magazine** comes out each month on the fifteenth.

さっそく 早速〔副〕

sassoku〔adv〕**at once, immediately, right away**

¶買ってきたくつを早速はいて出かけました。(Katte kita kutsu o *sassoku* haite dekakemashita.)

¶ I put on the shoes I had just bought and went out.

¶手紙を出したら、早速返事が来ました。(Tegami o dashitara, *sassoku* henji ga kimashita.)

¶ [I] received a **prompt** response to the letter [I] sent.

さっと〔副〕

satto〔adv〕**quickly, suddenly, all of a sudden**

¶その青年はさっと立って、老人に席を譲りました。(Sono seinen wa *satto* tatte, rōjin ni seki o yuzurimashita.)

¶ That youth **quickly** got up and offered his seat to an elderly person.

¶そのねこはわたしの姿を見ると、さっとベッドの下に隠れました。(Sono neko wa watashi no sugata o miru to, *satto* beddo no shita ni kakuremashita.)

¶ That cat **dashed** under the bed and hid as soon as it saw me.

さっぱり〔副、〜する〕

sappari〔adv, 〜*suru*〕**refreshing, refreshed; completely, entirely, not at all**

①[さわやかで気持ちのいい様子]
¶おふろに入ってさっぱりしました。(Ofuro ni haitte *sappari* shimashita.)

① [refreshing, refreshed]
¶ Taking a bath **refreshed** me.

②[まったく、全然]
¶試験は難しくて、さっぱりわかりませんでした。(Shiken wa muzukashikute, *sappari* wakarimasen deshita.)

② [completely, entirely, not at all]
¶ The exam was very difficult; I couldn't make **head or tail** of it.

¶このごろ山田さんから、さっぱり手紙が来ませんね。(Konogoro Yamada san kara, *sappari* tegami ga kimasen ne.)

¶ Recently there hasn't been a **single** letter from [Mr.] Yamada, has there?

*あとに打ち消しの言葉が来る。

*Used with the negative.

さて 〔接、感〕

1 〔接〕

① [前のことがらを受けて話を続け別の話題に移るときなどに使う]

¶経済の問題についてはこのぐらいにしまして、さて、次に教育の問題に移りたいと思います。(Keizai no mondai ni tsuite wa kono gurai ni shimashite, *sate*, tsugi ni kyōiku no mondai ni utsuritai to omoimasu.)

② [前のことがらを受けて本題などに移るときに使う]

¶朝晩かなり寒くなってきましたが、お変わりございませんか。さて、このたび1年間の予定で日本へ留学することになりました。(Asaban kanari samuku natte kimashita ga, okawari gozaimasen ka? *Sate*, kono tabi ichinenkan no yotei de Nihon e ryūgaku suru koto ni narimashita.)

2 〔感〕

¶さて、帰りましょうか。(*Sate*, kaerimashō ka?)

¶さて、これからどこへ行きましょうか。(*Sate*, kore kara doko e ikimashō ka?)

¶さて、困ったなあ。どうしよう。(*Sate*, komatta nā. Dō shiyō?)

＊これから何かをしようとして、相手に呼びかけたり自問したりするときに使う。

さとう 砂糖 〔名〕

¶砂糖は1キロいくらですか。(*Satō wa ichikiro ikura desu ka?*)

sate 〔conj, interj〕 **well, now**

1 〔conj〕

① [used when changing the subject of a conversation or other discourse]

¶ That concludes my remarks about economic matters. **Now** I would like to move on to educational matters.

② [used when moving on to the main topic of a conversation, discourse, or text]

¶ It's quite cold now in the mornings and the evenings, and I hope you are well. **Well then**, my news is that I'm going to go to Japan to study for a year (from a letter).

2 〔interj〕

¶ **Well**, shall we leave now?

¶ **Well**, where shall we go now?

¶ **Well**, that's awkward. What's best to do?

＊ Used to attract the attention of the listener or to question oneself when one is about to start doing something.

satō 〔n〕 **sugar**

¶ How much is **sugar** a kilo?

さばく 砂ばく〔名〕

¶砂ばくは雨が少なく、植物がほとんど生えません。(*Sabaku* wa ame ga sukunaku, shokubutsu ga hotondo haemasen.)

sabaku 〔n〕 **desert**

¶**Deserts** have little rain, and few plants grow there.

さび〔名〕

¶長い間使わなかったので、はさみに赤いさびがついてしまいました。(Nagai aida tsukawanakatta node, hasami ni akai *sabi* ga tsuite shimaimashita.)

sabi 〔u〕 **rust, tarnish**

¶The scissors 〚clippers, shears〛 haven't been used for a long time and have gotten **rusty** 〚The scissors weren't used for a long time and got **rusty**〛.

さびしい 寂しい〔形〕

① [にぎやかでない様子]

¶この辺は夜になると、急に寂しくなります。(Kono hen wa yoru ni naruto, kyū ni *sabishiku* narimasu.)

② [孤独な様子]

¶友達がいなくて、とても寂しいです。(Tomodachi ga inakute, totemo *sabishii* desu.)

¶田中さんはいつも寂しそうな顔をしています。(Tanaka san wa itsu mo *sabishisō* na kao o shite imasu.)

sabishii 〔adj〕 **deserted, lonely; lonely, lonesome**

① [deserted, lonely, desolate (about a place)]

¶At night this area quite suddenly becomes **deserted**.

② [lonely, lonesome (about one's feelings)]

¶[I] **am** very **lonely** as [I] don't have any friends.

¶[Miss] Tanaka always **looks sad and lonely**.

さびる〔動Ⅱ〕

¶このナイフはずいぶんさびていますね。(Kono naifu wa zuibun *sabite* imasu ne.)

sabiru 〔v Ⅱ〕 **to rust, to become rusty**

¶This knife is quite **rusty**, isn't it?

-さま -様〔尾〕

① [尊敬の意味を表す]

-sama 〔suf〕 **Mr., Mrs., Miss, Ms.; an honorific suffix added to names, occupations, etc.**

① [expresses respect]

338

王様 (ōsama) 神様 (kamisama)
お母様 (okāsama)
御主人様 (goshujinsama)

¶ 封筒の表に「山田太郎様」と書いて
あります。(Fūtō no omote ni "Yamada
Tarō sama" to kaite arimasu.)

② [丁寧の意味を表す]
御苦労さま (gokurōsama) ごちそうさ
ま (gochisōsama)

a king // God, a deity // mother //
(your) husband

¶ "Yamada Tarō-**sama**" is written on
the front of the envelope (i.e., **Mr.
Tarō Yamada**).

② [expresses politeness]
Thank you for your trouble (see also
the entry for *gokurōsama*) // Thank you
for the fine meal (see also the entry for
gochisōsama)

さまざま 〔形動、〜の〕

¶ 意見がさまざまでまとまりません。
(Iken ga samazama de matomarimasen.)
¶ 留学生はさまざまな国から来ていま
す。(Ryūgakusei wa samazama na kuni
kara kite imasu.)
⇒いろいろ **iroiro**

samazama 〔adj-v, 〜*no*〕 **various,
varied, diverse**

¶ Opinion **is divided**, and no
agreement has been reached.

¶ The foreign students are from **many
different** countries.

さむい 寒い 〔形〕
¶ 今日は寒いですね。(Kyō wa samui
desu ne.)
¶ 部屋が寒いので、ストーブをつけま
した。(Heya ga samui node, sutōbu o
tsukemashita.)
¶ だいぶ寒くなりましたね。(Daibu
samuku narimashita ne.)
⇔暑い **atsui**

samui 〔adj〕 **cold, chilly**
¶ **It's cold** today, isn't it?

¶ The room **was cold** so I turned on the
heater.

¶ It's turned quite **cold**, hasn't it?

さめる 覚める 〔動Ⅱ〕
¶ わたしは毎朝6時ごろに目が覚めま
す。(Watashi wa maiasa rokuji goro ni
me ga samemasu.)
¶ 大きな音で目が覚めました。
(Ookina oto de me ga samemashita.)

sameru 〔v Ⅱ〕 **wake up, awake**
¶ **I wake up** around six o'clock every
morning.

¶ [I] **was awakened** by a loud noise.

さめる 冷める 〔動Ⅱ〕

¶御飯が冷めないうちに、早く食べて
しまいなさい。(Gohan ga *samenai* uchi
ni, hayaku tabete shimainasai.)

¶おふろのお湯が冷めてしまったか
ら、もう一度沸かしましょう。(Ofuro
no oyu ga *samete* shimatta kara, mō ichido
wakashimashō.)

さよう 作用 〔名、〜する〕

電気の作用 (denki no *sayō*)

¶薬の作用で痛みが止まりました。
(Kusuri no *sayō* de itami ga
tomarimashita.)

さようなら 〔連〕

¶「さようなら。」と言って、駅前で山
田さんと別れました。("*Sayōnara*." to
itte, ekimae de Yamada san to
wakaremashita.)

さら 〔名〕

¶おさらを1枚持って来てください。
(O*sara* o ichimai motte kite kudasai)

さらいげつ さ来月 〔名〕

¶さ来月には家が完成する予定です。
(Saraigetsu ni wa ie ga kanseisuru yotei
desu.)

さらいしゅう さ来週 〔名〕

¶さ来週から2週間、海外旅行に行き
ます。(Saraishū kara nishūkan,
kaigairyokō ni iki masu.)

さらいねん 再来年 〔名〕

¶再来年から、海外に留学するつもり
です。(Sarainen kara, kaigai ni ryūgaku
suru tsumori desu.)

sameru 〔v Ⅱ〕 **cool off, get cold**

¶ Eat your food **before it gets cold**.

¶ The bath water **has cooled**; let me
heat it up again for you.

sayō 〔n, 〜*suru*〕 **working,
operation, effect, function**
the working of electricity

¶ The pain was relieved **by the
medicine**.

sayōnara 〔compd〕 **good-bye,
farewell**

¶ I parted from [Miss] Yamada in front
of the station saying "*Sayōnara*
〖**Good-bye**〗."

sara 〔n〕 **dish, plate, saucer, etc.**

¶ Please fetch **a plate**.

saraigetsu 〔n〕 **the month after
next**

¶ The house will be finished in two
months' time.

saraishu 〔n〕 **the week after next**

¶ I will be traveling abroad for two
weeks, leaving the week after next.

sarainen 〔n〕 **the year after next**

¶ I intend to study abroad the year after
next.

サラダ〔名〕

野菜サラダ（yasai-*sarada*）
¶晩御飯に肉やサラダを食べました。
（Bangohan ni niku ya *sarada* o
tabemashita.）

さらに 更に〔副〕

①〔もっと、いっそう〕
¶上田さんの病気は更に悪くなったそ
うです。（Ueda san no byōki wa *sarani*
waruku natta sō desu.）
②〔その上〕
¶学校で5時間勉強して、家へ帰って
から更に2時間勉強します。（Gakkō de
gojikan benkyō shite, ie e kaette kara
sarani nijikan benkyō shimasu.）

さる〔名〕

¶動物園へ行ってさるを見ました。
（Dōbutsuen e itte *saru* o mimashita.）

さわぐ 騒ぐ〔動Ⅰ〕

¶教室の中で騒いではいけません。
（Kyōshitsu no naka de *sawaide* wa
ikemasen.）
¶あのお酒を飲んで騒いでいる人はだ
れですか。（Ano osake o nonde *sawaide*
iru hito wa dare desu ka？）

さわる 触る〔動Ⅰ〕

¶そこに並べてある作品に触らないで
ください。（Soko ni narabete aru sakuhin
ni *sawaranaide* kudasai.）
¶汚い手で着物に触ったら、しかられ
ました。（Kitanai te de kimono ni
sawattara, shikararemashita.）

sarada〔n〕**salad**
(vegetable) **salad**
¶[I] had meat and **a salad** for dinner.

sarani〔adv〕**still more, further;
again; anew, afresh**
①[still more, further]
¶I hear that [Mrs.] Ueda's illness **has
worsened**.

②[again; anew, afresh]
¶[I] study five hours at school and then
return home and study two hours **more**.

saru〔n〕**monkey, ape**
¶[I] went to the zoo and saw **the
monkeys**.

sawagu〔vⅠ〕**be noisy, make a
disturbance, go on a spree**
¶One mustn't **be rowdy** in the
classroom.

¶Who is that drunk **making a
nuisance of [him]self?**

sawaru〔vⅠ〕**touch, handle, feel**
¶Please **don't touch** the works of art
on display there.

¶I was scolded for **touching** the
kimono with dirty hands.

さん 三 〔名〕

三人 (*san*nin) 三月 (*san*gatsu) 三年 (*san*nen) 三円 (*san*'en) 三軒 (*san*gen)

san 〔n〕 **three**

three persons // March // **three** years // **three** yen // **three** houses

-さん 〔尾〕

山田さん (Yamada *san*) お父さん (otō*san*) お医者さん (oisha*san*)

＊名前・職業などにつけて尊敬や親しみの意味を表す。より丁寧に言う場合には「-様 (sama)」を使う。

-san 〔suf〕 **Mr., Mrs., Miss, Ms.**

Mr. 〖**Mrs., Miss, Ms.**〗 Yamada // father // a doctor

＊Added to names, professions, etc., to indicate respect and a certain degree of familiarity. When speaking more politely, *-sama* is used.

さんか 参加 〔名、～する〕

参加者 (*sanka*sha) 参加国 (*sanka*koku)

¶あなたもこの研究会に参加しませんか。(Anata mo kono kenkyūkai ni *sanka* shimasen ka？)

sanka 〔n, ～*suru*〕 **participation**

a participant, a contestant // a **participating** nation

¶ Won't you **take part** in our study group?

さんかく 三角 〔名〕

三角形 (*sankak*kei)

sankaku 〔n〕 **triangle, triangular**

triangle, triangular

さんがつ 三月 〔名〕

sangatsu 〔n〕 **March**

さんぎょう 産業 〔名〕

産業が発達する (*sangyō* ga hattatsu suru)

¶あなたの国の主な産業は何ですか。(Anata no kuni no omo na *sangyō* wa nan desu ka？)

sangyō 〔n〕 **industry**

industry progresses

¶ What is the principal **industry** in your country?

さんこう 参考 〔名〕

参考書 (*sankō*sho)

¶この本は、わたしの研究にとても参考になります。(Kono hon wa, watashi no kenkyū ni totemo *sankō* ni narimasu.)

¶あなたの意見を参考にして、この計画を立てました。(Anata no iken o *sankō* ni shite, kono keikaku o tatemashita.)

sankō 〔n〕 **reference, consultation**

a **reference** book

¶ This book will be very **helpful** in my research.

¶ [I] drew up this plan taking your views **into consideration**.

さんせい　賛成〔名、〜する〕

sansei 〔n, 〜*suru*〕 **agreement, approval, support**

¶わたしもあなたの意見に賛成です。
(Watashi mo anata no iken ni *sansei* desu.)

¶ **I am in agreement** with your view.

¶この計画に賛成した人はあまりいません。(Kono keikaku ni *sansei* shita hito wa amari imasen.)

¶ Few **have given their approval** to this plan.

⇔反対 hantai

さんそ　酸素〔名〕

sanso 〔n〕 **oxygen**

サンダル〔名〕

sandaru 〔n〕 **sandal**

¶夏はサンダルをはいている女性が多いです。(Natsu wa *sandaru* o haiteiru josei ga ooi desu.)

¶ Many women wear sandals in the summer.

サンドイッチ〔名〕

sandoicchi 〔n〕 **sandwich**

¶今日のお昼はサンドイッチを食べました。(Kyō no ohiru wa *sandoicchi* o tabemashita.)

¶ I ate sandwiches for lunch today.

ざんねん　残念〔形動〕

zannen 〔adj-v〕 **regrettable, disappointing**

¶もう少し早く来れば秋子さんに会えたのに、残念でしたね。(Mō sukoshi hayaku kureba Akiko san ni aeta noni, *zannen* deshita ne.)

¶ **It's a pity** you didn't arrive a little earlier—you could have met Akiko.

¶残念ながら、今日の会には出席できません。(*Zannen* nagara, kyō no kai ni wa shusseki dekimasen.)

¶ **Regrettably**, I won't be able to attend today's meeting.

さんぶつ　産物〔名〕

sanbutsu 〔n〕 **product, produce**

¶この地方の主な産物はコーヒーです。(Kono chihō no omo na *sanbutsu* wa kōhii desu.)

¶ The principal **product** of this region is coffee.

¶東京のデパートでも京都の産物を買うことができます。(Tōkyō no depāto de mo Kyōto no *sanbutsu* o kau koto ga dekimasu.)

¶ One can buy Kyoto **products** in Tokyo department stores.

さんぽ 散歩 〔名、〜する〕

¶これから散歩に行きませんか。
(Kore kara *sanpo* ni ikimasen ka？)
¶公園を散歩していたら、友達に会い
ました。(Kōen o *sanpo* shite itara,
tomodachi ni aimashita.)

sanpo 〔n, 〜*suru*〕 **walk, stroll**

¶ Won't you come **for a walk** now?

¶ While **walking** in the park. [I] ran
across a friend.

し

し 四 [名]
四月 (*shi*gatsu) 四角 (*shi*kaku) 四方 (*shi*hō) 四季 (*shi*ki)
⇒四 yon

shi 〔n〕 **four**

April // square, a square // the **four** quarters; all directions // the **four** seasons

し 死 [名]
¶父の手紙で母の死を知りました。 (Chichi no tegami de haha no *shi* o shirimashita.)

shi 〔n〕 **death**

¶ I learned of **the death** of my mother in a letter from my father.

し 詩 [名]
詩人 (*shi*jin)
¶わたしは詩を作って、みんなの前で読みました。(Watashi wa *shi* o tsukutte, minna no mae de yomimashita.)

shi 〔n〕 **poem, poetry**
a poet

¶ I wrote **a poem** and read it aloud in front of everyone.

し [助]
¶今日は天気もいいし、暖かいから、どこかへ遊びに行きましょう。(Kyō wa tenki mo ii *shi*, atatakai kara, doko ka e asobi ni ikimashō.)

¶秋子さんは性格も明るいし、親切なので、みんなから好かれています。(Akiko san wa seikaku mo akarui *shi*, shinsetsu nanode, minna kara sukarete imasu.)

¶風もないし、波も静かだし、海水浴にはとてもいい日でした。(Kaze mo nai *shi*, nami mo shizuka da *shi*, kaisuiyoku ni wa totemo ii hi deshita.)

¶雨も降っているし、行くのはやめましょう。(Ame mo futte iru *shi*, iku no wa yamemashō.)

shi 〔part〕 **and, moreover, besides**

¶ Let's go somewhere, as it's so nice **and** warm out today.

¶ Everyone likes Akiko, as she's so cheerful **and** kind.

¶ What with the lack of wind **and** the calm seas, it was a very good day for going swimming.

¶ **And besides** it's raining—let's not go.

345

＊普通、二つ以上のことがらを対等の関係で並列して述べるときに使う。またあとのことがらに対して理由などを表すことが多い。

＊*Shi* is usually used to list two or more items of equal standing. It often gives the reason, etc., for what follows.

じ- 次- 〔頭〕

次回 (*ji*kai) 次週 (*ji*shū)

ji- 〔pref〕 **next, the following**

next time // **next** week

(-)じ (-)字 〔名、尾〕

(-)ji 〔n, suf〕 **written character, letter, ideograph, handwriting**

1 〔名〕

漢字 (kan*ji*) ローマ字 (rōma*ji*) 文字 (mo*ji*)

¶田中先生は字が上手です。(Tanaka sensei wa *ji* ga jōzu desu.)

1 〔n〕

a Chinese **character**, *kanji* // roman **letters** // written **characters**

¶ Professor Tanaka has good **handwriting**.

2 〔尾〕

¶漢字を三百字ぐらい習いました。(Kanji o sanbyaku *ji* gurai naraimashita.)

2 〔suf〕

¶ [I] learned 〚have learned〛 about three hundred *kanji*.

-じ -時 〔尾〕

¶今、何時ですか。(Ima, nan*ji* desu ka？)

¶授業は4時に終わります。(Jugyō wa yo*ji* ni owarimasu.)

-ji 〔suf〕 **o'clock; the counter for the hour**

¶ What **time** is it now?

¶ Class ends at four **o'clock**.

-じ -次 〔尾〕

第一次世界大戦 (daiichi*ji*-sekaitaisen)
二次試験 (ni*ji*-shiken)

-ji 〔suf〕 **a suffix indicating order**

World War **I** //the **second** examination

しあい 試合 〔名〕

¶今日の午後、ピンポンの試合があります。(Kyō no gogo, pinpon no *shiai* ga arimasu.)

¶テニスの試合をして、負けてしまいました。(Tenisu no *shiai* o shite, makete shimaimashita.)

shiai 〔n〕 **match, game, tournament**

¶ There is a ping-pong **match** this afternoon.

¶ [I] lost [my] tennis **match**.

しあわせ 幸せ〔名、形動〕

幸せを願う（*shiawase* o negau）幸せ
な家庭（*shiawase* na katei）

¶あなたはよいお子さんを持って幸せ
ですね。（Anata wa yoi okosan o motte
shiawase desu ne.）

¶上田さんは、いつもにこにこして幸
せそうです。（Ueda san wa, itsu mo
nikoniko shite *shiawasesō* desu.）

シーツ〔名〕

¶寝るときには布団の上にシーツを敷
いて寝ます。（Neru toki ni wa futon no
ue ni *shiitsu* o shiite nemasu.）

しお 塩〔名〕

塩辛い（*shio*karai）

¶この料理は塩で味をつけます。
（Kono ryōri wa *shio* de aji o tsukemasu.）

しか〔助〕

¶その部屋にはわたし一人しかいませ
んでした。（Sono heya ni wa watashi
hitori *shika* imasen deshita.）

¶食べ物はもうこれだけしかありませ
ん。（Tabemono wa mō kore dake *shika*
arimasen.）

＊いつも打ち消しの言葉を伴って、そ
れだけと限る意味を表す。「だけしか
（dake shika）」は特に強い限定を表す。
⇒だけ **dake**

しかく 四角〔名、形動〕

四角なテーブル（*shikaku* na tēburu）真
四角（ma*shikaku*）

＊「四角い（shikakui）」（形）という
言葉もある。

---

shiawase 〔n, adj-v〕 **happiness,
fortune, good luck, blessing**

wish someone **good luck** // a **happy**
home

¶ You **are fortunate** in having such
nice children.

¶ [Mrs.] Ueda **seems to be quite happy**
－[she] is always smiling.

shiitsu 〔n〕 **(bed)sheet**

¶ [I] sleep with **a sheet** spread on top
of [my] *futon*.

shio 〔n〕 **salt**

salty, too salty

¶ This dish is seasoned with **salt**.

shika 〔part〕 **only, no more than**

¶ There was **no one but** me in that
room.

¶ This is **all there is** to eat.

＊ *Shika* is always used with the
negative; it indicates that that is all
there is. For special stress *dake shika* is
used.

shikaku 〔n, adj-v〕 **a square, a
rectangle**

a **four-cornered** table // square, a true
square

＊ The adjectival form *shikakui* can
also be used.

しかく　資格〔名〕

① [身分・地位など]

¶上田さんは今度大使の資格でA国へ行きました。(Ueda san wa kondo taishi no *shikaku* de Ē-koku e ikimashita.)

② [ある身分や地位を得るのに必要な条件]

¶医者の資格を取るには、国の試験に合格しなければなりません。(Isha no *shikaku* o toru ni wa, kuni no shiken ni gōkaku shinakereba narimasen.)

¶こんなことも知らないのでは、先生としての資格はありませんね。

(Konna koto mo shiranai no de wa, sensei to shite no *shikaku* wa arimasen ne.)

しかし〔接〕

¶今日はいい天気です。しかし、あまり暖かくはありません。(Kyō wa ii tenki desu. *Shikashi*, amari atatakaku wa arimasen.)

¶あの学生は頭はいいのです。しかし、努力が足りません。(Ano gakusei wa atama wa ii no desu. *Shikashi*, doryoku ga tarimasen.)

⇒けれども **keredomo**

しかた　仕方〔名〕

¶漢字の勉強の仕方を教えてください。(Kanji no benkyō no *shikata* o oshiete kudasai.)

¶子供にあいさつの仕方を教えてやりました。(Kodomo ni aisatsu no *shikata* o oshiete yarimashita.)

shikaku 〔n〕 capacity, status; qualification, credential, competency

① [capacity, status]

¶ This time [Mr.] Ueda went to Country A **in the capacity** of ambassador.

② [qualification, credential, competency]

¶ One must pass a national examination in order **to qualify** as a physician.

¶ Anyone not knowing this sort of thing has no **right** to call [him]self a teacher.

shikashi 〔conj〕 however, but

¶ It's a nice day today. **However**, it is on the cool side (literally, is not very warm).

¶ That student is quite bright **but** lacks application.

shikata 〔n〕 way, method, means

¶ Please tell [me] **how** to study *kanji*.

¶ [I] taught the children **the way** to give greetings.

しかたがない〔連〕

shikata ga nai 〔compd〕 **cannot be helped, have no choice, be inevitable; cannot stand, be unbearable**

① [どうすることもできない様子]

① [cannot be helped, have no choice, be inevitable, be no use to]

¶なくしてしまったものはしかたがありません。これからは注意してください。(Nakushite shimatta mono wa *shikata ga arimasen*. Kore kara wa chūi shite kudasai.)

¶**What's lost is lost.** Just be more careful in the future.

¶バスがなくなってしまいました。しかたがないから、タクシーで帰りましょう。(Basu ga nakunatte shimaimashita. *Shikata ga nai* kara, takushii de kaerimashō.)

¶There are no more buses. **We have no choice** but to take a taxi home.

→やむをえない **yamu o enai**

② [我慢できない様子]

② [cannot stand, be unbearable]

¶暑くてしかたがないから、窓を開けましょう。(Atsukute *shikata ga nai* kara, mado o akemashō.)

¶Let's open a window—it's **unbearably** hot in here.

¶あの人は日本へ行ってみたくてしかたがないのです。(Ano hito wa Nihon e itte mitakute *shikata ga nai* no desu.)

¶[He] **is dying** to go to Japan.

＊「～てしかたがない（～te shikata ga nai)」の形で使う。

＊Used in the pattern "*-te shikata ga nai*."

しがつ 四月〔名〕

shigatsu 〔n〕 **April**

しかも〔接〕

shikamo 〔conj〕 **moreover, furthermore; and yet, nevertheless**

¶この国は土地も狭く、しかも人口が多いです。(Kono kuni wa tochi mo semaku, *shikamo* jinkō ga ooi desu.)

¶This country is not only small **but also** heavily populated.

¶この料理は安くて、しかもおいしいです。(Kono ryōri wa yasukute, *shikamo* oishii desu.)

¶This food is cheap and good **too**.

¶一生懸命勉強して、しかも入学でき
ないときは、あきらめるよりしかたが
ありません。(Isshōkenmei benkyō shite,
shikamo nyūgaku dekinai toki wa,
akirameru yori shikata ga arimasen.)
＊前のことがらを受けて、更にあとの
ことがらをつけ加えるときに使う。前
のことがらとあとのことがらが同じよ
うなときには、前のことがらだけでは
なく、そのうえにというような意味を
表し、前のことがらとあとのことがら
とが対比的な関係にあるときには、前
のことがらにかかわらず、なおという
ような意味を表す。

¶ One has no choice but to accept it as
hopeless when one studies hard **but
nevertheless** fails one's school
entrance exams.

＊*Shikamo* is used when adding
something to what has been said.
When the two items are of the same
nature the meaning is "moreover, in
addition," but when they are in
opposition the meaning is "in spite of,
nevertheless."

しかる〔動 I〕

shikaru 〔v I〕 scold, reprimand,
lecture

¶お母さんがいたずらした子供をし
かっています。(Okāsan ga itazura shita
kodomo o *shikatte* imasu.)

¶ The child who played the trick **is
being scolded** by its mother.

¶宿題をやらなかったので、先生にし
かられました。(Shukudai o yaranakatta
node, sensei ni *shikararemashita*.)

¶ My teacher **reprimanded** me for not
doing my homework.

(-)じかん (-)時間〔名、尾〕

(-)jikan 〔n, suf〕 time; an hour

1〔名〕

1〔n〕

①[ある一定の時の長さ]
時間がない (*jikan* ga nai)

① [time, period]
have no **time**, be pressed for **time**

¶この仕事は時間がかかりそうです。
(Kono shigoto wa *jikan* ga kakarisō
desu.)

¶ It looks like this job will take **time**.

¶食事までにはまだじゅうぶん時間が
あります。(Shokuji made ni wa mada
jūbun *jikan* ga arimasu.)

¶ There is still lots of **time** until
mealtime.

¶その放送の時間は午後8時から9時 ま
でです。(Sono hōsō no *jikan* wa gogo
hachiji kara kuji made desu.)

¶ **The time** of that broadcast is 8-9 PM

②[時刻]

② [time, the hour]

時間に間に合う（*jikan* ni maniau）時間に遅れる（*jikan* ni okureru）時間を守る（*jikan* o mamoru）

be in **time** for // be late // be on **time**, be punctual

→時刻 **jikoku**

③［何かをするために区切った一定の時の長さ］

③ [time, a set time for something]

時間割り（*jikan*wari）自由時間（jiyū-*jikan*）

a **time**table, schedule //free **time**

¶理科の時間に実験をしました。（Rika no *jikan* ni jikken o shimashita.）

¶ [We] performed an experiment during science **class**.

2〖尾〗

2〖suf〗 the counter for hours

¶毎日5時間ぐらい勉強します。（Mainichi go*jikan* gurai benkyō shimasu.）

¶ [I] study about five **hours** daily.

しき 四季〖名〗

shiki〖n〗 the four seasons

¶わたしは四季の中で、春がいちばん好きです。（Watashi wa *shiki* no naka de, haru ga ichiban suki desu.）

¶ Of **the four seasons**, I like spring the best.

じき 時期〖名〗

jiki〖n〗 time, season

¶もう桜の時期は過ぎました。（Mō sakura no *jiki* wa sugimashita.）

¶ The cherry **season** is already over.

¶勉強には秋が最も良い時期でしょう。（Benkyō ni wa aki ga mottomo yoi *jiki* deshō.）

¶ Autumn is probably the best **season of the year** for studying.

(-)しき (-)式〖名、尾〗

(-)shiki〖n, suf〗 ceremony; method, style, type

1〖名〗

1〖n〗 ceremony

入学式（nyūgaku*shiki*）卒業式（sotsugyō*shiki*）

an entrance **ceremony, a ceremony** for newly admitted students // a graduation **ceremony**, commencement **exercises**

¶「結婚式は何時から始まりますか。」（Kekkon*shiki* wa nanji kara hajimarimasu ka?）「式は10時から始まります。」（*Shiki* wa jūji kara hajimarimasu.）

¶ "What time does **the wedding** start?" "At ten o'clock."

2〖尾〗

2〖suf〗 method, style, type

351

ヘボン式ローマ字
（Hebonshiki-romaji）

¶ このテープレコーダーは旧式だけど使いやすいです。（Kono tēpurekōdā wa kyūshiki dakedo tsukaiyasui desu.）

the Hepburn **system** of romanization

¶ This tape recorder is an old model but is very easy to use.

じぎょう　事業〔名〕

事業団（jigyōdan）事業家（jigyōka）

¶ 彼は新しい事業を始めました。
（Kare wa atarashii jigyō o hajimemashita.）

¶ 彼はその事業に成功しましたか。
（Kare wa sono jigyō ni seikō shimashita ka？）

jigyō 〔n〕 **enterprise, undertaking; business, industry**

a **business** association // **an entrepreneur, industrialist**

¶ He has embarked upon a new **enterprise** 〚He embarked upon a new **enterprise**〛.

¶ Did he succeed in that **undertaking?**

しきりに〔副〕

① [同じことが繰り返して起こる様子]
¶ 最近、この辺でしきりに事故が起きます。（Saikin, kono hen de shikirini jiko ga okimasu.）

② [同じことがずっと続いて起こる様子]
¶ しきりに電話のベルがなっているのに、だれも出ません。（Shikirini denwa no beru ga natte iru noni, dare mo demasen.）

③ [熱心に繰り返す様子]
¶ 山田さんがしきりに勧めるので、この本を買いました。（Yamada san ga shikirini susumeru node, kono hon o kaimashita.）

shikirini 〔adv〕 **frequently, often; constantly, incessantly; eagerly, intently**

① [frequently, often, repeatedly]
¶ Recently there have been **many** traffic accidents around here.

② [constantly, incessantly, in rapid succession]
¶ The telephone **keeps on** ringing but no one answers.

③ [eagerly, intently, earnestly, keenly]
¶ [I] bought this book because [Miss] Yamada **kept on** recommending it to [me].

しく　敷く〔動 I〕

① [じゅうたん・布団・小石などを平らに広げる]

shiku 〔v I〕 **spread, lay out; lay (a railroad), pave**

① [spread, lay out]

¶この部屋には赤いじゅうたんが敷いてあります。(Kono heya ni wa akai jūtan ga *shiite* arimasu.)

¶もう遅いから、布団を敷いて寝ましょう。(Mō osoi kara, futon o *shiite* nemashō.)

②[鉄道などを敷設する]

¶来年はこの辺まで鉄道が敷かれるそうです。(Rainen wa kono hen made tetsudō ga *shikareru* sō desu.)

¶This room **has** red carpeting.

¶It's late—let's **lay out** the *futon* and go to bed.

②[lay (a railroad), pave]

¶They say the railroad **will be extended** up to here next year.

しげき 刺激 〔名、〜する〕

shigeki 〔n, 〜*suru*〕 **stimulus, irritant; stimulation, excitement**

①[人間・生物の感覚に外から働きかけて何かの変化を起こさせること]
刺激を与える (*shigeki* o ataeru) 刺激を受ける (*shigeki* o ukeru)

①[stimulus, impetus, irritant, incentive. incitement]
give **a stimulus** // receive **a stimulus**

¶コーヒーは胃を刺激するから、あまりたくさん飲まないほうがいいです。(Kōhii wa i o *shigeki* suru kara, amari takusan nomanai hō ga ii desu.)

¶Coffee is **a stimulant which irritates** the stomach so it's best not to drink too much of it.

②[人間の心に働きかけて何かを感じさせること]

②[stimulation, excitement]

¶わたしは刺激のない田舎の生活にあきました。(Watashi wa *shigeki* no nai inaka no seikatsu ni akimashita.)

¶I got 〚am〛 tired of life in the country with its lack of **stimulation**.

しげる 茂る 〔動 I〕

shigeru 〔v I〕 **grow thick, be luxuriant, be overgrown**

¶道の両側には木が茂っています。(Michi no ryōgawa ni wa ki ga *shigette* imasu.)

¶Both sides of the road are **heavily forested**.

しけん 試験 〔名、〜する〕

shiken 〔n, 〜*suru*〕 **examination, test**

入学試験 (nyūgaku-*shiken*) 試験を受ける (*shiken* o ukeru)

a school entrance **examination** // take **an exam**

¶来週、英語の試験があります。(Raishū, eigo no *shiken* ga arimasu.)

¶There is an English **test** next week.

¶中村さんは試験に合格しました。
(Nakamura san wa *shiken* ni gōkaku
shimashita.)

¶ [Miss] Nakamura passed **the exam**.

しげん 資源 〔名〕
天然資源 (tennen-*shigen*) 石油資源
(sekiyu-*shigen*)

shigen 〔n〕 **resources**
natural **resources** // oil **resources**

¶日本は資源の少ない国です。(Nihon
wa *shigen* no sukunai kuni desu.)

¶ Japan is a country poor in **natural
resources**.

じけん 事件 〔名〕

jiken 〔n〕 **matter, affair, incident,
event**

¶今日、銀行の前で人が殺されるとい
う事件が起こりました。(Kyō, ginkō
no mae de hito ga korosareru to iu *jiken* ga
okorimashita.)

¶ Today there was **an incident** in front
of the bank in which a person was
killed.

¶わたしはその事件には関係がありま
せん。(Watashi wa sono *jiken* ni wa
kankei ga arimasen.)

¶ I don't have anything to do with that
matter.

じこ 事故 〔名〕
自動車事故 (jidōsha-*jiko*) 交通事故
(kōtsū-*jiko*)

jiko 〔n〕 **accident**
an auto **accident** // a traffic **accident**

¶電車の事故で学校に遅れました。
(Densha no *jiko* de gakkō ni
okuremashita.)

¶ [I] was late for school because of a
train **accident**.

¶彼は車を運転していて、まだ一度も
事故を起こしていません。(Kare wa
kuruma o unten shite ite, mada ichido mo
jiko o okoshite imasen.)

¶ He hasn't had a single **accident** in all
the time he's been driving.

じこ 自己 〔名〕
自己中心 (*jiko*-chūshin) 自己批判
(*jiko*-hihan) 自己満足 (*jiko*-manzoku)
自己宣伝 (*jiko*-senden) 自己紹介
(*jiko*-shōkai) 自己主張 (*jiko*-shuchō)

jiko 〔n〕 **oneself, self, ego**
self-centeredness, **self**-ishness // **self**-
criticism // **self**-satisfaction // **self**-
advertisement // **self**-introduction //
self-assertion

¶自己を知ることは難しいです。(Jiko
o shiru kotowa muzukashii desu.)

¶ It is difficult to know **oneself**.

じこく 時刻 〔名〕
時刻表 (*jikoku*hyō)

jikoku 〔n〕 **time, hour**
a **time**table, schedule

¶ただ今の時刻は9時5分です。

（Tadaima no *jikoku* wa kuji gofun desu.）

¶急げば約束の時刻に間に合います。

（Isogeba yakusoku no *jikoku* ni maniaimasu.）

⇒(-)時間(-)jikan

しごと　仕事〔名〕

① [働くこと]

¶仕事は5時に終わります。（*Shigoto* wa goji ni owarimasu.）

¶昨日は夜10時まで仕事をしました。（Kinō wa yoru jūji made *shigoto* o shimashita.）

② [職業]

¶あなたの仕事は何ですか。（Anata no *shigoto* wa nan desu ka？）

③ [事業]

¶このごろ、どうも仕事がうまくいきません。（Konogoro, dōmo *shigoto* ga umaku ikimasen.）

じじつ　事実〔名〕

事実を話す（*jijitsu* o hanasu）事実を伝える（*jijitsu* o tsutaeru）

¶その物語は事実を基にして書かれています。（Sono monogatari wa *jijitsu* o moto ni shite kakarete imasu.）

しじゅう〔副〕

¶あの人はしじゅう何か食べていますね。（Ano hito wa *shijū* nani ka tabete imasu ne.）

¶子供がしじゅう仕事の邪魔をして困ります。（Kodomo ga *shijū* shigoto no jama o shite komarimasu.）

¶ **The time** is now 9:05.

¶ If [you] hurry, [you] can get there by the appointed **time**.

shigoto 〔n〕 **working, employment; job, occupation; work, a task, one's duties**

① [working, employment, labor]

¶ **Work** ends at five o'clock.

¶ [I] **worked** until ten o'clock last night.

② [job, occupation]

¶ What **do you do?**

③ [work, a task, one's duties]

¶ Things aren't going well **at work** recently.

jijitsu 〔n〕 **fact, actuality, the truth**

tell **the truth** // report **the facts**

¶ That story is based on **fact**.

shijū 〔adv〕 **from start to finish, all the time, continually, very often, frequently**

¶ [He] is **always** eating something, isn't [he]?

¶ [I] am bothered by the children **continually** interrupting [my] work.

じしゅう　自習〔名、〜する〕

自習時間 (jishu-jikan)
¶先生が御病気でお休みですから、静かに自習してください。(Senseiga gobyōki de oyasumi desu kara, shizuka ni *jishū* shite kudasai.)

jishū 〔n, 〜*suru*〕 **study, independent study, teaching oneself**
study hours
¶As the teacher is absent today due to illness, please **study** quietly **by yourselves**.

ししゅつ　支出〔名、〜する〕

¶今月は収入が10万円で支出が7万円でしたから、3万円残りました。(Kongetsu wa shūnyū ga jūman'en de *shishutsu* ga nanaman'en deshita kara, sanman'en nokorimashita.)
¶物価が上がって、支出が増えました。(Bukka ga agatte, *shishutsu* ga fuemashita.)
⇔収入 shūnyū

shishutsu 〔n, 〜*suru*〕 **expenditure, expenses, outlay, disbursement**
¶My income for this month was 100 thousand yen and **my expenditures** 70 thousand yen so I have 30 thousand yen left.

¶Prices have gone up so **[my] expenses** have increased.

じしょ　辞書〔名〕

¶言葉の意味がわからないときは辞書を引きます。(Kotoba no imi ga wakaranai toki wa *jisho* o hikimasu.)
¶この言葉は辞書に出ていません。(Kono kotoba wa *jisho* ni dete imasen.)
⇒辞典 jiten

jisho 〔n〕 **dictionary**
¶When [I] come across words whose meaning [I] don't know, [I] look them up in **the dictionary**.
¶This word doesn't appear in **the dictionary**.

じじょう　事情〔名〕

日本事情 (Nihon-*jijō*)
¶彼は家庭の事情で学校をやめました。(Kare wa katei no *jijō* de gakkō o yamemashita.)
¶それには何か事情があるらしいです。(Sore ni wa nani ka jijiō ga aru rashii desu.)

jijō 〔n〕 **circumstances, conditions, situation, state of things**
the state of affairs in Japan
¶He quit school for family **reasons**.

¶It seems that there is some **reason** for that.

じしん　自信〔名〕

自信がつく（jishin ga tsuku）自信を失う（jishin o ushinau）

¶試験に合格する自信がありません。（Shiken ni gōkaku suru jishin ga- arimasen.）

¶もっと自信を持って、がんばってください。（Motto jishin o motte, ganbatte kudasai.）

jishin 〔n〕 **(self-)confidence**

gain **confidence** //lose **confidence**

¶ **I am not sure** I will pass the exam.

¶ Keep going—**you can do it** (literally, Have **confidence** and hang on in there)!

じしん　地震〔名〕

地震が起こる（jishin ga okoru）地震が起きる（jishin ga okiru）

¶今朝、大きい地震がありました。（Kesa, ookii jishin ga arimashita.）

¶今度の地震で大きな被害が出ました。（Kondo no jishin de ookina higai ga demashita.）

jishin 〔n〕 **earthquake**

an **earthquake** takes place // an **earthquake** takes place

¶ There was a large **earthquake** this morning.

¶ The last **earthquake** caused extensive damage.

しずか　静か〔形動〕

①［うるさい音や声が聞こえない様子］

¶みんな寝てしまって、寮の中は静かになりました。（Minna nete shimatte, ryō no naka wa shizuka ni narimashita.）

¶図書館では、静かにしなければなりません。（Toshokan de wa, shizuka ni shinakereba narimasen.）

→うるさい urusai

②［おだやかな様子］

¶今日は海が静かです。（Kyo wa umi ga shizuka desu.）

¶夕方になって、風が静かになりました。（Yūgata ni natte, kaze ga shizuka ni narimashita.）

shizuka 〔adj-v〕 **quiet, still; calm, tranquil**

① [quiet, still, silent]

¶ With everyone asleep, the dormitory fell **silent**.

¶ One must **be quiet** in the library.

② [calm, tranquil, peaceful]

¶ The sea **is calm** today.

¶ The wind **died down** in the evening 〖The wind **has died down** from the evening〗.

しずむ　沈む〔動Ⅰ〕

①［太陽・月などが地平線などに隠れる］

shizumu 〔v I〕 **set, go down; sink, be submerged**

① [set, go down]

¶日が西に沈みました。(Hi ga nishi ni *shizumimashita.*)

② [物が水面などから下の方へ動いて見えなくなる]

¶台風で船が沈んでしまいました。(Taifū de fune ga *shizunde* shimaimashita.)

↔浮く **uku**

¶ The sun **set** in the west.

② [sink, be submerged]

¶ The ship **sank** in the typhoon.

しせい 姿勢 [名]

姿勢がいい (*shisei ga ii*) 姿勢が悪い (*shisei ga warui*)

¶楽な姿勢で話を聞いてください。(Raku na *shisei* de hanashi o kiite kudasai.)

shisei [n] **posture, pose, attitude, stance, carriage**

have a fine **posture** // have a poor **posture**

¶ Please **make yourself comfortable** and listen to what I have to say.

しぜん 自然 [名]

¶日本人は自然を愛する気持ちが強いです。(Nihonjin wa *shizen* o aisuru kimochi ga tsuyoi desu.)

¶夏休みには都会を離れ、自然の中で過ごすことにしています。(Natsuyasumi ni wa tokai o hanare, *shizen* no naka de sugosu koto ni shite imasu.)

shizen [n] **nature; natural**

¶ The Japanese have a strong love of **nature**.

¶ [I] make it a practice to leave the city and live in the midst of **nature** during [my] summer holidays.

しぜんに 自然に [副]

¶薬をつけなくても、傷は自然に治りました。(Kusuri o tsukenakute mo, kizu wa *shizen ni* naorimashita.)

¶日本に住んでいる間に、日本語が自然にわかるようになりました。(Nihon ni sunde iru aida ni, Nihongo ga *shizen ni* wakaru yō ni narimashita.)

＊「自然と (shizen to)」という言い方もある。

shizen ni [adv] **naturally, spontaneously, automatically, instinctively, of itself**

¶ The injury 〚cut, bite, scrape, etc.〛 healed **by itself** without putting any medication on it.

¶ Comprehension of Japanese **just came to me** while I was living in Japan.

＊Variant: *shizen to.*

しそう　思想〔名〕
思想家（shisōka）社会主義思想
（shakaishugi-shisō）
¶この本は日本の近代思想について書いたものです。（Kono hon wa Nihon no kindai-shisō ni tsuite kaita mono desu.）

shisō 〔n〕 thought, idea, ideology
a thinker // socialist thought
¶ This book is about modern Japanese thought.

しそん　子孫〔名〕
¶わたしは子孫に財産を残すつもりはありません。（Watashi wa shison ni zaisan o nokosu tsumori wa arimasen.）
⇔先祖 senzo

shison 〔n〕 a descendant, offspring, posterity
¶ I do not intend to leave an estate to my offspring.

した　下〔名〕

shita 〔n〕 under, below; beneath, underneath; lower, below; the lower part, the bottom; down, downwards

① [位置が低い所]
¶テーブルの下にねこがいます。
（Tēburu no shita ni neko ga imasu.）
② [物の内側]
¶あの人はセーターの下にシャツを3枚も着ています。（Ano hito wa sētā no shita ni shatsu o sanmai mo kite imasu.）
③ [年齢・地位・程度などが低いこと]

① [under, below]
¶ There is a cat under the table.

② [beneath, underneath]
¶ [He] is wearing three shirts under [his] sweater.

③ [lower, below (in age, status, degree, etc.)]

¶田中さんはわたしより三つ下です。
（Tanaka san wa watashi yori mittsu shita desu.）
¶このクラスは難しすぎるので、下のクラスに入れてください。（Kono kurasu wa muzukashisugiru node, shita no kurasu ni irete kudasai.）
⇔上 ue

¶ [Mr.] Tanaka is three years younger than I am.

¶ This class is too difficult; please put me in a lower one.

した　舌〔名〕
¶「舌を出してみなさい。」と、医者が言いました。（"Shita o dashite minasai." to, isha ga iimashita.）

shita 〔n〕 tongue
¶ The doctor said, "Put out your tongue, please."

じだい 時代 〔名〕

時代劇 (jidaigeki) 時代遅れ
(jidaiokure) 学生時代 (gakusei-jidai)
明治時代 (Meiji-jidai) 大正時代
(Taishō-jidai)

¶ この物語の時代はいつごろですか。
(Kono monogatari no jidai wa itsu goro
desu ka？)

¶ あの人のおじいさんの時代には、あ
の店はたいへん有名でした。(Ano hito
no ojiisan no jidai ni wa, ano mise wa
taihen yūmei deshita.)

jidai 〔n〕 **period, age**

a **costume** play, **historical** drama // out-of-**date**, behind **the times** // student **days** // the Meiji **era** //the Taishō **era**

¶ What is **the period** of this story?

¶ In **the time** of [his] grandfather, that shop 〖restaurant, etc.〗 was very famous.

しだいに 次第に 〔副〕

¶ 2学期になって、勉強が次第に難し
くなってきました。(Nigakki ni natte,
benkyō ga shidai ni muzukashiku natte
kimashita.)

¶ 夜になってから、風は次第に強くな
りました。(Yoru ni natte kara, kaze wa
shidai ni tsuyoku narimashita)

shidai ni 〔adv〕 **gradually**

¶ The coursework has **gradually** become 〖**gradually** became〗 more difficult in the second semester.

¶ The wind **gradually** increased from nightfall.

したがう 従う 〔動Ⅰ〕

① [ついて行く]
¶ わたしたちは、案内の人に従って工
場を見学しました。(Watashitachi wa,
annai no hito ni shitagatte kōjō o kengaku
shimashita.)

② [命令・規則・意見などのとおりに
する]
¶ あなたの意見に従って、この計画は
やめることにしました。(Anata no iken
ni shitagatte, kono keikaku wa yameru
koto ni shimashita.)

shitagau 〔v I〕 **follow, accompany; obey, comply with, agree to; in proportion to, according to, as**

① [follow, accompany]
¶ We toured the factory, **following** the guide.

② [obey, comply with, agree to, accept]

¶ **In accordance with** your views, [we] have decided against this project.

¶規則には従わなければなりません（Kisoku ni wa *shitagawanakereba* narimasen.）

¶ One **must abide** by the rules.

③ [一つのことがらが進むにつれて他のことがらが起こることを表す]

③ [in proportion to, according to, as]

¶収入が増えるにしたがって、税金も多くなります。（Shūnyū ga fueru ni *shitagatte*, zeikin mo ooku narimasu.）

¶ Taxes go up **in proportion to** income.

¶台風が近づくにしたがって、風が強くなってきました。（Taifū ga chikazuku ni *shitagatte*, kaze ga tsuyoku natte kimashita.）

¶ **As** the typhoon comes closer, the wind has become stronger 〚**As** the typhoon came closer, the wind became stronger〛.

*「〜にしたがって（〜ni shitagatte）」の形で使う。

*Used in the pattern "〜 *ni shitagatte*."

したぎ 下着〔名〕

shitagi 〔n〕 **underwear, underclothes**

¶わたしは毎日下着を替えます。（Watashi wa mainichi *shitagi* o kaemasu.）

¶ I put on fresh **underwear** every day.

したく 支度〔名、〜する〕

shitaku 〔n, ~*suru*〕 **preparations, arrangements**

¶食事の支度ができました。（Shokuji no *shitaku* ga dekimashita.）

¶ Dinner 〚lunch, breakfast〛 **is ready**.

¶今、出かける支度をしているところです。（Ima, dekakeru *shitaku* o shite iru tokoro desu.）

¶ Right now **I'm getting ready** to go out.

したしい 親しい〔形〕

shitashii 〔adj〕 **close, friendly, intimate**

¶山田さんはわたしの親しい友達です。（Yamada san wa watashi no *shitashii* tomodachi desu.）

¶ [Miss] Yamada is a **close** friend of mine.

¶わたしはあの人とはあまり親しくしていません。（Watashi wa ano hito to wa amari *shitashiku* shite imasen.）

¶ I am not particularly **close** to [him].

しち 七〔名〕

shichi 〔n〕 **seven**

七人（*shichi*nin）七時間（*shichi*jikan）

seven persons // **seven** hours

361

＊「なな（nana）」とも言う。

＊Variant: *nana*.

しちがつ　七月〔名〕

shichigatsu〔n〕 July

-しつ　-室〔尾〕
教室（kyō*shitsu*）病室（byō*shitsu*）寝室（shin*shitsu*）温室（on*shitsu*）図書室（tosho*shitsu*）地下室（chika*shitsu*）

-shitsu〔suf〕 **room(s)**
a class**room** // a sick**room**, hospital**room**, ward, infirmary // a bed**room** // a green**house** // a library // a basement, an underground **room**

しっかり〔副、〜と、〜する〕

shikkari〔adv, 〜to, 〜*suru*〕 **strong, solid, firm; be strong-minded, be stouthearted; reliable, sound**

① [堅固な様子、強い様子]
¶この箱はずいぶんしっかりしていますね。（Kono hako wa zuibun *shikkari* shite imasu ne.）
¶しっかりと持っていないと、落としますよ。（*Shikkari* to motte inai to, otoshimasu yo.）

① [strong, solid, firm; firmly, tightly]
¶This is a very **solid** box, isn't it?

¶You will drop that if you don't take a **firm** grip on it.

② [気をひきしめる様子]

¶入学試験が近いですから、しっかり勉強してください。（Nyūgakushiken ga chikai desu kara, *shikkari* benkyō shite kudasai.）
¶このくらいの傷はなんでもないです。しっかりしなさい。（Kono kurai no kizu wa nan demo nai desu. *Shikkari* shinasai.）

② [be strong-minded, be stouthearted, keep up one's nerve, brace oneself]
¶The entrance exam is coming soon so you'd better **buckle down** and study hard.

¶This is hardly any injury at all. **Take a hold of yourself**〚Pull yourself together〛.

③ [人の性質や考え方が間違いなく信用できる様子]
¶田中さんの奥さんはとてもしっかりした人です。（Tanaka san no okusan wa totemo *shikkari* shita hito desu.）

③ [reliable, sound, of firm character]
¶Mr. Tanaka's wife is a person **of firm character**〚has her feet firmly on the ground〛.

じっけん　実験〔名、〜する〕
実験室（*jikken*shitsu）実験に成功する（*jikken* ni seikō suru）

jikken〔n, 〜*suru*〕 **experiment, test**
a laboratory // succeed in **an experiment**

¶化学の実験で石けんを作りました。
（Kagaku no *jikken* de sekken o tsukurimashita.）
¶その理論が正しいかどうか実験してみました。（Sono riron ga tadashii ka dō ka *jikken* shite mimashita.）

¶ [I] made soap in a laboratory **experiment** for chemistry class.

¶ [I] tried **to test** whether that theory was correct or not.

じつげん 実現〔名、〜する〕

jitsugen 〔n, 〜*suru*〕 **realize, actualize, materialize, come true**

¶この計画の実現には、たいへんなお金がかかります。（Kono keikaku no *jitsugen* ni wa, taihen na okane ga kakarimasu.）
¶日本に留学できて、やっと長い間の夢が実現しました。（Nihon ni ryūgaku dekite, yatto nagai aida no yume ga *jitsugen* shimashita.）
¶いつ月旅行が実現するでしょうか。
（Itsu tsukiryokō ga *jitsugen* suru deshō ka？）

¶ It will cost a lot **to implement** this plan.

¶ [I] was finally **able to realize** my long-held dream and go to school in Japan.

¶ When do you suppose travel to the moon **will become a reality?**

じっこう 実行〔名、〜する〕

jikkō 〔n, 〜*suru*〕 **carry out, put into practice, execute, realize**

¶その計画は実行が難しいです。
（Sono keikaku wa *jikkō* ga muzukashii desu.）
¶あの人は言ったことは必ず実行します。（Ano hito wa itta koto wa kanarazu *jikkō* shimasu.）

¶ That plan will be difficult **to implement**.

¶ [He] always **delivers on** what [he] says 〚**does** what he says he will〛.

じっさい 実際〔名、副〕

jissai 〔n, adv〕 **truth, actuality; really, actually**

1〔名〕
¶彼の話は実際とはだいぶ違います。
（Kare no hanashi wa *jissai* to wa daibu chigaimasu.）
¶彼はああ言っていますが、実際はどうでしたか。（Kare wa ā itte imasu ga, *jissai* wa dō deshita ka？）

1〔n〕
¶ His story is quite different from **the actual facts of the matter**.

¶ That's what he says, but what's **the real story?**

¶習った日本語を実際に話す機会がなくて残念です。（Naratta Nihongo o *jissai* ni hanasu kikai ga nakute zannen desu.）

2〔副〕

¶この問題には実際困っています。（Kono mondai ni wa *jissai* komatte imasu.）

¶ It's a shame I don't have any opportunity to **actually** speak Japanese after having studied it.

2〖adv〗

¶ [I] **really** don't know what to do about this problem〚I am **really** in a fix due to this problem〛.

じっしゅう　実習〔名、〜する〕

実習生（*jisshū*sei）教育実習（kyōiku-*jisshū*）実習費（*jisshū*hi）

¶実習の経験はたいへん役に立ちます。（Jisshū no keiken wa taihen yaku ni tachimasu.）

¶今、病院で実習しています。（Ima, byōin de *jisshū* shite imasu.）

jisshū 〖n, 〜*suru*〗 **practice, practical training, on-the-job training**
a trainee, apprentice, intern //
practice teaching, **student** teaching //
a **practice** fee, **training** fee
¶ **On-the-job training** is very useful.

¶ [I] am **an intern** at a hospital.

じっと〔副、〜する〕

①［体を動かさないで静かにしている様子］

¶あの子は少しもじっとしていません。（Ano ko wa sukoshi mo *jitto* shite imasen.）

②［苦しいこと・痛いことなどに耐える様子］

¶手術は痛かったが、じっと我慢しました。（Shujutsu wa itakatta ga, *jitto* gaman shimashita.）

③［視線や考えなどをほかに向けない様子］

¶彼はじっとその絵を見ていました。（Kare wa *jitto* sono e o mite imashita.）

jitto 〖adv, 〜*suru*〗 **quietly; patiently, stoically; steadily, fixedly**
① [quietly, without moving]

¶ That child is never **still** for a moment.

② [patiently, stoically]

¶ The operation was painful but I **stoically** bore the pain.

③ [steadily, fixedly, intently, concentratedly]

¶ He **was staring** at that painting.

¶彼女はじっと何かを考えているようでした。(Kanojo wa *jitto* nani ka o kangaete iru yō deshita.)

¶ It looked like she was **intently** thinking about something.

じつに　実に 〔副〕

jitsu ni 〔adv〕 truly, really, indeed, very, awfully

¶あの人は実にきれいですね。(Ano hito wa *jitsu ni* kirei desu ne.)

¶ She is **really** beautiful.

¶あの映画は実におもしろいです。(Ano eiga wa *jitsu ni* omoshiroi desu.)

¶ That movie is **really** interesting.

じつは　実は 〔副〕

jitsu wa 〔adv〕 really, actually, in fact, as a matter of fact, to tell the truth

¶実は、お願いがあるのですが...。(Jitsu wa, onegai ga aru no desu ga...)

¶ **Actually**, I have a favor to ask of you....

¶「どうして学校をやめるのですか。」(Dōshite gakkō o yameru no desu ka?)「実は、父が亡くなって働かなければならなくなったからです。」(Jitsu wa, chichi ga nakunatte hatarakanakereba naranaku natta kara desu.)

¶ "Why are you quitting school?" "**The fact is** my father has died and I have to go to work."

しっぱい　失敗 〔名、〜する〕

shippai 〔n, ~*suru*〕 failure, error, mistake

試験に失敗する (shiken ni *shippai* suru) 事業に失敗する (jigyō ni *shippai* suru)

fail an exam // **fail** in a business undertaking

¶同じ失敗を二度と繰り返さないように注意しなさい。(Onaji *shippai* o nido to kurikaesanai yō ni chūi shinasai.)

¶ Be careful not to make the same **mistake** twice.

¶この計画は完全に失敗しました。(Kono keikaku wa kanzen ni *shippai* shimashita.)

¶ This project was 〔is〕 a complete **failure**.

⇔成功 seikō

しつもん　質問 〔名、〜する〕

shitsumon 〔n, ~*suru*〕 question, questioning

¶質問はありませんか。(*Shitsumon* wa arimasen ka?)

¶ Are there any **questions**?

¶次の質問に答えてください。(Tsugi no *shitsumon* ni kotaete kudasai.)

¶質問してもよろしいですか。(*Shitsumon* shite mo yoroshii desu ka？)

¶ Please answer the following **questions**.

¶ May I ask **a question?**

しつれい　失礼〔名、形動、〜する〕

shitsurei 〔n, adj-v, 〜*suru*〕 **rudeness, impoliteness, discourtesy**

①〔人の気持ちを不愉快にさせるようなことを言ったりしたりすること〕
¶お客様に失礼なことをしてはいけませんよ。(Okyakusama ni *shitsurei* na koto o shite wa ikemasen yo.)
¶人の手紙を黙って読むのは失礼です。(Hito no tegami o damatte yomu no wa *shitsurei* desu.)

① [rudeness, impoliteness, discourtesy]

¶ One shouldn't **be rude** to a guest 〚customer〛.

¶ **It's rude** to read someone else's letters without permission.

②〔相手にすまないという気持ちを表す〕
¶お名前を間違えて失礼しました。(Onamae o machigaete *shitsurei* shimashita.)

② [used to indicate one is sorry]

¶ **I'm very sorry** to have mistaken your name.

③〔人に何かを尋ねるときの言葉〕
¶失礼ですが、どなた様でいらっしゃいますか。(*Shitsurei* desu ga, donata sama de irasshaimasu ka？)
*普通「失礼ですが、 …(Shitsurei desu ga, ...)」の形で使う。

③ [used to preface a question to someone]

¶ **Excuse me**, but could I have your name please?

*Usually used in the pattern "*Shitsurei desu ga...*"

④〔別れるときのあいさつの言葉〕
¶お先に、失礼します。(Osaki ni *shitsurei* shimasu.)

④ [used when parting from someone]

¶ Well, **I must be going** now 〚Goodbye〛 (literally, **Excuse me** for leaving before you).

じてん　事典〔名〕
百科事典 (hyakka-*jiten*) 医学事典 (igaku-*jiten*)

jiten 〔n〕 **encyclopedia**
an encyclopedia // a medical **encyclopedia**

じてん　辞典〔名〕

国語辞典（kokugo-*jiten*）漢和辞典
（kanwa-*jiten*）英和辞典（eiwa-*jiten*）和
英辞典（waei-*jiten*）
⇒辞書 jisho

jiten 〔n〕 **dictionary**
a Japanese-language **dictionary** // a
Japanese-language Chinese character
dictionary // an English-Japanese
dictionary // a Japanese-English
dictionary

じてんしゃ　自転車〔名〕

¶自転車に乗れますか。（Jitensha ni
noremasu ka？）
¶自転車で学校へ通っています。
（Jitensha de gakkō e kayotte imasu.）

jitensha 〔n〕 **bicycle**
¶Can you ride **a bicycle?**

¶[I] go to school by **bicycle.**

しどう　指導〔名、〜する〕

指導者（*shidō*sha）技術指導（gijutsu-
shidō）
¶わたしは田中先生の指導を受けて、
この研究を完成しました。（Watash
wa Tanaka sensei no *shidō* o ukete kono
kenkyū o kansei shimashita.）
¶おおぜいの学生を指導するのは、た
いへんでしょうね。（Oozei no gakusei
o *shidō* suru no wa, taihendeshō ne.）

shidō 〔n, 〜*suru*〕 **guidance,
leadership, direction, coaching**
a leader, director, coach, adviser //
technical **guidance**
¶I completed this research under **the
guidance** of Professor Tanaka.

¶It must be hard **to be responsible for
〚to teach〛** so many students.

じどうしゃ　自動車〔名〕

自動車事故（*jidōsha*-jiko）自動車旅行
（*jidōsha*-ryoko）自動車に乗る（*jidōsha*
ni noru）自動車を運転する（*jidōsha* o
unten suru）
¶自動車の運転ができますか。
（*Jidōsha* no unten ga dekimasu ka？）
¶道の真ん中で自動車が故障しまし
た。（Michi no mannaka de *jidōsha* ga
koshō shimashita.）

jidōsha 〔n〕 **automobile, car,
motorcar**
an **auto** accident // a **car** trip // ride in
a car // drive **a car**

¶Can you drive?

¶**A car** broke down 〚has broken
down〛 in the middle of the road.

しなもの　品物〔名〕

¶この店の品物には値段がついていま
せんね。（Kono mise no *shinamono* ni
wa nedan ga tsuite imasen ne.）

¶この店には安くてよい品物がたくさ
んあります。（Kono mise ni wa yasukute
yoi *shinamono* ga takusan arimasu.）

shinamono〔n〕**article, goods, wares**

¶There are no prices on **the merchandise** in this shop.

¶This shop has many fine **articles** that are inexpensively priced.

しぬ　死ぬ〔動Ⅰ〕

交通事故で死ぬ（kōtsū-jiko de *shinu*）

¶母が死んだのは、わたしが6歳の時
でした。（Haha ga *shinda* no wa, watashi
ga rokusai no toki deshita.）

¶苦しくて何度も死のうと思ったこと
があります。（Kurushikute nando mo
shinō to omotta koto ga arimasu.）

shinu〔v Ⅰ〕**die, pass away**

die in a traffic accident

¶My mother **died** when I was six years old.

¶There have been many times that I've suffered so much that **I've wanted to die.**

しはい　支配〔名、～する〕

支配者（*shihai*sha）支配人
（*shihai*nin）

¶この国は長い間、A国の支配を受け
ていました。（Kono kuni wa nagai aida,
Ē-koku no *shihai* o ukete imashita.）

shihai〔n, ～*suru*〕**control, rule, government, domination, management**

a ruler, master, governor // a manager, an executive

¶For a long time this country was under **the rule** of Country A.

しばい　芝居〔名〕

¶あした、芝居を見に行きませんか。
（Ashita, *shibai* o mi ni ikimasen ka？）

shibai〔n〕**play, drama, theatrical performance**

¶Would you like to go to **the theater** with [me] tomorrow?

しばしば〔副〕

¶わたしは医者にたばこを吸わないよ
うにしばしば注意されました。
（Watashi wa isha ni tabako o suwanai yō
ni *shibashiba* chūi saremashita.）

¶会社を辞めようと思ったこともしば
しばありました。（Kaisha o yameyō to
omotta koto mo *shibashiba* arimashita.）

shibashiba〔adv〕**often, frequently, many times**

¶I was **repeatedly** warned by my doctor not to smoke.

¶I thought **several times** about quitting my job.

しばふ　芝生 [名]

¶天気がよかったので、公園の芝生の上に座って本を読みました。(Tenki ga yokatta node, kōen no *shibafu* no ue ni suwatte hon o yomimashita.)

しばらく [副]

① [少しの間]
¶この仕事が終わるまで、しばらくお待ちください。(Kono shigoto ga owaru made, *shibaraku* omachi kudasai.)
¶山田さんはしばらくして帰ってきました。(Yamada san wa *shibaraku* shite kaette kimashita.)
② [やや長い間]
¶父からしばらく手紙が来ません。(Chichi kara *shibaraku* tegami ga kimasen.)
¶しばらく会わないうちにずいぶん大きくなりましたね。(*Shibaraku* awanai uchi ni zuibun ookiku narimashita ne.)
¶昨日、山田さんにしばらくぶりに会いました。(Kinō, Yamada san ni *shibaraku* buri ni aimashita.)

しばる　縛る [動 I]

ひもで縛る (himo de *shibaru*)

じびき　字引 [名]　☞辞書 jisho

じぶん　自分 [名]

自分自身 (*jibun*-jishin)
¶彼はいつも自分のことしか考えません。(Kare wa itsu mo *jibun* no koto shika kangaemasen.)

---

shibafu 〔n〕 **lawn, patch of grass**
¶As it was a nice day [I] read a book sitting on **the grass** in the park.

shibaraku 〔adv〕 **a little while, a moment; quite a while, for a long time**
① [a little while, a moment]
¶Please wait **a moment** while I finish up this job.

¶[Miss] Yamada stayed there **a little while** and then came home.

② [quite a while, for a long time]
¶There hasn't been a letter from my father **for quite a while**.

¶**It's been a long time** since I've seen you—[you]'ve really grown a lot, haven't [you]?
¶Yesterday [I] met [Miss] Yamada for the first time **in a long while**.

shibaru 〔v I〕 **tie, bind, fasten**
fasten with string 〚twine, cord, a strap, etc.〛

jibiki 〔n〕　☞jisho

jibun 〔n〕 **self, oneself**
oneself, by oneself
¶He never thinks of anyone 〚anything〛 but **himself**.

¶自分の物は自分でかたづけてください。(Jibun no mono wa *jibun* de katazukete kudasai.)

¶自分かってなことはしないでください。(Jibunkatte na koto wa shinaide kudasai.)

¶ Please put away your things **yourself**.

¶ Please don't do anything on **your own** authority 〖without consulting others〗.

しぼる 絞る〔動 I〕

¶手ぬぐいをよく絞ってから干してください。(Tenugui o yoku *shibotte* kara hoshite kudasai.)

shiboru〔v I〕**wring, squeeze, press**

¶ Please **wring out** the (hand) towel thoroughly before hanging it up.

しぼる 搾る〔動 I〕

¶わたしは父に牛の乳の搾り方を教えてもらいました。(Watashi wa chichi ni ushi no chichi no *shiborikata* o oshiete moraimashita.)

shiboru〔v I〕**milk(a cow, etc.)**

¶ My father taught me how **to milk** a cow.

しほん 資本〔名〕
資本家 (*shihon*ka)

¶その事業を始めるのには、大きな資本が要ります。(Sono jigyō o hajimeru no ni wa, ookina *shihon* ga irimasu.)

¶この会社の資本金は 20 億円です。(Kono kaisha no *shihon*kin wa nijūokuen desu.)

shihon〔n〕**capital, funds**
a capitalist, financier

¶ A large **capital** is needed to begin that enterprise.

¶ This company **is capitalized** at 2 billion yen.

しほんしゅぎ 資本主義〔名〕

shihonshugi〔n〕**capitalism**

しま 島〔名〕
島国 (*shima*guni)

¶小さな島の間を船が通っていきます。(Chiisana *shima* no aida o fune ga tootte ikimasu.)

shima〔n〕**island**
an island nation

¶ A ship is passing between 〖among〗 the small **islands**.

しまい 姉妹〔名〕

¶春子さんは三人姉妹のいちばん下です。(Haruko san wa sannin *shimai* no ichiban shita desu.)
⇒兄弟 kyōdai

shimai〔n〕**sisters**

¶ Haruko is the youngest of three **sisters**.

しまう 〔動 I〕

① [外にあるものを中に入れる]

¶これを机の引き出しにしまっておいてください。（Kore o tsukue no hikidashi ni *shimatte* oite kudasai.）

② [かたづける]

¶辞書を使ったら、元の所へしまいなさい。（Jisho o tsukattara, moto no tokoro e *shimainasai*.）

（〜て）しまう 〔連〕

① [動作・作用が完了することを表す]

¶宿題の作文をもう書いてしまいました。（Shukudai no sakubun o mō kaite *shimaimashita*.）

¶この本はゆうべ全部読んでしまいましたから、お返しします。（Kono hon wa yūbe zenbu yonde *shimaimashita* kara, okaeshi shimasu.）

¶昨日買ったパンはもう全部食べてしまいました。（Kinō katta pan wa mō zenbu tabete *shimaimashita*.）

¶残っている仕事を片づけてしまってから、うちへ帰るつもりです。（Nokotte iru shigoto o katazukete *shimatte* kara, uchi e kaeru tsumori desu.）

② [自分の意志に反してある動作・作用が行われ残念だという気持ちなどを表す]

¶花びんを落して、割ってしまいました。（Kabin o otoshite watte *shimaimashita*.）

¶かわいがっていた鳥がとうとう死んでしまいました。（Kawaigatte ita tori ga tōtō shinde *shimaimashita*.）

shimau 〔v I〕 put away; put back

① [put away]

¶ Please **put** this **away** in the desk drawer.

② [put back]

¶ **Put** the dictionary **back** after using it.

(-te)shimau 〔compd〕 finish, end, bring to a close; end up 〜ing, go and 〜

① [finish, end, bring to a close]

¶ [I] already **finished** writing the assigned composition.

¶ I'll give this book back to you now-I **finished** reading it last night.

¶ [I]'ve **eaten up** all the bread 〚rolls, etc.〛 [I] bought yesterday.

¶ [I] plan to go home after **finishing up** the remaining work.

② [end up 〜ing, go and 〜; expresses regret at something that happened against one's will]

¶ The vase **fell and broke**.

¶ The bird [we] were so fond of **died**.

¶父に買ってもらった時計をなくしてしまいました。(Chichi ni katte moratta tokei o nakushite *shimaimashita.*)

¶ **I lost** the watch my father bought for me.

¶台風で庭の木や草花が倒れてしまいました。(Taifū de niwa no ki ya kusabana ga taorete *shimaimashita.*)

¶ Trees and flowers in the garden 〚yard〛 **were blown over** in the typhoon.

＊「(〜て) しまう ([〜te] shimau)」は「〜ちゃう (〜chau)」、「(〜で) しまう ([〜de] shimau)」は「〜じゃう (〜jau)」とも言う。「(〜て) しまった ([〜te] shimatta)」は、「〜ちゃった (chatta)」、「(〜で) しまった ([〜de] shimatta)」は「〜じゃった (jatta)」とも言う。「食べちゃう (tabechau)」「読んじゃう (yonjau)」「終わっちゃった (owatchatta)」「死んじゃった (shinjatta)」など。

＊(*-te*) *shimau* is contracted to *-chau* and (*-de*) *shimau* to *-jau*; (*-te*) *shimatta* becomes *-chatta* and (*-de*) *shimatta* becomes *-jatta*. Thus one has the forms *tabechau* (from *tabete shimau*), *yonjau* (*yonde shimau*), *owatchatta* (*owatte shimatta*), *shinjatta* (*shinde shimatta*), etc.

しまつ 始末 〖名、〜する〗

shimatsu 〖n, 〜*suru*〗 **circumstances, state of affairs; manage, deal with, settle, look after**

始末をつける (*shimatsu* o tsukeru)

settle a matter, wind something up

¶自分が使った物は自分で始末しなさい。(Jibun ga tsukatta mono wa jibun de *shimatsu* shinasai.)

¶ **Put back** yourself what you have used 〚Don't make others **straighten up** after you〛.

しまる 閉まる 〖動 I〗

shimaru 〖v I〗 **shut, close**

¶戸が閉まっています。(To ga *shimatte* imasu.)

¶ The door **is closed**.

¶あの店は7時に閉まります。(Ano mise wa shichiji ni *shimarimasu.*)

¶ That shop **closes** at seven o'clock.

⇔開く **aku**

じまん 自慢 〖名、〜する〗

jiman 〖n, 〜*suru*〗 **boast, be proud of**

¶これが父の自慢の花びんです。(Kore ga chichi no *jiman* no kabin desu.)

¶ This vase is my father's **pride and joy**.

¶彼はいつも自分の娘を自慢しています。（Kare wa itsu mo jibun no musume o *jiman* shite imasu.）

¶ He is always **boasting about** his daughter.

じみ 地味〔形動〕

¶この着物は若い娘には少し地味でしょう。（Kono kimono wa wakai musume ni wa sukoshi *jimi* deshō.）

¶わたしは地味な色のほうが好きです。（Watashi wa *jimi* na iro no hō ga sukidesu.）

⇔派手 hade

jimi 〔adj-v〕 plain, quiet, sober, restrained, conservative

¶ This kimono is a little **on the conservative side** for a young lady.

¶ I like **subdued** colors.

じむ 事務〔名〕

事務員（*jimu*in）事務室（*jimu*shitsu）事務所（*jimu*sho）

¶わたしは事務関係の仕事を探しています。（Watashi wa *jimu*-kankei no shigoto o sagashite imasu.）

¶彼は事務の能力があります。（Kare wa *jimu* no nōryoku ga arimasu.）

jimu 〔n〕 business matters, office work, desk work

a clerk, **clerical** worker // a clerical office, **administrative** office // an office, **business** premises

¶ I am looking for an **office** job 〚**administrative** position〛.

¶ With his eye for detail he is good at **office work**.

しめい 氏名〔名〕

¶ここに氏名、年齢、住所を書いてください。（Koko ni *shimei*, nenrei, jūsho o kaite kudasai.）

⇒名前 namae

shimei 〔n〕 name, full name

¶ Please write **your name**, age, and address here.

しめす 示す〔動Ｉ〕

¶その場所を地図で示して教えてください。（Sono basho o chizu de *shimeshite* oshiete kudasai.）

¶口で言うだけでなく、態度で示してください。（Kuchi de iu dake de naku, taido de *shimeshite* kudasai.）

shimesu 〔v I〕 show, indicate, express, point out

¶ Please **show me** where it is on the map.

¶ Don't just say it, but **look like you mean it** too.

しめる 閉める 〔動〕

¶窓を閉めてください。(Mado o *shimete* kudasai.)

¶夜9時に店を閉めます。(Yoru kuji ni mise o *shimemasu*.)

⇔開ける akeru

shimeru 〔v II〕 **shut, close**

¶ Please **close** the window.

¶ [I] **close** the shop at 9 PM.

しめる 締める 〔動 II〕

帯を締める (obi o *shimeru*)

¶田中さんは赤いネクタイを締めています。(Tanaka san wa akai nekutai o *shimete* imasu.)

shimeru 〔v II〕 **tie, fasten, tighten, put on**

put on an obi

¶ [Mr.] Tanaka **is wearing** a red necktie.

しめる 湿る 〔動 I〕

¶三日も雨がやまないため、畳まで湿ってきました。(Mikka mo ame ga yamanai tame, tatami made *shimette* kimashita.)

¶マッチが湿っていて、火がつきません。(Matchi ga *shimette* ite, hi ga tsukimasen.)

shimeru 〔v I〕 **become damp, dampen, moisten**

¶ As it hasn't stopped raining for three days, even the *tatami* mats **are damp**.

¶ The match **is damp** and won't light.

しも 霜 〔名〕

霜が降りる (*shimo* ga oriru)

¶屋根が霜で白くなっています。(Yane ga *shimo* de shiroku natte imasu.)

shimo 〔n〕 **frost**

frost falls

¶ The roof is white with **frost**.

じゃ 〔接〕 ☞では dewa

ja 〔conj〕 ☞dewa

しゃかい 社会 〔名〕

社会生活 (*shakai*-seikatsu) 社会問題 (*shakai*-mondai)

¶わたしはみんなが幸せになれる社会をつくるために働きたいです。(Watashi wa minna ga shiawase ni nareru *shakai* o tsukuru tame ni hatarakitai desu.)

shakai 〔n〕 **society; the world**

community life, **social** life // a **social** problem

¶ I want to work for the creation of a**society** where all can be happy.

¶学校を卒業して社会に出たら、社会
人としての責任があります。(Gakkō o
sotsugyō shite *shakai* ni detara, *shakai*jin
to shite no sekinin ga arimasu.)

¶ When one graduates from school and
goes out into **the world** one has the
responsibilities of **an adult member
of society**.

しゃかいしゅぎ 社会主義 〔名〕

shakaishugi 〔n〕 **socialism**

しゃしょう 車掌 〔名〕

shashō 〔n〕 **conductor**

¶最近は、車掌のいないバスが多くな
りました。(Saikin wa, *shashō* no inai
basu ga ooku narimashita.)

¶ Recently buses without **conductors**
have increased.

¶電車に乗っていると、車掌が切符を
調べに来ました。(Densha ni notte iru
to, *shashō* ga kippu o shirabe ni
kimashita.)

¶ While [I] was on the train, **the
conductor** came looking at everyone's
tickets.

しゃしん 写真 〔名〕

shashin 〔n〕 **photograph**

写真を写す (*shashin* o utsusu) 写真を
撮る (*shashin* o toru)

take **a photograph** // take **a
photograph**

¶わたしは田中さんに写真を写しても
らいました。(Watashi wa Tanaka san ni
shashin o utsushite moraimashita.)

¶ I had [Miss] Tanaka take **my picture**.

¶この写真はとてもよく撮れています
ね。(Kono *shashin* wa totemo yoku
torete imasu ne.)

¶ This **photo** came out well, didn't it?

¶この間のパーティーの写真を早く見
せてください。(Konoaida no pātī no
shashin o hayaku misete kudasai.)

¶ I would like to see the pictures that
were taken at the party the other day.

しゃちょう 社長 〔名〕

shachō 〔n〕 **company president,
head of a firm**

¶山田さんはこの会社の社長です。
(Yamada san wa kono kaisha no *shachō*
desu.)

¶ [Mr.] Yamada is **the president** of
this company.

シャツ 〔名〕

shatsu 〔n〕 **undershirt, shirt,
T-shirt, knit shirt, etc.**

¶山田さんは赤いシャツを着ていま
す。(Yamada san wa akai *shatsu* o kite
imasu.)

¶ Mr. Yamada is wearing a red **shirt**.

じゃま 邪魔 〔名、形動、～する〕

仕事の邪魔をする（shigoto no *jama* o suru）

¶ラジオの音が邪魔になって、勉強ができません。（Rajio no oto ga *jama* ni natte, benkyō ga dekimasen.）

¶午後、お邪魔してもよろしいでしょうか。（Gogo, o*jama* shite mo yoroshii deshō ka？）

jama 〔n, adj-v, ～*suru*〕 **hindrance, obstruction, intrusion**

hinder someone's work

¶ The sound of the radio **is interfering** with my studying.

¶ May I **intrude on you** 〖**come and see you**〗 this afternoon?

じゅう 十 〔名〕

jū 〔n〕 **ten**

じゆう 自由 〔名、形動〕

① [何の統制・制限も受けない様子]
自由時間（*jiyū*-jikan）自由行動（*jiyū*-kōdō）自由経済（jiyu-keizai）自由主義（*jiyū*-shugi）出版の自由（shuppan no *jiyū*）表現の自由（hyōgen no *jiyū*）

¶作文の題は自由ですから、あしたまでに書いてきてください。（Sakubun no dai wa *jiyū* desu kara, ashita made ni kaite kite kudasai.）

② [思うとおりに行動する様子]

¶田中さんは英語もフランス語も自由に話せます。（Tanaka san wa Eigo mo Furansugo mo *jiyū* ni hanasemasu.）

jiyū 〔n, adj-v〕 **freedom; freely**

① [freedom, liberty]
free time // **freedom** of movement; having a **free** hand // a **free** economy // **liberal**ism //**freedom** of the press // **freedom** of expression

¶ Please write a composition by tomorrow on **any** topic **you desire.**

② [freely, as one likes, without restraint]
¶ [Mrs.] Tanaka speaks both English and French **fluently.**

-じゅう -中 〔尾〕

① [その期間ずっと]

¶昨日は一日中本を読んでいました。（Kinō wa ichinichi*jū* hon o yonde imashita.）

¶子供の病気が心配で、一晩中起きていました。（Kodomo no byōki ga shinpai de, hitoban*jū* okite imashita.）

-jū 〔suf〕 **through, throughout; everywhere**

① [through, throughout, in the course of]
¶ [I] was reading books **all** day yesterday.

¶ [I] was up **all** night with worry over [my] sick child.

¶この島は一年中いい天気です。（Kono shima wa ichinenjū ii tenki desu.）
②[ある場所全体、どこでも]
¶日本中の人がそのテレビ番組を見ました。（Nihonjū no hitoga sono terebi-bangumi o mimashita.）
¶世界中の人々が平和を願っています。（Sekaijū no hitobito ga heiwa o negatte imasu.）

¶This island has good weather **throughout** the year.
② [everywhere, throughout]
¶People **all over** Japan watched that television program.

¶People **everywhere** in the world want peace.

しゅうい 周囲〔名〕

shūi 〔n〕 **circumference, surroundings, environs**

¶この湖の周囲は約20キロあります。（Kono mizuumi no *shūi* wa yaku nijikkiro arimasu.）
¶この村は周囲を山に囲まれています。（Kono mura wa *shūi* o yamani kakomarete imasu.）

¶**The circumference** of this lake is about 20 kilometers.

¶This village **is surrounded** by mountains 〚hills〛.

じゅういちがつ 十一月〔名〕

jūichigatsu 〔n〕 **November**

しゅうかく 収穫〔名、〜する〕

shūkaku 〔n、〜*suru*〕 **harvest, crop, yield**

¶今年の麦の収穫は予想以上でした。（Kotoshi no mugi no *shūkaku* wa yosō ijō deshita.）
¶この国では1年に2度米が収穫できます。（Kono kuni de wa ichinen ni nido kome ga *shūkaku* dekimasu.）

¶This year's wheat 〚barley〛 **crop** surpassed expectation.

¶Rice yields two **crops** a year in this country.

じゅうがつ 十月〔名〕

jūgatsu 〔n〕 **October**

しゅうかん 習慣〔名〕

shūkan 〔n〕 **custom, convention, habit, practice**

¶国によって習慣が違います。（Kuni ni yotte *shūkan* ga chigaimasu.）
¶わたしは夜遅くまで起きているのが習慣になってしまいました。（Watashi wa yoru osoku made okite iru no ga *shūkan* ni natte shimaimashita.）

¶**Customs** differ from country to country.

¶I have gotten into **the habit** of staying up late at night.

-しゅうかん -週間 〔尾〕

¶ 1週間は7日です。(Is*shūkan* wa nanoka desu.)

¶ 日本語の授業は1週間に何時間ありますか。(Nihongo no jugyō wa is*shūkan* ni nanjikan arimasu ka？)

-shūkan 〔suf〕 **a week**

¶ One **week** is seven days.

¶ How many hours **a week** is Japanese class?

しゅうきょう 宗教 〔名〕

宗教家 (*shūkyō*ka)

¶ あなたが信じている宗教は何ですか。(Anata ga shinjite iru *shūkyō* wa nan desuka？)

shūkyō 〔n〕 **religion**

a person **of the cloth** (a priest, nun, minister, etc.), **religious** leader, scholar of **religion**

¶ What **religion** do you belong to?

しゅうごう 集合 〔名、〜する〕

集合時間 (*shūgō*-jikan) 集合場所 (*shūgō*-basho)

¶ あした、8時に駅に集合してください。(Ashita, hachiji ni eki ni *shūgō* shite kudasai.)

shūgō 〔n, 〜*suru*〕 **gathering, meeting, assembly**

rendezvous time // **rendezvous** point

¶ Please **assemble** at the station tomorrow at eight o'clock.

しゅうしゅう 収集 〔名、〜する〕

¶ 弟は珍しい切手の収集をしています。(Otōto wa mezurashii kitte no *shūshū* o shite imasu.)

¶ 海岸へ行って、いろいろな貝を収集してきました。(Kaigan e itte, iroiro na kai o *shūshū* shite kimashita.)

shūshū 〔n, 〜*suru*〕 **collection, collecting**

¶ My younger brother **collects** rare stamps.

¶ [I] **gathered** various seashells at the shore.

じゅうしょ 住所 〔名〕

¶ ここに住所と名前を書いてください。(Koko ni *jūsho* to namae o kaite kudasai.)

¶ すみませんが、住所を教えていただけませんか。(Sumimasen ga, *jūsho* o oshiete itadakemasen ka？)

jūsho 〔n〕 **address**

¶ Please write your name and **address** here.

¶ Excuse me, but could you give me **your address** please?

しゅうしょく　就職〔名、〜する〕

¶おじが就職の世話をしてくれました。(Oji ga *shūshoku* no sewa o shite kuremashita.)
¶わたしは卒業したら、銀行に就職するつもりです。(Watashi wa sotsugyō shitara, ginkō ni *shūshoku* suru tsumori desu.)

shūshoku 〔n, 〜*suru*〕 looking for employment, finding employment
¶ My uncle helped me **find a job**.

¶ I want **to work** in a bank after graduation.

ジュース〔名〕

いちごジュース (ichigo-*jūsu*) みかんジュース (mikan-*jūsu*) りんごジュース (ringo-*jūsu*) 野菜ジュース (yasai-*jūsu*)

jūsu 〔n〕 juice, fruit drinks
strawberry **juice** // mandarin orange **juice** // apple **juice** // vegetable **juice**

じゅうたく　住宅〔名〕

住宅地 (*jūtaku*chi) 住宅街 (*jūtaku*gai) 住宅問題 (*jūtaku*-mondai) 住宅難 (*jūtaku*nan)
¶都会では住宅がたいへん不足しています。(Tokai de wa *jūtaku* ga taihen fusoku shite imasu.)
¶あの建物は1階が店で、2階から上が住宅です。(Ano tatemono wa ikkai ga mise de, nikai kara ue ga *jūtaku* desu.)

jūtaku 〔n〕 house, residence
a **residential** area // a **residential** street, **residential** block // the **housing** problem // a **housing** shortage
¶ There is a severe shortage of **housing** in the cities.

¶ That building has shops on the first floor and **living quarters** from the second floor upward.

しゅうちゅう　集中〔名、〜する〕

集中講義 (*shūchū*-kōgi)
¶日本の人口の約10パーセントが東京に集中しています。(Nihon no jinkō no yaku jippāsento ga Tōkyō ni *shūchū* shite imasu.)

shūchū 〔n, 〜*suru*〕 concentration; concentrated, intensive
an **intensive** course
¶ Approximately 10 percent of the population of Japan **is concentrated** in Tokyo.

しゅうてん 終点 〔名〕

¶わたしはこの電車で終点まで行きます。(Watashi wa kono densha de *shūten* made ikimasu.)
¶この線は東京が終点です。(Kono sen wa Tōkyō ga *shūten* desu.)

shūten 〔n〕 terminus, end of the line

¶I take this train to **the end of the line**.

¶This line **ends** at Tokyo Station.

じゅうどう 柔道 〔名〕

柔道初段 (*jūdō* shodan)

¶柔道を習っています。(Jūdō o naratte imasu.)
¶柔道の先生を紹介してください。

(Jūdō no sensei o shōkai shite kudasai.)

jūdō 〔n〕 judo

shodan, the first grade of black belt in **judo**

¶[I] am studying **judo**.

¶Could you please give me the name of a **judo** teacher?

じゅうにがつ 十二月 〔名〕

jūnigatsu 〔n〕 December

しゅうにゅう 収入 〔名〕

収入が多い (*shūnyū* ga ooi) 収入が少ない (*shūnyū* ga sukunai)
¶わたしの1か月の収入は10万円です。(Watashi no ikkagetsu no *shūnyū* wa jūman'en desu.)
¶あなたはその収入で生活ができますか。(Anata wa sono *shūnyū* de seikatsu ga dekimasu ka？)
⇔支出 shishutsu

shūnyū 〔n〕 income, earnings, revenue

have a large **income** // have a small **income**

¶My monthly **income** is a hundred thousand yen.

¶Can you live on that **income?**

じゅうぶん 〔副、形動〕

¶旅行の費用は五万円でじゅうぶんでしょう。(Ryokō no hiyō wa goman'en de *jūbun* deshō.)
¶冬の登山にはじゅうぶんな準備が必要です。(Fuyu no tozan ni wa *jūbun* na junbi ga hitsuyō desu.)

jūbun 〔adv, adj-v〕 enough, suffident

¶Fifty thousand yen **should be enough** to cover the cost of the trip.

¶It is necessary to make **thorough** preparations for mountain climbing in the winter.

¶お体にじゅうぶん気をつけてください。(Okarada ni *jūbun* ki o tsukete kudasai.)

¶ Please take **good** care of yourself.

じゅうよう 重要 〔形動〕
重要書類 (*jūyō*-shorui)

jūyō 〔adj-v〕 **important**
important documents; **classified** papers

¶これは非常に重要な問題です。
(Kore wa hijō ni *jūyō* na mondaidesu.)

¶ This is a matter of great **importance**.

¶彼の実験はこの研究にとってたいへん重要です。(Kare no jikken wa kono kenkyū ni totte taihen *jūyō* desu.)

¶ His experiment **is crucial** for this research.

しゅうり 修理 〔名、〜する〕
修理代 (*shūri*dai)

shūri 〔n, 〜*suru*〕 **repairs, mending**
a **repair** charge

¶時計が壊れたので、修理に出しました。(Tokei ga kowareta node, *shūri* ni dashimashita.)

¶ As [my] watch 〖clock〗 was broken I took it **to be repaired**.

¶これを修理するには、1週間ぐらいかかりますよ。(Kore o *shūri* suru ni wa, isshūkan gurai kakarimasu yo.)

¶ It will take about a week **to repair** this.

しゅかんてき 主観的 〔形動〕
主観的な見方 (*shukanteki* na mikata)

shukanteki 〔adj-v〕 **subjective**
a **subjective** outlook

¶あの人の考えは主観的すぎます。
(Ano hito no kangae wa *shukanteki*sugimasu.)

¶ [His] thinking is too **subjective**.

⇔客観的 kyakkanteki

-しゅぎ -主義 〔尾〕

民主主義 (minshu*shugi*) 自由主義
(jiyū*shugi*) 共産主義 (kyōsan*shugi*)
社会主義 (shakai*shugi*)

-shugi 〔suf〕 **-ism, principle, doctrine**
democra**cy** // liberal**ism** // commun**ism** // social**ism**

じゅぎょう 授業 〔名、〜する〕

授業中 (*jugyō*chū) 授業時間 (*jugyō*-jikan) 授業料 (*jugyō*-ryō)

jugyō 〔n, 〜*suru*〕 **teaching, a class**
during **school** hours; during **class** // **school** hours; **class** periods // tuition

¶土曜にも授業がありますか。(Doyō ni mo *jugyō* ga arimasu ka？)

¶ Are there **classes** on Saturday too?

¶日本語の授業は9時に始まります。
（Nihongo no *jugyō* wa kuji ni
hajimarimasu.）

¶ Japanese **class** starts at nine o'clock.

しゅくだい 宿題〔名〕

shukudai 〔n〕 **homework,
assignment**

¶山田先生は毎日宿題を出します。
（Yamada sensei wa mainichi *shukudai* o
dashimasu.）

¶ Professor Yamada assigns
homework every day.

¶宿題をやってくるのを忘れました。
（*Shukudai* o yatte kuru no o
wasuremashita.）

¶ [I] forgot to do **[my] homework**.

しゅじゅつ 手術〔名、〜する〕

shujutsu 〔n, 〜*suru*〕 **operation,
surgery**

¶去年、わたしは胃の手術を受けまし
た。（Kyonen, watashi wa i no *shujutsu* o
ukemashita.）

¶ I had a stomach **operation** last year.

¶この病気は手術しなければ治りませ
ん。（Kono byōki wa *shujutsu*
shinakereba naorimasen.）

¶ This disorder requires **surgery**.

しゅしょう 首相〔名〕

shushō 〔n〕 **prime minister,
premier**

¶次の首相にはだれがなるでしょう。
（Tsugi no *shushō* ni wa dare ga naru
deshō？）

¶ [I] wonder who the next **prime
minister** will be.

しゅじん 主人〔名〕

shujin 〔n〕 **husband; master;
proprietor, landlord, employer**

①[夫]
¶「御主人はいらっしゃいますか。」
（Go*shujin* wa irasshaimasu ka？）「主人
はちょっと出かけております。（*Shujin*
wa chotto dekakete orimasu.）

① [husband]
¶ "Is **your husband** there?"
"No, **he**'s out right now."

＊他人に話す場合、自分の夫のことを
「主人（shujin）」と言い、他人の夫の
ことを「御主人（goshujin）」と言う。
→夫 otto

＊When talking with others, one refers
to one's own husband as *shujin* and to
someone else's husband as *goshujin*.

②[飼い主]

② [master]

¶あの犬は、毎日駅まで主人を迎えに行きます。(Ano inu wa, mainichi eki made *shujin* o mukae ni ikimasu.)

③ [店主]

¶旅館の主人が玄関でわたしたちを迎えてくれました。(Ryokan no *shujin* ga genkan de watashitachi o mukaete kuremashita.)

¶ That dog goes to the station every day to meet **its master**.

③ [proprietor, landlord, employer]

¶ **The proprietor** of the Japanese inn greeted us in the entryway.

しゅだん　手段 〔名〕

¶目的はたいへんいいが、手段が問題です。(Mokuteki wa taihen ii ga, *shudan* ga mondai desu.)

¶科学は平和を実現する手段として用いなければなりません。(Kagaku wa heiwa o jitsugen suru *shudan* to shite mochiinakereba narimasen.)

shudan 〔n〕 way, means, measure

¶ It is a very worthy end but there is a problem with **the means** being used 〚that you plan to use〛.

¶ Science must be utilized as **a means** of achieving peace.

しゅちょう　主張 〔名、〜する〕

¶わたしの主張は間違っているでしょうか。(Watashi no *shuchō* wa machigatte iru deshō ka？)

¶あの人は自分の考えばかりを主張して、ほかの人の意見を聞きません。(Ano hito wa jibun no kangae bakari o *shuchō* shite, hoka no hito no iken o kikimasen.)

shuchō 〔n, 〜*suru*〕 one's opinion, one's point; insist, assert, claim, stress, advocate

¶ Is my **view** on this wrong?

¶ [He] only **pushes forward** [his] own views without listening to those of anyone else.

しゅっせき　出席 〔名、〜する〕

出席者 (*shusseki*sha)　出席簿 (*shusseki*bo)　出席が悪い (*shusseki* ga warui)

¶出席を取りますから、返事をしてください。(*Shusseki* o torimasu kara, henji o shite kudasai.)

shusseki 〔n, 〜*suru*〕 attendance, presence

persons **attending**, those **present** // a **roll** book // have a poor **attendance** record

¶ I'm going to take **the roll** now; please answer when I call your name.

¶あしたの会議に出席しますか。
（Ashita no kaigi ni *shusseki* shimasu
ka？）
⇔欠席 kesseki

¶ **Will you be attending** tomorrow's
meeting?

しゅっぱつ 出発〔名、〜する〕

¶出発の日は3月 30 日に決まりまし
た。（*Shuppatsu* no hi wa sangatsu
sanjūnichi ni kimarimashita.）
¶6時に出発しますから、遅れないよ
うにしてください。（Rokuji ni
shuppatsu shimasu kara, okurenai yō ni
shite kudasai.）
⇔到着 tōchaku

shuppatsu 〔n, 〜*suru*〕 **departure,
starting out**

¶ The **departure** date has been fixed at
March 30.

¶ **[We]'re leaving** at six o'clock—
please don't be late.

しゅっぱん 出版〔名、〜する〕

出版社（*shuppan*sha）
¶中村さんの書いた小説が出版される
ことになりました。（Nakamura san no
kaita shōsetsu ga *shuppan* sareru koto ni
narimashita.）

shuppan 〔n, 〜*suru*〕 **publication,
publishing**
a **publishing** company
¶ [Mrs.] Nakamura's novel has been
chosen **for publication**.

しゅと 首都〔名〕

¶日本の首都は東京です。（Nippon no
shuto wa Tōkyō desu.）

shuto 〔n〕 **capital, capital city,
metropolis**
¶ **The capital** of Japan is Tokyo.

しゅみ 趣味〔名〕

¶あなたの趣味は何ですか。（Anata no
shumi wa nan desu ka？）
¶私の趣味は絵を見ることです。
（Watashi no *shumi* wa e o miru koto
desu.）

shumi 〔n〕 **hobby, interest, liking,
taste**
¶ What are your **hobbies**?

¶ My hobby is looking at paintings.

しゅるい 種類〔名〕

¶この山にはいろいろな種類の鳥がい
ます。（Kono yama ni wa iroiro na *shurui*
no tori ga imasu.）

shurui 〔n〕 **kind, sort, type**
¶ There are many different **sorts** of
birds on this mountain.

¶りんごにも種類がたくさんありま
す。(Ringo ni mo *shurui* ga takusan
arimasu.)

¶ There are many different **kinds** of
apples, too.

(-)じゅん (-)順 〔名、尾〕

1 〔名〕

¶背の高い順に並んでください。(Se
no takai *jun* ni narande kudasai.)

2 〔尾〕

番号順 (bangō*jun*) 年齢順
(nenrei*jun*) 成績順 (seiseki*jun*)

(-)jun 〔n, suf〕 order, sequence

1 〔n〕

¶ Please line up **in order** by height,
from tallest to shortest.

2 〔suf〕

numerical **order** // **in order** of age // **in
order** of grades achieved

じゅんじょ 順序 〔名〕

¶みんなにわかるように順序よく話し
てください。(Minna ni wakaru yōni
junjo yoku hanashite kudasai.)

¶漢字を書くときは、正しい順序で書
きなさい。(Kanji o kaku toki wa,
tadashii *junjo* de kakinasai.)

junjo 〔n〕 order, sequence, procedure

¶ Please talk **systematically** so
everyone will understand.

¶ When writing kanji, write the strokes
in the correct **order**.

じゅんばん 順番 〔名〕

¶順番に並んでください。(Junban ni
narande kudasai.)

¶タクシー乗り場でおおぜいの人が順
番を待っています。(Takushii-noriba de
oozei no hito ga *junban* o matte imasu.)

junban 〔n〕 turn, order

¶ Please line up **in order**.

¶ Many people are waiting **their turn**
at the taxi stand.

じゅんび 準備 〔名、〜する〕

¶じゅうぶんな準備をして、山に登り
ました。(Jūbun na *junbi* o shite, yama ni
noborimashita.)

¶今、試験の準備で忙しいです。
(Ima, shiken no *junbi* de isogashii desu.)

junbi 〔n, 〜suru〕 preparations

¶ [I] climbed the mountain after
preparing fully.

¶ [I]'m busy now **preparing** for exams.

しよう 使用 〔名、〜する〕

¶今、この部屋は使用できません。
(Ima, kono heya wa *shiyō* dekimasen.)

shiyō 〔n, 〜suru〕 use, employment, application

¶ This room is not available **for use** at
the present time.

¶現在、新聞などで使用されている漢字はどのくらいありますか。(Genzai, shinbun nado de *shiyō* sarete iru kanji wa dono kurai arimasu ka？)

¶ About how many *kanji* are presently **in use** in the newspaper and the like?

しょうかい 紹介 〔名、～する〕
自己紹介 (jiko-*shōkai*) 紹介状 (*shōkai*jō)

shōkai 〔n, ～*suru*〕 **introduction**
a self-**introduction** // a letter of **introduction**

¶山田さんは、わたしを田中さんに紹介してくれました。(Yamada san wa, watashi o Tanaka san ni *shōkai* shite kuremashita.)

¶ [Mr.] Yamada **introduced** me to [Mr.] Tanaka.

¶みなさんに御紹介します。こちらが田中さんです。(Minasan ni go*shōkai* shimasu. Kochira ga Tanaka san desu.)

¶ I'd like **to introduce someone** to all of you now. This is [Mrs.] Tanaka.

しょうがくせい 小学生 〔名〕

shōgakusei 〔n〕 **pupil in elementary school**

¶うちの子はまだ小学生です。(Uchi no ko wa mada *shōgakusei* desu.)

¶ Our child **is still in elementary school**.

しょうがつ 正月 〔名〕

shōgatsu 〔n〕 **the New Year, the New Year's holidays; January**

¶母と姉がお正月の料理を作っています。(Haha to ane ga o*shōgatsu* no ryōri o tsukutte imasu.)

¶ My mother and (older) sister are fixing food for **the New Year's holidays**.

＊「1月 (ichigatsu)」の意味であるが、特に1月1日から1月7日ごろまでをさす場合が多い。

＊*Shōgatsu* originally had the meaning of January but usually refers to the period of January 1-7.

しょうがっこう 小学校 〔名〕

shōgakkō 〔n〕 **elementary school**

¶あの子供たちは小学校の生徒です。(Ano kodomotachi wa *shōgakkō* no seito desu.)

¶ Those children are **elementary school** students.

¶小学校の何年生から漢字を習いますか。(Shōgakkō no nannensei kara kanji o naraimasu ka？)

¶ In what grade of **elementary school** do students first study *kanji*?

しょうがない 〔連〕
☞しかたがない **shikata ga nai**

shō ga nai 〔compd〕
☞**shikata ga nai**

しょうぎょう 商業 〔名〕

商業学校 (*shōgyō*-gakkō)
¶大阪は昔から商業の盛んな所です。(Oosaka wa mukashi kara *shōgyō* no sakan na tokoro desu.)

shōgyō 〔n〕 **commerce, trade, business**

a **commercial** school
¶ Osaka has been an active **commercial** center since ancient times.

しょうきょくてき 消極的 〔形動〕

¶彼はたいへん消極的で、自分からはあまり意見を言いません。(Kare wa taihen *shōkyokuteki* de, jibun kara wa amari iken o iimasen.)
⇔積極的 sekkyokuteki

shōkyokuteki 〔adj-v〕 **negative, passive**

¶ He **is** very **passive** and rarely states a personal opinion.

じょうけん 条件 〔名〕

¶条件が悪いので、あの仕事はやめました。(Jōken ga warui node, ano shigoto wa yamemashita.)
¶どんな条件であのアパートを借りましたか。(Donna *jōken* de ano apāto o karimashita ka？)

jōken 〔n〕 **term, condition, stipulation**

¶ I quit that job because **the terms of employment** were poor.

¶ On what **terms** did you rent that apartment?

しょうこ 証拠 〔名〕

¶あの人がお金を盗んだという証拠がありますか。(Ano hito ga okane o nusunda to iu *shōko* ga arimasuka？)
¶御飯が食べられないというのは、どこか体が悪い証拠です。(Gohan ga taberarenai to iu no wa, doko ka karada ga warui *shōko* desu.)

shōko 〔n〕 **evidence, proof**

¶ Is there **any proof** that [he] stole the money?

¶ Your not being able to eat is **an indication** that something is physically wrong with you.

しょうじき 正直 〔名、形動〕

¶山田さんは正直な人です。(Yamada san wa *shōjiki* na hito desu.)
¶うそをつかないで正直に話しなさい。(Uso o tsukanaide *shōjiki* ni hanashinasai.)

shōjiki 〔n, adj-v〕 **honest, upright; honestly, frankly**

¶ [Miss] Yamada is an **honest** person.

¶ Tell **the truth** now without any lying.

じょうしき　常識〔名〕

常識外れ（*jōshiki*hazure）非常識
（hi*jōshiki*）

¶こんなことは常識です。（Konna
koto wa *jōshiki* desu.）

¶あの人は常識がありません。（Ano
hito wa *jōshiki* ga arimasen.）

jōshiki〔n〕**common sense**

contrary to **common sense,** absurd //
senseless, absurd, preposterous

¶ This sort of thing is **a matter of
common sense**〚is **common
knowledge**〛.

¶ [He] doesn't have **good sense**.

じょうじゅん　上旬〔名〕

¶わたしは8月の上旬に旅行に出かけ
ます。（Watashi wa hachigatsu no *jōjun*
ni ryokō ni dekakemasu.）
⇒中旬 chūjun　下旬 gejun

jōjun〔n〕**the first third of the
month**

¶ I will be leaving on a trip in **early
August.**

しょうじょ　少女〔名〕

¶わたしは少女時代を外国で過ごしま
した。（Watashi wa *shōjo*-jidai o gaikoku
de sugoshimashita.）
⇔少年 shōnen

shōjo〔n〕**young girl, girl**

¶ I lived abroad when I was **a young
girl**.

じょうず　上手〔形動〕

¶日本語が上手になりたいです。
（Nihongo ga *jōzu* ni naritai desu.）
¶あの子はピアノが上手ですね。
（Ano ko wa piano ga *jōzu* desu ne.）
⇔下手 heta
⇒うまい umai

jōzu〔adj-v〕**skill, proficiency**

¶ I want to become **good at** Japanese.

¶ That child plays the piano **well,**
doesn't it?

しょうせつ　小説〔名〕

長編小説（chōhen-*shōsetsu*）短編小説
（tanpen-*shōsetsu*）歴史小説（rekishi-
shōsetsu）推理小説（suiri-*shōsetsu*）小
説家（*shōsetsu*ka）

¶ゆうべは宿題をやらないで、小説を
読んでいました。（Yūbe wa shukudai o
yaranaide, *shōsetsu* o yonde imashita.）

shōsetsu〔n〕**novel, story, fiction**

a full-length **novel** // a short **story** // an
historical **novel** // detective **fiction** // **a
novelist**

¶ [I] didn't do [my] homework last
night but read **a novel** instead.

¶わたしは父の一生を小説に書きたいと思っています。（Watashi wa chichi no isshō o *shōsetsu* ni kakitai to omotte imasu.）

¶I would like to write about my father's life in **the form of a novel**.

しょうたい　招待 〔名、〜する〕

招待状（*shōtai*jō）招待を受ける（*shōtai* o ukeru）

shōtai 〔n, 〜*suru*〕 **invitation**
(written) **invitation** // receive **an invitation**

¶今晩の食事に山田さんを招待しましょう。（Konban no shokuji ni Yamada san o *shōtai* shimashō.）

¶**Let's invite** [Miss] Yamada to dinner tonight.

¶わたしは田中さんの結婚式に招待されました。（Watashi wa Tanaka san no kekkonshiki ni *shōtai* saremashita.）

¶I received **an invitation** to [Mr.] Tanaka's wedding.

⇒招く **maneku**

じょうたい　状態 〔名〕

経済状態（keizai-*jōtai*）健康状態（kenkō-*jōtai*）精神状態（seishin-*jōtai*）

jōtai 〔n〕 **state, condition, situation, state of affairs**
economic **conditions**, financial **situation** // **state** of health // mental **state, state** of mind

¶この建物はたいへん古くて危険な状態です。（Kono tatemono wa taihen furukute kikenna *jōtai* desu.）

¶This building is very old and in a hazardous **condition**.

¶あんな状態では試験に合格しないでしょう。（Anna *jōtai* de wa shiken ni gōkaku shinai deshō.）

¶Considering **that** (i.e., his illness, his lack of preparation, etc.), [he] probably won't pass the exam.

じょうだん　冗談 〔名〕

¶あの人はよく冗談を言って、人を笑わせます。（Ano hito wa yoku *jōdan* o itte, hito o warawasemasu.）

jōdan 〔n〕 **joke, pleasantry**
¶[He] is often **joking** and making people laugh.

¶今の話は冗談ではなく、本当のことです。（Ima no hanashi wa *jōdan* de wa naku, hontō no koto desu.）

¶That wasn't **a joke**, it's the truth.

しょうち　承知 〔名、〜する〕

①[よく知っていること]

shōchi 〔n, 〜*suru*〕 **know, be aware of; consent, agree to, accept**
① [know, be aware of]

¶そのことは承知しています。（Sono koto wa *shōchi* shite imasu.）

¶ [I] **am aware** of that.

② [他の人の依頼・要求・願いなどを引き受けたり聞き入れたりすること]

② [consent, agree to, accept]

¶「この仕事をあしたまでにやってください。」（Kono shigoto o ashita made ni yatte kudasai.）「はい、承知しました。」（Hai, *shōchi* shimashita.）

¶ "Please have this job done by tomorrow."
"**All right**."

¶父がわたしたちの結婚を承知しないので、困っています。（Chichi ga watashitachi no kekkon o *shōchi* shinai node, komatte imasu.）

¶ We have a problem as my father **objects** to our marriage.

しょうてん　商店〔名〕

商店街（*shōten*gai）

shōten 〔n〕 **store, shop**

a **shopping** street, a **shopping** district

¶この通りは商店がたくさんあって、いつもにぎやかです。（Kono toori wa *shōten* ga takusan atte, itsu mo nigiyaka desu.）

¶ This street has lots of **shops** and is always bustling.

¶この辺りの商店は毎週月曜日が休みです。（Kono atari no *shōten* wa maishū getsuyōbi ga yasumi desu.）

¶ **The shops** around here are closed every Monday.

しょうとつ　衝突〔名、〜する〕

shōtotsu 〔n, 〜*suru*〕 **collision; conflict, clash**

① [車などが強くぶつかること]

① [collision]

¶バスとタクシーが衝突して、けが人が出ました。（Basu to takushii ga *shōtotsu* shite, keganin ga demashita.）

¶ A bus and taxi **collided** and some people were injured.

② [立場・意見などが激しく対立すること]

② [conflict, clash, discord]

¶親と意見が衝突して、田中さんは家を出ていきました。（Oya to iken ga *shōtotsu* shite, Tanaka san wa ie o dete ikimashita.）

¶ [Mr.] Tanaka **fought** with [his] parents and moved out.

しょうねん　少年 〔名〕

¶わたしがまだ少年だったころ、よくこの川で魚を捕って遊びました。
（Watashi ga mada *shōnen* datta koro, yoku kono kawa de sakana o totte asobimashita.）
⇔少女 **shōjo**

shōnen 〔n〕 **a boy, a youth**

¶ When I was still **a boy**, [we] often went fishing in this river.

しょうばい　商売 〔名、〜する〕

① [利益を目的として物の売買をすること]
¶田中さんは商売が上手です。
（Tanaka san wa *shōbai* ga jōzu desu.）
② [仕事、職業]
¶あの人の商売は何ですか。（Ano hito no *shōbai* wa nan desu ka？）

shōbai 〔n, 〜*suru*〕 **trade, business, commerce; occupation, calling, trade**

① [trade, business, commerce]

¶ [Mr.] Tanaka has a good head for **business**.

② [occupation, calling, tradc]

¶ What **line of business** is [he] in?

しょうひん　商品 〔名〕

商品見本（*shōhin*-mihōn）
¶この商品は外国から輸入したものです。（Kono *shōhin* wa gaikoku kara yunyū shita mono desu.）

shōhin 〔n〕 **commodity, goods, wares, merchandise**

a **trade** sample, sample **ware**

¶ This **merchandise** is imported.

しょうぶ　勝負 〔名、〜する〕

¶その試合はなかなか勝負がつきませんでした。（Sono shiai wa nakanaka *shōbu* ga tsukimasen deshita.）

shōbu 〔n, 〜*suru*〕 **victory or defeat; match, game, contest**

¶ That game 〚match〛 could have **gone either way** until the very end.

じょうぶ　丈夫 〔形動〕

① [体が健康な様子]
¶体を丈夫にするために毎日運動をしています。（Karada o *jōbu* ni suru tame ni mainichi undō o shite imasu.）
② [物などがしっかりしている様子]
丈夫なくつ下（*jōbu* na kutsushita）

jōbu 〔adj-v〕 **healthy, hardy; strong, substantial, tough**

① [healthy, hardy, robust]

¶ [I] exercise every day in order to **build up** [my] health.

② [strong, substantial, tough]

durable socks

¶このかばんはとても丈夫です。
（Kono kaban wa totemo *jōbu* desu.）

¶ This suitcase 〚bag, briefcase, etc.〛 is very **solidly built**.

しょうめい　証明〔名、〜する〕

shōmei 〔n, 〜*suru*〕 proof, evidence, corroboration

証明書（*shōmei*sho）身分証明書
（mibun-*shōmei*sho）

a certificate, diploma // an identification card, identification papers

¶わたしがそこにいなかったことは、山田さんが証明してくれます。
（Watashi ga soko ni inakatta koto wa, Yamada san ga *shōmei* shite kuremasu.）

¶ [Mr.] Yamada **will confirm** that I wasn't there.

しょうめん　正面〔名〕

shōmen 〔n〕 the front, the front part, face, facade

¶正面から撮ったあなたの写真を送ってください。（*Shōmen* kara totta anata no shashin o okutte kudasai.）

¶ Please send a **full-face** photograph.

¶正面に見える高い建物がわたしの会社です。（*Shōmen* ni mieru takai tatemono ga watashi no kaisha desu.）

¶ The tall building you can see **in front of you** is my office.

しょうゆ　しょう油〔名〕

shōyu 〔n〕 soy sauce

¶焼いた魚にしょう油をかけて食べました。（Yaita sakana ni *shōyu* o kakete tabemashita.）

¶ [I] put **soy sauce** on the grilled fish before eating it.

しょうらい　将来〔名〕

shōrai 〔n〕 the future, in time, some time

¶あなたは将来何になるつもりですか。（Anata wa *shōrai* nani ni naru tsumori desu ka？）

¶ What do you want to be **when you grow up?**

¶わたしたちは将来の希望について話し合いました。（Watashitachi wa *shōrai* no kibō ni tsuite hanashiaimashita.）

¶ We talked about our hopes for **the future**.

しょうりゃく　省略〔名、〜する〕

shōryaku 〔n, 〜*suru*〕 abbreviation, omission, abridgment

以下省略（ika *shōryaku*）

the rest **has been omitted**

¶どうしてそうなったかという説明は省略して、結論だけ言います。
（Dōshite sō natta ka to iu setsumei wa *shōryaku* shite, ketsuron dake iimasu.）

しょうわ　昭和〔名〕

¶昭和50年は西暦 1975 年です。（*Shōwa* gojūnen wa seireki senkyūhyaku-nanajūgonen desu.）
¶わたしは昭和 30 年に生まれました。（Watashi wa *Shōwa* sanjūnen ni umaremashita.）

しょくぎょう　職業〔名〕

¶あの人の職業は何ですか。（Ano hito no *shokugyō* wa nan desu ka？）
＊「職業を探す（shokugyō o sagasu）」「職業を失う（shokugyō o ushinau）」は普通「職を探す（shoku o sagasu）」「職を失う（shoku o ushinau）」と言う。

しょくじ　食事〔名、〜する〕

食事代（*shokuji*dai）
¶わたしは毎朝7時に食事をします。（Watashi wa maiasa shichiji ni *shokuji* o shimasu.）
¶今晩、わたしは食事に招かれています。（Konban, watashi wa *shokuji* ni manekarete imasu.）

しょくどう　食堂〔名〕

①〔食事をする部屋〕
¶台所の隣に食堂があります。（Daidokoro no tonari ni *shokudō* ga arimasu.）

¶ **I will pass over** an explanation of why it turned out that way and only state my conclusions.

shōwa 〔n〕 **Showa; the name given to the era beginning in 1926**
¶ **Showa** 50 equals 1975.

¶ I was born in **Showa** 30 (1955).

shokugyō 〔n〕 **occupation, calling, trade**
¶ What **does** [he] **do?**

＊*Shokugyō o sagasu* (look for a job, seek employment) and *shokugyō o ushinau* (lose one's job, be put out of work) are shortened to *shoku o sagasu* and *shoku o ushinau*.

shokuji 〔n, ～*suru*〕 **meal, dinner; have a meal, dine**
board, **eating** expenses
¶ **I eat breakfast** every morning at seven o'clock.

¶ I have been invited out **for dinner** tonight.

shokudō 〔n〕 **dining hall; restaurant, eating place**
① 〔dining hall, dining room, cafeteria〕
¶ **The dining room** is next to the kitchen.

② [食事をする店]

¶学校の近くにある食堂は、いつも学生でいっぱいです。(Gakkō no chikaku ni aru *shokudō* wa, itsu mo gakusei de ippai desu.)

② [restaurant, eating place, diner]

¶ **Eating places** near a school are always filled with students.

しょくぶつ 植物 〔名〕

植物園 (*shokubutsu*en) 高山植物 (kōzan-*shokubutsu*)

¶この山にはいろいろな種類の植物が生えています。(Kono yama ni wa iroiro na shurui no *shokubutsu* ga haete imasu.)

shokubutsu 〔n〕 **plant, plant life, vegetation**

botanical garden(s) // alpine **plant(s)**

¶ Many different **plants** are growing on this mountain.

しょくりょう 食料 〔名〕

食料品 (*shokuryō*hin)

¶いつも日曜日に1週間分の食料を買っておきます。(Itsu mo nichiyōbi ni isshūkanbun no *shokuryō* o katte okimasu.)

¶このデパートの食料品売り場は、いつも人でいっぱいです。(Kono depāto no *shokuryō*hin-uriba wa, itsu mo hito de ippai desu.)

shokuryō 〔n〕 **food, foodstuffs, provisions**

food, an article of **food, groceries**

¶ I always buy a week's **groceries** on Sunday.

¶ The **food** floor of this department store is always crowded.

じょし 女子 〔名〕

女子大 (*joshi*dai) 女子学生 (*joshi*gakusei) 女子用 (*joshi*yō) 女子寮 (*joshi*ryō)

¶このクラスは男子4名、女子3名です。(Kono kurasu wa danshi yonmei, *joshi* sanmei desu.)

¶体育の時間は男子と女子に分かれます。(Taiiku no jikan wa danshi to *joshi* ni wakaremasu.)

⇔男子 danshi

joshi 〔n〕 **girl, woman, female**

a **women's** college // a **female** student, a coed // **women's,** for use by **women** // a **women's** 〚**girls**〛 dormitory

¶ There are four boys 〚**men**〛 and three **girls** 〚**women**〛 in this class.

¶ Physical education classes are divided into male and **female** sections.

じょせい 女性 〔名〕

¶この店では女性の物しか売っていません。(Kono mise de wa *josei* no mono shika utte imasen.)

¶働く女性はだんだん多くなっています。(Hataraku *josei* wa dandan ooku natte imasu.)

⇔男性 dansei

josei 〔n〕 **woman, women**

¶This shop sells only **women's** goods.

¶The number of working **women** is gradually increasing.

しょるい 書類 〔名〕

¶あしたの会議に必要な書類を作りました。(Ashita no kaigi ni hitsuyō na *shorui* o tsukurimashita.)

¶机の上にある書類を整理しておいてください。(Tsukue no ue ni aru *shorui* o seiri shite oite kudasai.)

shorui 〔n〕 **document(s), paper(s)**

¶[I] prepared **the papers** necessary for the meeting tomorrow.

¶Please put **the papers** on the desk in order.

しらせる 知らせる 〔動Ⅱ〕

¶今度こちらに来るときは知らせてください。(Kondo kochira ni kuru toki wa shirasete kudasai.)

shiraseru 〔v Ⅱ〕 **acquaint, inform**

¶Let me know next time you're this way.

しらべる 調べる 〔動Ⅱ〕

¶わからない言葉は辞書で調べなさい。(Wakaranai kotoba wa jisho de *shirabenasai.*)

¶日本の宗教について調べたいのですが、どんな本がいいでしょうか。(Nihon no shūkyō ni tsuite *shirabetai* no desuga, donna hon ga ii deshō ka？)

¶うちじゅう調べてみましたが、その本は見つかりませんでした。(Uchijū *shirabete* mimashita ga, sono hon wa mitsukarimasen deshita.)

¶どろぼうが警官に調べられています。(Dorobō ga keikan ni *shiraberarete* imasu.)

shiraberu 〔v Ⅱ〕 **investigate, study, examine, check, search, look up**

¶**Look up** any words you don't know in the dictionary.

¶**I want to study** about Japanese religion. What books should I use?

¶**I looked** all over the house but couldn't find that book.

¶The police **are interrogating** the thief.

しりあい 知り合い 〔名〕

¶あの方とはお知り合いですか。(Ano kata to to wa o*shiriai* desu ka？)

¶あの大学にはわたしの知り合いがおおぜいいます。(Ano daigaku ni wa watashi no *shiriai* ga oozei imasu.)

shiriai 〔n〕 **acquaintance**

¶ Do you **know** [him]?

¶ I have many **acquaintances** at that university.

しりつ 私立 〔名〕

¶私立の学校は国立や公立より授業料が高いです。(*Shiritsu* no gakkō wa kokuritsu ya kōritsu yori jugyōryō ga takai desu.)

¶中村さんは私立大学を卒業しました。(Nakamura san wa *shiritsu*daigaku o sotsugyō shimashita.)

⇒国立 kokuritsu 公立 kōritsu

shiritsu 〔n〕 **private, nongovernmental**

¶ Tuition is higher at **private** schools than at national and other public ones.

¶ [Miss] Nakamura graduated from a **private** university.

しりょう 資料 〔名〕

研究資料 (kenkyū-*shiryō*) 資料を集める (*shiryō* o atsumeru)

¶図書館に行けば、古い時代の資料がたくさんありますよ。(Toshokan ni ikeba, furui jidai no *shiryō* ga takusan arimasu yo.)

shiryō 〔n〕 **material(s), data**

research **materials** // collect **data**, gather **material**

¶ If you go to the library, you will find much **material** on olden times.

しる 知る 〔動 I〕

① [わかる]

¶ 「あなたは日本語を知っていますか。」(Anata wa Nihongo o *shitte* imasu ka？)「いいえ、知りません。」(Iie, *shirimasen.*)

② [知り合いである]

¶わたしは田中さんをよく知っています。(Watashi wa Tanaka san o yoku *shitte* imasu.)

③ [気がつく]

shiru 〔v I〕 **know; be acquainted with someone; notice, realize**

① [know, be informed of, find out]

¶ "Do you **know** Japanese?" "No, **I don't.**"

② [be acquainted with someone, know someone]

¶ I **know** [Mr.] Tanaka quite well.

③ [notice, realize, be aware of]

396

¶あの人はお金を落としたのを知らずに行ってしまいました。(Anohito wa okane o otoshita no o *shirazu* ni itte shimaimashita.)

¶ [She] walked on **without noticing** that [she] had dropped some money.

しるし 印 〔名〕
○印 (maru*jirushi*) ×印 (batsu*jirushi*) 目印 (me*jirushi*)

shirushi 〔n〕 **mark, sign**
a circle (used to indicate that an item is correct or chosen) // an X, a cross (used to indicate that an item is wrong or not chosen) // mark, sign, landmark, earmark

¶わからない言葉に印をつけて、あとで先生にききます。(Wakaranai kotoba ni *shirushi* o tsukete, ato de sensei ni kikimasu.)

¶ [I] **mark** the words [I] don't understand and ask the teacher about them later.

しろ 白 〔名〕
白のシャツ (*shiro* no shatsu)
白黒フイルム (*shiro*kuro-firumu)

shiro 〔n〕 **white**
a **white** shirt // black-and-**white** film

しろい 白い 〔形〕
¶山田さんは白いシャツを着ています。(Yamada san wa *shiroi* shatsu o kite imasu.)

shiroi 〔adj〕 **white**
¶ Mr. Yamada is wearing a **white** shirt.

¶あなたの髪の毛もずいぶん白くなりましたね。(Anata no kaminoke mo zuibun *shiroku* narimashita ne.)

¶ Your hair has turned quite **white** 〚**gray**〛 too.

-じん -人 〔尾〕
アメリカ人 (Amerika*jin*) 中国人 (Chūgoku*jin*) ドイツ人 (Doitsu*jin*) フランス人 (Furansu*jin*) イギリス人 (Igirisu*jin*) インド人 (Indo*jin*) 日本人 (Nihon*jin*) スペイン人 (Supein*jin*) タイ人 (Tai*jin*) 外人 (gai*jin*) 外国人 (gaikoku*jin*) 知識人 (chishiki*jin*) 現代人 (gendai*jin*)

-jin 〔suf〕 **person, persons**
American(s), // a 〚the〛 Chinese // German(s) // a Frenchman 〚Frenchwoman〛, the French // an Englishman 〚Englishwoman〛, the English //Indian(s) (from India) // a 〚the〛 Japanese // a Spaniard, the Spanish // a Thai, the Thais // a foreigner // a foreigner // an intellectual // a contemporary, a modern **person**

¶あの人は何人ですか。(Ano hito wa nani*jin* desu ka?)

¶ What **nationality** is that person?

しんかんせん 新幹線 〔名〕

shinkansen 〔n〕 the Shinkansen, the bullet train

¶東京から大阪まで新幹線で約3時間です。(Tōkyō kara Oosaka made *shinkansen* de yaku sanjikan desu.)

¶あなたは新幹線に乗ったことがありますか。(Anata wa *shinkansen* ni notta koto ga arimasu ka?)

¶ It takes approximately three hours from Tokyo to Osaka on **the Shinkansen**.

¶ Have you ever ridden on **the Shinkansen?**

しんけい 神経 〔名〕

shinkei 〔n〕 a nerve; nerves, sensitivity

① [動物の体内にあって運動・知覚などをつかさどる器官]

① [a nerve]

¶彼は運動神経が発達していて、スポーツは何でも上手です。(Kare wa undō-*shinkei* ga hattatsu shite ite, supōtsu wa nan demo jōzu desu.)

¶ His **reflexes** are fast so he is good at all sports.

¶神経を抜いたから、歯の痛みはなくなりました。(*Shinkei* o nuita kara, ha no itami wa nakunarimashita.)

¶ **The nerve** was extracted so [my] tooth stopped [[has stopped]] hurting.

②[心の働き]
神経が鋭い (*shinkei* ga surudoi) 神経が鈍い (*shinkei* ga nibui)

② [nerves, sensitivity]
sensitive, thin-skinned, nervous, jumpy // insensitive, thick-skinned, dull, stolid

¶あの人は無神経な人だから、周りの人の気持ちなど気にしません。(Ano hito wa mu*shinkei* na hito dakara, mawari no hito no kimochi nado ki ni shimasen.)

¶ [He]'s **thick-skinned** and doesn't care about the feelings of other people.

しんごう 信号 〔名〕

shingō 〔n〕 signal, sign, traffic light

¶道を渡るときには、信号をよく見て渡りましょう。(Michi o wataru toki ni wa, *shingō* o yoku mite watarimashō.)

¶ Please be sure to look at **the light** when crossing the street.

¶信号が赤ですから、車をとめなさい。(*Shingō* ga aka desu kara, kuruma o tomenasai.)

¶ Stop the car! **The light** is red.

じんこう 人口 〔名〕

人口調査 (jinkō-chōsa) 人口問題
(jinkō-mondai)

¶あなたの国の人口はどのくらいです
か。(Anata no kuni no jinkō wa dono
kurai desu ka？)

¶この町の人口は今も増え続けていま
す。(Kono machi no jinkō wa ima mo
fuetsuzukete imasu.)

jinkō 〔n〕 **population**

a census //the **population** problem

¶ What is **the population** of your
country?

¶ **The population** of this city
continues to increase.

しんさつ 診察 〔名、〜する〕

¶この病院は9時から診察が始まりま
す。(Kono byōin wa kuji kara shinsatsu
ga hajimarimasu.)

¶体のぐあいが悪いので、お医者さん
に診察してもらいました。(Karada no
guai ga warui node, oishasan ni shinsatsu
shite moraimashita.)

shinsatsu 〔n, 〜suru〕 **medical
examination**

¶ **Consultations** start at nine o'clock at
this hospital.

¶ I wasn't feeling well so I **went to the
doctor**.

じんじゃ 神社 〔名〕

¶今度の旅行では古い神社やお寺を見
て歩きました。(Kondo no ryokō de wa
furui jinja ya otera o mite arukimashita.)

¶毎年、お正月には神社へお参りに行
きます。(Mainen, oshōgatsu ni wa jinja
e omairi ni ikimasu.)

jinja 〔n〕 **Shinto shrine**

¶ On [my] trip this time [I] visited
ancient **shrines** and temples.

¶ Every year [I] make a **shrine** visit
during the New Year holiday season.

しんじゅ 真珠 〔名〕

¶わたしは母から真珠の指輪をもらい
ました。(Watashi wa haha kara shinju
no yubiwa o moraimashita.)

shinju 〔n〕 **pearl(s)**

¶ My mother gave me a **pearl** ring.

しんじる 信じる 〔動Ⅱ〕

① [確信する]
¶わたしは田中さんの成功を信じてい
ます。(Watashi wa Tanaka san no seikō
o shinjite imasu.)

shinjiru 〔v Ⅱ〕 **be sure, be
confident of; believe, trust;
have faith**

① [be sure, be confident of]
¶ I **am sure** [Mr.] Tanaka will succeed.

② [信用する]
¶わたしは山田さんを信じています。
（Watashi wa yamada san o *shinjite*
imasu.）
¶あの人の言うことは信じられませ
ん。（Ano hito no iu koto wa
shinjiraremasen.）
③ [信仰する]
¶わたしは神を信じています。
（Watashi wa kami o *shinjite* imasu.）

② [believe, trust]
¶ I **trust** [Mrs.] Yamada.

¶ **You can't believe** what [he] says.

③ [believe in, have faith]
¶ I **believe in** God.

じんせい 人生 [名]

人生観 （*jinsei*kan）　人生相談
（*jin-sei*sōdan）

¶人生の目的は何ですか。（Jinsei no
mokuteki wa nan desu ka？）

jinsei [n] **human life**

view of **life**, one's attitude toward **life** //
counseling, seeking advice about
personal problems
¶ What is the purpose of **life?**

しんせつ 親切 [名、形動]

¶田中さんはとても親切な方です。
（Tanaka san wa totemo *shinsetsu* na kata
desu.）
¶交番で道を尋ねたら、親切に教えて
くれました。（Kōban de michi o
tazunetara, *shinsetsu* ni oshiete
kuremashita.）
¶御親切を心から感謝します。
（Go*shinsetsu* o kokoro kara kansha
shimasu.）

shinsetsu [n, adj-v] **kind, kindly,
friendly**
¶ [Mrs.] Tanaka is very **kind**.

¶ When I stopped and asked at the
police box, they **very obligingly** told
me the way.

¶ Thank you very much for **your
kindness**.

しんせん 新鮮 [形動]

¶これは今海で捕れたばかりの新鮮な
魚です。（Kore wa ima umi de toreta
bakari no *shinsen* na sakana desu.）
¶山の新鮮な空気を胸いっぱい吸いま
した。（Yama no *shinsen* na kūki o mune
ippai suimashita.）

shinsen [adj-v] **fresh, new**
¶ This fish is **fresh** from the sea.

¶ [I] took a deep breath of the **fresh**
mountain air.

しんぞう　心臓 〔名〕
心臓病　(*shinzō*byō)
¶心臓の手術はたいへん難しいそうです。(*Shinzō* no shujutsu wa taihen muzukashii sō desu.)
¶入学試験の発表の時には、心臓がどきどきしました。(Nyūgaku-shiken no happyō no toki ni wa, *shinzō* ga dokidoki shimashita.)

shinzō 〔n〕 the heart
heart disease
¶ I understand that **heart** surgery is very difficult.
¶ **My heart** was pounding 〚was in my throat〛 when the school entrance exam results were announced.

しんだい　寝台 〔名〕
寝台車　(*shindai*sha)
¶寝台が堅くて、ゆうべはよく眠れませんでした。(*Shindai* ga katakute, yūbe wa yoku nemuremasen deshita.)
⇒ベッド **beddo**

shindai 〔n〕 bed, berth
a **sleeping** car (on a train)
¶ **The bed** was hard so I didn't sleep well last night.

しんちょう　身長 〔名〕
¶わたしは身長が 170 センチあります。(Watashi wa *shinchō* ga hyakunanajissenchi arimasu.)

shinchō 〔n〕 stature, height
¶ I am 170 centimeters **tall**.

しんとう　神道 〔名〕

shintō 〔n〕 Shinto, Shintoism

しんぱい　心配 〔名、〜する〕
¶両親に心配をかけないようにしなさい。(Ryōshin ni *shinpai* o kakenai yō ni shinasai.)
¶飛行機は安全ですから、心配はいりません。(Hikōki wa anzen desu kara, *shinpai* wa irimasen.)

shinpai 〔n, 〜*suru*〕 worry, anxiety, concern, fear
¶ Don't cause your parents **worry**.
¶ There's no need for **fear**－flying is safe.

しんぶん　新聞 〔名〕
新聞社　(*shinbun*sha)　新聞記者　(*shinbun*-kisha)　新聞紙　(*shinbun*shi)
¶あなたは日本語の新聞が読めますか。(Anata wa Nihongo no *shinbun* ga yomemasu ka？)

shinbun 〔n〕 newspaper
a **newspaper** publisher, **newspaper** office // a **newspaper** reporter, journalist // a **newspaper**
¶ Can you read **a newspaper** written in Japanese?

¶毎朝、少年が新聞を配達してくれます。(Maiasa, shōnen ga *shinbun* o haitatsu shite kuremasu.)

¶A paperboy brings **my paper** each morning.

しんぽ 進歩 〔名、〜する〕

shinpo 〔n, 〜*suru*〕 **progress, advancement**

進歩的な考え (*shinpo*teki na kangae)

a **progressive** idea

¶最近、日本語がだいぶ進歩しましたね。(Saikin, Nihongo ga daibu *shinpo* shimashita ne.)

¶[Your] Japanese **has** greatly **improved** recently.

¶20世紀になって、科学が非常に進歩しました。(Nijisseiki ni natte, kagaku ga hijō ni *shinpo* shimashita.)

¶Science **has made** great **strides** in the 20th century.

しんよう 信用 〔名、〜する〕

shin'yō 〔n, 〜*suru*〕 **confidence, trust, reliance, faith, credit**

信用できる (*shin'yō* dekiru) 信用を得る (*shin'yō* o eru) 信用を失う (*shin'yō* o ushinau)

trustworthy, reliable, reputable // win **someone's confidence** // lose **someone's confidence**

¶山田さんは社長に信用があります。(Yamada san wa shachō ni *shin'yō* ga arimasu.)

¶[Mr.] Yamada enjoys **the confidence** of the company president.

¶あの人はよくうそをつくから、だれにも信用されません。(Ano hito wa yoku uso o tsuku kara, dare ni mo *shin'yō* saremasen.)

¶No one **trusts** [him] as [he] often lies.

しんるい 親類 〔名〕

shinrui 〔n〕 **a relative, a relation**

¶お正月には、親類の人たちがみんなうちに集まりました。(Oshōgatsu ni wa, *shinrui* no hitotachi ga minna uchi ni atsumarimashita.)

¶**My relatives** gathered at my home over the New Year's holidays.

しん- 新- 〔頭〕

shin- 〔pref〕 **new, modern**

新年 (*shin*nen) 新製品 (*shin*seihin) 新婚 (*shin*kon) 新人 (*shin*jin) 新入生 (*shin*nyūsei) 新学期 (*shin*gakki)

the New Year, a **new** year // a **new** product, a **newly issued** product // **newly** wed // a **new**comer, a **new** face, a rookie // a **new** student, freshman // a **new** school term

す

す 酢 〔名〕

¶ 料理に酢を使いすぎたので、すっぱくなってしまいました。(Ryōri ni *su* o tsukaisugita node, suppaku natte shimaimashita.)

su 〔n〕 **vinegar**

¶ [I] put too much **vinegar** in the dish so it is 〖was〗 on the sour side.

す 巣 〔名〕

ねずみの巣 (nezumi no *su*) くもの巣 (kumo no *su*) 巣を作る (*su* o tsukuru) ¶ この木の上には鳥の巣があります。(Kono ki no ue ni wa tori no su ga arimasu.)

su 〔n〕 **nest, beehive, cobweb, etc.**

a rat's **nest**, a mouse **nest** // a cobweb // build **a nest**, to nest

¶ There's a bird's **nest** in the top of this tree.

ず 図 〔名〕

① [物の形や状態を絵やグラフなどで表したもの]
天気図 (tenki*zu*)
¶ 先生が黒板に図をかいて、発音の説明をしてくださいました。(Sensei ga kokuban ni *zu* o kaite, hatsuon no setsumei o shite kudasai mashita.)
② [土地の様子などを言葉によらないでわかりやすくかいたもの]
地図 (chi*zu*) 案内図 (annai*zu*)

¶ 交番で道を尋ねたら、図をかいて教えてくれました。(Kōban de michi o tazunetara, *zu* o kaite oshiete kuremashita.)

zu 〔n〕 **drawing, diagram; map, plan**

① [drawing, diagram, figure, graph]

a weather **map**, a weather **chart**
¶ The teacher draw **a diagram** on the board and explained the pronunciation.

② [map, plan]

a **map** // a guide **map**, a **map** for visitors
¶ When I asked the way at a police box they drew **a map** for me.

ず 〔助動〕

¶ 昨日は、どこへも行かずに家で本を読んでいました。(Kinō wa, doko e mo ika*zu* ni ie de hon o yonde imashita.)

-zu 〔auxil〕 **a negative verb ending**

¶ Yesterday [I] **didn't go** anywhere but stayed home and read books.

403

¶勉強もせずに、どこへ行っていたん
ですか。（Benkyō mo se*zu* ni, doko e itte
ita n desu ka？）

＊「する（suru）」を「ない（nai）」で
打ち消す場合には「しない（shinai）」
となるが、「ず（zu）」で打ち消す場合
には「せず（sezu）」となる。

¶ Where did you go **before finishing**
your studying?

＊The negative of *suru* formed with
-*nai* is *shinai* but the negative
formed with -*zu* is *sezu*.

すいえい　水泳〔名、〜する〕

¶午後はプールで水泳をします。
（Gogo wa pūru de *suiei* o shimasu.）
¶わたしはスポーツの中では水泳が得
意です。（Watashi wa supōtsu no naka de
wa *suiei* ga tokui desu.）
⇒泳ぐ oyogu

suiei 〔n, 〜*suru*〕 **swimming, a
swim**
¶ [I] **will swim** in the pool in the
afternoon.
¶ The sport I'm strongest at is
swimming.

すいさん　水産〔名〕

水産物（*suisan*butsu）水産大学
（*suisan*daigaku）
¶日本は海に囲まれているので、水産
業が盛んです。（Nihon wa umi ni
kakomarete iru node, *suisan*gyō ga sakan
desu.）

suisan 〔n〕 **marine, fisheries**
marine products // a **fisheries** college

¶ As Japan is surrounded by the sea, it
has an active **fishing** industry.

すいそ　水素〔名〕

suiso 〔n〕 **hydrogen**

すいどう　水道〔名〕

¶ここは電気も水道もない山奥です。
（Koko wa denki mo *suidō* mo nai
yamaoku desu.）

suidō 〔n〕 **water service, running
water; waterway, channel**
¶ Here deep in the mountains there is
neither electricity nor **running water**.

ずいぶん〔副〕

¶このお菓子はずいぶん甘いですね。
（Kono okashi wa *zuibun* amai desu ne.）
¶あの人は若い時ずいぶん苦労をした
そうです。（Ano hito wa wakai toki
zuibun kurō o shita sō desu.）

zuibun 〔adv〕 **fairly, quite, very**
¶ This cake 〖confection, etc.〗 is **quite**
sweet, isn't it?
¶ I hear [he] underwent **much** hardship
in [his] youth.

すいへい　水平〔名、形動〕
水平線（*suihei*sen）
¶コップの中の水の表面は、いつも水平です。（Koppu no naka no mizu no hyōmen wa, itsu mo *suihei* desu.）
¶はかりは水平に置かなければなりません。（Hakari wa *suihei* ni okanakereba narimasen.）

suihei〔n, adj-v〕**horizontal, level**
the horizon; a **horizontal** line
¶ The top of water in a glass is always **on the horizontal**.

¶ Scales should be placed **on a level**.

すいよう（び）　水曜（日）〔名〕

suiyō(bi)〔n〕**Wednesday**

すう　吸う〔動 I〕
息を吸う（iki o *suu*）
¶ここでたばこを吸ってもいいですか。（Koko de tabako o *sutte* mo iidesu ka?）

suu〔v I〕**inhale, smoke, sip, suck**
take a breath, breathe in
¶ May **I smoke** here?

すうがく　数学〔名〕
数学者（*sūgaku*sha）
¶わたしは将来、大学で数学を研究しようと思っています。（Watashi wa shōrai, daigaku de *sūgaku* o kenkyū shiyō to omotte imasu.）

sūgaku〔n〕**mathematics**
a mathematician
¶ I would like to do advanced studies in **mathematics** at the university sometime.

すうじ　数字〔名〕
¶1から10までの数字が黒板に書いてあります。（Ichi kara jū made no *sūji* ga kokuban ni kaite arimasu.）

sūji〔n〕**figure, numeral**
¶ **The numbers** from one to ten are written on the blackboard.

スーツケース〔名〕
¶このスーツケースはとても丈夫です。（Kono *sūtsukēsu* wa totemo jōbu desu.）

sūtsukēsu〔n〕**suitcase**
¶ This suitcase is very strong.

スープ〔名〕
¶スープが冷めないうちに飲んでください。（*Sūpu* ga samenai uchi ni nonde kudasai.）

sūpu〔n〕**soup**
¶ Please eat **your soup** before it gets cold.

すう(-)　数(-)〔名、頭〕
1〔名〕
数字（*sū*ji）数学（*sū*gaku）

sū(-)〔n, pref〕**a number; several**
1〔n〕a number, a figure
a figure, a numeral // mathematics

¶この大学の学生数はどのくらいです
か。(Kono daigaku no gakuseisū wa
dono kurai desu ka?)

¶ **How many** students are there at this
university?

2 〔頭〕
数日 (sūjitsu) 数時間 (sūjikan) 数千
人 (sūsennin)

2 〔pref〕 several
a few days, **several** days // **a few**
hours, **several** hours // **thousands** of
people

¶その会には外国人も数人来ていまし
た。(Sono kai ni wa gaikokujin mo sūnin
kite imashita.)

¶ **Several** foreigners came to that party
〖meeting〗.

*4、5、6ぐらいの数をさすことが多
い。

*Sū- usually indicates around four,
five, or six.

すえ 末 〔名〕

sue 〔n〕 **the end, the close; last
child; result**

① [ある期間の終わりのころ]
今月の末 (kongetsu no sue)
¶東京では、桜の花は三月の末か四月
の初めに咲きます。(Tōkyō de wa,
sakura no hana wa sangatsu no sue ka
shigatsu no hajime ni sakimasu.)

① [the end, the close]
the end of this month, **late** this month
¶ In Tokyo the cherry blossoms come
out at **the end** of March or the
beginning of April.

② [いちばん下の子]
末っ子 (suekko) 末の娘 (sue no
musume)

② [last child]
the **youngest** child (of a family) // the
youngest daughter (in a family)

③ [あることをしたあと・結果]
¶いろいろ考えた末、その仕事を引き
受けることにしました。(Iroiro
kangaeta sue, sono shigoto o hikiukeru
koto ni shimashita.)

③ [result, the end of an action]
¶ **After** much thought [I] decided to
accept that work.

スカート 〔名〕

sukāto 〔n〕 **a skirt**

¶秋子さんは赤いスカートをはいてい
ます。(Akiko san wa akai sukāto o haite
imasu.)

¶ Akiko is wearing a red **skirt**.

すがた 姿 〔名〕

sugata 〔n〕 **figure, shape, form;
(make one's) appearance,
(show) oneself; personal
appearance, dress, posture**

① [体や物の形・かっこう]

① [figure, shape, form]

¶姉は自分の姿を鏡に映して見ています。(Ane wa jibun no *sugata* o kagami ni utsushite mite imasu.)

¶My older sister is regarding **her reflection** in the mirror.

②[見えたり見えなかったりする生物などの体]

②[(make one's) appearance, (show) oneself]

¶会の終わるころ、田中さんはやっと姿を現しました。(Kai no owaru koro, Tanaka san wa yatto *sugata* o arawashimashita.)

¶[Mr.] Tanaka finally **showed up** when the party 〚meeting〛 was almost over.

③[身なり、服装]

③[personal appearance, guise, dress, pose, posture]

¶こんな姿では恥ずかしくて、みんなの前に出られません。(Konna *sugata* de wa hazukashikute, minna no mae ni deraremasen.)

¶I am embarrassed to go out in front of everyone **dressed like this**.

すかれる 好かれる 〚動Ⅱ〛
☞好く **suku**

sukareru 〚v Ⅱ〛　　☞**suku**

すき 好き 〚形動〛

suki 〚adj-v〛 **like, be fond of**

¶わたしが好きな先生は山田先生です。(Watashi ga *suki* na sensei wa Yamada sensei desu.)

¶My **favorite** teacher is [Mr.] Yamada.

¶わたしはこのごろ肉より魚のほうが好きになりまた。(Watashi wa konogoro niku yori sakana no hō ga *suki* ni narimashita.)

¶Recently I have come to **like** fish better than meat.

¶わたしは旅行が大好きです。(Watashi wa ryokō ga dai*suki* desu.)

¶I **love** to travel.

¶わたしはあなたが好きです。(Watashi wa anata ga *suki* desu.)

¶I **love** you 〚I **like** you **very much**〛.

⇔きらい **kirai**

-すぎ -過ぎ 〚尾〛

-sugi 〚suf〛 **after, past; over-**

①[ある時間・年齢などを超えていること]

①[after, past]

二十歳過ぎの娘 (hatachi *sugi* no musume)

a young lady **over** 20 years of age

¶今、9時5分過ぎです。(Ima, kuji gofun *sugi* desu.)

¶It is now five minutes **past** 9.

¶午前中は忙しいから、お昼過ぎに来てください。(Gozenchū wa isogashii kara, ohiru *sugi* ni kite kudasai.)

¶[I]'ll be busy during the morning so please come in the afternoon.

②[ある動作・状態などのちょうどよい程度を超えること]

②[over-]

¶食べすぎは胃によくありません。(Tabe*sugi* wa i ni yoku arimasen.)

¶**Over**eating is bad for the stomach.

¶健康のため、たばこの吸いすぎに注意しましょう。(Kenkō no tame, tabako no sui*sugi* ni chūi shimashō.)

¶For the sake of one's health one should beware of smoking **too much**.

スキー〔名〕 ## sukii 〔n〕 skiing, skis

スキーをする(*sukii* o suru)
  to ski

¶冬のスポーツでは、わたしはスキーがいちばん好きです。(Fuyu no supōtsu de wa, watashi wa *sukii* ga ichiban suki desu.)

¶**Skiing** is my favorite winter sport.

すきやき〔名〕 ## sukiyaki 〔n〕 sukiyaki

¶友達が来たので、牛肉や野菜などを買ってきて、すきやきにして食べました。(Tomodachi ga kita node, gyūniku ya yasai nado o katte kite, *sukiyaki* ni shite tabemashita.)

¶Some friends came by so [we] bought beef and vegetables and made *sukiyaki* for dinner.

すぎる 過ぎる〔動Ⅱ〕 ## (-)sugiru 〔v Ⅱ〕 pass by, go past; pass, elapse; exceed, go too far, over-

①[通過する]

①[pass by, go past]

¶京都はさっき過ぎました。(Kyōto wa sakki *sugimashita*.)

¶We **went through** Kyoto a little while ago.

¶急行列車が勢いよく走り過ぎていきました。(Kyūkō-ressha ga ikioi yoku hashiri*sugite* ikimashita.)

¶The express train **sped by**.

②[時間などが経過する]

②[pass, elapse]

¶この研究を始めてから、もう3年過ぎました。(Kono kenkyū o hajimete kara, mō sannen *sugimashita*.)

¶Three years **have passed** since [I] started this research.

408

¶ 父が死んでから、半年過ぎました。
(Chichi ga shinde kara, hantoshi
sugimashita.)

③ [ある動作・状態などのちょうどよ
い程度を超える]

¶ これは高すぎます。もっと安いのは
ありませんか。(Kore wa taka*sugimasu*.
Motto yasui no wa arimasen ka？)

¶ 勉強をしすぎて、頭が痛くなりまし
た。(Benkyō o shi*sugite*, atama ga itaku
narimashita.)

すく 好く 〔動 I〕
¶ 山田さんは性格がいいので、みんな
から好かれています。(Yamada san wa
seikaku ga ii node, minna kara *sukarete*
imasu.)

¶ だれからも好かれるような人になり
たいです。(Dare kara mo *sukareru* yō
na hito ni naritai desu.)

＊「好かれる（sukareru）」の形で使う
ことが多い。

すく 〔動 I〕

¶ おなかがすきました。(Onaka ga
sukimashita.)

¶ このレストランはいつもすいていま
す。(Kono resutoran wa itsu mo *suite*
imasu.)

¶ 汽車はこんでいましたか、すいてい
ましたか。(Kisha wa konde imashita ka,
suite imashita ka？)

すぐ 〔副〕

① [時間のかからない様子、ただちに]
¶ 田中さんに手紙を出したら、すぐ返
事が来ました。(Tanaka san ni tegami o
dashitara, *sugu* henji ga kimashita.)

¶ Half a year **has** 〚**had**〛 **passed** since
the death of my father.

③ [exceed, go too far, over-]

¶ This is **too** expensive. Don't you have
anything cheaper?

¶ [I] got 〚have gotten〛 a headache
from studying **too much**.

suku 〔v I〕 **like, be fond of**
¶ As [Mr.] Yamada is such a nice
person, [he] **is well liked** by everyone.

¶ I want to become a person **liked** by
all.

＊Generally used in the form *sukareru*.

suku 〔v I〕 **become empty,
vacant, less crowded**
¶ [I] am 〚was〛 **hungry**.

¶ This restaurant **is never crowded**.

¶ Was the train crowded or **were there
plenty of seats?**

sugu 〔adv〕 **at once, immediately;
easily, readily; right (here)**
① [at once, immediately]
¶ [I] received a **prompt** reply to [my]
letter to [Mr.] Tanaka.

¶待っているから、すぐ来てくださ
い。(Matte iru kara, *sugu* kite kudasai.)
＊「すぐに（sugu ni）」の形でも使う。
②[ものごとが簡単に行われる様子]
¶交番できいたら、上田さんのうちは
すぐわかりました。(Kōban de kiitara,
Ueda san no uchi wa *sugu*
wakarimashita.)
¶買ったばかりのおもちゃが、すぐ壊
れてしまいました。(Katta bakari no
omocha ga, *sugu* kowarate
shimaimashita.)
＊「すぐに（sugu ni）」の形でも使う。
③[距離などのごく近い様子]
¶山田さんの家は駅のすぐ近くです。
(Yamada san no ie wa eki no *sugu*
chikaku desu.)
¶うちのすぐそばに公園があります。
(Uchi no *sugu* soba ni kōen ga arimasu.)

すくう 救う〔動Ⅰ〕
¶田中さんは川に落ちた子供を救った
ので、両親から感謝されました。
(Tanaka san wa kawa ni ochita kodomo o
sukutta node, ryōshin kara kansha
saremashita.)
¶このお金は、気の毒な子供たちを救
うために使われます。(Kono okane wa,
kinodoku na kodomotachi o *sukuu* tame ni
tsukawaremasu.)

すくない 少ない〔形〕

¶このクラスは女の人が少ないです
ね。(Kono kurasu wa onna no hito ga
sukunai desu ne.)
¶今年は、去年より雨が少なかったで
す。(Kotoshi wa, kyonen yori ame ga
sukunakatta desu.)

¶ Please come **right away**－I'll be
waiting for you.
*Also used in the form *sugu ni*.
② [easily, readily]
¶ [I] found [Miss] Ueda's place **easily**
after inquiring at the police box.

¶ The toy [I] had just bought **soon**
broke 〖The toy I just bought has
already broken〗.

*Also used in the form *sugu ni*.
③ [right (here), just (there)]
¶ [Mrs.] Yamada's house is **close by**
the station.

¶ There is a park **nearby** my home.

sukuu 〔vⅠ〕 **rescue, save, help**
¶ [Mr.] Tanaka **rescued** a child that
had fallen into the river and received
the gratitude of its parents.

¶ This money will be used **to help**
unfortunate children.

sukunai 〔adj〕 **few, little, limited,
scarce**
¶ There **are few** women in this class.

¶ There **was less** rain this year than last
year.

¶山田さんは家にいることが少ないよ
うです。(Yamada san wa ie ni iru koto
ga *sukunai* yō desu.)
　⇔多い ooi

すくなくとも　少なくとも〔副〕

¶あしたのパーティーには少なくとも
100人は集まるでしょう。(Ashita no
pātii ni wa *sukunakutomo* hyakunin wa
atsumaru deshō.)
¶この仕事を完成するには、少なくと
も1か月はかかります。(Kono shigoto
o kansei suru ni wa, *sukunakutomo*
ikkagetsu wa kakarimasu.)

すぐれる　優れる〔動Ⅱ〕

¶あの学生は成績がたいへん優れてい
ます。(Ano gakusei wa seiseki ga taihen
sugurete imasu.)
¶あの人は非常に優れた技術を持って
います。(Ano hito wa hijō ni *sugureta*
gijutsu o motte imasu.)

スケート〔名〕

スケートをする (*sukēto* o suru)
¶山田さんはスキーよりスケートのほ
うが上手です。(Yamada san wa sukii
yori *sukēto* no hō ga jōzu desu.)

スケジュール〔名〕

¶旅行のスケジュールを作りました。
(Ryokō no *sukejūru* o tsukurimashita.)
¶来年のスケジュールはまだわかりま
せん。(Rainen no *sukejūru* wa mada
wakarimasen.)

¶ It seems that [Mr.] Yamada spends
little time at home.

sukunakutomo 〔adv〕 **at least, at
the very least**

¶ **No less** than a hundred persons
should show up at the party tomorrow.

¶ It will take **at least** a month to finish
this job.

sugureru 〔v Ⅱ〕 **be excellent, be
superior**

¶ That student has **excellent** grades.

¶ [He] is **superbly** skilled at it.

sukēto 〔n〕 **skating, skates**
to skate

¶ [Miss] Yamada is better at **skating**
than skiing.

sukejūru 〔n〕 **schedule, program,
plan**

¶ [I] made out **an itinerary** for the trip.

¶ [We] don't know **the schedule** for
next year yet.

すごい〔形〕

¶ゆうべはすごい雨でしたね。(Yūbe wa *sugoi* ame deshita ne.)

¶電車はすごくこんでいました。(Densha wa *sugoku* konde imashita.)

すこし 少し〔副〕

① [数量が少ない様子、程度が低い]

¶わたしは朝御飯は少ししか食べません。(Watashi wa asagohan wa *sukoshi* shika tabemasen.)

¶今日は頭が少し痛いです。(Kyō wa atama ga *sukoshi* itai desu.)

② [時間が短い様子]

¶それでは、少し休みましょう。(Soredewa, *sukoshi* yasumimashō.)

¶もう少したったら、田中さんが来ると思います。(Mō *sukoshi* tattara, Tanaka san ga kuru to omoimasu.)

③ [距離が短い様子]

¶駅はこの道をもう少し行った所です。(Eki wa kono michi o mō *sukoshi* itta tokoro desu.)

④ [全然、何も]

¶あの人は少しも日本語が話せないようです。(Ano hito wa *sukoshi* mo Nihongo ga hanasenai yō desu.)

¶わたしは山田さんが大阪へ行ったことを、少しも知りませんでした。(Watashi wa yamada san ga Oosaka e itta koto o, *sukoshi* mo shirimasen deshita.)

*「少しも～ない(sukoshimo～nai)」の形で使う。

sugoi 〔adj〕 **terrible, dreadful, terrific, amazing, great, wonderful**

¶ That was **really some** rain last night, wasn't it?

¶ The train was **terribly** crowded.

sukoshi 〔adv〕 **a little, somewhat; a moment, a little while; a little way; (not) at all,(not) a bit**

① [a little, a few, a little bit, somewhat]

¶ I have only a **small** breakfast.

¶ I have a **slight** headache today 〚My head is a **little** sore today〛.

② [a moment, a little while]

¶ Well, let's take a **short** break.

¶ I think [Mr.] Tanaka will be here **shortly**.

③ [a little way, a short distance]

¶ The station is **a little farther** down this street.

④ [(not) at all, (not) a bit]

¶ It seems [he] can't speak Japanese **at all**.

¶ I had no idea **whatsoever** that [Mr.] Yamada had gone to Osaka.

*Used in the pattern "*sukoshi mo* ～ (-) *nai*."

すごす　過ごす〔動Ⅰ〕

¶昨日は休みだったので、一日じゅう子供と遊んで過ごしました。（Kinō wa yasumi datta node, ichinichijū kodomo to asonde *sugoshimashita*.)

¶では、夏休みを楽しくお過ごしください。（Dewa, natsuyasumi o tanoshiku o*sugoshi* kudasai.)

すし〔名〕

¶おなかがすいたので、すし屋でおすしを食べました。（Onaka ga suita node, *sushi*ya de o*sushi* o tabemashita.)

すじ　筋〔名〕

① [筋肉の繊維・血管など]

¶この肉は筋が多くて、おいしくありません。（Kono niku wa *suji* ga ookute, oishiku arimasen.)

② [細長い線の模様、しま]

¶その縦に青い筋の入っている布を見せてください。（Sono tate ni aoi *suji* no haitte iru nuno o misete kudasai.)

③ [話の組み立て]

¶その小説の筋を簡単に話してください。（Sono shōsetsu no *suji* o kantan ni hanashite kudasai.)

すずしい　涼しい〔形〕

¶昼間は暑かったが、夕方になって涼しくなりました。（Hiruma wa atsukatta ga, yūgata ni natte *suzushiku* narimashita.)

¶ここは夏は涼しく冬は暖かい、とてもいい所です。（Koko wa natsu wa *suzushiku* fuyu wa atatakai, totemo ii tokoro desu.)

sugosu 〔vⅠ〕 **pass (time), spend (time)**

¶ [I] had the day off yesterday so [I] **spent** the whole day playing with [my] children.

¶ Well, be sure and **have** a pleasant summer vacation.

sushi 〔n〕 **sushi**

¶ [I] was hungry so [I] had some *sushi* at a *sushi* shop.

suji 〔n〕 **muscle; line, stripe; plot**

① [muscle, tendon, vein, fiber, string]

¶ This meat isn't very good—it's too **stringy**.

② [line, stripe]

¶ Please show me that cloth with the vertical blue **stripe**.

③ [plot, story]

¶ Please give a brief synopsis of the **plot** of that novel.

suzushii 〔adj〕 **cool**

¶ It was hot during the day but **cooled off** in the evening [**has cooled off** from the evening].

¶ The summers **are cool** here and the winters warm, making it a very pleasant area.

すすむ 進む〔動Ⅰ〕

susumu 〔vⅠ〕 **advance, go forward; progress, advance; be fast, gain time**

① [前へ行く]

① [advance, go forward]

¶ もう少し前へ進みなさい。(Mō sukoshi mae e *susuminasai*.)

¶ **Move** a little farther **forward**.

¶ この前の授業はどこまで進みましたか。(Kono mae no jugyō wa doko made *susumimashita* ka？)

¶ How far **did we get** in our lesson last time?

② [進歩する、進行させる]
進んだ考え (*susunda* kangae) 進んだ文化 (*susunda* bunka)

② [progress, advance, improve]
an **advanced** way of thinking // an **advanced** culture

¶ この国の農業技術はたいへん進んでいます。(Kono kuni no nōgyōgijutsu wa taihen *susunde* imasu.)

¶ Agricultural techniques **are** very **advanced** in this country.

③ [時計が正しい時刻より早くなる]

③ [be fast, gain time]

¶ この時計は1日に5分進みます。(Kono tokei wa ichinichi ni gofun *susumimasu*.)

¶ This watch 〖clock〗 **gains** five minutes a day.

すすめる 進める〔動Ⅱ〕

susumeru 〔vⅡ〕 **advance, put forward; promote, further**

① [前方に行かせる、正しい時刻より前にする)]

① [advance, put forward]

¶ この時計は15分進めてあります。(Kono tokei wa jūgofun *susumete* arimasu.)

¶ This watch 〖clock〗 **is** 15 minutes **fast**.

② [はかどらせる、進行させる]

② [promote, further, speed up]

¶ 雨の日が多くて、工事が進められません。(Ame no hi ga ookute, kōji ga *susumeraremasen*.)

¶ There have been many rainy days, **hindering the progress** of the construction.

すすめる 勧める〔動Ⅱ〕

susumeru 〔vⅡ〕 **recommend, advise**

¶ わたしはみんなにその会に参加するように勧めています。(Watashi wa minna ni sono kai ni sanka suru yōni *susumete* imasu.)

¶ I **recommend** that everyone participate in that club.

¶ 山田さんに保険に入ることを勧められました。(Yamada san ni hoken ni hairu koto o *susumeraremashita*.)

¶ [Mr.] Yamada **recommended** that I take out insurance.

ずつ 〔助〕

zutsu 〔part〕 **each, respectively**

① [それぞれが同じ数量であるという意味を表す]

① [indicates each is the same amount]

¶ りんごが一つしか残っていなかったので、二人で半分ずつ食べました。(Ringo ga hitotsu shika nokotte inakatta node, futari de hanbun *zutsu* tabemashita.)

¶ As there was only one apple left, [we] **each** ate half of it.

¶ 3人の子供に1000円ずつ小遣いをやりました。(Sannin no kodomo ni sen'en *zutsu* kozukai o yarimashita.)

¶ [I] gave **each** of the three children a thousand yen allowance.

② [同程度の数量が繰り返されるという意味を表す]

② [indicates a repetition of the same amount]

¶ わたしは日本語を毎日5時間ずつ1年間勉強しました。(Watashi wa Nihongo o mainichi gojikan *zutsu* ichinenkan benkyō shimashita.)

¶ I studied Japanese five hours a day for a year.

¶ わたしは今2週間に1回ずつ病院に通っています。(Watashi wa ima nishūkan ni ikkai *zutsu* byōin ni kayotte imasu.)

¶ I am receiving treatment at the hospital every other week.

¶ 最近、少しずつ太ってきて困っています。(Saikin, sukoshi *zutsu* futtote kite komatte imasu.)

¶ Lately I have been putting on weight **little by little** and don't know what to do about it.

＊数や量を表す言葉につく。

＊Added to words expressing number or amount.

すっかり 〔副〕

sukkari 〔adv〕 **all, entirely, wholly; quite, utterly, completely**

① [全部、残らず、すべて]

① [all, entirely, wholly]

¶ パーティーの準備はすっかりできています。(Pātii no junbi wa *sukkari* dekite imasu.)

¶ **All** the preparations for the party are done now.

¶雨に降られて、すっかりぬれてしまいました。(Ame ni furarete, *sukkari* nurete shimaimashita.)

¶ [I] got soaked **to the skin** in the rain.

② [完全に、全く]

② [quite, utterly, completely]

¶わたしはあなたとの約束をすっかり忘れていました。(Watashi wa anata to no yakusoku o *sukkari* wasurete imashita.)

¶ I **completely** forgot about my appointment〚date〛with you.

¶一日休んだら、疲れがすっかりとれました。(Ichinichi yasundara, tsukare ga *sukkari* toremashita.)

¶ One day's rest has **completely** relieved [my] fatigue〚One day's rest **completely** relieved my fatigue〛.

ずっと〔副〕

zutto〔adv〕**by far, much more; long, far; all the time, throughout, all along; direct, straight, all the way**

① [比べてみて大きな違いのある様子]

① [by far, much more]

¶今日は昨日よりずっと暖かいですね。(Kyō wa kinō yori *zutto* atatakai desu ne.)

¶ It's **much** warmer today than yesterday, isn't it?

¶駅へ行くには、この道のほうがずっと近いですよ。(Eki e iku ni wa, kono michi no hō ga *zutto* chikai desu yo.)

¶ This road is **much** shorter for going to the station.

② [時間の隔たりがある様子]

② [long, far]

ずっと昔のこと (*zutto* mukashi no koto)

something **far** in the past

¶わたしがそのことを知ったのは、ずっとあとのことでした。(Watashi ga sono koto o shitta no wa, *zutto* ato no koto deshita.)

¶ I learned that **long** afterwards.

③ [初めから終わりまで続いている様子]

③ [all the time, throughout, all along]

¶わたしは東京に来てから、ずっとおじの家にいます。(Watashi wa Tōkyō ni kite kara, *zutto* oji no ie ni imasu.)

¶ I've been living at my uncle's **ever since** I came to Tokyo.

¶数年間、ずっとこの辞書の仕事をしてきたので、たいへん疲れました。(Sūnenkan, *zutto* kono jisho no shigoto o shite kita node, taihen tsukaremashita.)

¶ [I] am very tired after working on this dictionary for several years.

416

すっぱい 〔形〕

¶わたしはレモンのようなすっぱい果物は好きではありません。（Watashi wa remon no yō na *suppai* kudamono wa suki de wa arimasen.）

suppai 〔adj〕 **sour, acid, tart**

¶I don't like **sour** fruits like lemons.

すでに 既に 〔副〕

¶わたしが訪ねた時には、既に田中さんは出かけたあとでした。（Watashi ga tazuneta toki ni wa, *sudeni* Tanaka san wa dekaketa ato deshita.）

¶山田さんはこのことを既に知っていました。（Yamada san wa kono koto o *sudeni* shitte imashita.）

sudeni 〔adv〕 **already, previously, before**

¶When I went to see [her], [Mrs.] Tanaka had **already** left.

¶[Miss] Yamada **already** knew this.

すてる 捨てる 〔動Ⅱ〕

¶道路にごみを捨てないでください。（Dōro ni gomi o *sutenaide* kudasai.）

¶このねこはだれが捨てたのでしょうか。（Kono neko wa dare ga *suteta* no deshō ka？）

⇒拾う hirou

suteru 〔v Ⅱ〕 **throw away, discard, abandon, desert**

¶Please **don't litter** in the street.

¶I wonder who **abandoned** this cat.

ステレオ 〔名〕

¶ステレオが壊れてしまったので、来週、新しいのを買いに行きます。（Sutereo ga kowarete shimatta node, raishū, atarashii no o kai ni ikimasu.）

sutereo 〔n〕 **stereo**

¶The stereo has broken down so I am going to buy a new one next week.

ストーブ 〔名〕

電気ストーブ（denki-*sutōbu*）ガスストーブ（gasu-*sutōbu*）石油ストーブ（sekiyu-*sutōbu*）

¶寒くなりましたから、ストーブをつけましょうか。（Samuku narimashita kara, *sutōbu* o tsukemashō ka？）

sutōbu 〔n〕 **heater, stove**

an electric **heater** // a gas **heater** // a kerosene **heater**

¶It's gotten cold in here—shall I turn on **the heater?**

417

¶暑すぎますね。ストーブの火を消しましょう。(Atsusugimasu ne. *Sutōbu* no hi o keshimashō.)

¶ It's too hot. Let's turn off **the heater**.

すな 砂 〔名〕

¶目に砂が入って痛いです。(Me ni *suna* ga haitte itai desu.)

¶子供たちが庭で砂遊びをしています。(Kodomotachi ga niwa de *suna*asobi o shite imasu.)

suna 〔n〕 **sand, grit**

¶ My eye hurts because I've gotten **sand** in it.

¶ The children are playing in **the sand** out in the yard.

すなお 〔形動〕

¶あの子はすなおな子で、親や先生の言うことをよくききます。(Ano ko wa *sunao* na ko de, oya ya sensei no iu koto o yoku kikimasu.)

¶悪いことをしたのだから、すなおに謝りなさい。(Warui koto o shita no da kara, *sunao* ni ayamarinasai.)

sunao 〔adj-v〕 **mild, docile, honest, frank, guileless**

¶ That is an **obedient** child who minds [his] parents and teachers.

¶ You did wrong so apologize **with good grace**.

すなわち 〔接〕

¶わたしの高校では、40 パーセントの人、すなわち5人に2 人の人が大学に行きます。(Watashi no kōkō de wa, yonjippāsento no hito, *sunawachi* gonin ni futari no hito ga daigaku ni ikimasu.)

¶日本の人口の10パーセントが、首都すなわち東京に集中しています。(Nihon no jinkō no jippāsento ga, shuto *sunawachi* Tōkyō ni shūchū shite imasu.)

＊前のことがらを更に別の言葉で説明したり言い換えたりするときに使う。

sunawachi 〔conj〕 **namely, that is**

¶ Forty percent, **that is**, two out of five, of the students at my high school go on to college.

¶ Ten percent of the population of Japan is concentrated in the capital, **that is**, in Tokyo.

＊Used when explaining or expressing in different words what came before.

すばらしい 〔形〕

¶今日はすばらしい天気で、富士山がよく見えます。(Kyō wa *subarashii* tenki de, Fujisan ga yoku miemasu.)

subarashii 〔adj〕 **wonderful, splendid, grand, excellent**

¶ It's a **marvelous** day today—one can see Mount Fuji clearly.

¶山田さんはすばらしい成績で学校を卒業しました。(Yamada san wa *subarashii* seiseki de gakkō o sotsugyō shimashita.)

¶ [Miss] Yamada graduated from school with a **brilliant** academic record.

スピード〔名〕

スピードを出す(*supiido* o dasu)

¶この辺は道が狭いから、スピードを落として、注意しながら運転してください。(Kono hen wa michi ga semai kara, *supiido* o otoshite, chūi shinagara unten shite kudasai.)

supiido 〔n〕 speed

speed up, pick up **speed**

¶ The streets around here are narrow so please drive **slowly** and carefully.

スプーン〔名〕

¶スプーンでスープを飲みます。(*Supūn* de sūpu o nomimasu.)

supūn 〔n〕 spoon

¶ One eats soup with **a spoon**.

すべて〔名、副〕

1〔名〕

¶ここにあるすべてのおもちゃは外国製です。(Koko ni aru *subete* no omocha wa gaikokusei desu.)

¶あの人はすべての点でわたしより優れています。(Ano hito wa *subete* no ten de watashi yori sugurete imasu.)

2〔副〕

¶旅行の準備はすべて終わりました。(Ryokō no junbi wa *subete* owarimashita.)

subete 〔n, adv〕 all, everything; entirely

1 〔n〕

¶ **All** of the toys here are foreignmade.

¶ [He] is in **every** way my superior.

2 〔adv〕

¶ The preparations for the journey are 〚were〛 **all** complete.

すべる　滑る〔動Ⅰ〕

¶駅の階段で滑ってけがをしました。(Eki no kaidan de *subette* kega o shimashita.)

¶道が凍っていて滑りやすいから、気をつけてください。(Michi ga kootte ite *suberi*yasui kara, ki o tsukete kudasai.)

suberu 〔vⅠ〕 slip, slide

¶ [I] **slipped** on the station stairs and hurt [my]self.

¶ Please be careful—the road is icy and **slippery**.

スポーツ〔名〕

¶わたしはスポーツではテニスとピンポンが好きです。（Watashi wa *supōtsu* de wa tenisu to pinpon ga suki desu.）

supōtsu〔n〕**a sport, sports**

¶My favorite **sports** are tennis and ping-pong.

ズボン〔名〕

ズボンを脱ぐ（*zubon* o nugu）
¶田中さんはいつも茶色のズボンをはいています。（Tanaka san wa itsu mo chairo no *zubon* o haite imasu.）

zubon〔n〕**trousers, pants**

take off **one's trousers**
¶Mr. Tanaka always wears brown **trousers**.

すみ 炭〔名〕

¶炭で魚を焼きます。（*Sumi* de sakana o yakimasu.）

sumi〔n〕**charcoal**

¶[I] grill fish over **charcoal**.

すみ〔名〕

¶切手は普通、封筒の左上のすみにはります。（Kitte wa futsū, fūtō no hidariue no *sumi* ni harimasu.）
¶部屋のすみからすみまで捜しましたが、かぎは見つかりませんでした。（Heya no *sumi* kara *sumi* made sagashimashita ga, kagi wa mitsukarimasen deshita.）

sumi〔n〕**corner, nook**

¶Stamps are usually placed at the top left **corner** of the envelope.

¶[I] searched **every inch** of the room but couldn't find the keys.

すみません〔連〕

¶お待たせして、本当にすみませんでした。（Omatase shite, hontō ni *sumimasen* deshita.）
¶すみませんが、その荷物を取っていただけませんか。（*Sumimasen* ga, sono nimotsu o totte itadakemasen ka？）
⇒ごめんなさい **gomen nasai**

sumimasen〔compd〕**Excuse me, pardon me, I'm sorry, thank you; a phrase used when calling attention to oneself, asking something, apologizing, or expressing gratitude**

¶**I'm** very **sorry** to have kept you waiting.

¶**I'm sorry to trouble you**, but could you please hand me that package〚bag, etc.〛?

すむ 済む〔動Ⅰ〕

¶会議は4時に済みました。(Kaigi wa yoji ni *sumimashita*.)

¶仕事が済んだら、コーヒーでも飲みに行きましょう。(Shigoto ga *sundara*, kōhii demo nomi ni ikimashō.)

sumu 〔v Ⅰ〕 **end, be concluded**

¶ The meeting 〚conference〛 **ended** at four o'clock.

¶ Let's go have some coffee **after** work.

すむ 住む〔動Ⅰ〕

¶田中さんは今、大阪に住んでいます。(Tanaka san wa ima, Oosaka ni *sunde* imasu.)

¶兄は両親といっしょに住んでいます。(Ani wa ryōshin to issho ni *sunde* imasu.)

sumu 〔v Ⅰ〕 **live, reside, dwell**

¶ [Mrs.] Tanaka **is** now **living** in Osaka.

¶ My (elder) brother **is living** with our parents.

すもう 相撲〔名〕

相撲をとる (*sumō* o toru)

¶相撲は日本で人気のあるスポーツです。(*Sumō* wa Nihon de ninki no aru supōtsu desu.)

sumō 〔n〕 **sumo, sumo wrestling**

wrestle with

¶ *Sumo* is a popular sport in Japan.

スリッパ〔名〕

¶今まで使っていたスリッパが古くなってしまったので、新しいのを買いました。(Imamade tsukatte ita *surippa* ga furuku natte shimatta node, atarashii no o kaimashita.)

surippa 〔n〕 **slipper**

¶ Since the slippers that I was using were getting worn out, I bought some new ones.

する〔動Ⅲ〕

① [動作を行う]
¶今日はすることがたくさんあります。(Kyō wa *suru* koto ga takusan arimasu.)

¶あなたは日曜日にはいつも何をしていますか。(Anata wa nichiyōbi ni wa itsu mo nani o *shite* imasu ka？)

② [ある仕事などに従事する]

suru 〔v Ⅲ〕 **do; perform (a job); make; cost; pass, elapse**

① [do]

¶ [I] have many things **to do** today.

¶ What do you usually **do** on Sunday?

② [perform (a job), engage in]

¶田中さんはタクシーの運転手をしています。(Tanaka san wa takushii no untenshu o *shite* imasu.)

¶ [Mr.] Tanaka **is** a taxi driver.

¶姉は小学校の先生をしています。(Ane wa shōgakkō no sensei o *shite* imasu.)

¶ My (elder) sister **is** an elementary school teacher.

③ [人をあるものにならせる、ある地位につける]

③ [make, make into]

¶中村さんは息子さんを将来医者にするつもりだそうです。(Nakamura san wa musukosan o shōrai isha ni *suru* tsumori da sō desu.)

¶ I hear that [Mr.] Nakamura plans for [his] son **to become** a doctor.

¶山田さんをクラスの委員にしましょう。(Yamada san o kurasu no iin ni shimashō.)

¶ **Let's make** [Miss] Yamada the class representative.

④ [物をほかの形に変える、ほかの用途に使う]

④ [make, change, convert]

¶一万円札を千円札十枚にしてください。(Ichiman'ensatsu o sen'ensatsu jūmai ni *shite* kudasai.)

¶ Please **give me** 10 one-thousand yen bills for this ten-thousand yen bill.

¶あの人は本をまくらにして寝ています。(Ano hito wa hon o makura ni *shite* nete imasu.)

¶ [He] is sleeping **using** a book as a pillow.

⑤ [何かを感じる]

⑤ [make, produce, have]

¶この花はとてもいいにおいがします。(Kono hana wa totemo ii nioi ga *shimasu*.)

¶ This flower **is** very sweet-**smelling**.

¶二階で大きな音がしました。(Nikai de ookina oto ga *shimashita*.)

¶ There **was a** loud **noise** on the second floor.

*「〜がする(〜ga suru)」の形で使う。

*Used in the pattern "〜 *ga suru*."

⑥ [ものごとをある状態にならせる]

⑥ [make into a certain condition or state]

¶よく聞こえないから、ラジオの音をもう少し大きくしてください。(Yokukikoenai kara, rajio no oto o mō sukoshi ookiku *shite* kudasai.)

¶ Please **turn** the radio **up** a little—it's too low to hear.

¶部屋をきれいにしましょう。(Heya o kirei ni *shimashō*.)

¶ **Let's clean up** the room 〖apartment〗.

⑦ [ものごとがある状態である、ある性質を持っている]

⑦ [have, be in a certain condition or state]

円い形をしたテーブル (marui katachi o *shita* tēburu)

a round table

¶彼は大きな手をしています。(Kare wa ookina te o *shite* imasu.)

¶ He **has** big hands.

¶上田さんは怒った顔をして、部屋を出ていきました。(Ueda san wa okotta kao o *shite*, heya o dete ikimashita.)

¶ [Mrs.] Ueda left the room **with** an angry look on [her] face.

¶その果物はどんな色をしていますか。(Sono kudamono wa donna iro o *shite* imasu ka？)

¶ What color **is** that fruit?

⑧ [人などに対してある態度をとる]

⑧ [do, be]

¶おとなしくしていれば、お菓子を上げます。(Otonashiku *shite* ireba, okashi o agemasu.)

¶ If you **behave** yourself, I'll give you a sweet.

¶お年寄りには親切にしてあげましょう。(Otoshiyori ni wa shinsetsu ni *shite* agemashō.)

¶ Everyone **should be** kind to the elderly.

¶わたしが病気の時、上田さんはとても優しくしてくれました。(Watashi ga byōki no toki, Ueda san wa totemo yasashiku *shite* kuremashita.)

¶ When I was ill [Miss] Ueda **was** very kind to me.

⑨ [値段を表す]

⑨ [cost]

¶その時計はいくらしましたか。(Sono tokei wa ikura *shimashita* ka？)

¶ How much did that watch 〖clock〗 **cost?**

¶この部屋は一泊二万円もするそうです。(Kono heya wa ippaku niman'en mo *suru* sōdesu.)

¶ They say that this room **costs** twenty thousand yen a day.

⑩ [時間が経過する]

⑩ [pass, elapse]

¶もう少しすると、御飯ですよ。(Mō sukoshi *suru* to, gohan desu yo.)

¶ Dinner 〖lunch, breakfast, etc.〗 will be ready **in** a little while.

¶あと1か月すれば卒業です。(Ato ikkagetsu *sureba* sotsugyō desu.)

¶ It's only a month **until** graduation.

*「すると（suru to）」「すれば
（sureba）」「したら（shitara）」の形で、
未来のことを言うときに使う。

⑪ [決める]

¶お飲み物は何にしますか。
(Onomimono wa nan ni *shimasu* ka？)

¶来月、京都へ旅行することにしまし
た。(Raigetsu, Kyōto e ryokō suru koto
ni *shimashita*.)

*名詞の場合は「名詞＋にする（ni
suru）」、動詞の場合は「動詞（連体の
形）＋ことにする（koto ni suru）」の形
で使う。

⑫ [これから動作を行う状態であるこ
とを表す]

¶うちを出ようとすると、雨が降って
きました。(Uchi o deyō to *suru* to, ame
ga futte kimashita.)

¶今、あなたに電話しようとしていた
ところです。(Ima, anata ni denwa shiyō
to *shite* ita tokoro desu.)

*「動詞（う・ようの形）＋とする
（to suru）」の形で使う。

＊「する（suru）」はある名詞や副詞に
ついて動詞を作る。「勉強（benkyō）」
は「勉強する（benkyō suru）」、「ぼん
やり（bon'yari）」は、「ぼんやりする
（bon'yari suru）」となる。

すると〔接〕

①[前のことがらを受けてその時その
場面で起こったことがらや気づいたこ
とがらなどをあとに続けるときに使う]

¶電気が暗くなりました。すると、ど
こからか静かな音楽が流れてきまし
た。(Denki ga kuraku narimashita.

*Used in the patterns "*suru to*,"
"*sureba*," and "*shitara*" to refer to a
future happening.

⑪ [decide]

¶ What **will you have** to drink?

¶ [I] **have decided** to take a trip to
Kyoto next month.

*For nouns, used in the pattern "noun
+ *ni suru*." For verbs, used in the
pattern "verb (dictionary form) + *koto
ni suru*."

⑫ [try to, be about to]

¶ **As I was leaving** the house it started
to rain.

¶ **I was just now trying to** telephone
you.

*Used in the pattern "verb (-*ō* 〚-*yō*〛
form) + *to suru*."

＊*Suru* combines with certain nouns
and adverbs to form a new verb. For
example *benkyō* (study, studying)
becomes *benkyō suru* (to study) and
bon'yari (absentmindedness) becomes
bon'yari suru (to act absentmindedly).

suruto 〚conj〛 **thereupon, just
then; then, if so**

① [thereupon, just then, and then]

¶ The lights were lowered. **And then**
soft music could be heard drifting on
the air.

Suruto, doko kara ka shizuka na ongaku ga nagarete kimashita.)

¶ ドアを開けました。すると、部屋に知らない人が立っていました。(Doa o akemashita. *Suruto*, heya ni shiranai hito ga tatte imashita.)

*普通、前の文も「すると（suruto）」のあとの文も動詞の過去・完了を表す「たの形」が来る。また、あとに話し手が自分の意志で決めることができるような内容の文は来ない。「ドアの前に立ちました。すると、ドアが開きました。(Doa no mae ni tachimashita. Suruto, doa ga akimashita.)」はいいが、「ドアの前に立ちました。すると、ドアを開けました。(Doa no mae ni tachimashita. Suruto, doa o akemashita.)」とは言えない。

② [前のことがらを受けてそのことから当然起こると考えられることなどを言うときに使う]

¶「大きな台風が近づいているそうです。」(Ookina taifū ga chikazuite iru sō desu.)「すると、あしたは出発は無理ですね。」(*Suruto*, ashita wa shuppatsu wa muri desu ne.)

するどい 鋭い〔形〕

① [とがっている、よく切れる]

¶ 書きやすいように鉛筆の先を鋭くしておきました。(Kakiyasui yō ni enpitsu no saki o *surudoku* shite okimashita.)

¶ このナイフは先が鋭いから、気をつけて使いなさい。(Kono naifu wa saki ga *surudoi* kara, ki o tsukete tsukainasai.)

② [頭の働きが速い]

¶ I opened the door. **And** a stranger was standing there inside the room.

*Usually the verbs in both clauses are in the *-ta* form expressing past or completed action. The clause with *suruto* does not express something decided by the will of the speaker. Thus "*Doa no mae ni tachimashita. Suruto, doa ga akimashita*" (I stood in front of the door. And then the door opened) is possible, but one cannot say * " *Doa no mae ni tachimashita. Suruto, doa o akemashita*" (I stood in front of the door. And then I opened the door).

② [then, if so, in that case, if that's the case]

¶ "I hear a large typhoon is approaching."
"**If that's so**, [we] won't be able to leave on [our] trip tomorrow."

surudoi 〔adj〕 **pointed, sharp; quick, smart**

① [pointed, sharp]

¶ [I] **sharpened** the pencils so they would be easy to write with.

¶ Please be careful as this knife is **sharply pointed**.

② [quick, smart, shrewd, acute, keen]

¶田中さんはとても頭の鋭い人です。
(Tanaka san wa totemo atama no *surudoi* hito desu.)

¶ [Mr.] Tanaka is very **quick-witted** 〚has a **keen** intelligence〛.

すわる　座る〔動 I〕

suwaru 〔v I〕 **sit down, take a seat**

¶どうぞ、ここに座ってください。
(Dōzo, koko ni *suwatte* kudasai.)

¶ Please **sit down** here.

¶日本の旅館では、畳に座って御飯を食べます。(Nihon no ryokan de wa, tatami ni *suwatte* gohan o tabemasu.)

¶ In a Japanese-style inn one eats **sitting** on the *tatami*-mat floor.

せ

せ 背 〔名〕

① [背中]
背にかごを負う （se ni kago o ou）
② [身長、物の高さ]
背が伸びる （se ga nobiru）
¶ 上田さんは背が高いですね。（Ueda san wa *se* ga takai desu ne.）
¶ 田中さんのほうが、わたしより5センチ背が低いです。（Tanaka san no hōga, watashi yori gosenchi *se* ga hikui desu.）
¶ 門のそばに背の高い木が2本あります。（Mon no soba ni *se* no takai ki ga nihon arimasu.）
＊「背 (sei)」とも言う。
→背 sei

se 〔n〕 the back; height, stature

① [the back]
carry a basket on **one's back**
② [height, stature]
grow taller
¶ [Mr.] Ueda **is tall**, isn't [he]?

¶ [Miss] Tanaka is five centimeters **shorter** than I am.

¶ There are two **tall** trees near the gate.

＊Variant: *sei*.

せい 背 〔名〕

背が低い人 （*sei* ga hikui hito）
¶ このクラスでは、だれがいちばん背が高いですか。（Kono kurasu de wa, dare ga ichiban *sei* ga takai desu ka？）
¶ あの背の高い木は何という名前ですか。（Ano *sei* no takai ki wa nan to iu namae desu ka？）
＊「背 (se)」とも言う。
⇒背 se

sei 〔n〕 height, stature

a **short** person
¶ Who is the **tallest** student in this class?

¶ What is the name of that **tall** tree?

＊Variant: *se*.

せい 〔名〕

¶ 風邪を引いたせいか、頭が痛いです。（Kaze o hiita *sei* ka, atama ga itai desu.）
¶ この事業に失敗したのは、山田さんのせいです。（Kono jigyō ni shippai shita no wa, yamada san no *sei* desu.）

sei 〔n〕 be due to ～, because of ～, be the fault of ～

¶ I have a headache, perhaps **from** a cold.

¶ [Mr.] Yamada **is to blame** for the failure of this project.

-せい -製 〔尾〕

① [物が作られた国や会社などを表す]

¶わたしはアメリカ製の万年筆を持っています。（Watashi wa Amerika*sei* no mannenhitsu o motte imasu.）

¶Ａ社製の時計はたいへんいいです。（Ē-sha*sei* no tokei wa taihen ii desu.）

② [材料を表す]

¶ナイロン製のくつ下は、絹のくつ下より丈夫だそうです。（Nairon*sei* no kutsushita wa, kinu no kutsushita yori jōbu da sō desu.）

せいかく 正確 〔形動〕

¶この時計は正確ですか。（Kono tokei wa *seikaku* desu ka？）

¶この言葉はなかなか正確に発音できません。（Kono kotoba wa nakanaka *seikaku* ni hatsuon dekimasen.）

せいかく 性格 〔名〕

① [人の性質]

性格がいい（*seikaku* ga ii）性格が似ている（*seikaku* ga nite iru）

¶あの二人は性格が合わないから、けんかばかりしています。（Ano futari wa *seikaku* ga awanai kara, kenka bakari shite imasu.）

¶明るい性格の人はみんなに好かれます。（Akarui *seikaku* no hito wa minna ni sukaremasu.）

② [ものの性質]

¶それとこれとは、問題の性格が違います。（Sore to kore to wa, mondai no *seikaku* ga chigaimasu.）

-sei 〔suf〕 make, manufacture

① [indicates the place of manufacture or the manufacturer]

¶I own an American-**made** fountainpen.

¶The watches 〖clocks〗 **made** by Company A are very good.

② [indicates the raw material]

¶They say that **nylon** socks 〖stockings〗 are stronger than silk ones.

seikaku 〔adj-v〕 accurate, precise, exact, correct

¶Is this clock **right**?

¶[I] just can't pronounce this word **right**.

seikaku 〔n〕 character, personality; character, nature

① [(human) character, personality]

be a good person // have similar **personalities**

¶Those two **are incompatible** and are always fighting.

¶**Sunny** persons are liked by all.

② [character, nature (of things)]

¶These two matters are completely different **in nature**.

せいかつ 生活〔名、〜する〕

家庭生活（katei-*seikatsu*）生活費（*seikatsu*hi）

¶月給が安くて、生活が苦しいです。（Gekkyū ga yasukute, *seikatsu* ga kurushii desu.）

¶わたしは外国で生活したことがありません。（Watashi wa gaikoku de *seikatsu* shita koto ga arimasen.）

seikatsu 〔n, 〜*suru*〕 life, existence, livelihood, living

family **life**, domestic **life** // **living** expenses, the cost of **living**

¶ [My] wages are low and it's hard to make ends meet.

¶ I have never **lived** abroad.

-せいき -世紀〔尾〕

紀元前3世紀（kigenzen san*seiki*）20世紀（nijis*seiki*）

-seiki 〔suf〕 century

the third **century** B.C. // the 20th **century**

せいきゅう 請求〔名、〜する〕

請求書（*seikyū*sho）請求を受ける（*seikyū* o ukeru）

¶本屋から本代の請求が来ました。（Hon'ya kara hondai no *seikyū* ga kimashita.）

¶あの人に請求しても、お金がないのですから、払えないと思いますよ。（Ano hito ni *seikyū* shite mo, okane ga nai no desu kara, haraenai to omoimasu yo.）

seikyū 〔n, 〜*suru*〕 demand, request, claim, application

a bill // receive a bill, be billed

¶ **A bill** came from the bookstore.

¶ **Even if you demand payment** from [him], I don't think [he] has the money to pay you.

ぜいきん 税金〔名〕

¶父は税務署へ税金を納めに行きました。（Chichi wa zeimusho e *zeikin* o osame ni ikimashita.）

zeikin 〔n〕 a tax

¶ My father has gone to the tax office to pay **our taxes**.

せいけつ 清潔〔名、形動〕

¶この食堂はとても清潔です。（Kono shokudō wa totemo *seiketsu* desu.）

¶中村さんはいつも清潔なシャツを着ています。（Nakamura san wa itsu mo *seiketsu* na shatsu o kite imasu.）

seiketsu 〔n, adj-v〕 clean, neat, pure

¶ This eating place is very **clean and neat**.

¶ [Mr.] Nakamura is always wearing a **clean** shirt.

せいげん　制限〔名、〜する〕

制限時間 (seigen-jikan)

¶この会の会員には、年齢の制限はありません。(Kono kai no kaiin ni wa, nenrei no *seigen* wa arimasen.)

¶飛行機に載せる荷物は、20キロに制限されています。(Hikōki ni noseru nimotsu wa, nijikkiro ni *seigen* sarete imasu.)

seigen 〔n, 〜*suru*〕 **restriction, limitation, limit**

a time **limit**

¶There is no **minimum or maximum** age for members of this club 〚association, society〛.

¶The luggage of air passengers **is restricted** to 20 kilos.

せいこう　成功〔名、〜する〕

¶実験は大成功でした。(Jikken wa dai*seikō* deshita.)

¶御成功を祈ります。(Go*seikō* o inorimasu.)

¶人間はついに月へ行くことに成功しました。(Ningen wa tsuini tsuki e iku koto ni *seikō* shimashita.)

⇔失敗 shippai

seikō 〔n, 〜*suru*〕 **success**

¶The experiment was a great **success**.

¶I wish you **success**.

¶Humanity finally **succeeded** in going to the moon.

せいさく　製作〔名、〜する〕

製作費 (*seisaku*hi) 製作所 (*seisaku*jo)

¶この工場では、農業機械を製作しています。(Kono kōjō de wa, nōgyō-kikai o *seisaku* shite imasu.)

¶この映画は、日本文化を紹介するために製作されたものです。(Kono eiga wa, Nihon-bunka o shōkai suru tame ni *seisaku* sareta mono desu.)

seisaku 〔n, 〜*suru*〕 **manufacture, production**

the **production** cost // a factory, a plant

¶This factory **manufactures** farm machinery.

¶This movie **was made** in order to introduce Japanese culture to others.

せいさく　政策〔名〕

外交政策 (gaikō-*seisaku*) 経済政策 (keizai-*seisaku*) 農業政策 (nōgyō-*seisaku*) 政策を立てる (*seisaku* o tateru)

seisaku 〔n〕 **policy**

foreign **policy** // economic **policy** // agricultural **policy** // formulate **a policy**

¶この国の政府は、外国製品の輸入について厳しい政策をとっています。
(Kono kuni no seifu wa, gaikokuseihin no yunyū ni tsuite kibishii *seisaku* o totte imasu.)

¶The government of this country is taking a hard **line** on foreign imports.

せいさん　生産 〔名、〜する〕

生産高 (*seisan*daka) 生産者 (*seisan*sha) 生産技術 (*seisan*-gijutsu)

seisan 〔n, 〜*suru*〕 **production**
the output, the yield // **a producer, a maker** // **manufacturing** techniques, **industrial** technology

¶この工場では、一日何台の自動車が生産されているのですか。(Kono kōjō de wa, ichinichi nandai no jidōsha ga *seisan* sarete iru no desu ka？)

¶How many cars **are produced** a day at this plant?

¶静岡県はお茶の生産地として有名です。(Shizuoka-ken wa ocha no *seisan*chi to shite yūmei desu.)

¶Shizuoka Prefecture is famous as a tea-**producing** center.

せいじ　政治 〔名〕

政治家 (*seiji*ka) 政治運動 (*seiji*-undō)

seiji 〔n〕 **politics, political affairs, government**
a politician, a statesman // a political movement; a political campaign

¶この国の政治家は立派な政治を行っています。(Kono kuni no *seiji*ka wa rippa na *seiji* o okonatte imasu.)

¶**The politicians** in this country are conducting **the affairs of state** well.

せいしき　正式 〔名、形動〕

seishiki 〔n, adj-v〕 **formal, official, regular, full-dress**

¶それは結婚式のときに着る正式な服ではありません。(Sore wa kekkonshiki no toki ni kiru *seishiki* na fuku de wa arimasen.)

¶That is not **proper** dress for a wedding.

¶田中さんが社長になるといううわさがあったが、今日正式に発表がありました。(Tanaka san ga shachō ni naru to iu uwasa ga atta ga, kyō *seishiki* ni happyō ga arimashita.)

¶There had been a rumor that [Mr.] Tanaka would be the next company president, and that was **officially** announced today.

431

せいしつ 性質 〔名〕

seishitsu 〔n〕 nature, temperament; property, quality, character

① [人が生まれつき持っている感情や考え方]

¶「山田さんはどんな性質の人ですか。」(Yamada san wa donna *seishitsu* no hito desu ka？)「山田さんは、とてもおとなしい人です。」(Yamada san wa totemo otonashii hito desu.)

① [nature, temperament, disposition]

¶ "What **is** [Mr.] Yamada **like?**" "[He]'s very mild-mannered."

② [ものごとに本来備わっている特色]

¶ 木綿と絹とは性質が違います。(Momen to kinu to wa *seishitsu* ga chigaimasu.)

¶ このことは問題の性質上みんなに知らせないほうがいいでしょう。(Kono koto wa mondai no *seishitsu*jō minna ni shirasenai hō ga ii deshō.)

② [property, quality, character, nature]

¶ Cotton and silk are different **in nature**.

¶ Because of **its nature**, this matter should probably be kept secret.

せいしょ 聖書 〔名〕

seisho 〔n〕 the Bible, the Scriptures

旧約聖書 (kyūyaku-*seisho*) 新約聖書 (shin'yaku-*seisho*)

the Old **Testament** // the New **Testament**

¶ わたしが子供の時、母がよく聖書を読んでくれました。(Watashi ga kodomo no toki, haha ga yoku *seisho* o yonde kuremashita.)

¶ When I was small my mother often read to me from **the Bible**.

せいしん 精神 〔名〕

seishin 〔n〕 mind, spirit, soul, will

精神病 (*seishin*byō) 精神力 (*seishin*ryoku) 精神的 (*seishin*teki)

mental illness // spiritual strength; the power of **the mind** // spiritual, mental, moral

¶ あの人は精神が異常のようです。(Ano hito wa *seishin* ga ijō no yō desu.)

¶ 田中さんは、どんな苦しみにも負けない強い精神を持っています。(Tanaka san wa, donna kurushimi ni mo makenai tsuyoi *seishin* o motte imasu.)

¶ [He] appears to be not in [his] right **mind**.

¶ [Mrs.] Tanaka has a strong **spirit** such that [she] is not defeated no matter what hardship [she] might meet.

せいせき　成績〔名〕

成績が悪い（seiseki ga warui）成績が上がる（seiseki ga agaru）

¶あまり勉強しなかったので、成績が下がりました。（Amari benkyō shinakatta node, seiseki ga sagarimashita.）
¶試験の成績がよかったので、先生にほめられました。（Shiken no seiseki ga yokatta node, sensei ni homeraremashita.）

seiseki 〔n〕 result, record, showing, score

do poorly at school, get poor **grades**; make a poor **showing** (in business, etc.) // show a better **record** (in school, business, etc.)

¶ [My] **grades** fell as [I] didn't study very much.

¶ My teacher praised me for my good **mark** on the exam.

せいちょう　成長〔名、〜する〕
¶太郎君は立派に成長して医者になりました。（Tarō kun wa rippa ni seichō shite isha ni narimashita.）
¶この会社は戦後、急に成長したのです。（Kono kaisha wa sengo, kyū ni seichō shita no desu.）

seichō 〔n, 〜suru〕 growth

¶ Tarō **has grown** into a fine man and is now a doctor 〚Tarō **grew** into a fine man and became a doctor〛.
¶ This company **grew** rapidly in the postwar period.

せいちょう　生長〔名、〜する〕
¶暖かい所では、草や木の生長が速いです。（Atatakai tokoro de wa, kusa ya ki no seichō ga hayai desu.）

seichō 〔n, 〜suru〕 growth

¶ Grasses and trees **grow** rapidly in warm climates.

せいと　生徒〔名〕

小学校の生徒（shōgakkō no seito）
¶わたしは中学校の生徒に英語を教えています。（Watashi wa chūgakkō no seito ni Eigo o oshiete imasu.）

seito 〔n〕 student, pupil, schoolboy, schoolgirl

an elementary school **student**
¶ I am teaching English to junior high school **students**.

せいど　制度〔名〕
教育制度（kyōiku-seido）選挙制度（senkyo-seido）

seido 〔n〕 system

a school **system** // an electoral **system**

¶来年から新しい奨学金の制度が作られます。(Rainen kara atarashii shōgakukin no *seido* ga tsukuraremasu.)

¶ There will be a new **system** for scholarships starting next year.

せいねん　青年〔名〕

seinen 〔n〕 **a youth, young people, the younger generation, a young man**

¶青年時代に、できるだけ多くの本を読んでおいたほうがいいですよ。(*Seinen*-jidai ni, dekiru dake ooku no hon o yonde oita hō ga ii desu yo.)

¶ It is best to read as many books as possible during **one's youth**.

¶山田さんの息子さんは、もう立派な青年になりました。(Yamada san no musukosan wa, mō rippa na *seinen* ni narimashita.)

¶ [Mr.] Yamada's son has grown into a fine **young man**.

せいねんがっぴ　生年月日〔名〕

seinengappi 〔n〕 **one's date of birth**

¶名前と生年月日をここに書いてください。(Namae to *seinengappi* o koko ni kaite kudasai.)

¶ Please write your name and **date of birth** here.

せいひん　製品〔名〕

seihin 〔n〕 **a product, manufactured goods**

電気製品（denki-*seihin*）繊維製品（sen'i-*seihin*）外国製品（gaikoku*seihin*）

electrical **products** // textile **goods** // foreign-made **articles**

¶あなたの会社では、どういう製品を作っているのですか。(Anata no kaisha de wa, dōiu *seihin* o tsukutte iru no desu ka?)

¶ What kind of **goods** does your company make?

せいふ　政府〔名〕

seifu 〔n〕 **the government**

日本政府（Nihon-*seifu*）

the Japanese **government**

¶政府は今年の予算を決めました。(*Seifu* wa kotoshi no yosan o kimemashita.)

¶ **The government** has decided this year's budget.

せいぶつ　生物〔名〕

¶生物を大きく分けると、動物と植物になります。(*Seibutsu* o ookiku wakeru to, dōbutsu to shokubutsu ni narimasu.)
¶この地球には、数えられないくらい多くの生物がいます。(Kono chikyu ni wa, kazoerarenai kurai ooku no *seibutsu* ga imasu.)

seibutsu〔n〕**a living creature, life**

¶**Living creatures** can be broadly divided into plants and animals.

¶The number of **living creatures** on earth is beyond count.

せいめい　生命〔名〕

生命保険（*seimei*-hoken)
¶戦争で多くの生命が失われました。(Sensō de ooku no *seimei* ga ushinawaremashita.)

seimei〔n〕**life, existence, the soul**

life insurance
¶Much **life** was lost in the war.

せいよう　西洋〔名〕

西洋人（*seiyō*jin)　西洋史（*seiyō*shi)
¶この辺には西洋風の建物が並んでいます。(Kono hen ni wa *seiyō*fū no tatemono ga narande imasu.)
⇔東洋 tōyō

seiyō〔n〕**the West, the Occident**

a Westerner // **Western** history
¶There are many **Western**-style buildings (i.e., homes) around here.

せいり　整理〔名、〜する〕

交通整理（kōtsū-*seiri*)
¶お客が来るので、部屋の中を整理しました。(Okyaku ga kuru node, heya no naka o *seiri* shimashita.)
¶このノートはまだ整理してありませんから、読みにくいかもしれませんよ。(Kono nōto wa mada *seiri* shite arimasen kara, yominikui ka mo shiremasen yo.)

seiri〔n, 〜*suru*〕**arranging, adjustment, regulation, putting in order**

traffic **control**
¶[I] **straightened up** the room as a guest is 『was』 coming.

¶These notes **aren't edited** yet so they may be hard to read.

せいれき　西暦〔名〕

¶わたしは西暦 1936 年に生まれました。(Watashi wa *seireki* senkyūhyaku-sanjūrokunen ni umaremashita.)

seireki〔n〕**the Christian era, A.D.**

¶I was born in 1936.

セーター〔名〕

¶上田さんは黒いセーターを着ています。(Ueda san wa kuroi *sētā* o kite imasu.)

¶寒ければ、セーターを着なさい。(Samukereba, *sētā* o kinasai.)

sētā〔n〕**sweater**

¶ [Miss] Ueda is wearing a black **sweater**.

¶ Put on **a sweater** if you're cold.

せかい 世界〔名〕

世界一 (*sekai*ichi) 世界史 (*sekai*shi)

¶世界でいちばん高い山はエベレストです。(*Sekai* de ichiban takai yama wa Eberesuto desu.)

sekai〔n〕**the world, the earth, the globe**

the greatest in **the world** // **world** history

¶ The highest mountain in **the world** is Mount Everest.

せき 席〔名〕

席を離れる (*seki* o hanareru) 席へもどる (*seki* e modoru) 席を立つ (*seki* o tatsu)

¶席に着いてください。(*Seki* ni tsuite kudasai)

¶電車はこんでいて、席がありませんでした。(Densha wa konde ite, *seki* ga arimasen deshita.)

⇒座席 **zaseki**

seki〔n〕**seat, one's place**

leave **one's seat** 〚**desk**〛 // return to **one's seat** 〚**desk**〛 // get up from **one's seat**

¶ Please take **your seat(s)**.

¶ The train was crowded; there were no empty **seats**.

せき〔名〕

¶よくせきをしますね。風邪を引いたのですか。(Yoku *seki* o shimasu ne. Kaze o hiita no desu ka?)

¶ゆうべは一晩じゅうせきが出て、眠れませんでした。(Yūbe wa hitobanjū *seki* ga dete, nemuremasen deshita.)

seki〔n〕**cough, coughing**

¶ You **are coughing** a lot. Have you caught a cold?

¶ I was up all last night **with a cough**.

せきたん 石炭〔名〕

石炭産業 (*sekitan*-sangyō)

sekitan〔n〕**coal**

the **coal** industry

せきどう 赤道〔名〕

¶赤道に近づくにしたがって、だんだん暑くなります。(*Sekidō* ni chikazuku ni shitagatte, dandan atsuku narimasu.)

sekidō〔n〕**the equator**

¶ It gets hotter and hotter as one nears **the equator**.

436

せきにん 責任 〔名〕

責任者（*sekinin*sha）責任を果たす
（*sekinin* o hatasu）責任をとる（*sekinin* o toru）

¶この事業が失敗したのは、わたしの責任です。(Kono jigyō ga shippai shita no wa, watashi no *sekinin* desu.)

¶仕事を引き受けたら、責任を持ってやらなければなりません。(Shigoto o hikiuketara, *sekinin* o motte yaranakereba narimasen.)

sekinin 〔n〕 **responsibility, obligation, duty**

the person **in charge** // fulfill **one's responsibility**, do **one's duty** // take **responsibility** for

¶ I **am responsible** for the failure of this undertaking.

¶ If you accept a job you must take on **the responsibility** for it.

せきゆ 石油 〔名〕

石油ストーブ（*sekiyu*-sutōbu）

¶今では、石炭より石油のほうが多く使われています。(Ima de wa, sekitan yori *sekiyu* no hō ga ooku tsukawarete imasu.)

sekiyu 〔n〕 **petroleum, kerosene**

a **kerosene** heater

¶ Nowadays **oil** is used more widely than coal.

せけん 世間 〔名〕

¶世間を騒がせたどろぼうも、ついに捕まりました。(*Seken* o sawagaseta dorobō mo, tsuini tsukamarimashita.)

¶わたしは世間を離れて、一人で山の中で暮らしたいです。(Watashi wa *seken* o hanarete, hitori de yama no naka de kurashitai desu.)

seken 〔n〕 **world, people, the public, society**

¶ The thief that **everyone** was talking about has finally been caught 〖was caught in the end〗.

¶ I would like to leave **the world** behind and go live alone in the mountains.

せっかく 〔副、〜の〕

① [あることのためにわざわざ努力するという意味を表す]

¶せっかく来たのに、田中さんは留守でした。(*Sekkaku* kita noni, Tanaka san wa rusu deshita.)

sekkaku 〔adv, 〜*no*〕 **specially, on purpose, with much trouble; precious; kindly**

① [specially, on purpose, expressly, with much trouble, at great pains]

¶ Even though [I] **came all the way** to see [him], [Mr.] Tanaka wasn't at home.

¶せっかく日本に来たのですから、もう一年日本で勉強したいと思います。(*Sekkaku* Nihon ni kita no desu kara, mō ichinen Nihon de benkyō shitai to omoimasu.)

¶ As I have **come all the way** to Japan, I would like to study here one more year.

¶せっかくの努力がむだになりました。(*Sekkaku* no doryoku ga muda ni narimashita.)

¶ **All** [our] efforts were 〖have been〗 in vain.

② [めったになくて貴重だという意味を表す]

② [precious, long-awaited]

¶せっかくの日曜日なのに、朝から用事ができてゆっくり休めませんでした。(*Sekkaku* no nichiyōbi na noni, asa kara yōji ga dekite yukkuri yasumemasen deshita.)

¶ Even though it was Sunday, I had various things to do from morning on so I couldn't just relax and take it easy.

¶せっかくの旅行だから、みんな参加することにしましょう。(*Sekkaku* no ryokō da kara, minna sanka suru koto ni shimashō.)

¶ Let's all be sure to go on the trip as **it's not something we can do every day**.

③ [相手の好意に感謝の気持ちを表しながらその意に添えないことを表す]

③ [kindly]

¶せっかくの御招待ですが、あいにく用事があって行けません。(*Sekkaku* no goshōtai desu ga, ainiku yōji ga atte ikemasen.)

¶ **It's very kind** of you to invite me, but unfortunately I have another appointment and won't be able to go.

¶せっかくですが、あしたの会には出席できません。(*Sekkaku* desu ga, ashita no kai ni wa shusseki dekimasen.)

¶ **Thank you** for asking me, but I won't be able to attend tomorrow's meeting 〖gathering, get-together, etc.〗.

せっきょくてき 積極的 〔形動〕

sekkyokuteki 〔adj-v〕 **positive, active, vigorous, aggressive**

積極的な人 (*sekkyokuteki* na hito)

an **aggressive** person

¶積極的な御意見をどうぞお出しください。(*Sekkyokuteki* na goiken o dōzo odashi kudasai.)

¶ Please **don't hesitate** to give your opinions.

¶田中さんはこの仕事に積極的に参加しています。(Tanaka san wa kono shigoto ni *sekkyokuteki* ni sanka shite imasu.)
⇔消極的 shōkyokuteki

¶ [Miss] Tanaka is taking an **active** part in this work.

せっけん 石けん〔名〕

¶石けんで顔を洗います。(*Sekken* de kao o araimasu.)

sekken〔n〕**soap**

¶ [I] wash [my] face with **soap**.

ぜったい 絶対〔副〕

¶このことは絶対にほかの人に話さないでくださいね。(Kono koto wa *zettai* ni hoka no hito ni hanasanaide kudasai ne.)

¶わたしはその意見には絶対反対です。(Watashi wa sono iken ni wa *zettai* hantaidesu.)

＊「絶対に(zettai ni)」の形でも使う。

zettai〔adv〕**absolutely, unconditionally, positively**

¶ Please be **absolutely sure** not to speak of this to anyone.

¶ I am **unconditionally** opposed to that position.

＊Also used in the form *zettai ni*.

せつび 設備〔名、〜する〕

暖房設備(danbō-*setsubi*)冷房設備(reibō-*setsubi*)

¶このホテルは設備がよくありません。(Kono hoteru wa *setsubi* ga yoku arimasen.)

setsubi〔n, 〜*suru*〕**equipment, facilities, accommodations, arrangements**
heating **facilities** // air conditioning

¶ **The accommodations** at this hotel are poor.

せつめい 説明〔名、〜する〕

¶田中先生の説明はとてもわかりやすいです。(Tanaka sensei no *setsumei* wa totemo wakariyasui desu.)

¶その言葉の意味をもう一度説明してください。(Sono kotoba no imi o mō ichido *setsumei* shite kudasai.)

setsumei〔n, 〜*suru*〕**explanation, interpretation, elucidation**

¶ Professor Tanaka's **explanations** are very easy to understand.

¶ Please **explain** again the meaning of that word.

せなか　背中 〔名〕

¶おふろで中村さんに背中を洗っても
らいました。（Ofuro de Nakamura san ni
senaka o aratte moraimashita.）

ぜひ 〔副〕

¶ぜひ、わたしのうちへ遊びに来てく
ださい。（Zehi, watashi no uchi e asobi
ni kite kudasai.）
¶日本へ行ったら、ぜひ京都へ行って
みたいと思っています。（Nihon e
ittara, *zehi* Kyōto e itte mitaito omottei
masu.）

せびろ　背広 〔名〕

¶昨日、冬用の背広をクリーニングに
出しました。（Kinō, fuyuyō no *sebiro* o
kurīningu ni dashimashita.）

せまい　狭い 〔形〕

¶この部屋は狭いですね。（Kono heya
wa *semai* desu ne.）
¶この道は狭くて自動車が通れませ
ん。（Kono michi wa *semakute* jidōsha ga
tooremasen.）
⇔広い hiroi

セメント 〔名〕

¶セメントに砂などを混ぜて水を加え
ると、コンクリートができます。
（*Semento* ni suna nado o mazete mizu o
kuwaeru to, konkuriito ga dekimasu.）

せる 〔助動〕

① [他に対してある行為を実現するよ
うに仕向ける意味を表す]

senaka 〔n〕 **the back**

¶ [Mr.] Nakamura washed **my back** at
the public bath.

zehi 〔adv〕 **without fail, by all
means**

¶ **Do** come and visit me at home some
time.

¶ If I go to Japan, I want **by all means**
to visit Kyoto.

sebiro 〔n〕 **suit**

¶ I took my winter suit to the cleaners
yesterday.

semai 〔adj〕 **narrow, small,
limited, restricted, cramped**

¶ This room **is small**, isn't it?

¶ This street is **too narrow** for cars.

semento 〔n〕 **cement**

¶ One makes concrete by mixing sand
and the like with **cement** and then
adding water.

-seru 〔auxil〕 **a verb ending
expressing the causative, etc.**

① [make do, cause to do, have do]

¶病気をして、両親を心配させました。(Byōki o shite, ryōshin o shinpai *sasemashita*.)

¶ [I] **caused** worry to [my] parents with [my] illness.

¶先生が学生に本を読ませます。(Sensei ga gakusei ni hon o yoma*semasu*.)

¶ The teacher **has** the students read the book.

¶病気が治ったばかりですから、あまり無理な運動はさせないほうがいいです。(Byōki ga naotta bakari desu kara, amari muri na undō wa sa*senai* hō ga ii desu.)

¶ As [he] has just recovered from [his] illness, you **should not let** [him] exercise too strenuously.

②[他の人がある行為をするのを許容あるいは黙認する意味を表す]

② [let do, allow to do]

¶子供を夜遅くまで外で遊ばせておくのはよくないです。(Kodomo o yoru osoku made soto de asoba*sete* oku no wa yoku nai desu.)

¶ You shouldn't **let** the children play outside until so late at night.

¶今年は、娘が希望していた海外旅行に行かせることにしました。(Kotoshi wa, musume ga kibō shite ita kaigai-ryokō ni ika*seru* koto ni shimashita.)

¶ [We]'ve decided **to let** [our] daughter travel abroad this year as she has been wanting to do.

＊Ⅰ型動詞とⅢ型動詞の「する(suru)」につく。

＊-*seru* is added to Type I verbs and the Type III verb *suru* (→*saseru*).

⇒させる **saseru**

ゼロ〔名〕 ☞零 rei

zero ☞rei

せわ 世話〔名、〜する〕

sewa 〚n, 〜*suru*〛 **care; help, assistance; kind offices**

¶お母さんは赤ちゃんの世話で忙しいです。(Okāsan wa akachan no *sewa* de isogashii desu.)

¶ The mother is busy **taking care of** her baby.

¶わたしは今おじの世話になっています。(Watashi wa ima oji no *sewa* ni natte imasu.)

¶ I am now **being looked after** by my uncle.

¶田中さんのお世話で、この会社に勤めることになりました。(Tanaka san no o*sewa* de, kono kaisha ni tsutomeru koto ni narimashita.)

¶ I got my job at this company through **the kind offices** of [Mr.] Tanaka.

せん　千〔名〕
千円（sen'en）千人（sennin）数千キロ
（sūsenkiro）

sen 〔n〕 **a thousand**
a thousand yen // **a thousand**
persons // **thousands** of kilometers;
thousands of kilos

(-)せん　(-)線〔名、尾〕

1〔名〕
① [筋]
¶鉛筆で紙に線を引きます。（Enpitsu
de kami ni sen o hikimasu.）
②[細長いもの]
電線（densen）線路（senro）

2〔尾〕
山の手線（Yamanotesen）中央線
（Chūōsen）国際線（kokusaisen）国内
線（kokunaisen）

(-)sen 〔n, suf〕 **line; wire, line,
track, route;(train or air)line**
1〔n〕
① [line]
¶ [I] draw **a line** on paper with a pencil.

② [wire, line, track, route]
an electric **wire**, a telephone **line**, a
telegraph **wire** // a railroad **track**
2 〔suf〕 (train or air) line
the Yamanote **Line** // the Chuo **Line** //
a plane going overseas // **a plane**
flying within the country

せんきょ　選挙〔名、〜する〕
選挙権（senkyoken）選挙運動（senkyo-
undō）
¶上田さんは選挙でクラスの委員に選
ばれました。（Ueda san wa senkyo de
kurasu no iin ni erabaremashita.）
¶大統領は選挙をして選びます。
（Daitōryō wa senkyo o shite erabimasu.）

senkyo 〔n, 〜suru〕 **election**
the franchise, suffrage, the right **to
vote** // an **election** campaign
¶ [Miss] Ueda **was elected** to be one of
the class officers.

¶ The nation's president is chosen in **an
election**.

せんげつ　先月〔名〕
¶わたしの誕生日は先月の二十日でし
た。（Watashi no tanjōbi wa sengetsu no
hatsuka deshita.）
¶わたしは先月日本に来ました。
（Watashi wa sengetsu Nihon ni
kimashita.）

sengetsu 〔n〕 **last month**
¶ My birthday was the twentieth of **last
month**.

¶ I came to Japan **last month**.

せんご　戦後 〔名〕

¶戦後、東京の町は大きく変わりました。(*Sengo*, Tōkyō no machi wa ookiku kawarimashita.)

⇔戦前 **senzen**

sengo 〔n〕 **postwar, after World War II**

¶ Tokyo changed greatly **after the war** 〚**after World War II**〛.

せんこう　専攻 〔名、～する〕

¶山田さんの専攻は何ですか。(Yamada san no *senkō* wa nan desu ka？)

¶わたしは大学で日本文学を専攻しました。(Watashi wa daigaku de Nihon-bungaku o *senkō* shimashita.)

senkō 〔n, ～*suru*〕 **special study, one's academic speciality, one's major**

¶ What is [Mr.] Yamada's **speciality** 〚**majot**〛?

¶ I **majored** in Japanese literature in college.

ぜんこく　全国 〔名〕

¶この放送は日本全国どこでも聞けます。(Kono hōsō wa Nihon-*zenkoku* doko demo kikemasu.)

¶東京へは全国から学生が集まってきます。(Tōkyō e wa *zenkoku* kara gakusei ga atsumatte kimasu.)

zenkoku 〔n〕 **the whole country, national**

¶ This broadcast can be heard **anywhere** in Japan.

¶ Students flock to Tokyo from **all over the country**.

せんじつ　先日 〔名〕

¶先日、田中さんに会いました。(*Senjitsu*, Tanaka san ni aimashita.)

¶先日は子供がたいへんお世話になり、ありがとうございました。(*Senjitsu* wa kodomo ga taihen osewa ni nari, arigatō gozaimashita.)

⇒この間 **konoaida**

scnjitsu 〔n〕 **the other day, a few days ago, lately**

¶ [I] met [Mrs.] Tanaka **the other day**.

¶ Thank you very much for your kindness to my child **the other day**.

せんしゅ　選手 〔名〕

¶中村さんはテニスの選手です。(Nakamura san wa tenisu no *senshu* desu.)

senshu 〔n〕 **player, athlete**

¶ [Mr.] Nakamura **is on the** tennis **team**.

443

¶田中さんはオリンピックの選手に選ばれました。(Tanaka san wa orinpikku no *senshu* ni erabaremashita.)

¶ [Miss] Tanaka was chosen **to compete** in the Olympics.

せんしゅう 先週 〔名〕

senshū 〔n〕 **last week**

¶先週の月曜日は何日でしたか。(*Senshū* no getsuyōbi wa nannichi deshita ka？)

¶ What date was Monday **last week?**

¶先週、わたしは友達と旅行しました。(*Senshū*, watashi wa tomodachi to ryokō shimashita.)

¶ I went on a trip with friends **last week**.

せんせい 先生 〔名〕

sensei 〔n〕 **a teacher; a term of address or respect for teachers, doctors, artists, lawyers, etc.**

① [学校の教師、学問や芸術など特別な知識・技能などを教える人]

① [teacher at a school, a teacher of some scholarly or artistic knowledge or skill]

数学の先生 (sūgaku no *sensei*)

a mathematics **teacher**

¶あの人は小学校の先生です。(Ano hito wa shōgakkō no *sensei* desu.)

¶ [He] is an elementary school **teacher**.

¶山田さんの奥さんは生け花の先生です。(Yamada san no okusan wa ikebana no *sensei* desu.)

¶ Mr. Yamada's wife **teaches** *ikebana*.

② [教師・医者・芸術家・弁護士などに呼びかける場合に使う言葉]

② [term of address for teachers, doctors, artists, lawyers, etc.]

¶先生、この言葉の意味を説明していただけませんか。(*Sensei*, kono kotoba no imi o setsumei shite itadakemasen ka？)

¶ **Sir** 〚**Ma'am**〛, could you please explain the meaning of this word?

¶先生、わたしはいつ退院できますか。(*Sensei*, watashi wa itsu taiin dekimasu ka？)

¶ **Doctor**, when will I be able to go home from the hospital?

③ [教師・医者・芸術家・弁護士などの名前につけて尊敬の気持ちを表す]

③ [term of respect added to the names of teachers, doctors, artists, lawyers, etc.]

¶わたしは田中先生に日本語を習っています。(Watashi wa Tanaka *sensei* ni Nihongo o naratte imasu.)

¶ I am studying Japanese with **Professor** Tanaka.

¶山田先生は国立病院の内科の先生です。(Yamada *sensei* wa kokuritsubyōin no naika no *sensei* desu.)

¶ **Dr.** Yamada is a physician in the department of internal medicine at a national hospital.

せんぜん 戦前 〔名〕

senzen 〔n〕 **prewar, before World War II**

¶わたしは戦前からここに住んでいます。(Watashi wa *senzen* kara koko ni sunde imasu.)
⇔戦後 sengo

¶ I've been living here since **before the war**.

ぜんぜん 全然 〔副〕

zenzen 〔adv〕 **wholly, entirely; not at all**

¶初めて日本へ来た時には、日本語が全然わかりませんでした。(Hajimete Nihon e kita toki ni wa, Nihongo ga *zenzen* wakarimasen deshita.)

¶ When I first came to Japan I didn't know **any** Japanese **at all**.

¶山田さんが病気だったことは全然知りませんでした。(Yamada san ga byōki datta koto wa *zenzen* shirimasen deshita.)

¶ **I had no idea** that [Mrs.] Yamada was ill.

¶たばこをやめようとしましたが、全然だめでした。(Tabako o yameyō to shimashita ga, *zenzen* dame deshita.)

¶ I tried to stop smoking but it was a **complete** failure.

＊あとに打ち消しの言葉や否定的な意味の言葉が来る。

＊Followed hy words or expressions negative in form or sense.

せんぞ 先祖 〔名〕

senzo 〔n〕 **ancestor, forefather, ancestry**

先祖代々 (*senzo*daidai)

(a home, business, etc.) in the family for generations

¶わたしは先祖のお墓へお参りに行きました。(Watashi wa *senzo* no ohaka e omairi ni ikimashita.)
⇔子孫 shison
⇒祖先 sosen

¶ I visited my **family** graves.

せんそう 戦争 〔名、～する〕

sensō 〔n, ～*suru*〕 **war, warfare, hostilities, a battle**

戦争が始まる (*sensō* ga hajimaru) 戦争に行く (*sensō* ni iku)

a **war** breaks out // go off to **war**

¶ A国とB国は今戦争をしています。
（Ē-koku to Bii-koku wa ima *sensō* o shite imasu.）

¶ Country A and Country B are presently **at war** with each other.

ぜんたい　全体〔名〕

¶ この問題については、あしたクラス全体の意見をまとめて先生に報告します。（Kono mondai ni tsuite wa, ashita kurasu *zentai* no iken o matomete sensei ni hōkoku shimasu.）

¶ 自分のことだけでなく、社会全体のことも考えなければいけません。（Jibun no koto dake de naku, shakai *zentai* no koto mo kangaenakereba ikemasen.）

zentai 〔n〕 **whole, entire, general**

¶ Tomorrow I will get the opinion of the **whole** class concerning this matter and report it to the teacher.

¶ One must think not of oneself alone, but of **the whole** of society.

せんたく　洗たく〔名、～する〕

洗たく機（*sentaku*ki）洗たく物（*sentaku*mono）

¶ 今日は天気がいいので、洗たくをしようと思います。（Kyō wa tenki ga ii node, *sentaku* o shiyō to omoimasu.）

¶ この汚れは洗たくしてもきれいになりません。（Kono yogore wa *sentaku* shite mo kirei ni narimasen.）

sentaku 〔n, ～*suru*〕 **wash, washing, laundry**
a **washing** machine // a **washing**, the **laundry**

¶ I think **I'll do the wash** today as the weather is so nice.

¶ This dirt 〚spot, stain〛 won't **wash out** completely.

-センチ〔尾〕

¶ 1メートルは100センチです。（Ichimētoru wa hyaku*senchi* desu.）

-senchi 〔suf〕 **centimeter(s)**

¶ One meter is 100 **centimeters**.

せんでん　宣伝〔名、～する〕

¶ あの会社は新しい製品の宣伝を盛んにしています。（Ano kaisha wa atarashii seihin no *senden* o sakan ni shite imasu.）

¶ テレビで宣伝していたカメラはこれですか。（Terebi de *senden* shite ita kamera wa kore desu ka？）

senden 〔n, ～*suru*〕 **publicity, advertisement, propaganda**

¶ That company is extensively **advertising** its new products.

¶ Is this the camera **advertised** on television?

ぜんぶ 全部 〔名〕

¶男の子が5人、女の子が3人、子供は全部で8人います。(Otoko no ko ga gonin, onna no ko ga sannin, kodomo wa *zenbu* de hachinin imasu.)

¶この家は古いから、一部だけではなく全部直さなければなりません。(Kono ie wa furui kara, ichibu dake de wa naku *zenbu* naosanakereba narimasen.)

⇒一部 **ichibu**

senpūki 〔n〕 **electric fan**

zenbu 〔n〕 **all, whole, entire, total**

¶ There are eight children **in all**—five boys and three girls.

¶ As this house is old it will have to **all** be rebuilt, not just a part of it.

せんぷうき 扇風機 〔名〕

¶暑いですね。扇風機をつけましょう。(Atsui desu ne. *Senpūki* o tsukemashō.)

senpūki 〔n〕 **electric fan**

¶ It's hot, isn't it? Let's turn on **the fan**.

せんめんじょ 洗面所 〔名〕

¶朝起きると、まず洗面所で顔を洗います。(Asa okiru to, mazu *senmenjo* de kao o araimasu.)

senmenjo 〔n〕 **lavatory, washroom**

¶ After getting up in the morning [I] first of all wash my face in **the bathroom**.

せんもん 専門 〔名〕

専門家 (*senmon*ka)

¶私の専門は経済です。(Watashi no *senmon* wa kcizai desu.)

senmon 〔n〕 **speciality, special subject of study, profession**

a specialist, an expert, a professional

¶ I specialize in economics.

せんろ 線路 〔名〕

¶汽車は線路を走ります。(Kisha wa *senro* o hashirimasu.)

senro 〔n〕 **railroad track, line, rails**

¶ The train runs along **the track**.

ぜん- 全- 〔頭〕

① [すべての]
全財産 (*zen*-zaisan) 全国民 (*zen*-kokumin)

② [あるもののすべて]
全国 (zenkoku) 全校 (zenkō) 全世界 (*zen*-sekai)

③ [全部で]

zen- 〔pref〕 **whole, entire; all; complete**

① [whole, entire]
total assets // the **whole** nation, **all** the people

② [all (of a certain thing)]
the **whole** country, nation**wide**, national // **all** the school // the **whole** world, **throughout** the world

③ [complete]

447

全10巻の百科事典（*zen*-jikkan no hyakka-jiten）　　an encyclopedia **complete** in 10 volumes

そ

そう 沿う〔動Ⅰ〕

¶川に沿って歩いていきました。
（Kawa ni *sotte* aruite ikimashita.）

¶電車はしばらく海岸に沿って走りました。（Densha wa shibaraku kaigan ni *sotte* hashirimashita.）

*普通「〜に沿って（〜ni sotte）」の形で使う。

そう〔副〕

① [話し相手の行動の様子などをさし示す]

¶そう急いでも、汽車にはもう間に合いませんよ。（*Sō* isoide mo, kisha ni wa mō maniaimasen yo.）

¶そうあわてては、転びますよ。（*Sō* awatete wa, korobimasu yo.）

② [ものごとの状態について話し相手などが考えている程度をさし示す]

¶この小説はそうおもしろくないです。（Kono shōsetsu wa *sō* omoshiroku nai desu.）

¶今日はお金がそうないから、買い物はしないことにしましょう。（Kyō wa okane ga *sō* nai kara, kaimono wa shinai koto ni shimashō.）

*あとに打ち消しの言葉が来る。話し相手または広く人々が期待したり予想したりしている程度には達していないという意味を表すときに使う。

③ [文脈の上で話し相手の言ったものごとをさし示したり前に述べて話し相手にわかっているものごとの状態をさし示したりする]

sou〔v Ⅰ〕 along, by, parallel to

¶[I] walked **along** the river.

¶The train ran for some distance **parallel to** the coast.

*Usually used in the pattern "〜 *ni sotte*."

sō〔adv〕 so, like that, that way

① [so, like that, that way; used concerning the actions of the listener]

¶Even hurrying **like that**, you won't be able to catch the train.

¶Don't rush around **so**—you'll fall down.

② [so, so much; used concerning the thinking of the listener]

¶This novel isn't **all that** interesting.

¶I don't have **all that** much money with me today; let's not go shopping.

*Followed by the negative. Used when expressing the idea that something isn't as much as the listener or as people in general might think.

③ [so, that; indicates something that has been talked about by the listener or already mentioned and understood by the listener]

¶「失礼ですが、中村さんでいらっしゃいますか。」(Shitsurei desu ga, Nakamura san de irasshaimasu ka？)「はい、そうです。」(Hai, *sō* desu.)

¶「山田さんは病気だそうです。」(Yamada san wa byōki da *sō* desu.)「そうですか。」(*Sō* desu ka.)

¶「伊豆の海岸は水もきれいだし、波も静かです。」(Izu no kaigan wa mizu mo kirei da shi, nami mo shizuka desu.)「そういう海岸なら、わたしも行ってみたいです。」(*Sō*iu kaigan nara, watashi mo itte mitai desu.)

⇒こう **kō**　ああ **ā**　どう **dō**

¶ "Pardon me, but would you be [Mr.] Nakamura?"
"Yes, **that's right**."

¶ "I heard that [Miss] Yamada is ill."
"Is **that so**?"

¶ "The sea is calm and the water clean along the Izu coast."
"I'd like to go to **that sort** of place."

ぞうか　増加 〔名、〜する〕

zōka 〔n, ~*suru*〕 **increase, gain, rise**

¶ 車の増加が空気を汚す原因の一つになっています。(Kuruma no *zōka* ga kūki o yogosu genin no hitotsu ni natte imasu.)

¶ このごろ、日本語を習う外国人の数が増加してきました。(Konogoro, Nihongo o narau gaikokujin no kazu ga *zōka* shite kimashita.)

⇔減少 **genshō**
⇒増える **fueru**

¶ **The increase** in the number of automobiles is one cause of air pollution.

¶ The number of foreigners studying Japanese **has increased** recently.

そうこ　倉庫 〔名〕

sōko 〔n〕 **warehouse, storehouse**

¶ 倉庫にいっぱい米が入っています。(*Sōko* ni ippai kome ga haitte imasu.)

¶ あまり使わない物は、倉庫にしまっておきます。(Amari tsukawanai mono wa, *sōko* ni shimatte okimasu.)

¶ **The warehouse** is filled with rice.

¶ Articles not often used are put away in **the storehouse**.

そうごう　総合 [名、〜する]

総合病院（sōgō-byōin）総合大学（sōgō-daigaku）総合雑誌（sōgō-zasshi）

¶今までに出た意見を総合して考えると、どうなるでしょうか。（Ima made ni deta iken o sōgō shite kangaeru to, dō naru deshō ka？）

¶一つ一つの専門的な研究よりも、総合的な研究が必要です。（Hitotsu hitotsu no senmonteki na kenkyū yori mo, sōgōteki na kenkyū ga hitsuyō desu.）

sōgō [n, 〜*suru*] **all-around, overall, comprehensive, synthetic**

a **general** hospital // a university // a **general** magazine

¶ So what do we have if **we put together all** the opinions expressed so far?

¶ Rather than individual, specialized research, **comprehensive, crossdisciplinary** work is needed.

そうじ　掃除 [名、〜する]

¶この公園はいつもきれいに掃除がしてあって、気持ちがいいですね。（Kono kōen wa itsu mo kirei ni sōji ga shite atte, kimochi ga ii desu ne.）

¶わたしは毎日部屋を掃除しています。（Watashi wa mainichi heya o sōji shiteimasu.）

sōji [n, 〜*suru*] **cleaning, sweeping**

¶ This park **is kept** so **clean** and nice that it is always a pleasure to be here.

¶ I **clean** my room 〚apartment〛 every day.

そうぞう　想像 [名、〜する]

¶これは百年後の日本を想像してかいた絵です。（Kore wa hyakunengo no Nihon o sōzō shite kaita e desu.）

¶朝の電車は、あなたが想像できないくらいこみます。（Asa no densha wa, anata ga sōzō dekinai kurai komimasu.）

sōzō [n, 〜*suru*] **imagination, conjecture, guess**

¶ This is a picture **visualizing** what Japan will be like in a hundred years.

¶ The morning trains are **unimaginably** crowded.

そうだ [助動]

① [ほかの人などから聞いて知ったという意味を表す]

sō da 〚auxil〛 **they say, I hear; seem, appear, look like; threaten to, be likely to**

① [they say, I hear]

¶天気予報によると、あしたは雨が降るそうです。(Tenki-yohō ni yoru to, ashita wa ame ga furu *sō* desu.)

¶息子がお世話になったそうで、ありがとうございます。(Musuko ga osewa ni natta *sō* de, arigatō gozaimasu.)

¶上田さんは最近忙しいそうです。(Ueda san wa saikin isogashii *sō desu*.)

¶田中さんは病気だそうです。(Tanaka san wa byōki da *sō desu*.)

②[現在そのように見えるという意味を表す]

¶このお菓子はおいしそうですね。(Kono okashi wa oishi*sō* desu ne.)

¶心配そうな顔をしていますね。どうしたんですか。(Shinpai*sō* na kao o shite imasu ne. Dō shita n desu ka？)

¶このナイフはよく切れそうですね。(Kono naifu wa yoku kire*sō* desu ne.)

*形容詞・形容動詞、状態を表す動詞などにつく。ただし形容詞「よい(yoi)」「ない(nai)」につく場合は、それぞれ「よさそうだ(yosasō da)」「なさそうだ(nasasō da)」の形になる。「このネクタイがよさそうですから、これを買いましょう。」(Kono nekutai ga yosasō desu kara, kore o kaimashō.)「その映画はあまりおもしろくなさそうです。」(Sono eiga wa amari omoshiroku nasasō desu.)

③[今にもそのようになる様子だという意味を表す]

¶雨が降りそうな天気ですね。(Ame ga furi*sō* na tenki desu ne.)

¶わたしは病気で死にそうになったことがあります。(Watashi wa byōki de shini*sō ni* natta koto ga arimasu.)

¶ The weather report **says** we will have rain tomorrow.

¶ **I understand** that you have done a lot for my son. Thank you very much.

¶ **I hear** that [Mr.] Ueda has been quite busy recently.

¶ **I hear** that [Mrs.] Tanaka is ill.

②[seem, appear, look like]

¶ These sweets 〚cakes, candies, etc.〛 **look** good, don't they?

¶ **You look** worried. Is something wrong?

¶ This knife **looks** sharp.

*Added to adjectives, adjectiveverbs, verbs expressing conditions, etc. When added to the adjectives *yoi* and *nai*, the resulting forms are *yosasō da* and *nasasō da*. as in "*Kono nekutai ga yosasō desu kara, kore o kaimashō*" (This tie looks nice—let's buy it) and "*Sono eiga wa amari omoshiroku nasasō desu*" (That movie doesn't look very interesting).

③[threaten to, be likely to]

¶ **It looks like** rain, doesn't it?

¶ I was once so sick that I was **on the point of** death.

＊丁寧に言う場合「そうです（sō desu）」となる。

＊*Sō desu* is used instead of *sō da* when speaking politely.

そうだん　相談〔名、〜する〕

¶あなたに相談があるんですが…。（Anata ni *sōdan* ga aru n desuga…）
¶父と相談してから、決めたいと思います。（Chichi to *sōdan* shite kara, kimetai to omoimasu.）

sōdan 〔n, 〜*suru*〕 consultation, conference, talk
¶ There is something I would like **to talk** with you about.
¶ I want **to consult** with my father before deciding.

そうりだいじん　総理大臣〔名〕
☞首相 shushō

sōridaijin 〔n〕　　☞shushō

そえる　添える〔動 II〕

¶手紙に写真を添えて送りました。（Tegami ni shashin o *soete* okurimashita.）
¶贈り物に花を添えて、秋子さんに上げました。（Okurimono ni hana o *soete*, Akiko san ni agemashita.）

soeru 〔v II〕 add, attach, accompany
¶ [I] **enclosed** a photograph in [my] letter.
¶ [I] gave flowers to Akiko **along with** a present.

ソース〔名〕

¶この料理はソースをかけて食べると、おいしいですよ。（Kono ryōri wa *sōsu* o kakete taberu to, oishii desu yo.）

sōsu 〔n〕 sauce, Worcestershire sauce
¶ This dish is good with **a sauce**.

-そく　-足〔尾〕

3足（san*zoku*）8足（has*soku*）10足（jis*soku*）
¶わたしはくつを2足買いました。（Watashi wa kutsu o ni*soku* kaimashita.）

-soku 〔suf〕 a pair (of shoes, socks, etc.)
three **pair(s)** // eight **pair(s)** // ten **pair(s)**
¶ I bought two **pairs** of shoes.

そくたつ　速達〔名〕

手紙を速達にする（tegami o *sokutatsu* ni suru）
¶この手紙を速達で出してください。（Kono tegami o *sokutatsu* de dashite kudasai.）

sokutatsu 〔n〕 special delivery
send a letter **special delivery**
¶ Please have this letter sent **special delivery**.

453

¶ 父から速達が届きました。（Chichi kara *sokutatsu* ga todokimashita.）

¶ A letter 〖parcel, etc.〗 came **special delivery** from my father.

そくど 速度 〔名〕

sokudo 〔n〕 **speed, velocity**

速度が速い（*sokudo* ga hayai）速度が遅い（*sokudo* ga osoi）

at high **speed** // at low **speed**

¶ あそこから道が狭くなっていますから、車の速度を落としてください。（Asoko kara michi ga semaku natte imasu kara, kuruma no *sokudo* o otoshite kudasai.）

¶ The road narrows there so please **slow down** (said to the driver of a taxi or other car).

そこ 底 〔名〕

soko 〔n〕 **bottom; depths**

① [容器などの下の面]

① [bottom, sole, riverbed]

びんの底（bin no *soko*）くつの底（kutsu no *soko*）

the bottom of a bottle // **the sole** of a shoe

¶ 割れやすい物は、箱の底のほうには入れないで、上のほうに入れてください。（Wareyasui mono wa, hako no *soko* no hō ni wa irenaide, ue no hō ni irete kudasai.）

¶ Please put easily broken items towards the top of the box, not the **bottom**.

② [地面や水面から下の深い所]

② [depths, bowels]

¶ 海の底に潜って、沈んだ船を調べました。（Umi no *soko* ni mogutte, shizunda fune o shirabemashita.）

¶ [They] dived **deep** into the sea and looked over the sunken ship.

¶ 地の底で石炭を掘っています。（Chi no *soko* de sekitan o hotte imasu.）

¶ Coal is mined **deep** in the earth.

そこ 〔代〕

soko 〔pron〕 **that place, there, that**

① [話し手にとって少し隔たりのある関係にある所をさし示す]

① [that place, there, that; indicates a place somewhat far from the speaker]

¶ 「そこに鉛筆がありますか。」（*Soko* ni enpitsu ga arimasu ka？）「はい、ここに鉛筆があります。」（Hai, koko ni enpitsu ga arimasu.）

¶ "Is there a pencil **there?**" "Yes, there's a pencil here."

¶ 「テニスはどこでしましょうか。」（Tenisu wa doko de shimashō ka？）「そこの庭でしましょう。」（Soko no niwa de shimashō.）

¶ "Where shall we play tennis?" "Let's play in **that** yard **there**."

*話し手にとって少し隔たりのある関係にある所は話し相手に身近な所である場合が多い。なお、話し手からも話し相手からも少し隔たりのある所をさし示すこともある。

② [文脈の上で前に述べて話し相手にもよくわかっていると認める所をさし示す]

¶ 伊豆の海岸に別荘があります。そこからは富士山がとてもきれいに大きく見えます。(Izu no kaigan ni bessō ga arimasu. *Soko* kara wa Fujisan ga totemo kirei ni ookiku miemasu.)

*文脈の上で前に述べてある所を話し相手に身近な関係にある所としてさし示すのに使う。つまり、その所を共通の話題の所として取り扱うものである。

③ [文脈の上で前に述べて話し相手にもよくわかっていると認める場面などをさし示す]

¶ お金を落として困っていると、そこへちょうど上田さんが来ました。
(Okane o otoshite komatte iru to, *soko* e chōdo Ueda san ga kimashita.)

④ [文脈の上で前に述べて話し相手によくわかっていると認めることがらの問題とすべき点・状態などをさし示す]

¶ 「向こうに着いたら、すぐ旅館を探さなければなりません。」(Mukō ni tsuitara, sugu ryokan o sagasanakereba narimasen.)「もしなかったらどうしましょうか。」(Moshi nakattara dō shimashō ka?)「そこまではまだ考えていません。」(*Soko* made wa mada kangaete imasen.)

*Often this place somewhat far from the speaker is close to the listener. Sometimes it is somewhat distant from both of them.

② [there, that place; refers to a place which has been talked about and is known to the listener]

¶ [We] have a country place on the Izu coast. From **there** you get a very nice view of Mount Fuji—it looks very close and large.

*Used to refer to a place known to the listener which has already been talked about. That is, it is treated as a common topic of conversation between the speaker and the listener.

③ [indicates a time, situation, etc., already talked about and regarded as known to the listener]

¶ [I] had lost [my] money and didn't know what to do **when** [Mr.] Ueda happened to come by.

④ [that; indicates an item already talked about and points it out as a problem]

¶ "[We] will have to look for an inn after arriving there."
"What will [we] do if there aren't any free rooms?"
"[I] haven't thought **that far** yet."

¶先生、今おっしゃった、そこのところをもっと詳しく説明してください。(Sensei, ima osshata, *soko* no tokoro o motto kuwashiku setsumei shite kudasai.)

*話し相手の述べたことがらの問題とすべき点なども受けてさし示す。

⇒ここ **koko**　あそこ **asoko**　どこ **doko**

¶ [Sir], please explain **that** in more detail (said to a professor or teacher).

*Treats as a problem a matter condition, etc., talked about by the listener.

そしき　組織 〔名、〜する〕

soshiki 〔n, 〜*suru*〕 organization, structure, system

¶今度、会社の組織が少し変わりました。(Kondo, kaisha no *soshiki* ga sukoshi kawarimashita.)

¶この委員会は、10名で組織されています。(Kono iinkai wa, jūmei de *soshiki* sarete imasu.)

¶ **The organizational structure** of the company has changed somewhat recently.

¶ This committee 〚commission, board, panel〛 **is made up** of 10 persons.

そして 〔接〕

soshite 〔conj〕 then, and then; and, and now

① [前のことがらを受けて次に起こることをあとで述べるときに使う]

¶わたしは昨日銀座へ買い物に行きました。そして、これを買いました。(Watashi wa kinō Ginza e kaimono ni ikimashita. *Soshite*, kore o kaimashita.)

② [ことがらを並べて言うときなどに使う]

¶昨日は天気もよく、そして、波も静かでした。(Kinō wa tenki mo yoku, *soshite*, nami mo shizuka deshita.)

¶兄は医者になりました。そして、弟は先生になりました。(Ani wa isha ni narimashita. *Soshite*, otōto wa sensei ni narimashita.)

¶田中さんは毎晩遅くまで働きました。そして、病気になってしまいました。(Tanaka san wa maiban osoku made

① [then, and then]

¶ I went to Ginza to shop yesterday **and** bought this.

② [and, and now]

¶ The weather was nice yesterday, **and** the sea 〚lake〛 was calm.

¶ My older brother is 〚became〛 a doctor. **And** my younger brother is 〚became〛 a teacher.

¶ [Mr.] Tanaka worked until late every night **and** became 〚has now becomes〛 ill.

hatarakimashita. *Soshite*, byōki ni natte
shimaimashita.)

*前のことがらと同じようなことがら
や対比的なことがらを並べるとき、ま
た前のことがらの結果を述べるときな
どに使う。

*Used when stating something similar
to, in contrast to, or the result of what
was stated earlier.

そせん 祖先 〔名〕

¶人間の祖先はさるだと言われていま
す。（Ningen no *sosen* wa saru da to
iwarete imasu.）

¶日本人の祖先はどこから来たのです
か。（Nihonjin no *sosen* wa doko kara
kita no desu ka？）
⇔先祖 senzo

sosen 〔n〕 ancestor, forefather

¶ It is said that human beings **are
descended from** apes.

¶ Where did **the ancestors** of the
Japanese come from?

そだつ 育つ 〔動Ⅰ〕

¶わたしは東京で生まれ、東京で育ち
ました。（Watashi wa Tōkyō de umare,
Tōkyō de *sodachimashita*.）

¶寒い所では、みかんは育ちません。
（Samui tokoro de wa, mikan wa
sodachimasen.）

sodatsu 〔vⅠ〕 grow up, be
brought up, be raised

¶ I was born and **raised** in Tokyo.

¶ Mandarin oranges **can't be grown** in
a cold climate.

そだてる 育てる 〔動Ⅱ〕

¶母が一人でわたしたちを育ててくれ
ました。（Haha ga hitori de watashitachi
o *sodatete* kuremashita.）

¶父は菊の花を大事に育てています。
（Chichi wa kiku no hana o daiji ni
sodatete imasu.）

sodateru 〔vⅡ〕 bring up, raise,
rear

¶ My mother **brought** us **up** all by
herself.

¶ My father carefully **tends to** his
chrysanthemums.

そちら 〔代〕

①〔話し手にとって少し隔たりのある
関係にある方向をさし示す〕

sochira 〔pron〕 there, over there;
your place; that person; that
one, the other one; you, your
family

① 〔there, over there; indicates a place
somewhat separated from the speaker〕

457

¶そちらを見ないで、こちらを見てください。(*Sochira* o minaide, kochira o mite kudasai.)

¶ Please look here, not **there**.

¶もう少しそちらへおつめください。(Mō sukoshi *sochira* e otsume kudasai.)

¶ Please move a little more in **that direction**.

¶「エレベーターはどこにありますか。」(Erebētā wa doko ni arimasu ka？)「そちらの方でございます。」(*Sochira* no hō de gozaimasu.)

¶ "Where is the elevator?" "It is **over there**."

*話し手にとって少し隔たりのある関係にある方向は、話し相手に対しては身近な関係にある方向である場合が多い。したがって、話し相手に身近な関係にある方向をさす場合が多い。

*In many cases a place somewhat separated from the speaker is close to the listener. Therefore *sochira* frequently indicates a direction or place close to the listener.

②[話し相手に対して身近な関係にある方向に存在する所などをさし示す]

② [your place; refers to a place, etc., physically close to the listener]

¶こちらはもう桜が咲いていますが、そちらはまだ寒いでしょうね。(Kochira wa mō sakura ga saite imasu ga, *sochira* wa mada samui deshō ne.)

¶ The cherry blossoms are already out here but it must still be cold **there where you are**.

*話し相手に対して身近な関係にある方向は話し手にとっては少し隔たりのある関係にある方向になる。例えば、東京にいる人が北海道にいる人に対して言う場合には北海道のことについては、「あちら (achira)」とは言わないで「そちら (sochira)」と言う。

*Used for a place or direction close for the listener but somewhat far for the speaker. For example, someone in Tokyo speaking to someone in Hokkaido will refer to Hokkaido as *sochira* and not as *achira*.

③[話し相手に身近な関係にある方向にいる人をさし示す]

③ [that person; used to refer to a person close to the listener]

¶こちらは中村さんで、そちらが山田さんです。(Kochira wa Nakamura san de, *sochira* ga yamada san desu.)

¶ This is [Miss] Nakamura and **that** is [Miss] Yamada.

*「そちらの方 (sochira no kata)」とも言う。

*Variant: *sochira no kata*.

④[話し相手に身近な関係にある方向に存在するものごとをさし示す]

④ [that one, the other one; indicates something close to the listener]

¶わたしはこちらの万年筆よりそちら
のほうがいいです。（Watashi wa
kochira no mannenhitsu yori *sochira* no
hō ga ii desu.）
⑤[話し相手をさし示す]

¶このことについて、そちらの御意見
はいかがでしょうか。（Kono koto ni
tsuite, *sochira* no goiken wa ikaga deshō
ka？）
＊「そっち（sotchi）」とも言うが、
「そちら（sochira）」のほうが丁寧な言
葉である。
⇒こちら **kochira**　あちら **achira**
どちら **dochira**

¶ I prefer **that fountain pen** to this one.

⑤[you, your family, your side;
indicates the listener and those
associated with the listener]
¶ What is **your** opinion concerning this
matter?

＊*Sotchi* is also used but *sochira* is
more polite.

そつぎょう　卒業〔名、〜する〕
卒業式（*sotsugyō*shiki）卒業生
（*sōtsugyō*sei）

¶わたしは今年の三月に大学を卒業し
ます。（Watashi wa kotoshi no sangatsu
ni daigaku o *sotsugyō* shimasu.）
¶卒業後は、新聞社に勤めたいと思っ
ています。（*Sotsugyō*go wa, shinbunsha
ni tsutometai to omotte imasu.）
⇔入学 **nyūgaku**

sotsugyō 〔n, 〜*suru*〕 **graduation**
a **graduation** ceremony,
commencement exercises //
a **graduate, alumni**
¶ I **will graduate** from college this
March.

¶ I would like a newspaper job after
graduating.

そっくり〔副〕

¶この魚は骨までそっくり食べられま
す。（Kono sakana wa hone made *sokkuri*
taberaremasu.）
¶持っているお金をそっくり田中さん
に貸しました。（Motte iru okane o
sokkuri Tanaka san ni kashimashita.）

sokkuri 〔adv〕 **wholly, entirely,
altogether, all**
¶ **All** of this fish can be eaten, even the
bones.

¶ I loaned **all** the money I had on me to
[Mr.] Tanaka.

そっくり〔形動、〜の〕

¶春子さんはお母さんにそっくりな顔をしています。(Haruko san wa okāsan ni *sokkuri* na kao o shite imasu.)

¶山田さんはお兄さんと声がそっくりですね。(Yamada san wa oniisan to koe ga *sokkuri* desu ne.)

そっち〔代〕　☞そちら sochira

そっと〔副、〜する〕

① [静かに何かをする様子]
¶赤ちゃんが寝ているから、そっと歩きなさい。(Akachan ga nete iru kara, *sotto* arukinasai.)

② [相手に気づかれずに何かをする様子]
¶犬が子を産んだから、そっと見てごらんなさい。(Inu ga ko o unda kara, *sotto* mite goran nasai.)

③ [そのままにしておく様子]
¶寝ているなら、そっとしておきましょう。(Nete iru nara, *sotto* shite okimashō.)

そで〔名〕

半そで (han*sode*)　長そで (naga*sode*)

¶手を洗っている時、シャツのそでがぬれてしまいました。(Te o aratte iru toki, shatsu no *sode* ga nurete shimaimashita.)

そと　外〔名〕

¶ドアの外にだれかいますよ。
(Doa no *soto* ni dare ka imasu yo.)
¶外はとても寒いです。
(*Soto* wa totemo samui desu.)

sokkuri 〔adj-v, 〜no〕 be exactly like, be just like

¶Haruko's face is **an exact replica** of her mother's.

¶Mr. Yamada's voice **is just like** his older brother's.

sotchi 〔pron〕　☞sochira

sotto 〔adv, 〜suru〕 quietly, softly; secretly, stealthily; (leave) as is

① [quietly, softly, lightly]
¶Walk **quietly** as the baby is asleep.

② [secretly, stealthily]

¶The dog has had her puppies—**be careful** so she doesn't see us looking.

③ [(leave) as is]
¶If [he]'s asleep, let's **leave [him] alone**.

sode 〔n〕 sleeve

short **sleeves**, short-**sleeved** // long **sleeves**, long-**sleeved**

¶[My] shirt **sleeves** got wet when [I] washed [my] hands.

soto 〔n〕 outside, the exterior, outdoors

¶There's someone **at** the door!

¶It's very cold **outside**.

¶このみかんは外側は腐っています
が、中は大丈夫です。(Kono mikan wa
*soto*gawa wa kusatte imasu ga, naka wa
daijōbu desu.)
⇔内 uchi　中 naka

その〔連体〕

①[話し手とものごととの少し隔たり
のある関係をさし示す]
その人（*sono* hito）その方（*sono*
kata）
¶「この本はだれのですか。」(Kono
hon wa dare no desu ka？)「その本はわ
たしのです。」(*Sono* hon wa watashi no
desu.)
¶あなたの前にあるそのはさみを取っ
てください。(Anata no mae ni aru *sono*
hasami o totte kudasai.)
*話し手とものごととの少し隔たりの
ある関係は、話し相手に対しては身近
な関係になる場合が多い。したがっ
て、話し相手とものごととの身近な関
係をさし示すことが多い。
②[文脈の上で前に述べたものごとと
話し相手との身近な関係をさし示す]

¶「ここを新宿へ行くバスが通ります
か。」(Koko o Shinjuku e iku basu ga
toorimasu ka？)「はい、通ります。」
(Hai, toorimasu.)「そのバスは池袋駅
の前に止まりますか。」(*Sono* basu wa
Ikebukuro-eki no mae ni tomarimasu
ka？)
¶りんごは5月に花が咲きます。そのあ
とに小さい実がたくさんなります。
(Ringo wa gogatsu ni hana ga sakimasu.
Sono ato ni chiisai mi ga takusan
narimasu.)

sono〔attrib〕**that; the one in
question, the very**

① [that; indicates something some
what far from the speaker]
that person **there** // **that** person **there**
(more polite)
¶ "Whose book is this?"
"**That** book is mine."

¶ Please hand me **those** scissors there
in front of you.

*Often what is somewhat far from the
speaker is close to the listener.
Therefore *sono* often indicates
something close to the listener.

② [that, the one in question, the very;
indicates a matter already mentioned or
associated with the listener]
¶ "Does the bus going to Shinjuku pass
by here?"
"Yes, it does."
"Does **it** stop at Ikebukuro Station?"

¶ Apple trees blossom in May. After
that lots of small apples appear.

¶ The outside of this mandarin orange
is rotten but the inside is all right.

*文脈の上で前に述べて話し相手にわかっているものごとは話し相手に身近な関係にあるので、その関係をさし示すのに使う。また話し相手の言ったり、関係したりしていることがらを受けて、それをさし示す場合にも使う。

⇒この **kono**　あの **ano**　どの **dono**

*Since something mentioned previously and known by the listener is close to the listener, *sono* is used to indicate that relationship. It is also used to indicate something said by the listener or associated with him or her.

そば〔名〕

¶ 机のそばに本箱があります。
(Tsukue no *soba* ni honbako ga arimasu.)
¶ わたしはいつも辞書をそばに置いて勉強しています。(Watashi wa itsu mo jisho o *soba* ni oite benkyō shite imasu.)

soba 〔n〕 beside; near, in the vicinity

¶ There is a bookcase **next to** the desk.

¶ I always study with a dictionary **at my side**.

そば〔名〕

¶ 昼御飯はおそばにしました。
(Hirugohan wa o*soba* ni shimashita.)
¶ このそば屋でそばを食べましょう。
(Kono *soba*ya de *soba* o tabemashō.)

soba 〔n〕 *soba*, buckwheat noodles

¶ [I] had *soba* for lunch.

¶ Let's have *soba* at this *soba* shop.

そふ 祖父〔名〕

¶ わたしの祖父は今年 80 歳ですが、今でもとても元気です。(Watashi no *sofu* wa kotoshi hachijissai desu ga, ima demo totemo genki desu.)
⇔祖母 **sobo**
⇒おじいさん **ojiisan**

sofu 〔n〕 one's grandfather

¶ My **grandfather** is 80 years old this year, but he's still quite vigorous.

そぼ 祖母〔名〕

¶ あなたのおばあさんとわたしの祖母は、昔同じ学校に行っていたのだそうですね。(Anata no obāsan to watashi no *sobo* wa, mukashi onaji gakkō ni itte ita no da sō desu ne.)
⇔祖父 **sofu**
⇒おばあさん **obāsan**

sobo 〔n〕 one's grandmother

¶ I hear that your grandmother and **my grandmother** long ago once went to the same school.

そまつ　粗末〔形動〕

① [材料や作り方が悪い様子]
¶粗末な食事でも、みんなで食べればおいしいですね。（Somatsu na shokuji demo, minna de tabereba oishii desu ne.）
¶粗末な物ですが、どうぞ…。
（Somatsu na mono desu ga, dōzo...）
② [大切にしない様子、むだにする様子]
¶物を粗末にしてはいけません。
（Mono o somatsu ni shite wa ikemasen.）

¶一円のお金でも粗末に使ってはいけません。（Ichien no okane demo somatsu ni tsukatte wa ikemasen.）

そめる　染める〔動Ⅱ〕
¶白い生地を青く染めました。（Shiroi kiji o aoku somemashita.）
¶山田さんは髪の毛を染めています。
（Yamada san wa kaminoke o somete imasu.）

そら　空〔名〕

青空（aozora）
¶雨がやんで、空が晴れてきました。
（Ame ga yande, sora ga harete kimashita.）

そる〔動Ⅰ〕
¶顔を洗ってから、ひげをそります。
（Kao o aratte kara, hige o sorimasu.）

それ〔代〕

① [話し手にとって少し隔たりのある関係にあるものごとをさし示す]

---

somatsu 〔adj-v〕 **coarse, crude, inferior; careless, rough, wasteful**

① [coarse, crude, inferior]
¶ Even **plain** food tastes good when eaten together with others.

¶ It is **nothing fine** but please take it (said when giving someone a present).
② [careless, rough, wasteful]

¶ You shouldn't handle things **roughly** 〖You should handle things with due respect〗.
¶ One shouldn't **waste** even a penny.

someru 〔v Ⅱ〕 **dye, tint, color**
¶ [I] **dyed** the white cloth blue.

¶ [Mr.] Yamada **dyes** [his] hair.

sora 〔n〕 **the sky, the heaven, the skies, the air**
the blue **sky**, blue **skies**; open-**air**
¶ The rain has stopped and **the skies** have cleared 〖The rain stopped and **the skies** cleared〗.

soru 〔v Ⅰ〕 **shave, get a shave**
¶ [I] **shave** after washing [my] face.

sore 〔pron〕 **that; it, the one in question; that time, then**
① [that; indicates something somewhat distant from the speaker]

¶「それは何ですか。」(*Sore* wa nan desu ka？)「これは日本語の本です。」(Kore wa Nihongo no hon desu.)

¶「このりんごはおいしいですよ。」(Kono ringo wa oishii desu yo.)「では、それを五つください。」(Dewa, *sore* o itsutsu kudasai.)

*話し手にとって少し隔たりのある関係にあるものごとは話し相手に対しては身近な関係にあるものごとである場合が多い。

②[文脈の上で前に述べたものごとを話し手にとって少し隔たりのある関係にあるものとしてさし示す]

¶わたしはこの間新しいカメラを買いました。今度の旅行にはそれを持って行くつもりです。(Watashi wa konoaida atarashii kamera o kaimashita. Kondo no ryokō ni wa *sore* o motte iku tsumori desu.)

¶「上田さん、顔色がよくありませんね。どうしたのですか。」(Ueda san, kaoiro ga yoku arimasen ne. Dō shita no desu ka？)「体のぐあいが悪いのです。」(Karada no guai ga warui no desu.)「それはいけませんね。」(*Sore* wa ikemasen ne.)

*文脈の上で前に述べて話し相手によくわかっていると認めるものごとをさし示すのに使う。また、話し相手が言ったことや関係していることをさし示す。

③[文脈の上で前に述べた話し相手に関係のあることがらの成立した時をさし示す]

¶ "What is **that?**"
"This is a Japanese book."

¶ "These apples are very good."
"Well, give me five of them."

*Often what is somewhat distant from the speaker is close to the person addressed.

② [it, the one in question; points to something previously mentioned as something which is somewhat distant from the speaker]

¶ I have recently bought a new camera. I plan to take **it** with me on the coming trip.

¶ "You look pale, [Miss] Ueda. Is something the matter?"
"I don't feel well."
"**That**'s too bad."

*Used to refer to something previously mentioned and treated as well known to the listener. Also used to indicate things said by the listener or concerning him or her.

③ [that time, then; indicates the time of something mentioned earlier which has some connection with the listener]

¶中村さんは今年の四月に東京に出て
きました。それまで、両親から離れて
暮らしたことはありませんでした。
(Nakamura san wa kotoshi no shigatsu ni
Tōkyō ni dete kimashita. *Sore* made,
ryōshin kara hanarete kurashita koto wa
arimasen deshita.)

⇒これ **kore**　あれ **are**　どれ **dore**

¶ [Mr.] Nakamura came to Tokyo this
April. Before **that** [he] had never lived
away from [his] parents.

それから〔接〕

① [前のことがらに続いてあとに起こ
ることがらを述べるときに使う]

¶わたしは買い物をして、それから、
あなたのうちへ行きます。(Watashi
wa kaimono o shite, *sorekara*, anata no
uchi e ikimasu.)

¶田中さんは10年も留学していまし
た。それから、帰ってきて、大学の先
生になったそうです。(Tanaka san wa
jūnen mo ryūgaku shite imashita.
Sorekara, kaette kite, daigaku no sensei ni
natta sō desu.)

② [前のものごとと同じようなものご
とをあとにつけ加えるときに使う]

¶わたしの部屋にはラジオ、テレビ、
それから、冷蔵庫もあります。
(Watashi no heya ni wa rajio, terebi,
sorekara, reizōko mo arimasu.)

¶鉛筆を2本ください。それから、ノー
トもください。(Enpitsu o nihon
kudasai. *Sorekara*, nōto mo kudasai.)

sorekara〔conj〕**after that, and
then; and, and also**

① [after that, and then; used when
something happens after something
else]

¶ I will do some shopping **and then** go
to your home.

¶ [Mr.] Tanaka studied abroad for 10
years. **And then** [he] became a college
professor after returning home,
according to what I hear.

② [and, and also; used when adding
similar items to what has already been
said]

¶ There is a radio, television, **and also**
a refrigerator in my room〘apartment〙.

¶ Two pencils please. **And** a notebook
too.

それぞれ〔名、副〕

1〔名〕

sorezore〔n, adv〕**each, severally,
respectively**

1〘n〙

¶人には、それぞれの考えがあります。(Hito ni wa, *sorezore* no kangae ga arimasu.)

2〔副〕

¶兄弟でも、それぞれ性格が違います。(Kyōdai demo, *sorezore* seikaku ga chigaimasu.)

¶ Different people have **different** ways of thinking.

2 〖adv〗

¶ Even brothers have **their own** characters.

それで〔接〕

① [前のことがらを受けて当然だと考えられる結果をあとに続けるときに使う]

¶中村さんは10年フランスに住んでいました。それで、フランス語が上手なのです。(Nakamura san wa jūnen Furansu ni sunde imashita. *Sorede*, Furansugo ga jōzu na no desu.)

¶お母さんが病気なのです。それで、あの子は元気がないのです。(Okāsan ga byōki na no desu. *Sorede*, ano ko wa genki ga nai no desu.)

*普通あとに「〜なさい（〜nasai）」などの命令、「〜てください（〜te kudasai)」などの依頼などの言い方は来ない。

② [相手の話を受けて更に先に話を促すときに言う言葉]

¶「昨日、田中さんを見舞いに行きました。」(Kinō, Tanaka san o mimai ni ikimashita.)「それで、田中さんのぐあいはどうでしたか。」(*Sorede*, Tanaka san no guai wa dō deshita ka?)

¶「汽車に間に合いませんでした。」(Kisha ni maniaimasen deshita.)「それで、あなたはどうしましたか。」(*Sorede*, anata wa dō shimashita ka?)

sorede 〔conj〕 **therefore, consequently, accordingly; and, and then**

① [therefore, consequently, accordingly]

¶ [Mrs.] Nakamura lived for 10 years in France. **Therefore** [she] speaks French well.

¶ [His] mother is ill. **That's why** that child is in low spirits.

*Usually not followed by commands with *-nasai*, requests with *-te kudasai*, etc.

② [and, and then, thereupon]

¶ "[I] paid a sick call on [Mr.] Tanaka yesterday."
"**And** how was [he]?"

¶ "I missed the train."
"What did you do **then?**"

466

それでは〔接〕

① [相手の話を受けてそれを根拠として自分の考え・判断などを述べるときに使う]

¶あなたも行くんですか。それでは、わたしも行きましょう。(Anata mo ikun desu ka? *Soredewa*, watashi mo ikimashō.)

¶「いいレストランを知っていますよ。」(Ii resutoran o shitte imasu yo.)「そうですか。それでは、いつか連れていってください。」(Sō desu ka. *Soredewa*, itsu ka tsurete itte kudasai.)

② [何かを始めたり終えたり別れたりするときに使う]

¶それでは、これから授業を始めます。(*Soredewa*, kore kara jugyō o hajimemasu.)

¶それでは、これで終わります。(*Soredewa*, kore de owarimasu.)

¶それでは、さようなら。また、あした…。(*Soredewa*, sayōnara. Mata, ashita…)

＊「それじゃ(soreja)」とも言う。

⇒では dewa

それとも〔接〕

¶コーヒーにしますか。それとも、紅茶にしますか。(Kōhii ni shimasu ka? *Soretomo*, kōcha ni shimasu ka?)

¶あしたはテニスをしますか。それとも、勉強しますか。(Ashita wa tenisu o shimasu ka? *Soretomo*, benkyō shimasu ka?)

＊前のことがらとあとに述べることがらのうち、どちらかを選ぶときに使う。普通「～か。それとも、～か。

soredewa 〔conj〕 **if so; well, well then**

① [if so, if that is the case, in that case]

¶ Are you going? **Then** I'll go too.

¶ "I know a good restaurant."
"Really? **If that's the case**, please take me there some time."

② [well, well then]

¶ **Well**, let's start class now.

¶ **Well**, let's stop here (said in a class, meeting, etc.).

¶ **Well**, good-bye. See you tomorrow.

＊Variant: *soreja*.

soretomo 〔conj〕 **or, or else**

¶ Which would you like—coffee **or** tea?

¶ Are you going to play tennis tomorrow? **Or** are you going to study?

＊Used when presenting a choice of two items. Usually used in the pattern "～ *ka? Soretomo, ～ ka?*"

（〜ka？ Soretomo, 〜ka？）」の形で使う。

それに〔接〕

¶今日は頭が痛いし、それに、せきも出ます。（Kyō wa atama ga itai shi, *soreni*, seki mo demasu.）

¶あしたは雨が降るでしょう。それに、風も強いでしょう。（Ashita wa ame ga furu deshō. *Soreni*, kaze mo tsuyoi deshō.）

＊前のことがらを受けて、更に同じようなことがらをつけ加えるときに使う。

それほど〔副〕

¶このテープレコーダーはもう古いので、それほど音がよくありません。（Kono tēpurekōdā wa mō furui node, *sorehodo* oto ga yoku arimasen.）

そろう〔動 I〕

①〔二つ以上のものが同じになる、合う〕

¶歌の練習をしていますが、なかなかみんなの声がそろいません。（Uta no renshū o shite imasu ga, nakanaka minna no koe ga *soroimasen*.）

②〔必要なものが集まる〕

¶この学校にはいい先生がそろっています。（Kono gakkō ni wa ii sensei ga *sorotte* imasu.）

¶みんなそろったから、会を始めましょう。（Minna *sorotta* kara, kai o hajimemashō.）

soreni 〔conj〕 **on top of that, in addition to that, what is more, moreover, besides**

¶ I have a headache today and, **what is more**, a cough.

¶ It will probably rain tomorrow. **And in addition to that** there will probably be strong winds.

＊ Used when adding something similar to what has already been said.

sorehodo 〔adv〕 **so, that, less of,**

¶ The quality of the sound is not so good because this tape recorder is very old.

sorou 〔v I〕 **be uniform, match; be all present, assemble, become complete**

① [be uniform, be even, match]

¶ We have practiced the song, but somehow **can't sing it in perfect harmony**.

② [be all present, assemble, become complete]

¶ This school **has gathered together** a fine set of teachers.

¶ Everyone **has arrived now** so let's start the meeting 〚party〛.

そろえる 〔動Ⅱ〕

① [二つ以上のものを同じようにする、合わせる]
¶服とハンドバッグの色をそろえました。(Fuku to handobaggu no iro o *soroemashita*.)
¶みんなで声をそろえて言ってください。(Minnade koe o *soroete* itte kudasai.)

② [全部集める]

¶図書館には、日本語の教科書が全部そろえてあります。(Toshokan ni wa, Nihongo no kyōkasho ga zenbu *soroete* arimasu.)
¶必要な物を言ってください。あしたまでにそろえておきます。(Hitsuyō na mono o itte kudasai. Ashita made ni *soroete* okimasu.)

そろそろ 〔副〕

① [もうすぐ何かが行われる様子]
¶4時ですね。そろそろ出かけましょう。(Yoji desu ne. *Sorosoro* dekakemashō.)
¶そろそろ父が帰ってくるころです。(*Sorosoro* chichi ga kaette kuru koro desu.)
② [動作をゆっくり静かにする様子]
¶山田さんは足にけがをしているので、そろそろ歩いています。(Yamada san wa ashi ni kega o shite iru node, *sorosoro* aruite imasu.)
* 「そろそろと（sorosoroto）」の形でも使う。

soroeru 〔v Ⅱ〕 make uniform, match up; get ready, put in order, complete, collect

① [make uniform, make even, match up]
¶[I] **matched** the color of [my] handbag to [my] outfit.

¶Please say it aloud **together**.

② [get ready, put in order, complete, collect]
¶**A complete set** of Japanese textbooks is in the library.

¶Please tell me what you need. I'll **have it ready** for you by tomorrow.

sorosoro 〔adv〕 soon, by and by; (move)slowly, leisurely

① [soon, by and by]
¶It's four o'clock. Let's be going **soon**.

¶**It's getting to be** the time my father returns home.

② [(move) slowly, leisurely]
¶[Mr.] Yamada **is inching along** as [his] leg 〖foot〗 is hurt.

*Variant: *sorosoro to*.

そん 損 〔名、形動、〜する〕

損害 (songai)

¶ 事業に失敗して、百万円の損をしました。(Jigyō ni shippai shite, hyakuman'en no *son* o shimashita.)

¶ わたしは話し方が下手だから、いつも損をしています。(Watashi wa hanashikata ga heta da kara, itsu mo *son* o shite imasu.)

¶ そんなつまらない絵に高いお金を出すのは損ですよ。(Sonna tsumaranai e ni takai okane o dasu no wa *son* desu yo.)

⇔ 得 toku

son 〔n, adj-v, 〜*suru*〕 **loss, damage, disadvantage**
damage, a loss

¶ [I] had a business failure and **lost** a million yen.

¶ I **suffer the handicap** of being a poor speaker.

¶ **It will be your loss** if you pay so much for such a poor painting.

そんけい 尊敬 〔名、〜する〕

¶ あなたがいちばん尊敬している人はだれですか。(Anata ga ichiban *sonkei* shite iru hito wa dare desu ka?)

¶ 山田先生は立派な方なので、学生に尊敬されています。(Yamada sensei wa rippa na kata na node, gakusei ni *sonkei* sarete imasu.)

sonkei 〔n, 〜*suru*〕 **respect, esteem**

¶ Who is the person you **respect** the most?

¶ As Professor Yamada is such a fine person, [he] **is highly regarded** by all [his] students.

そんざい 存在 〔名、〜する〕

¶ あなたは神の存在を信じますか。(Anata wa kami no *sonzai* o shinjimasu ka?)

¶ そんな名前の町は東京には存在しませんよ。(Sonna namae no machi wa Tōkyō ni wa *sonzai* shimasen yo.)

sonzai 〔n, 〜*suru*〕 **existence, being**

¶ Do you believe in **the existence** of God?

¶ **There isn't** any town of that name in Tokyo.

そんな 〔連体〕

① [話し相手に身近な関係にあるものごとの状態などをさし示す]

¶ 先生にそんな失礼な言い方をしてはいけません。(Sensei ni *sonna* shitsurei na iikata o shite wa ikemasen.)

sonna 〔attrib〕 **such, that sort of, like that, that**

① [such, that sort of, like that; used to indicate the nature of something associated with the listener]

¶ You shouldn't speak **so** rudely to your teacher 〚the doctor〛.

¶そんなふうに乱暴に扱ってはいけません。(Sonna fū ni ranbō ni atsukatte wa ikemasen.)

*話し相手の言動などの状態をさし示すのに使う。場面や文脈の上でその状態のわかっているときには、例えば「そんな失礼な言い方 (sonna shitsurei na iikata)」の代わりに、「失礼な (shitsurei na)」を省いて「そんな言い方 (sonna iikata)」と言う場合もある。

②[文脈の上で話し相手の言ったものごとやその状態などをさし示したり前に述べて話し相手にわかっているものごとやその状態などをさし示したりする]
¶「山田さんという人を知っていますか。」(Yamada san to iu hito o shitte imasu ka?)「いいえ、そんな人は知りません。」(Iie, sonna hito wa shirimasen.)
¶ときどき国の母に会いたいと思います。そんなときにはよく手紙を書きます。(Tokidoki kuni no haha ni aitai to omoimasu. Sonna toki ni wa yoku tegami o kakimasu.)
⇒こんな konna　あんな anna　どんな donna

そんなに〔副〕

①[話し相手の言動に関係のあるものごとの様子などをさし示す]

¶そんなに急いで、どこへ行くんですか。(Sonna ni isoide, doko e iku n desu ka?)

¶ You shouldn't be **so** rough with it.

*Used to indicate the nature of the speech, behavior, etc., of the person addressed. When understood from the situation or context, the phrase might be shortened so that, for example, *sonna shitsurei na iikata* (such an impolite way of talking) becomes *sonna iikata* (such a way of talking).
② [that; indicates something previously mentioned and known to the listener, something the listener said earlier, etc.]

¶ "Do you know [Mr.] Yamada?" "No, I don't know **[him]**" (literally, **such** a person).

¶ Sometimes I miss my mother back home. I often write letters at times **like that**.

sonna ni 〔adv〕 **so, so much, like that;(not)very,(not)so**
① [so, so much, like that; indicates something concerning the speech or behavior of the person addressed, etc.]
¶ Where are you going in **such** a hurry?

¶そんなにあわてなくても、じゅうぶ
ん間に合いますよ。（Sonna ni
awatenakute mo, jūbun maniaimasu yo.)
¶上田さんはそんなに偉くなりました
か。（Ueda san wa *sonna ni* eraku
narimashita ka？）
②[ものごとの状態について話し相手
などが考えている程度をさし示す]

¶「富士山に登るのはたいへんです
か。」（Fujisan ni noboru no wa taihen
desu ka？）「途中までバスで行けます
から、そんなにたいへんではありませ
ん。」（Tochū made basu de ikemasu kara,
sonna ni taihen de wa arimasen.)
¶「バスの止まる所から駅まで遠いで
すか。」（Basu no tomaru tokoro kara eki
made tooi desu ka？）「いいえ、そんな
に遠くないです。」（Iie, *sonna ni* tooku
nai desu.)
¶「あなたは背が高いですね。 180
センチぐらいありますか。」（Anata wa
sei ga takai desu ne. Hyakuhachijissenchi
gurai arimasu ka？）「いいえ、そんなに
高くありません。 175 センチで
す。」（Iie, *sonna ni* takaku arimasen.
Hyakunanajūgosenchi desu.)
*あとに打ち消しの言葉が来る。話し
相手または広く人々が期待したり予想
したりしているほどではないという意
味を表すときに使う。
⇒こんなに **konna ni** あんなに **anna
ni** どんなに **donna ni**

¶ You will make it in plenty of time
without rushing around so 〚getting in
such a panic〛.
¶ Has [Mr.] Ueda become **such** a big
name?

② [(not) very, (not) so; indicates the
listener's opinion of some degree or
quantity]
¶ "Is it hard to climb Mount Fuji?"
"No, one can go partway by bus so it's
not **all that** hard."

¶ "Is it far to the station from where the
bus stops?"
"No, it's not **so** far."

¶ "You're really tall. Are you 180
centimeters tall?"
"No, I'm not **that** tall. I'm 175
centimeters tall."

*Followed by the negative. Used when
stating that something is not as much
as the listener or people in general
might think.

た

た　田 [名]

¶この辺は畑より田のほうが多いです。(Kono hen wa hatake yori *ta* no hō ga ooi desu.)

¶米は田で作ります。(Kome wa *ta* de tsukurimasu.)

た [助動]

① [過去・経験・回想などを表す]

¶「あなたは咋日新宿へ行きましたか。」(Anata wa kinō Shinjuku e ikimashi*ta* ka?)「はい、行きました。」(Hai, ikimashi*ta*.)

¶わたしはあの映画を5回も見ました。(Watashi wa ano ciga o gokai mo mimashi*ta*.)

¶ゆうべはたいへん暑かったですね。(Yūbe wa taihen atsuka*tta* desu ne.)

¶若いころの上田先生は、とても怖い先生でした。(Wakai koro no Ueda sensei wa, totemo kowai sensei deshi*ta*.)

② [完了を表す]

¶「もう、昼御飯を食べましたか。」(Mō hirugohan o tabemashi*ta* ka?)「いいえ、まだ食べていません。」(Iie, mada tabete imasen.)

¶今、授業が終わったところです。(Ima, jugyō ga owa*tta* tokoro desu.)

¶あした学校へ行った時、本をお返しします。(Ashita gakkō e i*tta* toki, hon o okaeshi shimasu.)

ta [n] rice field, rice paddy

¶ Around here there is more land in **rice paddies** than under dry cultivation.

¶ Rice is grown in **rice paddies**.

-ta [auxil] **a verb ending expressing past action, completed action, etc.**

① [expresses action in the past, an experience, a recollection, etc.]

¶ "**Did you go** to Shinjuku yesterday?" "Yes, **I did**."

¶ **I've seen** that movie five times.

¶ **It was** very hot last night, wasn't it?

¶ [Mr.] Ueda **was** a very forbidding teacher when [he] was young.

② [expresses completed action]

¶ "**Have you** already **eaten** lunch?" "No, I haven't eaten yet."

¶ Class just **ended**.

¶ [I] will return the book when [I] **go** to school tomorrow.

473

③ [期待したり予想したりしたことな
どが実際に起こったことを表す]

¶財布はやっぱり引き出しの中にあり
ました。(Saifu wa yappari hikidashi no
naka ni arimashi*ta*.)
¶あ、バスが来ましたよ。(A！basu
ga kimashi*ta* yo.)

④ [忘れたことを思い出したり不確か
なことを確かめるとき言う]

¶あしたは数学の試験がありました
ね。(Ashita wa sūgaku no shiken ga
arimashi*ta* ne.)
¶あなたは田中さんの息子さんでした
ね。(Anata wa Tanaka san no musukosan
deshi*ta* ne.)
¶上田さんはあしたフランスへ行くん
でしたね。(Ueda san wa ashita Furansu
e iku n deshi*ta* ne.)

*動作などを表す動詞の場合は「動詞
(連体の形)＋の（ん）でした (no
[n] deshita)」の形になる。

⑤ [ものごとの性質や状態を表す]

太った人 (futot*ta* hito) とがった鉛筆
(togat*ta* enpitsu) 黒板にかいた絵
(kokuban ni kai*ta* e) 砂糖を入れたコー
ヒー (satō o ire*ta* kōhii)
¶あの眼鏡をかけた人はだれですか。
(Ano megane o kake*ta* hito wa dare desu
ka？)

③ [used when something one has been
expecting or waiting for actually
happens]
¶ The wallet *was* in the drawer after all.

¶ Oh, the bus **is here**!

④ [used when remembering something
one has forgotten or when confirming
something one is unsure about]
¶ **There's** a math exam tomorrow, isn't
there?

¶ Now, **you're** [Mr.] Tanaka's son,
aren't you?

¶ **Wasn't** [Miss] Ueda going to leave
for France tomorrow?

*In the case of a verb expressing an
action, etc., the pattern "verb
(dictionary form) + *no* [[*n*]] *deshita*" is
used.
⑤ [used to express the nature or state
of something]
a **fat** person // a **sharpened** pencil // a
picture **drawn** on the blackboard //
coffee **sweetened** with sugar

¶ Who is that person **wearing** glasses?

¶川に沿った道を歩いていきました。
(Kawa ni sotta michi o aruite
ikimashita.)

¶ [I] walked along the road **running
parallel** to the river.

*名詞を修飾する形で使われ、「〜てい
る（〜te iru）」「〜てある（〜te aru）」と
置き換えることができる。

*Used modifying a noun. Can be
replaced by *-te iru* or *-te aru*.

⑥[条件を表す]

⑥ [used to express some stipulation]

¶春になったら、旅行をしましょう。
(Haru ni nattara, ryokō o shimashō.)

¶ Let's take a trip **in** the spring.

¶もし高かったら、買いません。
(Moshi takakattara, kaimasen.)

¶ **If** it's expensive [I] won't buy it.

¶雨だったら、行きません。(Ame
dattara, ikimasen.)

¶ **If** it rains [I] won't go.

*いつも「〜たら（ば）（〜tara
〔ba〕）」の形で使う。

*Always used in the *-tara* 〖*-ba*〗 form.

→たら **tara**

だ〔助動〕

da 〔auxil〕 **is, are**

①[あるものがある類に属するもので
あるという関係を表すのに使う]

① [indicates something is in a
particular category]

¶それは日本語の本だ。(Sore wa Ni-
hongo no hon *da*.)

¶ That **is** a book written in Japanese.

¶田中さんは学生だ。(Tanaka san wa
gakusei *da*.)

¶ [Mr.] Tanaka **is** a student.

¶山田さんは学生ではない。(Yamada
san wa gakusei *de* wa nai.)

¶ [Miss] Yamada **is not** a student.

¶この建物は病院で、あの建物は学校
だ。(Kono tatemono wa byōin *de*, ano
tatemono wa gakkō *da*.)

¶ This building **is** a hospital, and that
one **is** a school.

②[あるものがあるものと一致するも
のであるという関係を表すのに使う]

② [indicates that one thing equals
another]

¶ここは銀座だ。(Koko wa Ginza *da*.)

¶ This **is** the Ginza.

¶このクラスでいちばん背の高い人は
山田さんだ。(Kono kurasu de ichiban se
no takai hito wa Yamada san *da*.)

¶ The tallest person in this class **is**
[Mr.] Yamada.

¶この小説の作者は中村さんだ。(Ko-
no shōsetsu no sakusha wa Nakamura san
da.)

¶ The author of this novel **is** [Miss]
Nakamura.

③ [あるものがある空間に存在するという関係を表するのに使う]

¶「お母さんは今どこにいる。」(Okāsan wa ima doko ni iru？)「お母さんは台所だ。」(Okāsan wa daidokoro *da*.)

¶ 山田先生の研究室はあの建物の2階だ。(Yamada sensei no kenkyūshitsu wa ano tatemono no nikai *da*.)

¶ 郵便局は駅の前だ。(Yūbinkyoku wa eki no mae *da*.)

④ [人などがある動作を続けているという時間的な関係を表すのに使う]

¶「先生は。」(Sensei wa？)「先生は今授業中だ。」(Sensei wa ima jugyō-chū *da*.)

¶「お父さんはいる。」(Otōsan wa iru？)「父は今旅行中だ。」(Chichi wa ima ryokōchū *da*.)

¶ 上田さんは今食事中だと思います。(Ueda san wa ima shokujichū *da* to omoimasu.)

*「先生は今授業だ。(Sensei wa ima jugyō da.)」「父は今旅行だ。(Chichi wa ima ryokō da.)」「上田さんは今食事だと思います。(Ueda san wa ima shokuji da to omoimasu.)」とも言う。

⑤ [ものごとのある事態やものごとがある状態にあることなどを表すのに使う]

¶ 昨日は一日じゅう雨だった。(Kinō wa ichinichijū ame **datta**.)

¶ あした雨なら、旅行には行きません。(Ashita ame *nara*, ryokō ni wa ikimasen.)

③ [indicates a person or thing exists in a certain space]

¶ "Where is your mother now?" "She's in the kitchen."

¶ Professor Yamada's office 〚study room, laboratory〛 **is** on the second floor of that building.

¶ The post office **is** in front of the station.

④ [indicates a person or thing is in the course of doing some action]

¶ The professor 〚teacher〛? [He] **is** in class now.

¶ "Is your father there?" "No, **he's** away on a trip now."

¶ I believe that [Mrs.] Ueda **is** atlunch 〚dinner〛 now.

*One can also omit -*chū* and say "*Sensei wa ima jugyō da* ," "*Chichi wa ima ryokō da* ," or "*Ueda san wa ima shokuji da to omoimasu.*"

⑤ [indicates the situation or condition of someone or something]

¶ **It rained** all day yesterday.

¶ **If it rains** tomorrow [we] won't go on [our] trip.

¶ 田中さんは病気だから今日は来ないよ。(Tanaka san wa byōki *da*kara kyōwa konai yo.)

¶ 今日は学校が休みなので、映画を見に行こうと思っています。(Kyō wa gakkō ga yasumi *na* node, eiga o mini ikō to omotte imasu.)

＊ものごとの関係や病態などについての確定的な判断を表すのに使う。丁寧に言う場合には、「です（desu）」となる。

＊「だ（da）」は「終止の形」、「で（de）」「なら（ば）（nara［ba］）」「なので（na node）」は「接続の形」、「だった（datta）」は「たの形」、「で（は）ない（de［wa］nai）」は「ないの形」である。

⇒です desu　だろう darō　なら nara

たい 対〔名〕

¶ 日本対アメリカのバレーボールの試合はあした行われます。(Nihon *tai* Amerika no barēbōru no shiai wa ashita okonawaremasu.)

¶ 試合は4対3で、わたしたちのチームが勝ちました。(Shiai wa yon *tai* san de, watashitachi no chiimu ga kachimashita.)

たい〔助動〕

¶ 水が飲みたいです。(Mizu ga nomi*tai* desu.)

¶ 何も食べたくありません。(Nani mo tabe*taku* arimasen.)

¶ 芝居を見に行きたかったら、連れていってあげます。(Shibai o mi ni iki*takattara*, tsurete itte agemasu.)

¶ わたしは一度日本へ行ってみたいです。(Watashi wa ichido Nihon e itte mi*tai* desu.)

¶ [Mr.] Tanaka won't be coming today as [he] is sick.

¶ As there **is** no school today, I think I'll go to see a movie.

＊ Used to express definite conclusions about a condition, situation, or relationship. When one speaks politely, *da* becomes *desu*.

＊ The sentence-final form is *da*; continuative forms are *de*, nara *[ba]* and *na node*; the -*ta* form is *datta*; and the negative form is *de [wa] nai*.

tai 〔n〕 **versus, against**

¶ The **Japan-U.S.** volleyball game is tomorrow.

¶ Our team won the game with a score of 4 **to** 3.

-**tai** 〔auxil〕 **want to, feel like ~ing**

¶ **I want** a drink of water.

¶ **I don't want** anything to eat.

¶ I'll take you **if you'd like** to go see a play.

¶ I **would like** to go to Japan at least once.

477

＊ある行為や事態の実現を希望する意味を表す。普通は話し手の希望を表すが、質問する場合や相手の心情を推量する場合や相手がそういう希望を持っているということが判断できる場合には話し手以外の人の場合にも使う。
「あなたも今度の旅行にはいっしょに行きたいでしょう。(Anata mo kondo no ryokō ni wa issho ni ikitai deshō？)」
「今度の旅行に行きたい人はもういませんか。(Kondo no ryokō ni ikitai hito wa mō imasen ka？)」「芝居を見に行きたかったら、連れていってあげます。(Shibai o mi ni ikitakattara, tsurete itte agemasu.)」
⇒たがる **tagaru**

＊Used to refer to wanting to do something. Generally *-tai* refers to the speaker's wishes but it can also be used for the desires of others when asking a question, when guessing the feelings of another, or when one can judge that another has certain feelings. For example, "*Anata mo kondo no ryokō ni wa issho ni ikitai deshō?*" (You want to come with us on the trip too, don't you?); "*Kondo no ryokō ni ikitai hito wa mō imasen ka?*" (Aren't there any others who want to come on the trip?); or "*Shibai o mi ni ikitakattara, tsurete itte agemasu*" (I'll take you if you'd like to go see a play).

だい 題 〔名〕

dai 〔n〕 **title; subject, theme**

¶あの本の題は何でしたか。(Ano hon no *dai* wa nan deshita ka？)

¶ What is 〚was〛 **the title** of that book?

¶「日本」という題で作文を書きました。("Nihon" to iu *dai* de sakubun o kakimashita.)

¶ [I] wrote a composition on **the theme**, "Japan."

だい 第 〔頭〕

dai 〔pref〕 **Number~**

¶今日は第3課を勉強しました。(Kyō wa *dai*sanka o benkyō shimashita.)

¶ Today [we] studied Lesson 3.

(-)だい (-)台 〔名、尾〕

(-)dai 〔n, suf〕

stand, pedestal, dais, platform; units, sets

1 〔名〕

1 〔n〕

stand, pedestal, base, table, platform, bench, block

¶この台に乗って、たなの上の物を取ってください。(Kono *dai* ni notte, tana no ue no mono o totte kudasai.)

¶ Please stand on this **footstool** and take down something 〚everything〛 on the shelf for me.

2 〔尾〕

2 〔suf〕

units, sets; the counter for relatively large manufactured items such as cars, bicycles, television sets, radios and sewing machines

¶東京の自動車は全部で何台ぐらいあ りますか。（Tōkyō no jidōsha wa zenbu de nan*dai* gurai arimasu ka？）

¶ About **how many** automobiles are there in Tokyo?

¶わたしの家にはテレビが一台もあり ません。（Watashi no ie ni wa terebi ga ichi*dai* mo arimasen.）

¶ There isn't even one television **set** in my house.

-だい -代〔尾〕

部屋代（heya*dai*）下宿代 （geshuku*dai*）本代（hon*dai*）洗たく代 （sentaku*dai*）バス代（basu*dai*）タクシ ー代（takushii*dai*）

-dai〔suf〕**charge, fee**
room **rent** // a boardinghouse **charge** // a book **bill** // a laundry **charge** // a bus **fare** // a taxi **fare**

¶食事代は一か月いくらかかります か。（Shokuji *dai* wa ikkagetsu ikura kakarimasu ka？）

¶ How much do you **pay for meals** a month〚How much will **meals cost** a month〛?

たいいく 体育〔名〕

体育の日（*taiiku* no hi）

¶今日の体育の授業は体育館で行いま す。（Kyō no *taiiku* no jugyō wa *taiiku*kan de okonaimasu.）

taiiku〔n〕**physical training, physical education**
Sports Day

¶ Today's **gym** class will be in **the gym**.

だいいちに 第一に〔副〕

¶日本へ行ったら、まず第一に京都へ 行きたいと思っています。（Nihon e ittara, mazu *daiichi ni* Kyōto e ikitai to omotte imasu.）

daiichi ni〔adv〕**first, first of all**
¶ When I go to Japan, I want to go to Kyoto **first of all**.

¶まず第一に健康に気をつけなければ なりません。（Mazu *daiichi ni* kenkō ni ki o tsukenakereba narimasen.）

¶ One should take care of one's health **above all else**.

たいいん 退院〔名、～する〕

¶田中さんは昨日退院したそうです。
(Tanaka san wa kinō *taiin* shita sō desu.)
¶病気が重いので、いつ退院できるか
わかりません。(Byōki ga omoi node,
itsu *taiin* dekiru ka wakarimasen.)
⇔入院 nyūin

taiin 〔n, ～*suru*〕 **leave the hospital, discharge from the hospital**
¶I hear that [Mrs.] Tanaka **came home from the hospital** yesterday.
¶As [his] illness is quite serious, it is unclear when [he] will be able **to leave the hospital**.

たいかい 大会〔名〕

全国大会 (zenkoku-*taikai*)
¶東京で人口問題についての世界大会
が開かれました。(Tōkyō de
jinkōmondai ni tsuite no sekai-*taikai* ga
hirakaremashita.)

taikai 〔n〕 **mass meeting, rally, general meeting; conference, convention; meet, tournament**
a national **convention**
¶A world **conference** concerning the population problem opened〖has opened〗in Tokyo.

たいかく 体格〔名〕

¶上田さんはとてもいい体格をしてい
ます。(Ueda san wa totemo ii *taikaku* o
shite imasu.)
¶スポーツをすると、体格がよくなり
ます。(Supōtsu o suru to, *taikaku* ga
yoku narimasu.)

taikaku 〔n〕 **physique, physical constitution,(body)build**
¶[Mr.] Ueda has a fine **build**.

¶**One's constitution** improves if one participates in sports.

だいがく 大学〔名〕

大学生 (*daigaku*sei) 大学に入る
(*daigaku* ni hairu) 大学を出る
(*daigaku* o deru) 国立大学 (kokuritsu-
daigaku) 私立大学 (shiritsu-*daigaku*)
大学院 (*daigaku*in)
¶わたしはA大学の学生です。
(Watashi wa E-*daigaku* no gakusei
desu.)

daigaku 〔n〕 **college, university**
a **college**〖**university**〗student, an undergraduate // enter **college** // graduate from **college** // a national **university** // a private **university** 〖**college**〗// graduate **school**
¶I am a student at **University A** 〖**College A**〗.

¶わたしは 1975 年に大学を卒業しました。(Watashi wa senkyū-hyaku-nanajūgonen ni *daigaku* o sotsugyō shimashita.)

¶ I graduated from **college** in 1975.

だいきん 代金 〔名〕

daikin 〔n〕 **price, charge, bill**

¶わたしはまだ本の代金を払っていません。(Watashi wa mada hon no *daikin* o haratte imasen.)

¶ I haven't paid my book **bill** yet.

¶代金を先にいただきます。(*Daikin* o saki ni itadakimasu.)

¶ Please **pay** in advance 〚now〛.

＊普通、物を買って払う金のことをいう。

＊Usually refers to the money used to pay for something.

たいくつ 退屈 〔名、形動、～する〕

taikutsu 〔n, adj-v, ～*suru*〕 **tedious, dull, boring**

退屈な話 (*taikutsu* na hanashi)

a **boring** talk

¶何もすることがないので退屈です。(Nani mo suru koto ga nai node *taikutsu* desu.)

¶ [I] **am bored** as there is nothing to do.

¶話がおもしろくないので、みんな退屈そうな顔をしています。(Hanashi ga omoshiroku nai node, minna *taikutsu*sō na kao o shite imasu.)

¶ Everyone **looks bored** as the lecture isn't very interesting.

たいざい 滞在 〔名、～する〕

taizai 〔n, ～*suru*〕 **stay, visit, sojourn**

¶いつまでこちらに御滞在ですか。(Itsu made kochira ni go*taizai* desu ka?)「1週間ぐらい滞在する予定です。」(Isshūkan gurai *taizai* suru yotei desu.)

¶ "How long **will you be staying** here?"
"I plan **to stay** about a week."

¶滞在期間をもう1年延ばすつもりです。(*Taizai*-kikan o mō ichinen nobasu tsumori desu.)

¶ I intend to extend **my stay** for an additional year.

たいし 大使 〔名〕

taishi 〔n〕 **ambassador**

大使館 (*taishi*kan) 駐日アメリカ大使 (chūnichi-Amerika*taishi*)

an embassy // the American **ambassador** to Japan

だいじ　大事〔名、形動〕
大事な用事（*daiji* na yōji）

¶どうぞ、体を大事にしてください。
（Dōzo, karada o *daiji* ni shite kudasai.）
¶これは父の大事にしている花びんです。（Kore wa chichi no *daiji* ni shite iru kabin desu.）

daiji〔n, adj-v〕**important, precious**
important business, an **important** engagement

¶Please **take good care** of yourself.

¶This is a vase **treasured** by my father.

たいして　大して〔副〕
¶この料理は大しておいしくありません。（Kono ryōri wa *taishite* oishiku arimasen.）
¶今度の試験は大して難しくありませんでした。（Kondo no shiken wa *taishite* muzukashiku arimasen deshita.）
＊あとに打ち消しの言葉が来る。

taishite〔adv〕**(not)very,(not)much**
¶This food isn't **very** good.

¶The last test wasn't **particularly** difficult.

＊Used with the negative.

たいじゅう　体重〔名〕
¶今、わたしの体重は50キロです。
（Ima, watashi no *taijū* wa gojikkiro desu.）
¶病気をしたので、体重が軽くなりました。（Byōki o shita node, *taijū* ga karuku narimashita.）

taijū〔n〕**one's body weight**
¶I presently **weigh** 50 kilos.

¶[I] lost **weight**〚have lost **weight**〛 due to illness.

たいしょう　対象〔名〕
¶これは高校生を対象とした雑誌です。（Kore wa kōkōsei o *taishō* to shita zasshi desu.）
¶わたしは戦後の日本経済を研究の対象としています。（Watashi wa sengo no Nihon-keizai o kenkyū no *taishō* to shite imasu.）

taishō〔n〕**object, subject, target**
¶This magazine **is aimed** at high school students.

¶**The subject** of my research is the postwar Japanese economy.

たいしょう　大正〔名〕

大正時代（*taishō*-jidai）

taishō〔n〕**Taisho; the name of a Japanese emperor and of his reign from 1912 to 1926**
the **Taisho** period

だいじょうぶ 大丈夫 〔形動〕

① [心配する必要のない様子]

¶この水を飲んでも大丈夫ですか。
(Kono mizu o nonde mo *daijōbu* desu ka？)

¶お体はもう大丈夫ですか。(Okarada wa mō *daijōbu* desu ka？)

② [間違いのない確かな様子]

¶大丈夫、あしたは天気ですよ。(*Daijōbu*, ashita wa tenki desu yo.)

*語幹だけで副詞的にも使う。

daijōbu 〔adj-v〕 safe; certain

① [safe, free from danger, all right]

¶ **Is it safe** to drink this water?

¶ **Are you recovered** now (literally, Is your body **all right** now)?

② [certain, sure]

¶ **Don't worry**. The weather will be fine tomorrow.

*Sometimes *daijōbu* alone is used adverbially.

だいじん 大臣 〔名〕

総理大臣 (sōri*daijin*) 文部大臣
(monbu*daijin*) 大蔵大臣 (ookura-
daijin) 外務大臣 (gaimu*daijin*)

daijin 〔n〕 (government)minister

the prime **minister** // the **minister** of education // the **minister** of finance // the **minister** of foreign affairs

たいする 対する 〔動Ⅲ〕

① [向かう、相手とする]

¶目上の人に対しては、丁寧な言葉を使わなければなりません。(Meue no hito ni *taishite* wa, teinei na kotoba o tsukawanakereba narimasen.)

¶最近、子供の親に対する態度が変わってきました。(Saikin, kodomo no oya ni *taisuru* taido ga kawatte kimashita.)

② [あるものごとに関する]

¶この問題に対する意見は、ほかにありませんか。(Kono mondai ni *taisuru* iken wa, hoka ni arimasen ka？)

¶わたしは日本文化に対して興味があります。(Watashi wa Nihon-bunka ni *taishite* kyōmi ga arimasu.)

*普通「〜に対する (〜ni taisuru)」の形で使う。

taisuru 〔vⅢ〕 toward, to, against; concerning, in regard to

① [toward, to, against, as opposed to, in comparison with]

¶ One should use polite language **toward** one's superiors.

¶ In recent years there has been a change in the attitude of children **toward** their parents.

② [concerning, in regard to]

¶ Are there any other opinions **concerning** this matter?

¶ I have an interest **in** Japanese culture.

*Usually used in the pattern "〜*ni taisuru*."

たいせつ　大切〔形動〕

① [大事な様子]

大切なもの（*taisetsu* na mono）大切な
人（*taisetsu* na hito）大切な問題
（*taisetsu* na mondai）

¶石油は現在、非常に大切なものに
なっています。（Sekiyu wa genzai, hijō
ni *taisetsu* na mono ni natte imasu.）

¶外国語を話すときは、発音が大切で
す。（Gaikokugo o hanasu toki wa,
hatsuon ga *taisetsu* desu.）

② [丁寧に扱う様子、大事にする様子]

¶体を大切にしてください。（Karada o
taisetsu ni shite kudasai.）

¶資源は大切に使いましょう。（Shigen
wa *taisetsu* ni tsukaimashō.）

たいそう　体操〔名、〜する〕

ラジオ体操（rajio-*taisō*）

¶わたしは毎朝体操をしています。
（Watashi wa maiasa *taisō* o shite imasu.）

だいたい〔名〕

¶だいたいのことはわかりました。
（*Daitai* no koto wa wakarimashita.）

¶仕事はだいたい終わりました。
（Shigoto wa *daitai* owarimashita.）

¶わたしも、あなたとだいたい同じ意
見です。（Watashi mo, anata to *daitai*
onaji iken desu.）

＊副詞的に使われることが多い。

たいてい〔副、〜の〕

① [ほとんどの場合]

---

taisetsu 〔adj-v〕 **important,
serious, valuable; to value, prize**

① [important, serious, grave, valuable,
precious]

treasure, valuables // an **important**
person, a **beloved** person // a **serious**
problem

¶ Oil is presently an extremely
valuable commodity.

¶ Pronunciation **is important** when
speaking a foreign language.

② [to value, prize]

¶ Please **take good care of** yourself.

¶ We should **value** our natural
resources **and use** them **carefully**.

taisō 〔n, 〜*suru*〕 **gymnastics,
athletic exercises**

radio **calisthenics**

¶ I do **exercises** every morning.

daitai 〔n〕 **outline, gist; generally,
on the whole**

¶ **For the most part I** understand.

¶ The work is **practically** finished.

¶ I have **substantially** the same
opinion as you.

＊Often used adverbially.

taitei 〔adv, 〜*no*〕 **usually,
generally, mostly; almost all,
most**

① [usually, generally, mostly]

¶日曜日はたいてい家にいます。
(Nichiyōbi wa *taitei* ie ni imasu.)

¶ [I] am **generally** at home on Sunday.

¶あなたはたいてい何時ごろ起きますか。(Anata wa *taitei* nanji goro okimasu ka？)

¶ What time do you **usually** get up?

② [大部分]

② [almost all, most]

¶たいていの学生は歩いて学校へ来ます。(*Taitei* no gakusei wa aruite gakkō e kimasu.)

¶ **The majority** of students walk to school.

¶ここにある本はたいてい読みました。(Koko ni aru hon wa *taitei* yomimashita.)

¶ [I] have read **almost all** of the books here.

たいど　態度 〔名〕

taido 〔n〕 **attitude, stance, manner**

¶田中さんは授業中の態度が悪かったので、先生にしかられました。
(Tanaka san wa jugyōchū no *taido* ga warukatta node, sensei ni shikararemashita.)

¶ The teacher reprimanded [Mr.] Tanaka for [his] poor **attitude** during class.

¶賛成か反対か、態度をはっきりしなさい。(Sansei ka hantai ka, *taido* o hakkiri shinasai.)

¶ Make clear **where you stand**, for it or against it.

だいとうりょう　大統領 〔名〕

daitōryō 〔n〕 **president (of a country)**

副大統領 （fuku-*daitōryō*） 大統領夫人 （*daitōryō* fujin）

a vice-**president** // the First Lady

だいどころ　台所 〔名〕

daidokoro 〔n〕 **kitchen**

台所用品 （*daidokoro*yōhin）

kitchenware

¶母は台所で夕食の支度をしています。(Haha wa *daidokoro* de yūshoku no shitaku o shite imasu.)

¶ My mother is in **the kitchen** fixing dinner.

だいひょう　代表 〔名、～する〕

daihyō 〔n, ～*suru*〕 **representative**

① [多くの人に代わって意見などを述べること、またその人]

① [representative, delegate]

代表者 （*daihyō*sha） 学生の意見を代表する （gakusei no iken o *daihyō* suru）

a representative, a delegate // **represent** student opinion

¶山田さんがクラスの代表に選ばれました。(Yamada san ga kurasu no *daihyō* ni erabaremashita.)

¶ [Miss] Yamada was elected as the class **representative**.

②[一つまたは一部分によってその全体を表すこと、またそのもの]

② [representative, typical]

代表的な作品 (*daihyō*teki na sakuhin)

a **representativeh** work (of art, literature, etc.)

¶自動車は日本の代表的な輸出品です。(Jidōsha wa Nihon no *daihyō*teki na yushutsuhin desu.)

¶ Automobiles are **representative** Japanese exports.

だいぶ〔副〕

daibu〔adv〕**greatly, much, very**

¶病気はもうだいぶよくなりました。(Byōki wa mō *daibu* yoku narimashita.)

¶ [My] illness is **much** better.

¶田中さんとはだいぶ長い間会っていません。(Tanaka san to wa *daibu* nagai aida atte imasen.)

¶ [I] haven't met [Miss] Tanaka in **quite** a long time.

たいふう 台風〔名〕

taifū〔n〕**typhoon**

台風が来る (*taifū* ga kuru)

a **typhoon** approaches; a **typhoon** strikes

¶日本では、八月の下旬から九月の上旬にかけて台風が多いです。(Nihon de wa, hachigatsu no gejun kara kugatsu no jōjun ni kakete *taifū* ga ooi desu.)

¶ **Typhoons** are frequent in Japan in late August and early September.

¶台風でたくさんの家が壊れました。(*Taifū* de takusan no ie ga kowaremashita.)

¶ Many homes were destroyed in **the typhoon**.

だいぶぶん 大部分〔名〕

daibubun〔n〕**most of, majority of**

¶宿題は大部分終わりました。(Shukudai wa *daibubun* owarimashita.)

¶ [I] have finished **most** of the homework.

¶大部分の学生はもう帰りました。(*Daibubun* no gakusei wa mō kaerimashita.)

¶ **Most** of the students have already left.

⇒一部分 ichibubun

タイプライター〔名〕

和文タイプライター（wabun-*taipuraitā*）英文タイプライター（eibun-*taipuraitā*）タイプライターを打つ（*taipuraitā* o utsu）

＊「タイプ（taipu）」とも言う。

たいへん〔副、形動〕

1〔副〕

¶ 今日はたいへん疲れました。（Kyō wa *taihen* tsukaremashita.）

¶ 妹はバナナがたいへん好きです。（Imōto wa banana ga *taihen* suki desu.）

¶ 田中さんは試験の成績にたいへん満足しています。（Tanaka san wa shiken no seiseki ni *taihen* manzoku shite imasu.）

2〔形動〕

① [重大である様子、程度が普通ではない様子]

¶ あっ、たいへんだ。隣が火事だ。（A'！ *Taihen* da. Tonari ga kaji da.）

¶ 今、東京に大地震が来たらたいへんです。（Ima, Tōkyō ni oojishin ga kitara *taihen* desu.）

¶ 「会社のお金を落としてしまいました。」（Kaisha no okane o otoshite shimaimashita.）「それはたいへんなことをしましたね。」（Sore wa *taihen* na koto o shimashita ne.）

② [何かをするのに非常な苦労をしたり努力をしたりする様子]

¶ 「富士山に登るのはたいへんですか。」（Fujisan ni noboru no wa *taihen* desuka？）「いいえ、途中までバスで行けますから、そんなにたいへんではありません。」（Iie, tochū made basu de

---

taipuraitā 〔n〕 **typewriter**

a Japanese-character **typewriter** // a roman-letter **typewriter** // to type

＊Variant: *taipu*.

taihen 〔adv, adj-v〕 **very, greatly; serious, grave; hard, difficult**

1 〖adv〗 very, greatly, awfully

¶ Today **really** tired me out.

¶ My younger sister is **very** fond of bananas.

¶ [Mr.] Tanaka is **fully** satisfied with [his] mark on the exam.

2 〖adj-v〗

① [serious, grave, horrible, terrible]

¶ **My God!** There's a fire next door!

¶ **It would be disastrous** if a major earthquake should strike present-day Tokyo.

¶ "I lost some company money." "Oh, **how terrible**."

② [hard, difficulti]

¶ **"Is it difficult** to climb Mount Fuji?" "No, you can go partway by bus so **it's not** so **bad**."

ikemasu kara, sonna ni *taihen* de wa arimasen.)

¶ 会議の資料を作っていたので、ゆうべは寝ませんでした。」(Kaigi no shiryō o tsukutte ita node, yūbe wa nemasen deshita.)「それはたいへんでしたね。」(Sore wa *taihen* deshita ne.)

¶ "I was up all night preparing papers for the meeting〚conference〛." "That's **really hard** on you" (literally, That was **terrible**).

たいよう　太陽〔名〕

¶ 地球は太陽の周りを回っています。(Chikyū wa *taiyō* no mawari o mawatte imasu.)

taiyō 〔n〕 **the sun**

¶ The earth revolves around **the sun**.

たいら　平ら〔形動〕

¶ 平らな道が遠くまで続いています。(*Taira* na michi ga tooku made tsuzuite imasu.)

¶ 山をけずって平らにすれば、もっと家が建てられます。(Yama o kezutte *taira* ni sureba, motto ie ga tateraremasu.)

taira 〔adj-v〕 **flat, even, level**

¶ The **flat** road stretches out into the distance.

¶ If the bill **were leveled**, more houses could be built.

たいりく　大陸〔名〕

¶ 日本はアジア大陸の東にあります。(Nihon wa Ajia-*tairiku* no higashi ni arimasu.)

¶ 北アメリカ大陸と南アメリカ大陸はつながっています。(Kitaamerika-*tairiku* to Minamiamerika-*tairiku* wa tsunagatte imasu.)

tairiku 〔n〕 **continent**

¶ Japan lies to the east of the Asian **continent**.

¶ **The continents** of North and South America are joined together.

たいりつ　対立〔名、〜する〕

¶ 意見の対立は、話し合いで解決したほうがいいです。(Iken no *tairitsu* wa, hanashiai de kaiketsu shita hō ga ii desu.)

¶ 意見が激しく対立して、会議はなかなか終わりませんでした。(Iken ga hageshiku *tairitsu* shite, kaigi wa nakanaka owarimasen deshita.)

tairitsu 〔n, 〜*suru*〕 **opposition, confrontation**

¶ It is best to resolve **differences** of opinion through discussion.

¶ The meeting dragged on due to **the clash** of opinion.

だい- 大- 〔頭〕

① [大きい]
大会社 (*dai*gaisha) 大企業 (*dai*kigyō) 大事件 (*dai*jiken) 大劇場 (*dai*gekijō)

② [優れた、立派な]
大音楽家 (*dai*ongakka) 大学者 (*dai*gakusha) 大人物 (*dai*jinbutsu)

③ [程度がはなはだしい]
大きらい (*dai*kirai) 大成功 (*dai*seikō) 大賛成 (*dai*sansei)
¶わたしは魚が大好きです。(Watashi wa sakana ga *dai*suki desu.)

たえず 絶えず 〔副〕

¶水道のせんがよく閉まらないので、絶えず水が流れています。(Suidō no sen ga yoku shimaranai node, *taezu* mizu ga nagarete imasu.)
¶うちの母は絶えず文句を言っています。(Uchi no haha wa *taezu* monku o itte imasu.)

たおす 倒す 〔動 I〕

¶掃除をしていて、花びんを倒してしまいました。(Sōji o shite ite, kabin o *taoshite* shimaimashlta.)
¶台風でたくさんの木が倒されました。(Taifū de takusan no ki ga *taosaremashita*.)

タオル 〔名〕

タオルで顔をふく (*taoru* de kao o fuku) 湯上がりタオル (yuagari*taoru*)

---

dai- 〔pref〕 **large; great; extreme**

① [large, big, great]
a **large** company // a **large** enterprise 〚corporation, company〛 // a **major** incident // a **large** theater

② [great, outstanding]
a **great** musician // an **eminent** scholar // a **great** person, an **outstanding** personality

③ [extreme degree]
hate, detest // a **great** success // **fully** approve of something
¶ I **love** fish.

taezu 〔adv〕 **constantly, continually, without interruption**
¶ The faucet doesn't close tightly so it's **perpetually** dripping.

¶ My mother is **always** complaining.

taosu 〔vI〕 **throw down, knock down**
¶ [I] **knocked over** a vase while cleaning.

¶ Many trees **were blown over** in the typhoon.

taoru 〔n〕 **towel, toweling**
wipe one's face with **a towel** // a bath **towel**

たおれる　倒れる〔動Ⅱ〕

¶昨日の地震でたくさんの家が倒れました。(Kinō no jishin de takusan no ie ga *taoremashita*.)

¶山田さんは気を失って倒れました。(Yamada san wa ki o ushinatte *taoremashita*.)

たかい　高い〔形〕

①[下から上までの長さが大きい様子、ものの位置が上の方にあって地面などから離れている様子]

高い木（*takai* ki）背が高い（se ga *takai*）

¶あの高い建物は何ですか。(Ano *takai* tatemono wa nan desu ka?)

¶世界でいちばん高い山はエベレストです。(Sekai de ichiban *takai* yama wa Eberesuto desu.)

¶日が高く昇っています。(Hi ga *takaku* nobotte imasu.)

⇔低い hikui

②[買うのに金が多くかかる様子]

¶この紙は1枚50円ですか。高いですね。(Kono kami wa ichimai gojūen desu ka? *Takai* desu ne.)

¶あまり高ければ買いません。(Amari *takakereba* kaimasen.)

⇔安い yasui

③[声・音が大きく聞こえる様子、音階が上である様子]

高い音（*takai* oto）

¶隣の部屋から高い笑い声が聞こえてきます。(Tonari no heya kara *takai* waraigoe ga kikoete kimasu.)

taoreru 〔vII〕 **fall, fall down, collapse**

¶ Many houses **were destroyed** in the earthquake yesterday.

¶ [Mr.] Yamada lost consciousness and **fell to the floor** 〚ground〛.

takai 〔adj〕 **high, tall; expensive; loud, high-pitched; elevated; exalted**

① [high, tall]

a **tall** tree // (a person is) **tall**

¶ What is that **tall** building over there?

¶ The **highest** mountain in the world is Mount Everest.

¶ The sun is **high** in the sky.

② [expensive, high-priced]

¶ This paper is 50 yen a sheet? **It's expensive**, isn't it?

¶ [I] won't buy it **if it's** too **expensive**.

③ [loud, high-pitched]

a **loud** sound

¶ [I] can hear someone laughing **loudly** next door.

¶春子さんの声は高いです。（Haruko san no koe wa *takai* desu.）

¶ Haruko's voice **is high-pitched**.

⇔低い **hikui**

④ [温度・熱などの数値が大きい]
温度が高い（ondo ga *takai*）気圧が高い（kiatsu ga *takai*）

④ [high, elevated]
the temperature **is high** //the atmospheric pressure **is high**

¶山田さんは熱が高くて、学校を休みました。（Yamada san wa netsu ga *takakute*, gakkō o yasumimashita.）

¶ [Miss] Yamada stayed home from school with a **high** fever.

⇔低い **hikui**

⑤ [身分などが上である様子]
地位が高い（chii ga *takai*）

⑤ [high, exalted, superior]
have a **high** social standing; have a **high** position

⇔低い **hikui**

たがい 互い [名]

tagai [n] **mutual, reciprocal, each other's, one another's**

¶世界各国の人々がお互いを理解し合うのが平和にとって大切なことです。（Sekai kakkoku no hitobito ga o*tagai* o rikai shiau no ga heiwa ni totte taisetsu na koto desu.）

¶ **Mutual** understanding among the peoples of the world is important for world peace.

¶いっしょに生活するためには、お互いが気をつけなければなりません。（Issho ni seikatsu suru tame ni wa, o*tagai* ga ki o tsukenakereba narimasen.）

¶ People living together must be considerate **of each other**.

＊普通「お互い（otagai）」の形で使う。

＊ Usually used in the form *otagai*.

たがいに 互いに [副]

tagai ni [adv] **mutually, reciprocally**

¶わたしたちはお互いに助け合って生活しています。（Watashitachi wa o*tagai ni* tasukeatte seikatsu shite imasu.）

¶ We live helping **one another**.

¶二人は互いに自分の国の言葉を教え合いました。（Futari wa *tagai ni* jibun no kuni no kotoba o oshieaimashita.）

¶ The two taught **each other** their own respective language.

たかさ 高さ [名]

takasa [n] **height; expensiveness**

① [上へのびている程度]

① [height]

¶わたしは背の高さが弟と同じくらいです。（Watashi wa se no *takasa* ga otōto to onaji kurai desu.）

¶富士山の高さはどのくらいですか。（Fujisan no *takasa* wa dono kurai desu ka？）

②［金のかかる程度］

¶東京の物価の高さには驚きました。（Tōkyō no bukka no *takasa* ni wa odorokimashita.）

⇒-さ **-sa**

¶ I am roughly the same **height** as my younger brother.

¶ How **high** is Mount Fuji?

② [expensiveness]

¶ [I] was surprised at the **high** prices in Tokyo.

だから〔接〕

¶昨日はひどい雨でした。だから、どこへも行きませんでした。（Kinō wa hidoi ame deshita. *Dakara*, doko e mo ikimasen deshita.）

¶彼は毎晩酒を飲んでいました。だから、病気になったのです。（Kare wa maiban sake o nonde imashita. *Dakara*, byōki ni natta no desu.）

＊前に述べた理由を受けて、その帰結をあとに続けるときに使う。丁寧に言う場合には「ですから（desukara）」を使う。

dakara 〔conj〕 **accordingly, therefore**

¶ It was raining heavily yesterday. **Therefore** [I] didn't go anywhere.

¶ He drank every night. **Therefore** he became ill.

＊Used when stating the result or conclusion for a cause given earlier. When speaking more politely, *desukara* is used instead.

たがる〔助動〕

¶田中さんはカメラを買いたがっています。（Tanaka san wa kamera o kai*tagatte* imasu.）

¶妹は日本へ行きたがっています。（Imōto wa Nihon e iki*tagatte* imasu.）

¶犬が外へ出たがっています。（Inu ga soto e de*tagatte* imasu.）

＊普通、話し手・話し相手以外の者があることをしたいと希望していることを客観的な立場から観察して述べる場

-tagaru 〔auxil〕 **want to, be eager to, be apt to**

¶ [Mr.] Tanaka **wants** to buy a camera.

¶ My younger sister **wants** to go to Japan.

¶ The dog **wants** to go outside.

＊Usually expresses an objective judgment about what someone other than the speaker or the listener wants

合に使う。「～たがっている（～
tagatte iru)」の形で使うことが多い。
しかし、過去のことについて自分の心
情を回想的に述べる場合や、相手にも
自分の希望していることがわかってい
ると判断する場合には、話し手のこと
についても使う。また、話し相手の心
情がよくわかっている状態のときに
は、話し相手のことについても使われ
ることがある。「わたしは子供のこ
ろ、よく学校を休みたがって親を困ら
せました。(Watashi wa kodomo no
koro, yoku gakkō o yasumitagatte oya o
komarasemashita.)」「わたしが行きた
がっていることを知っていながら、中
村さんは連れていってくれませんでし
た。(Watashi ga ikitagatte iru koto o
shitte inagara, Nakamura san wa tsurete
itte kuremasen deshita.)」「あなたが行き
たがっていることはよくわかります
が、今度は無理です。(Anata ga
ikitagatte iru koto wa yoku wakarimasu
ga, kondo wa muri desu.)」

⇒たい **tai** -がる **-garu**

たく 炊く 〔動 I〕
御飯を炊く (gohan o *taku*)

だく 抱く 〔動 I〕

¶ 女の子が人形を抱いています。
(Onna no ko ga ningyō o *daite* imasu.)
¶ ちょっと赤ちゃんを抱かせてくださ
い。(Chotto akachan o *dakasete*
kudasai.)

たくさん 〔副、～の〕

① [数や量が多い]

to do; it is not used about others when
speaking politely. Generally used in the
pattern "-*tagatte iru*." However, it can
also be used about the speaker's own
desires when recollecting how one felt
in the past or when judging that
another understands one's desires. It
can also be used concerning the
listener's desires when the speaker
knows well how the listener is feeling.
For example, "*Watashi wa kodomo no
koro, yoku gakkō o yasumitagatte oya
o komarasemashita*" (When I was
young I often troubled my parents with
my desire to stay home from school);
"*Watashi ga ikitagatte iru koto o shitte
inagara, Nakamura san wa tsurete itte
kuremasen deshita*" (Even though [he]
knew I wanted to go, [Mr.] Nakamura
didn't take me along); or "*Anata ga
ikitagatte iru koto wa yoku
wakarimasu ga, kondo wa muri desu*"
(I realize you want to go but it's
impossible this time).

taku 〔vI〕 **boil, cook**
boil rice

daku 〔v I〕 **embrace, hold in one's
arms**
¶ The little girl **is holding** a doll.

¶ Please **let me hold** the baby for a
moment.

takusan 〔adv, ～no〕 **much, plenty,
a great many; enough, sufficient**
① [much, plenty, a great many, a large
quantity]

493

¶ここにりんごがたくさんあります。
(Koko ni ringo ga *takusan* arimasu.)

¶この川には魚がたくさんいます。
(Kono kawa ni wa sakana ga *takusan* imasu.)

¶広場にたくさんの人が集まってきました。(Hiroba ni *takusan* no hito ga atsumatte kimashita.)

②[じゅうぶんである、それ以上いらない]

¶「もう少しいかがですか。」(Mō sukoshi ikagadesu ka？)「もうたくさんいただきました。」(Mō *takusan* itadakimashita.)

¶There are **a lot** of apples here.

¶This river **abounds** with fish.

¶There is 〖was〗 **a throng** of people gathered in the plaza.

②[enough, sufficient]

¶"Would you like a little more?" "No, thank you. I've had **plenty**."

タクシー〔名〕

タクシーで行く (*takushii* de iku)

¶わたしは駅からタクシーに乗って帰ります。(Watashi wa eki kara *takushii* ni notte kaerimasu.)

takushii〔n〕**taxi**

go by **taxi**

¶I will take **a taxi** home from the station.

たけ 竹〔名〕

竹の子 (*take*noko) 竹やぶ (*take*yabu)
竹細工 (*take*zaiku) 竹かご (*take*kago) 竹で編んだざる (*take* de anda zaru)

take〔n〕**bamboo**

a **bamboo** shoot // a **bamboo** grove // **bamboo**ware // a **bamboo** basket // a **bamboo** sieve

たけ 丈〔名〕

¶このズボンは丈が短すぎます。
(Kono zubon wa *take* ga mijikasugimasu.)

take〔n〕**length, height, stature**

¶These trousers 〖pants, slacks〗 are too **short**.

だけ〔助〕

①[それ以外にはないという限定の意味を表す]

¶その問題ができなかったのはわたしだけでした。(Sono mondai ga de-kinakatta no wa watashi *dake* deshita.)

dake〔part〕**only, no more than; as much as**

① [only, no more than]

¶I was the **only** one who couldn't do that problem.

¶旅行にはクラスの学生の半分だけが
参加しました。(Ryokō ni wa kurasu no
gakusei no hanbun *dake* ga sanka
shimashita.)

¶たくさんのりんごの中から、おいし
そうなのだけを選んで買いました。
(Takusan no ringo no naka kara, oishisō
na no *dake* o erande kaimashita.)

*「〜だけが (〜dake ga)」「〜だけを
(〜dake o)」は「が (ga)」「を (o)」
を省略して使うことが多い。「学生の
半分だけ参加しました。(Gakusei no
hanbun dake sanka shimashita.)」「おい
しそうなのだけ選んで買いました。
(Oishisōna no dake erande kaimashita.)」

*少ないということを強調したいとき
は、「だけ (dake)」よりも「〜しか〜
ない (〜shika 〜nai)」を使う。「鉛筆
は一本だけあります。(Enpitsu wa
ippon dake arimasu.)」と言うより、「鉛
筆は一本しかありません。(Enpitsu wa
ippon shika arimasen.)」と言う。

②[ものごとの程度の限界を表す]
¶成功するかどうかわかりませんが、
できるだけ努力してみます。(Seikō
suru ka dō ka wakarimasen ga, dekiru
dake doryoku shite mimasu.)

¶この花を欲しいだけ持って行っても
いいですよ。(Kono hana o hoshii *dake*
motte itte mo ii desu yo.)

たしか　確か〔副、形動〕

1 〔副〕

¶ **Only** half of the students in the class
went on the trip.

¶ Among many apples, [I] picked out
and bought **only** the ones that looked
good.

*The particles *ga* and *o* of "〜 *dake*
ga" and "〜 *dake o*" are often omitted:
"*Gakusei no hanbun dake sanka
shimashita*"; "*Oishisō na no dake
erande kaimashita.*"

*When one wants to emphasize the
smallness of the quantity, the pattern
"〜 *shika -nai*" is used rather than
dake. For example, "*Enpitsu wa ippon
shika arimasen*" (I have only one
pencil) is more emphatic than "*Enpitsu
wa ippon dake arimasu.*"

② [as much as]
¶ I don't know if I'll succeed or not, but
I'll try **as hard as** I can.

¶ You may take **as many** of these
flowers as you'd like.

tashika 〔adv, adj-v〕 **probably, I
think; certain, certainly;
accurate, exact; reliable,
trustworthy**

1 〔adv〕 probably, I think, if I am
correct

¶山田さんがうちへ来たのは、確か先月でした。(Yamada san ga uchi e kita no wa, *tashika* sengetsu deshita.)

¶ If I remember correctly, it was last month that [Mr.] Yamada visited [our] home.

¶上田さんは確か先月会社を辞めたはずですよ。(Ueda san wa *tashika* sengetsu kaisha o yameta hazu desu yo.)

¶ I think that it was last month that [Miss] Ueda quit the company.

2〔形動〕

2 【adj-v】 certain; exact; reliable

¶あの人の言うことは確かです。(Ano hito no iu koto wa *tashika* desu.)

¶ You can believe what [he] says.

¶父が何時に帰ってくるか、確かな時間はわかりません。(Chichi ga nanji ni kaette kuru ka, *tashika* na jikan wa wakarimasen.)

¶ I don't know exactly what time my father will return home.

¶あの人は確かに上田さんです。(Ano hito wa *tashika* ni Ueda san desu.)

¶ I'm certain that is [Mrs.] Ueda.

たしかめる 確かめる〔動Ⅱ〕

tashikameru 〔vII〕 make sure, check, verify

¶これが正しいかどうか確かめてください。(Kore ga tadashii ka dō ka *tashikamete* kudasai.)

¶ Please check whether this is correct or not.

¶飛行機が到着する時間を電話で確かめました。(Hikōki ga tōchaku suru jikan o denwa de *tashikamemashita*.)

¶ [I] verified the arrival time of the airplane on the telephone.

たす 足す〔動Ⅰ〕

tasu 〔vI〕 add

¶1足す1は2です。(Ichi *tasu* ichi wa ni desu.)

¶ One plus one is two.

¶味が薄いので、しょう油を足しました。(Aji ga usui node, shōyu o *tashimashita*.)

¶ The flavor was too weak so [I] added some soy sauce.

⇔引く hiku

だす 出す〔動Ⅰ〕

dasu 〔vI〕 put out, put forth; present, submit; produce, yield

① [何かを中から外に移す]

① [put out, take out, bring out]

ポケットから財布を出す (poketto kara saifu o *dasu*) 本だなから本を出す (hondana kara hon o *dasu*)

take one's wallet out of one's pocket // take a book from the bookshelf

¶あまりうるさいので、ねこを外へ出しました。(Amari urusai node, neko o soto e *dashimashita*.)

↔入れる **ireru**

② [前の方などへ伸ばす、突き出す]
足を前に出す (ashi o mae ni *dasu*)

¶電車の窓から手を出すと危ないですよ。(Densha no mado kara te o *dasu* to abunai desu yo.)

③ [ほかの所へ行かせる]
子供を使いに出す (kodomo o tsukai ni *dasu*)

④ [車や船などをその仕事に就かせる]
舟を海に出す (fune o umi ni *dasu*) 臨時列車を出す (rinji-ressha o *dasu*)

⑤ [手紙や荷物などを目的の所に向けて送る]
小包を出す (kozutsumi o *dasu*) 野菜を市場に出す (yasai o ichiba ni *dasu*)

¶今朝、お母さんに手紙を出しました。(Kesa, okāsan ni tegami o *dashimashita*.)

¶冬服をクリーニングに出しました。(Fuyufuku o kuriiningu ni *dashimashita*.)

⑥ [出版する、掲載する]
経済学の本を出す (keizaigaku no hon o *dasu*) 雑誌を出す (zasshi o *dasu*) 新聞に広告を出す (shinbun ni kōkoku o *dasu*)

¶今度、日本文化についての論文を雑誌に出しました。(Kondo, Nihon-bunka ni tsuite no ronbun o zasshi ni *dashimashita*.)

⑦ [広く人の目に触れるようにする]
掲示を出す (keiji o *dasu*) 看板を出す (kanban o *dasu*)

¶ **I put** the cat **out** because it was so noisy 〚such a nuisance〛.

② [stretch out, stick out]
stretch one's legs **out**

¶ It is dangerous to **put** one's hand **out** of a train window.

③ [send somewhere]
send a child on an errand

④ [run, put out (a train, boat, etc.)]
put a ship **out** to sea // **run** a special train

⑤ [send, post, forward letters, freight, etc.]
send a parcel // **send** vegetables to market

¶ **I mailed** a letter to my mother this morning.

¶ [I] **sent** the winter clothing to the cleaners.

⑥ [publish, print, insert]
publish 〚**have published**〛 an economics book // **publish** a magazine // **insert** an ad in the newspaper

¶ Recently [I] had an article of [mine] about Japanese culture **appear** in a magazine.

⑦ [put up, hang out, hoist]
put up a notice // **put up** a signboard 〚shingle〛

⑧ [渡す、提出する]

願書を出す (gansho o *dasu*)　欠席届を出す (kessekitodoke o *dasu*)

¶ 書き終わった人は出してください。(Kakiowatta hito wa *dashite* kudasai.)

⑨ [問題などを課する]

¶ 先生はいつも宿題をたくさん出します。(Sensei wa itsu mo shukudai o takusan *dashimasu*.)

⑩ [発生させる、発する]

火事を出す (kaji o *dasu*)

¶ そんなに大きな声を出さないでください。(Sonna ni ookina koe o *dasanaide* kudasai)

¶ 父は熱を出して寝ています。(Chichi wa netsu o *dashite* nete imasu.)

⑪ [更に増加させる]

¶ あまりスピードを出しては危ないですよ。(Amari supiido o *dashite* wa abunai desu yo.)

¶ もっと元気を出して歩いてください。(Motto genki o *dashite* aruite kudasai.)

⑫ [提供してもてなす]

お茶を出す (ocha o *dasu*)　お菓子を出す (okashi o *dasu*)　ビールを出す (biiru o *dasu*)

-だす〔尾〕

¶ 雨が降りだしました。(Ame ga furi-*dashimashita*.)

¶ 汽車が動きだしました。(Kisha ga ugoki *dashimashita*.)

¶ 赤ん坊が急に泣きだしました。(Akanbō ga kyu ni naki*dashimashita*.)

---

⑧ [present, submit, hand in]

make an application in writing // **give** written notice of one's absence

¶ Will those who have finished writing please **hand in** their papers 〚forms. etc.〛.

⑨ [assign, set (someone a problem, etc.)]

¶ Our teacher always **assigns** us lots of homework.

⑩ [issue, give forth, produce]

start a fire

¶ Please **don't speak** in such a loud voice.

¶ My father is in bed **with** a fever.

⑪ [put forth, increase]

¶ It's dangerous **to go too fast**.

¶ Please walk **putting more spirit into it**.

⑫ [put out, offer, serve]

offer (green) tea // **serve** a sweet // **serve** beer

-dasu 〚suf〛 **start -ing**

¶ It **has started** to rain 〚It **started** to rain〛.

¶ The train **started** to move.

¶ The baby suddenly **started** to cry 〚**burst out** crying〛.

＊「動詞（基幹の形）＋だす（dasu）」
の形で使う。

＊Used in the pattern "verb (stem
form) + -*dasu*."

たすう　多数〔名〕

多数決（*tasū*ketsu）

¶この考えに多数の人が賛成しまし
た。（Kono kangae ni *tasū* no hito ga
sansei shimashita.）

tasū 〔n〕 **a large number; a
majority**

a **majority** decision, decision **by
majority**

¶ **A majority** agreed with this view.

たすける　助ける〔動Ⅱ〕

① [救助する]
¶上田さんは川に落ちた子供を助けま
した。（Ueda san wa kawa ni ochita
kodomo o *tasukemashita*.）
¶「助けてくれ。」という叫び声がしま
した。（"*Tasukete* kure！" to iu
sakebigoe ga shimashita.）
② [困っている人や苦しんでいる人な
どに力を貸してやる]
¶わたしは体の不自由な人を助けるた
めに働きたいと思います。（Watashi
wa karada no fujiyū na hito o *tasukeru*
tame ni hatarakitai to omoimasu.）
③ [手伝う]
¶上田さんはお兄さんの仕事を助けて
います。（Ueda san wa oniisan no
shigoto o *tasukete* imasu.）

tasukeru 〔vII〕 **save, rescue; give
relief to; help, aid**

① [save, rescue]
¶ [Mr.] Ueda **rescued** a child that had
fallen in the river.

¶ There was a voice crying out, "**Help,
help!**"

② [give relief to, help someone in
trouble]
¶ I want to work **to help** the physically
handicapped.

③ [help, aid, support]
¶ [Mr.] Ueda **helps** [his] older brother
in his work.

たずねる　尋ねる〔動Ⅱ〕

¶交番で道を尋ねました。（Kōban de
michi o *tazunemashita*.）

tazuneru 〔vII〕 **ask, inquire**

¶ [I] **asked** the way at a police box.

たずねる　訪ねる〔動Ⅱ〕

¶あした、息子の家を訪ねようと思っ
ています。（Ashita, musuko no ie o
tazuneyō to omotte imasu.）

tazuneru 〔vII〕 **call on, visit, pay a
visit to**

¶ I plan **to go visit** my son tomorrow.

¶昨日の夜、田中さんが訪ねてきました。(Kinō no yoru, Tanaka san ga *tazunete* kimashita.)

¶ [Miss] Tanaka **called on [us]** yesterday evening.

ただ〔副〕

tada〔adv〕**merely, solely, only, alone**

¶母親は、毎日ただ息子の勉強のことばかり心配しています。(Hahaoya wa, mainichi *tada* musuko no benkyō no koto bakari shinpai shite imasu.)

¶ Every day the mother does **nothing but** worry about her son's studies.

＊「だけ（dake）」「ばかり（bakari）」「しか（shika）」などといっしょに使うことが多い。

＊ Often used with *dake, bakari, shika,* etc.

ただ〔名〕

tada〔n〕**free, without charge**

¶今晩の映画会はただです。(Konban no eigakai wa *tada* desu.)

¶ The movie showing this evening **is free**.

¶この入場券をただで上げます。(Kono nyūjōken o *tada* de agemasu.)
⇒無料 **muryō**

¶ I'd like you to have this admission ticket (to a concert, play, exhibition, etc.) **free of charge**.

たたかう　戦う〔動Ⅰ〕

tatakau〔vI〕**contest, play; fight, struggle against**

①〔試合をする〕
¶AチームはBチームと戦って勝ちました。(Ē-chiimu wa Bii-chiimu to *tatakatte* kachimashita.)

① [contest, play]
¶ Team A **played** Team B and won.

②〔戦争をする〕
¶青年たちは民族の独立と自由のために戦いました。(Seinentachi wa minzoku no dokuritsu to jiyū no tame ni *tatakaimashita*.)

② [fight, struggle against]
¶ The youths **fought** for liberty and their country's independence.

たたく〔動Ⅰ〕

tataku〔vI〕**strike, hit, knock, slap, etc.**

手をたたく（te o *tataku*）肩をたたく（kata o *tataku*）ドアをたたく（doa o *tataku*）

clap one's hands // **tap** someone on the shoulder; massage someone's shoulders by **tapping** with one's fists // **knock** on a door

¶だれかが戸をたたいていますよ。(Dare ka ga to o *tataite* imasu yo.)

¶ Someone **is knocking** at the door.

500

¶子供は悪いことをして、お母さんに
おしりをたたかれました。(Kodomo
wa warui koto o shite, okāsan ni oshiri o
tatakaremashita.)

¶ The children did something bad and
were spanked by their mother.

ただしい　正しい〔形〕

① [間違いがない様子]
正しい発音 (*tadashii* hatsuon)
¶正しい答えには〇、間違っている答
えには×をつけなさい。(*Tadashii*
kotae ni wa maru, machigatte iru kotae ni
wa batsu o tsukenasai.)

② [守るべきことに外れない様子]

正しい人 (*tadashii* hito) 正しい行い
(*tadashii* okonai)
¶小さな子供には、何が正しいことな
のかわかりません。(Chiisana kodomo
ni wa, nani ga *tadashii* koto na no ka
wakarimasen.)

tadashii 〔adj〕 **right, correct; right,
upright, just, honest**

① [right, correct, exact, accurate]
the **correct** pronunciation
¶ Mark **correct** answers with a circle
and wrong ones with an *X*.

② [right, upright, just, honest, proper,
lawful]
a **just** person // **right** conduct

¶ Small children don't know **right** from
wrong.

たたみ　畳〔名〕
¶畳の材料は何ですか。(Tatami no
zairyō wa nan desu ka?)

tatami 〔n〕 *tatami* **mat**
¶ What is *tatami* made from?

たたむ　畳む〔動 I〕
ハンカチを畳む (hankachi o *tatamu*)
布団を畳む (futon o *tatamu*)
¶毛布をきちんと畳んでください。
(Mōfu o kichinto *tatande* kudasai.)
¶シーツや下着を畳んで、引き出しに
しまいました。(Shiitsu ya shitagi o
tatande, hikidashi ni shimaimashita.)

tatamu 〔vI〕 **fold, fold up**
fold a handkerchief // **fold up** *futon*
bedding, **put away** the bedding
¶ Please **fold** the blankets **up** neatly.

¶ [I] **folded up** the sheets and
underwear and put them away in the
drawers.

たち〔尾〕

わたしたち (watashi*tachi*) 子供たち
(kodomo*tachi*) あなたたち

-tachi 〔suf〕 **a suffix indicating the
plural**
us, we, our // child**ren** // you (plural) //
those people // students

（anata*tachi*）あの人たち（ano
hito*tachi*）学生たち（gakusei*tachi*）
＊人などの複数を表す。

＊Indicates the plural; used for human
beings and sometimes animals.

たちあがる　立ち上がる〔動 I〕

いすから立ち上がる（isu kara
tachiagaru）
¶足がしびれて、立ち上がることがで
きませんでした。（Ashi ga shibirete,
tachiagaru koto ga dekimasen deshita.）

tachiagaru〔vI〕**stand up, get to
one's feet**
to rise from one's seat

¶My leg had gone to sleep so that I
had difficulty **getting up**.

たちば　立場〔名〕

¶自分のことばかり考えないで、相手
の立場も考えなさい。（Jibun no koto
bakari kangaenaide, aite no *tachiba* mo
kangaenasai.）

tachiba〔n〕**position, standpoint,
point of view**

¶Don't just think of yourself—put
yourself **in the place** of the other
person as well.

たちまち〔副〕

¶客がおおぜいだったので、料理はた
ちまちなくなってしまいました。
（Kyaku ga oozei datta node, ryōri wa
tachimachi nakunatte shimaimashita.）
¶飛行機はたちまち雲の中に見えなく
なりました。（Hikōki wa *tachimachi*
kumo no naka ni mienaku narimashita.）

tachimachi〔adv〕**in an instant, in
a flash, at once, immediately**
¶As there were many guests the food
quickly disappeared.

¶The plane **suddenly** disappeared
from view behind a cloud.

たつ　建つ〔動 I〕

¶東京には高いビルが次々に建ってい
ます。（Tōkyō ni wa takai biru ga
tsugitsugi ni *tatte* imasu.）
¶この家が建ってから、もう 30 年に
なります。（Kono ie ga *tatte* kara, mō
sanjūnen ni narimasu.）

tatsu〔vI〕**be built, stand**
¶Tall buildings **are going up** one after
the other in Tokyo.

¶Thirty years have passed since this
house **was erected**.

たつ　立つ〔動 I〕

① 〔縦にまっすぐになる、立ち上がる〕

tatsu〔vI〕**stand, stand up; leave,
depart**
① 〔stand, stand up, be put up〕

502

¶田中さん、ちょっと立ってくださ
い。(Tanaka san, chotto *tatte* kudasai.)

¶電車がこんでいたので、ずっと立っ
ていました。(Densha ga konde ita node,
zutto *tatte* imashita.)

¶「ここで泳いではいけません。」とい
う立て札が立っています。("Koko de
oyoide wa ikemasen." to iu tatefuda ga
tatte imasu.)

②[感情などがたかぶる]

¶悪口を言われて、腹が立ちました。
(Warukuchi o iwarete, hara ga
tachimashita.)

*普通「腹が立つ(hara ga tatsu)」の形
で使う。

③[出発する]

¶東京を朝の7時に立って、正午にこ
ちらに着きました。(Tōkyō o asa no
shichiji ni *tatte*, shōgo ni kochira ni
tsukimashita.)

¶ [Mr.] Tanaka, **stand up** a moment
please!

¶ [I] **stood** all the way as the train was
crowded.

¶ A sign **is up** reading "No swimming
here."

② [get angry, lose one's temper]

¶ [I] was insulted and **got angry**.

*Usually used in the pattern "*hara ga
tatsu*."

③ [leave, depart, start, set out]

¶ [We] **left** Tokyo at seven in the
morning and arrived here at noon.

たつ 〔動Ⅰ〕

¶日本語を習い始めてから、もう1年
たちました。(Nihongo o naraihajimete
kara, mō ichinen *tachimashshita*.)

tatsu 〔vⅠ〕 **pass, pass by, elapse**

¶ A year **has passed** since [I] started
studying Japanese.

たっする 達する 〔動Ⅲ〕

¶5時間も登って、ようやく山の頂上
に達しました。(Gojikan mo nobotte,
yōyaku yama no chōjō ni *tasshimashita*.)

¶先月は工場の生産が目標に達しませ
んでした。(Sengetsu wa kōjō no seisan
ga mokuhyō ni *tasshimasen* deshita.)

tassuru 〔vⅢ〕 **reach, arrive at,
attain, achieve**

¶ [We] at last **reached** the top of the
mountain after five hours of climbing.

¶ Factory production **failed to reach**
the target figure last month.

たて 縦 〔名〕

縦10センチ横5センチの紙(*tate
jissenchi yoko gosenchi no kami*)

tate 〔n〕 **length, height; vertical,
lengthwise**

paper 10 centimeters **long** and 5
centimeters wide

¶日本語には、縦書きと横書きの二つ の書き方があります。（Nihongo ni wa, *tate*gaki to yokogaki no futatsu no kakikata ga arimasu.）

¶Japanese can be written two ways — **up and down** or left to right.

⇔横 **yoko**

たてもの 建物〔名〕

¶あの建物は何ですか。（Ano *tatemono* wa nan desu ka？）

¶外は暑いですが、この建物の中は涼 しいです。（Soto wa atsui desu ga, kono *tatemono* no naka wa suzushii desu.）

tatemono 〔n〕 **a building**

¶What is that **building** over there?

¶It's hot outside but cool inside this **building**.

たてる 立てる〔動Ⅱ〕

① [横になっていた物や倒れていた物 を起こす、縦にまっすぐな状態にする] 国旗を立てる（kokki o *tateru*）

¶「芝生に入らないでください。」とい う札が立ててあります。（"Shibafu ni hairanaide kudasai." to iu fuda ga *tatete* arimasu.）

② [計画や予定を考えて作る] 案を立てる（an o *tateru*）予定を立てる （yotei o *tateru*）

¶もう夏休みの旅行の計画を立てまし たか。（Mō natsuyasumi no ryokō no keikaku o *tatemashita* ka？）

③ [声や音を出す] 声を立てる（koe o *tateru*）

¶赤ちゃんが寝ていますから、大きな 音を立てないでください。（Akachan ga nete imasu kara, ookina oto o *tatenaide* kudasai.）

④ [感情などをたかぶらせる] ¶山田さんは、田中さんが約束を守ら なかったので、たいへん腹を立ててい ます。（Yamada san wa, Tanaka san ga

tateru 〔vII〕 **erect, raise; form, establish**

① [erect, raise, put up]

raise the national flag

¶A sign **is up** reading "Keep off the grass."

② [form, establish, lay down]

frame a plan // **map out** a program

¶**Have** [you] **planned** [your] summer vacation trip yet?

③ [raise (a voice), make (a noise)]

cry out, **raise** one's voice

¶The baby is sleeping so please **don't make** any loud noises.

④ [be angry, lose one's temper]

¶[Mr.] Yamada **is** very **angry** because [Mr.] Tanaka broke [his] promise.

yakusoku o *tatete* imasu.)

*普通「腹を立てる（hara o tateru）」の形で使う。

*Generally used in the pattern "*hara o taeru*."

たてる 建てる〔動Ⅱ〕

¶田中さんは最近家を建てました。（Tanaka san wa saikin ie o *tatemashita*.）
¶このお寺は約500年前に建てられました。（Kono otera wa yaku gohyakunen mae ni *tateraremashita*.）

tateru〔vⅡ〕 **build, construct, erect**

¶ [Mr.] Tanaka **has** recently **built** a house.
¶ This temple **was erected** approximately five hundred years ago.

たとい〔副〕 ☞たとえ tatoe

tatoi〔adv〕 ☞**tatoe**

たとえ〔名〕

たとえ話（*tatoe*banashi）
¶わかりにくいことでも、たとえを使うとわかりやすいです。（Wakarinikui koto demo, *tatoe* o tsukau to wakariyasui desu.）

tatoe〔n〕 **simile, metaphor, fable, parable, proverb, example, illustration**
fable, allegory, parable
¶ Even something hard to understand is easier to understand if one uses **an example**.

たとえ〔副〕

¶たとえ両親に反対されても、わたしはあの人と結婚します。（*Tatoe* ryō-shin ni hantai sarete mo, watashi wa ano hito to kekkon shimasu.）
¶たとえ雨が降っても、ハイキングには出かけます。（*Tatoe* ame ga futte mo, haikingu ni wa dekakemasu.）

*普通「たとえ～ても（tatoe～te mo）」の形で使う。「たとい（tatoi）」とも言う。

tatoe〔adv〕 **if, even if, although, supposing that, granted that**

¶ I would marry [him] **even if** my parents were opposed.

¶ [I] will go hiking **even if** it should rain.

* Usually used in the pattern "*tatoe ～ -te mo*." The form *tatoi* is also used.

たとえば 例えば〔副〕

¶わたしは、古い町、例えば京都のような所に住みたいです。（Watashi wa,

tatoeba〔adv〕 **for example, for instance, such as**
¶ I would like to live in an old place **such as** Kyoto.

furui machi, *tatoeba* Kyōto no yōna tokoro ni sumitai desu.)

¶ 料理に味をつけるものにはいろいろあります。**例えば**、塩、砂糖、しょう油などです。（Ryōri ni aji o tsukeru mono ni wa iroiro arimasu. *Tatoeba*, shio, satō, shōyu nado desu.）

¶ There are various seasonings used in cooking. **For example**, salt, sugar, soy sauce, etc.

たな〔名〕

本だな（hon*dana*）たなから物を降ろす（*tana* kara mono o orosu）

¶ この箱をたなに上げてください。（Kono hako o *tana* ni agete kudasai.）

tana 〔n〕 **shelf, shelves, rack**

a book**shelf**, a book**case** // take an article from **a shelf**

¶ Please put this box on **the shelf**.

たにん 他人〔名〕

① ［ほかの人］

¶ 他人の迷惑になるようなことはしないでください。（*Tanin* no meiwaku ni naru yō na koto wa shinaide kudasai.）

② ［血縁関係のない人］

¶ あの二人はとてもよく似ていますが、他人なのです。（Ano futari wa totemo yoku nite imasu ga, *tanin* na no desu.）

tanin 〔n〕 **another person, others; unrelated persons**

① ［another person, others］

¶ Please don't do anything that will inconvenience **others**.

② ［persons unrelated by blood］

¶ Although those two look a lot alike, **they are unrelated** to each other.

たね 種〔名〕

¶ 庭に花の種をまきました。（Niwa ni hana no *tane* o makimashita.）

¶ このぶどうには種がありません。（Kono budō ni wa *tane* ga arimasen.）

tane 〔n〕 **seed, pit, stone**

¶ ［I］ sowed flower **seed** in the garden.

¶ These are **seed**less grapes.

たのしい 楽しい〔形〕

¶ 今日のパーティーはとても楽しかったです。（Kyō no pātii wa totemo *tanoshikatta* desu.）

¶ これから歌を歌って、楽しく過ごしましょう。（Kore kara uta o utatte, *tanoshiku* sugoshimashō.）

tanoshii 〔adj〕 **pleasant, happy, delightful, enjoyable**

¶ Today's party was a lot of **fun**.

¶ Let's have **a good time** singing songs now.

たのしみ 楽しみ〔名、形動〕

¶昔の友達に会うのが楽しみです。
（Mukashi no tomodachi ni au no ga *tanoshimi* desu.）

tanoshimi 〔n, adj-v〕 **amenity, comfort, amusement, enjoyment**

¶ I am looking forward to seeing old friends.

たのしむ 楽しむ〔動Ⅰ〕

¶上田さんは一人で音楽を聞いて楽しんでいます。（Ueda san wa hitori de ongaku o kiite *tanoshinde* imasu.）
¶夏休みには、山に登ったり海で泳いだりして楽しもうと思っています。（Natsuyasumi ni wa, yama ni nobottari umi de oyoidari shite *tanoshimō* to omotte imasu.）

tanoshimu 〔vI〕 **enjoy oneself, take pleasure in**

¶ [Mr.] Ueda **is having a good time** listening to music by [him]self.

¶ I plan **to enjoy** summer vacation climbing mountains, swimming at the shore, and so forth.

たのむ 頼む〔動Ⅰ〕
¶田中さんに頼んで、お金を貸してもらいました。（Tanaka san ni *tanonde*, okane o kashite moraimashita.）
¶友達にノートを貸してくれと頼んだら、断られました。（Tomodachi ni nōto o kashite kure to *tanondara*, kotowararemashita.）

tanomu 〔vI〕 **ask, request**

¶ When I asked [him], [Mr.] Tanaka loaned me some money.

¶ I asked a friend to loan me [her] notes, but [she] refused.

たばこ〔名〕

¶わたしはたばこを吸いません。
（Watashi wa *tabako* o suimasen.）

tabako 〔n〕 **tobacco, cigarettes, cigars**

¶ I don't **smoke**.

たび 旅〔名〕

汽車の旅（kisha no *tabi*）空の旅（sora no *tabi*）旅人（*tabi*bito）旅をする（*tabi* o suru）
¶この仕事が終わったら、しばらく旅に出るつもりです。（Kono shigoto ga owattara, shibaraku *tabi* ni deru tsumori desu.）
⇒旅行 ryokō

tabi 〔n〕 **traveling, travel, journey, trip**

a train **trip** // a plane **trip** // a traveler, a tourist // travel, make a journey, take a trip

¶ I plan to go **traveling** for some time after this job is over.

507

たび〔名〕

¶わたしはこの写真を見るたびに、子供のころを思い出します。(Watashi wa kono shashin o miru *tabi* ni, kodomo no koro o omoidashimasu.)

¶定期券を買わないで、電車に乗るたびに切符を買います。(Teikiken o kawanaide, densha ni noru *tabi* ni kippu o kaimasu.)

tabi 〔n〕 **time, occasion, whenever**

¶I remember my childhood days **whenever** I look at this photo.

¶[I] haven't bought a commuter's pass; [I] buy a ticket **each time** [I] take the train.

たびたび〔副〕

¶小学生のころ病気で学校をたびたび休みました。(Shōgakusei no koro byōki de gakkō o *tabitabi* yasumimashita.)

¶たびたびお邪魔して申し訳ありません。(*Tabitabi* ojama shite mōshiwake arimasen.)

tabitabi 〔adv〕 **often, frequently, time after time**

¶[I] was **frequently** absent from school due to illness when [I] was in elementary school.

¶I am sorry to bother you 〖interrupt your work〗 **so often**.

たぶん〔副〕

¶あしたはたぶんいい天気でしょう。(Ashita wa *tabun* ii tenki deshō.)

¶山田さんはひどい風邪で、今日はたぶん来ないでしょう。(Yamada san wa hidoi kaze de, kyō wa *tabun* konai deshō.)

＊「～でしょう（～deshō）」「～だろう（～darō）」などがあとに来ることが多い。

tabun 〔adv〕 **probably, most likely**

¶**Chances are** it will be a nice day tomorrow.

¶As [Mr.] Yamada has a bad cold, [he] will **probably** not come today.

＊Generally followed by ～ *deshō* ,～ *darō*, etc.

たべもの　食べ物〔名〕

¶あなたは食べ物ではどんなものが好きですか。(Anata wa *tabemono* de wa donna mono ga suki desu ka？)

¶わたしはきらいな食べ物はありません。(Watashi wa kirai na *tabemono* wa arimasen.)

⇒飲み物 nomimono

tabemono 〔n〕 **food, a dish, foodstuff, edibles**

¶What **foods** do you like?

¶I have no dislikes in **food**.

たべる　食べる 〔動Ⅱ〕
¶あなたは朝御飯を何時ごろ食べますか。(Anata wa asagohan o nanji goro *tabemasu* ka？)
¶わたしは昨日さしみを食べました。(Watashi wa kinō sashimi o *tabemashita*.)

taberu 〔vⅡ〕 eat
¶ What time **do you eat** breakfast?
¶ I **ate** *sashimi* yesterday.

たま　弾 〔名〕
ピストルの弾 (pisutoru no *tama*) 鉄砲の弾 (teppō no *tama*)

tama 〔n〕 bullet, shell, shot
a pistol **bullet** // a gun 〚rifle〛 **bullet**

たま　球 〔名〕
電気の球 (denki no *tama*) 野球の球 (yakyū no *tama*) 球を打つ (*tama* o utsu)

tama 〔n〕 ball, bulb, globe
an electric light **bulb** // **a ball** for baseball // hit 〚bat〛 **a ball**

たま　玉 〔名〕
目玉 (me*dama*) 眼鏡の玉 (megane no *tama*) 十円玉 (jūen*dama*)

tama 〔n〕 ball, bead, lens, drop, jewel, etc.
the eye**ball** // an eyeglass **lens** // a 10-yen **coin**

たまご　卵 〔名〕
生卵 (nama*tamago*) 卵焼き (*tamago*yaki) ゆで卵 (yude*tamago*) 半熟卵 (hanjuku*tamago*) 卵を産む (*tamago* o umu) 卵がかえる (*tamago* ga kaeru)

tamago 〔n〕 egg
an raw **egg** // an omelet // a boiled **egg** // a soft-boiled **egg** // lay **an egg**, spawn // **an egg** hatches

たまに 〔副〕

tama ni 〔adv〕 occasionally, now and then, at times, once in a while

¶わたしはたまに映画を見に行きます。(Watashi wa *tama ni* eiga o mi ni ikimasu.)
¶山田さんはたまにしか図書館へ行きません。(Yamada san wa *tama ni* shika toshokan e ikimasen.)

¶ I **occasionally** go to see a movie.
¶ [Mr.] Yamada **seldom** goes to the library.

たまる〔動 I〕

① [物が一つの所に少しずつ集まってたくさんになる]

¶大雨が降ったので、道路に水がたまってしまいました。(Ooame ga futta node, dōro ni mizu ga *tamatte* shimaimashita.)

② [貯金などが多くなる]

¶お金がたまったら、旅行に行きたいと思っています。(Okane ga *tamattara*, ryokō ni ikitai to omotte imasu.)

③ [仕事や支払いなどがかたづかないで残る]

アパート代がたまる (apātodai ga *tamaru*)

¶病気で会社を休んだので、仕事がたまってしまいました。(Byōki de kaisha o yasunda node, shigoto ga *tamatte* shimaimashita.)

だまる 黙る〔動 I〕

① [何も言わない、話さない]

¶わたしがあいさつしたのに、あの人は黙って行ってしまいました。(Watashi ga aisatsu shita noni, ano hito wa *damatte* itte shimaimashita.)

¶このことは、ほかの人には黙っていてください。(Kono koto wa, hoka no hito ni wa *damatte* ite kudasai.)

② [前もって何も言わない、断らない]

¶あの人は黙って学校を休みました。(Ano hito wa *damatte* gakkō o yasumimashita.)

---

tamaru 〔vI〕 **gather, collect, accumulate; save, be saved; be in arrears, be overdue**

① [gather, collect, accumulate]

¶ There **are** 〖were〗 **puddles** in the street after the heavy rains.

② [save, be saved]

¶ **When I have** enough money **saved** I want to go on a trip.

③ [be in arrears, be overdue]

be behind on the rent

¶ [I] **am behind** in [my] work as [I] had to take time off sick.

---

damaru 〔v I〕 **be silent, don't speak; without notice, without permission**

① [be silent, don't speak]

¶ Even though I greeted [her], [she] left **without a word**.

¶ Please **don't say anything** about this matter to anyone else.

② [without prior notice, without permission]

¶ [He] stayed home from school **without any explanation**.

¶タイプライターを黙って持って行かないでください。(Taipuraitā o *damatte* motte ikanaide kudasai.)

¶ Please don't move the typewriter **without getting permission**.

ため〔名〕

tame 〔n〕 **in order to, to; because of, owing to; good, benefit**

① [目的を表す]

① [in order to, to]

¶わたしは日本文学を勉強するために日本語を習っています。(Watashi wa Nihon-bungaku o benkyō suru *tame* ni Nihongo o naratte imasu.)

¶ I am learning Japanese **so that** I can study Japanese literature.

¶山田さんは、家を建てるためにお金をためています。(Yamada san wa, ie o tateru *tame* ni okane o tamete imasu.)

¶ [Mr.] Yamada is saving money **in order** to build a house.

② [理由・原因を表す]

② [because of, owing to, on account of]

¶病気のため学校を休みました。(Byōki no *tame* gakkō o yasumimashita.)

¶ [I] stayed home from school **due to** illness.

¶不注意のため試験に失敗しました。(Fuchūi no *tame* shiken ni shippai shimashita.)

¶ [I] failed the exam **because of** carelessness.

¶バスが遅れたために遅刻しました。(Basu ga okureta *tame* ni chikoku shimashita.)

¶ [I] am 『was』 late **because** the bus was delayed.

③ [役に立つこと・利益になることを表す]

③ [good, advantage, benefit, sake]

¶これはとてもためになる本です。(Kore wa totemo *tame* ni naru hon desu.)

¶ This is a very **instructive** book.

¶上田さんは会社のために夜遅くまで働いています。(Ueda san wa kaisha no *tame* ni yoru osoku made hataraite imasu.)

¶ [Mr.] Ueda works late at night **for the benefit** of [his] company.

だめ〔形動〕

dame 〔adj-v〕 **useless; no good; hopeless, impossible; must, must not**

① [むだ、効果がない様子]

① [useless, vain, unavailing]

¶やってみましたが、だめでした。(Yatte mimashita ga, *dame* deshita.)

¶ I tried to do it but **it was no good**.

¶いくらあの人に注意してもだめで
す。(Ikura ano hito ni chūi shite mo
dame desu.)

② [役に立たない様子]
¶このラジオは古くてもうだめです。
(Kono rajio wa furukute mō *dame* desu.)

③ [望みがない様子]
¶中村さんはＡ大学を受けましたが、
だめらしいです。(Nakamura san wa Ē-
daigaku o ukemashita ga, *dame* rashii
desu.)

④ [それをしてはいけないという意味
を表す]
¶「あした休んでもいいですか。」
(Ashita yasunde mo ii desu ka？)「だめ
です。」(*Dame* desu.)
¶約束を守らなくてはだめですよ。
(Yakusoku o mamoranakute wa *dame*
desu yo.)
¶もっと早起きしなければだめです
よ。(Motto hayaoki shinakereba *dame*
desu yo.)

ためす 試す [動Ⅰ]
¶機械が直ったかどうか試してみま
しょう。(Kikai ga naotta ka dō ka
tameshite mimashō.)
¶漢字の力を試すためにテストしま
しょう。(Kanji no chikara o *tamesu*
tame ni tesuto shimashō.)

ためる [動Ⅱ]

①[物を一つの所に少しずつ集めてた
くさんにする]

¶ **It's no use** no matter how much one
admonishes [him].

② [no good]
¶This radio is old and **not good for
anything**.

③ [hopeless, impossible]
¶[Mr.] Nakamura took the entrance
examination for University A, but it
seems [he] **was unsuccessful**.

④ [must, must not (do something)]

¶"Is it all right if I take the day off
tomorrow?"
"No, it isn't."

¶ **One must** keep one's promises.

¶ **You must** get up earlier.

tamesu 〔vI〕 **try, attempt, test**
¶ Let's **try out** the machine 〘device,
apparatus, mechanism〙 and see if it's
all right now after being fixed.
¶ Let's have a test **to see** how strong
you are in *kanji*.

tameru 〔vII〕 **accumulate, amass;
save, store up; run up(a bill),
leave undone**
① [accumulate, amass, collect, gather]

¶この地方では雨水をためておいて、それを飲んでいるそうです。(Kono chihō de wa amamizu o *tamete* oite, sore o nonde iru sō desu.)

¶ I hear that in this area **they save** rainwater and use it for drinking water.

② [貯金などを多くする]

② [save, store up]

¶お金をためて、テープレコーダーを買うつもりです。(Okane o *tamete*, tēpurekōdā o kau tsumori desu.)

¶ I intend **to save** my money and buy a tape recorder.

③ [仕事や支払いなどをかたづけないで残す]

③ [run up (a bill), leave undone]

部屋代をためる (heyadai o *tameru*)

let one's rent **fall in arrears, owe** rent

たより 便り〔名〕

tayori 〔n〕 **correspondence, a letter, word, news**

¶兄からはこのごろ便りが全然ありません。(Ani kara wa konogoro *tayori* ga zenzen arimasen.)

¶ I haven't **heard anything** from my (older) brother lately.

¶息子さんから便りがありますか。(Musukosan kara *tayori* ga arimasu ka？)

¶ **Do you hear regularly** from your son?

⇔手紙 tegami

たよる 頼る〔動Ⅰ〕

tayoru 〔vI〕 **depend on, rely on, trust to**

¶あの人は親に頼らないで、自分で働いて大学を卒業しました。(Ano hito wa oya ni *tayoranaide*, jibun de hataraite daigaku o sotsugyō shimashita.)

¶ [He] worked [his] way through college **without leaning** on [his] parents.

¶わたしは兄を頼って東京に来ました。(Watashi wa ani o *tayotte* Tōkyō ni kimashita.)

¶ I came to Tokyo **counting on the assistance** of my older brother.

たら〔助動〕

-tara 〔auxil〕 **when, if; a verb ending expressing the conditional**

① [前件が成立した場合にはそれに伴って後件が成立するという関係を表す]

① [indicates that the second clause will be realized if or when the first clause is realized]

¶春になったら、旅行するつもりです。(Haru ni nat*tara*, ryokō suru tsumori desu.)

¶ I plan to travel **in** the spring.

¶安かったら買ってもいいですが、高かったら買いません。(Yasukat*tara* katte mo ii desu ga, takakat*tara* kaimasen.)

¶ [I] might buy it **if** it's inexpensive but [I] won't buy it **if** it's expensive.

¶暑かったら、上着を脱いでもいいですよ。(Atsukat*tara*, uwagi o nuide mo ii desu yo.)

¶ You may remove your jacket **if** you're hot.

¶車だったら10分で行けます。(Kuruma dat*tara* jippun de ikemasu.)

¶ It takes 10 minutes **by** car.

¶あした雨が降ったら、旅行には行きませんか。(Ashita ame ga fut*tara*, ryokō ni wa ikimasen ka？)「いいえ、雨が降っても、行きます。」(Iie, ame ga futte mo, ikimasu.)

¶ "**If** it rains tomorrow will you give up on your trip?"
"No, [I]'ll go even if it rains."

→ば **ba**

②［前件がもし成立していた場合には後件も成立するという関係を表す］

② [indicates that the second clause would have been realized if the first clause had been realized]

¶もう少し背が高かったら、バスケットボールをやっていたと思います。(Mō sukoshi se ga takakat*tara*, basukettobōru o yatte ita to omoimasu.)

¶ I think [I] would have played basketball **if** [I] had been a little taller.

¶お医者さんがもう少し早く来てくれたら、父は助かったのに。(Oishasan ga mō sukoshi hayaku kite kure*tara*, chichi wa tasukatta noni.)

¶ My father's life could have been saved **if only** the doctor had come a little sooner.

＊前件には実際には成立しなかったことが来る。

＊The first clause was not actually realized.

→ば **ba**　なら **nara**

③［願望や示唆などの意味を表す］
¶学生の時にもっと勉強していたらと思います。(Gakusei no toki ni motto benkyō shite itara to omoimasu.)

③ [expresses a wish or suggestion]
¶ **I wish I had** studied more when I was a student.

¶ 頭が痛いんでしょう。今日は学校を休んだら。（Atama ga itai n deshō？ Kyō wa gakkō o yasun*dara*？）

→ば **ba**

④ [前件が行われた時に後件が成立したという関係を表す]

¶ 山田さんと話をしていたら、上田さんが来ました。（Yamada san to hanashi o shite i*tara*, Ueda san ga kimashita.）

¶ 銀座を歩いていたら、偶然小学校の時の友達に会いました。（Ginza o aruite i*tara*, gūzen shōgakkō no toki no tomodachi ni aimashita.）

*後件には過去・完了を表す「たの形」が来る。

→と **to**

⑤ [前件の成立をきっかけとして後件が成立するという関係を表す]

¶ 一人の赤ちゃんが泣きだしたら、ほかの赤ちゃんまで泣きだしました。（Hitori no akachan ga nakidashi*tara*, hoka no akachan made nakidashimashita.）

¶ 部屋の電気をつけたら、窓からたくさんの虫が入ってきました。（Heya no denki o tsuke*tara*, mado kara takusan no mushi ga haitte kimashita.）

*前件と後件の主語は異なる。後件には過去・完了を表す「たの形」が来る。

→と **to**

⑥ [前件の成立によって後件のことがらに気づくという関係を表す]

¶ 箱を開けたら、りんごが五つありました。（Hako o ake*tara*, ringo ga itsutsu arimashita.）

¶ You have a headache, don't you? **Why don't you** stay home from school today?

④ [indicates that the second clause is realized when the first clause takes place]

¶ [Mr.] Ueda came **while** I was talking with [Mrs.] Yamada.

¶ I ran into a friend from my elementary school days **when** I was walking along the Ginza.

*The *-ta* form expressing past or completed action is found in the second clause.

⑤ [indicates that the second clause takes place because of the first clause]

¶ **When** one baby started crying the others started crying too.

¶ **When** [I] turned on the lights inside the room lots of insects flew in through the window.

*The two clauses have different subjects. The *-ta* form expressing past or completed action is found in the second clause.

⑥ [indicates that what comes in the second clause is noticed when the first clause is realized]

¶ [I] opened the box **and** found five apples.

¶台風のあと庭へ出てみたら、木や花が倒れていました。(Taifū no ato niwa e dete mi*tara*, ki ya hana ga taorete imashita.)

¶ **When** [I] went out into the yard 〚garden〛 after the typhoon, blownover trees and flowers were lying on the ground.

¶山の頂上に着いたら、遠くに海が見えました。(Yama no chōjō ni tsui*tara*, tooku ni umi ga miemashita.)

¶ **When** [we] got to the top of the mountain, [we] were able to see the ocean in the distance.

*後件には「あった (atta)」「～ていた (～te ita)」「見えた (mieta)」などの状態・作用を表す言葉のほかに「音がした (oto ga shita)」「においがした (nioi ga shita)」などの感覚を表す言葉も使い、前件によって後件のことがらに気づくという関係を表す。前件の主語と後件の主語は異なる。

*The relationship of one being aware of the second clause because of the first clause is expressed by the use in the second clause of words expressing condition or process like *atta, -te ita* and *mieta*; words concerning the physical senses like *oto ga shita, nioi ga shita*; and so on. The subjects of the two clauses are different.

→と **to**

⑦ [話題とすることがらを提示するのに使う]

⑦ [used to point out the topic]

¶「田中さんはどこにいますか。」(Tanaka san wa doko ni imasu ka？)「田中さんだったら、図書室にいますよ。」(Tanaka san dat*tara*, toshoshitsu ni imasu yo.)

¶ "Where is [Mr.] Tanaka?"
"**[Mr.] Tanaka**? Oh, [he]'s in the library."

¶「辞書はどこにあるか知りませんか。」(Jisho wa doko ni aru ka shirimasen ka？)「辞書だったら、あのテーブルの上にありますよ。」(Jisho dat*tara*, ano tēburu no ue ni arimasu yo.)

¶ "Do you know where the dictionary is?"
"**It's** over there on the table."

*普通「名詞＋だったら (dattara)」の形で使う。

*Generally used in the pattern "noun + *dattara*."

→なら **nara**

-だらけ〔尾〕

-darake 〔suf〕 **filled with ～, covered with ～**

どろだらけ (doro*darake*) 傷だらけ (kizu*darake*) 血だらけ (chi*darake*) ごみだらけ (gomi*darake*)

covered with mud // **covered with** injuries; **covered with** scars // **covered with** blood, bloodstained // **full of** trash, littered

¶この計算は間違いだらけです。(Ko-no keisan wa machigai*darake* desu.)

¶本がほこりだらけになってしまいました。(Hon ga hokori*darake* ni natte shimaimashita.)

¶ These figures are **full of** mistakes.

¶ The books have gotten **all** dusty.

たり〔助〕

¶昨日は、映画を見たり買い物をしたりしました。(Kinō wa, eiga o mi*tari* kaimono o shi*tari* shimashita.)

¶海で泳いだり貝を拾ったりして遊びました。(Umi de oyoi*dari* kai o hirot*tari* shite asobimashita.)

＊普通「～たり ～たりする（～tari ～tari suru）」の形で使う。動作を例示的に述べて代表させ、その他の動作もあることを表す。「ぶ（bu）」「ぐ（gu）」「む（mu）」「ぬ（nu）」で終わる I 型動詞のあとに「たり（tari）」が来る場合には「だり（dari）」となる。

-tari 〔part〕 now ～ now ～; now ～ and then ～; sometimes ～ sometimes ～

¶ Yesterday I **saw** a movie, **went** shopping, **etc.**

¶ [I] relaxed at the shore, **sometimes** swimming **and sometimes** picking up shells.

＊ Usually used in the pattern "*-tari* ～ -*tari suru.*" It cites actions as representative examples and implies there were other actions as well. *-tari* changes to *-dari* in the case of Type I verbs ending in *-bu, -gu, -mu,* or *-nu.*

たりる　足りる〔動 II〕

¶時間が足りなくて、最後の問題はできませんでした。(Jikan ga *tarinakute*, saigo no mondai wa dekimasen deshita.)

¶生活費は 1 か月 10 万円では足りません。(Seikatsuhi wa ikkagetsu jūman'en de wa *tarimasen*.)

tariru 〔vII〕 **be enough, be sufficient, suffice**

¶ [I] **ran out** of time and wasn't able to do the last question.

¶ One hundred thousand yen a month **is not enough** to live on.

だれ〔代〕

¶あの人はだれですか。(Ano hito wa *dare* desu ka?)

¶これはだれの本ですか。(Kore wa *dare* no hon desu ka?)

dare 〔pron〕 **who, whom, whose; no one, someone, anyone, everyone**

¶ **Who** is that person?

¶ **Whose** book is this?

¶これはだれが書きましたか。(Kore wa *dare* ga kakimashita ka?)

¶あなたはだれに会いたいのですか。(Anata wa *dare* ni aitai no desu ka?)

¶「教室の中にだれかいますか。」(Kyōshitsu no naka ni *dare* ka imasu ka?)「いいえ、だれもいません。」(Iie, *dare* mo imasen.)

¶この図書館は、だれでも入ることができます。(Kono toshokan wa, *dare* demo hairu koto ga dekimasu.)

¶このことは、だれにも言わないでください。(Kono koto wa, *dare* ni mo iwanaide kudasai.)

だろう 〔助動〕

¶あしたはたぶん雨だろう。(Ashita wa tabun ame *darō*.)

¶わたしが行かなくても、田中さんは行くだろう。(Watashi ga ikanakute mo, Tanaka san wa iku *darō*.)

¶母はもうすぐ帰ってくるだろうと思います。(Haha wa mō sugu kaette kuru *darō* to omoimasu.)

＊名詞・動詞・形容詞・形容動詞・ある種の助動詞・助詞「の」などについて、推測の意味を表す。

⇒でしょう **deshō** だ **da**

(-)だん (-)段 〔名、尾〕

1 〔名〕
本箱の上の段、下の段 (honbako no ue no *dan*, shita no *dan*) 寝台車の上の段 (shindaisha no ue no *dan*)

2 〔尾〕
① [階段などを数えるときに使う]

¶ **Who** wrote this?

¶ **Who** do you want to see?

¶ "Is there **anyone** in the classroom?" "No, there's **nobody** there."

¶ **Anyone** can enter this library.

¶ Please don't say anything about this matter to **anyone**.

darō 〔auxil〕 **perhaps, will probably, I think**

¶ It **will probably** rain tomorrow.

¶ [Mrs.] Tanaka **will probably** go even if I don't.

¶ My mother **should** be back soon.

＊Used after nouns, verbs, adjectives, adjective-verbs, certain auxiliaries, and the particle *no* to express conjecture or supposition.

(-)dan 〔n, suf〕 **step, rung; grade, rank**

1 〔n〕 step, rung, deck, tier
the upper **shelf**, lower **shelf** of a bookcase // the upper **berth** in a train sleeping car

2 〔suf〕
① [the counter for stairs, steps]

¶危ないから、階段は1段ずつ降りなさい。(Abunai kara, kaidan wa ichi*dan* zutsu orinasai.)

②[柔道や碁などで強さの程度によって与えられる資格]
¶山田さんは柔道2段です。(Yamada san wa jūdō ni*dan* desu.)

-だん -団〔尾〕

選手団 (senshu*dan*)
¶その事故については、調査団を作って調べています。(Sono jiko ni tsuite wa, chōsa*dan* o tsukutte shirabete imasu.)

たんい 単位〔名〕
¶日本では、長さの単位はメートルを、重さの単位はグラムを使っています。(Nihon de wa, nagasa no *tan'i* wa mētoru o, omosa no *tan'i* wa guramu o tsukatte imasu.)

たんご 単語〔名〕
¶わたしはまだ日本語の単語を少ししか知りません。(Watashi wa mada Nihongo no *tango* o sukoshi shika shirimasen.)
¶単語帳を作って勉強しています。(*Tango*chō o tsukutte benkyō shite imasu.)

たんさんガス 炭酸ガス〔名〕

だんし 男子〔名〕
¶このクラスは男子ばかりです。(Kono kurasu wa *danshi* bakari desu.)
¶男子の学生より女子学生のほうが、よく勉強するようです。(*Danshi* no gakusei yori joshi-gakusei no hō ga, yoku benkyō suru yō desu.)
⇔女子 joshi

¶That's dangerous; go down the stairs one **step** at a time.

②[the counter for grades or ranks as in judo, *go*, etc.]
¶[Miss] Yamada holds a *nidan* 〖the second **rank**〗 in judo.

-dan 〔suf〕 body, group, organization
sports team 〖squad, group〗
¶A study **group** 〖inquiry commission〗 has been formed and is investigating that accident.

tan'i 〔n〕 a unit, a denomination
¶**The unit** of length in use in Japan is the meter and **the unit** of weight is the gram.

tango 〔n〕 word(s), vocabulary
¶My Japanese **vocabulary** is still very limited.

¶[I] study keeping a notebook of new **vocabulary**.

tansan-gasu 〔n〕 carbon dioxide

danshi 〔n〕 boy, man, male
¶This class is all **male**.

¶It seems that female students study harder than **male** students.

たんしょ 短所 〔名〕

¶人にはだれでも長所と短所があります。（Hito ni wa dare demo chōsho to *tansho* ga arimasu.）
⇔長所 chōsho
⇒欠点 ketten

tansho 〔n〕 defect, fault, shortcoming, weak point

¶ Everyone has **weak** and strong **points**.

だんじょ 男女 〔名〕

男女平等（*danjo*-byōdō）男女共学（*danjo*-kyōgaku）男女同権（*danjo*-dōken）
¶学生は男女合わせて 20 名です。（Gakusei wa *danjo* awasete nijūmei desu.）
¶この会社は、男女で給料の差がありません。（Kono kaisha wa, *danjo* de kyūryō no sa ga arimasen.）

danjo 〔n〕 man and woman, male and female, both sexes

equality of **the sexes** // **co**education // equal rights **for men and women**

¶ **Male and female**, there are 20 students in all.

¶ There is no difference in pay **according to sex** in this company.

たんじょうび 誕生日 〔名〕

¶わたしの誕生日は 3 月 3 日です。（Watashi no *tanjōbi* wa sangatsu mikka desu.）
¶今晩、山田さんの誕生日のお祝いをします。（Konban, Yamada san no *tanjōbi* no oiwai o shimasu.）

tanjōbi 〔n〕 one's birthday

¶ My **birthday** is March 3.

¶ Tonight [we]'re having a **birthday** celebration for [Miss] Yamada.

ダンス 〔名〕

社交ダンス（shakō-*dansu*）フォークダンス（fōku-*dansu*）ダンスパーティー（*dansu*-pātii）ダンス音楽（*dansu*-ongaku）ダンスをする（*dansu* o suru）

dansu 〔n〕 dance, dancing

social 〚ballroom〛 **dancing** // a folk **dance**, folk **dancing** // a **dance** party // **dance** music // **to dance**

たんすう 単数 〔名〕

⇔複数 fukusū

tansū 〔n〕 singular number, the singular

だんせい 男性 〔名〕

¶今の社会は男性中心です。（Ima no shakai wa *dansei* chūshin desu.）

dansei 〔n〕 male

¶ Present-day society is **male** oriented.

¶これは男性用のシャツです。（Kore wa *danseiyō* no shatsu desu.）
⇔女性 josei

だんたい　団体〔名〕

政治団体（seiji-*dantai*）宗教団体（shūkyō-*dantai*）団体旅行（*dantai*-ryokō）
¶団体で旅行するのはとても楽しいです。（*Dantai* de ryokō suru no wa totemo tanoshii desu.）

だんだん〔副〕

¶だんだん寒くなってきました。（*Dandan* samuku natte kimashita.）
¶日本語の勉強がだんだん難しくなってきました。（Nihongo no benkyō ga *dandan* muzukashiku natte kimashita.）

だんぼう　暖房〔名、～する〕

暖房のある部屋（*danbō* no aru heya）暖房がきく（*danbō* ga kiku）暖房をつける（*danbō* o tsukeru）
¶うちには暖房設備が何もありません。（Uchi ni wa *danbō*-setsubi ga nani mo arimasen.）
¶この部屋は、暖房しているから暖かいです。（Kono heya wa, *danbō* shite iru kara atatakai desu.）
⇔冷房 reibō

¶This is a **men's** shirt.

dantai 〔n〕 group, party; organization, association
a political **organization** // a religious **body** // a **group** tour, traveling **in a party**
¶It is very pleasant to travel **with others**.

dandan 〔adv〕 **increasingly; step by step, gradually**
¶It has **gradually** gotten colder and colder.
¶[My] Japanese studies have **gradually** gotten more difficult.

danbō 〔n, ～*suru*〕 **heating**
a room with **heat** // can be **heated**; is well **heated** // turn on **the heat**
¶There is no **heating** system in my home.
¶This room is warm because **the heat is on**.

ち

ち　血 〔名〕

血が出る (*chi* ga deru) 血が止まる
(*chi* ga tomaru) 鼻血 (*hanaji*)

chi 〔n〕 blood

bleed // stop **bleeding** // a nose**bleed**

ちいさい　小さい 〔形〕

① [形などが大きくない様子]
小さい花 (chisai hana)
¶このくつはわたしには小さいです。
(Kono kutsu wa watashi ni wa *chiisai*
desu.)
② [程度などが低い様子]
小さい声 (*chiisai* koe)
¶ラジオの音をもう少し小さくしてく
ださい。(Rajio no oto o mō sukoshi
chiisaku shite kudasai.)
③ [年齢が少ない]
¶小さい時のことはよく覚えていませ
ん。(*Chiisai* toki no koto wa yoku oboete
imasen.)
⇔大きい **ookii**
⇒小さな **chiisana**

chiisai 〔adj〕 **small, little; young**

① [small (in size); too small]
a **small** flower
¶ These shoes **are too small** for me.

② [small (in degree, etc.)]
a **low** voice
¶ Please **turn** the radio **down** a little
bit.

③ [low in age, young]
¶ [I] don't remember things from when
[I] **was little** very well.

ちいさな　小さな 〔連体〕

小さな花 (*chiisana* hana) 小さな手
(*chiisana* te) 小さな家 (*chiisana* ie)
⇔大きな **ookina**
⇒小さい **chiisai**

chiisana 〔attrib〕 **small, little**

a **small** flower // a **small** hand // a
small house

ちか　地下 〔名〕

地下水 (*chika*sui) 地下道 (*chika*dō)
地下室 (*chika*shitsu) 地下街
(*chika*gai) 地下鉄 (*chika*tetsu)
地下2階 (*chika* nikai)

chika 〔n〕 **underground,
subterranean**

underground water, groundwater // an
underpass, an **underground**
passage // **a basement** // an
underground shopping center // a
subway // a second **basement**

¶ここは地下 150 メートルぐらい掘らないと、水が出ません。(Koko wa *chika* hyakugojūmētoru gurai horanai to, mizu ga demasen.)

¶You have to drill **down** about 150 meters here to hit water.

¶地下で働く人もいます。(*Chika* de hataraku hito mo imasu.)

¶There are people who work **underground**.

⇔地上 **chijō**

ちかい 近い〔形〕

chikai〔adj〕 **near, close to; nearly, soon; almost**

①［距離的に離れていない］

①[near, close to]

¶あなたのうちは学校から近いですか。(Anata no uchi wa gakkō kara *chikai* desu ka?)

¶Is your home **near** the school?

↔遠い **tooi**

②［時間的にあまり離れていない、間もない］

②[nearly, soon, in a short time]

¶近いうちにまた会いましょう。(*Chikai* uchi ni mata aimashō.)

¶Let's meet again **soon**.

¶もう 12 時に近いです。(Mō jūniji ni *chikai* desu.)

¶It's **almost** twelve o'clock.

¶あの人は、日本へ来てからもう2年近くなります。(Ano hito wa, Nihon e kite kara mō ninen *chikaku* narimasu.)

¶It's **nearly** two years since [he] came to Japan.

③［数量などがそれより少し足りないがそれとほとんど同じぐらいである］

③[almost, nearly, close to (the same amount)]

¶会場に千人近い人が集まってきました。(Kaijō ni sennin *chikai* hito ga atsumatte kimashita.)

¶**Close to** a thousand persons came to the auditorium〖theater, hall, etc.〗.

ちがい 違い〔名〕

chigai〔n〕 **difference; mistake**

①［違うこと、差があること］

①[difference, discrepancy]

¶兄弟でもこんなに性格の違いがあります。(Kyōdai demo konna ni seikaku no *chigai* ga arimasu.)

¶Even though they are brothers, they have such **different** personalities.

¶姉とわたしは三つ違いです。(Ane to watashi wa mittsu *chigai* desu.)

¶There is a three-year **difference** in age between my elder sister and myself.

②［間違えること］

②[mistake]

523

計算違い (keisan*chigai*) 思い違い (omoi*chigai*)

¶それはわたしの考え違いでした。 (Sore wa watashi no kangae*chigai* deshita.)

miscalculation // a misunderstanding, misapprehension

¶I was mistaken.

ちがいない 違いない [連]

¶あ、あれは山田さんに違いありません。(A! Are wa Yamada san ni *chigai arimasen*.)

¶田中さんは必ず来るに違いありません。(Tanaka san wa kanarazu kuru ni *chigai ariamsen*.)

chigai nai [compd] certainly, undoubtedly; it is certain that, there is no doubt that

¶Oh, look! Surely that's [Mrs.] Yamada.

¶There's no doubt that [Mr.] Tanaka will come.

ちがう 違う [動 I]

① [同じでなくなる、相違する]
大きさが違う (ookisa ga *chigau*) 重さが違う (omosa ga *chigau*) 意見が違う (iken ga *chigau*)

¶習慣は国によって違います。
(Shūkan wa kuni ni yotte *chigaimasu*.)

② [間違う]
¶この字は違っていますよ。(Konoji wa *chigatte* imasu yo.)

¶電話番号が違っています。
(Denwabangō ga *chigatte* imasu.)

③ [あることがらを否定するのに使う]
¶「これはあなたのですか。」(Kore wa anata no desu ka?)「いいえ、違います。」(Iie, *chigaimasu*.)

chigau [v I] differ; be wrong; no, not

① [differ, vary]
be different in size // be different in weight // have differing opinions

¶Customs differ from country to country.

② [be wrong, mistaken]
¶This (written) character 〖letter, kanji. etc.〗 is wrong.

¶You have the wrong number (said on the telephone).

③ [no, not; used to deny something]
¶"Is this yours?"
"No, it's not."

ちかく 近く [名]

① [距離的に離れていない所]
¶わたしは学校の近くに住んでいます。(Watashi wa gakkō no *chikaku* ni sunde imasu.)

chikaku [n] close, nearby; shortly, before long; nearly, almost

① [close, nearby]
¶I live near the school.

¶この近くに郵便局はありませんか。
(Kono *chikaku* ni yūbinkyoku wa arimasen ka？)

¶ Isn't there a post office **nearby**?

⇔遠く **tooku**
→付近 **fukin**

② [時間的にあまり離れていないこと]

② [shortly, before long]

¶もう12時近くです。(Mō jūniji *chikaku* desu.)

¶ It's **nearly** twelve o'clock.

¶1時間近く待ったのに、山田さんはまだ来ません。(Ichijikan *chikaku* matta noni, Yamada san wa mada kimasen.)

¶ Even though I've waited **nearly** an hour, [Mrs.] Yamada still hasn't come.

③ [数量などがそれより少し足りないがそれとほとんど同じぐらいであること]

③ [nearly, almost]

¶千人近くの人が会場に集まりました。(Sennin *chikaku* no hito ga kaijō ni atsumarimashita.)

¶ **Nearly** a thousand people came to the auditorium 〖hall, theater, etc.〗.

¶この時計は10万円近くしました。(Kono tokei wa jūman'en *chikaku* shimashita.)

¶ This watch cost **almost** a hundred thousand yen.

¶食費と部屋代で、1か月8万円近くかかります。(Shokuhi to heyadai de, ikkagetsu hachiman'en *chikaku* kakarimasu.)

¶ Room and board take **close to** eighty thousand yen a month.

ちかごろ 近ごろ 〔名〕

chikagoro 〔n〕 **recently, nowadays**

¶近ごろ、山田さんから手紙が来ませんね。(*Chikagoro*, Yamada san kara tegami ga kimasen ne.)

¶ There haven't been any letters **recently** from [Miss] Yamada.

¶近ごろの学生はあまり勉強しません。(*Chikagoro* no gakusei wa amari benkyō shimasen.)

¶ Students don't study very hard **nowadays**.

ちかづく 近づく 〔動Ⅰ〕

chikazuku 〔v I〕 **approach, come near**

¶船がこちらへ近づいてきました。(Fune ga kochira e *chikazuite* kimashita.)

¶ The ship **is** 〖**was**〗 **approaching**.

¶試験の日が近づいてきました。(Shiken no hi ga *chikazuite* kimashita.)

¶ The day of the examination **has** 〖**had**〗 **drawn near**.

ちかてつ 地下鉄 〔名〕

¶わたしは地下鉄で東京駅へ行きました。（Watashi wa *chikatetsu* de Tōkyō-eki e ikimashita.）

ちから 力 〔名〕

① [体力]
力がない（*chikara* ga nai） 力が強い（*chikara* ga tsuyoi） 力が弱い（*chikara* ga yowai）
¶あの人は体が小さいのに、力があります。（Ano hito wa karada ga chiisai noni, *chikara* ga arimasu.）

② [能力・学力など]
力がある（*chikara* ga aru） 力がない（*chikara* ga nai）
¶わたしは日本語を話す力がまだ弱いです。（Watashi wa Nihongo o hanasu *chikara* ga mada yowai desu.）

ちきゅう 地球 〔名〕
¶地球は太陽の周りを回っています。（*Chikyū* wa taiyō no mawari o mawatte imasu.）

ちこく 遅刻 〔名、〜する〕

¶朝寝坊して、学校に遅刻しました。（Asanebō shite, gakkō ni *chikoku* shimashita.）

ちしき 知識 〔名〕
¶大学で専門的な知識を身につけたいと思っています。（Daigaku de senmonteki na *chishiki* o mi ni tsuketai to omotte imasu.）
¶わたしは、日本文学についての知識はほとんどありません。（Watashiwa,

---

chikatetsu 〔n〕 **subway**

¶I went to Tokyo Station on **the subway**.

chikara 〔n〕 **strength, force; ability, proficiency**

① [strength, force]
weak // strong // weak

¶Even though small, [he] **is strong**.

② [ability, proficiency]
be able // be incapable; be powerless

¶**I can't speak** Japanese **well** yet.

chikyū 〔n〕 **the earth, the globe**
¶**The earth** revolves around the sun.

chikoku 〔n, 〜*suru*〕 **lateness, being late**

¶[I] overslept and was **late for** school.

chishiki 〔n〕 **knowledge**
¶I want to obtain a specialized **education** at a university.

¶I have hardly any **knowledge** at all of Japanese literature.

Nihon-bungaku ni tsuite no *chishiki* wa
hotondo arimasen.)

ちじょう 地上 〔名〕

¶地下鉄を降りて、エスカレーターで
地上に出ました。(Chikatetsu o orite,
esukarētā de *chijō* ni demashita.)
⇔地下 **chika**

---

chijō 〔n〕 **aboveground, ground
level**

¶[I] got off the subway and took the
escalator up to **the surface**.

ちず 地図 〔名〕
日本地図（Nihon-*chizu*）世界地図
(sekai-*chizu*)
¶地図で探しましたが、その町は載っ
ていませんでした。(*Chizu* de sagashimashita ga, sono machi wa notte
imasen deshita.)
¶駅からあなたのうちまでの地図をか
いてください。(Eki kara anata no uchi
made no *chizu* o kaite kudasai.)

---

chizu 〔n〕 **map**
a map of Japan // a world **map**

¶[I] looked for that town on **the map**,
but it wasn't there.

¶Please draw me **a map** of the way
from the station to your place.

ちち 父 〔名〕
¶わたしは父に手紙を書きました。
(Watashi wa *chichi* ni tegami o
kakimashita.)
＊自分の父親のことを他人に話す場合
に使う。直接、父親に呼びかける場合
や、他人の父親のことを言う場合は、
「お父さん（otōsan）」「お父様
（otōsama）」と言う。
⇔母 **haha**
⇒お父さん **otōsan**

---

chichi 〔n〕 **father**
¶I wrote a letter to **my father**.

＊Used to refer to one's own father
when speaking with others. When
directly addressing one's father or referring to someone else's father, *otōsan* or *otōsama* is used instead.

ちぢむ 縮む 〔動Ⅰ〕

¶このシャツはナイロン製ですから、
洗っても縮みません。(Kono shatsu wa
naironsei desu kara, aratte mo
chijimimasen.)

---

chijimu 〔v Ⅰ〕 **shrink, contract,
be shortened**
¶As this shirt is made of nylon, **it
won't shrink** when washed.

527

ちぢめる 縮める〔動Ⅱ〕

¶このズボンは長すぎますから、少し縮めてください。(Kono zubon wa nagasugimasu kara, sukoshi *chijimete* kudasai.)

¶お金が足りなくなったので、日本にいる期間を縮めなければなりません。(Okane ga tarinaku natta node, Nihon ni iru kikan o *chijimenakereba* narimasen.)

ちっとも〔副〕

¶漢字は難しくて、ちっとも覚えられません。(Kanji wa muzukashikute, *chittomo* oboeraremasen.)

ちほう 地方〔名〕

① [ある広がりをもつ地域]
¶この地方は、夏は雨があまり降りません。(Kono *chihō* wa, natsu wa ame ga amari furimasen.)

② [田舎]
¶地方へ行くと、空気がきれいです。(*Chihō* e iku to, kūki ga kirei desu.)

ちゃ 茶〔名〕

お茶を飲む (ocha o nomu) お茶を入れる (oha o ireru) 濃いお茶 (koi o*cha*)

¶お茶をどうぞ。(Ocha o dōzo.)

¶お茶でも飲みに行きませんか。(*Ocha* demo nomi ni ikimasen ka?)

¶秋子さんのうちでお茶とお菓子をごちそうになりました。(Akiko san no uchi de o*cha* to okashi o gochisō ni narimashita.)

chijimeru 〔v Ⅱ〕 shorten, contract, reduce

¶ Please **shorten** these trousers a littie as they are too long.

¶ **I must reduce** my stay in Japan since I am running out of money.

chittomo 〔adv〕 for a moment, in the least

¶ Since kanji is very difficult, I can**not** memorize the characters **at all**.

chihō 〔n〕 district, region; the provinces, the country

① [district, region, area]
¶ It doesn't rain very much in the summer in this **area** 〚**around** here, in these **parts**〛.

② [the provinces, the country]
¶ The air is clean in **the country**.

cha 〔n〕 (green)tea

drink **tea** // fix **tea** // strong **tea**

¶ Please have **some tea** (said when handing a cup of tea to someone).

¶ How about going somewhere for **some tea** (or other light refreshment)?

¶ I was treated to **tea** and a sweet at Akiko's.

ちゃいろ 茶色 〔名〕

¶山田さんは茶色のズボンをはいています。(Yamada san wa *chairo* no zubon o haite imasu.)

chairo 〔n〕 **brown, light brown**

¶ [Mr.] Yamada is wearing **brown** trousers.

ちゃわん 茶わん 〔名〕

湯飲み茶わん (yunomi-*jawan*) コーヒー茶わん (kōhii-*jawan*) 茶わんを割る (*chawan* o waru) 御飯を茶わんに盛る (gohan o *chawan* ni moru)

¶茶わんにお茶をついで飲みました。(*Chawan* ni ocha o tsuide nomimashita.)

chawan 〔n〕 **(rice)bowl, (tea)cup**

a tea**cup** // a coffee **cup** // break a **cupbowl** // dish rice out into **a bowl**

¶ [I] poured (green) tea into **the cup** and drank it.

-ちゃん 〔尾〕

¶みゆきちゃん、もう宿題は終わりましたか。(Miyukichan, mō shukudai wa owari mashita ka?)

-chan 〔suf〕 **suffix for a personal name especially for a kid's name**

¶ Miyuki-*chan*, have you finished your homework?

ちゃんと 〔副、〜する〕

①〔きちんと、きれいに〕

¶上田さんの部屋はいつもちゃんとかたづけてあります。(Ueda san no heya wa itsu mo *chanto* katazukete arimasu.)

¶田中さんはいつもちゃんとネクタイを締めています。(Tanaka san wa itsu mo *chanto* nekutai o shimete imasu.)

②〔すっかり、完全に〕

¶出発の用意はちゃんとできています。(Shuppatsu no yōi wa *chanto* dekite imasu.)

¶部屋代は、毎月ちゃんと払っています。(Heyadai wa, maitsuki *chanto* haratte imasu.)

⇒きちんと **kichinto**

chanto 〔adv, 〜*suru*〕 **properly, exactly; perfectly, duly**

① [properly, exactly, neatly, in good order]

¶ [Miss] Ueda's room is always **neat**.

¶ [Mr.] Tanaka always **neatly** wears a tie.

② [perfectly, duly]

¶ **Everything is ready** for [our] departure.

¶ [I] pay [my] rent **punctually** 〚**regularly**〛 every month.

-ちゅう -中 〔尾〕

①〔あるものの中〕

-chū 〔suf〕 **in, within; during**

① [in, within (something)]

空気中 (kūkichū) 血液中
(ketsueki*chū*)

② [ある時間の間]
午前中 (gozenchū) 今週中
(konshūchū)

¶ 今月中には日本へ行きたいと思って
います。(Kongetsuchū ni wa Nihon e
ikitai to omotte imasu.)

③ [あることをしている間]
勉強中 (benkyōchū) 仕事中
(shigotochū) 食事中 (shokujichū)
使用中 (shiyōchū)

¶ 先生は今、授業中です。(Sensei wa
ima, jugyōchū desu.)

¶ 山田さんに電話をかけましたが、話
し中でした。(Yamadasan ni denwa o
kakemashita ga hanashichū deshita.)

ちゅうい 注意 〔名、～する〕

① [何かをするときなどにそれが順調
にいくようにいろいろな点によく気を
つけること]
注意深い (*chūi*bukai) 不注意
(fu*chūi*)

¶ 交通信号に注意しながら、道を渡り
ました。(Kōtsū-shingō ni *chūi*
shinagara, michi o watarimashita.)

¶ これから話すことは大事ですから、
注意して聞いてください。(Korekara
hanasu koto wa daiji desu kara, *chūi* shite
kiite kudasai.)

② [悪いことなどが起こらないように
前もってじゅうぶんに気をつけること]

in the air // **in** the blood

② [during, while]
in the morning; **all through** the
morning // **during** this week; **all** this
week

¶ I want to go to Japan **sometime** this
month.

③ [during, under, in progress]
to be studying; **while** studying // to be
at work; **while** at work // to be dining;
while dining // **in** use

¶ The professor is **in** class now.

¶ I telephoned [Mr.] Yamada, but the
line was **busy**.

chūi 〔n, ～*suru*〕 **attention;
caution; warning**

① [attention; pay attention, be careful
(when doing something)]

careful; attentive // careless; inattentive

¶ [They] crossed the street **paying
heed** to the traffic signal.

¶ What I am going to say now is
important so please listen **carefully**.

② [caution; be careful, keep watch (to
prevent something bad from
happening)]

¶寒くなりましたから、風邪を引かないように注意してください。(Samuku narimashita kara, kaze o hikanai yō ni *chūi* shite kudasai.)

¶冬の山は危ないですから、注意してください。(Fuyu no yama wa abunai desu kara, *chūi* shite kudasai.)

③ [言動などについてその人に気をつけるように言うこと]

注意を与える (*chūi* o ataeru)

¶成績が下がったので、先生に注意されました。(Seiseki gasagatta node, sensei ni *chūi* saremashita.)

¶バスの運転手さんが、「窓から手を出さないでください。」とお客に注意しました。(Basu no untenshusan ga, "Mado kara te o dasanaide kudasai." to okyaku ni *chūi* shimashita.)

ちゅうおう　中央〔名〕

¶町の中央から四方に道が延びています。(Machi no *chūō* kara shihō ni michi ga nobite imasu.)

ちゅうがくせい　中学生〔名〕

¶弟は中学生です。(Otōto wa *chūgakusei* desu.)

ちゅうがっこう　中学校〔名〕

¶弟は中学校へ通っています。(Otōto wa *chūgakkō* e kayotte imasu.)

＊「中学校 (*chūgakkō*)」を略して「中学 (chūgaku)」とも言う。

ちゅうしゃ　注射〔名、〜する〕

予防注射 (yobō-*chūsha*) 注射を打つ (*chūsha* o utsu)

¶ It has gotten colder so please **be careful** not to catch a cold.

¶ Mountains are dangerous in the winter so please **take care**.

③ [warning; to advise, to warn]

give **advice**; give **a warning**

¶ [I] **was warned** by my teacher as [my] grades had fallen.

¶ The bus driver **warned** the passenger, saying "Please don't put your hand out of the window."

chūō〔n〕 center, middle, heart

¶ Streets extend in all directions from **the center** of the town.

chūgakusci〔n〕 junior high school student

¶ My younger brother is **a junior high school student**.

chūgakkō〔n〕 junior high school, lower secondary school

¶ My younger brother is in **junior high school**.

＊*Chūgakkō* is sometimes abbreviated to *chūgaku*.

chūsha〔n, 〜*suru*〕 injection, shot

a preventive **injection**, an inoculation // give **an injectionshot**

¶看護婦さんは腕に注射をしてくれました。(Kangofusan wa ude ni *chūsha* o shite kuremashita.)

¶ The nurse gave me **an injection** in the arm.

ちゅうしゃ 駐車 〔名、～する〕

chūsha 〔n, ～*suru*〕 **(automobile) parking**

駐車場（*chūsha*jyo）駐車禁止（chūshakinshi）

a **parking** zone, a **parking** lot // No **Parking**

¶ここに駐車しないでください。(Koko ni *chūsha* shinaide kudasai.)

¶ Please **don't park** here.

ちゅうし 中止 〔名、～する〕

chūshi 〔n, ～*suru*〕 **discontinue, suspend, stop, call off**

¶試合は雨のため中止になりました。(Shiai wa ame no tame *chūshi* ni narimashita.)

¶ The game **was called off** because of rain.

¶わたしは忙しくなったので、外国へ行くのを中止しました。(Watashi wa isogashiku natta node, gaikoku e iku no o *chūshi* shimashita.)

¶ **I called off** my trip abroad because I am 〖was〗 so busy.

ちゅうじゅん 中旬 〔名〕

chūjun 〔n〕 **the middle third of the month**

¶わたしは9月の中旬に旅行する予定です。(Watashi wa kugatsu no chūjun ni ryokō suru yotei desu.)

¶ I plan to take a trip in **mid**-September.

⇒上旬 jōjun 下旬 gejun

ちゅうしん 中心 〔名〕

chūshin 〔n〕 **center, core; heart, crux, nucleus**

①〔物・所などの真ん中〕

① [center, core, middle]

円の中心（en no *chūshin*）台風の中心（taifū no *chūshin*）

the middle of a circle // **the center** of a typhoon

¶町の中心に住んでいますから便利です。(Machi no *chūshin* ni sunde imasu kara benri desu.)

¶ It's convenient for me living in the **center** of the town.

②〔最も重要な点、重要な役割をする人〕

② [heart, crux, nucleus]

問題の中心（mondai no *chūshin*）

the heart of the problem

¶上田さんが中心となって、この研究会を作りました。(Ueda san ga *chūshin* to natte, kono kenkyūkai o tsukurimashita.)

¶ This study group was formed **centering around** [Mr.] Ueda.

ちゅうもん 注文 〔名、〜する〕

¶どんな料理を注文しましょうか。(Donna ryōri o *chūmon* shimashō ka？)

¶電話でも注文できますか。(Denwa de mo *chūmon* dekimasu ka？)

¶手紙で注文すれば、すぐ送ってくれます。(Tegami de *chūmon* sureba, sugu okutte kuremasu.)

chūmon 〔n, 〜*suru*〕 order; request

¶ What dishes **shall we order?**

¶ Can one **place an order** by telephone?

¶ **If you order** by mail, they will send it right away.

ちゅうもく 注目 〔名、〜する〕

¶彼の研究は世界じゅうから注目されています。(Kare no kenkyū wa sekaijū kara *chūmoku* sarete imasu.)

¶日本の経済的な発展は、他の国々から注目されています。(Nihon no keizaiteki na hatten wa, ta no kuniguni kara *chūmoku* sarete imasu.)

chūmoku 〔n, 〜*suru*〕 attention, notice

¶ His research **has attracted attention** throughout the world.

¶ Other nations **are watching** Japan's economic growth **with interest**.

-ちょう -長 〔尾〕
校長 (kōchō) 課長 (kachō) 社長 (shachō) 会長 (kaichō) 議長 (gichō)

-chō 〔suf〕 head, director, etc.
a (school) **principal** // a (section) **chief** // a (company) **president** // a (committee) **chairman**; a (society) **president** // a **chairman** (of a representative assembly); a **leader** of a meeting

ちょうさ 調査 〔名、〜する〕

人口調査 (jinkō-*chōsa*) 調査用紙 (*chōsa* yōshi)

¶警察が今、この事故の原因を調査しています。(Keisatsu ga ima, kono jiko no gen'in o *chōsa* shite imasu.)

chōsa 〔n, 〜*suru*〕 investigation, research
a census // a questionnaire

¶ The police are now **investigating** the cause of this accident.

¶調査の結果、事故の原因がわかりました。(*Chōsa* no kekka, jiko no gen'in ga wakarimashita.)

¶ **Investigation** revealed the cause of the accident 〚Upon **investigation**, the cause of the accident was identified〛.

ちょうし 調子 〔名〕
chōshi 〔n〕 **tone, pitch; condition**

① [音の高低]
声の調子が高い (koe no *chōshi* ga takai)

① [tone, pitch (of sound)]
a voice is high-**pitched**

¶山田さんの歌はいつも調子が外れています。(Yamada san no uta wa itsu mo *chōshi* ga hazurete imasu.)

¶ [Mrs.] Yamada always sings **off key**.

¶このピアノは音の調子がおかしいです。(Kono piano wa oto no *chōshi* ga okashii desu.)

¶ This piano is **out of tune**.

② [状態、ぐあい]

② [condition, state]

¶今日は体の調子がいいです。(Kyō wa karada no *chōshi* ga ii desu.)

¶ I feel very **well** today.

¶この機械は調子が悪いですね。(Kono kikai wa *chōshi* ga warui desu ne.)

¶ Something **is wrong** with this machine.

ちょうしょ 長所 〔名〕
chōsho 〔n〕 **strong point, advantage**

¶だれにも長所と短所があります。(Dare ni mo *chōsho* to tansho ga arimasu.)

¶ Everyone has their **strong points** and weak points.

¶この機械の長所は取り扱いが簡単だということです。(Kono kikai no *chōsho* wa toriatsukai ga kantan da to iu koto desu.)

¶ **The strong point** of this machine is its ease of handling.

⇔短所 tansho
⇒欠点 ketten

ちょうど 〔副〕
chōdo 〔adv〕 **exactly, precisely; just right**

① [過不足のない様子]

① [exactly, precisely]

¶今、ちょうど6時です。(Ima, *chōdo* rokuji desu.)

¶ It's **exactly** six o'clock now.

¶「その本はいくらでしたか。」(Sono hon wa ikura deshita ka?)「ちょうど千円でした。」(Chōdo sen'en deshita.)

¶ "How much was that book?" "**Exactly** a thousand yen."

② [ぐあいよく、都合よく、折よく]

② [just right]

¶「おふろのお湯はぬるくないですか。」(Ofuro no oyu wa nuruku nai desu ka?)「ちょうどいいです。」(Chōdo ii desu.)

¶ "Isn't the bathwater a little too cool?" "No, it's **just** right."

¶ この洋服はわたしにちょうどよく合っています。(Kono yōfuku wa watashi ni chōdo yoku atte imasu.)

¶ This piece of clothing is a **perfect** fit on me.

¶ ちょうどよいところへ来てくれました。(Chōdo yoi tokoro e kite kuremashita.)

¶ You couldn't have come at a **better** time 〖You have come at **exactly** the right time〗.

ちょうめん 帳面 〔名〕
☞ノート nōto

chōmen 〔n〕　☞**nōto**

チョーク 〔名〕

chōku 〔n〕 chalk

¶ チョークで黒板に漢字を書いてください。(Chōku de kokuban ni kanji o kaite kudasai.)

¶ Please write the kanji on the blackboard with **chalk**.

¶ 白いチョークを1本取ってください。(Shiroi chōku o ippon totte kudasai.)

¶ Please hand me a piece of white **chalk**.

ちょきん 貯金 〔名、〜する〕

chokin 〔n, 〜**suru**〕 savings

¶ 郵便局から貯金を下ろしてきました。(Yūbinkyoku kara chokin o oroshite kimashita.)

¶ [I] withdrew [my] **savings** from the post office.

¶ わたしは毎月1万円ずつ貯金しています。(Watashi wa maitsuki ichiman'en zutsu chokin shite imasu.)

¶ **I save** ten thousand yen every month.

ちょくせつ 直接 〔名〕

chokusetsu 〔n〕 direct, immediate, personal

¶ わたしが上田さんに直接きいてみます。(Watashi ga Ueda san ni chokusetsu kiite mimasu.)

¶ I will **personally** ask [Miss] Ueda.

¶このガラスのなべは、直接火にかけても大丈夫です。(Kono garasu no nabe wa, *chokusetsu* hi ni kakete mo daijōbu desu.)
⇔間接 **kansetsu**

¶It is safe to put this glass pot **directly** on the burner.

ちょくせん 直線 〔名〕

¶ものさしを使って、直線を引きました。(Monosashi o tsukatte, chokusen o hikimashita.)
⇔曲線 **kyokusen**

chokusen 〔n〕 **straight line**

¶I drew **a straight line** using a ruler 〖measuring sticks〗.

ちょっと 〔副〕

①[時間が短い様子]
¶疲れたから、ちょっと休みましょう。(Tsukareta kara, *chotto* yasumimashō.)
¶ちょっと待ってください。(*Chotto* matte kudasai.)
②[ものごとの程度などがわずかな様子]
¶もうちょっとゆっくり話してください。(Mō *chotto* yukkuri hanashite kudasai.)
¶ちょっと値段が高すぎます。もう少し安いのはありませんか。(*Chotto* nedan ga takasugimasu. Mō sukoshi yasui no wa arimasen ka?)

chotto 〔adv〕 **for a moment; a little bit**
①[for a moment, a short time]
¶[I'm] tired; let's rest **a little while**.

¶Please wait **a moment**.

②[a little bit, slightly]

¶Please speak **a little bit** more slowly.

¶That is **a little** too expensive. Don't you have anything a little cheaper?

ちり 地理 〔名〕

①[世界の地形・気候・生物・都市・産業・交通などの様子]
地理学 (*chiri*gaku)
¶上田さんは中学校の地理の先生です。(Ueda san wa chūgakkō no *chiri* no sensei desu.)
②[ある土地の様子]

chiri 〔n〕 **geography; topography, geographical features**
①[geography]

(the science of) **geography**
¶[Mr.] Ueda teaches **geography** in junior high school.

②[topography, geographical features (of a certain area)]

¶兄は東京の地理に詳しいです。（Ani wa Tōkyō no *chiri* ni kuwashii desu.）

¶ My older brother **knows his way around** Tokyo (physically).

ちる 散る〔動Ⅰ〕

① [花や葉が落ちる]

¶桜はもう散ってしまいました。（Sakura wa mō *chitte* shimaimashita.）

② [集中しない、心が落ち着かない]

¶隣がうるさいので、気が散って勉強ができません。（Tonari ga urusai node, ki ga *cihtte* benkyō ga dekimasen.）

＊「気が散る（ki ga *chiru*）」の形で使う。

chiru 〔vⅠ〕 fall, scatter

① [(flowers, leaves) fall, scatter]

¶ The cherry blossoms have all **fallen**.

② [be distracted]

¶ **I can't concentrate** on my studies because they are so noisy next door.

＊Used in the pattern "*ki ga chiru*."

つい〔副〕

① [時間や距離などがほんのちょっとである様子]

¶ 山田さんには、つい先日学校で会ったばかりです。（Yamada san ni wa, *tsui* senjitsu gakkō de atta bakari desu.）

¶ わたしのうちは、ついそこです。（Watashi no uchi wa, *tsui* soko desu.）

② [うっかり何かをする様子]

¶ わたしは甘い物が好きなので、つい食べすぎてしまいます。（Watashi wa amai mono ga suki na node, *tsui* tabesugite shimaimasu.）

¶ あまり忙しかったので、友達に電話するのをつい忘れてしまいました。（Amari isogashikatta node, tomodachi ni denwa suru no o *tsui* wasurete shimaimashita.）

ついたち 一日〔名〕

¶ 今日は三月一日です。（Kyō wa sangatsu *tsuitachi* desu.）

⇒ 日 -ka

ついて〔連〕

¶ あなたは日本で何について勉強するつもりですか。（Anata wa Nihon de nani ni *tsuite* benkyō suru tsumori desu ka？）

tsui 〔adv〕 only, just; inadvertently, unintentionally

① [only, just]

¶ I met [Mr.] Yamada at school **just** the other day.

¶ My home is **just** over there.

② [inadvertently, unintentionally, by chance]

¶ Because of my sweet tooth I always eat too many of them 〚too much of it〛 **before I know it**.

¶ I was so busy that I forgot to call my friend.

tsuitachi 〔n〕 the first day of the month

¶ Today is March **1**.

tsuite 〔compd〕 about, on, concerning, in regard to

¶ **What** do you plan to study in Japan?

¶ 今日は、あなたがたの国について作文を書いてください。（Kyō wa, anatagata no kuni ni *tsuite* sakubun o kaite kudasai.）

＊いつも「〜について（〜ni tsuite）」の形で使う。

ついでに〔副〕

¶ 銀行へ行ったついでに、郵便局へ寄って切手を買って来ました。（Ginkō e itta *tsuide ni*, yūbinkyoku e yotte kitte o katte kimashita.）

ついに〔副〕

① ［いろいろな過程を経て最後にある事態になるという意味を表すときに使う］

¶ 何時間も急な山道を登って、ついに頂上に着きました。（Nanjikan mo kyū na yamamichi o nobotte, *tsuini* chōjō ni tsukimashita.）

¶ 実験はついに成功しました。（Jikken wa *tsuini* seikō shimashita.）

¶ 丈夫だった上田さんもついに病気で入院したそうです。（Jōbu datta Ueda san mo *tsuini* byōki de nyūin shita sō desu.）

＊普通あとに過去・完了を表す「たの形」がきて、喜び・失望・あきらめなどの感情を表すことが多い。「とうとう（tōtō）」が事態が成立するまでの過程に重点があるのに対し、事態の成立そのものに重点がある。

¶ Today please write a composition **about** your native countries.

＊Always used in the pattern "〜 *ni tsuite*."

tsuide ni 〔adv〕 **while, in passing, at the same time**

¶ **On the way** to the bank [I] stopped off at the post office and bought some stamps.

tsuini 〔adv〕 **at last, finally; in the end, after all**

① [at last, finally, ultimately; used when an event takes place after various stages]

¶ After hours of climbing up the steep mountain trail, [we] **at last** reached the summit.

¶ The experiment **finally** succeeded 〚has **finally** succeeded〛.

¶ I hear that even the hardy [Mr.] Ueda was **ultimately** sick and in the hospital 〚has **in the end** become sick and is in the hospital〛.

＊Usually followed by a verb in the *-ta* form expressing past or completed action and often used with expressions of emotion such as joy, disappointment, resignation, etc. In the case of *tōtō* the emphasis is on the process leading up to the event but for *tsuini* it is on the event itself.

②[前と同じ状態が続いて新しい事態が起こらないことが確定したときに使う]

¶1時間待ったが、田中さんはついに来ませんでした。(Ichijikan matta ga, Tanaka san wa *tsuini* kimasen deshita.)
¶時計がなくなったので、一生懸命捜しましたが、ついに見つかりませんでした。(Tokei ga nakunatta node, isshōkenmei sagashimashita ga, *tsuini* mitsukarimasen deshita.)
*普通あとに「〜ませんでした(〜masen deshita)」の形か、否定的な意味の言葉の過去・完了を表す「たの形」が来る。
⇒とうとう **tōtō**

つうじる 通じる〔動II〕

①[道などがある場所に続く]
¶この道は学校の前に通じています。(Kono michi wa gakkō no mae ni *tsūjite* imasu.)
②[交通や通信などがある所などとつながる]
鉄道が通じる (tetsudō ga *tsūjiru*)
¶電話が通じません。どうしたのでしょう。(Denwa ga *tsūjimasen*. Dō shita no deshō?)
③[相手にわかってもらえる]
¶わたしの下手な英語では、とてもアメリカでは通じないでしょう。(Watashi no heta na Eigo de wa, totemo Amerika de wa *tsūjinai* deshō.)

②[in the end, after all; used when the preexisting state continues and one sees that some new event has not taken place]

¶[I] waited an hour but **in the event** [Mr.] Tanaka didn't come.

¶[I] searched all over for [my] missing watch but it **never** turned up.

*Usually followed by a verb in the -*masen deshita* form or a verb in the *-ta* form expressing past or completed action and expressing a negative meaning.

tsūjiru〔vII〕**pass, run; lead to, connect with; be understood, be comprehended; via, through the medium of**
①[pass, run]
¶This street **passes** in front of the school.

②[lead to, connect with]

have train **service**
¶The phone **is dead.** I wonder what happened.

③[be understood, be comprehended]
¶With my poor command of English I probably **wouldn't be able to make myself understood** at all in the United States.

¶あの人には冗談を言っても通じません。(Ano hito ni wa jōdan o itte mo *tsūjimasen*.)

¶ [He] doesn't have any sense of humor—[he] **never understands the point** of a joke (literally, Even if you tell him a joke he **won't understand** it).

④ [全体にわたってという意味を表す]
¶一年を通じて今月がいちばん雨が多いです。(Ichinen o *tsūjite* kongetsu ga ichiban ame ga ooi desu.)

④ [throughout]
¶ **Of all** the year, this month has the most rainfall.

*いつも「〜を通じて（〜o tsūjite）」の形で使う。

*Always used in the pattern "〜 *o tsūjite*."

⑤ [あるものを媒介としてという意味を表す]
¶そのニュースはラジオを通じて全国に放送されました。(Sono nyūsu wa rajio o *tsūjite* zenkoku ni hōsō saremashita.)

⑤ [via, through the medium of]
¶ That news was broadcast to the whole country **on** the radio.

*いつも「〜を通じて（〜o tsūjite）」の形で使う。

*Always used in the pattern "〜 *o tsūjite*."

つうしん 通信 〔名、〜する〕

tsūshin 〔n, 〜*suru*〕 **communication(s), news, information**

通信社 (*tsūshin*sha)
¶最近、科学の進歩によって通信の方法が発達しました。(Saikin, kagaku no shinpo ni yotte *tsūshin* no hōhōga hattatsu shimashita.)

a **news** agency, a **wire** service
¶ The advance of science in recent years has resulted in improved means of **communication**.

¶台風のため、九州地方との通信ができなくなりました。(Taifū no tame, Kyūshū-chihō to no *tsūshin* ga dekinaku narimashita.)

¶ **Communications** with the Kyushu region were 〚are〛 cut off due to the typhoon.

つうち 通知 〔名、〜する〕

tsūchi 〔n, 〜*suru*〕 **notice, notification, communication**

¶来週の会議の通知はもう届きました。(Raishū no kaigi no *tsūchi* wa mō todokimashita ka？)

¶ Have you been **notified** of the meeting next week?

¶あしたの会が延期になったことをみんなに通知してください。(Ashita no kai ga enki ni natta koto o minna ni *tsūchi* shite kudasai.)

¶ Please **inform** everyone that tomorrow's meeting has been postponed.

つうやく 通訳 〔名、〜する〕

同時通訳 (dōji-*tsūyaku*)

¶彼女の職業は通訳です。(Kanojo no shokugyō wa *tsūyaku* desu.)

tsūyaku 〔n, 〜*suru*〕 **interpretation, an interpreter**

simultaneous **interpretation**

¶ She is a professional **interpreter**.

つかう 使う 〔動Ⅰ〕

¶この紙は何に使いますか。(Kono kami wa nan ni *tsukaimasu* ka？)

¶塩を使って、料理に味をつけます。(Shio o *tsukatte*, ryōri ni aji o tsukemasu.)

¶英語を使わないで、日本語で話してください。(Eigo o *tsukawanaide*, Nihongo de hanashite kudasai)

¶お金をむだに使ってはいけません。(Okane o muda ni *tsukatte* wa ikemasen.)

⇒用いる **mochiiru**

tsukau 〔vI〕 **use, make use of, employ**

¶ What is this paper **used for?**

¶ Salt **is used** to flavor food.

¶ Please **don't use** English—speak in Japanese.

¶ One shouldn't **waste** money.

つかまえる 捕まえる 〔動Ⅱ〕

¶警官がどろぼうを捕まえました。(Keikan ga dorobō o *tsukamaemashita*.)

¶子供たちが川で魚を捕まえています。(Kodomotachi ga kawa de sakana o *tsukamaete* imasu.)

tsukamaeru 〔vII〕 **capture, arrest; catch, grab**

¶ The police **arrested** the thief.

¶ The children **are catching** fish at the river (with a net or in their hands).

つかむ 〔動Ⅰ〕

① [指で強く持つ]

tsukamu 〔vI〕 **grab, grip, hold; grasp, have a firm hold of; grasp, apprehend**

① [grab, grip, hold]

¶田中さんはわたしの腕をつかんで離しませんでした。(Tanaka san wa watashi no ude o *tsukande* hanashimasen deshita.)

¶このひもの端をしっかりつかんでいてください。(Kono himo no hashi o shikkari *tsukande* ite kudasai.)

② [確実にとらえて自分のものにする] 機会をつかむ (kikai o *tsukamu*) 幸福をつかむ (kōfuku o *tsukamu*)

③ [要点・意味などを把握する]

¶わたしはこの文の意味をつかむことができません。(Watashi wa kono bun no imi o *tsukamu* koto ga dekimasen.)

つかれる 疲れる〔動II〕

¶今日は仕事が忙しくて、たいへん疲れました。(Kyō wa shigoto ga isogashikute, taihen *tsukaremashita*.)

¶疲れたら、少し休んでください。(*Tsukaretara*, sukoshi yasunde kudasai.)

つき 月〔名〕

① [1年を12に分けたその一つ]

¶一年じゅうでいちばん寒い月は何月ですか。(Ichinenjū de ichiban samui *tsuki* wa nangatsu desu ka?)

② [衛星]

¶空に円いきれいな月が出ています。(Sora ni marui kirei na *tsuki* ga dete imasu.)

つぎ 次〔名〕

¶この次の日曜日にテニスをしませんか。(Kono *tsugi* no nichiyōbi ni tenisu o shimasen ka?)

¶わたしは次の駅で降ります。(Watashi wa *tsugi* no eki de orimasu.)

¶ [Mr.] Tanaka **took hold** of my arm and wouldn't let go of it.

¶ Please **take a** firm **hold** on the end of this string 〚twine, cord, etc.〛.

② [grasp, have a firm hold on] **seize** an opportunity // **don't let** happiness **slip** through one's fingers

③ [grasp, apprehend]

¶ I can't **grasp** the meaning of this passage.

tsukareru 〔vII〕 **be tired, become tired**

¶ [I]'m very **tired** as it was quite busy at work today.

¶ Please rest a bit **if you're tired.**

tsuki 〔n〕 **a month; the moon**

① [a month]

¶ What is the coldest **month** of the year?

② [the moon]

¶ There's a lovely full **moon** up in the sky.

tsugi 〔n〕 **next, following, coming**

¶ Would you like to play tennis this **coming** Sunday?

¶ I am getting off at the **next** station.

¶わたしが今いちばん欲しいものはカメラで、その次に欲しいものは時計です。（Watashi ga ima ichiban hoshii mono wa kamera de, sono *tsugi* ni hoshii mono wa tokei desu.）

¶ The thing I want most right now is a camera and, **after that**, a watch.

つく　着く〔動Ⅰ〕

tsuku〔vI〕**arrive, get to; take, occupy**

①[目的の場所に達する]
¶１週間前にそちらに送った小包はもう着きましたか。（Isshūkan mae ni sochira ni okutta kozutsumi wa mō *tsukimashita* ka？）

① [arrive, get to, reach]
¶ Has the parcel [I] mailed you a week ago **arrived** yet?

¶日本に着いたら、すぐあなたに手紙を書きます。（Nihon ni *tsuitara*, sugu anata ni tegami o kakimasu.）

¶ [I] will write you a letter soon after **[my] arrival** in Japan.

②[ある位置に身を置く]
¶席に着いてください。（Seki ni *tsuite* kudasai.）

② [take, occupy, take one's position]
¶ Please **take** your seats.

つく〔動Ⅰ〕

tsuku〔vI〕**stick to, be stained; be attached to, belong to; follow, accompany; be established, take root; be lighted, come on**

①[あるものが何かの表面に付着する]
¶この切手の裏にはのりがついています。（Kono kitte no ura ni wa nori ga *tsuite* imasu.）

① [stick to, be stained]
¶ This stamp **has** glue on the back.

¶手にインクがついてしまいました。（Te ni inku ga *tsuite* shimaimashita.）

¶ [My] hand **got stained** with ink.

②[あるものが何かに加わる]
¶この日本語の教科書の後ろには、日本の地図と漢字の表がついています。（Kono Nihongo no kyōkasho no ushiro ni wa, Nihon no chizu to kanji no hyō ga *tsuite* imasu.）

② [be attached to, belong to]
¶ This Japanese textbook **has** a map of Japan and a table of *kanji* in the back.

¶わたしのかばんにはかぎがついていません。（Watashi no kaban ni wa kagi ga *tsuite* imasen.）

¶ My suitcase 〚briefcase, bag, etc.〛 **doesn't have** a lock on it.

③ [何かがあるもののそばにいて離れない]

¶ この犬は駅からずっとわたしについてきました。（Kono inu wa eki kara zutto watashi ni *tsuite* kimashita.）

¶ 旅行の時は上田さんがついて案内してくれるそうです。（Ryokō no toki wa Ueda san ga *tsuite* annai shite kureru sō desu.）

④ [決まる、定まる]

話がつく（hanashi ga *tsuku*）解決がつく（kaiketsu ga *tsuku*）

¶ 1年間考えましたが、やっと会社をやめる決心がつきました。（Ichinenkan kangaemashita ga, yatto kaisha o yameru kesshin ga *tsukimashita.*）

⑤ [感覚器官に感じられる]

¶ 看板は人の目につくような所に出さなければだめです。（Kanban wa hito no me ni *tsuku* yō na tokoro ni dasanakereba dame desu.）

⑥ [スイッチなどが入る、点火する]

火がつく（hi ga *tsuku*）

¶ 部屋に電燈がついています。（Heya ni dentō ga *tsuite* imasu.）

⑦ [注意が行き届く、あることがらを意識する]

¶ 山田さんはよく気がつく人です。（Yamada san wa yoku ki ga *tsuku* hito desu.）

¶ 学校へ行く途中本を忘れたことに気がつきました。（Gakkō e iku tochū hon o wasureta koto ni ki ga *tsukimashita.*）

*いつも「気がつく（ki ga tsuku）」の形で使う。

⑧ [言う]

③ [follow, accompany]

¶ This dog **has followed me** all the way from the station.

¶ I hear that [Mr.] Ueda **will accompany us** on the trip and act as guide.

④ [be established, take root]
come to an understanding, **reach** an agreement // settle a matter, **reach** a solution

¶ I thought it over for a year and finally **made up my mind** to quit my job.

⑤ [be sensed]
¶ Signboards must be placed where they **will catch the eye**.

⑥ [be lighted, come on]
catch fire
¶ The lights **are on** in the room.

⑦ [notice]

¶ [Mr.] Yamada **is** very **considerate**.

¶ When [I] was partway to school [I] **realized** that [I] had forgotten the book.

*Always used in the pattern "*ki ga tsuku*."

⑧ [say, speak]

¶うそをつかないで本当のことを言いなさい。(Uso o *tsukanaide* hontō no koto o iinasai.)

¶ **No lies** now—tell the truth.

*普通「うそをつく (uso o tsuku)」の形で使う。

*Usually used in the pattern "*uso o tsuku* (tell a lie)."

つくえ 机 〔名〕

tsukue 〔n〕 **desk**

¶机の上に本と鉛筆があります。(*Tsukue* no ue ni hon to enpitsu ga arimasu.)

¶ There are books and pencils on **the desk**.

つくす 尽くす 〔動 I〕

(-)tsukusu 〔vI〕 **exhaust, use up; exert oneself, make efforts**

全力を尽くす (zenryoku o *tsukusu*)

exert all one's powers

¶食べ物は全部食べ尽くしてしまいました。(Tabemono wa zenbu *tabetsukushite* shimaimashita.)

¶ [We] **ate up** 〚**have eaten up**〛 all the food.

¶わたしの言いたいことはもう言い尽くしました。(Watashi no iitai koto wa mō *iitsukushimashita*.)

¶ I've **said everything** I have to say (literally, want to say) 〚I **said everything** I had to say〛.

つくる 作る 〔動 I〕

tsukuru 〔vI〕 **make; raise, grow; make, create, compose; form, establish**

① [材料を使って物をこしらえる]

① [make, prepare]

¶紙で人形を作ります。(Kami de ningyō o *tsukurimasu*.)

¶ [I] **will make** a doll out of paper.

¶わたしは料理を作るのが好きです。(Watashi wa ryōri o *tsukuru* no ga suki desu.)

¶ I like **to cook**.

② [栽培する]

② [raise, grow]

野菜を作る (yasai o *tsukuru*)

raise vegetables

¶この村では、米を作る人より花を作る人のほうが多いです。(Kono mura de wa, kome o *tsukuru* hito yori hana o *tsukuru* hito no hō ga ooi desu.)

¶ In this village more people **raise** flowers than **grow** rice.

③ [芸術作品などを産み出す]
文を作る (bun o *tsukuru*)

③ [make, create, compose]
write a text, **compose** a sentence

¶上田さんの作った詩を見せてもらいました。(Ueda san no *tsukutta* shi o misete moraimashita.)

④ [今まで無かったものを新しく考えだしたりこしらえたりする]

記録をつくる (kiroku o *tsukuru*) 規則をつくる (kisoku o *tsukuru*)

¶田中さんは友達と日本文学の研究会をつくるつもりです。(Tanaka san wa tomodachi to Nihon-bungaku no kenkyūkai o *tsukuru* tsumori desu.)

つくる 造る 〔動 I〕

船を造る (fune o *tsukuru*) 酒を造る (sake o *tsukuru*)

¶山田さんは自分の家に大きな庭を造りました。(Yamada san wa jibun no ie ni ookina niwa o *tsukurimashita*.)

つける 漬ける 〔動 II〕

¶洗濯物がひどく汚れていたので、1日水に漬けておきました。(Sentakumono ga hidoku yogorete ita node, ichinichi mizu ni tsukete okimashita.)

つける 〔動 II〕

① [あるものを何かの表面に付着させる]

¶パンにバターをつけて食べます。(Pan ni batā o *tsukete* tabemasu.)

¶けがをしたので、足に薬をつけました。(Kega o shita node, ashi ni kusuri o *tsukemashita*.)

② [あるものを何かに添えたり加えたりする、留めて離れない状態にする]

¶ [Miss] Ueda showed me the poem [she] **wrote** 〖I was shown the poem Miss Ueda **wrote**〗.

④ [form, establish, found]

set a new record // **set up** rules

¶ [Mr.] Tanaka plans **to found** a group of [his] friends to study Japanese literature.

tsukuru 〔vI〕 **make, manufacture, construct**
build a ship // **brew** sake

¶ [Mr.] Yamada **laid out** a large garden at [his] home.

tsukeru 〔n〕 **soak**
¶ Since the laundry was so dirty, I soaked it in water for a day.

tsukeru 〔vII〕 **apply, put on; add, attach; set, price, assign; turn on, light; enter, put down**
① [apply, put on]

¶ **I butter** bread 〖toast, rolls, etc.〗 and eat it.
¶ [I] hurt [my] leg 〖foot〗 so [I] **put** some medication 〖ointment, etc.〗 on it.

② [add, attach, append]

¶ 次の漢字に仮名をつけなさい。
(Tsugi no kanji ni kana o tsukenasai.)

¶ ボタンが取れたからつけてくださ
い。(Botan ga toreta kara tsukete
kudasai.)

③ [決める、定める]
値段をつける（nedan o tsukeru）点数を
つける（tensū o tsukeru）

¶ 赤ん坊が生まれたので、父に名前を
つけてもらいました。(Akanbō ga
umareta node, chichi ni namae o tsukete
moraimashita.)

④ [スイッチなどを入れる、点火する]
電燈をつける（dentō o tsukeru）ラジオ
をつける（rajio o tsukeru）テレビをつ
ける（terebi o tsukeru）

¶ マッチでたばこに火をつけました。
(Matchi de tabako ni hi o tsukemashita.)

⑤ [注意する]
¶ 道を歩くときは車に気をつけましょ
う。(Michi o aruku toki wa kuruma ni ki
o tsukemashō.)

*いつも「気をつける（ki o tsukeru）」
の形で使う。

⑥ [書く]
〇印をつける（marujirushi o tsukeru）

¶ わたしは毎日日記をつけています。
(Watashi wa mainichi nikki o tsukete
imasu.)

つごう　都合〔名〕

都合がいい（tsugō ga ii）都合が悪い
（tsugō ga warui）

¶ 今日の午後、御都合はどうでしょう
か。(Kyō no gogo gotsugō wa dō deshō
ka？)

¶ **Write** *kana* **alongside** the following
kanji.

¶ Please **sew on** this button which has
come off.

③ [set, price, assign, give]
put a price **on** something // **assign** a
mark

¶ We had a baby and asked my father
to think of a good name **for it**.

④ [turn on, light]
turn on the light, **turn on** an electric
light // **turn on** the radio // **turn on** the
television

¶ [I] **lighted** the cigarette with a match.

⑤ [be careful, pay attention to]
¶ **One must watch out** for cars when
walking along the road.

*Always used in the pattern "*ki o
tsukeru*."

⑥ [enter, put down, keep]
mark with a circle

¶ I **make** a diary entry every day.

tsugō 〔n〕 **convenience;
circumstances**

be convenient // be inconvenient

¶ Would this afternoon **be convenient**
for you?

¶都合が悪くて、その会には出席できません。(*Tsugō ga warukute, sono kai ni wa shusseki dekimasen.*)

¶ That meeting 〚gathering, etc.〛 is **at a bad time** for [me] so [I] won't be able to attend.

つたえる 伝える〔動 II〕

tsutaeru 〔vII〕 **convey, tell; hand down, bequeath; introduce; transmit, conduct**

① [伝言する]

¶「あしたは学校が休みです。」と山田さんに伝えてください。("Ashita wa gakkō ga yasumi desu." to Yamada san ni *tsutaete* kudasai.)

¶奥さんにどうぞよろしくお伝えください。(Okusan ni dōzo yoroshiku *otsutae* kudasai.)

② [昔から今まで受け継いできている]

¶この話はこの地方に昔から伝えられているものです。(Kono hanashi wa kono chihō ni mukashi kara *tsutaerarete* iru mono desu.)

③ [学問・芸術・宗教・制度などを外国から持って来る]

¶漢字は中国から日本に伝えられたものです。(Kanji wa Chūgoku kara Nihon ni *tsutaerareta* mono desu.)

④ [電気・音・熱などをほかに移す]

熱を伝える (netsu o *tsutaeru*)

¶銅は電気をよく伝えます。(Dō wa denki o yoku *tsutaemasu*.)

① [convey, tell, report]

¶ Please **tell** [Miss] Yamada that there will be no school tomorrow.

¶ Please **convey** my best regards to your wife.

② [hand down, bequeath, leave]

¶ This tale **has been handed down** in this region from long-ago generations.

③ [introduce]

¶ *Kanji* **were introduced** into Japan from China.

④ [transmit, conduct]

conduct heat

¶ Copper is a good **conductor** of electricity.

つたわる 伝わる〔動 I〕

tsutawaru 〔vI〕 **spread, circulate; be handed down, come down; be transmitted, be conveyed; come across, go along**

① [人を通してあることが広がる]

ニュースが伝わる (nyūsu ga *tsutawaru*)

① [spread, circulate]

news **travels**

¶そのうわさは、たちまち町じゅうに伝わりました。(Sono uwasa wa, tachimachi machijū ni *tsutawarimashita*.)

② [昔から今に受け継がれてきている]
¶古くからこの地方に伝わる話を集めて本を作りました。(Furuku kara kono chihō ni *tsutawaru* hanashi o atsumete hon o tsukurimashita.)

③ [電気・音・熱などが移る]

電気が伝わる (denki ga *tsutawaru*)
¶隣のうちのピアノの音がここまで伝わってきます。(Tonari no uchi no piano no oto ga koko made *tsutawatte* kimasu.)

④ [一方から他方へあるものに沿って移る]
¶どろぼうは窓を伝わって部屋に入ったらしいです。(Dorobō wa mado o *tsutawatte* heya ni haitta rashii desu.)

つち 土 〔名〕
¶土を掘って木を植えました。(*Tsuchi* o hotte ki o uemashita.)

つづく 続く 〔動Ⅰ〕
¶天気のよい日が1か月も続いています。(Tenki no yoi hi ga ikkagetsu mo *tsuzuite* imasu.)
¶高い山がどこまでも続いています。(Takai yama ga doko made mo *tsuzuite* imasu.)

つづける 続ける 〔動Ⅱ〕

¶休まないで仕事を続けてください。(Yasumanaide shigoto o *tsuzukete* kudasai.)

¶ That rumor **spread** quickly throughout the town.

② [be handed down, come down]
¶ [I] collected tales **handed down** from olden times in this region and made them into a book.

③ [be transmitted, be conveyed, be carried]
electricity **is conducted**
¶ The sound of the piano next door **carries over** to here.

④ [come across, go along]

¶ It appears that the thief entered the room 〚apartment〛 **by** the window.

tsuchi 〔n〕 **earth, soil, the ground**
¶ [I] dug a hole in **the ground** and planted a tree.

tsuzuku 〔vI〕 **continue, go on, last**
¶ The fine weather **has continued** for a month now.

¶ The tall mountains **extend** as far as the eye can see.

tsuzukeru 〔vII〕 **continue, keep up, go on**
¶ Please **continue** working without taking a break.

¶山田先生は休まずに、2時間続けて授業をしました。(Yamada sensei wa yasumazu ni, nijikan *tsuzukete* jugyō o shimashita.)

¶ Professor Yamada **went on** teaching for two hours without a break.

つつむ 包む〔動Ⅰ〕

tsutsumu 〔vI〕 **wrap, do up(a parcel), cover, envelop in**

¶デパートで買い物をすると、きれいな紙に包んでくれます。(Depāto de kaimono o suru to, kirei na kami ni *tsutsunde* kuremasu.)

¶ When one buys an article at a department store, they **wrap it up** in attractive paper.

つとめる 努める〔動Ⅱ〕

tsutomeru 〔vII〕 **strive, endeavor, try hard, make an effort**

¶できるだけ勉強するように努めなさい。(Dekiru dake benkyō suru yō ni *tsutomenasai*.)

¶ **Try** to study as much as possible.

¶みんながこの問題の解決に努めています。(Minna ga kono mondai no kaiketsu ni *tsutomete* imasu.)

¶ All **are striving** to solve this problem.

つとめる 勤める〔動Ⅱ〕

tsutomeru 〔vII〕 **be employed, hold a post, work for**

¶兄は会社に勤めています。(Ani wa kaisha ni *tsutomete* imasu.)

¶ My older brother **has an office job**.

¶わたしは卒業したら、銀行に勤めたいと思っています。(Watashi wa sotsugyō shitara, ginkō ni *tsutometai* to omotte imasu.)

¶ **I would like a position** at a bank after graduating.

つな 綱〔名〕

tsuna 〔n〕 **rope, line, cord, cable**

綱を引く (*tsuna* o hiku) 太い綱 (futoi *tsuna*)

pull **a rope** // a thick **rope**

つなぐ〔動Ⅰ〕

tsunagu 〔vI〕 **tie, fasten; connect, link**

①[ある物を綱やひもで結んで離れないようにする]

① [tie, fasten, chain, tether]

¶犬をつないでおいてください。(Inu o *tsunaide* oite kudasai.)

¶ Please keep the dog **tied up**.

¶ボートが岸につないであります。
(Bōto ga kishi ni *tsunaide* arimasu.)

¶The boat **is moored** to the bank.

②［離れているものを一つに結ぶ］

②[connect, link, join]

¶わたしは妹と手をつないで公園を散歩しました。(Watashi wa imōto to te o *tsunaide* kōen o sanpo shimashita.)

¶My (younger) sister and I walked in the park **hand in hand**.

¶この電話を社長室につないでください。(Kono denwa o shachōshitsu ni *tsunaide* kudasai.)

¶Please **put** this call **through** to the director's office.

つねに 常に〔副〕

tsune ni 〔adv〕 **always, ordinarily, customarily, usually**

¶わたしは病気をしないように常に注意しています。(Watashi wa byōki o shinai yō ni *tsune ni* chūi shite imasu.)

¶I **habitually** take care not to become ill.

¶あの人は常にわたしの意見に反対します。(Ano hito wa *tsune ni* watashi no iken ni hantai shimasu.)

¶[He] **always** opposes my views.

(-)つぶ (-)粒〔名、尾〕

(-)tsubu 〔n, suf〕 **a grain, a drop, etc.**

1〔名〕
米粒 (kome*tsubu*)

1 〔n〕
a grain of rice

¶煙突から出る煙は炭のような粒が集まったものです。(Entotsu kara deru kemuri wa sumi no yō na *tsubu* ga atsumatta mono desu.)

¶The smoke coming from the smokestack is like a conglomeration of charcoal **particles**.

2〔尾〕

2 〔suf〕

¶この薬を食事のあとで二粒ずつ飲んでください。(Kono kusuri o shokuji no ato de futa*tsubu* zutsu nonde kudasai.)

¶Please take two **drops** of this medicine after each meal.

¶この花の種は二、三粒いっしょにまきます。(Kono hana no tane wa ni, san*tsubu* issho ni makimasu.)

¶The seeds of this flower are planted in **twos** and **threes**.

つぶす〔動 I〕

tsubusu 〔vI〕 **crush, smash, mash, break**

¶じゃがいもをつぶして、サラダを作りました。(Jagaimo o *tsubushite*, sarada o tsukurimashita.)

¶[I] **mashed** potatoes and made a salad.

つぶれる〔動〕

¶かごを落としたので、卵がつぶれて
しまいました。(Kago o otoshita node,
tamago ga *tsuburete* shimaimashita.)

¶地震でたくさんの家がつぶれまし
た。(Jishin de takusan no ie ga
tsuburemashita.)

tsubureru〔vII〕**be crushed,
smashed, destroyed**

¶The eggs **smashed** when [I] dropped
the basket.

¶Many houses **were destroyed** in the
earthquake.

つま 妻〔名〕

¶わたしは妻と子供を連れて旅行に出
ました。(Watashi wa *tsuma* to kodomo
o tsurete ryokō ni demashita.)

＊結婚した男女の女のほうをさす言
葉。自分の妻のことを他人に話す場合
には、普通「家内 (kanai)」と言う。

⇔夫 otto

⇒家内 kanai　奥さん okusan

tsuma〔n〕**a wife**

¶I went on a trip with **my wife** and
children.

＊Indicates the female spouse in a
married couple. When speaking of
one's own wife to others, one usually
uses *kanai* instead.

つまらない〔形〕

① [おもしろくない]

¶あの映画はつまらなかったです。
(Ano eiga wa *tsumaranakatta* desu.)

¶話がつまらないので、眠くなりまし
た。(Hanashi ga *tsumaranai* node,
nemuku narimashita.)

② [価値がない]

¶これはわたしがかいたつまらない絵
ですが、どうぞ部屋に掛けてくださ
い。(Kore wa watashi ga kaita
tsumaranai e desu ga, dōzo heya ni kakete
kudasai.)

tsumaranai〔adj〕**uninteresting,
dull; trifling, worthless**

① [uninteresting, dull, monotonous,
boring]

¶That movie **was boring**.

¶The speech **was uninteresting** so [I]
became sleepy.

② [trifling, worthless]

¶This is **just something** I painted
myself but please hang it in your room
if you'd like.

つまり〔副〕

¶山田さんが言いたいのは、つまり秋
子さんと結婚したいということです。
(Yamada san ga iitai no wa, *tsumari*

tsumari〔adv〕**in brief, in other
words**

¶**In short**, what Mr. Yamada is trying
to say is that he wants to marry Akiko.

Akiko san to kekkon shitai to iu koto
desu.)
¶お花見というのは、つまり桜の花を
見ながらお酒を飲んだり、ごちそうを
食べたりすることです。(Ohanami to
iu no wa, *tsumari* sakura no hana o
minagara osake o nondari, gochisō o
tabetari suru koto desu.)

¶ **In other words**, *ohanami* refers to
eating and drinking while viewing the
cherry blossoms.

つまる 詰まる 〔動 I〕

tsumaru 〔vI〕 **be full, be crammed; be stopped up, be obstructed**

① [ある空間にものがいっぱいになる]
¶かばんに本がいっぱい詰まっていま
す。(Kaban ni hon ga ippai *tsumatte*
imasu.)

① [be full, be crammed, be stuffed]
¶ The bag 〚briefcase, etc.〛 **is crammed** full of books.

② [ふさがって通じなくなる]

② [be stopped up, be obstructed, be clogged]

¶風邪をひいて、鼻が詰まりました。
(Kaze o hiite, hana ga *tsumarimashita*.)

¶ [I] caught a cold and now [my] nose **is all stuffed up**.

つみ 罪 〔名〕

tsumi 〔n〕 **crime, sin, offense, guilt, blame, punishment**

¶人を殺すと重い罪になります。(Hito
o korosu to omoi *tsumi* ni narimasu.)

¶ Murder brings a severe **punishment**.

つむ 積む 〔動 I〕

tsumu 〔vI〕 **pile up, stack; load, take on board**

① [重ねる]
¶机の上に本が積んであります。
(Tsukue no ue ni hon ga *tsunde*
arimasu.)

① [pile up, stack]
¶ Books **are piled up** on the desk.

② [荷を載せる]
¶荷物を車に積みました。(Nimotsu o
kuruma ni *tsumimashita*.)

② [load, take on board]
¶ [I] **loaded up** the car.

つめ 〔名〕

tsume 〔n〕 **a nail, a claw**

つめを切る (*tsume* o kiru) つめが伸び
る (*tsume* ga nobiru)

trim **one's nails** // **one's nails** grow out

-づめ -詰め〔尾〕

かん詰め（kan*zume*）びん詰め
（bin*zume*）四百字詰めの原稿用紙
（yonhyakuji*zume* no genkōyōshi）

¶友達が箱詰めのみかんを送ってくれ
ました。（Tomodachi ga hako*zume* no
mikan o okutte kuremashita.）

-zume 〔suf〕 **a suffix indicating
being packed in or filled up**

canned goods, canning, canned //
bottled goods, bottling, bottled // 400-
character writing paper (for writing
Japanese)

¶My friend sent me some **boxed**
mandarin oranges.

つめたい 冷たい〔形〕

¶冷たい水を飲みました。（*Tsumetai*
mizu o nomimashita.）

¶このビールは冷蔵庫から出したばか
りですから、冷たいですよ。（Kono
biiru wa reizōko kara dashita bakari desu
kara, *tsumetai* desu yo.）

⇔熱い **atsui**

tsumetai 〔adj〕 **cold, cool**

¶[I] drank some **cold** water.

¶This beer **is chilled**—it's right out of
the refrigerator.

つめる 詰める〔動Ⅱ〕

¶お菓子をその箱に詰めてください。
（Okashi o sono hako ni *tsumete* kudasai.）

¶あとの人が乗れませんから、もう少
し奥に詰めてください。（Ato no hito
ga noremasen kara, mō sukoshi oku ni
tsumete kudasai.）

tsumeru 〔vⅡ〕 **stuff, cram, move
closer**

¶Please **put** the candy〚cake, sweets〛
in that box.

¶Please **move** to the rear so there will
be room for those getting on (said by
the driver on a bus, etc.).

つもり〔名〕

¶あなたは夏休みに何をするつもりで
すか。（Anata wa natsuyasumi ni nani o
suru *tsumori* desu ka？）

¶わたしは日本へ行って経済学を勉強
するつもりです。（Watashi wa Nihon e
itte keizaigaku o benkyō suru *tsumori*
desu.）

tsumori 〔n〕 **intention, purpose,
motive**

¶What do you **intend** to do during
summer vacation〚your summer
holidays〛?

¶**I plan** to go to Japan and study
economics.

つもる　積もる〔動Ⅰ〕

¶昨日降った雪が庭に積もっています。(Kinō futta yuki ga niwa ni *tsumotte* imasu.)

tsumoru 〔vI〕 accumulate, pile up

¶ The snow that fell yesterday **is lying deep** on the ground in the yard.

つゆ　梅雨〔名〕

¶日本では、6月から7月の中ごろまで梅雨の季節です。(Nihon de wa, rokugatsu kara shichigatsu no nakagoro made *tsuyu* no kisetsu desu.)

tsuyu 〔n〕 the rainy season

¶ **The rainy season** in Japan falls from June to mid-July.

つよい　強い〔形〕

tsuyoi 〔adj〕 **strong, powerful; violent, strong; stout, healthy; be good at; resistant, tolerant**

①[力・技などが優れている様子]
¶山田さんはたいへん力が強いから、この重い荷物を持ってもらいましょう。(Yamada san wa taihen chikara ga *tsuyoi* kara, kono omoi nimotsu o motte moraimashō.)

① [strong, powerful]
¶ [Mr.] Yamada **is** very **strong**—let's have [him] carry this heavy load 〖bag, etc.〗.

¶わたしの学校は野球が強いです。(Watashi no gakkō wa yakyū ga *tsuyoi* desu.)

¶ My school **is strong** in baseball.

②[激しい様子、程度がはなはだしい様子]
強い雨 (*tsuyoi* ame)

② [violent, strong, intense, sharp]
a **heavy** rain

¶山の方から突然風が強く吹いてきました。(Yama no hō kara totsuzen kaze ga *tsuyoku* fuite kimashita.)

¶ A **sharp** wind suddenly started 〖has suddenly started〗 blowing in from the mountains.

③[体などが丈夫な様子]
足が強い (ashi ga *tsuyoi*)

③ [stout, healthy, robust]
be a **good** walker

¶スポーツをして、強い体を作りましょう。(Supōtsu o shite, *tsuyoi* karada o tsukurimashō.)

¶ Let's all build **strong** constitutions by participating in sports.

④[得意である様子]
数学に強い (sūgaku ni *tsuyoi*)

④ [be good at]
be good at mathematics

¶上田さんば英語に強いです。(Ueda san wa Eigo ni *tsuyoi* desu.)

¶ [Miss] Ueda **is very good** at English.

*いつも「〜に強い（〜ni tsuyoi）」の
形で使う。
⑤ [ものごとに耐える力がある様子]
¶ナイロンは水には強いですが、火に
は弱いです。（Nairon wa mizu ni wa
tsuyoi desu ga, hi ni wa yowai desu.）
¶わたしは暑さには強いですから、夏
は好きです。（Watashi wa atsusa ni wa
tsuyoi desu kara, natsu wa suki desu.）
*いつも「〜に強い（〜ni tsuyoi）」の
形で使う。
⇔弱い yowai

つらい〔形〕
¶あなたと別れるのは、とてもつらい
ことです。（Anata to wakareru no wa,
totemo *tsurai* koto desu.）
¶ゆうべ遅く寝たので、今朝は起きる
のがつらかったです。（Yūbe osoku
neta node, kesa wa okiru no ga *tsurakatta*
desu.）

つり〔名〕
¶細かいお金がないから、すみません
が一万円でおつりをください。
（Komakai okane ga nai kara, sumimasen
ga, ichiman'en de o*tsuri* o kudasai.）

つり〔名〕
つり糸（*tsuri*ito）
¶中村さんの趣味はつりです。
（Nakamura san no shumi wa *tsuri* desu.）

つる〔動Ｉ〕
¶海でつってきた魚を料理して食べま
した。（Umi de *tsutte* kita sakana o ryōri
shite tabemashita.）

*Always used in the pattern "〜 *ni
tsuyoi*."
⑤ [resistant, tolerant]
¶ Nylon **stands up** against water but is
highly combustible.

¶ As I **don't feel** the heat, I like
summer.

*Always used in the pattern "〜 *ni
tsuyoi*."

tsurai 〔adj〕 **hard, trying, painful**
¶ **It is** very **painful** to say goodbye to
you.

¶ Since [I] went to bed late last night **it
was hard** to get up this morning.

tsuri 〔n〕 **change(from a
purchase)**
¶ I'm sorry but I don't have anything
smaller than this ten-thousand yen bill
to pay with (literally, please give me
the change out of ten thousand yen).

tsuri 〔n〕 **fishing**
fishing line
¶ [Mr.] Nakamura's hobby is **fishing**.

tsuru 〔vI〕 **fish, catch**
¶ [I] cooked and ate the fish [I] **caught**
at the ocean.

つれる　連れる〔動Ⅱ〕

¶わたしは毎朝犬を連れて散歩をします。（Watashi wa maiasa inu o *tsurete* sanpo shimasu.）

¶先週の日曜日、弟を連れて映画を見に行きました。（Senshū no nichiyōbi, otōto o *tsurete* eiga o mi ni ikimashita.）

＊自分より目下の者や動物といっしょに行く場合に使う。

tsureru〔vII〕 bring, take, be accompanied by

¶ I go for a walk **with** the dog every morning.

¶ **I took** my younger brother to a movie last Sunday.

＊Used when one goes somewhere with an animal or a person lower in status than oneself.

て

て 手 〔名〕

右手 (migi*te*) 左手 (hidari*te*) 両手 (ryō*te*) 手を挙げる (*te* o ageru) 手を振る (*te* o furu) 手をたたく (*te* o tataku)

¶御飯を食べる前には、手を洗いましょう。(Gohan o taberu mae ni wa, *te* o araimashō.)

て 〔助〕

① [前のことがらとあとのことがらが並列の関係にあることを表す]
¶田中さんは背が高くて、目が大きくて、髪が長いです。(Tanaka san wa se ga takaku*te*, me ga ookiku*te*, kami ga nagai desu.)
¶あの白い服を着て眼鏡をかけた人はだれですか。(Ano shiroi fuku o ki*te* megane o kaketa hito wa dare desu ka?)
② [前のことがらとあとのことがらが対比の関係にあることを表す]
¶ここは夏は涼しくて、冬は暖かいです。(Koko wa natsu wa suzushiku*te*, fuyu wa atatakai desu.)
¶兄は太っていて、弟のほうはやせています。(Ani wa futotte i*te*, otōto no hō wa yasete imasu.)
③ [ものごとが次々に成立するという関係を表す]

te 〔n〕 **hand, arm**

the right **hand**, to the right, right-**handed** // the left **hand**, to the left, left-**handed** // both **hands**, with both hands; both **arms** // raise **one's hand**, hold up **one's hands**; raise **one's hand** against someone; give up // wave **one's hand** // clap **one's hands**
¶ One should wash **one's hands** before eating.

-te 〔part〕 **a particle used to form the -te form of the verb**

① [indicates that items are in a parallel relationship]
¶ [Mr.] Tanaka **is tall, has** large eyes, **and** has long hair.

¶ Who is that person **dressed** in white **and** wearing glasses?

② [indicates that items are in opposition to each other]
¶ It **is cool** here in summer **but** warm in winter.

¶ My older brother **is fat but** my younger brother is thin.

③ [indicates that items follow each other in sequence]

¶わたしは毎朝、7時に起きて、顔を洗って、御飯を食べて、8時に家を出ます。（Watashi wa maiasa, shichiji ni oki*te*, kao o arat*te*, gohan o tabe*te*, hachiji ni ie o demasu.）

¶ Every morning I **get up** at seven o'clock, **wash** my face, **eat** breakfast, **and leave** the house at eight o'clock.

¶この道をまっすぐ行って、右へ曲がると、駅の前に出ます。（Kono michi o massugu it*te*, migi e magaru to, eki no mae ni demasu.）

¶ If you **go** straight along this street **and** then turn right, you will come out in front of the station.

④ [ものごとが時間的に前後しているという関係を表す]

④ [indicates chronological order]

¶あなたは日本へ来てから、もう何年になりますか。（Anata wa Nihon e ki*te* kara, mō nannen ni narimasu ka？）

¶ How many years have you been in Japan (literally, How many years has it been **since you came** to Japan)?

¶わたしは朝新聞を読んでから、学校へ行きます。（Watashi wa asa shinbun o yon*de* kara, gakkō e ikimasu.）

¶ I go to school in the morning **after reading** the newspaper.

¶北海道へは5年前に行って以来、行っていません。（Hokkaidō e wa gonen mae ni it*te* irai, itte imasen.）

¶ [I] haven't been to Hokkaido **since going** there five years ago.

＊普通「から (kara)」「以来 (irai)」「以後 (igo)」などといっしょに使う。

＊Usually used with *kara, irai, igo,* etc.

⑤ [二つの動作・作用が同時に行われるという関係を表す]

⑤ [indicates that two items occur simultaneously]

¶考えごとをして歩いていたら、自動車にひかれそうになりました。（Kangaegoto o shi*te* aruite itara, jidōsha ni hikaresō ni narimashita.）

¶ **While** walking along **deep in thought,** [I] was almost hit by a car.

¶選手は手を振って入場してきました。（Senshu wa te o fut*te* nyūjō shite kimashita.）

¶ The players came onto the field 〚court, ice, etc.〛 **waving** their hands.

¶川の水は音を立てて流れています。（Kawa no mizu wa oto o tate*te* nagarete imasu.）

¶ The water in the river is flowing along **burbling**.

*動作・作用の主体は同じである。

→ながら **nagara**

⑥ [原因と結果の関係を表す]

¶昨日は頭が痛くて、学校を休みました。(Kinō wa atama ga itaku*te*, gakkō o yasumimashita.)

¶この荷物は重くて、わたしには持てません。(Kono nimotsu wa omoku*te*, watashi ni wa motemasen.)

¶雨にぬれて、風邪を引いてしまいました。(Ame ni nure*te*, kaze o hiiteshimaimashita.)

*普通、「て（*te*)」のあとには「～う［よう］（～u［yo]）」などの意志、「～なさい（～nasai）」などの命令、「～てもいい（te mo ii）」などの許可、「～てください（～*te* kudasai）」などの依頼などの言い方は来ない。

→ので **node**　から **kara**

⑦ [前のことがらがあとのことがらの手段・方法となっているという関係を表す]

¶遅くなったから、タクシーに乗って帰りました。(Osoku natta kara, takushii ni not*te* kaerimashita.)

¶わからない言葉は辞書を引いて調べなさい。(Wakaranai kotoba wa jisho o hii*te* shirabenasai.)

⑧ [前のことがらがあとのことがらの行なわれる状態であることを表す]

*The subject of the two clauses is the same.

⑥ [indicates a cause-and-effect relationship]

¶ [I] stayed home from school yesterday **with** a headache.

¶ This load 〚package, case, etc.〛 **is so heavy that** I can't carry it alone.

¶ [I] **got wet** in the rain **and** caught a cold.

*Generally this -*te* is not followed by statements of intention with -*ō* 〚-*yō*〛, orders with -*nasai*, statements of permission with -*te mo ii*, requests with -*te kudasai*, etc.

⑦ [used when the -*te* clause is the way or means of accomplishing the following clause]

¶ As it was late [I] **went** home **by** taxi (literally, **by riding** in a taxi).

¶ **Look** words you don't understand **up** in the dictionary (literally, Investigate words you don't understand **by looking them up** in the dictionary).

⑧ [used when the -*te* clause describes the condition or state in which the following clause occurs]

¶ 中村さんは昨日赤いセーターを着て町を歩いていました。(Nakamura san wa kinō akai sētā o ki*te* machi o aruite imashita.)

¶ Yesterday [Mr.] Nakamura was walking around town **wearing** a red sweater.

¶ 転びますから、そんな重い荷物を持って走らないでください。
(Korobimasu kara, sonna omoi nimotsu o mot*te* hashiranaide kudasai.)

¶ Please don't run **while carrying** such a heavy load 〚package, etc.〛—you'll fall.

⑨ [前のことがらがあとのことがらの判断のよりどころであることを表す]

⑨ [used when the -*te* clause forms the basis of the following clause]

¶ 今年は去年に比べて、だいぶ暑いです。(Kotoshi wa kyonen ni kurabe*te*, daibu atsui desu.)

¶ This year is quite hot **compared** to last year.

¶ 電話の声から考えて、田中さんはたいへん心配しているようです。
(Denwa no koe kara kangae*te*, Tanakasan wa taihen shinpai shite iru yōdesu.)

¶ **Judging** from [his] voice on the telephone, [Mr.] Tanaka is very worried.

→と **to** ば **ba**

⑩ [前のことがらが成立するとあとのことがらも成立するという関係を表す]

⑩ [indicates the second clause is realized when the first clause is realized]

¶ 兄弟はわたしを入れて5人です。
(Kyōdai wa watashi o ire*te* gonin desu.)

¶ **Including** myself, there are five of us children.

¶ 3に2を足して、いくつになりますか。(San ni ni o tashi*te*, ikutsu ni narimasu ka？)

¶ How much is two **plus** three (literally, three **plus** two)?

→と **to** ば **ba** たら **tara**

⑪ [あとのことがらが前のことがらから予期されることとは逆の結果であるという関係を表す]

⑪ [indicates the second clause is the opposite of what might be expected from the first clause]

¶ 隣に住んでいて、あの人とは話をしたこともありません。(Tonari ni sunde i*te*, ano hito to wa hanashi o shita koto mo arimasen.)

¶ [I] **live** next door to [him], **but** [I]'ve never talked with [him].

¶そんなにたくさんのお金をもらって
いて、まだ足りないのですか。（Sonna
ni takusan no okane o moratte *ite*, mada
tarinai no desu ka？）

→のに **noni**

＊二つのことがらを結び合わせる役目
をするが、前のことがらとあとのこと
がらとの意味内容の関係によっていろ
いろの意味が生じてくる。

＊動詞の「ての形」のあとに補助動詞
「いる（iru）」「ある（aru）」「おく
（oku）」「みる（miru）」「しまう
（shimau）」「いく（iku）」「くる
（kuru）」「あげる（ageru）」「もらう
（morau）」「くれる（kureru）」などを続
けて、動詞にいろいろな意味をつけ加
える。

＊動詞の「終止の形」の語尾が「ぶ
（bu）」「ぐ（gu）」「む（mu）」「ぬ
（nu）」で終わるⅠ型動詞のあとに「て
（te）」が来る場合には「で（de）」とな
る。

で 〔助〕

① [動作などの行われる場所を表す]

¶昼御飯はどこで食べましょうか。
（Hirugohan wa doko *de* tabemashō ka？）
¶日本では、車は道の左側を走りま
す。（Nihon *de* wa, kuruma wa michi no
hidarigawa o hashirimasu.）

② [ある限定的な時間・空間などの範
囲を表す]

¶世界でいちばん高い山はエベレスト
です。（Sekai *de* ichiban takai yama wa
Eberesuto desu.）

¶ **You're getting** all that money **and**
it's still not enough?

＊*-te* serves to join together two items
but has many different meanings
depending on the context and the
meaning of those two items.

＊When the *-te* form of a verb is
followed by such helping verbs as *iru,
aru, oku, miru, shimau, iku, kuru,
ageru, morau,* or *kureru*, different
meanings result. (See also the
individual entries for these helping
verbs.)

＊*-te* becomes *-de* in the case of Type I
verbs ending in *-bu* (*yobu→yonde*), *-gu*
(*oyogu→oyoide*), *-mu*(*yomu→yonde*),
or *-nu*(*shinu→shinde*).

de 〔part〕 **in, at, by**

① [indicates the place where an action
occurs]

¶ **Where** shall we eat lunch?

¶ **In** Japan automobiles run on the left-
hand side of the road.

② [pinpoints a time period or physical
space]

¶ The highest mountain **in** the world is
Mount Everest.

¶一年じゅうでいちばん寒い月はいつ
ですか。(Ichinenjū *de* ichiban samui
tsuki wa itsu desu ka？)

¶ Which is the coldest month **in** the
year?

③ [手段・方法・材料などを表す]
タクシーで行く (takushii *de* iku) 鉛筆
で書く (enpitsu *de* kaku) 日本語で話す
(Nihongo *de* hanasu)

③ [indicates means, method, material]
go **by** taxi // write **with** a pencil //
speak **in** Japanese

¶あなたの国まで航空便で何日ぐらい
かかりますか。(Anata no kuni made
kōkūbin *de* nannichi gurai kakarimasu
ka？)

¶ How many days does it take things
sent airmail to get to your country?

¶この花は紙でできています。(Kono
hana wa kami *de* dekite imasu.)

¶ This flower is made **out of** paper.

④ [原因・理由などを表す]
¶わたしは病気で学校を休みました。
(Watashi wa byōki *de* gakkō o
yasumimashita.)

④ [indicates cause, reason]
¶ I stayed home from school **due to**
illness.

¶今、外国へ行く準備でとても忙しい
です。(Ima, gaikoku e iku junbi *de*
totemo isogashii desu.)

¶ [I] am very busy now **with**
preparations for going abroad.

⑤ [限定的な状態を表す]
¶みんなで先生の家へ行きましょう。
(Minna *de* sensei no ie e ikimashō.)

⑤ [indicates an exclusive agent]
¶ Let's **all** go to [our] teacher's house
together.

¶わたしはゆうべ寂しい道を一人で
帰ってきました。(Watashi wa yūbe
sabishii michi o hitori *de*
kaettekimashita.)

¶ Last night I came home **alone**
through the deserted streets.

⑥ [時間・値段・数量などの限定を表
す]
¶この仕事は1日でできます。(Kono
shigoto wa ichinichi *de* dekimasu.)

⑥ [indicates boundaries of time, value,
quantity]
¶ This job can be done **in** one day.

¶もう1週間で夏休みが来ます。(Mō
isshūkan *de* natsuyasumi ga kimasu.)

¶ **In** one week summer vacation will be
here.

¶この時計は1万円で買いました。
(Kono tokei wa ichiman'en *de*
kaimashita.)

¶ [I] bought this watch 〚clock〛 **for** ten
thousand yen.

¶この鉛筆は2本で50円です。(Kono enpitsu wa nihon *de* gojūen desu.)

＊「こちらは銀行で、あちらは病院です。(Kochira wa ginkō de, achira wa byōin desu.)」の「で (de)」は、助動詞「だ (da)」の「接続の形」である。

¶These pencils are **2 for** 50 yen.

＊The *de* in a sentence like "*Kochira wa ginkō de, achira wa byōin desu*" (This is a bank and that is a hospital) is the *-te* form of *da*.

てあらい　手洗い〔名〕

¶ちょっとお尋ねしますが、お手洗いはどこですか。(Chotto otazune shimasu ga, o*tearai* wa doko desu ka？)
⇒便所 **benjo**　トイレ **toire**

tearai 〔n〕 **lavatory, rest room, Ladies' Room, Men's Room**

¶Excuse me, but could you please tell me where **the rest rooms** are?

ていきけん　定期券〔名〕

¶わたしはいつも6か月の定期券を買います。(Watashi wa itsu mo rokkagetsu no *teikiken* o kaimasu.)
＊「定期 (teiki)」とも言う。

teikiken 〔n〕 **commuting pass, season pass**

¶I always buy a six-month **commuter's pass**.

＊Variant: *teiki*.

ていこう　抵抗〔名、～する〕

抵抗を受ける (*teikō* o ukeru)
¶あの人たちは、外国の軍隊が来た時抵抗して戦った人たちです。(Ano hitotachi wa, gaikoku no guntai ga kita toki *teikō* shite tatakatta hitotachi desu.)

teikō 〔n, ～*suru*〕 **resistance, opposition**

meet with **opposition**

¶They **resisted** and fought when the foreign troops came.

ていど　程度〔名〕

① [他のものと比べた場合の度合い]
程度が違う (*teido* ga chigau) 程度が低い (*teido* ga hikui)
¶この問題は、中学生には程度が高すぎませんか。(Kono mondai wa, chūgakusei ni wa *teido* ga takasugimasen ka？)
② [だいたいの距離・時間・量などを表す]

teido 〔n〕 **grade, standard, level; degree, extent**

① [grade, standard, level]
differ in **degree**, differ in **quality** // be of a low **standard**

¶Isn't this problem **too difficult** for middle school students?

② [degree, extent]

¶旅行の費用は5万円程度でしょう。
（Ryokō no hiyō wa goman'en *teido* deshō.）
¶この問題について5枚程度のレポートを書いてください。（Kono mondai ni tsuite gomai *teido* no repōto o kaite kudasai.）

¶ The expenses for the trip **shouldn't exceed** fifty thousand yen.

¶ Please write a report **of about** five pages about this matter.

ていねい　丁寧 〔形動〕

① [礼儀正しい]
¶帽子をとって、丁寧にあいさつしました。（Bōshi o totte, *teinei* ni aisatsu shimashita.）
¶先生には丁寧な言葉を使います。（Sensei ni wa *teinei* na kotoba o tsukaimasu.）
②[親切で行き届いている様子]
¶上田先生はいつも丁寧に教えてくださいます。（Ueda sensei wa itsu mo *teinei* ni oshiete kudasaimasu.）
③[注意してものごとをする様子]
¶もっと字を丁寧に書きなさい。（Motto ji o *teinei* ni kakinasai.）

teinei 〔adj-v〕 **polite; conscientious; careful**

① [polite, civil, courteous]
¶ [He] raised [his] hat and gave a **polite** greeting.

¶ [I] use **polite** language toward [my] teacher.

② [conscientious, thorough]
¶ Professor Ueda always teaches **conscientiously** 〚explains **thoroughly**〛.

③ [careful]
¶ Please write more **carefully** 〚**clearly**〛.

ていりゅうじょ　停留所 〔名〕

¶この辺りにバスの停留所はありませんか。（Kono atari ni basu no *teiryūjo* wa arimasen ka?）

teiryūjo 〔n〕 **stopping place, stop, station**

¶ Is there a bus **stop** around here?

テープ 〔名〕

カセットテープ （kasetto-*tēpu*）

tēpu 〔n〕 **tape, magnetic tape; paper streamer**

a cassette **tape**

テーブル 〔名〕

¶テーブルの上をかたづけてください。（*Tēburu* no ue o katazukete kudasai.）

tēburu 〔n〕 **a table**

¶ Please clear off **the table**.

テープレコーダー〔名〕

¶テープレコーダーは、音や声を何度も繰り返して聞けるので便利です。
(*Tēpurekōdā* wa oto ya koe o nando mo kurikaeshite kikeru node benri desu.)

でかける 出かける〔動Ⅱ〕

旅行に出かける（ryokō ni *dekakeru*）散歩に出かける（sanpo ni *dekakeru*）買い物に出かける（kaimono ni *dekakeru*）

¶今、父は仕事で出かけています。
(Ima, chichi wa shigoto de *dekakete* imasu.)

¶そろそろ出かけましょうか。
(Sorosoro *dekakemashō* ka？)

てがみ 手紙〔名〕

¶母に手紙を書きました。(Haha ni *tegami* o kakimashita.)

¶この手紙を出してきてください。
(Kono *tegami* o dashite kite kudasai.)

⇒便り tayori

てき 敵〔名〕

敵と戦う（*teki* to tatakau）敵を追う（*teki* o ou）

¶敵が来たので、村の人たちはみんな逃げました。(*Teki* ga kita node, mura no hitotachi wa minna nige mashita.)

-てき -的〔尾〕

¶わたしには科学的な知識がないから、この本を読んでも全然わからないでしょう。(Watashi ni wa kagaku*teki* na chishiki ga nai kara, kono hon o yonde mo zenzen wakaranai deshō.)

¶富士山は男性的な山だと思いませんか。(Fujisan wa dansei*teki* na yama da to omoimasen ka？)

---

tēpurekōdā〔n〕**a tape recorder**

¶ **Tape recorders** are handy because they make it possible to listen to recorded sounds and voices over and over again.

dekakeru〔v Ⅱ〕**go out, start out**

set out on a journey // **go out** for a walk // **go out** shopping

¶ My father **is out** at work now.

¶ Let's **be off**.

tegami〔n〕**a letter, mail**

¶ I wrote **a letter** to my mother.

¶ Please go and mail this **letter** for me.

teki〔n〕**enemy, foe**

fight with **the enemy** // pursue **the enemy**

¶ Everyone in the village fled because **the enemy** was coming.

-teki〔suf〕**-ic, -ical**

¶ Since I don't know anything **about** science I probably couldn't understand this book even if I did try to read it.

¶ Don't you think Mount Fuji is a "**masculine**" (i.e., sharp and rugged vs. gently rounded) mountain?

¶部屋の中を徹底的に調べてみましたが、わたしのお金は見つかりませんでした。（Heya no naka o tetteiteki ni shirabete mimashita ga, watashi no okane wa mitsukarimasen deshita.）

¶教育的な立場から見れば、子供にまんがばかり見せるのはよくないと思います。（Kyōikuteki na tachiba kara mireba, kodomo ni manga bakari miseru no wa yoku nai to omoimasu.）

＊普通、名詞について形容動詞の語幹を作り、あるものについての、ある性質を持つ、ある状態にある、あることをする上での、などの意味を表す。

¶ I searched the room thoroughly but couldn't find my money.

¶ From an educational standpoint, I don't think it's good for children to only watch cartoons.

＊ -teki generally converts a noun to an adjective-verb and conveys the meaning of having a certain character, being in a certain state, etc.

テキスト〔名〕 tekisuto 〔n〕 textbook

¶今までに使った日本語のテキストはたくさんあるので、全部は覚えていません。（Imamade ni tsukatta nihongo no tekisuto wa takusan aru node, zenbu wa oboete imasen.）

¶ Since I studied many Japanese textbooks, I don't remember them all.

てきとう 適当〔形動〕 tekitō 〔adj-v〕 fit, suitable, proper, appropriate

¶適当な例を挙げて説明してください。（Tekitō na rei o agete setsumei shite kudasai.）

¶ Please explain using an appropriate example.

¶下宿したいのですが、なかなか適当な部屋が見つかりません。（Geshuku shitai no desu ga, nakanaka tekitō na heya ga mitsukarimasen.）

¶ I'd like to live in a boardinghouse but am having a hard time finding a suitable place.

できる〔動 II〕 dekiru 〔v II〕 can, be able to; be made; be ready; be made of; grow, produce; be skilled

① [あることをする能力がある、あることをすることが可能である]

① [can, be able to, be possible]

運転ができる（unten ga dekiru）泳ぎができる（oyogi ga dekiru）運転できる（unten dekiru）

be able to drive // be able to swim // be able to drive

¶ あなたは日本語を話すことができますか。(Anata wa Nihongo o hanasu koto ga *dekimasu* ka？)

¶ あの人はフランス語ができるそうです。(Ano hito wa Furansugo ga *dekiru* sō desu.)

¶ 今日は波が荒いから、泳ぐことができません。(Kyō wa nami ga arai kara, oyogu koto ga *dekimasen*.)

② [ものごとが生じる、発生する]

家ができる (ie ga *dekiru*) 赤ん坊ができる (akanbō ga *dekiru*)

¶ 用事ができたので、遊びに行けなくなりました。(Yōji ga *dekita* node, asobi ni ikenaku narimashita.)

¶ 近くに新しい駅ができました。(Chikaku ni atarashii eki ga *deki-mashita*.)

③ [準備が終わる、完成する]

¶ 食事の用意ができました。(Shokuji no yōi ga *dakimashita*.)

¶ 立派な論文ができましたね。(Rippa na ronbun ga *dekimashita* ne.)

④ [作られる]

¶ このテーブルは木でできています。(Kono tēburu wa ki de *dekite* imasu.)

⑤ [生産される]

米ができる (kome ga *dekiru*)

¶ 寒い地方ではみかんができません。(Samui chihō de wa mikan ga *dekimasen*.)

⑥ [学問・才能などが優れている、成績がいい]

よくできる子供 (yoku *dekiru* kodo-mo) できない生徒 (*dekinai* seito)

¶ **Can** you speak Japanese?

¶ I hear that [he] **knows** French.

¶ [We] **cannot** go swimming today as the sea is rough.

② [be made, be produced, come into existence]

build a house // **have** a baby

¶ Something **has come up** so I can't visit you.

¶ A new station **has been built** nearby.

③ [be ready, be completed]

¶ The meal **is ready**.

¶ **You've written** a fine paper 〚essay, article, thesis〛here.

④ [be made of]

¶ This table **is made of** wood.

⑤ [grow, produce]

to grow rice

¶ Mandarin oranges **can't be grown** in cold regions.

⑥ [be skilled, be proficient, be good at]

an **able** 〚**bright**〛child // a **poor** student

¶あの学生はたいへんよくできます。
（Ano gakusei wa taihen yoku *dekimasu*.）

¶試験はよくできましたか。（Shiken wa yoku *dekimashita* ka？）

⑦ [可能なかぎり]

¶できるだけ早く来てください。
（*Dekiru* dake hayaku kite kudasai.）

＊「できるだけ（dekirudake）」「できるかぎり（dekiru kagiri）」の形で使う。

でぐち　出口 〔名〕

¶出口はどちらですか。（*Deguchi* wa dochira desu ka？）

⇔入り口 **iriguchi**

でしょう 〔助動〕

¶あしたは雨が降るでしょう。（Ashita wa ame ga furu *deshō*.）

¶田中さんは間もなく来るでしょう。
（Tanaka san wa mamonaku kuru *deshō*.）

＊「だろう（darō）」の丁寧な言葉。

⇒だろう **darō**

です 〔助動〕

¶これは本です。（Kore wa hon *desu*.）

¶わたしは田中です。（Watashi wa Tanaka *desu*.）

¶昨日はいい天気でした。（Kinō wa ii tenki *deshita*.）

¶この鉛筆はだれのですか。（Kono enpitsu wa dare no *desu* ka？）

＊「だ（da）」の丁寧な言葉。

⇒だ **da**

テスト 〔名〕

¶昨日の数学のテストはとても難しかったです。（Kinō no sūgaku no *tesuto* wa totemo muzukashikatta desu.）

¶ That is an **excellent** student.

¶ **Did you do well** on the exam?

⑦ [to the extent possible, as ~ as possible]

¶ Please come as soon **as possible** ⟦as soon **as you can**⟧.

＊Used in the patterns "*dekiru dake*" and "*dekiru kagiri*."

deguchi 〔n〕 **exit**

¶ Which way is **the exit**?

deshō 〔auxil〕 **perhaps, will probably, I think**

¶ It **will probably** rain tomorrow.

¶ **I think** [Mr.] Tanaka will come soon.

＊*Deshō* is a more polite form of *darō*.

desu 〔auxil〕 **is, are**

¶ This **is** a book.

¶ **I am** [Miss] Tanaka ⟦My name **is** Tanaka⟧.

¶ The weather **was** fine yesterday.

¶ Whose pencil **is** this?

＊*Desu* is a more polite form of *da*.

tesuto 〔n〕 **test**

¶ Yesterday's math test was very difficult.

でたらめ〔名、形動〕

でたらめな答え（*detarame* na kotae）
¶あの人の言うことはでたらめで信用できません。（Ano hito no iu koto wa *detarame* de shin'yō dekimasen.）
¶でたらめを言っては困ります。（*Detarame* o itte wa komarimasu.）
¶このたなの本はでたらめに並べてあります。（Kono tana no hon wa *detarame* ni narabete arimasu.）

detarame 〔n, adj-v〕 **random, irresponsible, hit-or-miss, nonsense**
a **brandom** answer
¶ That person talks **irresponsibly**. You can't trust anything [he] says.

¶ It won't do for you to talk **so carelessly**.

¶ The books on this shelf are arranged **haphazardly**.

てちょう 手帳〔名〕

¶わたしは約束したことや予定などはいつも手帳に書いておきます。（Watashi wa yakusoku shita koto ya yotei nado wa itsu mo *techō* ni kaite okimasu.）

techō 〔n〕 **notebook, memorandum book**
¶ I always note appointments, scheduled events, etc., in **a pocket schedule**.

てつ 鉄〔名〕

鉄橋（*tek*kyō）鉄砲（*tep*pō）鉄筋（*tek*kin）

¶この機械は鉄でできています。（Kono kikai wa *tetsu* de dekite imasu.）

tetsu 〔n〕 **iron, steel**
an **iron** bridge, a railway bridge // a gun, firearms // an **iron** reinforcing bar 〚rod〛.
¶ This machine 〚device, mechanism〛 is made of **steel**.

てっきょう 鉄橋〔名〕

¶汽車が鉄橋を渡っています。（Kisha ga *tekkyō* o watatte imasu.）
¶この川には鉄橋が架かっています。（Kono kawa ni wa *tekkyō* ga kakatte imasu.）

tekkyō 〔n〕 **iron bridge, railway bridge**
¶ The train is passing over **a bridge**.

¶ This river is spanned by **an iron railway bridge**.

てつだい 手伝い〔名〕

¶今日はお客さんがいらっしゃるので、姉は台所で母の手伝いをしています。（Kyō wa okyakusan ga irassharu node, ane wa daidokoro de haha no *tetsudai* o shite imasu.）

tetsudai 〔n〕 **help, assistance**
¶ My (older) sister **is helping** our mother in the kitchen as we expect guests today.

てつだう　手伝う〔動Ⅰ〕

¶山田さん、すみませんが、この仕事を手伝ってください。（Yamada san, sumimasen ga, kono shigoto o *tetsudatte* kudasai.）

¶お金の計算を中村さんに手伝ってもらいました。（Okane no keisan o Nakamura san ni *tetsudatte* moraimashita.）

tetsudau 〔vI〕 **help, assist**

¶ I'm sorry to trouble you, [Mr.] Yamada, but could you please **help me** with this job?

¶ [Miss] Nakamura **helped me** with the monetary calculations.

てつづき　手続き〔名、～する〕

¶入学の手続きは3月20日までです。（Nyūgaku no *tetsuzuki* wa sangatsu hatsuka made desu.）

¶外国旅行の手続きは、全部旅行会社がやってくれました。（Gaikoku-ryokō no *tetsuzuki* wa, zenbu ryokō-gaisha ga yatte kuremashita.）

tetsuzuki 〔n, ～*suru*〕 **procedure, formalities, steps**

¶ The entrance **procedures** for the university are to be completed by March 20.

¶ The travel agency took care of all **the paperwork** for [my] trip abroad.

てつどう　鉄道〔名〕

¶この町が発展したのは、50年前に鉄道が通ってからです。（Kono machi ga hatten shita no wa, gojūnen mae ni *tetsudō* ga tootte kara desu.）

tetsudō 〔n〕 **railroad, railway**

¶ The development of this city dates from when **the railroad** came to it 50 years ago.

テニス〔名〕

テニスの試合（*tenisu* no shiai）

¶父は若い時にはよくテニスをしたそうです。（Chichi wa wakai toki ni wa yoku *tenisu* o shita sō desu.）

tenisu 〔n〕 **tennis**

a **tennis** match

¶ I hear that my father often played **tennis** when he was young.

テニスコート〔名〕

¶私たち夫婦が初めて会ったのは、あのテニスコートです。（Watashitachi fūfu ga hajimete atta no wa ano tenisu kōto desu.）

tenisukōto 〔n〕 **tennis court**

¶ The first time the two of us met, was at that tennis court.

てぬぐい 手ぬぐい〔名〕

手ぬぐいで手をふく（*tenugui* de te o fuku）

ては〔助〕

① [ものごとが繰り返し行われることを表す]
¶川に落ちたボールは、浮かんでは沈みながら流れていきました。（Kawa ni ochita bōru wa, ukan*de wa* shizuminagara nagarete ikimashita.）
¶父はよく新宿へ寄ってはお菓子を買ってきてくれます。（Chichi wa yoku Shinjuku e yot*te wa* okashi o katte kite kuremasu.）
② [仮定または既定の条件を表す]

¶こんな所で泳いでは危ないですよ。（Konna tokoro de oyoi*de wa* abunai desu yo.）
¶そんなに夜も寝ないで勉強しては、体をこわしますよ。（Sonna ni yoru mo nenaide benkyō shi*te wa*, karada o kowashimasu yo.）
¶芝生の中に入ってはいけません。（Shibafu no naka ni hait*te wa* ikemasen.）
¶危ないですから、走っている車の中から手を出してはだめです。（Abunai desu kara, hashitte iru kuruma no naka kara te o dashi*te wa* dame desu.）
¶こう寒くては我慢ができません。（Kō samuku*te wa* gaman dekimasen.）

tenugui 〔n〕 hand towel, washcloth(usually refers to a cotton cloth of traditional size and pattern)

wipe one's hands on **a hand towel**

-te wa 〔part〕 a particle making a verbal phrase into the topic

① [used to indicate something happens repeatedly]
¶ The ball that fell in the river was carried away alternately **floating** and sinking.

¶ My father often **stops by** in Shinjuku and brings back sweets.

② [used when expressing denial or restriction]
¶ It's dangerous **to swim** in this sort of spot.

¶ You'll get sick **studying** like that going without sleep at night.

¶ It is forbidden **to walk** on the grass.

¶ **Don't stick** your hand or arm **out** of a moving car—it's dangerous.

¶ I can't stand it **when it's** this **cold**.

*否定すべきこと、禁止すべきことなどを提示する場合が多い。「～てはいけない（～te wa ikenai）」「～てはだめだ（～te wa dame da）」「～ては我慢できない（～te wa gaman dekinai）」などの形で使うことが多い。

→（～ては）いけない（～te wa）ikenai

＊「ては（te wa）」は「ちゃ（cha）」、「では（de wa）」は「じゃ（ja）」とも言う。

Usually used when indicating that something is denied or forbidden. Frequently used in the patterns "-te wa ikenai*," "*-te wa dame da*," "*-te wa gaman dekinai*," etc.

＊Sometimes *-te wa* becomes *-cha* and *-de wa* becomes *-ja*.

では〔接〕 / dewa 〚conj〛 well, well then

①[相手の話を受けてそれを根拠として自分の考え・判断などを述べるときに使う]

①[well then, in that case; used to state a conclusion or judgment of the speaker based on what the other has said]

¶「いつ旅行に行きましょうか。」（Itsu ryokō ni ikimashō ka？）「わたしはいつでもいいですよ。」（Watashi wa itsu demo ii desu yo.）「では、今度の日曜日にしましょう。」（*Dewa*, kondo no nichiyōbi ni shimashō.）

¶ "When shall we leave on our trip?" "Anytime is fine with me." **"Well then,** let's make it next Sunday."

¶「何をお飲みになりますか。」（Nani o onomi ni narimasu ka？）「わたしは、コーヒーを飲みます。」（Watashi wa kōhii o nomimasu.）「では、わたしもコーヒーにしましょう。」（*Dewa*, watashi mo kōhii ni shimashō.）

¶ "What will you have to drink?" "I'll have coffee." **"Then** I'll have coffee too."

②[何かを始めたり終えたりまたは別れたりするときに使う言葉]

②[well, so, now; used at a time of transition or parting]

¶では、これから会議を開きます。（*Dewa*, kore kara kaigi o hirakimasu.）

¶ **Well,** let's start the meeting now.

¶では、本日はこれで終わります。（*Dewa*, honjitsu wa kore de owarimasu.）

¶ **Well,** this will be all for today.

¶では、お先に失礼します。（*Dewa*, osaki ni shitsurei shimasu.）

¶ **Well,** I'll be leaving now 〚**Well,** good-bye now〛.

＊「わたしは日本人ではありません。(Watashi wa Nihonjin de wa arimasen.)」の「で (de)」は助動詞であり、「日本では、車は道の左側を走ります。(Nihon de wa, kuruma wa michi no hidarigawa o hashirimasu.)」の「で (de)」は助詞である。

＊「じゃ (ja)」とも言う。
⇒それでは soredewa

＊In a sentence like "*Watashi wa Nihonjin de wa arimasen*" (I am not a Japanese), *de* is part of the copula. In a sentence like "*Nihon de wa, kuruma wa michi no hidarigawa o hashirimasu*" (Cars run on the left-hand side of the road in Japan), *de* is a particle.

＊Variant: *ja*.

デパート〔名〕

¶母はデパートへ買い物に行きました。(Haha wa *depāto* e kaimono ni ikimashita.)

¶デパートではいろいろな物を売っています。(*Depāto* de wa iroiro na mono o utte imasu.)

depāto 〔n〕 **department store**

¶My mother has gone shopping at **a department store**.

¶They sell various things in **a department store**.

てぶくろ 手袋〔名〕

手袋をする (*tebukuro* o suru) 手袋をはめる (*tebukuro* o hameru) 革の手袋 (kawa no *tebukuro*)

tebukuro 〔n〕 **gloves, mittens**

wear **gloves** // put on **gloves** // leather **gloves**

てほん 手本〔名〕

¶先生が黒板に書いた字を手本にして、漢字を習います。(Sensei ga kokuban ni kaita ji o *tehon* ni shite, kanji o naraimasu.)

¶お手本のとおりにきれいに書いてください。(*Otehon* no toori ni kirei ni kaite kudasai.)

tehon 〔n〕 **model, example**

¶We learn *kanji* using the ones our teacher writes on the blackboard for **our model**.

¶Please write it carefully following **the sample**.

ても〔助〕

①[前件とはかかわりなく後件が成立するという関係を表す]
¶あなたがいくら待っても、春子さんは来ないでしょう。(Anata ga ikura matte *mo*, Haruko san wa konai deshō.)

-te mo 〔part〕 **no matter how, however, even if**

①[indicates that the second clause is realized unrelated to the first clause]
¶**No matter** how long you wait, Haruko probably won't be coming.

¶「あしたは雨が降ったら、行きませんか。」(Ashita wa ame ga futtara, ikimasen ka?)「いいえ、雨が降っても、行くつもりです。」(Iie, ame ga fut*te mo*, iku tsumori desu.)

¶勉強はつらくても、我慢しなければなりませんよ。(Benkyō wa tsuraku*te mo*, gaman shinakereba narimasen yo.)

*普通、後件には「〜でしょう（〜deshō)」などの推量、「〜う［よう］(〜u［yō])」などの意志、「〜なければならない（〜nakereba naranai)」などの義務などの言い方が来る。また、後件には過去・完了を表す「たの形」は来ない。

→と **to**　ば **ba**　たら **tara**

② [前件から期待されることは逆の結果が後件で成立するという関係を表す]

¶この子はいくらしかっても勉強しません。(Kono ko wa ikura shikat*te mo* benkyō shimasen.)

¶田中さんは、わたしが呼んでも返事もしませんでした。(Tanaka san wa, watashi ga yon*de mo* henji mo shimasen deshita.)

*既に成立したことがらを言い、そのことがらから当然期待される結果とは逆のことをあとに続ける場合に使う。

③ [前件は実際には成立しなかったことを述べてその成立とはかかわりなく後件が成立するという関係を表す]

¶上田さんがあの大学の入学試験を受けても、合格できなかったでしょう。(Ueda san ga ano daigaku no

¶ "Will you put off going tomorrow if it rains?"
"No, I plan to go **even if** it rains."

¶ **Even if** studying is hard, you must keep at it.

*Usually followed in the second clause by suppositions with 〜*deshō*, statements of intent with *-ō* 〚*-yō*〛, of obligation with *-nakereba naranai*, etc. The *-ta* form of the verb expressing past or completed action is not found in the second clause.

② [indicates that the second clause is the opposite of what might be expected from the first clause]
¶ This child won't study **no matter** how much [he] is scolded.

¶ **Even though** I called to [him], [Mr.] Tanaka didn't answer.

*Used when stating something that has already happened in the first clause and following it with a result opposite to what is expected or natural.
③ [used when the first clause is something that didn't actually happen; indicates that the second clause is realized unrelated to it]
¶ **Even if** [Mr.] Ueda had taken the entrance exam for that university, [he] probably wouldn't have passed it.

nyūgakushiken o uke*te mo*, gōkaku dekinakatta deshō.)

¶ もし雨が降っても、昨日は出かけるつもりでした。(Moshi ame ga fut*te mo*, kinō wa dekakeru tsumori deshita.)

¶ I planned to go out yesterday **even in the case of** rain.

¶「お金があれば、車を買いましたか。」(Okane ga areba, kuruma o kaimashita ka?)「いいえ、お金があっても、車は買いませんでした。」(Iie, okane ga at*te mo*, kuruma wa kaimasen deshita.)

¶ "Would you have bought a car if you had had the money for it?" "No, I would not have bought a car **even if** I had had the money."

*普通、後件には「〜でしょう（〜deshō)」などの推量、「〜う［よう］（〜u［yō]）などの意志などの言い方が来る。また、過去・完了を表す「たの形」を使う。

*Usually followed in the second clause by suppositions with 〜 *deshō*, statements of intent with -*ō* 〚-*yō*〛, etc. The -*ta* form of the verb expressing past or completed action is also used.

⇔と **to**　ば **ba**　たら **tara**

④ [許可の意味を表す]
¶ あしたは休んでもいいです。(Ashitawa yasun*de mo* ii desu.)

④ [expresses permission]
¶ You **may** have tomorrow off.

¶ 鉛筆で書いてもかまいません。(Enpitsu de kai*te mo* kamaimasen.)

¶ You **may** write it in pencil.

*「〜てもいい（〜te mo ii)」「〜てもかまわない（〜te mo kamawanai)」の形で使う。

*Used in the patterns "-*te mo ii* ," "-*te mo kamawanai*."

⇔（〜ては）いけない（〜**te wa**）**ikenai**
→（〜ても）いい（〜**te mo**）**ii**　（〜ても）かまわない（〜**temo**）**kamawanai**

⑤ [不必要の意味を表す]
¶ そんなに急がなくてもいいです。(Sonna ni isoganaku*te mo* ii desu.)

⑤ [indicates something is unnecessary]
¶ **There's no need** to be in such a hurry.

¶ お金は今すぐ払わなくてもかまいません。(Okane wa ima sugu harawanaku*te mo* kamaimasen.)

¶ **You don't have** to pay right this moment.

＊「〜なくてもいい（〜nakute mo ii）」
「〜なくてもかまわない（〜nakute mo
kamawanai）」の形で使う。
⇔（〜ては）いけない（〜te wa）
ikenai
→**ii**（〜ても）いい（〜te mo）　（〜
ても）かまわない（〜temo）
kamawanai
＊「〜たって（〜tatte）」「〜だって
（〜datte）」とも言う。

＊Used in the patterns "-*nakute mo ii* ,"
"-*nakute mc kamawanai*."

＊Variants: -*tatte*, -*datte*.

でも〔助〕

① [特別な例を挙げて他の場合ももちろんであるという意味を表す]

¶それは子供でもできます。（Sore wa
kodomo *demo* dekimasu.）

¶高い山の上には夏でも雪があります。（Takai yama no ue ni wa natsu *demo*
yuki ga arimasu.）

② [前のことがらに関係なくあとのことがらが実現することを表す]

¶試合は雨でも行われます。（Shiai wa
ame *demo* okonawaremasu.）

¶今からでも遅くはありません。（Ima
kara *demo* osoku wa arimasen.）

③ [軽く一例として挙げる場合に使う]

¶コーヒーでも飲みませんか。（Kōhii
demo nomimasen ka？）

¶日曜日にでも見に行きましょうか。
（Nichiyōbi ni *demo* mi ni ikimashō ka？）

④ [すべての]
いつでも（itsu *demo*）どこでも（doko
demo）何でも（nan *demo*）
何年でも（nannen *demo*）

demo〔part〕 even; even if, even though; or the like; all

① [even; indicates that a condition is
true in exceptional circumstances and
so is of course true at other times]

¶ **Even** a child can do that.

¶ There is snow on the top of high
mountains **even** in the summer.

② [even, even if, even though;
indicates something will be realized
regardless of something else]

¶ The game will take place **even in the
case** of rain.

¶ It isn't too late **even** now.

③ [or the like, maybe; used to lightly
suggest something]

¶ How about some coffee **or
something?**

¶ Why don't we go to see it on, **say,**
Sunday?

④ [all]
at **any** time, always // **any**where,
everywhere // **any**thing, **every**thing //
for **however many** years, forever

¶そんなことはだれでも知っています。（Sonna koto wa dare *demo* shitte imasu.）

¶どんな難しいことでもわかります。（Donna muzukashii koto *demo* wakarimasu.）

*疑問の言葉といっしょに使う。

¶ **Everyone** knows that.

¶ [He] knows **everything**, no matter how difficult.

*Used with interrogatives.

てら 寺 〔名〕

¶京都や奈良には、有名な古いお寺がたくさんあります。（Kyōto ya Nara ni wa, yūmei na furui o*tera* ga takusan arimasu.）

tera 〔n〕 **Buddhist temple**

¶ There are many famous ancient **temples** in Kyoto and Nara.

てらす 照らす 〔動 I〕

¶月の光が辺りを明るく照らして、とても美しい夜です。（Tsuki no hikari ga atari o akaruku *terashite*, totemo utsukushii yoru desu.）

¶車のライトを照らして、合図をしました。（Kuruma no raito o *terashite*, aizu o shimashita.）

terasu 〔vI〕 **shine on, light up, illuinmate**

¶ Brightly **lit** by the moonlight, this is a perfectly lovely evening.

¶ [They] signaled by **turning on the car lights**.

てる 照る 〔動 I〕

¶雨がやんで、雲の間から日が照ってきました。（Ame ga yande, kumo no aida kara hi ga *tette* kimashita.）

teru 〔vI〕 **shine**

¶ The rain has stopped and the sun has startcd **shining** from behind the clouds.

でる 出る 〔動 II〕

①〔家の中などから外に行く〕
部屋を出る（heya o *deru*）学校の門を出る（gakkō no mon o *deru*）会社を4時に出る（kaisha o yoji ni *deru*）外に出る（soto ni *deru*）庭に出る（niwa ni *deru*）

¶父は3時にうちを出ました。（Chichi wa sanji ni uchi o *detemashita*.）

↔入る **hairu**

deru 〔v II〕 **go out, come out; leave; appear**

① [go, out, come out]
go out of a room // **come through** the school gate // **leave** the office at four o'clock // **go** outside // **go out** into the garden 〚yard〛

¶ My father **left** the house at three o'clock.

② [学校を卒業する・家を去る・会社
を辞めるなどの意味を表す]
¶わたしは2年前に大学を出ました。
(Watashi wa ninen mae ni daigaku o
demashita.)

② [graduate (from school), leave
(home), quit (work)]
¶I **graduated** from college two years
ago.

③ [出発する]
旅行に出る (ryokō ni *deru*)
¶この汽車は何時に出ますか。(Kono
kisha wa nanji ni *demasu* ka？)
¶もう船が出る時間です。(Mō fune ga
deru jikan desu.)

③ [start, leave, depart]
leave on a trip
¶What time does this train **leave?**
¶It's time for the ship **to depart**.

④ [現れる]
木の芽が出る (ki no me ga *deru*)
¶山の上に月が出ました。(Yama no ue
ni tsuki ga *demashita*.)

④ [appear, come out]
a tree **buds**
¶The moon **has appeared** 〖The moon
appeared〗 over the mountain.

⑤ [出席する、出勤する]
¶わたしは今日の会議には出られませ
ん。(Watashi wa kyō no kaigi ni wa
deraremasen.)
¶わたしはあしたの日曜日にも会社へ
出ます。(Watashi wa ashita no nichiyōbi
ni mo kaisha e *demasu*.)

⑤ [be present, attend]
¶**I can't attend** today's meeting.

¶**I will go to work** even tomorrow,
Sunday.

⑥ [出版される、掲載される]
新刊本が出る (shinkanbon ga *deru*)
¶この言葉は辞書に出ていません。
(Kono kotoba wa jisho ni *dete* imasen.)
¶今日の新聞にA国の大地震のことが
出ていました。(Kyō no shinbun ni
Ēkoku no oojishin no koto ga *dete*
imashita.)

⑥ [be published, be issued]
a new book **will be published**
¶This word **isn't listed** in the
dictionary.
¶News of a large earthquake in
Country A **appeared** in today's
newspaper.

⑦ [生じる、発生する、流れ出る]
¶風邪を引いて、熱が出ました。
(Kaze o hiite, netsu ga *demashita*.)
¶どうしたんですか。足から血が出て
いますよ。(Dō shita n desu ka？ Ashi
kara chi ga *dete* imasu yo.)

⑦ [occur, break out, arise]
¶I caught a cold and **had** 〖**have**〗 a
fever.
¶What happened? Your leg 〖foot〗 **is
bleeding!**

⑧ [ある所に到達する]

⑧ [lead to, come out]

¶この道をまっすぐ行くと、駅の前に出ます。（Kono michi o massugu iku to, eki no mae ni *demasu*.）

¶ If you go straight along this street, **you'll come out** in front of the station.

テレビ〔名〕

¶わたしは毎晩テレビを見ます。（Watashi wa maiban *terebi* o mimasu.）

terebi〔n〕**television, television set**

¶ I watch **television** every night.

てん　天〔名〕

天と地（*ten* to chi）天気（*ten*ki）晴天（sei*ten*）雨天（u*ten*）

ten〔n〕**the heavens, the sky; Heaven**

heaven and earth // the weather // the blue **sky** // rainy **weather**

(-)てん　(-)点〔名、尾〕

(-)ten〔n, suf〕**point, dot; marks, grades; point, respect, detail; points, score**

1〔名〕
①[小さい印や句読点など]
点と線（*ten* to sen）

1〔n〕
①[point, dot]
points and lines

¶長い文は読みにくいので、文の区切りのところに点を打ちます。（Nagai bun wa yominikui node, bun no kugiri no tokoro ni *ten* o uchimasu.）

¶ As long sentences are hard to read, [we] punctuate them with **commas** at natural breaks.

②[成績、評価]
点がいい（*ten* ga ii）点が悪い（*ten* ga warui）点が甘い（*ten* ga amai）点が辛い（*ten* ga karai）

②[marks, grades]
have good **marks** // have bad **marks** // be liberal in **marking** // be strict in **marking**

③[特に問題になる部分・ところ]
問題点（mondai*ten*）

③[point, respect, detail]
the problem **point**, **the point** at issue

¶この点について何か御質問はありませんか。（Kono *ten* ni tsuite nani ka goshitsumon wa arimasen ka？）

¶ Are there any questions about this **point**〚in this **regard**〛?

2〔尾〕
¶「試験の成績は何点ぐらいでしたか。」（Shiken no seiseki wa nan*ten* gurai deshita ka？）「80 点でした。」（Hachijit*ten* deshita.）

2〔suf〕points, score
¶ "What was **your mark** on the exam?" "I got an 80."

-てん -店 〔尾〕

商店 (shōten) 書店 (shoten) 売店
(baiten)

-ten 〔suf〕 **shop, store**

a shop, store // a bookstore // a stand,
stall, concession

てんいん 店員 〔名〕

¶あのデパートの店員さんはとても
親切です。(Ano depāto no *tenin*san wa
totemo shinsetsu desu.)

tenin 〔n〕 **salesperson**

¶ The salespersons at that department
store are very kind.

てんき 天気 〔名〕

① [晴れ・曇り・雨などの空模様]
天気予報 (*tenki*-yohō)
¶明日はいい天気になるでしょう。
(Asu wa ii *tenki* ni naru deshō.)
② [いい天気]
¶あした天気なら行きます。(Ashita
tenki nara ikimasu.)

tenki 〔n〕 **the weather; fine
weather**

① [the weather]
weather forecast
¶ **The weather** will probably be nice
tomorrow.
② [fine weather]
¶ If it is **a nice day** tomorrow [I] will
go.

でんき 電気 〔名〕

① [電燈]
¶暗くなったので、電気をつけまし
た。(Kuraku natta node, *denki* o
tsukemashita.)
¶最後に部屋を出る人は電気を消して
ください。(Saigo ni heya o deru hito wa
denki o keshite kudasai.)
② [電燈をつけたり物を動かしたりす
るエネルギーの一つ]
電気製品 (*denki*-seihin) 電気洗濯機
(*denki*-sentakuki) 電気冷蔵庫 (*denki*-
reizōko) 電気スタンド (*denki*-
sutando)
¶アイロンに電気が通じません。
(Airon ni *denki* ga tsūjimasen.)

denki 〔n〕 **electric light; electricity**

① [electric light]
¶ [I] turned on **the lights** as it had
gotten dark.

¶ Will the last person to leave the room
please turn off **the lights**.

② [electricity]

an **electrical** appliance // an **electric**
washing machine // an **electric**
refrigerator // an **electric** lamp

¶ This iron is broken; **the electricity**
doesn't flow through it.

でんしゃ 電車 〔名〕

densha 〔n〕 train(run by electricity), streetcar

電車に乗る（densha ni noru）電車を降りる（densha o oriru）電車で行く（densha de iku）電車賃（den-shachin）

get on **a train** // get off **a train** // go by **train** // a **train** fare

¶東京の電車はいつもこんでいます。（Tōkyō no densha wa itsu mo konde imasu.）

¶ **The trains** in Tokyo are always crowded.

てんじょう 天井 〔名〕

tenjō 〔n〕 ceiling

¶この家は天井が高いので、広く感じます。（Kono ie wa tenjō ga takai node, hiroku kanjimasu.）

¶ This house has high **ceilings**, giving it a feeling of great space.

でんせん 伝染 〔名、～する〕

densen 〔n, ～suru〕 contagious, infectious

¶各地に伝染病が流行しています。（Kakuchi ni densenbyō ga ryūkō shite imasu.）

¶ **Epidemics** have broken out in various districts.

¶この病気は伝染するので、注意してください。（Kono byōki wa densen suru node, chūi shite kudasai.）

¶ This disease **is contagious** so please take care.

でんち 電池 〔名〕

denchi 〔n〕 electric battery

電池が切れる（denchi ga kireru）電池を新しいのと取り替える（denchi o atarashii no to torikaeru）

a **battery** goes dead // replace a **battery** with a new one

でんとう 電燈 〔名〕

dentō 〔n〕 electric light, electric lamp

電燈をつける（dentō o tsukeru）電燈を消す（dentō o kesu）

turn on **an electric light** // turn off **an electric light**

¶部屋に電燈がついているから、だれかいると思います。（Heya ni dentō ga tsuite iru kara, dare ka iru to omoimasu.）

¶ Since **a light** is on in the room, I think someone is there.

てんのう 天皇 〔名〕

tennō 〔n〕 the Emperor

583

てんぷら〔名〕

¶魚と野菜のてんぷらを食べました。
（Sakana to yasai no *tenpura* o tabemashita.）

¶てんぷらはえびがいちばんおいしいですね。（*Tenpura* wa ebi ga ichiban oishii desu ne.）

でんぽう　電報〔名〕

電報を打つ（*denpō* o utsu）電報で知らせる（*denpō* de shiraseru）

¶日本に着いたら、すぐ電報を打ちます。（Nihon ni tsuitara, sugu *denpō* o uchimasu.）

てんらんかい　展覧会〔名〕

¶今度の日曜日に絵の展覧会に行きませんか。（Kondo no nichiyōbi ni e no *tenrankai* ni ikimasen ka？）

でんわ　電話〔名、〜する〕

電話料金（*denwa*-ryōkin）公衆電話（kōshū-*denwa*）電話帳（*denwa*chō）国際電話（kokusai*denwa*）電話で話す（*denwa* de hanasu）電話をかける（*denwa* o kakeru）電話を切る（*denwa* o kiru）電話口へ呼び出す（*denwa* guchi e yobidasu）

¶あなたのうちの電話番号を教えてください。（Anata no uchi no *denwa*bangō o oshiete kudasai.）

¶上田さん、田中さんから電話です。（Ueda san, Tanaka san kara *denwa* desu.）

¶もしもし、上田さんは今ほかの電話に出ていますから、ちょっとお待ちください。（Moshi moshi, Ueda san wa ima hoka no *denwa* ni dete imasu kara, chotto omachi kudasai.）

tenpura 〔n〕 tempura

¶ [I] had fish and vegetable *tempura*.

¶ The shrimp *tempura* is best, isn't it?

denpō 〔n〕 telegram

send **a telegram** // inform by **telegram**

¶ [I] will send [you] **a telegram** without delay upon arrival in Japan.

tenrankai 〔n〕 exhibition, show

¶ Would you like to go to **an exhibition** of paintings next Sunday?

denwa 〔n, 〜*suru*〕 telephone

a **telephone** bill, a **telephone** charge // a public **telephone**, a pay **phone** // a **telephone** book, a **telephone** directory // an overseas **telephone** call // talk on **the telephone** // make a **telephone** call, **telephone** someone // hang up **the phone** // call someone to **the telephone**

¶ Please tell me your home **telephone** number.

¶ [Mr.] Ueda, there's **a telephone call** for you from [Miss] Tanaka.

¶ Hello, [Mr.] Ueda is now on another **line**. Please wait a moment.

¶電話を切らずにおいてください。
(*Denwa* o kirazu ni oite kudasai.)

¶さきほど、田中さんから電話があり
ました。(Sakihodo, Tanaka san kara
denwa ga arimashita.)

¶今、話し中で電話が通じません。
(Ima, hanashichū de *denwa* ga
tsūjimasen.)

¶何か用があったら、わたしに電話を
ください。(Nani ka yō ga attara, watashi
ni *denwa* o kudasai.)

¶またあとで電話します。(Mata ato de
denwa shimasu.)

¶ Please **hold the line**.

¶ There was **a telephone call** [for you]
a little while ago from [Mrs.] Tanaka.

¶ I **can't get through** to [him] now;
the line is busy.

¶ Give me **a call** if there's anything I
can do for you.

¶ **I will call** again later.

と 戸 〔名〕

戸を開ける (*to* o akeru) 戸を閉める
(*to* o shimeru)

¶ 玄関の戸が開いていますから、閉め
てください。(Genkan no *to* ga aite
imasu kara, shimete kudasai.)

と 〔助〕

① [動作の相手を表す]

¶ わたしは昨日駅で上田さんと会いま
した。(Watashi wa kinō eki de Ueda san
to aimashita.)

¶ 妹は山田さんと結婚しました。
(Imōto wa Yamada san *to* kekkon
shimashita.)

*「と (to)」は相手を必要とする動作
を表す動詞の前についてその相手を表
し、動作を行う者とその相手との相互
の行為であることを表す。「田中さん
と話す (Tanaka san to hanasu)」はわた
しが田中さんと話し合う意味である。
これに対し、「に (ni)」は動作が相手
に対して一方的に行われることを表
し、「田中さんに話す (Tanaka san ni
hanasu)」はわたしが田中さんに一方的
に話す意味である。したがって、「会
う (au)」「話す (hanasu)」「相談する
(sōdan suru)」などは「と (to)」でも
「に (ni)」でもその相手を表すことが
できるが、一方的働きかけの関係では
ない「結婚する (kekkon suru)」「けん
かする (kenka suru)」などの動詞には
「と (to)」しか使えない。

→に ni

to 〔n〕 **door, sliding door, shutter**

open **a door** // close **a door**

¶ Please close the entryway **door**.

to 〔part〕 **to, with; with, together
with**

① [indicates the object of an action]

¶ I met [Mrs.] Ueda at the station
yesterday.

¶ My (younger) sister married Mr.
Yamada.

*This *to* is used with verbs where the
action requires another person, and it
indicates the mutual nature of that
action. "*Tanaka san to hanasu*" (I
speak with Mr. Tanaka) means that the
speaker talks mutually with Mr.
Tanaka. The use of *ni*, on the other
hand, indicates the one-way nature of
the action so that "*Tanaka san ni
hanasu*" means "I speak to Mr.
Tanaka." Consequently, for verbs such
as *au* (meet), *hanasu* (talk), and *sōdan
suru* (consult), either *to* or *ni* can be
used; but with verbs expressing an
action that must be done mutually,
such as *kekkon suru* (marry) or *kenka
suru* (quarrel), one can only use *to*.

②[いっしょに動作をする相手を表す]

¶あした、母とデパートへ行きます。
（Ashita haha *to* depāto e ikimasu.）

¶昨日、友達といっしょに映画を見に行きました。（Kinō, tomodachi *to* issho ni eiga o mi ni ikimashita.）

③[比較・異同などの基準を表す]

¶今年の夏は去年と比べると、たいへん暑いです。（Kotoshi no natsu wa kyonen *to* kuraberu to, taihen atsui desu.）

¶昔と違って、今はおおぜいの日本人が外国旅行をするようになりました。（Mukashi *to* chigatte, ima wa oozeino Nihonjin ga gaikoku-ryokō o suru yō ni narimashita.）

④[ものごとの成り行き・変化などの結果を表す]

¶心配していたことが事実となりました。（Shinpai shite ita koto ga jijitsu *to* narimashita.）

*いつも「～となる（～to naru）」の形で使う。

→に ni

⑤[言ったり考えたりすることの内容を表すときに使う]

¶あしたはいい天気だと思います。（Ashita wa ii tenki da *to* omoimasu.）

¶「ありがとう」は、あなたの国の言葉で何と言いますか。（"Arigatō" wa, anata no kuni no kotoba de nan *to* iimasuka？）

②[indicates the person one does something with]

¶ I will go **with** my mother to a department store tomorrow.

¶ [I] went to see a movie **with** a friend yesterday.

③[indicates the standard for a comparison, difference, etc.]

¶ It's very hot this summer compared **to** last summer.

¶ In a change **from** the past, many Japanese now travel abroad.

④[indicates an outcome, result, etc.]

¶ What I was afraid would happen actually happened 〖has actually happened〗.

*Always used in the pattern "～ *to naru*."

⑤[used when reporting what is said or thought]

¶ I think it will be a nice day tomorrow.

¶ How do you say "Thank you" in your language?

*「言う（iu）」「書く（kaku）」「思う（omou）」などの動詞の前につく。

⑥ [立場・資格などを表す]

¶上田さんは大使としてアメリカへ行きました。（Ueda san wa taishi *to* shite Amerika e ikimashita.）

¶山田さんは医者としてよりも政治家として有名です。（Yamada san wa isha *to* shite yori mo seijika *to* shite yūmei desu.）

*いつも「〜として（〜to shite）」の形で使う。

⑦ [ある動作・作用がこれから行われる状態にあることを表す]

¶うちを出ようとしたら、雨が降りだしました。（Uchi o deyō *to* shitara, ame ga furidashimashita.）

¶芝居が終わって幕が下りようとした時、大きな拍手が起こりました。（Shibai ga owatte maku ga oriyō *to* shita toki, ookina hakushu ga okorimashita.）

*いつも「動詞（う・ようの形）＋とする（to suru）」の形で使う。

→する **suru**

⑧ [ものごとの様子を表すときに使う]

¶子供は母親の手をしっかりと握りました。（Kodomo wa hahaoya no te o shikkari *to* nigirimashita.）

¶急がずにゆっくりと歩いてください。（Isogazu ni yukkuri *to* aruite kudasai.）

---

*Used before the verbs *iu, kaku, omou,* etc.

⑥ [indicates a position, qualification, etc.]

¶ [Mr.] Ueda went to the United States **as** ambassador.

¶ [Mr.] Yamada is better known **as** a politician than **as** a physician.

*Always used in the pattern "∼ *to shite*."

⑦ [indicates that some action or operation is about to take place or was about to take place]

¶ It started to rain **as I was about** to go out.

¶ The audience burst into applause as the play ended and the curtain **was on the point** of coming down.

Always used in the pattern "verb (-ō* 〖*-yō*〗 form) + *to suru*."

⑧ [used to indicate a state or condition]

¶ The child **tightly** grasped [her] mother's hand.

¶ Please walk **slowly** without hurrying.

*副詞などにつけることが多い。

*Generally used with an adverb, etc.

と 〔助〕 **to** 〔part〕 **and**

¶朝御飯はパンと牛乳とサラダを食べ
ました。(Asagohan wa pan *to* gyū-nyū
to sarada o tabemashita.)

¶[I] had bread 〖toast, a roll, etc.〗,
milk, **and** salad for breakfast.

¶かばんの中には本とノートしかあり
ません。(Kaban no naka ni wa hon *to*
nōto shika arimasen.)

¶There is only a book **and** a notebook
in the briefcase 〖bag, etc.〗.

*いくつかのものごとのすべてを対等
の関係で並べて言うときに使う。

＊Used when stating all relevant items;
the items are on the same level. (See
also the entry for *ya*.)

と 〔助〕 **to** 〔part〕 **when, whenever, if, even
if**

① [前件が成立するとそれに伴ってい
つも後件が成立するという関係を表す]

① [indicates that the second clause is
always realized when the first clause is
realized]

¶春になると、花が咲きます。(Haru
ni naru *to*, hana ga sakimasu.)

¶Flowers bloom **in** the spring.

¶5に4を足すと、9になります。(Go
ni yon o tasu *to*, kyū ni narimasu.)

¶Four **plus** five (literally, five **plus**
four) is nine.

¶この道を左に曲がると、駅の前に出
ます。(Kono michi o hidari ni magaru
to, eki no mae ni demasu.)

¶**If** you turn left from this street, you
will come out in front of the station.

¶わたしはこの歌を聞くと、子供のこ
ろのことを思い出します。(Watashi
wa kono uta o kiku *to*, kodomo no koro no
koto o omoidashimasu.)

¶I am reminded of my childhood
whenever I hear this song.

¶わたしは若い時はお酒を飲むと、気
持ちが悪くなりました。(Watashi wa
wakai toki wa osake o nomu *to*, kimochi
ga waruku narimashita.)

¶When I was young I always felt sick
whenever I drank *sake*.

¶「船に乗ると、気持ちが悪くなりま
すか。(Fune ni noru *to*, kimochi ga
waruku narimasu ka?)「いいえ、船に
乗っても、大丈夫です。」(Iie, fune ni
notte mo, daijōbu desu.)

¶"Do you get seasick **on board** a
ship?"
"No, I don't get seasick while I'm **on
board** a ship."

*真理や習慣的なことがらを表すとき
よく使い、後件が過去・完了を表す
「たの形」のときは過去の習慣を表
す。また後件には、「〜う［よう］（〜
u［yō]）」などの意志、「〜なさい（〜
nasai）」などの命令、「〜てください
（〜te kudasai）」などの依頼などの言い
方は来ない。

⇒ば **ba**　たら **tara**　ても **te mo**

② [前件に既に成立していることがら
を述べてその条件のもとで後件が成立
するという関係を表す]

¶そんなひどいことを言うと、許しま
せんよ。(Sonna hidoi koto o iu *to*,
yurushimasen yo.)

¶これから寒くなると思うと、いやに
なります。(Kore kara samuku naru to
omou *to*, iya ni narimasu.)

→たら **tara**

③ [前件の動作に引き続いて後件の動
作を行うという関係を表す]

¶田中さんは部屋に入ると、電話をか
けました。(Tanaka san wa heya ni hairu
to, denwa o kakemashita.)

¶上田さんは手紙を書くと、すぐ出か
けました。(Ueda san wa tegami o kaku
to, sugu dekakemashita.)

*前件と後件の主語は同じで、両方と
も意志的な動作であることが多い。ま
た、後件には過去・完了を表す「たの
形」が来る。

④ [前件の動作・作用が行われた時ま
たはその直後に後件の動作・作用が行
われるという関係を表す]

*Often used concerning something
factual or habitual; if it is followed by a
verb in the *-ta* form expressing past or
completed action, it expresses habitual
action in the past. In the second clause
one does not find statements of intent
with *-ō* 〖*-yō*〗, orders with *-nasai*,
requests with *-te kudasai*, etc.

② [indicates that the first clause is
already realized and the second clause
is realized based on that]

¶ I can't forgive **your saying** such a
terrible thing.

¶ It's depressing **to think** about its
getting colder from now on.

③ [indicates that the action of the
second clause continues from that of
the first clause]

¶ [Mr.] Tanaka **came in** the room **and**
made a telephone call.

¶ [Miss] Ueda left soon **after writing** a
letter.

*Generally the subjects of the two
clauses are the same, and both clauses
express a voluntary or intentional
action. The verb in the second clause is
in the *-ta* form expressing past or
completed action.

④ [indicates that the action or
operation in the second clause takes
place at the same time as or soon after
that of the first clause]

¶ 電車が止まると、乗っている人が降り始めました。(Densha ga tomaru *to*, notte iru hito ga orihajimemashita.)

¶ The train **stopped and** passengers started to get off.

¶ 庭を散歩していると、母がわたしを呼びました。(Niwa o sanpo shiteiru *to*, haha ga watashi o yobimashita.)

¶ My mother called to me **as I was** walking in the garden 〚yard〛.

¶ 家を出ようとすると、雨が降りだしました。(Ie o deyō to suru *to*, ame ga furidashimashita.)

¶ It started to rain **just as** I was leaving the house.

*前件と後件の主語は異なる。後件には過去・完了を表す「たの形」が来る。

*The two clauses have different subjects. The verb in the second clause is in the *-ta* form expressing past or completed action.

→たら **tara**

⑤ [前件の成立をきっかけとして後件が成立するという関係を表す]

⑤ [indicates the second clause is realized based on the realization of the first clause]

¶ 「うるさい。」と言うと、山田さんはラジオの音を小さくしました。("Urusai ! *to* iu *to*, Yamada san wa rajio no oto o chiisaku shimashita.)

¶ **When** [I] cried out that it was too noisy, [Mr.] Yamada turned down the radio.

¶ 男の子が女の子を押すと、女の子は転んでしまいました。(Otoko no ko ga onna no ko o osu *to*, onna no ko wa koronde shimaimashita.)

¶ The boy **pushed** the girl **and** she fell.

*普通、前件と後件の主語は異なる。後件には過去・完了を表す「たの形」が来る。

*Generally the two clauses have different subjects. The verb in the second clause is in the *-ta* form expressing past or completed action.

→たら **tara**

⑥ [前件の成立によって後件のことがらに気づくという関係を表す]

⑥ [indicates that what comes in the second clause is noticed through the realization of the first clause]

¶ ふと空を見上げると、飛行機が飛んでいました。(Futo sora o miageru *to*, hikōki ga tonde imashita.)

¶ **When** [I] happened to look up at the sky, there was an airplane flying there.

¶ 川のそばまで来ると、子供たちが泳いでいるのが見えました。(Kawa no soba made kuru *to*, kodomotachi ga oyoide iru no ga miemashita.)

¶ **When** [I] came up to the river, [I] could see children swimming there.

と

¶長いトンネルを抜けると、雪国でした。（Nagai tonneru o nukeru *to*, yukiguni deshita.）

¶びんのふたを開けると、いやなにおいがしました。（Bin no futa o akeru *to*, iya na nioi ga shimashita.）

*後件には「あった（atta）」「～ていた（～te ita）」「見えた（mieta）」などの状態・作用を表す言葉のほかに「音がした（oto ga shita）」「においがした（nioi ga shita）」などの感覚を表す言葉も使い、前件によって後件のことがらに気づくという関係を表す。前件の主語と後件の主語は異なる。

→たら tara

⑦ [評価などを導くことを表す]
¶この病気を治すには、まずたばこをやめるといいです。（Kono byōki o naosu ni wa, mazu tabako o yameru *to* ii desu.）

¶君も早く結婚しないといけませんね。（Kimi mo hayaku kekkon shinai *to* ikemasen ne.）

*「～といい（～to ii）」「～といけない（～to ikenai）」「～とだめだ（～to dame da）」などの形で使う。

→ば ba

⑧ [前件が後件のことがらの出どころとなっているという関係を表す]
¶今朝の新聞によると、昨日北海道で地震があったそうです。（Kesa no shinbun ni yoru *to*, kinō Hokkaidō de jishin ga atta sō desu.）

¶山田さんの話だと、秋子さんは来月結婚するそうです。（Yamada san no hanashi da *to*, Akiko san wa raigetsu kekkon suru sō desu.）

¶ **On** coming out of the long tunnel [we] were in snow country.

¶ **When** [I] opened the top of the bottle, a terrible smell emerged.

*The relationship of what comes in the second clause being noticed by means of what comes in the first clause is expressed by using in the second clause words indicating a state or process such as *atta*, *-te ita*, or *mieta*, words concerning the physical senses such as *oto ga shita* or *nioi ga shita*, etc. The subjects of the two clauses are different.

⑦ [used to introduce a judgment, etc.]
¶ To get over this illness **you should** first of all stop smoking.

¶ **You should** hurry up and get married too.

*Used in the patterns "～ *to ii*," "～ *to ikenai*," "～ *to dame da*," etc.

⑧ [indicates that the first clause is the grounds for the second clause]
¶ **According to** the newspaper this morning, there was an earthquake in Hokkaido yesterday.

¶ **According to** [Mrs.] Yamada, Akiko is going to get married next month.

⑨ [前件のことがらにかかわらず後件のことがらが成立するという関係を表す]

¶人が何と言おうと、わたしは平気です。(Hito ga nan to iō *to*, watashi wa heiki desu.)

¶行こうと行くまいとわたしの自由です。(Ikō *to* ikumai *to* watashi no jiyū desu.)

*普通「～う［よう］（～u［yō]）」「～まい（mai）」などの言葉に続く。

⑨ [indicates that the second clause is realized unconnected to the first clause]

¶I don't care what others **may say**.

¶**Whether I go or not** is for me to decide.

*Usually used with -*ō* [[-*yō]]*, -*mai*, etc.

-ど -度 〔尾〕

① [回数などを表すのに使う]

¶もう一度言ってください。(Mō ichi-*do* itte kudasai.)

② [温度などの程度を表す]

¶ここでは夏の気温は普通 30 度ぐらいになります。(Koko de wa natsu no kion wa futsū sanjū*do* gurai ni narimasu.)

-do 〔suf〕 **times; degrees**

① [the counter for number of times]

¶Please say it **once** again.

② [the counter for degrees of temperature, etc.]

¶The temperature here in the summer is usually around 30 **degrees**.

ドア 〔名〕

ドアを開ける (*doa* o akeru) ドアを閉める (*doa* o shimeru)

¶ドアにかぎを掛けました。(*Doa* ni kagi o kakemashita.)

doa 〔n〕 **door**

open **the door** // close **the door**

¶[I] locked **the door**.

とい 問い 〔名〕

問いを出す (*toi* o dasu)

¶次の問いに答えなさい。(Tsugi no *toi* ni kotaenasai.)

toi 〔n〕 **question, inquiry**

ask **a question**

¶Answer the following **questions**.

トイレ 〔名〕

¶このトイレは清潔で気持ちがいいです。(Kono *toire* wa seiketsu de kimochi ga ii desu.)

⇒便所 **benjio** 手洗い **tearai**

toire 〔n〕 **toilet, rest room**

¶This **rest room** is nice and clean.

どう〔副〕

① [話し手にとってものごとの不明な内容・状態などを表す]

¶「あしたの天気はどうでしょうか。」（Ashita no tenki wa *dō* deshō ka？）「たぶんいい天気でしょう。」（Tabun ii tenki deshō.）

¶「あしたの音楽会にいらっしゃいますか。」（Ashita no ongakkai ni irasshaimasu ka？）「まだどうするか決めていません。」（Mada *dō* suru ka kimete imasen.）

¶「上田さん、今日はどうかしたのですか。元気がありませんね。」（Ueda san, kyō wa *dō* ka shita no desu ka？ Genki ga arimasen ne.）「体のぐあいが悪いのです。」（Karada no guai ga warui no desu.）

¶この言葉はどういう意味ですか。（Kono kotoba wa *dō* iu imi desu ka？）

¶山田さんは来るかどうかわかりません。（Yamada san wa kuru ka *dō* ka wakarimasen.）

② [話し相手の意向や状態などを尋ねるのに使う]

¶わたしはこの夏に北海道へ行きます。どうですか。いっしょに行きませんか。（Watashi wa kono natsu ni Hokkaidō e ikimasu. *Dō* desu ka？ Issho ni ikimasen ka？）

¶「上田さん、あなたはテニスはどうですか。」（Ueda san, anata wa tenisu wa *dō* desu ka？）「見るのは好きですが、自分ではやりません。」（Miru no wa suki desu ga, jibun de wa yarimasen.）

dō 〔adv〕 how, what

① [how, what]

¶ "I wonder **what** the weather **will be like** tomorrow."
"It will probably be fine."

¶ "Are you going to the concert 〚recital〛 tomorrow?"
"I haven't decided yet **what** I'll do."

¶ "Is **something the matter** today, [Mr.] Ueda? You seem to be a little low."
"Yes, I don't feel well."

¶ **What** is the meaning of this word?

¶ I don't know **whether** [Miss] Yamada will come or not.

② [what, how; used to inquire into the intentions or situation of the listener]

¶ I'm going to Hokkaido this summer. **How about it?** Won't you go with me?

¶ "Do you play tennis, [Mrs.] Ueda?"
"I like to watch, but I don't play it myself."

¶「けがをしたそうですが、どうです
か。」(Kega o shita sō desu ga, *dō* desu
ka?)「おかげさまで、だいぶよくな
りました。」(Okagesama de, daibu yoku
narimashita.)

*普通「どうですか(dō desu ka)」の形
で使う。

→いかが ikaga

⇒こう kō　そう sō　ああ ā

どういたしまして〔連〕

¶「どうもありがとうございました。」
(Dōmo arigatō gozaimashita.)「いいえ、
どういたしまして。」(Iie, *dō
itashimashite*.)

とういつ　統一〔名、〜する〕

国を統一する (kuni o *tōitsu* suru)

¶クラスの意見を統一するのは難しい
です。(Kurasu no iken o *tōitsu* suru no
wa muzukashii desu.)

どうぐ　道具〔名〕

台所道具 (daidokoro-*dōgu*)
¶テーブルの上の勉強道具をかたづけ
てください。(Tēburu no ue no benkyō-
dōgu o katazukete kudasai.)
¶道具があれば、自分でラジオが直せ
ます。(*Dōgu* ga areba, jibun de rajio ga
naosemasu.)

どうさ　動作〔名〕

¶年を取ると、だんだん動作が鈍くな
ります。(Toshi o toru to, dandan *dōsa*
ga nibuku narimasu.)

¶ "I heard you were hurt. **How are
you?**"
"Much better, thank you."

*Usually used in the pattern "*dō desu
ka.*"

dōitashimashite 〔compd〕 **not at
all, don't mention it, you're
welcome**

¶ "Thank you very much." "Oh no, **not
at all**."

tōitsu 〔n, 〜*suru*〕 **unified, uniform,
united, concerted; unify, unite**
unify a country, **bring** a country
under a single rule
¶ It is difficult to get a **unified** (school)
class opinion.

dōgu 〔n〕 **instrument, implement,
utensil, tool**
kitchen**ware**
¶ Please clear away the study **things** on
the table.

¶ If I had **the tools**, I could repair the
radio myself.

dōsa 〔n〕 **action, movement,
bearing**
¶ As one ages, one becomes
progressively slower **in movement**.

とうじ 当時〔名〕

¶わたしが小学生だった当時は、まだこの辺はとても静かでした。(Watashi ga shōgakusei datta *tōji* wa, mada kono hen wa totemo shizuka deshita.)

¶両親が結婚したのは戦後間もなくですが、その当時は食べ物もあまりなかったそうです。(Ryōshin ga kekkon shita no wa sengo mamonaku desu ga, sono *tōji* wa tabemono mo amari nakatta sō desu.)

tōji 〔n〕 **at that time**

¶ This was still a very quiet area **when** I was in elementary school.

¶ My parents got married soon after the war ended; I hear food was scarce **then**.

どうじ 同時〔名〕

① [同じ時]
¶二人が着いたのは、ほとんど同時でした。(Futari ga tsuita no wa, hotondo *dōji* deshita.)

¶発車のベルが鳴り終わると同時に、ドアが閉まりました。(Hassha no beru ga nariowaru to *dōji* ni, doa ga shimarimashita.)

② [あることがらと共に]
¶この本はおもしろいと同時にためになります。(Kono hon wa omoshiroi to *dōji* ni tame ni narimasu.)

¶この計画には、よい点もあると同時に悪い点もあります。(Kono keikaku ni wa, yoi ten mo aru to *dōji* ni warui ten mo arimasu.)

dōji 〔n〕 **at the same time; while**

① [at the same time, simultaneously]
¶ The two arrived almost **simultaneously**.

¶ The doors closed **the moment** the departure bell stopped ringing.

② [while, along with]
¶ This book is **both** interesting and instructive.

¶ This plan has bad points **as well as** good points.

どうして〔副〕

① [なぜ]
¶昨日はどうして学校を休んだのですか。(Kinō wa *dōshite* gakkō o yasunda no desu ka?)

¶あの人が来ないのは、どうしてでしょう。(Ano hito ga konai no wa, *dōshite* deshō?)

dōshite 〔adv〕 **why; how**

① [why]
¶ **Why** did you stay home from school yesterday?

¶ I wonder **why** [he] doesn't 〖hasn't〗 come.

*理由などをたずねるときに使う言葉。

→なぜ naze

② [どのようにして、どういう方法で]

¶夏休みをどうして過ごそうかと考えています。(Natsuyasumi o *dōshite* sugosō ka to kangaete imasu.)

どうしても〔連〕

① [どういうふうにしても、どのように考えても]

¶この問題はどうしてもわかりません。(Kono mondai wa *dōshite mo* wakarimasen.)

¶あの人と結婚するのはどうしてもいやです。(Ano hito to kekkon suru no wa *dōshite mo* iya desu.)

*あとに打ち消しまたは否定的な意味の言葉が来る。

② [必ず、どんなことがあっても]

¶この試合には、どうしても勝ちたいんです。(Kono shiai ni wa, *dōshite mo* kachitai n desu.)

¶昨日は学校を休んだので、今日はどうしても行かなければなりません。(Kinō wa gakkō o yasunda node, kyō wa *dōshite mo* ikanakereba narimasen.)

どうじょう 同情〔名、〜する〕

¶わたしたちは、地震で被害を受けた人たちに同情して、お金を集めて送りました。(Watashitachi wa, jishin de higai o uketa hitotachi ni *dōjō* shite, okane o atsumete okurimashita.)

---

*Used when asking the reason for something.

② [how, by what means, in what way]

¶ I am thinking about **how** to spend summer vacation.

dōshite mo 〔compd〕 **whatever one may do; no matter what, at any cost**

① [whatever one may do, by no means]

¶ I can't understand this problem **no matter what I do**.

¶ **I hate the very thought of** marrying that person.

*Followed by a negative or words having a negative sense.

② [no matter what, at any cost, must]

¶ I am determined to win this match 〖game〗 **no matter what**.

¶ Since I stayed home from school yesterday, I must **by all means** go today.

dōjō 〔n, 〜*suru*〕 **sympathy, compassion**

¶ **Sympathizing** with those who had suffered in the earthquake, we collected and sent off money to them.

とうぜん　当然 〔副、形動、〜の〕

¶大学生なら、当然これくらいのこと
は知っていなければなりません。
（Daigakusei nara, *tōzen* kore kurai no
koto wa shitte inakereba narimasen.）
¶夜遅く寝れば、朝眠いのは当然で
す。（Yoru osoku nereba, asa nemui no
wa *tōzen* desu.）
⇔あたりまえ atarimae

tōzen 〔adv, adj-v, 〜no〕 **naturally,
as a matter of course, of
course, necessarily, in the
nature of things**

¶As a university student, [you] should
of course be familiar with something
like this.

¶If you go to bed late, **of course** you
will be sleepy in the morning.

どうぞ 〔副〕

¶どうぞお入りください。（*Dōzo* ohairi
kudasai.）
¶わたしは山田です。どうぞよろし
く。（Watashi wa Yamada desu. *Dōzo*
yoroshiku.）

dōzo 〔adv〕 **please, kindly**

¶**Please** come in.

¶My name is Yamada. **I'm pleased to
make your acquaintance**.

とうちゃく　到着 〔名、〜する〕

¶弟が乗った飛行機は、今夜8時に到
着します。（Otōto ga notta hikōki wa,
kon'ya hachiji ni *tōchaku* shimasu.）
¶11時に着く予定の列車は、事故の
ため1時間遅れて到着します。
（Jūichiji ni tsuku yotei no ressha wa, jiko
no tame ichijikan okurete *tōchaku*
shimasu.）
⇔出発 shuppatsu

tōchaku 〔n, 〜*suru*〕 **arrival; arrive,
reach**

¶The plane my (younger) brother is on
will arrive tonight at eight o'clock.

¶The train scheduled to arrive at
eleven o'clock will be delayed an hour
due to an accident.

とうとう 〔副〕

① [いろいろな過程を経て最後にある
事態になるという意味を表すときに使
う]
¶長い間の研究がとうとう完成しまし
た。（Nagai aida no kenkyū ga *tōtō* kansei
shimashita.）

tōtō 〔adv〕 **at last, finally; in the
end, after all**

① [at last, finally, ultimately; used
when something happens after various
stages]

¶The research of so many years
〖months〗 was 〖is〗 **finally** complete.

¶田中さんはお酒ばかり飲んでいたので、とうとう病気になってしまいました。(Tanaka san wa osake bakari nonde ita node, *tōtō* byōki ni natte shimaimashita.)

¶ [Mr.] Tanaka did nothing but drink and **ultimately** [he] became ill 〚**in the end** he has become ill〛.

¶夢中になって本を読んでいたら、とうとう夜が明けてしまいました。(Muchū ni natte hon o yonde itara, *tōtō* yo ga akete shimaimashita.)

¶ While [I] was absorbed in reading [my] book a new day dawned.

*普通あとに過去・完了を表す「たの形」が来、喜び・あきらめ・驚きなどの感情を表すことが多い。「ついに(tsuini)」が事態の成立に重点があるのに対し、事態が成立するまでの過程に重点がある。

*Usually followed by a verb in the *-ta* form expressing past or completed action and often followed by an expression of emotion such as joy, resignation, surprise, etc. In the case of *tōtō* the emphasis is on the process leading up to a particular event while for *tsuini* it falls on the event itself.

②[前と同じ状態が続いて新しい事態が起こらないことが確定したときに使う]

② [in the end, after all; used when a preexisting state continues and one sees that a new event didn't happen]

¶一日じゅう待っていたのに、山田さんはとうとう来ませんでした。(Ichinichijū matte ita noni, Yamada san wa *tōtō* kimasen deshita.)

¶ Even though I waited all day, **in the end** [Mr.] Yamada never showed up.

¶忙しくてとうとうその映画を見に行けませんでした。(Isogashikute *tōtō* sono eiga o mi ni ikemasen deshita.)

¶ [I] was busy and wasn't able to go see that film **after all**.

*普通あとに「～ませんでした(～masen deshita)」の形か、否定的な意味の言葉の過去・完了を表す「たの形」が来る。

*Usually followed by a verb in the *-masen deshita* form or a verb in the *-ta* form expressing past or completed action and expressing a negative meaning.

⇒ついに **tsuini**

とうふ 豆腐 [名]

tōfu [n] **tofu, bean curd**

¶豆腐は大豆から作ります。(*Tōfu* wa daizu kara tsukurimasu.)

¶ **Tofu** is made from soybeans.

どうぶつ 動物 〔名〕

動物園 (*dōbutsu*en) 動物学 (*dō-butsu*gaku)

dōbutsu 〔n〕 **animal**

a zoo // zoology

とうめい 透明 〔形動〕

¶この酒のびんは透明だから、色も飲んだ量もよくわかります。(Kono sake no bin wa *tōmei* da kara, iro mo nonda ryō mo yoku wakarimasu.)

¶この湖の水は透明で、底の方もよく見えます。(Kono mizuumi no mizu wa *tōmei* de, soko no hō mo yoku miemasu.)

tōmei 〔adj-v〕 **transparent, clear**

¶ Since this bottle is made of **clear** glass, one can clearly see the color of the liquor and tell how much one has drunk.

¶ The water of this lake **is so clear** that one can see the bottom.

どうも 〔副〕

① [どうしても、どのようにやってみても]

¶どうもうまく発音できません。(*Dōmo* umaku hatsuon dekimasen.)

¶この文の意味はどうもよくわかりません。(Kono bun no imi wa *dōmo* yoku wakarimasen.)

*あとに打ち消しまたは否定的な意味の言葉が来る。

② [どう考えてもはっきりしないが]

¶あの人には、どうもどこかで会ったような気がします。(Ano hito ni wa, *dōmo* doko ka de atta yō na ki ga shimasu.)

③ [たいへん、ほんとうに]

¶どうもありがとうございます。(*Dōmo* arigatō gozaimasu.)

¶どうも失礼しました。(*Dōmo* shitsurei shimashita.)

dōmo 〔adv〕 **no matter how hard one tries; somehow; very, quite**

① [no matter how hard one tries, no matter what one does]

¶ **I just** can't pronounce it right.

¶ **I just** can't seem to understand the meaning of this sentence.

*Followed by a negative or words having a negative sense.

② [somehow]

¶ **Somehow** I feel I've met that person before somewhere.

③ [very, quite, really]

¶ Thank you **very much**.

¶ I beg your pardon 〚I'm **very** sorry; Thank you for your time, etc.〛.

とうよう 東洋 〔名〕

東洋史 (*tōyō*shi) 東洋人 (*tōyō*jin)

tōyō 〔n〕 **the East, the Orient**

Oriental history // an **Oriental**

¶東洋の文化は、西洋の文化とはいろ
いろな点で違います。(*Tōyō* no bunka
wa, seiyō no bunka to wa iroiro na ten de
chigaimasu.)
⇔西洋 **seiyō**

¶ **Oriental** culture differs from
Western culture in various respects.

どうろ 道路 〔名〕

広い道路 (hiroi *dōro*) 狭い道路
(semai *dōro*)
¶今の時間は、道路がたいへんこんで
います。(Ima no jikan wa, *dōro* ga
taihen konde imasu.)

dōro 〔n〕 **road, street, highway**

a wide **street** // a narrow **street**

¶ **The roads** are very crowded at this
time of the day.

とお 十 〔名〕

① [10 個]
¶かごの中にりんごが十あります。
(Kago no naka ni ringo ga *too* arimasu.)
② [10 歳]
¶息子は十で、娘は八つになりまし
た。(Musuko wa *too* de, musume wa
yattsu ni narimashita.)

too 〔n〕 **10; 10 years old**

① [10, 10 items]
¶ There are **10** apples in the basket.

② [10 years old]
¶ My son **is 10** and my daughter has
turned eight.

とおい 遠い 〔形〕

¶わたしのうちは学校から遠いので、
毎日自転車で通っています。(Watashi
no uchi wa gakkō kara *tooi* node, mainichi
jitensha de kayotte imasu.)
¶海岸はここからあまり遠くないで
す。(Kaigan wa koko kara amari *tooku*
nai desu.)
⇔近い **chikai**

tooi 〔adj〕 **far, distant, remote**

¶ As the school **is far** from my home, I
commute there every day by bicycle.

¶ The shore **isn't far** from here.

とおか 十日 〔名〕

① [日付を表す]
十月十日 (jūgatsu *tooka*)
② [日数を表す]
十日間 (*tooka*kan) 十日前
(*tooka*mae) 十日後 (*tooka*go)
⇒-日 **-ka**

tooka 〔n〕 **the tenth of the month;
10 days**

① [the tenth of the month]
October 10
② [10 days]
for **10 days, 10-days'** time // **10 days**
ago, **10 days** earlier // **10 days** from
now, **10 days** later

とおく 遠く〔名〕

¶危ないから、遠くへ遊びに行っては
いけませんよ。(Abunai kara, *tooku* e
asobi ni itte wa ikemasen yo.)
¶この船は魚を捕るために、遠くの海
へ出かけていきます。(Kono fune wa
sakana o toru tame ni, *tooku* no umi e
dekakete ikimasu.)
⇔近く chikaku

とおす 通す〔動Ｉ〕

①[一方からもう一方へ通過させる]
¶すみませんが、ちょっと前を通して
ください。(Sumimasen ga, chotto mae o
tooshite kudasai.)
¶ガラスは光を通します。(Garasu wa
hikari o *tooshimasu*.)
②[部屋などへ案内する]
¶お客様を座敷にお通ししました。
(Okyakusama o zashiki ni *otooshi*
shimashita.)
③[あることを初めから終わりまで続
ける]
¶上田さんは小学校、中学校、高等学
校をずっと１番で通しました。(Ueda
san wa shōgakkō, chūgakkō, kōtōgakkō o
zutto ichiban de *tooshimashita*.)

とおり 通り〔名〕

①[道路]
大通り (oo*doori*)
¶この通りをまっすぐ行くと、右側に
交番があります。(Kono *toori* o
massuguikuto, migigawa ni kōban ga
arimasu.)

---

tooku 〔n〕 **a distant place; far
away, in the distance**
¶ You mustn't play **too far away**— it's
dangerous.

¶ This ship sails to **distant** seas to fish.

toosu 〔vI〕 **let pass, pass through;
show in, usher; persist in, keep
at**
① [let pass, pass through]
¶ Excuse me, I'd like **to be let by**
please.

¶ Glass **admits** light.

② [show in, usher]
¶ [I] **showed** our guest into the parlor
〖our customer into the Japanesestyle
room〗.

③ [persist in, keep at, continue, carry
through]
¶ [Miss] Ueda **remained** first in the
class throughout elementary, junior
high and high school.

toori 〔n〕 **road, street; street
traffic; way, as, like**
① [road, street]
a main **road**, thoroughfare
¶ If you go straight down this **street**,
there will be a police box on the right.

② [人・車の往来]
人通り (hito*doori*)
¶駅の前のこの道は、いつも車の通りが多いです。(Eki no mae no kono michi wa, itsu mo kuruma no *toori* ga ooi desu.)

② [street traffic, coming and going]
pedestrian **traffic**
¶ **Traffic** is always heavy on this road in front of the station.

③ [同じ状態]
¶わたしが初めに歌いますから、あとでそのとおりに歌ってください。(Watashi ga hajime ni utaimasu kara, ato de sono *toori* ni utatte kudasai.)
¶わたしが言うとおりに発音してください。(Watashi ga iu *toori* ni hatsuon shite kudasai.)

③ [way, as, like]
¶ I'll sing it first—then you please sing it the same **way**.
¶ Please listen and pronounce it **like** I do.

とおり 〔尾〕

① [種類などを表す]
¶この漢字には三とおりの読み方があります。(Kono kanji ni wa mi*toori* no yomikata ga arimasu.)

-toori 〔suf〕 kind, sort; approximately, roughly; that way, like that
① [kind, sort]
¶ There are three different **ways** of reading this *kanji*.

② [だいたい、ざっと]
¶彼が会社を辞めた理由は、ひととおり聞いて知っています。(Kare ga kaisha o yameta riyū wa, hito*toori* kiite shitte imasu.)
¶桜はもう九分どおり咲いていました。(Sakura wa mō kubu*doori* saite imashita.)

② [approximately, roughly]
¶ I've heard **in a general way** his reasons for quitting his job.
¶ The cherry blossoms are 〚were〛 **almost** in full bloom.

③ [そのようであることを表す]
予想どおり (yosō *doori*)
¶仕事は計画どおりに進んでいます。(Shigoto wa keikaku *doori* ni susunde imasu.)
*いつも「～どおり (～doori)」の形で使う。

③ [that way, like that]
as expected
¶ The work is proceeding **according to** schedule.
*Always used in the pattern "～ -*doori*."

とおる　通る〔動Ⅰ〕

① [道を過ぎていく]
¶どちらの道を通って帰りましょうか。(Dochira no michi o *tootte* kaerimashō ka？)
¶このバスは新宿を通りますか。(Kono basu wa Shinjuku o *toorimasu* ka？)

② [一方からもう一方へ抜けて出る]
¶風がよく通るのでここは涼しいです。(Kaze ga yoku *tooru* node koko wa suzushii desu.)
¶針の穴が小さくて、糸が通りません。(Hari no ana ga chiisakute, ito ga *toorimasen*.)

③ [認められる、合格する]
意見が通る (iken ga *tooru*)
¶田中さんは試験に通らなかったようです。(Tanaka san wa shiken ni *tooranakatta* yō desu.)

とか〔助〕

① [同じようなものごとや動作について例を挙げて言う場合に使う]
¶タイとかベトナムとかいう暑い国では、1年に2回米が取れるそうです。(Tai *toka* Betonamu *toka* iu atsui kuni de wa, ichinen ni nikai kome ga toreru sō desu.)
¶勉強ばかりしないで、テニスをするとかピンポンをするとか、運動もしなさい。(Benkyō bakari shinaide, tenisu o suru *toka* pinpon o suru *toka*, undō mo shinasai.)

② [聞いたことや自分の記憶などが不確かなときに使う]

---

tooru 〔vI〕 **pass, go by; pass through; pass(an exam), prevail**

① [pass, go by]
¶ Which streets shall **we take** on our return?

¶ Does this bus **go through** Shinjuku?

② [pass through]
¶ It's cool here as there's a good breeze **passing through**.

¶ **I can't thread** this needle—its eye is too small.

③ [pass (an exam), prevail]
an opinion **wins out**
¶ It seems that [Mr.] Tanaka **did not pass** [his] exam.

toka 〔part〕 **and ~ and the like**

① [used when citing similar things as examples]
¶ I understand two rice crops a year are possible in hot countries **such as** Thailand, Vietnam, **and the like**.

¶ Don't spend all your time studying—play tennis **or** ping-pong **or** take **some other** physical exercise.

② [used when one is not sure of what one has heard, of one's memory, etc.]

¶さっき山田さんとかいう人から電話がありましたよ。(Sakki Yamada san *toka* iu hito kara denwa ga arimashita yo.)

¶ There was a telephone call a little while ago from someone called Yamada **or something like that**.

とかい 都会〔名〕

tokai 〔n〕 city, the town

¶夏休みには都会を離れて、田舎へ行くつもりです。(Natsuyasumi ni wa *tokai* o hanarete, inaka e iku tsumori desu.)
⇒田舎 **inaka**

¶ During summer vacation I intend to get out of **the city** and go to the country.

とかす 溶かす〔動Ⅰ〕

tokasu 〔vI〕 melt, dissolve, liquefy; melt down, smelt

¶金属を溶かすためには高い温度が必要です。(Kinzoku o *tokasu* tame ni wa takai ondo ga hitsuyō desu.)

¶ High temperatures are necessary **to melt** metals.

とき 時〔名〕

toki 〔n〕 time; the time

①[時間]

① [time, hour]

¶小説がおもしろかったので、時がたつのを忘れて読んでいました。(Shōsetsu ga omoshirokatta node, *toki* ga tatsu no o wasurete yonde imashita.)

¶ The novel was so interesting that lost track of **time**.

②[何かが行われる時刻]

② [the time, the moment, when]

¶食事をしている時、友達が来ました。(Shokuji o shite iru *toki*, tomodachi ga kimashita.)

¶ A friend came **while** [I] was eating.

¶ちょうど家に帰った時、田中さんから電話がかかってきました。(Chōdo ie ni kaetta *toki*, Tanaka san kara denwa ga kakatte kimashita.)

¶ [I] got a telephone call from [Miss] Tanaka **just as** [I] arrived home.

③[時期・季節・時代など]

③ [time, age, period, season]

¶この大きな木は、おじいさんが子供の時植えたのだそうです。(Kono ookina ki wa, ojiisan ga kodomo no *toki* ueta no da sōdesu.)

¶ I understand this big tree was planted by my grandfather **when** he was a child.

¶暑い時は物が腐りやすいから、気をつけてください。(Atsui *toki* wa mono ga kusariyasui kara, ki o tsukete kudasai.)

¶ Things easily go bad **during** hot weather so please be careful.

④ [場合]

¶非常のときはここから外に出てくだ さい。(Hijō no *toki* wa koko kara soto ni dete kudasai.)

¶わたしは困ったときにはいつも田中 先生に相談します。(Watashi wa komatta *toki* ni wa itsu mo Tanaka sensei ni sōdan shimasu.)

④ [time, occasion, case]

¶ **In case of** emergency please exit from here.

¶ I always consult Professor Tanaka **when** I have a problem.

ときどき 〔副〕

¶わたしはときどき映画を見に行きま す。(Watashi wa *tokidoki* eiga o mi ni ikimasu.)

¶田舎にいる母がときどき訪ねてきて くれます。(Inaka ni iru haha ga *tokidoki* tazunete kite kuremasu.)

tokidoki 〔adv〕 sometimes, once in a while, occasionally, at times

¶ I **sometimes** go to see a movie.

¶ **Once in a while** my mother comes from the country to visit me.

とく 解く 〔動Ⅰ〕

① [結んであったものをほどく]

¶ひもを解いて、箱を開けてみまし た。(Himo o *toite*, hako o akete mimashita.)

② [わからなかった筋道を明らかにし 疑問や問題の答えを見つける]

¶この問題を解いた人は手を挙げてく ださい。(Kono mondai o *toita* hito wa te o agete kudasai.)

toku 〔vI〕 untie, undo, unfasten; solve, work out

① [untie, undo, unfasten, loosen]

¶ [I] **unfastened** the string 〚twine, ete. 〛 and opened up the box.

② [solve, work out, answer]

¶ Will those who **have answered** this question please raise their hands.

とく 得 〔名、形動、～する〕

¶100円の物を 80 円で買ったので、 20 円の得をしました。(Hyakuen no mono o hachijūen de katta node, nijūen no *toku* o shimashita.)

¶これは安くていい品物ですから、 買ったほうが得ですよ。(Kore wa yasukute ii shinamono desu kara, katta hō ga *toku* desu yo.)

toku 〔n, adj-v, ～*suru*〕 profit, gain, advantage, benefit

¶ As I bought a 100-yen article for 80 yen, **I saved** 20 yen.

¶ Buying this merchandise **will be to your advantage** as it is inexpensive and of good quality.

⇔損 son

どく 毒 〔名〕

毒虫 (*doku*mushi) 毒へび (*doku*hebi)
毒ガス (*doku*gasu)

¶このきのこには毒があります。
(Kono kinoko ni wa *doku* ga arimasu.)

doku 〔n〕 **poison**

a **poisonous** insect // a **poisonous**
snake // a **toxic** gas

¶ This mushroom **is poisonous**.

とくい 得意 〔名、形動〕

① [自慢する様子]
¶山田さんは先日の試験の成績がよ
かったので、得意になっています。
(Yamada san wa senjitsu no shiken no
seiseki ga yokatta node, *tokui* ni natte
imasu.)
② [上手にできる]
¶わたしは物理や化学より生物のほう
が得意です。(Watashi wa butsuri ya
kagaku yori seibutsu no hō ga *tokui*
desu.)

tokui 〔n, adj-v〕 **vanity, boasting;
one's forte, one's strong point**

① [vanity, boasting, pride]
¶ [Mr.] Yamada **is suffering a swelled
head** over [his] good mark on the exam
last week.

② [one's forte, strong point, specialty]
¶ **I'm better** at biology than physics or
chemistry.

とくちょう 特徴 〔名〕

¶あの人の字には特徴があるので、す
ぐわかります。(Ano hito no ji ni wa
tokuchō ga aru node, sugu wakarimasu.)
¶彼の顔の特徴はよく覚えていません
が、確か目の大きい人だったと思いま
す。(Kare no kao no *tokuchō* wa yoku
oboete imasen ga, tashika me no ookii hito
datta to omoimasu.)

tokuchō 〔n〕 **special feature,
characteristic, trait**

¶ [He] has a **distinctive** handwriting
easily identifiable as [his].

¶ I don't remember **the particular
features** of his face but I think he had
large eyes.

とくに 特に 〔副〕

¶田中さんはいろいろなスポーツがで
きますが、特にテニスが上手です。
(Tanaka san wa iroiro na supōtsu ga
dekimasu ga, *tokuni* tenisu ga jōzu desu.)

tokuni 〔adv〕 **especially,
particularly, in particular**

¶ [Mr.] Tanaka can play several
different sports but [he] is **especially**
good at tennis.

¶わたしは果物の中で特にりんごが好きです。（Watashi wa kudamono no naka de *tokuni* ringo ga suki desu.）

¶ Among fruits, I **particularly** like apples.

とくべつ 特別 〔形動、〜の〕

tokubetsu 〔adj-v, 〜no〕 **special, extraordinary, uncommon, exceptional**

¶二、三日の旅行ですから、特別な準備はいりません。（Ni, sannichi no ryokō desu kara, *tokubetsu* na junbi wa irimasen.）

¶ It's only a two- or three-day trip so no **special** preparations are necessary.

¶ここは特別の部屋ですから、一般の人は使用できません。（Koko wa *tokubetsu* no heya desu kara, ippan no hito wa shiyō dekimasen.）

¶ This is a **special** room not for use by the general public.

どくりつ 独立 〔名、〜する〕

dokuritsu 〔n, 〜*suru*〕 **independence, freedom**

独立国（*dokuritsu*koku）独立運動（*dokuritsu*-undō）独立戦争（*dokuritsu*-sensō）

a **sovereign** nation, an **independent** state // an **independence** movement // the American **Revolution**; a war for **independence**

¶わたしたちは民族独立のために戦いました。（Watashitachi wa minzoku-*dokuritsu* no tame ni tatakaimashita.）

¶ We fought for **self-determination**.

¶あの人は独立心が強いです。（Ano hito wa *dokuritsu*shin ga tsuyoi desu.）

¶ [He] has a strong spirit of **independence** 〚He is a very **independent** person〛.

とけい 時計 〔名〕

tokei 〔n〕 **clock, watch, timepiece**

腕時計（ude*dokei*）柱時計（hashira-*dokei*）置時計（oki*dokei*）目覚まし時計（mezamashi-*dokei*）

wrist**watch** // wall **clock** // table **clock**, mantel **clock** // alarm **clock**

¶この時計は5分進んでいますよ。（Kono *tokei* wa gofun susunde imasu yo.）

¶ This **clock** 〚**watch**〛 is five minutes fast.

とける 溶ける 〔動Ⅱ〕
① 〔液体の中に他の物が入り全体が液体のようになる〕

tokeru 〔vⅡ〕 **dissolve; melt, fuse**
① 〔dissolve〕

¶砂糖は水に溶けます。（Satō wa mizu ni *tokemasu*.）

¶ Sugar **dissolves** in water.

②[金属が熱せられて液体のようになる]

②[melt, fuse]

¶鉄をつくる工場で溶けた鉄を初めて見ました。（Tetsu o tsukuru kōjō de *toketa* tetsu o hajimete mimashita.）

¶ [I] first saw **molten** iron at a steel plant.

とける 解ける〔動Ⅱ〕

tokeru 〔vII〕 **come loose, untied, undone; be solved, be resolved, work out; melt, thaw, run**

①[結んであったものがほどける]

①[come loose, untied, undone]

¶靴のひもが解けないように、きつく結びました。（Kutsu no himo ga *tokenai* yō ni, kitsuku musubimashita.）

¶ [I] tied [my] shoelaces tightly so they **wouldn't come undone**.

②[わからない筋道が明らかになり問題の答えが見つかる]

②[be solved, be resolved, work out]

なぞが解ける（nazo ga *tokeru*）

a puzzle **is solved, find the answer to a puzzle**

③[固体が液体になる]

③[melt, thaw, run]

¶春になって、雪が解けてきました。（Haru ni natte, yuki ga *tokete* kimashita.）

¶ The snow **has melted** with the coming of spring〖The snow **melted** with the coming of spring〗.

どこ〔代〕

doko 〔pron〕 **where; what place, whereabouts**

①[話し手にとって不明な所を表す]

①[where]

¶〔どこが玄関ですか。〕（*Doko* ga genkan desu ka?）「あそこが玄関です。」（Asoko ga genkan desu.）

¶ "**Where** is the entryway?"
"It's over there."

¶「あなたの学校はどこにありますか。」（Anata no gakkō wa *doko* ni arimasu ka?）「わたしの学校は京都にあります。」（Watashi no gakkō wa Kyōto ni arimasu.）

¶ "**Where** is your school?"
"It's in Kyoto."

¶「あなたの国はどこですか。」（Anata no kuni wa *doko* desu ka?）「わたしの国は日本です。」（Watashi no kuni wa Nihon desu.）

¶ "**What** country are you from?"
"I am from Japan."

¶「あなたはどこの大学に行っていますか。」（Anata wa *doko* no daigaku ni itte imasu ka？）「わたしはA大学に行っています。」（Watashi wa Ē-daigaku ni itte imasu.）

¶ "**What** university do you go to?"
"I go to University A."

¶どこでもいいから、遊びに行きましょう。（*Doko* demo ii kara, asobi ni ikimashō.）

¶ Let's go out somewhere, **anywhere**.

¶わたしは、今日は、どこへも行かずに一日じゅう勉強しようと思っています。（Watashi wa kyō wa, *doko* e mo ikazu ni ichinichijū benkyō shiyō to omotte imasu.）

¶ I'm planning to study all day today without going **anywhere**.

*助詞「でも（demo）」がつくと全面的な肯定を表す。また、助詞「も（mo）」がつくと、全面的な肯定または全面的な否定を表す。

*_Doko demo_ (anywhere, everywhere) is affirmative in meaning. _Doko mo_ (anywhere, everywhere; nowhere) can be affirmative or negative depending on the context.

②[話し手にとって当面するものごとの不明な点・部分・範囲・状態などを表す]

② [what place, whereabouts]

¶「昨日はどこまで勉強しましたか。」（Kinō wa *doko* made benkyō shimashita ka？）「50ページまで勉強しました。」（Gojippēji made benkyō shimashita.）

¶ "**How far** did [you] study yesterday?"
"[We] studied up to page 50."

¶「顔色がよくありませんね。どこか悪いのですか。」（Kaoiro ga yoku arimasen ne. *Doko* ka warui no desu ka？）「今朝から胃が痛いのです。」（Kesa kara i ga itai no desu.）

¶ "You look pale. Is **anything** the matter?"
"My stomach has been hurting since this morning."

¶あなたの研究はどこまで進んでいますか。（Anata no kenkyū wa *doko* made susunde imasuka？）

¶ **How far** have you progressed in your research?

⇒ここ **koko** そこ **soko** あそこ **asoko**

610

とこや　床屋〔名〕

¶床屋へ行って髪を短く切ってもらいました。(*Tokoya* e itte kami o mijikaku kitte moraimashita.)

＊「理髪店（rihatsuten）」とも言う。

ところ　所〔名〕

① [場所]

¶どこか景色のいい所へ旅行に行きたいです。(Doko ka keshiki no ii *tokoro* e ryokō ni ikitai desu.)

¶眼鏡を置いた所を忘れてしまいました。(Megane o oita *tokoro* o wasurete shimaimashita.)

② [ものの存在する場所、その近く]

¶門の所で待っています。(Mon no *tokoro* de matte imasu.)

¶郵便局の所で待っていてください。(Yūbinkyoku no *tokoro* de matte ite kudasai.)

③ [人の存在する場所・家庭・その人のもと]

¶昨日、山田さんは上田さんの所に泊まりました。(Kinō, Yamada san wa Ueda san no *tokoro* ni tomarimashita.)

¶授業が終わったら、先生の所へ行ってください。(Jugyō ga owattara, sensei no *tokoro* e itte kudasai.)

④ [住所]

¶この紙にお所とお名前をお書きください。(Kono kami ni o*tokoro* to onamae o okaki kudasai.)

⑤ [部分、点]

tokoya 〔n〕 **barber, barbershop**

¶I went to **the barber** and got a haircut.

＊Another word for "barbershop" is *rihatsiaen*.

tokoro 〔n〕 **place, spot; one's home, where one is; one's address; point, section; time, moment**

① [place, spot]

¶I want to take a trip **somewhere** with good scenery.

¶[I] have forgotten **where** [I] put [my] glasses.

② [where something is or near there]

¶[He] is waiting **at** the gate.

¶Please wait **at** the post office.

③ [one's home, where one is]

¶[Mr.] Yamada stayed at [Mr.] Ueda's **place** last night.

¶Please go see **your teacher** after class is over.

④ [one's address]

¶Please write your name and **address** on this paper.

⑤ [point, section, part]

¶わからないところがあったらきいて
ください。(Wakaranai *tokoro* ga attara
kiite kudasai.)

¶何でもすぐにあきてしまうのがあな
たの悪いところです。(Nan demo sugu
ni akite shimau no ga anata no warui
tokoro desu.)

⑥ [ある動作・作用がこれから起こる
という状態にあることを表す]

¶今、出かけるところです。(Ima,
dekakeru *tokoro* desu.)

¶これから御飯を食べるところです。
(Kore kara gohan o taberu *tokoro* desu.)

*「動詞（連体の形）＋ところ
(tokoro)」の形で使う。

⑦ [ある動作・作用が行われた直後の
状態であることを表す]

¶会議は今始まったところです。
(Kaigi wa ima hajimatta *tokoro* desu.)

¶父は今家を出たところです。(Chichi
wa ima ie o deta *tokoro* desu.)

*「動詞（たの形）＋ところ
(tokoro)」の形で使う。

⑧ [ある動作・作用が継続中の状態で
あることを表す]

¶わたしは今日本語の勉強をしている
ところです。(Watashi wa ima Nihongo
no benkyō o shite iru *tokoro* desu.)

¶田中さんは先生の所に話しに行って
いるところです。(Tanaka san wa
sensei no tokoro ni hanashi ni itte iru
tokoro desu.)

*「動詞（ての形）＋いる (iru) ＋と
ころ (tokoro)」の形で使う。

¶ Please ask if there's **something** you
don't understand.

¶ Becoming quickly bored is a bad
point of yours.

⑥ [indicates that something is on the
point of happening]

¶ [I]'m **just about** to go out now.

¶ [We]'re **just about** to eat at the
moment.

*Used in the pattern "verb (dictionary
form) + *tokoro*."

⑦ [indicates that something has just
happened]

¶ The meeting has **just now** begun.

¶ My father **just** left the house **a
moment ago**.

Used in the pattern "verb (-ta* form) +
tokoro."

⑧ [indicates that something is in the
course of taking place]

¶ I'm studying my Japanese **just now**.

¶ [Mr.] Tanaka is **now** talking with
[his] teacher (literally, has gone to talk
with his teacher and is **now** talking
with him).

Used in the pattern "verb (-te* form) +
iru + *tokoro*."

ところが〔接〕

¶妹はすぐ帰ると言って出かけました。ところが、3時間もたつのにまだ帰りません。(Imōto wa sugu kaeru to itte dekakemashita. *Tokoroga*, sanjikan mo tatsu noni mada kaerimasen.)

¶このおもちゃはたいへん高かったです。ところが、少し使っただけでもう壊れてしまいました。(Kono omocha wa taihen takakatta desu. *Tokoroga*, sukoshi tsukatta dake de mō kowarete shimaimashita.)

＊前のことがらを受けて、そのことがらに反するようなことがらをあとに続けるときに使う。普通あとに「〜なさい（〜nasai）」などの命令、「〜てください（〜te kudasai）」などの依頼、「〜う（よう）（〜u [yō]）」などの意志などの言い方は来ない。

ところで〔接〕

¶ところで、最近田中さんに会いましたか。(*Tokorode*, saikin Tanaka san ni aimashita ka?)

¶毎日いいお天気ですね。ところで、奥さんの御病気はいかがですか。(Mainichi ii otenki desu ne. *Tokorode*, okusan no gobyōki wa ikaga desu ka?)

＊話題を変えるときなどに使う。

とざん　登山〔名、〜する〕

¶山田さんの趣味は登山です。(Yamada san no shumi wa *tozan* desu.)

¶天気の悪いときに登山するのは危険です。(Tenki no warui toki ni *tozan* suru no wa kiken deshita.)

tokoroga 〔conj〕 **however, but, and yet, on the contrary**

¶ When my (younger) sister went out, she said she'd be back soon. **However,** it's been three hours and she hasn't gotten back yet.

¶ This toy was very expensive. **Nevertheless** it broke after being used only a little while.

＊ Used when stating something opposed to what came earlier. Usually it is not followed by orders with *-nasai*, requests with *-te kudasai*, statements of intent with *-ō* 〖*-yō*〗 etc.

tokorode 〔conj〕 **by the way, incidentally**

¶ **By the way,** have you seen [Mr.] Tanaka recently?

¶ We've been enjoying nice weather, haven't we? **And** how is your wife's illness?

＊ Used when changing the subject, etc.

tozan 〔n, 〜*suru*〕 **mountain climbing, an ascent of a mountain**

¶ [Mr.] Yamada's hobby is **mountain climbing**.

¶ It is dangerous **to go mountain climbing** in bad weather.

とし 年〔名〕

① [1年]
年の初め (toshi no hajime) 年の暮れ
(toshi no kure) 年が明ける (toshi ga
akeru)
¶ 1月1日に新しい年を迎えます。
(Ichigatsu tsuitachi ni atarashii toshi o
mukaemasu.)
② [年齢]
年を取る (toshi o toru) 年上
(toshiue) 年下 (toshishita)
¶ 兄はわたしより三つ年が上です。
(Ani wa watashi yori mittsu toshi ga ue
desu.)

としより 年寄り〔名〕

¶ 年寄りには席を譲りましょう。
(Toshiyori ni wa seki o yuzurimashō.)
→ 老人 rōjin

としょかん 図書館〔名〕

¶ 授業のないときには、図書館へ行っ
て勉強します。 (Jugyō no nai toki ni
wa, toshokan e itte benkyō shimasu.)

とじる 閉じる〔動II〕

目を閉じる (me o tojiru)
¶ 本を閉じて、黒板の方を見てくださ
い。 (Hon o tojite, okuban no hō o mite
kudasai.)
⇔ 開ける akeru
⇒ 開く hiraku

とち 土地〔名〕

¶ 山田さんは学校のそばに土地を買っ
て、家を建てました。 (Yamada san wa
gakkō no soba ni tochi o katte, ie o
tatemashita.)

---

toshi 〔n〕 a year; age, years old

① [a year]
the beginning of **the year** //
the **year**-end // a new **year** begins

¶ [We] welcome the New **Year** on
January 1.

② [age, years old]
to age, grow older // (someone) older //
(someone) younger

¶ My (older) brother is three **years**
older than me.

toshiyori 〔n〕 an old person, the
aged

¶ One should offer one's seat to **the
elderly**.

toshokan 〔n〕 library

¶ When [I] don't have class [I] go to
the library and study.

tojiru 〔vII〕 shut, close

close one's eyes
¶ Please **close** your books and look at
the blackboard.

tochi 〔n〕 land, piece of land

¶ [Mr.] Yamada bought **land** near the
school and built a house there.

とちゅう 途中〔名〕

¶ 昨日、家へ帰る途中本屋に寄って、この本を買ってきました。（Kinō, ie e kaeru *tochū* hon'ya ni yotte, kono hon o katte kimashita.）

¶ 郵便局は学校へ行く途中にあります。（Yūbinkyoku wa gakkō e iku *tochū* ni arimasu.）

どちら〔代〕

① [話し手にとって不明な方向を表す]

¶「病院はどちらでしょうか。」（Byōin wa *dochira* deshō ka？）「病院はあちらです。」（Byōin wa achira desu.）

¶「東京はどちらですか。」（Tōkyō wa *dochira* desu ka？）「東京はこちらです。」（Tōkyō wa kochira desu.）

＊「どっち（dotchi）」とも言うが、「どちら（dochira）」のほうが丁寧な言葉である。

② [話し手にとって不明な方向にある所を表す]

¶「あなたのおうちはどちらですか。」（Anata no ouchi wa *dochira* desu ka？）「わたしのうちは新宿です。」（Watashi no uchi wa Shinjuku desu.）

¶「あなたはどちらの国からおいでになりましたか。」（Anata wa *dochira* no kuni kara oide ni narimashita ka？）「わたしは日本から来ました。」（Watashi wa Nihon kara kimashita.）

＊「どこ（doko）」よりも丁寧な言葉。

③ [話し手にとって不明な人を表す]

¶ 失礼ですが、どちら様ですか。（Shitsurei desu ga, *dochira* sama desu ka？）

＊いつも「どちら様（dochirasama）」の形で使う。

---

tochū 〔n〕 **on the way, midway**

¶ **On** [my] **way** home yesterday [I] stopped by at the bookstore and bought this book.

¶ There is a post office **on the way** to school.

dochira 〔pron〕 **where; who; which**

① [which way, where]

¶ "**Which way** is the hospital?" "It's that way."

¶ "**Which direction** is Tokyo?" "It's this direction."

＊*Dotchi* is also used, but *dochira* is more polite.

② [where]

¶ "**Where** do you live?" "I live in Shinjuku."

¶ "**What** country are you from?" "I am from Japan."

＊*Dochira* is more polite than *doko*.

③ [who]

¶ Might I ask **your name**, please (literally, **Who** are you)?

＊Always used in the pattern *dochira sama*.

*「だれ（dare）」と言うよりも丁寧な言い方である。「どなた（donata）」「どなた様（donata sama）」などとも言う。

④ [二つのものごとの中から一つのものを選ぶときに使う]

¶「上田さんと中村さんとどちらが背が高いですか。」（Ueda san to Nakamura san to *dochira* ga sei ga takai desu ka？）「上田さんのほうが、中村さんより背が高いです。」（Ueda san no hō ga, Nakamura san yori sei ga takai desu.）

¶「あなたは魚と肉とどちらが好きですか。」（Anata wa sakana to niku to *dochira* ga suki desu ka？）「わたしはどちらも好きです。」（Watashi wa *dochira* mo suki desu.）

¶「作文を書くのに題は書かなくてもいいですか。」（Sakubun o kaku no ni dai wa kakanakute mo ii desu ka？）「書いても書かなくてもいいです。どちらでもいいです。」（Kaite mo kakanakute mo ii desu. *Dochira* demo ii desu.）

*助詞「でも（demo）」がつくと、全面的な肯定を表す。助詞「も（mo）」がつくと、全面的な肯定または全面的な否定を表す。

*「どっち（dotchi）」とも言うが、「どちら（dochira）」のほうが丁寧な言葉である。
⇒こちら **kochira**　そちら **sochira**　あちら **achira**

とっきゅう　特急〔名〕

¶あの駅は急行はとまりますが、特急は、とまりません。（Ano eki wa kyūkō

Dochira is more polite than *dare*. *Donata* and *donata sama* are also used as polite forms of *dare*.

④ [which, which one]

¶ "**Who** is taller, [Mr.] Ueda or [Mr.] Nakamura?"
"[Mr.] Ueda is taller than [Mr.] Nakamura."

¶ "**Which** do you like better, fish or meat?"
"I like **both of them**."

¶ "Is it all right not to write down the title when writing a composition?"
"You may write it down or not write it down. **Either** will be fine."

Dochira demo (either, whichever) is affirmative in meaning. *Dochira mo* (both, either; neither) can be affirmative or negative depending on the context.

Dotchi is also used, but *dochira* is more polite.

tokkyū 〔n〕 a limited express train
¶ The express stops at that station but **the limited express** doesn't.

wa tomarimasu ga, *tokkū* wa
tomarimasen.)

とつぜん 突然 〔副〕

¶突然、大きな音がしたので、びっくりしました。(*Totsuzen*, ookina oto ga shita node, bikkuri shimashita.)

¶夜遅く突然友達が訪ねてきました。(Yoru osoku *totsuzen* tomodachi ga tazunete kimashita.)

どっち〔代〕 ☞どちら dochira

とって〔連〕

¶それはわたしにとって大事な問題です。(Sore wa watashi ni *totte* daiji na mondai desu.)

¶あなたにとって成功とはいったい何ですか。(Anata ni *totte* seikō to wa ittai nan desu ka?)

＊いつも「〜にとって（〜ni totte）」の形で使う。

とても〔副〕

①[非常に]

¶この料理はとてもおいしいですね。(Kono ryōri wa *totemo* oishii desu ne.)

¶電車はとてもこんでいました。(Densha wa *totemo* konde imashita.)

②[どんなにしても]

¶こんなに重い荷物は、とても一人では持てません。(Konna ni omoi nimotsu wa, *totemo* hitori de wa motemasen.)

¶山田さんはとても50歳には見えません。(Yamada san wa *totemo* gojissai ni wa miemasen.)

---

totsuzen 〔adv〕 **suddenly, all at once, unexpectedly**

¶[I] was startled by the **sudden** loud noise.

¶Late at night a friend paid [me] a **surprise** visit.

dotchi 〔pron〕 ☞**dochira**

totte 〔compd〕 **for, to, with**

¶That is an important matter **to** me.

¶What is success **for** you 〚What is your idea of success〛?

＊Always used in the pattern "〜 *ni totte*."

totemo 〔adv〕 **very, extremely, terribly; by no means, utterly**

① [very, extremely, terribly]

¶This dish is **very** good.

¶The train was **terribly** crowded.

② [by no means, utterly]

¶A heavy package 〚load〛 like this **can't possibly** be carried by one person 〚I **can't possibly** carry something so heavy by myself〛.

¶[Mr.] Yamada doesn't look **at all** like he's 50 years old.

*あとに打ち消しの言葉や否定的な意味の言葉が来る。

*Followed by words or expressions negative in form or sense.

とどく 届く〔動Ⅰ〕

todoku 〔vI〕 **reach, get to; arrive, be received**

① [あるものがある場所に達する]
¶このたなは高すぎて手が届きません。(Kono tana wa takasugite te ga *todokimasen*.)

① [reach, get to, carry to]
¶This shelf is too high for me **to reach**.

¶どんなに大きな声を出しても、川の向こうまでは届かないでしょう。(Donna ni ookina koe o dashite mo, kawa no mukō made wa *todokanai* deshō.)

¶No matter how loud one shouts, one's voice probably **won't carry** to the other side of the river.

② [品物などが送り先に着く]
¶今朝、母から小包が届きました。(Kesa, haha kara kozutsumi ga *todokimashita*.)

② [arrive, be received]
¶A package from my mother **came** this morning.

とどける 届ける〔動Ⅱ〕

todokeru 〔vII〕 **deliver, send, forward**

¶あなたに頼まれた手紙は、昨日中村さんに届けました。(Anata ni tanomareta tegami wa, kinō Nakamura san ni *todokemashita*.)

¶You asked me to give [Mr.] Nakamura a letter. **I gave** it to [him] yesterday.

¶デパートで買った家具はあした届けてくれます。(Depāto de katta kagu wa ashita *todokete* kuremasu.)

¶The furniture [I] bought at the department store **will be delivered** tomorrow.

どなた〔代〕

donata 〔pron〕 **who, whom**

¶あの方はどなたですか。(Ano kata wa *donata* desuka?)

¶**Who** is that person?

¶失礼ですが、どなた様でいらっしゃいますか。(Shitsureidesu ga, *donata* sama de irasshaimasu ka?)

¶Excuse me, but may I ask **your name** please (literally, **who** are you)?

*「だれ（dare）」の丁寧な言い方。

*_Donata_ is a more polite form of *dare*.

となり　隣〔名〕

¶兄は今隣の部屋で本を読んでいます。(Ani wa ima *tonari* no heya de hon o yonde imasu.)

¶田中さんの隣にいる人はだれですか。(Tanaka san no *tonari* ni iru hito wa dare desu ka?)

とにかく〔副〕

¶結果はどうなるかわかりませんが、とにかくがんばってやってみましょう。(Kekka wa dō naru ka wakarimasen ga, *tonikaku* ganbatte yatte mimashō.)

¶山田さんはうちにいないかもしれませんが、とにかく行ってみましょう。(Yamada san wa uchi ni inai ka mo shiremasen ga, *tonikaku* itte mimashō.)

⇒ともかく **tomokaku**

どの〔連体〕

どの人（*dono* hito）どの方（*dono* kata）

¶「中村さんのはどのかばんですか。」(Nakamura san no wa *dono* kaban desu ka?)「あの大きなかばんです。」(Ano ookina kaban desu.)

¶お金はどのくらい持って行けばいいでしょうか。(Okane wa *dono* kurai motte ikeba ii deshō ka?)

¶「どのくらい日本語を習っていますか。」(*Dono* kurai Nihongo o na-ratte imasu ka?)「約1年です。」(Yaku ichinen desu.)

¶どの本でもいいですから、読みたい本をお持ちなさい。(*Dono* hon demo ii desu kara, yomitai hon o omochinasai.)

tonari 〔n〕 next, next-door, neighboring

¶My (older) brother is presently reading a book in the **next** room.

¶Who is the person **next to** [Mr.] Tanaka?

tonikaku 〔adv〕 anyway, at any rate, in any case

¶[I] don't know how it will turn out but **at any rate** [I]'ll take a try at it.

¶[Miss] Yamada might not be home, but let's go and see if [she] is **anyway**.

dono 〔attrib〕 which, what who, **which** one // who, **which** one (polite)

¶"**Which** suitcase 〚briefcase, bag, etc. is yours, [Miss] Nakamura 〚**Which** suitcase is Miss Nakamura's〛?" "It's that large one over there."

¶**How much** money should [I] take with [me]?

¶"**How long** have you been studying Japanese?" "About one year."

¶Take a book you would like to read, **any one** of them.

¶どの問題もみんな難しかったです。
(*Dono* mondai mo minna muzuka-shikatta
desu.)

＊話し手にとって不明なものごと・数
量・程度などを表すのに使う。「どの
(dono) ＋名詞＋でも (demo)」の形は
全面的な肯定を表す。「どの (dono)
＋名詞＋も (mo)」の形は、全面的な
肯定または全面的な否定を表す。

⇒この **kono**　その **sono**　あの **ano**

¶ **All** of the problems were difficult.

＊The pattern "*dono* + noun + *demo*"
(whichever, any, every) is affirmative
in meaning. The pattern "*dono* + noun
+ *mo*" (every; no, none) can be
affirmative or negative depending on
the context.

とびだす　飛び出す〔動 I〕

¶子供が急に道路へ飛び出しました。
(Kodomo ga kyū ni dōro e
tobidashimashita.)
¶兄は会社に遅れそうになったので、
あわてて家を飛び出していきました。
(Ani wa kaisha ni okuresō ni natta node,
awatete ie o *tobidashite* ikimashita.)

tobidasu 〔vI〕 **run out, rush out;
jump out**

¶ A child suddenly **ran out** 〖has
suddenly **run out**〗 into the road.

¶ In danger of being late to work, my
(older) brother hurriedly **rushed out** of
the house.

とぶ　飛ぶ〔動 I〕

¶白い鳥が海の上を飛んでいます。
(Shiroi tori ga umi no ue o *tonde* imasu.)
¶飛行機が西の方へ飛んでいきまし
た。(Hikōki ga nishi no hō e *tonde*
ikimashita.)

tobu 〔vI〕 **fly, take to the air**

¶ White birds **are flying** over the ocean.

¶ The airplane **flew off** into the west.

トマト〔名〕

トマトを作る (*tomato* o tsukuru)　トマ
トがなる (*tomato* ga naru)

tomato 〔n〕 **tomato**

grow **tomatoes** // **a tomato plant** bears
fruit

とまる　泊まる〔動 I〕

①[宿をとる]
¶日本を旅行するときは、ホテルでは
なく旅館に泊まることにしています。
(Nihon o ryokō suru toki wa, hoteru de
wa naku ryokan ni *tomaru* koto ni shite
imasu.)

tomaru 〔vI〕 **stay the night,
lodge; lie at anchor**

① [stay the night, lodge]
¶ When [I] am traveling in Japan I
make it a practice **to stay** in Japanese-
style inns rather than hotels.

② [船が港に入っている]
¶港には日本の船だけでなく外国の船も泊まっています。(Minato ni wa Nihon no fune dake de naku gaikoku no fune mo *tomatte* imasu.)

とまる 止まる [動 I]

① [動いたり進んだりしているものなどが動かなくなる]
¶車が山田さんの家の前で止まりました。(Kuruma ga Yamada san no ie no mae de *tomarimashita*.)
¶あの時計は止まっていますよ。(Ano tokei wa *tomatte* imasu yo.)
② [続いている状態が終わりになったり続くはずのものが一時続かなくなったりする]
¶あしたの午後10時から水道の水が止まるそうです。(Ashita no gogo jūji kara suidō no mizu ga *tomaru* sō desu.)
¶薬をつけてしばらくすると、足の血が止まりました。(Kusuri o tsukete shibaraku suru to, ashi no chi ga *tomarimashita*.)
③ [鳥や虫が何かにつかまって休む]
¶あの木に止まっている白い鳥は何という鳥ですか。(Ano ki ni *tomatte* iru shiroi tori wa nan to iu tori desu ka？)
¶ちょうちょうが赤い花に止まっています。(Chōchō ga akai hana ni *tomatte* imasu.)

とめる 止める [動 II]

① [動いたり進んだりしているものなどを動かなくする]

② [lie at anchor]
¶ There are foreign as well as Japanese ships **at anchor** in the harbor.

tomaru 〔vI〕 stop, halt; stop, cease, be suspended; perch

① [stop, halt; something stops moving]

¶ The automobile 〖taxi〗 **stopped** in front of [Mr.] Yamada's house.

¶ That clock 〖watch〗 **has stopped running**.
② [stop, cease, be suspended; a state ends or something stops temporarily]

¶ I hear that water service **will be suspended** from ten o'clock tomorrow night.
¶ [My] leg 〖foot〗 **stopped** bleeding a little while after [I] put the medication 〖ointment, etc.〗 on it.

③ [perch]
¶ What is the name of the white bird **in** that tree over there?

¶ A butterfly **is alight** on the red flower.

tomeru 〔vII〕 stop, bring to a stop; stop, be off; dissuade, hold back, stop, forbid

① [stop, bring to a stop, turn off; stop something moving]

¶手を挙げて、タクシーを止めました。（Te o agete, takushii o *tomemashita*.)

¶ [I] **stopped** a taxi by raising [my] hand.

¶その機械を止めてください。（Sono kikai o *tomete* kudasai.)

¶ Please **stop** that machine.

②[続いている状態などを終わりにさせたり続くはずのものを一時的に続かなくさせる]

② [stop, be off; bring a condition to a close or temporarily stop something]

¶歯の痛みを止める薬がありますか。（Ha no itami o *tomeru* kusuri ga arimasu ka?）

¶ Do you have anything to take **to relieve** a toothache?

¶あした、工事のために電気を一時止めます。（Ashita, kōji no tame ni denki o ichiji *tomemasu*.)

¶ The electricity **will be off** for a time tomorrow due to construction.

③[何かをしていたりこれからしようとするのをやめさせる]

③ [dissuade, hold back, stop, forbid]

¶医者にたばこを止められました。（Isha ni tabako o *tomeraremashita*.)

¶ The doctor **forbid me to** smoke.

¶お母さんは子供のいたずらを止めました。（Okāsan wa kodomo no itazura o *tomemashita*.)

¶ The mother **stopped** her child from playing pranks.

¶酔った人が石を車に投げようとしたので、上田さんが止めました。（Yotta hito ga ishi o kuruma ni nageyō to shita node, Ueda san ga *tomemashita*.)

¶ [Mr.] Ueda **dissuaded** the drunk from throwing stones at cars.

とめる 留める〔動Ⅱ〕

tomeru〔vⅡ〕**fasten, put in place, fix**

¶姉がシャツのボタンを留めてくれました。（Ane ga shatsu no botan o *tomete* kuremashita.)

¶ My (older) sister **buttoned** my shirt for me.

¶その地図が壁から落ちないようにしっかり留めておいてください。（Sono chizu ga kabe kara ochinai yō ni shikkari *tomete* oite kudasai.)

¶ Please **fix** that map firmly onto the wall so it won't fall down.

とめる 泊める〔動Ⅱ〕

¶昨晩は雨がひどく降ったので、山田さんの家に泊めてもらいました。
（Sakuban wa ame ga hidoku futta node, Yamada san no ie ni *tomete* moraimashita.）

とも 友〔名〕 ☞友達 tomodachi

-とも〔尾〕

① [あるものが全部そうであることを表す]
¶わたしたち夫婦は二人とも甘いものが大好きです。（Watashitachi fūfu wa futari*tomo* amai mono ga daisuki desu.）
¶わたしたちの学校はテニスの試合で男女とも優勝しました。（Watashitachi no gakkō wa tenisu no shiai de danjo*tomo* yūshō shimashita.）

② [だいたいの限界を表す]
¶昨日、ここに集まった人は少なくとも 30 名以上でした。（Kinō, koko ni atsumatta hito wa sukunaku*tomo* sanjūmei ijō deshita.）
¶遅くとも10時までには帰るつもりです。（Osoku*tomo* jūji made ni wa kaeru tsumori desu.）

ともかく〔副〕

① [あることは一応別にして]
¶日本人ならともかく、外国人が日本語を間違えるのはあたりまえでしょう。（Nihonjin nara *tomokaku*, gaikokujin ga Nihongo o machigaeru no wa atarimae deshō.）

---

tomeru 〚vⅡ〛 **lodge, give shelter, put up for the night**

¶ As it was raining so hard last evening, **I stayed the night** at [Mr.] Yamada's.

tomo 〚n〛 ☞**tomodachi**

-tomo 〚suf〛 **both, all**

① [both, all, neither]

¶ My husband 〚wife〛 and I **both** have a sweet tooth.

¶ Our school won **both** the men's and women's tennis matches.

② [indicates broad limits]
¶ **At the very least** there were over 30 persons gathered here yesterday.

¶ I plan to return home by ten o'clock **at the latest**.

tomokaku 〚adv〛 **setting aside, apart from; at any rate, in any case**

① [setting aside, apart from]
¶ **Leaving** the Japanese themselves **out of the question**, it is only to be expected that foreigners should make mistakes in Japanese.

¶成功するかしないかはともかく、一
生懸命努力してみなさい。(Seikō
suru ka shinai ka wa *tomokaku*,
isshōkenmei doryoku shite minasai.)

*普通「〜はともかく(〜wa
tomokaku)」「〜ならともかく(〜nara
tomokaku)」の形で使う。

②[問題はいろいろあるがひとまず次
のことはしようというような意味を表
す]

¶山田さんは行かないかもしれません
が、ともかく旅行のことは知らせてお
きました。(Yamada san wa ikanai ka
mo shiremasen ga, *tomokaku* ryokō no
koto wa shirasete okimashita.)

→とにかく **tonikaku**

ともだち 友達 〔名〕
友達になる (*tomodachi* ni naru)
¶わたしと田中さんとは親しい友達で
す。(Watashi to Tanaka san to wa
shitashii *tomodachi* desu.)

どよう(び) 土曜(日) 〔名〕

とり 鳥 〔名〕

鳥が鳴く (*tori* ga naku)
¶鳥がたくさん山の方へ飛んでいきま
す。(*Tori* ga takusan yama no hō e tonde
ikimasu.)

とりあげる 取り上げる 〔動Ⅱ〕

①[手に取って持ち上げる]
¶山田さんは机の上の新聞を取り上げ
て読み始めました。(Yamada san wa
tsukue no ue no shinbun o *toriagete*
yomihajimemashita.)

②[意見・申し出を採用・受理する]

¶ **Don't worry about** whether you will
succeed or not, but just do your best.

*Usually used in the patterns "〜*wa
tomokaku*" and "〜*nara tomokaku*."

② [at any rate, in any case, anyway]

¶ [Miss] Yamada might not be going
but **at any rate** I told [her] about the
trip.

tomodachi 〔n〕 friend
become **a friend** of, make **friends** with
¶ [Mr.] Tanaka and I are close **friends**.

doyō(bi) 〔n〕 Saturday

tori 〔n〕 bird, fowl; chicken,
poultry
a bird cries 〚peeps, honks, crows, etc.〛
¶ A flock of **birds** is flying toward the
mountains.

toriageru 〔vⅡ〕 take up, pick up;
accept, adopt; take away, seize
① [take up, pick up]
¶ [Mrs.] Yamada **picked up** the
newspaper on the desk and started to
read it.

② [accept, adopt, listen to]

¶会議でわたしの意見は取り上げられませんでした。(Kaigi de watashi no iken wa *toriageraremasen* deshita.)

③ [持っている物を奪い取る]

¶兄は妹の持っていたおもちゃを取り上げてしまいました。(Ani wa imōto no motte ita omocha o *toriagete* shimaimashita.)

¶ The meeting **rejected** my opinion.

③ [take away, seize, confiscate]

¶ The boy **took** a toy **away** from his younger sister.

とりあつかう　取り扱う〔動 I〕

¶外国へ送る小包は、大きな郵便局でなければ取り扱いません。(Gaikoku e okuru kozutsumi wa, ookina yūbinkyoku de nakereba *toriatsukaimasen*.)

¶郵便局では電報を取り扱っていますか。(Yūbinkyoku de wa denpō o *toriatsukatte* imasu ka?)

toriatsukau 〔vI〕 **treat, handle, deal with**

¶ Only larger post offices **handle** parcels being sent abroad.

¶ Does the post office **handle** telegrams?

とりかえる　取り替える〔動 II〕

¶シャツが汚れたので、新しいのに取り替えました。(Shatsu ga yogoreta node, atarashii no ni *torikaemashita*.)

¶ラジオの部品が壊れたので、新しいのに取り替えました。(Rajio no buhin ga kowareta node, atarashii no ni *torikaemashita*.)

torikaeru 〔vII〕 **exchange, change**

¶ [My] shirt was dirty so [I] **changed** into a clean one.

¶ The radio part was broken so **I replaced it** with a new one.

とりにく　鶏肉〔名〕

¶まず、鶏肉を食べやすい大きさに切ってください。(Mazu, *toriniku* o tabeyasui ōkisa ni kitte kudasai.)

toriniku 〔n〕 **chicken**

¶ To begin with, cut the chicken into individual portions.

どりょく　努力〔名、～する〕

努力家 (*doryoku*ka)

¶努力すれば、だれでも上手になれます。(*Doryoku* sureba, dare demo jōzu ni naremasu.)

doryoku 〔n, ～*suru*〕 **effort, endeavor; strive**

a hard worker, an industrious person

¶ Anyone can become good at it if they really **apply themselves**.

¶努力したので、いい成績がもらえました。(*Doryoku* shita node, ii seiseki ga moraemashita.)

¶ [He] was able to receive good grades because [he] **worked hard**.

とる 取る〔動Ⅰ〕

toru 〔vI〕 **take, take hold of; get, gather; obtain, win; engage, reserve; pick up, fetch; rob, steal; charge, ask; take, eat; obtain, extract; remove, take away**

① [手に持つ、握る、つかむ]

① [take, hold, take hold of]

¶山田さんは机の上の本を取って読み始めました。(Yamada san wa tsukue no ue no hon o *totte* yomihajimemashita.)

¶ [Mr.] Yamada **picked up** the book on the desk and started to read it.

¶すみませんが、そこの新聞を取ってくださいませんか。(Sumimasen ga, soko no shinbun o *totte* kudasaimasen ka?)

¶ Excuse me, but could you please **hand me** that newspaper?

② [自然にある物や栽培した物を得る]
貝を取る (kai o *toru*) 果物を取る (kudamono o *toru*)

② [get, gather, pick]
gather shells, **dig out** shellfish // **pick** fruit

¶今年は天気が悪くて、米はあまり取れませんでした。(Kotoshi wa tenkiga warukute, kome wa amari *toremasen* deshita.)

¶ The rice **crop is poor** this year due to bad weather.

③ [自分の努力によって何かを得る]

③ [obtain, win]

¶英語の試験で100点を取りました。(Eigo no shiken de hyakuten o *torimashita*.)

¶ [I] **got** a score of 100 on the English test.

¶田中さんは働きながら勉強を続けて、先生の資格を取りました。
(Tanaka san wa hatarakinagara benkyō o tsuzukete, sensei no shikaku o *torimashita*.)

¶ [Miss] Tanaka continued [her] studies while working and **earned** [her] teaching credentials.

④ [席や部屋を予約して得る]
ホテルの部屋を取る (hoteru no heyao *toru*)

④ [engage, reserve, book]
book a hotel room

626

¶あしたの芝居の席は取りました。
（Ashita no shibai no seki wa
torimashita.）

¶ [I]'ve **reserved** a seat for the play tomorrow.

⑤ [預けた物などを引き取る]

⑤ [pick up, fetch]

¶これから駅に預けた荷物を取りに行きます。（Kore kara eki ni azuketa nimotsu o *tori* ni ikimasu.）

¶ [I]'m going to go now **to pick up** the package 〖bags, items, etc.〗 [I] checked at the station.

⑥ [他人の物を盗む]

⑥ [rob, steal]

¶どろぼうにお金を取られてしまいました。（Dorobō ni okane o *torarete* shimaimashita.）

¶ A thief **took** my money.

⑦ [お金などを払わせる]
月謝を取る（gessha o *toru*） 税金を取る（zeikin o *toru*）

⑦ [charge, ask]
charge monthly tuition // **impose** a tax

¶昨日パーティーへ行ったら、会費を千円取られました。（Kinō pātii e ittara, kaihi o sen'en *toraremashita*.）

¶ [I] **had to pay** a thousand yen toward expenses at the party yesterday.

⑧ [食物などを体にとり入れる]
栄養を取る（eiyō o *toru*）

⑧ [take, eat]
eat nourishing food

¶おなかのぐあいが悪くて、昨日から食事を取っていません。（Onaka no guai ga warukute, kinō kara shokuji o *totte* imasen.）

¶ [I] **haven't eaten** since yesterday because of stomach trouble.

⑨ [ある物から有用な成分を抜き出す]

⑨ [obtain, extract]

¶塩は海水から取っています。（Shio wa kaisui kara *totte* imasu.）

¶ Salt **is obtained** from salt water.

¶これは何から取った油ですか。
（Kore wa nani kara *totta* abura desu ka？）

¶ What kind of oil is this (literally, From what has this oil **been extracted**)?

⑩ [必要ないものなどを取り除く]
痛みを取る（itami o *toru*） 熱を取る（netsu o *toru*） 疲れを取る（tsukare o *toru*）

⑩ [remove, take away]
relieve pain // **drive off** a fever // **relieve** fatigue

¶寝るときには眼鏡を取ります。
（Neru toki ni wa megane o *torimasu*.）

¶ [I] **take off** [my] glasses when [I] go to bed.

¶もうすぐ田の草を取らなければなりません。(Mō sugu ta no kusa o *toranakereba* narimasen.)

¶ Soon [we] will have **to weed** the rice field.

⑪ [年齢などを重ねる]

¶だれでも一年に一つずつ年を取ります。(Dare demo ichinen ni hitotsu zutsu toshi o *torimasu*.)

⑪ [age]

¶ Everyone **gets** a year **older** each year.

⑫ [ノートしたりメモをつけたりする]

ノートをとる(nōto o *toru*)

¶メモをとりながら先生の話を聞きました。(Memo o *torinagara* sensei no hanashi o kikimashita.)

⑫ [take (notes, etc.)]

take notes

¶ [I] listened to the professor and **took** notes on [his] talk.

とる 捕る 〔動Ⅰ〕

生け捕る(ike*doru*)

¶昨日捕った魚は池に入れてあります。(Kinō *totta* sakana wa ike ni iretearimasu.)

¶ねこがねずみを捕ってきました。(Neko ga nezumi o *totte* kimashita.)

toru 〔vt〕 **catch, take, seize**

capture alive

¶ The fish [we] **caught** yesterday are in the pond 〖pool〗.

¶ The cat brought back a mouse it **had caught**.

とる 撮る 〔動Ⅰ〕

写真を撮る(shashin o *toru*)

¶あそこで映画を撮っているから、行ってみましょう。(Asoko de eiga o *totte* iru kara, itte mimashō.)

toru 〔vt〕 **take (a picture), film**

take a photograph

¶ **They're filming** a movie over there—let's go watch.

どれ 〔感〕

¶どれ、見せてごらん。(*Dore*, misete goran.)

＊何かを見せてもらうときなどに相手に言う言葉。

dore 〔interj〕 **well, come, now**

¶ Let me see it, **will you?**

＊ Said when wanting to be shown something or the like.

どれ 〔代〕

¶「あなたの本はどれですか。」(Anata no hon wa *dore* desu ka?)「わたしの本はこれです。」(Watashi no hon wa kore desu.)

dore 〔pron〕 **which**

¶ **"Which** is your book?" "It's this one."

¶「東京の地図はどれですか。」
(Tōkyō no chizu wa *dore* desu ka？)「東京の地図はあれです。」(Tōkyō no chizu wa are desu.)

¶ "**Which** is a map of Tokyo?"
"It's that one."

¶どれでもあなたの好きなものを取りなさい。(*Dore* demo anata no suki na mono o torinasai.)

¶ Take **whichever** you like.

¶どれもみんな好きです。(*Dore* mo minna suki desu.)

¶ I like **all of them**.

¶どれもあまり好きではありません。(*Dore* mo amari suki de wa arimasen.)

¶ I don't like **any of them** very well.

＊普通、三つ以上のものごとの中から一つを選ぶときに使う。助詞「も(mo)」がつくと全面的な肯定または全面的な否定を表す。助詞「でも(demo)」がつくと全面的な肯定を表し、選択が自由であることを表す。
⇒これ kore　それ sore　あれ are

＊Usually used when choosing one out of three or more items. *Dore mo* (any, all, every; none, no) can be affirmative or negative in meaning depending on the context. *Doredemo* (any, any one, whichever) is affirmative in meaning; it indicates a freedom of choice.

とれる　撮れる〔動Ⅱ〕

toreru〔vⅡ〕**(a photograph)is taken, come out**

¶この写真はきれいに撮れていますね。(Kono shashin wa kirei ni *torete* imasu ne.)

¶ This photo **came out** well, didn't it?

とれる　取れる〔動Ⅱ〕

toreru〔vⅡ〕**be obtained, be yielded; be made from, yield; be relieved of; be interpreted; come off**

①[自然にある物や栽培した物が得られる]
りんごが取れる（ringo ga *toreru*）

①[be obtained, be yielded]

have a crop of apples, apples **are grown**

¶今年は米がたくさん取れて、農家の人たちも喜んでいるそうです。
(Kotoshi wa kome ga takusan *torete*, nōka no hitotachi mo yorokonde iru sōdesu.)

¶ I hear that the farmers are happy this year because of the large rice **crop**.

②[ある物から有用な成分を抽出できる]

②[be made from, yield]

629

¶海水から塩が取れます。(Kaisui kara shio ga *toremasu*.)

¶ Salt **is obtained** from salt water.

¶この花の種から油が取れますか。(Kono hana no tane kara abura ga *toremasu* ka?)

¶ **Can** oil **be extracted** from the seeds of this flower?

③ [必要ないものなどがなくなる]
熱が取れる (netsu ga *toreru*) 疲れが取れる (tsukare ga *toreru*)

③ [be relieved of]
one's fever **falls** // **be relieved of** one's fatigue

¶薬を飲んだら、傷の痛みが取れました。(Kusuri o nondara, kizu no itami ga *toremashita*.)

¶ The medicine [I] took **relieved** [me] of the pain from the wound.

④ [理解できる、解釈できる]
¶田中さんの返事は、行きたいともとれるし行きたくないとも取れます。(Tanaka san no henji wa, ikitai to mo *toreru*shi ikitaku nai to mo *toremasu*.)

④ [be interpreted, be taken]
¶ [Mr.] Tanaka's answer **can be taken to mean** either that [he] wants to go or that [he] doesn't want to go.

⑤ [ある物についていた物が離れて落ちる]
¶シャツのボタンが取れそうですよ。(Shatsu no botan ga *toresō* desu yo.)

⑤ [come off]

¶ The shirt button **is about to come off**.

¶子供が引っぱったので、人形の手が取れてしまいました。(Kodomo ga hippatta node, ningyō no te ga *torete* shimaimashita.)

¶ The arm of the doll **came off** when the child pulled on it.

どろぼう 〔名〕

dorobō 〔n〕 thief

¶留守中にどろぼうに入られました。(Rusuchū ni *dorobō* ni hairaremashita.)

¶ My home **was broken into** when no one was there.

どんどん 〔副〕

dondon 〔adv〕 rapidly, steadily

¶物価がどんどん上がっています。(Bukka ga *dondon* agatte imasu.)

¶ Prices are rising **rapidly**.

¶どんどん進むので、予習がたいへんです。(*Dondon* susumu node, yoshū ga taihen desu.)

¶ As [we] are moving ahead so **rapidly**, preparing [our] lessons is a real task.

＊「どんどんと (dondon to)」とも言う。

＊*Dondon to* is also used.

どんな〔連体〕

¶「あなたはどんなスポーツが好きで
すか。」(Anata wa *donna* supōtsu ga suki
desu ka?)「わたしはテニスがいちば
ん好きです。」(Watashi wa tenisu ga
ichiban suki desu.)

¶「山田さんは山でけがをしたそうで
す。」(Yamada san wa yama de kega o
shita sō desu.)「どんなぐあいなので
しょうか。」(*Donna* guai na no deshō
ka?)

¶おいしそうですね。どんな材料で作
りましたか。(Oishisō desu ne. *Donna*
zairyō de tsukurimashitaka?)

¶「どんな質問でもいいですか。」
(*Donna* shitsumon demo ii desu ka?)
「はい、どんな質問でもいいです。」
(Hai, *donna* shitsumon demo ii desu.)

¶あの人にきけば、どんなことでもわ
かります。(Ano hito ni kikeba, *donna*
koto demo wakarimasu.)

＊話し手にとって不明なものごとの内
容・状態などを表す。「どんな
(donna) ＋名詞＋でも (demo)」の形
で全面的な肯定を表す。

⇒こんな **konna** そんな **sonna**
あんな **anna**

どんなに〔副〕

① [ものごとの状態・数量などの程度
を強調して表すときに使う]

¶外国語が自由に話せたら、どんなに
いいでしょう。(Gaikokugo ga jiyū ni
hanasetara, *donna ni* ii deshō.)

---

donna 〔attrib〕 **what, what sort of,
what kind of**

¶ "**What** sports do you like?"
"I like tennis best."

¶ "I hear that [Mr.] Yamada was hurt in
the mountains."
"I wonder **how** [he] is."

¶ That dish looks very good. **What**
ingredients is it made from?

¶ "Is **whatever** question all right?"
"Yes, please ask **any** question at all."

¶ That person knows the answer to
anything you might ask.

＊The pattern "*donna* + noun + *demo*"
(any ～, every ～) is affirmative in
meaning. It indicates something
incompletely known to the speaker.

donna ni 〔adv〕 **how, to what
extent; however, no matter how**

① [how, to what extent, how much]

¶ **How** nice it would be to be able to
speak a foreign language fluently!

¶戦争中みんながどんなに苦労した
か、今のあなたがたにはわからないで
しょう。(Sensōchū minna ga *donna
ni* kurō shita ka, ima no anata gata ni wa
wakaranai deshō.)

②[ものごとの状態・数量などの限り
ない程度を仮定して表すときに使う]

¶どんなにお金があっても、テレビは
買いませんか。(*Donna ni* okane ga atte
mo, terebi wa kaimasen ka ?)

¶どんなに急いでも、汽車には間に合
いません。(*Donna ni* isoide mo, kisha ni
wa maniaimasen.)

*いつも「どんなに～ても(donna ni ～
te mo)」の形で使い、あとに否定的な
言葉が来る。

→いくら **ikura**

⇒こんなに **konna ni** そんなに **sonna
ni** あんなに **anna ni**

トンネル [名]

¶汽車はトンネルを出て、海のそばを
走っていきました。(Kisha wa *tonneru*
o dete, umi no soba o hashitte
ikimashita.)

¶ You people today cannot imagine
how much everyone suffered during
the war.

② [however, no matter how]

¶ You wouldn't buy a television set **no
matter how much** money you had?

¶ **However much** [you] hurry, [you]
won't be able to catch the train.

*Always used in the pattern "*donna ni
～-te mo*." Followed by words or
expressions having a negative sense.

tonneru [n] **tunnel**

¶ The train emerged from **the tunnel**
and ran along beside the sea.

な

な〔助〕

① [感動などの気持ちを表す]

¶ああ、いい天気だな。（Ā, ii tenki da *na*.）

¶あの花はきれいだな。（Ano hana wa kirei da *na*.）

*「なあ（nā）」とも言う。

② [禁止の気持ちを表す]

¶かぎを忘れるな。（Kagi o wasureru*na*.）

¶部屋に入るな。（Heya ni hairu*na*.）

*動詞（終止の形）に続く。

ない〔助動〕

¶本を見ないで、もう一度言ってください。（Hon o mi*naide*, mō ichido itte kudasai.）

¶今度の旅行にあなたがいっしょに行けなくて残念です。（Kondo no ryokō ni anata ga issho ni ike*nakute* zannen desu.）

¶勉強しなければ、日本語が上手になりません。（Benkyō shi*nakereba*, Nihongo ga jōzu ni narimasen.）

¶あした雨が降らなかったら、テニスをしに行きましょう。（Ashita ame ga fura*nakattara*, tenisu o shi ni ikimashō.）

ない〔形〕

① [存在しない]

¶机の上には何もない。（Tsukue no ue ni wa nani mo *nai*.）

na 〔part〕 a sentence-final particle used as an intensifier or to express prohibition

① [acts as an intensifier]

¶ **What a** nice day!

¶ **What a** lovely flower 〖**How** lovely that flower is〗!

*Variant: *nā*.

② [expresses prohibition]

¶ **Don't** forget your key 〖**Don't** forget to lock up〗.

¶ **Don't** go 〖come〗 in the room.

*Used immediately after a verb in the dictionary form.

-nai 〔auxil〕 a negative ending added to the stem of verbs

¶ Please say it once again **without** looking at your book.

¶ It's too bad that you **can't** go along with [us] on the coming trip.

¶ You will not become good a Japanese **if you don't** study.

¶ Let's go play tennis tomorrow **if it doesn't** rain.

nai 〔adj〕 do not exist; do not have; not

① [do not exist]

¶ There **is nothing** on the desk.

¶その本が図書館にあるかないかわかりません。(Sono hon ga toshokan ni aru ka *nai* ka wakarimasen.)

¶ [I] do not know if that book is in the library or **not**.

⇔ある **aru**

② [所有しない]

¶今お金がないから、あとで払います。(Ima okane ga *nai* kara, ato de haraimasu.)

② [do not have]

¶ [I] will pay later because [I] **don't have** the money for it now.

¶うちに電話がないので、不便です。(Uchi ni denwa ga *nai* node, fuben desu.)

¶ [My] **not having** a telephone is inconvenient.

↔ある **aru**

③ [状態を表す言葉などを打ち消す]

¶今日はあまり寒くないです。(Kyō wa amari samuku *nai* desu.)

③ [not]

¶ **It's not** so cold today.

¶その映画はおもしろくなかったです。(Sono eiga wa omoshiroku *nakatta* desu.)

¶ That movie **wasn't** interesting.

¶たぶんあの人は日本人ではないでしょう。(Tabun ano hito wa Nihonjin de wa *nai* deshō.)

¶ [He] probably **isn't** Japanese.

* 「それは日本語の本ではない。(Sore wa Nihongo no hon de wa nai.)」を丁寧に言うときには「それは日本語の本ではありません。(Sore wa Nihongo no hon de wa arimasen.)」と言う。

*The polite way of saying "*Sore wa Nihongo no hon de wa nai*" (That book is not written, in Japanese) is "*Sore wa Nihongo no hon de wa ari masen.*"

-ない -内 〔尾〕

学校内 (gakkō*nai*) 時間内 (jikan*nai*) 東京都内 (Tōkyōto*nai*) 日本国内 (Nihonkoku*nai*)

-nai 〔suf〕 **within**

within the school // **within** the allotted time // **within** Tokyo, **inside** Tokyo // **within** Japan, **inside** Japan

ないかく 内閣 〔名〕

内閣総理大臣 (*naikaku*sōridaijin) 内閣が倒れる (*naikaku* ga taoreru) 内閣が替わる (*naikaku* ga kawaru)

naikaku 〔n〕 **(government) cabinet**

the prime minister, the premier // **a cabinet** falls // **the cabinet** changes

¶昨日、新しい内閣が誕生しました。(Kinō, atarashii *naikaku* ga tanjō shimashita.)

¶ A new **cabinet** came into being yesterday.

ナイフ〔名〕

ないよう　内容〔名〕

① [話や文章などの中身]
書類の内容（shorui no *naiyō*）

¶その手紙の内容を教えてください。
（Sono tegami no *naiyō* o oshiete
kudasai.）

② [価値のある中身]
¶形式だけで内容のない会議でした。
（Keishiki dake de *naiyō* no nai kaigi
deshita.）
¶この論文は題名は立派ですが、内容
がありません。（Kono ronbun wa
daimei wa rippa desu ga, *naiyō* ga
arimasen.）

ナイロン〔名〕
ナイロン製のくつ下（*nairon*sei no
kutsushita）

なお〔副〕

① [更に、いっそう]

¶この本も難しいが、その本はなお難
しいです。（Kono hon mo muzukashii
ga, sono hon wa *nao* muzukashii desu.）
¶わたしも背が高いが、兄のほうがな
お高いです。（Watashi mo se ga takai
ga, ani no hō ga *nao* takai desu.）
② [やはり、依然、引き続いて]
¶母は 90 歳ですが、今もなお元気で
す。（Haha wa kyūjissai desu ga, ima mo
nao genki desu.）

なおす　直す〔動Ⅰ〕

① [正しくする]

naifu 〔n〕 **knife**

naiyō 〔n〕 **content(s), import; sub
stance, depth**

① [content(s), import]
the contents of a document 〚of
paperwork〛
¶ Please tell me **what** that letter **says**.

② [substance, depth]
¶ It was a meeting for show alone
without any **real substance**.

¶ This thesis 〚paper, dissertation〛 has
a fine-sounding title but has no **depth**
to it.

nairon 〔n〕 **nylon**
nylon socks

nao 〔adv〕 **more, further, still
more, less, still less; still, yet**
① [(more, further, still more, less, still
less]
¶ This book is difficult but that one is
even more difficult.

¶ I am tall but my older brother is **still**
taller.

② [still, yet]
¶ My mother is 90 years old but she
still enjoys good health.

(-)naosu 〔v Ⅰ〕 **correct; repair,
mend; do over again**
① [correct]

¶先生は学生の間違いを直します。
(Sensei wa gakusei no machigai o *naoshimasu*.)

¶The teacher **corrects** the students' mistakes.

②[修繕する]

②[repair, mend]

¶ラジオが壊れたので、電気屋さんに直してもらいました。(Rajio ga kowareta node, denkiyasan ni *naoshite* moraimashita.)

¶As the radio was broken, I had it **fixed** at the electric appliance shop.

③[改めて何かをする]

③[do over again]

¶この文章はもう一度書き直してください。(Kono bunshō wa mō ichido kaki*naoshite* kudasai.)

¶Please **rewrite** this sentence.

なおす 治す〔動I〕

naosu 〔vI〕 **cure, heal**

病気を治す (byōki o *naosu*)

cure an illness

¶虫歯は早く治したほうがいいですよ。(Mushiba wa hayaku *naoshita* hōga ii desu yo.)

¶It is best to have cavities **cared for** early.

なおる 直る〔動I〕

naoru 〔vI〕 **be corrected, be reformed; be repaired**

①[正しくなる]

①[be corrected, be reformed]

¶悪い習慣はなかなか直りません。(Warui shūkan wa nakanaka *naorimasen*.)

¶Bad habits are hard **to break**.

②[修繕してよくなる]

②[be repaired, be set to rights, be restored]

¶壊れていたテレビが直りました。(Kowarete ita terebi ga *naorimashita*.)

¶The broken television set **has been fixed**.

なおる 治る〔動I〕

naoru 〔vI〕 **recover, get well, get better, heal**

病気が治る (byōki ga *naoru*)

recover from an illness

¶風邪はもう治りましたか。(Kaze wa mō *naorimashita* ka?)

¶**Are you over** your cold 〚case of the flu〛 now?

なか 仲〔名〕

naka 〔n〕 **relations, relationship**

仲が悪い (*naka* ga warui)

be on bad **terms** with someone

¶あの二人はとても仲がいいです。(Ano futari wa totemo *naka* ga ii desu.)

¶Those two **are very close**.

¶先週、仲のいい友達と音楽会に行きました。(Senshū, *naka no ii tomodachi to ongakkai ni ikimashita.*)

¶ Last week [I] went to a concert 〚recital〛 with a **good** friend.

なか 中 〔名〕

naka 〔n〕 inside; among, of

① [あるものの内部]

① [inside, interior]

¶寒いから、家の中に入りましょう。(Samui kara, ie no *naka* ni hairimashō.)

¶ As it's cold let's go on **inside** the house.

¶この袋の中には、何が入っていますか。(Kono fukuro no *naka* ni wa, nani ga haitte imasu ka?)

¶ What's **inside** this bag?

↔外 **soto**

② [ある範囲のうち]

② [among, of]

¶わたしは果物の中でりんごがいちばん好きです。(Watashi wa kudamono no *naka* de ringo ga ichiban suki desu.)

¶ **Of** fruits, I like apples best 〚My favorite fruit is the apple〛.

ながい 長い 〔形〕

nagai 〔adj〕 long; prolonged

① [もののある点からある点までの間隔が大きい]

① [long (spatial), too long]

¶長い鉛筆と短い鉛筆が2本ずつあります。(*Nagai* enpitsu to mijikai enpitsu ga nihon zutsu arimasu.)

¶ There are two **long** pencils and two short pencils.

② [時間の間隔が大きい]

② [long (temporal), prolonged]

¶わたしは長い間アメリカに住んでいました。(Watashi wa *nagai* aida Amerika ni sunde imashita.)

¶ I lived in the United States for a **long** time.

⇔短い **mijikai**

ながさ 長さ 〔名〕

nagasa 〔n〕 length

¶その橋の長さはどのくらいですか。(Sono hashi no *nagasa* wa dono kurai desu ka?)

¶ **How long** is that bridge 〚What is **the length** of that bridge〛?

⇒-さ **-sa**

ながす 流す 〔動Ⅰ〕

nagasu 〔v I〕 pour, let flow

¶ここに水を流さないでください。(Koko ni mizu o *nagasanaide* kudasai.)

¶ Please **don't run** the water here 〚Please **don't get** this place wet〛.

¶わたしは悲しい映画を見て、涙を流しました。(Watashi wa kanashii eiga o mite, namida o *nagashimashita*.)

¶ **I cried** at the sad movie.

なかなか〔副〕

nakanaka 〔adv〕 considerably, quite; not easily, not readily

① [かなり、相当に]

① [considerably, quite, rather, very]

¶この本はなかなかおもしろいです。(Kono hon wa *nakanaka* omoshiroi desu.)

¶This book is **quite** interesting.

¶この問題はなかなか難しいです。(Kono mondai wa *nakanaka* muzukashii desu.)

¶This problem is **quite** difficult.

② [容易でない、期待どおりにならない]

② [not easily, not readily]

¶この問題は難しくて、なかなかできません。(Kono mondai wa muzukashikute, *nakanaka* dekimasen.)

¶This (test or homework) question is difficult and **not easily** answered.

¶バスがなかなか来ません。(Basu ga *nakanaka* kimasen.)

¶The bus **is long** in coming.

*あとに打ち消しの言葉が来る。

*Used with the negative.

なかま 仲間〔名〕

nakama 〔n〕 colleagues, associates, set, circle

¶その子には仲間がおおぜいいます。(Sono ko ni wa *nakama* ga oozei imasu.)

¶That child has a wide **circle of acquaintances**.

¶先週、会社の仲間と旅行しました。(Senshū, kaisha no *nakama* to ryokō shimashita.)

¶Last week [I] went on a trip with **people** from work.

ながめる〔動Ⅱ〕

nagameru 〔v Ⅱ〕 look at, watch; look out over, overlook

① [見つめる]

① [look at, watch, see]

¶その人は同じ絵を30分もながめていました。(Sono hito wa onaji e o sanjippun mo *nagamete* imashita.)

¶That person **was looking at** the same picture for 30 minutes.

② [見渡す]

② [look out over, overlook]

¶山の上から下の町をながめました。(Yama no ue kara shita no machi o *nagamemashita*.)

¶[I] **surveyed** the town below from the top of the mountain.

ながら〔助〕

① [ある動作を行う一方で他の動作も行うという意味を表す]

¶ わたしはいつも音楽を聞きながら仕事をします。(Watashi wa itsu mo ongaku o kikinagara shigoto o shimasu.)

¶ テレビを見ながら勉強してはいけません。(Terebi o minagara benkyō shite wa ikemasen.)

¶ 山田さんは働きながら大学を卒業しました。(Yamada san wa hatarakinagara daigaku o sotsugyō shimashita.)

*二つの動作の主体は同じである。

② [ある動作・状態とそれと相いれない他の動作・状態とがともに成立するという関係を表す]

¶ あの人はそのことを知っていながら教えてくれませんでした。(Ano hito wa sono koto o shitte inagara oshiete kuremasen deshita.)

¶ あの人は「はい、はい。」と言いながら、いつも頼んだことをしてくれません。(Ano hito wa "Hai, hai." to iinagara, itsu mo tanonda koto o shite kuremasen.)

*普通、二つの動作・状態の主体は同じである。

③ [断りや前置きなどを表すのに使う]

¶ 残念ながら、用事があって、あしたのパーティーには出席できません。(Zannennagara, yōji ga atte, ashita no pātii ni wa shusseki dekimasen.)

¶ 失礼ながら、ラジオの音をもう少し小さくしていただけませんか。(Shitsureinagara, rajio no oto o mō

-nagara 〔part〕 while, as; though

① [while, as, at the same time that]

¶ I always listen to music while I work (literally, I always work **while** listening to music).

¶ One shouldn't watch television while studying (literally, One shouldn't study **while** watching television).

¶ [Mr.] Yamada worked [his] way through college.

*The subject of the two clauses is the same.

② [though, yet, in spite of]

¶ **Even though** [he] knew that, [he] didn't tell [me] about it.

¶ **In spite of** agreeing to it, [he] never does what [he]'s asked to do.

*Usually the subject of the two clauses is the same.

③ [used when refusing or in a preliminary remark]

¶ I'm sorry (literally, **although** it's a shame) but something has come up so that I will be unable to attend the party tomorrow.

¶ Excuse me (literally, **although** it's rude) but could you please turn your radio down a little bit?

sukoshi chiisaku shite itadakemasen ka？）

ながれ　流れ〔名〕

¶この川はずいぶん流れが急ですね。
（Kono kawa wa zuibun *nagare* ga kyū desu ne.）

¶車の流れが激しくて、道の向こう側へ渡れません。（Kuruma no *nagare* ga hageshikute, michi no mukōgawa e wataremasen.）

nagare 〔n〕 **flow, stream, current**

¶This is a very rapidly **running** river.

¶**Traffic** is so heavy that one can't cross to the other side of the road.

ながれる　流れる〔動Ⅱ〕

① [液体が低い方へ行く]
¶町の中を川が流れています。（Machi no naka o kawa ga *nagarete* imasu.）

② [水に浮いて行く]
¶川に木の葉が落ちて、流れていきました。（Kawa ni ki no ha ga ochite, *nagarete* ikimashita.）

nagareru 〔vⅡ〕 **stream, flow, run; float, be carried away**

① [stream, flow, run, drain]
¶A river **runs** through the town 〚city〛.

② [float, be carried away]
¶Tree leaves fell into the river and **were carried away**.

なく　泣く〔動Ⅰ〕

¶赤ちゃんが泣いていますよ。
（Akachan ga *naite* imasu yo.）

¶母が死んだ時、わたしは一日じゅう泣きました。（Haha ga shinda toki, watashi wa ichinichijū *nakimashita*.）

naku 〔vⅠ〕 **cry**

¶The baby **is crying**!

¶I **cried** all day long when my mother died.

なく　鳴く〔動Ⅰ〕

¶庭で鳥が鳴いています。（Niwa de tori ga *naite* imasu.）

¶秋になると、虫が盛んに鳴きます。
（Aki ni naru to, mushi ga sakan ni *nakimasu*.）

naku 〔vⅠ〕 **(birds, insects) cry, sing; (animals) bark, roar, mew, etc.**

¶A bird **is singing** in the yard 〚garden〛.

¶When autumn comes one hears **the sound** of many insects.

なぐさめる　慰める〔動Ⅱ〕

① [人を勇気づける]

nagusameru 〔vⅡ〕 **comfort, console, cheer up; soothe**

① [comfort, console, cheer up]

¶試験に落ちた友達を慰めてあげました。(Shiken ni ochita tomodachi o *nagusamete* agemashita.)

② [心をやわらげる]

¶音楽はわたしたちの心を慰めてくれます。(Ongaku wa watashitachi no kokoro o *nagusamete* kuremasu.)

なくす 〔動 I〕

① [紛失する]

¶友達から借りた本をなくしてしまいました。(Tomodachi kara karita hon o *nakushite* shimaimashita.)

¶昨日なくした財布がまだ見つかりません。(Kinō *nakushita* saifu ga mada mitsukarimasen.)

② [ない状態にする]

¶交通事故をなくすように、みんなで注意しましょう。(Kōtsū-jiko o *nakusu* yō ni, minna de chūi shimashō.)

¶こんな悪い規則はなくしたほうがいいです。(Konna warui kisoku wa *nakushita* hō ga ii desu.)

なくてはならない 〔連〕
☞**なければならない** -nakereba naranai

なくなる 亡くなる 〔動 I〕

¶上田さんは、昨日病気で亡くなりました。(Ueda san wa, kinō byōki de *nakunarimashita*.)

＊「死ぬ (shinu)」の丁寧な言葉。人間以外の動物には使わない。

⇒死ぬ **shinu**

なくなる 〔動 I〕

① [尽きる、使い果たす]

¶ I tried **to cheer up** a friend who had failed an exam.

② [soothe]

¶ Music **soothes** our souls.

nakusu 〔v I〕 **lose; get rid of**

① [lose, be deprived of]

¶ [I] **lost** 〖**have lost**〗 the book [I] borrowed from a friend.

¶ The wallet [I] **lost** yesterday still hasn't been found.

② [get rid of, do away with]

¶ Everyone should work **to eliminate** traffic accidents.

¶ It would be best **to get rid of** such a bad rule.

-nakute wa naranai 〔compd〕
☞**-nakereba naranai**

nakunaru 〔v I〕 **pass away, die**

¶ [Mr.] Ueda **passed away** yesterday due to illness.

＊*Nakunaru* is the polite form of *shinu*. It is used only for human beings.

nakunaru 〔v I〕 **run low, run out, be used up; be lost, be gone, be missing**

① [run low, run out, be used up]

¶時間がなくなりましたから、今日の講義はこれで終わります。(Jikan ga *nakunarimashita* kara, kyō no kōgi wa kore de owarimasu.)

¶ Today's lecture will end here as we have **run out** of time.

¶たばこがなくなったから、買ってきてください。(Tabako ga *nakunatta* kara, katte kite kudasai.)

¶ I have **run out** of cigarettes— please go buy me some.

②[見当たらなくなる]

② [be lost, be gone, be missing]

¶わたしのかさがなくなりました。(Watashi no kasa ga *nakunarimashita*.)

¶ My umbrella **is missing**.

なげる 投げる〔動Ⅱ〕

nageru 〔v Ⅱ〕 **throw, pitch, fling**

¶子供がボールを投げています。(Kodomo ga bōru o *nagete* imasu.)

¶ The children **are playing catch**.

¶池の中に石を投げないでください。(Ike no naka ni ishi o *nagenaide* kudasai.)

¶ Please **don't throw** stones 〚pebbles〛 into the pond 〚pool〛.

なければならない〔連〕

-nakereba naranai 〔compd〕 **must**

¶友達と約束したから、10時までに駅へ行かなければなりません。(Tomodachi to yakusoku shita kara, jūji made ni eki e ika*nakereba narimasen*.)

¶ [I] **must** go to the station by ten o'clock as [I] have an appointment with a friend.

¶日本の大学に入るためには、まず日本語を勉強しなければなりません。(Nihon no daigaku ni hairu tame ni wa, mazu Nihongo o benkyō shi*nakereba narimasen*.)

¶ In order to enter a Japanese university one **must** first learn Japanese.

＊「〜なくてはならない（〜nakute wa naranai)」とも言う。

＊ Variant: *-nakute wa naranai*.

⇒ならない **naranai**

なさい〔動Ⅰ〕

(-)nasai 〔v Ⅰ〕 **an imperative form**

¶もう遅いから、うちへ帰りなさい。(Mō osoi kara, uchi e kaeri*nasai*.)

¶ It's late; **you'd better** go home.

¶もっと一生懸命勉強しなさい。(Motto isshōkenmei benkyō shi*nasai*.)

¶ **You'd better** study harder.

＊「なさる（nasaru）」の「命令の
形」。命令するときには普通この形を
使う。

＊*Nasai* is the imperative form of
nasaru; this is the form usually used
for imperatives.

なさる〔動Ⅰ〕

¶夏休みはどうなさいますか。
(Natsuyasumi wa dō *nasaimasu* ka？)
¶お食事は何になさいますか。
(Oshokuji wa nan ni *nasaimasu* ka？)
¶どうぞ、御心配なさらないでくださ
い。(Dōzo, goshinpai *nasaranaide*
kudasai.)
＊「する（suru）」の尊敬語。「ますの
形」は「なさいます（nasaimasu）」と
なる。
⇒する suru

nasaru〔vⅠ〕do

¶ What are you going **to do** during
summer vacation?

¶ What would **you like** for dinner
〚lunch, breakfast〛?

¶ Please **don't** worry about it.

＊*Nasaru* is the honorific form of *suru*.
The *-masu* form is *nasaimasu*.

なし〔名〕

nashi〔n〕pear, pear tree

なぜ〔副〕

¶あなたはなぜ昨日学校を休んだので
すか。(Anata wa *naze* kinō gakkō o
yasunda no desu ka？)
¶「なぜ、大学へ行かなかったのです
か。」(*Naze*, daigaku e ikanakatta no desu
ka？)「奨学金がもらえなかったから
です。」(Shōgakukin ga moraenakatta
kara desu.)
⇒どうして dōshite

naze〔adv〕why, for what reason

¶ **Why** were you absent from school
yesterday?

¶ "**Why** didn't [you] go to college?"
"Because [I] couldn't get any financial
aid."

なぜなら〔接〕

¶「わたしは大学へは行けませんでし
た。なぜなら、うちが貧乏だったから
です。(Watashi wa daigaku e wa
ikemasen deshita. *Nazenara*, uchi ga
binbō datta kara desu.)」
¶今年は米があまり取れませんでし
た。なぜなら、夏の間気温が低かった
からです。(Kotoshi wa kome ga amari

nazenara〔conj〕because, for, the reason is

¶ I couldn't go to college. **That's
because** I came from a poor family.

¶ The rice crop was poor this year. **The
reason is that** temperatures were low
during the summer.

toremasen deshita. *Nazenara*, natsu no aida kion ga hikukatta kara desu.)

＊前のことがらを受けて、あとにその理由や根拠などを言うときに使う。「なぜならば（nazenaraba）」とも言う。また「なぜかと言えば（naze ka to ieba）」「どうしてかと言うと（dō shite ka to iu to）」という言い方もある。

＊普通「なぜなら、〜からです（nazenara, 〜kara desu）」の形で使う。

＊Used when giving the reason for or background behind something previously stated. *Nazenaraba* is also used, as are *naze ka to ieba* and *dōshite ka to iu to*.

＊Usually used in the pattern "*Nazenara*, 〜 *kara desu*."

なつ 夏 〔名〕
夏休み（*natsu*yasumi）

natsu 〔n〕 **summer**
summer vacation

なつかしい 懐かしい 〔形〕

¶学校時代のことを懐かしく思い出します。（Gakkō-jidai no koto o *natsukashiku* omoidashimasu.）

¶中村さんは留学した時のことを懐かしそうに話してくれました。（Nakamura san wa ryūgaku shita toki no koto o *natsukashisō* ni hanashite kuremashita.）

natsukashii 〔adj〕 **dear, beloved, feel a yearning for, feel nostalgic about**

¶ I have **fond** memories of my student days.

¶ [Miss] Nakamura spoke **nostalgically** about the time [she] was studying abroad.

など 〔助〕

① [同じようなものごとを列挙するときに使う]
¶この店では本やノートや鉛筆などを売っています。（Kono mise de wa hon ya nōto ya enpitsu *nado* o utte imasu.）

¶わたしは映画や芝居などはあまり好きではありません。（Watashi wa eiga ya shibai *nado* wa amari suki de wa arimasen.）

＊普通「〜や〜や〜など（〜ya 〜 ya 〜 nado）」の形で使い、列挙するものがそれだけに限らないことを表す。

nado 〔part〕 **and the like, etc.; or the like**

① [and the like, etc.; used when citing things of the same sort]

¶ This shop sells books, notebooks, pencils, **and so forth**.

¶ I am not very fond of movies, plays, **and the like**.

＊Usually used in the pattern "〜*ya*〜*ya* 〜*nado*"; indicates that there are other items in addition to those cited.

②[ものごとを一例として挙げるとき
に使う]

¶「日本語を勉強するのに何かいい本
はありませんか。」(Nihongo o benkyō
suru no ni nani ka ii hon wa arimasen
ka？)「そうですね。この本などいか
がですか。」(Sō desu ne. Kono hon *nado*
ikaga desu ka？)

¶お疲れになったでしょう。お茶など
いかがですか。(Otsukare ni nattadeshō.
Ocha *nado* ikaga desu ka？)

③[否定的な気持を込めてあるもの
ごとを取り上げて言うときに使う]

¶山田さんはうそなどつく人ではあり
ません。(Yamada san wa uso *nado*
tsuku hito de wa arimasen.)

¶こんなまずい料理など、とても食べ
られません。(Konna mazui ryōri *nado*,
totemo taberaremasen.)

*普通、あとに打ち消しの言葉や否定
的な意味の言葉が来る。

＊「なんか (nan ka)」とも言う。

なな 七〔名〕 ☞**七 shichi**

ななつ 七つ〔名〕

①[7個]

¶卵はあと七つ残っています。
(Tamago wa ato *nanatsu* nokotte imasu.)

②[7歳]

¶娘は今年七つになります。(Musume
wa kotoshi *nanatsu* ni narimasu.)

ななめ 斜め〔名〕

¶道路を斜めに渡るのは危険です。
(Dōro o *naname* ni wataru no wa kiken
desu.)

②[or the like; used when citing
something as an example]

¶ "Can you tell me some good books
for studying Japanese?"
"Well, how about **something like** this
book?"

¶ You must be tired. How about some
tea **or something?**

③ [or the like, such a thing as; used
when citing something in a denial]

¶ [Mr.] Yamada isn't a liar.

¶ There's no way anyone could eat
such terrible food.

*Usually followed by words negative
in form or sense.

＊ Variant: *nan ka*.

nana〔n〕☞**shichi**

nanatsu〔n〕 seven; seven years
of age

① [seven (items)]

¶ There are **seven** eggs left.

② [seven years of age]

¶ My daughter will be **seven** this year.

naname〔n〕 oblique, slanting,
diagonal

¶ It is dangerous **not to take the
shortest path** when crossing the street.

645

¶船が風で斜めに傾きました。(Fune ga kaze de *naname* ni katamukimashita.)

¶ The boat **listed** in the wind.

なにか 何か〔連〕

nani ka 〔compd〕 **something, anything**

¶そこに何かありますか。(Soko ni *nani ka* arimasu ka?)

¶ Is there **anything** there?

¶何か欲しい物がありますか。(*Nani ka* hoshii mono ga arimasu ka?)

¶ Is there **anything** you'd like?

¶台所にパンか何かがあると思います。(Daidokoro ni pan ka *nani ka* ga aru to omoimasu.)

¶ I think there is bread 〚rolls, etc.〛 or **something** in the kitchen.

なにも 何も〔連〕

nani mo 〔compd〕 **nothing, not anything**

¶ここには何もありません。(Koko ni wa *nani mo* arimasen.)

¶ There is **nothing** here.

¶デパートで何も買いませんでした。

¶ [I] didn't buy **anything** at the department store.

(Depāto de *nani mo* kaimasen deshita.)

＊あとに打ち消しの言葉が来る。

＊ Used with the negative.

なに(-) 何(-)〔代、頭〕

nani(-) 〔pron, pref〕 **what**

1〔代〕

1 〔pron〕

¶そこに何がありますか。(Soko ni *nani* ga arimasu ka?)

¶ **What** is that there?

¶あなたは食べ物では何が好きですか。(Anata wa tabemono de wa *nani* ga suki desu ka?)

¶ **What** foods do you like?

¶朝、起きてから何をしますか。(Asa, okite kara *nani* o shimasu ka?)

¶ **What** do you do in the morning after you get up?

2〔頭〕

2 〔pref〕

何語 (*nani*go) 何色 (*nani*iro) 何人 (*nani*jin) 何曜日 (*nani*yōbi)
⇒何(-)nan(-)

what language // what color // what nationality // what day of the week

なのか 七日〔名〕

nanoka 〔n〕 **the seventh of the month; seven days**

①[日付を表す]
七月七日 (shichigatsu *nanoka*)

① [the seventh of the month]
July 7

②[日数を表す]

② [seven days]

¶一週間は七日です。(Isshūkan wa *nanoka* desu.)

＊「なぬか (nanuka)」と言うこともある。

⇒-日 -ka

なま 生〔名〕

生魚 (*namazakana*) 生卵 (*namatamago*) 生野菜 (*namayasai*)

¶あなたは魚を生で食べることができますか。(Anata wa sakana o *nama* de taberu koto ga dekimasu ka？)

¶生の野菜をもっとたくさん食べなさい。(*Nama* no yasai o motto takusan tabenasai.)

なまえ 名前〔名〕

¶わたしの名前は中村です。(Watashi no *namae* wa Nakamura desu.)

¶わたしは犬に「コロ」という名前をつけました。(Watashi wa inu ni "Koro" to iu *namae* o tsukemashita.)

なまける 怠ける〔動Ⅱ〕

¶一郎は勉強を怠けて、遊んでばかりいます。(Ichirō wa benkyō o *namakete*, asonde bakari imasu.)

¶仕事を怠けてはいけません。(Shigoto o *namakete* wa ikemasen.)

なみ 波〔名〕

波が高い (*nami* ga takai) 波が荒い (*nami* ga arai)

¶この海岸は波が静かです。(Kono kaigan wa *nami* ga shizuka desu.)

なみだ 涙〔名〕

涙を流す (*namida* o nagasu) 涙をこぼす (*namida* o kobosu) 涙が出る (*namida* ga deru)

¶ One week is **seven days**.

＊Variant: *nanuka*.

nama 〔n〕 **raw, uncooked**

raw fish // a **raw** egg // **raw** vegetables; a salad

¶ Can you eat **raw** fish?

¶ Eat more **raw** vegetables!

namae 〔n〕 **name; given name**

¶ My **name** is Nakamura.

¶ I **named** my dog Koro.

namakeru 〔v Ⅱ〕 **be idle, be lazy, neglect**

¶ Ichirō **is neglecting** his studies and doing nothing but playing around.

¶ You mustn't **slight** your work.

nami 〔n〕 **wave, surf**

the waves are high, **the sea** is rough // **the waves** are high, **the sea** is rough

¶ **The sea** is calm at this beach.

namida 〔n〕 **a tear**

shed **tears**, weep // shed **tears** // **tears** fall, **tears** come to one's eyes

¶その人は目に涙を浮かべて、別れの
あいさつをしました。(Sono hito wa
me ni *namida* o ukabete, wakare no
aisatsu o shimashita.)

¶ [He] said [his] farewell with **tears** in
[his] eyes.

なら〔助動〕

nara 〔auxil〕 **if; as for**

① [前件が成立することを想定して現
在の話し手の立場や判断などを後件で
述べるという関係を表す]

① [if, provided that; used when the
speaker states a conclusion, etc., based
on a stipulation in the first clause]

¶あなたが行くなら、わたしも行くこ
とにします。(Anata ga iku *nara*,
watashi mo iku koto ni shimasu.)

¶ **If** you are going, I will go too.

¶この本をお読みになるなら、お貸し
しましょう。(Kono hon o oyomi ni naru
nara, okashi shimashō.)

¶ I will lend you this book **if** you are
interested in reading it.

¶あしたお暇なら、わたしの家へ来て
ください。(Ashita ohima *nara*, watashi
no ie e kite kudasai.)

¶ Please come visit me tomorrow **if**
you are free.

¶頭が痛いなら、早く帰って休んだほ
うがいいですよ。(Atama ga itai *nara*,
hayaku kaette yasunda hō ga ii desu yo.)

¶ **If** you have a headache you had
better go home early and rest.

*後件には普通、話し手の「～う［よ
う］（～u［yō］）」などの意志、「～な
さい（～nasai）」などの命令、「～て
ください（～te kudasai）」などの依頼、
「～ほうがいい（～hō ga ii）」などの勧
告などの言い方が来る。また、後件の
ことがらの成立のほうが前件のことが
らの成立より時間的に早い。「山田さ
んが来たら、わたしは帰ります。
(Yamada san ga kitara, watashi wa
kaerimasu.)」の場合には、山田さんが
来てからわたしが帰るという意味であ
るが、「山田さんが来るなら、わたし
は帰ります。(Yamada san ga kuru nara,
watashi wa kaerimasu.)」の場合には、
山田さんが来る前にわたしが帰るとい
う意味になる。

*In the second clause the speaker
usually expresses an intention with *-ō*
〚*-yō*〛, a command with *-nasai*, a
request with *-te kudasai*, a
recommendation with ～ *hō ga ii*, etc.
Also, the time of the second clause is
earlier than that of the first, *nara*-
clause. Thus "*Yamada san ga kitara,
watashi wa kaerimasu*" (I will leave
when Mr. Yamada comes) means that I
will go after [Mr.] Yamada comes, but
"*Yamada san ga kuru nara, watashi
wa kaerimasu*" (If Mr. Yamada is
coming, I will leave) means that I will
leave before [Mr.] Yamada comes.

② [前件がもし成立していた場合には後件も成立するという関係を表す]

¶もう少し背が高かったなら、どんなによかったでしょう。(Mō sukoshi sei ga takakatta *nara*, donna ni yokatta deshō.)

¶お医者さんがもう少し早く来てくれたなら、父は助かったのに。
(Oishasan ga mō sukoshi hayaku kite kureta *nara*, chichi wa tasukatta noni.)

*前件は実際には成立しなかったことがらが来る。「～たなら（～ta nara)」の形で使う。

→ば **ba** たら **tara**

③ [話題とすることがらを提示するのに使う]

¶その問題なら、もう解決しました。
(Sono mondai *nara*, mō kaiketsu shimashita.)

¶「お兄さんはいらっしゃいますか。」(Oniisan wa irasshaimasu ka？)「兄なら今床屋へ行っていますよ。」(Ani *nara* ima tokoya e itte imasu yo.)

→たら **tara**

*助動詞「だ（da)」の「接続の形」である。「ならば（naraba)」とも言うが、普通「なら（narara)」の形で使う。

ならう 習う 〔動Ⅰ〕

¶わたしは今ピアノを習っています。
(Watashi wa ima piano o *naratte* imasu.)

¶日本語を習うのはたいへんですか。
(Nihongo o *narau* no wa taihen desu ka？)

② [if; indicates that the second clause would have been realized if the first clause had been realized]

¶ How nice it would have been **if** [I] were a little taller.

¶ **If** only the doctor had come sooner, my father's life could have been saved.

*The first clause wasn't actually realized. Used in the pattern "-*ta nara*."

③ [as for; used to indicate the topic]

¶ Oh, that problem has already been resolved.

¶ "Is your older brother there?" "Oh, he's gone to the barbershop."

* *Nara* is the connective form of the auxiliary *da*. *Naraba* is also used but *nara* is the more usual form.

narau 〔v I〕 **learn, study, be taught**

¶ I am presently **taking** piano **lessons**.

¶ Is Japanese hard **to learn?**

ならない〔連〕

① [禁止の意味を表す]

¶酒を飲んではならない。(Sake o nonde wa *naranai*.)

¶うそをついてはなりません。(Uso o tsuite wa *narimasen*.)

*「動詞（ての形）＋は（wa）＋ならない（naranai）」の形で使う。

② [義務や当然の意味を表す]

¶友達と約束したから、10時までに駅へ行かなければなりません。

(Tomodachi to yakusoku shita kara, jūji made ni eki e ikanakereba *narimasen*.)

¶あしたまでに宿題を出さなくてはなりません。(Ashita made ni shukudai o dasanakute wa *narimasen*.)

*「〜なければならない（〜nakerebanaranai）」「〜なくてはならない（〜nakute wa naranai）」の形で使う。

⇒なければならない nakereba naranai

ならば〔助動〕　☞なら nara

ならぶ　並ぶ〔動Ⅰ〕

¶わたしは田中さんと並んで座りました。(Watashi wa Tanaka san to *narande* suwarimashita.)

¶道の両側にはいろいろな店が並んでいます。(Michi no ryōgawa ni wa iroiro na mise ga *narande* imasu.)

ならべる　並べる〔動Ⅱ〕

¶机を1列に並べてください。

(Tsukue o ichiretsu ni *narabete* kudasai.)

naranai 〔compd〕 must not, should not; must, should, ought

① [must not, should not]

¶ You **shouldn't** drink.

¶ One **shouldn't** tell lies.

*Used in the pattern "verb (-*te* form) + *wa* + *naranai*."

② [must, should, ought, have to]

¶ [I] **have to** be at the station by ten o'clock as [I] have an appointment with a friend.

¶ The homework **has to** be handed in by tomorrow.

*Used in the patterns "-*nakereba naranai*" and "-*nakute wa naranai*."

naraba 〔auxil〕　☞nara

narabu 〔v〕 I be in a row, stand in line

¶ I sat down **next to** [Mrs.] Tanaka.

¶ Various shops **line** both sides of the street.

naraberu 〔v Ⅱ〕 arrange, place side by side, display

¶ Please **arrange** the desks in one row.

¶本だなには本がきちんと並べてあります。(Hondana ni wa hon ga kichinto *narabete* arimasu.)

¶ The books **are in** good **order** 〚**are arranged** nicely〛 in the bookcase.

なる　鳴る〔動 I〕

naru 〚v I〛 **sound, ring, peal, strike, boom, etc.**

¶電話のベルが鳴っています。(Denwa no beru ga *natte* imasu.)

¶ The telephone **is ringing**.

¶ベルが鳴って授業が終わりました。(Beru ga *natte* jugyō ga owarimashita.)

¶ Class ended with **the ringing** of the bell.

なる〔動 I〕

naru 〚v I〛 **bear fruit, be in fruit**

¶このみかんの木には、あまり実がなりません。(Kono mikan no ki ni wa, amari mi ga *narimasen*.)

¶ This mandarin orange tree **isn't bearing** very well.

なる〔動 I〕

naru 〚v I〛 **become, grow, turn**

¶春になると、桜が咲きます。(Haru ni *naru* to, sakura ga sakimasu.)

¶ When spring **comes**, the cherry blossoms will come out 〚Cherry trees blossom in the spring〛.

¶3時になったら、少し休みましょう。(Sanji ni *nattara*, sukoshi yasumimashō.)

¶ Let's take a break **at** three o'clock.

¶上田さんは将来医者になりたいそうです。(Ueda san wa shōrai isha ni *naritai* sō desu.)

¶ I understand that [Miss] Ueda **wants to become** a doctor.

¶太陽が昇って、辺りが急に明るくなりました。(Taiyō ga nobotte, atari ga kyū ni akaruku *narimashita*.)

¶ It suddenly **became** light with the rising of the sun.

¶この辺は夜になると、静かになります。(Kono hen wa yoru ni *naru* to, shizuka ni narimasu.)

¶ It's quiet here **at** night.

¶一生懸命練習したので、だいぶ上手に日本語が話せるようになりました。(Isshōkenmei renshū shita node, daibu jōzu ni Nihongo ga hanaseru yō ni *narimashita*.)

¶ As [he] practiced hard, [he] **can now** speak Japanese quite well.

＊名詞の場合は助詞「に（ni）」のあと
に続き、形容詞・形容動詞の場合は
「連用の形」に続く。また動詞の場合
には「動詞（連体の形）＋ように
（yōni）＋なる（naru）」の形になる。

＊*Naru* is used with the particle *ni*
after nouns and adjective-verbs and
with the *-ku* form of adjectives. When
used with another verb, the pattern
"verb (dictionary form) + *yō ni* + *naru*"
is used.

なるべく 〔副〕

¶なるべく早く来てください。
（*Narubeku* hayaku kite kudasai.）
¶なるべくゆっくり話してください。
（*Narubeku* yukkuri hanashite kudasai.）

narubeku 〔adv〕 **as ～ as possible**

¶ Please come **as** quickly **as possible**.

¶ Please speak **as** slowly **as possible**.

なるほど 〔副〕

¶なるほど、そういう考えもあるんで
すね。（*Naruhodo* sōiu kangae mo aru n
desu ne.）

naruhodo 〔n〕 **I get it., indeed,
doubtless**

¶ Indeed, there is such a way of
thinking.

なれる 慣れる 〔動Ⅱ〕

¶わたしは日本の生活にもう慣れまし
た。（Watashi wa Nihon no seikatsu ni
mō *naremashita*.）
¶慣れれば、この仕事も楽になるで
しょう。（*Narereba*, kono shigoto mo
raku ni naru deshō.）

nareru 〔v Ⅱ〕 **get used to, be
accustomed to, become
experienced in**

¶ I am now **acclimated** to life in Japan.

¶ [You] will find this job easier once
[you] **get more used to it**.

なれる 〔動Ⅱ〕

¶この犬はわたしによくなれていま
す。（Kono inu wa watashi ni yoku *narete*
imasu.）

nareru 〔v Ⅱ〕 **become tame, be
domesticated**

¶ This dog is quite **good with me**.

なわ 〔名〕

なわ跳び（*nawa*tobi）

nawa 〔n〕 **rope (made of straw or
hemp)**

to be jumping **rope**

なんか 〔助〕　☞など nado

nanka 〔part〕　☞**nado**

なんでも 何でも 〔連〕

¶何でも好きな物を買ってあげましょう。(*Nan demo* suki na mono o katte agemashō.)

¶何でもいいから、質問してください。(*Nan demo* ii kara, shitsumon shite kudasai.)

なん(-) 何(-) 〔代、頭〕

1 〔代〕

¶あれは何ですか。(Are wa *nan* desu ka？)

¶これは何の薬ですか。(Kore wa *nan* no kusuri desu ka？)

¶あの方は何というお名前ですか。(Ano kata wa *nan* to iu onamae desu ka？)

2 〔頭〕

何匹 (*nan*biki) 何本 (*nan*bon) 何秒 (*nan*byō) 何台 (*nan*dai) 何月 (*nan*gatsu) 何時 (*nan*ji) 何時間 (*nan*jikan) 何か月 (*nan*kagetsu) 何回 (*nan*kai) 何年 (*nan*nen) 何日 (*nan*nichi) 何人 (*nan*nin) 何十人 (*nan*jūnin) 十何人 (jū*nan*nin) 何千人 (*nan*zennin) 何分 (*nan*pun) 何週間 (*nan*shūkan) 何足 (*nan*zoku)

⇒何(-) nani(-)

---

nan demo 〔compd〕 **anything, whatever**

¶ I will buy you **whatever** you want.

¶ Please ask **whatever** questions you may have.

nan(-) 〔pron, pref〕 **what; what, how many**

1 〔pron〕 what

¶ **What** is that?

¶ **What** is this medicine?

¶ **What** is that gentleman's 〖lady's〗 name?

2 〔pref〕 what, how many

how many (cats, dogs, etc.) // how many (cigarettes, bottles, etc.) // how many seconds // how many (cars, machines, etc.) // what month // what time, when // how many hours // how many months // how many times // how many years; what year // how many days; what day // how many people // how many tens of persons // 10-**odd** people // how many thousands of persons // how many minutes // how many weeks // how many pairs (of socks, shoes, etc.)

に

に 二 〔名〕
二階 (*ni*kai) 二番め (*ni*banme)

に 〔助〕

① [ものごとが存在しているところまたある状態で存在しているところなどを表す]
¶ 机の上に日本語の本があります。
(Tsukue no ue *ni* Nihongo no hon ga arimasu.)
¶ わたしは東京に住んでいます。
(Watashi wa Tōkyō *ni* sunde imasu.)
¶ 空に白い雲が浮かんでいます。(Sora *ni* shiroi kumo ga ukande imasu.)
¶ この道をまっすぐ行くと、左手に海が見えます。(Kono michi o massugu iku to, hidarite *ni* umi ga miemasu.)
¶ りんごにはいろいろな種類があります。(Ringo *ni* wa iroiro na shurui ga arimasu.)

② [移動などの方向や到達するところまた移動したものの存在するところなどを表す]

バスに乗る (basu *ni* noru) 山に登る (yama *ni* noboru)
¶ わたしは毎朝8時に学校に来ます。
(Watashi wa maiasa hachiji ni gakkō *ni* kimasu.)
¶ この道をまっすぐ行って、二つめの角を左に曲がると、駅の前に出ます。
(Kono michi o massugu itte, futatsume no

---

ni 〔n〕 **two**

the **second** floor // the **second** one, **second**

ni 〔part〕 **in, on, at, to, into, by, from, with, for**

① [in, on; indicates where something exists or where it exists in a certain condition, etc.]
¶ There is a Japanese book **on** the desk.

¶ I live **in** Tokyo.

¶ A white cloud is floating **in** the sky.

¶ If you go straight along this road, you will be able to see the ocean **on** the left.

¶ There are various types **of** apples.

② [in, at; indicates the direction or stopping place of a movement, the present location of something that had been moving, etc.]
ride a bus; get **on** a bus // climb a mountain

¶ I come **to** school every day at eight o'clock.

¶ If you go straight along this street and turn left at the second corner, you will come out **in** front of the station.

kado o hidari *ni* magaru to, eki no mae *ni* demasu.)

¶ わたしはゆうべ10時に東京駅に着きました。（Watashi wa yūbe jūji ni Tōkyō-eki *ni* tsukimashita.）

¶ I arrived **at** Tokyo Station last night at ten o'clock.

*移動の方向を特に意識して言う場合には「へ（e）」を使うこともある。
→へ e

*Sometimes *e* is used rather than *ni* when one is particularly conscious of the direction of the movement.

③ [ある動作の成立の結果の存在するところなどを表す]

③ [in, on; indicates the location of the result of an action]

¶ 庭にすみれの花を植えました。
（Niwa *ni* sumire no hana o uemashita.）

¶ [I] planted violets **in** the garden 〚yard〛.

¶ この紙にあなたの名前と生年月日を書いてください。（Kono kami *ni* anata no namae to seinengappi o kaite kudasai.）

¶ Please write your name and date of birth **on** this paper.

¶ 壁に日本の地図がはってあります。
（Kabe *ni* Nihon no chizu ga hatte arimasu.）

¶ There is a map of Japan fastened **on** the wall.

④ [ものごとの成り行き・変化などの結果を表す]

④ [to, into; indicates the result of a course of events, a change, etc.]

¶ 夕方から雨は雪になりました。
（Yūgata kara ame wa yuki *ni* narimashita.）

¶ In the evening the rain changed **into** snow.

¶ みかんは 11 月ごろになると、黄色になっておいしくなります。（Mikan wa jūichigatsu goro *ni* naru to, kiiro *ni* natte oishiku narimasu.）

¶ Mandarin oranges turn orange and become better-tasting around November.

¶ わたしは将来医者になるつもりです。（Watashi wa shōrai isha *ni* naru tsumori desu.）

¶ My future plan is to become a doctor.

¶交通信号が青から赤に変わりました。(Kōtsū-shingō ga ao kara aka *ni* kawarimashita.)

¶The traffic light turned from green **to** red.

→と **to**

⑤ [ものごとを決めたり選んだり変化させたりするその結果を表す]

⑤ [indicates the result of deciding, choosing, changing something, etc.]

¶今日はこれで終わりにします。(Kyō wa kore de owari *ni* shimasu.)

¶Let's stop here today.

¶わたしは来月京都に行くことにしました。(Watashi wa raigetsu Kyōto ni iku koto *ni* shimashita.)

¶I've decided to go to Kyoto next month.

¶わたしはコーヒーにします。(Watashi wa kōhii *ni* shimasu.)

¶Coffee for me, please.

¶子供は人形を患者にして、注射をしたり、薬を飲ませたりして遊んでいます。(Kodomo wa ningyō o kanja *ni* shite, chūsha o shitari, kusuri o nomasetari shite asonde imasu.)

¶The children are playing, pretending a doll is a patient and giving it shots, making it take medicine, and so forth.

⑥ [動作・作用の行われる時や場合などを表す]

⑥ [at, in, on; indicates the time or occasion when an action or process takes place]

¶わたしは毎朝7時に起きます。(Watashi wa maiasa shichiji *ni* okimasu.)

¶I get up **at** seven o'clock each morning.

¶あなたは夏休みにどこかへ行きますか。(Anata wa natsuyasumi *ni* doko ka e ikimasu ka?)

¶Are you going to go somewhere **during** summer vacation?

¶この地方では春の初めによく強い風が吹きます。(Kono chihō de wa haru no hajime *ni* yoku tsuyoi kaze ga fukimasu.)

¶There are often strong winds in this region **in** early spring.

¶お金は物を売ったり買ったりするときにいつも使うものです。(Okane wa mono o uttari kattari suru toki *ni* itsu mo tsukau mono desu.)

¶Money is something that is always used **when** buying and selling.

⑦ [動作などの向けられる相手・対象などを表す]

¶わたしは昨日国の母に手紙を書きました。(Watashi wa kinō kuni no haha *ni* tegami o kakimashita.)

¶わたしは今日山田さんに会います。(Watashi wa kyō Yamada san *ni* aimasu.)

¶漢字は、今から千七百年ぐらい前に日本に伝えられたものです。(Kanji wa, ima kara sennanahyakunen gurai mae ni Nihon *ni* tsutaerareta mono desu.)

¶わたしは上田さんには本当に親しみを感じます。(Watashi wa Ueda san *ni* wa hontō ni shitashimi o kanjimasu.)

⑧ [動作や状態の根拠・よりどころなどを表す]

¶雨にぬれた木の葉が、朝日にきらきら光っています。(Ame *ni* nureta konoha ga, asahi *ni* kirakira hikatte imasu.)

¶旗が風に静かに揺れています。(Hata ga kaze *ni* shizuka ni yurete imasu.)

¶今朝の天気予報によると、午後は晴れるそうです。(Kesa no tenki-yohō *ni* yoru to, gogo wa hareru sō desu.)

⑨ [ほかのものが影響を受ける動作・作用の主体や動作の出所を表す]

¶わたしは先生にほめられました。(Watashi wa sensei *ni* homeraremashita.)

¶昨日、雨に降られて風邪を引いてしまいました。(Kinō, ame *ni* furarete kaze o hiite shimaimashita.)

⑦ [to, toward, for; indicates the object of an action, etc.]

¶ Yesterday I wrote a letter **to** my mother back home.

¶ I am meeting [Miss] Yamada today.

¶ Kanji were introduced **to** Japan about 1,700 years ago.

¶ I really feel close **to** [Mrs.] Ueda.

⑧ [by, from, with; indicates the source of an action, condition, etc.]

¶ The leaves wet **by** the rain are shining **in** the morning sun.

¶ The flag 〚banner, pennant〛 is gently fluttering **in** the wind.

¶ **According to** this morning's weather report, it will be clear 〚will clear up, will stop raining〛 this afternoon.

⑨ [by, from, with; indicates the source, or performer of an action or operation that affects another]

¶ I received a compliment **from** my teacher.

¶ Yesterday I got wet **in** the rain and caught a cold.

¶わたしは小学校の時、山田先生に教わりました。（Watashi wa shōgakkō no toki, Yamada sensei *ni* osowarimashita.）

¶旅行先でお金が足りなくなって、友達に借りました。（Ryokōsaki de okane ga tarinaku natte, tomodachi *ni* karimashita.）

⑩ [ほかの者から影響を受けて行う動作の主体を表す]

¶先生は正しく言えるようになるまで、何度も同じことを学生に言わせます。（Sensei wa tadashiku ieru yō ni naru made, nando mo onaji koto o gakusei *ni* iwasemasu.）

¶母は今赤ん坊にミルクを飲ませています。（Haha wa ima akanbō *ni* miruku o nomasete imasu.）

⑪ [行く・来るなどの動作の目的を表す]

¶姉は八百屋へりんごを買いに行きました。（Ane wa yaoya e ringo o kai *ni* ikimashita.）

¶母はデパートへ買い物に行きました。（Haha wa depāto e kaimono *ni* ikimashita.）

¶わたしは日本へ文学の勉強に来ました。（Watashi wa Nihon e bungaku no benkyō *ni* kimashita.）

¶わたしはこれから新宿にいる友達の所へ遊びに行きます。（Watashi wa kore kara Shinjuku ni iru tomodachi no tokoro e asobi *ni* ikimasu.）

¶ When I was in elementary school, I was taught **by** [Mr.] Yamada.

¶ I ran out of money while traveling and borrowed some **from** a friend.

⑩ [indicates the performer of an act caused by someone else]

¶ The teacher makes the students say the same thing over and over until they can say it correctly.

¶ My mother is now nursing the baby.

⑪ [for, to; indicates the purpose of an act such as going or coming somewhere]

¶ My elder sister went 〚has gone〛 to the fruit and vegetable store **to** buy some apples.

¶ My mother went 〚has gone〛 shopping at the department store.

¶ I came to Japan **to** study literature.

¶ I am now going **to** visit a friend at [his] place in Shinjuku.

*「動詞（基幹の形）＋に（ni）」の形と「名詞＋に（ni）」の形とがある。

⑫ [動作の行われる目的などを表す]

¶「この機械は何に使いますか。」
(Kono kikai wa nan *ni* tsukaimasu ka？)
「この機械は紙を切るのに使います。」
(Kono kikai wa kami o kiru no *ni* tsukaimasu.)

¶大学に入るためにはもっと勉強しなければなりません。(Daigaku ni hairu tame *ni* wa motto benkyō shinakereba narimasen.)

¶外国の文化を正しく理解するには、その国に住むのがいちばんです。
(Gaikoku no bunka o tadashiku rikai suru *ni* wa, sono kuni ni sumu no ga ichiban desu.)

*「動詞（連体の形）＋に（ni）」の形や「動詞（連体の形）＋の（no）＋に（ni）」の形や「名詞＋に（ni）」の形などがある。

⑬ [比較・異同・評価などの基準を表す]

¶わたしのうちは駅に近いです。
(Watashi no uchi wa eki *ni* chikai desu.)

¶山田さんはお母さんによく似ています。(Yamada san wa okāsan *ni* yoku nite imasu.)

¶たばこは体に悪いです。(Tabako wa karada *ni* warui desu.)

⑭ [割合・割り当てなどの基準を表す]

*Used in the patterns "verb (stem form) + *ni*" and "noun + *ni*."

⑫ [for, to; indicates the purpose or objective of an act]

¶ "What is this device 〚machine〛 used **for?**"
"It is **for** cutting paper."

¶ **To** get into college, [you] must study harder.

¶ The best course **for** correctly understanding a foreign culture is to go and live in that country.

*Used in the patterns "verb (dictionary form) + *ni* ," "verb (dictionary form) + *no* + *ni* ," "noun + *ni* ," etc.

⑬ [to, for; indicates the criterion of a comparison, difference, evaluation, etc.]
¶ My home is near the station.

¶ [Miss] Yamada looks a lot like [her] mother.

¶ Smoking is bad **for** the health.

⑭ [per, at, for; indicates the basic unit of a rate, apportioning, etc.]

¶ 紙は一人に二枚ずつ渡してくださ
い。(Kami wa hitori *ni* nimai zutsu
watashite kudasai.)

¶ Please give **each** person two sheets
of paper.

¶ わたしは一か月に一度床屋へ行きま
す。(Watashi wa ikkagetsu *ni* ichido
tokoya e ikimasu.)

¶ I go to the barber **once** a month.

¶ わたしは一日おきにおふろに入りま
す。(Watashi wa ichinichi oki *ni* ofuro ni
hairimasu.)

¶ I take a bath **every other** day.

⑮ [動作・作用・状態などの様子を表
す]

⑮ [indicates the condition of an
action, operation, state, etc.]

¶ 本は横に一列に並べてください。
(Hon wa yoko *ni* ichiretsu *ni* narabete
kudasai.)

¶ Please lay the books down **in** a single
row.

¶ わたしは辞書を引かずに日本語の新
聞が読めるようになりました。
(Watashi wa jisho o hikazu *ni* Nihongo no
shinbun ga yomeru yō ni narimashita.)

¶ I have become 〚became〛 able to read
a Japanese newspaper **without**
consulting a dictionary.

¶ 仕事は予定どおりにうまくいってい
ます。(Shigoto wa yotei doori *ni* umaku
itte imasu.)

¶ The work is progressing well and **on**
schedule.

⑯ [ある能力をもっている主体を表す]

⑯ [indicates a person having a certain
ability]

¶ この問題はわたしにはわかりませ
ん。(Kono mondai wa watashi *ni* wa
wakarimasen.)

¶ I don't understand this problem.

¶ わたしにはとてもあんな難しい本は
読めません。(Watashi *ni* wa totemo
anna muzukashii hon wa yomemasen.)

¶ I could never read such a difficult
book.

¶ あの人にできることなら、わたしに
もできると思います。(Ano hito *ni*
dekiru koto nara, watashi *ni* mo dekiru to
omoimasu.)

¶ If [he] can do it, I think that I can, too.

にあう 似合う〔動Ⅰ〕

¶その洋服はあなたによく似合います
よ。(Sono yōfuku wa anata ni yoku
niaimasu yo.)

におい〔名〕

いいにおい (ii *nioi*) いやなにおい
(iya na *nioi*) 臭いにおい (kusai *nioi*)
においをかぐ (*nioi* o kagu)
¶台所からおいしそうなにおいがして
きました。(Daidokoro kara oishisō na
nioi ga shite kimashita.)

におう〔動Ⅰ〕

¶この花はあまりにおいませんね。
(Kono hana wa amari *nioimasen* ne.)
¶ガスがもれていませんか。においま
すよ。(Gasu ga morete imasen ka?
Nioimasu yo.)

にがい 苦い〔形〕

¶この薬は苦いですね。(Kono kusuri
wa *nigai* desu ne.)
¶濃いコーヒーは苦くて飲めません。
(Koi kōhii wa *nigakute* nomemasen.)

にがつ 二月〔名〕

にぎやか〔形動〕

¶市場はいつもにぎやかです。(Ichiba
wa itsu mo *nigiyaka* desu.)
¶ここはずいぶんにぎやかな所です
ね。(Koko wa zuibun *nigiyaka* na tokoro
desu ne.)

にく 肉〔名〕

肉屋 (*niku*ya) 牛肉 (gyū*niku*) 鳥肉
(tori*niku*)

niau 〔vⅠ〕 become, suit, match well

¶That outfit **looks** very **nice** on you.

nioi 〔n〕 smell, odor, scent

a nice **odor** // an unpleasant **smell** // an
offensive **smell** // smell something

¶**The aroma** of something good
drifted out 〖is drifting out〗 from the
kitchen.

niou 〔vⅠ〕 smell, give off a smell, be fragrant, stink

¶This flower **doesn't have** much smell.

¶Is that gas leaking? **It smells** like it.

nigai 〔adj〕 bitter

¶This medicine **is bitter**, isn't it?

¶Strong coffee **is too bitter** for [me] to
drink.

nigatsu 〔n〕 February

nigiyaka 〔adj-v〕 lively, bustling, flourishing, noisy

¶The market is always **crowded and bustling**.

¶This is a very **lively** place.

niku 〔n〕 meat, flesh

a **meat** shop, a butcher's, a butcher //
beef // (dressed) chicken, fowl

661

¶豚肉を 100 グラムください。
(Butaniku o hyakuguramu kudasai.)

¶ Please give me one hundred grams of **pork**.

¶この肉は柔らかくておいしいです。
(Kono niku wa yawarakakute oishii
desu.)

¶ This **meat** is nice and tender.

-にくい 〔尾〕

-nikui 〔suf〕 hard to ～, difficult to ～

¶この字はたいへん書きにくいです。
(Kono ji wa taihen kakinikui desu.)

¶ This character is very **difficult** to write.

¶その本の題は長くて覚えにくいです。(Sono hon no dai wa nagakute
oboenikui desu.)

¶ The title of that book is long and **hard** to remember.

⇔-やすい -yasui

にげる 逃げる 〔動Ⅱ〕

nigeru 〔vⅡ〕 run away, flee, escape

¶ねこが魚を取って逃げました。
(Neko ga sakana o totte nigemashita.)

¶ The cat took the fish and **ran off** with it.

¶警官は逃げるどろぼうを追いかけました。(Keikan wa nigeru dorobō o
oikakemashita.)

¶ The policeman chased after the **fleeing** thief.

にごる 濁る 〔動Ⅰ〕

nigoru 〔vⅠ〕 become muddy, impure, cloudy

¶雨で川の水が濁っています。(Ame
de kawa no mizu ga nigotte imasu.)

¶ The river **is muddy** after the rain.

にし 西 〔名〕

nishi 〔n〕 west

西側 (nishigawa) 西の風 (nishi no
kaze)

the **western** side // a **west** wind, a wind from **the west**

¶太陽は東から出て、西に沈みます。
(Taiyō wa higashi kara dete, nishi ni
shizumimasu.)

¶ The sun rises in the east and sets in **the west**.

⇔東 higashi

-にち -日 〔尾〕

-nichi 〔suf〕 the counter used for days of the month and for days

①[日付を表す]
¶今日は2月 11 日です。(Kyō wa
nigatsu jūichinichi desu.)

① [the counter for days of the month]
¶ Today is February **11**.

662

＊「11 日 (jūichinichi)」以降は「14 日 (jūyokka)」、「20 日 (hatsuka)」、「24 日 (nijūyokka)」を除いて、すべて「〜にち (〜nichi)」と言う。

②［日数を表す］

¶今日は一日じゅう忙しかったです。(Kyō wa ichinichijū isogashikatta desu.)

¶もう四、五日待ってください。(Mōshi-gonichi matte kudasai.)

⇒-日 -ka

にちよう（び） 日曜（日）〔名〕

にっき 日記〔名〕

¶わたしは毎日日記をつけています。(Watashi wa mainichi nikki o tsukete imasu.)

にっぽん 日本〔名〕 ☞日本 Nihon

にほん 日本〔名〕

日本人 (Nihonjin) 日本語 (Nihongo) 日本料理 (Nihon-ryōri)

＊「にっぽん (Nippon)」とも言う。

にもつ 荷物〔名〕

¶わたしの荷物はこのかばんとかさだけです。(Watashi no nimotsu wa kono kaban to kasa dake desu.)
¶ホテルに着くと、ボーイが荷物を部屋まで運んでくれました。(Hoteru ni tsuku to, bōi ga nimotsu o heya made hakonde kuremashita.)

にゅういん 入院〔名、〜する〕

入院生活 (nyūin-seikatsu)

---

*-nichi is added to all the days of the month above 10 with the exception of the 14th (jūyokka), the 20th (hatsuka), and the 24th (nijūyokka).

② [the counter for days]

¶ [I] was busy all **day** today.

¶ Please wait four or five **days** longer.

nichiyō(bi) 〔n〕 Sunday

nikki 〔n〕 diary, journal

¶ I make a **diary** entry every day.

Nippon 〔n〕 ☞Nihon

Nihon 〔n〕 Japan

a Japanese, the Japanese // the Japanese language // Japanese cooking, Japanese food.

＊Variant: Nippon.

nimotsu 〔n〕 load, burden, baggage, goods, freight, cargo, one's belongings, etc.

¶ I have only this bag 〖suitcase, briefcase, etc.〗 and umbrella **with me**.

¶ When [we] arrived at the hotel, the bellboy took **[our] luggage** up to the room.

nyūin 〔n, 〜suru〕 admission to a hospital, hospitalization

one's days **while in the hospital**

¶長い間入院していましたが、あした やっと退院できるようになりました。 （Nagai aida *nyūin* shite imashita ga, ashita yatto taiin dekiru yō ni narimashita.）

¶田中さんはあした入院するそうで す。（Tanaka san wa ashita *nyūin* suru sō desu.）

⇔退院 **taiin**

¶ [I] have **been in the hospital** for a long time but tomorrow [I] can finally go home.

¶ I hear that [Mrs.] Tanaka is **going into the hospital** tomorrow.

にゅうがく 入学〔名、～する〕

入学式（*nyūgaku*shiki）入学試験 （*nyūgaku*-shiken）入学願書（*nyūgaku*-gansho）

¶わたしの息子は今年小学校に入学し ました。（Watashi no musuko wa kotoshi shōgakkō ni *nyūgaku* shimashita.）

⇔卒業 **sotsugyō**

nyūgaku 〔n, ～*suru*〕 **entrance or admission into some sort of school**

an **entrance** ceremony // a (school) **entrance** exam // application for **admission** (to a school)

¶ My son **entered** elementary school this year.

ニュース〔名〕

¶わたしは毎朝ラジオのニュースを聞 きます。（Watashi wa maiasa rajio no *nyūsu* o kikimasu.）

¶山田さんが結婚したというニュース を知っていますか。（Yamada san ga kekkon shita to iu *nyūsu* o shitte imasu ka？）

nyūsu 〔n〕 **news**

¶ I listen to **the news** on the radio every morning.

¶ Did you hear **the news?** [Miss] Yamada has gotten married.

にゅう- 入-〔頭〕

入場（*nyū*jō）入場券（*nyū*jōken）入 荷（*nyū*ka）入港（*nyū*kō）入国 （*nyū*koku）

nyū- 〔pref〕 **a prefix meaning entering**

admission, entrance // a ticket of admission, entry ticket // the receipt of goods // entry (into a port) // entry into a country, immigration

---

にる 似る〔動Ⅱ〕

¶あなたはお母さんに顔がよく似てい ますね。（Anata wa okāsan ni kao ga yoku *nite* imasu ne.）

niru 〔v Ⅱ〕 **resemble, look like, sound like**

¶ Your face **looks** a lot **like** your mother's.

¶兄弟だから、声がとても似ていま
す。(Kyōdai da kara, koe ga totemo *nite*
imasu.)

¶ As [they] are brothers, [their] voices
are a lot **alike**.

にる 煮る〔動Ⅱ〕

¶今晩は野菜を煮て食べましょう。
(Konban wa yasai o *nite* tabemashō.)
¶この魚は煮るより焼いたほうがおい
しいです。(Kono sakana wa *niru* yori
yaita hō ga oishii desu.)

niru 〔v Ⅱ〕 **boil, cook**

¶ Let's have **boiled** 〖**cooked**〗
vegetables tonight.

¶ This fish is better grilled than **boiled**
〖**poached**〗.

にわ 庭〔名〕

¶庭に花が咲いています。(*Niwa* ni
hana ga saite imasu.)
¶わたしの家の庭は狭いです。
(Watashi no ie no *niwa* wa semai desu.)

niwa 〔n〕 **garden, yard**

¶ Flowers are blooming in **the garden**.

¶ **The yard** at my house is small.

にわとり 鶏〔名〕

niwatori 〔n〕 **chicken(s)**

-にん -人〔尾〕

-nin 〔suf〕 **a suffix indicating a
person; the counter for people**

①[その仕事をする人、その状態にあ
る人を表す]
病人（byō*nin*）けが人（kega*nin*）保証
人（hoshō*nin*）

① [indicates a person doing a
particular job or action or a person in a
particular state]
a sick **person**, a patient, an invalid // an
injured **person**, the wounded // a
guarantor, a sponsor, a reference

②[人数を表す]
¶「御兄弟は何人ですか。」(Gokyōdai
wa nan*nin* desu ka?)「兄が一人と姉が
二人、わたしを入れて四人です。」
(Ani ga hitori to ane ga futari, watashi o
irete yo*nin* desu.)
＊「一人（ichinin）」「二人（ninin）」と
は言わないで、「一人（hitori）」「二人
（futari）」と言う。「四人（shinin）」と
言わないで「四人（yonin）」と言う。

② [the counter for people]
¶ "**How many** brothers and sisters do
you have?"
"I have one older brother and two older
sisters so there are **four of us** in all."

*Irregular forms are *hitori* (one person)
and *futari* (two persons). Also, "four
persons" is *yonin*, not **shinin*.

にんき　人気〔名〕

¶山田先生は学生に人気があります。
（Yamada sensei wa gakusei ni *ninki* ga arimasu.）

¶あなたの国でいちばん人気のあるスポーツは何ですか。（Anata no kuni de ichiban *ninki* no aru supōtsu wa nan desu ka？）

にんぎょう　人形〔名〕

¶妹は人形を欲しがっています。
（Imōto wa *ningyō* o hoshigatte imasu.）

にんげん　人間〔名〕

① [ひと]
¶人間は考える動物です。（*Ningen* wa kangaeru dōbutsu desu.）
② [人柄]
¶あの人は正直な人間です。（Ano hito wa shōjiki na *ningen* desu.）

にんずう　人数〔名〕

¶このクラスの人数は何人ですか。
（Kono kurasu no *ninzū* wa nannin desu ka？）

ninki 〔n〕 popularity; popular

¶ Professor Yamada **is popular** with students.

¶ What sport is most **popular** in your country?

ningyō 〔n〕 doll, puppet

¶ My younger sister wants **a doll**.

ningen 〔n〕 a human being, humanity; character, personality

① [a human being, humanity]
¶ **Humans** are thinking creatures 〚animals with the power of reason〛.
② [character, personality]
¶ [He] is naturally honest.

ninzū 〔n〕 the number of persons

¶ **How many are there** in this class?

ぬ

ぬう 縫う 〔動 I 〕

¶わたしは自分で着物を縫います。
（Watashi wa jibun de kimono o
nuimasu.)

nuu 〔v I〕 **sew, stitch**

¶ I **make** my own clothes.

ぬく 抜く 〔動 I 〕

くぎを抜く（kugi o *nuku*）毛を抜く
（ke o *nuku*）草を抜く（kusa o *nuku*）歯
を抜く（ha o *nuku*）
¶もう一本ビールのせんを抜きましょ
うか。（Mō ippon biiru no sen o
nukimashō ka？）

nuku 〔v I〕 **pull out, extract,
remove**

pull out a nail 〖spike, etc.〗 // **pull out**
a hair // to weed, **pull out** weeds // **pull
out** 〖**extract**〗 a tooth

¶ Shall I open another bottle of beer
(literally, **take** the cap **off**)?

ぬぐ 脱ぐ 〔動 I 〕

服を脱ぐ（fuku o *nugu*）ズボンを脱ぐ
（zubon o *nugu*）くつ下を脱ぐ
（kutsushita o *nugu*）
¶日本の家では、普通くつを脱いで部
屋に上がります。（Nihon no ie de wa,
futsū kutsu o *nuide* heya ni agarimasu.）
⇔着る kiru はく haku

nugu 〔v I〕 **take off (an item of
clothing)**

undress // **take off** one's pants
〖trousers, slacks〗 // **take off** one's
socks 〖stockings〗

¶ In Japan one usually **takes off** one's
shoes at the door before going inside.

ぬける 抜ける 〔動 II 〕

① [離れて取れる]
髪の毛が抜ける（kaminoke ga nukeru）
歯が抜ける（ha ga *nukeru*）
② [あるべきものが脱落する]

¶この本は1ページ抜けています。
（Kono hon wa ippēji *nukete* imasu.）
③ [もれる、なくなる]

nukeru 〔v II〕 **come out, fall off;
be missing, be omitted; escape,
leak**

① [come out, fall off, become loose]
one s hair **falls out**, one's hair **thins** // a
tooth **comes out**

② [be missing, be omitted, be left out,
be lacking]

¶ This book **is missing** a page.

③ [escape, leak, be gone]

¶タイヤの空気が抜けています。
(Taiya no kūki ga *nukete* imasu.)

¶ The air **is leaking** from the tire 〖The tire is flat〗.

ぬすむ 盗む〔動Ⅰ〕

¶昨日店にどろぼうが入って、100万円盗んでいきました。(Kinō mise ni dorobō ga haitte, hyakuman'en *nusunde* ikimashita.)

¶わたしは電車の中で財布を盗まれました。(Watashi wa densha no naka de saifu o *nusumaremashita*.)

nusumu 〖v I〗 **steal, rob**

¶ Burglars broke into my store 〖the store where I work〗 yesterday and **stole** a million yen.

¶ I **had** my wallet **stolen** on the train.

ぬの 布〔名〕

布切れ（*nuno*gire）布地（*nuno*ji）布製（*nuno*sei）

nuno 〖n〗 **cloth**

a piece of **cloth** // **cloth, fabric** // **cloth**, made of **cloth**

ぬる 塗る〔動Ⅰ〕

¶パンにバターを塗って食べます。(Pan ni batā o *nutte* tabemasu.)

¶この腰掛けはペンキを塗ったばかりです。(Kono koshikake wa penki o *nutta* bakari desu.)

nuru 〖v I〗 **to paint, varnish, plaster, etc.**

¶ [I] eat **buttered** bread 〖toast, rolls, etc.〗.

¶ This bench 〖seat, chair, stool, etc.〗 has just **been painted**.

ぬるい〔形〕

¶早く飲まないと、コーヒーがぬるくなります。(Hayaku nomanai to, kōhii ga *nuruku* narimasu.)

nurui 〖adj〗 **tepid, lukewarm, not hot enough**

¶ [Your] coffee will **get cold** if [you] don't hurry up and drink it.

ぬれる〔動Ⅱ〕

¶かさを持って行かなかったので、雨にぬれてしまいました。(Kasa o motte ikanakatta node, ame ni *nurete* shimaimashita.)

¶ぬれたシャツを着ていると、風邪を引きます。(*Nureta* shatsu o kite iru to, kaze o hikimasu.)

nureru 〖v II〗 **get wet, be wet, be damp**

¶ [I] didn't have an umbrella with [me] so [I] **got wet** in the rain.

¶ You will catch cold if you wear a **wet** shirt.

ね

ね 根 [名]

木の根 (ki no *ne*) 草の根 (kusa no *ne*) 根が出る (*ne* ga deru) 根が生える (*ne* ga haeru) 根が伸びる (*ne* ga nobiru)

ね [助]

① [相手に同意を求めたり念を押したりする意味を表す]

¶あしたはきっと来てくださいね。(Ashita wa kitto kite kudasai *ne*.)

¶あなたが田中さんですね。(Anata ga Tanaka san desu *ne*.)

② [感嘆したり驚いたりする気持ちなどを表す]

¶このりんごは高いですね。(Kono ringo wa takai desu *ne*.)

¶秋子さんはきれいな人ですね。(Akiko san wa kirei na hito desu *ne*.)

③ [自分はそう思うという軽い主張の気持ちを表す]

¶空がこんなに暗いから、夕方は雨になると思いますね。(Sora ga konna ni kurai kara, yūgata wa ame ni naru to omoimasu *ne*.)

¶この魚は腐っているようですから、食べないほうがいいですね。(Kono sakana wa kussatte iru yō desu kara, tabenai hō ga ii desu *ne*.)

¶夕食のため豚肉を買います。牛肉は高いですからね。(Yūshoku no tame butaniku o kaimasu. Gyūniku wa takai desu kara *ne*.)

ne [n] **root(s)**

the roots of a tree 〘shrub〙 // **the roots** of grass 〘an herb, a weed〙 // take **root**; **the roots** are exposed // take **root** // **the roots** spread

ne [part] **isn't it, doesn't it, don't you; I suppose, I believe; you see, you know**

① [used to invite the concurrence of the listener or for emphasis]

¶ Now you will come tomorrow, **won't you?**

¶ You **must be** [Mr.] Tanaka.

② [used to express one's admiration, wonder, surprise, etc.]

¶ **My**, these apples are expensive!

¶ Isn't Akiko pretty!

③ [used to lightly stress that something is the speaker's opinion]

¶ I believe it will rain this evening—the skies are so dark now.

¶ This fish seems to have gone bad. [We]'d better not eat it.

¶ I'm going to buy pork for dinner—beef is so expensive, **you know**.

④ [ちょっと考える気持ちを表す]

¶「映画を見に行きませんか。」（Eiga o mi ni ikimasen ka？）「そうですね。今度の日曜日なら大丈夫です。」（Sō desu *ne.* Kondo no nichiyōbi nara daijōbu desu.）

*質問に答える場合、「そうね（sō ne）」「そうですね（sō desu ne）」の形で使うことが多い。

*「ねえ（nē）」と言う場合もある。

④ [used when thinking something over]

¶ "Won't you come see a movie?" **"Let's see.** I could go next Sunday."

*Ne is often used in the patterns "*Sō ne* ," "*Sō desu ne*" when answering a question.

* Variant: *nē.*

ねがい　願い〔名〕
negai 〔n〕 desire, wish; request

① [希望]
平和の願い（heiwa no *negai*）

② [依頼]
¶これからもよろしくお願いします。（Kore kara mo yoroshiku o*negai* shimasu.）

① [desire, wish, hope]
hopes for peace, **a desire** for peace

② [request]
¶ **I hope** to continue to receive your kind offices on my behalf (a set polite expression).

ねがう　願う〔動 I〕
negau 〔v I〕 desire, wish, hope for; request, implore

① [希望する]
¶みんなが世界の平和を願っています。（Minna ga sekai no heiwa o *negatte* imasu.）

② [頼む]
¶絵に手を触れないように願います。（E ni te o furenai yō ni *negaimasu.*）

① [desire, wish, hope for]
¶ All **hope** 〚**pray**〛 for world peace.

② [request, implore]
¶ **Kindly refrain** from touching the paintings.

ネクタイ〔名〕
nekutai 〔n〕 necktie, tie

ネクタイを締める（*nekutai* o shime-ru）ネクタイを外す（*nekutai* o hazusu）

¶いいネクタイをしていますね。（Ii *nekutai* o shite imasu ne.）

tie **a necktie** // unite **a necktie**, take off **a tie**

¶ That's a nice **tie** you have on.

ねこ〔名〕
neko 〔n〕 cat

ねじ〔名〕

ねじを締める（neji o shimeru）ねじを外す（neji o hazusu）
¶機械のねじが外れました。（Kikai no neji ga hazuremashita.）
¶毎晩、寝る前に時計のねじを巻きます。（Maiban, neru mae ni tokei no neji o makimasu.）

neji 〔n〕 **screw**

turn **a screw**, screw // unscrew

¶ **A screw** has come off〚is coming off〛the machine.
¶ [I] **wind** [my] watch〚clock〛every night at bedtime.

ねじる〔動Ⅰ〕

¶そんなにねじったら、腕が折れます。（Sonna ni nejittara, ude ga oremasu.）

nejiru 〔vⅠ〕 **twist, wrench, wring**

¶ **If you twist** [my] arm like that, you'll break it.

ねずみ〔名〕

nezumi 〔n〕 **mouse, rat**

ねだん　値段〔名〕

¶このくつの値段はいくらですか。（Kono kutsu no nedan wa ikura desu ka？）
¶この品物には値段がついていませんね。（Kono shinamono ni wa nedan ga tsuite imasen ne.）

nedan 〔n〕 **price, cost**

¶ What is **the price** of these shoes?

¶ There's no **price** on this merchandise.

ねつ　熱〔名〕

①[熱さを感じさせるもとになるもの]
¶太陽の熱で水が温かくなりました。（Taiyō no netsu de mizu ga atatakaku narimashita.）
¶ナイロンは熱に弱いです。（Nairon wa netsu ni yowai desu.）
②[体の温度]
熱がある（netsu ga aru）熱が下がる（netsu ga sagaru）熱を計る（netsu o hakaru）
¶子供が風邪を引いて熱を出しました。（Kodomo ga kaze o hiite netsu o dashimashita.）

netsu 〔n〕 **heat; temperature, fever**
① [heat]
¶ The water was warmed by **the sun**.

¶ Nylon has a low **heat** tolerance.

② [temperature, fever]
run **a temperature**, have **a fever** // **one's fever** goes down // take **one's temperature**

¶ The child has caught a cold and is running **a temperature**〚The child caught a cold and had **a fever**〛.

671

ねっしん　熱心〔形動〕

¶あした試験があるので、学生はみんな熱心に勉強しています。(Ashita shiken ga aru node, gakusei wa minna *nesshin* ni benkyō shite imasu.)

¶中村さんは仕事に熱心な人です。(Nakamura san wa shigoto ni *nesshin* na hito desu.)

ねむい　眠い〔形〕

眠くなる (*nemuku* naru)

¶ゆうべはあまりよく眠れなかったので、今日は眠いです。(Yūbe wa amari yoku nemurenakatta node, kyō wa *nemui* desu.)

¶田中さんは眠そうな顔をしています。(Tanaka san wa *nemusō* na kao o shite imasu.)

ねむる　眠る〔動Ⅰ〕

¶赤ちゃんはよく眠っています。(Akachan wa yoku *nemutte* imasu.)

¶一晩じゅう、眠らないで勉強しました。(Hitobanjū, *nemuranaide* benkyō shimashita.)

¶ゆうべはよく眠れましたか。(Yūbe wa yoku *nemuremashita* ka？)

ねらう〔動Ⅰ〕

¶ねこがねずみをねらっています。(Neko ga nezumi o *neratte* imasu.)

ねる　寝る〔動Ⅱ〕

① 〔眠る〕

¶あなたはいつも何時ごろ寝ますか。(Anata wa itsu mo nanji goro *nemasu* ka？)

---

nesshin 〔adj-v〕 **enthusiastic, eager, earnest, dedicated**

¶ All the students are studying **hard** as they have an exam tomorrow.

¶ [Mr.] Nakamura is a **hard** worker.

nemui 〔adj〕 **be sleepy**

become **sleepy**

¶ **I'm sleepy** today because I didn't sleep very well last night.

¶ [Mrs.] Tanaka **looks sleepy**.

nemuru 〔v Ⅰ〕 **sleep, fall asleep**

¶ The baby **is sleeping** soundly.

¶ [I] **stayed up** all night studying.

¶ **Did you sleep** well last night?

nerau 〔v Ⅰ〕 **aim at, set one's sights on, stalk**

¶ The cat **is stalking** a mouse.

neru 〔v Ⅱ〕 **sleep, go to sleep; be ill in bed; lie down**

① 〔sleep, go to sleep, go to bed〕

¶ What time do you **go to bed** each night?

672

¶わたしは夜寝る前に歯をみがきます。（Watashi wa yoru *neru* mae ni ha o migakimasu.）

② [病気で休む]

¶父は風邪を引いて寝ています。（Chichi wa kaze o hiite *nete* imasu.）

③ [体を横にする]

¶山田さんは寝ながら本を読んでいます。（Yamada san wa *nenagara* hon o yonde imasu.）

¶ I brush my teeth before **going to bed** at night.

② [be ill in bed, be confined to bed]

¶ My father **is in bed** with a cold.

③ [lie down, be lying down]

¶ [Mr.] Yamada **is lying down** and reading a book.

-ねん -年 〔尾〕

¶わたしは 1930 年に生まれました。（Watashi wa senkyūhyakusanjū*nen* ni umaremashita.）

¶ 弟は小学校3年です。（Otōto wa shōgakkō san*nen* desu.）

-nen 〔suf〕 **year**

¶ I was born in 1930.

¶ My younger brother is in the third **year** of elementary school.

ねんど 年度 〔名〕

昨年度（saku*nendo*）来年度（rai*nendo*）新年度（shin*nendo*）年度末（*nendo*matsu）

¶日本では、4月に新しい年度が始まります。（Nihon de wa, shigatsu ni atarashii *nendo* ga hajimarimasu.）

¶今年度の予算はどのくらいですか。（Kon*nendo* no yosan wa dono kurai desu ka？）

nendo 〔n〕 **year, term, fiscal year, school year**

last **year**, the previous **fiscal year** // next **year**, the coming **fiscal year** // the new **year** 〚fiscal year〛 // the end of **the year** 〚fiscal year〛

¶ In Japan the new fiscal 〚academic〛 **year** begins in April.

¶ What is the budget for the current **fiscal year?**

ねんりょう 燃料 〔名〕

¶自動車の燃料は普通はガソリンです。（Jidōsha no *nenryō* wa futsū wa gasorin desu.）

nenryō 〔n〕 **fuel**

¶ Gasoline is **the fuel** usually used in automobiles

ねんれい 年齢 〔名〕

¶ここに住所、氏名、年齢を書いてください。（Koko ni jūsho, shimei, *nenrei* o kaite kudasai.）⇒年 **toshi**

nenrei 〔n〕 **age, years**

¶ Please write your name, address and **age** here.

の

の〔助〕

① [前の名詞などがあとに来る名詞などをいろいろな意味で修飾限定する]

東京の地図 (Tōkyō *no* chizu) 子供のくつ (kodomo *no* kutsu) 日本語の先生 (Nihongo *no* sensei)

¶これはわたしの本です。(Kore wa watashi *no* hon desu.)

¶あれは木の机です。(Are wa ki *no* tsukue desu.)

¶母からの手紙が今日着きました。(Haha kara *no* tegami ga kyō tsukimashita.)

*普通「名詞＋の (no) ＋名詞」の形で使うが、「名詞＋助詞＋の (no) ＋名詞」の形で使うこともある。「母からの手紙 (haha kara no tegami)」は「母から来た手紙 (haha kara kita tegami)」の意味である。

② [前の名詞があとに来る動作や状態などを表す名詞に対してその主体や目的である関係を表す]

¶子供がお父さんの帰りを待っています。(Kodomo ga otōsan *no* kaeri o matte imasu.)

¶学校に着いた時、授業の始まりのベルが鳴っていました。(Gakkō ni tsuita toki, jugyō *no* hajimari no beru ga natte imashita.)

no〔part〕 **of, for, by, in, on**

① [indicates that the noun or other words preceding it modifies or restricts in some way the noun following it]
a map **of** Tokyo // children**'s** shoes // a teacher **of** Japanese

¶This is **my** book.

¶That is a **wooden** desk.

¶A letter **from** my mother arrived today.

*Usually used in the pattern "noun + *no* + noun" but can also be used in the pattern "noun + particle + *no* + noun." *Haha kara no tegami* (a letter from my mother) is equivalent to *haha kara kita tegami* (a letter coming from my mother).

② [indicates that the noun preceding it is the subject or object of the action, state, etc., expressed in the noun following it]

¶The children are waiting for 〚looking forward to〛 the return **of** their father.

¶When [I] arrived at school, the bell for the beginning **of** class was ringing.

¶ようやく日本語の読み書きができるようになりました。（Yōyaku Nihongo *no* yomikaki ga dekiru yō ni narimashita.）

¶ [I] have finally become〖I finally became〗able to read and write Japanese.

¶南の海の水の青さはすばらしかった。（Minami no umi no mizu *no* aosa wa subarashikatta.）

¶ The blue **of** the water of the southern sea was wonderful〖The southern sea was a marvelous blue〗.

＊「お父さんの帰り（otōsan no kaeri）」は「お父さんが帰る（otōsan ga kaeru）」、「授業の始まり（jugyō no hajimari）」は「授業が始まる（jugyō ga hajimaru）」、「日本語の読み書き（Nihongo no yomikaki）」は「日本語を読んだり書いたりする（Nihongo o yondari kaitari suru）」、「南の海の水の青さ（minami no umi no mizu no aosa）」、は「南の海の水が青い（minami no umi no mizu ga aoi）」という意味を表す。

＊In the above sentences *otōsan no kaeri* (the father's return) = *otōsan ga kaeru* (the father returns), *jugyō no hajimari* (the start of class) = *jugyō ga hajimaru* (class starts), *Nihongo no yomikaki* (the reading and writing of Japanese) = *Nihongo o yondari kaitari suru* (to read and write Japanese), and *minami no umi no mizu no aosa* (the blue of the water of southern seas) = *minami no umi no mizu ga aoi* (the water of southern seas is blue).

③[動詞や形容詞・形容動詞などが名詞を修飾する形で使われる場合その動作や状態の主体や対象などを表す]

③[indicates the subject or object of a verb, adjective, or adjective-verb in a noun phrase]

¶上田さんの乗っていた車が事故を起こしました。（Ueda san *no* notte ita kuruma ga jiko o okoshimashita.）

¶ The car that [Mr.] Ueda was riding in caused an accident.

¶天気のいい日にはよく散歩します。（Tenki *no* ii hi ni wa yoku sanpo shimasu.）

¶ [I] often take a walk on days when the weather is nice.

¶おすしのきらいな人はいませんか。（Osushi *no* kirai na hito wa imasen ka？）

¶ Is there anyone here who doesn't like *sushi*?

＊この場合の「の（no）」は「が（ga）」と置き換えられる。

＊This particular *no* can be replaced by *ga*.

の〔助〕

no〔part〕 **one; that, those; thing, matter**

①[所属その他いろいろな意味で関係のあるものごとを表す]

① [one; stands in for something previously mentioned]

¶「このペンはだれのですか。」（Kono pen wa dare *no* desu ka？）「わたしのです。」（Watashi *no* desu.）

¶「大きいりんごは100円で、小さいのは70円です。」（Ookii ringo wa hyakuen de, chiisai *no* wa nanajūen desu.）「では、その100円のを5個ください。」（Dewa, sono hyakuen *no* o goko kudasai.）

*前の名詞に関係のあるものごとが場面や文脈によってわかっているときに使う。「だれの（dare no）」は「だれのペン（dare no pen）」、「わたしの（watashi no）」は「わたしのペン（watashi no pen）」、「100円の（hyakuen no）」は、「100円のりんご（hyakuen no ringo）」の意味である。

②[前に来る動詞や形容詞・形容動詞の表すことがらに関係のあるものごとを表す]

¶あそこに並んでいるのは、バスに乗る人たちです。（Asoko ni narande iru *no* wa, basu ni noru hitotachi desu.）

¶本がたくさん並んでいますが、いちばんおもしろいのはどれですか。（Hon ga takusan narande imasu ga, ichiban omoshiroi *no* wa dore desu ka？）

*前に来る動詞や形容詞・形容動詞の表すことがらに関係のあるものごとが場面や文脈によってわかっているときに使う。「あそこに並んでいるの（asoko ni narande iru no）」は「あそこに並んでいる人たち（asoko ni narande iru hitotachi）」、「おもしろいの（omoshiroi no）」は「おもしろい本（omoshiroi hon）」の意味である。

¶ "**Whose** pen is this?"
"It's **mine**."

¶ "The large apples are a hundred yen and the small **ones** are seventy yen."
"Well, please give me five of the hundred yen **ones**."

*Used when the thing related to a previous noun is understood from the situation or context. In the above sentences *dare no* (whose) = *dare no pen* (whose pen), *watashi no* (mine) = *watashi no pen* (my pen), and *hyakuen no* (the hundred yen ones) = *hyakuen no ringo* (the hundred yen apples).

② [that, those; stands for something related to the verb, adjective, adjective-verb, or phrase preceding it]

¶ **The people** lined up over there are waiting for the bus (literally, **What** is lined up over there is people who are to board the bus).

¶ There are lots of books here. Which is the most interesting **one?**

*Used when the thing related to the verb, adjective, adjective-verb, or phrase coming before is understood from the situation or context. In the above sentences *asoko ni narande iru no* (that which is lined up over there) = *asoko ni narande iru hitotachi* (the people who are lined up over there), and *omoshiroi no* (the interesting one) = *omoshiroi hon* (an interesting book).

③ [前に来る動詞や形容詞・形容動詞の表すことがらを名詞のような働きにするときに使う]

¶ 寒い日に外へ出るのはいやです。
(Samui hi ni soto e deru *no* wa iya desu.)

¶ 山田さんが向こうから急いで来るのが見えました。(Yamada san ga mukō kara isoide kuru *no* ga miemashita.)

¶ このアパートは狭いのが欠点です。
(Kono apāto wa semai *no* ga ketten desu.)

④ [見聞きしたことに対する事情や根拠などを尋ねるときに使う]

¶ 「どうかしたのですか。顔色が悪いですね。」(Dō ka shita *no* desu ka？ Kaoiro ga warui desu ne.)「ええ、頭が痛いのです。」(Ee, atama ga itai no desu.)

¶ 「テレビを買わないのですか。」
(Terebi o kawanai *no* desu ka？)「ええ、お金がないのです。」(Ee, okane ga nai no desu.)

*「ん (n)」とも言う。「～の［ん］か (～no ［n］ ka)」「～の［ん］ですか (～no ［n］ desu ka)」の形で使う。

⑤ [ものごとに対する事情や根拠などを説明するのに使う]

¶ 「田中さんは今度の旅行には行かないそうですね。」(Tanaka san wa kondo no ryokō ni wa ikanai sō desu ne.)「田中さんは病気なのだそうです。」
(Tanaka san wa byōki na *no* da sō desu.)

¶ テレビを買いたいのですが、お金がありません。(Terebi o kaitai *no* desu ga, okane ga arimasen.)

③ [thing, matter, the fact that; used to make the preceding verb, adjective, adjective-verb, or phrase into a noun]

¶ I dislike **going out** on cold days 〚**Going out** on cold days is unpleasant〛.

¶ [I] saw [Miss] Yamada **come hurrying** in my direction.

¶ **The smallness** of this apartment is a drawback 〚One disadvantage of this apartment is **its smallness**〛.

④ [used when inquiring about something one has observed]

¶ "Is something wrong? You look pale." "Yes, I have a headache."

¶ "You aren't going to buy a television?"
"That's right. [I] don't have the money for it."

*This *no* is sometimes shortened to *n*. Used in the patterns "~ *no* 〚*n*〛 *ka*" and "~ *no* 〚*n*〛 *desu ka*."

⑤ [used when explaining about something]

¶ "1 hear that [Mr.] Tanaka isn't coming on the next trip."
"They say [he]'s ill."

¶ I want to buy a television set but I don't have the money for it.

*「ん (n)」とも言う。「〜の [ん] だ (〜no [n] da)」「〜の [ん] です (〜no [n] desu)」の形で使う。

*This *no* is sometimes shortened to *n*. Used in the patterns "〜 *no* ⟦*n*⟧ *da*" and "〜 *no* ⟦*n*⟧ *desu*."

の 〔助〕

① [質問するときに使う]
¶その映画、どこで見たの。(Sono eiga, doko de mita *no*？)
¶昨日はどこへ行ったの。(Kinō wa doko e itta *no*？)
¶今日は忙しいの。(Kyō wa isogashii *no*？)
*文末のイントネーションが上がる。

② [あることがらの事情や根拠などを説明するのに使う]
¶今日はおなかが痛いの。だから、あまり食べたくないわ。(Kyō wa onaka ga itai *no*. Dakara, amari tabetakunai wa.)
¶「今度の旅行には行かないの。」(Kondo no ryokō ni wa ikanai no？)「ええ、来週から試験が始まるの。」(Ee, raishū kara shiken ga hajimaru *no*.)
*文末のイントネーションが下がる。

*「のよ (no yo)」とも言う。
＊主に女性や子供が使うが、男性もかなり使うようになった。普通、目上の人には使わない。

no 〔part〕 **a sentence-ending particle**

① [used when asking a question]
¶ Where did [you] see that movie?

¶ Where did [you] go yesterday?

¶ Are [you] busy today?

*With this use of *no*, there is a rise in intonation at the end of the sentence.
② [used when explaining about something]
¶ I have a stomachache today. That's why I don't feel much like eating.

¶ "You aren't going on the coming trip?"
"That's right. Exams start next week."

*With this use of *no*, there is a falling intonation at the end of the sentence.
*Variant: *no yo*.
＊Mainly used by women and children but also used by men quite a bit now. Usually not used towards those of higher status.

のうか 農家 〔名〕

① [農民の住んでいる家]
¶畑の向こうに農家が1軒見えます。(Hatake no mukō ni *nōka* ga ikken miemasu.)
② [農業で生活している家庭]

nōka 〔n〕 **farmhouse; farm family, farmer**

① [farmhouse]
¶ **A farmhouse** is in sight across the field.

② [farm family, farmer]

¶わたしは農家に生まれました。
（Watashi wa nōka ni umaremashita.）

のうぎょう 農業 〔名〕
農業高校（nōgyō-kōkō）農業技術者
（nōgyō-gijutsusha）
¶この国の農業技術はかなり進んでい
ます。（Kono kuni no nōgyō-gijutsu wa
kanari susunde imasu.）

nōgyō 〔n〕 **agriculture, farming**
an **agricultural** high school // an
agricultural expert
¶ **Farming** methods are quite advanced
in this country.

のうりつ 能率 〔名〕
能率がいい（nōritsu ga ii）能率が悪い
（nōritsu ga warui）能率が上がる
（nōritsu ga agaru）能率が下がる
（nōritsu ga sagaru）
¶コンピューターのおかげで、事務の
能率がたいへん上がりました。
（Konpyūtā no okage de, jimu no nōritsu
ga taihen agarimashita.）

nōritsu 〔n〕 **efficiency**
be efficient // be inefficient // become
efficient // become inefficient
¶ Thanks to computers, [our] office
efficiency has been 〖was〗 greatly in
creased.

のうりょく 能力 〔名〕
能力がある（nōryoku ga aru）能力が
ない（nōryoku ga nai）
¶あの人は、すばらしい計算の能力を
持っています。（Ano hito wa, subarashii
keisan no nōryoku o motte imasu.）
¶わたしの能力では、この仕事はでき
ません。（Watashi no nōryoku de wa,
kono shigoto wa dekimasen.）

nōryoku 〔n〕 **ability, capability, capacity**
able, capable, competent // incapable,
incompetent
¶ [He] has a marvelous **head** for
figures.

¶ This job is beyond my **abilities**.

ノート 〔名〕
①〔ノートブック、帳面〕
¶かばんの中には本やノートなどが
入っています。（Kaban no naka ni wa
hon ya nōto nado ga haitte imasu.）
②〔書き留めること〕
ノートをとる（nōto o toru）

nōto 〔n〕 **notebook; notes**
① [notebook]
¶ The briefcase 〖bag, etc.〗 contains
books, **notebooks**, etc.

② [notes]
take **notes**

のこす 残す〔動Ⅰ〕

① [余らせる]
¶食べ物は残さないで全部食べなさい。(Tabemono wa *nokosanaide* zenbu tabenasai.)
② [後にとどめる]
¶田中さんは家族を残して、一人で外国へ行きました。(Tanaka san wa kazoku o *nokoshite*, hitori de gaikoku e ikimashita.)

のこる 残る〔動Ⅰ〕

① [余る]
¶昨日のごちそうがまだたくさん残っています。(Kinō no gochisō ga mada takusan *nokotte* imasu.)
¶残った御飯を捨てないでください。(*Nokotta* gohan o sutenaide kudasai.)
② [後までその場所にいる]
¶中村さんはまだ会社に残って仕事をしています。(Nakamura san wa mada kaisha ni *nokotte* shigoto o shite imasu.)

のせる 載せる〔動Ⅱ〕

① [物を何かの上に置く]
¶この箱の上には、何も載せないでください。(Kono hako no ue ni wa, nani mo *nosenaide* kudasai.)
¶机の上に載せておいた万年筆を知りませんか。(Tsukue no ue ni *nosete* oita mannenhitsu o shirimasen ka？)
② [新聞や本などに掲載する]
¶この小説は何という雑誌に載せるのですか。(Kono shōsetsu wa nan to iu zasshi ni *noseru* no desu ka？)

nokosu 〔v I〕 **leave, set aside; leave, leave behind**
① [leave, set aside]
¶ Clean up your plate(s).

② [leave, leave behind]
¶ [Mr.] Tanaka **left** [his] family **behind** and went abroad alone.

nokoru 〔v I〕 **remain, be left; remain, stay**
① [remain, be left, be left over]
¶ There **is** still a lot of food **left** from yesterday's party 〚dinner, etc.〛.

¶ Please don't throw out the **leftover** rice 〚**the leftovers**〛.
② [remain, stay, stay on]
¶ [Mr.] Nakamura is **still** at the office working.

noseru 〔v II〕 **place on; record, mention**
① [place on, set on, lay on]
¶ Please **don't put** anything **on** top of this box 〚case, casket, chest, etc.〛.

¶ Do you know what happened to the fountain pen I left **on** the desk?

② [record, mention, publish, carry]
¶ What magazine is this novel going **to be published** in?

のせる　乗せる〔動Ⅱ〕

¶わたしはおばあさんをバスに乗せて
あげました。（Watashi wa obāsan o basu
ni *nosete* agemashita.）

のぞく　除く〔動Ⅰ〕

① [不必要なものなどを取り去る]
¶この中から腐ったみかんを除いて、
いいみかんだけ残してください。
（Kono naka kara kusatta mikan o *nozoite*,
ii mikan dake nokoshite kudasai.）
② [ある範囲から外す]
¶その計画にはわたしを除いてみんな
が賛成しました。（Sono keikaku ni wa
watashi o *nozoite* minna ga sansei
shimashita.）

のぞく〔動Ⅰ〕

① [窓やすき間などから向こうを見る]

¶窓から部屋の中をのぞきました。
（Mado kara heya no naka o
nozokimushita.）
② [ちょっと見る、何かの一部分を見
る]
¶試験のときには、隣の人の答えをの
ぞいてはいけません。（Shiken no toki
ni wa, tonari no hito no kotae o *nozoite* wa
ikemasen.）

のち　後〔名〕

¶今日の天気は晴れ後曇りです。（Kyō
no tenki wa hare *nochi* kumori desu.）
¶また後ほどお電話します。（Mata
nochi hodo odenwa shimasu.）

noseru 〔v Ⅱ〕 carry, take on board, place on board (a train, bus, etc.)
¶ I **helped** the old lady **onto** the bus.

nozoku 〔v Ⅰ〕 remove, eliminate; exclude, except, omit
① [remove, eliminate, get rid of]
¶ Please **take out** the spoiled mandarin oranges and leave just the good ones here.

② [exclude, except, omit]
¶ All approved the plan **except for** me.

nozoku 〔v Ⅰ〕 take a look; peek, take a peek
① [take a look, look out, look in, peer at]
¶ I **looked** through the window into the room.

② [peek, take a peek, peep]

¶ One mustn't **look at** the answers of the person next to one during an exam.

nochi 〔n〕 after, afterwards, later, in future
¶ The weather for today will be clear, **later** cloudy.
¶ I will call again **later** (polite, spoken on the telephone).

ので〔助〕

¶雨が降っているので、今日はテニスができません。(Ame ga futte iru *node*, kyō wa tenisu ga dekimasen.)

¶ゆうべ遅くまで起きていたので、今日はとても眠いです。(Yūbe osoku made okite ita *node*, kyō wa totemo nemui desu.)

¶暑いので、上着を脱いで仕事をしました。(Atsui *node*, uwagi o nuide shigoto o shimashita.)

¶部屋が静かなので、落着いて勉強ができました。(Heya ga shizuka na *node*, ochitsuite benkyō ga dekimashita.)

¶日曜日なので、今日は電車がすいています。(Nichiyōbi na *node*, kyō wa densha ga suite imasu.)

＊前件が原因となり、後件がその結果として成立するという原因結果の関係を表す。普通、後件には結果としての客観的な言い方が来る。

⇒から **kara**

のど〔名〕

¶風邪を引いて、のどが痛いです。(Kaze o hiite, *nodo* ga itai desu.)

¶のどが渇いたから、お茶が飲みたいです。(*Nodo* ga kawaita kara, ocha ga nomitai desu.)

のに〔助〕

¶あの人はこんなに暑いのに、セーターを着ています。(Ano hito wa konna ni atsui *noni*, sētā o kite imasu.)

¶今日は日曜日なのに、学校へ行くのですか。(Kyō wa nichiyōbi na *noni*, gakkō e iku no desu ka？)

---

node 〔part〕 **as, because, on account of, owing to**

¶ [We] can't play tennis today—it's raining.

¶ [I] was up until late last night **so** [I] am very sleepy today.

¶ **It was so hot that** [I] took off [my] suit jacket and worked in [my] shirt sleeves.

¶ [I] was able to settle down and study **as** the room was quiet.

¶ The trains aren't crowded today **because** it's Sunday.

＊Expresses a cause-and-effect relationship, with the cause stated in the first, *node*-clause and the effect in the second clause. Usually this result or effect is stated objectively.

nodo 〔n〕 **throat, voice**

¶ I have a sore **throat** from a cold.

¶ I'm **thirsty** and would like some (green) tea to drink.

noni 〔part〕 **though, although, in spite of**

¶ [He] is wearing a sweater **even though** it is so hot.

¶ Are you going to school today **even though** it's Sunday?

¶みんな遊んでいるのに、あの人だけ勉強しています。（Minna asonde iru *noni*, ano hito dake benkyō shite imasu.）

¶一生懸命に勉強したのに、大学の入学試験にとうとう受かりませんでした。（Isshōkenmei ni benkyō shita *noni*, daigaku no nyūgaku-shiken ni tōtō ukarimasen deshita.）

＊前件のことがらと後件のことがらとの相いれない関係を表す。予期することがらと反対のことがらが起こるような場合に使う。後件には、「〜う（よう）（〜u［yō］）」などの意志。「〜なさい（〜nasai）」などの命令、「〜てください（〜te kudasai）」などの依頼、「〜てもいい（〜te mo ii）」などの許可などの言い方は来ない。

のばす 延ばす〔動Ⅰ〕

¶試験の時間を少し延ばしてください。（Shiken no jikan o sukoshi *nobashite* kudasai.）

¶用事ができたので、旅行の出発を1日延ばしました。（Yōji ga dekita node, ryokō no shuppatsu o ichinichi *nobashimashita*.）

のばす 伸ばす〔動Ⅰ〕

背中を伸ばす（senaka o *nobasu*）才能を伸ばす（sainō o *nobasu*）

¶本はたなの上の方にあるので、手を伸ばしても届きません。（Hon wa tana no ue no hō ni aru node, te o *nobashite* mo todokimasen.）

¶ [He] alone is studying **while** everyone else is taking the day off.

¶ **In spite** of studying hard, in the end [I] didn't pass [my] university entrance exams.

＊Used when the first clause and the second clause are not in conformity with each other, such as when the opposite of what would be expected has happened. The second clause does not end with an expression of intent such as -ō ⟦-yō⟧, an order with -nasai, a request with -te kudasai or a giving of permission such as -te mo ii.

nobasu 〚v Ⅰ〛 **postpone, delay, extend, prolong**

¶ Please **give** us a little **more time** for the exam.

¶ Something came up so [I] **postponed** [my] departure date a day.

nobasu 〚v Ⅰ〛 **lengthen, extend, stretch, spread out, unbend**

stretch, straighten up // **develop** one s abilities, **cultivate** one's talent

¶ Since the book is towards the top of the bookcase [I] can't reach it.

のはら　野原〔名〕

¶山を越えると、広い野原がありま
す。(Yama o koeru to, hiroi *nohara* ga
arimasu.)

nohara 〔n〕 field, plain, plains

¶There is a broad **plain** on the other
side of the mountain.

のびる　延びる〔動Ⅱ〕

¶昼休みの時間が 15 分延びました。
(Hiruyasumi no jikan ga jūgofun
nobimashita.)

¶会議が延びて夕方までかかってしま
いました。(Kaigi ga *nobite* yūgata made
kakatte shimaimashita.)

nobiru 〔v Ⅱ〕 be postponed, be
delayed, be prolonged

¶The noon break **has been extended**
by 15 minutes.

¶The meeting **stretched out** into the
evening.

のびる　伸びる〔動Ⅱ〕

①[長くなる]
¶髪が伸びたので、床屋へ行きまし
た。(Kami ga *nobita* node, tokoya e
ikimashita.)

¶中学生になって、子供の背が急に伸
びました。(Chūgakusei ni natte,
kodomo no se ga kyū ni *nobimashita*.)

¶この木は１年に5センチぐらい伸びま
す。(Kono ki wa ichinen ni gosenchi
gurai *nobimasu*.)

②[能力などが発達する]
¶去年に比べて今年は成績がずいぶん
伸びました。(Kyonen ni kurabete
kotoshi wa seiseki ga zuibun
nobimashita.)

nobiru 〔v Ⅱ〕 extend, lengthen,
increase, grow; advance, make
progress

①[extend, lengthen, increase, grow]
¶[My] hair **grew out** and [I] went to
the barber's.

¶The child's height suddenly **shot up**
after [he] entered middle school.

¶This tree **grows** about five
centimeters a year.

②[advance, make progress]
¶Compared to last year, this year's
record **has improved** considerably.

のぼり　上り〔名〕

①[下から上へ移ること、上り坂]
¶この道はあの木の所から上りになり
ます。(Kono michi wa ano ki no tokoro
kara *nobori* ni narimasu.)

nobori 〔n〕 ascent, rise, going
up; train bound for a major city

①[ascent, rise, going up]
¶This road starts **going uphill** from
that tree over there.

② [地方から中心的な所へ行く汽車・電車]

上り列車（*noboriressha*）

⇔下り **kudari**

② [train going from the country into a major city]

the **ingoing** train, the **up** train

のぼる 登る〔動Ⅰ〕

¶わたしはまだその山に登ったことがありません。（Watashi wa mada sono yama ni *nobotta* koto ga arimasen.）

¶子供が木に登って遊んでいます。（Kodomo ga ki ni *nobotte* asonde imasu.）

noboru 〔vⅠ〕 **climb**

¶I haven't **climbed** that mountain yet.

¶The children are playing, **climbing** trees.

のぼる 上る〔動Ⅰ〕

¶その階段は上るのがたいへんです。（Sono kaidan wa *noboru* no ga taihen desu.）

⇔下る **kudaru**

noboru 〔vⅠ〕 **climb, go up, mount, ascend**

¶**Climbing** those stairs is hard work.

のぼる 昇る〔動Ⅰ〕

¶東の空に太陽が昇りました。（Higashi no sora ni taiyō ga *noborimashita*.）

noboru 〔vⅠ〕 **rise**

¶The sun **rose** in the eastern skies.

のみもの 飲み物〔名〕

¶飲み物は何がいいですか。（*Nomimono* wa nani ga ii desu ka?）

⇒食べ物 **tabemono**

nomimono 〔n〕 **a drink, a beverage**

¶What would you like **to drink?**

のむ 飲む〔動Ⅰ〕

水を飲む（mizu o *nomu*） 酒を飲む（sake o *nomu*） 薬を飲む（kusuri o *nomu*）

¶ビールを飲みに行きませんか。（Biiru o *nomi* ni ikimasen ka?）

nomu 〔vⅠ〕 **drink, swallow**

drink water, **have a drink** of water // **take** a drink; **drink** sake // **take** medicine

¶Won't you come and **have** some beer with [us]?

のり〔名〕

のりではる（*nori* de haru） のりをつける（*nori* o tsukeru）

nori 〔n〕 **paste, starch**

paste on, fasten with **paste** // apply **paste**, paste together

¶切手にのりをつけて封筒にはります。(Kitte ni *nori* o tsukete fūtō ni harimasu.)

¶ [I] **paste** the stamp on the envelope.

のりかえ 乗り換え〔名〕

norikae 〔n〕 **transfer, change (of train, plane, bus, etc.)**

¶電車で行くと、乗り換えが多くてめんどうです。(Densha de iku to, *norikae* ga ookute mendō desu.)

¶ The large number of **transfers** is a nuisance when one goes there by train.

のりかえる 乗り換える〔動Ⅱ〕

norikaeru 〔v Ⅱ〕 **to transfer, change (trains, planes, buses, etc.)**

¶東京駅へ行くのには、どこで乗り換えたらいいですか。(Tōkyō-eki e iku no ni wa, doko de *norikaetara* ii desu ka?)

¶ Where **should I transfer** in order to go to Tokyo Station?

¶次の駅で乗り換えてください。(Tsugi no eki de *norikaete* kudasai.)

¶ Please **transfer** at the next station.

のりもの 乗り物〔名〕

norimono 〔n〕 **vehicle, conveyance**

¶乗り物には、汽車、電車、船、飛行機、自動車などがあります。(*Norimono* ni wa, kisha, densha, fune, hikōki, jidōsha nado ga arimasu.)

¶ Types of **vehicles** include trains 〚steam and electric trains〛, ships, airplanes, automobiles and the like.

のる 載る〔動Ⅰ〕

noru 〔v Ⅰ〕 **lie on, be on top of; be recorded, be mentioned**

① [何かの上に置いてある]
¶机の上に載っている辞書を取ってください。(Tsukue no ue ni *notte* iru jisho o totte kudasai.)

① [lie on, be on top of, rest on]
¶ Please hand me the dictionary **sitting** on the desk.

② [新聞や本などに掲載される]

② [be recorded, be mentioned, appear, be published (in a newspaper, book, etc.)]

¶この言葉は辞書に載っていません。(Kono kotoba wa jisho ni *notte* imasen.)

¶ This word **isn't in** the dictionary.

¶今朝の新聞にあなたの国のことが載っていました。(Kesa no shinbun ni anata no kuni no koto ga *notte* imashita.)

¶ There was **something** about your country **in** the newspaper this morning.

686

のる 乗る〔動Ⅰ〕

①[人などが乗り物などで移動する]
電車に乗る（densha ni *noru*）　自動車に乗る（jidōsha ni *noru*）　馬に乗る（uma ni *noru*）

¶ このバスは乗る時に料金を払います。（Kono basu wa *noru* toki ni ryōkin o haraimasu.）

②[人や動物などが台などの上に上る]
¶ いすの上に乗ってたなの物を取りました。（Isu no ue ni *notte* tana no mono o torimashita.）

noru〔vⅠ〕ride, get on, board; step on, mount

① [ride, get on, board, take (a vehicle)]
ride a train; **board** a train // **ride** in a car; **get in** a car // **ride** a horse; **mount** a horse

¶ With this type of bus, one pays when **getting on**.

② [step on, mount (a platform, etc.)]
¶ [I] **stepped** up on the chair and took something off the shelf.

は

は 葉〔名〕

¶秋には木の葉が散ります。（Aki ni wa ko no ha ga chirimasu.）

は 歯〔名〕

歯ブラシ（haburashi）歯医者（haisha）歯みがき（hamigaki）虫歯（mushiba）練り歯みがき（nerihamigaki）歯が生える（ha ga haeru）歯が抜ける（ha ga nukeru）

¶毎朝歯をみがきます。（Maiasa ha o migakimasu.）

¶急に歯が痛くなりました。（Kyū ni ha ga itaku narimashita.）

は〔助〕

①［ものごとを特定的に取り上げてそれについて述べるときに使う］

¶わたしは学生です。（Watashi *wa* gakusei desu.）

¶バスの停留所はどこですか。（Basu no teiryūjo *wa* doko desu ka？）

¶日本は地震が多いです。（Nihon *wa* jishin ga ooi desu.）

¶この本は、昨日駅前の本屋で買いました。（Kono hon *wa*, kinō ekimae no hon'ya de kaimashita.）

¶昨日はいい天気でしたね。（Kinō *wa* ii tenki deshita ne.）

*「だれ（dare）」「どれ（dore）」「何（nani）」などの疑問の言葉のあとにはつかない。「どなたは田中さんですか。（Donata wa Tanaka san desu ka？）」とは言わないで、「田中さんはどなた

ha 〔n〕 **leaf**

¶ Tree **leaves** fall in the autumn.

ha 〔n〕 **tooth, teeth**

a **tooth**brush // a dentist //**tooth**paste, **tooth** powder // a decayed **tooth**, **tooth** with a cavity //**tooth**paste // cut a **tooth**, teethe //lose **a tooth**, lose **one's teeth**

¶ [I] brush **[my] teeth** every morning.

¶ I suddenly got a **tooth**ache 〖**My teeth** suddenly started to hurt〗.

wa 〔part〕 **a particle indicating the topic of a sentence, etc.**

① [used to indicate the topic]

¶ I am a student.

¶ Where is **the bus stop?**

¶ There are a lot of earthquakes **in Japan**.

¶ [I] bought **this book** yesterday at the bookstore in front of the station.

¶ It was a nice day **yesterday**, wasn't it?

*Wa is not used after interrogatives such as *dare, dore*, or *nani*. One says *"Tanaka san wa donata desu ka"* (Which one of you is Mr. Tanaka?) and not * *"Donata wa Tanaka san desu ka."*

ですか。（Tanaka san wa donata desu
ka?）」と言う。

② [ものごとを対比的にまたは区別し
て取り上げて述べるときに使う]

¶ わたしはりんごは好きですが、みか
んはきらいです。（Watashi wa ringo *wa*
suki desu ga, mikan *wa* kirai desu.）

¶ 風は吹いていますが、雨は降ってい
ません。（Kaze *wa* fuite imasu ga, ame
wa futte imasen.）

¶ あの山には登らないでください。
（Ano yama ni *wa* noboranaide kudasai.）

¶ 田中さんはテレビは見ないそうで
す。（Tanaka san wa terebi *wa* minai sō
desu.）

＊「あの山には（Ano yama ni wa）」や
「田中さんは（Tanaka san wa）」の文で
は、文中に直接対比されているものは
ないが、ほかの山には登ってもよいが
あの山だけはという気持ち、テレビは
見なくてもラジオは聞くというような
対比の気持ちが感じられる。また、一
般的に否定の文には「は（wa）」が使
われることが多い。述語が名詞・形容
動詞の否定の文は「～ではありません
（～de wa arimasen）」となる。「暑く
は、ありません。（Atsuku wa
arimasen.）」「行こうとは思いません。
（Ikō to wa omoimasen.）」「学校へは行き
ません。（Gakkō e wa ikimasen.）」「ま
だ、話してはいません。（Mada,
hanashite wa imasen.）」「いい天気では
ありません。（Ii tenki de wa

② [used when contrasting or
distinguishing items]

¶ I like **apples** but dislike **mandarin
oranges**.

¶ **The wind** is blowing but it is not
raining.

¶ Please don't climb **that mountain**.

¶ I hear that **[Mr.] Tanaka** doesn't
watch television.

＊In the case of *ano yama ni wa* and
Tanaka san wa in the sentences above,
a contrast is implied such that one may
climb other mountains but not that
particular one or that even though Mr.
Tanaka doesn't watch television he
listens to the radio. Also, in general *wa*
is the particle used in negative
sentences; the predicate for the
negative of a noun or adjective-verb is
~ *de wa arimasen*. Other examples of
negative sentences with *wa* are "*Atsuku
wa arimasen*" (It's not hot), "*Ikō to wa
omoimasen*" (I don't have any intention
of going), "*Gakkō e wa ikimasen*" (I'm
not going to school), "*Mada hanashite
wa imasen*" (I haven't talked with them
about it yet), "*Ii tenki de wa arimasen*"
(It's not very nice weather), and "*Amari

arimasen.)」「あまり元気ではありません。(Amari genki de wa arimasen.)」

genki de wa arimasen" (He's somewhat downcast).

ば 場〔名〕

¶その場にいなかったので、詳しいことはわかりません。(Sono *ba* ni inakatta node, kuwashii koto wa wakarimasen.)

¶皆が集まっているから、この場で決めましょう。(Mina ga atsumatte iru kara, kono *ba* de kimemashō.)

ba 〔n〕 place; occasion

¶ I wasn't **there** so I don't know any details.

¶ Since everyone is present, let's decide it **here and now**.

ば〔助〕

① [前件が成立する場合には後件が成立するという関係を表す]

¶春になれば、花が咲きます。(Haru ni nare*ba*, hana ga sakimasu.)

¶2に3を足せば、5になります。(Ni ni san o tase*ba*, go ni narimasu.)

¶天気がよければ、汽車の窓から富士山が見えます。(Tenki ga yokere*ba*, kisha no mado kara Fujisan ga miemasu.)

¶「あした雨が降れば、旅行には行きませんか。」(Ashita ame ga fure*ba*, ryokō ni wa ikimasen ka?)「いいえ、雨が降っても行きます。」(Iie, ame ga futte mo ikimasu.)

¶安ければ、りんごを五つ買ってきてください。(Yasukere*ba*, ringo o itsutsu katte kite kudasai.)

¶父はお酒を飲めば、歌を歌いました。(Chichi wa osake o nome*ba*, uta o utaimashita.)

*普通、前件と後件の主語が同じで、しかも前件が動作を表す動詞の場合は、後件には「〜う［よう］（〜u ［yō］)」などの意志、「〜なさい（〜nasai)」などの命令、「〜てください（〜te kudasai)」などの依頼、「〜ては

-ba 〔part〕 if, when

① [indicates something happens when another thing happens]

¶ **When** spring comes, flowers will bloom.

¶ Two plus three is five (literally, *If* you add three to two it is five).

¶ **When** the weather is good, one can see Mount Fuji from the train window.

¶ "Will you give up (literally, not go on) your trip **if** it rains tomorrow?" "No, I will go even if it rains."

¶ **If** they are cheap, please buy five apples.

¶ My father used to sing **when** he drank *sake*.

*Usually when the subjects of bothclauses are the same and the verb of the -*ba* clause indicates an action, the -*ba* clause is *not* followed by an expression of desire (-*ō* 〖-*yō*〗, etc.), an order (-*nasai*, etc.), a request (-*te*

いけない（〜te wa ikenai）」などの禁止などの言い方は来ない。「安ければ、りんごを五つ買ってきてください。（Yasukereba, ringo o itsutsu katte kite kudasai.）」という文は前件が状態を表す形容詞であるから言えるが、「お酒を飲めば、歌を歌いなさい。（Osake o nomeba, uta o utainasai.）」とは言えない。また、後件が動詞の過去・完了を表す「たの形」のときは過去の習慣を表す。

→と **to**　たら **tara**　ても **te mo**

② [前件がもし成立していた場合には後件も成立するという関係を表す]

¶ 父が病気にならなければ、大学をやめなくてもよかったのですが。（Chichi ga byōki ni naranakereba, daigaku o yamenakute mo yokatta no desu ga.）

¶ 背がもう少し高ければ、バレーボールの選手になっていたと思います。（Sei ga mō sukoshi takakereba, barēbōru no senshu ni natte ita to omoimasu.）

＊前件には実際には成立しなかったことがらが来る。

→たら **tara**　なら **nara**

③ [願望や示唆などの意味を表す]

¶ 学生の時にもっと勉強していればと思いました。（Gakusei no toki ni motto benkyō shite ireba to omoimashita.）

¶ 料理はまだたくさんあるから、もっとめしあがれば。（Ryōri wa mada takusan aru kara, motto meshiagareba？）

→たら **tara**

④ [[評価などを導くことを表す]]

---

kudasai, etc.), or a prohibition (*-te wa ikenai*, etc.). "*Yasukereba, ringo o itsutsu katte kite kudasai*" is possible because the *-ba* clause is an adjective indicating a condition, but a sentence like *"*Osake o nomeba, uta o utainasai*" is not possible. Further, when the second clause is in the *-ta* form expressing past or completed action, then the *-ba* clause indicates habitual action in the past.

② [indicates something would have happened if another thing had happened]

¶ **If** my father hadn't become ill, I wouldn't have had to leave the university.

¶ I think [I] would have become a volleyball player **if** [I] had been a little taller.

*In this case, the *-ba* clause expresses something that didn't actually happen.

③ [indicates desire, a suggestion, etc.]
¶ **I wished** then that **I had** studied more in my student days.

¶ Since there is still lots of food left, **won't you** have some more?

④ [introduces or invites a judgment, evaluation, etc.]

¶どんなカメラを選べばいいか教えて
ください。(Donna kamera o erabe*ba* ii
ka oshiete kudasai.)

¶Please tell me what camera I **should**
choose.

¶大学に入るためには、もっと勉強し
なければいけませんよ。(Daigaku ni
hairu tame ni wa, motto benkyō
shinakere*ba* ikemasen yo.)

¶You **must** study harder in order to be
able to enter a university.

*「～ばいい（～*ba* ii)」「～ばいけな
い（～*ba* ikenai)」などの形で使う。

*Used in the patterns "-*ba ii* ," "-*ba
ikenai* ," etc.

⑤ [前件に既に成立していることを述
べてその条件のもとで後件が成立する
という関係を表す]

⑤ [indicates something happens based
on something that has already
happened]

¶ここまで送っていただけば、あとは
一人で帰れます。(Koko made okutte
itadakere*ba*, ato wa hitori de kaeremasu.)

¶**Now that you have** come with me
up to here, I can go the rest of the way
by myself.

¶あなたにそう言われれば、そんな気
がします。(Anata ni sō iwarere*ba*, sonna
ki ga shimasu.)

¶**When** you say that, I feel that it is so.

⑥ [前件のことがらが成立する場合そ
れに比例して後件のことがらの程度も
進むという関係を表す]

⑥ [indicates something happens in
proportion to something else]

¶物価が上がれば上がるほど生活が苦
しくなります。(Bukka ga agare*ba*
agaru hodo seikatsu ga kurushiku
narimasu.)

¶**The more** prices rise, the harder it is
to make ends meet.

¶アパートは部屋が広ければ広いほど
高くなります。(Apāto wa heya ga
hirokere*ba* hiroi hodo takaku
narimasu.)

¶Apartments are more expensive **the
larger** the rooms are.

*「～ば～ほど（～*ba*～hodo)」の形で
使う。

*Used in the pattern "verb or adjective
(-*ba* form) + verb or adjective
(dictionary form) + *hodo*."

⑦ [類似したものごとを列挙するとき
に使う]

⑦ [used when citing similar things]

¶上田さんの部屋にはラジオもあれば
テレビもあります。(Ueda san no heya
ni wa rajio mo are*ba* terebi mo arimasu.)

¶There's a television in [Miss] Ueda's
room **as well as** a radio.

¶中村さんは英語も話せばフランス語も話します。(Nakamura san wa Eigo mo hanase*ba* Furansugo mo hanashimasu.)

¶ [Mr.] Nakamura speaks **not only** English **but** French as well.

→し shi

⑧ [前件が後件のことがらの出どころとなっているという関係を表す]

¶ラジオの天気予報によれば、午後からは雨が降るそうです。(Rajio no tenki-yohō ni yore*ba*, gogo kara wa ame ga furu sō desu.)

*「～によれば（～ni yore*ba*)」の形で使う。

→と to

⑧ [indicates that something is the source for another thing]

¶ **According to** the weather report on the radio, it's going to rain in the afternoon.

*Used in the pattern "～*ni yoreba*."

ばあい 場合 〔名〕

baai 〔n〕 **case, occasion, time; situation, circumstances**

① [ものごとの起こるとき、ある状態になったとき]

① [occasion, time]

¶雨が降った場合にはピクニックに行きません。(Ame ga futta *baai* ni wa pikunikku ni ikimasen.)

¶ **In the case** of rain, [we] won't go on the picnic.

¶困った場合には、わたしに相談してください。(Komatta *baai* ni wa, watashi ni sōdan shite kudasai.)

¶ Please consult me **when** you are troubled.

② [その時の事情]

② [circumstances, situation]

¶場合によっては、あした来られないかもしれません。(*Baai* ni yotte wa, ashita korarenai ka mo shiremasen.)

¶ I might not be able to come tomorrow depending on **circumstances**.

-パーセント 〔尾〕

-pāsento 〔suf〕 **percent**

¶4分の1は 25 パーセントです。(Yonbun no ichi wa nijūgo*pāsento* desu.)

¶ One-fourth is 25 **percent**.

¶地震のときでもここにいれば、100パーセント安全です。(Jishin no toki demo koko ni ireba, hyaku*pāsento* anzen desu.)

¶ It is 100 **percent** safe here, even in the case of an earthquake.

パーティー〔名〕

¶昨日のパーティーはとても楽しかったです。(Kinō no *pātii* wa totemo tanoshikatta desu.)

¶来週の日曜日に誕生日のパーティーをしますから、ぜひおいでください。(Raishū no nichiyōbi ni tanjōbi no *pātii* o shimasu kara, zehi oide kudasai.)

pātii 〔n〕 **a party**

¶ **The party** yesterday was a lot of fun.

¶ Please be sure to come to the birthday **party** next week Sunday.

はい 灰〔名〕

¶たばこの灰はここに入れてください。(Tabako no *hai* wa koko ni irete kudasai.)

¶ストーブの灰を掃除してください。(Sutōbu no *hai* o sōji shite kudasai.)

hai 〔n〕 **ash, ashes**

¶ Please put your cigarette **ashes** in this.

¶ Please clean **the ashes** from the stove.

はい〔感〕

¶「これは日本語の本ですか。」(Kore wa Nihongo no hon desu ka?)「はい、そうです。」(*Hai*, sō desu.)

¶「そこに辞書がありますか。」(Soko ni jisho ga arimasu ka?)「はい、あります。」(*Hai*, arimasu.)

＊「ええ (ee)」より丁寧な言葉。

⇔いいえ **iie**

⇒ええ **ee**

hai 〔interj〕 **yes**

¶ "Is this book written in Japanese?" "**Yes**, it is."

¶ "Is there a dictionary over there?" "**Yes**, there is."

＊*Hai* is more polite than *ee*.

-はい -杯〔尾〕

1杯 (ip*pai*) 2杯 (ni*hai*) 3杯 (san*bai*) 4杯 (yon*hai*) 5杯 (go*hai*) 6杯 (rop*pai*) 7杯 (nana*hai*) 8杯 (hap*pai*) 9杯 (kyū*hai*) 10杯 (jip*pai*)

¶「お砂糖を何杯入れましょうか。」(Osatō o nan*bai* iremashō ka?)

-hai 〔suf〕 **the counter for cups, glasses, or spoonfuls of something**

1 glassful 〚cupful, spoonful〛 // 2 glassfuls // 3 glassfuls // 4 glassfuls // 5 glassfuls // 6 glassfuls // 7 glassfuls // 8 glassfuls // 9 glassfuls // 10 glassfuls

¶ "How many **spoonfuls** 〚cups〛 of sugar should I put in?" "Please put in two **spoonfuls** 〚cups〛."

「2杯入れてください。」(Ni*hai* irete kudasai.)

-ばい (-)倍 〔名、尾〕

1 〔名〕
¶2の倍は4です。(Ni no *bai* wa yon desu.)

2 〔尾〕
¶物価が以前の3倍になりました。(Bukka ga izen no san*bai* ni narimashita.)

(-)bai 〖n, suf〗 **double; times**

1 〖n〗 double
¶ **Twice** two is four.

2 〖suf〗 times, -fold
¶ Prices are three **times** what they were formerly.

はいいろ 灰色 〔名〕
¶灰色のズボンを買いました。(*Haiiro* no zubon o kaimashita.)
¶空が曇って灰色になりました。(Sora ga kumotte *haiiro* ni narimashita.)

haiiro 〖n〗 **gray, ash colored**
¶ [I] bought a pair of **gray** slacks.
¶ The sky has clouded over 〚The sky clouded over〛 and turned **a gray color**.

はいけん 拝見 〔名、〜する〕
¶切符を拝見します。(Kippu o *haiken* shimasu.)

haiken 〖n, 〜*suru*〗 **see, look**
¶ Please let me take a look at your ticket.

はいざら 灰ざら 〔名〕
¶灰ざらはどこですか。(*Haizara* wa doko desu ka?)

haizara 〖n〗 **ashtray**
¶ Where is **the ashtray?**

はいたつ 配達 〔名、〜する〕
牛乳配達 (gyūnyū-*haitatsu*) 新聞配達 (shinbun-*haitatsu*) 郵便配達 (yūbin-*haitatsu*)
¶このテーブルをあした配達してください。(Kono tēburu o ashita *haitatsu* shite kudasai.)
¶郵便は一日に何回配達されますか。(Yūbin wa ichinichi ni nankai *haitatsu* saremasu ka?)

haitatsu 〖n, 〜*suru*〗 **delivery**
milk **delivery** // newspaper **delivery** // mail **delivery**
¶ Please **deliver** this table tomorrow.
¶ How many times is the mail **delivered** a day?

パイナップル 〔名〕

painappuru 〖n〗 **pineapple**

はいゆう 俳優 〔名〕
映画俳優 (eiga-*haiyū*) かぶき俳優 (kabuki-*haiyū*)

haiyū 〖n〗 **actor, actress**
a film **actor**, film **actress** // a kabuki **player**

¶あの俳優の名前を知っていますか。（Ano *haiyū* no namae o shitte imasu ka？）

¶ Do you know the name of that **actor**〚**actress**〛?

¶あの俳優はたいへん人気があります。（Ano *haiyū* wa taihen ninki ga arimasu.）

¶ That **actor**〚**actress**〛 is very popular.

はいる 入る〔動Ⅰ〕

hairu〔vⅠ〕**enter, come in; contam; loin; receive; begin**

① [外から中に移る]
家の中に入る（ie no naka ni*hairu*）玄関を入る（genkan o *hairu*）門を入る（mon o *hairu*）

① [enter, come in]
come inside the house // **come into** the entryway // **come in** the gate

¶夕方おふろに入ります。（Yūgata ofuro ni *hairimasu*.）

¶ [I] **take** a bath in the evenings.

↔出る **deru**

② [あるものが区切られた所に入れてある]

② [contain, hold]

¶この箱の中に何が入っていますか。（Kono hako no naka ni nani ga *haitte* imasu ka？）

¶ What's **in** this box?

③ [組織や団体などに加わる]
大学に入る（daigaku ni *hairu*）会社に入る（kaisha ni *hairu*）仲間に入る（nakama ni *hairu*）

③ [join, enter]
enter a university //**join** a company, **go to work** for a company // **join** others in something, **mix** with others

¶わたしはテニス部に入りました。（Watashi wa tenisubu ni *hairimashita*.）

¶ I **joined** the tennis club.

④ [あるものが自分のものになる]
手に入る（te ni *hairu*）お金が入る（okane ga *hairu*）

④ [get, receive]
obtain, be obtained, **come into** one's possession // **come into** money, be paid

¶今日はボーナスが入りました。（Kyō wa bōnasu ga *hairimashita*.）

¶ [I] **received** [my] bonus today.

⑤ [ある時刻・時期になる]
梅雨に入る（tsuyu ni *hairu*）夜に入る（yoru ni *hairu*）

⑤ [begin, set in]
enter the rainy season // **become** evening, night **falls**

¶8月に入って急に暑くなりました。（Hachigatsu ni *haitte* kyū ni atsuku narimashita.）

¶ It has suddenly gotten hot **since the beginning** of August〚It suddenly got hot **from the beginning** of August〛.

はえ 〔名〕

¶はえが1匹飛んでいます。（*Hae ga ippiki tonde imasu.*）

¶この町にはあまりはえがいません。（*Kono machi ni wa amari hae ga imasen.*）

＊「はい（hai）」とも言う。

はえる 生える 〔動Ⅱ〕

¶庭に草がたくさん生えてきました。（*Niwa ni kusa ga takusan haete kimashita.*）

¶赤ん坊の歯が生えました。（*Akanbō no ha ga haemashita.*）

はか 墓 〔名〕

墓場（*haka*ba） 墓参り（*haka*mairi）

¶お寺の後ろにお墓があります。（*Otera no ushiro ni ohaka ga arimasu.*）

¶先祖のお墓にお参りしました。（*Senzo no ohaka ni omairi shimashita.*）

ばか 〔名、形動〕

ばか者（*baka*mono） ばかにする（baka ni suru）

¶あの人はクラスのみんなにばかにされています。（*Ano hito wa kurasu no minna ni baka ni sarete imasu.*）

はがき 〔名〕

絵はがき（*ehagaki*） 年賀はがき（nenga-*hagaki*） 往復はがき（ōfuku-*hagaki*） 郵便はがき（yūbin-*hagaki*）

¶はがきを5枚ください。（*Hagaki o gomai kudasai.*）

¶友達にはがきを出しました。（*Tomodachi ni hagaki o dashimashita.*）

はかり 〔名〕

はかりで量る（*hakari* de hakaru）

---

hae 〔n〕 fly

¶**A fly** is buzzing around.

¶There aren't very many **flies** in this town.

＊Variant: *hai*.

haeru 〔v Ⅱ〕 grow, sprout

¶A lot of weeds **have appeared** in the yard.

¶The baby **has cut** its first teeth.

haka 〔n〕 grave, tomb

graveyard, cemetery // visit to **a grave**

¶There are **graves** behind the temple.

¶[I] visited the family **tombs**.

baka 〔n, adj-v〕 fool; stupidity

a fool // look down on, make fun of, hold in contempt

¶That person **is looked down upon** by the whole class.

hagaki 〔n〕 postcard

a picture **postcard** // a New Year's **(post)card** // a double **postcard** with a card for replying // **a postcard**

¶Five **postcards**, please.

¶[I] sent **a postcard** to a friend.

hakari 〔n〕 scales, balance

weigh on **a scale**

¶ 牛肉をはかりにかけて、100グラムずつに分けてください。(Gyūniku o *hakari* ni kakete, hyakuguramu zutsu ni wakete kudasai.)

¶ Please weigh the beef on **the scale** and divide it into hundred-gram portions.

ばかり〔助〕

① [数量を表す言葉についてだいたいの分量・程度などを表す]

¶ すみませんが、5分ばかり待ってください。(Sumimasen ga, gofun *bakari* matte kudasai.)

¶ 1万円ばかり貸していただけないでしょうか。(Ichiman'en *bakari* kashite itadakenai deshō ka？)

② [ものごとがそれだけであるという限定の意味を表す]

¶ 田中さんは自分の意見ばかり言って、人の意見を聞きません。(Tanaka san wa jibun no iken *bakari* itte, hito no iken o kikimasen.)

¶ 山田さんは英語ばかりでなく、フランス語も話せます。(Yamada san wa Eigo *bakari* de naku, Furansugo mo hanasemasu.)

¶ あの人は遊んでばかりいて勉強しません。(Ano hito wa asonde *bakari* ite benkyō shimasen.)

*「名詞＋ばかり（*bakari*）」「動詞（連体の形）＋ばかり（*bakari*）」「動詞（ての形）＋ばかり（*bakari*）＋いる（iru）」の形で使う。

③ [ある動作がいつでも行われるような状態にあることを表す]

¶ 夕食はもういつでも食べられるばかりになっています。(Yūshoku wa mō itsu demo taberareru *bakari* ni natte imasu.)

bakari 〔part〕 about; only; just

① [about, approximately (following expressions of quantity)]

¶ I'm sorry, but could you please wait **around** five minutes?

¶ Could you lend me ten thousand yen **or so?**

② [only]

¶ [Miss] Tanaka **only** gives [her] own opinions and won't listen to those of others.

¶ [Mrs.] Yamada speaks **not only** English but also French.

¶ [He] **only** plays and never studies.

*Used in the patterns "noun + *bakari* ," "verb (dictionary form) + *bakari* ," "verb (-*te* form) + *bakar* + *iru*."

③ [indicates that one can start doing something at any time]

¶ Dinner **is ready**; we can start eating at any time.

*「動詞（連体の形）＋ばかり
（*bakari*)」などの形で使う。
④ [ある動作が行われて間もない状態
にあることを表す]
¶ 父は今帰ってきたばかりです。
（Chichi wa ima kaette kita *bakari* desu.)
¶ わたしは日本語を習い始めたばかり
で、まだ上手に話せません。（Watashi
wa Nihongo o naraihajimeta *bakari* de,
mada jōzu ni hanasemasen.)
*「動詞（たの形）＋ばかり
（*bakari*)」の形で使う。

*Used in the pattern "verb (dictionary
form) + *bakari* ," etc.
④ [just, just now, only, only now]

¶ Father has **just now** come home.

¶ I have **just** started to learn Japanese
and cannot speak it well yet.

*Used in the pattern "verb (-*ta* form) +
bakari."

はかる　測る〔動 I〕
面積を測る（menseki o *hakaru*)
¶ 池の深さを測ってみました。（Ike no
fukasa o *hakatte* mimashita.)

hakaru 〔v I〕 measure
measure the area
¶ [I] **measured** the depth of the pond.

はかる　量る〔動 I〕
目方を量る（mekata o *hakaru*)
¶ 体重を量ったら、60キログラムあ
りました。（Taijū o *hakattara*,
rokujikkiroguramu arimashita.)

hakaru 〔v I〕 measure
weigh something 〚someone〛
¶ When **I weighed** myself 〚him, her〛,
my 〚his, her〛 weight was 60 kilos.

はかる　計る〔動 I〕
身長を計る（shinchō o *hakaru*)
¶ 熱を計ったら 39 度ありました。
（Netsu o *hakattara* sanjūkudo
arimashita.)

hakaru 〔v I〕 measure
measure someone's height
¶ When **I took** [my] temperature, it
was 39 degrees.

はく　掃く〔動 I〕
ほうきで庭を掃く（hōki de niwa o
haku)
¶ 神社の周りは、いつもきれいに掃い
てあります。（Jinja no mawari wa, itsu
mo kirei ni *haite* arimasu.)

haku 〔v I〕 sweep
sweep the garden 〚yard〛 with a broom

¶ The grounds of a shrine are
alwaysnicely **swept**.

はく 〔動 I〕

¶ くつ下をはかないで、くつをはきました。(Kutsushita o *hakanaide*, kutsu o *hakimashita*.)
¶ 彼女はいつもズボンをはいています。(Kanojo wa itsu mo zubon o *haite* imasu.)
⇔脱ぐ nugu

haku 〔v I〕 **put on, wear (something below the waist)**
¶ [I] **put on** shoes **without putting on** socks.

¶ She always **has on** slacks.

はくし 博士 〔名〕

¶ 田中教授は文学博士です。(Tanaka kyōju wa bungaku-*hakushi* desu.)
¶ 田中博士の講義はたいへんおもしろいです。(Tanaka *hakushi* no kōgi wa taihen omoshiroi desu.)
＊「博士 (hakase)」とも言う。

hakushi 〔n〕 **doctor, holder of a doctorate**
¶ Professor Tanaka **has a doctorate** in literature.
¶ **Dr.** Tanaka's lectures are very interesting.

＊Variant: *hakase*.

ばくはつ 爆発 〔名、〜する〕
① [物質の体積が急激に増大して飛び散り破壊力を出すこと]
¶ 工場で爆発が起こりました。(Kōjō de *bakuhatsu* ga okorimashita.)
¶ ガス爆発で、家が壊れました。(Gasu-*bakuhatsu* de, ie ga kowaremashita.)
② [不満などが急に表に現れること]
¶ ついに国民の不満が爆発しました。(Tsuini kokumin no fuman ga *bakuhatsu* shimashita.)

bakuhatsu 〔n, 〜*suru*〕 **explosion**
① [physical explosion]

¶ **An explosion** occurred at the factory.

¶ The house was destroyed in a gas **explosion**.

② [explosion of discontent, etc.]
¶ Finally the discontent of the people **exploded**.

はくぶつかん 博物館 〔名〕
¶ 国立博物館はどこですか。(Kokuritsu-*hakubutsukan* wa doko desu ka？)
¶ 日曜日に博物館へ見学に行きました。(Nichiyōbi ni *hakubutsukan* e kengaku ni ikimashita.)

hakubutsukan 〔n〕 **museum**
¶ Where is the National **Museum?**

¶ [We] went to **the museum** on Sunday.

はげしい 激しい〔形〕

激しい風（*hageshii* kaze）

¶雨が激しく降ってきました。（Ame ga *hageshiku* futte kimashita.）

¶ここは交通が激しいから気をつけてください。（Koko wa kōtsū ga *hageshii* kara ki o tsukete kudasai.）

hageshii〔adj〕**strong, intense, severe**

a **strong** wind

¶ It has started to rain **heavily**〖It started to rain heavily〗.

¶ Please be careful as the traffic **is heavy** here.

はげます 励ます〔動Ⅰ〕

¶先生は試験に落ちた学生を励ましました。（Sensei wa shiken ni ochita gakusei o *hagemashimashita*.）

¶「がんばりなさい。」と友達に励まされました。（"Ganbarinasai." to tomodachi ni *hagemasaremashita*.）

hagemasu〔vⅠ〕**encourage, cheer up**

¶ The teacher **tried to cheer up** the students who had failed the exam.

¶ **I was encouraged** by my friends with the word "*Ganbarinasai*."

(-)はこ (-)箱〔名、尾〕

1〔名〕

本箱（hon*bako*）

¶その箱の中に何が入っていますか。（Sono *hako* no naka ni nani ga haitte imasu ka？）

2〔尾〕

¶たばこを二箱買ってきてください。（Tabako o futa*hako* katte kite kudasai.）

(-)hako〔n, suf〕**box, case, package, container**

1〔n〕

box, case, package a book**case**

¶ What is in that **box**?

2〔suf〕the counter for packages or cases of something

¶ Please buy me two **packs** of cigarettes.

はこぶ 運ぶ〔動Ⅰ〕

¶重い物は車で運びましょう。（Omoi mono wa kuruma de *hakobimashō*.）

¶この荷物をわたしの部屋へ運んでください。（Kono nimotsu o watashi no heya e *hakonde* kudasai.）

hakobu〔vⅠ〕**carry, transport**

¶ **Let's take** the heavy things by car〖taxi, van, truck, etc.〗.

¶ Please **take** this luggage〖these bags, boxes, etc.〗to my room.

はさみ〔名〕

¶はさみで紙を切ります。（*Hasami* de kami o kirimasu.）

hasami〔n〕**scissors, shears**

¶ One cuts paper with **scissors**.

¶このはさみはよく切れます。(Kono *hasami* wa yoku kiremasu.)

¶ These **scissors** cut well.

はさむ〔動Ⅰ〕

¶料理をはしではさんで食べます。(Ryōri o hashi de *hasande* tabemasu.)

¶写真を本の間にはさんでおきました。(Shashin o hon no aida ni *hasande* okimashita.)

hasamu〔v Ⅰ〕**put between, insert**

¶ [We] **pick up** food **between** [our] two chopsticks and eat it.

¶ [I] **put** the photo away **between** the leaves of a book.

はし 橋〔名〕

橋を架ける (*hashi* o kakeru)

¶この橋を渡って、向こう側に行きましょう。(Kono *hashi* o watatte, mukōgawa ni ikimashō.)

hashi〔n〕**bridge**

build **a bridge**

¶ Let's cross this **bridge** to the other side.

はし 端〔名〕

¶危ないから、道の端を歩きましょう。(Abunai kara, michi no *hashi* o arukimashō.)

¶このひもの端を持ってください。(Kono himo no *hashi* o motte kudasai.)

hashi〔n〕**end, tip, edge**

¶ Let's walk along **the edge** of the road to be safe (literally, because it's dangerous).

¶ Please hold **the end** of this string 〚cord, band, ribbon, etc.〛.

はし〔名〕

¶あなたははしで食べることができますか。(Anata wa *hashi* de taberu koto ga dekimasu ka?)

¶はしが使えませんから、フォークをください。(*Hashi* ga tsukaemasen kara, fōku o kudasai.)

hashi〔n〕**chopsticks**

¶ Can you eat with **chopsticks?**

¶ Please give me a fork—I can't use **chopsticks**.

はじ 恥〔名〕

¶みんなの前で恥をかきました。(Minna no mae de *haji* o kakimashita.)

¶子供が悪いことをすれば、親の恥になります。(Kodomo ga warui koto o sureba, oya no *haji* ninarimasu.)

haji〔n〕**shame, disgrace, humiliation**

¶ [I] **disgraced** [myself] in front of everyone.

¶ [I] If a child does something bad, it **brings shame** to its parents.

はじまる　始まる〔動Ｉ〕

¶次の授業は３時に始まります。
（Tsugi no jugyō wa sanji ni
hajimarimasu.）
¶会議はいつ始まりましたか。（Kaigi
wa itsu *hajimarimashita* ka？）
⇔終わる **owaru**

hajimaru 〔vI〕 **begin, commence**

¶ The next class **starts** at three o'clock.

¶ When did the meeting **start?**

はじめ　始め〔名〕

¶始めから終わりまで、みんな熱心に
彼の話を聞きました。（*Hajime* kara
owari made, minna nesshin ni kare no
hanashi o kikimashita.）
¶あの映画の始めのほうはあまりおも
しろくありません。（Ano eiga no
hajime no hō wa amari omoshiroku
arimasen.）
⇔終わり **owari**

hajime 〔n〕 **beginning, outset**

¶ Everyone listened to his talk 〚story〛
intently from **beginning** to end.

¶ **The first part** of that movie isn't
very interesting.

はじめ　初め〔名〕

¶３月の初めに試験があります。
（Sangatsu no *hajime* ni shiken ga
arimasu.）
¶夏の初めに旅行します。（Natsu no
hajime ni ryokō shimasu.）
⇔終わり **owari**

hajime 〔n〕 **the beginning, the
start**

¶ There's an exam **early** in March.

¶ [I] will go on a trip at **the beginning**
of the summer.

はじめて　初めて〔副〕

¶今年の夏、初めて富士山に登りまし
た。（Kotoshi no natsu, *hajimete* Fujisan
ni noborimashita.）
¶今日、初めて日本語で電話しまし
た。
（Kyō, *hajimete* Nihongo de denwa
shimashita.）

hajimete 〔adv〕 **for the first time**

¶ This summer [I] climbed Mount Fuji
for the first time.

¶ Today [I] made [my] **first** telephone
call in Japanese.

はじめまして　初めまして〔連〕

¶初めまして、どうぞよろしく。

(*Hajimemashite*, dōzo yoroshiku.)

hajimemashite 〔compd〕 **an expression used when meeting someone for the first time**

¶ **How do you do?** I'm pleased to make your acquaintance.

はじめる　始める〔動Ⅱ〕

① [ものごとを開始する]
¶さあ、勉強を始めましょう。(Sā, benkyō o *hajimemashō*.)
¶今日は10ページから始めます。(Kyō wa jippēji kara *hajimemasu*.)
② [ある動作・作用が始まることを表す]
¶桜の花が咲き始めました。(Sakura no hana ga saki*hajimemashita*.)
¶9月から日本語を習い始めました。(Kugatsu kara Nihongo o narai*hajimemashita*.)
*「動詞（基幹の形）＋始める (hajimeru)」の形で使う。
⇔終える oeru

(-)hajimeru 〔vⅡ〕 **start (something);start ~ing**

① [start (something)]
¶ Well, **let's start** class.

¶ Today [we] **will be starting** from page 10.

② [start ~ing, start to ~]

¶ The cherry blossoms **have started** to bloom.

¶ [I] **started** studying Japanese in September.

*Used in the pattern "verb (stem form) + *-hajimeru*."

ばしょ　場所〔名〕

① [所、位置]
¶ここが事故のあった場所です。(Koko ga jiko no atta *basho* desu.)
¶わたしのうちは買い物に便利な場所にあります。(Watashi no uchi wa kaimono ni benri na *basho* ni arimasu.)
② [人などのいる所、席]
¶会場へ早く行って、場所を取っておいてください。(Kaijō e hayaku itte, *basho* o totte oite kudasai.)

basho 〔n〕 **place**

① [place, location, position]
¶ This is **the place** where the accident was.

¶ My home is in **a location** convenient for shopping.

② [place, seat]
¶ Please go to the auditorium 〚theater, hall, etc.〛 early and save **seats** for [us].

はしら　柱〔名〕

電信柱 (denshin*bashira*)

hashira 〔n〕 **pillar, column, post, pole**

a telephone **pole**, electric **pole**

¶暗かったので柱に頭をぶつけました。(Kurakatta node *hashira* ni atama o butsukemashita.)

¶ As it was dark, [I] bumped my head on **a pillar**.

¶子供が柱の周りを回って遊んでいます。(Kodomo ga *hashira* no mawari o mawatte asonde imasu.)

¶ The children are playing running around **the pole** 〖**pillar**〗.

はしる 走る〔動Ⅰ〕

① [人や動物などが足を速く動かして行く]

犬が走る (inu ga *hashiru*) 馬が走る (uma ga *hashiru*)

¶遅くなったので、駅へ走っていきました。(Osoku natta node, eki e *hashitte* ikimashita.)

hashiru 〔vI〕 run

① [(animals and people) run]

a dog **runs** // a horse **gallops**

¶ As [I] was late, [I] **ran** to the station.

②[船や車などが速い速度で進む]

ヨットが水の上を走る (yottoga mizu no ueo *hashiru*) 急行列車が走る (kyūkō-ressha ga *hashiru*)

¶町の中を車がたくさん走っています。(Machi no naka o kuruma ga takusan *hashitte* imasu.)

② [(vehicles) run, proceed at speed]

a yacht **sails through** the water // an express train **runs**

¶ There **is** much **traffic** in the city.

はず〔名〕

① [ものごとの経過などから言って当然そうなる事情にあるということを表す]

¶この漢字はもう習ったのだから、読めるはずですよ。(Kono kanji wa mō naratta no da kara, yomeru *hazu* desu yo.)

¶この道をまっすぐ行けば、大通りに出るはずです。(Kono michi o massugu ikeba, oodoori ni deru *hazu* desu.)

¶「飛行機は何時にここを出発することになっていますか。」(Hikōki wa nanji ni koko o shuppatsu suru koto ni natte imasu ka？）「ちょうど12時に出

hazu 〔n〕 ought to, should, be supposed to, be expected to

① [ought to, should; indicates that something ought to be or is expected to be so]

¶ Since you've already studied this kanji, you **should** be able to read it.

¶ If you go straight along this street, you **ought to** come out at a major thoroughfare.

¶ "What time is the plane scheduled to depart?"
"It **is due to** take off at twelve o'clock sharp."

発するはずです。」（Chōdo jūniji ni
shuppatsu suru *hazu* desu.)
②［当然なこととして予定されている
ことなどが実現に至らなかったような
場合に使う］
¶上田さんは今年の4月に大学を卒業
するはずだったが、都合で1年延ばし
たそうです。（Ueda san wa kotoshi no
shigatsu ni daigaku o sotsugyō suru *hazu*
datta ga, tsugō de ichinen nobashita
sōdesu.)
¶飛行機は12時にここに到着するは
ずでしたが、霧のため遅れるそうで
す。（Hikōki wa jūniji ni koko ni tōchaku
suru *hazu* deshita ga, kiri no tame okureru
sōdesu.)
*「はずだった（hazu datta）」の形で使
うことが多い。
③［常識的に考えてとてもそういうこ
とはありえないということを表す］

¶子供にそんな重い物が持てるはずは
ありません。（Kodomo ni sonna omoi
mono ga moteru *hazu* wa arimasen.)
¶2か月日本語を習っただけで、こんな
難しい本が読めるはずはありません。
（Nikagetsu Nihongo o naratta dake de,
konna muzukashii hon ga yomeru *hazu* wa
arimasen.)
*普通「はずはない（hazu wa nai）」の
形で使う。

バス〔名〕

バスに乗る（*basu* ni noru）バスを降り
る（*basu* o oriru）
¶バスの停留所はどこですか。（*Basu*
no teiryūjo wa doko desu ka?)
¶このバスはどこ行きですか。（Kono
basu wa doko yuki desu ka?)

②[ought to have, should have;
indicates that something that was
expected to take place didn't]
¶ [Mr.] Ueda **was supposed to**
graduate from college this April, but I
hear that's been postponed one year due
to personal circumstances.

¶ The plane **was supposed to** land here
at twelve o'clock, but I hear it's been
delayed due to fog.

*Usually used in the pattern
"~ *hazu datta*."
③[cannot be, hardly be possible that;
indicates that something cannot be so
according to common sense, etc.]
¶ A child **can hardly be expected** to
be able to carry something that heavy.

¶ **No one can** read such a difficult
book after having studied Japanese for
only two months.

*Usually used in the pattern
"~ *hazu wa nai*."

basu 〔n〕 **bus**
take **a bus** // get off **a bus**

¶ Where is the **bus** stop?

¶ Where does this **bus** go (that is, its
final destination)?

はずかしい　恥ずかしい〔形〕

¶こんなに易しい質問に答えられなくては、恥ずかしいです。(Konna ni yasashii shitsumon ni kotaerarenakute wa, *hazukashii* desu.)
¶恥ずかしくて、顔が赤くなりました。(*Hazukashikute*, kao ga akaku narimashita.)
¶少女は恥ずかしそうに下を向きました。(Shōjo wa *hazukashisō* ni, shita o mukimashita.)

hazukashii 〔adj〕 **be ashamed, be embarrassed, be shy; be shameful, be disgraceful**

¶[I] **am ashamed** 〚**embarrassed**〛 not to be able to answer such a simple question.

¶[I] blushed **out of shame** 〚**embarrassment**〛.

¶The young girl looked **shyly** downward.

はずす　外す〔動Ⅰ〕
¶時計を外して、机の上に置きました。(Tokei o *hazushite*, tsukue no ue ni okimashita.)
¶ちょっと眼鏡を外してください。(Chotto megane o *hazushite* kudasai.)

hazusu 〔vⅠ〕 **take off**

¶[I] **took off** [my] watch and placed it on the desk.

¶Please **take off** your glasses a moment.

パスポート〔名〕
¶外国へ旅行するときには、パスポートが必要です。(Gaikoku e ryokō suru toki ni wa, *pasupōto* ga hitsuyō desu.)

pasupōto 〔n〕 **passport**

¶**A passport** is necessary when traveling abroad.

はずれる　外れる〔動Ⅱ〕

①[取れて離れる]

¶ボタンが外れました。(Botan ga *hazuremashita*.)
¶戸が外れてしまいました。(To ga *hazurete* shimaimashita.)
②[予想やくじなどが当たらない]
くじが外れる (kuji ga *hazureru*)
¶今日の天気予報は外れました。(Kyō no tenki-yohō wa *hazuremashita*.)

hazureru 〔vⅡ〕 **come off, get loose; miss, go wide; depart from**

① [come off, get loose, get out of place, be dislocated]
¶The button **has come undone**.

¶The door **has come off its hinges**.

② [miss, go wide, be beside the point]
hold a **losing ticket** in a lottery
¶Today's weather report **was off the mark**.

¶彼の予想はよく外れます。（Kare no yosō wa yoku *hazuremasu*.）

¶ He is often **disappointed in** his expectations.

↔当たる **ataru**

③ [正しいものごとからそれる]

③ [depart from, be contrary to, be out of line]

歌の調子が外れる（uta no chōshi ga *hazureru*）

to sing **out of** tune

¶規則に外れたことをしてはいけません。（Kisoku ni *hazureta* koto o shite wa ikemasen.）

¶ One mustn't do anything **against** the rules.

はた 旗 [名]

¶祭日には家の前に旗を立てます。（Saijitsu ni wa ie no mae ni *hata* o tatemasu.）

hata [n] **flag, banner**

¶ [We] fly **a flag** in front of the house on holidays.

¶子供が旗を振っています。（Kodomo ga *hata* o futte imasu.）

¶ The children are waving **flags**.

バター [名]

¶パンにバターをつけて食べます。（Pan ni *batā* o tsukete tabemasu.）

batā [n] **butter**

¶ [I] **butter** bread and eat it.

はだか 裸 [名]

hadaka [n] **nude; denuded, uncovered**

① [着物などを着ないで全身を出している姿]

① [nude, naked body]

¶男の子が裸で遊んでいます。（Otoko no ko ga *hadaka* de asonde imasu.）

¶ A boy is playing **without any clothes on**.

② [覆いなどのない様子、またその姿]

② [denuded, uncovered]

裸馬（*hadaka*uma）

a **barebacked** horse

¶裸の電燈に触ると熱いです。（*Hadaka* no dentō ni sawaru to atsui desu.）

¶ A **naked** electric bulb is hot to the touch.

はたけ 畑 [名]

hatake [n] **cultivated field, dry field**

麦畑（mugi*batake*） 野菜畑（yasai*batake*）

a wheat ⟦barley⟧ **field** // a vegetable **field**

¶この畑では何を作っていますか。
（Kono *hatake* de wa nani o tsukutte imasu ka？）

¶この村では田より畑のほうが多いです。（Kono mura de wa ta yori *hatake* no hō ga ooi desu.）

¶ What are you growing in this **field**?

¶ This village has more **dry fields** than paddy fields.

はだし 〔名〕

¶砂浜をはだしで走りました。

（Sunahama o *hadashi* de hashirimashita.）

¶くつ下を脱いで、はだしになりました。（Kutsushita o nuide, *hadashi* ni narimashita.）

hadashi 〔n〕 **bare feet, barefooted**

¶ [I] ran **barefoot** along the sandy beach.

¶ I took off [my] socks and went **barefoot**.

はたす 果たす 〔動 I〕

約束を果たす（yakusoku o *hatasu*）
使命を果たす（shimei o *hatasu*）

¶彼はやっと目的を果たしました。

（Kare wa yatto mokuteki o *hatashimashita*.）

¶責任を果たして安心しました。

（Sekinin o *hatashite* anshin shimashita.）

hatasu 〔v I〕 **achieve, accomplish, realize, discharge, fulfill**

carry out one's promises //
accomplish one' s mission

¶ He finally **achieved** his objective.

¶ I am relieved **to have fulfilled** my responsibility 〖**discharged** my obligation〗.

はたち 二十歳 〔名〕

¶弟は今年二十歳になりました。

（Otōto wa kotoshi *hatachi* ni narimashita.）

¶日本の法律では二十歳から大人です。（Nihon no hōritsu de wa *hatachi* kara otona desu.）

hatachi 〔n〕 **20 years of age**

¶ My younger brother became **20 years old** this year.

¶ In Japanese law one becomes an adult at **20**.

はたらき 働き 〔名〕

①〔働いて仕事をすること〕
働き者（*hataraki*mono）

hataraki 〔n〕 **work; working, action; ability**

① 〔work, labor〕
a good **worker**, a hard**working** person

¶働きが過ぎると、病気になってしまいますよ。(*Hataraki* ga sugiru to, byōki ni natte shimaimasu yo.)

¶ If you **work** too much, you will become ill.

② [あるものの機能・作用など]

② [working, function, operation, action]

胃の働き (i no *hataraki*) 薬の働き (kusuri no *hataraki*)

the function 〚**working**〛 of the stomach // **the action** of a medicine

¶あの人は頭の働きが鋭いです。(Ano hito wa atama no *hataraki* ga surudoidesu.)

¶ [He] is sharp-**witted** 〚has a keen **intelligence**〛.

③ [仕事をする才能、仕事をして収入などを得る能力]

③ [ability (to do a job), capability (of getting a good income)]

働きのある人 (*hataraki* no aru hito)

an able 〚resourceful〛 person, a good provider

¶中村さんはあまり働きがないので、生活が苦しいです。(Nakamura san wa amari *hataraki* ga nai node, seikatsu ga kurushii desu.)

¶ Because [Mr.] Nakamura **is a poor provider**, they have trouble making ends meet.

はたらく 働く 〔動 I〕

hataraku 〔v I〕 **to work, labor; to work, function**

① [仕事をする、収入を得るために労働する]

① [to work, labor]

¶母は毎日よく働きます。(Haha wa mainichi yoku *hatarakimasu*.)

¶ My mother **works** hard every day.

¶兄は銀行で働いています。(Ani wa ginkō de *hataraite* imasu.)

¶ My older brother **works** at a bank.

② [あるものが機能する]

② [to work, function, operate]

頭がよく働かない (atama ga yoku *hatarakanai*) 引力が働く (inryoku ga *hataraku*)

one's head **is sluggish** // gravity **comes into play** 〚operation〛

はち 八 〔名〕

hachi 〔n〕 **eight**

はちがつ 八月 〔名〕

hachigatsu 〔n〕 **August**

-はつ -発 〔尾〕

-hatsu 〔suf〕 **departing (from ~, at ~)**

¶東京発の電車に乗りました。(Tōkyō *hatsu* no densha ni norimashita.)

¶ [I] took the train **leaving from** Tokyo.

¶5時発の急行で行きましょう。(Goji *hatsu* no kyūkō de ikimashō.)

¶ Let's go on the five o'clock express.

はつおん 発音 〔名、〜する〕

¶あの人はたいへん発音がいいです。(Ano hito wa taihen *hatsuon* ga iidesu.)

先生、もう一度発音してください。(Sensei, mō ichido *hatsuon* shite kudasai.)

hatsuon 〔n, 〜*suru*〕 **pronunciation**

¶ [He] has very good **pronunciation** 〖has hardly any accent〗.

¶ Please **pronounce** it again (said to one's teacher or professor).

はつか 二十日 〔名〕

① [日付を表す]
¶わたしの誕生日は五月二十日です。(Watashi no tanjōbi wa gogatsu *hatsuka* desu.)

② [日数を表す]
¶病気で二十日も学校を休みました。(Byōki de *hatsuka* mo gakkō o yasumimashita.)

hatsuka 〔n〕 **the 20th of the month; 20 days**

① [the 20th of the month]
¶ My birthday is May **20**.

② [20 days]
¶ [I] stayed home from school **20 days** due to illness.

はっきり 〔副、〜する〕

¶名前ははっきり書いてください。(Namae wa *hakkiri* kaite kudasai.)

¶今日は富士山がはっきり見えます。(Kyō wa Fujisan ga *hakkiri* miemasu.)

¶ゆうべあまり寝なかったので、今日は頭がはっきりしません。(Yūbe amari nenakatta node, kyō wa atama ga *hakkiri* shimasen.)

＊「はっきりと（hakkiri to）」とも言う。

hakkiri 〔adv, 〜*suru*〕 **clearly, distinctly**

¶ Please write your name **clearly**.

¶ Mount Fuji can be seen **clearly** today.

¶ My head **is fuzzy** today as I didn't get much sleep last night.

＊Variant: *hakkiri to*.

はっけん 発見 〔名、〜する〕

¶アメリカ大陸はだれが発見しましたか。(Amerika-tairiku wa dare ga *hakken* shimashita ka？)

hakken 〔n, 〜*suru*〕 **discovery**

¶ Who **discovered** the American continent?

¶早くがんの薬が発見されるといいで
すね。(Hayaku gan no kusuri ga *hakken*
sareru to ii desu ne.)

¶ I hope that a drug for cancer **will be
discovered** soon.

はっこう 発行〔名、〜する〕
発行所(*hakkō*jo)発行者(*hakkō*sha)

hakkō〔n, 〜*suru*〕**publish, issue
publisher** (company) // **publisher**
(person within a publishing company
in charge of the publication of a given
book)

¶その本は来月発行される予定です。
(Sono hon wa raigetsu *hakkō* sareru yotei
desu.)

¶ That book is scheduled **to be
published** next month.

¶この雑誌は毎週発行されます。
(Kono zasshi wa maishū *hakkō*
saremasu.)

¶ This magazine **comes out** monthly.

はったつ 発達〔名、〜する〕

hattatsu〔n, 〜*suru*〕**development,
advance, progress**

¶この国は工業が発達しています。
(Kono kuni wa kōgyō ga *hattatsu*
shiteimasu.)

¶ This country has an **advanced**
industry.

¶この辺も交通が発達して便利になり
ました。(Kono hen mo kotsū ga *hattatsu*
shite benri ni narimashita.)

¶ Transportation **has advanced** in this
area and it has become more
convenient to live here.

はってん 発展〔名、〜する〕

hatten〔n, 〜*suru*〕**expansion,
growth**

¶駅ができてからこの辺は急に発展し
ました。(Eki ga dekite kara kono hen wa
kyū ni *hatten* shimashita.)

¶ This area suddenly **developed** after
the building of the station.

¶この会社は海外へも発展していま
す。(Kono kaisha wa kaigai e mo *hatten*
shite imasu.)

¶ This company **is expanding** overseas
as well.

はっぴょう 発表〔名、〜する〕

happyō〔n, 〜*suru*〕
announcement, making public

¶みんなの前で自分の意見を発表しま
した。(Minna no mae de jibun no iken o
happyō shimashita.)

¶ [I] **set forth** my opinion in front of
everyone.

¶あした、試験の結果が発表されま
す。(Ashita, shiken no kekka ga *happyō*
saremasu.)

¶ The results of the exam **will be
announced** tomorrow.

はつめい 発明 〔名、～する〕

発明家 (*hatsumei*ka)

¶だれがラジオを発明しましたか。
(Dare ga rajio o *hatsumei* shimashita
ka？)

¶電話が発明されて、たいへん便利に
なりました。(Denwa ga *hatsumei*
sarete, taihen benri ni narimashita.)

hatsumei 〔n, ～*suru*〕 **invention**

an inventor

¶ Who **invented** the radio?

¶ **The invention** of the telephone has
made life very convenient.

はで 派手 〔形動〕

¶彼はいつも派手なシャツを着ていま
す。(Kare wa itsu mo *hade* na shatsu o
kite imasu.)

¶この服はわたしには派手ですか、地
味ですか。(Kono fuku wa watashi ni wa
hade desu ka, jimi desu ka？)

⇔地味 **jimi**

hade 〔adj-v〕 **showy, gaudy, flashy**

¶ He always wears a rather **loud**
〖**bright, splashy**〗 shirt.

¶ Is this outfit **too young** 〖**gay**〗 or too
old 〖**subdued**〗 for me?

はな 鼻 〔名〕

¶子供が転んで、鼻にけがをしまし
た。(Kodomo ga koronde, *hana* ni kega
o shimashita.)

¶あの子はよく鼻血を出します。(Ano
ko wa yoku *hana*ji o dashimasu.)

hana 〔n〕 **nose**

¶ The child fell and injured **[his] nose**.

¶ That child often has **nose**bleeds.

はな 花 〔名〕

花見 (*hana*mi)

¶春になって、庭に花が咲きだしまし
た。(Haru ni natte, niwa ni *hana* ga
sakidashimashita.)

¶花びんの花が枯れました。(Kabin no
hana ga karemashita.)

hana 〔n〕 **flower, blossom**

cherry-blossom viewing

¶ With the coming of spring, **flowers**
started to bloom in the garden.

¶ **The flowers** in the vase have
withered.

はな〔名〕

¶風邪を引いたので、はなが出て困ります。(Kaze o hiita node, *hana* ga dete komarimasu.)

¶はなをかみなさい。(*Hana* o kaminasai.)

hana 〔n〕 **nasal mucus**

¶ I caught a cold and am now troubled by **a runny nose**.

¶ Blow **your nose**.

はなし 話〔名〕

① [自分の感じていることや考えていることなどを人に言うこと]
¶今、父はお客さんと話をしています。(Ima, chichi wa okyakusan to *hanashi* o shite imasu.)

② [相談・交渉など]
話がまとまる (*hanashi* ga matomaru)
¶ちょっと話があるんですが…。(Chotto *hanashi* ga aru n desu ga…)

③ [物語など]
昔話 (mukashi*banashi*)

hanashi 〔n〕 **talk; consultation; story**

① [talk, conversation, speech]

¶ My father is now **talking** with a guest 〚customer〛.

② [consultation, negotiations]
come to an agreement

¶ There is **something I would like to talk with you about**.

③ [story, tale]
a legend, folk**tale**

はなす 離す〔動 I〕

① [二つのものの間をあける]
ハンドルから手を離す (handorukara teo *hanasu*) 間を離す (aida o *hanasu*)
机と机を離す (tsukue to tsukue o *hanasu*)

② [視線を外してほかの方を見る]
¶赤ん坊から目を離さないでください。(Akanbō kara me o *hanasanaide* kudasai.)

hanasu 〔v II〕 **separate, divide; remove one's eyes from**

① [separate, divide two things]
take one's hand(s) **off** the handle 〚steering wheel, handlebar, doorknob, etc.〛 // **move** two things **apart** 〚**further apart**〛 // **move** the desks **apart**

② [remove one's eyes from]
¶ Please **don't take your eyes off** the baby 〚Please **keep your eyes on** the baby〛.

はなす 放す〔動 I〕

小鳥を放す (kotori o *hanasu*)
¶池に魚を放しました。(Ike ni sakana o *hanashimashita*.)

hanasu 〔v I〕 **let go, release**

set a small bird **free**
¶ [I] **let** the fish **loose** in the pond 〚pool.〛

はなす 話す〔動Ⅰ〕

¶ 留学のことをお父さんに話しましたか。（Ryūgaku no koto o otōsan ni *hanashimashita* ka？）

¶ 日本語を話すことができますか。（Nihongo o *hanasu* koto ga dekimasuka？）

hanasu 〔vⅠ〕 **talk, speak, discuss, tell**

¶ Did you **talk with** your father about studying abroad?

¶ Can you **speak** Japanese?

はなれる 離れる〔動Ⅱ〕

① [二つのものの間の距離が開く]
¶ ここから5キロほど離れた所に池があります。（Koko kara gokiro hodo *hanareta* tokoro ni ike ga arimasu.）
② [ある場所から遠ざかる]
東京を離れる（Tōkyō o *hanareru*）席を離れる（seki o *hanareru*）
③ [いっしょであったものの間に距離ができる]
¶ あの学生たちは親と離れて生活しています。（Ano gakuseitachi wa oya to *hanarete* seikatsu shite imasu.）

hanareru 〔vⅡ〕 **be apart from; leave, depart; separate from**

① [be apart from, be at a distance from]
¶ There is a pond five kilometers **away** 〖**at a distance of** five kilometers from here〗.
② [leave, depart]
leave Tokyo // **step away from** one's seat 〖desk〗
③ [separate from, part from]

¶ Those students are living **away from** home (literally, **away from** their parents).

はね 羽〔名〕
¶ 鳥は羽を広げて飛びます。（Tori wa *hane* o hirogete tobimasu.）
¶ つるは羽にけがをしていました。（Tsuru wa *hane* ni kega o shite imashita.）

hane 〔n〕 **wing**

¶ Birds spread their **wings** and fly.

¶ The crane had an injured **wing**.

はね 羽根〔名〕
赤い羽根（akai *hane*）羽根つき（*hane*tsuki）
¶ 羽根布団を買いました。（*Hane*buton o kaimashita.）

hane 〔n〕 **feather, down**

a red **feather** // battledore and shuttlecock

¶ [I] bought a **down-filled** quilt 〖futon, coverlet〗.

はねる 跳ねる〔動Ⅱ〕

① [飛び上がる、おどり上がる]

haneru 〔vⅡ〕 **leap, jump; spatter, splash**

① [leap, jump, spring, prance]

715

馬が跳ねる（uma ga *haneru*）

② [水やどろなどが飛び散る]

¶ どろ水が跳ねてズボンが汚れました。（Doromizu ga *hanete* zubon ga yogoremashita.）

a horse **bucks**

② [spatter, splash]

¶ Muddy water **spattered** [my] trousers and dirtied them.

はは 母 [名]

¶ 母は今年60歳です。（*Haha* wa kotoshi rokujissai desu.）

¶ 母の料理が懐かしいです。（*Haha* no ryōri ga natsukashii desu.）

＊自分の母親のことを他人に話す場合に使う。直接、母親に呼びかける場合や、他人の母親のことを言う場合は、「お母さん（okāsan）」「お母様（okāsama）」と言う。

⇔父 chichi

⇒お母さん okasan

haha [n] **mother**

¶ **My mother** is 60 years old this year.

¶ I am homesick for **my mother's** cooking.

＊Used to refer to one's own mother when talking with others. When directly addressing one's own mother or referring to someone else's mother, *okāsan* or *okāsama* is used.

はば 幅 [名]

¶ この川の幅は何メートルぐらいありますか。（Kono kawa no *haba* wa nanmētoru gurai arimasu ka？）

¶ この道の幅は狭いですね。（Kono michi no *haba* wa semai desu ne.）

haba [n] **width, breadth, range**

¶ How many meters **wide** is this river?

¶ This street is narrow, isn't it?

はぶく 省く [動]

¶ ここでは詳しい説明は省きます。（Koko de wa kuwashii setsumei wa *habukimasu*.）

¶ 重要でないところは省いてください。（Jūyō de nai tokoro wa *habuite* kudasai.）

habuku [v I] **omit, leave out, skip**

¶ At this time **I will dispense with** a detailed explanation.

¶ Please **skip over** unimportant parts.

はめる [動Ⅱ]

指輪をはめる（yubiwa o *hameru*）

¶ 秋子さんは革の手袋をはめています。（Akiko san wa kawa no tebukuro o *hamete* imasu.）

hameru [v I] **put on, pull on, wear (ring, gloves, etc.)**

put on a ring

¶ Akiko **is wearing** leather gloves.

はやい 速い 〔形〕

足が速い（ashi ga *hayai*） 流れが速い（nagare ga *hayai*）

¶船より飛行機のほうが速いです。（Fune yori hikōki no hō ga *hayai* desu.）

¶もっと速く歩きましょう。（Motto *hayaku* arukimashō.）

⇔遅い osoi

はやい 早い 〔形〕

①［ある基準・比較の時間より前である］

¶わたしは毎日早く寝て、早く起きます。（Watashi wa mainichi *hayaku* nete, *hayaku* okimasu.）

¶上田さんは中村さんよりいつも早く学校へ来ます。（Ueda san wa Nakamura san yori itsu mo *hayaku* gakkō e kimasu.）

②［ある基準の時間までには間がある］

¶出発にはまだ早いから、コーヒーでも飲みましょう。（Shuppatsu ni wa mada *hayai* kara, kōhii demo nomimashō.）

¶9時ですから、寝るにはまだ早いです。（Kuji desu kara, neru ni wa mada *hayai* desu.）

⇔遅い osoi

はやさ 速さ 〔名〕

¶新幹線の速さはどのくらいですか。（Shinkansen no *hayasa* wa dono kurai desu ka？）

⇒-さ -sa

はやし 林 〔名〕

¶林の中で鳥が鳴いています。（*Hayashi* no naka de tori ga naite imasu.）

hayai 〔adj〕 **fast, quick**

be a **fast** walker 〚runner〛 // a **rapid** stream, a **fast** current

¶Airplanes **are faster** than ships.

¶Let's walk **faster**.

hayai 〔adj〕 **early**

① [early; be earlier than a set time]

¶I go to bed **early** and get up **early** every day.

¶[Miss] Ueda always comes to school **earlier** than [Mrs.] Nakamura.

② [early, too early, too soon; there is still time before a set time]

¶**There's** still **some time left** before departure so let's have some coffee or something.

¶As it's nine o'clock, it's still **too early** to go to bed.

hayasa 〔n〕 **speed, rapidity**

¶What is **the speed** of the Shinkansen 〚bullet train〛?

hayashi 〔n〕 **wood, woods, grove**

¶A bird is singing in **the woods**.

¶山や林の写真を写しました。（Yama ya *hayashi* no shashin o utsushimashita.）

¶ [I] took pictures of mountains and **woods**.

はやる〔動 I〕

hayaru 〔v I〕 **be prevalent; be popular, be in fashion**

¶悪い風邪がはやっています。（Warui kaze ga *hayatte* imasu.）

¶今、若い人の間ではどんな歌がはやっていますか。（Ima, wakai hito no aida de wa donna uta ga *hayatte* imasu ka？）

¶ There's a bad flu virus **going around** now.

¶ What sorts of songs **are popular** among young people now?

はら 腹〔名〕

hara 〔n〕 **stomach; spirit**

① [胃や腸の部分]
腹が痛い（*hara* ga itai）腹が減る（*hara* ga heru）腹がすく（*hara* ga suku）腹をこわす（*hara* o kowasu）
*丁寧に言うときは、普通「おなか（onaka）」と言う。

① [stomach, abdomen]
have a **stomach**ache, have a pain in **one's stomach** // be hungry // be hungry // upset **one's stomach**
*Onaka is more polite than *hara*.

②[気持ち・感情などを表す]
腹が立つ（*hara* ga tatsu）
¶上田さんはそれを聞いて、たいへん腹を立てました。（Ueda san wa sore o kiite, taihen *hara* o tatemashita.）

② [spirit, heart, mind, intention]
lose **one's temper**, be angry
¶ When [Mr.] Ueda heard that, [he] **became** very **angry**.

はらう 払う〔動 I〕

harau 〔v I〕 **pay; clear away, brush off**

①[代金などを相手に渡す]
¶食事代はわたしが払います。（Shokujidai wa watashi ga *haraimasu.*）
¶もう授業料を払いましたか。（Mō jugyōryō o *haraimashita* ka？）

① [pay]
¶ I'll **pay** the restaurant bill.

¶ **Have you paid** your tuition yet?

②[たたいたりして取り除く]
¶ブラシで洋服のほこりを払いました。（Burashi de yōfuku no hokori o *haraimashita.*）
¶オーバーの雪を払って家に入りました。（Ōbā no yuki o *haratte* ie ni hairimashita.）

② [clear away, sweep away, brush off]
¶ [I] **removed** lint from [my] suit 〚dress, etc.〛with a brush.

¶ [I] **brushed** the snow off of [my] overcoat and came into the house.

はり 針〔名〕

¶この針に糸を通してください。
(Kono *hari* ni ito o tooshite kudasai.)
¶時計の針が5時を指しています。
(Tokei no *hari* ga goji o sashite imasu.)

hari 〘n〙 **needle, pin, (clock) hands, indicator**

¶ Please thread this **needle** for me.

¶ **The hands** of the clock 〚watch〛 show five o'clock.

はる 張る〔動 I〕

①[伸び広がる、伸ばし広げる]
幕を張る (maku o *haru*) 帆を張る
(ho o *haru*) 木が根を張る (ki ga ne o *haru*)
¶川のそばにテントを張りました。
(Kawa no soba ni tento o *harimashita*.)
②[一面に覆う]
¶池に氷が張りました。(Ike ni koori ga *harimashita*.)
③[綱や糸などを引き渡す]
糸を張る (ito o *haru*)
¶そこは綱を張って人が入れないようにしてあります。(Soko wa tsuna o *hatte* hito ga hairenai yō ni shite arimasu.)

haru 〘v I〙 **stretch out, spread out; cover; stretch, extend**

① [stretch out, spread out]
stretch out a curtain // **unfurl** a sail // a tree is **deep-rooted**

¶ [I] **pitched** a tent beside the river.

② [cover]

¶ The pond **is** 〚**was**〛 **covered** with ice.

③ [stretch, extend]
stretch a thread between two points

¶ That area **is roped off** so no one can enter.

はる 春〔名〕
¶冬が過ぎて、春が来ました。(Fuyu ga sugite, *haru* ga kimashita.)
¶春と秋とどちらが好きですか。
(*Haru* to aki to dochira ga suki desu ka？)

haru 〘n〙 **spring, springtime**

¶ Winter is over and **spring** has come.

¶ Which do you like better, **spring** or fall?

はる〔動 I〕
¶この手紙に切手をはって出してください。(Kono tegami ni kitte o *hatte* dashite kudasai.)
¶壁にきれいな紙をはりましょう。
(Kabe ni kirei na kami o *harimashō*.)

haru 〘v I〙 **stick, paste, affix**

¶ Please **put** a stamp on this letter and mail it.

¶ **Let's put** some pretty wallpaper **up** on the walls.

はれ 晴れ〔名〕

¶あしたは晴れ後曇りでしょう。
（Ashita wa *hare* nochi kumori deshō.）
¶晴れの日には、ここから富士山が見えます。（*Hare* no hi ni wa, koko kara Fujisan ga miemasu.）
⇒曇り **kumori**

hare〔n〕**fair weather**

¶Tomorrow will probably be **fair**, later cloudy.

¶On a **clear** day one can see Mount Fuji from here.

はれる 晴れる〔動Ⅱ〕

¶午後はたぶん晴れるでしょう。
（Gogo wa tabun *hareru* deshō.）
¶今日はよく晴れて、いいお天気になりました。（Kyō wa yoku *harete*, ii otenki ni narimashita.）
⇒曇る **kumoru**

hareru〔v Ⅱ〕**become clear, clear up**

¶**It will** probably **become clear** in the afternoon.

¶**It's cleared up** nicely and become a fine day today.

はん 判〔名〕

¶ここに判を押してください。（Koko ni *han* o oshite kudasai.）
¶この領収書には判がありません。
（Kono ryōshūsho ni wa *han* ga arimasen.）
＊「判こ（hanko）」とも言う。

han〔n〕**stamp, seal, seal impression**

¶Please stamp **your seal** here.

¶This receipt does not bear **a seal**.

＊Variant: *hanko*.

ばん 晩〔名〕

朝から晩まで（asa kara *ban* made）晩御飯（*ban*gohan）前の晩（mae no *ban*）毎晩（mai*ban*）
¶あしたの晩、中村さんがうちに来ます。（Ashita no *ban*, Nakamura san ga uchi ni kimasu.）
¶一晩じゅう寝ないで起きていました。（Hito*ban*jū nenaide okite imashita.）

ban〔n〕**evening, night**

from morning to **night** // supper // the **night** before // every **night**

¶[Mr.] Nakamura is coming to [our] house tomorrow **evening**.

¶I was up all **night** without getting any sleep at all.

ばん 番〔名、尾〕

1〔名〕

(-)ban〔n, suf〕**watch, guard; order, one's turn; number, place**

1〔n〕

① [見張りなどをすること]
番人 (bannin) 番犬 (banken) 留守番
(rusuban)

¶あの店は、いつも子供が番をしてい
ます。(Ano mise wa, itsu mo kodomo ga
ban o shite imasu.)
② [順序や順番を表す]
¶次は田中さんの読む番です。(Tsugi
wa Tanaka san no yomu *ban* desu.)
2 〖尾〗
1番 (ichiban) 2番 (niban)
¶3番めの妹は今年15歳です。
(Sanbanme no imōto wa kotoshi jūgosai
desu.)

パン 〖名〗

¶わたしは毎朝パンを食べてコーヒー
を飲みます。(Watashi wa maiasa *pan* o
tabete kōhii o nomimasu.)

-はん -半 〖尾〗
¶今、9時半です。(Ima, kuji *han*
desu.)
¶もう2時間半働きました。(Mō
nijikan *han* hatarakimashita.)

はんい 範囲 〖名〗

¶試験の範囲を教えてください。
(Shiken no *han'i* o oshiete kudasai.)
¶地震で広い範囲に被害が出ました。
(Jishin de hiroi *han'i* ni higai ga
demashita.)

ハンカチ 〖名〗
ハンカチで手をふく (*hankachi* de te o
fuku)

① [watch over, guard]
a **watch**man, **guard** // a **watch**dog //
guarding an empty house against theft,
fire, etc.

¶ That shop is always **tended** by
children.

② [order, one's turn]
¶ Next it is [Miss] Tanaka's **turn** to
read.

2 〖suf〗 number, placef
Number 1 // **Number** 2
¶ My **third** younger sister is 〘will be〙
15 years old this year.

pan 〖n〗 **bread, toast, rolls, buns,**
etc.
¶ I have **bread** 〘**toast, croissants,**
rolls, etc.〙 and coffee every morning.

-han 〖suf〗 **half**
¶ It's now 9:30.

¶ [I]'ve already worked for two and **a**
half hours.

han'i 〖n〗 **extent, scope, bounds,**
limits
¶ Please tell us what the exam **will**
cover.
¶ The earthquake caused damage over
a wide **area**.

hankachi 〖n〗 **handkerchief**
wipe one's hands on **a handkerchief**

¶いつもハンカチを2枚持っています。
(Itsu mo *hankachi* o nimai motte imasu.)

¶ [I] always carry two **handkerchiefs** with [me].

パンク〔名、〜する〕

panku 〔n, 〜*suru*〕 **a puncture, a blowout**

¶自動車のタイヤがパンクしました。
(Jidōsha no taiya ga *panku* shimashita.)

¶ A tire **blew out** on the car.

ばんぐみ 番組〔名〕

bangumi 〔n〕 **program**

ラジオ番組（rajio-*bangumi*）

a radio program

¶今夜は、おもしろいテレビ番組があ
りますか。(Kon'ya wa, omoshiroi terebi-*bangumi* ga arimasu ka？)

¶ Are there any interesting television **programs** on this evening?

ばんごう 番号〔名〕

bangō 〔n〕 **number**

電話番号（denwa-*bangō*）番号をつけ
る（*bangō* o tsukeru）

a telephone **number** // assign a **number** to

¶あなたの部屋の番号は何番ですか。
(Anata no heya no *bangō* wa nanban desu ka?)

¶ What is **the number** of your room?

はんしゃ 反射〔名、〜する〕

hansha 〔n, 〜*suru*〕 **(physical) reflection**

¶鏡は光を反射します。(Kagami wa hikari o *hansha* shimasu.)

¶ Mirrors **reflect** light.

¶月は太陽の光を反射して光っていま
す。(Tsuki wa taiyō no hikari o *hansha* shite hikatte imasu.)

¶ The moon shines **reflecting** the rays of the sun.

はんせい 反省〔名、〜する〕

hansei 〔n, 〜*suru*〕 **self-examination, reflection, reconsideration**

¶あの人は悪いことをしても、少しも
反省しません。(Ano hito wa warui koto o shite mo, sukoshi mo *hansei* shimasen.)

¶ Even when [he] does something bad, [he] **has no second thoughts** whatsoever.

はんたい 反対〔名、〜する〕

hantai 〔n, 〜*suru*〕 **reverse, opposite; opposition, objection**

①[あることに対して逆の関係にある
こと]

① [the reverse, opposite, contrary]

反対の方向（*hantai* no hōkō）駅の反対
側（eki no *hantai*gawa）

the **opposite** direction // the **other** side of the station

② [ある意見や立場などに逆らうこと]
¶わたしはその考えに反対です。
(Watashi wa sono kangae ni *hantai* desu.)
¶父に反対されて留学をあきらめました。(Chichi ni *hantai* sarete ryūgaku o akiramemashita.)
↔賛成 sansei

② [opposition, objection]
¶I **am opposed** to that idea.

¶I gave up studying abroad as my father **was against it**.

はんだん 判断 〔名、〜する〕

¶どちらがいいか判断に迷っています。(Dochira ga ii ka *handan* ni mayotteimasu.)
¶それがいいか悪いかは、自分で判断してください。(Sore ga ii ka warui ka wa, jibun de *handan* shite kudasai.)

handan 〔n, 〜suru〕 **judgment, decision**
¶I am having trouble **deciding** which would be better.

¶Please **judge** for yourself whether that is good or bad.

はんつき 半月 〔名〕

¶日本へ来るのが予定より半月遅れました。(Nihon e kuru no ga yotei yori *hantsuki* okuremashita.)
¶この半月の間に病気がずいぶんよくなりました。(Kono *hantsuki* no aida ni byōki ga zuibun yoku narimashita.)

hantsuki 〔n〕 **half a month, a half month**
¶[My] coming to Japan was **a half month** later than planned.

¶In the past **half month** [my] illness has greatly improved.

はんとう 半島 〔名〕
¶あの半島の周りを船で回りました。(Ano *hantō* no mawari o fune de mawarimashita.)
¶日本でいちばん大きい半島は紀伊半島です。(Nihon de ichiban ookii *hantō* wa Kii-*hantō* desu.)

hantō 〔n〕 **peninsula**
¶[I] went around that **peninsula** by boat.

¶The biggest **peninsula** in Japan is the Kii **Peninsula**.

はんとし 半年 〔名〕

¶日本に来てからもう半年になります。(Nihon ni kite kara mō *hantoshi* ni narimasu.)

hantoshi 〔n〕 **half a year, a half year**
¶**Half a year** has already passed since [I] came to Japan.

¶半年後に結婚します。(*Hantoshi*go ni kekkon shimasu.)

¶ I will get married in **half a year**.

ハンドバッグ 〔名〕

handobaggu 〔n〕 **handbag, purse, pocketbook**

ハンドバッグを開ける (*handobaggu* o akeru)

open **a handbag**

¶新しいハンドバッグを買いました。(Atarashii *handobaggu* o kaimashita.)

¶ [I] bought a new **handbag**.

＊「ハンドバック (handobakku)」とも言う。

＊Variant: *handobakku*.

ハンドル 〔名〕

handoru 〔n〕 **doorknob, doorhandle; steering wheel**

①[ドアの取っ手]

① [doorknob, door handle]

¶ハンドルを回してドアを開けました。(*Handoru* o mawashite doa o akemashita.)

¶ [I] turned **the doorknob** and opened the door.

②[自動車などの手で握って回す部分]

② [steering wheel, handlebar]

¶ハンドルを左に切って、前から来る車をよけました。(*Handoru* o hidari ni kitte, mae kara kuru kuruma o yokemashita.)

¶ Turning **the wheel** to the left, [I] avoided hitting the oncoming car.

はんにち 半日 〔名〕

hannichi 〔n〕 **half a day, a half day**

¶仕事は半日で終わりました。(Shigoto wa *hannichi* de owarimashita.)

¶ The work was finished in **half a day**.

¶土曜には半日だけ働きます。(Doyō ni wa *hannichi* dake hatarakimasu.)

¶ [I] only work **half a day** on Saturday.

はんばい 販売 〔名、～する〕

hanbai 〔n, ～*suru*〕 **sales, selling**

販売店 (*hanbai*ten) 自動販売機 (jidō*hanbai*ki)

a shop, store // a **vending** machine

¶あの薬屋では化粧品の販売もしています。(Ano kusuriya de wa keshōhin no *hanbai* mo shite imasu.)

¶ That drugstore also **sells** cosmetics.

¶汽車の中でもお弁当を販売していますか。(Kisha no naka de mo obentō o *hanbai* shite imasu ka？)

¶ Are box lunches **on sale** on the train?

724

はんぶん 半分 〔名〕

¶りんごを半分ずつ食べましょう。

（Ringo o *hanbun* zutsu tabemashō.）

¶これを半分に分けてください。

（Kore o *hanbun* ni wakete kudasai.）

hanbun 〔n〕 half

¶ Let's each have **half** of the apple.

¶ Please divide this **in half**.

ひ

ひ 日 〔名〕

hi 〔n〕 **sun; sunlight; daytime; day**

① [太陽]

① [sun]

¶ 日は東から昇って、西に沈みます。
(*Hi* wa higashi kara nobotte, nishi ni shizumimasu.)

¶ **The sun** rises in the east and sets in the west.

② [日光]

② [sunlight]

日当たりがいい (*hi*atari ga ii)

be **sunny**, get much **sunlight**

¶ ぬれた服を日に干しましょう。
(Nureta fuku o *hi* ni hoshimashō.)

¶ Let's dry the wet clothes in **the sun**.

¶ 海に行ったので、日に焼けました。
(Umi ni itta node, *hi* ni yakemashita.)

¶ [I] got **sun**burned 〚tanned〛 at the ocean.

¶ ここはよく日が当たります。(Koko wa yoku *hi* ga atarimasu.)

¶ It's nice and **sunny** here 〚This spot gets lots of **sunshine**〛.

③ [昼間の時間]

③ [day, daytime]

¶ だんだん日が短くなりました。
(Dandan *hi* ga mijikaku narimashita.)

¶ **The days** gradually got shorter.

¶ 夏は日が長くなります。(Natsu wa *hi* ga nagaku narimasu.)

¶ **The days** are longer in the summer.

④ [1 日、24 時間]

④ [day, 24 hours]

ある日 (aru *hi*) その日 (sono *hi*) 次の日 (tsugi no *hi*) 天気のよい日 (tenki no yoi *hi*)

one **day**, a certain **day** //that **day** // the next **day** // a nice **day**, a clear **day**

ひ 火 〔名〕

hi 〔n〕 **fire, flame**

¶ たばこの火を貸してください。
(Tabako no hi o kashite kudasai.)

¶ Please give me **a light**.

¶ ガスの火を消してください。(Gasu no hi o keshite kudasai.)

¶ Please turn off the gas **burner**.

¶ ストーブの火をつけました。(Sutōbu no hi o tsukemashita.)

¶ [I] **lighted** the stove 〚heater〛.

-ひ -費 〔尾〕
交通費（kōtsū*hi*） 生活費（seikatsu*hi*）
会費（kai*hi*） 旅費（ryo*hi*）

¶ 食費は一か月いくらぐらいかかります
か。（Shoku*hi* wa ikkagetsu ikura gurai
kakarimasu ka？）

-hi 〔suf〕 **expenses, cost**

carfare, transportation **expenses** // living **expenses** // a fee (for a party, outing, etc.), membership **fee**, membership **dues** // travel **expenses**

¶ How much are food **expenses** 〚is board〛 a month?

ピアノ 〔名〕
¶ 妹 がピアノを弾いています。
（Imōto ga *piano* o hiite imasu.）
¶ 山田さんはピアノが上手です。
（Yamada san wa *piano* ga jōzu desu.）

piano 〔n〕 **piano**

¶ My (younger) sister is playing **the piano**.
¶ [Mrs.] Yamada plays **the piano** well.

ビール 〔名〕
ビールびん（*biiru*bin） ビールを飲む
（*biiru* o nomu）
¶ ビールを1本ください。（*Biiru* o
ippon kudasai.）

biiru 〔n〕 **beer**

a **beer** bottle // drink **beer**

¶ A bottle of **beer**, please.

ひえる 冷える 〔動〕

① [寒くなる、寒く感じる]

体が冷える（karada ga *hieru*）
¶ 今晩はずいぶん冷えますね。
（Konban wa zuibun *hiemasu* ne.）
② [冷たくなる]
¶ 冷えたビールがありますか。（*Hieta*
biiru ga arimasu ka？）

hieru 〔v II〕 **grow cold, become chilled**

① [it becomes cold or chilly, one feels cold or chilly]
one's body **is chilled**
¶ **It's** very **chilly** this evening, isn't it?

② [something becomes cold, chilled]
¶ Is there any **cold** beer?

ひがい 被害 〔名〕
被害地（*higai*chi）
¶ 台風のため、各地に大きな被害があ
りました。（Taifū no tame, kakuchi ni
ookina *higai* ga arimashita.）
¶ 昨日の交通事故の被害者は 30 歳ぐら
いの男の人でした。（Kinō no kōtsūjiko

higai 〔n〕 **damage, harm, injury**

the **afflicted** region, the **affected** area
¶ The typhoon caused great **damage** in many places.

¶ **The victim** of yesterday's traffic accident was a male of about 30 years.

no *higai*sha wa sanjissai gurai no otoko no
hito deshita.)

ひかく 比較 〔名、〜する〕

AとBを比較する（ē to bii o *hikaku*
suru）

¶ いろいろな店の値段を比較して、い
ちばん安い店で買い物をしました。
（Iroiro na mise no nedan o *hikaku* shite,
ichiban yasui mise de kaimono o
shimashita.）

⇒比べる **kuraberu**

ひがし 東 〔名〕

東側（*higashi*gawa）東風
（*higashi*kaze）

¶ 太陽は東から出て、西に沈みます。
（Taiyō wa *higashi* kara dete, nishi ni
shizumimasu.）

¶ 風が東から西に吹いています。
（Kaze ga *higashi* kara nishi ni fuite
imasu.）

⇔西 **nishi**

ひかり 光 〔名〕

¶ 月の光が明るく照っていました。
（Tsuki no *hikari* ga akaruku tette
imashita.）

¶ 電気が消えたので、ろうそくの光で
勉強しました。（Denki ga kieta node,
rōsoku no *hikari* de benkyō shimashita.）

ひかる 光る 〔動 I〕

ダイヤモンドが光る（daiyamondo ga
hikaru）

¶ 空には星が光っています。（Sora ni
wa hoshi ga *hikatte* imasu.）

¶ 遠くで何か光りましたが、何でしょ
うか。（Tooku de nani ka *hikarimashita*
ga, nan deshō ka？）

---

hikaku 〔n, 〜*suru*〕 **comparison**
to compare A with B

¶ [I] **compared** the prices at various
shops and did [my] shopping at the
cheapest one.

higashi 〔n〕 **east**
the **eastern** side // an **easterly** wind, a
wind from the east

¶ The sun rises in **the east** and sets in
the west.

¶ The wind is blowing from **east** to
west.

hikari 〔n〕 **light, illumination, glow**
¶ The moon **was shining** brightly.

¶ The electricity went out so [I] studied
by **the light** of a candle.

hikaru 〔v I〕 **shine, be luminous**
a diamond **sparkles**

¶ A star **is** 〚Stars **are**〛 **shining** in the
sky.

¶ Something **flashed** in the distance.

-ひき -匹 〔尾〕

1匹 (ip*piki*) 2匹 (ni*hiki*)
3匹 (san*biki*) 4匹 (yon*hiki*)
5匹 (go*hiki*) 6匹 (rop*piki*)
7匹 (nana*hiki*) 8匹 (hap*piki*)
9匹 (kyū*hiki*) 10匹 (jip*piki*)

¶ この池には魚が何匹ぐらいいます
か。(Kono ike ni wa sakana ga nan*biki*
gurai imasu ka？)

ひきうける 引き受ける 〔動〕

¶ 案内係は、わたしが引き受けます。
(Annaigakari wa, watashi ga
hikiukemasu.)
¶ そんな難しいことを引き受けて大丈
夫ですか。(Sonna muzukashii koto o
hikiukete daijōbu desu ka？)

ひきだし 引き出し 〔名〕

¶ 机の左の引き出しの中からはさみを
出してください。(Tsukue no hidari no
hikidashi no naka kara hasami o dashite
kudasai.)
¶ 引き出しを開けたら、ちゃんと閉め
てください。(*Hikidashi* o aketara,
chanto shimete kudasai.)

ひく 引く 〔動 I〕

① [物などを自分の手もとに引き寄せ
る]
ドアの取っ手を引く (doa no totteo
hiku)
¶ このひもを引くと、電気がつきま
す。(Kono himo o *hiku* to, denki ga
tsukimasu.)
⇔押す osu

-hiki 〔suf〕 the counter for animals, fish, insects

one cat 〖dog. goldfish, ant. etc.〗 // two
cats // three cats //four cats // five
cats // six cats // seven cats // eight
cats // nine cats //ten cats

¶ **How many** fish are there in this
pond 〖pool〗?

hikiukeru 〔v II〕 undertake, take charge of

¶ I'll **take on** the job of handling the
information desk.

¶ **You've taken** that **on**, but are you
sure you can handle such a difficult
task?

hikidashi 〔n〕 drawer, chest of drawers

¶ Please fetch the scissors from the left
drawer of the desk.

¶ If you pull out **a drawer** thenplease
close it again.

hiku 〔v I〕 pull; lead; subtract; look up; cite; install

① [pull by hand, draw]

pull on the door handle

¶ If **you pull on** this cord, the light will
come on.

② [車などを引っ張る]
馬がそりを引く　(uma ga sori o *hiku*)
¶重い荷物を積んだ車を引いたので、腕が痛くなりました。(Omoi nimotsu o tsunda kuruma o *hiita* node, ude ga itaku narimashita.)

② [pull, haul, tow]
a horse **pulls** a sleigh
¶ [My] arms are sore because [I] **pulled** a cart piled with a heavy load.

③ [導く]
¶お年寄りの手を引いて、会場を案内しました。(Otoshiyori no te o *hiite*, kaijo o annai shimashita.)

③ [lead]
¶ **Taking** the elderly person by the hand. [I] showed [him] around the grounds 〖convention area, exhibition hall, auditorium, etc.〗.

④ [減らす]
¶5から3を引くと、2になります。(Go kara san o *hiku* to, ni ni narimasu.)
¶あの店では、どの品物も1割引いて売っています。(Ano mise de wa, dono shinamono mo ichiwari *hiite* utte imasu.)
⇔足す tasu

④ [subtract, deduct, discount]
¶ Three **from** five is two.

¶ At that shop they sell everything at a 10 percent **discount**.

⑤ [風邪などにかかる]
¶風邪を引いて寝ています。(Kaze o *hiite* nete imasu.)

⑤ [catch a cold, the flu, etc.]
¶ [I] am in bed **with** a cold 〖the flu〗.

⑥ [辞書などから探しだす]
¶辞書を引いて、言葉の意味を調べました。(Jisho o *hiite*, kotoba no imi o shirabemashita.)

⑥ [look up in a dictionary, etc.]
¶ [I] **looked up** the meaning of a word in the dictionary.

⑦ [引用する]
¶先生は例を引いて説明しました。(Sensei wa rei o *hiite* setsumei shimashita.)

⑦ [cite, quote, refer to]
¶ The teacher explained **with** an example.

⑧ [電燈・ガスなどを家の中に導き入れる]
電話を引く　(denwa o *hiku*)　水道を引く (suidō o *hiku*)　ガスを引く　(gasu o *hiku*)

⑧ [install electricity, gas, etc.]

install a telephone // **have** water pipes **laid** //**lay on** gas

⑨ [線などを長くかく]
線を引く　(sen o *hiku*)

⑨ [draw a line, sketch, etc.]
draw a line

ひく 弾く 〔動Ⅰ〕

¶彼はギターを弾いて歌いました。
(Kare wa gitā o *hiite* utaimashita.)
¶子供が上手にピアノを弾きました。
(Kodomo ga jōzu ni piano o
hikimashita.)

hiku 〔vⅠ〕 **play (a stringed instrument)**

¶ He **played** the guitar and sang.

¶ The child **played** the piano well.

ひくい 低い 〔形〕
① [下から上までの長さが小さい、も
のの位置が地面などからあまり上の方
にない様子]
低い木（*hikui* ki）背が低い（se ga
hikui)
¶あの低い山は何と言いますか。(Ano
hikui yama wa nan to iimasu ka？)
¶白い鳥が低く飛んでいきました。
(Shiroi tori ga *hikuku* tonde ikimashita.)
② [声・音が小さく聞こえる様子、音
階が下である様子]
低い音（*hikui* oto）
¶二人は低い声で話しているので、何
を話しているかわかりません。(Futari
wa *hikui* koe de hanashite iru node, nani o
hanashite iru no ka wakarimasen.)
¶田中さんの声は低いです。(Tanaka
san no koe wa *hikui* desu.)
③ [温度や熱などの数値が小さい]
気圧が低い（kiatsu ga *hikui*)
¶ここは一年じゅう温度が低いから、
植物の生長が遅いです。(Koko wa
ichinenjū ondo ga *hikui* kara, shokubutsu
no seichō ga osoi desu.)
④ [身分などが下である様子]
地位が低い（chii ga *hikui*)
⇔高い **takai**

hikui 〔adj〕 **short; low**

① [short, low]

a **short** tree // **be short** of stature

¶ What is that **low** mountain called?

¶ The white bird flew away **close to the ground**.

② [low volume, low pitch]

a **low** sound; a **low-pitched** sound

¶ As the two are speaking in **low** voices, I can't hear what they're talking about.

¶ [Mr.] Tanaka has a **low-pitched** voice.

③ [be low on a scale]
low atmospheric pressure

¶ The temperatures **are low** here the year round so plant growth is slow.

④ [low, humble]
be low in position, **be low** in social standing

ひげ〔名〕

ひげが伸びる（*hige* ga nobiru）ひげを伸ばす（*hige* o nobasu）

¶田中さんのひげは立派ですね。
（Tanaka san no *hige* wa rippa desu ne.）
¶忙しくて二、三日ひげをそりませんでした。（Isogashikute ni-sannichi *hige* o sorimasen deshita.）

ひこうき　飛行機〔名〕

¶飛行機に乗ったことがありますか。
（*Hikōki* ni notta koto ga arimasu ka？）
¶飛行機は西の方へ飛んでいきました。（*Hiikōki* wa nishi no hō e tonde ikimashita.）

ひこうじょう　飛行場〔名〕

¶今日、羽田飛行場に着きました。
（Kyō, Haneda-*hikōjō* ni tsukimashita.）
¶中村さんは飛行場へ友達を迎えに行きました。（Nakamura san wa *hikōjō* e tomodachi o mukae ni ikimashita.）
⇔空港 kūkō

ひざ〔名〕

¶ひざを曲げて座りました。（*Hiza* o magete suwarimashita.）
¶ひざにちょっとけがをしました。
（*Hiza* ni chotto kega o shimashita.）

ビザ〔名〕

¶アメリカへ行くのにビザを取りました。（Amerika e iku no ni *biza* o torimashita.）

hige 〔n〕 **moustache, beard, whiskers**

one's beard 〚moustache〛 growslonger // to let one's beard 〚moustache〛 grow
¶ Mr. Tanaka has a fine **beard** 〚moustache; beard and moustache〛.
¶ [I] was so busy [I] didn't **shave** for two or three days.

hikōki 〔n〕 **airplane, aircraft**
¶ Have you ever ridden in **an airplane?**

¶ **The airplane** flew away toward the west.

hikōjō 〔n〕 **airport, airfield**
¶ [I] arrived at Haneda **Airport** today.

¶ [Mrs.] Nakamura went to **the airport** to meet a friend.

hiza 〔n〕 **knee, lap**
¶ [I] bent **[my] knees** and sat down.

¶ [I] injured **[my] knee** slightly.

biza 〔n〕 **visa**
¶ I obtained **a visa** to go to the United States.

ひさしぶり 久しぶり〔名〕

¶久しぶりに昔の友達に会いました。
(*Hisashiburi* ni mukashi no tomodachi ni
aimashita.)
¶久しぶりですね。お元気ですか。
(*Hisashiburi* desu ne. Ogenki desu ka？)

hisashiburi 〔n〕 **after a long time;
an expression used when
meeting someone after some
time has passed**

¶ [I] met an old friend **after a long
separation**.

¶ It's been **a long time**, hasn't it? How
are you doing?

びじゅつ 美術〔名〕
美術品（*bijutsu*hin）美術館
（bijutsukan）
¶わたしは日本の美術について研究し
たいと思っています。(Watashi wa
Nihon no *bijutsu* ni tsuite kenkyū shitai to
omotte imasu.)

bijutsu 〔n〕 **art**
a work of **art** // an **art** museum

¶ I would like to do research
concerning Japanese **art**.

ひじょう 非常〔名〕
非常口（*hijō*guchi）非常時（*hijō*ji）

¶非常の場合には、ここから出てくだ
さい。(*Hijō* no baai ni wa, koko kara
dete kudasai.)

hijō 〔n〕 **emergency,
extraordinary situation**
emergency exit // **an emergency,
crisis**

¶ In case of **emergency,** please go out
this way 〚from here〛.

ひじょうに 非常に〔副〕
¶試験は非常に難しかったです。
(Shiken wa *hijō ni* muzukashikatta
desu.)
¶今日は非常に寒いです。(Kyō wa
hijō ni samui desu.)

hijō ni 〔adv〕 **extremely, greatly**
¶ The exam was **extremely** difficult.

¶ It's **terribly** cold today.

ひたい 額〔名〕
¶ハンカチで額の汗をふきました。
(Hankachi de *hitai* no ase o fukimashita.)
¶子供の時、額にけがをしました。
(Kodomo no toki, *hitai* ni kega o
shimashita.)

hitai 〔n〕 **forehead, brow**
¶ [I] wiped the sweat from **[my]
forehead** with a handkerchief.
¶ [I] hurt [my]self on **the forehead**
when [I] was a child.

733

ひだり 左 〔名〕

左足 (hidariashi) 左手 (hidarite)

¶日本では車は左側を通ります。
(Nihon de wa kuruma wa hidarigawa o toorimasu.)

¶あの銀行の左の建物は何ですか。
(Ano ginkō no hidari no tatemono wa nan desu ka?)

⇔右 migi

hidari 〔n〕 **left**

the **left** foot 〚leg〛 // the **left** hand 〚arm〛; **left**-hand

¶In Japan traffic runs on **the left**.

¶What is the building to **the left** of that bank?

びっくりする 〔動Ⅲ〕

¶急に犬がほえだしたので、どろぼうはびっくりして逃げました。(Kyū ni inu ga hoedashita node, dorobō wa bikkuri shite nigemashita.)

¶考えていた以上に値段が高くてびっくりしました。(Kangaete ita ijō ni nedan ga takakute bikkuri shimashita.)

bikkuri suru 〔v Ⅲ〕 **be surprised, amazed, frightened**

¶The thief **was frightened** by the sudden barking of the dog and fled.

¶I was very surprised because the prices were much higher than expected.

ひっこし 引っ越し 〔名、～する〕

¶中村さんの引っ越しの手伝いをしました。(Nakamura san no hikkoshi no tetsudai o shimashita.)

¶引っ越しの荷物はどのくらいありますか。(Hikkoshi no nimotsu wa dono kurai arimasu ka?)

hikkoshi 〔n, ～suru〕 **moving, house moving**

¶[I] helped [Miss] Nakamura **move**.

¶How much property do you have **to be moved?**

ひっこす 引っ越す 〔動Ⅰ〕

¶来月、大学の近くに引っ越します。
(Raigetsu, daigaku no chikaku ni hikkoshimasu.)

¶あの人はよく引っ越しますね。(Ano hito wa yoku hikkoshimasu ne.)

hikkosu 〔v Ⅰ〕 **move (house)**

¶Next month [I] **will move** near to the university.

¶[He] **moves** a lot.

ひつじ 羊 〔名〕

羊を飼う (hitsuji o kau)

hitsuji 〔n〕 **sheep**

raise **sheep**

¶ 羊はたいへんおとなしい動物です。
(*Hitsuji* wa taihen otonashii dōbutsu desu.)

¶ **Sheep** are very docile animals.

ぴったり 〔副、〜する〕

① [すき間なくつく様子]
¶ 戸をぴったり閉めてください。(To o *pittari* shimete kudasai.)
② [よく合う様子]
¶ この服はあなたにぴったりです。
(Kono fuku wa anata ni *pittari* desu.)

pittari 〔adv, 〜*suru*〕 **tightly; exactly**

① [tightly]
¶ Please close the door **tightly**.
② [exactly, to a tee]
¶ This outfit is **exactly right** for you 〚is **a perfect fit** on you〛.

ひっぱる 引っ張る 〔動 I〕

¶ このひもを強く引っ張ってください。(Kono himo o tsuyoku *hippatte* kudasai.)
¶ 車が故障したので、綱をつけて引っ張りました。(Kuruma ga koshō shita node, tsuna o tsukete *hipparimashita*.)

hipparu 〔v I〕 **pull, drag, tug**

¶ Please **pull** hard on this string 〚cord, band, strap, etc.〛.

¶ The car wouldn't run so [we] **towed** it with a cable 〚rope, line〛.

ひつよう 必要 〔名、形動〕

¶ そんなことをする必要はありません。(Sonna koto o suru *hitsuyō* wa arimasen.)
¶ このお金で必要な物を買ってください。(Kono okane de *hitsuyō* na mono o katte kudasai.)
¶ 研究のために日本語が必要です。
(Kenkyū no tame ni Nihongo ga *hitsuyō* desu.)

hitsuyō 〔n, adj-v〕 **need, necessity; necessary, essential**

¶ There is no **need** to do such a thing.

¶ Please buy something you **need** with this money.

¶ Japanese **is essential** to [my] research.

ひてい 否定 〔名、〜する〕

否定的な意見 (*hitei*teki na iken)
¶ それは事実ですから否定しません。
(Sore wa jijitsu desu kara *hitei* shimasen.)
⇔ 肯定 **kōtei**

hitei 〔n, 〜*suru*〕 **denial**

a **dissenting** view
¶ [I] **don't deny** that that is so.

ひと 人〔名〕

hito 〔n〕 **person, people; other people, others**

① [人間]

男の人 (otoko no *hito*) 女の人 (onna no *hito*) いい人 (ii *hito*) 悪い人 (warui *hito*)

¶あそこに人が何人いますか。(Asoko ni *hito* ga nannin imasu ka？)

② [ほかの人、他人]

¶田中さんは人のことを全然考えません。(Tanaka san wa *hito* no koto o zenzen kangaemasen.)

¶人をばかにしてはいけません。(*Hito* o baka ni shite wa ikemasen.)

① [person, people, human beings]

a man // a woman // a good **person** // a bad **person**

¶ How many **people** are there over there?

② [other people, others]

¶ [Mrs.] Tanaka doesn't think of **other people** at all 〖show any consideration for **others**〗.

¶ One mustn't make fun of **others**.

ひどい〔形〕

hidoi 〔adj〕 **severe, intense; cruel, harsh**

① [程度が激しい、はなはだしい]

¶ひどい風でかさがこわれました。(*Hidoi* kaze de kasa ga kowaremashita.)

¶バスがひどくこんでいました。(Basu ga *hidoku* konde imashita.)

② [残酷な、情けがない、被害などがはなはだしい]

¶人を自動車でひいて逃げてしまうようなひどい人がいます。(Hito o jidōsha de hiite nigete shimau yō na *hidoi* hito ga imasu.)

¶台風のためにひどい目に遭いました。(Taifū no tame ni *hidoi* me ni aimashita.)

① [severe, intense, heavy, terrible]

¶ [My] umbrella broke in the **strong** wind.

¶ The bus was **terribly** crowded.

② [cruel, harsh, hard]

¶ There are people **terrible** enough to run away after hitting someone with their car.

¶ [I] suffered **greatly** 〖had a **terrible** experience〗 because of the typhoon.

ひとしい 等しい〔形〕

hitoshii 〔adj〕 **equal, identical, equivalent, similar, like**

¶ＡとＢは長さが等しいです。(Ē to bii wa nagasa ga *hitoshii* desu.)

¶そんなやり方はどろぼうに等しいです。(Sonna yarikata wa dorobō ni *hitoshii* desu.)

¶ A and B **are equal** in length.

¶ That's **tantamount to** thievery 〖That **amounts to** thievery〗.

ひとつ 一つ〔名〕

① [1 個]
¶このりんごは一ついくらですか。
(Kono ringo wa *hitotsu* ikura desu ka？)
② [1 歳]
¶この子は一つになったばかりです。
(Kono ko wa *hitotsu* ni natta bakari
desu.)

hitotsu 〔n〕 one, one item; one
　year of age
① [one item]
¶ How much are these apples **apiece**?

② [one year of age]
¶ This child has just turned **one year
old**.

ひとつき 一月〔名〕

¶部屋代は一月いくらですか。
(Heyadai wa *hitotsuki* ikura desu ka？)
¶胃の手術をして、一月以上入院しま
した。(I no shujutsu o shite, *hitotsuki* ijō
nyūin shimashita.)

hitotsuki 〔n〕 one month

¶ How much is **one month's** rent?

¶ [I] had a stomach operation and was
hospitalized for over **a month**.

ひとり 独り〔名〕

独り者（*hitori*mono) 独りぼっち
(*hitori*botchi)
¶あの人はまだ独りです。(Ano hito
wa mada *hitori* desu.)

hitori 〔n〕 alone, single

an **unmarried** person // all **by oneself**,
all **alone**
¶ [He] is still **single**.

ひとり 一人〔名〕

¶あの人は子供が一人しかありませ
ん。(Ano hito wa kodomo ga *hitori* shika
arimasen.)
¶費用は一人千円です。(Hiyō wa *hitori*
sen'en desu.)
¶今年の夏は一人で旅行しました。
(Kotoshi no natsu wa *hitori* de ryokō
shimashita.)
¶一人で荷物を全部運びました。
(*Hitori* de nimotsu o zenbu
hakobimashita.)

hitori 〔n〕 one person

¶ [He] has only **one** child.

¶ The cost is a thousand yen **per
person**.

¶ [I] went on a trip **by [my]self** this
summer.

¶ [I] transferred all of the load
〖baggage, bags〗 **by [my]self**.

ひにち 日にち〔名〕

① [ものごとを行う日、期日]
¶旅行の日にちを決めましょう。
(Ryokō no *hinichi* o kimemashō.)

hinichi 〔n〕 day, date; days, time
① [day, date, set date]
¶ Let's set **a date** for the trip.

¶会議の日にちと場所をメモしておい
てください。（Kaigi no *hinichi* to basho
o memo shite oite kudasai.）

¶ Please make a note of **the day(s)** and
place of the meeting 〚conference〛.

②[あることをするまでの日数]

② [days, time (before something)]

¶出発までにはまだ日にちがありま
す。（Shuppatsu made ni wa mada *hinichi*
ga arimasu.）

¶ There's still **time** before the departure
date.

¶試験までもうあまり日にちがありま
せん。（Shiken made mō amari *hinichi* ga
arimasen.）

¶ There's not much **time** left before the
examination.

③[あることをするのに要する日数]

③ [days, time (required to do
something)]

¶この仕事を完成するのには、ずいぶ
ん日にちがかかりそうです。（Kono
shigoto o kansei suru no ni wa, zuibun
hinichi ga kakarisō desu.）

¶ It looks like it will take a long **time**
to complete this work.

ひねる〔動 I〕

hineru〔v I〕 twist, bend

①[物を手などでねじって回す]

① [twist, turn]

¶水道のせんをひねっても水が出ませ
ん。（Suidō no sen o *hinette* mo mizu ga
demasen.）

¶ No water comes out when **you turn**
the faucet **on**.

②[よい工夫をするためにいろいろと
考えをめぐらす]

② [twist, turn, bend, incline (one's
head), rack (one's brains)]

¶頭をひねって考えましたが、いい考
えが浮かびません。（Atama o *hinette*
kangaemashita ga, ii kangae ga
ukabimasen.）

¶ [I] **racked** [my] brains but didn't have
any good ideas.

ひびく 響く〔動 I〕

hibiku〔v I〕 sound, resound,
reverberate; echo

①[音などが辺りに伝わる]

① [sound, resound, reverberate]
the waterfall makes a **booming** sound

滝の音が響く（taki no oto ga *hibiku*）

¶工事の音が響いてきてうるさいで
す。（Kōji no oto ga *hibiite* kite urusai
desu.）

¶ The construction sounds are very
loud and jarring.

②[音などが反響する]

② [echo]

¶トンネルの中では声が響きます。
（Tonneru no naka de wa koe ga
hibikimasu.)

¶ Voices **echo** in the tunnel.

ひひょう　批評 〔名、〜する〕

¶新しい本の批評が新聞に出ていま
す。（Atarashii hon no *hihyō* ga shinbun
ni deteimasu.)

¶彼はその小説を厳しく批評しまし
た。（Kare wa sono shōsetsu o kibishiku
hihyō shimashita.)

hihyō 〔n, 〜*suru*〕 **criticism, review**

¶ **Reviews** of new books appear in the
newspaper.

¶ He severely **criticized** that novel.

ひふ　皮膚 〔名〕

皮膚病　（*hifu*byō）皮膚科　（*hifu*ka）

¶この子は皮膚が弱いので困ります。
（Kono ko wa *hifu* ga yowai node
komarimasu.)

¶日に焼けて皮膚が赤くなりました。
（Hi ni yakete *hifu* ga akaku narimashita.)

hifu 〔n〕 **skin**

a **skin** disease // **dermatology,
dermatology** department

¶ This child has a delicate **skin** and we
don't know what to do.

¶ [I] burned in the sun and [my] **skin**
turned red.

ひま　暇 〔名、形動〕

① [何かをする時間]
¶忙しくて本を読む暇もありません。
（Isogashikute hon o yomu *hima* mo
arimasen.)

② [何もしなくてもいい時間、あいて
いる時間]
¶今度の日曜はお暇ですか。（Kondo
no nichiyō wa o*hima* desu ka？）
¶暇なときは何をしていますか。
（*Hima* na toki wa nani o shite imasu
ka？）
¶お暇でしたら、遊びにいらっしゃっ
てください。（O*hima* deshitara, asobi ni
irasshatte kudasai.)

hima 〔n, adj-v〕 **time; leisure,
leisure time**

① [time (to do something)]
¶ [I]'m so busy [I] don't have **the time**
to read books.

② [leisure, leisure time, free time]

¶ **Are you free** this Sunday?

¶ What do you do in **your spare time?**

¶ **If you aren't doing anything,** please
come and visit me.

ひみつ 秘密 〔名、形動〕

¶これはまだ秘密ですから、ほかの人には話さないでください。（Kore wa mada *himitsu* desu kara, hoka no hito ni wa hanasanaide kudasai.）

¶会社の秘密は守ってください。（Kaisha no *himitsu* wa mamotte kudasai.）

himitsu 〔n, adj-v〕 **secret**

¶ This is still **a secret** so please don't tell anyone else.

¶ Please keep our business **secrets** safe.

ひも 〔名〕

¶くつのひもが切れてしまいました。（Kutsu no *himo* ga kirete shimaimashita.）

¶この小包をひもで縛ってください。（Kono kozutsumi o *himo* de shibatte kudasai.）

himo 〔n〕 **string, cord, braid, band, ribbon, tape, strap, lace, etc.**

¶ [My] shoe**laces** broke.

¶ Please tie up this parcel with **string** 〚**cord, twine**, etc.〛.

ひゃく 百 〔名〕

hyaku 〔n〕 **one hundred**

ひやす 冷やす 〔動Ⅰ〕

¶ビールを冷やしておいてください。（Biiru o *hiyashite* oite kudasai.）

¶熱があるから、氷で頭を冷やしてください。（Netsu ga aru kara, koori de atama o *hiyashite* kudasai.）

hiyasu 〔vⅠ〕 **cool, ice, refrigerate**

¶ Please put the beer in the refrigerator 〚cooler〛 to **get cold**.

¶ Since [she] has a fever, please **cool** [her] head with an ice pack.

ひょう 表 〔名〕

時間表（jikan*hyō*）時刻表（jikoku*hyō*）予定表（yotei*hyō*）動詞の活用表（dōshi no katsuyō*hyō*）

¶1か月の予定を表にしました。（Ikkagetsu no yotei o *hyō* ni shimashita.）

¶調査の結果を表にまとめてください。（Chōsa no kekka o *hyō* ni matomete kudasai.）

hyō 〔n〕 **table, schedule, chart, list, diagram**

schedule // **schedule** of arrivals and departures // **program, schedule** // **table** of verb conjugations

¶ [I] made a one-month **schedule** (in tabular form).

¶ Please put the results of the survey into **tabular form**.

ひよう 費用 〔名〕

¶旅行の費用はいくらぐらいかかりますか。(Ryokō no *hiyō* wa ikura gurai kakarimasu ka？)

¶費用を計算してみましょう。(*Hiyō* o keisan shite mimashō.)

hiyō 〔n〕 expense, cost

¶How much will **the expenses** for the trip be?

¶Let's calculate **the expenses**.

-びょう -秒 〔尾〕

¶1分は 60 秒です。(Ippun wa rokujūbyō desu.)

-byō 〔suf〕 a second (of time)

¶One minute is 60 **seconds**.

びょういん 病院 〔名〕

¶田中さんは三日に一度病院に通っているそうです。(Tanaka san wa mikka ni ichido *byōin* ni kayotte iru sō desu.)

¶その病気は、大きな病院で診てもらったほうがいいですよ。(Sono byōki wa, ookina *byōin* de mite moratta hō ga ii desu yo.)

byōin 〔n〕 hospital, clinic

¶I hear that [Miss] Tanaka is being treated at **the hospital** once every three days.

¶With that illness, you had better be treated at a large **hospital**.

びょうき 病気 〔名〕

病気になる（*byōki* ni naru）病気にかかる（*byōki* ni kakaru）病気が治る（*byōki* ga naoru）病気を治す（*byōki* o naosu）重い病気（omoi *byōki*）軽い病気（karui *byōki*）

¶山田さんの病気はもうよくなりましたか。(Yamada san no *byōki* wa mō yoku narimashita ka？)

¶お父さんの御病気はいかがですか。(Otōsan no go*byōki* wa ikaga desu ka?)

¶病気で学校を1週間休みました。(*Byōki* de gakkō o isshūkan yasumimashita.)

byōki 〔n〕 illness, disease

become **ill** 〚sick〛 // become **ill** 〚sick〛 // get well, recover from **an illness** 〚disease〛 // cure **a disease** // a serious **illness** 〚disease〛 // a slight **illness**

¶Has [Mrs.] Yamada's **illness** become better yet?

¶How is your **(sick)** father?

¶[I] was absent from school for one week due to **illness**.

ひょうげん 表現 〔名、〜する〕

表現の自由（*hyōgen* no jiyū）

hyōgen 〔n, 〜*suru*〕 expression

freedom of **expression**

¶自分の考えを正確に表現するのは難しいことです。(Jibun no kangae o seikaku ni *hyōgen* suru no wa muzukashii koto desu.)

¶ It is difficult **to** precisely **express** one's thoughts.

ひょうじゅん　標準〔名〕

標準語 (*hyōjun*go)

¶田中さんのうちの赤ちゃんは標準よりかなり大きいそうです。(Tanaka san no uchi no akachan wa *hyōjun* yori kanari ookii sōdesu.)

¶彼の成績は標準以下です。(Kare no seiseki wa *hyōjun* ika desu.)

hyōjun 〔n〕 **standard, norm**

the **standard** language

¶ I hear that the Tanaka baby is considerably larger than **the norm**.

¶ His grades are 〖business record is〗 **substandard**.

ひょうばん　評判〔名〕

¶あの先生はたいへん評判がいいです。(Ano sensei wa taihen *hyōban* ga ii desu.)

¶新しい社長の評判はどうですか。(Atarashii shachō no *hyōban* wa dōdesu ka?)

hyōban 〔n〕 **reputation, public estimation, popularity**

¶ That teacher **is highly spoken of** 〖That teacher **is very popular**〗.

¶ What does everyone **think of** the new president of the company?

ひょうめん　表面〔名〕

① [物の外側の部分]

¶月の表面には穴がたくさんあります。(Tsuki no *hyōmen* ni wa ana ga takusan arimasu.)

② [外に現れたところ、うわべ]

¶彼は表面は穏やかですが、心の中では怒っているでしょう。(Kare wa *hyōmen* wa odayaka desu ga, kokoro no naka de wa okotte irudeshō.)

hyōmen 〔n〕 **surface; exterior**

① [surface]

¶ There are many holes in **the surface** of the moon.

② [exterior, outward appearance]

¶ He is **outwardly** calm, but inwardly he's probably angry 〖He is calm **on the outside**, but I bet he's angry on the inside〗.

ひらがな〔名〕

¶漢字の読み方をひらがなで書きました。(Kanji no yomikata o *hiragana* de kakimashita.)

hiragana 〔n〕 **hiragana, the hiragana syllabary**

¶ [I] wrote the readings of the kanji in **hiragana**.

¶ローマ字でなくひらがなで書いてください。(Rōmaji de naku *hiragana* de kaite kudasai.)

⇒かな **kana**　カタカナ **katakana**

ひらく 開く〔動I〕

① [閉じていたものがあく]
風で戸が開く (kaze de to ga *hiraku*)
¶桜の花が開きました。(Sakura no hana ga *hirakimashita*.)

② [閉じてあったものをあける]
小包を開く (kozutsumi o *hiraku*)
¶では、本を開いて勉強を始めましょう。(Dewa, hon o *hiraite* benkyō o hajimemashō.)

③ [店などを新しく始める]
¶上田さんは駅のそばに果物屋を開きました。(Ueda san wa eki no soba ni kudamonoya o *hirakimashita*.)

④ [会などを行う]
¶今晩7時から研究会を開きます。(Konban shichiji kara kenkyūkai o *hirakimasu*.)

⇒閉じる **tojiru**

ひる 昼〔名〕

① [昼間]
¶昼も夜も休まずに働きました。(*Hiru* mo yoru mo yasumazu ni hatarakimashita.)
¶今日は昼寝をしました。(Kyō wa *hiru*ne o shimashita.)

⇔夜 **yoru**

② [正午]
昼休み (*hiru*yasumi)

¶ Please write it in **hiragana**, not roman letters.

hiraku 〖v I〗 open; open, start; hold (a meeting)

① [(something) opens]
the door **opens** in the wind
¶ The cherry blossoms **have opened**
〖The cherry blossoms **opened**〗.

② [open, undo]
open a parcel
¶ Well, let's **open** our books and start the lesson.

③ [open, start (a shop, etc.)]
¶ [Miss] Ueda **opened** a fruit store near the station.

④ [hold (a meeting, party, etc.)]
¶ The study meeting **will be held** this evening from seven o'clock.

hiru 〖n〗 daytime; noon, noontime; lunch

① [daytime]
¶ [I] worked nonstop **day** and night.

¶ [I] took **a nap** today.

② [noon, noontime, midday]
noon recess, **lunch** hour

¶彼はいつもお昼ごろ会社へ来ます。
（Kare wa itsu mo o*hiru* goro kaisha e
kimasu.）

¶He always comes to the office around
noon.

¶もう昼御飯を食べましたか。（Mō
*hiru*gohan o tabemashita ka？）

¶Have you eaten **lunch** yet?

③[昼御飯]

③[lunch, noon meal]

¶お昼は何にしますか。（O*hiru* wa nani
ni shimasu ka？）

¶What do you want to eat for **lunch?**

¶お昼はおそばにしましょう。（O*hiru*
wa osoba ni shimashō.）

¶Let's have soba for **lunch**.

ビル〔名〕

biru 〔n〕 **building, office building**

¶50階建ての高いビルが建ちました。
（Gojikkaidate no takai *biru* ga
tachimashita.）

¶A tall **building** 50 stories high has
been built.

ひるま 昼間〔名〕

hiruma 〔n〕 **day, daytime, during
the daytime**

¶彼は昼間働いて、夜学校へ行きま
す。（Kare wa *hiruma* hataraite, yoru
gakkō e ikimasu.）

¶He works **during the day** and goes
to school at night.

¶昼間からそんなにお酒を飲まないで
ください。（*Hiruma* kara sonna ni osake
o nomanaide kudasai.）

¶Please don't drink so much so **early
in the day** 〚**during the daytime**〛.

⇔夜 **yoru**

ひるやすみ 昼休み〔名〕

hiruyasumi 〔n〕 **lunch hour**

¶この会社の昼休みは12時から1時
までです。（Kono kaisha no *hiruyasumi*
wa jūniji kara ichiji made desu.）

¶The lunch hour in this company is
from twelve to one.

ひろい 広い〔形〕

hiroi 〔adj〕 **wide, broad, spacious**

¶あの家の庭は広いです。（Ano ie no
niwa wa *hiroi* desu.）

¶That house has a **large** garden
〚**extensive** yard〛.

¶この部屋はあまり広くありません。
（Kono heya wa amari *hiroku* arimasen.）

¶This room **isn't** very **big**.

⇔狭い **semai**

ひろう 拾う〔動Ⅰ〕

hirou 〔vⅠ〕 **pick up; find**

①[落ちているものなどを取り上げる]

①[pick up, gather, find]

¶ 道でお金を拾いました。(Michi de okane o *hiroimashita*.)

¶ [I] **found** some money in the street.

¶ 紙くずを拾って、この箱に入れてください。(Kamikuzu o *hirotte*, kono hako ni irete kudasai.)

¶ Please **pick up** the wastepaper and put it in this box.

⇔捨てる suteru

② [タクシーなどを呼び止めて乗る]

② [find, catch (a taxi, etc.)]

¶ 雨が降ってきたから、タクシーを拾いましょう。(Ame ga futte kita kara, takushii o *hiroimashō*.)

¶ It's started to rain—**let's take** a taxi.

ひろがる 広がる 〔動Ⅰ〕

hirogaru 〔v I〕 **spread, expand; spread, be disseminated**

① [空間的に大きくなる、広くなる]

① [spread, expand]

¶ 学校の前の道が広がりました。(Gakkō no mae no michi ga *hirogarimashita*.)

¶ The road **has been widened** in front of the school.

¶ 木の枝が四方に広がっています。(Ki no eda ga shihō ni *hirogatte* imasu.)

¶ The branches of the tree **are spreading out** in all directions.

② [ものごとがいろいろな人・場所などに及ぶ]

② [spread, be disseminated]

伝染病が広がる (densenbyō ga *hirogaru*)

a contagious disease **spreads**

¶ うわさが町じゅうに広がっています。(Uwasa ga machijū ni *hirogatte* imasu)

¶ The rumor **is spreading** throughout the town.

ひろげる 広げる 〔動Ⅱ〕

hirogeru 〔v Ⅲ〕 **extend, expand; open, spread out**

① [空間的に大きくする、広くする]

① [extend, expand, enlarge]

道の幅を広げる (michi no haba o *hirogeru*)

widen the road

¶ 店を広げて、きれいにしました。(Mise o *hirogete*, kirei ni shimashita.)

¶ [They] **enlarged** and fixed up the shop 〖restaurant, etc.〗.

② [開ける]

② [open, spread out, unfold]

¶ 地図を広げて、旅行の相談をしました。(Chizu o *hirogete*, ryokō no sōdan o shimashita.)

¶ **Spreading out** a map, [we] consulted about the trip.

¶本を広げたまま眠ってしまいました。(Hon o *hirogeta* mama nemutte shimaimashita.)

¶ [I] fell asleep with [my] book still **open**.

ひろさ 広さ 〔名〕

hirosa 〔n〕 **area, dimensions**

¶この家の広さはどのくらいですか。(Kono ie no *hirosa* wa dono kurai desu ka?)

¶ What is **the floor space** of this house?

⇔-さ -sa

ひろば 広場 〔名〕

hiroba 〔n〕 **open space, plaza, square**

¶駅の前に広場があります。(Eki no mae ni *hiroba* ga arimasu.)

¶ There is **a plaza** in front of the station.

¶広場に人がたくさん集まっています。(*Hiroba* ni hito ga takusan atsumatte imasu.)

¶ A lot of people are gathered in **the plaza**.

びん 〔名〕

bin 〔n〕 **bottle**

ビールびん (biiru*bin*) インクびん (inku*bin*) しょう油びん (shōyu*bin*) 空きびん (aki*bin*)

a beer **bottle** // an ink **bottle** // a soy sauce **bottle** // an empty **bottle**

びんせん 便せん 〔名〕

binsen 〔n〕 **letter paper**

¶文房具屋で便せんと封筒を買ってきてください。(Bunbōguya de *binsen* to fūtō o katte kite kudasai.)

¶ Please go buy me **letter paper** and envelopes at a stationery store.

びんぼう 貧乏 〔名、形動、〜する〕

binbō 〔n, adj-v, 〜*suru*〕 **poverty, poor**

貧乏な人 (*binbō* na hito) 貧乏になる (*binbō* ni naru)

a **poor** person // become **poor**

¶家が貧乏だったので、わたしは大学へ行けませんでした。(Ie ga *binbō* datta node, watashi wa daigaku e ikemasen deshita.)

¶ Since my family **was poor, I** was not able to go to college.

⇒貧しい **mazushii**

ピンポン 〔名〕

pinpon 〔n〕 **ping-pong, table tennis**

¶友達とピンポンをしました。(Tomodachi to *pinpon* o shimashita.)

¶ [I] played **ping-pong** with a friend.

746

ふ

-ぶ -部 〔尾〕

① [全体をいくつかに分けたもの]

¶この本は1部と2部に分かれています。(Kono hon wa ichibu to nibu ni wakarete imasu.)

② [組織の上での区分]

¶山田さんはA新聞社の写真部に勤めています。(Yamada san wa Ē-shinbunsha no shashinbu ni tsutomete imasu.)

③ [スポーツ・文化活動などのグループ]

野球部（yakyūbu）山岳部（sangakubu）スキー部（sukiibu）演劇部（engekibu）

④ [本や雑誌や新聞などを数えるのに使う]

¶この新聞は一部いくらですか。(Kono shinbun wa ichibu ikura desu ka?)

-ぶ -分 〔尾〕

① [温度の1度の10分の1の単位]

¶熱が 38 度5分あります。(Netsu ga sanjūhachido gobu arimasu.)

② [利率などの1割の10分の1の単位]

¶この商品は3割5分引きですから、買うと得です。(Kono shōhin wa sanwari gobu biki desu kara, kau to toku desu.)

-bu 〔suf〕 **part, section; division, department; club; copy**

① [part, section]

¶This book is divided into a **Part I** and a **Part II**.

② [organizational unit(department, division, section, etc.)]

¶ [Mrs.] Yamada works in the photography **department** of Newspaper A.

③ [school or company club (sports, cultural, etc.)]

a baseball **club** // a mountaineering **club** // a ski **club** // a drama **club**

④ [copy; the counter for copies of books, magazines, newspapers, etc.]

¶ How much is a **copy** of this newspaper?

-bu 〔suf〕 *bu*

① [one *bu* (= one-tenth of one degree of temperature)]

¶ [He] has a fever of 38.**5 degrees**.

② [one *bu* (=1% of interest, etc.)]

¶ Since this product is 35% off, it is a bargain.

ふあん　不安〔名、形動〕

¶試験に合格するかどうか不安です。
（Shiken ni gōkaku suru ka dō ka *fuan* desu.）
¶入試の結果がわかるまで不安な気持ちです。（Nyūshi no kekka ga wakaru made *fuan* na kimochi desu.）

fuan 〔n, adj-v〕 **anxiety, uncertainty, uneasiness**

¶ **I am worried** over whether [I] will pass the exam or not.

¶ **I will be anxious** until we find out the results of the entrance exam.

フィルム〔名〕

¶このカメラにフィルムを入れてください。（Kono kamera ni *firumu* o irete kudasai.）
¶カラーフィルムで写真を写しました。（Karā-*firumu* de shashin o utsushimashita.）

firumu 〔n〕 **film**

¶ Please put **film** in this camera.

¶ [I] took the photograph with color **film**.

ふうとう　封筒〔名〕

¶この手紙を封筒に入れて出してください。（Kono tegami o *fūtō* ni irete dashite kudasai.）
¶封筒と便せんをください。（*Fūtō* to binsen o kudasai.）

fūtō 〔n〕 **envelope**

¶ Please put this letter in **an envelope** and mail it.

¶ **Envelopes** and letter paper, please.

ふうふ　夫婦〔名〕

夫婦げんか（*fūfu*genka）新婚夫婦（shinkon*fūfu*）
¶あの二人は結婚して夫婦になりました。（Ano futari wa kekkon shite *fūfu* ni narimashita.）
¶夫婦そろって旅行しました。（*Fūfu* sorotte ryokō shimashita.）

fūfu 〔n〕 **husband and wife, a married couple**

a **marital** quarrel // newly**weds**

¶ Those two have married and formed **a couple**.

¶ Both **husband and wife** 〚**My husband/wife and I**〛 went on a trip together.

プール〔名〕

¶健康のために毎週プールで泳いでいます。（Kenkō no tame ni maishū *pūru* de oyoide imasu.）

pūru 〔n〕 **pool**

¶ I swim at the pool every week to keep fit.

748

ふえる 増える 〔動Ⅱ〕

¶体重が5キロ増えました。(Taijū ga gokiro *fuemashita.*)

¶このごろ、交通事故が増えています。(Konogoro, kōtsū-jiko ga *fuete imasu.*)

⇔減る **heru**
⇒増加 **zōka** 増す **masu**

フォーク 〔名〕

¶ナイフとフォークを買いました。(Naifu to *fōku* o kaimashita.)

¶食事のとき、はしとフォークとどちらを使いますか。(Shokuji no toki, hashi to *fōku* to dochira o tsukaimasu ka?)

ふかい 深い 〔形〕

① [表面から底までの距離が長い]
深い海 (*fukai* umi) 深い井戸 (*fukai* ido)

¶日本の周りの海でいちばん深い所はどこですか。(Nihon no mawari no umi de ichiban *fukai* tokoro wa doko desu ka?)

¶深い所では泳がないでください。(*Fukai* tokoro de wa oyoganaide kudasai.)

↔浅い **asai**

② [入り口から奥までの距離が長い]
山が深い (yama ga *fukai*)

¶一匹のしかが深い森の中に住んでいました。(Ippiki no shika ga *fukai* mori no naka ni sunde imashita.)

③ [学問や知識などがじゅうぶんにある様子]

¶彼はこの問題について深い知識を持っています。(Kare wa kono mondai ni tsuite *fukai* chishiki o motte imasu.)

fueru 〔v Ⅱ〕 **increase**

¶ [I] **gained** five kilos.

¶ Traffic accidents **are increasing** these days.

fōku 〔n〕 **fork**

¶ [I] bought knives and **forks**.

¶ Which do you use when you eat, chopsticks or **a fork?**

fukai 〔adj〕 **deep; dense; profound**

① [deep; far from top to bottom]
a **deep** sea // a **deep** well

¶ Where is the **deepest** point in the seas around Japan?

¶ Please don't swim where the water **is deep**.

② [deep, dense; far from front to back]
deep in the mountains

¶ A deer lived **deep** in the forest.

③ [deep, profound (knowledge, learning, etc.)]

¶ He possesses a **profound** knowledge concerning this problem.

④ [霧などが濃い]
深い霧 (*fukai* kiri)

④ [heavy, dense (fog, etc.)]
a **heavy** fog

⑤ [程度などが大きい]
注意深い (chū*ibukai*) 遠慮深い
(enryo*bukai*) 用心深い (yōjin*bukai*)
¶ 御親切を深く感謝します。
(Goshinsetsu o *fukaku* kansha shimasu.)

⑤ [deep, profound, intense, strong]
careful, attentive // reserved, modest,
shy // careful, cautious
¶ I am **profoundly** grateful for your
kindness to me.

ふかさ 深さ 〔名〕

¶ この湖の深さは200メートルありま
す。(Kono mizuumi no *fukasa* wa
nihyakumētoru arimasu.)

⇒-さ -sa

fukasa 〔n〕 **depth**

¶ This lake is two hundred meters **deep**.

ふきん 付近 〔名〕

¶ この付近に病院がありますか。
(Kono *fukin* ni byōin ga arimasu ka?)
¶ 駅の付近には店がたくさんありま
す。(Eki no *fukin* ni wa mise ga takusan
arimasu.)

⇒近く chikaku

fukin 〔n〕 **vicinity, neighborhood**

¶ Is there a hospital **near** here?

¶ There are many shops **around** the
station.

ふく 服 〔名〕

婦人服 (fujin*fuku*) 子供服
(kodomo*fuku*) 和服 (wa*fuku*) 洋服
(yō*fuku*)
¶ 母が新しい服を作ってくれました。
(Haha ga atarashii *fuku* o tsukutte
kuremashita.)
¶ 冬の服をクリーニングに出しまし
た。(Fuyu no *fuku* o kuriiningu ni
dashimashita.)

fuku 〔n〕 **dress, clothing, clothes**

women's **clothing** // children's
clothing // Japanese-style **clothing** //
Western-style **clothing**
¶ My mother made me some new
clothes.

¶ [I] sent the winter **clothing** to the
cleaners.

ふく 吹く 〔動 I〕

① [風などが動いて通りすぎる]
¶ 昨日は一日じゅう強い風が吹いてい
ました。(Kinō wa ichinichijū tsuyoi
kaze ga *fuite* imashita.)
② [口から息を勢いよく出す]

fuku 〔v I〕 **blow**

① [blow (the wind, etc.)]
¶ A strong wind **was blowing** all day
yesterday.

② [blow, breathe out]

¶ろうそくの火を吹いて消しました。
(Rōsoku no hi o *fuite* keshimashita.)
③［息で楽器などを鳴らす］
ハーモニカを吹く（hāmonika o *fuku*)
トランペットを吹く（toranpetto o *fuku*)

¶ [I] **blew** out the candle.

③ [play a wind instrument]
play on a harmonica // **blow** a trumpet

ふく〔動I〕
¶ハンカチで汗をふきました。
(Hankachi de ase o *fukimashita*.)
¶机の上が汚れているから、ふいてく
ださい。（Tsukue no ue ga yogorete iru
kara, *fuite* kudasai.)

fuku 〚v I〛 **wipe, mop**
¶ [I] **wiped** the sweat **off** with a
handkerchief.
¶ The desk top is dirty-please **wipe it
off**.

ふくざつ 複雑〔形動〕

¶複雑な漢字はまだ書けません。
(*Fukuzatsu* na kanji wa mada
kakemasen.)
¶あの人の話は複雑で、よくわかりま
せん。（Ano hito no hanashi wa *fukuzatsu*
de, yoku wakarimasen.)
⇒簡単 kantan

fukuzatsu 〚adj-v〛 **complicated,
involved**
¶ [I] can't write **complex** *kanji* yet.

¶ [His] stories〚lectures〛**are
complicated**, and I don't understand
them very well.

ふくしゅう 復習〔名、〜する〕

¶予習も復習も大切です。（Yoshū mo
fukushū mo taisetsu desu.)
¶家でよく復習してください。（Ie de
yoku *fukushū* shite kudasai.)
⇔予習 yoshū

fukushū 〚n, 〜*suru*〛 **review (of
lessons)**
¶ Both preparation and **review** of
lessons are important.
¶ Please **review** this well at home.

ふくすう 複数〔名〕
¶日本語には、単数と複数の区別はあ
まりありません。（Nihongo ni wa, tansū
to *fukusū* no kubetsu wa amari arimasen.)
¶あなたの国の言葉では、複数の形は
どう表しますか。（Anata no kuni no
kotoba de wa, *fukusū* no katachi wa dō
arawashimasu ka？)

fukusū 〚n〛 **plural**
¶ The distinction between singular and
plural isn't made very often in the
Japanese language.
¶ How is the **plural** form expressed in
your native language?

⇔単数 tansū

ふくむ 含む 〔動Ⅰ〕

¶海の水は塩分を含んでいます。(Umi no mizu wa enbun o *fukunde* imasu.)

¶このソースには何が含まれていますか。(Kono sōsu ni wa nani ga *fukumarete* imasu ka?)

fukumu 〖vI〗 contain

¶ Seawater **contains** salt.

¶ What **is in** this sauce?

ふくめる 含める 〔動Ⅱ〕

¶お客は子供を含めて15人です。(Okyaku wa kodomo o *fukumete* jūgonin desu.)

¶税金も含めて月給はいくらですか。(Zeikin mo *fukumete* gekkyū wa ikura desu ka?)

fukumeru 〖vII〗 include

¶ **Including** children, the guests 〚customers〛number 15 persons.

¶ How much is the monthly wage **including** tax?

ふくらむ 〔動Ⅰ〕

風船がふくらむ (fūsen ga *fukuramu*)

¶春になって、木の芽がふくらんできました。(Haru ni natte, ki no me ga *fukurande* kimashita.)

fukuramu 〖vI〗 swell, expand, bulge out

the balloon **is being inflated**

¶ Spring has come and the buds on the trees **are swelling.**

ふくれる 〔動Ⅱ〕

¶ビールをたくさん飲んだので、おなかがふくれました。(Biiru o takusan nonda node, onaka ga *fukuremashita.*)

fukureru 〖vII〗 swell out, expand

¶ My stomach **is bloated** 〚**full**〛 as I drank a lot of beer.

(-)ふくろ (-)袋 〔名、尾〕

1 〔名〕
ビニール袋 (biniiru-*bukuro*)　紙袋 (kami*bukuro*)

¶これを袋に入れてください。(Kore o *fukuro* ni irete kudasai.)

2 〔尾〕

¶お菓子を一袋買いました。(Okashi o hito *fukuro* kaimashita.)

(-)fukuro 〖n, suf〗 bag, sack; bagful, sackful

1 〖n〗 bag, sack
a plastic **bag**, vinyl **bag** // a paper **bag**

¶ Please put this in **a bag.**

2 〖suf〗 bagful, sackful; the counter for bags or sacks of something

¶ [I] bought **a bag** of candy.

ふく- 副- 〔頭〕

fuku- 〔pref〕 **assistant, deputy, acting, vice-, secondary, auxiliary**

副大統領 (*fuku*-daitōryō) 副社長 (*fuku*-shachō) 副読本 (*fuku*-dokuhon)

the vice-president (of a nation) // the **vice**-president (of a company) // a **supplementary** reader

ふこう 不幸 〔名、形動〕

fukō 〔n, adj-v〕 **unhappiness, sorrow; misfortune**

不幸な一生 (*fukō* na isshō)
¶彼は不幸にも交通事故に遭って、ひどいけがをしました。(Kare wa *fukō* ni mo kōtsū-jiko ni atte, hidoi kega o shimashita.)
⇔幸福 **kōfuku**

a life of **misery**, an **unhappy** lifetime
¶He **had the misfortune** to be seriously injured in a traffic accident.

ぶじ 無事 〔名、形動〕

buji 〔n, adj-v〕 **safe, well**

¶無事に日本に着きましたから、御安心ください。(*Buji* ni Nihon ni tsukimashita kara, goanshin kudasai.)
¶車はひどく壊れましたが、運転していた人は無事でした。(Kuruma wa hidoku kowaremashita ga, unten shite ita hito wa *buji* deshita.)

¶Please don't worry as 〖I am happy to inform you that〗 I have arrived **safely** in Japan.
¶The car was severely damaged, but the driver **escaped injury.**

ふしぎ 不思議 〔形動〕

fushigi 〔adj-v〕 **wonderful, strange, mysterious, curious**

¶日本ではなぜ牛肉がこんなに高いのか不思議です。(Nihon de wa naze gyūniku ga konna ni takai no ka *fushigi* desu.)
¶こんな簡単な問題がなぜ解決できないのか、それが不思議です。(Konna kantan na mondai ga naze kaiketsu dekinai no ka, sore ga *fushigi* desu.)
¶ひどい事故でしたが、不思議に彼は無事でした。(Hidoi jiko deshita ga, *fushigi* ni kare wa buji deshita.)

¶**It's strange** that beef should be so expensive in Japan.

¶**It's curious** that such a simple problem hasn't been solved.

¶It was a terrible accident, but **miraculously enough** he escaped injury.

ふじん　婦人〔名〕

婦人服（*fujin*fuku）婦人ぐつ
（*fujin*gutsu）婦人物（*fujin*mono）婦人
用（*fujin*yō）

¶この小説を書いたのはこちらのご婦
人です。（Kono shōsetsu o kaita no wa
kochira no go*fujin* desu.）

fujin 〔n〕 **woman, lady, female**

women's clothes // **women's** shoes //
an item for use by **women** // for
women, for use by **women**

¶ This is the lady who wrote this novel.

ふじん　夫人〔名〕

首相夫人（shushō *fujin*）

¶山田夫人と田中夫人が委員に選ばれ
ました。（Yamada *fujin* to Tanaka *fujin*
ga iin ni erabaremashita.）

fujin 〔n〕 **wife, Mrs.～**

the **wife** of the prime minister

¶ **Mrs**. Yamada and **Mrs**. Tanaka were
chosen to be on the committee.

ふそく　不足〔名、～する〕

¶料金が 50 円不足していますから、
そこで切手を買ってはってください。
（Ryōkin ga gojūen *fusoku* shite imasu
kara, soko de kitte o katte hatte kudasai.）

¶栄養が不足すると、病気になりま
す。（Eiyō ga *fusoku* suru to, byōki ni
narimasu.）

fusoku 〔n, ～*suru*〕 **insufficiency,
deficiency**

¶ It's 50 yen **short**; please buy a stamp
for it over there (literally, buy a stamp
over there and put it on).

¶ **Malnutrition** leads to illness.

ふた〔名〕

¶おふろのふたをしてください。
（Ofuro no *futa* o shite kudasai.）

¶びんのふたがなかなか開きません。
（Bin no *futa* ga nakanaka akimasen.）

futa 〔n〕 **cover, lid**

¶ Please put **the cover** back on the
bathtub.

¶ **The lid** of this bottle is difficult to
open.

ふだ　札〔名〕

① [文字などを書いて何かにつけたり
何かの印としたりする小さな紙や板な
ど]

名札（na*fuda*）荷札（ni*fuda*）

¶受付で番号札を受け取ってくださ
い。（Uketsuke de bangō*fuda* o uketotte
kudasai.）

fuda 〔n〕 **label, tag, nameplate;
charm, talisman**

① [label, tag, nameplate, ticket; small
piece of paper or wood with something
written upon it]

a name**plate**, place **card**, identification
tag // a baggage **tag**

¶ Please receive **a number** at the
reception desk.

②[災難などを受けないようにと神社
や寺などが出してくれるもの、お守り]

¶神社で交通安全のお札をもらってき
ました。(Jinja de kōtsū-anzen no o*fuda*
o moratte kimashita.)

ぶた　豚〔名〕

ぶたい　舞台〔名〕

①[音楽や劇などをする所]
¶舞台ではちょうど日本の踊りをやっ
ていました。(*Butai* de wa chōdo Nihon
no odori o yatte imashita.)

②[活躍する場]
¶この小説の舞台は京都です。(Kono
shōsetsu no *butai* wa Kyōto desu.)

ふたたび　再び〔副〕

¶再びお目にかかれるかどうかわかり
ませんね。(*Futatabi* ome ni kakareru ka
dō ka wakarimasen ne.)
¶再び同じ間違いを繰り返したくあり
ません。(*Futatabi* onaji machigai o
kurikaeshitaku arimasen.)

ふたつ　二つ〔名〕

①[2個]
¶りんごを二つください。(Ringo o
futatsu kudasai.)

②[2歳]
¶この子は今年二つになります。
(Kono ko wa kotoshi *futatsu* ni
narimasu.)

ぶたにく　豚肉〔名〕
¶わたしは牛肉より豚肉のほうが好き
です。(Watashi wa gyūniku yori
butaniku no hō ga suki desu.)

②[charm or talisman obtained at a
shrine or temple for protection against
misfortune]

¶[I] obtained **a charm** for traffic
safety at a shrine.

buta〔n〕**pig, hog**

butai〔n〕**stage**

①[theatrical stage]
¶They were just then doing Japanese
dancing on **the stage**.

②[stage of operations]
¶**The setting** of this novel is Kyoto.

futatabi〔adv〕**again, a second
time**

¶I don't know if we will ever be able to
meet **again**.

¶I don't want to make the same
mistake **twice**.

futatsu〔n〕**two**

①[two items]
¶Please give me **two** apples.

②[two years old]
¶This child will be **two years old** this
year.

butaniku〔n〕**pork**
¶I like **pork** better than beef.

ふたり 二人 〔名〕

¶二人でいっしょに来てください。
(*Futari* de issho ni kite kudasai.)

¶あの夫婦は子供が二人います。(Ano fūfu wa kodomo ga *futari* imasu.)

ふだん 〔名〕

ふだん着 (*fudan*gi)

¶今朝は、ふだんより1時間早く起きました。(Kesa wa, *fudan* yori ichijikan hayaku okimashita.)

¶ふだん勉強しないと、試験のときに困りますよ。(*Fudan* benkyō shinai to, shiken no toki ni komarimasu yo.)

ふつう 普通 〔名、形動〕

普通列車 (*futsū*-ressha)

¶朝御飯は普通7時ごろ食べます。(Asagohan wa *futsū* shichiji goro tabemasu.)

¶ここから駅までは普通に歩いて5分です。(Koko kara eki made wa *futsū* ni aruite gofun desu.)

ふつか 二日 〔名〕

① [日付]
¶今日は五月二日です。(Kyō wa gogatsu *futsuka* desu.)

② [日数]
¶風邪を引いて、二日間休みました。(Kaze o hiite, *futsuka*kan yasumimashita.)
⇒-日 -ka

ぶっか 物価 〔名〕

物価が高い (*bukka* ga takai) 物価が安い (*bukka* ga yasui) 物価が下がる (buuka ga sagaru)

---

futari 〔n〕 two persons, a couple

¶ Please come together, **the two of you**.

¶ That couple (husband and wife) have two children.

fudan 〔n〕 usual, ordinary

everyday clothing

¶ [I] got up an hour earlier than **usual** this morning.

¶ If you don't study **ordinarily**, you will have a hard time when you have an exam.

futsū 〔n, adj-v〕 usual, ordinary, regular

regular train; **local** train

¶ [I] **usually** eat breakfast around seven o'clock.

¶ At an **ordinary** pace it's a five-minute walk from here to the station.

futsuka 〔n〕 the second day of the month; two days

① [the second day of the month]
¶ Today is **the second** of May.

② [two days]
¶ [I] caught a cold and stayed home for **two days**.

bukka 〔n〕 prices (of goods)

prices are high // **prices** are low // **prices** are falling

¶また物価が上がって、生活が苦しくなりました。(Mata *bukka* ga agatte, seikatsu ga kurushiku narimashita.)

¶ **Prices** have gone up again, and it is hard to make ends meet.

ぶつかる〔動 I〕

① [当たる、突き当たる]
¶自動車が電車にぶつかって、けが人が出ました。(Jidōsha ga densha ni *butsukatte*, keganin ga demashita.)

② [出会う]
¶今、大きな問題にぶつかって困っています。(Ima, ookina mondai ni *butsukatte* komatte imasu.)

butsukaru 〔v I〕 **strike, hit, run into; come across, encounter**

① [strike, hit, run into]
¶ A car **ran into** a train; some persons were injured.

② [come across, encounter]
¶ [I] am now **confronted by** a large problem and don't know what to do.

ぶっきょう 仏教〔名〕

仏教を信じる(*bukkyō* o shinjiru) 仏教徒(*bukkyō*to) 仏教美術(bukkyō-bijutsu)

bukkyō 〔n〕 **Buddhism**

to believe in **Buddhism** // a **Buddhist** // **Buddhist** art

ぶつける〔動 II〕

¶頭をドアにぶつけてしまいました。(Atama o doa ni *butsukete* shimaimashita.)

¶ボールをぶつけて、ガラスを壊してしまいました。(Bōru o *butsukete*, garasu o kowashite shimaimashita.)

butsukeru 〔v II〕 **strike, hit**

¶ [I] **hit** [my] head on the door.

¶ [My] ball **struck** the window and broke it.

ぶっしつ 物質〔名〕

① [物体の実質]
¶ダイヤモンドは非常に硬い物質です。(Daiyamondo wa hijō ni katai *busshitsu* desu.)

② [精神に対するもの、金や品物など]
¶現代の社会は、物質的には豊かになったが、精神的には貧しくなったと言う人がいます。(Gendai no shakai wa, *busshitsu*teki ni wa yutaka ni natta ga,

busshitsu 〔n〕 **substance, matter; the material**

① [substance, matter]
¶ A diamond is an extremely hard **substance**.

② [the material (vs. the spiritual)]
¶ Some people say that contemporary society has become **materially** affluent but spiritually poor.

seishinteki ni wa mazushiku natta to iu
hito ga imasu.)

ふで 筆 〔名〕

¶筆で名前を書いてください。(*Fude
de namae o kaite kudasai.*)

¶あしたは、すみと筆を持って来てく
ださい。(*Ashita wa, sumi to fude o
motte kite kudasai.*)

fude 〔n〕 **writing brush, brush**

¶ Please write your name with **a brush**.

¶ Please bring ink and **brushes**
tomorrow.

ふと 〔副〕

¶駅に向かって歩いているうちに、ふ
と忘れ物をしたことに気がつきまし
た。(*Eki ni mukatte aruite iru uchi ni,
futo wasuremono o shita koto ni ki ga
tsukimashita.*)

¶ふと見ると、もう桜が咲いていまし
た。(*Futo miru to, mō sakura ga saite
imashita.*)

futo 〔adv〕 **suddenly, accidentally**

¶ As I was walking toward the station,
I suddenly realized that I had
forgotten something.

¶ When I **happened to** look that way, I
saw that the cherry blossoms were in
bloom.

ふとい 太い 〔形〕

太い木 (*futoi* ki) 太い腕 (*futoi* ude)

¶もっと太いひもはありませんか。
(*Motto futoi himo wa arimasen ka？*)

⇔細い **hosoi**

futoi 〔adj〕 **thick, broad**

a **thick** tree // a **big** arm

¶ Don't you have any **thicker** cord
〚rope, string, ribbon, etc.〛 than this?

ぶどう 〔名〕

¶私が一番好きな果物はぶどうです。
(*Watashi ga ichiban sukina kudamono wa
budō desu.*)

budō 〔n〕 **grape**

¶ My favorite fruit is grapes.

ふとる 太る 〔動Ⅰ〕

¶最近、少し太りました。(*Saikin,
sukoshi futorimashita.*)

¶太ったので、洋服が合わなくなりま
した。(*Futotta node, yōfuku ga awanaku
narimashita.*)

⇔やせる **yaseru**

futoru 〔v I〕 **put on weight, grow
stout**

¶ [I]'ve **put on** some **weight** lately.

¶ [I]'ve **put on weight** so that [my]
clothes don't fit anymore.

ふとん　布団〔名〕

掛け布団　(kake*buton*)　敷き布団
(shiki*buton*)　座布団　(za*buton*)　布団を
敷く　(*futon* o shiku)
¶寒いから、布団をもう一枚掛けてく
ださい。(Samui kara, *futon* o mō ichimai
kakete kudasai.)

futon〔n〕**futon, Japanese-style
bedding**
top **futon**, coverlet // bottom **futon**,
sleeping mat // *zabuton*, Japanese floor
cushion // lay out the **bedding**
¶It's cold so please put on one more
coverlet.

ふなびん　船便〔名〕

¶これを船便でお願いします。(Kore o
funabin de onegai shimasu.)
¶船便のほうが航空便より安いです。
(*Funabin* no hō ga kōkūbin yori yasui
desu.)
⇒航空便 **kōkūbin**

funabin〔n〕**sea mail, shipping
service**
¶Please send this by **sea mail**.

¶**Sea mail** is cheaper than airmail.

ふね　船〔名〕

船で旅行する　(*fune* de ryokō suru)
¶大きな船が港に着きました。
(Ookina *fune* ga minato ni tsukimashita.)

fune〔n〕**boat, ship**
travel by **boat**
¶A large **ship** has arrived in port　〖A
large **ship** arrived in port〗.

ぶひん　部品〔名〕

ラジオの部品　(rajio no *buhin*)　自動車
の部品　(jidōsha no *buhin*)　部品を取り
替える　(*buhin* o torikaeru)
＊「部分品　(bubunhin)」とも言う。

buhin〔n〕**parts, components**
radio **parts** // automobile **parts** // to
replace **a part**

＊Variant: *bubunhin*.

ぶぶん　部分〔名〕

一部分　(ichi*bubun*)　大部分
(dai*bubun*)　部分品　(*bubun*hin)

¶このくつは底の部分がゴムでできて
います。(Kono kutsu wa soko no *bubun*
ga gomu de dekite imasu.)
¶火事で建物の一部分が焼けました。
(Kaji de tatemono no ichi*bubun* ga
yakcmashita.)

bubun〔n〕**part, portion**
a **part** 〖**portion, section, installment**,
etc.〗 // a large **part**;
the majority // **parts, components**
¶**The sole** of these shoes is made of
rubber.

¶A **part** of the building was destroyed
by fire.

ぶぶんてき 部分的〔形動〕

¶この建物は、部分的に直せばまだ使えます。(Kono tatemono wa, bubunteki ni naoseba mada tsukaemasu.)

bubunteki〔adj-v〕**partly, partially**

¶This building can still be used if it is repaired **here and there**.

ふべん 不便〔名、形動〕

¶わたしの家は、駅から遠くて不便です。(Watashi no ie wa, eki kara tookute *fuben* desu.)

¶この辺は、店がなくて買い物に不便な所です。(Kono hen wa, mise ga nakute kaimono ni *fuben* na tokoro desu.)

⇔便利 benri

fuben〔n, adj-v〕**inconvenience**

¶My house **is inconvenient** as it is so far from the station.

¶This area **is inconvenient** for shopping as there are few shops.

ふむ 踏む〔動Ⅰ〕

¶花を踏まないように気をつけてください。(Hana o *fumanai* yō ni ki o tsukete kudasai.)

¶電車の中で足を踏まれました。(Densha no naka de ashi o *fumaremashita*.)

fumu〔v I〕**step on, tread on**

¶Please be careful **not to step on** the flowers.

¶Someone **stepped on** my foot in the train.

ふゆ 冬〔名〕

¶ここの冬はとても寒いです。(Koko no *fuyu* wa totemo samui desu.)

¶冬休みには京都へ旅行します。(*Fuyu*yasumi ni wa Kyōto e ryokō shimasu.)

fuyu〔n〕**winter**

¶**The winters** are very cold here.

¶[I] am going to travel to Kyoto during **winter** vacation.

ふりかえる 振り返る〔動Ⅰ〕

①[後ろを見る]

¶秋子さんは何度も振り返って手を振りました。(Akiko san wa nando mo *furikaette* te o furimashita.)

②[昔のことを思い出してみる]

¶子供のころを振り返ると、とても懐かしいです。(Kodomo no koro o *furikaeru* to, totemo natsukashii desu.)

furikaeru〔v I〕**look back, turn around; look back at, review**

①[look back, turn one's head, turn around]

¶Akiko **looked back**〚**turned around**〛many times and waved.

②[look back at, review past events]

¶**Thinking back over** my childhood, I feel very nostalgic.

ふる 振る〔動Ⅰ〕

① [ゆり動かす]

ハンカチを振る (hankachi o *furu*)

¶子供が電車の窓から手を振っています。 (Kodomo ga densha no mado kara te o *futte* imasu.)

② [漢字に読み方をつける]

¶次の漢字に仮名を振りなさい。 (Tsugi no kanji ni kana o *furinasai*.)

ふる 降る〔動Ⅰ〕

¶雨が降ってきました。 (Ame ga *futte* kimashita.)

¶あなたの国では雪が降りますか。 (Anata no kuni de wa yuki ga *furimasu* ka?)

ふるい 古い〔形〕

¶あの人の考えはもう古いです。 (Ano hito no kangae wa mō *furui* desu.)

¶この建物はずいぶん古くなりましたね。 (Kono tatemono wa zuibun *furuku* narimashita ne.)

⇔新しい atarashii

ふるえる 震える〔動Ⅱ〕

¶寒いので子供が震えています。 (Samui node kodomo ga *furuete* imasu.)

¶恐ろしくて、ひざが震えました。 (Osoroshikute, hiza ga *furuemashita*.)

プレゼント〔名、～する〕

¶クリスマスのプレゼントに何を上げましょうか。 (Kurisumasu no *purezento* ni nani o agemashō ka?)

⇒贈り物 okurimono

ふれる 触れる〔動Ⅱ〕

① [さわる]

---

furu 〔v I〕 **wave; give, attach**

① [wave]

wave one's handkerchief

¶ The children **are waving** their hands out of the window of the train.

② [write the reading alongside *kanji*]

¶ **Write** the readings in *kanja*alongside the following *kanji*.

furu 〔v I〕 **fall (rain, snow, etc.)**

¶ It has started **to rain**.

¶ **Does it snow** in your country?

furui 〔adj〕 **old; dated**

¶ [His] way of thinking **is behind the times**.

¶ This building **is** really **old** now, isn't it?

furueru 〔v II〕 **tremble, shiver, shake**

¶ The children **are shivering** because of the cold.

¶ My knees **were trembling** with tright.

purezento 〔n, ～*suru*〕 **present, gift**

¶ What shall [we] give [him] **for Christmas?**

fureru 〔v II〕 **touch, feel; touch on, mention**

① [touch, feel]

¶この作品に手を触れないでくださ
い。（Kono sakuhin ni te o *furenaide*
kudasai.）

¶ Please **don't touch** this work of art.

②［ついでに問題にする、言及する］

②［touch on, mention, allude to］

¶先生は講義の中で公害の問題に触れ
ました。（Sensei wa kōgi no naka de
kōgai no mondai ni *furemashita*.）

¶ The teacher 〚professor〛 **touched
upon** the problem of pollution in the
lecture.

ふろ〔名〕

furo〔n〕**bath**

ふろ場（*furo*ba）ふろ屋（*furo*ya）

bathroom (for taking a bath only) //
public **bath**

¶おふろが沸きました。（O*furo* ga
wakimashita.）

¶ **The bath** is heated 〚is ready〛.

¶おふろに入りました。（O*furo* ni
hairimashita.）

¶ I had **a bath**.

ぶん 文〔名〕

bun〔n〕**sentence; text; writing
style**

¶この言葉を使って短い文を作りなさ
い。（Kono kotoba o tsukatte mijikai *bun*
o tsukurinasai.）

¶ Make up a short **sentence** using this
word.

¶わたしは文が下手ですから、手紙を
書くのがきらいです。（Watashiwa *bun*
ga heta desu kara, tegami o kaku no ga
kirai desu.）

¶ I don't like writing letters since I am
not a good **writer**.

-ふん -分〔尾〕

-fun〔suf〕**the counter for minutes**

1分（ip*pun*）2分（ni*fun*）3分
（san*pun*）4分（yon*pun*）5分（go*fun*）
6分（rop*pun*）7分（nana*fun*）8分
（hap*pun*）9分（kyū-*fun*）10分
（jip*pun*）

one **minute** // two **minutes** //
three **minutes** // four **minutes** //
five **minutes** // six **minutes** //
seven **minutes** // eight **minutes** //
nine **minutes** // ten **minutes**

¶今、1時15分です。（Ima, ichiji
jūgo*fun* desu.）

¶ It's now 1:**15**.

¶家から駅まで歩いて10分です。（Ie
kara eki made aruite jip*pun* desu.）

¶ It's a 10-**minute** walk from the house
to the station.

-ぶん (-)分〔名、尾〕

(-)bun〔n, suf〕**share, portion;
amount; division, part, segment**

1〔名〕

1〔n〕

①［割り当てられたもの、持ち分］

¶電車の切符は、あなたの分も買って

あります。(Densha no kippu wa, anata

no bun mo katte arimasu.)

②［ある数に分けた中のいくつか］

3分の2 (sanbun no ni)

2 〖尾〗

3人分の料理 (sanninbun no ryōri)

¶今日、わたしは今月分の月給をもら

いました。(Kyō, watashi wa

kongetsubun no gekkyū o

moraimashita.)

① [share, portion]

¶ **Your** train ticket is bought too.

② [amount, percentage, number of shares of the whole]

two-**thirds**

2 〖suf〗 division, part, segment

three **servings** of food

¶ I received my pay **for this month** today.

ぶんか　文化 〖名〗

¶わたしは日本文化について勉強した

いと思っています。(Watashi wa Nihon-

bunka ni tsuite benkyō shitai to omotte

imasu.)

bunka 〖n〗 **culture, civilization**

¶ I want to study Japanese **culture**.

ぶんがく　文学 〖名〗

文学者 (*bungaku*sha) 日本文学

(Nihon-*bungaku*)

¶わたしは日本へ文学の勉強に来まし

た。(Watashi wa Nihon e *bungaku* no

benkyō ni kimashita.)

bungaku 〖n〗 **literature**

a person **of letters** // Japanese **literature**

¶ I came to Japan to study **literature**.

ぶんしょう　文章 〖名〗

文章を作る (*bunshō* o tsukuru)

¶山田さんは文章がたいへん上手で

す。(Yamada san wa *bunshō* ga taihen

jōzu desu.)

bunshō 〖n〗 **composition; writing style; sentence**

write a **composition**

¶ [Mr.] Yamada is a very good **writer**.

ぶんぽう　文法 〖名〗

¶日本語の文法はそんなに難しくあり

ません。(Nihongo no *bunpō* wa sonna ni

muzukashiku arimasen.)

bunpō 〖n〗 **grammar**

¶ Japanese **grammar** is not so difficult.

¶この文は文法的に間違っています。
（Kono bun wa *bunpō*teki ni machigatte imasu.）

¶This sentence is **grammatically** wrong.

ぶんぼうぐ　文房具〔名〕

¶文房具屋ではノートや鉛筆などを売っています。（*Bunbōgu* ya de wa nōto ya enpitsu nado o utte imasu.）

bunbōgu 〔n〕 **stationery, writing materials**

¶**Stationery** stores sell notebooks, pencils, etc.

ふ-　不-〔頭〕

不衛生（*fu*eisei）　不合格（*fu*gōkaku）
不可能（*fu*kanō）　不完全（*fu*-kanzen）
不健康（*fu*kenkō）　不規則（*fu*kisoku）
不公平（*fu*kōhei）　不満（*fu*man）
不都合（*fu*tsugō）　不運（*fu*un）

fu- 〔pref〕 **non-, un-**

insanitary conditions //
disqualification, failure, rejection //
impossibility // **in**completeness,
imperfection // poor health,
unhealthiness // **ir**regularity //
injustice, **un**fairness // **dis**satisfaction,
discontent // **in**convenience;
impropriety // **mis**fortune

¶この村は、まだ電気も水道もなくてたいへん不便です。（Kono mura wa, mada denki mo suidō mo nakute taihen *fu*ben desu.）

¶This village is very **inconvenient**; it doesn't have electricity or running water yet.

¶あの人は知っているのに、教えてくれませんでした。不親切な人です。（Ano hito wa shitte iru noni, oshiete kuremasen deshita. *Fu*shinsetsu na hito desu.）

¶Even though [he] knew that, [he] didn't tell me. [He]'s a very **inconsiderate** person.

＊多くの場合、次に来る言葉を反対の意味にする。

＊In most cases, adding *fu*- to a word gives it the opposite meaning.

へ

へ〔助〕

¶昨日、銀行へ行きました。

(Kinō, ginkō *e* ikimashita.)

¶道の真ん中へ出ないでください。

(Michi no mannaka *e* denaide kudasai.)

へいき　平気〔形動〕

¶彼は冬でもシャツだけで平気です。

(Kare wa fuyu demo shatsu dake de *heiki* desu.)

¶あの子は平気な顔でうそをつきました。(Ano ko wa *heiki* na kao de uso o tsukimashita.)

へいきん　平均〔名、〜する〕

¶クラスの平均点は何点ですか。

(Kurasu no *heikin*ten wa nanten desu ka？)

¶平均して一日に何時間勉強しますか。(*Heikin* shite ichinichi ni nanjikan benkyō shimasu ka？)

へいせい　平成〔名〕

¶平成14年は2002年です。(*Heisei* jūyonen wa nisenninen desu.)

¶私の子どもは平成10年に生まれました。(Watashi no kodomo wa *heisei* jūnen ni umare mashita.)

へいたい　兵隊〔名〕

¶村の若い人はみんな兵隊に行ってしまいました。(Mura no wakai hito wa minna *heitai* ni itte shimaimashita.)

e〔part〕 **to, toward, into**

¶[I] went **to** the bank yesterday.

¶Please don't go out **into** the middle of the street.

heiki〔adj-v〕 **calmness, unconcern, self-possession**

¶He **thinks nothing of** going about in his shirt-sleeves even in the winter.

¶That child **nonchalantly** 〖**boldfacedly, shamelessly**〗 told a lie.

heikin〔n, 〜*suru*〕 **average**

¶What was the **average** mark 〖**grade average**〗 of the class?

¶How many hours a day do you study **on the average?**

heisei〔n〕 **Heisei; the name given to the era beginning in 1989**

¶Heisei 14 is the year 2002.

¶My child was born in Heisei 10.

heitai〔n〕 **soldier, sailor**

¶The young people of the village have all gone away into **the military**.

¶戦争が終わって、兵隊はみんな帰ってきました。(Sensō ga owatte, *heitai* wa minna kaette kimashita.)

¶ With the end of the war, all of **the soldiers** returned 〚have returned〛 home.

へいわ 平和 〔名、形動〕

平和運動 (*heiwa*-undō) 世界平和 (sekai-*heiwa*)

heiwa 〔n, adj-v〕 **peace, harmony**

the **peace** movement // world **peace**

¶戦争が終わって、平和がもどってきました。(Sensō ga owatte, *heiwa* ga modotte kimashita.)

¶ **Peace** was 〚has been〛 restored with the ending of the war.

¶平和な家庭をつくりたいです。(*Heiwa* na katei o tsukuritai desu.)

¶ I want to create a **tranquil** home.

-ページ 〔尾〕

-pēji 〔suf〕 **a page**

¶10ページを開けてください。(Jip*pēji* o akete kudasai.)

¶ Please open your books to **page** 10.

¶わたしはこの本を50ページ読みました。(Watashi wa kono hon o gojip*pēji* yomimashita.)

¶ I have read 50 **pages** of this book.

へた 下手 〔形動〕

heta 〔adj-v〕 **unskillful, poor at, awkward**

¶上手な人も下手な人もみんないっしょに歌いました。(Jōzu na hito mo *heta* na hito mo minna issho ni utaimashita.)

¶ They all sang together, good singers and **bad** singers.

¶日本語がまだ下手なので、早く上手になりたいです。(Nihongo ga mada *heta* na node, hayaku jōzuni naritai desu.)

¶ As I'm still **poor at** Japanese, I want to become good at it as quickly as possible.

⇔上手 **jōzu**

⇒まずい **mazui**　うまい **umai**

べつ 別 〔名、形動〕

betsu 〔n, adj-v〕 **distinction; different, another**

① [分けること、区別]

① [distinction, classification]

¶この学校へは男女の別なく入学できます。(Kono gakkō e wa danjo no *betsu* naku nyūgaku dekimasu.)

¶ One can enter this school with no **distinction** by sex.

¶あなたの物は別にしてあります。(Anata no mono wa *betsu* ni shite arimasu.)

¶ The things for you 〚your things〛 are set aside **separately**.

② [ほか、同じでない]

¶今日は忙しいので、また別の日に来てください。(Kyō wa isogashii node, mata *betsu* no hi ni kitekudasai.)

¶この紙ではなく、別の紙に書いてください。(Kono kami de wa naku, *betsu* no kami ni kaite kudasai.)

② [different, another, separate]

¶ [I]'m busy today so please come again **another** day.

¶ Please don't write it on this paper but on a **separate** piece of paper.

ベッド 〔名〕

¶あの部屋にはベッドが二つ置いてあります。(Ano heya ni wa *beddo* ga futatsu oite arimasu.)

¶わたしはいつもベッドで寝ています。(Watashi wa itsu mo *beddo* de nete imasu.)

⇒寝台 shindai

beddo 〔n〕 bed

¶ There are two **beds** in that room.

¶ I always sleep in **a bed**.

べつに 別に 〔副〕

¶「何か御用ですか。」(Nani ka goyō desu ka?)「いいえ、別に用事はありません。」(Iie, *betsu ni* yōji wa arimasen.)

¶「なにか欲しい物がありますか。」(Nani ka hoshii mono ga arimasu ka？)「いいえ、別に。」(Iie, *betsu ni*.)

＊あとに打ち消しの言葉が来る。

betsu ni 〔adv〕 **(not) particularly**

¶ "Was there something you wanted to see me about?"

"No, **not particularly**."

¶ "Is there something you would like?"

"No, **nothing in particular**."

＊ Used with the negative.

へや 部屋 〔名〕

部屋代 (*heya*dai)

¶学校のそばに部屋を借りました。(Gakkō no soba ni *heya* o karimashita.)

¶わたしの部屋は2階にあります。(Watashi no *heya* wa nikai ni arimasu.)

heya 〔n〕 **room, apartment**

room rent, rent

¶ [I] rented **a room** 〚**apartment**〛 near the school.

¶ My **room** 〚**apartment**〛 is on the second floor.

へる 減る 〔動Ⅰ〕

人口が減る (jinkō ga *heru*)

¶病気で体重が5キロ減りました。(Byōki de taijū ga gokiro *herimashita*.)

heru 〔vⅠ〕 **decrease**

the population **decreases**

¶ [I] **lost** five kilos due to illness.

¶これ以上収入が減ると困ります。
(Kore ijō shūnyū ga *heru* to
komarimasu.)

¶I don't know what I'll do if my
income **decreases** any more than this.

⇔増える fueru

⇒増す masu　減少 genshō

ベル〔名〕

¶御用の方はこのベルを押してくださ
い。(Goyō no kata wa kono *beru* o oshite
kudasai.)

¶授業の終わりのベルが鳴りました。
(Jugyō no owari no *beru* ga
narimashita.)

beru 〔n〕 **bell**

¶Please ring this **bell** for service (a
written notice).

¶The end-of-class **bell** has rung.

へん　変〔形動〕

¶門の前に変な人がいます。(Mon no
mae ni *hen* na hito ga imasu.)

¶あの人は泣いたり笑ったりして、
今日は少し変です。(Ano hito wa
naitari warattari shite, kyō wa sukoshi *hen*
desu.)

hen 〔adj-v〕 **strange, odd**

¶There's a **strange-looking** person in
front of the gate.

¶[She] is acting a little **oddly** today,
laughing and crying and the like.

へん　辺〔名〕

¶彼のうちはどの辺ですか。(Kare no
uchi wa dono *hen* desu ka?)

¶この辺に電話がありますか。(Kono
hen ni denwa ga arimasu ka?)

hen 〔n〕 **locality, region,
neighborhood, vicinity**

¶In what **general vicinity** is his house?

¶Is there a telephone **around** here
〖**near** here〗?

ペン〔名〕

¶わたしはペンを3本持っています。
(Watashi wa *pen* o sanbon motte imasu.)

pen 〔n〕 **pen**

¶I have three **pens**.

へんか　変化〔名、～する〕

¶日本語の動詞の変化を習いました。
(Nihongo no dōshi no *henka* o
naraimashita.)

¶この国では、一年じゅう気温があま
り変化しません。(Kono kuni de wa,
ichinenjū kion ga amari *henka* shimasen.)

henka 〔n, ～*suru*〕 **change,
variation; inflection, conjugation**

¶[I] studied **the conjugations** of
Japanese verbs.

¶The temperature **doesn't change** very
much throughout the year in this
country.

ペンキ〔名〕
壁にペンキを塗る
(kabe ni *penki* o nuru)

penki 〔n〕 **(house) paint**
to paint a wall

べんきょう 勉強〔名、～する〕
¶あなたは何の勉強をしているのです
か。(Anata wa nan no *benkyō* o shite iru
no desu ka?)
¶日本語の勉強は難しいですか。
(Nihongo no *benkyō* wa muzukashii desu
ka?)
¶わたしは日本語を勉強しています。
(Watashi wa Nihongo o *benkyō* shite
imasu.)

benkyō 〔n, ～*suru*〕 **study**
¶ What are you **studying?**

¶ Is it hard **to learn** Japanese?

¶ I **am studying** Japanese.

へんこう 変更〔名、～する〕

¶スケジュールに変更があったら、す
ぐ連絡してください。(Sukejūru ni
henkō ga attara, sugu renraku shite
kudasai.)
¶出発の予定を変更しました。
(Shuppatsu no yotei o *henkō* shimashita.)

henkō 〔n, ～*suru*〕 **change,
alteration, modification**
¶ If there should be **any change** in the
schedule, please notify me without
delay.

¶ [I] **changed** [my] scheduled time
〖day〗 of departure.

へんじ 返事〔名、～する〕

① [呼びかけなどに対して答えること]
¶名前を呼んだら、返事をしてくださ
い。(Namae o yondara, *henji* o
shitekudasai.)
② [受けた手紙に対する答えの手紙]
¶家から手紙が来たので、すぐ返事を
出しました。(Ie kara tegami ga kita
node, sugu *henji* o dashimashita.)

henji 〔n, ～*suru*〕 **answer,
response, reply**
① [verbal response, answer]
¶ Please **answer** when your name is
called.

② [written reply]
¶ A letter came from home and [I] soon
answered it.

べんじょ 便所〔名〕
便所に行く (*benjo* ni iku)
¶すみませんが、便所はどこでしょう
か。(Sumimasen ga, *benjo* wa doko
deshō ka?)

benjo 〔n〕 **toilet, bathroom**
go to the bathroom
¶ Excuse me. Where is **the lavatory**
〖**Men's Room, Ladies' Room**, etc.
〗?

769

＊「便所（benjo）」と言うより「手洗い（tearai）」、「お手洗い（otearai）」、「トイレ（toire）」と言ったほうが感じがいい。
⇒手洗い **tearai** トイレ **toire**

＊*Tearai*, *otearai*, or *toire* sound better than *benjo*.

べんとう 弁当〔名〕

bentō 〔n〕 box lunch

弁当箱（*bentō*bako）
a **lunch** box

¶わたしは、毎日学校へお弁当を持って行きます。（Watashi wa, mainichi gakkō e o*bentō* o motte ikimasu.）

¶I take **my lunch** to school with me every day.

べんり 便利〔名、形動〕

benri 〔n, adj-v〕 convenience, convenient

¶わたしの家は駅の近くですから便利です。（Watashi no ie wa eki no chikaku desu kara *benri* desu.）

¶My house **is convenient** as it is near the station.

¶これは小さくて、持って歩くのに便利な辞書です。（Kore wa chiisakute, motte aruku no ni *benri* na jisho desu.）

¶This is a small dictionary **handy** to carry around with one.

¶鉄道ができてから、この町は便利になりました。（Tetsudō ga dekite kara, kono machi wa *benri* ni narimashita.）

¶This town has become **easier to get to** since the opening of the railway.

⇔不便 **fuben**

ほ

-ほ -歩 〔尾〕

1歩（ip*po*）2歩（ni*ho*）3歩（san*po*）
4歩（yon*ho*）5歩（go*ho*）6歩
（rop*po*）7歩（nana*ho*）8歩（hap*po*）
9歩（kyu*ho*）10歩（jip*po*）

¶ここからあそこまで何歩あります
か。（Koko kara asoko made nan*po*
arimasu ka？）
¶1歩前に出てください。（Ip*po* mae ni
dete kudasai.）

ほう 方 〔名〕

¶黒板の方を見てください。（Kokuban
no *hō* o mite kudasai.）
¶鳥が北の方へ飛んでいきます。（Tori
ga kita no *hō* e tonde ikimasu.）

ほう 〔名〕

①［ものごとを比べてそのうちの一つ
を取り上げて表すのに使う］
¶わたしはみかんよりりんごのほうが
好きです。（Watashi wa mikan yori
ringo no *hō* ga suki desu.）
¶ビールは冷たいほうがおいしいです
よ。（Biiru wa tsumetai *hō* ga oishii desu
yo.）
②［いくつかのものごとのうちで適当
で望ましいものごとを取り上げて表す
のに使う］
¶あなたはもっと運動をしたほうがい
いですよ。（Anata wa motto undō o shita
hō ga ii desu yo.）
¶ああいう危険な所へはあまり行かな
いほうがいいですよ。（Aiu kiken na

-ho 〖suf〗 **a step, a pace**

one **step** //two **steps** //three **steps** //
four **steps** // five **steps** // six **steps** //
seven **steps** // eight **steps** //
nine **steps** // ten **steps**

¶ How many **steps** is it from here to
there?

¶ Please take one **step** forward.

hō 〖n〗 **direction, way**

¶ Please look **toward** 〚**at**〛 the
blackboard.
¶ The bird is flying **toward** the north.

hō 〖n〗 **side, part; class, category**

① [side; indicates something singled
out from two or more alternatives]
¶ I like apples better than oranges
(literally, mandarin oranges).

¶ Beer tastes best cold.

② [used to indicate something singled
out as desirable to do]

¶ You should exercise more.

¶ It would be best not to go very much
to such dangerous places.

tokoro e wa amari ikanai *hō* ga ii desu
yo.)

*普通「ほうがいい（hō ga ii)」の形で
使う。

*Usually used in the pattern "〜 *hō ga
ii*."

③ [ものごとを二つの部類に分けて考
える場合どちらかといえばその一方に
属するということを表すのに使う]

③ [class, category; used when
assigning someone or something to one
of two categories]

¶ 中村さんはどちらかといえばまじめ
なほうです。（Nakamura san wa dochira
ka to ieba majime na *hō* desu.)

¶ [Mr.] Nakamura is on the serious side.

¶ この店の料理はおいしいほうです
よ。（Kono mise no ryōri wa oishii *hō*
desu yo.)

¶ The food at this restaurant 〚bar, etc.〛
is quite good.

ぼうえき 貿易 〔名、〜する〕

貿易商（*bōeki*shō）貿易港（*bōeki*kō）

bōeki 〚n, 〜*suru*〛 **trade, commerce**
a trader 〚**importer**, **exporter**〛 // a
trade port

¶ 最近、日本とアジアの国々との貿易
が盛んになりました。（Saikin, Nihon
to Ajia no kuniguni to no *bōeki* ga sakan
ni narimashita.)

¶ **Trade** has been flourishing between
Japan and other Asian countries
recently.

ほうこう 方向 〔名〕

hōkō 〚n〛 **direction, course;
course, aim, object**

① [進んでいく向き、方角]
風の方向（kaze no *hōkō*）

① [direction, course]
the direction of the wind

¶ 駅はどちらの方向ですか。（Eki wa
dochira no *hōkō* desu ka？）

¶ In which **direction** is the station?

¶ 東はこちらの方向だと思います。
（Higashi wa kochira no *hōkō* da to
omoimasu.)

¶ I think that east is this **way**.

② [目標・目的・方針など]

② [course, aim, object]

¶ 将来の方向はまだわかりません。
（Shōrai no *hōkō* wa mada wakarimasen.)

¶ I haven't decided on my future **course**
yet.

ほうこく 報告 〔名、〜する〕

報告書（*hōkoku*sho）調査報告（chōsa-
hōkoku）研究報告
（kenkyū*hōkoku*）

hōkoku 〚n, 〜*suru*〛 **report**
a written **report**, paper, transactions,
record // a **report** of an investigation,
surveyor's **report**, findings // a **report**
of research, research paper

¶わたしは、そのことについてまだ報
告を受けていません。(Watashi wa,
sono koto ni tsuite mada *hōkoku* o ukete
imasen.)

¶ I haven't yet received **a report**
concerning that matter.

¶そのことについては、社長に詳しく
報告しました。(Sono koto ni tsuite wa,
shachō ni kuwashiku *hōkoku* shimashita.)

¶ [I] made a full **report** concerning that
matter to the president of the company.

ぼうし 帽子 〔名〕

帽子をかぶる (*bōshi* o kaburu) 帽子を
とる (*bōshi* o toru)

bōshi 〔n〕 **hat, cap**
put on **a hat** // take off **a hat**

ほうしん 方針 〔名〕

教育方針 (kyōiku-*hōshin*)

¶来年度の方針を立てましょう。
(Rainendo no *hōshin* o tatemashō.)

¶政府の外交方針が発表されました。
(Seifu no gaikō-*hōshin* ga happyō
saremashita.)

hōshin 〔n〕 **course, policy**
educational **policy**

¶ Let's formulate **our policy** 〖map out
our course〗 for next year.

¶ The government's foreign **policy** has
been announced.

ほうそう 放送 〔名、〜する〕

放送番組 (*hōsō*-bangumi) 放送局
(*hōsō*kyoku) 海外放送 (kaigai-*hōsō*)

hōsō 〔n, 〜*suru*〕 **(radio, television)
broadcasting**
a **radio** program, **television** program //
a **broadcasting** station, **radio** or
television station // overseas
broadcasting, an overseas **broadcast**

¶午後1時からテレビで首相の放送が
あります。(Gogo ichiji kara terebi de
shushō no *hōsō* ga arimasu.)

¶ There will be a television **broadcast**
by the prime minister at 1 PM.

¶その事件はニュースで放送されまし
た。(Sono jiken wa nyūsu de *hōsō*
saremashita.)

¶ That incident **was broadcast** on the
news.

ほうほう 方法 〔名〕

¶わたしはいろいろな方法で実験を
やってみました。(Watashi wa iroiro na
hōhō de jikken o yatte mimashita.)

¶どの方法がいちばんいいですか。
(Dono *hōhō* ga ichiban ii desu ka？)

hōhō 〔n〕 **method, way**

¶ [I] conducted experiments using
various **methods**.

¶ Which **method** is best 〖What is the
best **way to do it**〗?

ほうぼう〔名〕

¶ほうぼう捜しましたが、時計は見つかりませんでした。(*Hōbō* sagashimashita ga, tokei wa mitsukarimasen deshita.)

¶日本へ行ったら、ほうぼうを旅行したいと思います。(Nihon e ittara, *hōbō* o ryokō shitai to omoimasu.)

hōbō 〔n〕 every direction, everywhere, here and there

¶ [I] searched **everywhere** for [my] watch, but [I] couldn't find it.

¶ When I go to Japan, I want to travel **all around**.

ほうめん 方面〔名〕

① [その方向に当たる地域]
¶東京方面へ行く人は、ここで乗り換えてください。(Tōkyō *hōmen* e iku hito wa, koko de norikaete kudasai.)

② [領域・分野など]
¶中村さんは文学の方面に詳しいです。(Nakamura san wa bungaku no *hōmen* ni kuwashii desu.)

¶その計画は各方面から注目されています。(Sono keikaku wa kaku*hōmen* kara chūmoku sarete imasu.)

hōmen 〔n〕 direction, district; field, aspect

① [direction, district]
¶ Persons going in **the direction** of Tokyo should transfer here.

② [field, aspect, sphere]
¶ [Mrs.] Nakamura is well acquainted with **the field** of literature.

¶ That project is attracting attention from all **sides**.

ほうもん 訪問〔名、～する〕

¶みんなで先生の家を訪問しました。(Minnade sensei no ie o *hōmon* shimashita.)

¶午後、社長を訪問する予定です。(Gogo, shachō o *hōmon* suru yotei desu.)

hōmon 〔n, ～*suru*〕 call, visit, interview

¶ We all **visited** our teacher's home together.

¶ [I] intend to **pay a call** on the president of the company in the afternoon.

ほうりつ 法律〔名〕

法律を守る (*hōritsu* o mamoru)
¶それは法律で禁止されています。(Sore wa *hōritsu* de kinshi sarete imasu.)

¶その法律を破ると、どうなりますか。(Sono *hōritsu* o yaburu to, dō narimasu ka?)

hōritsu 〔n〕 law

observe **the law**
¶ That is prohibited by **law**.

¶ What will happen to [me] if [I] break that **law**?

ほお〔名〕

¶子供がほおを赤くして走っています。(Kodomo ga *hoo* o akaku shite hashitte imasu.)

¶病気でだんだんほおがやせてきました。(Byōki de dandan *hoo* ga yasete kimashita.)

＊「ほほ (hoho)」とも言う。

ほか〔名〕

①[別の人・物・時・所などを表す]
¶この問題について、ほかの人はどう思っていますか。(Kono mondai ni tsuite, *hoka* no hito wa dō omotte imasu ka？)

¶この店は高いから、ほかの店で買いましょう。(Kono mise wa takai kara, *hoka* no mise de kaimashō.)

②[あるものごとを除いて]
¶東京にはあなたのほかに知っている人はいません。(Tōkyō ni wa anata no *hoka* ni shitte iru hito wa imasen.)

¶雨がひどかったので、上田さんとわたしのほかにはだれも来ませんでした。(Ame ga hidokatta node, Ueda san to watashi no *hoka* ni wa dare mo kimasen deshita.)

＊普通「〜ほかに（〜hoka ni）」の形で使い、あとに打ち消しの言葉が来る。
③[あるものごとだけでなくそれ以外に]
¶そのほかに質問はありませんか。(Sono *hoka* ni shitsumon wa arimasenka？)

---

hoo 〔n〕 **cheek(s)**

¶ The running children have rosy 〖reddened〗 **cheeks**.

¶ Due to illness [I] have gradually become quite hollow-**cheeked**.

＊Variant: *hoho*.

hoka 〔n〕 **other, another; except for, other than; besides, in addition to**

① [other, another]
¶ What do **the rest** of you think about this problem?

¶ This shop is expensive so let's buy it **somewhere else**.

② [except for, other than, but]
¶ I don't know anyone in Tokyo **but** you.

¶ As it was raining heavily, no one came **except** [Miss] Ueda and me.

*Usually used in the pattern " ～ *hoka ni*" followed by a negative.
③ [besides, in addition to]

¶ Are there **any other** questions?

¶ このクラスには、中国人のほかにアメリカ人もいます。(Konokurasu ni wa, Chūgokujin no *hoka* ni Amerikajin mo imasu.)

*普通「〜ほかに（〜hoka ni）」の形で使う。

¶ There are Americans **as well as** Chinese in this class.

*Usually used in the pattern "〜*hoka ni*."

ほがらか 朗らか〔形動〕

¶ 彼女はいつも朗らかです。(Kanojo wa itsu mo *hogaraka* desu.)
¶ 子供たちは大きな声で朗らかに笑いました。(Kodomotachi wa ookina koe de *hogaraka* ni waraimashita.)

hogaraka 〔adj-v〕 **cheerful, bright**

¶ She is always **cheerful**.

¶ The children laughed **merrily**.

ぼく〔代〕

君とぼく（kimi to *boku*）ぼくの家（*boku* no ie）
¶ ぼくはまだ学生です。(*Boku* wa mada gakusei desu.)
＊親しい相手に対して男性が使う。

boku 〔pron〕 **I**

you and **me** // **my** house

¶ **I** am still a student.

＊Used by men in conversation with close acquaintances.

ポケット〔名〕

ポケットに財布を入れる（*poketto* ni saifu o ireru）
¶ ポケットの中に何が入っていますか。(*Poketto* no naka ni nani ga haitte imasu ka？)

poketto 〔n〕 **pocket**

put one's wallet 〚change purse〛 in **one's pocket**

¶ What's in 〚your〛 pocket?

ほけん 保険〔名〕

保険会社（*hoken*-gaisha）保険金（*hoken*kin）健康保険（kenkō-*hoken*）生命保険（seimei-*hoken*）火災保険（kasai-*hoken*）

¶ どんな保険に入っていますか。(Donna *hoken* ni haitte imasu ka？)
¶ この車に保険を掛けましたか。(Kono kuruma ni *hoken* o kakemashita ka？)

hoken 〔n〕 **insurance**

insurance company // **insurance, insurance** money (that is, money paid to one by an insurance company) // health **insurance** // life **insurance** // fire **insurance**

¶ What kinds of **insurance** do you have?

¶ Have you taken out **insurance** on 〚**insured**〛 this car?

ほこり 〔名〕

ほこりを払う (hokori o harau)

¶あの部屋には、だいぶほこりがたまっています。(Ano heya niwa, daibu hokori ga tamatte imasu.)

hokori 〔n〕 **dust, lint**

brush off **dust** 〚**lint**〛

¶That room has gotten 〚is〛 very **dusty**.

ほし 星 〔名〕

星が出る (hoshi ga deru) 流れ星 (nagareboshi)

¶今夜は星がきれいです。(Kon'ya wa hoshi ga kirei desu.)

¶あの星はよく光っていますね。(Ano hoshi wa yoku hikatte imasu ne.)

hoshi 〔n〕 **star**

the stars come out // a shooting **star**, meteor

¶**The stars** are pretty tonight.

¶That **star** is shining brightly, isn't it?

ほしい 欲しい 〔形〕

¶新しいくつが欲しいです。(Atarashii kutsu ga hoshii desu.)

¶今は何も欲しくありません。(Ima wa nani mo hoshiku arimasen.)

hoshii 〔adj〕 **(I) want, desire**

¶**I want** some new shoes.

¶**I don't want** anything right now.

(〜て) ほしい 〔連〕

¶わたしの悪いところをはっきり言ってほしいんです。(Watashi no warui tokoro o hakkiri itte hoshii n desu.)

¶日曜にわたしの家に来てほしいのですが…。(Nichiyō ni watashi no ie ni kite hoshii no desu ga…)

(-te)hoshii 〔compd〕 **I want someone to 〜**

¶**I would like** you to frankly tell me my bad points.

¶**I would like** you to come to my house on Sunday if you can.

ほしょう 保障 〔名、〜する〕

安全保障 (anzen-hoshō) 老後の生活を保障する (rōgo no seikatsu o hoshō suru)

¶社会保障は現在大きな社会問題の一つになっています。(Shakai-hoshō wa genzai ookina shakai-mondai no hitotsu ni natte imasu.)

hoshō 〔n, 〜suru〕 **security, guarantee**

(national) **security** // **guarantee** the livelihood of the elderly

¶Social **security** is presently a major social problem.

ほしょう 保証 〔名、〜する〕

¶この時計には1年間の保証がついています。(Kono tokei ni wa ichinenkan no *hoshō* ga tsuite imasu.)

¶彼の正直なことはわたしが保証します。(Kare no shōjiki na koto wa watashi ga *hoshō* shimasu.)

¶入学には保証人が必要です。(Nyūgaku ni wa *hoshō*nin ga hitsuyō desu.)

hoshō 〔n, ~*suru*〕 **guarantee**

¶This watch 〚clock〛 has a one-year **guarantee**.

¶I **will vouch for** his honesty.

¶A sponsor 〚reference, guarantor〛 is necessary for admission to the school 〚college〛.

ほす 干す 〔動 I〕

¶庭に洗たく物を干しました。(Niwa ni sentakumono o *hoshimashita*.)

¶この干した魚を食べてみますか。(Kono *hoshita* sakana o tabete mimasu ka?)

hosu 〔v I〕 **dry**

¶[I] **dried** the laundry in the yard.

¶Will you try a taste of this **dried** fish?

ポスト 〔名〕

¶手紙をポストに入れました。(Tegami o *posuto* ni iremashita.)

posuto 〔n〕 **mailbox, postbox**

¶[I] dropped the letter in **the mailbox**.

ほそい 細い 〔形〕

¶細いひもで縛ると切れてしまいます。(*Hosoi* himo de shibaru to kirete shimaimasu.)

¶彼のズボンは細くて長いですね。(Kare no zubon wa *hosokute* nagai desu ne.)

⇔太い **futoi**

hosoi 〔adj〕 **thin, fine, slender, narrow**

¶It will break if you tie it with a **thin** string 〚cord〛.

¶His trousers are long and **slenderlegged**.

ボタン 〔名〕

① [洋服などの合わせる部分につけるもの]

ボタンをはめる (*botan* o hameru) ボタンをかける (*botan* o kakeru) ボタンを外す (*botan* o hazusu)

¶シャツのボタンがとれそうです。(Shatsu no *botan* ga toresō desu.)

botan 〔n〕 **button**

① [button (clothing)]

fasten **a button** // fasten **a button** // un**button** (something)

¶A **button** on [my] shirt is loose.

778

② [機械などを作動させるために押すもの]

¶エレベーターに乗って、7階のボタンを押しました。（Erebētā ni notte, nanakai no *botan* o oshimashita.）

ホテル〔名〕

¶駅のそばのホテルに泊まりました。（Eki no soba no *hoteru* ni tomarimashita.）

¶ホテルに部屋を予約しました。（*Hoteru* ni heya o yoyaku shimashita.）

ほど〔助〕

① [だいたいの量や程度を表す]
¶病気で1年ほど会社を休みました。（Byōki de ichinen *hodo* kaisha o yasumimashita.）

¶牛肉を 300 グラムほどください。（Gyūniku o sanbyakuguramu *hodo* kudasai.）

② [比較の基準のものごとを例に挙げてものごとの程度を表す]
¶今年は去年ほど寒くありません。（Kotoshi wa kyonen *hodo* samukuarimasen.）

¶ひらがなは漢字ほど複雑ではありません。（Hiraganawa kanji *hodo* fukuzatsu de wa arimasen.）

¶上田さんほど熱心な学生はいません。（Ueda san *hodo* nesshin na gakusei wa imasen.）

*普通「〜ほど〜ない（〜hodo〜nai）」の形で使う。
③ [二つのことがらのうち一方の程度の変化に応じて他方の程度も変化するという関係を表すのに使う]

② [button (mechanical)]

¶ [I] got in the elevator and pressed **the button** for the seventh floor.

hoteru 〔n〕 **hotel**

¶ [I] stayed at **a hotel** near the station.

¶ [I] reserved a room at **a hotel**.

hodo 〔part〕 **about, around; as~ as; the more ~ the more ~**
① [about, around]
¶ [I] stayed home from work for **about a year** due to illness.

¶ Please give me three hundred grams **or so** of beef.

② [as ~ as]

¶ This year is not **as** cold **as** last year.

¶ *Hiragana* aren't **as** complex **as** *kanji*.

¶ No one is **as** hardworking a student **as** [Mr.] Ueda〚You couldn't find another student **as** hardworking **as** Mr. Ueda〛.

*Usually used in the pattern "~*hodo* ~ *nai*."
③ [the more ~ the more]

779

¶ 早ければ早いほどいいです。
(Hayakereba hayai *hodo* ii desu.)

¶ The **sooner** the **better**.

¶ 勉強すればするほどおもしろくなります。(Benkyō sureba suru *hodo* omoshiroku narimasu.)

¶ **The more** you study **the more** interesting it is.

* 「〜ば〜ほど（〜ba〜hodo）」の形で使う。

*Used in the pattern "-*ba* 〜 *hodo*."

ほとんど〔名、副〕

hotondo 〔n, adv〕 **almost all; almost, nearly**

1 〔名〕

1 〔n〕 almost all

¶ 出席者のほとんどがそれに賛成しました。(Shussekisha no *hotondo* ga sore ni sansei shimashita.)

¶ **Almost all** of those present were in favor of that.

¶ ほとんどの学生がその会に出席しました。(*Hotondo* no gakusei ga sono kai ni shusseki shimashita.)

¶ **Almost all** of the students attended that meeting〚assembly, party〛.

2 〔副〕

2 〔adv〕 almost, nearly

¶ 病気はほとんどよくなりました。(Byōki wa *hotondo* yoku narimashita.)

¶ [I] am **almost completely** recovered from [my] illness.

¶ その仕事はほとんど終わりました。(Sono shigoto wa *hotondo* owarimashita.)

¶ That work is **nearly** finished.

ほね　骨〔名〕

hone 〔n〕 **bones, skeleton; trouble, pains, effort**

① [人・動物の体を支える堅い組織]

① [bones, skeleton]

¶ 転んで足の骨を折りました。(Koronde ashi no *hone* o orimashita.)

¶ [I] fell down and broke **a bone** in [my] leg〚foot〛.

¶ この魚は骨がたくさんあります。(Kono sakana wa *hone* ga takusan arimasu.)

¶ This fish has many **bones**.

② [苦労をする、世話をする]

② [trouble, pains, effort]

¶ 漢字の勉強はなかなか骨が折れます。(Kanji no benkyō wa nakanaka *hone* ga oremasu.)

¶ Studying kanji **takes much effort**〚*Kanji* are hard to learnt〛.

¶ 彼が骨を折ってくれたので成功しました。(Kare ga *hone* o otte kureta node seikō shimashita.)

¶ [We] succeeded because he **did so much** for [us].

＊「骨が折れる（honegaoreru）」「骨を折る（hone o oru）」の形で使うことが多い。

*Usually used in the patterns "*hone ga oreru*" and "*hone o oru*."

ほめる〔動〕

¶お母さんは子供をほめました。
(Okāsan wa kodomo o *homemashita*.)
¶学生は先生にほめられました。
(Gakusei wa sensei ni *homeraremashita*.)

homeru 〘v II〙 **praise**

¶ The mother **praised** the child.

¶ The student **was praised** by the teacher.

ほる 掘る〔動Ⅰ〕

¶庭に穴を掘って木を植えました。
(Niwa ni ana o *hotte* ki o uemashita.)
¶山を掘ってトンネルを作りました。
(Yama o *hotte* tonneru o tsukurimashita.)

horu 〘v I〙 **dig, bore, drill**

¶ [I] **dug** a hole in the garden 〚yard〛 and planted a tree.
¶ **They cut** a tunnel through the mountain.

ほろびる 滅びる〔動〕

国が滅びる（kuni ga *horobiru*）
¶その動物は日本ではもう滅びてしまいました。(Sono dōbutsu wa Nihon de wa mō *horobite* shimaimashita.)

horobiru 〘v II〙 **be ruined, perish**
a country **falls**

¶ That animal **has become extinct** in Japan.

ほん 本〔名〕

¶机の上に本が何冊ありますか。
(Tsukue no ue ni *hon* ga nansatsu arimasu ka？)
¶この本の5ページを開けてください。
(Kono *hon* no gopēji o akete kudasai.)

hon 〘n〙 **book**

¶ How many **books** are there on the desk?

¶ Please open this **book** to page 5.

-ほん -本〔尾〕

1本（ip*pon*）2本（ni*hon*）
3本（san*bon*）4本（yon*hon*）
5本（go*hon*）6本（rop*pon*）7本（nana*hon*）8本（hap*pon*）
9本（kyū*hon*）10本（jip*pon*）
¶そこに鉛筆が何本ありますか。
(Soko ni enpitsu ga nan*bon* arimasu ka？)

-hon 〘suf〙 **the counter for long, cylindrical objects**
one pen 〚pencil, piece of chalk, cigarette, bottle, etc.〛//two pens // three pens //four pens //five pens // six pens // seven pens // eight pens // nine pens //ten pens

¶ **How many** pencils are there there?

ほんだな　本棚〔名〕

¶私の部屋には本がたくさんあるので、そろそろ新しい本棚が欲しいです。(Watashi no heya ni wa hon ga takusan aru node, sorosoro atarashii *hondana* ga hoshii desu.)

hondana〔n〕**bookshelf**

¶Since I have so many books in my room, I want to buy a new bookshelf soon.

ほんとう　本当〔名〕

¶それは本当ですか。(Sore wa *hontō* desu ka？)

¶これは本当の話です。(Kore wa *hontō* no hanashi desu.)

⇒うそ **uso**

hontō〔n〕**true, really, authentic**

¶Is that **true**〖Is that **really so**〗?

¶This is a **true** story〖This is something that **really** happened〗.

ほんとうに　本当に〔副〕

¶今日は本当に暑いです。(Kyō wa *hontō ni* atsui desu.)

¶本当にありがとうございました。(*Hontō ni* arigatō gozaimashita.)

⇒まことに **makoto ni**

hontō ni〔adv〕**really, very**

¶It's **really** hot today.

¶Thank you **very much indeed**.

ほんやく　翻訳〔名、〜する〕

¶わたしは将来翻訳の仕事がしたいです。(Watashi wa shōrai *hon'yaku* no shigoto ga shitai desu.)

¶英語の小説を日本語に翻訳しました。(Eigo no shōsetsu o Nihongo ni *hon'yaku* shimashita.)

¶この劇はフランス語から日本語に翻訳されたものです。(Kono geki wa Furansugo kara Nihongo ni *hon'yaku* sareta mono desu.)

⇔訳す **yakusu**

hon'yaku〔n, 〜*suru*〕**translation**

¶In the future I want to do **translation** work.

¶[I] **translated** a novel from English into Japanese.

¶This play **has been translated** into Japanese from French.

ぼんやり〔副、〜と、〜する〕

①[ものごとのはっきりしない様子]
¶遠くの山がぼんやり見えます。(Tooku no yama ga *bon'yari* miemasu.)

bon'yari〔adv, 〜*to*, 〜*suru*〕**vague, unclear; abstracted, absentminded**

①[vague, obscure, unclear, foggy, etc.]
¶A distant mountain〖mountain range〗can be seen **dimly**.

¶眠くて頭がぼんやりしています。
（Nemukute atama ga *bon'yari* shite imasu.）

¶ I'm so sleepy **I can't think straight**.

② ［意識が集中しない様子、不注意な様子］

② [abstracted, absentminded, careless]

¶ ぼんやりしていて、かさをバスの中に忘れてしまいました。（*Bon'yari* shite ite, kasa o basu no naka ni wasurete shimaimashita.）

¶ **I absentmindedly** left my umbrella on the bus.

¶ ぼんやりしていて、簡単な計算を間違えました。（*Bon'yari* shite ite, kantan na keisan o machigaemashita.）

¶ **I carelessly** made a mistake in a simple calculation.

ま

ま- 真-〔頭〕

① [まことの、真実の]
真顔 (*ma*gao)
¶山田さんから真心のこもった贈り物をいただきました。(Yamada san kara *ma*gokoro no komotta okurimono o itadakimashita.)

② [純粋な、正確な、ちょうど]
真水 (*ma*mizu) 真冬 (*ma*fuyu) 真夜中 (*ma*yonaka) 真新しい (*ma*-atarashii) 真上 (*ma*ue) 真っ赤な花 (*ma*kka na hana) 真っ白な紙 (*ma*sshiro na kami) 部屋の真ん中 (heya no *ma*nnaka) 真ん丸い月 (*ma*nmarui tsuki)

¶真正面に見える建物が郵便局です。(*Ma*shōmen ni mieru tatemono ga yūbinkyoku desu.)

(-)ま (-)間〔名、尾〕

1〔名〕
① [物と物との間]

¶3メートルずつ間を置いて木を植えました。(Sanmētoru zutsu *ma* o oite ki o uemashita.)

② [時間、ひま]
¶約束の時間までには、まだちょっと間があります。(Yakusoku no jikan made ni wa, mada chotto *ma* ga arimasu.)
¶夢中で本を読んでいたら、いつの間にか朝になってしまいました。

ma-〔pref〕 true, genuine; just, exactly

① [true, genuine, pure]
serious look, a **straight** face
¶I received a gift from [Mrs.] Yamada with [her] **best** wishes.

② [just, exactly]
fresh water // **the dead** of winter, **midwinter** // **the middle** of the night, **the small hours** of the morning // **brand**-new // **right** above, **directly** overhead // crimson flower(s) // **snow**-white paper; blank paper // **the center** of the room // a **full** moon
¶The building you can see **straight** ahead of you is the post office.

(-)ma〔n, suf〕 space, interval; time, spare time; a room

1〔n〕
① [space, interval; the area between two things]
¶[I] planted trees three meters **apart**.

② [time, spare time, free time]
¶There's still a little **time left** before the appointment.

¶I was absorbed in a book and it was morning **before I knew it**.

784

（Muchū de hon o yonde itara, itsu no *ma* ni ka asa ni natte shimaimashita.）

③〔部屋〕

客間（kyaku*ma*）応接間（ōsetsu*ma*）
茶の間（chano*ma*）居間（i*ma*）六畳間
（rokujō*ma*）

2〔尾〕

¶わたしのアパートは二間しかありま
せん。（Watashi no apāto wa futa*ma*
shika arimasen.）

まあ〔副、感〕

1〔副〕

¶まあ、ゆっくりしてください。（*Mā*,
yukkuri shite kudasai.）

¶おいしいかどうかわかりませんが、
まあ食べてみてください。（Oishii ka
dō ka wakarimasen ga, *mā* tabete mite
kudasai.）

2〔感〕

¶まあ、びっくりした。（*Mā*, bikkuri
shita.）

＊普通、女の人が使う。

-まい -枚〔尾〕

シャツ1枚（shatsu ichi*mai*）はがき2枚
（hagaki ni*mai*）

¶このおさらは1枚500円です。（Kono
osara wa ichi*mai* gohyakuen desu.）

まいあさ 毎朝〔名〕

¶わたしは毎朝6時に起きます。
（Watashi wa *maiasa* rokuji ni
okimasu.）

③ [room, chamber]

drawing **room**, parlor // reception
room, parlor // living **room**, sitting
room // sitting **room**, living **room** // a
six-*tatami*-mat **room**

2 〖suf〗 room, chamber

¶ My apartment is made up of only two
rooms.

mā 〖adv, interj〗 **well, just; Oh!**

1 〖adv〗 well, just

¶ Please make yourself at home 〚Don't
hurry off so soon〛.

¶ It may not be any good, but please try
some.

2 〖interj〗 Oh!

¶ **What** a surprise!

＊ *Ma* is usually used by women.

-mai 〖suf〗 **sheet, piece, page,
etc.; the counter for thin, flat
objects**

one shirt // **two** postcards

¶ These plates are five hundred yen
each.

maiasa 〖n〗 **every morning, each
morning**

¶ I get up at six o'clock **each morning**.

まいにち 毎日 〔名〕

¶わたしは毎日ピアノの練習をします。（Watashi wa *mainichi* piano no renshū o shimasu.）

mainichi 〔n〕 every day, each day, daily

¶ I practice the piano **every day**.

まいばん 毎晩 〔名〕

¶彼は毎晩遅くまで勉強しています。（Kare wa *maiban* osoku made benkyo shite imasu.）

maiban 〔n〕 every evening, every night

¶ He studies late every night.

まいる 参る 〔動 I〕

① 〔行く、来る〕
¶「いつこちらへいらっしゃいますか。」（Itsu kochira e irasshaimasu ka？）「明日参ります。」（Asu *mairimasu*.）

¶先月こちらに参りました。（Sengetsu kochira ni *mairimashita*.）

¶行って参ります。（Itte *mairimasu*.）

*「行く（iku）」「来る（kuru）」の謙譲語。

② 〔行く、来る〕
¶すぐ車が参りますから、しばらくお待ちください。（Sugu kuruma ga *mairimasu* kara, shibaraku omachi kudasai.）

¶雨が降って参りました。（Ame ga futte *mairimashita*.）

*「行く（iku）」「来る（kuru）」の丁寧語。

③ 〔神社や寺に行って参拝する〕
¶お正月には神社にお参りします。（Oshōgatsu ni wa jinja ni *omairi* shimasu.）

mairu 〔v I〕 go, come; visit a temple or shrine

① [go, come]
¶ "When will you be coming here?" "**I will come** tomorrow."

¶ **I came** here last month.

¶ **I'm going** now (set expression used when going out from a place one is going to return to the same day).

Mairu is the humble form of *iku* and of *kuru*.

② [go, come]
¶ Please wait a moment. The car 〚taxi〛 **will be here** shortly.

¶ It **has started** to rain.

Mairu is the polite form of *iku* and of *kuru*.

③ [visit a shrine or temple]
¶ [We] **visit** a shrine at New Year's.

まい- 毎- 〔頭〕

毎週 (*mai*shū) 毎月 (*mai*tsuki) 毎年
(*mai*nen) 毎年 (*mai*toshi) 毎回
(*mai*kai) 毎日曜日 (*mai*nichiyōbi)

¶毎度ありがとうございます。(*Mai*do
arigatō gozaimasu.)

(-)まえ (-)前 〔名、尾〕

1 〔名〕
　① [顔や目の向いている方、ものの正
面]
駅前 (eki*mae*)
¶まっすぐ前の方を見てください。
(Massugu *mae* no hō o mite kudasai.)
¶前から3番めの人、立ってくださ
い。(*Mae* kara sanbanme no hito, tatte
kudasai.)
¶郵便局は銀行の前にあります。
(Yūbinkyoku wa ginkō no *mae* ni
arimasu.)
→後ろ ushiro
　② [あるものごとの初めの部分]
¶この映画は前のほうはあまりおもし
ろくありません。(Kono eiga wa *mae*
no hō wa amari omoshiroku arimasen.)
¶前の部分を理解してから先に進んで
ください。(*Mae* no bubun o rikai shite
kara saki ni susunde kudasai.)
→あと ato
　③ [ある時点を基にしてそれより早い
時]
¶今9時5分前です。(Ima kuji gofun *mae*
desu.)

mai- 〔pref〕 **every**, **each**, apiece

every week, weekly // **every** month,
monthly // **every** year, yearly // **every**
year, yearly // **every** time, **each** time //
every Sunday, **each** Sunday

¶ Thank you for your **continued**
patronage (said to regular customers in
stores, restaurants, etc.).

(-)mae 〔n, suf〕 **front; first part;
before; ago; serving, portion**

1 〔n〕
　① [front]

in front of the station
¶ Please look straight **ahead**.

¶ Will the person third from **the front**
please stand up.

¶ The post office is **in front of** the
bank.

　② [the first part]
¶ The **first** part of this movie isn't very
interesting.

¶ Please move on to the rest after full
comprehension of the **first** part.

　③ [before, previous; earlier than a
given time]
¶ It is now five **to** nine.

¶わたしは日本へ来る前に、少し日本語を勉強したことがあります。
(Watashi wa Nihon e kuru *mae* ni, sukoshi Nihongo o benkyō shita koto ga arimasu.)

④ [現在の時点より以前]

¶あなたは前に上田さんに会ったことがありますか。(Anata wa *mae* ni Ueda san ni atta koto ga arimasu ka？)
¶この前の日曜日にわたしは映画を見に行きました。(Kono *mae* no nichiyōbi ni watashi wa eiga o mi ni ikimashita.)

2 〔尾〕
一人前の料理 (ichinin*mae* no ryōri)

まかせる 任せる 〔動Ⅱ〕

¶この仕事はあなたに任せます。
(Kono shigoto wa anata ni *makasemasu.*)
¶どうしたらよいかは、あなたの判断に任せます。(Dō shitara yoi ka wa, anata no handan ni *makasemasu.*)

まがる 曲がる 〔動Ⅰ〕

① [ものがまっすぐでなくなる]
腰が曲がる (koshi ga *magaru*)
¶この木は枝が曲がるほどたくさんの実がなっています。(Kono ki wa eda ga *magaru* hodo takusan no mi ga natte imasu.)

② [進む向きを変える]
¶その角を右へ曲がると、交番があります。(Sono kado o migi e *magaru* to, kōban ga arimasu.)

③ [道などが折れている]

¶ I studied Japanese a little **before** coming to Japan.

④ [before, ago; earlier than the present time]

¶ Have you met [Mrs.] Ueda **before?**

¶ I went to see a movie **last** Sunday.

2 〖suf〗 serving, portion
a single **serving** (of a dish or meal)

makaseru 〖v Ⅱ〗 **entrust to, leave to**

¶ **I'll leave** this job **up to** you to do.

¶ **I'll leave it to you** to decide what is best to do.

magaru 〖v Ⅰ〗 **curve, be bent; turn; be crooked, bend**

① [curve, be bent]
have a **bent** back
¶ This tree is so laden with fruit that its branches **are bent down**.

② [to turn]
¶ If you **turn** right at that corner, you'll find a police box.

③ [be crooked, bend]

¶川の所で道が曲がっています。
（Kawa no tokoro de michi ga *magatte* imasu.）

¶ There is **a bend** in the road at the river.

まく 巻く 〔動Ⅰ〕

maku 〚vⅠ〛 **turn, wind, roll up; wind around**

① [ねじって回す]
ねじを巻く（neji o *maku*）
¶時計を巻くのを忘れたので、止まってしまいました。（Tokei o *maku* no o wasureta node tomatte shimaimashita.）

① [turn, wind, roll up]
turn a screw
¶ The clock 〚watch〛 stopped 〚has stopped〛 because [I] forgot **to wind** it.

② [周りに長いものをからみつける]
¶ナイフで手を切ったので、包帯を巻きました。（Naifu de te o kitta node, hōtai o *makimashita*.）

② [wind around]
¶ [I] cut [my] hand with a knife and **wrapped** a bandage **around it**.

まく 〔動Ⅰ〕

maku 〚vⅠ〛 **sow (seed); scatter, sprinkle**

① [種などを土の上におく]
¶種をまきましたが、まだ芽が出ません。（Tane o *makimashita* ga, mada me ga demasen.）

① [sow (seed)]
¶ [I] **seeded** it but nothing has come up yet.

② [広い範囲に散らす]
¶ほこりがひどいので、道に水をまきました。（Hokori ga hidoi node, michi ni mizu o *makimashita*.）

② [scatter, sprinkle]
¶ [I] **sprinkled** the road with water as it was so dusty.

(-)まく (-)幕 〔名、尾〕

(-)maku 〚n, suf〛 **(stage) curtain; act (of a play)**

1 〔名〕
幕が開く（*maku* ga aku）幕が下りる（*maku* ga oriru）幕を引く（*maku* o hiku）
¶壁に幕を張って映画を映しました。（Kabe ni *maku* o hatte eiga o utsushimashita.）

1 〚n〛 (stage) curtain
the curtain rises 〚opens〛 // the curtain falls 〚closes〛 // draw 〚raise〛 the curtain
¶ [We] put **a makeshift screen** across the wall and showed a movie.

2 〔尾〕
¶この芝居は5幕からなっています。（Kono shibai wa go*maku* kara natte imasu.）

2 〚suf〛 act (of a play)
¶ This play is composed of five **acts**.

まくら〔名〕

まくらをする（*makura o suru*）

¶まくらが高すぎて、よく眠れません
でした。（Makura ga takasugite, yoku
nemuremasen deshita.）

makura 〔n〕 **pillow**

use **a pillow**, rest one's head on **a pillow**

¶ [I] couldn't sleep well as **[my]** pillow
was too thick.

まける 負ける〔動Ⅱ〕

① [相手が強くて勝つことができない]
戦争に負ける（sensō ni *makeru*）敵に
負ける（teki ni *makeru*）
¶この次の試合には負けないようにがん
ばりましょう。（Kono tsugi no shiai
ni wa *makenai* yō ni ganbarimashō.）
⇔勝つ katsu
→敗れる yabureru
② [値段を安くする]
¶高すぎますね。もう少し負けてくだ
さい。（Takasugimasu ne. Mō sukoshi
makete kudasai.）
¶あの本屋では1割負けてくれるそう
です。（Ano hon'ya de wa ichiwari
makete kureru sō desu.）

makeru 〔v Ⅱ〕 **be defeated, lose; give a price reduction**

① [be defeated, lose]
lose a war // **be defeated** by the enemy,
lose to one's opponent

¶ Let's stick in there and **win** the next
game 〚match〛.

② [give a price reduction]
¶ It's too expensive. Please **come down**
a little.

¶ I hear that bookstore **gives a** 10
percent **price reduction**.

まげる 曲げる〔動Ⅱ〕

¶けがをして、足を曲げることができ
なくなりました。（Kega o shite, ashi o
mageru koto ga dekinaku narimashita.）
¶いくら力があっても、この鉄棒を曲
げることはできないでしょう。（Ikura
chikara ga atte mo, kono tetsubō o *mageru*
koto wa dekinai deshō.）

mageru 〔v Ⅱ〕 **to bend, curve, twist**

¶ I hurt myself and can't 〚couldn't〛
bend my leg.

¶ No matter how strong [he] may be, I
bet [he] can't **bend** this iron bar.

まご 孫〔名〕

¶山田さんは孫が3人います。
（Yamada san wa *mago* ga sannin imasu.）

mago 〔n〕 **grandchild, grandson, granddaughter**

¶ [Ms.] Yamada has three
grandchildren.

まことに〔副〕

¶遅くなって、まことに申し訳ありません。(Osoku natte, *makoto ni* mōshiwake arimasen.)
¶山田さんはまことに立派な方です。(Yamada san wa *makoto ni* rippa na kata desu.)
⇒本当に **hontō ni**

まじめ〔形動〕

① [誠実である、一生懸命に何かをする]
¶あの学生はとてもまじめです。(Ano gakusei wa totemo *majime* desu.)
¶今度入ってきた人は、まじめによく働きます。(Kondo haitte kita hito wa, *majime* ni yoku hatarakimasu.)
② [本気である]
まじめな顔をする (*majime* na kao o suru)
¶わたしがまじめに話しているのに、あの人は笑いました。(Watashi ga *majime* ni hanashite iru noni, ano hito wa waraimashita.)

ましょう〔助動〕

① [話し手の意志を表す]
¶重そうなかばんですね。お持ちしましょう。(Omosō na kaban desu ne. Omochi shi*mashō*)
¶あなたの切符も買っておきましょう。(Anata no kippu mo katte oki*mashō*)
② [勧誘を表す]

makoto ni 〔adv〕 really, truly, sincerely

¶ I'm **very** sorry to be late.

¶ [Mr.] Yamada is **really** a fine person.

majime 〔adj-v〕 steady, faithful, honest; serious, grave, earnest

① [steady, faithful, honest, sober]

¶ That student is very **serious** 〖**diligent**〗.

¶ [Our] new colleague is **serious** and a hard worker.

② [serious, grave, earnest]
have a **serious** look on one's face; keep a **straight** face

¶ [He] laughed even though I was talking **seriously**.

-mashō 〔auxil〕 a verb ending expressing the speaker's intent or an invitation

① [expresses the speaker's intent]
¶ That bag 〖suitcase, briefcase〗 looks heavy. **Let me** carry it for you.

¶ **Let me** buy your ticket too.

② [expresses an invitation or persuasion]

¶今夜、映画を見に行きましょう。
（Kon'ya, eiga o mi ni ikima*shō*.）

¶疲れましたね。お茶でも飲みましょうか。（Tsukaremashita ne. Ocha demo nomi*mashō* ka？）

⇒ます **masu**

まじる 交じる〔動 I〕

majiru 〔v I〕 **mix, mingle, be mixed, be blended**

¶男の子の中に女の子が一人交じって遊んでいます。（Otoko no ko no naka ni onna no ko ga hitori *majitte* asonde imasu.）

¶This book is written in **a mixture** of *kanji* and *kana*.

¶The children are playing, with one girl **joining** several boys.

¶この本は漢字とかなの交じった文で書いてあります。（Kono hon wa kanji to kana no *majitta* bun de kaite arimasu.）

まじる 混じる〔動 I〕

majiru 〔v I〕 **mix, mingle, be mixed, be blended**

¶この米には石が混じっています。（Kono kome ni wa ishi ga *majitte* imasu.）

¶There are stones **mixed in** with this rice.

¶あの人には西洋人の血が混じっています。（Ano hito ni wa seiyōjin no chi ga *majitte* imasu.）

¶[He] **has some** Western 〖Occidental, European〗 blood **in [him]**.

ます 増す〔動 I〕

masu 〔v I〕 **increase, rise; increase, raise**

① [増える、多くなる]

① [increase, rise, grow]

¶昨日の雨で川の水が増しました。（Kinō no ame de kawa no mizu ga *mashimashita*.）

¶The river **has risen** due to the rain yesterday.

¶人口が増すと、ますます食糧が不足してきます。（Jinkō ga *masu* to, *masumasu* shokuryō ga fusoku shite ki*masu*.）

¶As the population **increases**, the shortage of food deepens.

→増える **fueru**

② [増やす、多くする]

② [increase, raise, add to]

¶電報は5字増すごとに、料金が高くなります。（Denpō wa goji *masu* goto ni, ryōkin ga takaku narimasu.）

¶ The charge for a telegram goes up with each **additional** five characters.

ます〔助動〕

-masu 〔auxil〕 **a verb ending expressing politeness**

¶よく雨が降りますね。（Yoku ame ga furi*masu* ne.）

¶ **It's been raining** a lot lately, hasn't it?〚How it **rains**!〛

¶机の上に本があります。（Tsukue no ue ni hon ga ari*masu*.）

¶ **There is** a book on the desk.

¶机の上には何もありません。（Tsukue no ue ni wa nani mo ari*masen*.）

¶ **There is nothing** at all on the desk.

¶いっしょに遊びに行きませんか。（Issho ni asobi ni iki*masen* ka.）

¶ **Won't you go** out with [us]?

¶あしたは暇だから、わたしが行きます。（Ashita wa hima da kara, watashi ga iki*masu*.）

¶ Since I'm free tomorrow, I **will go**.

¶昨日、わたしはデパートへ行きました。（Kinō, watashi wa depāto e iki*mashita*.）

¶ Yesterday I **went** to a department store.

¶わたしは中国語が話せます。（Watashi wa Chūgokugo ga hanase*masu*.）

¶ I **can speak** Chinese.

¶わたしは日本語は話せません。（Watashi wa Nihongo wa hanase*masen*.）

¶ I **can't speak** Japanese.

¶わたしは日本人ではありません。（Watashi wa Nihonjin de wa ari*masen*.）

¶ I **am not** Japanese.

＊「ます（masu）」は、話し手の聞き手に対する丁寧な気持ちを表す。「よく雨が降るね。（Yoku ame ga furu ne.）」と言うよりは、「よく雨が降りますね。（Yoku ame ga furimasu ne.）」と言うほうが、丁寧な言い方である。また「わたしは日本人ではありません。（Watashi wa Nihonjin de wa arimasen.）」は、「わたしは日本人です。（Watashi wa Nihonjin desu.）」の打ち消しの言い方である。

＊*-masu* indicates the politeness of the speaker toward the listener. "*Yoku ame ga furimasu ne*" is more polite than "*Yoku ame ga furu ne*." "*Watashi wa Nihonjin de wa arimasen*" is the negative of "*Watashi wa Nihonjin desu*."

⇒ましょう mashō

まず〔副〕

¶まず、あなたから意見を言ってください。(*Mazu*, anata kara iken o itte kudasai.)

¶まず、初めに自己紹介をしましょう。(*Mazu*, hajime ni jiko-shōkai o shimashō.)

まずい〔形〕

①[おいしくない]

¶この料理はまずいですね。(Kono ryōri wa *mazui* desu ne.)
⇔おいしい oishii　うまい umai
②[下手だ]
¶これはたいへんまずい字ですね。(Kore wa taihen *mazui* ji desu ne.)
⇔うまい umai
→下手 heta

まずしい　貧しい〔形〕

¶あの子の家はとても貧しいです。(Ano ko no ie wa totemo *mazushii* desu.)
¶世界にはまだ貧しい生活をしている人がおおぜいいます。(Sekai ni wa mada *mazushii* seikatsu o shite iru hito ga oozei imasu.)
⇒貧乏 binbō

ますます〔副〕

¶雨がますます強く降ってきました。(Ame ga *masumasu* tsuyoku futte kimashita.)

mazu〔adv〕**first, first of all**

¶ Please state your opinions, starting with you **first**.

¶ **First**, let's start with selfintroductions.

mazui〔adj〕**unpalatable, unappetizing; poor, unskillful**

① [unpalatable, unappetizing, unsavory]

¶ This dish **tastes awful**.

② [poor, unskillful]

¶ This is a very **poorly written** character.

mazushii〔adj〕**poor, impoverished**

¶ That child's family **is** very **poor**.

¶ There are still a great number of people in the world who are living **in poverty**.

masumasu〔adv〕**more and more, still more, still less**

¶ The rain has become 〚became〛 **still** stronger.

¶2学期になったら、勉強がますます難しくなってきました。（Nigakki ni nattara, benkyō ga *masumasu* muzukashiku natte kimashita.）

¶わたしもますます元気ですから御安心ください。（Watashi mo *masumasu* genki desu kara goanshin kudasai.）

まぜる　混ぜる 〔動Ⅱ〕

¶砂糖に塩を混ぜないでください。（Satō ni shio o *mazenaide* kudasai.）

¶日本語に英語を混ぜて話すと、おかしいです。（Nihongo ni Eigo o *mazete* hanasu to, okashii desu.）

また 〔副、接〕

1 〔副〕

①[もう一度、再び]

¶どうぞまたおいでください。（Dōzo *mata* oide kudasai.）

¶山田さんはさっき食べたばかりなのに、また食べています。（Yamada san wa sakki tabeta bakari na noni, *mata* tabete imasu.）

②[同じく、やはり]

¶今日もまた雨です。（Kyō mo *mata* ame desu.）

¶今度の試験もまただめでした。（Kondo no shiken mo *mata* dame deshita.）

2 〔接〕

山また山が続く（yama *mata* yama ga tsuzuku）

¶あの人は医者でもあり、また小説家でもあります。（Ano hito wa isha de mo ari, *mata* shōsetsuka de mo arimasu.）

¶ The studies have become 〚became〛 **more** difficult **still** in the second semester.

¶ Don't worry about me as I am **still** going strong.

mazeru 〔v Ⅱ〕 mix, blend

¶ Please **don't mix** salt in with the sugar.

¶ It's strange when one **sprinkles** Japanese **with** English words.

mata 〔adv, conj〕 **again, once more; also, as well, likewise; and, moreover, while**

1 〖adv〗

① [again, once more]

¶ Please come **again** sometime.

¶ Even though [he] ate just a little while ago, [Mr.] Yamada is eating **again** now.

② [also, as well, likewise]

¶ It's rainy **again** today.

¶ [I] didn't do well on the exam this time **either**.

2 〖conj〗 and, moreover, besides; while, on the other hand

mountains rise up **one after the other**

¶ [He] is **both** a doctor and a novelist.

＊ものごとを列挙したり、また別のことをつけ加えたりするときに使う。

まだ〔副〕

① [その状態が続いている様子]

¶まだ雨が降っています。(*Mada* ame ga futte imasu.)
¶母はまだ帰ってきません。(Haha wa *mada* kaette kimasen.)
¶わたしは日本語がまだ下手です。(Watashi wa Nihongo ga *mada* heta desu.)
→もう **mō**

② [あまり時間がたっていない様子、わずかに]
¶汽車が走り出してから、まだ10分しかたっていません。(Kisha ga hashiridashite kara, *mada* jippun shika tatte imasen.)
¶わたしは日本へ来てまだ1年です。(Watashi wa Nihon e kite *mada* ichinen desu.)
→もう **mō**

③ [もっと、ほかにも]
¶仕事はまだたくさん残っています。(Shigoto wa *mada* takusan nokotte imasu.)
¶まだ見たい所はたくさんあります。(*Mada* mitai tokoro wa takusan arimasu.)

または〔接〕
¶2または3で割りきれる数 (ni *mata wa* san de warikireru kazu)
¶大学を卒業するまでに、日本語または中国語のどちらか一つを学ばなければなりません。(Daigaku o sotsugyō suru made ni, Nihongo *mata wa*

＊Used when listing items or when adding something else.

mada 〔adv〕 **still, yet; only; more, still**

① [still, yet; a certain condition is still in effect]
¶ It's **still** raining.

¶ My mother hasn't returned home **yet**.

¶ My Japanese **still** isn't very good.

② [only, barely]

¶ **Only** 10 minutes have passed since the departure of the train.

¶ It's **only** been one year since I came to Japan.

③ [more, still]
¶ There's **still** a lot of work to do.

¶ There are **still** a lot of places I want to go to see.

mata wa 〔conj〕 **or, either ~ or ~**
numbers that can be divided evenly by **either** two **or** three
¶ Before graduation from college one must study **either** Japanese **or** Chinese.

Chūgokugō no dochira ka hitotsu o
manabanakereba narimasen.)

¶ この建物の完成は今月中には無理
で、来月または再来月になるでしょ
う。(Kono tatemono no kansei wa
kongetsuchū ni wa muri de, raigetsu
mata wa saraigetsu ni naru deshō.)

＊二つのものごとのうち、どちらかで
あるときに使う。話すときには普通
「2か3 (ni ka san)」「日本語か中国語
(Nihongo ka Chūgokugo)」「来月か再来
月 (raigetsu ka saraigetsu)」などの言い
方をする。

¶ It will be impossible to complete this
building this month; it will probably be
done next month **or** the month after
that.

＊Used for one of two possibilities. In
speech *ka* is usually used, as in "*ni ka
san*," "*Nihongo ka Chūgokugo*,"
"*raigetsu ka saraigetsu*," etc.

まち 町〔名〕

machi 〔n〕 **town, city; street,
quarter**

① [人家が多く集まった所]
¶ わたしは田舎を出て町で働きたいで
す。(Watashi wa inaka o dete *machi* de
hatarakitai desu.)
¶ 昨日は町まで買い物に行きました。
(Kinō wa *machi* made kaimono ni
ikimashita.)

① [town, city; densely populated area]
¶ I want to leave the country and go to
the city to work.

¶ [I] went to **town** 〚**downtown**〛
yesterday to shop.

② [家がたくさん並んでいてにぎやか
な通り]
¶ 町を歩いていたら、山田さんに会い
ました。(*Machi* o aruite itara, Yamada
san ni aimashita.)
¶ 夕方の町は買い物をする人でたいへ
んにぎやかでした。(Yūgata no *machi*
wa kaimono o suru hito de taihen nigiyaka
deshita.)
⇒村 **mura**

② [street, quarter; lively street(s) with
many houses]
¶ I met [Mrs.] Yamada while walking
along **the street**.

¶ The night **streets** were bustling with
shoppers.

まちあわせる 待ち合わせる〔動 Ⅱ〕

machiawaseru 〔v Ⅱ〕 **meet,
arrange to meet, wait for**

¶ 山田さんと6時に東京駅で待ち合わ
せました。(Yamada san to rokuji ni
Tōkyō-eki de *machiawasemashita*.)

¶ [Miss] Yamada and [I] **met** at Tokyo
Station at six o'clock.

まちがい 間違い 〔名〕

① [誤り、正しくないこと]
¶次の文章の間違いを直しなさい。
(Tsugi no bunshō no *machigai* o
naoshinasai.)
② [異常なこと「事故など」]
¶子供の帰りが遅いが、何か間違いが
あったのではないでしょうか。
(Kodomo no kaeri ga osoi ga, nani ka
machigai ga atta no de wa nai deshō
ka?)

machigai 〔n〕 mistake, error; accident, mishap

① [mistake, error]
¶ Correct **the mistakes** in the next
sentence.

② [accident, mishap, trouble]
¶ The children are late coming home.
Could **something have happened?**

まちがいない 間違いない 〔連〕

¶あの学校が優勝するのは間違いな
い。(Ano gakkō ga yūshō suru no wa
machigai nai.)
¶お金はあしたまでに間違いなく返し
ます。(Okane wa ashita made ni
machigai naku kaeshimasu.)

machigai nai 〔compd〕 without fail, certainly, surely

¶ That school **is sure** to win.

¶ [I] will repay the money by tomorrow
without fail.

まちがう 間違う 〔動Ⅰ〕

① [違う、誤る]
¶この漢字は間違っていますよ。
(Kono kanji wa *machigatte* imasu yo.)
② [とりちがえる]
¶山田さんは、間違ってわたしの本を
持って行ってしまいました。
(Yamada san wa, *machigatte* watashi
no hon o motte itte shimaimashita.)

machigau 〔vⅠ〕 make a mistake, err; mistake, confuse

① [make a mistake, err]
¶ This *kanji* **is wrong**.

② [mistake, confuse]
¶ [Mr.] Yamada **mistakenly** went off
with my book.

まちがえる 間違える 〔動Ⅱ〕

① [誤る、違える]
¶どうも計算を間違えたようです。
(Dōmo keisan o *machigaeta* yō desu.)
② [とりちがえる]

machigaeru 〔vⅡ〕 make a mistake, err; mistake, confuse

① [make a mistake, err]
¶ There seems **to be a mistake** in these
figures.

② [mistake, confuse]

¶ホテルで部屋を間違えて、隣の部屋へ入ってしまいました。(Hoteru de heya o *machigaete*, tonari no heya e haitte shimaimashita.)

¶ I mistook the room next door for mine at the hotel and entered it by mistake.

まつ 待つ〔動Ⅰ〕

matsu〔v Ⅰ〕 **wait, look for**

¶ちょっと待ってください。(Chotto *matte* kudasai.)

¶ Please **wait** a moment.

¶わたしは毎日母からの手紙を待っています。(Watashi wa mainichi haha kara no tegami o *matte* imasu.)

¶ I **am looking for** a letter from my mother every day.

¶車を待たせてありますから、急いでください。(Kuruma o *matasete* arimasu kara, isoide kudasai.)

¶ Please hurry as the car 〚taxi〛 **is waiting**.

-まつ -末〔尾〕

-matsu〔suf〕 **the end of**

今月末 (kongetsu*matsu*) 週末 (shū-*matsu*) 年末 (nen*matsu*) 学期末 (gakki*matsu*)

the end of this month // the week**end** // the year-**end** // **the end** of the semester

まっか 真っ赤〔形動〕

makka〔adj-v〕 **very red, bright red, crimson**

真っ赤な太陽 (*makka* na taiyō) 真っ赤な口紅 (*makka* na kuchibeni)

a **blood-red** sun // **crimson** lipstick

¶恥ずかしくて、顔が真っ赤になりました。(Hazukashikute, kao ga *makka* ni narimashita.)

¶ [My] face turned **bright red** from embarrassment 〚shame〛.

まっくら 真っ暗〔形動〕

makkura〔adj-v〕 **total darkness, pitch dark**

¶電気が消えて、部屋の中が真っ暗になりました。(Denki ga kiete, heya no naka ga *makkura* ni narimashita.)

¶ The electricity went off and the room turned **pitch dark**.

¶遅くなって、真っ暗な道を一人で帰りました。(Osoku natte, *makkura* na michi o hitori de kaerimashita.)

¶ It was late and [I] went home alone through the **pitch-dark** streets 〚along the **pitch-black** road〛.

まっくろ 真っ黒 〔形動〕

¶中村さんの髪の毛は真っ黒です。
(Nakamura san no kaminoke wa *makkuro* desu.)
¶日に焼けて、顔が真っ黒になりました。(Hi ni yakete, kao ga *makkuro* ni narimashita.)

makkuro 〔adj-v〕 **deep black, jet black**

¶[Miss] Nakamura's hair is **jet black** 〖**raven black**〗.

¶[His] face is 〖was〗 **deeply tanned**.

まっさお 真っ青 〔形動〕

①[本当に青い様子]
真っ青な海 (*massao* na umi)
¶真っ青な空に白い雲が一つ浮かんでいます。(*Massao* na sora ni shiroi kumo ga hitotsu ukande imasu.)
②[顔色が悪く血の気のない様子]
¶山田さんは恐ろしさで真っ青になりました。(Yamada san wa osoroshisa de *massao* ni narimashita.)

massao 〔adj-v〕 **deep blue; deadly pale**

①[deep blue]
a **deep blue** sea
¶There is a single white cloud floating in the **deep blue** sky.

②[deadly pale]
¶[Mr.] Yamada **blanched** from fear.

まっしろ 真っ白 〔形動〕

¶山は雪で真っ白です。(Yama wa yuki de *masshiro* desu.)
¶庭に真っ白な菊の花が咲いています。(Niwa ni *masshiro* na kiku no hana ga saite imasu.)

masshiro 〔adj-v〕 **pure white**

¶The mountain is **white** with snow.

¶A **pure white** chrysanthemum is blooming in the garden 〖yard〗.

まっすぐ 〔副、形動〕

¶駅はこの道をまっすぐ行ったところにあります。(Eki wa kono michi o *massugu* itta tokoro ni arimasu.)
¶曲がった線でなく、まっすぐな線を引いてください。(Magatta sen de naku, *massugu* na sen o hiite kudasai.)

massugu 〔adv, adj-v〕 **straight, direct, upright**

¶The station is **straight** along this street.

¶Please draw a **straight** line, not a curved one.

まったく 全く 〔副〕

①[全然、完全に]

mattaku 〔adv〕 **entirely, utterly; truly, indeed**

①[entirely, utterly, totally]

¶あなたが病気だったことは、全く知りませんでした。(Anata ga byōki datta koto wa, *mattaku* shirimasen deshita.)

¶わたしの意見は田中さんの意見と全く同じです。(Watashi no iken wa Tanaka san no iken to *mattaku* onaji desu.)

②[実に、本当に]

¶毎日雨ばかり降って、全くいやになります。(Mainichi ame bakari futte, *mattaku* iya ni narimasu.)

¶全くあなたの言うとおりです。(*Mattaku* anata no iu toori desu.)

マッチ〔名〕

¶マッチを使うときは、火事にならないように気をつけてください。(Macchi o tsukau toki wa, kaji ni naranai yō ni ki o tsukete kudasai.)

まつり　祭り〔名〕

¶町は祭りでたいへんにぎやかです。(Machi wa *matsuri* de taihen nigiyaka desu.)

¶日本にはいろいろな祭りがあります。(Nihon ni wa iroiro na *matsuri* ga arimasu.)

まで〔助〕

朝から晩まで (asa kara ban *made*)

¶午前9時から午後5時まで会社にいます。(Gozen kuji kara gogo goji *made* kaisha ni imasu.)

¶今週の土曜日まで学校は休みです。(Konshū no doyōbi *made* gakkō wa yasumi desu.)

¶ゆうべは遅くまで起きていました。(Yūbe wa osoku *made* okite imashita.)

¶ I had **no idea whatsoever** that you were ill.

¶ I **completely** agree with [Mrs.] Tanaka.

② [truly, indeed, really]

¶ This rain every day is **really** depressing.

¶ You're **absolutely** right.

macchi 〔n〕 **match**

¶ Be careful when you use matches not to start a fire.

matsuri 〔n〕 **festival**

¶ The town is very gay and lively because of **the festival**.

¶ Japan has many different **festivals**.

made 〔part〕 **until, to, up to, as far as**

from morning **until** night

¶ I am at the office from 9 AM **to** 5 PM.

¶ School is off **through** this Saturday.

¶ [I] was up **until** late last night.

¶ここから駅まで何分ぐらいですか。
（Koko kara eki *made* nanpun gurai desu
ka？）

¶東京から大阪までは何キロぐらいあ
りますか。（Tōkyō kara Oosaka *made*
wa nankiro gurai arimasu ka？）

までに〔連〕

¶来月の十日までに、この仕事を終え
なければなりません。（Raigetsu no
tooka *made ni*, kono shigoto o oenakereba
narimasen.)

¶レポートは来週の土曜日までに出し
てください。（Repōto wa raishū no
doyōbi *made ni* dashite kudasai.)

まど 窓〔名〕

窓を開ける（*mado* o akeru）窓を閉め
る（*mado* o shimeru）

¶バスの窓から手を出さないでくださ
い。（Basu no *mado* kara te o dasanaide
kudasai.)

まとまる〔動Ⅰ〕

①[集まって一つになる]
¶組ごとにまとまって電車に乗ってく
ださい。（Kumi goto ni *matomatte*
densha ni notte kudasai.)
②[決まりがつく、解決がつく]

¶みんなの意見がようやくまとまりま
した。（Minna no iken ga yōyaku
matomarimashita.)
③[整理がつく、できあがる]

¶ How many minutes is it from here **to**
the station?

¶ How many kilometers is it from
Tokyo **to** Osaka?

made ni 〔compd〕 **by, not later
than, before**
¶ This job must be finished **by** the
tenth of next month.

¶ Please submit your report **by**
Saturday next week.

mado 〔n〕 **window**
open **the window** // close **the window**

¶ Please don't put your hands out **the
windows** of the bus.

matomaru 〔v Ⅰ〕 **be united; be
settled, be concluded; be in
order, take shape**
① [be united, be collected]
¶ Please **gather** in your groups
〚squads〛 and then board the train.

② [be settled, be concluded, come to
an agreement]
¶ **A uniformity** of opinion **was
achieved** at last.

③ [be in order, take shape]

¶論文がまとまったので、発表したいと思っています。(Ronbun ga *matomatta* node, happyō shitai to omotte imasu.)

¶ My thesis has finally **taken shape** and I'd like to make some sort of public presentation of it.

まとめる〔動Ⅱ〕

matomeru 〔v Ⅱ〕 **unite, unify; settle, conclude; put in order**

①[集めて一つにする]

① [unite, unify, collect]

¶紙くずをまとめて、ごみ箱に捨ててください。(Kamikuzu o *matomete*, gomibako ni sutete kudasai.)

¶ Please **collect** the scrap paper and discard it in the trash can.

②[決まりをつける、解決する]

② [settle, conclude, bring to a conclusion]

¶この話し合いをまとめるのは、とても難しいです。(Kono hanashiai o *matomeru* no wa, totemo muzukashii desu.)

¶ It will be very difficult **to bring** these negotiations **to a successful conclusion**.

③[整理する、完成する]

③ [put in order, arrange]

¶卒業までに論文をまとめなければなりません。(Sotsugyō made ni ronbun o *matomenakereba* narimasen.)

¶ [I] **must finish** my thesis by graduation.

まにあう 間に合う〔動Ⅰ〕

maniau 〔v Ⅰ〕 **be in time for; meet the purpose, be enough, do**

¶急げば、まだ9時15分発の汽車に間に合います。(Isogeba, mada kuji jūgofun hatsu no kisha ni *maniaimasu*.)

¶ If [you] hurry, **[you] can** still **make** the 9:15 train.

¶今度の旅行は、1万円あればじゅうぶん間に合います。(Kondo no ryokō wa, ichiman'en areba jūbun *maniaimasu*.)

¶ Ten thousand yen **will be** quite **enough** for the coming trip.

まね〔名、〜する〕

mane 〔n, 〜*suru*〕 **imitation, mimicry**

人のまねをする (hito no *mane* o suru)

imitate another; **follow suit**

¶上田さんは鳥の鳴き声のまねをするのが上手です。(Ueda san wa tori no nakigoe no *mane* o suru no ga jōzu desu.)

¶ [Mr.] Ueda is skilled at **imitating** bird calls.

¶先生の発音をよく聞いてまねしてください。(Sensei no hatsuon o yoku kiite *mane* shite kudasai.)

¶ Please listen carefully to the teacher's pronunciation and **copy it**.

まねく 招く〔動Ⅰ〕
客を招く (kyaku o *maneku*)
¶友達を招いて、いっしょに食事をしました。(Tomodachi o *maneite*, issho ni shokuji o shimashita.)
¶わたしたちは友達の結婚式に招かれました。(Watashitachi wa tomodachi no kekkonshiki ni *manekaremashita*.)
¶わたしは日本政府に招かれて日本へ来ました。(Watashi wa Nihon-seifu ni *manekarete* Nihon e kimashita.)
⇒招待 shōtai

maneku 〔v Ⅰ〕 **invite**
invite a guest
¶ [I] **invited** a friend and we had a meal together.

¶ We **were invited** to a friend's wedding.

¶ I came to Japan **on the invitation** of the Japanese government.

まねる〔動Ⅱ〕
¶この建物はフランスの建築をまねて造ったものです。(Kono tatemono wa Furansu no kenchiku o *manete* tsukutta mono desu.)

maneru 〔v Ⅱ〕 **imitate, copy**
¶ This building **is modeled** after the style of French architecture.

まぶしい〔形〕

¶まぶしくて目を開けていられません。(*Mabushikute* me o akete iraremasen.)
¶その部屋はまぶしいほど明るかった。(Sono heya wa *mabushii* hodo akarukatta.)

mabushii 〔adj〕 **dazzling, glaring, blinding**
¶ **It's so bright** one can't keep one's eyes open.

¶ That room was very bright, **almost too bright**.

まま〔名〕
¶くつをはいたまま部屋へ入ってはいけません。(Kutsu o haita *mama* heya e haitte wa ikemasen.)
¶あの人は家を出たまま帰ってきません。(Ano hito wa ie o deta *mama* kaette kimasen.)
¶この魚は生のまま食べられますか。(Kono sakana wa nama no *mama* taberaremasu ka？)

mama 〔n〕 **as is, as it stands**
¶ One mustn't enter the room with one's shoes **still on**.

¶ [He] left home and has **never** come back.

¶ Can this fish be eaten **raw**?

¶テーブルの上は、かたづけないでそ
のままにしておいてください。
(Tēburu no ue wa, katazukenaide sono
mama ni shite oite kudasai.)
＊「まま（mama）」の前に来る動詞は
「た形」を使うことが多い。

| ¶ Please don't put away the things on
the table but leave them **as they are**.

＊ Verbs before *mama* are usually in
the *-ta* form.

まめ 豆 〔名〕   mame 〔n〕 beans, peas, soybeans

¶今晩は豆を煮て食べましょう。
(Konban wa *mame* o nite tabemashō.)
¶しょう油は豆から造ります。(Shōyu
wa *mame* kara tsukurimasu.)

¶ Let's have boiled 〖cooked〗 **beans**
tonight.
¶ Soy sauce is made from **soybeans**.

まもなく 間もなく 〔副〕   mamonaku 〔adv〕 soon, presently, before long

¶父は間もなく帰ると思います。
(Chichi wa *mamonaku* kaeru to
omoimasu.)
¶試験が終わると間もなく夏休みで
す。(Shiken ga owaru to *mamonaku*
natsuyasumi desu.)

¶ My father should be home **shortly**.

¶ Summer vacation starts **soon** after the
exams are over.

まもる 守る 〔動Ⅰ〕   mamoru 〔vⅠ〕 protect; obey, observe

①［害を受けないように防ぐ］
¶国を守るのは国民の義務です。
(Kuni o *mamoru* no wa kokumin no gimu
desu.)
②［決めたことに従う］
規則を守る（kisoku o *mamoru*）
¶約束は必ず守ります。(Yakusoku wa
kanarazu *mamorimasu*.)
¶あの人は、いつも時間を守らないで
遅れてきます。(Ano hito wa, itsu mo
jikan o *mamoranaide* okurete kimasu.)

① [protect, guard]
¶ It is the duty of citizens **to defend**
their country.

② [obey, observe, fulfill]
keep to regulations, **observe** the rules
¶ [I] always **keep** [my] promises.

¶ [He] **is unpunctual** and always
comes late.

まよう 迷う 〔動Ⅰ〕   mayou 〔vⅠ〕 be lost, lose one's way; be in doubt, be bewildered

①［道がわからなくなる］

① [be lost, lose one's way]

¶わたしは山の中で道に迷ってしまいました。(Watashi wa yama no naka de michi ni *mayotte* shimaimashita.)

② [はっきり決心できない]

¶どちらの本を買ったらよいか迷っています。(Dochira no hon o kattara yoi ka *mayotte* imasu.)

¶日本にいようか、国へ帰ろうかと迷っています。(Nihon ni iyō ka, kuni e kaerō ka to *mayotte* imasu.)

¶ I **lost my way** on the mountain 〚in the mountains〛.

② [be in doubt, be bewildered, waver, vacillate]

¶ **I am not sure** which book to buy.

¶ I am debating 〚**trying to decide**〛 whether to stay in Japan or return to my native country.

まる 丸 〔名〕

¶次の文のうち正しいものに丸をつけなさい。(Tsugi no bun no uchi tadashii mono ni *maru* o tsukenasai.)

maru 〔n〕 **circle**

¶ Choose the correct sentences among the following and mark them with **a circle**.

まるい 丸い 〔形〕

丸い石 (*marui* ishi)
¶東の空に丸い月が出ました。
(Higashi no sora ni *marui* tsuki ga demashita.)

marui 〔adj〕 **round, circular, spherical**

a **round** stone 〚pebble, rock〛
¶ A **rounded** moon appeared in the eastern sky.

まるい 円い 〔形〕

円い窓 (*marui* mado) 円いテーブル (*marui* tēburu)
¶わたしたちは先生の周りに円く輪になって座りました。(Watashitachi wa sensei no mawari ni *maruku* wa ni natte suwarimashita.)

marui 〔adj〕 **round, circular, spherical**

a **round** window // a **round** table

¶ We sat **in a circle** around our teacher.

まるで 〔副〕

① [ちょうどそのとおり、似ている]
¶こんなぜいたくな生活はまるで夢のようです。(Konna zeitaku na seikatsu wa *marude* yume no yō desu.)

marude 〔adv〕 **just like, exactly; completely, perfectly, entirely**

① [just like, exactly, as if]
¶ Such a life of luxury is **just like** a dream.

¶あの人は、犬をまるで自分の子供のようにかわいがっています。（Ano hito wa, inu o *marude* jibun no kodomo no yō ni kawaigatte imasu.）

¶ [He] dotes on [his] dog **as if** it were [his] child.

*あとに「ようだ（yō da）」が来ることが多い。

*Often used with *yō da*.

② [全く、ぜんぜん]

② [completely, perfectly, entirely]

¶あの兄弟はまるで性格が違います。（Ano kyōdai wa *marude* seikaku ga chigaimasu.）

¶ Those brothers have **completely** different personalities.

¶わたしはそのことをまるで知りませんでした。（Watashi wa sono koto o *marude* shirimasen deshita.）

¶ I had **no** idea of that.

*あとに打ち消しの言葉や否定的な意味の言葉が来る。

*Followed by the negative or words or expressions having a negative sense.

まわす　回す〔動Ⅰ〕

mawasu 〖v Ⅰ〗 **turn, whirl; send on, pass round**

① [回転させる]

① [turn, whirl, spin]

¶時計の針を逆に回してはいけません。（Tokei no hari o gyaku ni *mawashite* wa ikemasen.）

¶ One mustn't **turn** the hands of a clock 〖watch〗 backwards.

② [順におくる]

② [send on, pass round, transfer]

¶この本を回しますから、順番に読んでください。（Kono hon o *mawashi-masu* kara, junban ni yonde kudasai.）

¶ Please read this book and **pass it on** to the next person.

まわり　周り〔名〕

mawari 〖n〗 **circumference, surroundings; vicinity**

① [周囲]

① [circumference, surroundings]

¶池の周りに木がたくさん植えてあります。（Ike no *mawari* ni ki ga takusan uete arimasu.）

¶ There are numerous trees planted **around** the pond.

② [あたり、付近]

② [vicinity, neighborhood]

¶駅の周りはとてもにぎやかです。（Eki no *mawari* wa totemo nigiyaka desu.）

¶ It's very lively **around** the station.

まわる　回る〔動Ⅰ〕

① [回転する]

¶月は地球の周りを回ります。(Tsuki wa chikyū no mawari o *mawarimasu*.)

② [順に行く、ものごとが次々に移る]

¶病院で診察の順番が回ってくるまで座って待っていました。(Byōin de shinsatsu no junban ga *mawatte* kuru made suwatte matte imashita.)

¶ほうぼうの図書館を回って探しましたが、その本は見つかりませんでした。(Hōbō no toshokan o *mawatte* sagashimashita ga, sono hon wa mitsukarimasen deshita.)

まん　万〔名〕

1万 (ichi*man*) 10万 (jū*man*) 100万 (hyaku*man*) 1000万 (sen*man*, [issen*man*])

まんいん　満員〔名〕

満員電車 (*man'in*-densha)

¶バスが満員で乗れませんでした。(Basu ga *man'in* de noremasen deshita.)

¶どこのホテルも満員でした。(Doko no hoteru mo *man'in* deshita.)

まんが　漫画〔名〕

¶中村さんは漫画が大好きです。(Nakamura san wa *manga* ga daisuki desu.)

まんぞく　満足〔名、形動、～する〕

① [自分の思うとおりになってこれでじゅうぶんだと思うこと]

mawaru 〖vⅠ〗 revolve, rotate; make a round

① [revolve, rotate, turn round]

¶ The moon **revolves** around the earth.

② [make a round, make a tour]

¶ [I] sat at the hospital and waited **for [my] turn** to be examined.

¶ [I] **went around to** several libraries but [I] couldn't find that book.

man 〖n〗 ten thousand

10,000 // 100,000 // 1,000,000 // 10,000,000

man'in 〖n〗 full, no vacancy, sold out, capacity

a **crowded** train, a **jam-packed** train

¶ The bus **was full** and I couldn't get on.

¶ Every hotel **was full up**.

manga 〖n〗 cartoon, comics, comic book, caricature

¶ [Mr.] Nakamura is very fond of comic magazines 〚adult comic books〛.

manzoku 〖n, adj-v, ～*suru*〗 satisfied, contented; perfect, complete, adequate

① [satisfied, contented]

¶わたしは今の生活でじゅうぶん満足です。（Watashi wa ima no seikatsu de jūbun *manzoku* desu.）

¶こんな安い給料では満足できません。（Konna yasui kyūryō de wa *manzoku* dekimasen.）

②[じゅうぶんである様子、完全である様子]

¶1か月5万円では満足な生活はできません。（Ikkagetsu goman'en de wa *manzoku* na seikatsu wa deki-masen.）

¶あの人は易しい質問にも満足に答えられません。（Ano hito wa yasashii shitsumon ni mo *manzoku* ni kotaeraremasen.）

まんなか　真ん中〔名〕

①[中心の辺り]

¶町の真ん中に公園があります。（Machi no *mannaka* ni kōen ga arimasu.）

②[上下・左右の両端からみてちょうど中間のところ]

¶このひもを真ん中から切ってください。（Kono himo o *mannaka* kara kitte kudasai.）

¶上の子は中学2年生で真ん中は小学校の6年生、下のは4年生です。（Ue no ko wa chūgaku ninensei de *mannaka* wa shōgakkō no rokunensei, shita no wa yonensei desu.）

まんねんひつ　万年筆〔名〕

¶この万年筆は使いやすいです。（Kono *mannenhitsu* wa tsukaiyasui desu.）

¶ I **am** fully **satisfied** with my present life.

¶ [I] **cannot be satisfied** with such low wages.

② [perfect, complete, adequate, proper]

¶ One cannot live **adequately** on fifty thousand yen a month.

¶ [He] cannot answer even easy questions **satisfactorily**.

mannaka 〔n〕 **center; middle, halfway**

① [center]

¶ There is a park in **the center** of town 〚in **the heart** of the city〛.

② [middle, halfway]

¶ Please cut this string **in the middle**.

¶ [Our] oldest child is in the second year of junior high school, **the middle child** in the sixth year of elementary school, and the youngest child in the fourth year of elementary school.

mannenhitsu 〔n〕 **fountain pen**

¶ This **fountain pen** is easy to use.

み

み 実〔名〕

① [草や木の果実]

¶庭の木に実がなりました。(Niwa no ki ni *mi* ga narimashita.)

② [努力の結果]

¶上田さんの努力は、立派に実を結びました。(Ueda san no doryoku wa, rippa ni *mi* o musubimashita.)

*「実を結ぶ (mi o musubu)」の形で使う。

みえる 見える〔動Ⅱ〕

① [目にうつる]

¶わたしの部屋から山が見えます。(Watashi no heya kara yama ga *miemasu*.)

¶向こうに見えるのが、わたしたちの学校です。(Mukō ni *mieru* no ga, watashitachi no gakkō desu.)

② [見ることができる]

¶ねこは夜でも目が見えます。(Neko wa yoru demo me ga *miemasu*.)

③ [そのように感じられる]

¶あの人は若く見えます。(Ano hito wa wakaku *miemasu*.)

みおくる 見送る〔動Ⅰ〕

¶友達を見送りに空港へ行きました。(Tomodachi o *miokuri* ni kūkō e ikimashita.)

みがく〔動Ⅰ〕

¶わたしは毎朝歯をみがきます。(Watashi wa maiasa ha o **migakimasu**.)

---

mi 〔n〕 fruit; result

① [fruit, nut, berry, seed]

¶ The trees in the yard 〚garden〛 are 〚were〛 in fruit.

② [result, fruit of one's labors]

¶ [Mr.] Ueda's efforts **paid off** 〚**have paid off**〛 handsomely.

*Used in the pattern "*mi o musubu*."

mieru 〔v Ⅱ〕 see, be visible; be able to see; look, appear, seem

① [see, be visible]

¶ **You can see** the mountains from my room 〚apartment〛.

¶ What **you see** over there is our school.

② [be able to see]

¶ Cats **can see** even at night.

③ [look, appear, seem]

¶ [She] **looks** younger than [she] is.

miokuru 〔v Ⅰ〕 see off

¶ [I] went to the airport **to see off** a friend.

migaku 〔v Ⅰ〕 polish, clean

¶ I **brush** my teeth every morning.

¶くつをみがいてください。（Kutsu o *migaite* kudasai.）

¶ Please **polish** my shoes.

みかん〔名〕

mikan 〘n〙 **mandarin orange, tangerine**

みぎ 右〔名〕

右手（*migi*te）右足（*migi*ashi）

¶日本では人は道の右側を歩きます。（Nihon de wa hito wa michi no *migi*gawa o arukimasu.）
⇔左 hidari

migi 〘n〙 **the right**

one's **right** hand 〚arm〛 // one's **right** foot 〚leg〛

¶ People walk on the **right-hand** side of the road in Japan.

みごと〔形動〕

¶これはみごとなりんごですね。（Kore wa *migoto* na ringo desu ne.）
¶公園の桜がみごとに咲きました。（Kōen no sakura ga *migoto* ni sakimashita.）
¶今度の計画はみごとに成功しました。（Kondo no keikaku wa *migoto* ni seikō shimashita.）

migoto 〘adj-v〙 **fine, excellent, superb, splendid, beautiful**

¶ This is a **superb** apple.

¶ The cherry blossoms in the park were 〚are〛 **in their full splendor**.

¶ The plan this time succeeded **beautifully**.

みじかい 短い〔形〕

①［もののある点からある点までの間隔が小さい］
¶このひもは短いです。（Kono himo wa *mijikai* desu.）
¶あの女の子は短いスカートをはいています。（Ano onna no ko wa *mijikai* sukāto o haite imasu.）
②［時間の間隔が小さい］
¶授業と授業の間に短い休みがあります。（Jugyō to jugyō no aida ni *mijikai* yasumi ga arimasu.）
③［忍耐力がない］

mijikai 〘adj〙 **short; brief**

① [short, too short]

¶ This string 〚cord, lace, band, ribbon, etc.〛 **is short** 〚**too short**〛.
¶ That girl is wearing a **short** skirt.

② [brief]

¶ There is a **short** break between classes.

③ [short-tempered]

811

¶あの人は気が短くてすぐ怒ります。
（Ano hito wa ki ga *mijikakute* sugu okorimasu.)

* 「気が短い（ki ga mijikai）」の形で使う。

⇔長い **nagai**

¶ [He] **is short-tempered** and angers very easily.

*Used in the pattern **"ki ga mijikai."**

ミシン〔名〕
ミシンで縫う（*mishin* de nuu）

mishin 〔n〕 **sewing machine**
sew on **a sewing machine**, sew by **machine**

みず 水〔名〕
水を飲む（*mizu* o nomu）
¶冷たい水を一杯ください。（Tsume-tai *mizu* o ippai kudasai.)
¶のどが渇いて、水が飲みたくなりました。（Nodo ga kawaite, *mizu* ga nomitaku narimashita.)

mizu 〔n〕 **(cold) water**
drink **water**
¶ Please give me a glass of cold **water**.

¶ [I] became thirsty and wanted **some water** to drink 〖I am thirsty and want **some water** to drink〗.

みずうみ 湖〔名〕
¶琵琶湖は日本でいちばん大きい湖です。（Biwako wa Nihon de ichiban ookii *mizuumi* desu.)
¶この湖はとても深いです。（Kono *mizuumi* wa totemo fukai desu.)

mizuumi 〔n〕 **lake**
¶ Lake Biwa is the largest **lake** in Japan.

¶ This **lake** is very deep.

みせ 店〔名〕

店が開いている（*mise* ga aite iru）店が閉まっている（*mise* ga shimatte iru）
¶あなたはどの店でその品物を買いましたか。（Anata wa dono *mise* de sono shinamono o kaimashita ka？）

mise 〔n〕 **store, office, firm, place of business, restaurant, coffee shop, bar, etc.**
be open, be open for business // be closed
¶ **Where** did you buy that merchandise?

みせる 見せる〔動Ⅱ〕
¶ちょっと、その新聞を見せてください。（Chotto, sono shinbun o *misete* kudasai.)

miseru 〔v Ⅱ〕 **show, let see**
¶ Please **let me see** that newspaper a moment.

¶本がないので、隣の人に見せてもらいました。(Hon ga nai node, tonari no hito ni *misete* moraimashita.)

¶ As I didn't have a copy of that book, I **looked at** the one of the person sitting next to me.

みそ〔名〕

みそしる（*misoshiru*）
¶みそは豆から造ります。(*Miso* wa mame kara tsukurimasu.)

miso〔n〕 **miso**

miso shiru, **miso** soup
¶ *Miso* is made from soybeans.

みたいだ〔助動〕

① [外観がほかのものに似ているという意味を表す]
¶あの岩は人の顔みたいです。(Ano iwa wa hito no kao *mitai desu*.)
¶マッチ箱みたいに小さな家ですね。(Matchibako *mitai ni* chiisana ie desu ne.)
② [そのように感じられる]
¶熱があって、風邪を引いたみたいです。(Netsu ga atte, kaze o hiita *mitai desu*.)
¶ 弟 のほうが 頭 がいいみたいです。(Otōto no hō ga atama ga ii *mitai desu*.)
③ [あるものごとを例として示す]

¶あしたも今日みたいにいい天気だといいですね。(Ashita mo kyō *mitai ni* ii tenki da to ii desu ne.)
¶あの人みたいに上手に日本語が話したいです。(Ano hito *mitai ni* jōzu ni Nihongo ga hanashitai desu.)

mitai da〔auxil〕 **like, similar to; seems, looks like; like, the same way**
① [like, similar to]

¶ That rock 〚crag〛 **looks like** a human face.

¶ It is a small, matchbox-**like** house.

② [seems, looks like]
¶ [I] have a fever; **it seems** [I]'ve caught a cold.

¶ **It seems** that the younger brother is smarter 〚smartest〛.

③ [like, the same way; used when citing something as an example]
¶ I hope that tomorrow will be another nice day **like** today.

¶ I would like to be able to speak Japanese well **like** [she] does.

みち 道〔名〕

道を間違える（*michi* o machigaeru）道が悪い（*michi* ga warui）道を尋ねる（*michi* o tazuneru）
¶交番で道をききました。(Kōban de *michi* o kikimashita.)

michi〔n〕 **road, street, way**

take the wrong **way** 〚**turning**〛 // **the roads** are bad // ask **the way**, ask for **directions**

¶ [I] asked **the way** at a police box.

¶学校へ行く道で、おじさんに会いました。(Gakkō e iku *michi* de, ojisan ni aimashita.)

¶**On [my] way** to school, [I] happened to meet my uncle.

みっか 三日 〔名〕

mikka 〔n〕 **the third of the month; three days**

① [日付を表す]
三月三日 (sangatsu *mikka*)

① [the third of the month]
March 3

② [日数を表す]
¶わたしは三日間の旅行をしました。(Watashi wa *mikka*kan no ryokō o shimashita.)
⇒-日 **-ka**

② [three days]
¶I went on a **three-day** trip.

みつかる 見つかる 〔動 I〕

mitsukaru 〔v I〕 **be found, be discovered**

¶なくした万年筆が見つかりました。(Nakushita mannenhitsu ga *mitsukarimashita*.)

¶The lost fountain pen **has been found**.

¶いいアパートを探していますが、なかなか見つかりません。(Ii apāto o sagashite imasu ga, nakanaka *mitsukarimasen*.)

¶[I] am looking for a nice apartment but **am having a hard time finding one**.

みつける 見つける 〔動 II〕

mitsukeru 〔v II〕 **find, discover**

¶友達の家を見つけるのに苦労しました。(Tomodachi no ie o *mitsukeru* no ni kurō shimashita.)

¶[I] had a hard time **finding** [my] friend's house.

¶先日、本屋で珍しい本を見つけました。(Senjitsu, hon'ya de mezurashii hon o *mitsukemashita*.)

¶[I] **discovered** a rare 〚unusual〛 book at the bookstore the other day.

みっつ 三つ 〔名〕

mittsu 〔n〕 **three, three items; three years old**

① [3個]
¶ここにりんごが三つあります。(Koko ni ringo ga *mittsu* arimasu.)

① [three, three items]
¶There are **three** apples here.

② [3歳]
¶うちの子はまだ三つです。(Uchi no ko wa mada *mittsu* desu.)

② [three years old]
¶Our child is only **three years old**.

みとめる 認める〔動Ⅱ〕

① [そうであると判断する]

¶田中さんは、自分の間違いをなかなか認めません。(Tanaka san wa, jibun no machigai o nakanaka *mitomemasen*.)

② [許す]

¶父はわたしの日本への留学を認めてくれませんでした。(Chichi wa watashi no Nihon e no ryūgaku o *mitomete* kuremasen deshita.)

みどり 緑〔名〕

緑色 (*midori*iro)

¶5月は木や草の緑がきれいです。(Gogatsu wa ki ya kusa no *midori* ga kirei desu.)

みな 皆〔名、副〕

1〔名〕

¶皆の意見が一致しました。(*Mina* no iken ga itchi shimashita.)

¶皆さん、お元気ですか。(*Minasan*, ogenki desu ka？)

2〔副〕

¶冷蔵庫の中の食べ物は皆食べてしまいました。(Reizōko no naka no tabemono wa *mina* tabete shimaimashita.)

⇒みんな minna

みなと 港〔名〕

¶船が港に入ってきました。(Fune ga *minato* ni haitte kimashita.)

¶荷物が港に着いたので、取りに行きました。(Nimotsu ga *minato* ni tsuita node, tori ni ikimashita.)

mitomeru 〔v Ⅱ〕 **recognize, admit; approve, grant**

① [recognize, admit]

¶[Mr.] Tanaka **doesn't** readily **admit** [his] own mistakes.

② [approve, grant]

¶My father **didn't approve** of my going to Japan to study.

midori 〔n〕 **green**

green, the color **green**

¶**The green** of the trees and grass is pretty in May.

mina 〔n, adv〕 **all, everyone; everything**

1 〔n〕 everyone

¶**Everyone** held the same view.

¶Are **you and your family all** well? 〖And how is **everyone** today?; Hello ladies and gentlemen〗.

2 〔adv〕 everything

¶[We] ate **everything** that was in the refrigerator.

minato 〔n〕 **harbor, port**

¶A ship has entered **the harbor** 〖A ship came into **the harbor**〗.

¶The freight 〖luggage〗 had arrived at **the harbor** so [I] went to pick it up.

みなみ 南 〔名〕

南の風 (minami no kaze)
¶バナナは南の国の果物です。
(Banana wa minami no kuni no kudamono desu.)
⇔北 kita

minami 〔n〕 south

south wind, a wind from **the south**
¶ The banana is a fruit grown in **southern** countries.

みのる 実る 〔動Ⅰ〕

①[実がつく]
¶秋になると、果物が実ります。(Aki ni naru to, kudamono ga minorimasu.)
¶天気がよかったので、稲がよく実りました。(Tenki ga yokatta node, ine ga yoku minorimashita.)
②[成果が上がる]
¶長い間の研究がやっと実りました。(Nagai aida no kenkyū ga yatto minorimashita.)

minoru 〔vⅠ〕 bear fruit, ripen; produce results

①[bear fruit, ripen]
¶ Fruit **ripens** in the fall.

¶ There **is** 〚**was**〛 a good rice **crop** because of the favorable weather.

②[produce results, bear fruit]
¶ The long months 〚years〛 of research finally **paid off** 〚**have** finally **paid off**〛.

みぶん 身分 〔名〕

身分証明書 (mibun-shōmeisho) 身分が高い (mibun ga takai) 身分が低い (mibun ga hikui)

mibun 〔n〕 social standing, rank, identity

identification, identification card 〚papers〛 // have a high **social standing** // have a low **social standing**

みほん 見本 〔名〕

見本市 (mihon'ichi)
¶見本を見て、買うか買わないか決めます。(Mihon o mite, kau ka kawanai ka kimemasu.)

mihon 〔n〕 sample, specimen, model, example

trade fair
¶ [I] will look at **a sample one** and decide whether or not to buy it.

みまい 見舞い 〔名〕

¶昨日、病気の友達のお見舞いに行きました。(Kinō, byōki no tomodachi no omimai ni ikimashita.)

mimai 〔n〕 an expression of sympathy, a condolence call or visit

¶ Yesterday [I] paid **a call** on a sick friend.

みみ 耳 〔名〕
耳が遠い (*mimi* ga tooi)

¶あの人は耳が聞こえません。(Ano hito wa *mimi* ga kikoemasen.)

mimi 〔n〕 **ear(s), hearing**
be hard of **hearing**, have difficulty in **hearing**
¶ [He] is **deaf**.

みやげ 土産 〔名〕

¶父が外国旅行の土産に時計を買ってきてくれました。(Chichi ga gaikoku ryokō no *miyage* ni tokei o katte kite kuremashita.)
¶友達のうちへお土産を持って行きました。(Tomodachi no uchi e o*miyage* o motte ikimashita.)

miyage 〔n〕 **souvenir, gift from one's travels**
¶ My father brought me a watch from his trip abroad.

¶ [I] took **a present** to my friend's home.

みょう 妙 〔形動〕
¶山田さんが妙な顔をしてこちらを見ていました。(Yamada san ga *myō* na kao o shite kochira o mite imashita.)
¶辺りが妙に静かになりました。(Atari ga *myō* ni shizuka ni narimashita.)

myō 〔adj-v〕 **strange, odd, singular**
¶ [Miss] Yamada looked over here with a **strange** look on [her] face.

¶ It fell **strangely** quiet.

みょうじ 名字 〔名〕
¶わたしの名字は田中で、名前は太郎です。(Watashi no *myōji* wa Tanaka de, namae wa Tarō desu.)
¶日本の名字で多いのは、鈴木、山田などです。(Nihon no *myōji* de ooi no wa, Suzuki, Yamada nado desu.)

myōji 〔n〕 **family name, surname**
¶ My **family name** is Tanaka and my given name is Tarō.

¶ **Surnames** frequent in Japan are Suzuki, Yamada, etc.

みょう- 明- 〔頭〕
明日 (*myō*nichi) 明後日 (*myō*gonichi) 明朝 (*myō*chō) 明晩 (*myō*ban)

myō- 〔pref〕 **tomorrow, the next**
tomorrow // the day after **tomorrow** // **tomorrow** morning // **tomorrow** evening, **tomorrow** night

みらい 未来〔名〕

¶未来の乗り物はどうなるでしょうか。(Mirai no norimono wa dō naru deshō ka?)
⇒現在 genzai 過去 kako

mirai 〔n〕 **future**

¶ What do you suppose the vehicles of **the future** will be like?

-ミリ〔尾〕

1ミリ (ichimiri) 10ミリ (jūmiri)

-miri 〔suf〕 **millimeter(s)**

one **millimeter** // 10 **millimeters**

みる 診る〔動Ⅱ〕

¶風邪がなかなか治らないので、医者に診てもらいました。(Kaze ga nakanaka naoranai node, isha ni mite moraimashita.)

miru 〔v Ⅱ〕 **see, consult**

¶ [I] **went to see** the doctor since [my] cold 〚case of the flu〛 didn't seem to be getting any better.

みる 見る〔動Ⅱ〕

miru 〔v Ⅱ〕 **see, look at; read, look through; examine, look up, try**

① [目で見る]
¶山田さんは部屋でテレビを見ています。(Yamada san wa heya de terebi o mite imasu.)

① [see, look at]
¶ [Miss] Yamada **is watching** television in [her] room.

¶昨日、わたしは映画を見に行きました。(Kinō, watashi wa eiga o mi ni ikimashita.)

¶ I went **to see** a movie yesterday.

② [読む]
¶毎朝、わたしは新聞を見てから、会社へ行きます。(Maiasa, watashi wa shinbun o mite kara, kaisha e ikimasu.)

② [read, look through]
¶ I go to work every morning after **taking a look** at the newspaper.

③ [調べる]

¶この言葉は、辞書を見ても意味がよくわかりません。(Kono kotoba wa, jisho o mite mo imi ga yoku wakarimasen.)

¶ちょっと料理の味を見てください。(Chotto ryōri no aji o mite kudasai.)

③ [examine, look over, look up, consult, test, try]
¶ I don't really understand the meaning of this word even after **looking it up** in the dictionary.

¶ Please **see what you think** of the flavoring of this dish.

818

(-て) みる 〔連〕

¶おいしいかどうか、食べてみてください。(Oishii ka dō ka, tabete *mite* kudasai.)

¶その人がいい人かどうか、会ってみなければわかりません。(Sono hito ga ii hito ka dō ka, atte *minakereba* wakarimasen.)

(-te)miru 〔compd〕 **try, have a try at, test**

¶Please taste it **and see** if it's any good.

¶You can't know what [he]'s like **unless you go ahead** and meet [him].

ミルク 〔名〕

¶コーヒーにミルクを入れて飲みます。(Kōhii ni *miruku* o irete nomimasu.)

⇔牛乳 gyūnyū

miruku 〔n〕 **(cow's) milk**

¶[I] take my coffee with **milk**.

みんしゅしゅぎ 民主主義 〔名〕

minshushugi 〔n〕 **democracy**

みんぞく 民族 〔名〕

少数民族 (shōsū-*minzoku*) 民族学 (*minzoku*gaku) 民族主義 (*minzoku*-shugi) 民族性 (*minzoku*sei)

minzoku 〔n〕 **people, race, nation**

a minority, a minority **race** // ethnology // **national**ism, **racial**ism // the character of **a** people, **racial** characteristics

みんな 〔名、副〕

1 〔名〕

¶みんなでいっしょに歌いましょう。(*Minna* de issho ni utaimashō.)

＊「皆さん (minasan)」とは言うが、「みんなさん (minnasan)」とは言わない。

2 〔副〕

¶宿題はみんな終わりました。(Shukudai wa *minna* owarimashita.)

⇒皆 mina

minna 〔n, adv〕 **all, everyone; everything**

1 〔n〕 everyone

¶Let's **all** sing together.

＊*Minasan* is possible but *minnasan is not.

2 〔adv〕 everything

¶[I] have finished **all** the homework.

む

む(-) 無(-) 〔名、頭〕

1 〔名〕

¶ 長い間の努力が無になってしまいました。(Nagai aida no doryoku ga *mu* ni natte shimaimashita.)

2 〔頭〕

無意味 (*mu*imi) 無関係 (*mu*kankei)

むいか 六日 〔名〕

① [日付を表す]

一月六日 (ichigatsu *muika*)

② [日数を表す]

¶ 病気で六日入院しました。(Byōki de *muika* nyūin shimashita.)

⇒-日 -ka

むかう 向かう 〔動 I〕

① [何かをするときにそのものを正面に見ることができる姿勢をとる]

鏡に向かう (kagami ni *mukau*) 壁に向かう (kabe ni *mukau*)

¶ 試験があるので、毎日3時間机に向かうことにしています。(Shiken ga aru node, mainichi sanjikan tsukue ni *mukau* koto ni shite imasu.)

*普通、「～に向かう（～ni mukau）」の形で使う。

② [相手とする、対する]

¶ その子は歩いてくる父親に向かって手を振りました。(Sono ko wa aruite kuru chichioya ni *mukatte* te o furimashita.)

---

mu(-) 〖n, pref〗 **nothing, nil, zero**

1 〖n〗

¶ [Our] work for so long a time was all **in vain** 〖has all been **in vain**〗.

2 〖pref〗

meaning**less** // **un**related; **un**concerned; irrelevant

---

muika 〖n〗 **the sixth day of the month; six days**

① [the sixth day of the month]

January **6**

② [six days]

¶ [I] was hospitalized **for six days** due to illness.

---

mukau 〖v I〗 **face; meet, confront; facing one; proceed, head toward**

① [face, be opposite to]

look in the mirror // **face** the wall

¶ I make it a rule to spend three hours a day **at** my desk preparing for my examinations.

*Usually used in the pattern "～ *ni mukau*."

② [meet, confront]

¶ The child waved **to** [his] approaching father.

*普通、「〜に向かう（〜ni mukau）」の形で使う。

③ [自分の方から見て]

¶向かって右が銀行です。（*Mukatte migi ga ginkō desu.*）

*普通、「向かって右（mukatte mi-gi）」「向かって左（mukatte hidari）」の形で使う。

④ [ある方向へ進む、ある状態に近づく]

¶田中さんは今大阪へ向かっているところです。（Tanaka san wa ima Oosaka e *mukatte* iru tokoro desu.）

¶山田さんの病気はいいほうに向かっているそうです。（Yamada san no byōki wa ii hō ni *mukatte* iru sō desu.）

*普通、「〜へ向かう（〜e mukau）」「〜に向かう（〜ni mukau）」の形で使う。

むかえる　迎える〔動Ⅱ〕

① [人の来るのを待ち受ける]

¶父は田中さんを迎えに駅に行きました。（Chichi wa Tanaka san o *mukae* ni eki ni ikimashita.）

¶友達はわたしを喜んで迎えてくれました。（Tomodachi wa watashi o yorokonde *mukaete* kuremashita.）

② [その時の来るのを待つ]

¶母はお正月を迎える準備で忙しいです。（Haha wa oshōgatsu o *mukaeru* junbi de isogashii desu.）

むかし　昔〔名〕

¶おじいさんは、わたしに昔のことを話してくれました。（Ojiisan wa, wata-

*Usually used in the pattern "〜 *ni mukau*."

③ [facing one, opposite one]

¶ The bank is **on your** right.

*Usually used in the patterns "*mukatte migi*" and "*mukatte hidari*."

④ [proceed, head toward, tend toward]

¶ [Mr.] Tanaka **is** now **on [his] way to** Osaka.

¶ I hear that [Mrs.] Yamada's illness **has taken a turn for** the better.

*Usually used in the patterns "〜 *e mukau*" and "〜 *ni mukau*."

mukaeru 〔v Ⅱ〕 meet, welcome; greet

① [meet, welcome, receive]

¶ My father went to the station **to meet** [Mr.] Tanaka.

¶ My friends **greeted** me happily.

② [greet; await a certain time]

¶ My mother is busy with preparations **for** the New Year's holidays.

mukashi 〔n〕 ancient times, former days, the past

¶ My grandfather told me about **past times**.

shi ni *mukashi* no koto o hanashite
kuremashita.)

¶ 昔々、ある所におじいさんとおばあ
さんがいました。(Mukashi *mukashi*,
aru tokoro ni ojiisan to obāsan ga
imashita.)

¶ **Once upon a time** there was an old
man and an old woman.

むぎ 麦 〔名〕

大麦 (oo*mugi*) 小麦 (ko*mugi*)

¶ ビールは大麦から造ります。(Biiru
wa oo*mugi* kara tsukurimasu.)

mugi 〔n〕 **wheat, barley**

barley // wheat

¶ Beer is made from **barley**.

(-)むき (-)向き 〔名、尾〕

1 〔名〕

¶ 机の向きを変えましょう。(Tsukue
no *muki* o kaemashō.)

2 〔尾〕

① 〔方向〕

¶ 南向きの部屋は、日がよく当たりま
す。(Minami *muki* no heya wa, hi ga
yoku atarimasu.)

② [適していること]

¶ この料理は子供向きですね。(Kono
ryōri wa kodomo *muki* desu ne.)

¶ 若い女の人向きの仕事があります
よ。(Wakai onna no hito *muki* no shigoto
ga arimasu yo.)

(-)muki 〔n, suf〕 **direction;
suitability**

1 〔n〕 direction, position

¶ Let's change **the position** of the
desks.

2 〔suf〕

① [direction, exposure]

¶ Rooms with a southern **exposure** are
sunny.

② [suitability]

¶ This meal 〚dish〛 is **for** children.

¶ There is a job available **for** a young
woman.

むく 向く 〔動Ⅰ〕

① [その方向に面する]

¶ わたしの部屋は南に向いています。
(Watashi no heya wa minami ni *muite*
imasu.)

② [体または顔をその方向へ回す]

下を向く (shita o *muku*)

¶ 写真を撮りますから、こちらを向い
てください。(Shashin o torimasu kara,
kochira o *muite* kudasai.)

muku 〔v I〕 **face; turn toward,
look toward; suit, be geared for**

① [face, front on]

¶ My room **faces** south.

② [turn toward, look toward]

look down, lower **one's gaze**

¶ Please **look** this way; I'm going to
take the photo now.

③ [適する]

¶この仕事は老人に向いています。
（Kono shigoto wa rōjin ni *muite* imasu.）

¶この服は若い人には向きません。
（Kono fuku wa wakai hito ni wa *mukimasen*.）

むく〔動 I〕

¶みかんの皮をむきました。（Mikan no kawa o *mukimashita*.）

¶わたしはりんごの皮をむかないで食べます。（Watashi wa ringo no kawa o *mukanaide* tabemasu.）

むける 向ける〔動 II〕

¶恥ずかしいので、顔を下に向けたまま黙っていました。（Hazukashii node, kao o shita ni *muketa* mama damatte imashita.）

¶大きな音がしたので、皆その方に目を向けました。（Ookina oto ga shita node, mina sono hō ni me o *mukemashita*.）

¶山田さんは秋子さんにカメラを向けて、写真を撮りました。（Yamada san wa Akiko san ni kamera o *mukete*, shashin o torimashita.）

むこう 向こう〔名〕

① [ある物を隔てた反対の側]
¶あの山の向こう側に湖があります。
（Ano yama no *mukō*gawa ni mizuumi ga arimasu.）

¶敵は川の向こうまで来ています。
（Teki wa kawa no *mukō* made kite imasu.）

③ [suit, be geared for]

¶ This job **is suitable** for an elderly person.

¶ This outfit **is too old** for someone young.

muku〔v I〕**peel, pare, skin**

¶ [I] **peeled** a mandarin orange.

¶ I eat apples **without paring** them.

mukeru〔v II〕**turn toward, point at**

¶ Embarrassed〚Ashamed〛, **I kept** my head **down** and remained silent.

¶ Everyone turned and looked **in the direction** of the loud noise.

¶ [Mr.] Yamada **aimed** the camera **at** Akiko and took her picture.

mukō〔n〕**the other side; in front of one; beyond; one's destination, over there**

① [the other side, the opposite side]
¶ There is a lake on **the other side** of that mountain.

¶ The enemy has advanced up to **the opposite side** of the river.

② [先の方、前の方、正面]

¶向こうから来るのは山田さんのようです。(*Mukō* kara kuru no wa Yamada san no yō desu.)

¶向こうに見えるのが富士山です。(*Mukō* ni mieru no ga Fujisan desu.)

③ [少し離れている所]

¶子供は向こうへ行って遊んでいなさい。(Kodomo wa *mukō* e itte asonde inasai.)

④ [行く先、話題になっている遠方の場所]

¶向こうに着いたら、手紙をください。(*Mukō* ni tsuitara, tegami o kudasai.)

¶「昨日、アメリカから帰ってきました。」(Kinō, Amerika kara kaette kimashita.)「向こうの生活はいかがでしたか。」(*Mukō* no seikatsu wa ikaga deshita ka？)

② [in front of one, the opposite direction]

¶ That seems to be [Mr.] Yamada coming towards us.

¶ **Over there** you can see Mount Fuji.

③ [beyond, over there; somewhat distant]

¶ Children, go play **over there**.

④ [one's destination, over there; a distant place that is being talked about]

¶ Please write [us] after you arrive **there**.

¶ "I arrived back from the United States yesterday."
"What was it like living **there?**"

むし 虫 〔名〕

¶虫に刺されてかゆいので、薬をつけました。(*Mushi* ni sasarete kayui node, kusuri o tsukemashita.)

¶庭で虫が鳴いています。(Niwa de *mushi* ga naite imasu.)

mushi 〔n〕 **insect, bug**

¶ I put some medication on an **insect** bite that was itching.

¶ **Insects** are singing in the garden 〚yard〛.

むしば 虫歯 〔名〕

¶甘いものをたくさん食べると、虫歯になります。(Amai mono o takusan taberu to, *mushiba* ni narimasu.)

¶虫歯が痛くて、ものが食べられません。(*Mushiba* ga itakute, mono ga taberaremasen.)

mushiba 〔n〕 **decayed tooth**

¶ One will get **cavities** if one eats a lot of sweets.

¶ **My bad tooth** aches so much that I can't eat.

むしろ〔副〕

¶わたしは甘い物よりむしろ辛い物の
ほうが好きです。(Watashi wa amai
mono yori *mushiro* karai mono no hō ga
suki desu.)
¶自分で木を買って作るよりむしろこ
の箱を買ったほうが安いです。(Jibun
de ki o katte tsukuru yori, *mushiro* kono
hako o katta hō ga yasui desu.)

mushiro 〔adv〕 **rather (than),
better, sooner**

¶ I like nonsweet 〚salty〛 foods **better
than** sweet ones.

¶ It will be cheaper to buy this box
〚chest, casket, case, etc.〛 **than** to buy
the wood and make it oneself.

むずかしい 難しい〔形〕

¶この本は難しくてわかりません。
(Kono hon wa *muzukashikute*
wakarimasen.)
¶日本語は難しいですか。(Nihongo
wa *muzukashii* desu ka？)
¶この事件の解決はなかなか難しそう
です。(Kono jiken no kaiketsu wa
nakanaka *muzukashisō* desu.)
⇔易しい yasashii

muzukashii 〔adj〕 **difficult, hard**

¶ This book **is so hard** that I can't
understand it.

¶ Is Japanese **difficult?**

¶ **It looks like** this incident **will be**
quite **difficult** to resolve.

むすこ 息子〔名〕
¶うちの息子は来年の3月に大学を卒
業します。(Uchi no *musuko* wa rainen
no sangatsu ni daigaku o sotsugyō
shimasu.)
¶山田さんは息子さんが一人と娘さん
が二人います。(Yamada san wa *musuko*
san ga hitori to musumesan ga futari
imasu.)
⇔娘 musume

musuko 〔n〕 **son, boy**

¶ Our **son** graduates from college in
March of next year.

¶ Ms Yamada has a son and two
daughters.

むすぶ 結ぶ〔動Ⅰ〕

①[糸・ひもなどをつなぎ合わせる、
ひもなどで締める]
糸を結ぶ(ito o *musubu*) ひもを結ぶ
(himo o *musubu*)

musubu 〔vⅠ〕 **tie, tie up; enter
into relations with, contract;
connect, link**
① [tie, tie up, fasten, bind, knot]

tie threads 〚lines〛 **together** // **tie**
shoelaces, **tie** a package with string, etc.

825

¶ネクタイはどのように結ぶのですか。(Nekutai wa dono yō ni *musubu* no desu ka？)

¶荷物をひもで結びましょう。(Nimotsu o himo de *musubimashō*.)

②[二つ以上のものの間に関係をつける]

¶二人はようやく結ばれて、来月結婚することになりました。(Futari wa yōyaku *musubarete*, raigetsu kekkon suru koto ni narimashita.)

③[離れている所の間に連絡をつける]

¶この島と東京を結ぶ船は、毎週土曜日に来ます。(Kono shima to Tōkyō o *musubu* fune wa, maishū doyōbi ni kimasu.)

¶ How does one **tie** a necktie?

¶ **Let's tie up** the package with cord 〚string, a strap, etc.〛.

② [enter into relations with, contract]

¶ The two have finally **gotten together** and will be married next month.

③ [connect, link]

¶ The ship **linking** this island with Tokyo comes every Saturday.

むすめ 娘 〔名〕

① [自分の女の子供]

¶いちばん上の娘は今年 18 です。(Ichiban ue no *musume* wa kotoshi jūhachi desu.)

⇔息子 musuko

② [若い未婚の女性]

¶道できれいな娘さんにあいさつされたが、だれだかわかりませんでした。(Michi de kirei na *musume*san ni aisatsu sareta ga, dare da ka wakarimasen deshita.)

musume 〔n〕 daughter; young unmarried girt or woman

① [daughter]

¶ My eldest **daughter** is 18 this year.

② [young unmarried girl or woman]

¶ A pretty **young lady** greeted me in the street but I don't know who she was.

むだ 〔名、形動〕

① [効果がない]

¶あの人にはいくら注意してもむだです。(Ano hito ni wa ikura chūi shite mo *muda* desu.)

muda 〔n, adj-v〕 useless, futile; wasteful

① [useless, futile, fruitless]

¶ **It's no use** no matter how many times one warns 〚reprimands〛 [him].

¶試験に落ちて、山田さんの努力もむだになりました。(Shiken ni ochite, Yamada san no doryoku mo *muda* ni narimashita.)
②[役に立たない使い方をする]
¶食べ物をむだにしてはいけません。(Tabemono o *muda* ni shite wa ikemasen.)
¶一日じゅう何もしないで、時間をむだに過ごしてしまいました。(Ichinichijū nani mo shinaide, jikan o *muda* ni sugoshite shimaimashita.)

むだん 無断〔名〕

¶あなたがいなかったので、無断で本を借りました。(Anata ga inakatta node, *mudan* de hon o karimashita.)
¶この池の魚を無断で捕ってはいけません。(Kono ike no sakana o *mudan* de totte wa ikemasen.)

むちゅう 夢中〔形動〕

¶このごろ、中村さんはカメラに夢中です。(Konogoro, Nakamura san wa kamera ni *muchū* desu.)
¶山田さんは夢中でテレビを見ています。(Yamada san wa *muchū* de terebi o mite imasu.)

むっつ 六つ〔名〕

①[6個]
¶ここにみかんが六つあります。(Koko ni mikan ga *muttsu* arimasu.)
②[6歳]
¶日本では六つで小学校に入学します。(Nihon de wa *muttsu* de shōgakkō ni nyūgaku shimasu.)

¶ All of [Mr.] Yamada's efforts **were in vain**—[he] failed [his] exam.

② [wasteful]
¶ One shouldn't **waste** food.

¶ [I] **wasted** my time doing nothing all day.

mudan 〚n〛 **without permission, without notice**
¶ You weren't here so I borrowed a book **without asking**.

¶ One mustn't fish in this pond **without permission**.

muchū 〚adj-v〛 **absorbed in, crazy about, abstracted**
¶ [Mr.] Nakamura is camera-**crazy** these days.

¶ [Mr.] Yamada **is absorbed** in a television program.

muttsu 〚n〛 **six, six items; six years old**
① [six, six items]
¶ There are **six** mandarin oranges here.

② [six years old]
¶ In Japan one enters elementary school at **six years of age**.

むね　胸〔名〕

¶先生はいつも胸のポケットにハンカチを入れています。(Sensei wa itsu mo *mune* no poketto ni hankachi o irete imasu.)

mune〔n〕**breast, chest, lungs, heart**

¶ [My] teacher 〖doctor〗 always has a handkerchief in his **breast** pocket.

むやみに〔副〕

¶むやみに食べると、おなかをこわしますよ。(Muyami ni taberuto, onaka o kowashimasu yo.)

¶むやみにお金を使ってはいけません。(Muyami ni okane o tsukatte wa ikemasen.)

muyami ni〔adv〕**immoderately, excessively, recklessly, indiscriminately**

¶ Eating **to excess** invites stomach trouble.

¶ You shouldn't **throw away** your money.

むら　村〔名〕

¶ここがわたしの生まれた村です。(Koko ga watashi no umareta *mura* desu.)

¶若い人は都会へ行ってしまい、村には年寄りと子供しかいません。(Wakai hito wa tokai e itte shimai, *mura* ni wa toshiyori to kodomo shika imasen.)

⇒町 **machi**

mura〔n〕**village**

¶ This is **the village** where I was born.

¶ The young people all leave for the city so that **the villages** are populated by the old and the very young.

むらさき　紫〔名〕

¶あの紫の花は何という名前ですか。(Ano *murasaki* no hana wa nan to iu namae desu ka？)

¶長い時間泳いでいたので、くちびるが紫色になりました。(Nagai jikan oyoide ita node, kuchibiru ga *murasaki*iro ni narimashita.)

murasaki〔n〕**purple**

¶ What is the name of that **purple** flower?

¶ As [he] was swimming for a long time, [his] lips turned 〖have turned〗 **blue** (literally, **purple**).

むり　無理〔名、形動〕

① [筋道が通らないこと、道理に合わないこと]

muri〔n, adj-v〕**unreasonable; impossible**

① [unreasonable, unwarrantable, unnatural]

¶2時間も待たされたんですから、あの人が怒るのも無理はありません。（Nijikan mo matasareta n desu kara, ano hito ga okoru no mo *muri* wa arimasen.)

¶ As [he] was kept waiting for two hours, **it's only natural** that [he] became angry.

¶あまり働かないで、お金をたくさん欲しいというのは無理です。（Amari hatarakanaide, okane o takusan hoshii to iu no wa *muri* desu.)

¶ **It's asking too much** to want a lot of money while not working much.

②[適当だと思われる程度を超えること、それを押し切ってすること]

② [impossible, forced, excessive, immoderate, too difficult]

¶病気のあとは無理をしないほうがいいです。（Byōki no ato wa *muri* o shinai hō ga ii desu.)

¶ It's best not **to overstrain oneself** after being ill.

¶お酒がきらいな人に無理にすすめてはいけません。（Osake ga kirai na hito ni *muri* ni susumete wa ikemasen.)

¶ One shouldn't **force** liquor on those who don't like to drink.

むりょう 無料 〔名〕

muryō 〔n〕 **free of charge**

¶6歳以下の子供はバスが無料です。（Rokusai ika no kodomo wa basu ga *muryō* desu.)

¶ The bus **is free** for children aged six and under.

¶500名に無料でせっけんを配りました。（Gohyakumei ni *muryō* de sekken o kubarimashita.)

¶ **Free** soap was distributed to five hundred persons.

⇔有料 **yūryō**

⇒ただ **tada**

め

め 芽 〔名〕

¶春になって、木や草が芽を出しました。（Haru ni natte, ki ya kusa ga *me* o dashimashita.）

(-)め (-)目 〔名、尾〕

1 〔名〕

① [ものを見る働きをする器官]
目を開ける（*me* o akeru）目を閉じる（*me* o tojiru）目薬（*me*gusuri）

¶目にごみが入って痛いです。（*Me* ni gomi ga haitte itai desu.）

② [目の働き、目でものを見ること]
¶ねこは暗いところでもよく目が見えます。（Neko wa kurai tokoro de mo yoku *me* ga miemasu.）

¶わたしは今朝6時に目を覚ましました。（Watashi wa kesa rokuji ni *me* o samashimashita.）

③ [思いがけないこと、好ましくないようなこと]
悲しい目にあう（kanashii *me* ni au）つらい目にあう（tsurai *me* ni au）いやな目にあう（iya na *me* ni au）

¶昨日はお金を盗まれて、ひどい目にあいました。（Kinō wa okane o nusumarete, hidoi *me* ni aimashita.）

④ [会う]
¶先日、お父様にお目にかかりました。（Senjitsu, otōsama ni o*me* ni kakarimashita.）

me 〔n〕 **sprout, bud**

¶ With the coming of spring, trees **budded** and grass **sprouted**.

(-)me 〔n, suf〕 **eye(s); eyesight, vision; -th, the counter for indicating order**

1 〔n〕

① [eye(s)]
open **one's eyes** // close **one's eyes** // **eye** medicine

¶ **[My] eye** hurts as there's some dirt in it.

② [eyesight, vision, look, glance]
¶ Cats **can see** well even in the dark.

¶ I **woke up** at six o'clock this morning.

③ [experience, bad experience]

suffer great sorrow, come to grief // have a bitter **experience**, suffer severely // have a humiliating **experience**

¶ I had a terrible **experience** yesterday—my money was stolen.

④ [see, meet]
¶ **I met** your father the other day.

¶このことについては、お目にかかっ
て直接申し上げます。（Kono koto ni
tsuite wa, *ome* ni kakatte chokusetsu
mōshiagemasu.）

2〔尾〕
1番め（ichiban*me*）10番め（jūban-
me）一つめ（hitotsu*me*）二つめ
（futatsu*me*）

¶右から3番めの人が上田さんです。
（Migi kara sanban*me* no hito ga Ueda san
desu.）

¶その駅はここから三つめです。
（Sono eki wa koko kara mittsu*me* desu.）

めい〔名〕
⇔おい oi

-めい -名〔尾〕

①[名前]
学校名（gakkō*mei*）会社名
（kaisha*mei*）
②[人数を数えるときの言葉]
数名（sū*mei*）15名（jūgo*mei*）

めいし 名刺〔名〕

めいじ 明治〔名〕

明治30年（*Meiji* sanjūnen）明治時代
（*Meiji*-jidai）

めいぼ 名簿〔名〕

¶新しい学生の名簿を作りました。
（Atarashii gakusei no *meibo* o
tsukurimashita.）

¶I will tell you about this matter **face-to-face**.

2 〖suf〗 -th
first // tenth // first // second

¶The person **third** from the right is [Miss] Ueda.

¶That station is the **third** one from here.

mei 〖n〗 niece

-mei 〖suf〗 **name; the counter for persons**
① [name]
a school **name** // a company **name**
② [the counter for persons]
several **persons** // 15 **persons**

meishi 〖n〗 **name card, business card**

meiji 〖n〗 **Meiji; the name of a Japanese emperor and of the era of his reign (1868—1912)**
Meiji 30 (1897) // the **Meiji** period

meibo 〖n〗 **list of names, register, roll**
¶[I] made up **a register** of new students.

めいれい　命令〔名、～する〕

¶父の命令でおじの家へ行きました。
（Chichi no *meirei* de oji no ie e
ikimashita.）
¶社長から外国へ行くように命令され
ました。（Shachō kara gaikoku e iku yō
ni *meirei* saremashita.）

meirei〔n, ～*suru*〕 order,
command, instructions

¶[I] went to my uncle's at **the
instruction** of my father.

¶[I] **was directed** to go abroad by the
president of the company.

めいわく　迷惑〔名、形動、～する〕

¶テレビの音が大きいと、近所の迷惑
になります。（Terebi no oto ga ookii to,
kinjo no *meiwaku* ni narimasu.）
¶御迷惑でしょうが、田中さんに会っ
た時この本を返してください。
（Go*meiwaku* deshō ga, Tanaka san ni atta
toki kono hon o kaeshite kudasai.）

meiwaku〔n, adj-v, ～*suru*〕
trouble, inconvenience,
annoyance, nuisance

¶Playing the television loud
inconveniences one's neighbors.

¶**I'm sorry to inconvenience you**, but
would you please return this book to
[Mr.] Tanaka when you see [him]?

めい-　名-〔頭〕

名人（*mei*jin）名演奏家（*mei*ensōka）
名画（*mei*ga）名曲（*mei*kyoku）名案
（*mei*an）

mei-〔pref〕 noted, celebrated,
distinguished

a **master**, an **expert** // a **master**
musician // a **famous** painting; an
excellent film // a **famous** musical
piece〖tune〗 // an **excellent** idea

-メートル〔尾〕

3メートル（san*mētoru*）

-mētoru〔suf〕 meter(s)

three **meters**

めかた　目方〔名〕

目方を量る（*mekata* o hakaru）目方が
増える（*mekata* ga fueru）目方が減る
（*mekata* ga heru）
¶病気のため、目方が10キロも減りま
した。（Byōki no tame, *mekata* ga jikkiro
mo herimashita.）
¶この荷物の目方はどのくらいです
か。（Kono nimotsu no *mekata* wa dono
kurai desu ka ？）

mekata〔n〕 weight

weigh something, weigh oneself // gain
weight // lose **weight**

¶Due to illness [I] lost 10 kilos.

¶How much does this load〖luggage,
freight〗 **weigh?**

めがね　眼鏡 〔名〕

眼鏡をかける（*megane* o kakeru）眼鏡を外す（*megane* o hazusu）

¶あの眼鏡をかけた人が田中さんです。（Ano *megane* o kaketa hito ga Tanaka san desu.）

megane 〔n〕 **glasses, eyeglasses**

wear **glasses** // take off **one's glasses**

¶ That person wearing **glasses** is [Mrs.] Tanaka.

めす　雌 〔名〕

⇔雄 osu

mesu 〔n〕 **female (animal)**

めずらしい　珍しい 〔形〕

① [たまにしかない]

¶東京で 12 月に雪が降るのは珍しいです。（Tōkyō de jūnigatsu ni yuki ga furu no wa *mezurashii* desu.）

¶今朝は珍しく早く起きました。（Kesa wa *mezurashiku* hayaku okimashita.）

② [目新しい]

¶動物園には珍しい動物がたくさんいます。（Dōbutsuen ni wa *mezurashii* dōbutsu ga takusan imasu.）

¶珍しい物をいただいてありがとうございました。（*Mezurashii* mono o itadaite arigatō gozaimashita.）

mezurashii 〔adj〕 **rare, infrequent; rare, unusual**

① [rare, infrequent]

¶ **It is rare** for snow to fall in Tokyo in December.

¶ [I] got up early today **for a change**.

② [rare, unusual, novel]

¶ There are many **rare** animals in the zoo.

¶ Thank you for the **lovely** (literally, **uncommon**) present.

めだつ　目立つ 〔動Ⅰ〕

¶上田さんは背が高いので、おおぜいの中でもよく目立ちます。（Ueda san wa se ga takai node, oozei no naka de mo yoku *medachimasu*.）

¶このクラスには目立ってよくできる人はいません。（Kono kurasu ni wa *medatte* yoku dekiru hito wa imasen.）

medatsu 〔v Ⅰ〕 **be conspicuous, stand out**

¶ As [Mr.] Ueda is tall, [he] **stands out** even in a crowd.

¶ There is no **conspicuously** outstanding student in this class.

833

めったに〔副〕

¶あの学生はめったに間違いをしませ
ん。(Ano gakusei wa *metta ni* machigai o
shimasen.)
¶この地方ではめったに地震は起こり
ません。(Kono chihō de wa *metta ni*
jishin wa okorimasen.)
＊あとに打ち消しの言葉が来る。

めでたい〔形〕

¶今日は娘が結婚するめでたい日で
す。(Kyō wa musume ga kekkon suru
medetai hi desu.)
¶上田さんはめでたく試験に合格しま
した。(Ueda san wa *medetaku* shiken ni
gōkaku shimashita.)

めん 綿〔名〕

綿のシャツ (*men* no shatsu)
⇒木綿 momen

(-)めん (-)面〔名、尾〕

1〔名〕
¶子供たちが動物の面をかぶって劇を
しました。(Kodomotachi ga dōbutsu no
men o kabutte geki o shimashita.)
2〔尾〕
¶今朝の新聞の第1面には飛行機事故
のことが出ていました。(Kesa no
shinbun no daiichi*men* ni wa hikōki-jiko
no koto ga dete imashita.)

めんきょ 免許〔名〕

自動車の運転免許 (jidōsha no unten-
menkyo)

めんせき 面積〔名〕

¶日本の面積は、 37 万平方キロメ
ートルです。(Nihon no *menseki* wa,
sanjūnanaman-heihōkiromētoru desu.)

---

metta ni 〔adv〕 **rarely, seldom**

¶ That student is **seldom** wrong.

¶ Earthquakes **are rare** in this area.

＊ *Metta ni* is used with the negative.

medetai 〔adj〕 **happy, auspicious**

¶ Today is the **happy** day of my
daughter's wedding.

¶ **Happily**, [Miss] Ueda passed the
exam.

men 〔n〕 **cotton**

a **cotton** shirt

(-)men 〔n, suf〕 **mask; page**

1 〔n〕 mask
¶ The children put on a play wearing
animal **masks**.

2 〔suf〕 page
¶ There was a story about an airplane
crash on the front **page** of the
newspaper this morning.

menkyo 〔n〕 **license, permit**

a **license** to drive a car, a driver's
license

menseki 〔n〕 **area**

¶ **The area** of Japan is 370,000 square
kilometers.

めんどう 〔名、形動〕

① [手数がかかる]

¶辞書を引くのがめんどうだから、友達に教えてもらいました。（Jisho o hiku no ga *mendō* da kara, tomodachi ni oshiete moraimashita.）

¶自分で料理を作るのは、とてもめんどうです。（Jibun de ryōri o tsukuru no wa, totemo *mendō* desu.）

② [世話をする]

¶あの子は妹のめんどうをよくみます。（Ano ko wa imōto no *mendō* o yoku mimasu.）

mendō 〔n, adj-v〕 **difficulty, bother; attention, care**

① [difficulty, bother, trouble, nuisance]

¶ I asked a friend about it as it's a **bother** to consult a dictionary.

¶ Doing one's own cooking **is a nuisance**.

② [attention, care]

¶ That child **takes** good **care of** [his] younger sister.

も

も〔助〕

① [前に述べたものごとと同類のもの
ごとであることを表す]

¶山田さんは先生です。上田さんも先
生です。(Yamada san wa sensei desu.
Ueda san *mo* sensei desu.)

¶あなたが行けば、わたしも行きま
す。(Anata ga ikeba, watashi *mo*
ikimasu.)

¶「これはいくらですか。」(Kore wa
ikura desu ka?)「それは100円です。」
(Sore wa hyakuen desu.)「じゃ、これ
は。」(Ja, kore wa?)「それも100円で
す。」(Sore *mo* hyakuen desu.)

¶「昨日、これをデパートで買いまし
た。」(Kinō, kore o depāto de kaimashita.)「その品物なら、スーパーマ
ーケットでも売っていますよ。」(Sono
shinamono nara, sūpāmāketto de *mo* utte
imasu yo.)

② [同類と認めるようなものごとを並
列するときに使う]

¶山田さんも中村さんも、もう帰りま
した。(Yamada san *mo* Nakamura san
mo, mō kaerimashita.)

¶わたしはひらがなも漢字も読めませ
ん。(Watashi wa hiragana *mo* kanji *mo*
yomemasen.)

¶雨も降ってきたし、風も強くなって
きました。(Ame *mo* futte kita shi, kaze
mo tsuyoku natte kimashita.)

mo 〔part〕 **also; both; as much as
that; even; neither ~ nor ~**

① [also, too; indicates someone or
something is the same sort as one
previously mentioned]

¶ [Mr.] Yamada is a teacher. [Mrs.]
Ueda is **also** a teacher.

¶ If you go, I'll go **too**.

¶ "How much is this?"
"That's a hundred yen."
"And this one?"
"That's **also** a hundred yen."

¶ "[I] bought this at a department store
yesterday."
"Oh, you can buy that at the
supermarket **too**."

② [both, either, neither; used when
citing items recognized as being alike]

¶ **Both** [Mr.] Yamada **and** [Miss]
Nakamura have already gone home.

¶ I can read **neither** *hiragana* **nor**
kanji.

¶ It has started to rain and the wind has
gotten stronger 〖It started to rain and
the wind picked up〗.

836

¶わたしはヨーロッパへもアメリカへも行ったことがありません。（Watashi wa Yōroppa e *mo* Amerika e *mo* itta koto ga arimasen.）

¶ I've never been to **either** Europe **or** the United States.

*「〜も〜も（〜mo〜mo）」の形で使う。

*Used in the pattern "〜 *mo* 〜 *mo*."

③[全面的な肯定または全面的な否定を表す]

③[indicates total affirmation or total negation]

¶山田さんは日曜日はいつもうちにいます。（Yamada san wa nichiyōbi wa itsu *mo* uchi ni imasu.）

¶ [Mr.] Yamada is **always** at home on Sunday.

¶わたしはみかんもりんごもどちらも好きです。（Watashi wa mikan mo ringo mo dochira *mo* suki desu.）

¶ I like **both** mandarin oranges and apples.

¶部屋にはだれもいません。（Heya ni wa dare *mo* imasen.）

¶ **Nobody** is in the room.

¶食べる物が何もありません。（Taberu mono ga nani *mo* arimasen.）

¶ There is **nothing** to eat.

¶この字引はどれも役に立ちません。（Kono jibiki wa dore *mo* yaku ni tachimasen.）

¶ **None** ⟦**Neither**⟧ of these dictionaries is of any use.

¶先月はだれからも手紙が来ませんでした。（Sengetsu wa dare kara *mo* tegami ga kimasen deshita.）

¶ There weren't any letters from **anyone** last month.

¶かぎはどこにもありません。（Kagi wa doko ni *mo* arimasen.）

¶ The keys are **nowhere** to be found.

¶国からは何の知らせも来ませんでした。（Kuni kara wa nan no shirase *mo* kimasen deshita.）

¶ There was **no** word of that from [my] native country ⟦hometown⟧.

*「何（nani）」「だれ（dare）」「どれ（dore）」「どちら（dochira）」「どこ（doko）」「いつ（itsu）」などの疑問の言葉につく。「どこにも（doko ni mo）」「だれからも（dare kara mo）」

Mo is added to interrogatives such as *nani, dare, dore, dochira, doko, itsu*, etc. It is sometimes used with other particles in between as in *doko ni mo, dare kara mo, doko kara mo*, etc. Also

「どこからも（doko kara mo）」などの
ように間に助詞が入ることもある。ま
た「何の（nan no）＋名詞＋も
（mo）」の形でも使う。

④ [主題としてものごとを提示するの
に使う]

¶長かった夏休みも終わって、あした
からまた学校が始まります。（Naga-
katta natuyasumi *mo* owatte, ashita kara
mata gakkō ga hajimarimasu.）

¶春が来て、富士山の雪も解け始めま
した。（Haru ga kite, Fujisan no yuki *mo*
tokehajimemashita.）

¶さっきまであんなに泣いていた赤ん
坊もようやく寝ました。（Sakki made
anna ni naite ita akanbō *mo* yōyaku
nemashita.）

*時の経過に伴って生起するような動
作・作用が起こる場合に、そのものご
とをある感慨をこめて取り上げるとき
に使う。夏休みもいつか終わり、春に
なると雪が解けるのは、時の経過に
伴って起こる動作・作用である。そう
したことが特に関心の深いものごとに
ついて起こる場合に、例えば、終わる
のはまだまだと思っていた夏休みもつ
いにとか、なかなか解けそうもない富
士山の雪もついにとかいうように、そ
のものごとを感慨をこめて取り上げる
ときに使う。

→は wa

⑤ [時間や数量などを表す言葉につい
てその時間や数量が予想外であるとい
う気持ちを表す]

used in the pattern "*nan no + noun +
mo*."

④ [used to indicate the subject matter]

¶ The long summer vacation has come
to an end, and school starts again
tomorrow.

¶ Spring has 〚had〛 come and the snow
on Mount Fuji has 〚had〛 started to
melt.

¶ The baby, crying so until a little
while ago, has finally fallen asleep.

*This *mo* is used when taking up with
some deep emotion acts or events
which happen naturally in the course of
time: summer vacation ending and
snow melting in the spring are things
that come about in the course of time.
Mo is used to cite such events when
one is particularly impressed or
affected, for example when the end of
summer vacation is suddenly upon one
when one wasn't expecting it or when
the snow on Mount Fuji which had
shown no signs of melting has
suddenly started to melt.

⑤ [as much as, as long as, as far as,
etc.; used with words indicating time
or amount when the total is larger than
expected]

¶雨はもう3日も降っています。（Ame wa mō mikka *mo* futte imasu.）

¶駅から学校まで歩いて20分もかかります。（Eki kara gakkō made aruite nijippun *mo* kakarimasu.）

¶おじさんはわたしに1万円もくれました。（Ojisan wa watashi ni ichiman'en *mo* kuremashita.）

*予想外に多いという気持ちなどを表す。あとに肯定の言い方が来る。

⑥ [時間や数量などの範囲や限界を表す]

¶それを買うのには1万円もあればじゅうぶんでしょう。（Sore o kau noni wa ichiman'en *mo* areba jūbun deshō.）

¶もうしばらく待ってください。10分もすれば彼は来ると思います。（Mō shibaraku matte kudasai. Jippun *mo* sureba kare wa kuru to omoimasu.）

*時間や数量などを表す言葉について、ある条件を述べるときに使う。

⑦ [ある極端な場合を取り上げてそのほかの場合も事情は同じであるという意味を表す]

¶立っていることもできないほど疲れました。（Tatte iru koto *mo* dekinai hodo tsukaremashita.）

¶恐ろしくて、声も出ませんでした。（Osoroshikute, koe *mo* demasen deshita.）

¶ It has been raining for three **whole** days now.

¶ It takes **all of** 20 minutes to walk from the station to school.

¶ My uncle gave me ten thousand yen!

*Used to express the feeling of something being unexpectedly large, etc. Followed by affirmative words or expressions.

⑥ [used to express the limits or parameters of a time or amount]

¶ Ten thousand yen should be enough to buy that.

¶ Please wait a little longer. He should be here in 10 minutes, I think.

*Used when stating some condition relating to words expressing time, amount, etc.

⑦ [even; used when citing an extreme case and indicating that something else is the same]

¶ [I]'m so tired [I] can't stand up much longer.

¶ [I] was so frightened [I] couldn't **even** speak.

¶もう半年も日本語を勉強したのに、まだひらがなも読めません。(Mō hantoshi mo Nihongo o benkyō shita noni, mada hiragana mo yomemasen.)

¶ Even though [I]'ve been studying Japanese for half a year now, [I] can't read **even** *hiragana* yet.

*あとに打ち消しの言葉が来る。

*Used with the negative.

→さえ **sae**

⑧ [あることがらを強調的に否定するのに使う]

⑧ [used to emphatically deny something]

¶外国へは一度も行ったことがありません。(Gaikoku e wa ichido mo itta koto ga arimasen.)

¶ [I]'ve never been abroad **even** a single time.

¶お金は今一円も持っていません。(Okane wa ima ichien mo motte imasen.)

¶ [I] don't have a **single** cent on me right now.

¶学生はまだ一人も来ていません。(Gakusei wa mada hitori mo kite imasen.)

¶ Not a **single** student is here yet.

*最小の意味を表す言葉につく。あとに打ち消しの言葉が来る。

*Added to words expressing the lowest possible amount. Used with the negative.

⑨ [あるものごとについて否定的な判断を続けて述べるのに使う]

⑨ [neither 〜 nor 〜 ; used to express a negative judgment about a series of items]

¶日本語は易しくも難しくもありません。(Nihongo wa yasashiku mo muzukashiku mo arimasen.)

¶ The Japanese language is **neither** easy **nor** difficult.

¶今日は暑くも寒くもありません。(Kyō wa atsuku mo samuku mo arimasen.)

¶ Today is **neither especially** hot **nor** cold.

¶映画は好きでもきらいでもありません。(Eiga wa suki de mo kirai de mo arimasen.)

¶ I don't **especially** like **or** dislike movies.

¶この言葉は英語でもドイツ語でもありません。(Kono kotoba wa Eigo de mo Doitsugo de mo arimasen.)

¶ This language is **neither** English **nor** German.

¶この本は田中さんのでも山田さんの
でもありません。（Kono hon wa Tanaka
san no de *mo* Yamada san no de *mo*
arimasen.）
*あとに打ち消しの言葉が来る。「〜も
〜も〜ない（〜mo 〜mo 〜nai）」の形
で使う。

¶ This book doesn't belong to **either**
[Miss] Tanaka **or** [Miss] Yamada.

*Used with the negative. Used in the
pattern "〜 *mo* 〜 *mo* -*nai*."

もう〔副〕

① [既に]
¶もう6時です。（*Mō* rokuji desu.）
¶上田さんはもう帰りました。（Ueda
san wa *mō* kaerimashita.）
¶日本へ来てから、もう10年になりま
す。（Nihon e kite kara, *mō* jūnen ni
narimasu.）
→まだ **mada**
② [間もなく]
¶弟はもう来ると思います。（Otōto
wa *mō* kuru to omoimasu.）
¶もうすぐ試験が始まります。（*Mō*
sugu shiken ga hajimarimasu.）
→まだ **mada**
③ [更に]
¶もう一度言ってください。
（*Mō* ichido itte kudasai.）
¶お茶をもう一杯いかがですか。
（Ocha o *mō* ippai ikaga desu ka？）

mō〔adv〕**already, yet; soon;
again**
① [already, yet]
¶ It's six o'clock **already**.
¶ [Mrs.] Ueda has **already** left for
home.
¶ I've **already** been in Japan for 10
years (literally, It's **already** 10 years
since I came to Japan).

② [soon, before long]
¶ I think my (younger) brother will be
here **soon**.
¶ The exam will **soon** start.

③ [again, another, more]
¶ Please say it once **again**.

¶ Would you like **another** cup of
(green) tea?

もうける〔動Ⅱ〕
お金をもうける（okane o *mōkeru*）
¶あの人は商売でずいぶんもうけたら
しいです。（Ano hito wa shōbai de
zuibun *mōketa* rashii desu.）

mōkeru〔v Ⅱ〕**profit, make money**
make money, make a profit
¶ It seems [he] **has done** very **well** in
business.

もうしあげる　申し上げる 〔動Ⅱ〕

¶このことについては、さっき申し上げたはずですが。(Kono koto ni tsuite wa sakki mōshiageta hazu desu ga.)

mōshiageru 〔vⅡ〕 **say, mention**

¶ I think I mentioned this matter a little while ago.

もうしこむ　申し込む 〔動Ⅰ〕

① [自分の希望などを相手に伝える]
¶社長に面会を申し込んだら、断られました。(Shachō ni menkai o *mōshikondara*, kotowararemashita.)

¶山田さんは春子さんに結婚を申し込んだらしいです。(Yamada san wa Haruko san ni kekkon o *mōshikonda* rashii desu.)

② [募集などに応じる]
¶あなたはもう研究会への参加を申し込みましたか。(Anata wa mō kenkyūkai e no sanka o *mōshikomimashita* ka?)

mōshikomu 〔vⅠ〕 **request, propose; apply for**

① [request, propose]
¶ **My request** for an interview with the company president was refused.

¶ It seems that Mr. Yamada **has proposed** to Haruko.

② [apply for]
¶ **Have you asked** if you could participate in the study meeting 〚**applied for** membership in the study group〛?

もうしわけない　申し訳ない 〔連〕

¶遅くなって申し訳ありません。
(Osoku natte *mōshiwake arimasen*.)
¶申し訳ないのですが、あしたの会議には出席できません。(*Mōshiwake* nai no desu ga, ashita no kaigi ni wa shusseki dekimasen.)

mōshiwake nai 〔compd〕 **a set expression of apology (literally, there's no excuse)**

¶ I'm terribly sorry to be late.

¶ I'm very sorry, but I won't be able to attend the meeting tomorrow.

もうす　申す 〔動Ⅰ〕
¶わたしは上田と申します。(Watashi wa Ueda to *mōshimasu*.)
¶皆様の御親切に対してお礼を申し上げます。(Minasama no goshinsetsu ni taishite orei o *mōshi*agemasu.)
＊「言う (iu)」の謙譲語。

mōsu 〔vⅠ〕 **say, call**
¶ My name is Ueda.

¶ I would like to thank all of you for your kindness.

＊*Mōsu* is the humble form of *iu*.

もうすぐ 〔副〕

¶もうすぐ、あの夫婦に子供が生まれます。(Mōsugu, ano fūfu ni kodomo ga umare masu.)

もうふ 毛布 〔名〕

¶寒いので、毛布を2枚掛けて寝ました。(Samui node, *mōfu* o nimai kakete nemashita.)

もえる 燃える 〔動Ⅱ〕

① [火が燃える]
¶火事でたくさんの家が燃えてしまいました。(Kaji de takusan no ie ga *moete* shimaimashita.)

② [盛んな気持ちが起こる]

¶希望に燃えて大学に入学しました。(Kibō ni *moete* daigaku ni nyūgaku shimashita.)

もくてき 目的 〔名〕

目的地 (*mokuteki*chi) 目的を果たす (*mokuteki* o hatasu)
¶わたしは日本文学を研究する目的で日本に来ました。(Watashi wa Nihon-bungaku o kenkyū suru *mokuteki* de Nihon ni kimashita.)
¶何の目的も持たないで大学へ入る人もいます。(Nan no *mokuteki* mo motanaide daigaku e hairu hito mo imasu.)

もくひょう 目標 〔名〕

目標を立てる (*mokuhyō* o tateru)

mōsugu 〔adv〕 **at any minute, soon**

¶The couple's baby will be born soon.

mōfu 〔n〕 **blanket**

¶As it was cold [I] slept with two **blankets**.

moeru 〔vⅡ〕 **burn; burn (with emotion)**

① [burn]
¶Many houses **burned down** in the fire.

② [burn, be aglow, be ablaze (with some emotion)]
¶[He] entered college **full of** hope.

mokuteki 〔n〕 **purpose, aim, objective**

one's destination // achieve **one's aim**, realize **one's objective**

¶I came to Japan **for the purpose** of studying Japanese literature.

¶There are those who enter college without any **purpose** whatsoever.

mokuhyō 〔n〕 **goal, target, objective, aim, mark**

set **a goal**

¶わたしの家は、大きな木を目標にして来ればすぐわかります。（Watashi no ie wa, ookina ki o *mokuhyō* ni shite kureba sugu wakarimasu.)

¶わたしは医学部へ入ることを目標に勉強しています。（Watashi wa igakubu e hairu koto o *mokuhyō* ni benkyō shite imasu.)

もくよう（び） 木曜（日）〔名〕

もぐる 潜る〔動 I〕

¶あの人たちは海に潜って、魚を捕っているのです。（Ano hitotachi wa umi ni *mogutte*, sakana o totte iru no desu.)

¶かえるは冬の間土の中に潜って過ごします。（Kaeru wa fuyu no aida tsuchi no naka ni *mogutte* sugoshimasu.)

もし〔副〕

¶もしあした雨が降ったら、テニスの試合はありません。（*Moshi* ashita ame ga futtara, tenisu no shiai wa arimasen.)

¶今度の日曜日にもし天気がよければ、山に行きます。（Kondo no nichiyōbi ni *moshi* tenki ga yokereba, yama ni ikimasu.)

¶もし食べたくないなら、食べなくてもいいですよ。（*Moshi* tabetaku nai nara, tabenakute mo ii desu yo.)

¶もしあの人が行かなくても、あなたは行きますか。（*Moshi* ano hito ga ikanakute mo, anata wa ikimasu ka？）

＊「もし（moshi）」は条件を表す「たら（tara）」「ば（ba）」「なら（nara）」「ても（te mo）」などとともに使う。

¶ You will soon find my house if you **look out for** a large tree.

¶ I am studying **with the goal** of getting into medical school.

mokuyō(bi) 〔n〕 **Thursday**

moguru 〔v I〕 **dive in, go in, go under, hole up in**

¶ Those men are **diving into** the ocean and catching fish.

¶ Frogs spend the winter **under** the ground.

moshi 〔adv〕 **if, provided that, in case of**

¶ There will be no tennis match tomorrow **if** it rains.

¶ [We] will go to the mountains next Sunday **if** the weather is nice.

¶ You don't have to eat **if** you don't want to.

¶ Are you going to go even **if** [he] doesn't?

＊*Moshi* is used together with expressions of condition such as *-tara, -ba, nara* and *-te mo*.

もじ 文字〔名〕

かな文字（kana*moji*）

¶世界には文字を持っていない民族もいます。（Sekai ni wa *moji* o motte inai minzoku mo imasu.）

moji 〔n〕 **letter, character**

the *kana***characters**

¶ There are peoples in the world without any **written language**.

もしもし〔感〕

① [電話で相手に話しかけるときの言葉]

¶もしもし、山田さんですか。わたしは田中ですが…。（Moshi moshi, Yamada san desu ka? Watashi wa Tanaka desu ga...）

② [知らない人などに対する呼びかけの言葉]

¶もしもし、ハンカチが落ちましたよ。（Moshi moshi, hankachi ga ochimashita yo.）

moshi moshi 〔interj〕 **Hello; Excuse me**

① [Hello; used when addressing someone on the telephone]

¶ **Hello**, is that [Mr.] Yamada? This is [Mr.] Tanaka.

② [Excuse me; used to address a stranger]

¶ **Excuse me!** You've dropped your handkerchief.

もす 燃す〔動Ⅰ〕

¶古い手紙や日記を燃しました。（Furui tegami ya nikki o *moshimashita*.）

¶マッチで火をつけて、紙を燃しました。（Matchi de hi o tsukete, kami o *moshimashita*.）

➡燃やす **moyasu**

mosu 〔vⅠ〕 **burn, put to the flame, ignite**

¶ [I] **burned** [my] old letters and diaries.

¶ [I] lit the paper with a match and **burned** it.

もちいる 用いる〔動Ⅱ〕

¶この機械には、新しい電池が用いられています。（Kono kikai ni wa, atarashii denchi ga *mochiirarete* imasu.）

⇒使う **tsukau**

mochiiru 〔vⅡ〕 **use**

¶ A new type of battery **is used** in this machine.

もちろん〔副〕

¶もちろん銀行は日曜日はお休みです。（*Mochiron* ginkō wa nichiyōbi wa oyasumi desu.）

mochiron 〔adv〕 **of course, needless to say**

¶ **Of course** banks are closed on Sunday.

845

¶山田さんは、英語はもちろんフランス語も話せます。(Yamada san wa, Eigo wa *mochiron* Furansugo mo hanasemasu.)

¶ [Miss] Yamada speaks French, **not to mention** English.

もつ　持つ〔動 I〕

motsu 〔v I〕 **hold, carry; have with one, own, possess; have, harbor; be in charge of, pay**

① [手に取る]

① [hold, carry, take]

¶この荷物は重くて、一人では持つことができません。(Kono nimotsu wa omokute, hitori de wa *motsu* koto ga dekimasen.)

¶ These bags〖packages, etc.〗are too heavy for one person **to carry**.

¶すみませんが、この荷物を持ってください。(Sumimasen ga, kono nimotsu o *motte* kudasai.)

¶ Could you please **carry** this bag 〖package, load, etc.〗for me?

② [身につける、所有する]

② [have with one, own, possess]

¶あなたは時計を持っていますか。(Anata wa tokei o *motte* imasu ka？)

¶ **Are you wearing** a watch〖**Do you own** a watch〗?

¶今、わたしはお金を持っていません。(Ima, watashi wa okane o *motte* imasen.)

¶ **I don't have** any〖that much〗money on me at the moment.

③ [心にいだく]

③ [have, harbor, cherish, be endowed with]

¶わたしは日本文化に興味を持っています。(Watashi wa Nihon-bunka ni kyōmi o *motte* imasu.)

¶ I'm interested (literally, **have** an interest) in Japanese culture.

④ [負担する、受け持つ]

④ [be in charge of, pay, stand]

¶山田先生はAクラスを持っています。(Yamada sensei wa Ē-kurasu o *motte* imasu.)

¶ Professor Yamada **is in charge of** Class A.

¶今度の旅行の費用は会社が持ってくれます。(Kondo no ryokō no hiyō wa kaisha ga motte kuremasu.)

¶ The company **will bear** the expenses of the coming trip.

もったいない〔形〕

mottainai 〔adj〕 **wasteful**

¶その鉛筆はまだ書けますから、捨てるのはもったいないです。(Sono

¶ That pencil can still be used; it's a **shame** to throw it away.

enpitsu wa mada kakemasu kara, suteru no wa *mottainai* desu.)

¶ 待っている時間がもったいないので、本を読んでいました。(Matte iru jikan ga *mottainai* node, hon o yonde imashita.)

¶ [I] read a book so as **not to waste** the time [I] spent waiting.

もっていく 持って行く〔連〕

motte iku 〔compd〕 **take, take along**

¶ 学校へ行くときは、このかばんを持って行きます。(Gakkō e iku toki wa, kono kaban o *motte ikimasu*.)

¶ [I] **take** this bag〚briefcase, etc.〛 when [I] go to school.

¶ これを山田さんのところへ持って行ってください。(Kore o Yamada san no tokoro e *motte itte* kudasai.)

¶ Please **take** this to [Mr.] Yamada.

もってくる 持って来る〔連〕

motte kuru 〔compd〕 **bring, fetch**

¶ その本をここに持って来てください。(Sono hon o koko ni *motte kite* kudasai.)

¶ Please **bring** that book to me.

¶ あなたに借りた本は、あした持って来ます。(Anata ni karita hon wa, ashita *motte kimasu*.)

¶ Tomorrow **I'll bring back** the book I borrowed from you.

もっと〔副〕

motto 〔adv〕 **more, further, longer**

¶ もっと一生懸命勉強しなさい。(*Motto* isshōkenmei benkyō shinasai.)

¶ Please study **harder**.

¶ もっと右の方へ寄ってください。(*Motto* migi no hō e yotte kudasai.)

¶ Please move **more** to the right.

¶ 上田さんは英語が上手ですが、山田さんはもっと上手です。(Ueda san wa Eigo ga jōzu desu ga, Yamada san wa *motto* jōzu desu.)

¶ [Miss] Ueda speaks English well, but [Miss] Yamada speaks it **still better**.

もっとも 最も〔副〕

mottomo 〔adv〕 **most, extremely**

¶ 富士山は日本で最も高い山です。(Fujisan wa Nihon de *mottomo* takai yama desu.)

¶ Mount Fuji is **the highest** mountain in Japan.

¶あなたの最も好きな食べ物は何ですか。(Anata no *mottomo* suki na tabemono wa nan desu ka?)

¶ What is your **favorite** food?

もっとも〔接〕

mottomo 〖conj〗 **however, though, indeed, of course**

¶わたしは日本料理が好きです。もっとも、生の魚は食べられませんが。(Watashi wa Nihon-ryōri ga suki desu. *Mottomo*, nama no sakana wa taberaremasen ga.)

¶ I like Japanese food. **However,** I can't eat raw fish.

¶私の兄弟はみんな頭がいいです。もっとも、私だけは例外です。(Watakushi no kyōdai wa minna atama ga ii desu. *Mottomo* watakushi dake wa reigai desu.)

¶ My brothers and sisters are all smart. **Of course,** I am the exception.

＊前のことがらを受けて、それに対する例外や条件をつけ加えたりするときに使う。

＊Used when adding some exception or condition to the previous statement.

もっとも〔形動〕

mottomo 〖adj-v〗 **reasonable, understandable, natural, justifiable**

¶2時間も待たされたんですから、あの人が怒るのももっともです。(Nijikan mo matasareta n desu kara, ano hito ga okoru no mo *mottomo* desu.)

¶ **It is only natural** that [he] was angry as [he] had been kept waiting for two hours.

¶朝から何も食べていないのなら、おなかがすくのはもっともです。(Asa kara nani mo tabete inai no nara, onaka ga suku no wa *mottomo* desu.)

¶ **Of course** you are hungry if you haven't eaten anything all day.

もと 元〔名〕

moto 〖n〗 **former; source, origin**

元首相 (*moto*-shushō)

a **former** prime minister

¶あの人は元小学校の先生でした。(Ano hito wa *moto* shōgakkō no sensei deshita.)

¶ [He] was **formerly** 〖**originally**〗 an elementary school teacher.

¶本を読み終わったら、元にもどしてください。(Hon o yomiowattara, *moto* ni modoshite kudasai.)

¶ Please put the book **back** when you are finished with it.

¶久しぶりに行った町は、元のままでした。(Hisashiburi ni itta machi wa, *moto* no mama deshita.)

もとめる 求める 〔動Ⅱ〕

① [要求する、相手に望む]
¶山田さんに意見を求めたら、黙っていました。(Yamada san ni iken o *motometara*, damatte imashita.)
¶あしたの会に出席を求められたのですが、都合が悪くて行けません。(Ashita no kai ni shusseki o *motomerareta* no desu ga, tsugō ga warukute ikemasen.)
② [欲しいものや人を探す]
¶二人は幸福を求めて旅に出ました。(Futari wa kōfuku o *motomete* tabi ni demashita.)
¶わたしの学校で、今英語の先生を求めています。(Watashi no gakkō de, ima Eigo no sensei o *motomete* imasu.)
③ [買う]
¶「それはどこでお求めになりましたか。」(Sore wa doko de o*motome* ni narimashita ka?)「Aデパートで買いました。」(Ē-depāto de kaimashita.)

もどる 〔動Ⅰ〕

① [元の所へ帰る]

¶自分の席にもどってください。(Jibun no seki ni *modotte* kudasai.)
¶弟は忘れ物を取りにもどってきました。(Otōto wa wasuremono o tori ni *modotte* kimashita.)
② [失ったものが返ってくる]

motomeru 〔vⅡ〕 **desire, request, demand; pursue, seek; buy**
① [desire, request, demand, ask for]
¶ [Mrs.] Yamada remained silent **when asked** for [her] opinion.

¶ [I] **was requested** to attend tomorrow's meeting 〚session〛 but circumstances will not permit my going.

② [pursue, seek, search for]
¶ The two took to the road **in search** of happiness.

¶ My school is now **looking for** an English teacher.

③ [buy, purchase]
¶ "Where did you **purchase** that?" "I got it at Department Store A."

modoru 〔vⅠ〕 **return, get back; return, revert**
① [return, get back; return to where one was originally]
¶ Please **return** to your seats.

¶ My (younger) brother **came back** to get something he had forgotten.

② [return, revert; something lost returns]

¶落とした財布がもどってきました。
(Otoshita saifu ga *modotte* kimashita.)
¶若い時は二度ともどってこないので
す。(Wakai toki wa nido to *modotte*
konai no desu.)

¶ [I] got back the wallet [I] had lost.

¶ The days of our youth can never be
retrieved 〖We are only young once〗.

もの　物〔名〕

mono 〔n〕 **thing, physical object;
quality; property**

① [物体、品物]
¶物を大切にしましょう。(*Mono* o
taisetsu ni shimashō.)
¶袋の中にはいろいろな物が入ってい
ます。(Fukuro no naka ni wa iroiro na
mono ga haitte imasu.)

① [thing, physical object, article]
¶ One should not be wasteful.

¶ Inside the bag are various **objects**.

② [品質]
¶少しは高くても、物のいいほうが得
です。(Sukoshi wa takakutemo, *mono* no
ii hō ga toku desu.)
*普通「物がいい（mono ga ii）」「物 が
悪い（mono ga warui）」の形で使 う。

② [quality]
¶ It pays to buy **things** of good quality
even though they may be a little more
expensive.

*Usually used in the patterns "*mono ga
ii*" and "*mono ga warui*."

③ [人・団体などに所属している物]

③ [property of a person, organization,
etc.]

¶これはあなたの物ですか。(Kore wa
anata no *mono* desu ka？)
¶あの建物はわたしの会社の物になり
ました。(Ano tate*mono* wa watashi no
kaisha no *mono* ni narimashita.)

¶ Is this **yours?**

¶ That building has come **into the
possession** of my company.

④ [ある対象を具体的にささないで一
般的にとらえて表すときに使う]
¶疲れているので、ものを言うのがめ
んどうです。(Tsukarete iru node, *mono*
o iu no ga mendō desu.)
¶あの人はものも食べないで、一日
じゅうラジオを作っています。(Ano
hito wa *mono* mo tabenaide, ichinichijū
rajio o tsukutte imasu.)
*その対象が具体的に何であるかは文
脈によって表される。

④ [used when referring to something
in general terms]
¶ Because I'm tired, it's a nuisance **to
talk**.

¶ [He] makes radios all day without
even **eating**.

*What is being referred to is made
clear by the context.

850

⑤ [ものごとの特性などについて言う
ときに使う]

¶ いい音楽というものは、人の心を楽
しくさせてくれます。(Ii ongaku to iu
mono wa, hito no kokoro o tanoshiku
sasete kuremasu.)

¶ この世界から戦争というものをなく
したいです。(Kono sekai kara sensō to
iu *mono* o nakushitai desu.)

*「～というもの (～to iu mono)」の形
で使う。「もの (mono)」は前の言葉の
本来の性格などを広く示す。

⑥ [そうするのが当然でありそうなる
のが自然であるという意味を表す]

¶ わからないときには人に聞くもので
すよ。(Wakaranai toki ni wa hito ni kiku
mono desu yo.)

¶ 行けないとなると、いっそう行きた
くなるものです。(Ikenai to naru to,
issō ikitaku naru *mono* desu.)

*「～ものだ (～mono da)」「～もので
す (～mono desu)」などの形で使う。

⑦ [感慨・感嘆などの意味を表す]

¶ よくこれまで我慢してきたものだ。
(Yoku kore made gaman shite kita *mono*
da.)

¶ 漢字を覚えるのは難しいものです
ね。(Kanji o oboeru no wa muzukashii
mono desu ne.)

¶ 子供なのに、こんな難しい本がよく
読めるものですね。(Kodomo na noni,
konna muzukashii hon ga yoku yomeru
mono desu ne.)

*「～ものだ (mono da)」「～ものです
(mono desu)」などの形で使う。

⑧ [過去にしばしば起こったことを回
想するときに使う]

⑤ [used when stressing the essential
nature of something]

¶ **Good music** gladdens the human
heart.

¶ I would like to see **such a thing** as
war eliminated from this world.

*Used in the pattern "～ *to iu mono*."
In this case *mono* broadly indicates the
essence of what precedes it.

⑥ [indicates that something is natural
or a matter of course]

¶ You **should ask** someone when you
don't understand something.

¶ When one can't go somewhere, **one
wants** to go there all the more.

*Used in the patterns "～ *mono da*"
and "～ *mono desu*."

⑦ [used when expressing admiration,
deep emotion, etc.]

¶ **[You]'ve done well** to stand it this
long 『You've been very patient about
it』.

¶ **It is difficult** to learn *kanji*, isn't it?

¶ **What a** clever child that is to be able
to read such a difficult book!

*Used in the patterns "～ *mono da*"
and "～ *mono desu*."

⑧ [used when referring to habitual
action in the past]

¶子供のころ、よくこの川で泳いだものです。(Kodomo no koro, yoku kono kawa de oyoida *mono* desu.)

¶ I used to swim in this river often when I was young.

¶学生時代、友達とよく飲みに行ったものです。(Gakusei-jidai, tomodachi to yoku nomi ni itta *mono* desu.)

¶ In my student days I often went drinking with friends.

＊「～たものだ（～ta mono da）」「～たものです（～ta mono desu）」の形で使う。「昔（mukashi）」「以前（izen）」「～のころ（～no koro）」のような過去を表す言葉といっしょに使うことが多い。

*Used in the patterns "-*ta mono da*," "-*ta mono desu*." It is often used with words indicating the past such as *mukashi, izen,* or ～ *no koro.*

もの 者〔名〕

怠け者 (namake*mono*)

¶わたしは山田という者ですが、御主人はいらっしゃいますか。(Watashi wa Yamada to iu *mono* desu ga, goshujin wa irasshaimasu ka？)

¶名前を呼ばれた者は、前へ出なさい。(Namae o yobareta *mono* wa, mae e denasai.)

mono 〔n〕 **person, somebody**

a lazy **person**, a lazybones

¶ I'm [Mr.] Yamada 〚This is Mr. Yamada speaking〛. Is your husband at home?

¶ Will **those** whose names are called please step forward.

ものがたり 物語〔名〕

源氏物語 (Genji*monogatari*)

¶おじいさんが昔の物語を話してくれました。(Ojiisan ga mukashi no *monogatari* o hanashite kuremashita.)

monogatari 〔n〕 **tale, story, novel**

The Tale of Genji

¶ My grandfather told me ancient **tales**.

ものさし〔名〕

¶どのくらいの長さか、ものさしで測ってごらんなさい。(Dono kurai no nagasa ka, *monosashi* de hakatte goran nasai.)

monosashi 〔n〕 **ruler, rule, a measure**

¶ Now you try to measure its length with **a ruler** 〚**yardstick**, etc.〛.

もめん 木綿〔名〕

木綿のシャツ (*momen* no shatsu) 木綿のくつ下 (*momen* no kutsushita) 木綿糸 (*momen*'ito)

momen 〔n〕 **cotton, cotton cloth**

a **cotton** shirt 〚**undershirt**〛 // **cotton** socks // **cotton** thread, **cotton** yarn

⇒綿 men

もも 桃〔名〕

桃の木（momo no ki）桃の花（momo no hana）

momo 〔n〕 **a peach, a peach tree**

a **peach** tree // a **peach** blossom

もやす 燃やす〔動Ⅰ〕

¶マッチで火をつけて、手紙を燃やしてしまいました。（Matchi de hi o tsukete, tegami o *moyashite* shimaimashita.）

¶木をたくさん燃やしながら、その周りでみんなで歌を歌いました。（Ki o takusan *moyashinagara*, sono mawari de minna de uta o utaimashita.）

⇒燃す mosu

moyasu 〔v Ⅰ〕 **burn, put to the flame, ignite**

¶ [I] lit the letter with a match and **burned** it.

¶ We sat and sang around the fire where **we burned** lots of wood.

もよう 模様〔名〕

¶この花びんの模様はとてもきれいですね。（Kono kabin no *moyō* wa totemo kirei desu ne.）

¶あの花の模様の着物を着ている人はだれですか。（Ano hana no *moyō* no kimono o kite iru hito wa dare desu ka?）

moyō 〔n〕 **pattern, design**

¶ **The design** on this vase is very pretty.

¶ Who is that woman wearing the **flowered** kimono?

もらう〔動Ⅰ〕

¶わたしは兄にお金をもらいました。（Watashi wa ani ni okane o *moraimashita*.）

¶わたしは友達から手紙をもらいました。（Watashi wa tomodachi kara tegami o *moraimashita*.）

＊普通、ある人が対等または目下の人などから与えられたものを受け取るという意味を表す。受け取る人の側に立って言うときに使う。与える人が目上の人である場合には「いただく（itadaku）」を使う。「わたしは先生か

morau 〔v Ⅰ〕 **receive, accept, get**

¶ I **got** some money from my older brother〖My older brother gave me some money〗.

¶ I **received** a letter from a friend.

＊Usually expresses the meaning of someone receiving something from a person of equal or lower status; used from the standpoint of the recipient. When the donor is of higher status, *itadaku* is used instead, as in "*Watashi*

ら日本語の本をいただきました。
（Watashi wa sensei kara Nihongo no hon o itadakimashita.）」

⇒いただく **itadaku**

（〜て）もらう〔連〕

¶わたしは父にくつを買ってもらいました。（Watashi wa chichi ni kutsu o katte *moraimashita*.）
¶わたしは山田さんに日本語を教えてもらいました。（Watashi wa Yamada san ni Nihongo o oshiete *moraimashita*.）
¶熱が高いから、医者に診てもらったほうがいいでしょう。（Netsu ga takai kara, isha ni mite *moratta* hō ga ii deshō.）

＊普通、ある人の動作によって、利益や恩恵を受けたり、または依頼してある動作をさせるようにしたりする意味を表す。利益を受けたり、依頼したりする人の側に立って言うときに使う。動作をする人が利益などを受ける人と同等か目下の人であるときに使う。動作をする人が目上の人である場合には「（〜て）いただく（［〜te］ita-daku）」を使う。「わたしは先生に本を貸していただきました。（Watashi wa sensei ni hon o kashite itadakimashita.）」

⇒（〜て）いただく（〜te）**itadaku**

もり 森〔名〕

¶この町は森に囲まれています。（Kono machi wa *mori* ni kakomarete imasu.）

wa sensei kara Nihongo no hon o itadakimashita" (I received a Japanese book from my teacher; My teacher gave me a Japanese book).

(-te)morau 〔compd〕 **receive the favor of something being done; have someone do something, have something done**

¶ My father **bought me** a pair of shoes.

¶ [Miss] Yamada **taught me** Japanese 〚Miss Yamada **was kind enough to teach me** Japanese〛.

¶ You have a high fever; you should **have** a doctor **look you over**.

＊ Usually expresses the meaning of receiving some benefit through the actions of another, or of requesting that something be done for one; used from the standpoint of the person receiving the benefit or of the person making the request. The person performing the act is of equal or lower status than the one receiving the benefit of that act. When the person performing the act is of higher status, (-*te*) *itadaku* is used instead, as in "*Watashi wa sensei ni hon o kashite itadakimashita*" (My teacher lent me a book; I borrowed a book from my teacher).

mori 〔n〕 **forest, woods**

¶ This town is encircled by **woodlands**.

¶森の中の道を通っていくと、きれいな 湖 が見えてきました。(Mori no naka no michi o tootte iku to, kirei na mizuumi ga miete kimashita.)

¶As [we] went along the road through **the forest**, a lovely lake came into view.

もる 漏る〔動Ⅰ〕

¶この家は古いので、雨が降ると漏ってきます。(Kono ie wa furui node, ame ga furu to *motte* kimasu.)

¶車からガソリンが漏っていますよ。(Kuruma kara gasorin ga *motte* imasu yo.)

moru〔v Ⅰ〕**leak, escape**

¶This house is old so that the roof **leaks** when it rains.

¶Hey, your car **is leaking** gasoline!

もん 門〔名〕

表門 (omote*mon*) 裏門 (ura*mon*) 門が開く (*mon* ga aku) 門を開ける (*mon* o akeru) 門を閉める (*mon* o shimeru)

¶学校の門はもう閉まっていました。(Gakkō no *mon* wa mō shimatte imashita.)

mon〔n〕**gate**

the front **gate**, main **entrance** // the rear **gate** // a **gate** opens // open a **gate** // close a **gate**

¶The school **gate** was already closed.

もんだい 問題〔名〕

① [質問]

問題を解く (*mondai* o toku)

¶次の問題に答えなさい。(Tsugi no *mondai* ni kotaenasai.)

¶今度の試験問題はとても難しかったです。(Kondo no shiken-*mondai* wa totemo muzukashikatta desu.)

② [解決すべきことがら]

¶都会では交通事故が大きな問題になっています。(Tokai de wa kōtsū-jiko ga ookina *mondai* ni natte imasu.)

¶人口問題の解決はたいへん難しいです。(Jinkō-*mondai* no kaiketsu wa taihen muzukashii desu.)

mondai〔n〕**question, problem; problem, issue**

① [question, problem (exam, homework, etc.)]

solve **a problem**

¶Answer the following **questions**.

¶The exam **questions** were very difficult this time.

② [problem, issue, matter]

¶Traffic accidents have become a major urban **problem**.

¶The population **problem** is very difficult to solve.

や

や〔助〕

¶ 机の上には、本やノートや鉛筆など
があります。（Tsukue no ue ni wa, hon
ya nōto *ya* enpitsu nado ga arimasu.）
¶ このクラスの学生はアメリカやフラ
ンスやタイなどいろいろな国から来て
います。（Kono kurasu no gakusei wa
Amerika *ya* Furansu *ya* Tai nado iroiro na
kuni kara kite imasu.）
＊いくつかあるものの中から、その一
部を列挙する場合に使う。
⇒と **to**

ya〔part〕 **and, or**

¶ There are books, notebooks, pencils,
and the like on the desk.

¶ The students in this class are from
many different countries such as the
United States, France, **and** Thailand.

＊ *Ya* is used when citing only part of a
set of items.

-や -屋〔尾〕

八百屋（yao*ya*）魚屋（sakana*ya*）菓子
屋（kashi*ya*）本屋（hon'*ya*）酒屋
（saka*ya*）文房具屋（bunbōgu*ya*）

-ya〔suf〕 **a suffix indicating a
store, shop, dealer, etc.**

a vegetable **store**, a grocer // a fish
shop, a fish **dealer** // a confectionery
store, a candy **shop**, a confectioner // a
book**store**, a book**seller** // a liquor
store, a wine **dealer**, a sake **brewery** //
a stationery **store**, a stationer

やあ〔感〕

¶ やあ、しばらく。お元気ですか。
（*Yā*, shibaraku. Ogenki desu ka？）

yā〔interj〕 **hi, hello**

¶ **Hello there!** How are you doing?

やおや 八百屋〔名〕

¶ 八百屋で野菜を買ってきてくださ
い。（*Yaoya* de yasai o katte kite
kudasai.）

yaoya〔n〕 **vegetable store, grocer**

¶ Please go buy some vegetables at the
vegetable store.

やがて〔副〕

¶ 山田さんも、やがて来るでしょう。
（Yamada san mo *yagate* kuru deshō.）

yagate〔adv〕 **soon, shortly,
nearly, after all**

¶ [Mrs.] Yamada should be here
shortly.

¶田中さんが外国へ行ってから、やがて1年になります。(Tanaka san ga gaikoku e itte kara, *yagate* ichinen ni narimasu.)

¶ **Nearly** one year has passed since [Mr.] Tanaka went abroad.

やかましい 〔形〕

¶隣の部屋がやかましくて、勉強ができません。(Tonari no heya ga *yakamashikute*, benkyō ga dekimasen.)

¶やかましい。静かにしろ。(*Yakamashii*. Shizuka ni shiro.)

yakamashii 〔adj〕 **noisy**

¶ **It's so noisy** in the room next door that [I] can't study.

¶ Quiet! Stop making **such a racket!** (literally, **You're too loud.** Be quiet!)

やく 焼く 〔動Ⅰ〕

① [火をつけて燃やす]
ごみを焼く (gomi o *yaku*)
¶この手紙はもう要らないから、焼いてください。(Kono tegami wa mō iranai kara, *yaite* kudasai.)

② [食べ物などに熱を加えて食べるのに適するようにする]
魚を焼く (sakana o *yaku*)
¶パンを焼いて、バターをつけて食べました。(Pan o *yaite*, batā o tsukete tabemashita.)

yaku 〔vⅠ〕 **burn, set on fire; roast**

① [burn, set on fire]
burn the trash
¶ [I] don't need this letter any more. Please **burn it**.

② [roast, broil, grill, bake, toast]

grill 〚**roast, broil**〛 fish
¶ [I] ate the bread 〚roll, muffin, etc.〛 **toasted** and buttered.

やく 役 〔名〕

① [務め、仕事上の地位]
上役 (uwa*yaku*) 役目 (*yaku*me)

¶田中さんは、その委員会でどんな役をしているのですか。(Tanaka san wa, sono iinkai de donna *yaku* o shite iru no desu ka?)

② [劇などに出てくる人物などの役割]
役者 (*yaku*sha) 主役 (shu*yaku*)
¶この劇の主人公の役は、だれがやるのですか。(Kono geki no shujinnkō no *yaku* wa, dare ga yaru no desu ka?)

yaku 〔n〕 **office, post; role, part; duty, function**

① [office, post, position]
a senior **official,** one's superior // duty, function
¶ What is [Mr.] Tanaka's **position** on that committee 〚commission, board〛?

② [role, part]
an actor, actress // the lead, leading **role**
¶ Who is playing **the lead** in this play?

③[割り当てられた仕事、引き受けた仕事]

¶京都の案内役は、わたしが引き受ます。（Kyōto no annai*yaku* wa, watashi ga hikiukemasu.）

③ [duty, function]

¶I will undertake **to act as** guide in Kyoto.

④[はたらき、有用であること]

役に立つ（*yaku* ni tatsu）役立つ（*yaku*datsu）

¶この道具は全然役に立ちません。（Kono dōgu wa zenzen *yaku*ni tachimasen.）

¶この辞書は、日本語を勉強するのにとても役立ちます。（Kono jisho wa, Nihongo o benkyō suru no ni totemo *yaku*dachimasu.）

*いつも「役に立つ（yaku ni tatsu）」「役立つ（yakudatsu）」の形で使う。

④ [use, service]

be **useful,** be of **use** // be **useful,** be of **use**

¶This tool 〚utensil, apparatus, appliance〛 is of no **use** whatsoever.

¶This dictionary is very **useful** for studying Japanese.

*Always used in the patterns "*yaku ni tatsu*" and "*yakudatsu.*"

やく 約〔連体〕

¶駅からうちまで、歩いて約15分です。（Eki kara uchi made, aruite *yaku* jūgofun desu.）

¶これで仕事も約半分終わりました。（Kore de shigoto mo *yaku* hanbun owarimashita.）

yaku 〔attrib〕 **about, nearly, approximately**

¶It is **roughly** a 15-minute walk from the station to my house.

¶This marks **more or less** the halfway point of the work.

やくしょ 役所〔名〕

市役所（shi*yakusho*）

¶わたしの兄は役所に勤めています。（Watashi no ani wa *yakusho* ni tsutomete imasu.）

¶外国へ行く手続きは、どこの役所でするのですか。（Gaikoku e iku tetsuzuki wa, doko no *yakusho* de suru no desuka？）

yakusho 〔n〕 **a government office** a city **hall**

¶My elder brother is in **government** service.

¶What **office** handles the paperwork for going abroad?

やくす 訳す〔動Ⅰ〕

①[ある国の言葉を別の国の言葉に直す]

yakusu 〔vⅠ〕 **translate**

① [translate from one language to another]

¶山田さんは日本の現代小説を英語に訳しています。(Yamada san wa Nihon no gendai-shōsetsu o Eigo ni *yakushite* imasu.)

② [古い言葉や難しい言葉をわかりやすい言葉に直す]

¶中村さんは源氏物語を現代語に訳しました。(Nakamura san wa Genjimonogatari o gendaigo ni *yakushimashita*.)

やくそく 約束 〔名、〜する〕

約束を守る (*yakusoku* o mamoru) 約束を破る (*yakusoku* o yaburu)

¶わたしは今晩友達と食事をする約束があります。(Watashi wa konban tomodachi to shokuji o suru *yakusoku* ga arimasu.)

¶山田さんと約束して、日曜日に映画を見に行くことにしました。(Yamada san to *yakusoku* shite, nichiyōbi ni eiga o mini iku koto ni shimashita.)

やける 焼ける 〔動 I〕

① [火で燃える]
¶火事で家が何軒も焼けました。(Kaji de ie ga nangen mo *yakemashita*.)

② [食べ物などが熱を加えられて食べるのに適するようになる]

¶肉が焼けましたよ。どうぞ、おあがりください。(Niku ga *yakemashita* yo. Dōzo, oagari kudasai.)

③ [日光などにあたって色が変わる]

¶ [Miss] Yamada **translates** contemporary Japanese novels into English.

② [render something in older or difficult language into language easier to understand]

¶ [Mr.] Nakamura **put** *The Tale of Genji* **into** modern Japanese.

yakusoku 〔n, 〜*suru*〕 **promise, agreement, appointment, engagement, date**

keep **a promise**; keep **an appointment** // break **a promise**; miss **an appointment**

¶ I have **a date** to have dinner with a friend tonight.

¶ **I promised** to go to a movie with [Mr.] Yamada on Sunday.

yakeru 〔v II〕 **burn, be burnt; be roasted; be sunburned, be suntanned**

① [burn, be burnt]
¶ Many houses **burned down** in the fire.

② [be roasted, grilled, broiled, baked, toasted]

¶ The meat is done 〖**grilled, roasted**, etc.〗. Please have some.

③ [be sunburned, be suntanned]

¶泳ぎに行って、顔が真っ黒に焼けました。(Oyogi ni itte, kao ga makkuro ni yakemashita.)

¶ [His] face **got browned** in the sun when [he] went swimming.

やさい 野菜〔名〕

¶わたしは畑でじゃがいもやキャベツやトマトなどの野菜を作っています。(Watashi wa hatake de jagaimo ya kyabetsu ya tomato nado no *yasai* o tsukutte imasu.)

yasai 〔n〕 **vegetable(s)**

¶ I grow **vegetables**—potatoes, cabbage, tomatoes, etc.—in a field.

やさしい 優しい〔形〕

¶田中さんは心の優しい人です。(Tanaka san wa kokoro no *yasashii* hito desu.)

¶入学試験に落ちてがっかりしていたら、山田さんが優しく慰めてくれました。(Nyūgaku-shiken ni ochite gakkari shite itara, Yamada san ga *yasashiku* nagusamete kuremashita.)

yasashii 〔adj〕 **gentle, tender, kindly, considerate**

¶ [Mr.] Tanaka is a **kindhearted** person.

¶ When [I] was downhearted at failing [my] college entrance exams, [Miss] Yamada **gently** comforted [me].

やさしい 易しい〔形〕

¶日本語は易しいですか。難しいです。(Nihongo wa *yasashii* desu ka? Muzukashii desu ka?)

¶問題が易しかったので、すぐできました。(Mondai ga *yasashikatta* node, sugu dekimashita.)

⇔難しい **muzukashii**

yasashii 〔adj〕 **easy, simple**

¶ **Is** Japanese **easy?** Or is it hard?

¶ The (test) problem **was easy** so [I] finished it quickly.

やすい 安い〔形〕

¶もっと安いのを見せてください。(Motto *yasui* no o misete kudasai.)

¶安ければ買いますが、高ければ買いません。(*Yasukereba* kaimasu ga, takakereba kaimasen.)

⇔高い **takai**

yasui 〔adj〕 **cheap, inexpensive**

¶ Please show me a **cheaper** one.

¶ [I] will buy it **if it's cheap** but not if it's expensive.

-やすい〔尾〕

¶田中さんの手紙は、字がきれいで読みやすいです。(Tanaka san no tegami wa, ji ga kirei de yomi*yasui* desu.)

¶夏は食べ物が腐りやすいです。(Natsu wa tabemono ga kusari*yasui* desu.)

⇔-にくい -nikui

やすみ 休み〔名〕

休み時間 (*yasumi*jikan) 昼休み (hiru*yasumi*)

¶あしたは学校が休みです。(Ashita wa gakkō ga *yasumi* desu.)

¶今日、山田先生は風邪でお休みです (Kyō, Yamada sensei wa kaze de o*yasumi* desu.)

やすむ 休む〔動 I〕

①[休息する、心や体を楽にする]

¶それでは、10分間休みましょう。(Soredewa, jippunkan *yasumimashō*.)

②[学校や会社などに行くことをやめる]

¶体のぐあいが悪いので、会社を休みました。(Karada no guai ga warui node, kaisha o *yasumimashita*.)

やせる〔動 II〕

¶中村さんはわたしよりやせています。(Nakamura san wa watashi yori *yasete* imasu.)

-yasui 〔suf〕 **be easy to~, be apt to~**

¶ [Miss] Tanaka's letters are written in an attractive and **easy-to-read** handwriting.

¶ Food goes bad **easily** in the summer.

yasumi 〔n〕 **a rest, a break; a holiday, vacation, time off**

work-**breaks**, the time **between classes** // the lunch **break**

¶ There is **no school** tomorrow.

¶ Professor Yamada **is out** today with a cold 〚the flu〛.

yasumu 〔v I〕 **rest, take a break; be absent from work, school, etc.**

① [rest, take a break]

¶ Well, **let's have a** 10-minute **break** now.

② [be absent from work, school, etc.]

¶ [I] **stayed home** from work as [I] don't 〚didn't〛 feel well.

yaseru 〔v II〕 **become thin, lose weight**

¶ [Mr.] Nakamura **is thinner** than I am.

¶わたしは病気をしてやせてしまいました。（Watashi wa byōki o shite *yasete* shimaimashita.）
⇔太る **futoru**

¶ I **lost weight** due to my illness.

やっつ 八つ〔名〕

① [8個]
¶ここに卵が八つあります。（Koko ni tamago ga *yattsu* arimasu.）
② [8歳]
¶今年、この子は八つになりました。（Kotoshi, kono ko wa *yattsu* ni narimashita.）

yattsu 〔n〕 **eight; eight years old**

① [eight, eight items]
¶ There are **eight** eggs here.

② [eight years old]
¶ This child turned **eight** this year.

やっと〔副〕

① [困難な状況に耐えたりその状態を打開するための努力などをしてある事態が実現することを表す]
¶1時間並んで、やっと汽車の切符買うことができました。（Ichijikan narande, *yatto* kisha no kippu o kau koto ga dekimashita.）
¶一生懸命走って、やっと電車に間に合いました。（Isshōkenmei hashitte, *yatto* densha ni maniaimashita.）
¶長い厳しい冬が終わって、やっと暖かい春になりました。（Nagai kibishii fuyu ga owatte, *yatto* atatakai haru ni narimashita.）
*普通、待ち望んでいた結果が実現したときに使う。あとに過去・完了を表す「たの形」が来ることが多い。「やっとのことで（yatto no kotode）」の形でも使う。
→ようやく **yōyaku**
② [あることがらが可能ではあるがじゅうぶんではないという意味を表す]

yatto 〔adv〕 **at last, finally; barely, narrowly, just**

① [at last, finally, with much effort]

¶ After standing in line for an hour [I] was **at last** able to buy a train ticket.

¶ [I] ran as hard as [I] could and **managed** to catch the train.

¶ Spring has **finally** come 〖**finally came**〗 after the long, hard winter.

*Usually used when some desired result has been achieved. Generally followed by the -*ta* form expressing past or completed action. Also used in the pattern "*yatto no koto de.*"

② [barely, narrowly, just]

¶あの部屋は狭くて、5人がやっと入れる広さです。(Ano heya wa semakute, gonin ga *yatto* haireru hirosa desu.)

*「～がやっとです（～ga yatto desu）」の形でも使う。「月給が安いので、自分一人が生活するのがやっとです。(Gekkyū ga yasui node, jibun hitori ga seikatsu suru no ga yatto desu.)」

やっぱり〔副〕 ☞**やはり yahari**

やど 宿〔名〕
¶1時間も歩いて、やっと宿を見つけました。(Ichijikan mo aruite, yatto *yado* o mitsukemashita.)
¶今晩はどこに宿をとりましょうか。(Konban wa doko ni *yado* o torimashō ka?)

やとう 雇う〔動Ⅰ〕
¶あそこの家はお金持ちで、お手伝いさんを3人も雇っています。(Asoko no ie wa okanemochi de, otetsudaisan o sannin mo *yatotte* imasu.)

やね 屋根〔名〕
¶あの赤い屋根の建物が郵便局です。(Ano akai *yane* no tatemono ga yūbinkyoku desu.)

やはり〔副〕

①[ほかの場合と同じように]
¶この言葉の意味がわからないので、山田さんにきいてみましたが、やはりわかりませんでした。(Kono kotoba no imi ga wakaranai node, Yamada san ni kiite mimashitaga, *yahari* wakarimasen deshita.)

¶ The room is small—it **barely** holds five persons.

*Also used in the pattern "～ *ga yatto desu*." For example, "*Gekkyū ga yasui node, jibun hitori ga seikatsu suru no ga yauo desu*" (My wages are barely enough for one person to live on).

yappari〔adv〕 ☞**yahari**

yado〔n〕 **lodging, inn, a room**
¶ After walking for a hour [we] finally found **a room** for the night.

¶ Where shall we seek **lodging** tonight?

yatou〔v Ⅰ〕 **employ, hire**
¶ That family is rich—they **have** three maids.

yane〔n〕 **roof**
¶ That building with a red **roof** is the post office.

yahari〔adv〕 **too, also, likewise; still, just the same; after all, as expected**
① [too, also, likewise]
¶ I didn't understand the meaning of this word so I asked [Mr.] Yamada but he didn't understand **either**.

¶山田さんは医者ですが、息子さんもやはり医者になりたいそうです。（Yamada san wa isha desu ga, musuko san mo *yahari* isha ni naritai sō desu.）

② [前の場合と同じように]

¶上田さんは今でもやはり小学校の先生をしていらっしゃいますか？（Ueda san wa ima demo *yahari* shōgakkō no sensei o shite irasshaimasu ka？）

¶去年の夏も暑かったですが、今年もやはり暑いですね。（Kyonen no natsu mo atsukatta desu ga, kotoshi mo *yahari* atsui desu ne.）

③ [予想していたとおりに]

¶わたしが思っていたとおり、やはりあの人はうそをついていました。（Watashi ga omotte ita toori, *yahari* ano hito wa uso o tsuite imashita.）

¶中村さんは試験に合格しないだろうと思っていましたが、やはりだめでした。（Nakamura san wa shiken ni gōkaku shinai darō to omotte imashita ga, *yahari* dame deshita.）

＊「やっぱり（yappari）」とも言う。

やぶる　破る〔動Ｉ〕

① [紙・布などを引き裂いたりする]

¶山田さんは怒って、手紙を破って捨てました。（Yamada san wa okotte, tegami o *yabutte* sutemashita.）

② [約束や決まりなどを守らない]

¶田中さんはわたしとの約束を破って、ついに来ませんでした。（Tanaka san wa watashi tono yakusoku o *yabutte*, tsuini kimasen deshita.）

③ [試合や勝負などで相手を負かす]

¶ [Mrs.] Yamada is a doctor and I hear [her] son wants to become a doctor **too**.

② [still, just the same]

¶ Is [Miss] Ueda **still** teaching in elementary school?

¶ It was hot last summer and it's hot **again** this year **too**.

③ [after all, as expected]

¶ It's just as I thought—[he] *was* lying.

¶ I thought [Mr.] Nakamura would fail the exam and that's **just** what happened.

＊Variant: *yappari*.

yaburu 〔v I〕 **tear, rip; break, violate; beat, defeat**

① [tear, rip]

¶ [Miss] Yamada angrily **tore up** the letter and threw it away.

② [break, violate]

¶ [Mr.] Tanaka never showed up for [his] appointment with me.

③ [beat, defeat]

¶テニスの試合で、AチームはBチームを破りました。(Tenisu no shiai de, Ē-chiimu wa Bii-chiimu o *yaburimashita*.)

やぶれる 破れる〔動 II〕

¶この紙はすぐ破れます。(Kono kami wa sugu *yaburemasu*.)
¶このシャツは少し破れていますが、まだ着られます。(Kono shatsu wa sukoshi *yaburete* imasu ga, mada kiraremasu.)

やぶれる 敗れる〔動 II〕
戦争に敗れる (sensō ni *yabureru*)
¶テニスの試合で、田中さんは山田さんに敗れました。(Tenisu no shiai de, Tanakasan wa yamada san ni *yaburemasita*.)
⇒負ける **makeru**

やま 山〔名〕
¶富士山は日本でいちばん高い山です。(Fujisan wa Nihon de ichiban takai *yama* desu.)
¶夏休みには山に登るつもりです。(Natsuyasumi ni wa *yama* ni noboru tsumori desu.)

やむ〔動 I〕
¶雨がやみました。(Ame ga *yamimashita*.)
¶風がやんで、辺りが静かになりました。(Kaze ga *yande*, atari ga shizuka ni narimashita.)

¶ Team A **beat** Team B at tennis.

yabureru 〖v II〗 **be torn, rip, be broken, wear out, become threadbare**

¶ This paper **tears** easily.

¶ This shirt **is** a little **worn** but it's still good (literally, can still be worn).

yabureru 〖v II〗 **be defeated, lose**
lose a war
¶ [Mr.] Tanaka **lost** the tennis match to [Mr.] Yamada.

yama 〖n〗 **mountain, peak, hill**
¶ Mount Fuji is the highest **mountain** in Japan.

¶ I plan to go **mountain** climbing during summer vacation.

yamu 〖v I〗 **stop, cease**
¶ The rain **has stopped**.

¶ It became 〚has become〛 quiet with **the dying away** of the wind.

やむをえず〔副〕

¶乗り物がなくなってしまったので、やむをえず歩いてうちに帰りました。
（Norimono ga nakunatte shimatta node, yamuoezu aruite uchi ni kaerimasita.）

やむをえない〔連〕

¶あしたの会議には、やむをえない用事で欠席させていただきます。
（Ashita no kaigi ni wa, *yamuoenai* yōji de kessekisasete itadakimasu.）
¶用事があって来られなければ、やむをえません。（Yōji ga atte korarenakereba, *yamuoemasen*.）
⇒しかたがない shikata ga nai

やめる　辞める〔動Ⅱ〕
¶中村さんは先月会社を辞めました。
（Nakamura san wa sengetsu kaisha o *yamemashita*.）

やめる〔動Ⅱ〕

①[続けてきたことを終わりにする]
¶今日の勉強は、これでやめることにしましょう。（Kyō no benkyō wa kore de *yameru* koto ni shimashō.）
¶たばこをやめようと思っているのですが、なかなかやめることができません。（Tabako o *yameyō* to omotte iru no desu ga, nakanaka *yameru* koto ga dekimasen.）
②[する予定でいたことをしないことにする]
¶風邪を引いたので、旅行に行くのをやめました。（Kaze o hiita node, ryokō ni iku no o *yamemashita*.）

yamuoezu 〔adv〕 **unavoidably, inevitably, of necessity**
¶ [I] **was forced** to walk home as nothing was running 〚as the trains and buses had stopped running for the night〛.

yamuoenai 〔compd〕 **unavoidable, inevitable, cannot be helped, beyond one's control**
¶ I will have to be absent from tomorrow's meeting due to **unavoidable** circumstances.

¶ **It can't be helped** if [you] have some business that prevents [you] from coming.

yameru 〔v Ⅱ〕 **quit, resign**
¶ [Mr.] Nakamura **quit** [his] job last month.

yameru 〔v Ⅱ〕 **stop, end; give up, quit**
① [stop, end]
¶ Let's **end** our lesson here today.

¶ **I'm trying to stop** smoking but it's hard to do.

② [give up, quit]

¶ [I] **gave up** on going on the trip because [I] caught a cold.

やる〔動 I〕

① [人や動植物などに物を与える]
¶わたしは弟に万年筆をやりました。
(Watashi wa otōto ni mannenhitsu o *yarimashita*.)
¶犬にえさをやってください。(Inu ni esa o *yatte* kudasai.)
¶夕方、植木に水をやりました。
(Yūgata, ueki ni mizu o *yarimashita*.)
*普通、ある人が同等または目下の人、動植物などにある物を与えるという意味を表す。与える人の側に立って言ときに使う。
→上げる ageru
② [ものごとをする、行う]
¶テニスをやりませんか。(Tenisu o *yarimasen* ka?)
¶おもしろい映画をやっているから、見に行きませんか。(Omoshiroi eiga o *yatte* iru kara, mi ni ikimasen ka?)
¶来週、田中先生の送別会をやる予定です。(Raishū, Tanaka sensei no sōbetsukai o *yaru* yotei desu.)
③ [ある職業に就く、仕事をする]
¶わたしの兄は本屋をやっています。
(Watashi no ani wa hon'ya o *yatte* imasu.)
④ [収入などを得て生活する]
¶あなたは1か月10万円でやっていけますか。(Anata wa ikkagetsu jūman'en de *yatte* ikemasu ka?)

(〜て) やる〔連〕

¶子供を動物園へ連れていってやりました。(Kodomo o dōbutsuen e tsurete itte *yarimashita*.)

yaru 〔v I〕 **give; do; work; make do, live on**

① [give]
¶I **gave** my younger brother a fountain pen.

¶Please **feed** the dog.

¶[I] **watered** the plants in the evening.

Yaru usually expresses the meaning of a person giving something to someone of equal or lower status or to an animal or plant. Used from the standpoint of the giver.

② [do, hold]
¶**Won't you play** tennis?

¶**There's** an interesting movie **on**. Won't you come with [me] to see it?

¶A farewell party for Professor 〖Doctor〗 Tanaka is scheduled for next week.

③ [work, perform]
¶My elder brother **runs** a bookstore.

④ [make do, live on]
¶Can you **live on** a hundred thousand yen a month?

(-te)yaru 〔compd〕 **do something for someone**
¶**I took** the children to the zoo.

¶わたしは妹にくつを買ってやりました。(Watashi wa imōto ni kutsu o katte yarimashita.)

¶ **I bought** shoes for my younger sister.

＊一般的に、相手のためにある動作をするという意味を表す。動作をする人側に立って言うときに使う。普通同等または目下の人などのためにある動作をするときに使う。

＊Generally indicates an act done for another person. Used from the standpoint of the performer of the act. Usually used for an act done for someone of equal or lower status.

⇒（〜て）あげる（〜te) **ageru**

やわらか 柔らか 〔形動〕

柔らかな手（*yawaraka* na te）柔らかな布団（*yawaraka* na futon)
→柔らかい **yawarakai**

yawaraka 〔adj-v〕 **soft, gentle, tender**

a **soft** hand // **soft** *futon* bedding

やわらかい 柔らかい 〔形〕

¶このパンは今焼いたばかりですから柔らかいですよ。(Kono pan wa ima yaita bakari desu kara *yawarakai* desu yo.)

yawarakai 〔adj〕 **soft, gentle, tender**

¶ This bread **is nice and moist** because it's freshly baked.

¶ゆうべは柔らかい布団でぐっすり眠りました。(Yūbe wa *yawarakai* futon de gussuri nemurimashita.)
→柔らか **yawaraka**

¶ [I] slept well last night on the **soft** *futon* bedding.

ゆ

ゆ 湯 〔名〕

① [水に熱を加えて熱くしたもの]
¶お湯を沸かして、お茶を入れましょ
う。(Oyu o wakashite, ocha o
iremashō.)
② [ふろ]
¶わたしは1日おきにお湯に入りま
す。(Watashi wa ichinichi oki ni oyu ni
hairimasu.)

ゆうがた 夕方 〔名〕
¶今日は、朝から夕方まで本を読んで
いました。(Kyō wa, asa kara yūgata
made hon o yonde imashita.)

ゆうき 勇気 〔名〕
勇気がある (yūki ga aru)
¶正しいことは、勇気を持って行いな
さい。(Tadashii koto wa, yūki o motte
okonainasai.)
¶彼は勇気を出して、独りで敵に向
かっていきました。(Kare wa yūki o
dashite, hitori de teki ni mukatte
ikimashita.)

ゆうしょう 優勝 〔名、〜する〕

優勝旗 (yūshōki) 優勝カップ (yūshō-
kappu)

¶山田さんはテニスの試合で優勝しま
した。(Yamada san wa tenisu no shiai de
yūshō shimashita.)

yu 〔n〕 hot water; a bath, a public
bath

① [hot water]
¶I'm going to heat **some water** and fix
(green) tea.

② [a bath, a public bath]
¶I take **a bath** every other day.

yūgata 〔n〕 evening, nightfall
¶[I] read books from morning to **night**
(that is, until **dark**) today.

yūki 〔n〕 courage, bravery
brave, courageous, hold
¶**Be brave** and do what is right!

¶He screwed up **his courage** and went
to face the enemy single-handedly.

yūshō 〔n, 〜suru〕 victory,
chaimpionship
a **championship** flag 〚banner,
pennant〛 // a **championship** cup, a
trophy
¶[Mr.] Yamada **won** the tennis match.

ゆうびん　郵便〔名〕

郵便局（*yūbin*kyoku）航空郵便
（kōkū-*yūbin*）郵便配達
（*yūbin*haitatsu）

¶郵便局へ行って、手紙を出しました。（*Yūbin*kyoku e itte, tegami o
dashimashita.）

¶この辺では、1日に2回郵便が配達されます。（Kono hen de wa, ichinichi ni
nikai *yūbin* ga haitatsu saremasu.）

yūbin〔n〕**mail, postal service**

the **post** office // air**mail** // **mail**
delivery; **mail**man

¶[I] went to the **post** office and mailed
a letter.

¶There are two **mail** deliveries a day
in this area.

ゆうべ〔名〕

¶ゆうべは8時ごろ寝ました。（*Yūbe*
wa hachiji goro nemashita.）

¶ゆうべ、うちの近くで火事がありました。（*Yūbe* uchi no chikaku de kaji ga
arimashita.）

yūbe〔n〕**last night, yesterday
evening**

¶[I] went to bed at around eight
o'clock **last night**.

¶There was a fire near my home **last
night**.

ゆうめい　有名〔形動〕

¶あの山が有名な富士山ですか。（Ano
yama ga *yūmei* na Fujisan desu ka？）

¶京都は古いお寺がたくさんあるので
有名です。（Kyōto wa furui otera ga
takusan aru node *yūmei* desu.）

yūmei〔adj-v〕**famous, well
known, celebrated**

¶Is that mountain the **famous** Mount
Fuji?

¶Kyoto **is known for** its large number
of ancient temples.

ゆうりょう　有料〔名〕

有料道路（*yūryō*-dōro）有料駐車場
（*yūryō*-chūshajō）

¶この駐車場は有料です。（Kono
chūshajō wa *yūryō* desu.）

⇔無料 **muryō**

yūryō〔n〕**toll ~, pay ~**

a **toll** road // a **pay** parking lot, a **pay**
parking garage

¶**You have to pay** to park here.

ゆう-　夕-〔頭〕

夕飯（*yū*han）夕方（*yū*gata）夕暮れ
（*yū*gure）夕焼け（*yū*yake）

yū-〔pref〕**evening**

evening meal, dinner // **evening** //
dusk, twilight // sunset, **evening** glow

ゆか　床〔名〕
¶川があふれて、床の上まで水が来ました。(Kawa ga afurete, *yuka* no ue made mizu ga kimashita.)

ゆかい　愉快〔形動〕
¶昨日のクラス会はたいへん愉快でした。(Kinō no kurasukai wa taihen *yukai* deshita.)
¶田中さんは愉快な人で、いつも冗談ばかり言っています。(Tanaka san wa *yukai* na hito de, itsu mo jōdan bakari itte imasu.)

ゆき　行き〔名〕
行き先（*yuki*saki）東京行きの電車（Tōkyō *yuki* no densha)
¶この汽車は大阪行きです。(Kono kisha wa Oosaka *yuki* desu.)
⇒行き iki

ゆき　雪〔名〕
雪が積もる（*yuki* ga tsumoru）雪が解ける（*yuki* ga tokeru）
¶雪が降って、1メートルも積もりました。(*Yuki* ga futte, ichimyōtoru mo tsumorimashita.)

ゆく　行く〔動〕　☞行く iku

ゆしゅつ　輸出〔名、〜する〕
輸出品（*yushutsu*hin）
¶日本は自動車やテレビをたくさん輸出しています。(Nihon wa jidōsha ya terebi o takusan *yushutsu* shite imasu.)
⇔輸入 yunyū

yuka 〔n〕 **the floor**
¶The river overflowed and the water came up over **the floor**.

yukai 〔adj-v〕 **pleasant, happy, delightful**
¶The class party〚reunion〛yesterday **was** a lot of **fun**.
¶[Mr.] Tanaka is a **cheerful** person—[he] is always cracking jokes.

yuki 〔n〕 **going, bound for destination** // a Tokyo train, a train **bound for** Tokyo
¶This train **is going to** Osaka.

yuki 〔n〕 **snow**
snow piles up on the ground // snow melts
¶**The snow** fell to a depth of one meter.

yuku 〔v I〕　☞**iku**

yushutsu 〔n, 〜*suru*〕 **exporting, exportation**
an export, **exported** goods
¶Japan **exports** a large number of automobiles and television sets.

ゆずる 譲る〔動Ⅰ〕

¶わたしは年寄りにはいつも席を譲ってあげます。（Watashi wa toshiyori ni wa itsu mo seki o *yuzutte* agemasu.）

yuzuru 〔v Ⅰ〕 **give way, make room; hand over, transfer**

¶I always **give up** my seat to elderly people.

ゆだん 油断〔名、～する〕

¶油断してかぎを掛けなかったら、どろぼうに入られました。（*Yudan* shite kagi o kakenakattara, dorobō ni hairaremashita.）

¶試験は易しいと思って油断していたら、難しくて全然できませんでした。（Shiken wa yasashii to omotte *yudan* shite itara, muzukashikute zenzen dekimasen deshita.）

yudan 〔n, ～*suru*〕 **carelessness, inattention, negligence**

¶[I] **carelessly** left the door unlocked and [we] were robbed.

¶I thought the test would be easy and **was caught unprepared** when it was difficult— couldn't answer anything at all.

ゆっくり〔副〕

① [急がない様子、速くない様子]
¶まだ日本語が下手なので、もっとゆっくり話してください。（Mada nihongo ga hetana node, motto *yukkuri* hanashite kudasai.）

¶おばあさんがゆっくり坂を上ってきます。（Obāsan ga *yukkuri* saka o nobotte kimasu.）

② [心や体がくつろぐ様子]
¶今日は、一日ゆっくり休みたいと思っています。（Kyō wa, ichinichi *yukkuri* yasumitai to omotte imasu.）

¶久しぶりに会ったのですから、今晩はゆっくり話をしましょう。（Hisashiburi ni atta no desu kara, konban wa *yukkuri* hanashi o shimashō.）

yukkuri 〔adv〕 **slowly; at one's leisure**

① [slowly]
¶Could you speak more slowly as I am not yet fluent in Japanese?

¶The old woman is **slowly** climbing up the hill toward [us].

② [at one's leisure, unhurriedly]
¶I want to **take it easy** and not do anything at all today.

¶As we haven't met in such a long time let's have a **nice, long** talk tonight.

ゆにゅう 輸入〔名、～する〕

輸入品（*yunyū*hin）

yunyū 〔n, ～*suru*〕 **importing, importation**

imports, **imported** goods

¶日本はA国から石油を輸入していま
す。(Nihon wa Ē-koku kara sekiyu o
yunyū shite imasu.)
⇔輸出 **yushutsu**

¶ Japan **imports** oil from Country A.

ゆび 指〔名〕

親指 (oya*yubi*) 人指し指
(hitosashi*yubi*) 中指 (naka*yubi*) 薬指
(kusuri*yubi*) 小指 (ko*yubi*) 指輪
(*yubi*wa)
¶足の指にけがをしました。(Ashi no
yubi ni kega o shimashita.)

yubi 〔n〕 **a finger, a toe**

the thumb; the big **toe** // the index
finger // the middle **finger** // the third
finger, the ring **finger** // the little
finger; the little **toe** // a ring (jewelry)

¶ [I] have injured **[my] toe(s)** 〚I
injured **my toe(s)**〛.

ゆめ 夢〔名〕

¶わたしはゆうべおもしろい夢を見ま
した。(Watashi wa yūbe omoshiroi *yume*
o mimashita.)

yume 〔n〕 **dream**

¶ I had an interesting **dream** last night.

ゆるす 許す〔動Ⅰ〕

① [願いなどを許可する]
¶両親が許してくれたので、日本へ留
学する事に決めました。(Ryōshin ga
yurushite kuretanode, Nihon e ryūgaku
suru koto ni kimemashita.)
② [罪や間違いなどをとがめない]
¶わたしが悪かったのです。許してく
ださい。(Watashi ga warukatta no desu.
Yurushite kudasai.)
¶あんなに謝っているのですから、今
度だけは許してあげましょう。(Anna
ni ayamatte iru no desu kara, kondo dake
wa *yurushite* agemashō.)

yurusu 〔vⅠ〕 **permit, approve;
forgive, pardon**
① [permit, approve, allow]
¶ I decided to study in Japan sincc my
parents **had given me their
permission**.

② [forgive, pardon, excuse]
¶ It was my fault. Please **forgive me**.

¶ **Let's forgive [him]** this one time as
[he] has apologized so profusely.

ゆれる 揺れる〔動Ⅱ〕

¶地震で家が激しく揺れました。
(Jishin de ie ga hageshiku *yuremashita*.)

yureru 〔vⅡ〕 **shake, tremble,
sway**
¶ The house **shook** violently in the
earthquake.

¶ この先はバスが揺れますから、御注意ください。(Kono saki wa basu ga *yuremasu* kara, gochūi kudasai.)

¶ Please be prepared for the coming **pitching** 〖**jolting, swaying**, etc.〗 of the bus (said by the driver, etc.).

よ

よ〔助〕

① [意志や感情や判断などを相手に印象づけて表したり念を押したりする場合に使う]

¶急ぎますから、わたしはもう帰りますよ。(Isogimasu kara, watashi wa mō kaerimasu *yo*.)

¶早くしないと遅れますよ。(Hayaku shinai to okuremasu *yo*.)

¶あの映画はとてもおもしろいですよ。(Ano eiga wa totemo omoshiroi desu *yo*.)

② [命令・依頼・勧誘などの気持ちを相手に訴える場合に使う]

¶そんなことをしてはいけませんよ。(Sonna koto o shite wa ikemasen *yo*.)

¶あした必ず来てくださいよ。(Ashita kanarazu kite kudasai *yo*.)

¶疲れたから、少し休みましょうよ。(Tsukareta kara, sukoshi yasumimashō *yo*.)

＊ 一般に丁寧に言う場合は男性も女性も「～ですよ (～desu yo)」「～ますよ (～masu yo)」の形を使う。名詞、形容動詞の語幹、助詞に直接「よ (yo)」が続く形は、女性だけが使う。「これはあなたの本よ。(Kore wa anata no hon yo.)」「この花きれいよ。(Kono hana kirei yo.)」「あした休みなのよ。(Ashita yasumi na no yo.)」男性は、「だ (da)」をつけて使う。「これは君の本だよ。(Kore wa kimi no hon da yo.)」「この花きれいだよ。(Kono hana kirei

yo 〔part〕 a sentence-final particle used for stress, etc.

① [used for emphasizing to the listener the force of one's intent, emotion, judgment, etc.]

¶ I'm leaving now as I'm in a hurry.

¶ You'll be late if you don't hurry!

¶ That movie is really interesting.

② [used to appeal to the listener as in an order, request, urging, etc.]

¶ You shouldn't do that!

¶ Now be sure to come tomorrow.

¶ I'm tired—let's take a break!

＊ When speaking politely generally used in the forms "～ *desu yo* ," "-*masu yo*" by both men and women. *Yo* directly follows a noun, adjectiveverb, or particle only in women's language. Examples are "*Kore wa anata no hon yo*" (This is *your* book), "*Kono hana kirei yo*" (What a pretty flower!), and "*Ashita yasumi na no yo*" (Tomorrow is a holiday; It's closed tomorrow). In men's language *da* is used before *yo*: "*Kore wa kimi no hon da yo*", "*Kono hana kirei da yo*"; and "*Ashita yasumi*

da yo.)」「あした休みなんだよ。
(Ashita yasumi na n da yo.)」形容詞に直接「よ（yo）」のつく形は、一般に男性が使う。「この本おもしろいよ。
(Kono hon omoshiroi yo.)」女性の場合は「この本おもしろいわよ（Kono hon omoshiroi wa yo.）」などと言う。

na n da yo." Using *yo* directly after an adjective is also generally done by men, as in "*Kono hon omoshiroi yo*" (This is really an interesting book). Women will say something like "*Kono hon omoshiroi wa yo*" instead.

よい〔形〕

① [正しい立派な様子]

¶ よいと思ったことは、勇気を持って実行しなさい。（*Yoi* to omotta koto wa yūki o motte jikkō shinasai.）

¶ 人の物を取るのはよくないことです。（Hito no mono o toru no wa *yoku* nai koto desu.）

↔悪い **warui**

② [善良である様子]

¶ 山田さんはとてもよい人ですね。
(Yamada san wa totemo *yoi* hito desu ne.)

↔悪い **warui**

③ [親しい様子]

¶ 春子さんと秋子さんはたいへん仲のよい友達です。（Haruko san to Akiko san wa taihen naka no *yoi* tomodachi desu.）

*普通「仲がよい（naka ga yoi）」の形で使う。

↔悪い **warui**

④ [ものごとの優れている様子]

¶ 上田さんは成績がたいへんよいそうです。（Ueda san wa seiseki ga taihen *yoi* sō desu.）

¶ この万年筆はあまりよくないです。
(Kono mannenhitsu wa amari *yoku* nai desu.)

yoi 〔adj〕 **good, right; nice; fine; all right**

① [good, right]

¶ You should be brave and do what you think **is right**.

¶ Taking things that belong to others **is not right**.

② [good, nice]

¶ [Mr.] Yamada is a **fine** person.

③ [good, close]

¶ Haruko and Akiko are **good** friends.

*Usually used in the pattern "*naka ga yoi*."

④ [good, fine, excellent]

¶ They say that [Miss] Ueda's record 〚grade(s)〛 is **excellent**.

¶ This fountain pen **isn't** very **good**.

⑤ [状態の好ましい様子、気持ちのよい様子]

病気がよくなる（byōki ga *yoku* naru）

¶ 天気がよい日には散歩をします。（Tenki ga *yoi* hi ni wa sanpo o shimasu.）

¶ あの店は感じのよい店ですね。（Ano mise wa kanji no *yoi* mise desu ne.）

¶ お酒を飲んだらよい気持ちになって、ゆうべは早く寝てしまいました。（Osake o nondara *yoi* kimochi ni natte, yūbe wa hayaku nete shimaimashita.）

↔悪い **warui**

⑥ [じゅうぶんである様子]

¶ 「ここから駅までどのくらいかかりますか。」（Koko kara eki made dono kurai kakarimasu ka？）「10分もあればよいと思います。」（Jippun mo areba *yoi* to omoimasu.）

¶ 今度の旅行には五千円も持って行けばよいでしょう。（Kondo no ryokō ni wa gosen'en mo motte ikeba *yoi* deshō.）

⑦ [同意や許可などの意味を表す]

¶ 時間はありますから、急がなくてもよいでしょう。（Jikan wa arimasu kara, isoganakute mo *yoi* deshō.）

¶ たばこを吸ってもよいですか。（Tabako o sutte mo *yoi* desu ka.）

* 「〜てもよい（〜te mo yoi）」の形で使う。

→（〜ても）いい（〜**te mo**）**ii**

* 「終止の形」「連体の形」のときには「いい（ii）」も使われる。

⇒いい **ii**

よう 用 〔名〕

用が済む（*yō* ga sumu）用を済ませる（*yō* o sumaseru）

---

⑤ [good, nice, pleasant]

one's illness gets **better**

¶ [I] go for a walk on **nice** days.

¶ That restaurant 〖coffee shop, shop, etc.〗 has a **good** atmosphere, doesn't it?

¶ Last night I was feeling **good** after having something to drink and I went to bed early.

⑥ [all right, enough]

¶ "How long does it take to get to the station from here?"

"It shouldn't take more than 10 minutes (literally, I think 10 minutes **will be enough**)."

¶ Five thousand yen **should be enough** for the coming trip.

⑦ [all right, may]

¶ There's still time so you **don't have to** hurry.

¶ **Do you mind** if I smoke?

*Used in the pattern "-*te mo yoi*."

*In the dictionary or plain form, the form *ii* is also used.

yō 〔n〕 **business, engagement, errand, things to do**

one's **business** is completed // finish one's **business**

¶用があるから、ちょっと来てください。(Yō ga aru kara, chotto kite kudasai.)

¶Please come here a minute—there's **something I want to see you about**.

¶何か御用でしょうか。(Nani ka goyō deshō ka？)

¶Is there **something I can do for you?**

⇒用事 yōji

よう 酔う〔動 I〕

you 〔v I〕 **get drunk; be seasick, carsick, etc.**

① [酒などを飲んで心や体が正常でなくなる]

① [get drunk, be intoxicated]

¶ゆうべはお酒を飲みすぎて、すっかり酔ってしまいました。(Yūbe wa osake o nomisugite, sukkari *yotte* shimaimashita.)

¶Last night [I] drank too much and **got drunk**.

② [乗り物に乗って気持ちが悪くなる]

② [be seasick, carsick, airsick, etc.]

¶わたしは車に弱くてすぐに酔ってしまうので、本当に困ります。(Watashi wa kuruma ni yowakute sugu ni *yotte* shimau node, hontō ni komarimasu.)

¶**I get carsick** very easily (more literally, I am susceptible to carsickness and **get carsick** very easily). It's really a nuisance.

¶海が荒れたので、すっかり船に酔ってしまいました。(Umi ga areta node, sukkari fune ni *yotte* shimaimashita.)

¶The sea was rough and [I] **got** very **seasick**.

よう〔助動〕

-yō 〔auxil〕 **a verb ending indicating intent, urging, etc.**

① [意志を表す]

① [indicates intent]

¶その荷物を持ってあげよう。(Sono nimotsu o motte age*yō*.)

¶**Let me carry** that package 〚bag, etc.〛 for you.

¶わたしはA大学の入学試験を受けようと思っています。(Watashi wa Ē-daigaku no nyūgaku-shiken o uke*yō* to omotte imasu.)

¶**I plan to take** the entrance exam for University A.

¶あなたはどんな勉強をしようとお考えですか。(Anata wa donna benkyō o shi*yō* to okangae desu ka？)

¶What **do you plan** to study?

¶上田さんは早くから東京へ来ようと思っていたそうです。(Ueda san wa omotte ita sō desu.)

¶I hear that [Mr.] Ueda **had wanted to come** to Tokyo for some time.

hayaku kara Tōkyō e koyō to omotte ita sō desu.)

*「～と思う（～to omou）」「～と考える（～to kangaeru）などといっしょに使うことが多い。

*Often used with ~ *to omou*, ~ *to kangaeru*, etc.

②[勧誘を表す]

②[indicates urging]

¶みんなでいっしょに御飯を食べようよ。(Minna de issho ni gohan o tabeyō yo.)

¶ **Let's** all **eat** together.

③[ある動作・作用がこれから行われるという意味を表す]

③[indicates that some action or operation is about to take place]

¶出かけようとしているところへ友達が訪ねて来ました。(Dekake yō to shite iru tokoro e tomodachi ga tazunete kimashita.)

¶ A friend came to visit [mel **just as [I] was about to go out**.

¶夜が明けようとするころ、わたしたちは出発しました。(Yo ga akeyō to suru koro, watashitachi wa shuppatsu shimashita.)

¶ We set out **as the sun was coming up**.

*「～ようとする（～yō to suru）」の形で使う。

*Used in the pattern "-yō to suru."

＊「よう（yō）」はⅠ型動詞以外の動詞につく。

＊-yō is added to verbs other than Type I verbs.

⇒う u

-よう -用〔尾〕

-yō 〔suf〕 use, service, for~

子供用自転車（kodomoyō-jitensha）

非常用の階段（hijōyō no kaidan）

a **child's** bicycle // a **fire** escape

ようい 用意〔名、～する〕

yōi 〔n, ~*suru*〕 preparation, arrangements, provisions

¶食事の用意ができました。(Shokuji no yōi ga dekimashita.)

¶ Dinner 〖lunch, breakfast〗 **is ready**.

¶旅行に行くのに、いくらぐらい用意したらいいでしょうか。(Ryokō ni iku no ni, ikura gurai yōi shitara ii deshō ka？)

¶ How much money **will [we] need** for the trip?

ようか 八日 〔名〕

① [日付を表す]
五月八日 (gogatsu *yōka*)

② [日数を表す]
八日前 (*yōka*mae)　八日後 (*yōka*go)

⇒-日 -ka

ようきゅう 要求 〔名、〜する〕

¶ あなたがたの要求には応じられません。(Anatagata no *yōkyū* ni wa ōjiraremasen.)

¶ 社長に月給を上げてくれるように要求しました。(Shachō ni gekkyū o agete kureru yō ni *yōkyū* shimashita.)

ようじ 用事 〔名〕

用事がない (*yōji* ga nai)　用事を済ませる (*yōji* o sumaseru)

¶ 用事がありますので、お先に失礼します。(*Yōji* ga arimasu node, osaki ni shitsurei shimasu.)

¶ 用事を済んだら、お茶を飲みに行きましょう。(*Yōji* ga sundara, ocha o nomi ni ikimashō.)

⇒用 yō

ようじん 用心 〔名、〜する〕

用心深い (*yōjin*bukai)

¶ 風邪を引かないように用心してください。(Kaze o hikanai yō ni *yōjin* shite kudasai.)

¶ 電車の中でお金を取られないように用心したほうがいいですよ。(Densha no naka de okane o torarenaiyō ni *yōjin* shita hō ga ii desu yo.)

yōka 〔n〕 **the eighth of the month; eight days**

① [the eighth of the month]
May **8**

② [eight days]
8 days ago, **8 days** earlier // **8 days** from now, **8 days** later

yōkyū 〔n, 〜*suru*〕 **demand, request, claim**

¶ [I] can't agree to your **demands**.

¶ [I] **asked** the company president for a raise in salary.

yōji 〔n〕 **business, errand, engagement, things to do**

have nothing **that needs to be attended to**, be free // settle **one's business**, finish **an errand**

¶ I'm sorry to leave early but I have **some other business** to see to.

¶ Let's go have some tea after you've finished up **your business**.

yōjin 〔n, 〜*suru*〕 **care, caution**

careful, cautious, prudent

¶ Please **be careful** not to catch a cold.

¶ It is advisable **to be on one's guard** against pickpockets while riding the train (literally, **be careful** one's money is not stolen).

ようす　様子〔名〕

yōsu〔n〕**state, circumstances;
appearance, looks**

① [ものごとの有様・状態]

① [state, circumstances]

¶病人の様子はどうでしたか。

¶ How was the patient?

（Byōnin no *yōsu* wa dō deshita ka？）

¶わたしはまだ日本の様子がよくわか
りません。（Watashi wa mada Nihon no
yōsu ga yoku wakarimasen.）

¶ I still don't understand Japan fully.

② [ものごとの情況などから判断され
る状態]

② [appearance, looks]

¶わたしがその話をしたら、田中さん
は驚いた様子でした。（Watashi ga
sono hanashi o shitara, Tanaka san wa
odoroita *yōsu* deshita.）

¶ [Mr.] Tanaka **seemed** surprised when
I mentioned that.

¶空が曇ってきて、今にも雨が降りそ
うな様子でした。（Sora ga kumotte kite,
ima ni mo ame ga furisō na *yōsu* deshita.）

¶ The sky darkened and **it looked like**
it would start raining at any moment.

ようだ〔助動〕

yō da〔auxil〕**like, as; seem like,
look like**

① [あるものごとがほかのものごとに
似ていることを表す]

① [like]

¶あの雲は人の顔のようですね。（Ano
kumo wa hito no kao no *yō desu* ne.）

¶ That cloud **is like** a person's face.

¶あの人は日本語を日本人のように上
手に話します。（Ano hito wa Nihongo o
Nihonjin no *yō ni* jōzu ni hanashimasu.）

¶ [He] speaks Japanese **like** a native
speaker.

② [あるものごとを例として示すこと
を表す]

② [like, such as]

¶わたしは、東京のようなにぎやかな
町より京都のような静かな町が好きで
す。（Watashi wa, Tōkyō no *yō na*
nigiyaka na machi yori Kyōto no *yō na*
shizuka na machi ga suki desu.）

¶ I like quiet cities **like** Kyoto better
than lively ones **like** Tokyo.

¶わたしは上田さんのような立派な医
者になりたいです。（Watashi wa Ueda
san no *yō na* rippa na isha ni naritai
desu.）

¶ I want to become a good doctor **like**
Dr. Ueda.

③ [推量・不確かな判断などを表す]

③ [look like, seem like, appear]

881

¶あしたは雨のようですよ。（Ashita wa ame no *yō desu* yo.）

¶ **It looks like** rain tomorrow.

¶山田さんは来月アメリカへ行くようです。（Yamada san wa raigetsu Amerika e iku *yō desu.*）

¶ **It seems that** [Miss] Yamada is going to the United States next month.

④ [あるものごとの内容が同じであることを表す]

④ [like, as]

¶中村さんの言うようにしてください。（Nakamura san no iu *yō ni* shite kudasai.）

¶ Please do **what** [Mr.] Nakamura tells you to.

¶以上のようなわけで、わたしは会社を辞めるつもりです。（Ijō no *yō na* wake de, watashi wa kaisha o yameru tsumori desu.）

¶ I plan to quit my job for the above reasons.

⑤ [方法などを表す]

⑤ [way, manner]

¶あなたのうちは駅からどのように行くのですか。（Anata no uchi wa eki kara dono *yō ni* iku no desu ka？）

¶ **How** do [I] get from the station to your home?

¶「この言葉は漢字でどのように書きますか。（Kono kotoba wa kanji de dono *yō ni* kakimasu ka？）「このように書きます。」（Kono *yō ni* kakimasu.）

¶ "**How** is this word written in *kanii*?" "It is written **like** this."

*普通「どのように（dono yō ni）」「このように（kono yō ni）」「そのように（sono yō ni）」「あのように（ano yō ni）」の形で使う。

*Usually used in the patterns "*dono yō ni,* "*kono yō ni ,*" "*sono yō ni ,*" and "*ano yō ni.*"

⑥ [あることを意識的に心がけて行うことを表す]

⑥ [make it a practice to]

¶病気になってからは、毎日牛乳を飲むようにしています。（Byōki ni natte kara wa, mainichi gyūnyū o nomu *yō ni* shite imasu.）

¶ Since becoming ill [I] **make it a practice** to drink milk every day.

¶いつも日本語だけで話すようにしています。（Itsu mo Nihongo dake de hanasu *yō ni* shite imasu.）

¶ [I] **make it a practice** to speak only Japanese.

¶ 毎日、予習と復習をするようにしく
ださい。(Mainichi, yoshū to fukushū o
suru *yō ni* shite kudasai.)

¶ Please **try** to prepare your lessons
and to review every day.

*普通「〜ようにする（〜yō ni suru）」
の形で使う。

*Usually used in the pattern "〜 *yō ni
suru*."

⑦ [目標や目的などを表す]

⑦ [in order to, so as to]

¶ 汽車の時間に間に合うように急いで
ください。(Kisha no jikan ni maniau *yō
ni* isoide kudasai.)

¶ Please hurry **so** you'll be in time for
the train.

¶ 肉が腐らないように冷蔵庫に入れて
おいてください。(Niku ga kusaranai *yō
ni* reizōko ni irete oite kudasai.)

¶ Please put the meat in the refrigerator
so it won't spoil.

*「ように（yō ni）」の前には動詞の
「ないの形」か、無意志性の動詞が来
ることが多い。

*This *yō ni* is generally preceded by a
verb in the -*nai* form or by a verb
expressing uncontrollable action.

⑧ [ある状態の変化の結果を表す]

⑧ [an effect]

¶ 日本へ来てから、日本語が上手に話
せるようになりました。(Nihon e kite
kara, Nihongo ga jōzu ni hanaseru *yō ni*
narimashita.)

¶ [I] **have become** good at Japanese
since coming to Japan.

¶ 早く100メートル泳ぐことができるよ
うになりたいです。(Hayaku
hyakumētoru oyogu koto ga dekiru *yō ni*
naritai desu.)

¶ I want **to become** able to swim a
hundred meters as soon as possible.

¶ 弟は高等学校に入ってから、一生
懸命勉強するようになりました。
(Otōto wa kōtōgakkō ni haitte kara,
isshōkenmei benkyō suru yō ni
narimashita.)

¶ My younger brother **has started** to
study hard since entering high school
〚My younger brother **started** to study
hard after entering high school〛.

*普通「〜ようになる（〜yō ni naru）」
の形で使う。

*Usually used in the pattern "〜 *yō ni
naru*."

⑨ [願望・要求・勧めなどの内容を表
すときに使う]

⑨ [used when expressing a desire,
request, recommendation, etc.]

¶ 早くよくなるようにお祈りしており
ます。(Hayaku yoku naru *yō ni* oinori
shite orimasu.)

¶ I hope [you] will be better soon (very
polite).

¶山田さんにあしたわたしのうちへ来るように言ってください。(Yamada san ni ashita watashi no uchi e kuru *yō ni* itte kudasai.)

¶ Please ask [Mr.] Yamada to come to my place tomorrow.

¶田中さんに本を返してくれるように頼みました。(Tanaka san ni hon o kaeshite kureru *yō ni* tanomimashita.)

¶ I asked [Miss] Tanaka to please return the book.

*あとに「言う（iu）」「話す（hanasu）」「頼む（tanomu）」「命令する（meirei suru）」「勧める（susumeru）」「祈る（inoru）」などの動詞が来る。

*Followed by verbs like *iu, hanasu, tanomu, meirei suru, susumeru, inoru,* etc.

＊丁寧に言う場合「ようです（yō desu)」となる。

＊When speaking politely, *yō desu* is used rather than *yō da*.

ようふく 洋服〔名〕

yōfuku 〔n〕 **Western clothes, a suit, a dress, etc.**

洋服だんす（*yōfuku-dansu*）

a wardrobe, a clothespress

¶田中さんはいつも茶色の洋服を着ています。(Tanaka san wa itsumo chairo no *yōfuku* o kite imasu.)

¶ [Mr.] Tanaka is always dressed in brown.

ようやく〔副〕

yōyaku 〔adv〕 **at last, finally, at length**

¶夕方になって、ようやく涼しい風が吹き始めました。(Yūgata ni natte, *yōyaku* suzushii kaze ga fukihajimemashita.)

¶ A cool breeze **finally** came up after it got dark 〚A cool breeze has **finally** come up since it has gotten dark〛.

¶上田さんは3度めの試験でようやく合格しました。(Ueda san wa sandome no shiken de *yōyaku* gōkaku shimashita.)

¶ [Mr.] Ueda **finally** passed the exam on [his] third try.

¶わたしは3年日本語を勉強して、ようやく新聞が読めるようになりました。(Watashi wa sannen Nihongo o benkyō shite, *yōyaku* shinbun ga yomeru yō ni narimashita.)

¶ After studying the language for three years, I can now **at last** 〚I **at last** became able to〛 read the newspaper in Japanese.

＊なかなか実現しない事態が、一定の時間を経過した後、実現するという意味を表す。普通、待ち望んでいた結果が実現したときに使う。

＊*Yōyaku* indicates that something difficult to achieve has at last been realized after the passage of a certain

＊あとに過去・完了を表す「たの形」が来ることが多い。「ようやくのことで（yōyaku no koto de）」の形でも使う。

⇒やっと **yatto**

よく 欲〔名〕

¶あの人はとても欲が深いです。（Ano hito wa totemo *yoku* ga fukai desu.）
¶あの人くらい欲のない人はいませんね。（Ano hito kurai *yoku* no nai hito wa imasen ne.）

よく 〔副〕

① [じゅうぶんに]
¶疲れていたので、ゆうべはよく眠りました。（Tsukarete ita node, yūbe wa *yoku* nemurimashita.）
¶交差点を渡るときは、よく注意してください。（Kōsaten o wataru toki wa, *yoku* chūi shite kudasai.）
② [しばしば、たびたび]
¶山田さんはよく図書館へ行きます。（Yamada san wa *yoku* toshokan e ikimasu.）
¶子供のころは、よくけんかをしたものです。（Kodomo no koro wa, *yoku* kenka o shita mono desu.）
③ [程度がはなはだしい様子]
¶春子さんはお姉さんと顔がよく似ています。（Haruko san wa onēsan to kao ga *yoku* nite imasu.）
¶このナイフはよく切れますね。（Kono naifu wa *yoku* kiremasu ne.）

period of time; this is usually a desired result.

＊Often followed by the -ta form expressing past or completed action. Also used in the pattern "*yōyaku no koto de*."

yoku 〔n〕 **greed, desire, want, passian**

¶[He] is very **greedy**.

¶[He] is a [man] of few **wants** (more literally, There are few people with as few **wants** as him).

yoku 〔adv〕 **well, fully; often; much**

① [well, fully, thoroughly, carefully]
¶I was tired so I slept **well** last night.

¶Please be **very** careful when crossing the Street.

② [often, frequently]
¶[Miss] Yamada **often** goes to the library.

¶[1] was in **a number of** fights during [my] childhood.

③ [much, a good deal]
¶Haruko looks **a lot** like her older sister.

¶This knife is **quite** sharp, isn't it?

④ [相手をほめたりねぎらったりする
ときに使う]

¶よくがんばりましたね。(*Yoku
ganbarimashita ne.*)

¶よくいらっしゃいました。(*Yoku
irasshaimashita.*)

よくじつ 翌日 〔名〕

¶土曜日に旅行に出かけて、翌日の日
曜日に帰ってきました。(Doyōbi ni
ryokō ni dekakete, *yokujitsu* no nichiyōbi
ni kaette kimashita.)

よける 〔動 II〕

¶自動車が来たから、よけないと危な
いですよ。(Jidōsha ga kita kara, *yokenai
to abunai desu yo.*)

よこ 横 〔名〕

① [物に向かって左右の方向]

¶あなたの横に座っている人は、横を
向いて写っていますね。(Anata no
yoko ni suwatte iru hito wa, *yoko* o muite
utsutte imasu ne.)

② [四角形で水平方向の辺、またその
長さ]

¶この紙を縦10センチ、横15センチの
大きさに切ってください。(Kono kami
o tate jissenchi, *yoko* jūgosenchi no ookisa
ni kitte kudasai.)

↔縦 tate

よごす 汚す 〔動 I〕

¶スープをこぼして、洋服を汚してし
まいました。(Sūpu o koboshite, yōfuku
o *yogoshite* shimaimashita.)

④ [used when praising or thanking
someone, etc.]

¶ You did **well** not to get discouraged.

¶ Welcome 〚I'm glad you could come〛.

yokujitsu 〔n〕 **the next day**

¶ I left on the trip on Saturday and
came back the **following** Sunday.

yokeru 〔v II〕 **avoid, keep away
from, dodge**

¶ **Look out** for that car! (literally, A car
is coming and it will be dangerous **if
you don't move away** from its path)

yoko 〔n〕 **side; width; sideways,
horizontally**

① [side, flank]

¶ The person sitting **next** to you in the
photo has **the side** of [her] face
towards the camera.

② [width, breadth]

¶ Please cut this paper so it's 10
centimeters long and 15 centimeters
wide.

yogosu 〔v I〕 **make dirty, stain,
soil, deface**

¶ [I] spilled some soup and **stained**
[my] clothes.

¶きれいな着物を着たのですから、汚さないように気をつけなさい。(Kirei na kimono o kita no desukara, *yogosanai* yō ni ki o tsukenasai.)

¶ Please be careful **not to dirty** that pretty *kimono* you're wearing.

よごれる 汚れる〔動Ⅱ〕

yogoreru 〔v Ⅱ〕 **become dirty, be soiled**

¶シャツが汚れたので、洗たくしました。(Shatsu ga *yogoreta* node, sentaku shimashita.)

¶ [I] washed the shirt as it **was dirty**.

¶どろ道を走ったので、車が汚れてしまいました。(Doromichi o hashitta node, kuruma ga *yogorete* shimaimashita.)

¶ The car **got dirty** on the muddy roads.

よさん 予算〔名〕

yosan 〔n〕 **estimate, estimated cost; budget**

①〔必要な費用を見積もること、また見積もった金額〕

① [estimate, estimated cost, personal budget]

¶家を買いたいのですが、予算が足りません。(Ie o kaitai no desu ga, *yosan* ga tarimasen.)

¶ [I] want to buy a house, but **[my] budget** doesn't permit it.

¶旅行にいくらかかるか、予算を立ててみましょう。(Ryokō ni ikura kakaruka, *yosan* o tatete mimashō.)

¶ Let's draw up **an estimate** of what the trip will cost.

②〔国家や地方公共団体などが1年間の収入と支出を見積もること〕

② [budget (for a government, etc.)]

¶来年度の予算はいつ決まりますか。(Rainendo no *yosan* wa itsu kimarimasu ka?)

¶ When will next year's **budget** be decided?

よしゅう 予習〔名、～する〕

yoshū 〔n, ～*suru*〕 **preparation of lessons**

¶あしたの予習はもう済みましたか。(Ashita no *yoshū* wa mō sumimashita ka?)

¶ Have you finished **preparing** for tomorrow's class(es) yet?

¶予習していったので、先生の話がよくわかりました。(*Yoshū* shite itta node sensei no hanashi ga yoku wakarimashita.)

¶ [I] understood what the teacher was talking about because [I] **had prepared** beforehand.

⇔復習 fukushū

よせる 寄せる〔動Ⅱ〕

¶机やいすを教室のすみに寄せてください。(Tsukue ya isu o kyoshitsu no sumi ni *yosete* kudasai.)

¶花びんをもう少し右へ寄せてみてください。(Kabin o mō sukoshi migi e *yosete* mite kudasai.)

よそう 予想〔名、～する〕

予想が当たる (*yosō* ga ataru) 予想が外れる (*yosō* ga hazureru)

¶この試合は、最後までどちらが勝つか予想できませんでした。(Kono shiai wa, saigo made dochiraga katsu ka *yosō* dekimasen deshita.)

¶わたしの予想どおり、山田さんは秋子さんと結婚しました。(Watashi no *yosō* doori, Yamada san wa Akiko san to kekkon shimashita.)

よっか 四日〔名〕

①[日付を表す]
一月四日 (Ichigatsu *yokka*)
②[日数を表す]
四日前 (*yokka*mae) 四日後 (*yokka*go)
⇒-日 -ka

よっつ 四つ〔名〕

①[4個]
¶ここにみかんが四つあります。
(Koko ni mikan ga *yottsu* arimasu.)
②[4歳]
¶この子は四つです。(Kono ko wa *yottsu* desu.)

yoseru〔v Ⅱ〕move aside, put aside, bring something near

¶ Please **move** the desks and chairs to the corner(s) of the classroom.

¶ Please **move** the vase a little to the right.

yosō〔n, ～*suru*〕expectation, forecast, estimate, supposition
one's expectations come true, fulfill one's expectations // be disappointed in **one's expectations**

¶ The outcome of this match **was unpredictable** until the very end.

¶ **As I expected**, Mr. Yamada married Akiko.

yokka〔n〕the fourth of the month; four days
① [the fourth of the month]
January 4
② [four days]
four days ago, **four days** earlier // **four days** from now, **four days** later

yottsu〔n〕four; four years old
① [four, four items]
¶ There are **four** mandarin oranges here.
② [four years of age]
¶ This child is **four years old**.

よてい　予定〔名、〜する〕

¶わたしは 30 日に東京へ行く予定です（Watashi wa sanjūnichi ni Tōkyō e iku *yotei* desu.）

¶今日の午後は何か予定がありますか。（Kyō no gogo wa nani ka *yotei* ga arimasu ka？）

¶汽車は予定どおりに上野に着きました。（Kisha wa *yotei* doori ni Ueno ni tsukimashita.）

よなか　夜中〔名〕

¶ゆうべ、夜中に近所で火事がありました。（Yūbe, *yonaka* ni kinjo de kaji ga arimashita.）

⇒夜 yoru

よのなか　世の中〔名〕

① [世間、社会]

¶あの人は幸せに育って、世の中の苦労を知らないようです。（Ano hito wa shiawase ni sodatte, *yononaka* no kurō o shiranai yō desu.）

② [時代]

¶今は昔と違って、世界のどこへでもすぐ行ける世の中です。（Ima wa mukashi to chigatte, sekai no doko e demo sugu ikeru *yononaka* desu.）

よぶ　呼ぶ〔動Ⅰ〕

① [大声で声をかける]

¶山田さんが「おおい。」とわたしを呼びました。（Yamada san ga "Ōi" to watashi o *yobimashita*.）

② [声をかけてそばに来させる]

yotei〔n, 〜*suru*〕**program, plan, schedule, prearrangement, expectation**

¶**I plan** to go to Tokyo on the thirtieth.

¶Do you have any **plans** for this afternoon?

¶The train arrived at Ueno **on schedule**.

yonaka〔n〕**at midnight, in the middle of the night**

¶There was a fire in [my] neighborhood **late** last night.

yononaka〔n〕**the world, society; the times, the age**

① [the world, society, life]

¶It seems that [he] had a happy childhood and has not yet experienced the grim realities **of life**.

② [the times, the age]

¶The present age differs from the past in that one can soon go anywhere in the world.

yobu〔vⅠ〕**call, call out; call over, draw over; summon, send for**

① [call, call out, hail]

¶Mr. Yamada **called out** to me, saying "Hey!"

② [call over, draw over]

¶母に呼ばれたので、急いで行きました。(Haha ni *yobareta* node, isoide ikimashita.)

③ [使いや手紙などをやって来させる]
¶すぐ医者を呼んでください。(Sugu isha o *yonde* kudasai.)

¶ [I] went to her quickly when [my] mother **called**.

③ [summon, send for, call for]
¶ Please **send for** a doctor right away.

よふかし 夜更かし〔名、〜する〕

yofukashi 〔n, 〜*suru*〕 **stay up late at night, keep late hours**

¶夜更かしをした次の日は、なかなか起きられません。(*Yofukashi* o shita tsugi no hi wa, nakanaka okiraremasen.)

¶ [I] have a hard time getting up the next day after **staying up late**.

¶夜更かしするのは、体によくありません。(*Yofukashi* suru no wa, karada ni yoku arimasen.)

¶ **Late hours** are had for the health.

よほう 予報〔名、〜する〕

yohō 〔n, 〜*suru*〕 **forecast, prediction**

¶天気予報によると、明日は雨が降るそうです。(Tenki-*yohō* ni yoruto, asu wa ame ga furu sō desu.)

¶ According to the weather **forecast**, there will be rain tomorrow.

よぼう 予防〔名、〜する〕

yobō 〔n, 〜*suru*〕 **prevention, protection; preventive**

予防注射 (*yobō*-chūsha)

an innoculation, vaccination, immunization

¶毎日歯をみがいて、虫歯を予防しましょう。(Mainichi ha o migaite, mushiba o *yobō* shimashō.)

¶ Everyone should brush their teeth every day **to ward off** cavities.

¶ダムを作ったり山に木を植えたりして、水害を予防します。(Damu o tsukuttari yama ni ki o uetari shite, suigai o *yobō* shimasu.)

¶ Flood **control** is done by building dams, planting trees on hillsides, and so on.

よほど〔副〕

yohodo 〔adv〕 **very, much, greatly**

¶ゆうべはよほど寒かったのでしょう。水道が凍っています。(Yūbe wa *yohodo* samukatta nodeshō. Suidō ga kootte imasu.)

¶ It must have gotten **exceptionally** cold last night. The water pipes have frozen.

¶息子は一度に五杯も御飯を食べました。よほどおなかがすいていたのでしょう。(Musuko wa ichido ni gohai mo gohan o tabemashita. Yohodo onaka ga suite ita no deshō.)

¶My son ate five bowls of rice at one sitting. He must have been **famished**.

よむ 読む 〔動 I〕

¶聞こえませんから、もっと大きな声で読んでください。(Kikoemasen kara, motto ookina koe de *yonde* kudasai.)

¶あなたは今、どんな本を読んでいますか。(Anata wa ima, donna hon o *yonde* imasu ka？)

yomu 〔v I〕 **read**

¶[I] can't hear you—please **read it** in a louder voice.

¶What books **are you reading** now?

よめ 嫁 〔名〕

嫁にもらう (*yome* ni morau) 嫁にやる (*yome* ni yaru) 息子の嫁 (musuko no *yome*) 花嫁 (hana*yome*)

¶春子さんは、お金持ちのところへお嫁に行ったそうですね。(Haruko san wa, okanemochi no tokoro e o*yome* ni itta sō desu ne.)

yome 〔n〕 **bride, wife, daughter-in-law**

marry (a woman) // give (one's daughter) in marriage // one's son's **wife**, one's daughter-in-law // **bride**

¶I hear that Haruko **married** into a wealthy family.

よやく 予約 〔名、～する〕

席を予約する (seki o *yoyaku* suru)

¶京都はこんでいますから、宿を予約していらっしゃるほうがいいですよ。(Kyōto wa konde imasu kara, yado o *yoyaku* shite irassharu hō ga ii desu yo.)

yoyaku 〔n, ～*suru*〕 **reservation, advance order**

book a seat

¶Kyoto is crowded so it would be best **to reserve** a room in advance.

よゆう 余裕 〔名〕

¶時間の余裕がありません。早くしてください。(Jikan no *yoyū* ga arimasen. Hayaku shite kudasai)

¶うちは貧乏ですから、そんな高い物を買う余裕はありません。(Uchi wa binbō desu kara, sonna takai mono o kau *yoyū* wa arimasen.)

yoyū 〔n〕 **margin, leeway**

¶There is no time **to spare**. Please hurry up 〖Please do it quickly〗.

¶We are poor so we **cannot afford** to buy anything that expensive.

より〔助〕

¶山田さんは中村さんより背が高いです。(Yamada san wa Nakamura san *yori* se ga takai desu.)

¶わたしは、りんごよりみかんのほうが好きです。(Watashi wa, ringo *yori* mikan no hō ga suki desu.)

yori 〔part〕 **than; from**

¶ [Mr.] Yamada is taller **than** [Mr.] Nakamura.

¶ I like mandarin oranges better **than** apples.

よる 寄る〔動Ⅰ〕

① [近づく]

¶もっとそばに寄って、よく見てください。(Motto soba ni *yotte*, yoku mite kudasai.)

② [立ち寄る、目的の所へ行く途中ついでにほかの所へ行く]

¶帰りにデパートに寄って、買い物をしてきました。(Kaeri ni depāto ni *yotte*, kaimono o shite kimashita.)

yoru 〔vⅠ〕 **approach, come near; drop by, stop off at**

① [approach, come near]

¶ Please **move closer** and take a better look.

② [drop by, stop off at]

¶ [I] **stopped off** at a department store on [my] way home and did some shopping.

よる 夜〔名〕

¶あなたは夜何時ごろ寝ますか。(Anata wa *yoru* nanji goro nemasu ka?)

¶父は毎日、夜遅くまで働いています。(Chichi wa mainichi, *yoru* osoku made hataraite imasu.)

⇔昼 hiru　昼間 hiruma

yoru 〔n〕 **night, evening, nighttime**

¶ What time do you go to bed **at night?**

¶ Every day my father works far into **the night**.

よる〔動Ⅰ〕

① [基づく]

¶天気予報によると、あしたもいい天気だそうです。(Tenki-yohō ni *yoru* to, ashita mo ii tennki da sō desu.)

¶山田さんの話によると、中村さんは入院したそうです。(Yamada san no hanashi ni *yoru* to, Nakamura san wa nyūin shita sō desu.)

② [ものごとのそれぞれの性質・事情などに応じてという意味を表す]

yoru 〔vⅠ〕 **based on, according to; depending on; by; due to**

① [based on, according to]

¶ **According to** the weather forecast, it will be a nice day tomorrow too.

¶ **According to** [Mr.] Yamada, [Miss] Nakamura has entered the hospital.

② [depending on]

¶国によって習慣や考え方が違います。(Kuni ni *yotte* shūkan ya kangaekata ga chigaimasu.)

¶ Customs and ways of thinking differ **from** country **to** country.

¶場合によっては、あしたは休むかもしれません。(Baai ni *yotte* wa, ashita wa yasumu ka mo shiremasen.)

¶ **Depending on** circumstances, [I] may take the day off 〖stay home〗 tomorrow.

③[あるものを手段とすることを表す]

③ [by, according to]

¶わたしたちは、毎日のいろいろなできごとを新聞やテレビによって知ります。(Watashitachi wa, mainichi no iroiro na dekigoto o shinbun ya terebi ni *yotte* shirimasu.)

¶ We are informed of what takes place each day **by** the newspaper and television.

④[あるものごとに原因があるということを表す]

④ [due to, owing to]

¶親の不注意によって、子供がけがをしたのです。(Oyano fuchūi ni *yotte*, kodomo ga kega o shita no desu.)

¶ The child's injury was **due to** its parents' carelessness.

¶たばこの火の不始末によって、大火事になりました。(Tabako no hi no fushimatsu ni *yotte*, ookaji ni narimashita.)

¶ The large fire **resulted from** the careless disposal of a cigarette butt.

＊いつも「～による（～ni yoru）」の形で使う。

＊ Always used in the patterns "～ *ni yoru*" and "～ *ni yotte*."

よろこぶ 喜ぶ〔動Ⅰ〕

yorokobu〔v I〕 **be glad, rejoice**

¶山田さんは試験に合格して喜んでいます。(Yamada san wa shiken ni gōkaku shite *yorokonde* imasu.)

¶ [Miss] Yamada **is happy** because [she] passed the exam.

¶秋子さんは、誕生日の贈り物をもらってとても喜んでいます。(Akiko san wa, tanjōbi no okurimono o moratte totemo *yorokonde* imasu.)

¶ Akiko **is very pleased** with her birthday presents.

¶その会には喜んで出席いたします。(Sono kai ni wa *yorokonde* shusseki itashimasu.)

¶ [I] **will take great pleasure** in attending that gathering 〖meeting〗.

よろしい〔形〕

yoroshii〔adj〕 **good, all right**

¶もう帰ってもよろしいでしょうか。(Mō kaette mo *yoroshii* deshō ka？)

¶ **May I** leave now?

893

¶よろしかったら、今日うちへいらっしゃいませんか。(*Yoroshikattara*, kyō uchi e irasshaimasen ka？)

＊「よい (yoi)」「いい (ii)」の改まった言い方。

よろしく〔副〕

① [今後の交際などを願うときのあいさつの言葉]

¶わたしは山田です。どうぞよろしく。(Watashi wa Yamada desu. Dōzo *yoroshiku*.)

＊普通「どうぞよろしく。(Dōzo yoroshiku.)」または「どうぞよろしくお願いします。(Dōzo yoroshiku onegai shimasu.)」の形で使う。

② [好意を伝えるときに使う]

¶それでは、これで失礼します。奥様によろしくお伝えください。

(Soredewa, kore de shitsurei shimasu. Okusama ni *yoroshiku* otsutae kudasai.)

よわい　弱い〔形〕

① [力・技などが劣っている様子]

¶弱い者をいじめてはいけません。

(*Yowai* mono o ijimete wa ikemasen.)

¶わたしの学校はテニスは強いですが、バスケットボールは弱いです。

(Watashi no gakkō wa tenisu wa tsuyoi desu ga, basukettobōru wa *yowai* desu.)

② [程度が低い様子]

¶嵐がだいぶ弱くなってきましたね。

(Kaze ga daibu *yowaku* natte kimashita ne.)

¶ **If it's convenient**, won't you come visit me today?

＊*Yoroshii* is the formal form of *yoi, ii*.

yoroshiku 〔adv〕 well, as one thinks fit; one's regards

① [well, as one thinks fit, at one's own discretion; used to express hopes for friendly relations or kind treatment into the future]

¶ My name is Yamada. **I'm pleased to meet you** (more literally, Please treat me **kindly**).

＊Usually used in the patterns "*Dōzo yoroshiku* ," "*Dōzo yoroshiku onegai shimasu*."

② [one's regards. one's best wishes]

¶ Well, I'll be going now. Please **remember me** to your wife.

yowai 〔adj〕 weak; frail; unskilled

① [weak in strength, technique, etc.]

¶ One shouldn't tease 〖bully〗 those **weaker** than oneself.

¶ My school is strong in tennis but **weak** in basketball.

② [weak, faint]

¶ The wind has become a lot **weaker**.

¶電気の光が弱いので、新聞の字がよく読めません。（Denki no hikari ga *yowai* node, shinbun no ji ga yoku yomemasen.）

¶The electric light **is so weak** that it is hard to read the newspaper.

③ [体などが丈夫でない様子]
足が弱い（ashi ga *yowai*）

③ [weak, frail]
be a walker **who tires easily**

¶田中さんは体が弱くて、よく病気をします。（Tanaka san wa karada ga *yowakute*, yoku byōki o shimasu.）

¶[Mr.] Tanaka **is quite delicate** and is frequently ill.

④ [不得意・苦手である様子]
数学に弱い（sūgaku ni *yowai*）

④ [weak, poor, unskilled]
be poor at mathematics

¶わたしは漢字に弱いです。（Watashi wa kanji ni *yowai* desu.）

¶**I am poor** at *kanji*.

*いつも「〜に弱い（〜ni yowai）」の形で使う。

*Always used in the pattern "〜 *ni yowai*."

⑤ [ものごとに対して抵抗力が少ない様子]
地震に弱い建物（jishin ni *yowai* tatemono）

⑤ [weak, have a low tolerance]

a building **easily damaged** by earthquake

¶この生地は熱に弱いです。（Kono kiji wa netsu ni *yowai* desu.）

¶This cloth **has little resistance** against heat.

¶わたしは船に弱いので、なるべく乗らないようにしています。（Watashi wa fune ni *yowai* node, narubeku noranai yō ni shite imasu.）

¶**I get seasick easily** so I avoid being on board boats.

*いつも「〜に弱い（〜ni yowai）」の形で使う。

*Always used in the pattern "〜 *ni yowai*."

⇔強い tsuyoi

よん 四〔名〕
四個（*yon*ko）四匹（*yon*hiki）

yon〔n〕**four**
four items // **four** animals (dogs, cats, cows, goldfish, etc.)

＊人数のときは「四人（yonin）」、時刻のときは「四時（yoji）」と言う。
⇒四 shi

＊Four persons is *yonin* and four o'clock is *yoji*.

ら

ラーメン〔名〕
¶食堂でラーメンを注文しました。
(Shokudō de rāmen o chūmon shimashita.)

raigetsu 来月〔名〕
来月の中旬 (raigetsu no chūjun)
¶来月、アメリカから友達が来る予定です。(Raigetsu, Amerika kara tomodachi ga kuru yotei desu.)

らいしゅう 来週〔名〕
¶来週の火曜日は何日ですか。
(Raishū no kayōbi wa nannichi desu ka?)
¶来週、わたしは京都へ行くつもりです。(Raishū, watashi wa Kyōto e iku tsumori desu.)

ライター〔名〕
ガスライター (gasu-raitā)
¶ライターでたばこに火をつけます。
(Raitā de tabako ni hi o tsukemasu.)

らいねん 来年〔名〕
来年の春 (rainen no haru)
¶上田さんは来年大学を卒業します。
(Ueda san wa rainen daigaku o sotsugyō shimasu.)

らく 楽〔名、形動〕

① [体や心に苦しさを感じない様子、安らかな様子]

rāmen 〔n〕 **Chinese noodle soup**
¶[I] ordered ***rāmen*** in a restaurant 〚the cafeteria〛.

raigetsu 〔n〕 **next month**
the middle of **next month**
¶A friend from the United States is scheduled to arrive **next month**.

raishū 〔n〕 **next week**
¶What date is Tuesday **next week?**

¶I plan to go to Kyoto **next week**.

raitā 〔n〕 **lighter, cigarette lighter**
a butane **lighter**
¶One uses **a lighter** to light cigarettes.

rainen 〔n〕 **next year**
next spring, the spring of **next year**
¶[Miss] Ueda graduates from college **next year**.

raku 〔n, adj-v〕 **relief, at one's ease; comfortable, well-off; easy, simple**
① [relief, ease from pain, comfortable, at one's ease]

¶注射をしたので、痛みが楽になりました。(Chūsha o shita node, itami ga *raku* ni narimashita.)

¶ The pain **was alleviated** by the shot.

② [経済的に余裕がある様子]

② [comfortable, well-off]

¶こんなに安い月給では、とても楽な生活はできません。(Konna ni yasui gekkyu de wa, totemo *raku* na seikatsu wa dekimasen.)

¶ There is no way one can live **in comfort** on such cheap wages.

¶物価が高いので、生活が楽ではありません。(Bukka ga takai node, seikatsu ga *raku* de wa arimasen.)

¶ Life **is not easy** with such high prices.

③ [易しくて苦労しなくてもよい様子]

③ [easy, simple]

¶今度の試験は案外楽にできました。(Kondo no shiken wa angai *raku* ni dekimashita.)

¶ The test this time was surprisingly **easy**.

¶外国語で毎日日記をつけるのは楽ではありません。(Gaikokugo de mainichi nikki o tsukeru no wa *raku* de wa arimasen.)

¶ **It is no easy task** to keep a daily diary in a foreign language.

らしい〔助動〕

rashii 〔auxil〕 **seem, appear, look like**

¶中村さんは留守らしいです。(Nakamura san wa rusu *rashii* desu.)

¶ **It seems** that [Mrs.] Nakamura isn't at home.

¶どうも風邪を引いたらしく、頭が痛いです。(Dōmo kaze o hiita *rashiku*, atama ga itai desu.)

¶ [My] head aches—**it feels like** [I]'ve caught a cold.

¶今度の試験は難しいらしいですよ。(Kondo no shiken wa muzukashii *rashii* desu yo.)

¶ **It sounds like** the next exam will be a hard one.

＊名詞、動詞、形容詞、形容動詞、ある種の助動詞などについて、ある根拠に基づいてものごとの状況や事態などを推定するという意味を表す。

＊*Rashii* is used with nouns, verbs, adjectives, adjective-verbs and certain auxiliaries. It expresses a supposition about a state or condition based on certain evidence.

-らしい〔尾〕

-rashii 〔suf〕 **be like, be worthy of**

男らしい顔 (otoko*rashii* kao) 女らしい態度 (onna*rashii* taido)

a manly face // a ladylike bearing, feminine deportment

¶今日は本当に春らしい天気です。

（Kyō wa hontō ni haru*rashii* tenki desu.）

¶ Today is a really spring**like** day.

ラジオ〔名〕

rajio〔n〕radio

ラジオをつける（*rajio* o tsukeru）ラジオを消す（*rajio* o kesu）

turn on **the radio** // turn off **the radio**

¶毎朝、ラジオのニュースを聞いてから学校へ行きます。（Maiasa, *rajio* no nyūsu o kiite kara gakkō e ikimasu.）

¶ I listen to the **radio** news each morning before going to school.

られる〔助動〕

-rareru〔auxil〕a verb ending expressing the passive, the potential, respect, etc.

① [受け身の意味を表す]

① [expresses the passive and suffering passive]

¶その学生は質問に上手に答えたので、先生にほめられました。（Sono gakusei wa shitsumon ni jōzu ni kotaeta node, sensei ni home*raremashita*.）

¶ That student **was praised** by the teacher for answering the question well.

¶わたしは大好きなお菓子を弟にみんな食べられてしまいました。（Watashi wa daisuki na okashi o otōto ni minna tabe*rarete* shimaimashita.）

¶ My younger brother **ate up** all of my favorite cakes〚candy, etc.〛(the suffering passive).

¶あしたは試験があるので、今日友達に来られると困ります。（Ashita wa shiken ga aru node, kyō tomodachi ni ko*rareru* to komarimasu.）

¶ As I have a test tomorrow it would be inconvenient if a friend **should come to visit me** today (the suffering passive).

② [可能の意味を表す]

② [expresses the potential]

¶この肉は腐っているので、食べられません。（Kono niku wa kusatte iru node, tabe*raremasen*.）

¶ This meat **can't be eaten**—it's rotten.

¶質問が難しかったので、わたしは答えられませんでした。（Shitsumon ga muzukashikatta node, watashi wa kotae*raremasen* deshita.）

¶ I **couldn't answer** as the question was very difficult.

③ [尊敬の意味を表す]

③ [expresses respect]

¶いつごろ日本へ来られたのですか。（Itsu goro Nihon e ko*rareta* no desu ka？）

¶ When **did you come** to Japan?

¶先生は毎朝何時ごろお宅を出られますか。(Sensei wa maiasa nanji goro otaku o de*raremasu* ka?)

④ [自発の意味を表す]

¶だんだん秋らしい様子が感じられるようになりました。(Dandan akirashii yōsu ga kanji*rareru* yō ni narimashita.)

＊Ⅱ型動詞とⅢ型動詞の「来る (kuru)」につく。Ⅰ型動詞とⅢ型動詞の「する (suru)」には「れる (reru)」がつく。

⇒れる reru

¶ What time **do you leave home** each morning, sir 〖ma'am〗? (said to a teacher, doctor, etc.)

④ [expresses autonomous action]

¶ It has gradually **come to look** like autumn.

＊-*rareru* is added to Type II verbs and to the Type III verb *kuru* (→*korareru*); -*reru* is added to Type I verbs and to the Type III verb *suru* (→*sareru*).

り

りえき　利益〔名〕

① [もうけ]
¶この本を売ると、20パーセントの利益があります。(Kono hon o uru to, nijippāsento no *rieki* ga arimasu.)
② [ためになること、得になること]
¶将来、何か社会の利益になることをしたいと思います。(Shōrai, nani ka shakai no *rieki* ni naru koto o shitai to omoimasu.)

りかい　理解〔名、〜する〕

¶新しい言葉は、辞書を引いて意味を正しく理解しなければいけません。
(Atarashii kotoba wa, jisho o hiite imi o tadashiku *rikai* shinakereba ikemasen.)
¶あの人の言うことは、どうもよく理解できません。(Ano hito no iu koto wa, dōmo yoku *rikai* dekimasen.)

りく　陸〔名〕

¶わたしは船を降りて陸に上がりました。(Watashi wa fune o orite *riku* ni agarimashita.)
¶海の広さは陸の広さの何倍ですか。
(Umi no hirosa wa *riku* no hirosa no nanbai desu ka?)

りくつ　理屈〔名〕

① [道理、ものごとがそうなるわけ]
理屈に合わない (*rikutsu* ni awanai)

---

rieki 〔n〕 profit; benefit, advantage
① [profit]
¶ There is a 20 percent **profit** on the sale of this book.

② [benefit, advantage]
¶ My future plans are to work for the public **good**.

rikai 〔n, 〜*suru*〕 understanding, comprehension
¶ Words new to you should be looked up in the dictionary so you correctly **grasp** their meaning.

¶ I just don't **understand** what [he] says.

riku 〔n〕 land, shore
¶ I alighted from the boat 〖ship〗 and stepped onto **the shore**.

¶ How many times is the area of the world's oceans larger than that of **the land**?

rikutsu 〔n〕 logic, reason; pretext, excuse
① [logic, reason]
illogical, irrational

¶あの人の言うことにも理屈はあります。（Ano hito no iu koto ni mo *rikutsu* wa arimasu.）

② [自分の考えを通すための理由づけ]
¶田中さんは理屈ばかり言って何もしません。（Tanaka san wa *rikutsu* bakari itte nani mo shimasen.）

¶ **There's something to** what [he] says too.

② [pretext, excuse]
¶ [Mr.] Tanaka is **all talk** and no action.

りこう 〔形動〕

¶この子はりこうな子供で、どの科目もよくできます。（Kono ko wa *rikō* na kodomo de, dono kamoku mo yoku dekimasu.）
¶危ない仕事は初めからしないほうがりこうです。（Abunai shigoto wa hajime kara shinai hō ga *rikō* desu.）

rikō 〔adj-v〕 **bright, intelligent, sensible, shrewd, smart**
¶ This child **is quite bright** and does well in every subject at school.

¶ **It is wiser** to refuse dangerous work from the outset.

りそう **理想** 〔名〕
高い理想（takai *risō*）理想的な家庭（*risō*teki na katei）
¶理想と現実とは違います。（*Risō* to genjitsu to wa chigaimasu.）

risō 〔n〕 **an ideal**
lofty **ideals** // a **model** home 〖family〗

¶ There is a gap between **the ideal** and actual reality.

-リットル 〔尾〕
1リットル（ichi*rittoru*）4リットル（yon*rittoru*）9リットル（kyū*rittoru*）

-rittoru 〔suf〕 **liter(s)**
one **liter** // four **liters** // nine **liters**

りっぱ **立派** 〔形動〕

① [堂々として美しい]

¶山田さんの家はずいぶん立派ですね。（Yamada san no ie wa zuibun *rippa* desu ne.）
¶会議で自分の意見を主張した時の中村さんの態度は立派でした。（Kaigi de jibun no iken o shuchō shita toki no Nakamura san no taido wa *rippa* deshita.）

rippa 〔adj-v〕 **fine, handsome, splendid; fine, excellent, superb**
① [fine, handsome, splendid, commanding]
¶ [Mr.] Yamada has a really **fine** house.

¶ [Mr.] Nakamura **was very impressive** while upholding [his] opinions at the meeting.

② [申し分ない様子]

立派な学者 (rippa na gakusha)

¶田中さんは大学を立派な成績で卒業しました。(Tanaka san wa daigaku o *rippa* na seiseki de sotsugyō shimashita.)

¶あの人はなかなか立派な英語を話します。(Ano hito wa nakanaka *rippa* na Eigo o hanashimasu.)

② [fine, excellent, superb, brilliant, admirable]

¶ [Miss] Tanaka graduated from college with a **fine** record.

¶ [He] speaks English **exceptionally well**.

りはつてん　理髪店 〔名〕
☞床屋 tokoya

rihatsuten 〔n〕　☞tokoya

りゆう　理由 〔名〕

¶あなたが学校をやめる理由は何ですか。(Anata ga gakkō o yameru *riyū* wa nan desu ka?)

¶上田さんは病気を理由に会社を休みました。(Ueda san wa byōki o *riyū* ni kaisha o yasumimashita.)

riyū 〔n〕 **reason, cause**

¶ What is your **reason** for quitting school?

¶ [Miss] Ueda stayed home from work **for reasons of** ill health.

りゅうがく　留学 〔名、〜する〕

留学生 (*ryūgaku*sei)

¶来年、わたしは日本へ留学するつもりです。(Rainen, watashi wa Nihon e *ryūgaku* suru tsumori desu.)

ryūgaku 〔n, 〜*suru*〕 **study abroad**

a student **studying abroad**, an **exchange** student

¶ I plan **to study** in Japan next year.

りゅうこう　流行 〔名、〜する〕

¶これが今年流行のネクタイです。(Kore ga kotoshi *ryūkō* no nekutai desu.)

¶悪い風邪が流行していますから、気をつけてください。(Warui kaze ga *ryūkō* shite imasu kara, ki o tsukete kudasai.)

ryūkō 〔n, 〜*suru*〕 **fashion, fad, popularity; prevalence**

¶ This is the type of necktie **in vogue** this year.

¶ Please be careful as a bad flu virus is **going around** now.

りょう　寮 〔名〕

¶わたしは学校の寮にいます。(Watashi wa gakkō no *ryō* ni imasu.)

ryō 〔n〕 **dormitory**

¶ I am living in a school **dormitory**.

¶山田さんは会社の寮に入りました。
（Yamada san wa kaisha no *ryō* ni
hairimashita.）

¶ [Mr.] Yamada has moved into a
company **dormitory**〚Mr. Yamada
moved into a company **dormitory**〛.

りょう　量〔名〕

ryō〔n〕**quantity, amount, volume**

¶砂糖の量はこのぐらいでいいです
か。（Satō no *ryō* wa kono gurai de ii
desu ka？）

¶ Is this enough sugar?

¶忙しすぎるから、来月から仕事の量
を少し減らすつもりです。
（Isogashisugiru kara, raigetsu kara shigoto
no *ryō* o sukoshi herasu tsumori desu.）

¶ I'm too busy so I plan to cut back on
my work **load** starting next month.

りよう　利用〔名、〜する〕

riyō〔n, 〜*suru*〕**use, utilize, make
good use of, exploit**

¶わたしは図書館を利用して、勉強し
ています。（Watashi wa toshokan o *riyō*
shite, benkyō shite imasu.）

¶ I avail myself of the library in my
studies.

¶余ったきれを利用して、人形の服を
作りました。（Amatta kire o *riyō* shite,
ningyō no fuku o tsukurimashita.）

¶ I used the leftover cloth to make
doll's clothes.

-りょう　-料〔尾〕

-ryō〔suf〕**charge, rate, fee,
allowance**

入場料（nyūjō*ryō*）電話料
（denwa*ryō*）使用料（shiyō*ryō*）授業
料（jugyō*ryō*）受験料（juken*ryō*）

an admission **fee** // the telephone
charge // a rental **fee** // tuition // an
examination **fee**

りょうがわ　両側〔名〕

ryōgawa〔n〕**both sides, either
side**

¶道の両側に店が並んでいます。
（Michi no *ryōgawa* ni mise ga narande
imasu.）

¶ There are shops on **both sides** of the
street.

りょうきん　料金〔名〕

ryōkin〔n〕**charge, rate, fee, fare,
toll**

電気料金（denki-*ryōkin*）ガス料金
（gasu-*ryōkin*）タクシー料金
（takushii*ryōkin*）

an electricity **bill** // a gas **bill** // a taxi
fare

¶ 子供の料金は大人の半分です。
（Kodomo no *ryōkin* wa otona no hanbun
desu.）

＊普通、何かをしてもらったり、使っ
たり、利用したりするときに払う金の
ことをいう。

りょうじ　領事〔名〕

領事館（*ryōji*kan）

りょうしゅうしょ　領収書〔名〕

¶ 買い物をして、領収書をもらいまし
た。（Kaimono o shite, *ryōshūsho* o
moraimashita.）

りょうしん　両親〔名〕

¶ 机の上に両親の写真が置いてありま
す。（Tsukue no ue ni *ryōshin* no shashin
ga oite arimasu.）

¶ あの子は小さい時に両親を亡くしま
した。（Ano ko wa chiisai toki ni *ryōshin*
o nakushimashita.）

りょうほう　両方〔名〕

¶ 山田さんは英語もフランス語も両方
上手です。（Yamada san wa Eigo mo
Furansugo mo *ryōhō* jōzu desu.）

¶ わたしは二つの学校の試験を受けて
両方とも受かりました。（Watashi wa
futatsu no gakkō no shiken o ukete
*ryōhō*tomo ukarimashita.）

りょうり　料理〔名、〜する〕

日本料理（Nihon-*ryōri*）中華料理
（Chūka-*ryōri*）フランス料理（Furansu-
ryōri）料理を作る（*ryōri* o tsukuru）

¶ The child's **fare** 〚admission **fee**〛 is
half that of adults.

＊Usually refers to the money paid
when one has something done for one,
uses something, etc.

ryōji 〔n〕 consul, consular
representative
a consulate

ryōshūsho 〔n〕 receipt
¶ [I] did some shopping and received **a
receipt**.

ryōshin 〔n〕 one's parents
¶ There is a photo of **[my] parents** on
[my] desk.

¶ That child lost **its parents** at an early
age.

ryōhō 〔n〕 both, both sides, both
parties
¶ [Mrs.] Yamada is good at **both**
English and French.

¶ I took the entrance exams for two
schools and passed **both** of them.

ryōri 〔n, 〜*suru*〕 cooking,
cuisine, food, dish
Japanese **cooking**, Japanese **food** //
Chinese **cooking**, Chinese **food** //
French **cuisine**, French **food** // fix **a
meal**

¶あなたはどんな料理が好きですか。（Anata wa donna *ryōri* ga suki desu ka？）

¶ What kind of **food** do you like?

¶山田さんの奥さんはとても料理が上手です。（Yamada san no okusan wa totemo *ryōri* ga jōzu desu.）

¶ Mr. Yamada's wife is an excellent **cook**.

りょう- 両- 〔頭〕

両手（*ryō*te）両足（*ryō*ashi）両国（*ryō*koku）

ryō- 〔pref〕 **both, two, a couple of**

both hands, **both** arms // **both** feet, **both** legs // **both** countries

りょかん 旅館 〔名〕

¶旅行するときは、ホテルより旅館に泊まるほうがおもしろいですよ。（Ryokō suru toki wa, hoteru yori *ryokan* ni tomaru hō ga omoshiroi desu yo.）

ryokan 〔n〕 **Japanese-style inn**

¶ When traveling in Japan it is more fun to stay at **a Japanese-style inn** than at a Western-style hotel.

りょこう 旅行 〔名、〜する〕

¶わたしは旅行が好きです。（Watashi wa *ryokō* ga suki desu.）

¶日本へ行ったら、ほうぼうを旅行したいです。（Nihon e ittara, hōbō o *ryokō* shitai desu.）

ryokō 〔n, 〜*suru*〕 **travel, journey, trip**

¶ I like **to travel**.

¶ If I go to Japan **I want to travel** extensively there.

りろん 理論 〔名〕

¶上田さんは物理学の新しい理論を発表しました。（Ueda san wa butsurigaku no atarashii *riron* o happyō shimashita.）

¶理論は立派ですが、実際にうまくいくでしょうか。（*Riron* wa rippa desu ga, jissai ni umaku iku deshō ka？）

riron 〔n〕 **theory**

¶ [Mr.] Ueda has made public a new **theory** in physics 〖Mr. Ueda made public a new **theory** in physics〗.

¶ It sounds fine **in theory** but will it actually work well in practice?

りんご 〔名〕

¶このりんごは一ついくらですか。（Kono *ringo* wa hitotsu ikura desu ka？）

ringo 〔n〕 **apple**

¶ How much are these **apples** apiece?

りんじ 臨時 〔名〕

① [定時でないこと]

rinji 〔n〕 **special, extraordinary; temporary, provisional**

① [special, extraordinary, extra, unscheduled, emergency]

905

臨時休業 (*rinji*-kyūgyō) **臨時列車** (*rinji*-ressha)

a **special** holiday; Closed Today // a **special** train

¶ あしたは臨時に休みます。(Ashita wa *rinji* ni yasumimasu.)

¶ [We] will be closed tomorrow.

¶ 臨時の収入がありました。(*Rinji* no shūnyū ga arimashita.)

¶ [I] had some **supplementary** income.

② [一時的なこと、間に合わせ]

② [temporary, provisional, interim]

¶ 今日は山田先生がお休みですから、臨時にわたしが教えます。(Kyō wa Yamada sensei ga oyasumi desu kara, *rinji* ni watashi ga oshiemasu.)

¶ I will be your **substitute** teacher today as Professor Yamada is absent.

る

るす　留守〔名〕

¶友達を訪ねましたが、留守で会えませんでした。（Tomodachi o tazunemashita ga, *rusu* de aemasen deshita.）

¶旅行に出かけるので、二、三日家を留守にします。（Ryokō ni dekakeru node, ni, sannichi ie o *rusu* ni shimasu.）

rusu 〔n〕 **absent, out**

¶ [I] went to visit a friend but [he] **wasn't at home**.

¶ The house **will be empty** for two or three days because [I] am going away on a trip.

れ

れい 零 〔名〕

零下10度 (*rei*ka jūdo)

¶昨日の試験で、零点を取ってしまいました。(Kinō no shiken de, *rei*ten o totte shimaimashita.)

rei 〔n〕 **zero**

10 degrees below **zero**, minus 10 degrees

¶ [I] got **a zero** on yesterday's test.

れい 例 〔名〕

¶先生は例を挙げて、学生にわかりやすく説明しました。(Sensei wa *rei* o agete, gakusei ni wakariyasuku setsumei shimashita.)

rei 〔n〕 **example**

¶ The teacher gave **an example** in order to explain in a way easy for the students to understand.

れい 礼 〔名〕

① [おじぎ]

¶先生が教室に入ってこられたので、学生は立って礼をしました。(Sensei ga kyōshitsu ni haitte korareta node, gakusei wa tatte *rei* o shimashita.)

② [謝意を表すこと]

お礼をする (o*rei* o suru)

¶お世話になったお礼に何か差し上げたいのですが。(Osewa ni natta o*rei* ni nani ka sashiagetai no desu ga.)

rei 〔n〕 **bow, salute; thanks**

① [bow, salute]

¶ The students stood and **bowed** when their teacher entered the classroom.

② [thanks, gratitude, appreciation]

give **a token of one's appreciation**; give **a reward**

¶ I want to give you something **in appreciation** for your kindness to me.

れいがい 例外 〔名〕

¶デパートはたいてい6時に閉まりますが、このデパートだけは例外で、7時まで開いています。(Depāto wa taitei rokuji ni shimarimasu ga, kono depāto dake wa *reigai* de, shichiji made aite imasu.)

¶例外のない規則はないと言われています。(*Reigai* no nai kisoku wa nai to iwarete imasu.)

reigai 〔n〕 **exception**

¶ Although department stores generally close at six o'clock, this one is **an exception** and stays open until seven.

¶ It is said that there is **an exception** to every rule (literally, that there is no rule without **an exception**).

908

れいぞうこ 冷蔵庫〔名〕

冷蔵庫にしまう (*reizōko ni shimau*)

¶牛乳が腐らないように冷蔵庫に入れておきます。(Gyūnyū ga kusaranai yō ni *reizōko* ni irete okimasu.)

reizōko 〔n〕 **refrigerator, freezer**

put away in the refrigerator 〚freezer〛

¶[We] keep the milk in the refrigerator so it won't spoil.

れいぼう 冷房〔名、〜する〕

¶この建物には冷房があります。

(Kono tatemono ni wa *reibō* ga arimasu.)

⇔暖房 **danbō**

reibō 〔n, 〜*suru*〕 **air conditioning**

¶This building has air conditioning.

レインコート〔名〕

¶雨が降りそうだから、レインコートを着ていきなさい。(Ame ga furisō da kara, *reinkōto* o kite ikinasai.)

reinkōto 〔n〕 **raincoat**

¶Wear a raincoat—it looks like rain.

れきし 歴史〔名〕

¶わたしは大学で日本の歴史を勉強しています。(Watashi wa daigaku de Nihon no *rekishi* o benkyō shite imasu.)

＊「日本の歴史 (Nihon no rekishi)」は「日本史 (Nihonshi)」、「世界の歴史 (sekai no rekishi)」は「世界史 (sekaishi)」、「東洋の歴史 (tōyō no rekishi)」は「東洋史 (tōyōshi)」、「西洋の歴史 (seiyō no rekishi)」は「西洋史 (seiyōshi)」と言う。

rekishi 〔n〕 **history**

¶I am studying Japanese history at college.

＊*Nihon no rekishi* (the history of Japan) is shortened to *Nihonshi*, *sekai no rekishi* (world history) to *sekaishi*, *tōyō no rekishi* (Oriental history) to *tōyōshi*, *seiyō no rekishi* (Western history) to *seiyōshi*, etc.

レコード〔名〕

レコードをかける (*rekōdo* o kakeru)

¶田中さんは、コーヒーを飲みながらレコードを聞いています。(Tanaka san wa, kōhii o nominagara *rekōdo* o kiite imasu.)

rekōdo 〔n〕 **(musical) record**

put on a record, play a record

¶[Miss] Tanaka is drinking coffee and listening to a record.

レストラン〔名〕

¶あの角のレストランで食事をしましょう。(Ano kado no *resutoran* de shokuji o shimashō.)

resutoran 〔n〕 **restaurant**

¶Let's eat at that restaurant on the corner.

(-)れつ (-)列 〔名、尾〕

1〔名〕

¶駅はたいへんこんでいて、切符を買う人が列を作っていました。(Eki wa taihen konde ite, kippu o kau hito ga *retsu* o tsukutte imashita.)

2〔尾〕

1列 (ichi*retsu*) 2列 (ni*retsu*) 前列 (zen*retsu*) 後列 (kō*retsu*)

れっしゃ 列車 〔名〕

貨物列車 (kamotsu-*ressha*)

¶駅に列車がとまっています。(Eki ni *ressha* ga tomatte imasu.)

レポート 〔名〕

¶宿題のレポートをあしたまでに出してください。(Shukudai no *repōto* o ashita made ni dashite kudasai.)

れる 〔助動〕

①[受身の意味を表す]

¶上田さんは宿題を忘れたので、先生にしかられました。(Ueda san wa shukudai o wasureta node, sensei ni shikara*remashita*.)

¶わたしは犬に手をかまれました。(Watashi wa inu ni te o kama*remashita*.)

¶買い物に行く途中で、雨に降られて困りました。(Kaimono ni iku tochūde, ame ni fura*rete* komarimashita.)

¶委員会は2階の会議室で開かれています。(Iinkai wa nikai no kaigishitsu de hiraka*rete* imasu.)

(-)retsu 〖n, suf〗 line, queue; row, column

1 〖n〗 line, queue

¶ The station was very crowded; people **were lined up** to buy tickets.

2 〖suf〗 row, column

one **row**, one **column** // two **rows**, two **columns** // the front **row** // the back 〖last〗 **row**

ressha 〖n〗 train

a freight **train**

¶ **A train** is stopped at the station.

repōto 〖n〗 report, research paper, term paper

¶ Please hand in **your papers** by tomorrow.

-reru 〖auxil〗 a verb ending expressing the passive, the potential, respect, etc.

① [expresses the passive and the suffering passive]

¶ [Miss] Ueda **was scolded** by [her] teacher for forgetting [her] homework.

¶ I **had** my hand **bitten** by a dog (the suffering passive).

¶ **I was caught** in the rain on my way shopping (the suffering passive).

¶ The committee 〖board〗 meeting **is being held** in the conference room on the second floor.

②[可能の意味を表す]

¶昨日は病気で学校に行かれませんで
した。(Kinō wa byōki de gakkō ni
ika*remasen* deshita.)

¶ゆうべはコーヒーを飲みすぎて、な
かなか眠れませんでした。(Yūbe wa
kōhii o nomisugite, nakanaka
nemu*remasen* deshita.)

*この場合はほとんどⅠ型動詞の可能
の形、例えば「行ける（ikeru）」「眠れ
る（nemureru）」を使う。また、「自動
車の運転をする（jidōsha no unten o
suru）」の「する（suru）」、「自動車を
運転する（jidōsha o unten suru）」の
「運転する（unten suru）」などのⅢ型動
詞の場合は、「自動車の運転ができる
（jidōsha no unten ga dekiru）」、「自動車
が運転できる（jidōsha ga unten
dekiru）」などと「できる（dekiru）」を
使う。

→できる dekiru

③[尊敬の意味を表す]

¶山田先生はもうお宅へ帰られました
か。(Yamada sensei wa mō otaku e
kaera*remashita* ka？)

¶いつ、そのニュースを聞かれたので
すか。(Itsu, sono nyūsu o kika*reta* no
desu ka？)

④[自発の意味を表す]

¶昔の写真を見ると、子供のころのこ
とが思い出されます。(Mukashi no
shashin o miru to, kodomo no koro no
koto ga omoidasa*remasu*.)

*Ⅰ型動詞とⅢ型動詞の「する
（suru）」につく。Ⅱ型動詞とⅢ型動詞
の「来る（kuru）」には「られる
（rareru）」がつく。

②[expresses the potential]

¶ Yesterday [I] was sick and **couldn't
go** to school.

¶ Last night I drank too much coffee
and **had a hard time getting to sleep**.

*The potential of almost all Type I
verbs is formed in this way, as in *ikeru*
(from *iku*) or *nemureru* (from *nemuru*).
In the case of constructions with the
Type III verb *suru*, such as *jidōsha no
unten o suru* (drive a car) or *jidōsha o
unten suru* (drive a car), *dekiru* is used:
jidōsha no unten ga dekiru (be able to
drive a car), *jidōsha ga unten dekiru*
(be able to drive a car).

③[expresses respect]

¶ **Has** Professor 〖Doctor〗 Yamada
already **left for home**?

¶ When **did you hear** that news?

④[expresses autonomous action]

¶ Looking at old photos **reminds** [me]
of [my] childhood.

* *-reru* is used with Type I verbs and
the Type III verb *suru* (→*sareru*); *-
rareru* is used with Type II verbs and
the Type III verb *kuru* (→*korareru*).

⇒られる **rareru**

れんあい 恋愛 〔名、～する〕

恋愛小説（*ren'ai*-shōsetsu）恋愛結婚

（*ren'ai*-kekkon）

¶恋愛して結婚する若い人が増えてい

ます。（*Ren'ai* shite kekkon suru wakai

hito ga fuete imasu.）

⇒恋 **koi**

れんしゅう 練習 〔名、～する〕

練習問題（*renshū*-mondai）

¶春子さんは毎日3時間ピアノを練習

しています。（Haruko san wa mainichi

sanjikan piano o *renshū* shite imasu.）

¶難しい発音でも、練習すれば上手に

なります。（Muzukashii hatsuon demo,

renshū sureba jōzu ni narimasu.）

れんらく 連絡 〔名、～する〕

¶長い間連絡がないので、どうしたの

かと心配していました。（Nagai aida

renraku ga nai node, dō shita no ka to

shinpai shite imashita.）

¶すぐ山田さんに電話で連絡してくだ

さい。（Sugu Yamada san ni denwa de

renraku shite kudasai.）

ren'ai 〔n, ～*suru*〕 **love**

a **love** story, a romance // a **love**

marriage (vs. an arranged marriage)

¶ The number of young people

marrying in **love** matches is increasing.

renshū 〔n, ～*suru*〕 **practice,**
rehearsal

exercises, **practice** problems

¶ Haruko **practices** the piano for three

hours every day.

¶ **If you practice**, you can master even

difficult pronunciations.

renraku 〔n, ～*suru*〕 **contact,**
communication, connection

¶ I hadn't **heard anything** from you for

a long time so I was worried about

what had happened to you.

¶ Please **telephone** [Mr.] Yamada right

away.

ろ

ろうか 廊下 〔名〕
¶廊下で話をしている人がいます。
（*Rōka* de hanashi o shite iru hito ga
imasu.）

ろうじん 老人 〔名〕

老人ホーム（*rōjin*-hōmu）
¶電車やバスの中では、老人に席を譲
りましょう。（Densha ya basu no naka
de wa, *rōjin* ni seki o yuzurimashō.）
⇒年寄り toshiyori

ろうそく 〔名〕
¶ろうそくに火をつけてください。
（*Rōsoku* ni hi o tsukete kudasai.）

ろうどう 労働 〔名、～する〕

労働者（*rōdō*sha）労働組合（*rōdō*-
kumiai）重労働（*jūrōdō*）労働時間
（*rōdō*-jikan）
¶この工場では1日8時間労働です。
（Kono kōjō de wa ichinichi hachijikan-
rōdō desu.）

ローマじ ローマ字 〔名〕

¶ひらがなは読めませんから、ローマ
字で書いてください。（Hiragana wa
yomemasen kara, *rōmaji* de kaite
kudasai.）

ろく 六 〔名〕

---

rōka 〔n〕 corridor, hall
¶ There are people talking in **the hall**.

rōjin 〔n〕 an old person, the
　　aged, the elderly
a home for **the aged**, an **old-age** home
¶ All should cooperate in offering train
and bus seats to **the elderly**.

rōsoku 〔n〕 candle
¶ Please light **the candle**.

rōdō 〔n, ～*suru*〕 labor, manual
　　labor
a laborer, a worker // a labor union //
heavy **labor** // **working** hours; man-
hours
¶ This factory has an eight-hour
workday.

rōmaji 〔n〕 roman letters, *romaji*
　　(roman letters used to
　　transcribe Japanese)
¶ [I] can't read *hiragana* so please write
it in **roman letters**.

roku 〔n〕 six

ろくおん 録音 〔名、〜する〕

録音機 (rokuonki)

¶自分の声をテープに録音して、発音の練習をします。(Jibun no koe o tēpu ni *rokuon* shite, hatsuon no renshū o shimasu.)

rokuon 〔n, 〜*suru*〕 **recording, make a recording of**
a **recorder**, a tape **recorder**, a **transcribing** machine
¶ [I] practice pronunciation by **taping** [my] own voice.

ろくがつ 六月 〔名〕

rokugatsu 〔n〕 **June**

ロケット 〔名〕

¶ロケットで月に行けるようになりました。(*Roketto* de tsuki ni ikeru yō ni narimashita.)

roketto 〔n〕 **rocket**
¶ It is now possible to go to the moon by **rocket**.

(-)ろん (-)論 〔名、尾〕

1 〔名〕

¶そのことについては、いろいろな論があります。(Sono koto ni tsuite wa, iroiro na *ron* ga arimasu.)

2 〔尾〕
世論 (se*ron*) 人生論 (jinsei*ron*) 文学論 (bungaku*ron*) 教育論 (kyōiku*ron*)

(-)ron 〔n, suf〕 **argument, debate, controversy; theory, opinion, view**

1 〔n〕 argument, debate; theory, opinion
¶ There are various **theories** concerning that 〔Opinion is divided on that question〕.

2 〔suf〕 theory, view
public **opinion** // one's **philosophy** of life // one's **views** on literature, a literary **theory** // educational **theory** 〔philosophy〕

ろんぶん 論文 〔名〕

卒業論文 (sotsugyō-*ronbun*) 博士論文 (hakushi-*ronbun*)
¶ 12 月の末までに論文を書かなければなりません。(Jūnigatsu no sue made ni *ronbun* o kakanakereba narimasen.)

ronbun 〔n〕 **essay, thesis, paper**
a graduation **thesis** // a doctoral **thesis**

¶ [I] must finish writing [my] **thesis** by the end of December.

わ

わ 輪 〔名〕

① [円形または円形のもの]
指輪（yubiwa）

¶わたしたちは、先生の周りに輪になって座りました。（Watashitachi wa, Sensei no mawari ni *wa* ni natte suwarimashita.）

② [車輪]
車の輪（kuruma no *wa*）

わ 〔助〕

① [独り言のような言い方で詠嘆・感動などを表す]

¶困ったわ。財布を落としたらしいの。（Komatta *wa*. Saifu o otoshita rashii no.）

¶重いわ、この荷物。（Omoi *wa*, kono nimotsu.）

¶あそこにおまわりさんがいるわ。道をきいてみましょう。（Asoko ni omawari san ga iru *wa*. Michi o kiite mimashō.）

② [話し手の主張や決意を表す]

¶あなたはさっき確かにそう言いましたわ。（Anata wa sakki tashika ni sō iimashita *wa*.）

¶もうやめるわ、こんな仕事。（Mō yameru *wa*, konna shigoto.）

¶もう休みますわ、疲れましたから。（Mō yasumimasu *wa*, tsukaremashita kara.）

＊一般に女性が使う。

wa 〔n〕 circle, ring, link; wheel

① [circle, ring, link, loop]
a ring (jewelry)

¶ We sat in **a circle** around our teacher.

② [wheel]
a car **wheel**

wa 〔part〕 a sentence-final particle used for emphasis, etc.

① [used to express emotion when talking to oneself]

¶ Oh, what shall I do? It looks like I've lost my wallet.

¶ My, this bag 〖parcel, etc.〗 is heavy.

¶ Oh, there's a policeman. I'll ask him for directions.

② [used to indicate the speaker's determination or to stress what is being said]

¶ I'm sure that's what you said a little while ago.

¶ That's it! I'm not going to do this work any more!

¶ I'm tired. I'm going to take a break now.

＊ This *wa* is generally used by women.

ワイシャツ〔名〕

¶このワイシャツは小さいので、もう少し大きいのを出してください。
（Kono *waishatsu* wa chiisai node, mō sukoshi ookii no o dashite kudasai.）

waishatsu 〔n〕 **white shirt, dress shirt**

¶Could you show me a larger shirt, as this one is too small?

わかい 若い〔形〕

¶山田さんの奥さんは若くてきれいです。（Yamada san no okusan wa *wakakute* kirei desu.）

¶田中さんは年より若く見えますね。（Tanaka san wa toshi yori *wakaku* miemasu ne.）

¶上田さんは、あなたよりいくつ若いんですか。（Ueda san wa, anata yori ikutsu *wakai* n desu ka？）

wakai 〔adj〕 **young, younger**

¶Mr. Yamada's wife is **young** and pretty.

¶[Mrs.] Tanaka doesn't look [her] age 〖looks **younger** than she actually is〗.

¶How many years **younger** than you is [Mr.] Ueda?

わかす 沸かす〔動Ⅰ〕

¶お湯を沸かして、コーヒーをいれましょう。（Oyu o *wakashite*, kōhii o iremashō.）

wakasu 〔vI〕 **boil, heat**

¶**I'm going to boil** water and fix some coffee.

わがまま〔名、形動〕

¶あの人はいつもわがままを言って、みんなを困らせます。（Ano hito wa itsumo *wagamama* o itte, minna o komarasemasu.）

¶独りっ子はどうしてもわがままになりやすいです。（Hitorikko wa dōshitemo *wagamama* ni nariyasui desu.）

¶わがままな人はみんなにきらわれます。（*Wagamama* na hito wa minna ni kirawaremasu.）

wagamama 〔n, adj-v〕 **selfish, selfcentered, self-indulgent, willful**

¶[He] is always inconveniencing others with [his] **self-centered** remarks.

¶It is easy for an only child to become **spoiled**.

¶**Selfish** persons are universally disliked.

わかる〔動Ⅰ〕

① [理解することができる、意味などが明らかになる]

wakaru 〔vI〕 **understand; know**

① [understand, comprehend, grasp]

¶あなたは日本語がわかりますか。
（Anata wa Nihongo ga *wakarimasu
ka*？）

¶ **Do you understand** Japanese?

¶わからない言葉は、辞書で調べてく
ださい。（*Wakaranai* kotoba wa, jisho de
shirabete kudasai.)

¶ Please look up in the dictionary any
words **you don't understand**.

②[知りたいと思うことなどを知るこ
とができる、見たり聞いたりして知る
ことができる]

② [know, learn, be known, be
identified]

¶いつ試験があるか、まだわかりませ
ん。（Itsu shiken ga aruka, mada
wakarimasen.)

¶ [We] **don't know** yet when there will
be a test.

¶田中さんの電話番号がわかります
か。（Tanaka san no denwa-bangō ga
wakarimasu ka？）

¶ **Do you know** [Miss] Tanaka's phone
number?

わかれる　別れる〚動Ⅱ〛

wakareru 〚v Ⅱ〛 **part, separate
from, divorce, split up, bid
farewell, leave**

¶わたしたちは「さようなら。」と言っ
て別れました。（Watashitachi wa
"Sayōnara." to itte *wakaremashita*.)

¶ We **parted**, saying "Good-bye."

¶わたしは家族と別れて、独りで東京
にいます。（Watashi wa kazoku to
wakarete, hitori de Tōkyō ni imasu.)
⇒会う au

¶ I **left** home and came to live alone in
Tokyo.

わかれる　分かれる〚動Ⅱ〛

wakareru 〚v Ⅱ〛 **split, be divided**

¶男と女に分かれて、ゲームをしまし
た。（Otoko to onna ni *wakarete*, gēmu o
shimashita.)

¶ [We] **split up** by sex and played
games.

¶ここをまっすぐ行くと、道が二つに
分かれています。（Koko o massugu
ikuto, michi ga futatsu ni *wakarete*
imasu.)

¶ If you go straight here the road
divides in two.

¶意見が分かれて、今日は結論が出ま
せんでした。（Iken ga *wakarete*, kyō wa
ketsuron ga demasen deshita.)

¶ Opinion **was divided** and no
conclusion was reached today.

917

わき〔名〕

① [腕のつけねの下の所]

¶山田さんがたくさんの本をわきに抱えて、こちらへ来ます。(Yamada san ga takusan no hon o *waki* ni kakaete, kochira e kimasu.)

② [すぐ近くの所、そば]

¶わたしの家は、学校のすぐわきにあります。(Watashi no ie wa, gakkō no sugu *waki* ni arimasu.)

わく 沸く〔動Ⅰ〕

¶お湯が沸きました。お茶にしましょう。(Oyu ga waki *mashita*. Ocha ni shimashō.)

¶おふろが沸きましたから、お入りください。(Ofuro ga *wakimashita* kara, ohairi kudasai.)

＊「水が沸く(mizu ga waku)」とは言わないで、「お湯が沸く(oyu ga waku)」と言う。

わけ〔名〕

① [ことがらや言葉などの意味・内容を表す]

¶この言葉のわけを字引で調べてみましたが、わかりませんでした。(Kono kotoba no *wake* o jibiki de shirabete mimashita ga, wakarimasen deshita.)

¶この文は何を言おうとしているのか、さっぱりわけがわかりません。(Kono bun wa nani o iō to shite iru no ka, sappari *wake* ga wakarimasen.)

② [理由・原因を表す]

---

waki 〔n〕 **armpit, under one's arm (s); beside, very close**

① [armpit, under one's arm(s)]

¶[Mr.] Yamada is coming this way carrying many books **under [his] arm**.

② [beside, very close]

¶My house is **very near** to the school.

waku 〔vⅠ〕 **boil, grow hot**

¶The water **is boiling**. Let's have some (green) tea.

¶The bath **is ready now**. Please go ahead and have a bath.

＊The expression *mizu ga waku is not used; instead one says *oyu ga waku*.

wake 〔n〕 **meaning, sense; reason, cause; circumstances, case**

① [meaning, sense]

¶[I] looked up this word in the dictionary but in the end didn't learn **its meaning**.

¶[I] can't make **head or tail** of this sentence.

② [reason cause, grounds]

¶あんなに仲のよかった夫婦が、どういうわけで離婚してしまったのでしょう。（Anna ni naka no yokatta fūfu ga, dōiu *wake* de rikon shite shimatta no deshō？）

¶なぜ学校をやめるのか、そのわけを話してください。（Naze gakkō o yameru noka, sono *wake* o hanashite kudasai.）

③ [当然のこととして納得できるという意味を表す]

¶「田中さんは試験に失敗したそうです。」（Tanaka san wa shiken ni shippai shita sō desu.）「やはりそうでしたか。全然勉強しなかったんですから、落ちるわけです。」（Yahari sō deshita ka. Zenzen benkyō shinakatta n desu kara, ochiru *wake* desu.）

¶田中さんはいつも人の悪口ばかり言っています。みんなにきらわれるわけです。（Tanaka san wa itsumo hito no warukuchi bakari itte imasu. Minna ni kirawareru *wake* desu.）

④ [事情やいきさつなどを説明するときに使う]

¶わたしはお金がなくて大学へ行けなかったわけですが、息子には行かせたいと思います。（Watashi wa okane ga nakute daigaku e ikenakatta *wake* desu ga, musuko ni wa ikasetai to omoimasu.）

¶月末には必ず返すと言うので、田中さんに5万円貸したわけです。ところが、もう2か月にもなるのに、まだ返してくれません。（Getsumatsu ni wa kanarazu kaesu to iu node, Tanaka san ni goman'en kashita *wake* desu. Tokoroga, mō nikagetsu ni mo maru noni, mada kaeshite kuremasen.）

¶ I wonder **how** that couple came to be divorced when they seemed to get along so well together.

¶ Please give me **your reasons** for wanting to quit school.

③ [used to indicate that something is natural or reasonable]

¶ "I hear that [Mr.] Tanaka failed the test."
"I thought [he] might. **It stands to reason** that one will fail if one doesn't study at all 〖**No wonder** he failed—he didn't study at all〗.

¶ [Mr.] Tanaka is always speaking ill of others. **That's why** [he]'s universally disliked.

④ [used when explaining the circumstances, etc.]

¶ I couldn't go to college myself **because of** insufficient funds, but I'd like to have my son go.

¶ I lent fifty thousand yen to [Mr.] Tanaka **because** [he] said [he] would pay it back without fail at the end of the month. However, two months have gone by and [he] still hasn't paid it back.

⑤ [簡単なこと・すぐできることなど
の意味を表す]

¶ 一日に漢字を五つ覚えるのは、わけ
ないことです。(Ichinichi ni kanji o
itsutsu oboeru no wa, *wake* nai koto
desu.)

¶ 機械でやれば、そんなことはわけな
くできます。(Kikai de yareba, sonna
koto wa *wake* naku dekimasu.)

* 「わけない（wake nai)」「わけはない
（wake wa nai)」の形で使う。

⑥ [不可能であるという意味を表す]

¶ いくら困っても、人の物を盗むわけ
にはいきません。(Ikura komatte mo,
hito no mono o nusumu *wake* ni wa
ikimasen.)

¶ お金がないので、あまり高い物を買
うわけにはいきません。(Okane ga nai
node, amari takai mono o kau *wake* ni wa
ikimasen.)

* いつも「わけにはいかない（wake ni
wa ikanai)」の形で使う。

⑦ [常識的に考えてとてもそういうこ
とはありえないことを表す]

¶ 山田さんはあんなによく勉強したん
ですから、試験に落ちるわけがありま
せん。(Yamada san wa anna ni yoku
benkyō shita n desu kara, shiken ni ochiru
wake ga arimasen.)

¶ 山田さんはいつも人に親切ですか
ら、みんなにきらわれるわけがありま
せん。(Yamada san wa itsumo hito ni
shinsetsu desu kara, minna ni kirawareru
wake ga arimasen.)

* いつも「わけがない「(wake ga nai)」
の形で使う。

⑤ [used to indicate that something is
easy or simple]

¶ **It's a simple matter** to memorize
five *kanji* a day.

¶ If you do it by machine it will be
done **in no time at all**.

*Used in the patterns "*wake nai*" and
"*wake wa nai*."

⑥ [used to indicate that something is
impossible]

¶ **There is no excuse** for stealing no
matter how difficult one's situation
might be.

¶ [I] don't have much money so [I]
can't possibly buy anything expensive.

*Always used in the pattern "*wake ni
wa ikanai*."

⑦ [used to indicate that something is
unreasonable or contrary to common
sense]

¶ [Miss] Yamada **cannot possibly** fail
the exam after studying so hard.

¶ [Mr.] Yamada is always kind to
others so **it cannot be** that [he] is
unpopular.

*Always used in the pattern "*wake ga
nai*."

⑧ [特にそのようなことはないという
意味を表す]

¶漢字ができないといっても、全然読
めないわけではありません。(Kanji ga
dekinai to itte mo, zenzen yomenai *wake*
de wa arimasen.)

¶わたしは魚はきらいですが、全然食
べないわけではありません。(Watashi
wa sakana wa kirai desu ga, zenzen
tabenai *wake* de wa arimasen.)

*いつも「わけではない (wake de wa
nai)」の形で使い、部分否定を表す。

わける 分ける〔動II〕

① [全体をいくつかの部分にする]
¶人数が多いので、二組に分けまし
た。(Ninzū ga ooi node, futakumi ni
wakemashita.)

② [分類する]
¶りんごを大きさによって3種類に分
けました。(Ringo o ookisa ni yotte
sanshurui ni *wakemashita*.)

③ [全体をいくつかにして人に与える]
¶りんごをたくさんいただいたので、
隣の家にも分けてあげました。
(Ringo o takusan itadaita node, tonari no
ie ni mo *wakete* agemashita.)

¶一本のたばこを二人で分けました。
(Ippon no tabako o futari de
wakemashita.)

わざわざ〔副〕

① [あることのために特別に苦労など
して何かを行う様子]
¶このセーターはわざわざわたしのた
めに編んでくださったのですか。

⑧ [used to indicate that something is
not the case]

¶ [I] don't have a good knowledge of
kanji, but **that isn't to say** that [I] can't
read them at all 〖but I can read them a
little bit〗.

¶ I don't like fish, but **it's not the case**
that I never eat it 〖but I do eat it
sometimes〗.

*Always used in the pattern "*wake de
wa nai*" it forms a partial negative.

wakeru 〔v II〕 **divide; separate,
sort; distribute, allot**

① [divide, part, split]
¶ As there were so many people [we]
were split up into two groups 〖teams〗.

② [separate, sort, classify]
¶ [I] **sorted** the apples into three
groups by size.

③ [distribute, allot, share]
¶ Someone gave [me] lots of apples so
[I] **gave some** to [my] next-door
neighbors.

¶ The two **split** a cigarette.

wazawaza 〔adv〕 **purposely,
expressly; take the trouble to**

① [purposely, expressly, specially]

¶ Did you knit this sweater **just for
me**?

（Kono sētā wa *wazawaza* watashi no tame ni ande kudasatta no desu ka？）

¶わたしが北海道へ行った時、上田さんは忙しいのに、わざわざホテルまで会いに来てくれました。（Watashi ga Hokkaidō e itta toki, Ueda san wa isogashii noni, *wazawaza* hoteru made ai ni kite kuremashita.）

¶ When I went to Hokkaido, [Mr.] Ueda **took the time** from [his] busy schedule to come see me at my hotel.

②[そのことをする必要がないのにそうと知りながら何かを行う様子]

②[take the trouble to, go out of one's way to]

¶近くの店で買えるのに、どうしてわざわざ遠くの店まで買いに行ったのですか。（Chikaku no mise de kaeru noni, dōshite *wazawaza* tooku no mise made kai ni itta no desu ka？）

¶ Why did you **make a special trip** to a more distant shop when you could have bought it nearby?

わずか〔副、形動、～の〕

wazuka 〔adv, adj-v, ～*no*〕 only a few, only a little, scanty, mere

¶うちから学校までは、わずか5分です。（Uchi kara gakkō made wa, *wazuka* gofun desu.）

¶ It's **only** five minutes to school from my home.

¶父が亡くなったのは、わたしがわずか三つの時でした。（Chichi ga nakunatta no wa, watashi ga *wazuka* mittsu no toki deshita.）

¶ My father died when I was **only** three years old.

¶夜遅くまで働いたのに、わずかのお金しかもらえませんでした。（Yoru osoku made hataraita noni, *wazuka* no okane shika moraemasen deshita.）

¶ Even though [I] worked until late at night on it, [I] only received a **trifling** payment for it.

わすれもの 忘れ物〔名〕

wasuremono 〔n〕 lost property, things left behind

¶忘れ物をしないように、もう一度持ち物を調べてください。（Wasuremono o shinai yō ni, mō ichido mochimono o shirabete kudasai.）

¶ Please check your belongings again, so as not to leave anything behind.

わすれる 忘れる〔動Ⅱ〕

① [覚えたことなどが思い出せない]
¶学生時代に習った外国語は、もうみんな忘れてしまいました。
(Gakuseijidai ni naratta gaikokugo wa, mō minna *wasurete* shimaimashita.)

② [うっかりして物をどこかに置いてきてしまう]
¶教室に日本語の本を忘れてきてしまいました。(Kyōshitsu ni Nihongo no hon o *wasurete* kite shimaimashita.)

わた 綿〔名〕

¶寒い所では冬は綿の入った着物を着ます。(Samui tokoro de wa fuyu wa *wata* no haitta kimono o kimasu.)
¶空には白い綿のような雲が浮かんでいます。(Sora ni wa shiroi *wata* no yō na kumo ga ukande imasu.)

わたくし 私〔代〕

¶私は皆様の御親切を決して忘れません。(*Watakushi* wa minasama no goshinsetsu o kesshite wasuremasen.)
＊「私（watakushi）」は、「わたし（watashi）」の丁寧な言い方で、改まったときに使う。

わたし〔代〕

¶わたしは山田です。(*Watashi* wa Yamada desu.)

わたす 渡す〔動Ⅰ〕

① [人から人へある物を移す]
¶田中さんが来たら、この手紙を渡してください。(Tanaka san ga kitara, kono tegami o *watashite* kudasai.)

wasureru 〔vⅡ〕 **forget, escape one's memory; forget, leave behind**

① [forget, escape one's memory]
¶ [I]'ve completely **forgotten** the foreign languages [I] learned in [my] student days.

② [forget, leave behind]

¶ [I] **accidentally left** my Japanese book in the classroom.

wata 〔n〕 **cotton, cotton wool**
¶ In cold areas they wear clothing padded with **cotton** in the winter.

¶ **Fleecy** white clouds are floating in the sky.

watakushi 〔pron〕 **I, myself, me, mine**
¶ I will never forget how kind all of you have been to me.

＊ *Watakushi* is the polite form of *watashi;* it is used on more formal occasions.

watashi 〔pron〕 **I, myself, me, mine**
¶ I'm [Mr.] Yamada.

watasu 〔vⅠ〕 **hand over; carry across**
① [hand over, deliver, give to]
¶ Please **give** this letter to [Mrs.] Tanaka when [she] comes.

② [こちら側から向こう側へあるもの
を送る]

¶ここには橋がないので、人々を船で
向こう岸に渡しています。(Koko ni
wa hashi ga nai node, hitobito o fune de
mukōgishi ni *watashite* imasu.)

② [carry across, take over]

¶There is no bridge here so people **are
ferried** to the other side by boat.

わたる 渡る〔動Ⅰ〕

川を渡る (kawa o *wataru*) 橋を渡る
(hashi o *wataru*)

¶本屋は交差点を渡ったところにあり
ます。(Hon'ya wa kōsaten o *watatta*
tokoro ni arimasu.)

¶冬になると、北からいろいろな渡り
鳥が日本に渡ってきます。(Fuyu ni
naru to, kita kara iroiro na *wataridori* ga
Nihon ni *watatte* kimasu.)

wataru 〔v I〕 **cross, go across**

cross a river // **cross** a bridge

¶The bookstore is **on the other side** of
the intersection.

¶In the winter various migratory birds
cross the sea to Japan from the north.

わらい 笑い〔名〕

笑い話 (*warai*banashi)

¶友達の話がおかしくて、しばらく笑
いが止まりませんでした。(Tomodachi
no hanashi ga okashikute shibaraku *warai*
ga tomari masen deshita.)

warai 〔n〕 **laugh, laughter, smile,
smiling**

a **funny** story

¶I couldn't stop laughing as my friend's
story was so funny.

わらう 笑う〔動Ⅰ〕

¶山田先生がおもしろいことを言った
ので、みんな大声で笑いました。
(Yamada sensei ga omoshiroi koto o itta
node, minna oogoe de *waraimashita*.)

warau 〔v I〕 **laugh, smile**

¶Professor Yamada said something
amusing and everyone **laughed** loudly.

-わり -割〔尾〕

3割 (san *wari*) 10割 (jū *wari*)

-wari 〔suf〕 **percentage (1 wari =
10%)**

30 percent // 100 percent

わりあい 割合〔名〕

¶あの学校の入学試験を受けて合格す
る人の割合は、30パーセントぐらい
でしょう。(Ano gakkō no

wariai 〔n〕 **rate, percentage,
proportion, ratio**

¶**The percentage** of persons passing
the exam for entrance to that school is
around 30 percent.

nyūgakushiken o ukete gōkaku suru hito no *wariai* wa, sanjippāsento gurai deshō.)

わりあいに 割合に 〔副〕

¶ このお菓子は割合においしいです
ね。(Kono okashi wa *wariai ni* oishii
desu ne.)
¶ あの学生は割合によく勉強します。
(Ano gakusei wa *wariai ni* yoku benkyō
shimasu.)
* 「割合（wariai)」「わりに（warini)」
とも言う。
⇒わりに **warini**

わりに 割に 〔連〕

¶ この店の料理は、安い割においしい
です。(Kono mise no ryōri wa, yasui
wari ni oishii desu.)
¶ あの学生は、勉強する割には成績が
よくないです。(Ano gakusei wa,
benkyō suru *wari ni* wa seiseki ga yoku
nai desu.)
¶ 山田さんは50歳の割には若く見えま
す。(Yamada san wa gojissai no *wari ni*
wa wakaku micmasu.)
* 「動詞・形容詞・形容動詞（連体の
形）＋割に（wari ni)」「名詞＋の
(no) ＋割に（wari ni)」の形で使う。

わりに 〔副〕

¶ 小さな店ですが、味はわりにいいで
すよ。(Chiisana mise desu ga, aji wa
warini ii desu yo.)
¶ 田中さんの家は駅からわりに近いで
す。(Tanaka san no ie wa eki kara *warini*
chikai desu.)

wariai ni 〔adv〕 **comparatively, relatively**

¶ This sweet 〖candy, cake〗 is **quite** good.

¶ That student studies **relatively** hard.

*Variants: *wariai, warini.*

wari ni 〔compd〕 **for, considering, relative to, in proportion to**

¶ The food here is quite good **considering** how cheap it is.

¶ That student's marks aren't so good **considering** how much [he] studies.

¶ [Mr.] Yamada looks younger than [his] 50 years.

*Used in the patterns "verb, adjective, or adjective-verb (dictionary form) + *wari ni*" and "noun + *no* + *wari ni*.

warini 〔adv〕 **comparatively, rather**

¶ It's just a small place, but the food is **quite** good.

¶ [Mr.] Tanaka's house is **relatively** close to the station.

＊「わりと（warito）」「割合に（wariai ni）」とも言う。

⇒割合に **wariai ni**

わる 割る〔動Ⅰ〕

①[まとまっているものをいくつかの部分にする]

¶ナイフでりんごを半分に割って、二人で食べました。（Naifu de ringo o hanbun ni *watte*, futari de tabemashita.）

②[固い物を壊す]

コップを割る（koppu o *waru*）窓ガラスを割る（madogarasu o *waru*）

¶花びんを落として割ってしまいました。（Kabin o otoshite *watte* shimaimashita.）

③[割り算をする]

¶4割る2は2です。（Yon *waru* ni wa ni desu.）

わるい 悪い〔形〕

①[道徳的・法律的に正しくない様子]

¶人の物を盗むのは悪いことです。（Hito no mono o nusumu no wa *warui* koto desu.）

¶花びんを壊したのはしかたがないが、悪いのはうそをついたことです。（Kabin o kowashita no wa shikata ga nai ga, *warui* no wa uso o tsuita koto desu.）

↔いい ii よい yoi

②[性質が善良でない様子]

¶世の中にはいい人もいるが悪い人もいるから、気をつけなければなりません。（Yononaka ni wa ii hito mo iru ga *warui* hito mo iru kara, ki o tsukenakereba narimasen.）

↔いい ii よい yoi

waru 〔vⅠ〕 divide; break; divide by

① [divide, cut, halve]

¶ [We] **cut** the apple in half with a knife and split it between the two of [us].

② [break crack, smash]

break a glass tumbler // **break** a window

¶ [I] dropped the vase and **it broke**.

③ [divide]

¶ Four **divided by** two is two.

warui 〔adj〕 bad, wrong; evil; inferior; in poor condition

① [bad, wrong, evil]

¶ **It is wrong** to steal something belonging to another.

¶ Breaking the vase couldn't have been helped, but **it was wrong** to lie about it.

② [bad, evil, wicked]

¶ There are **bad** people as well as good people in the world so one must be careful.

③ [人間関係がよくない様子]

¶ 山田さんと田中さんは仲が悪いそうです。(Yamada san to Tanaka san wa naka ga *warui* sō desu.)

*普通「仲が悪い（naka ga warui）」の形で使う。

↔いい ii　よい yoi

④ [ものごとが劣っている様子]

悪い品物（*warui* shinamono）頭が悪い（atama ga *warui*）

¶ 上田さんは3学期の成績がたいへん悪かったそうです。(Ueda san wa sangakki no seiseki ga taihen *warukatta* sō desu.)

↔いい ii　よい yoi

⑤ [状態などの好ましくない様子、気持ちのよくない様子]

気分が悪い（kibun ga *warui*）

¶ 天気が悪い日には散歩はしません。(Tenki ga *warui* hi ni wa sanpo wa shimasen.)

¶ 雨が降って、道が悪くなりました。(Ame ga futte, michi ga *waruku* narimashita.)

¶ お酒を飲んだら、気持が悪くなりました。(Osake o nondara, kimochi ga *waruku* narimashita.)

↔いい ii　よい yoi

⑥ [気の毒である、申し訳ない]

¶ みんなを待たせると悪いから、急いで行きましょう。(Minna o mataseru to *warui* kara, isoide ikimashō.)

¶ 忙しい時に来て悪かったですね。(Isogashii toki ni kite *warukatta* desu ne.)

③ [be on bad terms with]

¶ I hear that [Mr.] Yamada and [Mr.] Tanaka **don't get along well** with each other.

*Usually used in the pattern "*naka ga warui*."

④ [bad, inferior, poor]

inferior goods // be **slow**, be **slow**witted

¶ I hear that [Miss] Ueda's marks for the third term were very **poor**.

⑤ [be in poor condition]

feel **ill**

¶ [I] don't go for a walk on days when the weather **is poor**.

¶ The roads **were** 〖**are**〗 **bad** because of the rain.

¶ [I] felt 〖feel〗 **sick** after doing some drinking.

⑥ [be wrong, be at fault]

¶ Let's hurry as we **shouldn't** keep everyone waiting.

¶ [I]'m **sorry** to have disturbed you when you are so busy.

*会話の文の中で自分の行為が相手に迷惑をかけたり不都合な影響を及ぼしたりするときに使う。

*Used in conversation when one's actions have bothered or inconvenienced another.

われる　割れる〔動Ⅱ〕

¶ボールが当たって、窓ガラスが割れてしまいました。(Bōru ga atatte, madogarasu ga *warete* shimaimashita.)

¶スケートをしていたら、氷が割れて池の中へ落ちてしまいました。(Sukēto o shite itara, koori ga *warete* ike no naka e ochite shimaimashita.)

wareru 〖v Ⅱ〗 **split, break**

¶ The window **broke** when the ball hit it.

¶ When [I] was skating, the ice **cracked** and [I] fell into the pond.

われわれ〔代〕

¶われわれ学生にとって最も重要なことは勉強することです。(*Wareware* gakusei ni totte mottomo jūyō na koto wa benkyō suru koto desu.)

*「わたしたち（watashitachi）」より少しかたい感じの言葉。一体感を強めて言う場合に使う。女性は普通使わない。

wareware 〖pron〗 **we, us, our**

¶ Studying is the most important thing for us students.

* *Wareware* is a little more formal than *watashitachi*. It is used when stressing a sense of solidarity. It is not usually used by women.

を〔助〕

o 〖part〗 **a particle used with a direct object, the place a movement takes place or passes through, etc.**

① [動作の目的・対象などを表す]

¶わたしは小説を読むのが好きです。(Watashi wa shōsetsu *o* yomu no ga suki desu.)

¶上田さんはセーターを着ています。(Ueda san wa sētā *o* kite imasu.)

¶先生は学生に答えを言わせます。(Sensei wa gakusei ni kotae *o* iwasemasu.)

¶山田さんはときどき変な質問をして、先生を困らせます。(Yamada san wa tokidoki hen na shitsumon *o* shite, sensei *o* komarasemasu.)

① [indicates a direct object]

¶ I like reading novels 〖stories, fiction〗.

¶ [Miss] Ueda is wearing a sweater.

¶ The teacher calls on the students for their answers.

¶ [Mr.] Yamada sometimes pesters the teacher with odd questions.

② [移動の行われる場所や通過点など
を表す]
公園を散歩する（kōen o sanpo suru）

¶道の真ん中を歩いてはいけません。
（Michi no mannaka o aruite wa
ikemasen.）
¶その角を曲がると、郵便局がありま
す。（Sono kado o magaru to, yūbinkyoku
ga arimasu.）
*普通「行く（iku）」「通る（tooru）」
「歩く（aruku）」「散歩する
（sanposuru）」などの移動を表す動詞と
いっしょに使う。
③ [移動する動作の起点となる場所な
どを表す]
¶わたしは毎朝7時にうちを出て、学
校へ行きます。（Watashi wa maiasa
shichiji ni uchi o dete, gakkō e ikimasu.）
¶わたしは電車を降りて、バスで会社
まで行きます。（Watashi wa densha o
orite, basu de kaisha made ikimasu.）

② [indicates where a movement takes
place or passes through]
stroll **in** the park, take a walk **in** the
park
¶ One mustn't walk **in** the middle of the
road.

¶ If you turn that corner, you will find a
post office 〚There is a post office
around that corner〛.
*Generally used with verbs expressing
movement such as *iku* (go), *tooru* (pass
through), *aruku* (walk), or *sanpo suru*
(take a walk).
③ [indicates the starting point of a
moving action]
¶ I leave the house at seven o'clock
each morning and go to school.

¶ I get **off** the train and then take a bus
to the office.

ん〔助〕　☞の no

n 〔part〕　☞**no**

AN INTRODUCTION
TO JAPANESE GRAMMAR*

Compiled by Nobuko MIZUTANI

VI. VERBS

VII. KEIGO (POLITE LANGUAGE)

---

* This is intended to provide a practical overview of Japanese grammar for foreign students of Japanese. Further example sentences and usage notes can be found under the appropriate entries in the dictionary itself. For more detail, readers should consult reference works on the subject.

I. THE STRUCTURE OF JAPANESE SENTENCES

1. Sentences

1-1 A sentence usually consists of (1) a noun phrase, (2) a verb phrase, or (3) an adjective phrase.

    (1) *Nichiyōbi desu.*   (It is Sunday.)

    (2) *Kimashita.*   (I/You/He/She/It/We/They came.)

    (3) *Akai desu.*   (It is/They are red.)

1-2 When the subject needs to be mentioned, the particle **ga** is added to the noun or pronoun.

    *Tanaka san **ga** kimashita.*   (Mr./Mrs./Miss Tanaka came.)

1-3 When the topic needs to be mentioned, the particle **wa** is added to the noun or pronoun.

    *Kyō **wa** nichiyōbi desu.*   (Today is Sunday.)

    *Kono hana **wa** akai desu.*   (This flower is red.)

1-4 A verb phrase is often preceded by (1) an object or (2) an adverbial phrase.

    (1) **Hon o** *yomimashita.*   (I/You/He/She/We/They read **a book.**)

    (2) **Sanji ni** *kite kudasai.*   (Please come **at three o'clock.**)

2. Omission

2-1 Any of (1) the topic, (2) a verb phrase, (3) an object, and (4) an adverbial phrase are left out when they can be understood from the context.

    (1) Speaker A: *Kyō wa naniyōbi desu ka?* (What day of the week is it today?)
           Speaker B: *Nichiyōbi desu.* (It's Sunday.)

    (2) Speaker A: *Nanji goro ikimasu ka?* (What time are you going?)
           Speaker B: *Sanji goro.* (At around three.)

    (3) Speaker A: *Ano hon o kaimasu ka?* (Are you going to buy that book?)
           Speaker B: *Ee, kaimasu.* (Yes, I'm going to buy it.)

3. Word order

3-1 Modifiers precede what is modified.

    akai *hana*   (a **red** flower, **red** flowers)

    saite iru *hana*   (flowers **in bloom**)

> ***watashi ga mita*** *hana*   (flowers **that I saw**)

3-2 Particles are always added to other words and phrases.

> *ame* ***ga***   (**the** rain)
> *sen'en* ***shika***   (**only** a thousand yen)

3-3 Phrases can be reversed in order in conversation.

> *Kimashita yo, Yamada san ga.*   (Mr. Yamada came!)
> *Kirei desu ne, kono hana.*   (This flower is beautiful!)

4. Desu (the copula)

4-1 ***Desu,*** or the copula, is used either to form a phrase or to make an adjective phrase more polite.

> noun phrase: *Nichiyôbi* ***desu.***   (**It's** Sunday.)
> adjective phrase: *Akai* ***desu.***   (**It's** red.)

4-2 The negative form of *desu* is ***ja arimasen*** (informal).

> *Kyô wa nichiyôbi* ***ja arimasen.*** (Today **is not** Sunday.)

4-3 The past form of *desu* is ***deshita,*** and the past negative form is ***ja arimasen deshita*** (informal).

> *Nichiyôbi* ***deshita.*** (**It was** Sunday.)
> *Nichiyôbi* ***ja arimasen deshita.*** (**It wasn't** Sunday.)

4-4 ***Deshô*** is used to mean "it probably is" or "it probably will be."

> *Ashita wa ame* ***deshô.*** (Tomorrow **probably will** be rainy.)

The negative form of *deshô* is ***ja nai deshô*** (informal).

> *Ashita wa ame* ***ja nai deshô.*** (Tomorrow **probably will not** be rainy.)

4-5 ***Da*** is used instead of *desu* in familiar speech; it has the following forms.

da (present affirmative)	*Nichiyôbi* ***da.*** (**It is** Sunday.)
ja nai (present negative)	*Nichiyôbi* ***ja nai.*** (**It isn't** Sunday.)
datta (past affirmative)	*Nichiyôbi* ***datta.*** (**It was** Sunday.)
ja nakatta (past negative)	*Nichiyôbi* ***ja nakatta.*** (**It wasn't** Sunday.)
darô (probability)	*Nichiyôbi* ***darô.*** (**It probably will be** Sunday.)

5. Particles

5-1 Particles are used to indicate relations between words, phrases, and clauses; they also express the speaker's feelings.

5-2 Particles are divided into (1) case particles, (2) modifying particles, (3) connecting particles, and (4) sentence particles.

(1) **Case particles:** These are added to nouns and pronouns.

ga (subject)	*Ame* **ga** *futte imasu.* (It is raining.)
o (object)	*Hon* **o** *yomimashita.* (I read a book.)
ni (at, in, on)	*Tōkyō* **ni** *sunde imasu.* (I live **in** Tokyo.)
e (to, toward)	*Kaisha* **e** *ikimasu.* (I'm going **to** the office.)
no (of)	*Yamada san* **no** *hon desu.* (It's Mr.Yamada's book.)
to (and)	*Sore* **to** *kore o kudasai.* (Please give me this **and** that.)
de (by, with)	*Naifu* **de** *kirimashita.* (I cut it **with** a knife.)
kara (from)	*Uchi* **kara** *ichijikan kakarimasu.* (It takes an hour to go there **from** my house.)
yori (than)	*Kore wa are* **yori** *yasui desu.* (This is cheaper **than** that.)
ya (and)	*Tokei* **ya** *megane o kaimashita.* (I bought a watch, glasses, **and other things.**)
ka (or)	*Tanaka san* **ka** *Yoshida san ni tanomimasu.* (I will ask Mr. Tanaka **or** Mr. Yoshida to do it.)

(2) **Modifying particles:** These are used as modifiers.

wa (as for)	*Watashi* **wa** *sushi da.* (Give me *sushi*.)
mo (also, too)	*Biiru* **mo** *kudasai.* (Please give me some beer, **too.**)
demo (or something)	*Ocha* **demo** *nomimashō ka?* (Shall we have tea **or something?**)
shika (only)	*Sen'en* **shika** *arimasen.* (I have **only** a thousand yen.)

(3) **Connecting particles:** These are used to connect phrases and clauses.

ga (but, and)	*Sumimasen **ga**, chotto matte kudasaimasen ka?* (I am sorry, **but** would you wait a moment?)
kara (because, so)	*Jikan ga arimasen **kara**, yomemasen.* (I cannot read it **because** I have no time.)
ke(re)do(mo) (but)	*Takai **keredo**, kaimasu.* (It is expensive, **but** I will buy it.)
shi (and what's more)	*Hiroi **shi** shizuka desu.* (It's spacious **and** quiet.)
-tari (do A and B)	*Uta o utat**tari** odot**tari** shimashita.* (We sang songs **and** danced.)
-te, -de (used for making the *-te* form)	*Mado ga ai**te** imasu.* (The window **is open.**)
-te mo, -de mo (even if)	*Ame ga fut**te mo** ikimasu.* (I will go **even if** it rains.)
to (when)	*Yūgata ni naru **to** samuku narimasu.* (It becomes cold in the evening — literally, **when** it becomes evening.)
-nagara (while)	*Ocha o nomi**nagara** hanashimashita.* (We talked **while** having tea.)
node (so)	*Kuraku natta **node** shigoto o yamemashita.* (It became dark, **so** we stopped working.)
noni (although)	*Renshū shita **noni** umaku dekimasen deshita.* (**Although** I practiced hard, I couldn't do it well.)

(4) **Sentence particles:** These are added at the end of a sentence.

ka (question)	*Yamada san desu **ka?*** (Are you Mr. Yamada?)
ne (agreement)	*Ii otenki desu **ne.*** (Lovely day, isn't it?)
yo (emphasis)	*Kamaimasen **yo.*** (That's all right.)
na (monologue)	*Ii otenki da **na.*** (It's a lovely day.)
tomo (emphasis)	*Kekkō desu **tomo.*** (That's fine.)
no (question, familiar)	*Doko e iku **no?*** (Where are you going?)

II. NOUNS

1. Number

Most nouns are not distinguished as to number. However, some suffixes can be added to indicate the plural in the case of human beings.

-tachi	*kodomo**tachi*** (child**ren**)
-ra	*kodomo**ra*** (child**ren**)
-gata (honorific)	*sensei**gata*** (professor**s**)

2. Case

The case of nouns is usually indicated with particles (see I-5-2).

3. Gender

Nouns have no gender.

4. Form nouns

There are several nouns which have no concrete meaning and are always used in a phrase, preceded by modifiers. These are called form nouns; the most important ones are: **koto, tame, mono, wake, hō, tokoro, toki, mae, ato,** etc.

koto	*Mada tabeta **koto** ga arimasen*. (I have never tasted it.)
tame	*Daigaku ni hairu **tame** ni benkyō shite imasu*. (I am studying **in order** to enter college.)
mono	*Sonna koto o iu **mono** ja arimasen*. (You should not say such a thing.)

See also the entries for each of the form nouns in the dictionary.

III. PRONOUNS

1. List of pronouns

1-1 The following is a list of the most commonly used pronouns.

	singular	plural
1st person	*watashi*	*watashitachi*
		watashidomo (humble)
	boku (male, informal)	*bokutachi, bokura*
	atashi (female, informal)	*atashitachi*

936

2nd person	*anata*	*anatatachi*
		anatagata (honorific)
	kimi (male, informal)	*kimitachi, kimira*
3rd person	*ano hito*	*ano hitotachi*
	kare (he, informal)	*karera* (informal)
	kanojo (she, informal)	*kanojotachi* (informal)
	ano kata (honorific)	*ano katagata* (honorific)

1-2 There are several other pronouns used in polite or vulgar speech.

1-3 Pronouns are not used as frequently in Japanese as in English. They are left out when understood from the context.

> Speaker A: *Yamada san, kimashita ka?* (Did Mr. Yamada come?)
> Speaker B: *Ee, kimashita.* (Yes, he did.)

2. Other terms used as pronouns

2-1 Personal names are often used instead of pronouns.

> **Yamamoto san** *mo ikimasu ka?*
> (Are you going, too? — said to Yamamoto san.)
> *Kore,* **Yoshiko san** *no deshō?* (Isn't this yours? — said to Yoshiko, familiar.)

2-2 Nouns indicating position or status are also used instead of pronouns.

> **Okusan** *mo ikimasu ka?*
> (Are you going, too? — said to someone's wife.)
> **Shachō** *wa dochira ni osumai desu ka?* (Where do you live? — said to a director of a company.)

2-3 Kinship terms are also used instead of pronouns.

> **Otōsan** *mo iku?* (Are you going, too? — said to one's father.)

IV. DEMONSTRATIVES

1. *Ko/so/a/do*

There are four groups of demonstratives, or words used to point to someone or something: (1) the *ko-* group, (2) the *so-* group, (3) the *a-* group, and (4) the *do- group*.

the *ko-* group	the *so-* group	the *a-* group	the *do-* group
kore (this one)	*sore* (that one)	*are* (that one over there)	*dore* (which one)
kono (of this)	*sono* (of that)	*ano* (of that over there)	*dono* (which)
koko (this place)	*soko* (there)	*asoko* (over there)	*doko* (where)
kochira (this way)	*sochira* (that way)	*achira* (that way over there)	*dochira* (which way)
kotchi (this way)	*sotchi* (that way)	*atchi* (that way over there)	*dotchi* (which way)
kô (in this way)	*sô* (in that way)	*â* (in that way there)	*do* (in which way)
konna (like this)	*sonna* (like that)	*anna* (like that over there)	*donna* (what kind of)

2. The *ko-* group

The **ko-** group words are used for indicating something near the speaker.

> **Kore** *wa ikura desu ka?* (How much is **this?**)
> **Kono** *kasa, ikura desu ka?* (How much is **this** umbrella?)

3. The *so-* group

3-1 The **so-** group words are used for indicating something closer to the listener than to the speaker.

> **Soko** *ni aru hon o totte kudasai.* (Would you get me the book **near you?**)
> **Sochira** *no hô ga ookii desu ne.* (**That one** is bigger, isn't it?)

3-2 The **so-** group words are also used to refer to what has already been talked about or what the speaker has just heard.

> *Kinjo no kissaten e ikimashita.* **Soko** *de kôhii o nomimashita.* (I went to a nearby coffee shop. I had some coffee **there.**)
>
> Speaker A: *Kodomo ga netsu o dashimashita.* (My child has a fever.)
> Speaker B: **Sore** *wa ikemasen ne.* (**That**'s too bad.)

4. The *a-* group

4-1 The **a-** group words are used to refer to something at a distance from both the speaker and the listener.

> Speaker A: ***Are*** *wa nan deshô.* (I wonder what **that** is.)
>
> Speaker B: *A,* ***are*** *wa byôin desu.* (Oh, **that**'s a hospital.)

4-2 The **a-** group words are also used to refer to something that both the speaker and the listener have knowledge of.

> Speaker A: *Akutagawa no "Hana" o yomimashita.* (I read "Hana" by Akutaga-
> wa.)
>
> Speaker B: *A,* ***are*** *wa omoshiroi desu ne.* (Oh, **that** is a very interesting story, isn't it?)

5. The *do-* group

The **do-** group words are used to ask questions.

> *Kore wa* ***dô*** *sureba ii deshô.* (**How** should I handle this?)
>
> ***Donna*** *ongaku ga suki desu ka?* (**What types of** music do you like?)

V. ADJECTIVES

1. Types of adjectives

There are two types of adjectives: (1) true adjectives and (2) adjective-verbs.

2. True adjectives

2-1 The true adjectives, or **-*i* adjectives,** have the following forms.

dictionary form	*akai* (red)	*omoshiroi* (interesting)
-ku form	*akaku*	*omoshiroku*
-eba form	*akakereba*	*omoshirokereba*
plain past, affirmative	*akakatta*	*omoshirokatta*
plain past, negative	*akaku nakatta*	*omoshiroku nakatta*

2-2 In polite speech, **desu** is added to the dictionary form to form an adjective phrase.

Akai **desu.**	(**It is** red.)
Omoshiroi **desu.**	(**It is** interesting.)

939

2-3 The **-ku** form is used to make the negative form and the past negative form.

> **Akaku** *(wa) arimasen.*　　　　(It is not **red.**)
> **Akaku** *(wa) arimasen deshita.*　(It was not **red.**)

2-4 The **-ku** form is used adverbially.

> **Akaku** *narimashita.*　　　　(It became **red.**)
> **Hayaku** *kite kudasai.*　　　(Please come **quickly.**)

2-5 The **-ku** form followed by **-te** is used to connect adjective phrases with other phrases.

> **Akakute** *kirei desu.*　　　　(It is **red and** beautiful.)
> **Samukute** *komarimashita.*　(It was **so cold that** we had a difficult time.)

2-6 The **-eba** form is used to indicate the conditional.

> *akakereba*　　　　　(if it is red)
> *omoshirokereba*　　(if it is interesting)

2-7 The plain past form is used as is in familiar conversation, and **desu** is added in polite speech.

> *Akakatta.*　　　　　(It was red — familiar)
> *Akakatta desu.*　　(It was red — polite)

2-8 Among the true adjectives, those describing feelings are usually used to refer to the feelings of the speaker.

> **Ureshii desu. (I am happy.)**
> *Sono toki totemo* **kanashikatta desu. (I was** very **sad** at that time.)

When describing feelings in the second or the third person, one refers to the appearance, rather than the feeling itself; thus, (1) **-sō** (look like) or (2) **yō** (seem) is used.

> (1) **Ureshisō** *desu ne.* (You **look happy.**)
> *Tanaka san wa totemo* **kanashisō** *deshita.*
> 　　　(Miss Tanaka **looked** very **sad.**)
> (2) *Tanaka san wa* **sabishii yō** *desu.*
> 　　　(Miss Tanaka **seems to be lonely.**)

Or else, verbs rather than adjectives are used.

> *Tanaka san wa* **kanashinde imasu.** (Miss Tanaka **is sad.**)
> *Tanaka san wa* **sabishigatte imashita.** (Miss Tanaka **was lonely.**)

3. Adjective-verbs

3-1 The adjective-verbs, or *na* **adjectives,** have the following forms.

dictionary form	*shizuka* (quiet)	*genki* (healthy)
na form	*shizuka na*	*genki na*
de form	*shizuka de*	*genki de*
ni form	*shizuka ni*	*genki ni*

3-2 In polite speech, **desu** is added to the dictionary form to form an adjective phrase.

Shizuka **desu.**　　　　　　　(**It is** quiet.)

3-3 The *na* form is used when modifying a noun.

shizuka na *heya*　　　　　(a **quiet** room)
genki na *kodomo*　　　　　(a **healthy** child)

3-4 The **de** form is used to connect two adjective phrases.

Shizuka de *hiroi heya deshita.* (It was a **quiet and** spacious room.)
genki de *akarui shōnen*　　　(a **healthy and** cheerful boy)

3-5 The **ni** form is used adverbially.

Shizuka ni *heya o dete ikimashita.* (She went out of the room **quietly.**)
Kodomo wa sugu **genki ni** *narimashita.* (The child soon recovered — literally, became **healthy.**)

3-6 For the polite negative, polite past affirmative, polite past negative, plain past affirmative, and plain past negative, see desu (I.4).

VI. VERBS

1. Verbs and auxiliary verbs

Verbs are usually used with **jodōshi,** auxiliary verbs. In traditional Japanese grammar, *ikimashita* is explained as the combination of the verb *iku* and the auxiliary verbs *-masu* and *-ta*. But to make the explanation simpler, auxiliary verbs are included in with verbs in this discussion.

941

2. Conjugation

2-1 Verbs are divided into three classes, depending on how they are conjugated; these are (1) Type I verbs, (2) Type II verbs, and (3) Type III verbs.

2-2 Type I verbs, or **godan** verbs or **-u** verbs: This class includes verbs which end in **-u,** preceded either by one of the consonants **k, s, t, n, m, g,** and **b,** or by a vowel other than *e.*

yomu	(read)
kaku	(write)
kiru	(cut)
au	(meet)

The verb stem for the -*masu* form is made by changing the final **-u** of the dictionary form into **-i.**

yomu	*yomi-*	*yomimasu*
kaku	*kaki-*	*kakimasu*
kiru	*kiri-*	*kirimasu*
au	*ai-*	*aimasu*

2-3 Type II or **-ru verbs:** The dictionary forms of verbs in this group end in **-ru** preceded by **e** or **i.**

taberu	(eat)
miru	(see)
hajimeru	(begin)
kiru	(wear)

The verb stem for the -*masu* form is made by dropping the final **-ru.**

taberu	*tabe-*	*tabemasu*
miru	*mi-*	*mimasu*
hajimeru	*hajime-*	*hajimemasu*
kiru	*ki-*	*kimasu*

2-4 Type III verbs: There are two **Type III verbs, kuru** and **suru.**

kuru (come)	*ki-*	*kimasu*
suru (do)	*shi-*	*shimasu*

2-5 The following five verbs belong to **Type I,** but the final **-ru** of the dictionary form is changed into **-i** when making the **-masu** form.

942

kudasaru (give)	*kudasai-*	*kudasaimasu*
ossharu (say)	*osshai-*	*osshaimasu*
irassharu (be, go, come)	*irasshai-*	*irasshaimasu*
nasaru (do)	*nasai-*	*asaimasu*
gozaru (copula)	*gozai-*	*gozaimasu*

3. Polite and plain speech

3-1 Verbs are used in different forms depending on the level of speech. In polite speech *-masu* is added to the stem of verbs to indicate non-past (present and future), while verbs are used in their dictionary form in familiar speech. These two styles are called "polite" and "plain."

Yomimasu.	(I (will) read it — polite)
Yomu.	(I (will) read it — plain)

3-2 Verbs are used in their dictionary form when used as a modifier.

kore kara **yomu** *hon*	(a book that **I am going to read**)
watashi ga **yonda** *hon*	(a book that **I have read**)

4. The negative

4-1 To change verbs in the -masu form into the negative, change the **-masu** to **-masen.**

Ikimasu.	(I will go.)	*Ikimasen.*	(I will not go.)
Tabemasu.	(I will eat it.)	*Tabemasen.*	(I will not eat it.)

4-2 To change verbs in the plain form into the negative:

(1) Type I verbs: Replace the final vowel by **-anai.**

iku	*ikanai*
yomu	*yomanai*

For Type I verbs ending in a vowel plus **-u,** replace the final vowel by **-wanai.**

au (meet)	*awanai*
iu (say)	*iwanai*

For Type I verbs ending in *-tsu,* replace the **-tsu** by **-tanai.**

matsu (wait)	*matanai*

(2) Type II verbs: Replace the final **-ru** by **-nai.**

taberu	*tabenai*

(3) Type III verbs, *kudasaru,* etc.: Replace the final *-ru* by *-anai.* The plain negative form of *kuru* is *konai,* and that of *suru* is *shinai.*

(4) The plain negative form of the verb *aru* (to be) is *nai.*

5. The -te form

5-1 Verbs in the *-te* (or *-de*) form, or gerund, are used together with other verbs such as *iru, kuru,* and *kudasaru.*

> **Kaite** *imasu.*   (I am **writing** it.)
> **Kaite** *kudasai.*   (Please **write** it.)

5-2 Verbs in the *-te* form are also used to connect clauses.

> *Onaka ga* **suite,** *hatarakemasen.* (**I am so hungry that** I cannot work.)
> **Okite,** *shokuji o* **shite,** *dekakemashita.* (**I got up, had a meal, and** went out.)

5-3 The *-te* form is formed in the following way:

(1) Type I verbs: Change the dictionary form as follows.

-u	to	*-tte*	*kau*	(buy)	*katte*
-tsu	to	*-tte*	*matsu*	(wait)	*matte*
-ru	to	*-tte*	*agaru*	(go up)	*agatte*
-su	to	*-shite*	*hanasu*	(talk)	*hanashite*
-ku	to	*-ite*	*kiku*	(hear)	*kiite*
-gu	to	*-ide*	*isogu*	(hurry)	*isoide*
-bu	to	*-nde*	*yobu*	(call)	*yonde*
-mu	to	*-nde*	*yomu*	(read)	*yonde*
-nu	to	*-nde*	*shinu*	(die)	*shinde*
exception			*iku*	(go)	*itte*

(2) Type II verbs: Change the final *-ru* to *-te.*

taberu	*tabete*
miru	*mite*

(3) Type III verbs: For *kudasaru,* etc., change the final *-ru* to *-tte.*

kudasaru	*kudasatte*

For *kuru* and *suru,* change *kuru* to **kite** and *suru* to **shite.**

6. The *-ta* form

6-1 Verbs in the *-ta* (or *-da*) form are used to indicate either (1) that the action took place in the past or (2) that it has/had been completed.

(1) *Kinô wa ame ga* **furimashita**. (**It rained** yesterday.)

Sono kamera wa itsu **kaimashita** *ka?* (When **did you buy** that camera?)

(2) *Ima* **kita** *bakari desu*. (I have just **arrived**.)

Kai ni **itta** *toki mô urikirete imashita*. (When **I went** to buy it, it was sold out.)

6-2 To change verbs in the *-masu* form into the *-ta* form, change **-masu** to **-mashita** and **-masen** to **-masen deshita**.

ikimasu — ikimashita	*ikimasen — ikimasen deshita*
tabemasu — tabemashita	*tabemasen — tabemasen deshita*

6-3 To change verbs in the plain form into the *-ta* form, change the final **-e** of the *-te* form into **-a**.

iku	*itte*	*itta*
taberu	*tabete*	*tabeta*

6-4 To change verbs in the plain negative form into the *-ta* form, change the final **-nai** into **-nakatta**.

iku	*ikanai*	*ikanakatta*
taberu	*tabenai*	*tabenakatta*

7. Transitive and intransitive verbs

7-1 Verbs which are usually preceded by an object plus the particle **o** are called transitive, and verbs which never so occur are called intransitive.

mado **o** *akeru*	(open the window — transitive)
mado **ga** *aku*	(the window opens — intransitive)
Kitte **o** *atsumemashita*.	(I collected stamps — transitive)
Kitte **ga** *atsumarimashita*.	(Stamps have been collected — intransitive)

7-2 The following is a table of the most important sets of transitive and intransitive verbs.

		transitive	intransitive	
(1)	-eru/-aru(-waru)	shimeru	shimaru	(shut)
		kakeru	kakaru	(hang)
		kaeru	kawaru	(change)
(2)	-eru/-u	akeru	aku	(open)
		tsukeru	tsuku	(attach)
(3)	-asu/-u	dasu	deru	(put out)
		wakasu	waku	(boil)
(4)	-su/-ru	naosu	naoru	(repair)
		toosu	tooru	(pass)
(5)	-u/-eru	kesu	kieru	(extinguish)
		mosu	moeru	(burn)

7-3 Intransitive verbs are used with a noun plus **o** when referring to an action which takes place through, along, or from, a certain place.

> tooru   *Kono basu wa doko **o toorimasu** ka?* (What course does this bus **take** — literally, Where does this bus **go through?**)
>
> deru   *Kuji ni uchi **o demashita**.* (**I left** home at nine — literally, **I went out** of the house at nine.)

7-4 Transitive verbs in the **-te** form followed by **aru** express a state that has resulted from an action.

> tsukeru   *Dentō ga **tsukete arimasu**.* (The light **is on** — literally, The light **has been turned on.**)
>
> shimeru   *To ga **shimete arimasu**.* (The door **is closed** — literally, The door **has been closed.**)

8. The potential

8-1 The potential form is used to indicate that one can do something or that something can be done.

> *Nama no sakana wa **taberaremasen**.* (**I cannot eat** raw fish.)

8-2 The potential form is constructed as follows:

(1) Type I verbs: The final *-u* is replaced by *-eru.*

yomu	*yomeru* (can read)
kaku	*kakeru* (can write)

(2) Type II verbs: The final *-ru* is replaced by *-rareru.*

taberu	*taberareru* (can eat)
miru	*mirareru* (can see)

(3) Type III verbs such as *kudasaru*: The final *-u* is replaced by *-eru,* but these verbs are seldom used in the potential form. The potential form of **kuru** is **korareru,** and that of **suru** is **dekiru.**

8-3 To change the plain potential form into the *-masu* form, replace the final *-ru* by **-masu.**

yomu	*yomeru*	*yomemasu*
taberu	*taberareru*	*taberaremasu*

8-4 In sentences employing the potential form, an object is usually followed by **ga** rather than **o.**

Sakana **o** *taberu.* — Sakana **ga** *taberareru.*

Hon **o** *yomu.* — Hon **ga** *yomeru.*

In the negative, **ga** often changes into **wa.**

Sakana **ga** *taberareru.* — Sakana **wa** *taberarenai.*

Hon **ga** *yomemasu.* — Hon **wa** *yomemasen.*

9. The passive

9-1 Passive sentences are constructed by using a verb in the passive form, with the performer of the action indicated by the particle **ni.**

Haha ni shikararemashita. (**I was scolded by** my mother.)

9-2 The passive form is constructed in the following way:

(1) Type I verbs: The final *-u* is replaced by *-areru.*

yomu	*yomareru* (to be read)
kaku	*kakareru* (to be written)

(2) Type II verbs: The final *-ru* is replaced by *-rareru* (identical to the potential form).

taberu	*taberareru* (to be eaten)

| *miru* | *mirareru* (to be seen) |

(3) The passive of **kuru** is **korareru,** and that of **suru** is **sareru.** The irregular verbs like *kudasaru* are not usually used in the passive.

9-3　There are two kinds of passive sentences: those in the suffering passive and those in the non-suffering passive.

9-4　Sentences in the suffering passive imply that the speaker is unfavorably affected by the action described by the verb. The subject of these sentences is usually the speaker, whether explicitly indicated or not. When the subject needs to be stated, a phrase plus *wa* is used.

> *Ani ni* **naguraremashita.**　　　(I **was hit** by my brother.)
>
> *Kodomo* **wa** *tomodachi ni* **naguraremashita.** (My child **was hit** by his friend.)

When an action is described with a verb plus object, the object is followed by **o.**

> *Densha no naka de ashi* **o fumaremashita. (Someone stepped on** my foot in the train — literally, I **had** my foot **stepped on.)**

9-5　In the case of the suffering passive, intransitive verbs can also be used in the passive form.

> *Kaeri ni ame ni* **furaremashita. (It rained** on my way home — literally, **I was rained** on.)
>
> *Kodomo no toki chichi ni* **shinaremashita.** (My father **died** when I was a child.)

9-6　Sentences in the non-suffering passive are similar to passive sentences in English; they are usually used to report a fact without referring to an agent.

> *Shiken no kekka ga* **happyō saremashita.** (The results of the examination **were announced.)**
>
> *Sono hon wa raigetsu* **shuppan saremasu.** (That book **will be published** next month.)

10. The causative

10-1 The causative form is used to mean "someone makes or lets someone do something."

10-2　The causative form is constructed as follows:

(1) Type I verbs: The final **-u** is replaced by **-aseru.**

> *yomu*　　　　　　　*yomaseru* (cause someone to read)

| *kaku* | *kakaseru* (cause someone to write) |

If the Type I verb ends in two vowels, the final *-u* is replaced by *-waseru.*

| *kau* | *kawaseru* (cause someone to buy) |

(2) Type II verbs: The final *-ru* is replaced by *-saseru.*

| *taberu* | *tabesaseru* (cause someone to eat) |
| *miru* | *misaseru* (cause someone to see) |

(3) The causative form of **kuru** is **kosaseru** and that of **suru** is **saseru.** Irregular verbs like *kudasaru* are not used in the causative form.

10-3 Causative sentences are constructed in the following way.

(1) When an intransitive verb is used to describe an action, the person caused to do that action is indicated with the particle **o.**

Kodomo **o** *gakkō e* **ikasemashita.** (**I made** my child **go** to school.)

(2) When a transitive verb is used to describe an action, the person caused to do that action is indicated with **ni,** and the object of the action with **o.**

Kodomo **ni** *hon* **o** *yomasemashita.* (**I made** my child **read** a book.)

10-4 The causative form usually refers to making someone do something by force; it cannot be used when politely asking someone to do something.

10-5 The causative form followed by *-te kudasai* is used to mean "let me do something" or "allow me to do something."

Kono denwa o **taukawasete kudasai. (Please let me use** this telephone.)

10-6 The causative form followed by the passive ending *-rareru* indicates that someone is forced to do something.

| *yomu* | *yomaseru* | *yomaserareru* |

Hon o **yomaseraremashita.**   (**I was forced to read** a book.)

11. The conditional

11-1 The conditional is expressed by (1) the *-eba* form of a verb, (2) the *-tara* form of a verb, and (3) by adding the particle **to** to the dictionary form of a verb. These three roughly correspond to the English "if" or "when"; in some cases they can be used interchangeably but not in others.

11-2 The three conditional forms are constructed in the following way:

(1) The *-eba* form is made by replacing the final *-u* of the verb by *-eba.*
For adjectives the final *-i* is replaced by *-kereba.*

yomu	*yomeba*
taberu	*tabereba*
akai	*akakereba*

(2) The *-tara* form is made by adding *-ra* to the plain past form of both verbs and adjectives.

yomu	*yonda*	*yondara*
taberu	*tabeta*	*tabetara*
akai	*akakatta*	*akakattara*

(3) The *to* form is made by adding the particle *to* to the dictionary form of both verbs and adjectives.

yomu	*yomu to*
taberu	*taberu to*
akai	*akai to*

11-3 These three forms cannot be used interchangeably in the following cases:

(1) The *-eba* and *to* forms are not usually followed by a verb, phrase, or clause indicating past action.

wrong: * *Yomeba wakarirnashita.*

wrong: * *Yomu to wakarimashita.*

Instead, the *-tara* form is used.

right: **Yondara** (or *Yonde* **mitara**) *wakarimashita.*
(**When I read it,** I understood.)

(2) The *to* form cannot be followed by verbs indicating a request or invitation.

wrong: * *Jikan ga aru to tetsudatte kudasai.*

wrong: * *Jikan ga aru to issho ni ikimashō.*

wrong: * *Yasui to kaimasen ka?*

Instead, *-tara* is usually used.

right: *Jikan ga* **attara** *tetsudatte kudasai.* (Please help me **if you have** time.)

right: *Jikan ga* **attara** *issho ni ikimashō.* (Let's go together **if you have** time.)

right: **Yasukattara** *kaimasen ka?* (Would you want to buy it **if it were inexpensive?**)

(3) **To** and **-eba** indicate a general condition, while **-tara** is used for referring to a particular condition or circumstance.

*Jikan ga **aru to** dekimasu.* (One can do it **if one has** time.)

*Jikan ga **areba** dekimasu.* (One can do it **if one has** time.)

*Ashita jikan ga **attara** yarimasu.* (I will do it tomorrow **if I have** time.)

12. Commands

12-1 Commands are expressed either with the plain imperative form or with the **-nasai** form.

12-2 The plain imperative form is constructed in the following way:

(1) Type I verbs: Replace the final **-u** by **-e.**

yomu	*yome*
iku	*ike*

(2) Type II verbs: Replace the final **-ru** by **-ro.**

taberu	*tabero*
miru	*miro*

(3) The plain imperative form of **kuru** is **koi,** and that of **suru** is **shiro.**

12-3 The plain imperative form is not used in polite speech, except in indirect speech conveying someone's command.

*Sensei ga **yome** to osshaimashita.* (The professor told me **to read it.**)

12-4 To form the -nasai form, add **-nasai** to the stem of the verb.

yomu	*yominasai*
taberu	*tabenasai*
kuru	*kinasai*

12-5 The **-nasai** form is used when giving an order.

*Sā, mō **okinasai**.* (Now you **get up!**)

12-6 For expressing a request, **kudasai** is added to the **-te** form of the verb.

yomu	*yonde*	*yonde kudasai*
taberu	*tabete*	*tabete kudasai*

The negative request is constructed by adding **-de kudasai** to the plain negative form of the verb.

yomu	*yomanai*	*yomanaide kudasai*
taberu	*tabenai*	*tabenaide kudasai*

13. Desideratives

13-1 To mean "want to," **-tai** is added to the verb stem. This usually expresses the desires of the speaker.

> *Gakko e **ikitai** desu.*   (**I want to go** to school.)

13-2 When the verb used with *-tai* is a transitive verb, the object is indicated with **ga** rather than *o*.

> *Ocha **ga nomitai** desu.*   (**I want to drink** some tea.)

13-3 Verbs ending in **-tai** are conjugated in the same way as true adjectives (IV.2).

> *Ikitaku wa arimasen.*   (1 don't want to go — polite)
> *Ikitaku wa nai.*   (I don't want to go — plain)
> *Ikitakatta desu.*   (I wanted to go — polite)
> *Ikitakatta.*   (I wanted to go — plain)

13-4 To refer to wishes in the third person, **-tagaru** is added to the stem of the verb.

> *Kodomo wa gakkō e **ikitagatte** imasu.* (My child **wants to go** to school.)

13-5 Verbs ending in **-tagaru** are conjugated in the same way as Type I verbs.

> *Kodomo wa gakkō e **ikitagarimasen.*** (My child does **not want to go** to school — polite)
> *Kodomo wa gakkō e **ikitagaranai.*** (My child does **not want to go** to school — plain)

13-6 When **-tagaru** is used with a transitive verb, the object is indicated with the particle **o**.

> *Kodomo wa mizu **o nomitagatte** imasu.* (The child **wants to drink** some water.)

13-7 To refer to wishes in the second or third person, indirect expressions such as (1) **-sō** (look like), (2) **yō** (seem), and (3) **to iu** (say that ...) are used. This is the same as the expression of emotion with adjectives (V.2-8).

(1) *-sō:*

> *Ikita**sō** desu ne.* (You **look like** you want to go.)
> *Tanaka san mo ikita**sō** deshita.* (Miss Tanaka also **looked like** she wanted to go.)

(2) *yō:*

> *Tanaka san mo ikitai **yō** desu.* (**It seems** that Miss Tanaka wants to go, too.)

(3) *to iu*:

> *Tanaka san mo ikitai **to iimashita**.* (Miss Tanaka **said that** she wants to go, too.)

13-8 To politely refer to wishes in the second or third person, *-tai* and *-tagaru* are usually replaced by completely different expressions. For example, "*Irasshaimasu ka?*" (Would you like to go? — literally, Are you going?) is used rather than * *Ikitai desu ka?*; and "*Shachō ga oyobi desu*" (The director would like to see you — literally, The director is calling you) is used rather than * *Shachō ga aitagatte imasu*.

14. The volitional

14-1 To refer to one's intentions, the volitional form is used; this corresponds to the English "I will" or "I shall."

14-2 The volitional form is constructed in the following way:

(1) Type I verbs: The final *-u* is replaced by *-ō*.

iku	*ikō*
yomu	*yomō*

-tsu is replaced by *-tō*.

matsu	*matō*

(2) Type II verbs: The final *-ru* is replaced by *-yō*.

taberu	*tabeyō*
miru	*miyō*

(3) The volitional form of ***kuru*** is ***koyō*** and that of ***suru*** is ***shiyō***.

14-3 In polite speech the volitional form is followed by ***to omoimasu***, while in familiar speech it is used as is.

> *Ashita eiga o **miyō to omoimasu**.* (**I think I will go** to the movies tomorrow.)
>
> *Ashita eiga o **miyō**.* (**I think I will go** to the movies tomorrow.)

14-4 The volitional form is used for invitations in familiar speech.

> *Issho ni **ikō**.* (**Let's go** together.)

In polite speech, ***-mashō*** is used instead.

> *Issho ni **ikimashō**.*

14-5 The volitional form followed by **to suru** refers to an action which is about to take place.

> **Kaerō to shita** *toki ame ga furidashimashita*. (When **I was about to go back,** it started to rain.)

14-6 The volitional form followed by **to suru** is also used to mean "try to."

> **Tabeyō to shimashita** *ga, taberaremasen deshita*. (**I tried to eat it,** but I couldn't.)

15. Expressing appearance

15-1 To refer to appearance, (1) *rashii*, (2) *yō da*, and (3) *mitai da* are added to words, phrases, and clauses.

(1) **Rashii** is added to phrases and sentences; it is also added to verb phrases indicating the past tense.

> *Tanaka san mo iku* **rashii desu**. (**It seems that** Miss Tanaka also is going.)
>
> *Tanaka san mo itta* **rashii desu**. (**It seems that** Miss Tanaka also went.)

When **rashii** is added to a noun, it usually forms an adjective meaning "really like ..."

onna	*onna***rashii** (woman**ly**, lady**like**)
kodomo	*kodomo***rashii** (**just like** a child, innocent, lively, etc.)

(2) **Yō da** is also added to phrases and clauses; it is used as **yō desu** in polite speech.

> *Kekka ga happyō sareta* **yō desu**. (**It seems that** the results have been announced.)

Yō is conjugated in the same way as the adjective-verbs; **yō na** is used as a modifier, and **yō ni** is used as an adverb.

> *Wakatta* **yō na** *ki ga shimasu*. (**I feel that** I understand.)
>
> *Keikaku wa shippai shita* **yō ni** *miemasu*. (**It seems that** the plan has ended in failure.)

Yō da, preceded by the particle **no,** is used to describe a noun.

haru **no yō**	(**like** spring)
Haru **no yō desu**.	(**It is like** spring.)

954

Haru **no yô na** *hi deshita.* (It was **like** a day in spring.)

(3) **Mitai da** is also added to phrases and clauses; it is conjugated in the same way as the adjective-verbs.

Kyô wa haru **mitai da.** (**It is like** spring today.)
Kyô wa haru **mitai na** *hi da.* (Today is **like** a spring day.)
Kyô wa haru **mitai ni** *atatakai.* (It is warm **like** spring today.)

15-2 The above three are similar in meaning, but *yô da* sounds more formal, and *mitai da* sounds more familiar. For further differences, see the respective entries in the dictionary.

16. Helping verbs

16-1 Verbs are often added to the **-te** form of other verbs; verbs used in this way can be called "helping verbs."

16-2 *-te iru:*

A verb in the **-te** form plus **iru** refers either (1) to an action that goes on over a period of time, or (2) to the state resulting from an action.

(1) *Ima hon o* **yonde imasu.** (I **am** now **reading** a book.)
Sono toki ocha o **nonde imashita.** (I **was drinking** tea at that time.)

(2) *Dentô ga* **tsuite imasu.** (The light **is on.**)
Futari wa **kekkon shite imasu.** (The two **are married.**)

16-3 *-te aru:*

A transitive verb in the **-te** form plus **aru** refers to the state that has resulted from an action (See 7-4).

16-4 *-te shimau:*

A verb in the **-te** form plus **shimau** indicates either (1) that an action has been completed, or (2) that the speaker has regrets about the completion of the action.

(1) *Zenbu* **yonde shimaimashita** *kara, toshokan ni kaeshimasu.* (Since I **have finished reading** them all, I am going to return them to the library.)

(2) *Kabin o* **otoshite shimaimashita.** (I **dropped** the vase — and I **regret** it.)
Osoku **natte shimatte,** *sumimasen.* (I am sorry I **am so** late.)

955

16-5 *-te oku:*

A verb in the **-te** form plus **oku** refers to doing something for future use.

Mado o **akete okimashita.** (I **left** the window **open** — so that the air would circulate.)

Yoku **shirabete oite** *kudasai.* (Please **make** a thorough **investigation beforehand.**)

16-6 *-te miru:*

A verb in the **-te** form plus **miru** means "to try and see."

Oishii ka dō ka **tabete mimashō.** (I **will taste it** to see if it is good or not.)

Atte minakereba *wakarimasen.* (I cannot tell [what he is like] **unless I see** him in person.)

16-7 *-te iku:*

A verb in the **-te** form plus **iku** refers to a change taking place from the present into the future.

Dandan samuku **natte iku** *deshō.* (It **will become** colder and colder.)

16-8 *-te kuru:*

A verb in the **-te** form plus **kuru** indicates either (1) that a change has been taking place up to the present, or (2) that an action is done in the direction of the speaker.

(1) *Dandan samuku* **natte kimashita.** (It **has been getting** colder and colder.)

Kono kaisha ni nijūnenkan **tsutomete kimashita.** (I **have been working** for this company for 20 years.)

(2) *Mukō kara ookina kuruma ga* **chikazuite kimashita.** (A large car **came from** the opposite direction.)

Haha ga sētā o **okutte kimashita.** (My mother **sent** me a sweater.)

17. Narration

17-1 To quote someone's speech, **to iu** is used; what is quoted is described in plain form even in polite speech.

Yamada san wa iku **to itte** *imasu.* (Mr. Yamada **says that** he is going to go there.)

Tanaka san wa ongaku ga suki da **to itte** *imasu.* (Miss Tanaka **says that** she likes music.)

956

17-2 To change the sentence into the past tense, only the main verb is changed into the past.

> *Yamada san wa iku* **to iimashita.** (Mr. Yamada **said that** he was going to go there.)

17-3 If the verb in the quoted clause is in the past, as well as the main verb, the action took place prior to the time of the statement.

> *Yamada san wa itta* **to iimashita.** (Mr. Yamada **said that** he had gone there.)

17-4 To relate what the speaker thinks, **to omou** is used; the rules of 17-1 to 17-3 apply in this case also.

> *Yamada san wa iku* **to omoimasu. (I think that** Mr. Yamada is going to go there.)
>
> *Yamada san wa iku* **to omoimashita. (I thought that** Mr. Yamada was going to go there.)
>
> *Yamada san wa itta* **to omoimashita. (I thought that** Mr. Yamada had gone there.)

17-5 When the quoted part includes an interrogative, **ka** is added at the end of the quoted part.

> **Doko e iku ka** *iimasen deshita.* (He didn't tell me **where he was going.**)
>
> **Nani ga hoshii ka** *itte kudasai.* (Please tell me **what you want.**)

17-6 The rule of 17-5 also applies when such verbs as **shiru, wakaru, oshieru,** and **shiraseru** are used as the main verb.

> **Naze sonna koto o shita ka** *wakarimasen.* (I don't know **why he did such a thing.**)
>
> **Itsu dekiru ka** *shitte imasu ka?* (Do you know **when it will be completed?**)

18. Giving and receiving

18-1 The verbs describing the action of giving and receiving things — *ageru, sashiageru, yaru, morau, itadaku, kureru, kudasaru* — are used depending on the relations between the giver and the receiver.

18-2 **Giving:** Verbs referring to giving are used as follows:

957

ageru	give something to one's equals or inferiors
sashiageru	give something to one's superiors
yaru	give something to one's inferiors or animals

Tomodachi ni shashin o **agemashita.** (**I gave** a picture to my friend.)

Sensei ni shashin o **sashiagemashita.** (**I gave** a picture to the professor.)

Otōto ni shashin o **yarimashita.** (**I gave** a picture to my brother.)

18-3 **Receiving:** Verbs referring to receiving are used as follows:

morau	receive something from one's equals or inferiors
itadaku	receive something from one's superiors

Tomodachi ni/kara shashin o **moraimashita.** (**I received** a picture from my friend.)

Otōto ni/kara shashin o **moraimashita.** (**I received** a picture from my brother.)

Sensei ni/kara shashin o **itadakimashita.** (**I received** a picture from the professor.)

18-4 Giving something to the speaker: The following verbs are used only when the speaker or someone who can be identified with the speaker is given something.

kudasaru	one's superiors give something to the speaker
kureru	one's equals or inferiors give something to the speaker

Sensei ga shashin o **kudasaimashita.** (The professor **gave me** a picture.)

Tomodachi ga shashin o **kuremashita.** (My friend **gave me** a picture.)

Otōto ga shashin o **kuremashita.** (My brother **gave me** a picture.)

18-5 When these verbs are used as helping verbs, they refer to doing and receiving a favor in the same way as when they are used for giving and receiving physical objects.

Tomodachi no shigoto o **tetsudatte agemashita.** (**I helped** my friend with his work.)

Otōto no shigoto o **tetsudatte yarimashita.** (**I helped** my brother with his work.)

Tomodachi ni shigoto o **tetsudatte moraimashita.** (My friend **helped me** with my work — literally, **I received help** from my friend.)

Sensei ni shigoto o **tetsudatte itadakimashita.** (The professor **helped me** with my work.)

Sensei ga shigoto o **tetsudatte kudasaimashita.** (The professor **helped**

me with my work.)

*Tomodachi ga shigoto o **tetsudatte kuremashita**.* (My friend **helped me** with my work.)

In the case of *sashiageru*, the humble form "*o- ～suru*" is preferred.

*Sensei no shigoto o **otetsudai shimashita**.* (**I helped** the professor with his work.)

VII. KEIGO (POLITE LANGUAGE)

The Japanese language is used in different ways depending on to whom it is spoken and to whom one refers. ***Keigo,*** or polite language, refers to a linguistic style in Japanese used when speaking to and about someone politely. It is usually divided into three types: (1) honorific, (2) humble, and (3) polite.

1. Honorific language

1-1 Honorific language is used to refer to someone with respect; special prefixes, suffixes, verbs, and verb forms are used for this purpose.

1-2 Prefixes: The honorific prefixes ***o-*** and ***go-*** are used when referring to someone's belongings with respect.

o*taku*	(your house, his/her/their house)
o*shigoto*	(your work, his/her/their work)
go*kenkyū*	(your research, his/her/their research)

1-3 Suffixes: The honorific suffixes ***sama, san,*** and the like are used when referring to someone with respect.

go*shujin **sama***	(someone's husband)
*kodomo **san***	(someone's child(ren))

1-4 Verbs: Special verbs are used to refer to someone's actions with respect.

irassharu	(be, go, come)
ossharu	(say)
nasaru	(do)
meshiagaru	(eat, drink)
goran ni naru	(see)

1-5 Verb forms: Special verb forms are used to refer to someone's actions with respect.

(1) *o-* + verb stem + *ni naru*

      oyomi **ni naru**   (someone reads)

      ooshie **ni naru**   (someone teaches)

(2) The passive form of a verb is also used to show respect.

      *yom***areru**   (someone reads)

      *oshie***rareru**   (someone teaches)

2. Humble language

2-1 Special verbs are used to refer to the actions of oneself and one's family members in order to express a humble attitude.

oru	(be)
mairu	(go, come)
itadaku	(receive, eat, drink)
haiken suru	(see something)
ome ni kakaru	(see someone)
môshiageru	(tell someone)
ojama suru	(visit)
ukagau	(ask, hear, visit)

2-2 Special verb forms are used to refer to one's own actions; namely, *o-* + verb stem + *suru*.

      oyobi **suru**   (I call someone)

      omachi **suru**   (I wait for someone to come)

2-3 The special helping verbs *itasu* and *môshiageru* are also used.

      oyobi **itasu**   (I call someone)

      ohanashi **môshiageru**   (I tell it to someone)

3. Polite language

Polite forms are used in formal speech and conversation between persons who are not on familiar terms or when talking to one's superiors; the plain forms are used in conversation between family members, to good friends, and to one's inferiors.

Katakana Glossary

【ア】

アート	art
アートショー	art show
アートセンター	art center
アートフェア	art fair
アイス	ice
アイスクリーム	ice cream
アイスコーヒー	iced coffee
アイスティー	ice tea/iced tea
アイスホッケー	ice hockey
アイデア	idea
アイディア	idea
アイロン	iron
アウト	out
アウトドア	outdoor
アクセサリー	accessory
アクセス	access
アクセル	accelerator
アクセント	accent
アクティビティー	activity
アジア	Asia
アップ	up
アップルパイ	apple pie
アドバイス	advice/advise
アナウンサー	announcer
アニメ	animation/cartoon film
アニメーション	animation/cartoon film
アニメフェスティバル	animation festival
アパート	apartment house
アフリカ	Africa
アプローチ	approach
アマチュア	amateur
アメフト	American football
アメリカ	America
アメリカ人	American (person)
アラブ	Arab
アラビア語	Arabic (language)
アルカリ	alkali
アルコール	alcohol
アルジェリア	Algeria
アルジェリア人	Algerian (person)
アルバイト	part-time job/side job
アルバム	album
アルミ	aluminum
アワー	hour
アンケート	questionnaire
アンコール	encore
アンテナ	antenna

【イ】

イエス	yes
イエス	Jesus
イエローツナ	yellow tuna
イギリス	England/Great Britain
イギリス人	English (person)
イコール	equal
イスラエル	Israel
イスラム	Islam
イタリア	Italy
イタリアンアイス	Italian ice
イベント	event
イメージ	image
イヤホーン	earphone
イヤリング	earring
インキ	ink
インク	ink
インスタントラーメン	instant noodles
インターチェンジ	interchange
インターナショナル	international
インターネット	Internet
インターホン	interphone
インタビュー	interview
インテリ	intelligentsia
インド	India
インド人	Indian (person)
インドネシア	Indonesia
インドネシア語	Indonesian (language)
インドネシア人	Indonesian (person)
インフォメーション	information
インフルエンザ	influenza/flu
インフレ	inflation

【ウ】

ウイスキー	whisky
ウイルス	virus
ウーマン	woman
ウール	wool
ウエーター	waiter
ウエートレス	waitress
ウエスト	west
ウエスト	waist
ウエルカムダンス	welcome dance
ウォークマン	Walkman®
ウクライナ人	Ukrainian (person)

【エ】

エアコン	air conditioner
エアメール	airmail
エアログラム	aerogramme
エイズウォーク	AIDS walk
エキスパートシステム	expert system
エジプト	Egypt
エジプト人	Egyptian (person)
エスカレーター	escalator
エチケット	etiquette
エッセーコンテスト	essay contest
エネルギー	energy
エプロン	apron
エルエル教室	language laboratory
エレガント	elegant
エレクトーン	Electone®/ electronic organ
エレベーター	elevator/lift
エンジニア	engineer
エンジン	engine

【オ】

オイル	oil
オーケー	O.K.
オーケストラ	orchestra
オーストラリア	Australia
オーストラリア人	Australian (person)
オーディオ	audio
オーディション	audition
オートバイ	motor cycle
オートマチック	automatic
オートメーション	automation
オーバー	overcoat
オーバーコート	overcoat
オーバーする	over
オープン	open
オフィス	office
オリエンテーション	orientation
オリンピック	Olympic
オルガン	organ
オレンジ	orange
オレンジジュース	orange juice
オンライン	on-line

【カ】

カー	car
カーテン	curtain
カード	card
カーナビ	car navigation system
カーネーション	carnation
カーブ	curve
カーペット	carpet
ガイド	guide
ガイドブック	guidebook
カウンセラー	counselor
カウンター	counter
カカオ	cacao
カクテル	cocktail
ガス	gas
ガスサービスセンター	gas service center
ガスレンジ	gas range
カセット	cassette
ガソリン	gasoline
ガソリンスタンド	gas station
カタログ	catalog
カット	cut
カップ	cup
カテゴリー	category
カナダ	Canada
カナダ人	Canadian (person)
カヌー	canoe
カバー	cover
カフェー	cafe
カフェテリア	cafeteria
ガム	gum
ガムテープ	gum tape/packing tape
カムバック	comeback
カメラ	camera
カメラマン	cameraman
カラー	color
カラオケ	karaoke
ガラス	glass
カルテ	medical chart
ガレージ	garage
カレーライス	curry and rice
カレンダー	calendar
カロリー	calorie
カントリー	country
カントリー	country music
カンニング	cheating

【キ】

キー	key
キウイ	kiwi fruit
ギガ	gigabyte
キス	kiss
ギター	guitar
キック	kick
ギフト	gift
ギフトセンター	gift center
キャッシュカード	cash card/bank card
キャッシュサービス	cash service
キャッチ	catch
キャプテン	captain
キャリア	carrier
キャリア	career
ギャング	gangster/mafia
キャンセル	cancel
キャンパス	campus
キャンプ	camp
キャンプ場	campsite
キャンプファイア	campfire
キリスト教	Christian faith
キリン	giraffe
キロ（キログラム）	kilogram
キロ（キロメートル）	kilometer
キロ（キロメーター）	kilometer

【ク】

クイーン	queen
クイズ	quiz
クーラー	air conditioner
クール	cool
クッキー	cookie
クッキング	cooking
クラシック	classic
クラシック	classical music
クラス	class
グラス	glass
クラスメート	classmate
クラブ	club
グラフ	graph
グラム	gram
クラムソース	clam sauce
グランド	ground/field
クリーニング	cleaning
クリーム	cream
グリーン	green
クリスマス	Christmas
グループ	group
グレー	gray
グレープフルーツ	grapefruit
クレーン	crane
クレジットカード	credit card
クロール	crawl (stroke)

【ケ】

ケイ	kilobyte
ケイ	light vehicle
ケーキ	cake
ケース（場合・状況）	case
ケース（箱）	case
ゲーム	game
ゲスト	guest

【コ】

コインランドリー	coin laundry
コーク	Coke®
コース	course
コーチ	coach
コード	code
コード	cord
コート	court
コート	coat
コーナー	corner
コーヒー	coffee
コーラ	cola
コーラス	chorus
ゴール	goal
ゴールデンウイーク	Golden Week holidays
ゴールド	gold
ココア	cocoa
コック	cook
コップ	cup
コピー	copy
コマーシャル	commercial
コミュニケーション	communication
ゴム	rubber
コメント	comments
ゴルフ	golf
コレクション	collection
コンクール	contest/concours
コンクリート	concrete
コンサート	concert
コンセント	wall outlet/wall socket
コンタクト（レンズ）	contact lenses
コンテスト	contest
コントラスト	contrast
コントロール	control
コンパ	party
コンパス	compass
コンパニー	company
コンビニ	convenience store

コンピュータ	computer

【サ】

サーカス	circus
サークル	circle
サービス	service
サーブ	serve
サーフィン	surfing
サーベイ	survey
サイエンスフェア	science fair
サイクル	cycle
サイズ	size
サイダー	cider/soda pop
サイレン	siren
サイン	signature
サッカー	soccer/football
サボる	go on a go-slow/sabotage
サラダ	salad
サラリーマン	salaried worker
サンキュー	thank you
サングラス	sunglasses
サンタクロース	Santa Claus
サンダル	sandals
サンドイッチ	sandwich
サンプル	sample

【シ】

シーズン	season
シーツ	bed sheet
シーディー（CD）	compact disc
シート	sheet
シート	seat
ジーパン	jeans
ジーンズ	jeans
ジェット	jet
システム	system
シック	sick
シック	chic
シナリオ	scenario
シニア	senior
ジム	gym/gymnasium
ジャーナリスト	journalist
シャープペンシル	automatic pencil/mechanical pencil
シャーベット	sherbet/water ice
ジャケット	jacket
ジャズ	jazz
シャツ	shirt
シャツ	undershirt
シャッター	shutter
ジャパニーズナイト	Japanese night
ジャパニーズパーティー	Japanese party
ジャパニーズフェア	Japanese fair
ジャム	jam
シャワー	shower
ジャンパー	jumper
ジャンプ	jump
シャンプー	shampoo
ジャンボ	jumbo
ジャンル	genre
ジュース	juice
ショー	show
ショート	short
ショート	shortstop
ショーツ	shorts
ジョッギング	jogging
ショック	shock
ショッピングセンター	shopping center
ショッピングモール	shopping mall
ショップ	shop
シリーズ	series
シルバー	silver
シングル	single
シングル	single room

【ス】

スイス	Switzerland
スイッチ	switch
スウェーデン	Sweden
スーツ	suit
スーツケース	suitcase
スーパー	supermarket
スーパーマーケット	supermarket
スープ	soup
スカート	skirt
スカーフ	scarf
スキー	ski/skiing
スキートーナメント	ski tournament
スクール	school
スクリーン	screen
スケート	skate
スケジュール	schedule
スケッチ	sketch
スター	star
スタート	start
スタイル	style
スタジオ	studio
スタンド	stand
スチーム	steam
スチュワーデス	stewardess
ステーキ	steak
ステージ	stage
ステレオ	stereo
スト	strike
ストーブ	stove
ストッキング	stockings
ストップ	stop
ストライキ	strike
ストレス	stress
ストロー	straw
ストロボ	electric flash/strobe light
スニーカー	sneakers
スノーフェスティバル	snow festival
スパイスコーナー	spice corner
スパゲッティ	spaghetti
スピーカー	speaker
スピーチ	speech
スピード	speed
スプーン	spoon
スプリング	spring
スペイン	Spain
スペイン語	Spanish (language)
スペイン人	Spanish (person)
スペース	space
スポーツ	sport
スポーツカー	sports car
ズボン	pants
ズボン	trousers
スマート	smart
スライド	slide
スラックス	slacks
スリッパ	slippers

【セ】

セーター	sweater/jumper
セール	sale
セール	sail
セクション	section
セックス	sex
セット	set
ゼミ	seminar
セメント	cement
ゼリー	jelly
セレモニー	ceremony
ゼロ	zero
セロテープ	Scotch tape®
センス	sense
センター	center
センチ	centimeter
センチメートル	centimeter

セント cent

【ソ】

ソース	source
ソース	sauce
ソーセージ	sausage
ソーダ	soda
ソーター	sorter
ソックス	socks
ソファー	sofa
ソフト	soft
ソロ	solo

【タ】

タイ	Thailand
タイ	tie
ダース	dozen
ターミナル	terminal
ダイエット	diet
タイトル	title
ダイニングキッチン	eat-in kitchen/kitchen-diner
タイピスト	typist
タイプ	type
タイプライター	typewriter
タイマー	timer
タイミング	timing
タイム	time
タイム	time out
タイムリー	timely
タイヤ	tire
ダイヤ（ダイヤグラム）	diagram
ダイヤ（ダイヤモンド）	diamond
ダイヤル	dial
タイル	tile
ダウン	down
タオル	towel
タクシー	taxi
ダブル	double
ダブる	double
ダム	dam
タレント	talent
タレントショー	talent show
タワー	tower
タンゴ	tango
ダンス	dance
ダンスパーティー	dance party
ダンプ	dump
ダンボール（箱）	cardboard box/carton box

【チ】

チーズ	cheese
チーズケーキ	cheesecake
チーム	team
チームワーク	teamwork
チェス	chess
チェスクラブ	chess club
チェック	check
チェックアウト	check out
チェックイン	check in
チェンジ	change
チキン	chicken
チケット	ticket
チップ	chip
チャイム	chime
チャレンジ	challenge
チャンス	chance
チャンネル	channel
チョーク	chalk
チョコレート	chocolate

【ツ】

ツアー	tour
ツイン	twin

【テ】

ティーンエージャー	teenager
ティッシュペーパー	tissue paper
ディスク	disc/disk
ディスコ	disco
ティラミス	tiramisu
データ	data
デート	date
テープ	tape
テーブル	table
テープレコーダー	tape recorder
テーマ	theme
テキスト	text
デコレーション	decoration
デザート	dessert
デザイナー	designer
デザイン	design
テスト	test
デッサン	drawing
テニス	tennis
テニスコート	tennis court
デパート	department store
デモ	demo
デモンストレーション	demonstration
テレックス	telex
テレビ	television
テレビゲーム	video game
テレホンカード	telephone card
テント	tent
テンポ	tempo

【ト】

ドア	door
ドイツ	Germany
ドイツ語	German (language)
ドイツ人	German (person)
トイレ	toilet/restroom
トースト	toast
ドーナツ	donut
トーン	tone
トップ	top
トピック	topic
トマト	tomato
トマトソース	tomato sauce
ドライ	dry
ドライクリーニング	dry-cleaning
ドライバー	driver
ドライブ	drive
ドライブイン	drive-in
トラック	truck
トラック	track
ドラフト	draft
トラブル	trouble
トラベラーズチェック	traveler's check
ドラマ	drama
ドラマクラブ	drama club
ドラマナイト	drama night
トランク	trunk
トランジスタ（ー）	transistor
トランプ	cards
ドリル	drill
ドル	dollar
トレー	tray
トレーナー	sweatshirt
トレーニング	training
ドレス	dress
トン（1000KG）	ton
トンネル	tunnel

【ナ】

ナイター	night game
ナイフ	knife
ナイロン	nylon
ナプキン	napkin
ナンセンス	nonsense

ナンバー	number

【ニ】

ニックネーム	nickname
ニヤニヤ	grin
ニュアンス	nuance
ニュー	new
ニュージーランド	New Zealand
ニュース	news

【ネ】

ネガ	negative film
ネクタイ	necktie
ネックレス	necklace
ネット	net

【ノ】

ノイローゼ	nervous breakdown
ノー	no
ノート	note
ノック	knock

【ハ】

バー	bar
バーイ	bye
バーゲン	bargain
バーセント	percent
パーティー	party
パート	part-time worker
ハードディスク	hard disk
バーベキュー	barbecue
パーマ	permanent
バイオリン	violin
ハイキング	hiking
バイク	motorbike
バイト	part-time job
バイト	byte
パイナップル	pineapple
バイバイ	bye-bye/goodbye
ハイビスカス	hibiscus
パイプ	pipe
パイロット	pilot
バケツ	bucket
パジャマ	pajama
バス	bus
バス	bass
バス（ふろ）	bath
バスケットボール	basketball
パス	pass
パスタ	pasta
パスポート	passport
パソコン	personal computer
バター	butter
パターン	pattern
パチッ	flick
パチンコ	pachinko
バックハンド	backhand
バッグ	bag
バッジ	badge
バッテリー	battery
バット	bat
パトカー	patrol car
バドミントン	badminton
バナナ	banana
パノラマ	panorama
パパ	father/papa
ハム	ham
バラ	rose
バランス	balance
バレーボール	volleyball
バレンタインデー	Valentine's Day
パン	bread
バン	ban, bun, van
ハンガー	hunger
ハンガー	hanger
ハンカチ	handkerchief
パンク	flat tire
ハンサム	handsome
パンダ	panda
パンチ	punch
パンツ	pants
パンツ（下着）	underwear
バンド（ベルト）	band
ハンドバッグ	handbag
ハンドル	steering wheel
ハンバーガー	hamburger
ハンバーグ	hamburger
パンフレット	pamphlet
ハワイ	Hawaii

【ヒ】

ピアノ	piano
ヒーター	heater
ビーフカレー	beef curry
ビール	beer
ビールス	virus
ピクニック	picnic
ビザ	visa
ビジネス	business
ビジネスホテル	business hotel
ピストル	pistol
ビタミン	vitamin
ヒット	hit
ビデオ	video
ビデオカメラ	camcorder
ビデオプレーヤー	video player
ビニール	vinyl
ピラミッド	pyramid
ビル	building
ビルディング	building
ビン	bottle
ピンク	pink
ヒント	hint
ヒンズー	Hindu
ヒンズー語	Hindi
ピンポン	ping-pong

【フ】

ファーストネーム	first name
ファーストレディー	first lady
ファイト	fight
ファイル	file
ファスナー	fastener/zipper
ファックス	facsimile/fax
ファッション	fashion
ファン	fan
フィルター	filter
フィルム	film
ブーツ	boots
ブーム	boom
プール	pool
フェスティバル	festival
フェタチーニ	fettuccini
フェリー	ferry
フォーク	fork
フォーク	folk music
フォークダンス	folk dance
フォーム	form
ブザー	buzzer
フットボール	football
フュージョン	fusion
フライドチキン	fried chicken
フライパン	frying pan
ブラシ	brush
ブラジル	Brazil
ブラジル人	Brazilian (person)
ブラウス	blouse
ブラスバンド	brass band
プラス	plus
プラスチック	plastic

Katakana Glossary

プラットホーム	platform	ボタン	button
フランス	France	ホッケー	hockey
フランス語	French (language)	ホッチキス	stapler
フランス人	French (person)	ホット	hot
フランス料理	French cuisine	ポット	pot
プラン	plan	ホットドッグ	hot dog
フリー	free	ポップコーン	popcorn
プリパレーション	preparation	ポップス	pops
プリント	print	ポテトチップ	potato chip
ブルー	blue	ホテル	hotel
フルーツ	fruit	ボトル	bottle
プレーガイド	ticket agency	ボランティア	volunteer
ブレーキ	brake	ボルト	volt
プレゼンター	presenter	ボルト	bolt
プレゼンテーション	presentation	ホワイトデー	White Day
プレゼント	present	ホワイトボード	whiteboard
プレパレーションする	prepare	ポンド	pound
プロ	professional	ポンプ	pump
ブロー	blow-dry		
ブローチ	brooch	**【マ】**	
プログラム	program		
プロジェクト	project	マーカー	marker
プロポーザル	proposal	マーク	mark
プロポーズ	propose	マーケット	market
プロレス	professional wrestling	マイ〜(my)	my
フロント	front	マイク	mic
		マイクロホン	microphone
【ヘ】		マイナス	minus
		マスク	mask
ペア	pair	マスコミ	mass communication/mass media
ヘアムース	hair mousse		
ベークセール	bake sale	マスター	master
ページ	page	マッサージ	massage
ベース	base	マッシュルーム	mushroom
ベスト	best	マッチ	match
ベスト	vest	マット	mat, mattress
ベストセラー	bestseller	マナー	manner
ベッド	bed	マフラー	muffler
ペット	pet	ママ	mother/mama
ベテラン	veteran	マラソン	marathon
ペパロニ	pepperoni	マンゴー	mango
ベランダ	veranda/deck	マンション	apartment house
ヘリコプター	helicopter		
ベル	bell	**【ミ】**	
ベルト	belt		
ペルー	Peru	ミーティング	meeting
ペルー人	Peruvian (person)	ミートソース	meat sauce
ヘルメット	helmet	ミートローフ	meat loaf
ペン	pen	ミキサー	mixer
ペンキ	paint	ミシン	sewing machine
ベンチ	bench	ミス	miss
ペンチ	nipper	ミス	Miss
ペンパル	pen pal/pen friend	ミスプリント	misprint
		ミセス	Mrs
【ホ】		ミット	mitt
		ミュージカル	musical
ボイコット	boycott	ミュージック	music
ポイント	point	ミリ (メートル)	millimeter
ボウリング	bowling	ミルク	milk
ボーイ	boy		
ホース	hose	**【ム】**	
ポーズ	pose		
ボート	boat	ムード	mood/atmosphere
ボーナス	bonus		
ホーム	home	**【メ】**	
ホームシック	homesickness		
ホームステイ	home stay	メーカー	maker
ホームレス	homeless	メーク	make-up
ホール	hall	メーター	indicator/meter
ホール	hole	メートル	meter
ボール	ball	メガ	megabyte
ボールペン	ballpoint pen	メキシコ	Mexico
ポケット	pocket	メキシコ人	Mexican (person)
ポケベル	beeper/pager	メッセージ	message
ポジション	position	メディア	media
ポスター	poster	メディアルーム	media room
ポスト	mailbox	メニュー	menu
ホストファミリー	host family	メモ	memorandum
		メリーゴーランド	merry-go-round
		メロディー	melody

メロン	melon
メンバー	member

【モ】

モーター	motor
モーテル	motel
モダン	modern
モデル	model
モニター	monitor
モノレール	monorail

【ヤ】

ヤング	young

【ユ】

ユースホステル	youth hostel
ユーモア	humor
ユニーク	unique
ユニセフ	UNICEF
ユニホーム	uniform

【ヨ】

ヨーロッパ	Europe
ヨット	yacht/sailboat

【ラ】

ラーメン	Chinese-style noodles
ライス	rice
ライター	lighter
ライター	writer
ライト	light
ライト	right
ライン	line
ラグビー	rugby
ラケット	racket
ラジオ	radio
ラジカセ	radio cassette player
ラッシュ	rush
ラッシュアワー	rush hour
ラップトップ	laptop
ラベル	label
ランチ	lunch
ランニング	running
ランプ	lamp

【リ】

リード	lead
リクエスト	request
リサーチ	research
リサイクル	recycle
リスト	list
リズム	rhythm
リットル	liter
リポート	report
リボン	ribbon
リモコン	remote control

【ル】

ルーズ	loose
ルームメート	room-mate
ルール	rule

【レ】

レーンコート	raincoat
レース	race
レース	lace
レギュラー	regular
レクリエーション	recreation
レコード	record
レジャー	leisure
レストラン	restaurant
レセプション	reception
レッスン	lesson
レディー	lady
レバー	liver

レバー（取手）	lever
レベル	level
レポート	report
レモネード	lemonade
レモン	lemon
レンジ	cooking range
レンズ	lenses
レンタカー	rent-a-car/rental car
レントゲン	X-ray

【ロ】

ローストビーフ	roast beef
ロープ	rope
ロープウェー	aerial railway
ローマ字	Roman character
ローン	loan
ロケット	rocket
ロシア	Russia
ロシア語	Russian (language)
ロシア人	Russian (person)
ロッカー	locker
ロック	lock
ロック	rock
ロックコンサート	rock concert
ロビー	lobby
ロボット	robot
ロマンチック	romantic

【ワ】

ワープロ	word processor
ワイシャツ	dress shirt
ワイフ	wife
ワイン	wine
ワット	watt
ワッフル	waffle
ワンピース	dress
ワンルームマンション	one-room apartment

【＊】

CDプレーヤー	CD player
Tシャツ	T-shirt
でんしメール	e-mail

967

Alphabetical Index

【C】

cha	ちゃ	茶《名》
chairo	ちゃいろ	茶色《名》
-chan	- ちゃん	- ちゃん《尾》
chanto	ちゃんと	ちゃんと《副、～する》
chawan	ちゃわん	茶わん《名》
chi	ち	血《名》
chichi	ちち	父《名》
chigai	ちがい	違い《名》
chigai nai	ちがいない	違いない《連》
chigau	ちがう	違う《動Ⅰ》
chihō	ちほう	地方《名》
chiisai	ちいさい	小さい《形》
chiisana	ちいさな	小さな《連体》
chijimeru	ちぢめる	縮める《動Ⅱ》
chijimu	ちぢむ	縮む《動Ⅰ》
chijō	ちじょう	地上《名》
chika	ちか	地下《名》
chikagoro	ちかごろ	近ごろ《名》
chikai	ちかい	近い《形》
chikaku	ちかく	近く《名》
chikara	ちから	力《名》
chikatetsu	ちかてつ	地下鉄《名》
chikazuku	ちかづく	近づく《動Ⅰ》
chikoku	ちこく	遅刻《名、～する》
chikyū	ちきゅう	地球《名》
chiri	ちり	地理《名》
chiru	ちる	散る《動Ⅰ》
chishiki	ちしき	知識《名》
chittomo	ちっとも	ちっとも《副》
chizu	ちず	地図《名》
-chō	- ちょう	- 長《尾》
chōdo	ちょうど	ちょうど《副》
chokin	ちょきん	貯金《名、～する》
chōku	チョーク	チョーク《名》
chokusen	ちょくせん	直線《名》
chokusetsu	ちょくせつ	直接《名》
chōmen	ちょうめん	帳面《名》
chōsa	ちょうさ	調査《名、～する》
chōshi	ちょうし	調子《名》
chōsho	ちょうしょ	長所《名》
chotto	ちょっと	ちょっと《副》
-chū	- ちゅう	- 中《尾》
chūgakkō	ちゅうがっこう	中学校《名》
chūgakusei	ちゅうがくせい	中学生《名》
chūi	ちゅうい	注意《名、～する》
chūjun	ちゅうじゅん	中旬《名》
chūmoku	ちゅうもく	注目《名、～する》

chūmon	ちゅうもん	注文《名、～する》
chūō	ちゅうおう	中央《名》
chūsha	ちゅうしゃ	注射《名、～する》
chūsha	ちゅうしゃ	駐車《名、～する》
chūshi	ちゅうし	中止《名、～する》
chūshin	ちゅうしん	中心《名》

【D】

da	だ	だ《助動》
dai	だい	題《名》
dai	だい	第《頭》
(-)dai	(-) だい	(-) 台《名、尾》
-dai	- だい	- 代《尾》
dai-	だい -	大 -《頭》
daibu	だいぶ	だいぶ《副》
daibubun	だいぶぶん	大部分《名》
daidokoro	だいどころ	台所《名Ⅰ》
daigaku	だいがく	大学《名》
daihyō	だいひょう	代表《名、～する》
daiichi ni	だいいちに	第一に《副》
daiji	だいじ	大事《名、形動》
daijin	だいじん	大臣《名》
daijōbu	だいじょうぶ	大丈夫《形動》
daikin	だいきん	代金《名》
daitai	だいたい	だいたい《名》
daitōryō	だいとうりょう	大統領《名》
dakara	だから	だから《接》
dake	だけ	だけ《助》
daku	だく	抱く《動Ⅰ》
damaru	だまる	黙る《動Ⅰ》
dame	だめ	だめ《形動》
(-)dan	(-) だん	(-) 段《名、尾》
-dan	- だん	- 団《尾》
danbō	だんぼう	暖房《名、～する》
dandan	だんだん	だんだん《副》
danjo	だんじょ	男女《名》
dansei	だんせい	男性《名》
danshi	だんし	男子《名》
dansu	ダンス	ダンス《名》
dantai	だんたい	団体《名》
-darake	- だらけ	- だらけ《尾》
dare	だれ	だれ《代》
darō	だろう	だろう《助動》
dasu	だす	出す《動Ⅰ》
-dasu	- だす	- だす《尾》
de	で	で《助》
deguchi	でぐち	出口《名》
dekakeru	でかける	出かける《動Ⅱ》
dekiru	できる	できる《動Ⅱ》

(-)fukuro	(-)ふくろ	(-)袋《名、尾》	gaman	がまん	我慢《名、～する》
fukushū	ふくしゅう	復習《名、～する》	ganbaru	がんばる	がんばる《動Ⅰ》
fukusū	ふくすう	複数《名》	garasu	ガラス	ガラス《名》
fukuzatsu	ふくざつ	複雑《形動》	-garu	-がる	-がる《尾》
fumu	ふむ	踏む《動Ⅰ》	gasorin	ガソリン	ガソリン《名》
-fun	-ふん	-分《尾》	gasu	ガス	ガス《名》
funabin	ふなびん	船便《名》	-gatsu	-がつ	-月《尾》
fune	ふね	船《名》	-gawa	-がわ	-側《尾》
fureru	ふれる	触れる《動Ⅱ》	geijutsu	げいじゅつ	芸術《名》
furikaeru	ふりかえる	振り返る《動Ⅰ》	gejun	げじゅん	下旬《名》
furo	ふろ	ふろ《名》	geki	げき	劇《名》
furu	ふる	振る《動Ⅰ》	gekijō	げきじょう	劇場《名》
furu	ふる	降る《動Ⅰ》	gekkyū	げっきゅう	月給《名》
furueru	ふるえる	震える《動Ⅱ》	gēmu	ゲーム	ゲーム《名》
furui	ふるい	古い《形》	gendai	げんだい	現代《名》
fushigi	ふしぎ	不思議《形動》	gen'in	げんいん	原因《名》
fusoku	ふそく	不足《名、～する》	genjitsu	げんじつ	現実《名》
futa	ふた	ふた《名》	genkan	げんかん	玄関《名》
futari	ふたり	二人《名》	genki	げんき	元気《名、形動》
futatabi	ふたたび	再び《副》	genkin	げんきん	現金《名》
futatsu	ふたつ	二つ《名》	genryō	げんりょう	原料《名》
fūtō	ふうとう	封筒《名》	genshō	げんしょう	減少《名、～する》
futo	ふと	ふと《副》	genshō	げんしょう	現象《名》
futoi	ふとい	太い《形》	genzai	げんざい	現在《名》
futon	ふとん	布団《名》	geshuku	げしゅく	下宿《名、～する》
futoru	ふとる	太る《動Ⅰ》	getsuyō (bi)	げつよう(び)	月曜(日)《名》
futsū	ふつう	普通《名、形動》	gijutsu	ぎじゅつ	技術《名》
futsuka	ふつか	二日《名》	gimon	ぎもん	疑問《名》
fuyu	ふゆ	冬《名》	gimu	ぎむ	義務《名》

[G]

ga	が	が《助》	gin	ぎん	銀《名》
ga	が	が《助》	ginkō	ぎんこう	銀行《名》
ga	が	が《助》	giron	ぎろん	議論《名、～する》
gai	がい	害《名、～する》	gitā	ギター	ギター《名》
gaijin	がいじん	外人《名》	-go	-ご	-後《尾》
gaikō	がいこう	外交《名》	go-	ご-	御-《頭》
gaikoku	がいこく	外国《名》	go	ご	五《名》
gakkari suru	がっかりする	がっかりする《動Ⅲ》	(-)go	(-)ご	(-)語《名、尾》
gakki	がっき	学期《名》	-gō	-ごう	-号《尾》
gakki	がっき	楽器《名》	gobusata	ごぶさた	ごぶさた《名、～する》
gakkō	がっこう	学校《名》	gochisō	ごちそう	ごちそう《名、～する》
-gaku	-がく	-学《尾》	gogatsu	ごがつ	五月《名》
gakubu	がくぶ	学部《名》	gogo	ごご	午後《名》
gakumon	がくもん	学問《名、～する》	gohan	ごはん	御飯《名》
gakunen	がくねん	学年《名》	gokai	ごかい	誤解《名、～する》
gakusei	がくせい	学生《名》	gōkaku	ごうかく	合格《名、～する》
gakusha	がくしゃ	学者《名》	gōkei	ごうけい	合計《名、～する》
gakushū	がくしゅう	学習《名、～する》	gokurōsama	ごくろうさま	御苦労さま《連》
			gomen kuda-sai	ごめんください	ごめんください《連》

gomen nasai	ごめんなさい	ごめんなさい《連》
gomi	ごみ	ごみ《名》
gomu	ゴム	ゴム《名》
(-te)goran nasai	(～て)ごらんなさい	(～て)ごらんなさい《連》
goranninaru	ごらんになる	ご覧になる《動Ⅰ》
-goro	-ごろ	-ごろ《尾》
-goto	-ごと	-ごと《尾》
gozaimasu	ございます	ございます《連》
gozen	ごぜん	午前《名》
gozonji	ごぞんじ	ご存じ《名》
guai	ぐあい	ぐあい《名》
gunjin	ぐんじん	軍人《名》
guntai	ぐんたい	軍隊《名》
gurai	ぐらい	ぐらい《助》
-guramu	- グラム	- グラム《尾》
gūsū	ぐうすう	偶数《名》
gūzen	ぐうぜん	偶然《名、副、形動》
gyaku	ぎゃく	逆《名、形動》
(-)gyō	(-)ぎょう	(-)行《名、尾》
gyogyō	ぎょぎょう	漁業《名》
gyōji	ぎょうじ	行事《名》
gyūniku	ぎゅうにく	牛肉《名》
gyūnyū	ぎゅうにゅう	牛乳《名》

【H】

ha	は	葉《名》
ha	は	歯《名》
haba	はば	幅《名》
habuku	はぶく	省く《動》
hachi	はち	八《名》
hachigatsu	はちがつ	八月《名》
hadaka	はだか	裸《名》
hadashi	はだし	はだし《名》
hade	はで	派手《形動》
hae	はえ	はえ《名》
haeru	はえる	生える《動Ⅱ》
hagaki	はがき	はがき《名》
hagemasu	はげます	励ます《動Ⅰ》
hageshii	はげしい	激しい《形》
haha	はは	母《名》
hai	はい	灰《名》
hai	はい	はい《感》
-hai	- はい	- 杯《尾》
haiiro	はいいろ	灰色《名》
haiken	はいけん	拝見《名、～する》
hairu	はいる	入る《動Ⅰ》
haitatsu	はいたつ	配達《名、～する》
haiyū	はいゆう	俳優《名》
haizara	はいざら	灰ざら《名》

haji	はじ	恥《名》
hajimaru	はじまる	始まる《動Ⅰ》
hajime	はじめ	始め《名》
hajime	はじめ	初め《名》
hajimemashite	はじめまして	初めまして《連》
(-)hajimeru	はじめる	始める《動Ⅱ》
hajimete	はじめて	初めて《副》
haka	はか	墓《名》
hakari	はかり	はかり《名》
hakaru	はかる	測る《動Ⅰ》
hakaru	はかる	量る《動Ⅰ》
hakaru	はかる	計る《動Ⅰ》
hakken	はっけん	発見《名、～する》
hakkiri	はっきり	はっきり《副、～する》
hakkō	はっこう	発行《名、～する》
(-)hako	(-)はこ	(-) 箱《名、尾》
hakobu	はこぶ	運ぶ《動Ⅰ》
haku	はく	はく《動Ⅰ》
haku	はく	掃く《動Ⅰ》
hakubutsukan	はくぶつかん	博物館《名》
hakushi	はくし	博士《名》
hameru	はめる	はめる《動Ⅱ》
han	はん	判《名》
-han	- はん	- 半《尾》
hana	はな	はな《名》
hana	はな	鼻《名》
hana	はな	花《名》
hanareru	はなれる	離れる《動Ⅱ》
hanashi	はなし	話《名》
hanasu	はなす	離す《動Ⅰ》
hanasu	はなす	放す《動Ⅰ》
hanasu	はなす	話す《動Ⅰ》
hanbai	はんばい	販売《名、～する》
hanbun	はんぶん	半分《名》
handan	はんだん	判断《名、～する》
handobaggu	ハンドバッグ	ハンドバッグ《名》
handoru	ハンドル	ハンドル《名》
hane	はね	羽《名》
hane	はね	羽根《名》
haneru	はねる	跳ねる《動Ⅱ》
han'i	はんい	範囲《名》
hankachi	ハンカチ	ハンカチ《名》
hannichi	はんにち	半日《名》
hansei	はんせい	反省《名、～する》
hansha	はんしゃ	反射《名、～する》
hantai	はんたい	反対《名、～する》
hantō	はんとう	半島《名》
hantoshi	はんとし	半年《名》
hantsuki	はんつき	半月《名》

kōkan	こうかん	交換《名、～する》	koppu	コップ	コップ《名》
kokka	こっか	国家《名》	kore	これ	これ《代》
kokka	こっか	国歌《名》	kore kara	これから	これから《連》
kokki	こっき	国旗《名》	kōritsu	こうりつ	公立《名》
koko	ここ	ここ《代》	koro	ころ	ころ《名》
kōkoku	こうこく	広告《名、～する》	korobu	ころぶ	転ぶ《動Ⅰ》
kokonoka	ここのか	九日《名》	(-)korogaru	ころがる	転がる《動Ⅰ》
kokonotsu	ここのつ	九つ《名》	korosu	ころす	殺す《動Ⅰ》
kokoro	こころ	心《名》	kōsai	こうさい	交際《名、～する》
kokuban	こくばん	黒板《名》	kōsaten	こうさてん	交差点《名》
kōkūbin	こうくうびん	航空便《名》	koshi	こし	腰《名》
kokugai	こくがい	国外《名》	koshikakeru	こしかける	腰掛ける《動Ⅱ》
kokugo	こくご	国語《名》	kōshō	こうしょう	交渉《名、～する》
kokumin	こくみん	国民《名》	koshō	こしょう	故障《名、～する》
kokunai	こくない	国内《名》	koshō	こしょう	こしょう《名》
kokuritsu	こくりつ	国立《名》	kotae	こたえ	答え《名》
kokusai	こくさい	国際《名》	kotaeru	こたえる	答える《動Ⅱ》
kokuseki	こくせき	国籍《名》	kōtai	こうたい	交替《名、～する》
kokyū	こきゅう	呼吸《名、～する》	kotai	こたい	固体《名》
komakai	こまかい	細かい《形》	kōtei	こうてい	肯定《名、～する》
komaru	こまる	困る《動Ⅰ》	kōto	コート	コート《名》
kome	こめ	米《名》	koto	こと	こと《名》
komu	こむ	こむ《動Ⅰ》	kotoba	ことば	言葉《名》
-komu	-こむ	-込む《尾》	kōtōgakkō	こうとうがっこう	高等学校《名》
komugi	こむぎ	小麦《名》	kotori	ことり	小鳥《名》
kōmuin	こうむいん	公務員《名》	kotoshi	ことし	今年《名》
kona	こな	粉《名》	kotowaru	ことわる	断る《動Ⅰ》
konban	こんばん	今晩《名》	kōtsū	こうつう	交通《名》
konban wa	こんばんは	今晩は《連》	kowai	こわい	怖い《形》
kondo	こんど	今度《名》	kowareru	こわれる	壊れる《動Ⅱ》
kongetsu	こんげつ	今月《名》	kowasu	こわす	壊す《動Ⅰ》
kongo	こんご	今後《名》	koyomi	こよみ	暦《名》
konkuriito	コンクリート	コンクリート《名》	kōzō	こうぞう	構造《名》
konna	こんな	こんな《連体》	kozukai	こづかい	小遣い《名》
konna ni	こんなに	こんなに《副》	kozutsumi	こづつみ	小包《名》
konnan	こんなん	困難《名、形動》	ku	く	九《名》
konnichi	こんにち	今日《名》	kubaru	くばる	配る《動Ⅰ》
konnichi wa	こんにちは	今日は《連》	kubetsu	くべつ	区別《名、～する》
kono	この	この《連体》	kubi	くび	首《名》
kono mae	このまえ	この前《連》	kuchi	くち	口《名》
kono tsugi	このつぎ	この次《連》	kuchibiru	くちびる	くちびる《名》
konoaida	このあいだ	この間《名》	kudamono	くだもの	果物《名》
konogoro	このごろ	このごろ《名》	kudari	くだり	下り《名》
konsāto	コンサート	コンサート《名》	kudaru	くだる	下る《動Ⅰ》
konshū	こんしゅう	今週《名》	kudasai	ください	ください《動Ⅰ》
kon'ya	こんや	今夜《名》	(o- ～)kudasai	(お～)ください	(お～)ください《連》
kon'yaku	こんやく	婚約《名、～する》	(go- ～)kuda-sai	(ご～)ください	(御～)ください《連》
koori	こおり	氷《名》	(-te)kudasai	(～て)ください	(～て)ください《連》
kooru	こおる	凍る《動Ⅰ》			

migaku	みがく	みがく《動Ⅰ》
migi	みぎ	右《名》
migoto	みごと	みごと《形動》
mihon	みほん	見本《名》
mijikai	みじかい	短い《形》
mikan	みかん	みかん《名》
mikka	みっか	三日《名》
mimai	みまい	見舞い《名》
mimi	みみ	耳《名》
mina	みな	皆《名、副》
minami	みなみ	南《名》
minato	みなと	港《名》
minna	みんな	みんな《名、副》
minoru	みのる	実る《動Ⅰ》
minshushugi	みんしゅしゅぎ	民主主義《名》
minzoku	みんぞく	民族《名》
miokuru	みおくる	見送る《動Ⅰ》
mirai	みらい	未来《名》
-miri	- ミリ	- ミリ《尾》
miru	みる	診る《動Ⅱ》
miru	みる	見る《動Ⅱ》
(-te)miru	(- て)みる	(- て)みる《連》
miruku	ミルク	ミルク《名》
mise	みせ	店《名》
miseru	みせる	見せる《動Ⅱ》
mishin	ミシン	ミシン《名》
miso	みそ	みそ《名》
mitai da	みたいだ	みたいだ《助動》
mitomeru	みとめる	認める《動Ⅱ》
mitsukaru	みつかる	見つかる《動Ⅰ》
mitsukeru	みつける	見つける《動Ⅱ》
mittsu	みっつ	三つ《名》
miyage	みやげ	土産《名》
mizu	みず	水《名》
mizuumi	みずうみ	湖《名》
mo	も	も《助》
mō	もう	もう《副》
mochiiru	もちいる	用いる《動Ⅱ》
mochiron	もちろん	もちろん《副》
modoru	もどる	もどる《動Ⅰ》
moeru	もえる	燃える《動Ⅱ》
mōfu	もうふ	毛布《名》
moguru	もぐる	潜る《動Ⅰ》
moji	もじ	文字《名》
mōkeru	もうける	もうける《動Ⅱ》
mokuhyō	もくひょう	目標《名》
mokuteki	もくてき	目的《名》
mokuyō(bi)	もくよう(び)	木曜(日)《名》
momen	もめん	木綿《名》

momo	もも	桃《名》
mon	もん	門《名》
mondai	もんだい	問題《名》
mono	もの	物《名》
mono	もの	者《名》
monogatari	ものがたり	物語《名》
monosashi	ものさし	ものさし《名》
morau	もらう	もらう《動Ⅰ》
(-te)morau	(〜て)もらう	(〜て)もらう《連》
mori	もり	森《名》
moru	もる	漏る《動Ⅰ》
moshi	もし	もし《副》
moshi moshi	もしもし	もしもし《感》
mōshiageru	もうしあげる	申し上げる《動Ⅱ》
mōshikomu	もうしこむ	申し込む《動Ⅰ》
mōshiwake nai	もうしわけない	申し訳ない《連》
mōsu	もうす	申す《動Ⅰ》
mosu	もす	燃す《動Ⅰ》
mōsugu	もうすぐ	もうすぐ《副》
moto	もと	元《名》
motomeru	もとめる	求める《動Ⅱ》
motsu	もつ	持つ《動Ⅰ》
mottainai	もったいない	もったいない《形》
motte iku	もっていく	持って行く《連》
motte kuru	もってくる	持って来る《連》
motto	もっと	もっと《副》
mottomo	もっとも	もっとも《接》
mottomo	もっとも	もっとも《形動》
mottomo	もっとも	最も《副》
moyasu	もやす	燃やす《動Ⅰ》
moyō	もよう	模様《名》
mu(-)	む(-)	無 (-)《名、頭》
muchū	むちゅう	夢中《形動》
muda	むだ	むだ《名、形動》
mudan	むだん	無断《名》
mugi	むぎ	麦《名》
muika	むいか	六日《名》
mukaeru	むかえる	迎える《動Ⅱ》
mukashi	むかし	昔《名》
mukau	むかう	向かう《動Ⅰ》
mukeru	むける	向ける《動Ⅱ》
(-)muki	(-)むき	(-) 向き《名、尾》
mukō	むこう	向こう《名》
muku	むく	向く《動Ⅰ》
muku	むく	むく《動Ⅰ》
mune	むね	胸《名》
mura	むら	村《名》
murasaki	むらさき	紫《名》

muri	むり	無理《名、形動》
muryō	むりょう	無料《名》
mushi	むし	虫《名》
mushiba	むしば	虫歯《名》
mushiro	むしろ	むしろ《副》
musubu	むすぶ	結ぶ《動Ⅰ》
musuko	むすこ	息子《名》
musume	むすめ	娘《名》
muttsu	むっつ	六つ《名》
muyami ni	むやみに	むやみに《副》
muzukashii	むずかしい	難しい《形》
myō	みょう	妙《形動》
myō-	みょう-	明-《頭》
myōji	みょうじ	名字《名》

【N】

n	ん	ん《助》
na	な	な《助》
nado	など	など《助》
nagai	ながい	長い《形》
nagameru	ながめる	ながめる《動Ⅱ》
-nagara	ながら	ながら《助》
nagare	ながれ	流れ《名》
nagareru	ながれる	流れる《動Ⅱ》
nagasa	ながさ	長さ《名》
nagasu	ながす	流す《動Ⅰ》
nageru	なげる	投げる《動Ⅱ》
nagusameru	なぐさめる	慰める《動Ⅱ》
-nai	ない	ない《助動》
nai	ない	ない《形》
-nai	-ない	-内《尾》
naifu	ナイフ	ナイフ《名》
naikaku	ないかく	内閣《名》
nairon	ナイロン	ナイロン《名》
naiyō	ないよう	内容《名》
naka	なか	仲《名》
naka	なか	中《名》
nakama	なかま	仲間《名》
nakanaka	なかなか	なかなか《副》
-nakereba naranai	なければならない	なければならない《連》
naku	なく	泣く《動Ⅰ》
naku	なく	鳴く《動Ⅰ》
nakunaru	なくなる	亡くなる《動Ⅰ》
nakunaru	なくなる	なくなる《動Ⅰ》
nakusu	なくす	なくす《動Ⅰ》
-nakute wa naranai	なくてはならない	なくてはならない《連》
nama	なま	生《名》
namae	なまえ	名前《名》

namakeru	なまける	怠ける《動Ⅱ》
nami	なみ	波《名》
namida	なみだ	涙《名》
nan(-)	なん(-)	何(-)《代、頭》
nan demo	なんでも	何でも《連》
nana	なな	七《名》
naname	ななめ	斜め《名》
nanatsu	ななつ	七つ《名》
nani(-)	なに(-)	何(-)《代、頭》
nani ka	なにか	何か《連》
nani mo	なにも	何も《連》
nanka	なんか	なんか《助》
nanoka	なのか	七日《名》
nao	なお	なお《副》
naoru	なおる	直る《動Ⅰ》
naoru	なおる	治る《動Ⅰ》
(-)naosu	なおす	直す《動Ⅰ》
naosu	なおす	治す《動Ⅰ》
nara	なら	なら《助動》
naraba	ならば	ならば《助動》
naraberu	ならべる	並べる《動Ⅱ》
narabu	ならぶ	並ぶ《動Ⅰ》
naranai	ならない	ならない《連》
narau	ならう	習う《動Ⅰ》
nareru	なれる	なれる《動Ⅱ》
nareru	なれる	慣れる《動Ⅱ》
naru	なる	なる《動Ⅰ》
naru	なる	なる《動Ⅰ》
naru	なる	鳴る《動Ⅰ》
narubeku	なるべく	なるべく《副》
naruhodo	なるほど	なるほど《副》
(-)nasai	なさい	なさい《動Ⅰ》
nasaru	なさる	なさる《動Ⅰ》
nashi	なし	なし《名》
natsu	なつ	夏《名》
natsukashii	なつかしい	懐かしい《形》
nawa	なわ	なわ《名》
naze	なぜ	なぜ《副》
nazenara	なぜなら	なぜなら《接》
ne	ね	ね《助》
ne	ね	根《名》
nedan	ねだん	値段《名》
negai	ねがい	願い《名》
negau	ねがう	願う《動Ⅰ》
neji	ねじ	ねじ《名》
nejiru	ねじる	ねじる《動Ⅰ》
neko	ねこ	ねこ《名》
nekutai	ネクタイ	ネクタイ《名》
nemui	ねむい	眠い《形》

nemuru	ねむる	眠る《動Ⅰ》
-nen	-ねん	-年《尾》
nendo	ねんど	年度《名》
nenrei	ねんれい	年齢《名》
nenryō	ねんりょう	燃料《名》
nerau	ねらう	ねらう《動Ⅰ》
neru	ねる	寝る《動Ⅱ》
nesshin	ねっしん	熱心《形動》
netsu	ねつ	熱《名》
nezumi	ねずみ	ねずみ《名》
ni	に	に《助》
ni	に	二《名》
niau	にあう	似合う《動Ⅰ》
-nichi	-にち	-日《尾》
nichiyō(bi)	にちよう(び)	日曜(日)《名》
nigai	にがい	苦い《形》
nigatsu	にがつ	二月《名》
nigeru	にげる	逃げる《動Ⅱ》
nigiyaka	にぎやか	にぎやか《形動》
nigoru	にごる	濁る《動Ⅰ》
Nihon	にほん	日本《名》
nikki	にっき	日記《名》
niku	にく	肉《名》
-nikui	-にくい	-にくい《尾》
nimotsu	にもつ	荷物《名》
-nin	-にん	-人《尾》
ningen	にんげん	人間《名》
ningyō	にんぎょう	人形《名》
ninki	にんき	人気《名》
ninzū	にんずう	人数《名》
nioi	におい	におい《名》
niou	におう	におう《動Ⅰ》
Nippon	にっぽん	日本《名》
niru	にる	似る《動Ⅱ》
niru	にる	煮る《動Ⅱ》
nishi	にし	西《名》
niwa	にわ	庭《名》
niwatori	にわとり	鶏《名》
no	の	の《助》
no	の	の《助》
no	の	の《助》
nobasu	のばす	延ばす《動Ⅰ》
nobasu	のばす	伸ばす《動Ⅰ》
nobiru	のびる	延びる《動Ⅱ》
nobiru	のびる	伸びる《動Ⅱ》
nobori	のぼり	上り《名》
noboru	のぼる	登る《動Ⅰ》
noboru	のぼる	上る《動Ⅰ》
noboru	のぼる	昇る《動Ⅰ》
nochi	のち	後《名》
node	ので	ので《助》
nodo	のど	のど《名》
nōgyō	のうぎょう	農業《名》
nohara	のはら	野原《名》
nōka	のうか	農家《名》
nokoru	のこる	残る《動Ⅰ》
nokosu	のこす	残す《動Ⅰ》
nomimono	のみもの	飲み物《名》
nomu	のむ	飲む《動Ⅰ》
noni	のに	のに《助》
nori	のり	のり《名》
norikae	のりかえ	乗り換え《名》
norikaeru	のりかえる	乗り換える《動Ⅱ》
norimono	のりもの	乗り物《名》
nōritsu	のうりつ	能率《名》
noru	のる	載る《動Ⅰ》
noru	のる	乗る《動Ⅰ》
nōryoku	のうりょく	能力《名》
noseru	のせる	載せる《動Ⅱ》
noseru	のせる	乗せる《動Ⅱ》
nōto	ノート	ノート《名》
nozoku	のぞく	のぞく《動Ⅰ》
nozoku	のぞく	除く《動Ⅰ》
nugu	ぬぐ	脱ぐ《動Ⅰ》
nukeru	ぬける	抜ける《動Ⅱ》
nuku	ぬく	抜く《動Ⅰ》
nuno	ぬの	布《名》
nureru	ぬれる	ぬれる《動Ⅱ》
nuru	ぬる	塗る《動Ⅰ》
nurui	ぬるい	ぬるい《形》
nusumu	ぬすむ	盗む《動Ⅰ》
nuu	ぬう	縫う《動Ⅰ》
nyū-	にゅう-	入-《頭》
nyūgaku	にゅうがく	入学《名、～する》
nyūin	にゅういん	入院《名、～する》
nyūsu	ニュース	ニュース《名》

【O】

o-	お-	お-《頭》
o	を	を《助》
ōbā	オーバー	オーバー《名》
oba	おば	おば《名》
obāsan	おばあさん	おばあさん《名》
obasan	おばさん	おばさん《名》
oboeru	おぼえる	覚える《動Ⅱ》
oboreru	おぼれる	おぼれる《動Ⅱ》
ocha	おちゃ	お茶《名》
ochiru	おちる	落ちる《動Ⅱ》

otaku	おたく	お宅《名》
otearai	おてあらい	お手洗い《名》
oto	おと	音《名》
ōtobai	オートバイ	オートバイ《名》
otoko	おとこ	男《名》
otona	おとな	大人《名》
otonashii	おとなしい	おとなしい《形》
otōsan	おとうさん	お父さん《名》
otosu	おとす	落とす《動Ⅰ》
otōto	おとうと	弟《名》
ototoi	おととい	おととい《名》
ototoshi	おととし	おととし《名》
otto	おっと	夫《名》
ou	おう	追う《動Ⅰ》
owari	おわり	終わり《名》
(-)owaru	おわる	終わる《動Ⅰ》
oya	おや	親《名》
oya	おや	おや《感》
oyako	おやこ	親子《名》
oyasumi nasai	おやすみなさい	おやすみなさい《連》
ōyō	おうよう	応用《名、〜する》
oyogu	およぐ	泳ぐ《動Ⅰ》

【P】

painappuru	パイナップル	パイナップル《名》
pan	パン	パン《名》
panku	パンク	パンク《名、〜する》
-pāsento	-パーセント	-パーセント《尾》
pasupōto	パスポート	パスポート《名》
pātii	パーティー	パーティー《名》
-pēji	-ページ	-ページ《尾》
pen	ペン	ペン《名》
penki	ペンキ	ペンキ《名》
piano	ピアノ	ピアノ《名》
pinpon	ピンポン	ピンポン《名》
pittari	ぴったり	ぴったり《副、〜する》
poketto	ポケット	ポケット《名》
posuto	ポスト	ポスト《名》
purezento	プレゼント	プレゼント《名、〜する》
pūru	プール	プール《名》

【R】

raigetsu	らいげつ	来月《名》
rainen	らいねん	来年《名》
raishū	らいしゅう	来週《名》
raitā	ライター	ライター《名》
rajio	ラジオ	ラジオ《名》
raku	らく	楽《名、形動》
rāmen	ラーメン	ラーメン《名》
-rareru	られる	られる《助動》

rashii	らしい	らしい《助動》
-rashii	-らしい	-らしい《尾》
rei	れい	零《名》
rei	れい	例《名》
rei	れい	礼《名》
reibō	れいぼう	冷房《名、〜する》
reigai	れいがい	例外《名》
reinkōto	レインコート	レインコート《名》
reizōko	れいぞうこ	冷蔵庫《名》
rekishi	れきし	歴史《名》
rekōdo	レコード	レコード《名》
ren'ai	れんあい	恋愛《名、〜する》
renraku	れんらく	連絡《名、〜する》
renshū	れんしゅう	練習《名、〜する》
repōto	レポート	レポート《名》
-reru	れる	れる《助動》
ressha	れっしゃ	列車《名》
resutoran	レストラン	レストラン《名》
(-)retsu	(-)れつ	(-)列《名、尾》
rieki	りえき	利益《名》
rihatsuten	りはつてん	理髪店《名》
rikai	りかい	理解《名、〜する》
rikō	りこう	りこう《形動》
riku	りく	陸《名》
rikutsu	りくつ	理屈《名》
ringo	りんご	りんご《名》
rinji	りんじ	臨時《名》
rippa	りっぱ	立派《形動》
riron	りろん	理論《名》
risō	りそう	理想《名》
-rittoru	-リットル	-リットル《尾》
riyō	りよう	利用《名、〜する》
riyū	りゆう	理由《名》
rōdō	ろうどう	労働《名、〜する》
rōjin	ろうじん	老人《名》
rōka	ろうか	廊下《名》
roketto	ロケット	ロケット《名》
roku	ろく	六《名》
rokugatsu	ろくがつ	六月《名》
rokuon	ろくおん	録音《名、〜する》
rōmaji	ローマじ	ローマ字《名》
(-)ron	(-)ろん	(-)論《名、尾》
ronbun	ろんぶん	論文《名》
rōsoku	ろうそく	ろうそく《名》
rusu	るす	留守《名》
ryō	りょう	寮《名》
ryō	りょう	量《名》
-ryō	-りょう	-料《尾》
ryō-	りょう-	両-《頭》

990

totemo	とても	とても《副》
tótó	とうとう	とうとう《副》
totsuzen	とつぜん	突然《副》
totte	とって	とって《連》
tōyō	とうよう	東洋《名》
tozan	とざん	登山《名、〜する》
tōzen	とうぜん	当然《副、形動、〜の》
(-)tsubu	(-)つぶ	(-) 粒《名、尾》
tsubureru	つぶれる	つぶれる《動》
tsubusu	つぶす	つぶす《動Ⅰ》
tsūchi	つうち	通知《名、〜する》
tsuchi	つち	土《名》
tsugi	つぎ	次《名》
tsugō	つごう	都合《名》
tsui	つい	つい《副》
tsuide ni	ついでに	ついでに《副》
tsuini	ついに	ついに《副》
tsuitachi	ついたち	一日《名》
tsuite	ついて	ついて《連》
tsūjiru	つうじる	通じる《動Ⅱ》
tsukamaeru	つかまえる	捕まえる《動Ⅱ》
tsukamu	つかむ	つかむ《動Ⅰ》
tsukareru	つかれる	疲れる《動Ⅱ》
tsukau	つかう	使う《動Ⅰ》
tsukeru	つける	漬ける《動Ⅱ》
tsukeru	つける	つける《動Ⅱ》
tsuki	つき	月《名》
tsuku	つく	着く《動Ⅰ》
tsuku	つく	つく《動Ⅰ》
tsukue	つくえ	机《名》
tsukuru	つくる	作る《動Ⅰ》
tsukuru	つくる	造る《動Ⅰ》
(-)tsukusu	つくす	尽くす《動Ⅰ》
tsuma	つま	妻《名》
tsumaranai	つまらない	つまらない《形》
tsumari	つまり	つまり《副》
tsumaru	つまる	詰まる《動Ⅰ》
tsume	つめ	つめ《名》
tsumeru	つめる	詰める《動Ⅱ》
tsumetai	つめたい	冷たい《形》
tsumi	つみ	罪《名》
tsumori	つもり	つもり《名》
tsumoru	つもる	積もる《動Ⅰ》
tsumu	つむ	積む《動Ⅰ》
tsuna	つな	綱《名》
tsunagu	つなぐ	つなぐ《動Ⅰ》
tsune ni	つねに	常に《副》
tsurai	つらい	つらい《形》
tsureru	つれる	連れる《動Ⅱ》
tsuri	つり	つり《名》
tsuri	つり	つり《名》
tsuru	つる	つる《動Ⅰ》
tsūshin	つうしん	通信《名、〜する》
tsutaeru	つたえる	伝える《動Ⅱ》
tsutawaru	つたわる	伝わる《動Ⅰ》
tsutomeru	つとめる	努める《動Ⅱ》
tsutomeru	つとめる	勤める《動Ⅱ》
tsutsumu	つつむ	包む《動Ⅰ》
tsūyaku	つうやく	通訳《名、〜する》
tsuyoi	つよい	強い《形》
tsuyu	つゆ	梅雨《名》
tsuzukeru	つづける	続ける《動Ⅱ》
tsuzuku	つづく	続く《動Ⅰ》
-u	う	う《助動》

【U】

uchi	うち	内《名》
uchi	うち	うち《名》
uchiawaseru	うちあわせる	打ち合わせる《動Ⅱ》
ude	うで	腕《名》
udon	うどん	うどん《名》
ue	うえ	上《名》
ueru	うえる	植える《動Ⅱ》
ugokasu	うごかす	動かす《動Ⅰ》
ugoki	うごき	動き《名》
ugoku	うごく	動く《動Ⅰ》
uisukii	ウイスキー	ウイスキー《名》
ukabu	うかぶ	浮かぶ《動Ⅰ》
ukagau	うかがう	伺う《動Ⅰ》
ukeru	うける	受ける《動Ⅱ》
uketori	うけとり	受取《名》
uketoru	うけとる	受け取る《動Ⅰ》
uketsuke	うけつけ	受付《名》
uketsukeru	うけつける	受け付ける《動Ⅱ》
uku	うく	浮く《動Ⅰ》
uma	うま	馬《名》
umai	うまい	うまい《形》
umare	うまれ	生まれ《名》
umareru	うまれる	生まれる《動Ⅱ》
umeru	うめる	埋める《動Ⅱ》
umi	うみ	海《名》
umu	うむ	産む《動Ⅰ》
un	うん	うん《感》
un	うん	運《名》
unazuku	うなずく	うなずく《動Ⅰ》
undō	うんどう	運動《名、〜する》
unten	うんてん	運転《名、〜する》
ura	うら	裏《名》

urayamashii	うらやましい	うらやましい《形》	waru	わる	割る《動Ⅰ》
ureshii	うれしい	うれしい《形》	warui	わるい	悪い《形》
uriba	うりば	売り場《名》	wasuremono	わすれもの	忘れ物《名》
uru	うる	売る《動Ⅰ》	wasureru	わすれる	忘れる《動Ⅱ》
urusai	うるさい	うるさい《形》	wata	わた	綿《名》
ushi	うし	牛《名》	watakushi	わたくし	私《代》
ushinau	うしなう	失う《動Ⅰ》	wataru	わたる	渡る《動Ⅰ》
ushiro	うしろ	後ろ《名》	watashi	わたし	わたし《代》
uso	うそ	うそ《名》	watasu	わたす	渡す《動Ⅰ》
usui	うすい	薄い《形》	wazawaza	わざわざ	わざわざ《副》
uta	うた	歌《名》	wazuka	わずか	わずか《副、形動、～の》
utagau	うたがう	疑う《動Ⅰ》			
utau	うたう	歌う《動Ⅰ》		**【Y】**	
utsu	うつ	打つ《動Ⅰ》	ya	や	や《助》
utsu	うつ	撃つ《動Ⅰ》	-ya	-や	- 屋《尾》
utsukushii	うつくしい	美しい《形》	yā	やあ	やあ《感》
utsuru	うつる	移る《動Ⅰ》	yabureru	やぶれる	破れる《動Ⅱ》
utsuru	うつる	映る《動Ⅰ》	yabureru	やぶれる	敗れる《動Ⅱ》
utsuru	うつる	写る《動Ⅰ》	yaburu	やぶる	破る《動Ⅰ》
utsusu	うつす	写す《動Ⅰ》	yado	やど	宿《名》
utsusu	うつす	映す《動Ⅰ》	yagate	やがて	やがて《副》
utsusu	うつす	移す《動Ⅰ》	yahari	やはり	やはり《副》
uwagi	うわぎ	上着《名》	yakamashii	やかましい	やかましい《形》
uwasa	うわさ	うわさ《名、～する》	yakeru	やける	焼ける《動Ⅰ》
	【W】		yaku	やく	焼く《動Ⅰ》
			yaku	やく	役《名》
wa	は	は《助》	yaku	やく	約《連体》
wa	わ	輪《名》	yakusho	やくしょ	役所《名》
wa	わ	わ《助》	yakusoku	やくそく	約束《名、～する》
wagamama	わがまま	わがまま《名、形動》	yakusu	やくす	訳す《動Ⅰ》
waishatsu	ワイシャツ	ワイシャツ《名》	yama	やま	山《名》
wakai	わかい	若い《形》	yameru	やめる	やめる《動Ⅱ》
wakareru	わかれる	別れる《動Ⅱ》	yameru	やめる	辞める《動Ⅱ》
wakareru	わかれる	分かれる《動Ⅱ》	yamu	やむ	やむ《動Ⅰ》
wakaru	わかる	わかる《動Ⅰ》	yamuoenai	やむをえない	やむをえない《連》
wakasu	わかす	沸かす《動Ⅰ》	yamuoezu	やむをえず	やむをえず《副》
wake	わけ	わけ《名》	yane	やね	屋根《名》
wakeru	わける	分ける《動Ⅱ》	yaoya	やおや	八百屋《名》
waki	わき	わき《名》	yappari	やっぱり	やっぱり《副》
waku	わく	沸く《動Ⅰ》	yaru	やる	やる《動Ⅰ》
warai	わらい	笑い《名》	(-te)yaru	（～て）やる	（～て）やる《連》
warau	わらう	笑う《動Ⅰ》	yasai	やさい	野菜《名》
wareru	われる	割れる《動Ⅱ》	yasashii	やさしい	優しい《形》
wareware	われわれ	われわれ《代》	yasashii	やさしい	易しい《形》
-wari	- わり	- 割《尾》	yaseru	やせる	やせる《動Ⅱ》
wari ni	わりに	割に《連》	yasui	やすい	安い《形》
wariai	わりあい	割合《名》	-yasui	- やすい	- やすい《尾》
wariai ni	わりあいに	割合に《副》	yasumi	やすみ	休み《名》
warini	わりに	わりに《副》	yasumu	やすむ	休む《動Ⅰ》
			yatou	やとう	雇う《動Ⅰ》
			yatto	やっと	やっと《副》

Staff

Senior Editors (Japanese text)

MOCHIZUKI Kōitsu

KUMAZAWA Seiji

YOSHIOKA Hideyuki

SANADA Kazuko

Associate Editors (Japanese text)

SHIBATA Shunzō

IMADA Shigeko

NITOGURI Akira

Editorial Supervisor (English text)

MIZUTANI Nobuko

Translator (English text)

Janet M. ASHBY

Proofreaders (English text)

Janet M. ASHBY

Keith D. LEARMONTH

999

1000

BASIC JAPANESE-ENGLISH DICTIONARY

基礎日本語学習辞典（英語版）

1986年12月10日　　初版第1刷発行
1997年5月10日　　初版第9刷発行
2004年8月5日　　第2版第1刷発行

著作権者　　独立行政法人　国際交流基金
　　　　　　〒107-6021　東京都港区赤坂1-12-32
　　　　　　（アーク森ビル内）
　　　　　　連絡先　日本語国際センター制作事業課
　　　　　　〒330-0074　埼玉県さいたま市浦和区北浦和
　　　　　　　　　　　　　　　　　　　　　5－6－36

　　　　　　電話　048（834）1183

発 行 者　　田中久光

発 行 所　　株式会社　凡人社
　　　　　　〒102-0093　東京都千代田区平河町1－3－13
　　　　　　　　　　　　菱進平河町ビル

　　　　　　電話（03）3263－3959